ROUTLEDGE HANDBOOK ON CAPITAL PUNISHMENT

Capital punishment is one of the more controversial subjects in the social sciences, especially in criminal justice and criminology. Over the last decade or so, the United States has experienced a significant decline in the number of death sentences and executions. Since 2007, eight states have abolished capital punishment, bringing the total number of states without the death penalty to 19, plus the District of Columbia, and more are likely to follow suit in the near future (Nebraska reinstated its death penalty in 2016). Worldwide, 70 percent of countries have abolished capital punishment in law or in practice. The current trend suggests the eventual demise of capital punishment in all but a few recalcitrant states and countries. Within this context, a fresh look at capital punishment in the United States and worldwide is warranted.

The *Routledge Handbook on Capital Punishment* comprehensively examines the topic of capital punishment from a wide variety of perspectives. A thoughtful introductory chapter from experts Bohm and Lee presents a contextual framework for the subject matter, and chapters present state-of-the-art analyses of a range of aspects of capital punishment, grouped into five sections: (1) Capital Punishment: History, Opinion, and Culture; (2) Capital Punishment: Rationales and Religious Views; (3) Capital Punishment and Constitutional Issues; (4) The Death Penalty's Administration; and (5) The Death Penalty's Consequences.

This is a key collection for students taking courses in prisons, penology, criminal justice, criminology, and related subjects, and is also an essential reference for academics and practitioners working in prison service or in related agencies.

Robert M. Bohm, Ph.D., is Professor Emeritus of Criminal Justice at the University of Central Florida. He has published numerous books, book chapters, and journal articles in the areas of criminal justice and criminology. His books on capital punishment include *DEATHQUEST: An Introduction to the Theory and Practice of Capital Punishment in the United States, 5th ed.* (2017); *America's Experiment with Capital Punishment: Reflections on the Past, Present, and Future of the Ultimate Sanction, 3rd ed.* (with James R. Acker and Charles S. Lanier, 2014); *Capital Punishment's Collateral Damage* (2013); *The Past as Prologue: The Supreme Court's Pre-Modern Jurisprudence and Its Influence on the Supreme Court's Modern Death Penalty Decisions* (2012); *Ultimate Sanction: Understanding the Death Penalty Through Its Many Voices and Many Sides* (2010); *The Death Penalty Today* (2008); and *The Death Penalty in America: Current Research* (1991). Professor Bohm is a Fellow of the Academy of Criminal Justice Sciences (1999), and he previously served as the organization's president (1992–1993). He also is the recipient of the Academy's Founder's Award (2001) and Bruce Smith Sr. Award (2008).

Gavin Lee, Ph.D., is an Assistant Professor of Criminology at the University of West Georgia. His research interests include the death penalty, serial murder, and criminological theory. His work has been published in the *American Journal of Criminal Justice*; the *International Journal of Crime, Criminal Justice and Law*; and the *Southwestern Journal of Criminology*; and he has written several chapters in encyclopedia and edited works.

ROUTLEDGE HANDBOOK ON CAPITAL PUNISHMENT

Edited by Robert M. Bohm and Gavin Lee

LONDON AND NEW YORK

First published 2018
by Routledge

2 Park Square, Milton Park, Abingdon, Oxfordshire OX14 4RN
52 Vanderbilt Avenue, New York, NY 10017

Routledge is an imprint of the Taylor & Francis Group, an informa business

First issued in paperback 2018

Library of Congress Cataloging-in-Publication Data
Names: Bohm, Robert M., editor. | Lee, Gavin, 1970– editor.
Title: Routledge handbook on capital punishment /
[edited by] Robert M. Bohm and Gavin Lee.
Description: 1 Edition. | New York : Routledge, 2018. | Includes index.
Identifiers: LCCN 2017028733 | ISBN 9781138651579 (hardback) |
ISBN 9781315624723 (ebook)
Subjects: LCSH: Capital punishment—United States.
Classification: LCC HV8699.U5 R68 2018 | DDC 364.660973—dc23
LC record available at https://lccn.loc.gov/2017028733

ISBN: 978-1-138-65157-9 (hbk)
ISBN: 978-0-367-19937-1 (pbk)

Typeset in Bembo
by Apex CoVantage, LLC

This book is dedicated to the three great B's of death penalty scholarship: Hugo Adam Bedau (1926–2012), William J. Bowers (1935–2017), and David C. Baldus (1935–2011). Their immense contributions to death penalty research will forever serve as inspiration and guidance to all those who attempt to follow in their footsteps.

CONTENTS

Contents

CONTRIBUTOR BIOS

Sanaz Alasti is Associate Professor of Criminal Justice and Director of the Center for Death Penalty Studies at Lamar University: Texas State University. Alasti has completed her postdoctoral research at Harvard law school, and she is the author of seven books.

Maya Pagni Barak is an Assistant Professor of Criminology and Criminal Justice at the University of Michigan–Dearborn. She holds a Ph.D. in Justice, Law and Criminology from American University (2016). Her research brings together the areas of law, capital punishment, deviance, and immigration utilizing interdisciplinary approaches that span the fields of Criminology and Criminal Justice, Law and Society, and Anthropology. Prior to completing her Ph.D., she spent several years as a community organizer and continues to volunteer with and support immigrant justice and legal aid organizations.

Katherine J. Bennett earned her Ph.D. in Criminal Justice from Sam Houston State University, Huntsville, Texas in 1996. She is a full professor in the Department of Criminal Justice, Social, and Political Science at Armstrong State University in Savannah, Georgia. Research in legal areas, in addition to death penalty issues and juvenile life without parole analyses, include constitutional challenges related to juvenile curfews, cross gender searches of female inmates, and closed circuit testimony of child victims and witnesses. Other research and publications include measuring faculty attitudes toward guns on campus, citizen satisfaction survey research, job satisfaction among correctional executives, reintegrative shaming theory, and labeling and symbolic interactionism.

John D. Bessler teaches at the University of Baltimore School of Law and at the Georgetown University Law Center. He is the author of several books on capital punishment, including *Death in the Dark: Midnight Executions in America* (1997), *Cruel and Unusual: The American Death Penalty and the Founders' Eighth Amendment* (2012), and *The Death Penalty as Torture: From the Dark Ages to Abolition* (2017). He is also the editor of Justice Stephen Breyer's *Against the Death Penalty* (2016). His prior book, *The Birth of American Law: An Italian Philosopher and the American Revolution* (2014) was the recipient of the Scribes Book Award, a national award given out since 1961 for "the best work of legal scholarship published during the previous year." He has a B.A. in political science from the University of Minnesota, a J.D. from Indiana University–Bloomington, an M.F.A. degree from Hamline University, and a master's degree in international human rights law from Oxford University.

Kristie R. Blevins is a Professor in the School of Justice Studies at Eastern Kentucky University. She received her Ph.D. in Criminal Justice from the University of Cincinnati. Her research interests include corrections, crime prevention, wildlife crime, and the occupational reactions of criminal justice employees.

Eric Bronson is Associate Professor and Director of Criminal Justice program at Texas State University System, specializing in Corrections.

Kyle A. Burgason is an Assistant Professor of Criminal Justice Studies in the Department of Sociology at Iowa State University. His research interests include policing, ethics in criminal justice, race and crime, criminological theory, structural and cultural context of violent crime and victimization, capital punishment, and optimal foraging theory's applications to crime.

Cathleen Burnett is Professor Emerita at the University of Missouri Kansas City, having taught criminal justice and sociology for 34 years. Her numerous publications include *Wrongful Death Sentences: Rethinking Justice in Capital Cases* (2010), *The Failed Failsafe: The Politics of Executive Clemency, Texas Journal of Civil Rights and Civil Liberties,* (2003); and *Justice Denied: Clemency Appeals in Death Penalty Cases* (2002). She is a founding member of the Kansas City chapter of Missourians for Alternatives to the Death Penalty [MADP] and serves as on the statewide Board of Directors of MADP. In 1996, Dr. Burnett witnessed the Missouri execution of Jeff Sloan, CP #55, a person to whom she had been writing for a year and a half.

Leah Butler is pursuing a doctoral degree in Criminal Justice from the University of Cincinnati. She obtained a master's degree in Sociology from Ohio University in 2016 and bachelor's degrees in Sociology-Criminology and English from Ohio University in 2014. Her research interests include corrections, sexual victimization, and intimate partner violence.

John K. Cochran is Professor of Criminology at the University of South Florida. Professor Cochran earned his Ph.D. in Sociology at the University of Florida (1987). He has over 100 peer reviewed manuscripts, most of which involve tests of micro-social theories of criminal behavior and macro-social theories of crime and crime control. His current research interests involve tests of micro-social theories of criminal behavior. He is also continuing his work on issues associated with the death penalty.

Mark Costanzo is a professor of psychology at Claremont McKenna College and a member of the plenary faculty at Claremont Graduate University. He has published research on a variety of law-related topics, including police interrogations, false confessions, jury decision making, sexual harassment, attorney argumentation, alternative dispute resolution, and the death penalty. Professor Costanzo is author of the books *Forensic and Legal Psychology* (with Dan Krauss), *Just Revenge: Costs and Consequences of the Death Penalty*, and *Psychology Applied to Law*. He has coedited four books, including *Expert Psychological Testimony for the Courts* and *Violence and the Law*. Professor Costanzo has served as a consultant for more than 150 criminal cases and has provided expert testimony in state, federal, military, and juvenile courts. He has received outstanding teaching and mentoring awards from the American Psychology-Law Society, the Society for the Psychological Study of Social Issues, the Western Psychological Association, and the Society for the Teaching of Psychology.

Zoey Costanzo is a student at Cornell University majoring in Psychology and minoring in Law & Society. She is a research assistant in the Behavioral Analysis of Beginning Years (BABY) Lab and serves on the committee for sexual consent education. Her research interests include interviewing techniques for child victims and judgment and decision making in legal contexts.

David Crawford is the Director of community Outreach and Education at Death Penalty Focus, a nonprofit organization that educates the public about capital punishment. He received his B.A. in History at UC Santa Barbara and his M.A. in U.S. History at San Francisco State University.

Francis T. Cullen is Distinguished Research Professor Emeritus and a Senior Research Associate in the School of Criminal Justice at the University of Cincinnati. His recent works include *Correctional Theory: Context and Consequences* (2nd ed.), *Environmental Corrections: A New Paradigm for Supervising Offenders in the Community*, and *Communities and Crime: An Enduring American Challenge*. His current research focuses on rehabilitation as a correctional policy and on the organization of criminological knowledge. He is a Past President of both the American Society of Criminology and the Academy of Criminal Justice Sciences.

Deborah W. Denno, Ph.D., J.D., is the Arthur A. McGivney Professor of Law and Founding Director of the Neuroscience and Law Center at Fordham University School of Law. She has been researching and writing about execution methods for over 25 years. Seven different articles of Professor Denno's have been cited by the United States Supreme Court, some multiple times, and primarily in conjunction with her scholarship on lethal injection. In *Arthur v. Dunn*, No. 16-602 (U.S. Feb. 21, 2017) and in *Glossip v. Gross*, 135 S. Ct. 2726 (2015), Justice Sotomayor's dissent cited two different articles by Professor Denno. Likewise, in *Baze v. Rees*, 128 S. Ct. 1520 (2008), the court's first execution methods decision, Chief Justice Roberts' plurality opinion and the concurring opinions of Justices Alito, Stevens, and Breyer together cited four different articles by Professor Denno. One of Professor Denno's cited articles was *Lethal Injection Chaos Post-*Baze (*Georgetown Law Journal* (2014)), in which Professor Denno reported her unprecedented study of over 300 cases citing *Baze* and analyzed states' rapidly-changing lethal injection drug protocols. One of Professor Denno's latest articles (in 2016) advocates the use of the firing squad as an alternative method of execution in light of the *Glossip* court's mandate concerning execution method substitutes for lethal injection. In 2016, the Fordham Student Bar Association named Professor Denno Teacher of the Year. In 2007, the *National Law Journal* selected Professor Denno as one of its "Fifty Most Influential Women Lawyers in America."

Edna Erez is Professor of Criminology, Law, and Justice at the University of Illinois at Chicago. She has a law degree (LL.B) from the Hebrew University of Jerusalem and M.A. and Ph.D. in Criminology/Sociology from the University of Pennsylvania. Her areas of interest are criminology/ victimology and law and society/legal studies, and her research includes victims in justice proceedings, violence against women, and transnational crimes. Professor Erez has received over $2 million in research grants from state and federal agencies in the U.S. and overseas. Her publication record includes over 100 scholarly articles, book chapters, and research reports. She currently serves as Associate Editor of *Victims and Violence*, and Co-Editor of *International Review of Victimology*.

Douglas N. Evans is an Associate Professor of Criminal Justice at Mercy College and a Project Director at the Research and Evaluation Center, John Jay College of Criminal Justice. His research focuses on criminal stigmatization, barriers to reentry for the formerly incarcerated, the effects of incarceration on families, and education programs in prisons. He received his Ph.D. in Criminal Justice from Indiana University.

Diana Falco earned her Ph.D. in Criminology from Indiana University of Pennsylvania. She is currently a Senior Lecturer in the Department of Criminology & Criminal Justice at Niagara University. Her current research focuses on punitiveness, with an emphasis on public opinion for capital punishment, rehabilitation, and general views toward the punishment of offenders. She has published work on public support for the death penalty as well as on arbitrariness and the administration of the death penalty.

Wanda D. Foglia, J.D., Ph.D. is a Professor of Law and Justice Studies at Rowan University. She earned her J.D. and Ph.D. in Criminology from the University of Pennsylvania. She has published on deterrence and cognition and crime and, since becoming the coordinator for the Pennsylvania portion of the Capital Jury Project in 1996, her publications have been focused primarily on the death penalty. As a result of her death penalty research, Dr. Foglia has been asked to testify as an expert witness for the defense in over 30 capital cases in 17 states and in federal court about capital jury decision making.

Andrew Fulkerson, Ph.D., is the former Judge of the Greene County, Arkansas, District Court and deputy prosecuting attorney for the Second Judicial Circuit of Arkansas. He has also served as Special Justice of the Supreme Court of Arkansas. Fulkerson holds a B.A. and M.A. from Arkansas State University, a J.D. from the University of Arkansas, where he served as Associate Editor of the *Arkansas Law Review*, and a Ph.D. from the University of Portsmouth, U.K. He is a former member of the Arkansas Judicial Discipline and Disability Commission and past president of the Arkansas District Judges Council. Fulkerson now serves as professor of criminal justice for the Department of Criminal Justice and Sociology at Southeast Missouri State University.

O. Hayden Griffin, III, Ph.D., J.D. is an Assistant Professor in the Department of Justice Sciences at the University of Alabama at Birmingham. His research interests are drug policy, corrections, and law and society. He has published more than 20 peer-reviewed publications. His research has been published in *International Journal of Drug Policy*, *Journal of Research in Crime and Delinquency*, *Criminal Justice and Behavior*, and *Deviant Behavior*.

Catherine M. Grosso is an associate professor at the Michigan State University College of Law. Her interdisciplinary scholarship examines the role of race and other extralegal factors in criminal investigations, trials, and the administration of capital punishment. She teaches criminal procedure, capital punishment law, a seminar on criminal juries, and remedies. Her most recent work examines the persistent role of race in jury selection and in charging and sentencing decisions relating to capital punishment. Her ongoing National Science Foundation project with Professor Barbara O'Brien applies conversation analysis to assess ways in which race influences *voir dire* in capital cases. Professor Grosso is also the managing editor of the National Registry of Exonerations. Grosso received a bachelor's degree in International Studies with a Middle East concentration from Earlham College and a J.D. from University of Iowa College of Law.

Talia Roitberg Harmon obtained her Ph.D. from the School of Criminal Justice at the State University of New York at Albany. She is currently a full professor and chair of the Department of Criminal Justice and Criminology at Niagara University. Her major research focus currently is on the decline in death sentences and wrongful convictions in capital cases. She has published work on issues surrounding capital punishment including death qualification, capital commutations, and wrongful convictions in capital cases.

Robert Johnson is a professor of justice, law, and criminology at American University, editor and publisher of BleakHouse Publishing, and an award-winning author of books and articles on crime and punishment, including works of social science, law, poetry, and fiction. He has testified or provided expert affidavits in capital and other criminal cases in many venues, including U.S. state and federal courts, the U.S. Congress, and the European Commission of Human Rights. He is best known for his book, *Death Work: A Study of the Modern Execution Process*, which won the Outstanding Book Award of the Academy of Criminal Justice Sciences. Johnson is a Distinguished Alumnus of the Nelson A. Rockefeller College of Public Affairs and Policy, University at Albany, State University of New York.

George F. Kain, Ph.D., is a professor and chairman of the Division of Justice and Law Administration at Western CT State University, where he has taught for over 32 years. He is also a police commissioner for the Town of Ridgefield, CT, a position he has held for over 17 years. He holds a Ph.D. in criminal justice from the City University of New York, John Jay College of Criminal Justice. He has served as an adult probation officer for the state of Connecticut and a Connecticut Judicial Branch Administrator prior to beginning his full-time teaching career. He is the recipient of the 2010 Walt Everett Humanitarian Award, given by the Connecticut Network to Abolish the Death Penalty in Hartford, CT. For the last five years in the month of November, he has presented lectures in Italy, at an annual event titled "A World Without the Death Penalty: No Justice Without Life," sponsored by the Community of Sant' Egidio. He has also presented in Japan and in the Philippines, as well as in Oslo, Norway, at the *World Congress Against the Death Penalty* in 2016. He has testified before numerous state legislatures considering abolition of the death penalty for the last seven years, primarily in the role of a law enforcement officer who once supported capital punishment and who now fully supports abolition. He has recently begun a volunteer ministry with inmates at the Federal Correctional Institution in Danbury, CT.

Jeffrey L. Kirchmeier is Professor of Law at the City University of New York School of Law. He received his J.D. from the Case Western Reserve University School of Law in 1989 and his B.A. from Case Western Reserve University in 1984.

Kaleigh B. Laird is pursuing a Master of Science in Criminal Justice with a concentration in Theory and Research at the University of North Texas. She holds a Bachelor of Arts in Criminal Justice from the University of Southern Mississippi. Her research interests include capital punishment, jury behavior, and prisoner reentry.

Kathy Laster, S.J.D. (Columbia), M.A., LL.B. (University of Melbourne), is the Director of the Sir Zelman Cowen Centre at Victoria University in Melbourne, Australia. The Sir Zelman Cowen Centre undertakes projects in 'law and cultural diversity'. Laster has held senior academic positions in a number of Australian universities and has also served in leadership roles in the public, philanthropic, and government sectors. A distinguished academic, she has published widely in criminology and legal history (including the operation of the death penalty in Australia) as well as gender and multiculturalism and the law.

Dennis R. Longmire, Ph.D., has been a faculty member at the College of Criminal Justice since 1984 and is currently serving as its Director of Practice Development. His academic specialties include the death penalty, public perceptions of crime, criminality, and criminal justice, the classification of offenders, and criminological theory. He has published in numerous scholarly journals including *Criminology, Justice Quarterly, Crime and Delinquency*, and *Criminal Justice and Behavior*. He has also authored numerous publications and special reports that have helped inform criminal justice policy makers and legislators about key crime-related issues. Dr. Longmire recently served on the Board of Directors of the *Texas After Violence Project* (www.**texasafterviolence**.org) and was a Distinguished Lecturer at Eastern Kentucky University in 2003–04.

Stacy L. Mallicoat, Ph.D., is a Professor of Criminal Justice and Chair of the Division of Politics, Administration and Justice at California State University, Fullerton. Her research interests include issues of feminist criminology, criminal justice policy, and capital punishment. She is the author of several textbooks, including *Crime and Criminal Justice: Concepts and Controversies*. Her research has appeared journals such as Feminist Criminology, American Journal of Criminal Justice, and various edited volumes.

Kevin I. Minor is Foundation Professor of Justice Studies at Eastern Kentucky University. Over the last three decades, he has published extensively on the subjects of adult corrections and juvenile justice. Besides a focus on capital and other extremist punishments in the United States, his current scholarly interests include theoretical perspectives on crime and punishment as well as correctional law and staff issues.

Stephanie Mizrahi, Ph.D., is an Associate Professor of Criminal Justice at California State University, Sacramento. She holds a J.D. from McGeorge School of Law and an M.A. and Ph.D. from Washington State University. She teaches in the area of law, terrorism, homeland security, and emergency management. Her research and writing interests center around criminal procedure, terrorism, and homeland security policy. She is also proudly involved with the Academy of Criminal Sciences and the Western Association of Criminal Justice. She is the co-author of *Terrorism and Homeland Security: A Text-Reader*, with Dr. Timothy Capron.

Etta Morgan is Department Chair and Associate Professor of the Department of Criminal Justice and Sociology at Jackson State University. Morgan has served on the Undergraduate Curriculum Committee and the Distance Education Implementation Team, and is a member of the City of Jackson Re-Entry Task Force and Mission Mississippi.

Stacy K. Parker is Associate Professor of Criminal Justice at Muskingum University in Ohio. She earned her law degree from the West Virginia University College of Law in 1997 and spent most of her legal career working prosecutors' offices in Kanawha County and Jackson County, West Virginia, and Franklin County, Ohio. After nearly a decade practicing law, she returned to school and completed her Master of Science in Criminal Justice at the University of Cincinnati in 2007. Professor Parker's main area of study is the death penalty. She has presented the results of several of her studies at national conferences and has a few forthcoming publications. She is currently a board member of Ohioans to Stop Executions.

Lynn Pazzani is an Assistant Professor of Criminology at the University of West Georgia. Her research and teaching interests include gender, victimization, the death penalty, and sexual assault. She has published in *Violence Against Women* and has two articles on the death penalty in *American Journal of Criminal Justice*; one with Kyle A. Burgason and the other with Gavin Lee and Robert Bohm. She also recently coauthored *Sex Offenders: Crimes and Processing in the Criminal Justice System*.

Dale Recinella, J.D., M.T.S., (generally known as "Brother Dale" by the inmates he serves) has been involved for over 20 years in prison ministry as a chaplain handling virtually every population and every category of offenders. He has done cell-front ministry in long-term solitary confinement and on death row, as well as conducting deathwatch spiritual counseling in Florida's death house. He still ministers on death row and has witnessed numerous executions of those under his spiritual care over many years. He is a certified Catholic Correctional Chaplain serving under the Bishop of St. Augustine and the Pastor of St. Mary Mother of Mercy Parish in Macclenny, Florida. Chaplain Recinella is a licensed Florida lawyer and a graduate of the University of Notre Dame Law school and had a successful career in the financial industry before leaving to do prison ministry full time. He holds a Master's in Theological Studies in Catholic Pastoral Theology from Ave Maria University, Naples, Florida. His ministry work has received numerous recognitions, including the Humanitarian Award from the Franciscan Alumni Association and, at the request of the Catholic Bishops of Florida, the 2016 Holy Cross *Pro Ecclesia et Pontifice*, the highest papal honor a layperson can receive in the Catholic Church. He is a world-renowned author and presenter, whose latest manuscript, *When We Visit Jesus in Prison* (2016), was awarded first place in the category of "Resources for Ministry" by the Association of Catholic Publishers Awards. His first scholarly manuscript, *The Biblical Truth About America's Death Penalty* (2004), has been regarded as the "bible" among scholars who have studied religion and capital punishment.

Thomas J. Reidy, Ph.D., ABPP is a clinical and forensic psychologist in Monterey, California. He is Board Certified in Forensic Psychology by the American Board of Forensic Psychology and is a Fellow of the American Academy of Forensic Psychology. Dr. Reidy provides forensic psychological assessments and consultation for the military services, law enforcement agencies, and federal and state courts on a wide array of topics, primarily involving risk assessment, violence, and homicide. His numerous professional publications are related to criminal behavior and risk assessment for prison violence, particularly related to capital homicide offenders. He received the 1993 Nelson Butters Award from the National Academy of Neuropsychology for clinical research contributions to the field.

Matthew Robinson is Professor of Government and Justice Studies at Appalachian State University in Boone, North Carolina. He teaches and does research in the areas of criminological theory, crime prevention, social justice, capital punishment, duty control policy, and media studies. Robinson is the author of 18 books in the field and is Past President of the Southern Criminal Justice Association and Past President of the North Carolina Criminal Justice Association

Marla Sandys, Ph.D., is Associate Professor of Criminal Justice at Indiana University–Bloomington. She earned her doctorate in social psychology from the University of Kentucky. She is one of the original co-investigators of the Capital Jury Project, overseeing the Project in Kentucky (phase I of the Project) and Indiana (phase III of the Project). She has published on attitudes toward capital punishment, death qualification issues, jurors' responses to mitigation in capital cases, and capital juror decision making. Her current work focuses on support for the death penalty for persons who are severely mentally ill.

Jonathan R. Sorensen, Ph.D., is a Professor of Criminal Justice at East Carolina University. He also works as a trial consultant and expert witness. His research focuses on prison violence and capital punishment.

Carol S. Steiker is the Henry J. Friendly Professor of Law and Faculty Co-Director of the Criminal Justice Policy Program at Harvard Law School. She specializes in the broad field of criminal justice, where her work ranges from substantive criminal law to criminal procedure to institutional design, with a special focus on issues related to capital punishment. Recent publications address topics such as the relationship of criminal justice scholarship to law reform, the role of mercy in the institutions of criminal justice, and the likelihood of nationwide abolition of capital punishment. Her most recent book, *Courting Death: The Supreme Court and Capital Punishment,* co-authored with her brother Jordan Steiker of the University of Texas School of Law, was published by Harvard University Press in November 2016. Professor Steiker is a graduate of Harvard Law School, where she served as president of the *Harvard Law Review,* the second woman to hold that position in its then 99-year history. After clerking for Judge J. Skelly Wright of the D.C. Circuit Court of Appeals and Justice Thurgood Marshall of the U.S. Supreme Court, she worked as a staff attorney for the Public Defender Service for the District of Columbia, where she represented indigent defendants at all stages of the criminal process. In addition to her scholarly work, Professor Steiker has worked on pro bono litigation projects on behalf of indigent criminal defendants, including death penalty cases in the U.S. Supreme Court. She also has served as a consultant and expert witness on issues of criminal justice for nonprofit organizations and has testified before Congress and state legislatures.

Jordan M. Steiker is the Judge Robert M. Parker Chair in Law and Director of the Capital Punishment Center at the University of Texas School of Law. He served as a law clerk for the Honorable Louis Pollak, U.S. District Court (Eastern District of Pennsylvania) and Justice Thurgood Marshall of the United States Supreme Court. He has taught constitutional law, criminal law, and death penalty law at the University of Texas since 1990. His work focuses primarily on the administration of capital punishment in the United States, and he has written extensively on constitutional law, federal habeas corpus, and the death penalty. Professor Steiker has testified before state legislative committees addressing death penalty issues in Texas, including state habeas reform, clemency procedures, sentencing options in capital cases, and the availability of the death penalty for juveniles and persons with intellectual disabilities. He co-authored the report (with Carol Steiker) that led the American Law Institute to withdraw the death penalty provision from the Model Penal Code. Professor Steiker has also litigated extensively on behalf of indigent death-sentenced inmates in state and federal court, including in the U.S. Supreme Court.

H. Chris Tecklenburg is an assistant professor of political science at Armstrong State University in Savannah, Georgia. Chris earned a Bachelor of Arts degree in political science in 2002 and a Juris Doctorate degree from the University of South Carolina in 2005. After a brief two year career practicing law in Charleston, South Carolina, he attended the University of Florida, earning a master's degree in political science in 2010 and a Ph.D. in political science in 2013. His research interests, in addition to death penalty issues, include constitutional issues involving separation of powers, such as court curbing and jurisdiction stripping legislation, as well as examining congressional motivations behind judicial expansion.

Angela J. Thielo received her Ph.D. from the University of Cincinnati and is currently an Assistant Professor of Criminal Justice at the University of Louisville. Her main research interest is in correctional policy and practice. She has published works on the connection of public attitudes to public policy. Recently, she conducted a national survey of public support for offender rehabilitation and redemption.

Peggy M. Tobolowsky is a Professor of Criminal Justice at the University of North Texas. She is the author of the book, *Excluding Intellectually Disabled Offenders from Execution*, and several articles addressing issues concerning capital offenders' intellectual disability and execution competency. She received her J.D. degree from George Washington University in 1977.

Adam Trahan is an Associate Professor in the Department of Criminal Justice at the University of North Texas. He received his Ph.D. in Criminal Justice from Indiana University. His research interests include capital punishment, jury behavior, and public opinion.

James D. Unnever (Ph.D., Duke University) is a Professor of Criminology at the University of South Florida Sarasota-Manatee. Dr. Unnever was the Recipient of the Donal A.J. MacNamara Award by the Academy of Criminal Justice Sciences in 2009 for the best article published that year. The author of over 50 publications appearing in such journals as *Social Forces*, *Criminology*, *Social Problems*, *Journal of Research in Crime and Delinquency*, *Race and Justice*, and *Justice Quarterly*, his areas of expertise include race, racism, and crime, public opinion about crime-related issues including the death penalty, the testing of theories of crime, and school bullying. Among his most recent research is his book with Shaun Gabbidon, *A Theory of African American Offending: Race, Racism, and Crime*.

Alexander H. Updegrove is a doctoral student in the Criminal Justice and Criminology department at Sam Houston State University. His research focuses on vulnerable populations, including those facing the death penalty and the sexually exploited. His recent works have appeared in *Crime & Delinquency* and the *Journal of Criminal Justice and Law.*

Margaret Vandiver, Ph.D., is the author of *Lethal Punishment: Lynchings and Legal Executions in the South* and co-editor of *Tennessee's New Abolitionists,* in addition to numerous articles. Her main area of research interest is state and collective violence, ranging from the use of the death penalty in America to contemporary instances of genocide. In retirement, she intends to continue research on historical homicides and death penalty cases.

Anthony G. Vito is an Assistant Professor in the Department of Criminology at the University of West Georgia. He received his Ph.D. in Justice Administration in 2015 from the University of Louisville. His research areas include policing, drug use, capital punishment, race and crime, and the use of advanced statistics. His research has been published in multiple journals including *Policing: An International Journal of Police Strategies & Management,* the *American Journal of Criminal Justice,* and *Deviant Behavior.* He recently published an academic press book with Routledge (2016), *Racial Profiling: Using Propensity Score Matching to Examine Focal Concerns Theory.*

Gennaro F. Vito is a Professor and Chair in the Department of Criminal Justice at the University of Louisville. He also serves as a faculty member in the Administrative Officer's Course at the Southern Police Institute. He holds a Ph.D. in Public Administration from The Ohio State University. Active in professional organizations, he is a past President and Fellow of the Academy of Criminal Justice Sciences and recipient of its Bruce Smith Award. He has published on such topics as capital sentencing, police consolidation, police traffic stops, policing strategies for drug problems in public housing, attitudes toward capital punishment, and the effectiveness of criminal justice programs, such as drug elimination programs, drug courts, and drug testing of probationers and parolees. He is the co-author of nine textbooks in criminal justice and criminology including *Criminology: Theory, Research and Practice.*

Brenda L. Vogel earned her Ph.D. in Social Ecology with an emphasis is Criminology, Law, and Society in 1996 from University of California–Irvine. She currently serves as the Director of the School of Criminology, Criminal Justice, and Emergency Management at California State University, Long Beach. Her areas of research interest include public perceptions of law enforcement, criminological theory, and the death penalty. She has co-authored one book, *A Primer on Crime and Delinquency Theory,* with Robert Bohm, and has written numerous articles appearing in several journals including *Justice Quarterly, The Journal of Criminal Justice,* and the *Journal of Applied Psychology in Criminal Justice.*

Scott Vollum is Department Head and Associate Professor in The Department of Anthropology, Sociology & Criminology at the University of Minnesota, Duluth. At this time, his primary areas of academic interest and research are violence, the death penalty, restorative justice, media and crime, and moral disengagement. He is currently working on a variety of research projects including an evaluation of a restorative justice program for domestic violence offenders, an examination of death penalty attitudes and the impact of wrongful convictions in capital cases, and a qualitative study of people who kill. He is author of the book *Last Words and The Death Penalty: Voices of the Condemned and Their Co-Victims* and co-author of the book *The Death Penalty: Constitutional Issues, Commentaries and Case Briefs.* His previous research has been published in a variety of scholarly journals, his most recent ("Gender Politics and The Walking Dead: Gendered Violence and the Reestablishment of Patriarchy") in the journal *Feminist Criminology.* He lives in Duluth, MN, with his son Kai and their dogs Milo and Cooper.

Gordon P. Waldo, Ph.D., is a Professor Emeritus of the College of Criminology and Criminal Justice at Florida State University. He received his B.A. from the University of North Carolina at Chapel Hill and his M.A. and Ph.D. from The Ohio State University. He was on the faculty of the University of Southern California before coming to Florida State in 1968. Dr. Waldo's experience covers a wide range of activities related to academic criminology and the criminal justice system. This includes more than 50 years of university teaching, administration, and research as well as three years of practical experience working in the juvenile and adult criminal justice field. He has written more than 200 articles, books, professional papers, and grant reports, has served on the editorial boards of several journals, and has served as Director of the Florida State University Southeastern Correctional and Criminological Research Center (SCCRC), as well as several other criminology programs. He has served on or chaired several state and national task forces in the criminal justice area.

Tobias Winright, Ph.D., University of Notre Dame, is the Mäder Endowed Associate Professor of Health Care Ethics and an Associate Professor of Theological Ethics at Saint Louis University. Previously he was a correctional officer, a reserve police officer, and a police ethics instructor. His research focuses on bioethics, war and peace ethics, ecological ethics, and criminal justice ethics. From 2012 to 2017 he was co-editor of the *Journal of the Society of Christian Ethics*.

Vanessa Woodward Griffin is an Assistant Professor in the Department of Criminology at the University of West Georgia. Her research interests include sexual violence, campus crime, and corrections. Her work has been published in *Criminal Justice Review*, *Deviant Behavior*, and *Journal of Criminal Justice Education*.

INTRODUCTION

Robert M. Bohm and Gavin Lee

Introduction

The 37 chapters in this handbook present the latest research and thinking about capital punishment, or the death penalty, in the United States. The book is necessary because many people passionately support capital punishment even though they know little about it. Other people believe their understanding about capital punishment is informed, without knowing or believing that the information on which they rely is wrong; in short, they are misinformed. Thus, their death penalty opinions are based on erroneous beliefs about the sanction. This book aims to provide these people, and all those interested in the subject, with a current and comprehensive compendium of valid death penalty knowledge with the hope that their death penalty opinions will become informed by accurate and evidence-based information. Surely, the state's intentional taking of a human life should be based on an accurately informed understanding of the process by which those lives are taken, and its ramifications.

A citizenry accurately informed about the death penalty is important for a second reason. If a majority of citizens were opposed to the death penalty, then the U.S. Supreme Court might abolish it, basing such a decision on the "evolving standards of decency that mark the progress of a maturing society" doctrine (*Trop v. Dulles* 356 U.S. 86, 1958; *Weems v. United States* 217 U.S. 349, 1910). Death penalty opinion has been used by both state supreme courts and the U.S. Supreme Court as a measure of "evolving standards of decency" regarding what constitutes "cruel and unusual punishment" in state constitutions and under the Eighth Amendment of the U.S. Constitution. Decline in death penalty support was cited as such a measure in *Furman v. Georgia*, the 1972 landmark decision that abolished capital punishment in the United States for the first and only time. According to political science professor Frank Baumgartner and his colleagues, "the majority opinion in each major [U.S. Supreme Court] death penalty decision in the last century cited polling data by Gallup or other major survey houses in support of the ruling, whether for or against capital punishment" (Baumgartner, DeBoef, & Boydstun, 2008, p. 169).

If the U.S. Supreme Court were to abolish capital punishment, then the United States would no longer be a statistical outlier in this area among the world's nations. As of January 1, 2016, 102 countries in the world had abolished the death penalty for all crimes—the first time that a majority of the world's 196 countries are completely abolitionist (Amnesty International, 2016). In addition to the 102 countries that are totally abolitionist, another six countries are abolitionist for ordinary crimes only (Amnesty International, 2016). Those six countries still allow the death penalty for exceptional crimes, such as those committed under military law. Another 32 countries are abolitionist in practice

(Amnesty International, 2016). These countries "have not executed anyone during the last ten years and are believed to have a policy or established practice of not carrying out executions" (Amnesty International, 2016). In total, 140 countries, or more than 70% of all countries in the world, now are abolitionist either in law or practice. Only 58 countries retain the death penalty and use it at least occasionally (Amnesty International, 2016).

Of the 58 retentionist countries—nearly 30% of the world's countries—84% of them are located in Africa, the Middle East, the Caribbean, and South or Southeast Asia (Amnesty International, 2016). Few of them, however, regularly execute anyone. An examination of worldwide execution trends from 2005 through 2014 found that the bulk of executions during this period were conducted in only a handful of the same countries (see Bohm, 2017, pp. 178–179). Outside of the Middle East (and the countries of Iran, Saudi Arabia, Iraq, Pakistan, and Yemen), only four other countries have ranked in the top five executing countries from 2005 through 2014: China, North Korea, Sudan, and the United States.

Although the number of death sentences and executions in the United States has been declining dramatically in recent years, the United States remains notable for being the only Western country to use capital punishment more than occasionally. A U.S. citizenry knowledgeable about capital punishment may be the impetus to end the practice, so the United States could join our peer nations in its condemnation. Clearly, capital punishment is not a necessary component of a nation's criminal justice process and, one day, may become merely a relic of a more barbaric past.

Our profound thanks to the numerous authors who contributed their time and effort to this project and to the talented staff at Routledge who guided us along the way. Without their help this *Handbook on Capital Punishment* would not have been possible.

References

Amnesty International. (2016). *Death sentences and executions 2015*. Retrieved September 5, 2016 from www.amnesty.org/en/latest/research/2016/04/death-sentences-executions-2015/

Baumgartner, F. R., DeBoef, S. L., & Boydstun, A. E. (2008). *The decline of the death penalty and the discovery of innocence*. New York: Cambridge University Press.

Bohm, R. M. (2017). *DeathQuest: An introduction to the theory and practice of the death penalty in the United States* (5th ed.). New York: Routledge.

PART 1

Capital Punishment: History, Opinion, and Culture

A. History

1

THE AMERICAN DEATH PENALTY

A Short (But Long) History

John D. Bessler

An Indigenous (But Imported) Punishment

American executions, in one form or another, predate colonial times. In Native American cultures, tribal customs—as law professor Jeffrey Kirchmeier points out—"allowed for something comparable to the death penalty" (Kirchmeier, 2015, p. 45). Although Indian tribes had no formalized mechanisms, jails, or gallows to arrest, confine, try and convict, or punish murderers, by custom revenge belonged to the male relatives of a murdered victim. "Those kin," one historian explains, "lost face as cowards, and suffered enduring anxiety, if they failed to secure blood revenge, for no spirit of the murdered could rest or give his (or her) kin peace until avenged." "Ideally," that historian, Alan Taylor, notes, "the vengeful tracked down and dispatched the actual killer, who might flee but was expected to submit if found." For example, one missionary, David McClure, reported seeing "a confronted Iroquois murderer calmly sit down to sing his death song while the avenger smoked a pipe for twenty minutes before plunging a tomahawk into the singer's skull." If the actual killer could not be located, one of the killer's relatives might be singled out for revenge, sparking a blood feud between the affected families that tribal leaders felt compelled to address. "Rather than execute a murderer," Taylor explains, "the chiefs sought to restore harmony by persuading the kin of the dead to accept presents from the kin of the killer." This ancient practice—known as "covering the grave"—took place in public ceremonies and effectively forfeited the kin's right to seek revenge (Taylor, 2006, pp. 29–31, 139, 195, 260, 264, 298, 327).[1]

Native Americans despised colonial laws, with one eighteenth-century colonist, Guy Johnson, emphasizing that Indians were "universally averse to our modes of Capital punishment" (Taylor, 2006, p. 30). "Historically," another source explains, "Native American tribal members were governed more by societal taboos and traditions than by rules and laws" (Miller, 2012, p. 1198). In ancient Hawaii, for example, the *kapu* system cemented the social structure, with Hawaiians who offended the social order swiftly put to death for violating sacred prohibitions. As historian Joseph Mullins has explained of this "taboo" system: "Criminals and violators of *kapu* were punished by strangulation or clubbing. Sometimes abuses of power took place when an arrogant chief ordered the execution of a commoner who displeased him in some way" (Mullins, 1978, p. 5). Human sacrifices, another historian of Hawaii notes, "were often selected from *kauw* (outcast class), whose lives were destined to end as offerings for the gods" (Stone, 2015, p. 18). In *Captive Paradise: A History of Hawaii*, author James Haley observes: "The usual mode of dispatch was strangulation, often after the victim was tied to a tree." Other Hawaiians, he notes, were thrown from cliffs or burned for violating a *kapu* (Haley, 2014, pp. 18, 25, 36, 311).

Archaeological and other historical evidence confirms that Native Americans were frequently killed or put to death even before Europeans reached the New World. One analysis of 900 skeletons of Native Americans, all of whom died before the arrival of Columbus in 1492, revealed that 13.4% of hunter-gatherers (their skeletal remains distributed from South America to southern Canada) showed signs of violent trauma (Pinker, 2011, p. 51).[2] "At the Cahokia mound (east of St. Louis, Mo.)," one criminology text notes, "a male body, which the evidence indicates to have been a sacrifice (for wrongdoing?) among the American aborigines, was found face down as if he had struggled against being sacrificed" (Mueller and Adler, 1995, p. 68). In *Cahokia: Ancient America's Great City on the Mississippi*, anthropologist Timothy Pauketat—writing of the Native American city that flourished from around 1050 to 1400 AD—writes of what archaeologists discovered in burial mounds: "Many bodies buried together suggested to them planned killings, executions, or ceremonial sacrifices and a society characterized by inequality, power struggles, and social complexity." Among other things, the Cahokia site revealed scores of sacrificial victims, including bodies with severed arms and legs, eighteen bodies (many with fractured skulls) arranged in a circular pattern, and the skeleton of a woman whose arms and legs appear to have been bound (Pauketat, 2009, pp. 23, 27, 69–70, 102–103).

The archaeological evidence, despite the passage of time, is almost as clear as it is gruesome. At one Cahokia mound, dubbed Mound 72, it is believed many of the people buried there were ritualistically sacrificed, "probably to accompany one or more important individuals."[3] At that mound, archaeologists made this grisly discovery: "fifty-three sacrificed women, fifty-two of whom were young (most between the ages of fifteen and twenty-five)." "[I]t is likely," Pauketat writes, "they were poisoned or strangled or that their throats had been slit." In a forensic report, bioarchaeologist Jerome Rose lays out what he found in sacrificial pit tombs: "Evidence of violence also distinguishes these burials from the other mass graves. Three individuals had been decapitated prior to being thrown into the pit. The heads were thrown in before the burials were covered." Of the skeletons found, Pauketat summarizes the archaeological findings:

> The toes of many of the bodies "were in contact with the southern wall," indicating that the people had been standing on the southern rim of the open pit, facing their executioners, awaiting the death blows that came in rapid succession. Most shocking of all, the phalanges, or finger bones, of the prone skeletons dug into the fine white sand, indicating that death had not been instantaneous for some.
>
> *(Pauketat, 2009, pp. 65, 69–77)*

Native Americans reportedly "executed enemies by torture (and killed suspected witches among their own people)," a form of capital punishment, though their preferred methods of execution differed from those employed by European colonists (Taylor, 2006, p. 31; Meggs, 2012, p. 11).[4] The word "capital" itself derives from the Latin *caput*, meaning "head," with beheading, throughout history, associated with capital punishment and other forms of violent retaliation or vengeance (Latzer and McCord, 2010, p. 1). Indeed, scalping—the taking of part of the human head as a token of a battle's victory—regularly happened on American soil centuries ago. Some Native American warriors took all of the upper head's skin, including the ears, while others took only the crown with the victim's hair. According to one historian:

> Although the morbid practice of scalping is much mentioned in modern literature, the Native American tribes didn't practice it as often as described until the arrival of the white man and the "competition" they introduced. Bounties were paid by the early Europeans for "dead Indians" and scalps were often produced as the proof of death.

"In some tribes, particularly among certain Plains groups," another writer emphasizes, "decapitation persisted, and a severed head was considered an even greater trophy than a scalp or scalp lock" (Axelrod, 2009, p. 96; Burch, 2004, p. 235).

Stereotypes aside about early Native American use of scalping in warfare, it was—as has been noted—actually *European* colonists who initially offered monetary rewards for the taking of Indian scalps, no doubt encouraging reciprocal tribal conduct. For instance, during Pennsylvania's 1756 war with the Delaware, Pennsylvania's governor offered "130 Pieces of Eight"—a type of Spanish coin— for the scalp of "every Male Indian Enemy" above the age of 12, and "50 Pieces of Eight" for the scalp of "every Indian Woman, produced as evidence of their being killed." Scalping proliferated as Europeans pushed their way westward, though its use in the Americas—at least to some degree—predated the arrival of European settlers. "[I]n 1535," one source notes, "an early explorer, Jacques Cartier, reportedly met a party of Iroquois who showed him five scalps stretched on hoops, taken from their enemies, the Micmac" (Martin, 1998, p. 58; Carpenter, 2012, p. 131). In the 1500s, other European explorers— Hernando de Soto and Tristan de Luna—also took notice of scalping (Axelrod, 2009, p. 96).

Of course, Native American cultures are not monolithic—and they never have been. "Before the European exploration and colonial conquest of North America," David Baker, a scholar of tribal executions, writes, "the indigenous population consisted of more than 700 separate cultural units with deep-rooted civilizations." Whatever the precise origins of scalping or beheading, what is crystal clear is that executions—whether on a tribal leader's orders or after cursory trials—were often used *by* and *against* native peoples. For instance, it is known that the Powhatan Indians of Virginia made use of executions, with executioners cutting off the men's hair and hanging it in front of tribal rulers' homes before offenders were bound or had their bones broken. While still alive, offenders would then be thrown onto fires to die in the flames. In other instances, Indians were clubbed to death for disobedience or their heads were laid on an "altar or sacrificing stone" before being smashed. While most deaths were relatively quick, "notorious" enemies or trespassers faced longer, more painful deaths, with war captives tortured until they died. As Helen Rountree, a professor of anthropology at Old Dominion University, writes: "The usual Powhatan practice was to build a fire and then strip the captive and tie him either to a tree or to stakes. The execution was then carried out either by the town's women or by a man appointed for the job." According to Rountree's account of these grisly affairs: "Using sharp mussel shells, the executioners gradually flayed and cut off the limbs of the victim, throwing the pieces into the fire before the victim's eyes. At length the victim was disemboweled, which killed him" (Rountree, 1989, pp. 84, 114–117).

Both Indians and white settlers employed executions to intimidate their enemies and to make examples of those who transgressed social customs, laws, or norms. "The first execution of an American Indian," David Baker explains of the first known use of capital punishment by a colonizing power, "took place when military authorities beheaded Nepauduck in Connecticut in October 1639 for the murder of Abraham Finch, a white man" (Baker, 2007, pp. 315, 317, 320). In *The Death Penalty: An American History*, UCLA law professor Stuart Banner specifically references that execution, emphasizing:

> When tensions between colonists and Indians were running high, an Indian hanged for murdering a colonist might have his head "cutt off the next day and pitched upon a pole in the markett place," as was the case with Nepaupuck, convicted of murder in 1639, shortly after the initial settlement of New Haven.
>
> *(Banner, 2002, p. 74)*

As Professor Kirchmeier, of CUNY School of Law, notes of other executions that took place in the years to come: "In 1711, the first Native American woman to be executed under the laws of the white settlers, Waisoiusksquaw, was hanged in Connecticut for killing her husband. The first legal execution in the colony of North Carolina occurred on August 26, 1726, when the colony hanged the Native American George Sennecca for murder" (Kirchmeier, 2015, p. 46).

History is frequently written by conquerors, and European settlers of the New World—despite their own barbaric practices and their rampant abuse of Native peoples—were not shy about recording their own perceptions of the indigenous people they unabashedly called "savages." For example, in *The History of American Indians* (1775), a text full of racist language that propounded a then-popular theory that Native Americans were ancestors of the lost tribes of Israel, James Adair—a trader who lived and worked among Native Americans for four decades—made this observation: "The Indians strictly adhere more than the rest of mankind to that positive, unrepealed law of Moses, 'He who sheddeth man's blood, by man shall his blood be shed': like the Israelites, their hearts burn violently day and night without intermission, till they shed blood for blood." "They transmit," Adair wrote, "from father to son, the memory of the loss of their relation, or one of their own tribe or family, though it were an old woman—if she was either killed by the enemy, or by any of their own people." "If indeed the murder be committed by a kinsman, the eldest can redeem," Adair emphasized.

Adair's book was written in another time, when slavery was still lawful and in widespread use. A native of Ireland, Adair had traveled to North America and become a trader with Indians in the South, living amongst the Chickasaw before moving to South Carolina. But Adair's language, like the institution of slavery he observed first-hand, reflects the overt racial prejudice of that era. In his book, which contained a chapter titled "On the descent of the American Indians from the Jews," Adair quoted Old Testament verses and penned chapters on the "punishment of adultery" and "[t]heir several punishments." Middle-aged "savage Americans," Adair wrote, "assure us, that they remember when adultery was punished among them with death, by shooting the offender with barbed arrows," though Adair noted that "the severity of that law" had since been "moderated" by the tribes. Instead of death, he wrote, the punishment for a woman's adultery was for "the enraged husband accompanied by some of his relations" to beat her "most barbarously" and then to cut off "her hair and nose, or one of her lips." "[W]hen an Indian sheds human blood," Adair added, "it does not proceed from wantonness, or the view of doing evil, but solely to put the law of retaliation in force, to return one injury for another."

Adair's description of Native Americans was racially charged and depicts a punishment regime at times forgiving, yet at other times ferocious and incredibly violent and vindictive. "There never was any set of people," Adair wrote in *The History of American Indians*, carrying his own prejudices and picking his words from his own tradition, "who pursued the Mosaic law of *retaliation* with such a fixt eagerness as these Americans." "They are so determined in this point," he added of the eye-for-an-eye, life-for-a-life *lex talionis* mentality so typical of that age, "that formerly a little boy shooting birds in the high and thick corn-fields, unfortunately chanced slightly to wound another with his childish arrow; the young vindictive fox, was excited by custom to watch his ways with the utmost earnestness, till the wound was returned in as equal a manner as could be expected." "They forgive all crimes at the annual atonement of sins, except murder, which is always punished with death," Adair clarified in shifting from a discussion of corporal to capital punishments. "If an unruly horse belonging to a white man, should chance to be tied at a trading house and kill one of the Indians," Adair continued, "either the owner of the house, or the person who tied the beast there, is responsible for it, by their lex talionis."[5]

Early Native Americans—like Europeans in prior ages—thus engaged in retaliatory killing and gratuitous violence, however frequent or infrequent from decade to decade or in a particular locale. In *The Barbarous Years*, about the clash of Indian and British cultures from 1600 to 1675, Pulitzer Prize-winning historian Bernard Bailyn writes of how "brutality grew commonplace." "The desecration of bodies, so much a part of the Indians' search for reciprocity in warfare and diplomacy," he observes, "became for the Europeans a search for domination." Virginians, Bailyn notes, scalped Indians, "did not hesitate to decapitate their enemies in campaigns of terror," and "offered bounties" for the "capture and execution" of Indians. "Day after day," he adds,

> native allies seeking to demonstrate their fidelity and mutuality of interests with English power appeared in Boston with the severed heads and hands of their common enemies, gestures that the English took as signs of submission and of the legitimacy of their conquest.

As Bailyn concludes of this ultra-violent, seventeenth-century era: "Dismembered body parts—heads, hands, scalps, and torn-off strips of skin—had become commonplace objects among such gentle people as the Pilgrims, as they had been for centuries among such militant people as the Narragansetts" (Bailyn, 2012, pp. 502–503).

Capital punishment in the Americas, despite its precolonial use, was also imported from Europe, with its form (often hanging) highly influenced by European colonizers. The English "Bloody Code"—the collection of laws from America's mother country during the late 1600s to the early nineteenth century—made scores of crimes punishable by death. And such laws infused, and bled into, colonial life (Bessler, 2014a, pp. 96–97). "[D]uring the eighteenth century the number of capital crimes increased substantially from about fifty in 1700 to between 220 and 230 by 1800," notes one writer, pointing out that even the smallest of offenses—stealing turnips, damaging a fish pond, or cutting down a tree—could result in a death sentence. As that writer, Neville Twitchell, writes in *The Politics of the Rope*:

> The judiciary enthusiastically expanded the range of hanging offences, as guardians of the common law. Executions were carried out in public, and indeed were treated as holidays for some workers. People "flocked to Tyburn Tree as to the music hall or a sporting event." It was not unusual for children to be hanged.
>
> (*Twitchell, 2012, pp. 19–20*)

As another writer, Louis Palmer, emphasizes: "Anglo-American jurisprudence owes its understanding and acceptance of the death penalty to the common law of England." The judge-made *common law* was itself derived from—and said to reflect and embody—the customs or beliefs of the English people, at least as determined by early, execution-prone English jurists (Palmer, 1998, p. 7).

In fact, the European migrants to America's colonies all came from places where the death penalty was still in widespread use. In England, public executions at Tyburn and elsewhere were a regular feature of English society, as were corporal punishments inflicted in front of large crowds, even for relatively minor crimes (McKenzie, 2007). As the author of *Daily Life in 18th-Century England* describes these recurrent scenes:

> People exposed in the pillory were tormented by the crowd, sometimes for fun, sometimes out of genuine resentment of the crime. It was not unusual for the person pilloried to suffer death or maiming as a result of being pelted with stones, food, dirt, dead animals, and trash. Those not pilloried were sometimes branded, though the brander could be bribed to use a cold iron.

"The holiday mood only intensified when a hanging was scheduled," that book emphasizes, offering this description:

> In London, the procession began every six weeks at Newgate with the condemned—most of them younger than twenty-one—being loaded onto an open cart, accompanied by their coffins. They made their slow way westward to Tyburn, where the triangular gallows awaited them.

As that source continued:

> On the way, they stopped at taverns, drinking heavily and promising to pay the bill "when they came back." The crowd, which included workmen, pickpockets, food vendors, and apprentices on holiday (much to the dismay of their employers), drank too.
>
> (*Olsen, 1999, p. 216*)

To understand colonial practices, one must study European ones. In the fourth volume of Sir William Blackstone's *Commentaries on the Laws of England*, published in 1769, the Oxford jurist described how capital offenders were usually "hanged by the neck till dead," though he acknowledged that, "in very atrocious crimes," "other circumstances of terror, pain, or disgrace are superadded." For treason, Blackstone recounted, the prescribed punishment was "being drawn or dragged to the place of execution," with "high treason affecting the king's person or government" punishable by "embowelling alive, beheading, and quartering." Murderers were subject to "a public dissection," while women committing treason were "to be burned alive." The only consolation for such offenders, Blackstone noted, was that the person to be executed was often rendered unconscious before the brunt of the punishment was inflicted. As Blackstone wrote:

> [T]he humanity of the English nation has authorized, by a tacit consent, an almost general mitigation of such part of these judgments as savour of torture or cruelty: a sledge or hurdle being usually allowed to such traitors as are condemned to be drawn; and there being very few instances (and those accidental or by negligence) of any person's being embowelled or burned, till previously deprived of sensation by strangling.
>
> *(Bessler, 2012, p. 172)*

Blackstone's writings capture the prevailing Anglo-American sentiment of pre-Revolutionary War times as regards the death penalty. In his *Commentaries*, Blackstone—skeptical of the efficacy of death sentences for certain offenders yet living at a time when murderers and other felons were regularly executed—wrote this in 1769:

> [T]he pains of death, and perpetual disability in exile, slavery, or imprisonment, ought never to be inflicted, but when the offender appears *incorrigible*: which may be collected either from a repetition of minuter offenses; or from the perpetration of some one crime of deep malignity, which of itself demonstrates a disposition without hope or probability of amendment and in such cases it would be cruelty to the public, to defer the punishment of such a criminal, till he had an opportunity of repeating perhaps the worst of villanies.

Seeking to avoid executions where "the evil to be prevented is not adequate to the violence of the preventative," Blackstone cautioned, however: "A multitude of sanguinary laws (besides the doubt that may be entertained concerning the right of making them) do likewise prove a manifest defect either in the wisdom of the legislature, or the strength of executive power." "It is a kind of quackery in government, and argues a want of solid skill," Blackstone argued, "to apply the same universal remedy, the *ultimum supplicium*, to every case of difficulty." "It is, it must be owned," Blackstone emphasized, "much *easier* to extirpate than to amend mankind: yet that magistrate must be esteemed both a weak and a cruel surgeon, who cuts off every limb, which through ignorance or indolence he will not attempt to cure" (Bessler, 2012, p. 49).

The Death Penalty's Abolition (But not Entirely)

In colonial America, a wide variety of offenses were punishable by death, with biblical passages justifying the imposition of death sentences. For example, the Massachusetts "Body of Liberties," prepared by Rev. Nathaniel Ward and adopted in 1641, had 12 capital crimes—among them, murder, rebellion, adultery, bestiality, blasphemy, and witchcraft. Of those, 11 of the prohibited acts cited verses of the Bible as legal authority. One capital offense, justified on the basis of Deuteronomy and Exodus, provided that if "any man . . . shall have or worship any other god, but the lord god, he shall be put to death." Another provision read: "No man shall be forced by Torture to confesse any Crime against himselfe nor any other unlesse it be in some Capitall case, where he is first fullie convicted by cleare and suffient evidence to be guilty." Puritans in the Massachusetts Bay Colony had initially relied on magistrates' interpretations of the Bible to determine punishments, but in 1636 the General Court of Massachusetts had appointed a committee to "make a draught of lawes agreeable to the word of God," a written code based on a literal reading of the Old Testament. Massachusetts' 1641 Body of Liberties authorized the death penalty for a number of offenses, including religious and nonhomicidal crimes, although it simultaneously—and without apparent irony—provided: "For bodilie punishments we allow amongst us none that are inhumane Barbarous or cruel" (Green, 2015, pp. 84–85; The Massachusetts Body of Liberties, 1641).[6]

With Quakers migrating from England to the New World, not everyone in colonial America looked upon executions favorably. In the early 1680s, William Penn (1644–1718)—a noteworthy penal reformer and land grant recipient—settled in the colony of Pennsylvania and quickly put in place a novel, more progressive legal code that he and his fellow Quakers had drafted in England. Although Penn's "Great Law" of 1682 restricted the death penalty's use to treason and murder and replaced corporal punishments with fines, hard labor, and imprisonment in houses of correction, that legal regime only lasted a few decades. In fact, Penn's law was rescinded in favor of a much harsher criminal code—one modeled on traditional English practice—immediately after Penn's death in 1718. Its replacement: an Anglican Code that not only expanded the number of capital offenses but that made use of branding, mutilation, and other corporal punishments (Welch, 2011, p. 54; Bessler, 2014c, pp. 245–246). William Penn himself had once been incarcerated in London's notorious Newgate Prison, and he favored alternatives to such prisons. "Because he had been deeply impressed by Dutch workhouses (which were based on the English Bridewell system) during his tour of Holland," one textbook notes, "Penn decreed that, in Pennsylvania, all counties were to have workhouses." Though the "Great Law" was a milder code, that law—adopted on December 7, 1682—nonetheless continued to criminalize drunkenness, profanity, and sexual acts seen by seventeenth-century lawmakers as immoral (Miller, 2002, p. 1475). In the seventeenth and eighteenth century, pillories and whipping posts were still in widespread use in England and its colonies, with offenses like adultery punishable by death, branding or whipping, banishment, or (as Nathaniel Hawthorne's novel made famous) the scarlet letter (Edge, 2009, p. 8; Johnson, 1995, pp. 72–74; Kennedy-Andrews, 1999, p. 71).[7]

North American colonial codes varied by locale, but premeditated murder—that universally detested act—was a capital crime throughout England's colonies. While some northern codes did not punish crimes against property (e.g., arson, burglary, and robbery) with death, southern colonies (where slave populations were larger) used executions more frequently, regularly resorting to draconian English law and practice. Recidivist property offenders were subject to the death penalty in some places, and harsh bodily punishments—whether lethal or nonlethal—were a regular, if disquieting, feature of colonial life. Before Enlightenment figures in Europe began calling for the death penalty's abolition or curtailment in the 1760s, with some seeking "life-long servitude" as a substitute for executions, William Penn—many decades earlier—had anticipated that call for milder punishments. Still, the "Great Law" of 1682 infamously criminalized "the unnatural sin of Sodomy" with forfeiture of property, public whipping, and hard labor. After William Penn's death, the crimes of arson, burglary, highway robbery, maiming, manslaughter, rape, sodomy, and witchcraft—already punishable by death elsewhere—became capital crimes in Pennsylvania, too (McLennan, 2008, p. 24; Eskridge, 2008, p. 17).

In colonial times, even relatively small transgressions were capital offenses. "Virginia," Stuart Banner writes in his history of American executions,

> imposed the death penalty for all sorts of crimes relating to the tobacco trade—including embezzling tobacco, fraudulently delivering tobacco, altering inspected tobacco, forging inspectors' stamps, and smuggling tobacco—as well as for stealing hogs (upon a third conviction), receiving a stolen horse, and concealing property to defraud creditors.
>
> *(Banner, 2002, pp. 6–8)*

There were variations between English law and colonial justice, but both made use of executions. As one source, *A History of Colonial America*, puts it:

> The number of capital offenses was much smaller in the colonial codes than in the English statutes, but larger than in our laws today. In the early days, blasphemy was punishable by death in Connecticut, in New Haven, and in Maryland under the rule of the Catholic proprietors.
>
> *(Chitwood, 1961, p. 155)*

"Although the laws of colonial America were greatly influenced by the legal traditions of Great Britain," the *Encyclopedia of Crime and Punishment* notes, summarizing and taking stock of differences between English and colonial practices, "colonial charters and statutes did not simply mirror the laws of England" (Levinson, 2002, Vol. 1, p. 153).

But despite such variations in the law's application, jurists in colonial America, as in England, routinely resorted to both capital and corporal punishments. As *The Cambridge History of Law in America* notes:

> Colonial authorities aimed to inflict pain on the bodies and humiliation on the souls of criminal offenders. They inflicted whippings (sometimes at a whipping post and sometimes at a cart's tail), imposed time in the pillory (with or without additional duress from onlookers), branded, bored holes in tongues, defaced, and cropped ears.

"Whippings," that text continues, "were not simply painful; they were public." "Hanging," it emphasizes, "was not the most painful death authorities employed." According to that detailed history of American law:

> Some of the condemned were put to death by burning. Burning was apparently limited to crimes that the authorities considered outright attacks on the social order: witchcraft, wives committing petit treason, and slaves involved in (alleged) revolt. Some criminals were hung in chains, others were dissected.
>
> *(Meranze, 2008, pp. 187–188)*

Famously, the Salem witch trials of 1692, in which 185 individuals were accused of witchcraft, led to 19 hangings, one man being crushed to death by stones in an effort to make him testify, and four adults and several children dying in prison while in custody (Campbell, 2008, p. 17). The Salem witch trials, the subject of many books and plays, are now closely associated with injustice, mass hysteria, and superstition run amok (Schiff, 2015; Hill, 1995; Roach, 2002).[8]

The roots of America's death penalty are, in fact, intertwined with superstition, intolerance, and fear—and with slavery and the suppression of slave revolts. Four Quakers were put to death in Boston in the 1650s for their views (Adams, 2010, pp. 63, 68–69), and slaves were regularly brutalized and executed in antebellum America (Purvis, 1999, p. 312).[9] Large slave populations led to the development of slave codes in places such as South Carolina, Virginia, and New York, followed by other codes in New Jersey, Maryland, North Carolina, Delaware, Pennsylvania, and Georgia. In the Deep South, Louisiana's slave code authorized the use of capital punishment if a slave struck the slave master or a member of the slave owner's family. While South Carolina's 1696 code spoke of the "barbarous, wild, savage natures" of slaves, the punishment of those held in bondage—and subjected to such colonial codes—was often swift and severe. As Sally Hadden observes in *The Cambridge History of Law in America*: "Typically the first punishment for theft or possessing weapons was whipping, nose slitting, or ear cropping, whereas a second or third offense might merit branding or even death. Murder or insurrection could attract the death penalty immediately" (Hadden, 2008, pp. 269–270). These slave codes sought to prevent insurrections and terrorize slaves, with a Georgia law from 1767 making theft by a black person a capital crime and one from 1770 adding rape to the list of crimes for which a slave could be executed (Grant, 1993, p. 54).

During the Enlightenment, slavery—as well as torture and capital punishment—came under attack. "The issue of slavery was uncontroversial for an extremely long time," Carsten Anckar writes in *Determinants of the Death Penalty: A Comparative Study of the World*. "In fact," Anckar explains, "the legitimacy of slavery was not really questioned until the Age of Enlightenment in the writings of Montesquieu and Rousseau" (Anckar, 2004, p. 83). While Jean-Jacques Rousseau (1712–1778) wrote *The Social Contract* (1762) and *The Discourse on the Origin of the Foundation of Inequality among Men* (1775), Charles de Secondat, Baron de Montesquieu (1689–1755), became famous for his book, *The Spirit of the Laws* (1748). Both men opposed slavery, though neither advocated the complete abolition of capital punishment. The very first line of *The Social Contract*—"Man is born free, and everywhere he is in chains"—reflected Rousseau's philosophical opposition to slavery, but Rousseau saw a place for executions in the social compact he posited. And Montesquieu—a skeptic of death sentences, but not a proponent of their total abolition—wrote that the institution of slavery

> is not good by its nature; it is useful neither to the master nor to the slave: not to the slave, because he can do nothing from virtue; not to the master, because he contracts all sorts of bad habits from his slaves, because he imperceptibly grows accustomed to failing in all the moral virtues, because he grows proud, curt, harsh, angry, voluptuous, and cruel.
>
> *(Hinks & McKivigan, 2007, pp. 477–478, 583; Rodriguez, 1997, p. 556; Cohler, Miller & Stone, 1989, p. 246)*

Widely read in Europe and across the Atlantic, the writings of Rousseau and Montesquieu influenced many Enlightenment figures and lawmakers and—with their emphasis on human rights and opposition to tyranny—set the stage for the birth of the world's anti-death penalty movement.[10]

In *The Spirit of the Laws*, Montesquieu—the French jurist who studied laws around the globe—advocated proportionality between crimes and punishments and wrote about felons and executions. "Among ourselves, it is a great ill that the same penalty is inflicted on the highway robber and on the one who robs and murders," he editorialized in a section of his book titled "*On the just proportion between the penalties and the crime*." As Montesquieu wrote:

> It is the triumph of liberty when criminal laws draw each penalty from the particular nature of the crime. All arbitrariness ends; the penalty does not ensue from the legislator's capriciousness but from the nature of the thing, and man does not do violence to man.
>
> *(Rosen, 2003, pp. 145–146)*

In another section of his book titled "*On the simplicity of criminal laws in the various governments*," Montesquieu—the French political theorist who felt that executing deserters had not diminished desertion—further emphasized:

> [I]n moderate states where the head of even the lowest citizen is esteemed, his honor and goods are removed from him only after long examination; he is deprived of his life only when the homeland itself attacks it; and when the homeland attacks his life, it gives him every possible means of defending it.

As Montesquieu concluded that section of his book after discussing republics and monarchies: "Men are all equal in republican government; they are equal in despotic government; in the former, it is because they are everything; in the latter, it is because they are nothing" (Cohler, Miller, & Stone, 1989, pp. 75, 85, 91).

Although Montesquieu did not advocate the total abolition of capital punishment, his book nonetheless questioned long-held assumptions about the criminal law. It became a must-read text for enlightened thinkers and was an especially popular title among America's founders and framers.[11] As author Mart Grams writes in *The Great Experiment*:

> Like the ancient philosophers Aristotle and Cicero, Montesquieu believed that a system which divided and balanced the power of government among the different classes of society, as was done in Great Britain, was the best way to be sure that the government would not be dominated by a single social class.
>
> *(Grams, 2003, p. 77)*

"At the time of the American Revolution," notes another source, "few other theorists could rival Montesquieu's prestige in the English-speaking world." "During the debate about adopting the American Constitution," that collection of the French aristocrat's writings emphasizes, "both federalists and anti-federalists argued their cases on the basis of their respective interpretations of Montesquieu." On the specific issue of separation of powers, James Madison wrote that "[t]he oracle who is always consulted and cited upon this point is the celebrated Montesquieu" (Richter, 1990, p. 1).

It was not until the 1760s, with publication of the Italian philosopher Cesare Beccaria's book, *Dei delitti e delle pene* (1764), that an Enlightenment thinker proposed doing away with capital punishment entirely. Beccaria, an aristocrat from Milan, a recent law graduate of the University of Pavia, and an avid reader of Montesquieu's *Lettres persanes*, was just 26 years of age when his book first appeared in Italian. In it, Beccaria—a young man fascinated by mathematics and economics—openly acknowledged his debt to Montesquieu in his own runaway bestseller, a book that was quickly translated into French, English, and other major European languages. *On Crimes and Punishments*, as it was translated into English in 1767, forcefully called (as Montesquieu had) for proportion between crimes and punishments, but it also pushed for an end to executions and torture. In Europe, Beccaria's book was voraciously read by Voltaire and the French *philosophes*, as well as by English penal reformers like Jeremy Bentham and William Blackstone. As historian Elio Monachesi described Beccaria's essay, at first published anonymously for fear of persecution:

> The essay was a tightly reasoned devastating attack upon the prevailing systems for the administration of criminal justice. As such it aroused the hostility and resistance of those who stood to gain by the perpetuation of the barbaric and archaic penological institutions of the day.

"In order to appreciate the reason Beccaria's brief essay . . . created such excitement, enthusiasm and controversy," Monachesi explains, "one needs to recall the state of the criminal law in continental Europe at the time the essay first appeared" (Monachesi, 1956, pp. 439, 441).

Across the Atlantic, American founders such as Dr. Benjamin Rush, Thomas Jefferson, John Hancock, and James Wilson were equally absorbed by *On Crimes and Punishments*. They had felt the heavy hand of England's monarchy and its Parliament, and they rightfully felt that they were the victims of tyranny and oppression. "The existent criminal law of eighteenth century Europe was, in general, repressive, uncertain and barbaric," Monachesi notes of the then-prevailing system of justice, giving some sense of the eighteenth-century yoke constraining—and applied to—American colonists. As Monachesi writes of that eighteenth-century approach: "Torture, ingenious and horrible, was employed to wrench confessions from the recalcitrant. Judges were permitted to exercise unlimited discretion in punishing those convicted of crime. The sentences imposed were arbitrary, inconsistent and depended upon the status and power of the convicted." Given that signers of America's Declaration of Independence faced death sentences—indeed, drawing and quartering—for declaring independence from Great Britain, it is not surprising that they were fascinated by Beccaria's book. In fact, even years after the publication of *On Crimes and Punishments*, James Madison—in preparing a list of books for "the use of Congress"—included "Beccaria's works" in his 1783 catalog of recommended books (Monachesi, 1956, p. 441).

On Crimes and Punishments covered a wide array of topics, though its principal focus was the criminal law. In it, Beccaria—inspired by Montesquieu and others—argued that crimes are "distributed across a scale that moves imperceptibly by diminishing degrees from the highest to the lowest" and that "[i]f geometry were applicable to the infinite and obscure combinations of human actions, there would be a corresponding scale of punishments, descending from the most severe to the mildest" (Beccaria, 1775, p. 18). "If the same punishment is prescribed for two crimes and injure society in different degrees," Beccaria wrote, "then men will face no stronger deterrent from committing the greater crime if they find it in their advantage to do so" (Beccaria, 1775, p. 19). As one commentator later described the book's impact:

> The Marquis of Beccaria, in his treatise . . . seems to have awakened legislators from a trance, in 1764, by propounding the simple inquiry—*Ought not punishments to be proportioned to crimes, and how shall that proportion be established?* A matter, so apparently simple, seems not to have been thought of before.[12]

Citing Montesquieu and reenvisioning and adapting Rousseau's social contract theory, Beccaria argued that there were limits on a sovereign's right to punish individuals. In his chapter on the death penalty, he specifically wrote: "Who has ever willingly given up to others the authority to kill him? How on earth can the minimum sacrifice of each individual's freedom involve handing over the greatest of all goods, life itself?"[13]

In *On Crimes and Punishments*, Beccaria railed against "cruelty," "cruel punishments," "useless cruelty," "barbarous and useless torments," "cruel imbecility," and "those cruel formalities of justice" (Thomas, 2008, pp. 3, 43, 46, 100–101, 114; Bellamy, 1995, pp. 10–13, 66). As translated into English, he lamented "barbarous torments" and "useless severity" (Thomas, 2008, p. 4), then argued—explicitly citing his idol, Montesquieu—that "[e]very punishment, which does not arise from absolute necessity . . . is tyrannical" (Thomas, 2008, p. 7). "[T]here ought to be a fixed proportion between crimes and punishments," Beccaria implored (Thomas, 2008, p. 21), asking—and then answering—a series of questions for his readers: "Is the punishment of death really *useful*, or necessary for the safety or good order of society? Are tortures and torments consistent with *justice*, or do they answer the end proposed by the laws? Are the same punishments equally useful at all times?" (Thomas, 2008, p. 42). "Crimes," Beccaria advised, "are more effectually prevented by the *certainty*, than the *severity* of punishment" (Thomas, 2008, p. 98). "The swifter and closer to the crime a punishment is, the juster and more useful it will be," he emphasized, calling for "promptness of punishment" because "the smaller the lapse of time between the misdeed and the punishment, the stronger and more lasting the association in the human mind between the two ideas *crime* and *punishment*" (Bellamy, 1995). "In proportion as punishments become more cruel," Beccaria added, "the minds of men, as a fluid rises to the same height with that which surrounds it, grow hardened and insensible" (Thomas, 2008, p. 99).

The father of the world's anti-death penalty movement,[14] Beccaria pointedly questioned whether executions were really necessary for the security or good order of society? (Thomas, 2008, p. 26). "By what right," he pondered, "can men presume to slaughter their fellows?" (Thomas, 2008, p. 51). "It seems absurd to me," he wrote, "that the laws, which are the expression of the public will, and which execrate and punish homicide, should themselves commit one, and that to deter citizens from murder they should order a public murder" (Thomas, 2008, p. 55). The frontispiece to the third edition of *Dei delitti e delle pene*, published in 1765, used an image to illustrate one of the most important objectives of Beccaria's treatise (i.e., to replace executions with incarceration and hard labor). A copperplate engraving based on a sketch supplied by Beccaria, the frontispiece depicts an idealized figure, Justice, shunning an executioner. That executioner is carrying a sword and axe in his right hand and is trying to hand Justice a cluster of severed heads with his outstretched left hand. In rejecting the severed heads, Justice's gaze is instead transfixed on a pile of prisoner's shackles and worker's tools—the instruments symbolizing imprisonment and prison labor (Thomas, 2008, p. 2). It was hard labor—whether performed by convicts on Philadelphia streets or within the confines of prisons—that would later emerge in America as a viable alternative to harsh corporal punishments and executions (Siegel, 2011, p. 620).

Beccaria's book condemned the barbarity of state-sanctioned executions, viewing them as violative of natural law. "[S]overeignty and the laws," Beccaria wrote, "are nothing but the sum of the smallest portions of the personal liberty of each individual; they represent the general will, which is the aggregate of particular wills" (Thomas, 2008, p. 51). "Who has ever willingly given other men the authority to kill him?" he asked rhetorically (Thomas, 2008, p. 51), arguing that "the death penalty is not a *right*, but the war of a nation against a citizen" (Thomas, 2008, p. 52); see also (Beccaria, 1775, p. 103). In a chapter devoted exclusively to the death penalty, that centuries-old punishment, Beccaria wrote: "This futile excess of punishments, which have never made men better, has impelled me to consider whether the death penalty is really useful and just in a well-organized state" (Thomas, 2008, p. 51). "The death penalty," he contended, "is not useful because of the example of cruelty that it gives to men" (Thomas, 2008, p. 55). "If one were to raise the objection that in almost all ages and almost all nations the death penalty has been prescribed for some crimes," the Italian criminal-law theorist continued, "I would reply that this objection amounts to nothing in the face of the truth—against which there is no legal remedy—and that the history of mankind gives us the impression of a vast sea of errors, in which a few confused truths float about with large and distant gaps between them" (Thomas, 2008, pp. 56–57). If monarchs left "the ancient laws in place," Beccaria observed, "it is because of the infinite difficulty in stripping the venerated rust of many centuries from so many errors" (Thomas, 2008, p. 57).

For Beccaria, executions—the state's ultimate sanction—only brutalized societies. "If the passions or the necessities of war have taught us how to shed human blood," he believed, "the laws, which moderate the conduct of men, should not augment that cruel example, which is all the more baleful when a legal killing is applied with deliberation and formality" (Thomas, 2008, p. 55).[15] To persuade any skeptical readers, of which he knew there would be many, Beccaria posed a series of questions: "Can the cries of an unfortunate wretch rescue from time, which never reverses its course, deeds already perpetrated?" (Thomas, 2008, p. 26). "When reading history, who does not shudder with horror at the barbaric and useless tortures that have been cold-bloodedly invented and practiced by men who considered themselves wise?" (Thomas, 2008, p. 51).

> What must men think when they see wise magistrates and solemn ministers of justice, who with tranquil indifference have a criminal dragged with slow precision to his death, and as a poor wretch writhes in his last agonies while awaiting the fatal blow, the judge goes on with cold insensitivity—and perhaps even with secret satisfaction at his own authority—to savour the comforts and pleasures of life?
>
> *(Thomas, 2008, p. 56)*

In England, the "Bloody Code"—the pejorative label traditionally given to England's criminal laws, and once defended by the likes of Philip Yorke (1690–1764), 1st Earl of Hardwicke and a barrister who became Lord Chancellor—made the death penalty a central feature of England's criminal justice system (McLynn, 1989, pp. xi–xii, 257; Harris, 1847, pp. 130, 143, 159–161, 166, 232).

The impact of *On Crimes and Punishments* cannot be understated. Cesare Beccaria's book—the equivalent of a *New York Times* bestseller—was a tremendous success and sensation in Europe and throughout the Americas. It was read at colleges, serialized or excerpted in newspapers and magazines, incorporated into American poetry, and became the topic of a great deal of discussion by lawmakers and nonlawmakers alike (Bessler, 2018). Indeed, Beccaria was passionately quoted by John Adams in 1770 at the Boston Massacre trial in which Adams, the future American president but then a practicing lawyer, represented British soldiers accused of murder. "I am for the prisoners at the bar," Adams said in 1770 in open court,

> and shall apologize for it only in the words of the Marquis Beccaria: 'If by supporting the rights of mankind, and of invincible truth, I shall contribute to save from the agonies of death one unfortunate victim of tyranny, or ignorance, equally fatal, his blessings and tears of transport shall be sufficient consolation to me for the contempt of all mankind.'

John Quincy Adams later remarked on the "electrical effect" his father's words had in the courtroom (Bessler, 2014b, pp. 3–4, 95–100, 136). John Adams, the second U.S. President, and his son John Quincy Adams, the sixth U.S. President, both studied Italian, with John Quincy Adams—the man who so fiercely opposed slavery—later coming to oppose capital punishment, too (Bessler, 2014b, pp. 17, 108, 175–182, 502; Finkelman, 2014, p. 174; Wice, 2009, p. 86).

Beccaria's ideas about crafting clear and precise laws and reducing the severity of punishments found a fertile soil in America. Dr. Benjamin Rush—a signer of the Declaration of Independence—pushed for the outright abolition of the death penalty, while other Pennsylvanians sought to curtail executions for nonhomicide offenses. At Benjamin Franklin's house, Dr. Rush specifically invoked Beccaria's name in March 1787 in an address about public punishments. "The Duke of Tuscany, soon after the publication of the Marquis of Beccaria's excellent treatise upon this subject," Rush observed, "abolished death as a punishment for murder." In his native Pennsylvania, the death penalty—due in part to the efforts of William Bradford, James Madison's close friend from college and a highly respected Pennsylvania jurist who became the attorney general of the United States—was restricted in the 1780s and 1790s, though not abolished altogether as it had been in Tuscany in 1786 (just a year before the Constitutional Convention in Philadelphia). Bradford's influential 1793 essay, *An Enquiry How Far the Punishment of Death Is Necessary in Pennsylvania*, itself cites Beccaria's writings. In Philadelphia, lawyer James Wilson—an early associate justice of the U.S. Supreme Court and, like Dr. Rush, a signer of the Declaration of Independence—also repeatedly brought up Beccaria in his writings and law lectures (Bessler, 2014b, pp. 4–5, 164–176, 170–173).

Thomas Jefferson—the principal drafter of the Declaration of Independence—actually copied more than two dozen passages from Beccaria's book into his commonplace book, transcribing the words, in page after page, in the original Italian. In Virginia in the 1770s, Jefferson drafted a "Bill for Proportioning Crimes and Punishments in Cases Heretofore Capital"—the title of which is a tip of the hat to Beccaria's popular book. That bill, which James Madison, in the mid-1780s, fought to get enacted into law in their home state, itself cited Beccaria's slender treatise. Though the legislation Jefferson wrote, and that Madison urged the Virginia Legislature to pass, failed by a single vote, penal reform ultimately came to Virginia in the 1790s. It was, not surprisingly, another Beccaria disciple and admirer, George Keith Taylor, who led that successful effort in 1796. A prominent politician, Taylor was the brother-in-law of the soon-to-be U.S. Supreme Court Chief Justice John Marshall, of *Marbury v. Madison* fame. In the 1820s, toward the end of his life, in a clear reflection of the Italian philosopher's widespread influence, Jefferson wrote that Beccaria "had satisfied the reasonable world of the unrightfulness and inefficacy of the punishment of crimes by death" (Bessler, 2014b, pp. 190–91; Bessler, 2012, pp. 31–65; *Marbury v. Madison*, 1803).

Everywhere in colonial and early America, from Georgia to Massachusetts to Vermont, America's founders turned again and again to Beccaria's landscape-changing book for inspiration and guidance.

The Continental Congress, as a body, itself quoted these stirring words from Beccaria's book in 1774, just before the start of the Revolutionary War (1775–1783):

> In every human society there is an effort continually tending to confer on one part the height of power and happiness, and to reduce the other to the extreme of weakness and misery. The intent of good laws is to oppose this effort, and to diffuse their influence universally and equally.
>
> *(Bessler, 2014b, pp. 147–148)*

Beccaria's call for proportionate punishments, which dovetailed nicely with the founders' own desire to check tyrannical and abusive power, explicitly shows up in early American state constitutions. For example, Ohio's 1802 constitution—modeled on New Hampshire's 1784 constitution—contained this provision: "All penalties shall be proportioned to the nature of the offense. No wise legislature will affix the same punishment to the crimes of theft, forgery and the like, which they do to those of murder and treason." "[A] multitude of sanguinary laws," it continued, "are both impolitic and unjust: the true design of all punishment being to reform, not to exterminate mankind." Early American constitutions and declarations of rights also echo Beccaria's views on proportionality, equality of treatment, and maximizing people's happiness (Bessler, 2014b, pp. 256, 258, 263, 373).

A wide array of eighteenth- and nineteenth-century writings tell the story. "Long before the recent Revolution," then Pennsylvania Attorney General William Bradford emphasized of Beccaria's *On Crimes and Punishments* in a 1786 letter, "this book was common among lettered persons of Pennsylvania, who admired its principles without daring to hope that they could be adopted in legislation, since we copied the laws of England, to whose laws we were subject." Writing to Milanese botanist Luigi Castiglioni, then in Philadelphia as part of an extended tour of North America, Bradford spoke of the period of penal reform that followed the issuance of the Declaration of Independence:

> [A]s soon as we were free of political bonds, this humanitarian system, long admired in secret, was publicly adopted and incorporated by the Constitution of the State, which, spurred by the influence of this benign spirit, ordered the legislative bodies to render penalties less bloody and, in general, more proportionate to the crimes.
>
> *(Bessler, 2014a, p. 98)*

American lawmakers and jurists regularly lauded Beccaria's book, with Beccaria becoming one of the most quoted figures in the founding period.[16] One lawmaker and jurist, Nathaniel Chipman—a U.S. senator and chief justice of Vermont's Supreme Court—would later write of the Italian nobleman whose book so shaped American law: "The world is more indebted to the Marquis Beccaria, for his little treatise on Crimes and Punishments, than to all other writers on the subject" (Bessler, 2014b, pp. 259–260; Chipman, 1846).

American efforts to restrict or abolish capital punishment, whether inspired by Beccaria's writings or other advocates of abolition, thus began even before George Washington's presidency. Though he made use of executions as a military commander, Washington himself was not particularly enthralled with state-sanctioned killing. In a letter to the president of the Continental Congress on July 15, 1776, General George Washington took note of "[t]he Inhuman Treatment . . . and Murder of part of our People after their Surrender and Capitulation" at the Battle of The Cedars, a series of military skirmishes that took place during the Continental Army's invasion of Quebec. Several American prisoners-of-war had been murdered by Indians, and Captain George Forster, of England's Eighth Foot, had—according to accounts—failed to protect the captives. Washington called the failure to protect American prisoners "a flagrant violation of that Faith which ought to be held sacred by all civilized nations, and founded in the most Savage barbarity." As Washington wrote to the president of Congress:

> It highly deserved the severest reprobation, and I trust the Spirited Measures Congress have adopted upon the Occasion, will prevent the like in future: But if they should not, and the claims of humanity are disregarded, Justice and Policy will require recourse to be had to the Law of retaliation, however abhorrent and disagreeable to our natures in cases of Torture and Capital Punishments.

In other words, George Washington—America's first commander in chief—viewed executions as a last resort (Fitzpatrick, 1932, Vol. 5, pp. 279–280).

Since the founding of the United States of America in 1776, the country's death penalty has undergone some major changes, with the anti-death penalty movement's fortunes ebbing and flowing over time. The building of penitentiaries, beginning with the 1790 opening of Philadelphia's Walnut Street Prison, allowed states to curtail or move away from executions entirely. A slew of states constructed penitentiaries in the years and decades to come, with Congress passing the Three Prisons Act—authorizing the construction of a federal prison in Leavenworth, Kansas, as well as ones in Atlanta, Georgia, and McNeil Island, Washington—in 1891.[17] And as hard labor and life sentences came into vogue, lawmakers adjusted their penal codes. Michigan abolished the death penalty in 1846 and, in the 1850s, Rhode Island and Wisconsin followed suit. Although the Civil War put an abrupt stop to America's anti-gallows movement, two trends that began before that war continued unabated after its conclusion. In the 1830s, mandatory death sentences began to give way to discretionary ones, and public executions began to be replaced by executions conducted within the confines of jails or prisons or enclosures adjoining them. Those trends continued over the coming decades, with the last American public executions taking place in the 1930s. Beginning in the 1880s, American states also passed "gag" laws forbidding newspapers from reporting the details of executions and requiring that they be held at night, with laws often requiring executions "before the hour of sunrise." These developments led to executions gradually being removed from the public eye, with more than 80% of U.S. executions from 1977 to 1995—in an indication of the sweeping change away from public, daytime executions—taking place between 11:00 p.m. and 7:30 a.m (Latzer & McCord, 2010, p. 87; Bessler, 2014c, pp. 253–254, 257–258; Bessler, 1997, pp. 3–4, 46, 49).

In the late nineteenth century, the U.S. Supreme Court upheld the constitutionality of the firing squad and the electric chair (*Wilkerson v. Utah*, 1879; In re *Kemmler*, 1890). Although many American states, during the Progressive Era, thereafter abolished the death penalty, the bulk of them soon brought it back due to social unrest and fears of violent crime. As the authors of *America Without the Death Penalty: States Leading the Way* put it: "The Progressive Era in America was a period of numerous legal reforms, including the abolition of capital punishment. During this period, ten U.S. states abolished the death penalty (Arizona, Washington, Oregon, Colorado, Kansas, Tennessee, Missouri, South Dakota, North Dakota, and Minnesota), but only North Dakota and Minnesota failed to quickly reinstate this punishment" (Galliher, Koch, Keys, & Guess, 2002, p. 79). The countless legislative battles over capital punishment have centered, over time, on everything from the interpretation of the Bible to human rights, to deterrence and retribution, to wrongful convictions and DNA and forensic evidence, to efficacy and escalating costs, to tough alternatives to capital punishment, including life-without-parole sentences. As Justice William Brennan once wrote in a judicial opinion: "[F]rom the beginning of our Nation, the punishment of death has stirred acute public controversy." "The country," he observed, summarizing the intense and hard-fought public dispute, "has debated whether a society for which the dignity of the individual is the supreme value can, without a fundamental inconsistency, follow the practice of deliberately putting some of its members to death" (Burkhead, 2009, pp. 1–2).

In the debate over capital punishment, judges have played—and continue to play—a prominent role. In 1947, retired Supreme Court Justice Benjamin Cardozo—one in a long line of ever-hopeful death penalty opponents—was moved to write:

> I have faith . . . that a century or less from now, our descendants will look back upon the penal system of today with the same surprise and horror that fill our minds when we are told that only about a century ago one hundred and sixty crimes were visited under English law with the punishment of death, and that in 1801, a child of thirteen was hanged at Tyburn for the larceny of a spoon. Dark chapters are these in the history of law.

As Cardozo emphasized at that time:

> The future may judge us less leniently than we choose to judge ourselves. Perhaps the whole business of the retention of the death penalty will seem to the next generation, as it seems to many even now, an anachronism too discordant to be suffered, mocking with grim reproach all our clamorous professions of the sanctity of life.
>
> *(Burkhead, 2009, p. 142)*

While one of his successors, Justice Arthur Goldberg, argued in vain in 1963 for his Supreme Court colleagues to take up the question of the death penalty's constitutionality (Goldberg, 1986, p. 493), the Court itself had this to say on the subject in the 1971 case of *McGautha v. California*:

> In light of history, experience, and the present limitations of human knowledge, we find it quite impossible to say that committing to the untrammeled discretion of the jury the power to pronounce life or death in capital cases is offensive to anything in the Constitution.
>
> *(McGautha v. California, 1971)*

There have been some judicial victories for abolitionists. Starting in 1972, the U.S. Supreme Court began to question the propriety of executions and how death sentences were being meted out. In that year, in *Furman v. Georgia*, a bare majority of the Court struck down death penalty laws, as then applied, as violating the Eighth and Fourteenth Amendments (*Furman v. Georgia*, 1972). The Eighth Amendment's prohibition against "cruel and unusual punishments" had, ten years earlier during the era of the Warren Court, first been applied against the states by virtue of the Fourteenth Amendment (*Robinson v. California*, 1962). But while the Court's decision in *Gregg v. Georgia* (1976) upheld the death penalty's constitutionality after 35 states reenacted death penalty laws in *Furman*'s wake, the Court—in another case decided in that bicentennial year—simultaneously held that mandatory death sentences violated the Constitution. And following a three-justice dissent in *Rudolph v. Alabama* (1963) that questioned the constitutionality and disproportionality of death sentences for nonhomicidal rapists, the Court in *Coker v. Georgia* (1977) also found the death penalty to be unconstitutional for the rape of an adult woman where the victim was not killed.

Though only Justices William Brennan and Thurgood Marshall expressed the view that executions are *per se* unconstitutional (Mandery & Shemtob, 2014, pp. 711, 717), in the 1980s and the decades that followed, the U.S. Supreme Court continued to restrict the categories of death-eligible offenders. In *Enmund v. Florida* (1982), the Supreme Court held that the death penalty may not be imposed on a person who was a less culpable participant in a crime and who did not kill, attempt to kill, or intend to kill (*Enmund v. Florida*, 1982). In *Ford v. Wainwright* (1986), the Court held that the Eighth Amendment banned the execution of the insane. And in *Thompson v. Oklahoma* (1988), it barred the execution of offenders age 15 and under at the time of their crimes. Although the Court initially approved the execution of the intellectually disabled and 16- and 17-year-old offenders (*Penry v. Lynaugh* (1989); *Stanford v. Kentucky* (1989)), it later reversed course and outlawed those practices in *Atkins v. Virginia* (2002) and *Roper v. Simmons* (2005). While *Kennedy v. Louisiana* (2008) forbade the execution of nonhomicidal child rapists, an extension of its ruling in *Coker*, a more recent case—*Hurst v. Florida* (2016)—held that the Constitution requires that juries, not judges, find the aggravating factors necessary for the death penalty's imposition.

The U.S. Supreme Court has thus far rejected challenges to state lethal injection protocols in *Baze v. Rees* (2008) and *Glossip v. Gross* (2015). But the number of U.S. death sentences and executions has declined precipitously in the last decade, especially since the European Union banned the export of lethal injection drugs in 2011 (Ford, 2014).[18] For years now, there has been a shortage of lethal injection drugs in the United States (Horne, 2016), and the European Union has put in place a strict anti-torture regulation that reads in part: "Any export of goods which have no practical use other than for the purpose of capital punishment or for the purpose of torture and other cruel, inhuman or degrading treatment or punishment . . . shall be prohibited, irrespective of the origin of such equipment."[19] The May 2016 decision of Pfizer, the American drug company, to enforce its own ban on the sale of its drugs for use in lethal injections is bound to make it even more difficult than ever for U.S. states to carry out lethal injections. "Pfizer makes its products to enhance and save the lives of the patients we serve," the company said in a statement, adding: "Consistent with these values, Pfizer strongly objects to the use of its products as lethal injections for capital punishment" (Ford, 2016; Eckholm, 2016).

The Future (But Hard to Predict)

The U.S. Constitution's Eighth Amendment prohibits "cruel and unusual punishments,"[20] while the Fourteenth Amendment guarantees "equal protection of the laws" and makes the Eighth Amendment applicable to the states.[21] Since 1958, the U.S. Supreme Court has used the nonstatic "evolving standards of decency" test to evaluate Eighth Amendment claims and the constitutionality of punishments (Trop v. Dulles (1958), p. 101). The rationale: "The standard of extreme cruelty is not merely descriptive, but necessarily embodies a moral judgment. The standard itself remains the same, but its applicability must change as the basic mores of society change."[22] In adjudicating Eighth Amendment cases, the Court has been guided by "'objective indicia of society's standards, as expressed in legislative enactments and state practice with respect to executions.'"[23] The Court typically counts states using or prohibiting a practice, then tries to determine whether a "national consensus" against that practice exists. "It is not so much the number of these States that is significant," the Court has held, "but the consistency of the direction of change."[24] But, the Court has warned, "[c]onsensus is not dispositive." "Whether the death penalty is disproportionate to the crime committed depends as well upon the standards elaborated by controlling precedents and by the Court's own understanding and interpretation of the Eighth Amendment's text, history, meaning, and purpose," the Court held in *Kennedy v. Louisiana*, the case that outlawed the death penalty's use for nonhomicidal child rape.[25]

As to the death penalty's constitutionality, the closely divided opinion of the U.S. Supreme Court in *Glossip v. Gross* (2015) underscored the judicial and societal division on the issue. In that case, decided shortly before Justice Antonin Scalia's death, a bare, five-member majority upheld the constitutionality of Oklahoma's three-drug lethal injection protocol. And it did so in spite of the risk of botched executions from the use of midazolam, a drug death row inmates contended might fail to render them insensate and thus oblivious to physical pain at the moment of death. The petitioning death row inmates had asserted that Oklahoma's method of killing violated the Eighth Amendment because it created an unacceptable risk of severe pain. But the Court rejected that assertion, ruling that the inmates "failed to identify a known and available alternative method of execution that entails a lesser risk of pain, a requirement of all Eighth Amendment method-of-execution claims." The Court further emphasized: "the District Court did not commit clear error when it found that the prisoners failed to establish that

Oklahoma's use of a massive dose of midazolam in its execution protocol entails a substantial risk of severe pain" (*Glossip v. Gross*, 2015, pp. 2731–32). Notably, Pfizer's May 2016 announcement—coming in the wake of the *Glossip* decision—now forecloses the lawful use by correctional officials of seven drugs (among them, midazolam) previously used or considered for use in lethal injections (Eckholm, 2006).

The Court's majority opinion in *Glossip*, written by Justice Alito and joined by Chief Justice Roberts and Justices Scalia, Kennedy, and Thomas, drew two dissents. The first dissent, written by Justice Breyer and joined by Justice Ginsburg, called for the Court to take up the question of the death penalty's constitutionality. "[R]ather than try to patch up the death penalty's legal wounds one at a time," Justice Breyer wrote, "I would ask for full briefing on a more basic question: whether the death penalty violates the Constitution." "Today's administration of the death penalty," Breyer emphasized, "involves three fundamental constitutional defects: (1) serious unreliability, (2) arbitrariness in application, and (3) unconscionably long delays that undermine the death penalty's penological purpose." "Perhaps as a result," he added, "(4) most places within the United States have abandoned its use."[26] Justice Breyer's dissenting opinion pointed to evidence of wrongful convictions and exonerations; irrationality, geographic disparities, and racial and gender discrimination in the death penalty's application; and "excessively long periods of time that individuals typically spend on death row, alive but under sentence of death." As Breyer wrote before describing how rare executions had become since the 1970s: "In 2014, 35 individuals were executed. Those executions occurred, on average, nearly 18 years after a court initially pronounced its sentence of death."[27]

The second dissent, written by Justice Sotomayor and joined by Justices Ginsburg, Breyer, and Kagan, pointedly observed: "The State plans to execute petitioners using three drugs: midazolam, rocuronium bromide, and potassium chloride. The latter two drugs are intended to paralyze the inmate and stop his heart. But they do so in a torturous manner, causing burning, searing pain. It is thus critical that the first drug, midazolam, do what it is supposed to do, which is to render and keep the inmate unconscious." Justice Sotomayor found that Oklahoma's death row inmates had "presented ample evidence showing that the State's planned use" of midazolam "poses substantial, constitutionally intolerable risks." "Nevertheless," she wrote, "the Court today turns aside petitioners' plea that they at least be allowed a stay of execution while they seek to prove midazolam's inadequacy." "As a result," she stressed, in language that Justice Alito took umbrage to, "it leaves petitioners exposed to what may well be the chemical equivalent of being burned at the stake."[28] In his opinion, Justice Alito—on behalf of himself and those joining his majority opinion—replied: "[W]e find it appropriate to respond to the principal dissent's groundless suggestion that our decision is tantamount to allowing prisoners to be 'drawn and quartered, slowly tortured to death, or actually burned at the stake.' That is simply not true, and the principal dissent's resort to this outlandish rhetoric reveals the weakness of its legal arguments."[29]

The anomaly of American executions in the twenty-first century is that *nonlethal* corporal punishments have already been abandoned. America's penal system no longer uses ear cropping or the stocks, the pillory, or the whipping post, and America's judicial system would no longer tolerate the branding of criminals or other nonlethal bodily punishments. Indeed, in *Jackson v. Bishop*, the late Justice Harry Blackmun—then speaking for the U.S. Court of Appeals for the Eighth Circuit—wrote that the U.S. Constitution prohibited the whipping of Arkansas prisoners with a strap in order to maintain discipline. "[W]e have no difficulty in reaching the conclusion," Blackmun wrote for that federal appellate court, "that the use of the strap in the penitentiaries of Arkansas is punishment which, in this last third of the 20th century, runs afoul of the Eighth Amendment." "[T]he strap's use, irrespective of any precautionary conditions which may be imposed," he observed, "offends contemporary concepts of decency and human dignity and precepts of civilization which we profess to possess." "Corporal punishment," he concluded, "is degrading to the punisher and to the punished alike" (Bessler, 2013, pp. 297, 304, 430–33, 451; *Jackson v. Bishop* (1968), p. 579). While the Eighth Amendment has been held to require that prisoners be *protected* from harm, including future harm, the Supreme Court has *permitted* executions to go forward. Meanwhile, the Court has condemned prison overcrowding and the gratuitous beating of prisoners as Eighth Amendment violations. In one case, *Hope v. Pelzer* (2002), it described the handcuffing of a prisoner to a hitching post for seven hours, resulting in the inmate's dehydration, as an "obvious" Eighth Amendment violation (Bessler, 2014c, p. 245).

Increasingly, death sentences and executions are being seen as human rights violations and even tantamount to torture (Bessler, 2017a). Europe is now a death penalty-free zone, with Protocols No. 6 and 13 to the European Convention on Human Rights barring the death penalty's use in peacetime and wartime.[30] The U.S. Supreme Court has already described human dignity as the touchstone of the Eighth Amendment,[31] and the right to be free from cruelty and torture—as well as the right to human dignity and nondiscrimination—are universal rights.[32] While the American Bar Association has not taken a firm position against the death penalty, it has adopted a resolution calling into question the fairness of the death penalty's administration. Meanwhile, the American Law Institute—the leading independent organization dedicated to modernizing and improving the law—has stripped all of the death penalty provisions from the Model Penal Code.[33] And the American Medical Association—the county's leading doctors' organization—has determined that it is unethical for physicians to participate in executions. According to "Opinion 2.06—Capital Punishment" of the AMA's Code of Medical Ethics: "A physician, as a member of a profession dedicated to preserving life when there is hope of doing so, should not be a participant in a legally authorized execution."[34]

While the Italian philosopher Cesare Beccaria wrote about torture and capital punishment in separate chapters in *On Crimes and Punishments*, the modern death penalty is increasingly being seen through the lens of torture—a legal concept associated with the intentional infliction of severe pain or suffering, whether physical or mental in nature.[35] In a thematic report on the death penalty and the prohibition of torture made to the Third Committee of the 67th U.N. General Assembly on October 23, 2012, the U.N. Special Rapporteur on Torture, Juan Méndez, called upon states to consider whether the death penalty fails to respect the inherent dignity of the human person and amounts to cruel, inhuman and degrading treatment (CIDT) or torture.[36] "There is evidence," Méndez wrote,

> of an evolving standard within regional and local jurisprudence and state practice to frame the debate about the legality of the death penalty within the context of the fundamental concepts of human dignity and the prohibition of torture and CIDT.

As Méndez emphasized: "Regional and domestic courts have increasingly held that the death penalty, both as a general practice and through the specific methods of implementation and other surrounding circumstances, can amount to CIDT or even torture" (Méndez, 2012, p. 1).

While the U.S. Supreme Court has, to date, focused on the risk of *physical* pain at the time of a death row inmate's execution, the *psychological* pain and suffering associated with capital punishment—and the death penalty's dehumanizing effects—have yet to be fully considered by the Court. Justices Stephen Breyer and Ruth Bader Ginsburg—as with Justice John Paul Stevens before his retirement—want the Supreme Court to consider the constitutionality of prolonged stays on death row, but so far the Court has declined to review such a case despite numerous dissents from denials of certiorari calling for the Court to do so (Breyer, 2016).[37] While international law already strictly prohibits torture and forbids "mock"—or simulated—executions as torture, judicially sanctioned executions thus linger on despite the protestations of jurists like Justices Breyer and Ginsburg (Breyer, 2016). Meanwhile, Justice Anthony Kennedy expressed the Court's own ambivalence about executions in 2008. Writing for the Court in *Kennedy v. Louisiana*, Justice Kennedy—often described as the "swing vote" on cases coming before the nation's highest court—freely acknowledged: "When the law punishes by death, it risks its own sudden descent into brutality, transgressing the constitutional commitment to decency and restraint" (*Kennedy v. Louisiana*, 2008, p. 420).

Notes

1 See also Taylor (2006, p. 30) ("Murders involving a killer and killed from different nations were especially dangerous and called for special exertions by the chiefs of both peoples. Otherwise, the feud between families could escalate into a war between nations. During the fifteenth century, such bloody conflicts had nearly consumed the Iroquois nations, inducing them to form their confederacy, which primarily served to cover graves as an alternative to war."). Compare Taylor (2006, p. 195) ("The Indians of the Genesee apparently bristled at this unilateral assertion of settler justice, for the executions broke the custom of consulting with the chiefs and permitting them to atone for a killing by covering the grave with goods."); Taylor (2006, p. 29) ("[N]othing so appalled or alarmed Indians as the public hanging of one of their own people. Nothing more viscerally and immediately threatened Indian autonomy as a free people. To defend their sovereignty, Indians clung to their customary alternative: a ceremony known as 'covering the grave.'").

2 Citing Steckel and Wallis (2007).

3 Mound 72, Cahokia Mounds State Historic Site, http://cahokiamounds.org/mound/mound-72/.

4 Compare Elster (2004, p. 13) ("[t]he early colonists used hanging").

5 (Adair, 1775, pp. 90, 138, 141–143, 146–152, 285–286). This text was recently reprinted in 2013 by Cambridge University Press Adair (2013) (1775).

6 In 1639, settlers in Connecticut also wrote a document called "The Fundamental Orders" that provided that the General Assembly "shall have power to administer justice according to the Laws here established, and for want thereof according to the rule of the word of God" (Collier, 2003, pp. 205, 207).

7 See also Kohut (2010, p. 45) ("Nathaniel Hawthorne's book about colonial America, *The Scarlet Letter*, is about female adultery, which was, at the time, still a crime for women. The punishment was often to have the letter 'A' branded on their foreheads or permanently placed on their clothing so everyone who saw them knew that they were unfaithful to their husbands.").

8 See also Kumar (2004, p. 120) ("At least three American dramatists in 1951 and 1953 wrote plays about the Salem witch trials, all of which were oblique comments on the mass hysteria that seemed again to be sweeping America. Of these *The Crucible* is the most celebrated; its first production ran for nearly two hundred performances and it has already achieved the status of a modern classic.").

9 Table 18.4—Slave Conspiracies and Unrest within the Present Boundaries of the United States, 1657–1774.

10 The world's anti-death penalty movement has been traced to the writings of Cesare Beccaria in the 1760s—writings that inspired Americans to restrict or curtail the use of executions (Bessler, 2018). Beccaria, of course, had intellectual influences of his own. See Derrida (2012, Vol. 1, p. 212) ("Obviously, Beccaria himself had his teachers who were the teachers of the Enlightenment. He explicitly lays claim to the legacy of d'Alembert, Montesquieu, Diderot, Helvétius, Buffon, Hume, d'Holbach and especially Rousseau, even if he does not mention the latter and sometimes takes a distance from him here or there.").

11 Kingston (2009) (noting that America's founders "lifted their view of separation of powers" from Montesquieu's *The Spirit of Laws*); Howard (2011, p. 41) ("In 1748, the French Baron, Charles de Montesquieu, published *The Spirit of Laws*. That book is widely considered to be the most important analysis of government since the classics of Greece and Rome. It was well known to America's founders who incorporated some of Montesquieu's insights into the United States Constitution.").

12 Sargent (1856, p. 207).

13 In *The Social Contract* itself, Rousseau had defended capital punishment for criminals. In Chapter Five, "Of the Right of Life and Death," Rousseau had begun: "It is asked how individuals who have no right to dispose of their own life can transfer to the Sovereign this same right which they do not have. The question seems difficult to resolve only because it is badly put." According to Rousseau:

> The social treaty has the preservation of the contracting parties as its end. Whoever wills the end, also wills the means, and those means are inseparable from certain risks and even certain losses. Whoever wants to preserve his life at the expense of others ought also to give it up for them when necessary.

As Rousseau continued:

> The death penalty imposed on criminals can be looked upon from more or less the same point of view: it is in order not to become the victim of an assassin that one consents to die if one becomes an assassin oneself. Under this treaty, far from disposing of one's own life, one only thinks of guaranteeing it, and it should not be presumed that at the time any of the contracting parties is planning to get himself hanged. Gourevitch (1997), p. 64.

14 See Schabas (2013, p. 5); Bedau (1996, pp. 789, 805). ("The original impetus to abolish the death penalty two hundred years ago in Europe was fueled by Cesare Beccaria's little book, *On Crimes and Punishments*, and by Jeremy Bentham in England.")

15 Dr. Benjamin Rush—Thomas Jefferson's friend and correspondent—felt much the same way, saying capital punishment "lessens the horror of taking away human life" and thus "tends to multiply murders" (Banner, 2002, p. 104).

16 The number of citations to Beccaria in America's founding era is very large. *See generally* Bessler, 2014b; Bessler, 2018; compare Cornell (2006, p. 225, n. 19) ("slightly more than a third of all libraries in the period 1777–90 contained a copy of the essay by Beccaria favored by Jefferson"; "[i]n his study of the patterns of citation to various thinkers in published writings in the Founding era, Donald Lutz found that Beccaria accounted for about 1 percent of citations in the 1770s" and "3 percent in the 1780s").

17 E.g., Lewis (2009, p. 30) ("[Thomas] Eddy leaned heavily on the experience of Pennsylvania in constructing New York's first penitentiary. In April, 1796, he wrote for advice to Caleb Lownes, a Quaker iron-merchant who was an inspector of the Walnut Street Jail. Lownes responded with a long letter giving his views on penal discipline and containing detailed information about improvements being contemplated at the Philadelphia prison."); Cheli (2003, p. 9) ("Built in 1828 as the third prison in New York State, Sing Sing Prison rose from the rocky shores of the Hudson River and eventually became world famous. The first prison in New York, called Newgate, was built in 1797 and was located in Greenwich Village, New York City, near the present-day Christopher Street, also on the shores of the Hudson River."); Cheli (2003, p. 9) ("In 1816, a second prison called Auburn State Prison, located well upstate, was built. With Auburn, a new theory of prison administration was put into practice. The Auburn system implemented separate confinement at night and perpetual silence during the day. The prisoners worked in shops during the day and spent the nights in total darkness."); Roth (2010, p. 110) ("In 1829, Pennsylvania responded to the Auburn model with the opening of Eastern State Penitentiary, admitting its first prisoner on October 25. Often referred to simply as 'Cherry Hill' because it was built on the site of a cherry orchard, it was the largest building project in America up to that time."); Payne, Oliver & Marion (2016, p. 393) ("A number of other penitentiaries were built and opened during this time. Maryland and Massachusetts opened theirs in 1829, and Tennessee and Vermont followed in 1831. The next year, Georgia and New Hampshire opened their penitentiaries, and 'between 1834 and 1837 Louisiana and Missouri built penitentiaries, as did Ohio and New Jersey.' Going into the early 1840s, Mississippi, Alabama, Michigan, Indiana, and Illinois opened theirs."); Roth (2006, p. 279) (discussing the Three Prisons Act).

18 Referencing the 2011 export ban by the European Union.

19 Council Regulation (EC) No 1236/2005 of 27 June 2005 concerning trade in certain goods which could be used for capital punishment, torture or other cruel, inhuman or degrading treatment or punishment, http://eur-lex.europa.eu/LexUriServ/LexUriServ.do?uri=OJ:L:2005:200:0001:0019:EN:PDF.

20 U.S. Const., amend. VIII.

21 U.S. Const., amend. XIV; *Robinson v. California* (1962); Bessler, 2017b.

22 *Kennedy*, 554 U.S. at 419 (quoting *Furman*, 408 U.S. at 382 (Burger, C. J., dissenting)).

23 *Kennedy*, 554 U.S. at 421 (quoting *Roper*, 543 U.S. at 563).

24 *Kennedy*, 554 U.S. at 426; *Atkins*, 536 U.S. at 315.

25 *Kennedy*, 554 U.S. at 421.

26 *Glossip*, 135 S. Ct. at 2755–56 (Breyer, J., dissenting).

27 *Glossip*, 135 S. Ct. at 2756–64, 2772–76 (Breyer, J., dissenting).

28 *Glossip*, 135 S. Ct. at 2780–81 (Sotomayor, J., dissenting).

29 *Glossip*, 135 S. Ct. at 2746 (citing id. at 2795 [Sotomayor, J., dissenting]).

30 Protocol No. 6 to the Convention for the Protection of Human Rights and Fundamental Freedoms Concerning the Abolition of the Death Penalty, Art. 1 ("The death penalty shall be abolished. No one shall be condemned to such penalty or executed."); id., Art. 2 ("A State may make provision in its law for the death penalty in respect of acts committed in time of war or of imminent threat of war; such penalty shall be applied only in the instances laid down in the law and in accordance with its provisions."); Protocol No. 13 to the Convention for the Protection of Human Rights and Fundamental Freedoms, concerning the abolition of the death penalty in all circumstances, Art. 1 ("The death penalty shall be abolished. No one shall be condemned to such penalty or executed."); id., Art. 2 ("No derogation from the provisions of this Protocol shall be made under Article 15 of the Convention.").

31 *Brown v. Plata* (2011), p. 510 ("Prisoners retain the essence of human dignity inherent in all persons. Respect for that dignity animates the Eighth Amendment prohibition against cruel and unusual punishment."); *Woodson v. North Carolina* (1976), p. 304 ("While the prevailing practice of individualized sentencing determinations generally reflects simply enlightened policy rather than a constitutional imperative, we believe that in capital cases the fundamental respect for humanity underlying the Eighth Amendment . . . requires

consideration of the character and record of the individual offender and the circumstances of the particular offense as a constitutionally indispensable part of the process of inflicting the penalty of death."); *Gregg v. Georgia* (1976), p. 182 ("[T]he Eighth Amendment demands more than that a challenged punishment be acceptable to contemporary society. The Court also must ask whether it comports with the basic concept of human dignity at the core of the Amendment."); see also *Atiyeh v. Capps* (1981), p. 1315 (noting that *Trop v. Dulles* (1958), p. 100 "stated in dicta that the touchstone of the Eighth Amendment is 'nothing less than the dignity of man'").

32 Universal Declaration of Human Rights, United Nations G.A. Res. 217A(III), 3rd Sess., preamble & Arts. 2 & 5, U.N. Doc. A/RES/3/217 (1948).

33 Liptak (2010) ("Last fall, the American Law Institute, which created the intellectual framework for the modern capital justice system almost 50 years ago, pronounced its project a failure and walked away from it.").

34 Opinion 2.06—Capital Punishment, American Medical Association, www.ama-assn.org/ama/pub/physician-resources/medical-ethics/code-medical-ethics/opinion206.page?.

35 United Nations Convention Against Torture and Other Cruel, Inhuman or Degrading Treatment or Punishment, *adopted* Dec. 10, 1984, Treaty Doc. No. 100-200, 1465 U.N.T.S. 85.

36 "The Special Rapporteur's Thematic Report on the Death Penalty," *Anti-Torture Initiative*, http://antitorture.org/new-death-penalty/.

37 In June 2016, the U.S. Supreme Court briefly agreed to review whether prolonged stays on death row violate the Eighth Amendment guarantee against "cruel and unusual punishments." But the Court then declined to review that issue. See "Supreme Court to Hear Texas Death Penalty Cases Dealing with Racial Bias, Intellectual Disability," *Death Penalty Information Center*, www.deathpenaltyinfo.org/node/6475 ("The Court granted review on one of two issues presented in Bobby James Moore's petition for certiorari, whether a state may reject current medical standards in determining intellectual disability. It initially appeared to have granted review of a second issue as well, whether Moore's 'extraordinarily long' confinement on death row violates the Eighth Amendment ban on cruel and unusual punishment. However, in an updated order, the court clarified that it was limiting its review to only the intellectual disability question. Moore was sentenced to death more than 35 years ago, and has been diagnosed as intellectually disabled by medical professionals.").

References

Adair, J. (1775). *The history of the American Indians: Particularly those nations adjoining to the Mississippi, East and West Florida, Georgia, South and North Carolina, and Virginia.* London: Edward and Charles Dilly.

Adair, J. (2013). *The history of the American Indians: Particularly those nations adjoining to the Mississippi, East and West Florida, Georgia, South and North Carolina, and Virginia.* Cambridge: Cambridge University Press.

Adams, H. (2010). *An abridgement of the history of New-England.* Carlisle, MA: Applewood Books.

Anckar, C. (2004). *Determinants of the death penalty: A comparative study of the world.* New York: Routledge.

Axelrod, A. (2009). *Little-known wars of great and lasting impact: The turning points in our history we should know more about.* Beverly, MA: Fair Winds Press.

Bailyn, B. (2012). *The barbarous years: The conflict of civilizations, 1600–1675.* New York: Vintage Books.

Baker, D. V. (2007). American Indian executions in historical context. *Crim. Just. Studies, 20,* 315.

Banner, S. (2002). *The death penalty: An American history.* Cambridge, MA: Harvard University Press.

Beccaria, C. (1775). *An essay on crimes and punishments* (4th ed.). p. 103. Retrieved from http://archive.org/stream/essayoncrimespun1775becc#page/n3/mode/2up.

Bedau, H. A. (1996). Interpreting the eighth amendment: Principled vs. populist strategies. *T.M. Cooley L. Rev., 13,* 789.

Bellamy, R. (Ed.). (1995). *Beccaria: On Crimes and Punishments and other writings* (R. Davies, Trans.). Cambridge, UK: Cambridge University Press.

Bessler, J. D. (1997). *Death in the dark: Midnight executions in America.* Boston: Northeastern University Press.

Bessler, J. D. (2012). *Cruel and unusual: The American death penalty and the founders' Eighth Amendment.* Boston, MA: Northeastern University Press.

Bessler, J. D. (2013). The anomaly of executions: The cruel and unusual punishments clause in the 21st century. *Br. J. Am. Leg. Studies, 2,* 297.

Bessler, J. D. (2014a). The American enlightenment: Eliminating capital punishment in the United States. In L. Scherdin (Ed.), *Capital punishment: A hazard to a sustainable criminal justice system?* (pp. 96–97). Surrey, England: Ashgate.

Bessler, J. D. (2014b). The birth of American law: An Italian philosopher and the American revolution. Durham, NC: Carolina Academic Press.

Bessler, J. D. (2014c). The death penalty in decline: From colonial America to the present. *Crim. L. Bull., 50,* 245.

Bessler, J. D. (2017a). *The death penalty as torture: From the dark ages to abolition.* Durham, NC: Carolina Academic Press.

Bessler, J. D. (2017b). The inequality of America's death penalty: A crossroads for capital punishment at the intersection of the Eighth and Fourteenth Amendments. *Wash. & Lee L. Rev. Online.*, *72*, Issue 1. Retrieved at http://scholarlycommons.law.wlu.edu/cgi/viewcontent.cgi?article=1065&context=wlulr-online.

Bessler, J. D. (2018). *The celebrated marquis: An Italian noble and the making of the modern world.* Durham, NC: Carolina Academic Press.

Breyer, S. (2016). *Against the death penalty* (J. Bessler, ed.). Washington, DC: Brookings Institution Press.

Burch, M. (2004). *Making Native American hunting, fighting, and survival tools: The complete guide to creating arrowheads, axes, and other primitive implements.* Guilford, CT: The Lyons Press, 2004.

Burkhead, M. D. (2009). *A life for a life: The American debate over the death penalty.* Jefferson, NC: McFarland & Co.

Campbell, B. C. (2008). *Disasters, accidents, and crises in American history: A reference guide to the nation's most catastrophic events.* New York: Facts on File.

Carpenter, R. M. (2012). *American Indian history day by day: A reference guide to events.* Santa Barbara, CA: Greenwood.

Cheli, G. (2003). *Sing Sing prison.* Charleston, SC: Arcadia Publishing.

Chipman, D. (1846). *The life of Hon. Nathaniel Chipman, LL.D.* Boston: Charles C. Little and James Brown.

Chitwood, O. P. (1961). *A history of colonial America* (3rd ed.). New York: Harper & Brothers.

Cohler, A. M., Miller, B. C., & Stone, H. S. (Eds.). (1989). *Montesquieu, The Spirit of the Laws.* Cambridge: Cambridge University Press.

Collier, C. (2003). Why the first law school in the United States was established in Connecticut. *Int'l J. Legal Info.*, *31*, 205.

Cornell, S. (2006). *A well-regulated militia: The founding fathers and the origins of gun control in America.* Oxford: Oxford University Press.

Derrida, J. (2012). *The death penalty* (Vol. 1, P. Kamuf, Trans.). Chicago: The University of Chicago Press.

Eckholm, E. (2016, May 13). Pfizer blocks the use of its drugs in executions. *New York Times.*

Edge, L. B. (2009). *Locked up: A history of the U.S. prison system.* Minneapolis, MN: Twenty-First Century Books.

Elster, J. A. (Ed.). (2004). *The death penalty.* San Diego, CA: Greenhaven Press.

Eskridge, W. N., Jr. (2008). *Dishonorable passions: Sodomy laws in America, 1861–2003.* New York: Viking.

Finkelman, P. (2014). *Slavery and the founders: Race and liberty in the age of Jefferson* (3rd ed.). Armonk, NY: M.E. Sharpe.

Fitzpatrick, J. C. (Ed.). (1932). *The writings of George Washington from the original manuscript sources 1745–1799.* Washington, DC: Government Printing Office.

Ford, M. (2014, February 18). Can Europe end the death penalty in America? An EU export ban on lethal-injection drugs is making U.S. executions more difficult to perform. *The Atlantic.* Retrieved from www.theatlantic.com/international/archive/2014/02/can-europe-end-the-death-penalty-in-america/283790/

Ford, M. (2016, May 13). Pfizer v. lethal injections. *The Atlantic.*

Galliher, J. F., Koch, L. W., Keys, D. P., & Guess, T. J. (2002). *America without the death penalty: States leading the way.* Boston: Northeastern University Press.

Goldberg, A. J. (1986). Memorandum to the conference re: Capital punishment, October term, 1963. *S. Tex. L.J.*, *27*, 493.

Gourevitch, V. (Ed.). (1997). *Rousseau: The Social Contract and other later political writings* (V. Gourevitch, Trans.). Cambridge, UK: Cambridge University Press.

Grams, M. (2003). *The great experiment: The rights and duties of citizenship.* Raleigh, NC: Lulu.com.

Grant, D. L. (1993). *The way it was in the South: The black experience in Georgia.* Athens, GA: The University of Georgia Press.

Green, S. K. (2015). *Inventing a Christian America: The myth of the religious founding.* Oxford: Oxford University Press.

Hadden, S. E. (2008). The fragmented laws of slavery in the colonial and revolutionary eras. In M. Grossberg & C. Tomlins (Eds.), *The Cambridge history of law in America: Early America (1580–1815)* (p. 253). Cambridge: Cambridge University Press.

Haley, J. L. (2014). *Captive paradise: A history of Hawaii.* New York: St. Martin's Press.

Harris, G. (1847). *The life of Lord Chancellor Hardwicke* (Vol. 1). London: Edward Moxon.

Hill, F. (1995). *A delusion of Satan: The full story of the Salem witch trials.* Old Saybrook, CT: Tantor Media.

Hinks, P., & McKivigan, J. (Eds.). (2007). *Encyclopedia of antislavery and abolition.* Westport, CT: Greenwood Press.

Horne, J. (2016, May–June). Lethal injection drug shortage. *E-Newsletter, The Council of State Governments.* Retrieved from www.csg.org/pubs/capitolideas/enews/issue65_4.aspx.

Howard, J. A. (2011). *Christianity: Lifeblood of America's free society (1620–1945).* Bloomington, IN: Crossbooks Publishing.

Johnson, C. D. (1995). *Understanding The Scarlet Letter: A student casebook to issues, sources, and historical documents.* Westport, CT: The Greenwood Press.

Kennedy-Andrews, E. (Ed.). (1999). *Nathaniel Hawthorne: The Scarlet Letter.* New York: Columbia University Press.

Kingston, R. E. (Ed.). (2009) *Montesquieu and his legacy*. Albany: State University of New York Press.

Kirchmeier, J. L. (2015). *Imprisoned by the past: Warren McCleskey and the American death penalty*. Oxford: Oxford University Press.

Kohut, M. R. (2010). *When you have to go to prison: A complete guide for you and your family*. Ocala, FL: Atlantic Publishing Group.

Kumar, S. (2004). *The allegory of quest: A study in Arthur Miller's plays*. Delhi, India: Kalpaz Publications.

Latzer, B., & McCord, D. (2010). *Death penalty cases: Leading U.S. Supreme Court cases on capital punishment* (3rd ed.). Oxford: Butterworth-Heinemann.

Levinson, D. (Ed.). (2002). *Encyclopedia of crime and punishment*. Thousand Oaks, CA: Sage Publications.

Lewis, W. D. (2009). *From Newgate to Dannemora: The rise of the penitentiary in New York, 1796–1848*. Ithaca, NY: Cornell University Press.

Liptak, A. (2010, January 4). Group gives up death penalty work. *New York Times*.

Mandery, E. J., & Shemtob, Z. B. (2014). Supreme convolution: What the capital cases teach us about Supreme Court decision-making. *New Eng. L. Rev.*, *48*, 711.

Martin, P. (1998). Scalping: Fact & fantasy. In B. Bigelow & B. Peterson (Eds.), *Rethinking Columbus: The next 500 years* (p. 58). Milwaukee, WI: Rethinking Schools.

The Massachusetts Body of Liberties. (1641). Retrieved from https://history.hanover.edu/texts/masslib.html.

McKenzie, A. (2007). *Tyburn's martyrs: Execution in England, 1675–1775*. London: Hambledon Continuum.

McLennan, R. M. (2008). *The crisis of imprisonment: Protest, politics, and the making of the American penal state, 1776–1941*. Cambridge: Cambridge University Press.

McLynn, F. (1989). *Crime and punishment in eighteenth-century England*. London: Routledge.

Meggs, K. (2012). *99 nooses: Illinois justice at the end of a rope, 1779–1896*. Rockford, IL: Black Oak Media.

Méndez, J. E. (2012). The death penalty and the absolute prohibition of torture and cruel, inhuman, and degrading treatment or punishment. *American University Washington College of Law*. Retrieved from www.wcl.american.edu/hrbrief/20/1mendez.pdf.

Meranze, M. (2008) Penality and the colonial project: Crime, punishment, and the regulation of morals in early America. In M. Grossberg & C. Tomlins (Eds.), *The Cambridge history of law in America: Early America (1580–1815)* (p. 178) Cambridge: Cambridge University Press.

Miller, W. R. (Ed.). (2002). *The social history of crime and punishment in America: An encyclopedia*. Thousand Oaks, CA: Sage Publications.

Miller, W. R. (Ed.). (2012). *The social history of crime and punishment in America: An encyclopedia*. Thousand Oaks, CA: Sage Publications.

Monachesi, E. (1956). Pioneers in criminology IX—Cesare Beccaria (1738–1794). *J. Crim. L. Criminology & Pol. Sci.*, *46*, 439.

Mueller, G. O. W., & Adler, F. (1995). The emergence of criminal justice: Tracing the route to Neolithic times. In J. McCord & J. H. Laub (Eds.), *Contemporary masters in criminology* (p. 68). New York: Plenum Press.

Mullins, J. G. (1978). *Hawaiian journey: Images of yesteryear*. Honolulu, HI: Mutual Publishing.

Olsen, K. (1999). *Daily life in 18th-century England*. Westport, CT: Greenwood Press.

Palmer, L. J., Jr. (1998). *The death penalty: An American citizen's guide to understanding federal and state laws*. Jefferson, NC: McFarland & Co.

Pauketat, T. R. (2009). *Cahokia: Ancient America's Great City on the Mississippi*. New York: Penguin Books.

Payne, B. K., Oliver, W. M., & Marion, N. E. (2016). *Introduction to criminal justice: A balanced approach*. Thousand Oaks, CA: Sage Publications.

Pinker, S. (2011). *The better angels of our nature: Why violence has declined*. New York: Penguin Books.

Purvis, T. L. (1999). *Colonial America to 1763*. New York: Facts on File.

Richter, M. (Ed. & Trans.). (1990). *Montesquieu: Selected political writings*. Indianapolis, IN: Hackett Publishing Co.

Roach, M. K. (2002). *The Salem witch trials: A day-by-day chronicle of a community under siege*. Lanham, MD: Taylor Trade Publishing.

Rodriguez, J. P. (Ed.). (1997). *The historical encyclopedia of world slavery*. Santa Barbara, CA: ABC-CLIO.

Rosen, F. (2003). *Classical utilitarianism from Hume to Mill*. New York: Routledge.

Roth, M. P. (2006). *Prisons and prison systems: A global encyclopedia*. Westport, CT: Greenwood Press.

Roth, M. P. (2010). *Crime and punishment: A history of the criminal justice system* (2nd ed.). Belmont, CA: Wadsworth.

Rountree, H. C. (1989). *The Powhatan Indians of Virginia: Their traditional culture*. Norman: University of Oklahoma Press.

Sargent, L. M. (1856). *A sexton of the old school, dealings with the dead* (Vol. 1). Boston: Dutton and Wentworth.

Schabas, W. A. (2013). *The abolition of the death penalty in international law* (3rd ed.). Cambridge: Cambridge University Press.

Schiff, S. (2015). *The witches: Salem, 1692*. New York: Little, Brown and Co.

Siegel, L. J. (2011). *Criminology* (11th ed.). Belmont, CA: Cengage Learning.

Steckel, R., & Wallis, J. (2007). Stones, bones, and states: A new approach to the Neolithic revolution. http://www.nber.org/confer/2007/daes07/steckel.pdf.

Stone, S. C. S. (2015) *Yesterday in Hawai'i: A voyage through time* (2nd ed.). Honolulu, HI: Island Heritage Publishing.

Taylor, A. (2006). *The divided ground: Indians, settlers, and the northern borderland of the American revolution.* New York: Vintage Books.

Thomas, A. (Ed.) (2008). *Cesare Beccaria, On Crimes and Punishments and other writings.* Toronto: University of Toronto Press.

Twitchell, N. (2012). *The politics of the rope: The campaign to abolish capital punishment in Britain 1955–1969.* Bury St. Edmunds, England: Arena Books.

Welch, M. (2011). *Corrections: A critical approach* (3rd ed.). New York: Routledge.

Wice, P. B. (2009). *Presidents in retirement: Alone and out of office.* Lanham, MD: Lexington Books.

Cases Cited

Atkins v. Virginia, 536 U.S. 304 (2002).
Atiyeh v. Capps, 449 U.S. 1312 (1981).
Baze v. Rees, 553 U.S. 35 (2008).
Brown v. Plata, 563 U.S. 493 (2011).
Coker v. Georgia, 433 U.S. 584 (1977).
Enmund v. Florida, 458 U.S. 782 (1982).
Ford v. Wainwright, 477 U.S. 399 (1986).
Furman v. Georgia, 408 U.S. 238 (1972).
Glossip v. Gross, 135 S. Ct. 2726 (2015).
Gregg v. Georgia, 428 U.S. 153 (1976).
Hope v. Pelzer, 536 U.S. 730 (2002).
Hurst v. Florida, 135 S. Ct. 1531 (2016).
In re Kemmler, 136 U.S. 436 (1890).
Jackson v. Bishop, 404 F.2d 571 (8th Cir. 1968).
Kennedy v. Louisiana, 554 U.S. 407 (2008).
McGautha v. California, 402 U.S. 183 (1971).
Marbury v. Madison, 5 U.S. 137 (1803).
Penry v. Lynaugh, 492 U.S. 302 (1989).
Robinson v. California, 370 U.S. 660 (1962).
Roper v. Simmons, 543 U.S. 551 (2005).
Rudolph v. Alabama, 375 U.S. 889 (1963).
Stanford v. Kentucky, 492 U.S. 361 (1989).
Thompson v. Oklahoma, 487 U.S. 815 (1988).
Trop v. Dulles, 356 U.S. 86 (1958).
Wilkerson v. Utah, 99 U.S. 130 (1879).
Woodson v. North Carolina, 428 U.S. 280 (1976).

2

CAPITAL PUNISHMENT AND LYNCHING

Margaret Vandiver

Introduction

Lethal punishment has taken the lives of thousands of people in the United States. These killings fall into two categories, legal executions and illegal lynchings.[1] Questions about the relationship between the two have engaged scholars since at least the early years of the twentieth century (Cutler, 1905/1969, 1907; Bye, 1919) and continue to generate research. This chapter explores the relationship by addressing two main issues: the link between lynchings and executions during the lynching era, and the lingering influence of lynching on modern capital punishment.[2] Despite the striking resemblance between some executions and lynchings during the historic period, close examination reveals a complex and varied relationship between the two forms of lethal punishment. The brutal and immediate violence of lynchings appears to be in stark contrast with the highly bureaucratic and lengthy processes involved in the current administration of capital punishment; however, there are intriguing indications that the mob killings of the earlier period may continue to influence modern practices.

Scholarship on lynching has flourished in the past several decades (Pfeifer, 2014). Much of this work falls into the general categories of detailed case studies, historical examinations of geographical areas over long periods of time, and quantitative analyses. Case studies can illustrate both strong similarities and differences between the two forms of lethal punishment. All efforts to use statistical data to study the relationship between historic executions and lynchings are potentially flawed due to the fact that we do not have complete inventories of either practice. More recent efforts to trace the influence of historic lynchings on the modern administration of capital punishment face a difficult challenge in explaining the mechanism by which relatively rare historic events can continue to influence current outcomes, especially in the face of the enormous demographic changes in many of the areas where lynchings were most common.

Despite the many difficulties of the research and the limitations imposed by incomplete data, the issues explored in this chapter are important and timely. The death penalty in America faces legal and legislative challenges, while the pace of death sentences and executions is steeply declining. Although complete abolition is unlikely in the near future, capital punishment is in the midst of reevaluation and reforms that will shape whatever course the punishment subsequently follows. The practice of mass lynchings before jubilant crowds has ended in America, but the shadow cast by these killings is a long one, and their emotional resonance is still extremely strong. "Underground" lynchings, those carried out secretly by small groups or by posses of deputized white men, continue to influence our reactions to modern hate crimes and questionable killings by law enforcement (NAACP, 1940).

Lynchings and Historic Executions Compared

In February 1901, Fred King, suspected of the attempted rape of a young white woman, was escorted by local law enforcement officers from the Dyersburg, Tennessee, jail to the courthouse. A jury and judge heard evidence from the owner of the bloodhounds that had tracked King, from the former sheriff, and from a relative of the victim. King took the stand, and after initially denying the crime, he confessed. King was found guilty; after a pause for prayer, he was taken from the courtroom and immediately hanged (Dyersburg is aroused, 1901, February 18; One negro lynched, 1901, February 18; Lynched in light of day, 1901, February 19; Triple lynching was averted, 1901, February 19; Negro is missing, 1901, February 20; Vandiver, 2006, pp. 93–96).

Also in February 1901, Ike Fitzgerald was arrested for the rape of a white girl in nearby Lake County, Tennessee. Due to threats of lynching, he was removed from the local jail and put in the Dyersburg jail where Fred King was held. A month after King was hanged, Fitzgerald was returned to Lake County. His trial began upon his arrival and continued on the next day. After evidence was heard and the jury deliberated, he was hanged at once (Black brute, 1901, February 2; Dyersburg is aroused, 1901, February 18; One negro lynched, 1901, February 18; Triple lynching was averted, 1901, February 19; Negro is missing, 1901, February 20; Hung jury, 1901, March 18; Old story, 1901, March 18; Ike Fitzgerald hanged, 1901, March 18).

In 1902, Henry Wilson, suspected of the murder of a deputy sheriff in Sumterville, Florida, was tried in a courtroom filled with angry men, many of them carrying Winchester rifles. During the trial, at least one shot was fired inside the courtroom; the victim's brother and the sheriff threatened each other at gunpoint; the crowd surged toward the prisoner, leading the sheriff to threaten to use deadly force to protect Wilson; and the judge had the prisoner handcuffed to himself in order to safely escort him out of court. Wilson was hanged the next day (Squally times, 1902, April 2; Judge left bench, 1902, April 4; Henry hung, 1902, April 5; Murderer Henry hung, 1902, April 5; Rogers & Denham, 2001, p. 166–168; Vandiver, 2006, pp. 99–101).

Which of these cases were lynchings, and which were legal executions? The relatively orderly trial of Fred King was carried out by a mob whose members acted as judge, jury, executioners, and spectators. The riotous trial of Henry Wilson was legal and his execution was expedited by direct order of the governor of Florida. Ike Fitzgerald experienced both situations: he was legally tried, but when the jurors reported that they were unable to reach a verdict, the spectators in the courtroom seized him from the authorities and immediately lynched him.

Similarities

These cases illustrate the overlap that occurred between some lynchings and legal executions. Mobs made their power felt in legal as well as in illegal proceedings, and the authorities were often willing to abandon due process and deliberate speed in order to provide an execution that was technically carried out under law. As W. Fitzhugh Brundage noted, in some cases courts "punished with a disregard for evidence and a ferocity only a step removed from the so-called justice imposed by mobs" (Brundage, 1993, p. 71). Mobs sometimes imitated the forms of law and "patterned their proceedings . . . on the very judicial procedures they are characteristically said to flout" (Kaufman-Osborn, 2006, p. 35). It is hard to argue that the legal trial of Henry Wilson provided more due process than the illegal trial of Fred King. Indeed, after King's hanging, the mob took his suspected accomplice from the Dyersburg jail, questioned him, and then returned him to jail, having decided that the evidence was insufficient to justify lynching him. This action provides a contrast to that of the Lake County mob two weeks later, which responded to the hung jury in Ike Fitzgerald's case by dragging him out of court and hanging him.

Historic executions and lynchings have a number of obvious similarities. In both forms of collective lethal violence, people who had power, whether legitimately or not, decided that a person had committed an offense that deserved the infliction of death as punishment. Lynchings and early executions were generally carried out by local residents, in the county where the offense occurred, generally in public and attended by very large crowds. The clearest overlap between capital punishment and lynching occurs between these local public executions and lynchings carried out in front of large groups of spectators, although Michael Trotti cautions that there were important differences between the two (2011, pp. 207–208).

Similarities in Demographics and Location

During the height of the lynching era in the South, lynchings outnumbered legal executions; lynching constituted a "pervasive and semiofficial institution in the South" (Brundage, 1993, p. 3). Allen, Clubb, and Lacey provide statistics that allow comparisons of the frequency of legal and extralegal executions over a period of 40 years in ten Southern states (2008, Table 4.3).[3] Based on calculations from their figures, lynchings made up 58.7% of the total of legal and illegal executions between 1886 and 1895; 48.2% between 1896 and 1905; 41.6% between 1906 and 1915; and 45.5% between 1916 and 1925.

Comparisons of the demographics of those who died in both types of execution rely on incomplete data, but reveal similar patterns. Men were overwhelmingly the victims of both practices; women were fewer than 3% of persons lynched and fewer than 1% of those executed. African Americans were almost 88% of the victims of Southern lynch mobs and slightly over 76% of those legally executed (Tolnay & Beck, 1995; Espy & Smykla, no date; Trotti, 2011).[4]

Just over half the legal executions carried out by American states occurred in the 11 states of the former Confederacy in the years between 1930, when the federal government began to keep statistics, and 1967, after which an informal moratorium on executions extended until 1977. Some non-Southern states had very high numbers of executions, however, including California, Ohio, New York, and Pennsylvania. Clear regional and racial patterns are evident when executions for rape are broken out from the total; 87% of these executions took place in states of the former Confederacy and 89% of those executed for rape were African American men (Bureau of Justice Statistics, 1982, Tables 1 and 2).

Justifications for Lethal Punishment

It may be surprising to modern readers, but lynching had ardent supporters at all levels of white society. This support was not always abstract: there are many documented instances of prominent people participating in lynchings. Leon Litwack cites the 1911 lynching of Willis Jackson in South Carolina, in which the mob was led by a member of the state legislature, whose son, the local newspaper editor, also participated. Governor Cole Blease responded to the event by saying that far from trying to prevent lynchings, he would, if necessary, resign his office in order to lead the mob himself (Litwack, 1998, p. 296). As this example indicates, support for lynching was expressed at the highest levels of state government, with a number of Southern governors excusing, condoning, or even applauding lynching. To take two examples from Florida, Sydney J. Catts stated in response to an NAACP complaint about Florida's lynching record, "If any man, White or Black should dishonor one of my family he would meet my pistol square from the shoulder and every white man in the South, who is a red-blooded American, feels the same as I do." In 1937, Governor Fred P. Cone stated, "I think a man ought to be hung on a tree if he advocates overthrow of the government" (McGovern, 1982, pp. 12, 143).

Some defenders of lynching believed that direct popular justice provided something unavailable through the slower formal mechanisms of the law. The will of the people (meaning whites) as expressed through mob action was a direct and powerful form of democracy. In this view, the very fact that a mob acted precipitously against a suspect was proof that the offense deserved this response. The judgment of the people was not to be denied, and lynching was a sort of "lawless law" (Friedman, 1993, pp. 189–192). An example of this attitude was expressed by John Shackleford, local justice of the peace and a leader of a mob that lynched three slaves in Saline County, Missouri, in 1859. Writing to the local paper after the lynching, Shackleford justified the mob's actions by saying, "The law that is not based upon public opinion is but a rope of sand. An enlightened public opinion is the voice of God, and when brought into action it has a power and an energy that cannot be resisted" (quoted in Dyer, 1997, p. 93). An early study of lynching described the attitude common among white Southerners:

> the people consider themselves a law unto themselves. They make the laws; therefore they can unmake them. . . . To execute a criminal deserving of death is to act merely in their sovereign capacity, temporarily dispensing with their agents, the legal administrators of the law.
>
> *(Cutler, 1905, p. 269)*

Many of the arguments whites used to justify lynching were also used to support the death penalty. The suppression of crime was a major rationale for both forms of punishment, and death was believed to be a necessary retribution for certain crimes. Christopher Waldrep noted that in the early twentieth century, "Legal executions operated much as lynchings in the public mind" (2002, p. 162). There was significant overlap in the language used to describe legal executions and lynchings. Newspapers often referred to "mob law" and to "Judge Lynch." White Southern newspapers again and again commended mobs as "orderly," "quiet," and composed of the "best citizens," who were "resolute" and "determined" (Jean, 2005), words that seem more apt as descriptions of legal executions than of murders by mobs. Mob killings were often termed executions, while hasty court proceedings lacking due process protections were frequently called "legal lynchings," a term still in use (Bright, 1995; Jackson, Jackson, & Shapiro, 2001).

Supporters of lynching relied heavily on the assertion that the leniency of the courts made it necessary for the people to inflict punishment directly (Ayers, 1984, p. 246). They were not always wrong that many offenders escaped legal sanction, even in areas where functioning legal systems had long been established. Jeffrey Adler notes that the "nation's criminal justice system appeared paralyzed" in the early years of the twentieth century, which, in combination with rising violent crime, created public "panic about the failure of the criminal justice system" (2015, quotations from p. 36 and p. 38). A study of crime in Memphis between 1920 and 1925 found that 327 persons were arrested for murder in that period. Convictions were obtained in 109 (33%) of the cases, and the average sentence was 14.7 years; it is likely that offenders actually served significantly less (Bruce & Fitzgerald, 1929, p. 82). At times, clearly guilty defendants were not charged or were acquitted due to their own local popularity, prejudice against their victims, sympathy with their actions, or fear of reprisal (Montell, 1986; Lane, 1999). But these arguments in favor of lynching overlooked the fact that the courts acted with great severity and often with great speed when the victims of crime were white and the suspected offenders black—that is, in precisely the category of cases most likely to result in lynching. Few if any apologists for lynching argued in favor of increasing the lynching of whites for crimes against blacks, which were the cases most likely to be ignored by the courts; Leon Litwack noted that Southern courts "granted virtual immunity to whites accused of crimes against black men and women" (1999, p. 253).

Advocates of lynching also claimed that the law moved too slowly to satisfy the community's desire for vengeance in cases of egregiously offensive acts. Thus, opponents of lynching frequently argued that, in order to avoid mob killings, great speed was necessary in the imposition and execution of death sentences. Legal proceedings could occur at an astonishing pace. In 1920, John Hood Price, an African American man suspected of the murder of a white farmer, was captured, indicted, tried, condemned, and executed in St. Augustine, Texas, all within a span of 20 hours. The haste of the proceedings did not prevent a crowd of 2,000 people from arriving in time to witness his hanging (NAACP, 1920, p. 95; 2000 see Texas negro hanged, 1920, March 24). George Wright describes the 1906 case of Allen Mathias, who was protected from lynching only to face an inevitable execution: the townspeople built a scaffold before his trial. Mathias entered court at 7:08 p.m. and at once pled guilty; the jury was out 14 minutes in order to sign the verdict form; the judge imposed death and ordered immediate execution; Mathias arrived at the gallows at 7:40; his body was taken down at 8 p.m. (Wright, 1990, pp. 251–253). These are extreme examples, but many cases moved through the system with great speed. A study of death row in Texas found that the average length of time from arrival to execution was about a month and a half in the 1930s (Marquart, Ekland-Olson, & Sorensen, 1994, p. 95). As late as 1931, John Graham was executed in Florida only eight days after his trial (Vandiver, 2006, pp. 77–80).

Supporters of using the courts to avoid lynching seem to have overlooked that the authorities always had an alternative to legal lynchings: rather than rushing to execute potential mob victims before the mob could do so, officials could have turned the resources of the justice system toward the prosecution of persons who threatened, attempted, and carried out lynchings. While no federal statute covered lynching, some states did have laws against mob killings, and everywhere the crime could be prosecuted as murder under state homicide statutes (Chadbourn, 1933/1970; Zangrando, 1980; Waldrep, 2009). It is true that local juries generally acquitted even clearly guilty defendants in the few cases that came to trial. Still, even a failed attempt to prosecute might have had a beneficial effect. Evidence is scattered and fragmentary, but serious attempts to bring lynchers to justice may have had some local deterrent effect (Vandiver, 2012).

In summary, it is not difficult to identify cases in which the authorities prevented lynchings by promising the mob quick executions and then delivering on those promises. There are also documented instances in which mobs provided "trials" to their prisoners. That these trials were not entirely shows is indicated by the "acquittals" occasionally granted to prisoners tried by mobs. The fact that there was overlap and close similarity between a subset of lynchings and a subset of legal executions does not provide sufficient grounds for concluding that the two practices are simply variant forms of one phenomenon (unless that phenomenon is so broad as to be useless analytically). Before turning to the research on this issue, the differences between the two forms of lethal punishment are briefly described.

Differences

Despite the similarity between some cases of lynching and execution and the justifications for both, most legal and illegal executions were clearly distinguishable. As Stuart Banner noted in his history of the American death penalty, although the line between lynchings and legal executions "could be thin . . . everyone knew it existed. Participants and victims alike could tell the difference" (2002, p. 229). The cases described here illustrate this point.

Two African American men were put to death for allegedly raping white women in Dyer County, Tennessee, in 1916 and 1917. To protect Julius Morgan from a mob that was seeking to lynch him, the sheriff of Dyer County moved Morgan to jails in Jackson, Union City, and Nashville. At a hearing, Morgan was represented by three lawyers who requested and were granted a change of venue for his trial, due to the high level of local feeling against him. Morgan was tried and condemned by a Memphis jury; his lawyers appealed to the Tennessee Supreme Court and the governor met with a committee requesting a commutation of his sentence. Both the appeal and clemency request were denied, and Morgan was executed at the state prison in Nashville five and a half months after the crime. Morgan was the first prisoner to be executed in the electric chair in Tennessee. While in the state prison, Morgan was allowed visitors, religious services, and special meals; the warden gave orders that "his every wish should be granted if possible." His body was shipped to his mother in Arkansas (Negro is trailed, 1916, February 4; Negro dies, 1916, July 13; Vandiver, 2006, pp. 44–46).

Julius Morgan's experience contrasts sharply with that of Lation Scott, also an African American man suspected of the rape of a white woman in Dyer County, Tennessee, who was burned alive in downtown Dyersburg on Sunday morning, December 2, 1917. Scott had eluded capture for ten days, at which point law enforcement found him in a nearby county. Rather than taking him to a secure jail, officers transported him back toward Dyersburg. A mob abducted Scott some distance from

Dyersburg and brought him to the city. A "trial" was held by the mob, and Scott was quickly found guilty. Unprotected and undefended, Scott died an excruciating death prolonged by torture for over three hours. The crowd was estimated at seven to eight thousand people. "Some time Monday an undertaker shoveled up the ashes and the bones and buried them" (Scour Dyer, 1917, November 24; Burn negro at stake, 1917, December 3; Negro tortured, 1917, December 3; quotation from Tennessee lynching, 1917, December 8, p. 1; NAACP, 1918; Vandiver, 2006, pp. 96–98).

Types of Lynchings and Executions

The term lynching covers a heterogeneous range of behavior, ranging from quiet killings by a small group of disguised men to public events drawing thousands of spectators who sometimes posed for photographs. W. Fitzhugh Brundage classified lynch mobs into four types: The "mass mob," with over 50 participants, publicly and ceremoniously killed its victims; the posse, which had the legal right to capture and arrest suspects, but sometimes carried out lynchings; the organized "terrorist" mob, which acted secretly and often constituted an ongoing organization; and the "private" mob that sought vengeance for personal affronts and injuries (1993).[5] The character of legal executions changed greatly in the nineteenth and early twentieth century, as they were moved to central locations and carried out privately under state authority, often months or years after the crimes. Executions increasingly took on a bureaucratic character, with strict protocol and secrecy predominating.

Lynchings for Noncapital Crimes

A small but significant number of lynchings occurred in response to real or imagined violations of the racial caste system in the South (Brundage, 1993, pp. 53–58; Harris, 1995). These acts were not capital crimes and thus never could have resulted in death sentences.[6] A look at data for 1892, the year frequently cited as the peak of lynchings, reveals mob killings for the following noncapital or nonexistent offenses: Advising murder, arguing with white men, being the daughter of a murderer, being the father of a murderer, being the mother of arsonists, being the son of a murderer, being an outlaw, burglary, entering a woman's room, fraud, improper behavior with a white girl, injuring livestock, insulting white women, shooting a man, theft, voting Democratic (Hines & Steelwater, no date).

Brundage noted a 1917 case in Pierce County, Georgia, that illustrates how even the most trivial interaction could lead to mob violence. A 17-year-old black youth, Sandy Reeves, "dropped a nickel on the ground and his employer's three-year-old daughter picked it up . . . . Reeves snatched the coin away from the child and returned to work." The little girl threw a tantrum, her parents suspected assault, and Reeves was lynched (1993, p. 81). As late as 1955, a minor violation of racial etiquette in Mississippi cost 14-year-old Emmett Till his life (Anderson, 2015).

These cases are important because they show the way in which the terror created by lynching extended into every aspect of life. The death penalty could be imposed only after some semblance of a trial and conviction for a capital offense, but any minor infraction of the complex racial code, intentional or inadvertent, could trigger a lynching. Mundane daily encounters and interactions could flare into deadly violence. The fact that lynchings for minor caste violations were not common probably did little to diminish their power to terrorize. Such events were a searing demonstration of the lengths to which whites would go to enforce the racial hierarchy.

Protections Offered by Legal Trials

Legal proceedings were often shockingly rushed and openly biased, but they generally offered protection from prolonged physical torture and sometimes allowed for review and reconsideration of evidence. With the exception of some executions of slaves carried out by burning and other excruciating methods (Aguirre & Baker, 1999), Americans have generally sought ways of carrying out executions that minimize physical pain and avoid bodily mutilation (Banner, 2002, pp. 296–298; Garland, 2010, pp. 271–272). While most lynchings involved relatively quick deaths by hanging, nothing protected the victim from the extremes of torture if the mob decided to inflict them. Brundage noted that the "very existence of legal procedures imposed constraints, however limited, upon whites that neither tradition nor community sentiment imposed upon mobs" (1993, p. 257). A person facing near certain death at the hands of either a mob or the authorities might express a strong preference for a "decent," that is, legal hanging, as did Henry Wilson in Florida in 1902. As Steiker and Steiker note, during this time period, "state imposed death was *not* the worst, or even the most likely, fate that could befall one suspected of a capital crime" (2010, p. 655).

During the historic period of lynching, some capital trials were carried out with due process (at least by the standards of the time) and careful deliberation on evidence. After conviction, the condemned prisoner might have an appeal to the state supreme court; consideration of state convictions by federal courts was rare, but did occur in some cases. Governors commuted many more death sentences historically than is currently the case, so prisoners had reason to hope for relief. All forms of review slowed down the process, thus providing time for emotions to calm and tempers to cool and perhaps for exculpatory evidence to emerge. Many threatened lynchings were prevented (Beck, 2015); some cases that appeared headed straight for a lynching, might, after a legal trial, end with imprisonment or even exoneration (Acker, 2008; Carter, 1979; Vandiver, 2006, pp. 144–145).

Lynchings Were Illegal

Perhaps the most important way in which lynchings and executions differed lies in the obvious fact that lynchings were illegal. Executions revealed the ultimate power of law and the authorities over the life of citizens. Lynching, in contrast, revealed the weakness of law and the authorities, vividly demonstrating their inability to maintain order and to control violence. Even when the authorities were in sympathy or collusion with the mob, they risked losing status and power when they abrogated their formal responsibilities and appeared helpless to control events. As some in authority learned, mobs were volatile and dangerous and could turn their rage against targets other than the lynching victim. Bertram Wyatt-Brown observed, "Lynchings consciously defied the law and abstract justice and could result in an explosion of hatred, rage, and anarchy" (Wyatt-Brown, 1986, p. 189).

A dramatic example of this occurred in 1919 in Omaha, Nebraska. A mob attacked the courthouse in order to seize Will Brown, suspected of the rape of a white woman. The mayor addressed the mob, telling them that he would protect the prisoner even at the cost of his own life. The mob struck the mayor, dragged him down the street, put a rope around his neck, and were on the point of hanging him when someone intervened and saved his life. While the mayor lay unconscious in the hospital, the mob returned to the courthouse, set it on fire, shot at the sheriff and prisoners, forced their way into the building, captured Brown, and lynched him. Three people were killed, including Brown, the courthouse was ruined, and irreplaceable records were destroyed (Menard, 2010).

Better known is the reaction to the commutation of Leo Frank's death sentence by Governor John M. Slaton in Georgia in 1915. In a sensational trial marked by great public pressure for conviction and by anti-Semitism, Frank had been convicted for the murder of a young girl who worked for him in a pencil factory in Atlanta. Governor Slaton commuted the death sentence to life due to doubt of Frank's guilt. It was necessary to declare martial law and to call up the Georgia National Guard to protect the governor in his own home from repeated attacks by mobs. In what must be one of, if not the, most audacious and meticulously planned mob actions in U.S. history, a group that included influential and prominent men planned, organized, and carried out an attack on the state penitentiary. At the prison, the group cut telephone lines and disabled vehicles before quickly overcoming the warden and superintendent. Going straight to where Frank was housed, they dragged him from bed and into one of their seven waiting cars; "the vigilantes had needed but ten minutes to abduct the nation's most celebrated prisoner . . . . Not a shot was fired." Without interference from law enforcement they drove over 100 miles before lynching Frank near Marietta, Georgia (Oney, 2003, quotation from p. 562).

The men who planned and executed the Frank lynching fell somewhere on the spectrum between a mob, that is, a group that formed more or less spontaneously for a particular occasion and disbanded immediately after, and a vigilante group, with organizational structure, cohesion over time, and a broader agenda than a single attack. When lynchers were organized as ongoing vigilante groups, they could pose an even greater threat to established order than did the short lived mobs. James Denham describes the situation in ante-bellum Florida, where the authorities, struggling to maintain order under frontier conditions, encouraged the formation of quasi-legal vigilante groups, known as "regulators," to assist law enforcement in acting against organized bands of outlaws. These groups had some success in their initial mission but gradually became agents of terror and disorder in their own right. Denham concluded that the regulators left "a bloody legacy that would haunt the state" (Denham, 1997, pp. 185–204; quotation p. 204).

Violent attacks on the authorities were rare, but mobs could turn on the forces of law and order, many lynchings had the potential to turn into riots, and ongoing vigilante groups posed a particularly dangerous threat. Obviously no government could allow this kind of defiance and disorder to occur and continue to function. The *Nashville Tennessean* argued this point in an editorial in response to the lynching of Joseph Boxley in 1929:

> The state cannot tolerate any rival . . . . It alone has the right to judge those who violate its laws . . . . The mob defies every legal restraint and makes a mockery of our boasted system of jurisprudence . . . . We tolerate lynching at our own peril. The mob lapses into barbarism, turns back the clock of civilization and substitutes the long repudiated doctrine of private vengeance for public punishment.
>
> *(State again disgraced, 1929, May 31, p. 4)*

Concerns over violence and disorder included worries about their negative effects on business prospects and on the effort to attract residents. The *Florida Times-Union* wrote, after a double lynching in downtown Jacksonville,

> Without the highest respect and confidence in the workings of our courts no city can hope to prosper and progress as it should. We have prospered and we must continue to prosper, therefore every man among us must be strong in his advocacy of the enforcement of law and order.
>
> *(Mob violence condemned, 1919, September 10, p. 6)*

The local paper in Ocala voiced a similar complaint after the 1926 lynching of Chandler Colding: "most hurtful . . . just at a time when we are trying so hard to put Ocala forward by inviting wealthy, intelligence and a decent population by giving her a good name as a law abiding city" (Ocala getting a bad name, 1926, January 29, p. 1). Alabama business and political leaders expressed similar concerns after the lynching of two men and three women in Butler County in 1895 (Crudele, 1980). Writing about North Carolina, Claude Clegg notes that white leaders had

> endeavored to remake the image of the region in such a way as to encourage outside investments, technological improvements, white immigration, urban growth, and the consolidation of Democratic hegemony. Lynchings and other forms of lawlessness were now inimical
> ‚ to this particular view of modernity and prosperity.
>
> *(2010, pp. 156–157)*

Despite the fact that it was in the authorities' interests to control mob violence, legal action was rarely taken against lynchers. Even in the rare cases in which arrests and prosecutions did occur, convictions were very rarely attained (West, 1947; Vandiver, 2012; Vandiver, 2014). In Mississippi, a local prosecutor in 1959 refused to present evidence to a grand jury, and a federal grand jury in 1960 refused to return indictments for the lynching of Mack Charles Parker (Smead, 1986). The legal response to most cases ended with a finding by a coroner's jury that the victim had come to his death "at the hands of parties unknown." This occurred even when thousands of people had witnessed the killing and the names of some of the mob leaders were published in the local newspapers.

The Relationship Between Lynchings and Historical Executions

Most observers of the historical record of legal and extra-legal executions have assumed that there is a connection between the two types of lethal punishment, although there has been disagreement as to the form this relationship took. In broad terms, one view held that lynchings and executions were basically alternatives, while the other held that they were complementary forms of the same phenomenon. The first view would predict that as one form of lethal punishment rose, the other would fall. This negative association between lynching and execution is generally referred to as the substitution model. Tolnay and Beck explain this model as assuming "that a fixed amount of punishment is 'required' given the level of deviant behavior . . . . When formal mechanisms are sufficient to provide the required punishment, supplementary methods are not required." The second view predicts a positive relationship between lynchings and executions. This "reinforcement model" views lynchings and executions "as complementary methods of punishment rather than as alternatives" (Tolnay & Beck, 1995, quotations pp. 99, 100).[7]

Limitations of Data

We do not have complete inventories of executions during the years they were carried out under county authority, and we do not have complete inventories of lynching for any period. The federal government has compiled data on executions in all states from 1930 on, and many states have complete records of executions carried out in central prisons. Although it is incomplete, the best source for executions before they were centralized under state authority is the inventory compiled by Watt Espy (Espy and Smykla, no date).

The difficult challenges of identifying lynchings have been thoroughly discussed in the literature (Tolnay & Beck, 1995; Trotti, 2013; Vandiver, 2006; Vinikas, 1999). Michael Trotti describes lynchings as "a strange and difficult-to-nail-down subset of murder, and the evidence will never yield more than estimates of the numbers actually lynched" (2013, p. 377). Missed cases are likely to be different from those that have been identified: they are more likely to have occurred in earlier years, in rural areas, in areas without extant local newspapers, and to have involved smaller mobs. A further problem is that even meticulous efforts to gather complete and accurate information will include factual errors that are present in the sources used.

Most inventories of lynching start in the early 1880s, and we know very little about earlier decades; George Wright's work in Kentucky is an important exception, and his documentation of large numbers of cases from the 1860s and 1870s should caution us from concluding that lynchings were less common in earlier decades (1990). In addition, our knowledge of the geographic distribution of lynchings is influenced and perhaps distorted by the Southern focus of most of the research until recently.[8]

Qualitative Studies

Case studies of particular instances of lynching and execution provide "richly detailed, fluid accounts . . . squarely situated in their cultural contexts and centered on the behavior of real people" (Griffin, Clark, & Sandberg, 1997, p. 24). Where adequate sources are available, these studies can give a depth of understanding unrivaled by broader statistical work. The limitations of case studies as a basis for broad conclusions is obvious, however; we cannot know how representative individual cases are even of their own time and place, much less of other locations and time periods.

Several studies have examined cases within limited geographical areas and specific time periods. These studies differ in their conclusions about the relationship between executions and lynchings. George Wright, in his work on Kentucky, found that the decline in lynching in the state was due to a number of factors, including the use of capital punishment, which he termed "an especially pernicious extension of lynchings . . . . This practice . . . proved to be effective, and the number of death sentences carried out by the state grew in number and significance after 1900" (Wright, 1997, p. 251). Commenting on the United States as a whole, Pfeifer concluded that by 1940, "Rough justice was enacted no longer through lynching but through legal executions that combined legal forms, symbolically charged and arbitrary retributive justice, and white supremacy" (2004, p. 150). Based on his close study of lynching in Virginia and Georgia, however, W. Fitzhugh Brundage noted fundamental differences between "violence by state authorities . . . [and] most earlier lynchings" and cautioned that executions "should not be interpreted as the continuation of lynching under another guise" (1993, p. 255).

Vandiver (2006) found no clear pattern suggesting substitution in Shelby County (Memphis), Tennessee, or in the rural counties of northwest Tennessee, but concluded there was some support for the substitution hypothesis in Marion County, Florida, where officials quite deliberately used death sentences in an effort to bring an end to a long history of the lynching of black men for alleged sexual assaults on white women. The Florida officials were open and explicit in their goal to use quick executions to prevent threatened lynchings from succeeding. When John Graham was convicted in 1931, the superintendent of the state prison wrote a personal letter to the state official in charge of prisons, expressing the hope that "the Governor will issue the death warrant as quickly as possible and let us make an example out of this man." The governor obliged, and Graham was executed eight days after his trial. Less than four months later, another African American faced the same charges in Marion County and was convicted 14 days after his alleged crime. When the governor did not act quickly to set an execution date, the sheriff of Marion County wrote complaining that he had saved the man from lynching by assuring the people that "this negro would receive the same quick action as the one prior" and that he was afraid that unless the prisoner were executed quickly, the next such case would result in a lynching (2006, pp. 76–88, quotation on p. 83).

The effort to replace lynchings with executions took place not only through the actions of local officials and juries, but it seems to have occurred also at the level of state policy. During the Progressive Era, ten states abolished capital punishment, with eight reinstating it by the end of the 1930s. A study of these states concluded that "lynchings emerged as the most important common triggering event in reinstatement of the death penalty" (Galliher, Ray, & Cook, 1992, p. 574). In Colorado, for example, lynchings during the period of abolition created momentum for the rapid reinstatement of capital punishment (Galliher et al., 1992; LaBode, 2014). Abolition in Tennessee was fragile and partial, being based largely on the work of one highly respected advocate and applying only to murder, while rape remained a capital crime. Public sentiment never supported abolition, and after a number of lynchings, the death penalty was brought back, with Governor Albert H. Roberts announcing, "I verily believe that the passage of [the abolition bill] has been the contributing cause to the commission of the crime of murder and to the summary vengeance of the mob" (Vandiver, 2006, pp. 158–164, quotation p. 163).

Aggregate Data

Research using aggregate data has reached differing conclusions on the relationship between lynching and executions. In 1905, James Cutler concluded, "There is an indication that the upward tendency in [executions] since 1887 may have contributed to the downward tendency in [lynchings] since 1892" (p. 163–164). Writing in 1919, another early researcher, James Bye, concluded that his analysis "almost warrants the conclusion that the practice of lynching . . . bears no relation to the use of the death penalty at all" (Bye, 1919, p. 71).

James W. Clarke analyzed lynchings and legal executions of blacks, demonstrating that between 1890 and 1930 executions rose and lynchings fell (1998a, 1998b).[9] Clarke argued "perhaps the most important reason that lynching declined is that it was replaced by a more palatable form of violence," that is, legal executions (1998b, p. 284). Allen, Clubb, and Lacey's work on executions and lynchings of African Americans in ten Southern states concluded that the two "tended to be closely related. Those states with the highest African American lynching rates also tended to have the highest African American execution rates" between 1885 and 1896. This relationship weakened afterward, and by the period of 1916–1925 the two rates "were effectively unrelated" (2008, p. 88).

A problem with data aggregated at the national or regional level is that they can conceal local variations pointing to a more nuanced or even contradictory relationship. It is important to recall that executions were fairly common outside the South during the later years of the lynching era, when lynchings occurred almost exclusively in the South. It is difficult to understand theoretically how executions in New England, for instance, could have much influence on the behavior of Southern mobs. Data aggregated at the state level can also obscure important local variations and changing relationships over time. David Oshinsky notes, "On the surface, Mississippi appears to provide a textbook example of the substitution effect. Between 1882 and 1930, it experienced more lynchings (463) and fewer executions (239) than any other state in the Deep South. Yet these totals are deceiving, for they are not spread evenly over time. In the first decade of the twentieth century . . . Mississippi witnessed an absolute flood of lynching *and* legal executions" (Oshinsky, 1996, p. 209).

Multivariate Analysis

Several scholars have undertaken more sophisticated statistical analysis; their results give little support to the substitution hypothesis. Charles Phillips (1987) led this line of research with data from North Carolina from 1889–1918 to test three ways in which lynching and legal execution might be related. He examined the possibility that the two practices substituted for each other, implying that as one increased, the other would decrease. Or lynchings and executions might rise and fall together, because "both types of killings are driven by the same social tensions." Or an "alternative form of repression," such as the disenfranchisement of African Americans, might influence the relationship (p. 367). Phillips found a positive correlation between lynchings and executions of African Americans until 1903, but after that the relationship was weak and negative. Phillips interpreted these findings as support for his third hypothesis, arguing that the disenfranchisement of African Americans in North Carolina provided a means of social control that made lynching "a costly and unnecessary form of repression" (p. 372).

Phillips' study was replicated and extended by Beck, Massey, and Tolnay (1989) who lengthened the period of time under study to cover 1882 to 1930; used their own inventory of lynchings and Watt Espy's inventory of executions, which included those carried out under local authority; and included Georgia as well as North Carolina. Their analysis of the North Carolina data revealed little correlation between executions and lynchings of African Americans, nor did disenfranchisement show an effect. In Georgia, the authors found a small positive correlation between lynchings and executions before the disenfranchisement of black voters; after disenfranchisement, there was a decline in both forms of punishment.

Massey and Myers (1989) used Georgia data to study the relationship between lynching, execution, and imprisonment of black men between 1882 and 1935. Their study found "virtually no empirical support for the presence of a relationship" (p. 482) between these three forms of social control. The authors noted that their research covered only 54 years in one state and suggested that future research should examine broader geographic areas, should include areas in which there was a clear "break point," or division in time, between lynchings and executions (p. 483), and that both short-term events and long-term social processes should be included as possible factors.

Keil and Vito (2009) addressed the same question using data from Kentucky. They drew on the work of George Wright, whose historical analysis of executions and lynchings in the state, mentioned earlier, concluded that executions did substitute for lynchings. Keil and Vito used Wright's data on lynchings and executions, supplemented by Espy's inventory, to study the years 1866 to 1934. Their findings differed by the time periods examined. Over the entire period, they found that the lynchings of both blacks and whites were positively related to executions. Between 1910 and 1934, however, they found that the number of lynchings of blacks fell as the number of executions of blacks rose.

The most thorough and extensive statistical exploration of the relationship between legal and extralegal executions was carried out by Stewart E. Tolnay and E. M. Beck (1995). Using their own inventory of lynchings and Watt Espy's data on executions in ten Southern states, they used both time-series and cross-sectional analysis to examine the relationship between lynchings and executions of African Americans. Tolnay and Beck controlled for variables that might influence the outcome and analyzed both the full set of cases and the subset that included only lynching cases that could have been prosecuted as capital crimes. Both analyses found that "the overall effect of executions [on lynchings] falls far short of both sociological and statistical significance" (p. 105). Concerned that their aggregate data might obscure significant variations, Tolnay and Beck also did a cross-sectional analysis within five separate time periods. In all periods other than 1882–1889, there was a weak positive correlation between executions and lynchings; only in 1882–1889 was there a negative relationship that could be argued to support the substitution hypothesis (Table 4–5). Interestingly, lynchings of whites were strongly related to those of blacks within counties, indicating "that some counties were simply more prone to generalized mob violence than others" (p. 111).

Overall, Tolnay and Beck concluded:

> Neither the time-series analysis nor the cross-sectional approach suggest that a more vigorous implementation of the death penalty reduced the level of mob violence. Neither, however, is there strong evidence that formal and informal lethal sanctioning were driven by the same social forces. Rather, in light of the evidence, we must conclude that executions and lynchings were largely independent forms of social control in the South.
>
> *(p. 111)*

The substitution hypothesis has considerable intuitive appeal. Historical research provides case studies that certainly seem to support it, and some broader historical analyses reach the conclusion that capital punishment was substituted for lynching in some jurisdictions at certain times. Evidence for this relationship is not found in studies using multivariate statistical analysis at the state or regional level, however. It is important to keep in mind the imperfections of the data, particularly that on lynching; still, it is striking that five studies, covering several areas, varying time periods, and based on different data sources, have failed to find strong and consistent evidence of any statistical relationship between lynchings and executions. It is clear that the relationship between these two forms of lethal punishment is complex, and it is likely to be contingent on time periods and local factors.

The Influence of Lynchings on Modern Executions

Most of the research on connections between lynching and capital punishment focuses on the relationship between the two practices during the decades when both were common. A related issue concerns whether mob killings during the lynching era exert any influence on the current use of capital punishment. All the problems with lynching data described earlier hamper research focused on the present as well as on the historic era; however, inventories of modern executions are complete, and information on cases is far more detailed and reliable than is true of most historical case data.

The Historical and Modern Death Penalty

With the United States Supreme Court's approval of new death penalty statutes in 1976 in *Gregg v. Georgia*, capital punishment entered its modern era. The death penalty as it is used today is in some ways almost the opposite of the penalty during the lynching period. Space precludes detailed discussion of the changes in capital punishment, but a brief summary is necessary before reviewing research that examines connections between lynching and the current system of capital punishment. While these changes may seem to point toward a laudable concern for improving due process and for minimizing the physical pain of executions, in fact they have done little to ameliorate many problems, and indeed have increased others, including the emotional costs to defendants, their families, and victims' families occasioned by extraordinarily long stays on death row; exorbitant use of money, time, and resources on a small number of cases; and increasing discordance with the practices of most of the world's countries.

The scope of capital crimes and those eligible for capital prosecutions has narrowed. The modern death penalty is almost entirely reserved for intellectually competent adult defendants who are convicted of some form of aggravated first-degree murder. The numbers of capital jurisdictions, death sentences, and executions have all steeply decreased. Executions have dropped from a peak of 98 in 1999 to only 20 in 2016, and capital punishment remains on the books in only 31 states (four of which have a moratorium in place on executions), the federal government, and the military. Both death sentences and executions have fallen dramatically since the 1990s. Only five states carried out executions in 2016, and the vast majority of new death sentences are clustered in a tiny number of counties (Bureau of Justice Statistics, 2014; Death Penalty Information Center, 2016a; Death Penalty Information Center, 2016b; Death Penalty Information Center, 2016c; Dieter, 2013).

A striking characteristic of the modern death penalty is its emphasis on procedure. In sharp contrast to the historical system, modern cases undergo extensive appellate review at both the state and federal levels. This has resulted in prisoners spending vastly lengthened amounts of time on death row. The Bureau of Justice Statistics reported that the average length of time on death row for inmates executed in 2013 was 186 months, or over 15 years (2014, Table 10). A few prisoners have been on death row for more than 40 years (*Sireci v. Florida*, 2016). The execution of death sentences is highly bureaucratized, centralized, and secretive. While some rituals remain more or less stable—the last meal, the last words—in most ways, modern executions bear almost no resemblance to the local public executions of the past.

The differences between the premodern and modern death penalty are real and significant, but so are the enduring similarities. The issue of racial disparity is of particular relevance to the subject of this chapter. Modern death penalty laws were written to avoid the clear racial bias that had infected the penalty historically and to ensure that the harshest sentence would be reserved for the worst offenders and homicides. Extensive research has documented continuing problems in the imposition and administration of capital punishment,[10] however, including significant racial disparities, leading some to argue that modern capital punishment continues to be a form of "legal lynching."

Lynching and the Modern Death Penalty

Hugo Bedau (2002) noted a number of factors pointing to "the connection between yesterday's unlawful lynchings and today's lawful executions" (p. 117). Bedau listed seven such connections: the mentality that tolerated/demanded lynching is similar to that which tolerates/demands modern capital punishment; the geographic distribution of lynchings and modern executions is similar; shared lack of concern for due process; both practices involve community-approved violence by whites against African Americans; a common argument made by opponents of lynching was that legal executions would accomplish the same purpose; killings by posses fall in a midrange between lynching and "quasi-legal summary execution" (p. 118); proponents of lynching and of the modern death penalty system relied heavily on arguments for states' rights and against federal interference. David Garland lists a number of factors as well, including that capital punishment is "driven by local politics and populist politicians . . . imposed by lay people . . . it continues to be an occasion for political mobilization around demands for local sovereignty, traditional values, and popular justice." He concluded that "distinct echoes [of lynching] remain" (2010, p. 280).

A further disturbing similarity is evident in the gatherings of celebratory crowds outside prisons during modern executions, which are strongly reminiscent of the crowds that gathered at spectacle lynchings. In some instances, brutally racist signs and slogans have been prominent. These gatherings are unusual and have not involved the direct infliction of violence; still, the echoes are abundantly clear (Paredes & Purdum, 1990; Vandiver, Giacopassi, & Gathje, 2002, pp. 392–395; Von Drehle, 1995, pp. 393, 400).

Research

The lingering influence of lynching on modern society has been the subject of a number of recent studies focused on racially tinged practices. Studies have found connections between historic lynchings and certain current criminal justice practices including hate crimes enforcement (King, Messner, & Baller, 2009); growth rates in prison admissions (Jacobs, Malone, & Iles, 2012); imposition of death sentences (Jacobs, Carmichael, & Kent, 2005); and executions (Zimring, 2003). Other research has documented the connection between lynching and modern Southern homicide rates (Messner, Baller, & Zevenbergen, 2005); housing segregation (DeFina & Hannon, 2011); Ku Klux Klan mobilization (Cunningham & Phillips, 2007); and support for capital punishment among whites (Messner, Baumer, & Rosenfeld, 2006). This body of research strongly suggests that historical lynchings continue to influence modern society more or less directly and/or that some underlying phenomenon that played a role in lynching continues to exert an influence even in the late twentieth and early twenty-first centuries.

Several scholars have undertaken empirical research specifically testing whether the historical practice of lynching exerts any influence on the modern death penalty. Franklin Zimring (2003) made the intriguing and important observation that the regional distribution of modern executions is predicted more closely by the pattern of lynching than by the pattern of historical executions. Using NAACP data on lynchings between 1889 and 1918 and looking at executions between 1977 and 2000, he found a remarkable similarity of regional distribution: the South had 88% of the lynchings and 81% of the executions; the Midwest had 7% of the lynchings and 10% of the executions; the West had 5% of the lynchings and 8% of the executions; the Northeast had under 1% of both the lynchings and the executions. Zimring broke the analysis down to the state level and found variations within the regional pattern. Delaware, for example, had relatively few lynchings, but for a period of time under modern death penalty laws had a high number of executions. Mississippi and Tennessee both had many lynchings but had few modern executions.

Jacobs et al. (2005) tested whether a vigilante tradition in combination with a large minority population influenced the imposition of modern death sentences in the U.S. The authors strengthened their analysis by testing their hypotheses nationally with NAACP data and again with Tolnay and Beck's data for ten Southern states, predicting both African American death sentences and all death sentences. The authors found that "the interaction between prior lynchings and black threat [size of population] that predicted all death sentences offers modest support for a hypothesis that whites and blacks are more likely to receive this sentence in states with a vigilante tradition . . . . The coefficients on this interaction term were stronger when the analyses were restricted to black death sentences" (p. 672).

The frequency of modern capital sentencing varies tremendously by county, even within states that produce a high number of death sentences. Thus, the question of the influence of lynching needs to be examined at the county level as well as at state, regional, and national levels (Cohen, 2012). Tony Poveda (2006) studied this question in Virginia, using death sentences imposed in the state between 1978 and 2001. Poveda used Brundage's data on lynching and Espy's data for historical executions in order to test whether lynching, among other factors, influences current death sentencing in Virginia.

Poveda classified counties as "abolitionist" (having no death sentences or executions) or "retentionist" (having at least one death sentence or execution) and tested the "expectation that jurisdictional variations in death sentences and executions would be linked to slavery and lynching at the county level." He discovered no evidence for such an influence, finding that of his historical variables, "only the level of executions in the pre-*Furman* era (1908–62) was significant" (p. 432).

It is not only death sentences and executions that may continue to show the influence of lynching but the whole legal structure of modern capital punishment. David Garland argues that the "specter of lynching" has hung over the United States Supreme Court's death penalty jurisprudence, "a continuing historical force that imparts a peculiar shape to the contemporary institution" (2010, p. 280). Garland asserts that the court's particular concern has been to strip the modern death penalty of any resemblance to lynching, other than the continuing racial disparities in its imposition.

Clearly, much remains to be done in this line of research. Better and more complete inventories of lynchings and executions resulting from further historical research will allow greater confidence in the conclusions of quantitative studies. Various geographic divisions need to be studied, since research done at the regional and state levels risks obscuring the variety of local cultural areas, and research done at the county level presents difficulties associated with the statistical analysis of small numbers. Where sufficient records exist, it may be possible to trace the effects of particular lynchings on the criminal justice interactions of the descendants of the victim (Butterfield, 1995). Studies need to consider executions, death sentences, legislative developments, jurisprudence, and public opinion in order to capture the range of variables relevant to the death penalty that may be influenced by lynching. Although we need much more work before this line of inquiry can yield more than suggestive results, the research that has been done is sufficient to indicate the interest and timeliness of this topic.

Interpretations

Lynchings were rare events in the statistical sense. They often occurred in rural areas and sometimes were reported only in local papers or not at all. Even counties with exceptionally high numbers of lynchings averaged less than a case per year during the lynching era; most counties had few if any lynchings. By the 1930s, only a very small number of lynchings occurred annually. In the decades since, the South has been transformed demographically and economically and has experienced profound cultural changes. Few living individuals have direct experience of lynching and threatened lynchings.

Scholars who find evidence for the continuing influence of lynchings on modern practices thus face a steep challenge in interpreting their findings.[11] It appears that "remnants of history linger on in the nation's death penalty" (Kirchmeier, 2015, pp. 310–311), but, as Bailey and Tolnay ask, "How is it possible that events that occurred so far in the past can continue to influence American society in so many different ways, so many decades later?" (2015, pp. 29–30). Messner, Baller, and Zevenbergen clearly delineate the challenges facing researchers on this and related topics:

> Our theoretical interpretations are predicated upon intervening processes that cannot be examined directly, and thus we cannot claim to have demonstrated the full range of implied causal relationships . . . . At a theoretical level, an important task is to explain exactly how the brutal events of decades ago could be converted into cultural orientations capable of transmission over time to those with no direct experience with these events. At an empirical level, the daunting challenge that has frustrated scholars in this area for decades remains—how to locate theoretically meaningful measures of cultural orientations that are suitable for quantitative research.
>
> *(2005, pp. 650–651)*

Scholars have advanced a number of factors in tentative explanation, among them the legacy of slavery, the "code of honor" common in the South, the Southern "culture of violence," and the intense localism of Southern culture in combination with suspicion of formal authority and outside interference. Yet none of these seem entirely satisfactory, as is often the case when we try to explain specific actions by broad cultural influences.

As scholars continue this line of research, it will be necessary to reflect further on the mechanism or mechanisms through which rare historical events could plausibly continue to exert an influence. Katherine Stovel's concept of "local sequential patterns" may be helpful in this regard. Stovel studied the effect that a lynching had on subsequent lynchings in the same county, arguing that "the locally extraordinary meaning that resides in semi-rare events . . . shapes subsequent possibilities" (2001, p. 853). Stovel examined the "social trace of lynching" upon other lynchings (p. 865), but it may be that the "residue of past lynchings" (p. 866) she noted plays a role in increasing the likelihood of future lethal punishment in another form as well. Thomas Church's concept of "local legal culture" may also be useful, although it was developed in a very different context (1986). Church found that criminal courts exhibited "tenacity in maintaining existing ways of doing things" and a "uniform resistance to change" (p. 508). To some extent, of course, this is true of bureaucracies in general, but legal practitioners are well aware of the substantial differences in attitude and practice exhibited by various courts even in close geographical proximity, and how resistant these differences can be to change. It may be that the legal culture of courts is connected to the cultural and historical legacies of their locations, including the local history of mob violence.

Conclusion

It may seem questionable that a causal chain, even a tenuous one, can be traced from historical events to modern practices. At the same time, it is worth considering the inverse of that question: is it reasonable to think that lynching would have no residual effects? Ashraf Rushdy has eloquently stated this point:

> Consider this: for fifty years, between 1880 and 1930, an African American person was killed by a lynch mob at the rate of more than one a week . . . . How could we possibly expect that this kind of violence, its frequency, magnitude, and focus, would disappear without leaving its mark? A violent heritage, a history of regimented hatred and terrorism, does not go away without leaving a residue in the society that sanctioned it.
>
> *(2012, p. 138)*

Historian Joel Williamson made the same point when he referred to lynching as a wound, not a scar (1997). What Justice William Brennan called the "subtle and persistent influence of the past" that derives from "a historical legacy spanning centuries" is not something that disappears as those individuals with specific memories of the events die (*McCleskey v. Kemp*, 1987, p. 344). In ways we may not now be able precisely to specify, much less quantify, the hatred that fed lynching and the terror created by lynching do live on, and it is not surprising that this legacy may manifest itself in our remaining form of lethal punishment.

The central question addressed by this chapter is how lynching and capital punishment are related. But the lingering influence of lynching appears to be much broader than its role in the modern death penalty. The remarkable force retained by the imagery of lynching has come into painful focus as this chapter is being written. The Southern Poverty Law Center published a disturbing report documenting 867 "hate incidents" occurring in the first ten days after the presidential election of 2016. These incidents targeted a number of groups, including African Americans. The report states:

> In many anti-black incidents, references to lynching has been common. "Noose Tying 101" was written on a whiteboard at San Francisco State University, and a black doll was found hanging from a noose in an elevator at New York's Canisius College. A man in Kansas City,

Missouri, reported that a noose and swastika were spray-painted onto his car, and a young woman in New York City received a text message from a high school classmate reading, "Fuck u nigger bitch. Die. Painfully from a tree . . . . Or being dragged behind a pickup truck flying the confederate flag" . . . . In Brundidge, Alabama, an interracial couple found a gun target tacked to the front door of their restaurant with a pair of nooses hung on either side.

(2016, pp. 8, 9)

That people would choose images related to lynching in order to express their hatred of African Americans is a forceful indication that lynching has continuing symbolic power and cannot be dismissed as a currently irrelevant aspect of American history.

In response to the legacy of lynching, the Equal Justice Initiative has begun an effort to commemorate lynchings with historical markers, ceremonies, and the collection of soil samples from lynching sites (2015). This is done in the belief that "The era of racial terror calls for serious and informed reflection as well as public acknowledgment of the lives lost" (2015, p. 63). This call to reflect on lynching coincides with reevaluation of the utility and morality of the modern death penalty. Perhaps the lessons of the lynching era will inform that reevaluation and lead us at last to renounce collective killing.

Notes

1 The most widely used definition of lynching was adopted in 1940 by a group of anti-lynching activists. This definition considers that a lynching occurred if "there [is] legal evidence that a person has been killed, and that he met his death illegally at the hands of a group acting under the pretext of service to justice, race, or tradition" (quoted in Brundage, 1993, p. 17; Waldrep, 2000). Three or more people acting together constitutes a group. While this definition is not perfect, it is the one used by most modern researchers. Most cases of lynching clearly fall under this definition, although there are cases that are difficult to classify. Not all racially motivated homicides are lynchings, and not all lynchings were racially motivated.

2 By lynching era, I mean the period extending roughly from the end of Reconstruction through the mid-1930s. By modern executions, I mean those carried out under laws passed after the U.S. Supreme Court's 1972 decision *Furman v. Georgia* invalidated earlier statutes.

3 Allen et al. do not claim to have definitive counts either of executions or of lynchings. Still, these numbers provide a good base for rough comparisons. The 10 states included in these calculations are Alabama, Arkansas, Florida, Georgia, Louisiana, Mississippi, North Carolina, and South Carolina (using Tolnay and Beck's data), Virginia (using Brundage's data), and Texas (using a variety of sources). The years covered are 1886–1925.

4 Statistics on the gender and race of lynching victims come from Tolnay and Beck's data covering 1882–1930 in the states of Alabama, Arkansas, Florida, Georgia, Kentucky, Louisiana, Mississippi, North Carolina, South Carolina, and Tennessee. (These data are available online from Hines and Steelwater, Historical American Lynching Project). Legal executions of women are calculated from Watt Espy's data using national data for the same span of years as Tolnay and Beck. (An abbreviated version of Espy's data is available online from Espy and Smykla, Death Penalty Information Center. The full data are available through the Inter-University Consortium for Political and Social Research). Michael Trotti (2011) has supplemented Espy's data with extensive newspaper articles, and I draw on his numbers for the racial breakdown of executions. The dates covered are 1866–1920; the states are those of the Confederacy and Kentucky.

5 Lynchings by "mass mobs" are easily identifiable as lynchings. Although they were less frequent than other types of lynching, they had a greater impact through the publicity they generated (Garland, 2005, p. 807). This type of mob violence is generally called 'spectacle lynching'. Posse killings overlap with justified and unjustified killings by law enforcement and can be hard to classify. Terrorist mob killings and those by private mobs can be difficult to distinguish from other forms of murder.

6 There was one type of case in which a racial caste violation could result in capital charges: consensual sexual relations between African American men and white women could be interpreted and prosecuted as rape. Willie McGee was executed in Mississippi in 1951 for what many believed was a consensual relationship with a white woman (Heard, 2010).

7 The substitution and reinforcement hypotheses may underestimate the degree to which the two practices were intertwined. As James Campbell noted, capital punishment and lynching can be viewed as "mutually reinforcing" (2013, p. 128). Michael Pfeifer concluded that

the history of lynching and the history of the death penalty in the United States are deeply and hopelessly entangled. One cannot be separated or understood apart from the other, for lynching came from the early modern death penalty, and the modern death penalty came from lynching (2004, p. 152).

8 Researchers have begun documenting lynchings that occurred outside the South, particularly those of Mexicans, Mexican Americans, and Native Americans (Bessler, 2003; Campney, 2015; Carrigan & Webb, 2013; Leonard, 2002; Pfeifer, 2013).

9 Clarke noted that his data did not include executions under county authority (1998a, p. 169); thus, the number of legal executions in the earlier decades of his analysis are underestimated. The sharp rise in executions shown by his data is likely to be partly due to the omission of these early local executions. Clarke drew his estimates of the numbers of lynchings from the records of the Tuskegee Institute (1998a, Figure 11.2).

10 I do not summarize or cite to this body of research, as it is covered thoroughly by other chapters in this volume.

11 A similar interpretive challenge is raised by research connecting slavery to the modern death penalty (Vandiver, Giacopassi, & Lofquist, 2006; Vandiver, Giacopassi, & Curley, 2003).

References

2000 see Texas negro hanged. (1920, March 24). *El Paso Herald*, p. 2. Retrieved from http://chroniclingamerica.loc.gov

Acker, J. R. (2008). *Scottsboro and its legacy: The cases that challenged American legal and social justice*. Westport, CN: Praeger.

Adler, J. S. (2015). Less crime, more punishment: Violence, race, and criminal justice in early twentieth-century America. *The Journal of American History, 102*, 34–46.

Aguirre, A., & Baker, D. V. (1999). Slave executions in the United States: A descriptive analysis of social and historical factors. *Social Science Journal, 36*, 1–31.

Allen, H. W., Clubb, J. M., & Lacey, V. A. (2008). *Race, class, and the death penalty: Capital punishment in American history*. Albany: State University of New York Press.

Anderson, D. S. (2015). *Emmett Till: The murder that shocked the world and propelled the Civil Rights Movement*. Jackson: University Press of Mississippi.

Ayers, E. L. (1984). *Vengeance and justice: Crime and punishment in the 19th century American South*. New York: Oxford University Press.

Bailey, A. K., & Tolnay, S. E. (2015). *Lynched: The victims of Southern mob violence*. Chapel Hill: University of North Carolina Press.

Banner, S. (2002). *The death penalty: An American history*. Cambridge: Harvard University Press.

Beck, E. M. (2015). Judge Lynch denied: Combating mob violence in the American South, 1877–1950. *Southern Cultures, 21*, 117–139.

Beck, E. M., Massey, J. L., & Tolnay, S. E. (1989). The gallows, the mob, and the vote: Lethal sanctioning of blacks in North Carolina and Georgia, 1882 to 1930. *Law and Society Review, 23*, 317–331.

Bedau, H. A. (2002). Causes and consequences of wrongful convictions: An essay-review. *Judicature, 86*, 115–119.

Bessler, J. D. (2003). *Legacy of violence: Lynch mobs and executions in Minnesota*. Minneapolis: University of Minnesota Press.

Black brute. (1901, February 2). *Nashville Banner*, p. 1.

Bright, S. B. (1995). Discrimination, death and denial: The tolerance of racial discrimination in infliction of the death penalty. *Santa Clara Law Review, 35*, 433–483.

Bruce, A. A., & Fitzgerald, T. S. (1928–9). A study of crime in the city of Memphis, Tennessee. *Journal of Criminal Law, Criminology, and Police Sciences, 19*, 1–124.

Brundage, W. F. (1993). *Lynching in the New South: Georgia and Virginia, 1880–1930*. Urbana: University of Illinois Press.

Bureau of Justice Statistics. (1982). *Capital punishment 1981*. Washington, DC: U.S. Department of Justice. Retrieved from www.bjs.gov

Bureau of Justice Statistics. (2014). *Capital punishment, 2013-statistical tables*. Washington, DC: U.S. Department of Justice. Retrieved from www.bjs.gov

Burn negro at stake on Dyersburg square. (1917, December 3). [Memphis] *Commercial Appeal*, p. 1.

Butterfield, F. (1995). *All God's children: The Bosket family and the American tradition of violence*. New York: Alfred A. Knopf.

Bye, R. T. (1919). *Capital punishment in the United States*. Philadelphia: The Committee on Philanthropic Labor of Philadelphia Yearly Meeting of Friends.

Campbell, J. (2013). *Crime and punishment in African American history*. New York: Palgrave Macmillan.

Campney, B. M. S. (2015). *This is not Dixie: Racist violence in Kansas, 1861–1927*. Urbana: University of Illinois Press.

Carrigan, W. D., & Webb, C. (2013). *Forgotten dead: Mob violence against Mexicans in the United States, 1848–1928*. Oxford: Oxford University Press.

Carter, D. T. (1979). *Scottsboro: A tragedy of the American South*. Baton Rouge: Louisiana State University Press.

Chadbourn, J. H. (1970). *Lynching and the law*. Chapel Hill: University of North Carolina Press. (Original work published 1933).

Church, T. W. (1986). Examining local legal culture. *American Bar Foundation Research Journal, 10*, 449–518.

Clarke, J. W. (1998a). *The lineaments of wrath: Race, violent crime, and American culture*. New Brunswick, NJ: Transaction Publishers.

Clarke, J. W. (1998b). Without fear or shame: Lynching, capital punishment and the subculture of violence in the American South. *British Journal of Political Science, 28*, 269–289.

Clegg, C. A. (2010). *Troubled ground: A tale of murder, lynching, and reckoning in the New South*. Urbana: University of Illinois Press.

Cohen, G. B. (2012). McCleskey's omission: The racial geography of retribution. *Ohio State Journal of Criminal Law, 10*, 65–101.

Crudele, L. W. (1980). A lynching bee: Butler County style. *Alabama Historical Quarterly, 42*, 59–71.

Cunningham, D., & Phillips, B. T. (2007). Contexts for mobilization: Spatial settings and Klan presence in North Carolina, 1964–1966. *American Journal of Sociology, 113*, 781–814.

Cutler, J. E. (1907). Capital punishment and lynching. *Annals of the American Academy of Political and Social Science, 29*, 622–625.

Cutler, J. E. (1969). *Lynch-law: An investigation into the history of lynching in the United States*. Reprinted, New York: Negro Universities Press. (Original work published 1905).

Death Penalty Information Center. (2016a, December 9). *Facts about the death penalty*. Retrieved from www.deathpenaltyinfo.org

Death Penalty Information Center. (2016b, November 9). *States with and without the death penalty*. Retrieved from www.deathpenaltyinfo.org

Death Penalty Information Center. (2016c). *The death penalty in 2016: Year end report*. Retrieved from www.deathpenaltyinfo.org

Defina, R., & Hannon, L. (2011). The legacy of black lynching and contemporary segregation in the South. *Review of Black Political Economy, 38*, 165–181.

Denham, J. M. (1997). *"A rogue's paradise": Crime and punishment in antebellum Florida, 1821–1861*. Tuscaloosa: University of Alabama Press.

Dieter, R. C. (2013). *The 2% death penalty: How a minority of counties produce most death cases at enormous costs to all*. Washington, DC: Death Penalty Information Center. Retrieved from www.deathpenaltyinfo.org

Dyer, T. G. (1997). A most unexampled exhibition of madness and brutality: Judge Lynch in Saline County, Missouri, 1859. In W. F. Brundage (Ed.), *Under sentence of death: Lynching in the South* (pp. 81–108). Chapel Hill: University of North Carolina Press.

Dyersburg is aroused. (1901, February 18). [Memphis] *Commercial Appeal*, p. 1.

Equal Justice Initiative. (2015). *Lynching in America: Confronting the legacy of racial terror*. Montgomery, AL: Equal Justice Initiative. Retrieved from www.eji.org

Espy, M. W., & Smykla, J. O. (no date). *Executions in the U.S. 1608–2002: The espy file*. Retrieved from www.deathpenaltyinfo.org

Friedman, L. M. (1993). *Crime and punishment in American history*. New York: Basic Books.

Galliher, J. F., Ray, G., & Cook, B. (1992). Abolition and reinstatement of capital punishment during the Progressive Era and early 20th Century. *Journal of Criminal Law and Criminology, 83*, 538–576.

Garland, D. (2005). Penal excess and surplus meaning: Public torture lynchings in twentieth-century America. *Law and Society Review, 39*, 793–833.

Garland, D. (2010). *Peculiar institution: America's death penalty in an age of abolition*. Cambridge: Belknap Press of Harvard University Press.

Griffin, L. J., Clark, P., & Sandberg, J. C. (1997). Narrative and event: Lynching and historical sociology. In W. F. Brundage (Ed.), *Under sentence of death: Lynching in the South* (pp. 24–47). Chapel Hill: University of North Carolina Press.

Harris, J. W. (1995). Etiquette, lynching, and racial boundaries in Southern history: A Mississippi example. *American Historical Review, 100*, 387–410.

Heard, A. (2010). *The eyes of Willie McGee: A tragedy of race, sex, and secrets in the Jim Crow South*. New York: Harper.

Henry hung. (1902, April 5). *Ocala Evening Star*, p. 1.

Hines, E., & Steelwater, E. (no date). *Project HAL: Historical American Lynching Data Collection Project (based on data compiled by Stewart E. Tolnay and E.M. Beck)*. Retrieved from www.uncwil.edu/earsci/projectHAL.htm

Hung jury and lynching. (1901, March 18). [Memphis] *Commercial Appeal*, p. 1.

Ike Fitzgerald hanged. (1901, March 18). [Memphis] *Evening Scimitar*, p. 2.

Jackson, J. L., Dr., Jackson, J. L., Jr., & Shapiro, B. K. (2001). *Legal lynching: The death penalty and America's future*. New York: New Press.

Jacobs, D., Carmichael, J. T., & Kent, S. L. (2005). Vigilantism, current racial threat, and death sentences. *American Sociological Review, 70*, 656–677.

Jacobs, D., Malone, C., & Iles, G. (2012). Race and imprisonments: Vigilante violence, minority threat, and racial politics. *Sociological Quarterly, 53*, 166–187.

Jean, S. (2005). "Warranted" lynchings: Narratives of mob violence in white Southern newspapers, 1880–1940. *American Nineteenth Century History, 6*, 351–372.

Judge left bench to save prisoner. (1902, April 4). [Tampa] *Morning Tribune*, p. 1.

Kaufman-Osborn, T. V. (2006). Capital punishment as legal lynching? In C. J. Ogletree & A. Sarat (Eds.), *From lynch mobs to the killing state: Race and the death penalty in America* (pp. 20–54). New York: New York University Press.

Keil, T. J., & Vito, G. F. (2009). Lynching and the death penalty in Kentucky, 1866–1934: Substitution or supplement? *Journal of Ethnicity in Criminal Justice, 7*, 53–68.

King, R. D., Messner, S. F., & Baller, R. D. (2009). Contemporary hate crimes, law enforcement, and the legacy of racial violence. *American Sociological Review, 74*, 291–315.

Kirchmeier, J. L. (2015). *Imprisoned by the past: Warren McCleskey and the American death penalty*. Oxford: Oxford University Press.

Labode, M. (2014). The "stern, fearless settlers of the West": Lynching, region, and capital punishment in early twentieth-century Colorado. *Western Historical Quarterly, 45*, 389–409.

Lane, R. (1999). Murder in America: A historian's perspective. *Crime and Justice, 25*, 191–224.

Leonard, S. J. (2002). *Lynching in Colorado, 1859–1919*. Boulder: University Press of Colorado.

Litwack, L. F. (1998). *Trouble in mind: Black Southerners in the age of Jim Crow*. New York: Vintage Books.

Lynched in light of day. (1901, February 19). [Memphis] *Commercial Appeal*, p. 1.

Marquart, J. W., Ekland-Olson, S., & Sorensen, J. R. (1994). *The rope, the chair, and the needle: Capital punishment in Texas*. Austin: University of Texas Press.

Massey, J. L., & Myers, M. A. (1989). Patterns of repressive social control in post-Reconstruction Georgia. *Social Forces, 68*, 458–488.

McGovern, J. R. (1982). *Anatomy of a lynching: The killing of Claude Neal*. Baton Rouge: Louisiana State University Press.

Menard, O. D. (2010). Lest we forget: The lynching of Will Brown, Omaha's 1919 race riot. *Nebraska History, 91*, 152–165.

Messner, S. F., Baller, R. D., & Zevenbergen, M. P. (2005). The legacy of lynching and Southern homicide. *American Sociological Review, 70*, 633–655.

Messner, S. F., Baumer, E. P., & Rosenfeld, R. (2006). Distrust of government, the vigilante tradition, and support for capital punishment. *Law and Society Review, 40*, 559–590.

Mob violence condemned. (1919, September 10). [Jacksonville] *Florida Times-Union*, p. 6.

Montell, W. L. (1986). *Killings: Folk justice in the Upper South*. Lexington: University Press of Kentucky.

Murderer Henry hung by order of governor. (1902, April 5). [Tampa] *Morning Tribune*, p. 1.

NAACP. (1918, February). The burning at Dyersburg. *The Crisis, 15*, 178–183.

NAACP. (1920, June). Contrasts. *The Crisis, 20*, 95.

NAACP. (1940, January). Lynching goes underground: A report on a new technique. Papers of the NAACP, Part 7, Series A, Anti-lynching campaign, 1916–1950, reel 25, frames 0517–0577.

Negro dies in electric chair. (1916, July 13). *Nashville Banner*, p. 1.

Negro is missing. (1901, February 20). [Memphis] *Evening Scimitar*, p. 1.

Negro is trailed. (1916, February 4). [Dyersburg] *State Gazette*, p. 1.

Negro tortured and then burned. (1917, December 3). *Nashville Banner*, p. 2.

Ocala getting a bad name. (1926, January 29). *Ocala Banner*, p. 1.

Old story. (1901, March 18). *Nashville Banner*, p. 3.

One negro lynched. (1901, February 18). [Memphis] *Evening Scimitar*, p. 1.

Oney, S. (2003). *And the dead shall rise: The murder of Mary Phagan and the lynching of Leo Frank*. New York: Pantheon Books.

Oshinsky, D. M. (1996). *Worse than slavery: Parchman Farm and the ordeal of Jim Crow justice*. New York: Free Press.

Paredes, J. A., & Purdum, E. D. (1990). "Bye-bye Ted . . . ": Community response in Florida to the execution of Theodore Bundy. *Anthropology Today, 6,* 9–11.

Pfeifer, M. J. (2004). *Rough justice: Lynching and American society, 1874–1947.* Urbana: University of Illinois Press.

Pfeifer, M. J. (2013). *Lynching beyond Dixie: American mob violence outside the South.* Urbana: University of Illinois Press.

Pfeifer, M. J. (2014). At the hands of parties unknown? The state of the field of lynching scholarship. *The Journal of American History, 101,* 832–846.

Phillips, C. D. (1987). Exploring relations among forms of social control: The lynching and execution of blacks in North Carolina, 1889–1918. *Law and Society Review, 21,* 361–374.

Poveda, T. G. (2006). Geographic location, death sentences and executions in post-*Furman* Virginia. *Punishment and Society, 8,* 423–442.

Rogers, W. W., & Denham, J. M. (2001). *Florida sheriffs: A history, 1821–1945.* Tallahassee, FL: Sentry Press.

Rushdy, A. A. (2012). *The end of American lynching.* New Brunswick, NJ: Rutgers University Press.

Scour Dyer for negro. (1917, November 24). [Memphis] *News Scimitar,* p. 1.

Smead, H. (1986). *Blood justice: The lynching of Mack Charles Parker.* New York: Oxford University Press.

Southern Poverty Law Center. (2016). *Ten days after: Harassment and intimidation in the aftermath of the election.* Montgomery, AL: Southern Poverty Law Center. Retrieved from www.splcenter.org

Squally times in Sumter. (1902, April 2). *Ocala Evening Star,* p. 3.

State again disgraced. (1929, May 31). *Nashville Tennessean,* p. 4.

Steiker, C. S., & Steiker, J. M. (2010). Capital punishment: A century of discontinuous debate. *Journal of Criminal Law and Criminology, 100,* 643–689.

Stovel, K. (2001). Local sequential patterns: The structure of lynching in the Deep South, 1882–1930. *Social Forces, 79,* 843–880.

Tennessee lynching outrivals worst German atrocity. (December 8, 1917). [Baltimore] *Afro American,* p. 1.

Tolnay, S. E., & Beck, E. M. (1995). *A festival of violence: An analysis of Southern lynchings, 1882–1930.* Urbana: University of Illinois Press.

Triple lynching was averted. (1901, February 19). [Memphis] *Evening Scimitar,* p. 1.

Trotti, M. A. (2011). The scaffold's revival: Race and public execution in the South. *Journal of Social History, 45,* 195–224.

Trotti, M. A. (2013). What counts: Trends in racial violence in the postbellum South. *Journal of American History, 100,* 375–400.

Vandiver, M. (2006). *Lethal punishment: Lynchings and legal executions in the South.* New Brunswick, NJ: Rutgers University Press.

Vandiver, M. (2012). Two years of terror: Lynchings in north Florida, 1893–1895. *Criminal Law Bulletin, 48,* 515–536.

Vandiver, M. (2014). "Florida's shame": The Lake City lynching of 1911. *Criminal Law Bulletin, 50,* 831–849.

Vandiver, M., Giacopassi, D. J., & Curley, M. S. (2003). The Tennessee Slave Code: A legal antecedent to inequities in modern capital cases. *Journal of Ethnicity in Criminal Justice, 1,* 67–89.

Vandiver, M., Giacopassi, D. J., & Gathje, P. R. (2002). "I hope someone murders your mother!": An exploration of extreme support for the death penalty. *Deviant Behavior, 23,* 385–415.

Vandiver, M., Giacopassi, D. J., & Lofquist, W. (2006). Slavery's enduring legacy: Executions in modern America. *Journal of Ethnicity in Criminal Justice, 4,* 19–36.

Vinikas, V. (1999). "Specters in the past": The Saint Charles, Arkansas, lynching of 1904 and the limits of historical inquiry. *Journal of Southern History, 65,* 535–564.

Von Drehle, D. (1995). *Among the lowest of the dead: The culture of death row.* New York: Random House.

Waldrep, C. (2000). War of words: The controversy over the definition of lynching, 1899–1940. *Journal of Southern History, 66,* 75–100.

Waldrep, C. (2002). *The many faces of Judge Lynch: Extralegal violence and punishment in America.* New York: Palgrave Macmillan.

Waldrep, C. (2009). *African Americans confront lynching: Strategies of resistance from the Civil War to the Civil Rights era.* Lanham, MD: Rowman & Littlefield Publishers.

West, R. (1947, June 14). Opera in Greenville. *The New Yorker.* Retrieved from www.newyorker.com

Williamson, J. (1997). Wounds not scars: Lynching, the national conscience, and the American historian. *The Journal of American History, 83,* 1221–1253.

Wright, G. C. (1990). *Racial violence in Kentucky, 1865–1940: Lynchings, mob rule, and "legal lynchings".* Baton Rouge: Louisiana State University Press.

Wright, G. C. (1997). By the book: The legal executions of Kentucky blacks. In W. F. Brundage (Ed.), *Under sentence of death: Lynching in the South* (pp. 250–270). Chapel Hill: University of North Carolina Press.

Wyatt-Brown, B. (1986). *Honor and violence in the Old South.* New York: Oxford University Press.

Zangrando, R. L. (1980). *The NAACP crusade against lynching, 1909–1950.* Philadelphia: Temple University Press.
Zimring, F. E. (2003). *The contradictions of American capital punishment.* Oxford: Oxford University Press.

Cases Cited

Furman v. Georgia, 408 U.S. 238 (1972).
Gregg v. Georgia, 428 U.S. 153 (1976).
McCleskey v. Kemp, 481 U.S. 279. (1987).
Sireci v. Florida, 580 U.S. _____ (2016).

B. Opinion

3

PUBLIC OPINION ABOUT THE DEATH PENALTY

*Leah Butler, James D. Unnever, Francis T. Cullen,
and Angela J. Thielo*

The professional ideology of criminologists, which is generally progressive (Cullen & Gendreau, 2001), includes opposition to the death penalty. This position is long-standing. By the early 1960s, Garland (2010, p. 211) observes, "Criminologists and penologists declared themselves against capital punishment, describing it as inimical to the reformative approach of modern penology." Such views have persisted across time. Thus, a 2003 survey of criminologists found that about 7 in 10 (69%) favored suspending "the death penalty because innocent people are almost certainly on death row"; nearly 2 in 3 (63.7%) also stated that "Even if capital punishment was a deterrent, I would still oppose its use" (Cullen, Blevins, Pealer, Daigle, & Coleman, 2004, pp. 55–56). In support of this policy stance, scholars have been able to marshal substantial evidence questioning the utility of this sanction, in particular its deterrent effects and cost effectiveness (Fagan, 2016; Nagin & Pepper, 2012). A more stubborn challenge, however, has been posed by public opinion research that, since the late 1960s, has shown that a majority of Americans support capital punishment (Cullen, Fisher, & Applegate, 2000). If the democratic impulse—the "will of the people"—is to execute those convicted of murder, then calls to ban the death penalty risk charges of political correctness and academic elitism.

In her analysis of the origins and impact of surveys within the United States, Igo (2007) documents how opinion polls gained legitimacy in the 1900s. Notions of collecting social data were limited in the 1930s, with one historian noting that "it was commonplace that the United States had better statistics on pigs than on its unemployed people" (quoted in Igo, 2007, p. 3). A key feature of surveys was the implicit claim that America had become a mass society that could be studied as having *a public opinion*. Igo calls her book *The Averaged American* precisely because the project of pollsters was to capture, often in a single number, the attitudes of the typical citizen. The danger of this approach was that once publicized, survey results could be "influential . . . in bounding and enforcing perceptions of social reality" (2007, p. 22).

In this context, criminologists and other social scientists have sought to deconstruct how national opinions polls—most based on a single question—portray how the so-called American public views the death penalty. They would agree with Igo (2007, p. 22) that "We need to understand social scientific representations—of 'typical communities,' 'majority opinion,' and 'normal Americans'—not as reflections of the body politic but as an index of political and epistemological power." They can take some solace that Americans' support for capital punishment has declined in recent years. That aside, their project over the past several decades has been to show that public opinion about the death penalty cannot be captured by a single question that yields a single percentage figure (e.g., 70% of the public supports executing those convicted of murder). Rather, they make the important point that death penalty attitudes are complex and, in turn, that measuring this complexity requires a more sophisticated methodological approach.

Informed by this understanding, the current chapter starts by describing the level and trends in support for the death penalty in the United States based on the traditional one-question opinion poll. The second section then reviews the various ways in which research using more detailed survey methodology has challenged the finding that the American citizenry has unshakable support for executing offenders. In a related line of inquiry, the chapter then shows how any discussion of how "the" public views capital punishment is widely off the mark if race and the views of African Americans are not considered. As Igo (2007, p. 19) observes, surveys "placed new cultural emphasis on the center point, the scientifically derived mean and median." Such aggregation swamps and thus hides minority opinion—a worrisome possibility when studying any criminal justice policy issue in the United States, let alone the state's exercise of lethal force.

Declining Support for the Death Penalty

Support for the death penalty has not been stable over the past 80 years during which Gallup has polled the American public on this policy issue. According to Gallup, in 1937, 59% of the United States favored the death penalty for those convicted of murder (Death Penalty, 2017; see also Cullen et al., 2000, pp. 12–13). The percent of the population with favorable attitudes toward the death penalty rose to 68% by the time the next poll was conducted in 1953. However, favorability fell to 53% by 1956 and declined again—to 47%—the following year. Aside from a 6% uptick in support from 1957 to 1960, the percent of the public who favored capital punishment continued to drop over the early 1960s and reached its lowest point in the twentieth century—and to date—at 42% in 1966. This year also marks the only point in the past eight decades when more people opposed capital punishment (47%) than favored it.

In the late 1960s, however, support (as measured by the Gallup Poll) began to grow incrementally, reaching 57% of the American public by 1972 and continuing on an upward climb for two decades. However, after its peak at 80% in 1994, support for capital punishment has generally declined—with the exception of a period of slight increase from 2000 (66%) to 2003 (70%) (Death Penalty, 2017). For the past 13 years (from 2003 to 2016), public support for the death penalty has decreased each year. The most recent Gallup Poll (October 2016) places public favor for the death penalty at 60%, the lowest it has been since 1972.

The Gallup numbers are similar to those reported by other polls. Table 3.1 shows the trends in support for the death penalty for the Gallup Poll and the General Social Survey (GSS). The GSS also shows a period of overall increase in support for the death penalty for those convicted of murder from 1980 to 1994. According to the GSS, support peaked at 80% in 1994—the same peak year and level of support reported by Gallup. GSS data also show consistently shrinking support from 1994 to 2014. The most recent GSS (2014) places support at 65%—nearly the same as that of the Gallup Poll for 2014, which revealed support at 63%. Note that because the General Social Survey began in 1974, comparisons to the Gallup Poll data prior to this year are not possible.

Other national surveys are also relevant. Thus, the *CBS News* and *New York Times* poll also reports declining death penalty support from 1988 to 2014—from 78% to 60% (Backus, 2011). Similarly, the Pew Research Center shows a peak in support in 1994 (80%), followed by generally diminishing support for the next 20 years (Oliphant, 2016). In 2016, the Pew Research Center reported 49% support, the first time that this figure dipped below 50% since 1971 (Oliphant, 2016). These poll data reveal stability in death penalty attitudes over short periods of time; for example, in the Gallup Poll, the mean difference from one polling time to the next was approximately 3.6%. However, the data manifest larger changes over longer periods, such as the period of increase from the late 1960s to the early 1990s and the decline more recently. In other words, public opinion on capital punishment tends to shift gradually, not suddenly.

Table 3.1 Public Opinion About the Death Penalty and Punitiveness in Sentencing

Year	Percent Supporting the Death Penalty—Gallup Poll	Percent Supporting the Death Penalty—General Social Survey	Percent Who Believe the Courts Are Not Harsh Enough—General Social Survey
1937	60	—	—
1953	68	—	—
1956	53	—	—
1957	47	—	—
1960	53	—	—
1965	45	—	—
1966	42	—	—
1967	54	—	—
1969	51	—	—
1971	49	—	—
1972	50	—	73
1973	—	—	80
1974	—	66	84
1975	—	64	85
1976	66	70	87
1977	—	—	88
1978	62	71	90
1980	—	72	89
1981	66	—	—
1982	—	73	87
1983	—	78	90
1984	—	76	86
1985	74	79	87
1986	70	76	89
1987	—	69	83
1988	79	76	86
1989	—	—	88
1990	—	79	86
1991	76	76	84
1993	—	—	86
1994	80	80	89
1995	77	—	—
1996	—	78	85
1998	—	73	80
1999	71	—	—
2000	66	70	75
2001	68	—	—

(Continued)

Table 3.1 (Continued)

Year	Percent Supporting the Death Penalty—Gallup Poll	Percent Supporting the Death Penalty—General Social Survey	Percent Who Believe the Courts Are Not Harsh Enough—General Social Survey
2002	70	70	72
2003	67	—	—
2004	64	68	69
2005	64	—	—
2006	66	69	68
2007	69	—	—
2008	64	68	67
2009	65	—	—
2010	64	68	67
2011	61	—	—
2012	63	65	62
2013	60	—	—
2014	63	65	63
2015	61	—	—
2016	60	—	—

Sources: Gallup Poll data for 1937 to 2016 from *Death Penalty* (2017). Gallup Poll question, "Are you in favor of the death penalty for a person convicted of murder?" General Social Survey data for 1974 to 2014 from Smith, Marsden, Hout, and Kim (1972–2014). GSS death penalty poll question: "Do you favor or oppose the death penalty for persons convicted of murder?" GSS harsher courts question: "In general, do you think the courts in this area deal too harshly or not harshly enough with criminals?"

Cullen et al. (2000) point out that from the 1960s through the 1990s, "the public ostensibly [grew] more punitive" and suggest that this could "reflect core, deeply rooted cultural values that make Americans a punitive people" (pp. 13–14). The idea that support for the death penalty is rooted in overall punitiveness can be evaluated by comparing trends in punitive attitudes other than death penalty opinion. One comparison in particular suggests that the American people may be becoming less punitive in their views toward crime control.

Thus, a measure of punitiveness often cited is the public's response to this GSS question: "In general, do you think the courts in this area deal too harshly or not harshly enough with criminals?" Table 3.1 presents the trend in the percent of respondents stating that the courts are not harsh enough. Notably, our calculations reveal that the percent of the public who believe courts are "not harsh enough" is clearly correlated ($r = .656$) with the percent of the public who favor capital punishment for convicted murderers. In fact, the percent of those who believed courts are not harsh enough reached its highest level of the past three decades in 1994, the same year as the peak of capital punishment support. And since that time, the public's endorsement of harsher courts and the death penalty has demonstrated a general pattern of decline. This finding suggests that the diminishing support for capital punishment in recent years reflects a downward trend in punitive attitudes in general.

How does the American public's views of the death penalty compare to those held by citizens of other nations? A number of non-European nations report higher public support for capital punishment, such as Taiwan (83.27%), Pakistan (81.6%), and Thailand (78.63%) (Unnever, 2010, p. 473). Still, the lessening embrace of capital punishment in the United States is moving the nation closer to the

Table 3.2 Public Support for the Death Penalty in North America and Western Europe

Country	Percent Supporting the Death Penalty
United States	67.96
United Kingdom	50.29
Canada	47.88
France	41.75
Belgium	39.86
Netherlands	35.37
Finland	35.27
Luxembourg	32.8
Switzerland	25.1
Ireland	17.36

Sources: Public support for the death penalty data from the *Voice of the People Millennium Survey, 2000* conducted by the Gallup International Association as reported in Unnever (2010). Gallup Poll question: "Are you personally in favor or against the death penalty?"

views expressed in other advanced Western nations (see Garland, 2010), most of whom no longer permit the execution of offenders. Although dated, a useful comparison is possible from Unnever's (2010) analysis of the Gallup International Association *Voice of the People Millennium Survey* (see Table 3.2).

In 2000, 67.96% of the U.S. population supported the death penalty. By contrast, support for capital punishment in other Western countries fell near or below the 50% mark. As seen in Table 3.2, support for capital punishment ranged from 50.29% in the United Kingdom to only 17.36% in Ireland (Unnever, 2010). Since that time, available polls suggest that support for the death penalty has remained stable or has decreased in these nations (International Polls and Studies, 2017). For example, the most recent British Social Attitudes survey shows that, for the first time, the citizenry's support fell below the 50% mark, with 48% of the British public agreeing with the statement: "For some crimes, the death penalty is the most appropriate sentence." (Support for the Death Penalty Falls Below 50% for First Time, 2015). One exception appears to be Canada, where the 2012 Angus Reid public opinion poll found that 63% of Canadians supported reinstating the death penalty (Three-in-Five Canadians Would Bring Back Death Penalty, 2013). Still, it remains the case that Canada abolished capital punishment and recently has moved, after a lengthy period of Conservative Party leadership, in a more progressive direction under the administration of Prime Minister Justin Trudeau.

Beyond Global Attitudes

Even though approval for the death penalty has declined, national polls still show that more Americans support than oppose this sanction. In a democratic society, the claim of public support is a salient justification for pursuing a policy—in this case, the execution of convicted murderers. After all, there must be a compelling reason not to follow the "will of the people." For elected officials, doing so carries the potential risk of being voted out of office.

Scholars, however, have challenged the assumption that national polls using a single question can accurately capture the full complexity of the public's thinking about any issue, let alone the state's use of lethal force versus offenders. This is not to say that these polls are irrelevant and do not assess some attitudinal domain. Usually, it is argued that a single item taps into a *global attitude*—that is, an overall view or knee-jerk response about the death penalty. Roberts and Stalans (1997, p. 229) argue that these public sentiments are often based on faulty information and on "emotion and symbolic attitudes" as opposed to "rational reflection." Still, global attitudes are not irrelevant because they may be precisely what citizens themselves define as their "position" on the death penalty—being for or against it.

The difficulty occurs when polling results are publicized in the media and then reified as defining the level of public support for capital punishment. Researchers have attempted to deconstruct this social reality by showing that citizens' attitudes vary when given more information and asked to make decisions that are more policy focused. The resulting opinions are sometimes referred to as *specific attitudes* or as *public judgment* (see, e.g., Applegate, Cullen, Turner, & Sundt, 1996; Yanklovich, 1991). There is an implicit, if not explicit, assumption that specific attitudes are more accurate or represent a higher quality of opinion. This may or may not be the case (Yanklovich, 1991). What is clear, however, is that research in this tradition is capturing another side of public opinion that must be included when discussing whether, as is the case here, the public supports the death penalty.

In this context, scholars have explored the extent to which survey respondents favor the death penalty when asked to make more specific judgments. It is conceivable to develop ways to inflate such support, such as by asking whether citizens wish to execute an offender who sexually assaulted and strangled to death a young child. Still, the general finding of this research is that specific attitudes are less punitive than global attitudes, even at times to the point where support for capital punishment falls below 50%. Here, we illustrate four important areas of scholarship in which the research moved beyond the assessment of global attitudes: (1) support for the juvenile death penalty; (2) how support varies when the respondents can choose an alternative penalty, such as life in prison without parole; (3) the impact of more information about the death penalty on attitudes; and (4) how concerns about innocent people being executed affects death penalty support.

Juvenile Death Penalty

In 2005, with a 5–4 decision in *Roper v. Simmons*, the Supreme Court of the United States ruled the use of the death penalty on juveniles unconstitutional. Prior to this case, however, scholars engaged in research assessing public support for the execution of juveniles. One purpose of this line of inquiry was to demonstrate that global attitudes about capital punishment would not necessarily apply to wayward youths. When it came to the death penalty, age might matter and specify the claim that a majority of the American public favored the execution of offenders convicted of murder.

In fact, studies revealed that the public was less supportive of the use of the death penalty with juveniles as opposed to adults. Thus, in 2001, the General Social Survey found that 34% of Americans favored the death penalty for juveniles compared to 62% who favored the use of the death penalty with no offender age specification (Smith, 2001). Similarly, a 2002 national poll discovered that only 26% of Americans favored the death penalty for juveniles, whereas 70% favored the death penalty for a convicted murderer with no offender age specification (Jones, 2002).

This general finding, however, varied according to when and where polls were conducted. For example, in 1986, support for the death penalty for "juveniles over the age of fourteen convicted of murder," was only 25% in Cincinnati, Ohio and 30% in Columbus, Ohio (Skovron, Scott, & Cullen, 1989, p. 551). Surveys conducted in the early 1990s estimated higher levels of support for the execution of juveniles, including 51.4% support in a 1991 Oklahoma City survey (Grasmick, Bursik, & Blackwell, 1993) and 60% support in the national 1994 Gallup Poll (Moore, 2004). Other statewide polls in conservative contexts reported similar levels of support, with support for executing youths reaching 41% in Indiana (Sandys & McGarrell, 1995), 42% in Kentucky (Vito & Keil, 1998), and 53.5% in Tennessee (Moon, Wright, Cullen, & Pealer, 2000).

Even with this variation, the statistics just cited reveal that support for the juvenile death penalty still fell well below support for the adult death penalty. As Jones (2002, para. 36) concludes, based on the Gallup Poll, "Historically, Americans have been far less supportive of the death penalty for those under 21 than for adults." The gap between general death penalty support and juvenile death penalty support was 33% in 1936 and 24% in 1965. Writing in 2002—not long before the U.S. Supreme Court's decision—Jones noted that "the gap in support may be widening" (2002, para. 36). Indeed, by 2002, the cleavage in support for the death penalty for juveniles and for the death penalty in general had grown to 46% (Jones, 2002).

Given the consistently lower levels of support for capital punishment for youthful offenders relative to adult offenders, it is unsurprising that the public tends to favor other forms of punishment for juveniles over capital punishment. When presented as alternatives to the death penalty, Moon and colleagues (2000, p. 677) found that 64% of their sample "would prefer a sentence of life in prison without the possibility of parole" and that 80% "supported life in prison without parole, combined with work and restitution to the families of their victims." Similarly, in a study using vignettes, Applegate and Davis (2006) reported that a majority of the respondents preferred alternative sentences to the death penalty for juveniles. This same pattern is found in research conducted on sanctioning preferences for adult offenders—an issue to which we now turn.

Giving More Sentencing Options

As Cullen et al. (2009, p. 81) explain, national polls on public support for the death penalty usually provide a "'favor' response" that "identifies precisely what sanction the murderer will receive (death)" and an "'oppose' response" that "leaves the nature of the subsequent penalty unspecified and open to speculation." Herein lies an important problem with public opinion polls on the death penalty: The percentage of respondents who "favor" the death penalty may be influenced by the alternative sentences that the respondents believe lie within the "oppose" response. For example, if a death penalty is not imposed, the possibility exists that the offenders might receive a short sentence ("get off easily") or, in the least, be paroled at some point in their lives. The issue, then, is not simply whether Americans support the death penalty but whether they support this sanction versus some other clearly stated sentencing option.

In response to this methodological blind spot, scholars designed surveys that asked the respondents to choose between the death penalty and other sentencing options. Most notably, many of these surveys explored whether the respondents preferred capital punishment or a life sentence without a possibility of parole—a sanction known by its acronym, "LWOP." Others include various alternative sanctions that may be attractive to respondents. In either case, the alternative sentence options are typically those that would be considered less severe than the death penalty.

Importantly, this research discovered that the level of support for the death penalty is lower when alternative sentencing options are given than when only "favor" or "oppose" options are given. Thus, the National Crime Policy survey showed that, "Although 74.0 per cent of the sample favored the death penalty on the global question, support declined to just over half when the respondents could choose between the 'the death penalty' (53.5 per cent) and [LWOP] (46.5 per cent)" (Cullen et al., 2009, p. 82). The Gallup Poll has found similar results. Moore (2004, para. 5) reports that, "Over the past 20 years, support for the death penalty instead of life imprisonment has fluctuated between a low of 49% and a high of 61%," whereas the percent of the public who favor the death penalty (rather than oppose) fluctuated between 64% and 80% from 1984 to 2004.

Other researchers have demonstrated the significance of specificity in alternative sentences provided as poll responses. In addition to life imprisonment without the possibility for parole, some surveys include options for the addition of restitution as a sentence component. Notably, a now-classic 1989 survey of New York State residents found that 62% of respondents said they would accept a life sentence for a person convicted of murder in which there was "no possibility of parole ever" and the offender would "work in a prison industry where his earnings would go to the victim's family" as an alternative to the death penalty (Bohm, Flanagan, & Harris, 1990, p. 830). Further, while "72% of the New York poll respondents favored the death penalty for people convicted of murder," "only 32% would not support any alternative to the death penalty" (Bohm et al., 1990, p. 831).

Likewise, Bowers, Vandiver, and Dugan (1994) reported that, in general, "both eliminating parole and adding a restitution requirement increased public endorsement for a life sentence as an alternative to the death penalty" (p. 92). In this study, 56% and 57% of the respondents in New York and Nebraska, respectively, who "strongly favored" the death penalty chose life without parole plus restitution as an alternative (Bowers et al., 1994, p. 106). Other researchers have demonstrated similar results in terms of lower support for the death penalty when alternative sentences are provided relative to general attitudes (see Sandys & McGarrell, 1995; McGarrell & Sandys, 1996).

Taken together, these investigations revealed that the claim that a majority of Americans support capital punishment was a methodological artifact, not a definitive empirical fact. When survey respondents were asked to make a judgment between alternative sanctions, they tended to show a preference for nonlethal penalties. They seemed to see a life sentence without the possibility of parole providing an equivalent amount of justice and public safety. In particular, they preferred a sentence in which offenders engaged in restorative action, working to provide restitution to the victim's family. This finding does not mean that crimes do not exist for which a majority of Americans might endorse an offender's execution (see, e.g., Durham, Elrod, & Kinkade, 1996). But it does mean that public views on the death penalty are not rigidly fixed on a specific statistical figure. Instead, they tend to be flexible and shaped by the array of sentencing options that are included in the calculations that the respondents are permitted to make.

Giving More Information

Studies that present subjects with vignettes describing the crime and the victim, among other things, allow researchers to determine whether case-specific factors influence death penalty attitudes. For example, Applegate and Davis (2006, p. 60) showed that support for the death penalty for juvenile offenders varied across different "types" of murder, including "manslaughter, attempted murder, murder as an outcome of an argument," robbery murder, and robbery murder with additional aggravating circumstances. Using logistic regression, the "odds of a preferred punishment greater than 3 years on probation" was "nearly 54 times higher when a youth had committed a murder during a robbery and brutalized the victim" than for a youth who committed manslaughter (Applegate & Davis, 2006, p. 66). The researchers also found that subjects were more likely to assign the harshest punishments (life in prison, life in prison without parole, or the death penalty) to youths with a serious prior criminal record. These findings suggest that perceptions regarding the harm caused by the crime or the dangerousness of the criminal may influence whether the respondent favors—or does not favor—the death penalty for a specific offender. Nearly half of the respondents preferred "3 years of probation or less" for manslaughter, yet only 2.4% of respondents chose this sentence option for those convicted of robbery murder with aggravating circumstances (Applegate & Davis, 2006, p. 63). This finding may indicate a tendency for individuals' desire for the punishment to "fit" the seriousness of the crime.

The relationship between the severity of the crime and preference for the death penalty is also shown in research on attitudes toward the death penalty for those convicted of murder with no offender age specification. For example, Burgason and Pazzani (2014) surveyed respondents using 40 different homicide vignettes. They found that the respondents were more likely to choose the death penalty (instead of LWOP, a respondent-specified prison term, or another respondent-specified sentence) when "a rape was committed in conjunction with the murder" and when "a gun was used in the commission of the murder" (Burgason & Pazzani, 2014, p. 827). These two factors are both related to perceived harm done beyond the murder itself.

Additionally, characteristics of the victim, of the offender, and of the relationship between the two were also related to the respondents' selection of the death penalty. The death penalty was chosen more frequently when "negative information about the offender was known" and when "the victim and offender were strangers" (Burgason & Pazzani, 2014, p. 827). Negative information about the offender included "the offender being a male prostitute, having a number of previous convictions for violent robberies, having an affair, being a drug addict, being a gang member, begging for money and having large gambling debts" (Burgason & Pazzani, 2014, p. 824). The opposite effect, however, was found when negative information about the victim was presented. Thus, the respondents were less likely to select the death penalty when they were told that the victim was having an affair, was sleeping with someone who was having an affair, or was a gang member (Burgason & Pazzani, 2014, p. 824). This result implies that the sympathy-worthiness or blame-worthiness of the victim may influence the degree of punitiveness the respondent directs toward the offender. Again, support for capital punishment is not rigid but flexible. Information can be used to inflate or depress support for this penalty.

Researchers have also examined the effect of knowledge about the death penalty itself on attitudes toward the death penalty. These studies, sometimes referred to as tests of "the Marshall Hypotheses," often cite Thurgood Marshall's written opinion in *Furman v. Georgia* (1972). In determining whether a sentence is cruel and unusual and therefore unconstitutional under the Fourth Amendment, Marshall wrote that "it is imperative for constitutional purposes to attempt to discern the probable opinion of an informed electorate" (*Furman v. Georgia*, 1972). Thus, researchers have questioned whether the public is "informed" on the subject of the death penalty and whether providing information influences attitudes.

Bohm, Clark, and Aveni (1991) tested whether the subjects were knowledgeable about various facts concerning the death penalty, including whether the death penalty has "been abolished by a majority of Western European Nations," whether the death penalty has effectively reduced crime, the frequency of executions, disproportionate death penalty sentencing, and the levels of support for the death penalty. In this study, the respondents were "relatively uninformed about the death penalty" but were informed on some facts (e.g., "men have been more likely to be executed than women," "poor people who commit murder are more likely to be sentenced to death than rich people") (Bohm et al., 1991, p. 370). The study tested whether "increasing knowledge about the death penalty" resulted in greater opposition toward the death penalty (p. 370). The design compared an experimental group of undergraduate students who participated in a semester-long course on the death penalty with a control group of undergraduates who were "enrolled in other courses offered at the same time as the death penalty class" (p. 366). Bohm et al. (1991, p. 375) found that the death penalty class increased knowledge about capital punishment and "the percentage of experimental group subjects opposed to the death penalty following the [death penalty course] (56.3%) . . . was significantly greater than the percentage of subjects opposed prior to it (34.7%)." Although these results varied depending on the question used to measure support for the death penalty, the findings suggest that, on the aggregate level, providing information can increase opposition to the death penalty.

Another study found that university students who participated in a death penalty course were "much more knowledgeable or informed about the death penalty at the end of the semester" relative to a control group of students who participated in an introductory criminal justice course (Wright, Bohm, & Jamieson, 1995, p. 64). However, there was no significant change in support for the death penalty from pretest to posttest for either the experimental or control group. Conversely, Bohm and Vogel's (2004, p. 307) panel study in which participants took a course on capital punishment found that "support for the death penalty significantly diminished after exposure to the death penalty class." However, the change in opinion did not hold over time. Instead, it "rebounded to initial pretest levels two or three years later," and "after more than ten years, the data revealed small increases in support of the death penalty from the first follow-up period" (Bohm & Vogel, 2004, p. 307). More recent research has reported that providing information on the death penalty—specifically "information on both deterrence and innocence"—resulted in lower support for the death penalty among the respondents (Lambert, Camp, Clarke, & Jiang, 2011, p. 573). These mixed results suggest that Justice Marshall's hypothesis (expressed in *Furman v. Georgia*, 1972) may have been correct, but various factors may influence the degree to which information changes attitudes toward the death penalty and how long attitude changes last.

Considering Innocence

The 2002 Gallup Poll showed a majority of Americans supported the death penalty despite the fact that the majority of Americans also reported believing innocent people have been executed (Jones, 2002). Thus, Jones (2002, para. 26) noted that although "91% of Americans said they believed that an innocent person had been sentenced to the death penalty in the last twenty years," 72% still favored the death penalty. Similarly, based on the 2009 Gallup Crime Survey, Newport (2009, para. 7) observes: "For many Americans, agreement with the assertion that innocent people have been put to death does not preclude simultaneous endorsement of the death penalty." He goes on to note that 34% of Americans simultaneously "believe an innocent person has been executed" in the last five years and "support the death penalty in cases of murder" (2009, para. 7).

It is instructive, however, that the polls used by Jones (2002) and Newport (2009) were based on a question—"Are you in favor of the death penalty for a person convicted of murder?"—that did not include the option of LWOP. When this penalty alternative is available to the respondents, a preference for the death penalty declines. In their analysis of the 2003 Gallup Poll data, Unnever and Cullen (2005) found that "individuals who believed that innocent people have been executed were significantly less likely to support the death penalty" over life imprisonment without parole (p. 15). Moreover, the belief that innocent people have been executed was held by a majority (74.6%) of the respondents. These findings suggest that the more widespread the belief that innocent people have been executed becomes, the more Americans may support life imprisonment without the possibility of parole over the death penalty.

Other research involving innocence is similarly relevant. Thus, the 2001 National Crime Policy Survey found that 39% of the respondents said, "I would have to oppose the death penalty—if the death penalty means putting even one innocent person to death, we would be better off just giving all murderers life in prison" (Cullen et al., 2009, p. 86). In response to the same question, 19.2% of respondents said they "already oppose the death penalty," presumably regardless of whether innocent people have been executed (p. 86). As Cullen and colleagues conclude, when those who would oppose the death penalty if it were proven innocent people were executed are combined with "those who already have rejected capital punishment," 58.2% of the respondents would be "against future executions" (p. 85). An even larger majority of the respondents (69.1%) said that they would be in favor of suspending the death penalty "until we can make sure that only guilty people are executed" (Cullen et al., 2009, p. 86). This shows that the possibility of executing persons for crimes which they did not commit is an important consideration for a majority of Americans.

In summary, the widespread belief among Americans that innocent people have been executed highlights just one of the factors that shapes support for the death penalty. As seen, any claim that the "public supports capital punishment" based on the most highly publicized polls is problematic. Single-question polls that provide no sentencing options capture, at best, global attitudes about the execution of offenders. In reality, opinion about the death penalty is complex. Members of the public will shift their views when asked to make judgments in which they are directed to consider a range of policy-relevant factors. The U.S. Supreme Court decision barring juvenile executions was consistent with growing public sentiments opposing this practice. Perhaps most important, giving survey respondents the option to select LWOP shows that a meaningful portion of Americans are not wed to executing offenders if a suitable alternative exists. When the possibility of putting an innocent person to death must be confronted, the attractiveness of LWOP becomes even more salient. Still, it must be admitted that when asked to prescribe a penalty for an offender who has committed a heinous crime and has a long criminal past, Americans will consider imposing capital punishment. Flexibility means that attitudes can be inflated by some factors and depressed by others. One group in the United States, however, has manifested a more robust opposition to the death penalty. It is to this issue that we next turn.

The Salience of Race

The claim that "Americans" support the death penalty is based on a statistical average of the popula-tion as a whole. The very power of national polls is that they can seemingly capture "what the public thinks" in a single number (Igo, 2007). Headlines can be set forth with convincing certainty, such as "Two Thirds Continue to Support Death Penalty" (Newport, 2009). This kind of citation of polls can mask as much as it illuminates, especially if cleavages in public opinion are either ignored or buried in the details of an article that follows. With regard to capital punishment, this issue is consequential because overall statistics hide an important fact: A group historically oppressed by the criminal justice system—African Americans—have long supported the death penalty less than whites and now are clearly opposed to its use. The section below explores this salient issue in more detail.

The Racial Divide

Polls show that support for the death penalty differs across racial groups—particularly between blacks and whites. As of 2015, 39% of African Americans supported the death penalty compared to 68% of white Americans (Dugan, 2015). According to Unnever, Cullen, and Jonson (2008), this racial divide has persisted for decades (see also Unnever & Cullen, 2007a). From 1972 to 2006, the difference between the average percentage of whites (71.8%) and blacks (44.2%) who favor the death penalty was 27.6% (Unnever et al., 2008). A similar gap is found in the GSS data. Between 1974 and 2004, a 28.2% difference existed between the average percent of whites (77.5%) and blacks (49.3%) who support the death penalty (Unnever et al., 2008). Further, Unnever and Cullen (2005) note that the racial gap in death penalty support also exists when the survey design includes LWOP as an alterna-tive sentencing option. Their analysis of the 2003 Gallup Poll data found that "the predicted odds of African Americans supporting the death penalty instead of life imprisonment without the possibility of parole were less than one-third of the predicted odds of whites" (p. 20). Researchers have offered several explanations for the racial divide in death penalty support including (1) the social convergence hypothesis, (2) the state threat hypothesis, and (3) the racial animus or social threat hypothesis.

The first explanation—the social convergence hypothesis—posits that the relationship between race and support for the death penalty is spurious and lies not in race but in the structural differences between racial groups. In *The Declining Significance of Race*, Wilson (1980) argued that the racial dif-ferences between blacks and whites have been shaped by structural forces, particularly the economy and labor market, and that economic oppression is becoming more salient than racial oppression in American society. Thus, as Davis (2005) explains, this thesis suggests "as the significance of race declines in society it is reasonable to expect that race as an influence on the formation of public opin-ion will also decline." (p. 489). In his analysis of GSS data from 1976–1982 and 1993–1998, Davis (2005) concluded that "the magnitude of difference on most issues, other than those related to race, rarely constituted anything more than a gap in public opinion and not a gulf of chasm" (p. 487). This supports the social convergence hypothesis in terms of public opinion in general.

The extant empirical evidence, however, does not provide strong support for social convergence as it applies to support for the death penalty. Cochran and Chamlin (2006, p. 97) controlled for "differences in socioeconomic status achievements, subcultural orientations, political persuasion, reli-gion, right-to-life views, attitudes support for social welfare, views on distributive justice, perceptions about criminal justice, fear of crime, victimization experience, media exposure, punitiveness, [and] attribution styles." They found that none of these variables significantly accounted for racial differ-ences in support for the death penalty (Cochran & Chamlin, 2006). Likewise, Unnever and Cul-len (2007a) tested the social convergence theory—as it applies specifically to attitudes toward the death penalty—using GSS data from 1974–2002. They found little evidence to support the social convergence hypothesis. The racial divide persisted even when "class, confidence in government, conservative politics, and religious fundamentalism" were controlled, therefore suggesting that "race remains a master status that defines views on capital punishment" (Unnever & Cullen, 2007a, p. 147). In other words, the relationship between race and support for the death penalty cannot be explained away by taking other social factors into account. Instead, Unnever and Cullen (2007a) argue that "the social convergence of African Americans," in terms of attitudes toward sentencing, "may require a public atonement for the historical oppression of African Americans by the criminal justice system." (p. 149). This conclusion leads us to the second explanation for the racial divide in death penalty support, the state threat hypothesis.

The state threat hypothesis argues that African Americans have different attitudes about the death penalty than whites because "the state is perceived by African Americans not as neutral but rather as an institution that has traditionally protected the interests of the majority group and undermined their interests" and "the death penalty takes on special significance . . . [as] the ultimate weapon of state criminal justice power" (Unnever et al., 2008, p. 82). This thesis is supported by Unnever and Cullen's (2005, p. 20) finding that "over one-fourth (29%) of the racial divide in support for capital punishment can be attributed to differences in the degree to which African Americans and whites believe that innocent people have been executed and the death penalty is applied unfairly."

This finding suggests that the racial divide in death penalty support is rooted more in differential attitudes about criminal justice than in structural differences between racial groups. This explanation of how African Americans think about the death penalty makes sense in light of the facts that African Americans are disproportionately incarcerated (Unnever & Cullen, 2007a) and disproportionately sentenced to the death penalty (Steiker & Steiker, 2015; Unnever et al., 2008). They are also more likely than white Americans to believe that the death penalty is imposed unfairly (Unnever et al., 2008). While the state threat thesis focuses on why African Americans do not support the death penalty, the third explanation for the racial divide—the racial-animus, or "social threat" hypothesis—questions what drives the high percent of support among white Americans.

The Impact of Racial Animus

In a factorial analysis of the effect of victim and offender race on support for the death penalty, the subjects were most likely to say they would "definitely vote for the death penalty" for vignettes that describe a black offender killing a white victim (Applegate, Wright, Dunaway, Cullen, & Wooldredge, 1994, pp. 105, 108). More recently, Unnever and Cullen (2012) concluded that whites who "embrace the negative stereotype that African Americans are more prone to violence than members of their own race are significantly more likely to support capital punishment while controlling for other covariates" (p. 531). Whites who embraced the same negative stereotype about Hispanics were also significantly more likely to support the death penalty (Unnever & Cullen, 2012, p. 531). These findings, among others, support the claim that the racial animus white Americans hold toward black and Hispanic Americans explains the racial divide in support for the death penalty.

This idea is echoed in Chiricos, Welch, and Gertz's (2004) research that identified beliefs about whether blacks commit disproportionately more crime as a "significant predictor of punitiveness, independent of the influence of racial prejudice, conservativism, crime salience, southern residence and other factors" (p. 359). Given that this research focuses on white Americans' perceptions of criminality and violence among African Americans, it is sometimes referred to as the "social threat hypothesis" or "racial threat hypothesis" (Chiricos et al., 2004; Unnever & Cullen, 2007b, 2010a, 2010b, 2012).

In their analysis of the 2000 National Election Study (NES) data, Unnever and Cullen (2010a) test the racial-animus model against two other explanations for the source of death penalty support—the escalating crime-distrust model and the moral decline model. In this study, racial animus is measured using two scales: (1) a "Racial Resentment" scale that measured the degree to which respondents agreed to four statements related to attitudes about the work ethic of African Americans and whether or not African Americans face barriers to upward class mobility, and (2) a "Racial Stereotype" scale that measured the degree to which the respondents believed that African Americans are lazy or hardworking, unintelligent or intelligent, and untrustworthy or trustworthy (Unnever & Cullen, 2010a, p. 111). Religiosity, political orientation, authoritarianism, and demographic variables including age, gender, race, education, residence in the South, and residence in an urban area were controlled (Unnever & Cullen, 2010a). The analysis involved the regression of punitive attitudes (including a general measure of punitiveness toward criminals and a measure of death penalty support) on the two scales of the racial-animus model, controlling for covariates and demographic variables. The results indicated "that the *Racial Resentment* scale is one of the most substantive and consistent predictors for both indicators of punitiveness" (Unnever & Cullen, 2010a, p. 117, emphasis in original). This finding supports the theory that support for the death penalty (and punitive attitudes toward criminals in general) are at least in part influenced by racial animus toward African Americans.

In another analysis of the 2000 NES data, Unnever and Cullen (2007b) test whether support for the death penalty significantly differs between racist and nonracist whites. Unnever and Cullen measured racism using three scales, a "Jim Crow" racism scale, a "symbolic racism" scale, and a "White racism scale." With regard to the white racism scale, Unnever and Cullen argue that "the issue of white racism should be 'seen' from the perspective of African Americans" (2007b, p. 1285). Thus, the white racism measure "defines white racists as those whites who . . . viewed African Americans with more racial animosity than the average African American held for his or her own race," as derived from the symbolic racism scale (Unnever & Cullen, 2007b, p. 1285). Controlling for demographic characteristics and other covariates of death penalty support, the analysis revealed that "the white racism measure was one of the most robust predictors of the degree to which Americans supported the death penalty" (Unnever & Cullen, 2007b, p. 1290). Furthermore, African American and nonracist whites did not significantly differ in level of support for the death penalty when other variables were controlled (Unnever & Cullen, 2007b). This result suggests that in addition to the racial divide between blacks and whites, there is also a within-racial-group divide between racist and nonracist whites in support for the death penalty.

The impact of racial animus on support for the death penalty may have implications for the expression of attitudes in European nations, where recent events suggest animus toward immigrants is high. For example, Unnever et al. (2008) provide an international perspective of the relationship between racial animus and support for the death penalty. Their findings indicate that in Britain, France, Spain, and Japan, those, "who harbor racial or ethnic resentments were significantly and robustly more likely to support capital punishment" (p. 81). Other research has pointed out that racial inequality in the criminal justice system exists beyond the United States, and racial animus persists among Western Europeans, particularly toward immigrants (Pettigrew, 1998; Tonry, 1997; Unnever & Cullen, 2010b). Given recent events such as "Brexit," the rising popularity of white nationalist political parties, mass immigration due to the refugee crisis in the Middle East, and terrorist attacks in France, Germany, and other Western European countries, the salience of racial animus may be an important consideration for future research on international death penalty attitudes.

Conclusion: Two Futures

For much of the past half-century, one of the most powerful justifications for the continued use of lethal executions has been that the "American public supports capital punishment." This claim is both true and false. At certain points in time, the embrace of the death penalty, seemingly nourished by broader punitive sentiments, has reached high levels. Even when the citizenry's endorsement of this penalty has diminished—such as at the present time—it has often been the case that national single-question polls could be cited as showing that more Americans favored the death penalty than opposed it.

Still, as we have taken pains to demonstrate, public opinion is complicated and can only be measured fully by employing surveys that are informed by standard social science methodology. Research in this vein reveals that support for capital punishment varies according to the rating task that the respondents are asked to undertake, including information about the offense (e.g., crime, criminal, victim), the nature of capital punishment as an institution (e.g., the inevitability of executing innocent people), and the sentencing options considered (e.g., LWOP). And, as just reviewed, the large racial divide in support for the death penalty, rooted in part in white animus toward African Americans, calls the very legitimacy of "majority" support for the death penalty into question.

What does the future hold? Current events suggest two possibilities—the first of which seemed unlikely until the 2016 presidential election. We will call this the "Trump Future." Much of President Trump's popularity has been derived from his creating enemies—"the other"—to attack. The supposed "fake news" of the news media has emerged as the leading target of his administration. Still, his attempt to ban refugees and visitors from Muslim nations, his animus toward immigrants, and his constant claim to be a "law-and-order" president who will stop the "carnage" in Chicago and the U.S.'s mythical record high murder rate, all send the message that White America is suffering racial/ethnic threat. The pushback against his rhetoric and policies and the affirmation of multiculturalism suggest that his efforts to inflame the electorate may not work. At the same time, his resilient support among his core base, especially in Red States, could foster a renewed trumpeting of the death penalty among that segment of the public.

The second option we will call "The Better Angels of Our Nature Future"—a label that borrows the title of Stephen Pinker's (2011) classic work. Pinker has noted that the long-term trend in Western societies is away from violence, including the use of state violence to execute offenders. "Today," he observes, "capital punishment is widely seen as a human rights violation" (2011, p. 150). Even in the United States, the trend is toward more states abolishing the penalty or using it sparingly (Garland, 2010; Pinker, 2011). Consistent with these developments, recent national polls report declining support for capital punishment in the American public. More sophisticated studies have, as noted, shown how even this level of support is often contingent and not firm. As Pinker (2011, p. 151) suggests, one other consideration might, in the long run, undermine support for the death penalty: that which actually occurs when capital punishment is abolished. Pinker points out that the "countries of Western Europe, none of which execute people, have the lowest homicide rates in the world" (2011, p. 153). Our "better Angels" might well be inspired by this empirical reality. "It may be one of the many cases in which institutionalized violence was once see as indispensable to the functioning of a society," observes Pinker, "yet once it was abolished, the society managed to get along perfectly well without it" (p. 153).

References

Applegate, B. K., Cullen, F. T., Turner, M. G., & Sundt, J. L. (1996). Assessing public support for three-strikes-and-you're-out laws: Global versus specific attitudes. *Crime & Delinquency, 42,* 517–534.

Applegate, B. K., & Davis, R. K. (2006). Public views on sentencing juvenile murderers: The impact of offender, offense, and perceived maturity. *Youth Violence and Juvenile Justice, 4,* 55–74.

Applegate, B. K., Wright, J. P., Dunaway, R. G., Cullen, F. T., & Wooldredge, J. D. (1994). Victim-offender race and support for capital punishment: A factorial design approach. *American Journal of Criminal Justice, 18,* 95–115.

Backus, F. (2011, September 26). Support for the death penalty for convicted murderers at a 20-year low. *CBS News.* Retrieved from www.deathpenaltyinfo.org/documents/cbs_news_poll.pdf

Bohm, R. M., Clark, L. J., & Aveni, A. F. (1991). Knowledge and death penalty opinion: A test of the Marshall hypotheses. *Journal of Research in Crime and Delinquency, 28,* 360–387.

Bohm, R. M., Flanagan, T. J., & Harris, P. W. (1990). Current death penalty opinion in New York State. *Albany Law Review, 54,* 819–843.

Bohm, R. M., & Vogel, B. L. (2004). More than ten years after: The long-term stability of informed death penalty opinions. *Journal of Criminal Justice, 32,* 307–327.

Bowers, W. J., Vandiver, M., & Dugan, P. H. (1994). A new look at public opinion on capital punishment: What citizens and legislators prefer. *American Journal of Criminal Law, 22,* 77–150.

Burgason, K. A., & Pazzani, L. (2014). The death penalty: A multi-level analysis of public opinion. *American Journal of Criminal Justice, 39*, 818–838.

Chiricos, T., Welch, K., & Gertz, M. (2004). Racial typification of crime and support for punitive measures. *Criminology, 42*, 359–389.

Cochran, J. K., & Chamlin, M. B. (2006). The enduring racial divide in death penalty support. *Journal of Criminal Justice, 34*, 85–99.

Cullen, F. T., Blevins, K. R., Pealer, J. L., Daigle, L. E., & Coleman, M. E. (2004). *ACJS membership survey final report.* Cincinnati, OH: University of Cincinnati.

Cullen, F. T., Fisher, B. S., & Applegate, B. K. (2000). Public opinion about punishment and corrections. In M. Tonry (Ed.), *Crime and justice: A review of research* (Vol. 14, pp. 1–79). Chicago, IL: University of Chicago Press.

Cullen, F. T., & Gendreau, P. (2001). From nothing works to what works: Changing professional ideology in the 21st century. *Prison Journal, 81*, 313–338.

Cullen, F. T., Unnever, J. D., Blevins, K. R., Pealer, J. A., Santana, S. A., Fisher, B. S., & Applegate, B. K. (2009). The myth of public support for capital punishment. In J. Wood & T. Gannon (Eds.), *Public opinion and criminal justice: Context, practice and values* (pp. 73–95). Cullompton, UK: Willan.

Davis, T. J. (2005). The political orientation of blacks and whites: Converging, diverging, or remaining constant? *Social Science Journal, 42*, 487–498.

Death Penalty. (2017). *Gallup Inc.* Retrieved from www.gallup.com/poll/1606/death-penalty.aspx

Dugan, A. (2015). Solid majority continue to support death penalty. *Gallup Poll News Service.* Retrieved from www.gallup.com/poll/186218/solid-majority-continue-support-death-penalty.aspx

Durham, A. M., Elrod, H. P., & Kinkade, P. T. (1996). Public support for the death penalty: Beyond Gallup. *Justice Quarterly, 13*, 705–736.

Fagan, J. A. (2016). Capital punishment: Deterrent effects and capital costs. *Columbia Law School.* Retrieved from columbia.edu/law_school/communications/reports/summer06/capitalpunish

Garland, D. (2010). *Peculiar institution: America's death penalty in an age of abolition.* Cambridge, MA: Belknap Press of Harvard University Press.

Grasmick, H. G., Bursik, R. J., Jr., & Blackwell, B. S. (1993). Religious beliefs and public support for the death penalty for juveniles and adults. *Journal of Crime and Justice, 16*, 59–86.

Igo, S. E. (2007). *The averaged American: Surveys, citizens, and the making of a mass public.* Cambridge, MA: Harvard University Press.

International Polls and Studies. (2017). *Death penalty information center.* Retrieved from www.deathpenaltyinfo.org/international-polls-and-studies-0

Jones, J. (2002). The death penalty. *Gallup Poll News Service.* Retrieved from www.gallup.com/poll/9913/death-penalty.aspx

Lambert, E. G., Camp, S. D., Clarke, A., & Jiang, S. (2011). The impact of information on death penalty support, revisited. *Crime & Delinquency, 57*, 572–599.

McGarrell, E. F., & Sandys, M. (1996). The misperception of public opinion toward capital punishment: Examining the spuriousness explanation of death penalty support. *American Behavioral Scientist, 39*, 500–513.

Moon, M. M., Wright, J. P., Cullen, F. T., & Pealer, J. A. (2000). Putting kids to death: Specifying public support for juvenile capital punishment. *Justice Quarterly, 17*, 663–684.

Moore, D. W. (2004). Public divided between death penalty and life imprisonment without parole. *The Gallup Poll Tuesday Briefing, 9.* Retrieved from www.gallup.com/poll/11878/public-divided-between-death-penalty-life-imprisonment-without-parole.aspx

Nagin, D. S., & Pepper, J. V. (2012). *Deterrence and the death penalty.* Washington, DC: National Academy Press.

Newport, F. (2009). In U.S., two-thirds continue to support death penalty; little change in recent years despite international opposition. *Gallup Poll News Service.* Retrieved from www.gallup.com/poll/123638/in-u.s.-two-thirds-continue-support-death-penalty.aspx

Oliphant, B. (2016, September 29). *Support for death penalty lowest in more than four decades.* Retrieved from www.pewresearch.org/fact-tank/2016/09/29/support-for-death-penalty-lowest-in-more-than-four-decades/

Pettigrew, T. F. (1998). Reactions toward the new minorities of Western Europe. *Annual Review of Sociology, 24*, 77–103.

Pinker, S. (2011). *The better angels of our nature: Why violence has declined.* New York, NY: Penguin.

Roberts, J. V., & Stalans, L. J. (1997). *Public opinion, crime, and criminal justice.* Boulder, CO: Westview.

Sandys, M., & McGarrell, E. F. (1995). Attitudes toward capital punishment: Preference for the penalty or mere acceptance? *Journal of Research in Crime and Delinquency, 32*, 191–213.

Skovron, S. E., Scott, J. E., & Cullen, F. T. (1989). The death penalty for juveniles: An assessment of public support. *Crime & Delinquency, 35*, 546–561.

Smith, T. W. (2001). Public opinion on the death penalty for youths. *National Opinion Research Center.* Retrieved from http://citeseerx.ist.psu.edu/viewdoc/download?doi=10.1.1.489.3489&rep=rep1&type=pdf

Smith, T. W., Marsden, P., Hout, M., & Kim, J. (1972–2014). *General Social Surveys, 1972–2014 [machine-readable data file]* /Principal Investigator, Tom W. Smith; Co-Principal Investigator, Peter V. Marsden; Co-Principal Investigator, Michael Hout; Sponsored by National Science Foundation. -NORC ed.- Chicago: NORC at the University of Chicago [producer and distributor]. Data accessed from the GSS Data Explorer website at gssdataexplorer.norc.org

Steiker, C. S., & Steiker, J. M. (2015). The American death penalty and the (in)visibility of race. *University of Chicago Law Review, 82,* 243–294.

Support for the death penalty falls below 50% for first time. (2015, March 26). Retrieved from www.bsa.natcen.ac.uk/media-centre/archived-press-releases/bsa-32-support-for-death-penalty.aspx

Three-in-five Canadians would bring back death penalty. (2013, March). Retrieved from http://angusreidglobal.com/wp-content/uploads/2013/03/2013.03.20_Death_CAN.pdf

Tonry, M. (1997). Ethnicity, crime, and immigration. In M. Tonry (Ed.), *Crime and justice: A review of research* (Vol. 21, pp. 1–29). Chicago, IL: University of Chicago Press.

Unnever, J. D. (2010). Global support for the death penalty. *Punishment & Society, 12,* 463–484.

Unnever, J. D., & Cullen, F. T. (2005). Executing the innocent and support for capital punishment: Implications for public policy. *Criminology & Public Policy, 4,* 3–38.

Unnever, J. D., & Cullen, F. T. (2007a). Reassessing the racial divide in support for capital punishment: The continuing significance of race. *Journal of Research in Crime and Delinquency, 44,* 124–158.

Unnever, J. D., & Cullen, F. T. (2007b). The racial divide in support for the death penalty: Does white racism matter? *Social Forces, 85,* 1281–1301.

Unnever, J. D., & Cullen, F. T. (2010a). The social sources of Americans' punitiveness: A test of three competing models. *Criminology, 48,* 99–129.

Unnever, J. D., & Cullen, F. T. (2010b). Racial-ethnic intolerance and support for capital punishment: A cross-national comparison. *Criminology, 48,* 831–864.

Unnever, J. D., & Cullen, F. T. (2012). White perceptions of whether African Americans and Hispanics are prone to violence and support for the death penalty. *Journal of Research in Crime and Delinquency, 49,* 519–544.

Unnever, J., Cullen, F. T., & Jonson, C. (2008). Race, racism, and support for capital punishment. In M. Tonry (Ed.), *Crime and justice: A review of research* (Vol. 37, pp. 45–96). Chicago, IL: The University of Chicago Press.

Vito, G. F., & Keil, T. J. (1998). Elements of support for capital punishment: An examination of changing attitudes. *Journal of Crime and Justice, 21,* 17–36.

Wilson, W. J. (1980). *The declining significance of race: Blacks and changing American institutions* (2nd ed.). Chicago, IL: University of Chicago Press.

Wright, H. O., Bohm, R. M., & Jamieson, K. M. (1995). A comparison of uninformed and informed death penalty opinions: A replication and expansion. *American Journal of Criminal Justice, 20,* 57–87.

Yanklovich, D. (1991). *Coming to public judgment: Making democracy work in a complex world.* Syracuse, NY: Syracuse University Press.

Cases Cited

Furman v. Georgia, 408 U.S. 238 (1972).
Roper v. Simmons, 543 U.S. 551 (2005).

4

THE MARSHALL HYPOTHESES

John K. Cochran

The Eighth Amendment to the U.S. Constitution bans cruel and unusual punishment. Historically, especially with regard to capital punishment, the justices serving on the United States Supreme Court (USSC) have applied fixed, unchanging, absolutist interpretations of this protection. Punishments which were viewed as 'torturous', 'lingering', or 'unnecessarily cruel' were deemed unconstitutional; conversely, methods of execution, such as death by hanging, firing squad, the electric chair, etc., were not viewed as violating this protection (see *Wilkerson v. Utah*, 1878, *In re Kemmler*, 1890, and *Louisiana ex rel. Francis v. Resweber*, 1947). In *Weems v. U.S.* (1910), the USSC adopted a much different interpretation of cruel and unusual punishment. Rather than a fixed and unchanging definition of cruel and unusual punishment, the court asserted that a punishment which is "disproportionate" to the harm caused by the crime is "excessive" and, therefore, cruel and unusual. Then, in 1958 in *Trop v. Dulles*, the court determined that excessiveness and proportionality, as measuring sticks used to determine what constitutes a cruel and unusual punishment, were to be based on the application of the "evolving standards of decency that mark the progress of a civilized and maturing society" (p. 101).

But this new, more culturally relative interpretation of cruel and unusual punishment still begs the question: what are these "evolving standards decency?" With regard to the death penalty, the court has asserted that a variety of indicators are available by which one could gauge these evolving standards. Among these are the legislative record (e.g., if more states abolish the death penalty than retain it, then our standards may have evolved to a point that we no longer support the application of the death penalty to murder); likewise the sentencing patterns of judges and juries on capital cases could also indicate the evolving nature of these standards; so too could the charging decision of prosecutors. If prosecutors should cease to seek the death penalty in otherwise eligible cases, or should capital juries recommend and/or capital trial judges sentence offenders to life rather than death, then perhaps our standards of decency have evolved to a point that the death penalty is viewed as excessive. Another indicator of these evolving standards, though one that is considered to be much less compelling to the court, are the attitudes and opinions of the general public as expressed in public opinion polls on the issue.

Despite the court's rather modest interest in the salience of public opinion polls, Bohm (1998, 2003b) asserts that capital punishment continues to exist in the United States primarily because public opinion is so strongly supportive of it. National opinion polls conducted since the early 1970s consistently reveal that approximately 70% (ranging typically between 60% and 80%) of adult Americans have supported capital punishment in general. He argues that there are at least five ways in which the strong public support for capital punishment contributes to its continued use. First, state legislators are unlikely to be swayed against the death penalty when a majority of their constituency supports it. Second, strong public support for capital punishment might influence prosecutorial discretion to more aggressively seek the death penalty, perhaps even in cases they would otherwise be disinclined from doing so. Third, trial judges might feel pressured to impose death sentences even when it may not be appropriate and appellate judges might feel pressured to uphold these sentences due to their perceptions of strong public support. Fourth, governors might be more inclined to support death penalty legislation and sign execution warrants and less inclined to consider commutations and pardons for death row inmates if they perceived strong public support for capital punishment. Finally, and perhaps most importantly, strong public support for capital punishment might be used by justices of state supreme courts and the U.S. Supreme Court as a real-time indicator of "the evolving standards of decency" when determining whether or not the death penalty violates constitutional safeguards against "cruel and unusual punishment."

It is this fifth and final argument that has fueled the research reviewed in this chapter, for the USSC did cite declines in public support for capital punishment during the 1950s and 1960s in its landmark decision in *Furman v. Georgia* (1972, p. 329) invalidating all capital punishment statutes across the country. As Bohm (2003a, p. 34) pointed out, public opinion polling prior to the *Furman* decision was quite crude and simplistic and had undergone very little scrutiny. In fact, the published results of these polls were generally accepted as accurate indicators of public sentiment.

One of the first to critique these figures was Supreme Court Justice Thurgood Marshall. Marshall emphasized the importance of public opinion as a direct indicator of the "evolving standards of decency" necessary to assess the constitutionality of capital punishment under the Eighth Amendment. Marshall noted that a punishment was invalid if "popular sentiment abhors it" (*Furman v. Georgia*, 1972, p. 332) and that "[i]t is imperative for constitutional purposes to attempt to discern the probable opinion of an informed electorate" (*Furman v. Georgia*, 1972, p. 362, fn.145). He stressed, however, that the probative value of public sentiment regarding capital punishment was limited only to an informed or knowledgeable opinion. Marshall asserted that support for capital punishment was largely a function of a lack of knowledge or information about it, but, if fully informed, then "the great mass of citizens would conclude . . . that the death penalty is immoral and unconstitutional" (*Furman v. Georgia*, 1972, p. 363; c.f., Justice Powell's dissent in *Furman*, 1972, pp. 430–446). Marshall acknowledged one exception to this assumption; for those who support capital punishment under a retributive rationale, information about capital punishment would not be persuasive (*Furman v. Georgia*, 1972, p. 363).

Justice Marshall's assertions regarding the effects of information on public support for the death penalty opened a line of social science inquiry and spurned a flurry of empirical investigations of what are referred to as the "Marshall hypotheses." These hypotheses are as follows: (1) support for capital punishment is inversely associated with knowledge about it, (2) exposure to information about capital punishment produces sentiments in opposition to capital punishment, but (3) exposure to information about capital punishment will have no impact on those who support it for retributive reasons.

Tests of the Marshall Hypotheses

To date there are almost 30 published studies that have tested one or more of these hypotheses (Bohm, 1989, 1990; Bohm & Vogel, 1991, 1994, 2004; Bohm, Clark, & Aveni, 1990, 1991; Bohm, Vogel, & Maisto, 1993; Clarke, Lambert, & Whitt, 2000–01; Cochran & Chamlin, 2005; Cochran, Sanders, & Chamlin, 2006; Cox, 2013; Diaz & Garza, 2015; Ellsworth & Ross, 1983; Falco & Freiberger, 2011; Kennedy-Kollar & Mandery, 2010; LaChappelle, 2014; Lambert, Camp, Clarke, & Jiang, 2011; Lambert & Clarke, 2001; Lee, Bohm, & Pazzani, 2014; Longmire, 1996; Lord, Ross, & Lepper, 1979; Mallicoat & Brown, 2008; Michel & Cochran, 2011; Sandys, 1995; Sarat & Vidmar, 1976; Vidmar, Dittenhoffer, Mallicoat, & Buffington-Vollum, 2009; Wright, Bohm, & Jamieson, 1995). Table 4.1 presents a brief description of each study's methodological features and key findings.

Table 4.1 Description of Studies Testing the Marshall Hypotheses

Author(s) & Date:	Research Design:	Sample:	Experiment Stimulus:	Outcome Measure:	Key Findings:			
					M Hyp 1.	M Hyp 2.	M Hyp 3.	M Hyp 4.
Sarat and Vidmar (1976)	experimental: three treatment + control	181 adult residents of Amherst, MA	informative essays (utilitarian and/ or humanitarian)	change in death penalty support	supported	supported	supported	n .a.
Lord et al. (1979)	quasi-experimental: dp proponents vs. dp opponents	48 undergrad students	research briefs	death penalty support belief in deterrence polarization	not tested	not tested	not tested	biased assimilation.
Vidmar and Dittenhoffer (1981)	quasi-experimental: two-group pretest posttest	39 undergrad students	information materials	change in death penalty support	supported	supported	not tested	n. a.
Ellsworth and Ross (1983)	survey comparison of proponents to opponents	500 adult residents on N. California	nine knowledge statements.	death penalty support	supported	not tested	not tested	n. a.
Bohm (1989)	one-group pretest posttest	50 undergrad students	death penalty course	change in death penalty support	not tested	supported	not tested	n. a.
Bohm (1990)	quasi-experimental: two-group pretest posttest	109 undergrad students	death penalty course	change in death penalty support	not tested	supported	not tested	public commitment

(Continued)

Table 4.1 (Continued)

Author(s) & Date:	Research Design:	Sample:	Experiment Stimulus:	Outcome Measure:	Key Findings: M Hyp 1.	M Hyp 2.	M Hyp 3.	M Hyp 4.
Bohm et al. (1990)	quasi experimental: two-group pretest posttest	71 undergrad students	death penalty course	reasons for support	not tested	not supported	not tested	n. a.
Bohm et al. (1991)	quasi-experimental: two-group pretest posttest	272 undergrad students	death penalty course	change in death penalty support	supported	mixed support	supported	n. a.
Bohm and Vogel (1991)	quasi-experimental: two-group pretest posttest	105 undergrad students	death penalty course	change in death penalty support	not tested	supported	supported	racial var.
Bohm et al. (1993)	quasi-experimental: two-group pretest posttest w/follow-up	106 undergrad students	death penalty course	change in death penalty support and reasons for support	not tested	supported	not tested	rebounding
Bohm and Vogel (1994)	quasi-experimental: two-group pretest posttest	222 undergrad students	death penalty course	change in death penalty support	not tested	supported	not tested	bias. assim.
Sandys (1995)	one-group pretest posttest w/follow-up	23 undergrad students	death penalty course	change in death penalty support	not tested	supported	not tested	no rebound

Study	Design	Sample	Intervention	Dependent variable				
Wright et al. (1995)	quasi-experimental: two-group pretest posttest	106 undergrad students	death penalty course	change in death penalty support	supported	supported not	tested	n. a.
Longmire (1996)	one-group pretest posttest adults	representative sample of U.S. general population	eight statements support	change in death penalty	not tested	supported	not tested	n. a.
Clarke et al. (2000–01)	quasi experimental: three-group pretest posttest	730 undergrad students	three essays (deter., innocence, control)	change in death penalty support	not tested	limited support	not tested	n. a.
Lambert and Clarke (2001)	quasi experimental: three-group pretest posttest	730 undergrad students	three essays (deter., innocence, control)	change in death penalty support	not tested	limited support	not tested	n. a.
Bohm and Vogel (2004)	quasi-experimental: two-group pretest posttest w/ follow-up	69 undergrad students	death penalty course	change in death penalty support	not tested	supported	not tested	rebound
Cochran and Chamlin (2005)	one-group pretest posttest	70 undergrad students	death penalty course change in knowledge	change in death penalty support	supported	supported	not supported	n. a.

(Continued)

Table 4.1 (Continued)

Author(s) & Date:	Research Design:	Sample:	Experiment Stimulus:	Outcome Measure:	Key Findings:			
					M Hyp 1.	M Hyp 2.	M Hyp 3.	M Hyp 4.
Cochran et al. (2006)	one-group pretest: posttest students	365 undergrad change in knowledge	death penalty course support dp "myths"	change in death penalty "truths"	supported	supported	not tested	profiles
Mallicoat and Brown (2008)	survey comparison of proponents to opponents	340 undergrad students	8 information stmts.	reasons for death penalty support	not tested	supported	not tested	racial var. bias. assim. mutabillity
Vollum, Mallicoat, and Buffington-Vollum (2009)	one-group pretest posttest	927 undergrad students	6 information stmts.	death penalty support reasons for dp support	not tested	limited support	supported	mutability receptivity
Kennedy-Kollar and Mandery (2010)	experimental: two-group pretest posttest	187 undergrad students	pro-dp lecture or anti-dp lecture	death penalty support	not tested	opposite findings	not tested	n. a.
Falco and Freiburger (2011)	qualitative: focus groups	20 adults Indiana, PA	8 information stmts.	change in death penalty support	not tested	not supported	not tested	bias. assim.
Michel and Cochran (2011)	one-group pretest: posttest	365 undergrad students	death penalty course change in knowledge	change in death penalty support dp "myths"	supported	supported	supported	no demographical variation

Study	Design	Sample	Intervention	DV				demo. var.
Lambert, Camp, Clarke, and Jiang (2011)	quasi experimental: three-group posttest	730 undergrad. pretest students	3 essays (deter., innocence, control)	change in death penalty support	not tested	supported	not tested	
Cox (2013)	experimental: two-group test posttest	362 undergrad pretest students	5 dp scenarios	change in death penalty support	supported	not supported	not tested	n. a.
LaChappelle (2014)	one-group pretest: posttest students	216 undergrad support	5 information stmts.	change in death penalty	not tested	supported	not tested	n. a.
Lee et al. (2014)	quasi-experimental: Solomon four-group	338 undergrad students	death penalty course	change in death penalty support	supported	supported	not supported	n. a.
Diaz and Garza (2015)	quasi-experimental: four group pretest posttest	481 undergrad students	2 dp videos; reading material	change in death penalty support	not tested	Limited support	not tested	n. a.

While there are important variations in methodology across these studies, they tend to share several common methodological elements: (1) a pretest measure of attitudes toward capital punishment, (2) exposure to information about capital punishment, and (3) a posttest measure of death penalty attitudes. Sometimes a one-group pretest-posttest design is employed, more commonly a treatment (informed) group is compared quasi-experimentally to a nonequivalent comparison group, and occasionally to a randomly assigned control group. Most typically the subjects are undergraduate college students. The studies also tended to vary in both the quantity and quality of the exposure to capital punishment information.

Methodological Limitations to These Studies

No empirical study is without its limitations and imperfections, and this truism also applies to any body of research within a common area of inquiry, such as tests of the Marshall hypotheses. In the material to follow, a brief critique of the extant research literature testing the Marshall hypotheses is provided, and the various methodological weaknesses and limitations of this body of research are examined.

First, nearly all of the various tests of the Marshall hypotheses have been based on either a non-experimental design or a quasi-experimental design. Only three studies (Sarat & Vidmar, 1976; Kennedy-Kollar & Mandery, 2010; Cox, 2013) used true experimental designs in which subjects were randomly assigned to either the treatment/experimental group(s), who were exposed to information about capital punishment, or the control group. The random assignment of subjects to experimental and control groups permits the researchers to control for various threats to the study's internal validity. The study by Lee and his colleagues (2014) is unique in that it is the only test of the Marshall hypotheses to employ a Solomon 4-group quasi-experimental design; such a design permits the researchers to examine the degree, if any, to which exposure to the pretest may interact with the treatment and, in turn, threaten the external validity of the study.

But for the Sarat and Vidmar (1976); Kennedy-Kollar and Mandery (2010); and Cox (2013) studies, all of the other studies in this body of research employed either a quasi-experimental design (12 of 29 studies) or a nonexperimental design (14 of 29 studies); one study employed a qualitative, focus group approach (Falco & Freiburger, 2011). Quasi-experimental designs make use of treatment and comparison groups, but the subjects were not randomly distributed to these groups. As such, preexisting differences between these groups constitute a serious potential threat to the internal validity of the studies. More troubling is the fact that many of these studies did not even include a comparison group of any sort; instead, these studies employed simple between-measures or one-group pretest-posttest nonexperimental designs. The absence of a comparison group makes it impossible to determine whether any observed changes in death penalty support are a function of the treatment (exposure to information) or to some other factor(s).

Many of these studies have been conducted in areas without the death penalty or where no executions have taken place (Sarat & Vidmar, 1976; Lord et al., 1979; Vidmar & Dittenhoffer, 1981; Ellsworth & Ross, 1983). The results of these studies may be less salient because the studies were conducted at a place and time for which the death penalty is not a concrete reality for the study subjects, but instead it is just a conceptual abstraction (Lee et al., 2014). In addition, many the studies on this issue have been based on data collected no more recently than the mid-1990s (Bohm, 1989; 1990; Bohm & Vogel, 1991; 1994; Bohm Clark, & Aveni, 1990; 1991; Bohm, Vogel, & Maisto, 1993; Ellsworth & Ross, 1983; Longmire, 1996; Lord et al., 1979; Sandys, 1995; Sarat & Vidmar, 1976; Vidmar & Dittenhoffer, 1981; Wright et al., 1995). The 1970s and 1980s were a period of dramatically increasing public support for capital punishment. Moreover, numerous significant events related to the death penalty have occurred since this time, and these events, especially if coupled with thorough exposure to information about the death penalty, could very well have established a unique context for testing the Marshall hypotheses.

Bohm (2003a, pp. 186–192) outlined a number of these potentially influential events. These include (1) the 1997 American Bar Association resolution calling for a moratorium on capital punishment, (2) the 1997 requirement that Russia abolish the death penalty as a criterion for membership in the Council of Europe, (3) the joint campaign in 1999 of the Catholic Church and both Reformed and Conservative Jewish groups calling for the abolition of capital punishment, (4) legislative calls for a moratorium on capital punishment in 1999 in Connecticut, Illinois, Maryland, Montana, Nebraska, North Carolina, Pennsylvania, Washington, and other states, (5) actual moratoriums on executions imposed by Governor George Ryan of Illinois in 2000 and Governor Parris Glendening of Maryland in 2003, (6) the abolition of the death penalty in New Hampshire, New Jersey, New Mexico, and New York, (7) the global trend toward abolition—59 countries have abolished the death penalty since 1990, and only 19 of the 193 nation-state members of the United Nations continue to retain the death penalty, (8) numerous states enjoined from carrying out lethal injections by various federal courts, (9) the publications of the Liebman study establishing that two-thirds of all capital cases nationwide between 1973 and 1995 were contaminated by serious, reversible errors (Liebman, Fagan, & West, 2000) and the study by Scheck, Nuefeld, and Dwyer (2001) of the Innocence Project documenting numerous exonerations of wrongfully convicted criminals, (10) the U.S. Supreme Court rulings in *Atkins v. Virginia* (2002); *Ring v. Arizona* (2002); and *Roper v. Simmons* (2005) (11) public criticisms of the quality of lawyering in capital cases uttered by Justices O'Connor and Ginsberg, (12) the release in 2000 of a Justice Department report regarding racial disparities in capital sentencing, (13) the reintroduction to Congress of the Innocence Protection Act in 2001, (14) the formation of the politically conservative National Commission to Prevent Wrongful Executions, (15) the 2003 executive pardons and commutations granted by Illinois Governor Ryan to all persons sentenced to death, and (16) the United Nations' Commission on Human Rights condemnation of the United States for failing to abolish capital punishment. Given these events and many others, it is no surprise that many of the numerous public opinion polls taken over the past several years have indicated the lowest recorded levels of death penalty support since the mid-1960s and the greatest drop in support ever recorded (Bohm, 2003a, pp. 191–192). As such, the period of time from the mid-1990s to the present may constitute an especially unique time for tests of the Marshall hypotheses, a period or history effect in which the public's staunch support for the death penalty may have become especially receptive to information about capital punishment.

A third methodological concern with this body of research is that, but for four studies (Sarat & Vidmar, 1976; Ellsworth & Ross, 1983; Longmire, 1996; Falco & Freiberger, 2011), this body of scholarship has used college students as the subjects of the investigation. College students are not very representative of the general population and, thus, the results of these studies may not reasonably be extended to the general population; this is a problem of questionable external validity (i.e., the inability to generalize the findings to a broader population). The lack of generalizability in these studies begs the question why student samples continue to be used. The answers are that (1) student samples constitute perhaps the best method for exposing subjects to the experimental stimulus (rich and complete information about the death penalty over an extended period of time) and (2) college students constitute an easily accessible population such that the costs of the research in terms of time, money, and other resources are minimized. The four studies employing nonstudent samples were limited by the very restricted nature of the experimental stimulus they used (i.e., very limited information presented in a very brief window of time); only the Longmire study (1996) employed a nationally representative sample.

A fourth area of concern within this body of literature involves the measurement of the key independent variable, knowledge about the death penalty, or under experimental/quasi-experimental designs, how information about the death penalty is employed as a treatment/stimulus. These are questions of measurement validity. Is the measure/treatment accurate? What information constitutes the appropriate information? Is the information accepted as "objective facts" or is it debated and contested by the experts? How is the information delivered? How much is delivered? How much knowledge is needed to be considered informed? Has the information been too compressed? Is it unbiased? How nuanced is it? Could the context within which the information was delivered contaminate it? What is the duration of the exposure to this information? How are the subjects able to process it? Do they have an opportunity to discuss or challenge the information? How confident can we be that persons exposed to information have learned it and, as such, have become informed? How receptive are the subjects to this information? Do they accept or reject it? Are they open or closed to it? Are their attitudes malleable/mutable?

About three-fourths of the studies testing the Marshall hypotheses have employed college students as their subjects, of which 14 have been conducted within a college course on the death penalty (see especially studies by Bohm and his colleagues—see also Sandys (1995) and those by Cochran and his colleagues). As a context for this research, classes on the death penalty provide arguably the most superior treatment/stimulus condition for studies of this type. The information provided tends to be the least compressed, the environment of the semester-long classroom allows for consideration of important and nuanced facts and to provide opportunities for the information to be challenged, interrogated, discussed, and weighed. As such we are most confident in the validity of the treatment/stimulus provided by these studies, though these research designs are not without their limitations as well, especially the problem of "experimenter effects" (see Kennedy-Kollar & Mandery, 2010).

The remaining studies have used a variety of mechanisms for exposing their subjects to information about the death penalty. For instance, Sarat and Vidmar (1976) and the various studies by Clarke and his colleagues (Clarke et al., 2001; Lambert & Clarke, 2001; Lambert et al., 2011) exposed their subjects to death penalty information through the use of short essays. Others have utilized short information statements (Ellsworth & Ross, 1983; Longmire, 1996; Mallicoat & Brown, 2008; Vollum et al., 2009; Falco & Freiberger, 2011; LaChappelle, 2014). Finally, others have exposed their subjects to information about the death penalty via research briefs (Lord et al., 1979), lectures (Kennedy-Kollar & Mandery, 2010), scenarios (Cox, 2013), or via a variety of means (Vidmar & Dittenhoffer, 1981; Diaz & Garza, 2015). Because of the highly compressed nature of the death penalty information used as the treatment/stimulus in these studies, they are perhaps the most vulnerable to critiques about the measurement validity of their key independent variable.

The final area of methodological concern involves the measure of the dependent variable, death penalty support. Most typically, death penalty support is measured as the amount of change in death penalty support at posttest relative to its pretest level. Almost always, these measures of change in death penalty support involve conceptually abstract measures of death penalty support rather than situation-specific (see Ellsworth & Ross, 1983) or concrete reasons for support (Bohm et al., 1990). Some studies failed to measure a change in attitude (Sarat & Vidmar, 1976) or simply relied upon their respondents' claims of attitude change (Lord et al., 1979). Finally, nearly all of the studies measure death penalty support immediately following exposure to information; only a small handful of studies have examined the potentially enduring nature of exposure to information on death penalty attitude change (see Bohm et al., 1993; Bohm & Vogel, 2004; Sandys, 1995).

Common Findings in Tests of the Marshall Hypotheses

Perhaps because of the various differences and limitations in the research designs and methodologies that characterize this body of research, these studies tend to produce a rather mixed and inconsistent pattern of support for the three Marshall hypotheses. That is, informed opinion is less supportive of capital punishment; exposure to information occasionally reduces support for capital punishment; and retributivists do tend to be immune to the effects of information about capital punishment. Additional findings common to this body of research include: (1) death penalty information may be assimilated in a biased manner and, as such, exposure to information might polarize opinion; those opposed become more opposed while those who support the death penalty become more supportive upon exposure to information, (2) death penalty sentiments that have been publically pronounced are more resistant to change, (3) initial beliefs about the death penalty such as its general deterrent effect or marginal incapacitation effect are not changed by information on these issues, (4) when attitudes toward capital punishment change, the change is primarily due to information regarding racial disparities in justice and/or the execution of innocent persons, and finally (5) changed death penalty opinions tend to rebound to their original, preinformed positions; thus any effects of information on death penalty support/opposition are short-lived (Bohm, 1998, pp. 40–41, 2003a, pp. 43–44).

The first of the Marshall hypotheses argues that American citizens tend to support capital punishment because the public is uninformed about it. This hypothesis, when tested, takes one of two forms: (a) a measure of the degree to which subjects are informed at pretest, or (b) an assessment of the pretest correlation between death penalty knowledge and death penalty support. The former, less rigorous test simply assesses the extent of knowledge that the subjects have at the beginning of the study; the hypothesis is considered to be supported if the subjects show a level of knowledge deemed to be "low" by the researchers. The second and more rigorous form of testing this hypothesis requires evidence of a significant negative correlation between respondents' pretest level of knowledge and their pretest attitudes toward capital punishment. If death penalty supporters are found to be less informed/knowledgeable than death penalty opponents, then the hypothesis is considered to be supported. The majority of studies in this area of research have elected not to test it. Of the 12 studies that have, only the studies by Cochran and his colleagues (Cochran & Chamlin, 2005; Cochran et al., 2006; Michel & Cochran, 2011) have done so under the more rigorous version.

Sarat and Vidmar (1976) observed that American's pretest level of knowledge about the death penalty was rather low, with less than 60% correctly responding to five of the six knowledge items; the only knowledge item that a large majority (72%) of the respondents knew was that there were "people awaiting execution in the United States." Vidmar and Dittenhoffer (1981) and Ellsworth and Ross (1983) also observed low pretest levels of knowledge about the death penalty among their respondents. Ellsworth and Ross (1983) report that a substantial proportion of their subjects acknowledged being uninformed about capital punishment, and of those who attempted to answer knowledge items most were often incorrect. Ellsworth and Ross (1983, p. 142) concluded that Justice Marshall was correct in that the American public "knows little about the application and consequences of capital punishment." Moreover, they found both death penalty proponents and opponents to be "equally ignorant" about capital punishment. Bohm et al. (1991) also observed that their subjects generally lacked knowledge about the death penalty (see also Cox, 2013).

Wright et al. (1995) measured levels of death penalty knowledge at both pretest and posttest. They observed at pretest that their subjects were not well informed; on average their subjects correctly answered less than half (47%) of the knowledge items correctly. Conversely, at posttest, the treatment group should marked improvement in their levels of death penalty knowledge, while the comparison / untreated group showed no real improvement in their level of knowledge (see also Lee et al., 2014).

Cochran and Chamlin (2005) are unique in that they expressly tested this first Marshall hypotheses by examining the pretest correlation between death penalty knowledge and death penalty support among their sample of college students. While the pretest association between knowledge levels and abstract support for capital punishment was not significant, and thus, failed to support this hypothesis, they did observe that pretest knowledge levels were positively associated with the subjects' acceptance of death penalty "truths" ($r = .263$) and inversely correlated with their adherence to death penalty "myths" ($r = -.267$). That is, uninformed persons were more likely to adhere to death penalty myths at pretest while more informed persons tended to accept death penalty truths.

In sum, while only a small subset of these studies have tested the first of the three Marshall hypotheses, the hypothesis has been supported. As claimed by Justice Marshall, the public is not well informant about application and consequences of the death penalty in this country. This is a finding that has endured continuously since this area of scholarship was initiated in the late 1970s. However, support for this hypothesis under the more rigorous test has been less supportive. Ellsworth and Ross observed death penalty opponents to be equally as ignorant about the death penalty as death penalty proponents. Similarly, while Cochran and Chamlin (2005) observed significant correlations between death penalty knowledge at pretest and adherence to death penalty "myths," they failed to observe a statistically significant association between pretest knowledge levels and death penalty support as the Marshall hypotheses predict.

The most widely tested of the three Marshall hypotheses is the second hypothesis, which predicts levels of death penalty support to decrease (or opposition to increase) upon exposure to information about the application and consequences of capital punishment. Only two studies did not test this hypothesis (Lord et al., 1979; Ellsworth & Ross, 1983). Of those that have directly tested this hypothesis, only four studies failed to observe support for it (Bohm et al., 1990; Kennedy-Kollar & Mandery, 2010; Falco & Freiberger, 2011; Cox, 2013). Bohm et al. (1990) examined the effects of a death penalty course on college students' *reasons* for supporting the death penalty and observed that exposure to information did not produce a significant change in the subjects' reasons for support. Kennedy-Kollar and Mandery (2010) tested the effects of pro-death penalty information on change in death penalty opponents—a twist on the Marshall hypotheses in that they argued that pro-death penalty information could also influence death penalty attitudes, though in a manner directly opposite of that predicted by Justice Marshall. They observed support for their test of this inverted Marshall hypothesis. The Falco and Freiberger (2011) study is the only qualitative study conducted in this area. Their focus group approach showed little change in death penalty support after their groups discussed death penalty information presented to them. Rather than change their stance on capital punishment, their subjects instead tended to critique and reject the validity of the information. Finally, Cox (2013) is one of three true experiments to be conducted in this area of scholarship (see also Sarat & Vidmar, 1976; Kennedy-Kollar & Mandery, 2010). Cox observed that the degree of change in death penalty support did not differ significantly between the experimental and control groups. Conversely, Sarat and Vidmar (1976) did observe a significant decrease in death penalty support among the experimental group relative to the control group. Again, Kennedy-Kollar and Mandery (2010), the third experimental design, observed support for their inverted Marshall hypothesis, exposure to pro-capital punishment information increased death penalty support among the experimental group.

Despite these four studies that failed to observe support for the second Marshall hypothesis, all of the remaining studies have observed support for it. But the support is modest, with only small decreases in support and/or increases in opposition observed for those exposed to information about capital punishment. Often these changes in attitudes are within levels of support/opposition rather than across. That is, death penalty proponents support somewhat less so but tend not to oppose the death penalty, while death penalty opponents tend to oppose somewhat more so. Importantly, the effects of this exposure on attitude change is not of long duration, and most subjects rebound to their pretest levels of support after six months or so (see Bohm et al., 1993; Bohm & Vogel, 2004; c.f., Sandys, 1995). Finally, the effects of information on death penalty attitudes is not invariant across race or sex; that is, the effects of information on change in death penalty support are unequal between whites and blacks and between males and females (see Cochran et al., 2006; Mallicoat & Brown, 2008; Lambert et al., 2011; c.f. Michel & Cochran, 2011).

Other findings include the observation that public pronouncements of one's stand on capital punishment tend to make these attitudes malleable (Bohm, 1990) and that exposure to death penalty information may be assimilated in a manner that is biased by pretests positions (Lord et al., 1979; Bohm & Vogel, 1994; Mallicoat & Brown, 2008; Falco & Freiberger, 2011). In turn such biased assimilation information can lead to polarization of attitudes such that proponents may support more so and opponents may oppose more so upon exposure (Lord et al., 1979). All of these observation suggest that people may be variably receptive to information on the death penalty (i.e., open to some—value-expressive, and closed to other—pragmatic/utilitarian) and that their attitudes may also vary in their mutability (Vollum et al., 2009).

Justice Marshall anticipated such variability when he made his third hypothesis, predicting that those who held highly retributive positions would be most immune to the influence of information about the application and consequences of capital punishment. Only six studies have directly tested this hypothesis (Sarat & Vidmar, 1976; Bohm et al., 1991; Bohm & Vogel, 1991; Cochran & Chamlin, 2005; Vollum et al., 2009; Lee et al., 2014), and only the Cochran and Chamlin (2205) and Lee et al. (2014) studies failed to observe support for it.

Discussion

The "evolving standards of decency" is the primary test employed by the USSC to assess the legitimacy of capital punishment and public sentiment on capital punishment may arguably be the best real-time indicator of these standards. However, Justice Thurgood Marshall warned that we might care to be cautious with regard to our interpretation and use of public opinion polls regarding the death penalty. Marshall opined that the high levels of public support regularly observed for the death penalty is of little value because the public is generally uniformed about capital punishment. He added that the probative value of public sentiment regarding capital punishment should be limited only to an informed or knowledgeable opinion. Marshall asserted that support for capital punishment was largely a function of a lack of knowledge or information about it. However, if fully informed, "the great mass of citizens would conclude . . . that the death penalty is immoral and unconstitutional" (*Furman v. Georgia*, 1972, p. 363). The one exception to this assumption; for those who support capital punishment under a retributive rationale, information about capital punishment would not be persuasive (*Furman v. Georgia*, 1972, p. 363). These statements on public opinion and the death penalty have come to be known as the "Marshall hypotheses." These hypotheses are as follows: (1) support for capital punishment is negatively/inversely associated with knowledge about it, (2) exposure to information about capital punishment produces sentiments in opposition to capital punishment, but (3) exposure to information about capital punishment will have no impact on those who support it for retributive reasons.

To date there are almost 30 published studies that have tested one or more of these hypotheses (Bohm, 1989, 1990; Bohm & Vogel, 1991, 1994, 2004; Bohm et al., 1990, 1991; Bohm et al., 1993; Clarke et al., 2000–01; Cochran & Chamlin, 2005; Cochran et al., 2006; Cox, 2013; Diaz & Garza, 2015, Ellsworth & Ross, 1983; Falco & Freiburger, 2011; Kennedy-Kollar & Mandery, 2010; LaChappelle, 2014; Lambert et al., 2008; Lambert & Clarke, 2001; Lee et al., 2014; Longmire, 1996; Lord et al., 1979; Mallicoat & Brown, 2008; Michel & Cochran, 2011; Sandys, 1995; Sarat & Vidmar, 1976; Vidmar & Dittenhoffer, 1981; Vollum et al., 2009; Wright et al., 1995). While there are important variations in methodology across these studies, they tend to share several common methodological elements: (1) a pretest measure of attitudes toward capital punishment, (2) exposure to information about capital punishment, and (3) a posttest measure of death penalty attitudes.

Perhaps because of the various differences and limitations in the research designs and methodologies that characterize this body of research, these studies tend to produce a rather mixed and inconsistent pattern of support for the three Marshall hypotheses. That is, informed opinion is less supportive of capital punishment; exposure to information occasionally reduces support for capital punishment; and retributivists do tend to be relatively immune to the effects of information about capital punishment. Additional findings common to this body of research include: (1) death penalty information may be assimilated in a biased manner and, as such, exposure to information might polarize opinion; those opposed become more opposed while those who support the death penalty become more supportive upon exposure to information, (2) death penalty sentiments which have been publically pronounced are more resistant to change, (3) initial beliefs about the death penalty such as its general deterrent effect or marginal incapacitation effect are not changed by information on these issues, (4) when attitudes toward capital punishment change, the change is primarily due to information regarding racial disparities in justice and/or the execution of innocent persons, and finally (5) changed death penalty opinions tend to rebound to their original, preinformed positions; thus any effects of information on death penalty support/opposition are short-lived. In short, death penalty attitudes are malleable and exposure to information does play an important, albeit limited role in this attitude change, but what else is involved? What other social or psychological forces are also involved in attitude change? Relatedly, what kinds of death penalty attitudes are mutable, and who is more or less receptive to this information?

Future research in this area should consider moving the sampling frame out of the college classroom and into the general public, for it is the public's attitudes, not college students' attitudes, from which we are trying to gauge the "evolving standards of decency." The samples need to be large enough to test for racial/ethnic, gender, SES, and other forms of invariance in the effects of knowledge information exposure on change in death penalty sentiments. Moreover, these studies need to be designed around a true experimental design in which subjects are randomly assigned to treatment and control groups. The subjects' levels of knowledge about the application and consequences of the death penalty as well as their death penalty attitudes (both abstract and concrete) need to be assessed at pretest, posttest, and follow-up time periods. Doing so would permit an assessment of the effects of *change in knowledge* on *change in attitudes*. Finally, these studies should randomly vary the nature of the treatment condition (i.e., the quantity, quality, duration, and type of exposure to information about the death penalty) to allow for assessments of the effects of these variable forms of death penalty information. Herein lies the rub; how, under such a research design, can the researcher assure that information exposure is not biased/one-sided or too constrained/compressed and also allow for the respondents to question/interrogate the information and perhaps discuss it among themselves? Clearly, no single study is likely to be able to address all of these issues.

References

Bohm, R. M. (1989). The effects of classroom instruction and discussion on death penalty opinions: A teaching note. *Journal of Criminal Justice, 17*, 123–131.

Bohm, R. M. (1998). American death penalty opinions: Past, present, and future. In J. R. Acker, R. M. Bohm, & C. S. Lanier (Eds.), *America's experiment with capital punishment* (pp. 25–46). Durham, NC: Carolina Academic Press.

Bohm, R. M. (2003a). *Deathquest II: An introduction to the theory and practice of capital punishment in the United States.* Cincinnati, OH: Anderson.

Bohm, R. M. (2003b). American death penalty opinions: Past, present, and future. In J. R. Acker, R. M. Bohm, & C. S. Lanier (Eds.), *America's experiment with capital punishment* (2nd ed., pp. 27–54). Durham, NC: Carolina Academic Press.

Bohm, R. M., Clark, L. J., & Aveni, A. F. (1990). The influence of knowledge on reasons for death penalty opinions: An experimental test. *Justice Quarterly, 7*, 175–188.

Bohm, R. M., Clark, L. J., & Aveni, A. F. (1991). Knowledge and death penalty opinion: A test of the Marshall hypotheses. *Journal or Research in Crime and Delinquency, 28*, 360–387.

Bohm, R. M., & Vogel, B. L. (2004). More than ten years after: The long-term stability of informed death penalty opinions. *Journal of Criminal Justice, 32*, 307–327.

Bohm, R. M., & Vogel, R. E. (1991). Educational experiences and death penalty opinions: Stimuli that produce change. *Journal of Criminal Justice Education, 2*, 69–80.

Bohm, R. M., & Vogel, R. E. (1994). A comparison of factors associated with uninformed and informed death penalty opinions. *Journal of Criminal Justice, 22*, 125–143.

Bohm, R. M., Vogel, R. E., & Maisto, A. A. (1993). Knowledge and death penalty opinion: A panel study. *Journal of Criminal Justice, 21*, 29–45.

Clarke, A. W., Lambert, E., & Whitt, L. A. (2000). *Executing the innocent: The next step in the Marshall hypotheses.* NYU Review of Law & Social Change, 26, 309.

Cochran, J. K., & Chamlin, M. B. (2005). Can information change public opinion? Another test of the Marshall hypotheses. *Journal of Criminal Justice, 33*, 573–584.

Cochran, J. K., Sanders, B., & Chamlin, M. B. (2006). Profiles in change: An alternative look at the Marshall hypotheses. *Journal of Criminal Justice Education, 17*, 205–226.

Cox, A. K. (2013). Student death penalty attitudes: Does new information matter? *Journal of Criminal Justice Education, 24*, 443–460.

Diaz, S., & Garza, R. (2015). The Troy Davis effects: Does information on wrongful convictions affect death penalty opinions? *Journal of Ethnicity in Criminal Justice, 13*, 111–130.

Ellsworth, P. C., & Ross, L. (1983). Public opinion and capital punishment: A close examination of the views of abolitionists and retentionists. *Crime and Delinquency, 29*, 116–169.

Falco, D. L., & Freiberger, T. L. (2011). Public opinion and the death penalty: A qualitative approach. *The Qualitative Report, 16*, 830–847.

Kennedy-Kollar, D., & Mandery, E. J. (2010). Testing the Marshall hypothesis and its antithesis: The effect of biased information on death-penalty opinion. *Criminal Justice Studies, 23*, 65–83.

LaChappelle, L. (2014). Capital punishment in the era of globalization: A partial test of the Marshall hypothesis among college students. *American Journal of Criminal Justice, 39*, 839–854.

Lambert, E. G., Camp, S. D., Clarke, A., & Jiang, S. (2011). The impact of information on death penalty support, revised. *Crime and Delinquency, 57*, 572–599.

Lambert, E., & Clarke, A. (2001). The impact of information on an individual's support of the death penalty: A partial test of the Marshall hypothesis among college students. *Criminal Justice Policy Review, 12*, 215–234.

Lee, G. M., Bohm, R. M., & Pazzani, L. M. (2014). Knowledge and death penalty opinion: The Marshall hypotheses revisited. *American Journal of Criminal Justice, 39*, 642–659.

Liebman, J. S., Fagan, J., & West, V. (2000). A broken system: Error rates in capital cases, 1973–1995. *The Justice Project*. Retrieved from www.justice.policy.net/jpreport.html

Longmire, D. R. (1996). *Americans' attitudes about the ultimate weapon: Capital punishment*. In T. J. Flanagan & D. R. Longmire (Eds.), Americans view crime and justice: A national public opinion survey (pp. 93–108). "http://psycnet.apa.org/doi/10.4135/9781483326900.n7"http://dx.doi.org/10.4135/9781483326900.n7

Lord, C. G., Ross, L., & Lepper, M. R. (1979). Biased assimilation and attitude polarization: The effects of prior theories on subsequently considered evidence. *Journal of Personality and Social Psychology, 37*, 2098–2109.

Mallicoat, S. L., & Brown, G. C. (2008). The impact of race and ethnicity on student opinions of capital punishment. *Journal of Ethnicity in Criminal Justice, 6*, 255–280.

Michel, C., & Cochran, J. K. (2011). The effects of information on change in death penalty support: Race- and gender-specific extensions of the Marshall hypotheses. *Journal of Ethnicity in Criminal Justice, 9*, 291–313.

Sandys, M. (1995). Attitudinal change among students in a capital punishment class: It may be possible. *American Journal of Criminal Justice, 20*, 37–55.

Sarat, A., & Vidmar, N. (1976). Public opinion, the death penalty, and the Eighth Amendment: Testing the Marshall hypothesis. *Wisconsin Law Review, 17*, 171–206.

Scheck, B., Nuefeld, P., & Dwyer, J. (2001). *Actual innocence: When justice goes wrong and how to make it right*. New York: Penguin Putnam.

Vidmar, N., & Dittenhoffer, T. (1981). Informed public opinion and death penalty attitudes. *Canadian Journal of Criminology, 23*, 43–56.

Vollum, S., Mallicoat, S., & Buffington-Vollum, J. (2009). Death penalty attitudes in an increasingly critical climate: Value-expressive support and attitude mutability. *Southwest Journal of Criminal Justice, 5*, 221–242.

Wright, H. O., Jr., Bohm, R. M., & Jamieson, K. M. (1995). A comparison of uninformed and informed death penalty opinions: A replication and expansion. *American Journal of Criminal Justice, 20*, 57–87.

Cases Cited

Atkins, Virginia, 536 U.S. 304 (2002).

Furman, v. Georgia, 408 U.S. 238 (1972).

In re Kemmler, 136 U.S. 436 (1890).

Louisiana ex rel. Francis v. Resweber, 329 U.S. 459 (1947).

Ring, Arizona, 536 U.S. 584 (2002).

Roper v. Simmons, 543 U.S. 551 (2005).

Trop v. Dulles, 356 U.S. 86 (1958).

Weems v. United States, 217 U.S. 349 (1910).

Wilkerson v. Utah, 99 U.S. 130 (1878).

C. Culture

5

MEDIA AND CAPITAL PUNISHMENT

Matthew Robinson

Introduction

The death penalty, being the most severe of all criminal justice sanctions, is logically attractive to the media. The death penalty tends to make the news when high profile murderers are sentenced to death and when inmates are executed, as well as when problems with capital punishment lead to wrongful convictions and exonerations. Media coverage of capital punishment can reduce the popularity of the punishment (for example, where studies are covered that illustrate racial bias in the application of the punishment, as in the case of North Carolina), or when they illustrate the very real possibility that innocent people have been put to death (Unnever & Cullen, 2005). Yet, historically, media coverage has tended to increase support for the death penalty (for example, where a heinous murder against a particularly vulnerable victim like a child does *not* lead to an execution).

In the latter case, particularly repellent crimes tend to produce strong emotions such as vengeance that demand tough punishment to correct (Bandes, 2008). This might help explain why states that had once abolished capital punishment ultimately reinstated it (Koch, Wark, & Galliher, 2012). Garland (2002, p. 461) asserts that the way murder tends to be depicted in the media—from the news to films and beyond—almost demands an execution due to the simplistic nature of the way the crime is covered. The media depict "a dangerous, guilty offender" who will "pay the ultimate penalty for a freely-willed, evil act."

Add on to this fact that, generally speaking, the research shows that the greater one's exposure to criminal justice programming on television, the higher one's level of support for capital punishment (Chiricos, Padgett, & Gertz, 2000; Romer, Jamieson, & Aday, 2003). For example, viewing police reality television shows directly and indirectly (through greater fear of crime) increases support for capital punishment (Holbert, Shah, & Kwak, 2004), although program type matters (Britta & Noga-Styron, 2014). One study found that watching nonfictional crime shows decreases support for the criminal justice system, and this effect is mediated by fear. Further, watching crime dramas is associated with higher support for the death penalty, even though, in this study, this was *not* because of increased fear (Kort-Butler & Hartshorn, 2011).

This chapter will explore how the media cover capital punishment. While most focus is on the news media (e.g., when and how executions are discussed in the news), additional focus is placed on the death penalty in entertainment (e.g., television shows). After reading this material, you will better understand how capital punishment tends to be covered in the media, problems with this coverage, and the effects this coverage has on public opinion as well as actual policy.

Before this examination commences, it is important to note that the media undeniably play a significant role in how Americans view criminal justice generally, including capital punishment, because the typical American watches television an average of eight hours per day, lives in households that have more televisions than people, is nearly constantly connected to the Internet and electronic devices, and is bombarded with images and stories of crime including, most notably, murder (Haney, 2009). Further, most Americans are not victims of serious violent crime and have few interactions with criminal justice agencies, meaning media images of crime are often the only ones people experience.

Media Coverage of Murder and Death Penalty Trials

Murder is viewed by citizens and governments alike as the most heinous of all crimes. As such, it is of great interest to the news media, not to mention entertainment media such as television shows and movies. As explained by Bandes (2004, p. 587): "Death eligible crimes tend to be violent, high profile, and thus by definition newsworthy under the 'if it bleeds, it leads' criteria that govern media coverage decisions."

After a horrific crime, when an offender is apprehended and there is significant evidence of his or her guilt, media portrayals of the crime and key actors' reactions to it have enormous impact on public opinion and ultimately whether an aggravated murder leads to a death sentence (Bandes, 2004). This can lead either to pressure on prosecutors to seek a death sentence, which is typical, or to abandon it, which is far less common. An example of the first is the case of Scott Peterson, who was charged with capital murder after the disappearance of his young, pregnant wife. District Attorney Jim Brazelton's statement about the case represents the common response generated by the intense media coverage of the case: "This case cries out for the ultimate punishment . . . . I owe it to Lacie and [her unborn baby] Connor." Peterson was convicted and sentenced to death. He remains on California's death row, the largest in the country, although California has only executed six people this century, and none since 2006!

An example of the latter comes from the case of convicted murderer Karla Faye Tucker, who committed brutal murders with a pickaxe after a failed burglary/theft attempt. Bandes (2004) speculates that public sympathy for the woman after her conversion to Christianity and support from many well-known Christian leaders as well as celebrities impacted the Harris County, Texas prosecutors' reluctance to push her case forward. In spite of this, Tucker was ultimately executed. Both of these cases, incidentally, not only received widespread media attention but also ultimately led to numerous portrayals in entertainment media, from television shows to movies and books, even to music.

Many studies examine how the media cover the crime of murder, as well as how society reacts to it through criminal punishment. One such study, which examined death sentences in two Ohio newspapers, found that coverage of capital punishment varied greatly between the papers (Williams, 2007). This helps us understand why the effects of media coverage on public opinion is not as straightforward as you might believe, because how people feel about something will logically be impacted by where they get their news (Dardis, Baumgartner, Boydstun, De Boef, & Shen, 2008).

Still, most research shows that significant media coverage tends to increase support for capital punishment. Part of this is because criminal justice officials such as law enforcement officers and prosecutors are overrepresented as sources (Chermak, 1995; Miller & Hunt, 2008). Individuals in these groups tend to overwhelmingly support capital punishment (Caravelis & Robinson, 2013). Yet it is also because of how capital murders tend to get covered in the media. For example, a study of how capital murders were covered in a newspaper between 1992 and 1999 in Harris County, Texas, found that the coverage presented "a distorted reality in which brutal crimes . . . [were] committed by minority offenders against vulnerable, 'worthy' victims"; this was found to sustain support for the death penalty (Lin & Phillips, 2014, p. 934). In reality, the vast majority of murder is committed within the same race rather than across races, and in the smallest number of cases are victims particularly vulnerable (e.g., children, the elderly). By focusing on extreme and unusual murders, media coverage tends to create misconceptions of the typical murder in the U.S. (Robinson, 2012).

The significance of this last point cannot be overstated. National research on serious reversible error in capital cases finds that more error is common in states that have higher portions of African Americans (who tend to be depicted as more violent in the media), as well in places where the murder risk falls most heavily on whites compared with blacks (which fits the stereotypical murder covered in the press, in spite of the reality that the murder victimization rate is actually significantly higher among African Americans) (Liebman et al., 2002). Media mischaracterization of murder may thus play a role in serious, reversible error in death penalty cases. In short, greater pressure to seek the death penalty increases the odds of errors in the capital punishment process.

Further, there is evidence that pretrial publicity impacts decision making in capital cases. For example, one study found that death-qualified jurors (those who successfully pass through the voir dire jury selection process, in part because of their willingness to impose the death penalty), knew more facts of a highly publicized murder case than nonqualified jurors. Those death-qualified jurors were more likely to believe the defendant was guilty and that he should be sentenced to death (Butler, 2007). This raises the possibility that media coverage of crimes might predispose jurors to convict defendants in the first place.

Media Coverage of Death Sentencing

Additionally, when killers are sentenced to death, this is generally deemed newsworthy, and it inevitably impacts public perceptions of and support for the death penalty. The newsworthiness of capital punishment is not only because murder is viewed as the most serious crime but also because death sentences are so rare. Specifically, only about 1% of all killings nationwide lead to death sentences, and only about 2% of killings in states with the death penalty lead to death sentences (Death Penalty Information Center, 2016). This means that about 98% of killers in states that have the death penalty are *not* sentenced to death! Currently, only 30 states currently have the death penalty, along with the federal government and U.S. military, although only about ten states actively use it. Given these realities, you can understand how a death sentence might generally interest the media as well as the public. Figure 5.1 illustrates the states with and without the death penalty in the United States.

One thing is certain: coverage of crime, including murder and even capital cases, tends to be acontextual, meaning no context is provided to help readers, viewers, and listeners fully understand the situations that preceded and ultimately even led to murder. For example, a study of newspaper coverage of 26 defendants eligible for the death penalty after being charged with capital murder found that the papers focused disproportionately on characteristics of the crime (such as their level of heinousness, which is legally considered to be an *aggravating factor* making a death sentence more likely) (Haney & Greene, 2004). The papers also tended not to provide the context necessary for readers to understand the circumstances that produced the murders, including potential *mitigating factors* that would reduce the likelihood of death sentences. In this way, media coverage of murder can be thought of as biased in favor of the death penalty.

Finally, at least one study of elected sentencing judges involved in cases of serious violent crimes find that "press coverage magnifies the influence of voters' penal preferences on criminal sentencing decisions" (Lim, Snyder, & Stromberg, 2010: 20). This suggests the possibility that judges who know they need to be reelected are more likely to listen to jury recommendations, especially when cases receive a lot of coverage in the media. The U.S. Supreme Court requires a recommendation of death from a jury before a judge can sentence a defendant to death.

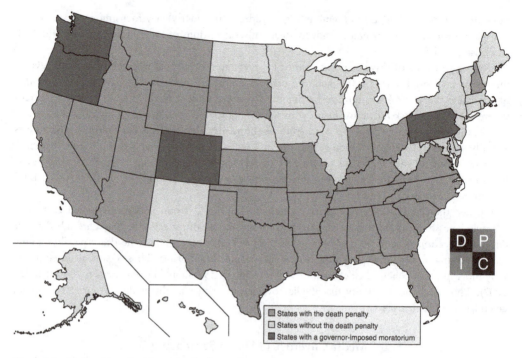

Figure 5.1   States with and without the death penalty as of August 18, 2016.
www.deathpenaltyinfo.org/states-and-without-death-penalty (Reproduced with permission)

Media Coverage of Executions

Executions, too, are often newsworthy, and they too are rare. Specifically, only 796 executions were carried out between 2000 and 2014, or 53 per year (or 4.4 per month) (Death Penalty Information Center, 2016). This is during a time when the nation experienced 235,935 murders, or an average of 15,729 murders per year (or 1,310.8 murders per month) (Disaster Center, 2016). Clearly, executions are extremely rare, especially when compared to the number of murders that happen each year. Figure 5.2 illustrates just how rare executions are, relative to murder.

The media are most interested in providing coverage of executions of widely known criminals such as serial killers like Ted Bundy or mass murderers like Timothy McVeigh. Bundy was a serial killer who murdered at least 30 people in numerous states in the 1970s. McVeigh killed 168 people by bombing the Alfred P. Murrah Federal Building in Oklahoma City in 1995. Offenders like Ted Bundy, Timothy McVeigh and others committed high-profile crimes that themselves generated immense media coverage; thus, you'd expect public interest to continue as a case processes its way through the criminal justice system to the actual execution. In these cases (and almost only these cases), the news media follow the cases beyond the arrest and investigation through the courtroom process, all the way until the final sentence is carried out. This allows the media to satisfy public demand to stay informed about these stories and also to continue to satisfy advertisers and generate profit by covering popular crime stories (Beale, 2006).

One of the most commonly discussed issues among students and some citizens is whether executions ought to be public (Hochstetler, 2001). It is possible that if executions were public, they might

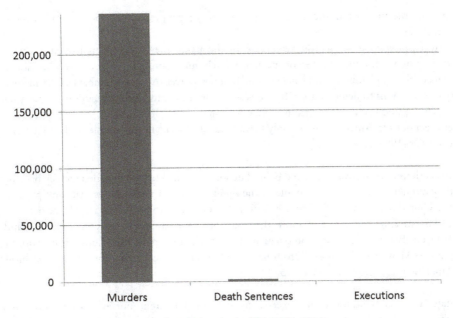

Figure 5.2 Murders, death sentences, and executions in the U.S., 2000–2014.

have a great crime preventive, or deterrent, effect. During the eighteenth century, a primary purpose of capital punishment was *deterrence*—instilling fear in citizens through punishment so that they would not violate the laws. Thus, it had to be carried out in public, in a large space so that many people could witness it, and during the day.

At the time, executions were preceded by lengthy speeches and sermons that focused public attention on sin and renunciation of it. Although it may seem strange when judged through today's lens, the execution ceremony provided the condemned with a chance at reintegration into society, even if it was only for a short time before his or her execution. The fact that repentance was important to people in the eighteenth century is another reason why the punishment was administered in public.

Yet, perceptions of unruly crowds in attendance meant public executions were no longer perceived as legitimate exercises of state power nor mechanisms to deliver a message of lawful retribution (Banner, 2003, p. 154). Over the next 100 years, every state hid its executions. Capital punishment historian John Bessler (1997, p. 4) claims that executions became private "[o]nly in response to a movement in the 1830s to abolish capital punishment, and to a growing concern among civic leaders that public executions were unwholesome spectacles." Further, "executions were seen as acts of violence that were likely to reflect badly on the larger community, harden the public, and demean the condemned" (Johnson, 1998, p. 40). When the electric chair was adopted by Florida, North Carolina, Oklahoma, and Texas in the early 1900s, the new method of death also necessitated indoor executions (Banner, 2003, p. 155).

The last public execution in the United States was in 1936 in Owensboro, Kentucky (Ryan, 1992). Between 10,000 and 20,000 people turned out to witness this public hanging, which was described by the press as a carnival type atmosphere (Banner, 2003). Decades after executions moved indoors, they still drew sizable crowds outside the jail. Eventually, however, the masses got their information from other sources, most notably the new 'penny presses', which meant people no longer had to attend executions to experience the details (Banner, 2003, p. 162). However, some states even passed laws barring the press from attending executions and/or printing detail about them in the papers (Bessler, 1997).

Today, executions are vastly different than in the past. They are hidden from the public and attended by only a limited number of spectators (including criminal justice officials but also family members of the condemned and of the victims' families, as well as some members of the media). The ability of executions to deter murder thus rests solely with the media; for executions to deter murder, people have to know about them from the news media.

Yet executions in America are not only private but also occur in the middle of the night. According to Bessler (1997, p. 81):

> Executions in America, conducted behind prison walls, are cloaked in added secrecy because they frequently occur in the middle of the night. Of the 313 executions that took place in the United States from 1977 to 1995, over 82 percent of them were carried out between 11:00 pm and 7:30 am, and more than half of them happened between midnight and 1:00 am. Because television audiences are largest when people return home from work or school—viewership levels peak from 8:00 to 11:00 pm—many executions occur after most Americans are already sound asleep.

It is state laws that typically require executions to be held at night, but even when this is not the case, prison wardens or other government officials generally prefer to hold executions in the middle of the night. This is often done because midnight (and later) is the safest time in the prison, where troublesome behaviors are least likely to occur. Further, midnight executions help "avoid unwanted protestors" and "ensure that enough time exists, because of possible last-minute stays and appeals, to carry out a death warrant—the legal document that lists a specific date on which the execution must occur" (Bessler, 1997, p. 82).

Today, almost all executions are thus unknown to nearly everyone. Dow and McNeese (2004, p. 149) agree, writing: "Executions in America are typically invisible. High profile executions are the exceptions that demonstrate the rule. When a particularly infamous murderer is put to death, such as Timothy McVeigh or Ted Bundy, the execution receives significant attention. Yet, in nearly all other cases, executions are banal." Even in those latter cases, Americans learn of executions only through the media.

Should American states resume public executions? Leighton (2009) argues that executions should either be televised or else capital punishment should be abolished. His argument rests of the claim that the government must be accountable to the people for its actions carried out in their names.

While some may argue that public executions—even if broadcast on television—would deter murder, there is literally no evidence that this is true (Robinson, 2008). Further, given the dominance of crime infotainment shown on television, we might expect executions to become seen as a form of entertainment alongside violent and gory movies.

A look at the top shows on television at the time of this writing shows that many of them prominently feature themes of crime and violence. According to Nielsen (2016), the top rated shows on network television (TV) include two shows about crime and murder (Navy Criminal Investigative Service [*NCIS*], and *NCIS: Los Angeles*), and a show about law and jury trials (*Bull*). Similarly, in terms of syndicated TV, the most popular shows include one featuring the civil law (*Judge Judy*), and another is one of the most popular and successful crime shows ever created (*Law & Order*). Several studies of *NCIS* and *Law & Order* have illustrated that these shows typically focus on violent crime, that they are highly unrealistic, and that they mislead viewers about the realities of crime and American criminal justice (Robinson, 2012).

In the 1990s, after Timothy McVeigh was convicted of the truck bombing that killed 168 people (including 19 children), he was sentenced to death by lethal injection by the federal government. According to Garland (2002), there was little if any debate in the media about whether McVeigh should be put to death but instead about whether his execution should be televised. Ultimately, his execution was only broadcast to via closed-circuit television to a single location where family members of those killed could watch. Incredibly, a mock execution of a man looking very similar to Timothy McVeigh is available for view on the Internet, illustrating the popularity of executions to many Americans.

Yet, only a small portion of executions are ever reported in the news. For example, Jacoby et al. (2008, p. 169) analyzed reports of executions imposed between 1977 and 2007 on network television, in national newspapers, and an in-state newspaper. The authors found that as executions became more common, coverage in the news became "less consistent, extensive, and prominent." In those states that had the most executions, newspapers regularly reported them, but the reports became shorter and less prominent even as executions increased. As for national news media coverage, "crimes with multiple victims, unusual offender characteristics, precedent-setting circumstances, unusual legal claims, or execution protocol violations" had the most coverage. This is consistent with the idea that the media are more attracted to the unusual rather than the usual. Recall that this tends to create misconceptions of crime and also may increase support for punitive responses such as the death penalty.

Amazingly, less than 7% of the executions that took place between 1977 and 2007 were covered on national television news. According to Jacoby and colleagues (2008, p. 184).

> Executions have disappeared almost entirely from network TV news—between 2001 and 2007 only 14 [3%] of the 416 executions carried out in the U.S. was reported by *any* of the major TV networks. During the same period *USA Today* reported only [3%] of executions.

Coverage in national newspapers was higher (*USA Today* and *New York Times* reported 20% and 48% of the executions, respectively). Further, while television news averaged only 15 reports per 100 executions, *USA Today* averaged 28 articles per 100 executions.

The average length of news reports on television was 140 seconds per execution. As for newspapers, reports were shorter in national newspapers than in newspapers with only coverage of in-state executions. Reports in the *New York Times* were longer than in the *USA Today* (366 words versus 37 words). Less than 5% of reports were reported on page one. Thus, executions in the news are even rarer than those in the real world.

Jacoby et al. (2008, pp. 184–195) explain why executions are not a high priority for news sources. They point out that, on television:

> a single broadcast contains only 8–10 stories. A huge number of national and international events occur each day from which TV news editors must chose no more than ten. Among these occurrences on a typical day would probably be bombings, accidents, or severe weather somewhere in the world resulting in many deaths, as well as political and economic events with important national and international consequences. In competition with news reports of such a large number of large-scale events, a news story about the death of a single criminal offender by lethal injection may, understandably, fail to survive an editor's cut.

Further, consider that since the average execution now occurs about 15 years after a crime, an execution following even a heinous crime will be of little interest to most people. The authors reason: "Stories that incorporate violent conflict, involve well-known persons, include graphic imagery, and allow for the reinforcement of traditional cultural values are preferred over more complex stories that may challenge the reader to reconsider widely held beliefs" (Jacoby et al., 2008, p. 169).

Hochstetler (2001) analyzed stories of executions in 50 large newspapers from January 1977 through February 1999. Of the 449 executions during this time, those who killed the most people received the greatest coverage. Further, sensational or unusual crimes received more attention. This is also consistent with the media's focus on the abnormal rather than the normal.

Another study examined 524 newspaper reports of 100 executions that occurred between January 1, 1990, and April 30, 2005. The authors (Miller & Hunt, 2008) found that defendant race had little effect on the mean articles per execution, although executions of minority defendants received slightly more coverage. Additionally, executions for crimes against white victims received more attention than those involving African-American victims. This, again, creates misconceptions in media consumers about murder, as blacks are significantly more likely than whites to be murdered.

According to the authors:

> Three factors had the largest impact on the number of reports. First, geography was a factor that influenced the coverage of an execution. Executions in non-southern states averaged 6.5 reports while those in southern states averaged 5.1. This is likely due to the fact that executions are more common in the south. Second . . . the number of victims impacted the amount of coverage an execution received. Cases with multiple victims averaged 7 reports while those with a single victim averaged 5. . . . Finally, the presence of some form of protest increased the number of reports. Executions that involved reports of collective protests averaged 6.2 articles per case while those without protest averaged 4.7.
>
> *(Miller & Hunt, 2008, p. 199)*

The later point reflects the reality that the media are attracted to conflict, as well as stories that feature clashes between opposing forces (Robinson, 2012).

In terms of what tends to be included in stories, nearly two-thirds of the stories (65%) included a summary of the details of the crime that led to the convictions and executions and almost half (48%) contained positive stories about the victims, whereas more than one-quarter (26%) contained negative stories about the condemned. And one-third (33%) discussed the criminal history of the condemned. This is all consistent with the idea of a media that is slanted toward the death penalty.

In addition, 60% of cases contained statements by criminal justice authorities, but only 12% contained statements by the defense; this is also consistent with the findings that media coverage tends to generally be pro-death penalty. Further, 26% contained statements by the victims' family and friends, whereas only 6% contained statements by the condemned inmate's family and friends. The authors suggest that "a primary function of reports of executions is to report justice being served" (Miller & Hunt, 2008, p. 202).

The authors explain how capital punishment stories in the media tend to be covered:

> Like telling a story, most of the reports began with the execution and then moved backwards to outline the original crime, then moving forward to explain the trial and appeals process that occurred prior to the execution. Included in most stories were details of the final hours and days of the condemned, including final appeals, final hours, and even the final meal.

According to the authors, "final meals of the condemned were often described in great detail, with one newspaper even including an entire story about condemned inmates' last meals." Stories also tended to provide some details of the actual execution, including the "condemned's final statement, describing the execution scene, reporting someone's satisfaction with the event, mentions of on-site protests, and/or descriptions of the defendant's death" (Miller & Hunt, 2008, p. 205).

Another study by Lipschultz and Hilt (1999, p. 250) of local television coverage of executions found that it tended to utilize powerful symbols (e.g., signs, candlelight vigils, heightened security, etc.) and

> did not attempt to bridge the gap between proponents and opponents of capital punishment. Bringing forth emotions in viewers surely increases viewership. Even in-studio experts focused on events at the prison scene, rather than the larger social issue of capital punishment.

This is consistent with the idea that media coverage of crime and criminal justice is actually meant to be entertaining, explaining why media corporations choose to continue to feature it so prominently in their programming.

Coverage of Death Row

Death row is, of course, private. Whereas television shows do exist to depict life in the nation's prisons—in infotainment format—nearly all of what happens on death row remains hidden from the public. Yet, according to LaChance (2007), two semi-public death penalty rituals persist in contemporary America—special, requested last meals of inmates (which are often reported in the news and can be examined on several websites), and final words spoken to those witnessing their executions. Both of these issues relate to people on death row, and the media occasionally focus on inmates on death row when they address those issues. The study by Miller and Hunt (2008), discussed earlier, of 524 newspaper reports of executions that occurred between 1889 and 2005, found that 50% contained the final statements of the condemned, and 25% contained references to the inmates' final meals.

LaChance (2007, p. 701) suggests that retaining and communicating final meals and final words of inmates tend to "reinforce a conception of those executed as autonomous actors, endowed with agency and individuality," meaning they are solely responsible for their behaviors. LaChance suggests murderers are thus portrayed as "self-made monsters who are intrinsically different by choice" rather than impacted by certain societal conditions, thereby possibly sustaining support for the death penalty among newspaper readers.

Haney (2009, p. 727) agrees that the dominant portrayal in the media of criminals, and violent murderers in particular, "reinforces a dominant cultural narrative about the origins of violent criminality—one that implies something about the nature of the persons who perpetrate such crimes and the societal policies that are needed to properly address them." This narrative, he suggests, depicts criminality "as entirely the product of free and autonomous choice-making [of the offender], unencumbered by past history or present circumstances." Offenders are dehumanized and demonized, characterized as abnormal, different, even unredeemable. The message to media consumers is "individuals alone are responsible for violent crime, and . . . extreme behavior stems entirely from deep-seated personal traits—depravity, narcissism, psychopathology, and the like." This means when people think about crime, including potential jurors in capital cases, they are less likely "to consider situational or contextual information in making judgments about others"—which produces more punitiveness, less consideration of mitigation, and a higher likelihood of imposing the death penalty (Haney, 2009, p. 728).

We'd thus expect the media to be particularly attracted to murder and death penalty cases when they are particularly unusual or abnormal. An analysis of 35 women on death row in the early 1990s supports this contention; it found that women were generally portrayed more favorably than men, consistent with the "chivalry hypothesis" that suggests women are treated more leniently in criminal justice than men (Belknap, 2001). Yet, lesbian murderers tended to be "over-represented in atypical death sentence cases," meaning that gay women offenders were more likely to be "depicted as manly and man-hating women . . . and who vent their rage and irrational desire for revenges through killing" (Farr, 2008, p. 49). The author suggests that when prosecutors portray female offenders in this light, it might impact sentencing decisions including a greater likelihood of being sentenced to death. This is consistent with research suggesting that, when women behave in ways that violate societal norms associated with the female gender, Americans react more harshly.

The "evil woman" hypothesis suggests that society will impose harsh punishments such as the death penalty on women when they do things outside what is viewed as normal for women (Belknap, 2001). The case of serial killer Eileen Wuornos is consistent with this expectation. Wuornos, killed at least seven men in Florida between 1989 and 1990 after a long criminal history

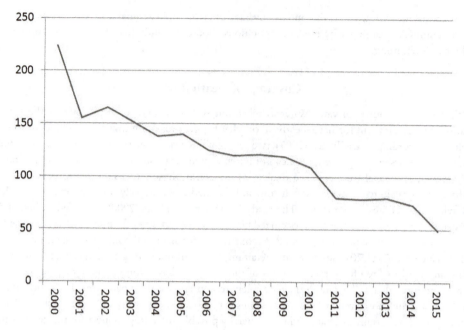

Figure 5.3   Death sentences in the U.S., 2000–2015.

spanning back nearly two decades. Wuornos shot all of her victims between two and nine times each after alleging that they tried to rape her while she hitchhiked in the state. Sentenced to death in 1992, she was executed in 2002. Wuornos's story has been featured widely in the mainstream media, including a highly rated and viewed Hollywood film called *Monster*, starring actress Charlize Theron.

In addition to studies such as these, media organizations also tend to focus on inmates when they are released from death row. Niven (2004) examined newspaper coverage of 16 inmates released from death rows in three Southern states, where executions are most common. He found that executed inmates received more coverage than those exonerated. Further, coverage of exonerees suggested that isolated mistakes produce errors rather than systematic failures. The "isolated mistake" frame was more than twice as common as the "systemic failure" frame, and some of the articles even framed the exonerations themselves as proof that the system works. Finally, newspaper stories on death row exonerees focused on life after release rather than experienced during incarceration, again by more than a two-to-one margin.

According to Niven (2004, p. 20), "those who were executed received more than three times as much coverage as exonerated people on death row, which is akin to giving three times as much coverage to the planes that land safely compared to the ones that crash." Niven thus concludes: "Cumulatively, this pattern serves to minimize the seriousness of the innocent on death row situation, and is consistent with media theories suggesting political coverage is generally supportive of moderatism/mainstream elite political thinking."

The framing of errors as isolated mistakes rather than systematic errors also creates misconceptions of the realities of capital punishment. In fact, in a study of error rates in capital cases across the country, Liebman, Jeffrey, Rifkind, and West found that the error rate of capital cases in the United States is 68%. This figure is based on a comprehensive study of 4,578 federal habeas corpus appeals in state capital cases between January 1, 1973 and October 2, 1995. The conclusion of the authors is that capital punishment in the United States is "collapsing under its own mistakes . . . a system that is wasteful and broken and needs to be addressed."

Some of the key findings of this report include:

- Nationally, the overall rate of prejudicial error was 68%—that is, "courts found serious, reversible error in nearly 7 of every 10 of the thousands of capital sentences that were fully reviewed during the period."
- Serious error was error substantially undermining the reliability of capital verdicts.
- Capital trials produce so many mistakes that it takes three judicial inspections to catch them, leaving grave doubt whether we do catch them all.
- State courts dismissed 47% of death sentences because of errors, and a later federal review dismissed 40% of the remaining cases.
- The most common errors found in the cases were (1) egregiously incompetent defense attorneys who missed evidence of the defendant's innocence or evidence that he or she did not deserve a death sentence and (2) suppression of evidence by police and prosecutors.
- Eighty-two percent of those whose death sentences were overturned by state courts were found to be deserving of less than a death sentence, and 7% were found to be innocent of the crimes for which they were convicted.
- Serious errors have been made in every year since the death penalty was reinstated, and more than half of all cases were found to be seriously flawed in 20 of the 23 study years.
- Serious errors are made in virtually every state that still executes people, and over 90% of these states make errors more than half of the time.
- In most cases, death row inmates wait for years for the lengthy review procedures needed to uncover all this error. Only then were their death sentences reversed.
- This much error, and the time needed to cure it, impose terrible costs on taxpayers, victims' families, the judicial system, and the wrongly condemned. And it renders unattainable the finality, retribution and deterrence that are the reasons usually given for having a death penalty.

The study just cited did receive significant media attention, likely influencing public opinion of capital punishment.

In the early twenty-first century, the number of exonerees from death row grew, causing increased concern among many citizens, including death penalty opponents and activists. In Niven's study, there was

> no significant increase in attention to the exonerated as their numbers have mounted . . . the results suggest attention to each additional exoneration has been largely flat. Overall, the exonerated can expect just under 32 articles featuring their plight, placed on average on page 8 and just under 672 words long.
>
> *(Niven, 2004, p. 24)*

Between 1976 through 2015, 150 people were released from death row in the United States. These are people who have had their convictions overturned and who were either acquitted at retrial, had all the charges dropped against them, or "were given an absolute pardon by the governor based on new evidence of innocence" (Death Penalty Information Center, 2016b).

Although some may view these exonerations as proof that "the system works," in fact there is now overwhelming evidence that innocent people have been executed in the United States. For example, consider the case of Cameron Willingham. Willingham was executed in the state of Texas in 2004 for starting a fire in his own home that killed his three children. According to the Death Penalty

Information Center (2006b), "four national arson experts have concluded that the original investigation of Willingham's case was flawed and it is possible the fire was accidental." They found "that prosecutors and arson investigators used arson theories that have since been repudiated by scientific advances."

The Death Penalty Information Center continues:

> Arson expert Gerald Hurst said, "There's nothing to suggest to any reasonable arson investigator that this was an arson fire. It was just a fire." Former Louisiana State University fire instructor Kendall Ryland added, "[It] made me sick to think this guy was executed based on this investigation. . . . They executed this guy and they've just got no idea—at least not scientifically—if he set the fire, or if the fire was even intentionally set.". . . Among the only other evidence presented by prosecutors during the trial was testimony from jailhouse snitch Johnny E. Webb, a drug addict on psychiatric medication, who claimed Willingham had confessed to him in the county jail. . . . Coincidentally, less than a year after Willingham's execution, arson evidence presented by some of the same experts who had appealed for relief in Willingham's case helped free Ernest Willis from Texas's death row. The experts noted that the evidence in the Willingham case was nearly identical to the evidence used to exonerate Willis.

Recent articles published in the media have concluded that Willingham was innocent (Grann, 2009; Mills, 2006). That major news entities, including an editorial in the *New York Times*, have covered this case is evidence that when a perceived wrong is serious enough, it will likely break into the mainstream press coverage (even in cases where it challenges mainstream institutions and practices like capital punishment).

Other cases of supposedly innocent individuals who have been executed have received some media coverage, but none near the level of Willingham. Still, they likely contribute to the shifts in public opinion in the US, away from capital punishment and toward alternatives such as life imprisonment without the possibility of parole (LWOP).

Media and Its Impact on Public Opinion

Scholars assert that unchecked media assertions of high levels of support for capital punishment among the public actually result in higher levels of support for capital punishment. For example, one study reported on the results of an experiment where people who read a typical media story on the death penalty which suggests very high, unqualified support tended to say they supported the death penalty more than people who read a more accurate portrayal of support for capital punishment that correctly pointed out that a very large number of Americans actually prefer alternatives to the death penalty such as LWOP (Niven, 2002). Therefore, even media stories about capital punishment opinion seem to impact public opinion of capital punishment.

Many studies exist to illustrate that media coverage of crime and criminal justice impact public policy by first impacting public opinion (Robinson, 2012). According to a study by Baumgartner, Linn, and Boydstun (2008), media coverage has become far more critical of the death penalty, focusing on issues of innocence, thereby lowering public support for the punishment and resulting in fewer death sentences nationally. In the words of the authors (Baumgartner et al., 2008, p. 33), the "recent shift in media coverage from pro-death penalty coverage focused on morality-and constitutionality-based frames to anti-death penalty coverage focused on the innocence frame was responsible for nearly as big a drop in death sentences as was the moratorium placed on capital punishment [by the U.S. Supreme Court] in 1972." Theirs was a study of death penalty coverage in the *New York Times* from 1960 through 2005, and stories of innocence increased dramatically in the late 1990s. Figure 5.4 illustrates the dramatic decline in death sentences since 2000.

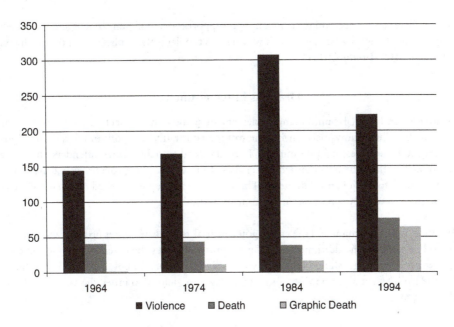

Figure 5.4   Violence, death, and graphic death in top films, 1964–1994.

In fact, Hayes (2013) argues that the media are highly responsible for "killing the death penalty." He suggests that Americans are conflicted about capital punishment because, even as a majority of them tend to say they support it,

> they worry that innocent people might be executed. And as the political debate has in the last two decades focused on wrongful convictions and death row exonerations, Americans have increasingly come to evaluate the death penalty in terms of its potential unfairness.

Hayes suggests this conflict is due in large part to the way media now cover capital punishment. He writes that a "shift in media coverage, which has highlighted problems in the death penalty's application, has encouraged the public to evaluate capital punishment in terms of fairness, especially the potential for innocent people to be sent to death row."

Yet an interesting study of pro-death penalty arguments on Internet websites found that the sites tend to ignore the complex issues surrounding numerous alleged problems with capital punishment and instead reduce arguments about the death penalty to issues of good versus evil. In the words of the author (Lynch, 2002, p. 213): "Once so reduced, no costs of capital punishment can outweigh the justice achieved by state executions in the rhetoric of pro-death activists and pundits." Lynch speculates that reading information on these websites will result in less empathy for accused and convicted murderers and unleashed and unrestrained criminal punishment.

The findings of this study about pro-death penalty arguments make sense when you consider research into public opinion on capital punishment more generally. This research shows that, as people become more aware of the alleged problems of capital punishment practice, they tend to become less supportive of it. This is not true for people who base their support largely on reasons related to retribution; these supporters tend to maintain their support for capital punishment and often become more supportive of it even when faced with very serious problems the application of the death penalty in the United States (Bohm, 2011).

Death as Entertainment

Finally, murder and capital punishment stories are frequently the subject of shows in the entertainment media. These shows necessarily (due to time constraints) simplify murder, criminal justice processing, and issues of capital punishment. They also tend to dehumanize offenders charged with murder as well as those being punished for crimes. Caldwell (2009) provides an example of how crime shows tend to dehumanize offenders: The *Law and Order* episode called "Teenage Wasteland" depicts an 18-year-old boy who beats an Asian man to death:

> When he is finally caught and the case is going to trial, the debate comes up as to whether he should be tried for the death penalty. When a prosecutor asks the detective who found the boy whether the court should convict a young, eighteen year-old boy, her reply is, "Where I come from, when a person does something that is so vicious, so cruel, the person forfeits the right to get older."

According to Caldwell, the death penalty is seen here "not an objective punishment from the court, but a subjective vendetta for the criminal's action." Caldwell adds:

> In this same episode, when the trial starts, the show focuses on the victim's tearful family. It shows the sickening pictures of the dead victim. Then the show focuses on the guilty eighteen year-old boy. His face is indifferent; his head is held high as if full of pride; there is no evidence that he is afraid of dying.

Later, the offender shows no emotion and is depicted as a dangerous person unworthy of help.

Caldwell provides another example, this time from the *Law and Order: Special Victims Unit* episode titled, "Execution." A detective in the show must try to gather information from a condemned inmate named Matthew Brodus. Caldwell describes Brodus as a sociopath, writing: "He is portrayed as daunting, diabolical and detached from reality." Prior to the detective's visit, he meets with a criminal psychiatrist who advises him to be safe and watch for signs of aggression. The psychiatrist says: "Pay attention to his eyes; serial killers have this stare; it's focused, it's like an animal's when it is hunting." This is obviously a very simplistic view of multiple murderers. This is reinforced when Brodus enters the cell with "a chilling appearance, with sharp features and a callous smile. He is obviously the villain."

During his interview with the detective, Brodus is depicted offering a lot of detail about "how much he enjoyed mutilating his victims." He is shown with no fear of dying, even though his execution is imminent. More amazingly, the detective is ultimate attacked by Brodus in the cell, forcing him to be restrained by three prison guards. Due to injuries from the violent interaction, Brutus must go to the hospital and thus his execution is delayed, infuriating the detective, who of course sees Brodus as a high danger to the innocent community.

Caldwell reviews episodes of other, similar shows, illustrating that this depiction of the cold-blooded, nonredeemable killer is common in crime shows. For example, in one episode of *Crime Scene Investigation* (CSI) titled, "DOA for a Day," the CSI unit is pursuing an active serial killer called "Suspect X." Graphic scenes depict mutilated bodies of the victims of "Suspect X," who has tortured her victims. After being captured by the police—and in fact, shot in the chest—the killer is asked, "What goes through your mind when you kill?" Her response, cold and matter of fact, is: "Besides playing God, pulling the trigger is like taking a deep breath of fresh air."

What is quite remarkable about these shows is that they are meant to be entertainment! And, based on ratings alone, the shows are highly popular, meaning that consumers are "buying" them. Logically, then, we can assume these shows have effects on what people tend to think about murder and murderers. Caldwell speculates that the shows also likely impact what people think about members of the criminal justice system. For example, police and prosecutors are depicted as good people working for justice, not influenced by politics or ideology or anything other than doing the right thing. They are what stands between orderly, functional society and crime-ridden danger zones across the country.

Other research on crime in the entertainment media illustrates that violence, murder, and graphic death have increased over time. For example, a study by Shipley and Cavender (2001) analyzed the five top-grossing films in a one year period over four decades (i.e., 1964, 1974, 1984, and 1994). The authors found that violence generally increased across the four decades. In 1964, the five top-grossing films contained a total of 144 violent acts (an average of 29 acts per film). In 1974, the five top-grossing films contained a total of 168 violent acts (an average of 34 acts per film). In 1984, the five top-grossing films contained a total of 307 violent acts (an average of 61 acts per film). In 1994, the five top-grossing films depicted a total of 223 violent acts (an average of 45 acts per film).

Instances of death also rose over time. In 1964, the five films showed a total of 41 deaths (an average of 8 deaths per film). In 1974, the five films showed a total of 44 deaths (an average of 9 deaths per film). In 1984, the five films showed 38 deaths (an average of 8 deaths per film). In 1994, the five films showed 76 deaths (an average of 15 deaths per film).

Graphic violence and graphic death also rose. Acts of graphic violence increased from 2 in 1964 to 12 in 1974 to 16 in 1984 to 64 in 1994. Graphic deaths increased from 0 in 1964 to 6 in 1974 to 10 in 1984 to 47 in 1994. This finding is consistent with claims that violence, graphic violence, and murder are becoming more common in the mainstream media. Potential implications for society, including increased violent behavior in society, are real possibilities.

However, acts of violence did not increase equally across all genres. Movies in two genres showed the most violence—action and disaster films. Another study of "slasher films" found that violent acts became more common, increasing from an average of 40 violent acts per film in 1980 to an average of 47 acts per film in 1985 to an average of 70 violent acts per film in 1989. Obviously, the violence in "slasher films" is graphic in nature, often showing very bloody attacks with major close-ups of injuries. Popular "slasher films" feature gruesome killers like Freddie Kruger (pictured from *Nightmare on Elm Street*), Jason Voorhies (from *Friday the 13th*), Michael Myers (from *Halloween*), and so many others.

Since the 1990s, it is certain that acts of violence and death have increased further. In fact, many of the best grossing films of today feature many acts of violence. Some even depict dozens if not hundreds of acts of violence, deaths, and graphic deaths. Olson (2013) compiled a list of deaths in films in order to demonstrate the deadliest films ever made based on "on-screen kills." The top 25 films show from 247 deaths (Rambo, 2008) to 836 (Lord of the Rings: Return of the Kings, 2003). The film *300* (released in 2007), which depicted bloody, gory, graphic deaths, came in at third, with 600 on-screen deaths. Interestingly, few of these movies ever feature the death penalty, but they very likely impact perceptions of murder, murderers, and the punishments they deserve based on their heinous acts. We might suspect that, as acts of graphic violence and death rise over time, people will likely become desensitized to death itself. This could lead to perhaps even disinterest in state-sanctioned killings, whether it be through war or even through capital punishment (Krahe, Moller, Huesman, Kirwil, & Felber, 2001; Thussu & Freedman, 2003; Scharrer, 2008).

Implication of Media Coverage of Capital Punishment

Media coverage of the realities of capital punishment may help change opinions in the United States. For example, increased coverage of innocent people being released from death row has helped weaken support of the death penalty, as noted earlier. An analysis of nearly 40,000 stories from the *Washington*

Post and Associated Press showed that support for capital punishment is directly impacted by media coverage including declining support in the face of problems with capital punishment practice (Fan, Keltner, & Wyatt, 2002). At least one national study, however, shows the latter effect to be partially dependent on race, meaning that African Americans are more likely than whites to change their opinion of capital punishment (Peffley & Hurwitz, 2007).

Yet a recent national poll conducted by the Pew Research Center shows that, for the first time since the 1960s, a majority of Americans no longer say they support the death penalty (only 49% answered "strongly favor" or "favor" the death penalty for persons convicted of murder?"). Figure 5.5 illustrates how support for the death penalty has begun to fall in the U.S., as measured in the Gallup Poll's question, "Are you in favor of the death penalty for a person convicted of murder?" As noted earlier, this is at least partially due to the way the media have been covering capital punishment in the past decade and longer. There is an increased focus by the media on problems with the application of capital punishment, including its excessive cost, alleged racial bias, and threat to the innocent.

Many are skeptical about whether this kind of critical coverage will continue, however, especially given the media's reliance on violence to sell both news and entertainment to "consumers." The "commercial interests that create and maintain" falsehoods about crime and criminal justice "are advanced by this emphasis on fear-arousing sensationalism" (Haney, 2009: 725). That is, media corporations are operated for profit, and whatever sells is what they will provide. Offering relentless coverage of crime and violence increases ratings and simultaneously keeps people in their seats watching—even if in fear—which guarantees higher exposure to consumers of the media to the advertising that pays for the programs we watch (Beale, 2006).

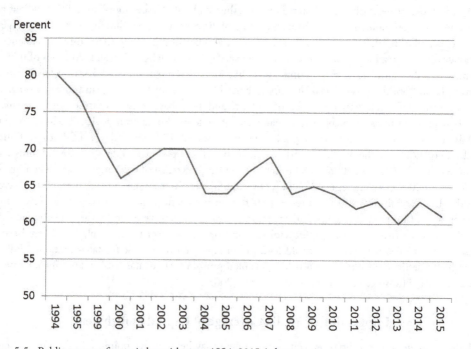

Figure 5.5 Public support for capital punishment, 1994–2015 (select years).

As long as the media continue to focus on crime and violence and to depict it the way they do, we can expect support for capital punishment to remain high. Haney (2009, p. 726) writes: "Intense public fear over violent crime, anxiety over the perceived threat of victimization, and fury directed at perpetrators can drive up support for the death penalty in general." Further, Haney (2009, p. 726) suggests it makes "fair administration of the death penalty" less likely. People become less concerned with and receptive to the mitigating factors that reduce the likelihood of imposing death sentences when they are constantly bombarded with images of the "monster," "thrill killer," "stone killer," rampage killer," "natural born killer," and so on.

In reality, homicides in the U.S. tend to be committed by people in the course of arguments, commission of felonies, by strangers, and in the context of gangs. However, they also occur among friends and acquaintances, in families, and even in intimate relationships. According to the Bureau of Justice Statistics (Cooper & Smith, 2011), homicide data from 1980 to 2008 show that, among homicides where the killer is known to authorities, only 22% of killers were strangers, whereas 78% were nonstrangers. This includes 49% of killers who were acquaintances of victims, 12% who were family members, 10% who were spouses, and 6% who were boyfriends/girlfriends. These data demonstrate that media depictions of homicide are highly inaccurate. Given that the public perceptions of crime, including homicide, come mostly from the media (because, thankfully, far less than 1% of Americans are murdered in any year or know someone who is), it makes sense that when people make decisions about what we should do to prevent murder they will tend to favor punitive approaches that offer the promise of public safety (Beale, 2006; Dowler, 2003).

Since studies illustrate that people tend to see criminal behavior as emanating from rational choices, making offenders morally and legally responsible for their behaviors, the death penalty appears to be a rational response to murder. And even though a large percentage of Americans favor prevention and rehabilitation as approaches to deal with crime generally, the same cannot be said of how we've historically tended to want to deal with violent offenders including murderers. Further, even though about twice as many Americans favor putting money toward reducing social and economic problems that lead to crime than toward deterring crime through more police and punishment, the same is not true when it comes to violent offenders, especially the worst of the worst depicted in the mainstream media (according to Opportunity Agenda, 2014). This could explain why majority opinion has been in favor of capital punishment from the 1960s until today, even in the face of significant problems with death penalty practice—excessive cost, wrongful conviction, and racial bias (Robinson, 2011). It might also help us understand why states in the U.S. continue to use capital punishment, even though nearly all of our allies have abandoned it.

In the not-too-distant future, when more and more states have abolished the death penalty, and executions have thus become even rarer, we will look back on the role played by the media. Scholars will likely conclude, first, that media coverage of violent crime and murder maintained a high level of support for the punishment. Yet, they will, second, probably conclude that increased media coverage of problems with capital punishment ultimately helped the nation move away from the death penalty.

References

Bandes, S. (2004). Fear factor: The role of the media in covering and shaping the death penalty. *Ohio State Journal of Criminal Law, 1*, 585–597.

Bandes, S. (2008). Repellent crimes and rational deliberation: Emotion and the death penalty. *Vermont Law Review, 33*, 489–526.

Banner, S. (2003). *The death penalty: An American primer*. Cambridge, MA: Harvard University Press.

Baumgartner, F., Linn, S., & Boydstun (2008). *The decline of the death penalty: How media framing changed capital punishment in America*. Retrieved from http://psfaculty.ucdavis.edu/boydstun/CV_and_Research_files/Baumgartner_Linn_Boydstun_Ch9_final_draft.pdf

Beale, S. (2006). The news media's influence on criminal justice policy: How market-driven news promotes punitiveness. *William & Mary Law Review, 48*(2), 397–481.

Belknap, J. (2001). *The invisible woman: Gender, crime, and justice.* Belmont, CA: Wadsworth.

Bessler, J. (1997). *Death in the dark: Midnight executions in America.* Boston, MA: Northeastern University Press.

Bohm, R. (2011). *DeathQuest: An introduction to the theory and practice of capital punishment in the United States.* New York: Routledge.

Britta, S., & Noga-Styron, K. (2014). Media consumption and support for capital punishment. *Criminal Justice Review, 39*(10), 81–100.

Butler, B. (2007). The role of death qualification in jurors' susceptibility to pretrial publicity. *Journal of Applied Social Psychology, 37*(1), 115–123.

Caldwell, R. (2009). Less human than human: American crime dramas' influence on capital punishment. *Interactions, 18*(2). Retrieved from https://itunes.apple.com/ca/book/less-human-than-human-american/id486195613?mt=11

Caravelis, C., & Robinson, M. (2013). Perceptions of capital punishment among law enforcement officers in North Carolina. *International Journal of Criminal Justice Sciences, 8*(2), 153–165.

Chermak, S. (1995). *Victims in the news: Crime and the American news media.* Boulder, CO: Westview Press.

Chiricos, T., Padgett, K., & Gertz, M. (2000). Fear, TV news, and the reality of crime. *Criminology, 38,* 755–786.

Cooper, A., & Smith, E. (2011). Homicide trends in the United States, 1980–2008. *U.S. Department of Justice, Office of Justice Programs, Bureau of Justice Statistics.* Retrieved from www.bjs.gov/content/pub/pdf/htus8008.pdf

Dardis, F., Baumgartner, F., Boydstun, A., De Boef, S., & Shen, F. (2008). Media framing of capital punishment and its impact on individuals' cognitive responses. *Mass Communication & Society, 11*(2), 115–140.

Death Penalty Information Center. (2006). *Additional innocence information, Executed but possibly innocent.* Retrieved from www.deathpenaltyinfo.org/article.php?scid=6&did=111#executed

Death Penalty Information Center. (2016a). *Executions in the United States.* Retrieved from http://deathpenaltyinfo.org/executions-united-states

Death Penalty Information Center. (2016b). *The innocence list.* Retrieved from http://deathpenaltyinfo.org/innocence-list-those-freed-death-row

Death Penalty Information Center. (2016c). *Sentencing.* Retrieved from http://deathpenaltyinfo.org/death-penalty-sentencing-information

Disaster Center. (2016). *U.S. crime rates 1960–2015.* Retrieved from www.disastercenter.com/crime/uscrime.htm

Dow, D., & McNeese, B. (2004). Invisible executions: A preliminary analysis of publication rates in death penalty cases in selected jurisdictions. *Texas Journal of Civil Liberties & Civil Rights, 8*(2), 149–173.

Dowler, K. (2003). Media consumption and public attitudes toward crime and justice: The relationship between fear of crime, punitive attitudes, and perceived police effectiveness. *Journal of Criminal Justice and Popular Culture, 10*(2), 109–126.

Fan, D., Keltner, K., & Wyatt, R. (2002). A matter of guilt or innocence: How news reports affect support for the death penalty in the United States. *International Journal of Public Opinion Research, 14,* 439–452.

Farr, K. (2008). Defeminizing and dehumanizing female murders: Depictions of lesbians on death row. *Women and Language, 24*(1), 49–66.

Garland, D. (2002). The cultural uses of capital punishment. *Punishment & Society, 4*(4), 459–487.

Grann, D. (2009, September 7). Trial by fire: Did Texas execute an innocent man? *The New Yorker.* https://www.newyorker.com/magazine/2009/09/07/trial-by-fire

Haney, C. (2009). Media criminology and the death penalty. *DePaul Law Review, 58*(3), 689–740.

Haney, C., & Greene, S. (2004). Capital constructions: Newspaper reporting in death penalty cases. *Analysis of Social Issues and Public Policy, 4*(1), 129–150.

Hayes, D. (2013, March 17). How the media is killing the death penalty. *Washington Post.* Retrieved from www.washingtonpost.com/news/wonk/wp/2013/03/17/how-the-media-is-killing-the-death-penalty/

Hochstetler, D. (2001). Reporting of executions in U.S. newspapers. *Journal of Crime & Justice, 24*(1), 1–13.

Holbert, R., Shah, D., & Kwak, N. (2004). Fear, authority, and justice: Crime-related TV viewing and endorsements of capital punishment and gun ownership. *Journal & Mass Communication Quarterly, 81*(2), 343–363.

Jacoby, J., Bronson, E., Wilczak, A., Mack, J., Suter, D., Xu, Q., & Rosenmerkel, S. (2008). The newsworthiness of executions. *Journal of Criminal Justice and Popular Culture, 15*(2), 168–188. Retrieved from www.albany.edu/scj/jcjpc/vol15is2/Jacoby_et_al.pdf

Johnson, R. (1998). *Death work: A study of the modern execution process.* Belmont, CA: Wadsworth.

Koch, L., Wark, C., & Galliher, J. (2012). *The death of the American death penalty: States still leading the way.* Boston, MA: Northeastern University Press.

Kort-Butler, L., & Hartshorn, K. (2011). Watching the detectives: Crime programming, fear of crime, and attitudes about the criminal justice system. *Sociological Quarterly, 52*(1), 36–55.

Krahe, B., Moller, I., Huesman, L., Kirwil, L., & Felber, J. (2001). Desensitization to media violence: Links with habitual media violence exposure, aggressive cognitions, and aggressive behavior. *Journal of Personality and Social Psychology, 100*(4), 630–646.

LaChance, D. (2007). Last words, last meals, and last stands: Agency and individuality in the modern execution process. *Law and Social Inquiry, 32*(3), 701–724.

Leighton, P. (2009). *Televising executions: An overview of the arguments.* Retrieved from http://paulsjusticepage.com/cjethics/6-emergingissues/tvexecutions.htm

Liebman, J., Fagan, J., Rifkind, S., & West, V., Davies, G., & Kiss, A. (2002). *A broken system, part II: Why there is so much error in capital cases, and what can be done about it?* Retrieved from http://www2.law.columbia.edu/brokensystem2/index2.html

Lim, C., Snyder, J., & Stromberg, D. (2010). The judge, the politician, and the press: Newspaper coverage and criminal sentencing across electoral systems. *American Economic Journal: Applied Economics, 7*(4), 103–135.

Lin, J., & Phillips, S. (2014). Media coverage of capital murder: Exceptions sustain the rule. *Justice Quarterly, 311*(5), 934.

Lipschultz, J., & Hilt, M. (1999). Mass media and the death penalty: Social construction of three Nebraska executions. *Journal of Broadcasting & Electronic Media, 43*(2), 236–253.

Lynch, M. (2002). Capital punishment as moral imperative: Pro-death-penalty discourse on the Internet. *Punishment & Society, 4*(2), 213–236.

Miller, K., & Hunt, S. (2008). Exit stage left: A dramaturgical analysis of media accounts of executions in America. *Journal of Criminal Justice and Popular Culture, 15*(2), 189–217. Retrieved from www.albany.edu/scj/jcjpc/vol15is2/MillerHunt.pdf

Mills, S. (2006, August 25). Cameron Todd Willingham case: Expert says fire for which father was executed was not arson. *Chicago Tribune.* http://articles.chicagotribune.com/2009-08-25/news/0908240429_1_cameron-todd-willingham-texas-forensic-science-commission-willingham-case

Nielsen. (2016). *Top 10 list.* Retrieved from www.nielsen.com/us/en/top10s.html

Niven, D. (2002). Bolstering an illusory majority: The effects of the media's portrayal of death penalty support. *Social Science Quarterly, 83*(3), 671–689.

Niven, D. (2004). Southern newspaper coverage of exonerations from death row. *Journal of Criminal Justice and Popular Culture, 11*(1), 20–31.

Olson, R. (2013). *Top 25 deadliest films of all time by on-screen death counts.* Retrieved from www.randalolson.com/2013/12/31/deadliest-films-of-all-time-by-on-screen-death-counts/

Opportunity Agenda. (2014). *An overview of public opinion and discourse on criminal justice issues.* Retrieved from https://opportunityagenda.org/files/field_file/2014.08.23-CriminalJusticeReport-FINAL_0.pdf

Peffley, M., & Hurwitz, J. (2007). Persuasion and resistance: Race and the death penalty in America. *American Journal of Political Science, 51*(4), 996–1012.

Robinson, M. (2008). *Death nation: The experts explain American capital punishment.* Upper Saddle River, NJ: Prentice Hall.

Robinson, M. (2011). Is capital punishment just? Assessing the death penalty using justice theory. *Journal of Theoretical and Philosophical Criminology, 3*(2), 27–66.

Robinson, M. (2012). *Media coverage of crime and criminal justice.* Durham, NC: Carolina Academic Press.

Romer, D., Jameison, K., & Aday, S. (2003). Television news and the cultivation of fear of crime. *Journal of Communications, 53*, 88–104.

Ryan, P. (1992). *The last public execution in America.* Retrieved from www.geocities.com/lastpublichang

Scharrer, E. (2008). Media exposure and sensitivity to violence in news reports: Evidence of desensitization? *Journalism & Mass Communication Quarterly, 85*(2), 291–310.

Shipley, W., & Cavender, G. (2001). Murder and mayhem at the movies. *Journal of Criminal Justice and Popular Culture, 9*(1), 1–14.

Thussu, D., & Freedman, D. (2003). *War and the media.* Thousand Oaks, CA: Sage Publications.

Unnever, J., & Cullen, F. (2005). Executing the innocent and support for capital punishment: Implications for public policy. *Criminology & Public Policy, 4*(1), 3–38.

Williams, M. (2007). How coverage of death sentences vary: A study of two Ohio newspapers. *Journal of Crime & Justice, 30*(2), 53–78.

6

POPULAR MEDIA AND THE DEATH PENALTY

A Critical Discourse Analysis of the Death Penalty in Film

Maya Pagni Barak

Firsthand, or even secondhand, experience with the death penalty: this begs the question—how do Americans obtain information about, and subsequently evaluate, the death penalty?

Apart from participating in an actual capital case, the closest one might come to the death penalty is observing it firsthand, yet the United States has long opposed public executions (Howells, Flanagan, & Hagan, 1995, p. 413). It follows, then, that the closest most Americans ever get to capital punishment is observing its representation in the media. As Garland (2010) points out:

> The death penalty is delivered by a legal process, but it is also a cultural performance. It is enacted by means of legal and administrative arrangements but also through dramatic forms and cultural figures. And if the legal forms determine capital punishment's application and constitutional validity, the cultural forms shape its broader social meanings, its popular authority, and its emotional appeal.
>
> *(p. 51)*

At times, reality portrayed on television and in film can be more accessible than reality in the world around us (Mutz & Nir, 2010). Moreover, individuals need not be actively trying to learn in order to take away lessons from the media they consume (Nielsen, Patel, & Rosner, 2013). Popular media serve as key sites of criminal justice knowledge acquisition for many Americans (see Surette, 2011), and capital punishment provides no exception. Capital punishment, as with other aspects of modern life, is "often 'mediated' through various forms of broadcasting, from newspapers and television to web sites and Twitter," (Kita & Johnson, 2014). Thus media provide viewers with framings, knowledge, and understandings of the death penalty, all of which may influence support for capital punishment (see Britto & Noga-Styron, 2014; Caldwell, 2009; Dardis, Baumgartner, Boydstun, & De Boef, 2008; Holbert, Shah, & Kwak, 2008; Howells et al., 1995; Kita & Johnson, 2014; Mutz & Nir, 2010; Slater, Rouner, & Long, 2006; Till & Vitouch, 2012). If the average American's understanding of capital punishment is derived primarily through media depictions (as opposed to empirical research),[1] then the content, style, and messages contained within such depictions are of great importance (Zimring, 2003). Just what does popular media tell us about the death penalty? More specifically, how is execution—both the physical and social act—interpreted, translated, and reproduced in film? In other words, what does death penalty film discourse look like?

Based on critical discourse analysis of execution scenes from *Manhattan Melodrama*, *A Place in the Sun*, *I Want to Live!*, *In Cold Blood*, and *Dead Man Walking*—five Oscar-winning films of the twentieth century—I argue that American death penalty films use strategic avoidance or emphasis of execution to reaffirm or contest the death penalty. Films that address execution more explicitly, those that discuss execution openly or that include graphic depictions of execution, challenge the death penalty. Films that "mask" or "hide" execution from the viewer by what is said or shown (or not) do not challenge the death penalty. Instead, such films often present a "rule of law" message wherein viewers may be encouraged to question specific applications of the death penalty but are discouraged and potentially dissuaded from questioning capital punishment's role in the American criminal justice system. Through strategic positioning of execution within death penalty films, death penalty discourse and, indeed, discourse about the American criminal justice system are created, translated, and (re)produced. The exploration of death penalty discourse[2] presented here exemplifies the role of popular film in ideological battles regarding the criminal justice system and has important implications for abolitionists and those who oppose the death penalty in its current form.

Assessing the Death Penalty in Film

Death penalty films have received limited academic attention, most of which has been based on critical analysis as opposed to empirical study. In general, this work addresses how execution is—or is not—portrayed in popular film, as well as its *potential* impacts on public opinion. While a thorough discussion of the impacts media can have on individual support for capital punishment is outside the parameters of this chapter, a brief review of the literature is useful in contextualizing the study of death penalty discourse in film.

A number of studies have demonstrated relationships between fiction and nonfiction media consumption and support of capital punishment. The majority of these studies focus on news and television as opposed to film and are centered around the impacts of general representations of the criminal justice system—not capital punishment. For instance, Dardis et al. (2008) demonstrate that the way in which coverage of capital punishment is framed in the news, in conjunction with individuals' preexisting attitudes, influences opinions of the death penalty; Slater et al. (2006) arrive at similar conclusions in the realm of television drama. Britto and Noga-Styron (2014), as well as Holbert et al. (2008), evidence that the consumption of crime television shows increases support for capital punishment; these findings hold even when controlling for support for the police. Mutz and Nir (2010) add nuance to such studies, finding that TV plots portraying the criminal justice system in a negative light reduce support for the death penalty, but note that these effects are influenced by the level of empathy individuals feel toward characters central to shows' plots (see also Till & Vitouch, 2012). In the realm of film, Till and Vitouch (2012) find that viewing negative portrayals of capital punishment in film reduces support for the death penalty; Howells et al. (1995) arrive at similar conclusions in relation to "documentary" representations of execution. On the contrary, Önder and Öner-Özkan (2003) find no relationship between viewing fictionalized capital punishment narratives and support for the death penalty. Similarly, in one of the earliest studies of media and capital punishment, Peterson and Thurston (1933) find no significant relationship between viewing films with capital punishment narratives and support for the death penalty.

For the purposes of this chapter, a close examination of literature exploring death penalty representation in film is required. The most prominent analysis of the death penalty in film is found in Austin Sarat's *When the State Kills: Capital Punishment and the American Condition* (2001). Offering an in-depth look at the films *Dead Man Walking, Last Dance,* and *The Green Mile,* Sarat (2001) argues that capital punishment as presented in mainstream film "distracts" from viewers' ability to accurately assess the death penalty. It does this by emphasizing the individual characteristics and personal responsibility of those sentenced to death, as well as "tricking" viewers into believing they are receiving an accurate representation of capital punishment and the American criminal justice system. Sarat (2001) insists that these films, despite offering up characters sentenced to death who are somewhat sympathetic, embody a "conservative cultural politics" that justifies—as opposed to challenges—capital punishment (see also Sarat, 1999).

Sarat's critique is important for several reasons. It explicitly links death penalty films with popular understandings of the death penalty. It suggests that even films that appear sympathetic toward the abolitionist cause may actually present rather conservative interpretations of crime and punishment. Sarat also implies that such conservative pro-capital punishment messages will be received and evaluated in the same manner by viewers, resulting in their support of, or at least failure to question, capital punishment. Yet such conclusions about the connection between these films and the American public's failure to challenge capital punishment are assumption—not fact. Without assessing death penalty film discourse and viewer reception in a systematic manner, Sarat's argument is weakened.

Presenting an alternative reading of these films, O'Sullivan (2003) argues that death penalty films of the 1990s—and specifically those analyzed by Sarat—actually contain strong anti-death penalty messages. O'Sullivan points out that Sarat's readings of the films ignores contradictory evidence and is "excessively literal," holding character dialogue to be representative of the film's world view (O'Sullivan, 2003). Finally, O'Sullivan (2003) stresses Sarat's failure to incorporate audience reception into his analysis and to properly address films' roles in perpetuating capital punishment.

Yet O'Sullivan is guilty of many of the same criticisms he levels upon Sarat. Like Sarat, O'Sullivan's analysis relies heavily upon his own perceptions of the films' messaging. For example, where Sarat reads *Dead Man Walking*'s portrayal of execution to be clinical and nonsadistic, O'Sullivan finds the portrayal of execution quite malevolent, provoking anti-death penalty sentiments (2003). Furthermore, O'Sullivan, too, selectively uses examples from the films to support his argument. However, O'Sullivan does attempt to incorporate audience reception and filmmaker intent in his analysis of the films. For example, O'Sullivan references box office grosses, highlights journalistic debates over capital punishment precipitated by the films under study, and notes several films' formal connections to the abolitionist movement (2003).

O'Sullivan is not alone in his oppositional reading of capital punishment stances in popular death penalty films. In "Celluloid Death: Cinematic Depictions of Capital Punishment," Harding (1995–1996) examines two popular films that center around execution—*Dead Man Walking* and *Last Light*. Specifically, Harding assesses the role of filmmaking techniques, story-lines, and character development in shaping viewer perceptions of capital punishment (1995–1996). Harding (1995–1996) stresses that both films offer rather realistic, nonsensationalized explorations of the death penalty while simultaneously presenting both the "major pros and cons" of capital punishment (p. 1179). Ultimately, Harding argues that the two films endorse an anti-death penalty stance, utilizing their plots to portray the condemned as monsters *and* human, as well as using filmmaking techniques to stress the inhumanity and purposelessness of execution (see also Caldwell, 2009).

Harding's analysis is important not so much for its reading of the specific death penalty films in question but more so for the way in which she contextualizes this analysis. Harding's exploration of the films is constrained to the realm of film messaging. Her analysis of messaging is grounded in a textual and cinematic reading of the films' screenplays and cinematic techniques. Thus, while not entirely objective, Harding's conclusions are grounded in tangible aspects of the films she studies—not just the "feelings" she gets while watching them.

In more recent work, Sarat addresses the issue of audience reception of death penalty films more directly. In "Scenes of Execution: Spectatorship, Political Responsibility, and State Killing in American Film," (Sarat et al., 2014) Sarat and a handful of young scholars build upon Sarat's earlier work. Utilizing the concept of "the gaze" and the political meaning attached to viewing execution in film, the authors argue that three central motifs of spectatorship characterize twentieth-century portrayals of execution in film: (1) viewer-as-audience, wherein the viewers are positioned as members of the audience to the execution; (2) viewer-as-privileged, wherein the viewer has "backstage" access to the "machinery of death"; and, (3) viewer-as-executed, wherein the film takes on the perspective of the character to be executed (Sarat et al., 2014). The authors claim that execution scenes not only "offer knowledge, induce anxiety, and invite empathy" but also ask viewers to consider their own responsibility for state executions, "turning the viewing experience into a moment of citizenship and, in so doing, [implicating] us all as authorizing agents of state executions" (Sarat et al., 2014, p. 716).

While the arguments laid forth by Sarat et al. (2014) are interesting and persuasive, they are grounded in assumptions regarding viewer reception. A philosophically interesting piece, the article lacks data reflecting audience or viewer experience in relation to death penalty cinema. This is problematic because the authors purport to shed light on the impact death penalty films have on individuals' perceptions of capital punishment.

Sarat et al. are not the only scholars to directly address audience reception of death penalty films. In "Deflecting the Political in the Visual Images of Execution and the Death Penalty Debate," George and Shoos (2005) provide a nuanced examination of the impact of real and fictional visual representations of execution. Beginning with the premise that images can "deflect" or "illuminate" the politics of an event depending upon their usage, the pair examine both lynching photos and Hollywood films with story-lines that center on execution in an attempt to assess their impact on political debates about capital punishment. The two argue that many depictions of execution in film, as well as historical accounts of execution, can be interpreted as either pro- or anti-death penalty depending upon viewer reception (George & Shoos, 2005).

Despite variation in methodologies and interpretations, the scholarly work explored here reveals film to be a powerful site of discourse construction on the death penalty. As Russell (1995) asserts in *Narrative Mortality: Death, Closure, and New Wave Cinema*, an exploration of the discourse of death in narrative cinema, the representation of death in film is comprised of both political and aesthetic parameters and the "ability to produce the spectacle of death is both a discourse of control and one of potential transgression" (1995, p. 46). Thus representations of death in film are more than mere representations—they are sociopolitical commentaries that serve to reinforce or challenge the status quo. For example, in discussing of the film *Beyond a Reasonable Doubt* (1956), Russell (1995) highlights the eventual censorship of director Fritz Lang's original conception of a key scene that was to include dragging a struggling man to his execution. Russell states that such censorship is indicative of institutional guilt and, moreover, that "implicit in this taboo is the realization that to see capital punishment is to condemn it" (1995, p. 46). Thus the "spectacle of death" produced, or in this case *not* produced, by *Beyond a Reasonable Doubt* becomes a discourse of control despite the director's desire for it to unfold as a site of transgression.

Russell's contributions are crucial to an exploration of death penalty discourse in film. Not only does Russell explicitly link film with discourse production, she also connects representations of death with sociopolitical discourse more specifically. Like Harding, Russell confines her analysis to an examination of film messaging grounded in film theory, shying away from speculation about audience reception. Yet this analysis is still more theoretical than applied, and it is important to remember that the aims of Russell's project are to examine death in film as opposed to examining capital punishment in film more specifically. Thus, while informative, Russell's work does not sufficiently address the question of the death penalty in film.

The works revisited here have produced critical interpretations of the death penalty in film that illuminate death penalty discourse, as well as the potential impacts of popular media on perception of capital punishment. These authors acknowledge—explicitly or implicitly—that the role of film in shaping public opinion is dependent upon a number of factors, including film style and aesthetics, filmmaker intent, studio censorship, and viewer reception. However, it is worth stressing that the aforementioned works do not offer a systematic analysis of execution in film.

A number of empirical avenues of study could address some of the shortcomings noted previously. For instance, filmmaker interviews or archival research could reveal the messages filmmakers hope to convey through their work. Of course, this may be incongruous with finished films (as in

Russell's example), as well as audience reception. Examinations of box office sales and awards could be used to measure film reception, yet this would not reveal filmmaker intent, audience impact, or anything about film discourse. Surveys of, or interviews with, individuals exposed to execution in film could capture death penalty discourse and its impacts as perceived by viewers just as analysis of user-generated movie reviews on various film sites, such as IMDB.com or RottenTomatoes.com, could. However, these methodological strategies would not capture long-term, time-lagged, or cumulative effects of death penalty films on public perceptions of capital punishment.[3] Furthermore, viewer perceptions would reveal the ways in which death penalty discourse is received but not the ways in which it is produced. As such, these one-sided strategies would be insufficient for explaining the relationship between discourse messaging and reception. As a first step toward understanding the role death penalty films play in larger conversations on capital punishment, I will now focus on the many ways in which language is used to create death penalty discourse in film.

The Films

The "universe" of American death penalty films—films in which the capital punishment serves as a central plot point—compiled for this project was created using various internet search engines and terms, as well as film websites. The initial list of study contained 42 films from 1932 to 1999. When examining these films by decade, a definitive pattern emerges that suggests recently renewed popularity of death penalty films (see O'Sullivan, 2003). From 1930 through 1959, a total of 19 death penalty films were released. Compare this to just one death penalty film released during the 1960s (*In Cold Blood*) and one released in the 1970s (*The Front Page*). The 1980s saw the release of three death penalty films. During the 1990s, however, the production of films depicting capital punishment began to rise significantly; there were a total 19 death penalty films released during this decade.

Steps were taken to ensure that only popular, fictional films with major capital punishment plot points were included for analysis (see Appendix A for detailed methodological discussion of film selection). The final list contains five films: *Manhattan Melodrama* (1934), *A Place in the Sun* (1951), *I Want to Live!* (1958), *In Cold Blood* (1967), and *Dead Man Walking* (1995).[4] *Manhattan Melodrama* (1934), is a "typical" 1930s crime drama that follows the friendship of two orphan boys as their lives take increasingly divergent paths. One boy, Edward 'Blackie' Gallagher (Clark Gable), becomes a criminal racketeer. The other boy, Jim Wade (William Powell), finds himself a district attorney running for governor. Despite different lifestyles, the two remain friends. Unbeknownst to Jim, Blackie commits murder to protect Jim's political campaign. Jim is forced to prosecute Blackie for the murder and asks for the electric chair. Blackie is eventually executed; however, the execution itself is not depicted.

A Place in the Sun (1951) follows the life of George Eastman (Montgomery Clift), a young, working class man torn between two women—a factory girl played by Shelley Winters and a socialite played by Elizabeth Taylor. George sees both women, eventually looking for a way to end his relationship with the factory girl when she becomes pregnant. Although George plots murder, he is unable to follow through. Instead, the factory girl accidentally drowns and, ironically, George is charged, convicted, and sentenced to death for her murder. George is last seen being led offscreen to his impending execution.

In the prison drama *I Want to Live!* (1958), Susan Hayward stars as real life Barbara Graham, a woman executed by the state of California in 1953. The film follows Barbara's trial, appeals, and imprisonment, all leading up to her execution. Unlike the executions in *Manhattan Melodrama* and *A Place in the Sun*, Barbara's execution is depicted in extreme detail. Throughout the film, Barbara is portrayed as innocent. In the end, we see Barbara suffocate, squirming within the gas chamber while dozens of reporters avidly watch from outside the large chamber window.

In Cold Blood (1967), an adaptation of the book by Truman Capote, tells the "true" story of Dick and Perry (Scott Wilson and Robert Blake), two young men convicted of murdering a family of four. The film follows the botched burglary and murder, as well as the men's capture, conviction, and executions. Although the viewer does not see Dick's hanging, Perry's execution is shown in its entirety—from preparation and harnessing through Perry's last walk and last words, to the moment his body free falls as the floor is pulled out from under him.

Based on the nonfiction book, *Dead Man Walking: An Eyewitness Account of the Death Penalty in the United States*, the film *Dead Man Walking* (1995) tells the story of Sister Helen Prejean (Susan Sarandon) and death row inmate Matthew Poncelet (Sean Penn). Sister Helen agrees to help Poncelet appeal his case and eventually becomes his spiritual counselor. On the day of his execution, Poncelet confesses his guilt to Sister Helen. Strapped to a medical table and connected to an IV drip, Poncelet shares his last words, stating that "killing is wrong, no matter who does it. Whether it's me or y'all or your government." His execution is depicted in graphic detail.

Death Penalty Discourse

Critical discourse analysis (CDA), originating within the fields of linguistics and anthropology, offers direct insight into the ways that capital punishment and execution are explicitly discussed, strategically implied, or outright avoided in death penalty films. CDA explores meaning-making as a semiotic, or linguistic, social process (Fairclough, 2011). Texts, defined broadly as "language use at the site and in the moment," are central to CDA (Fairclough, 2011, p. 11). Texts contain orders of discourse, or different types of meaning-making, which are examined to uncover patterns of linguistic workings that correspond with certain social practices and, together, operate in association with specific ideologies. Put another way, texts can be viewed as cultural objects that "embody social understandings" and "reflect, reinforce, challenge, and dismantle social orders" (Nielsen et al., 2013, p. 1). Thus discourse analysis reveals the (re)production of dominant, as well as oppositional, societal views and values.

When applying CDA to films, message encoding and decoding is as important as meaning-making. As Slater et al. (2006) highlight:

> Dramatic narratives tell stories that illustrate individual, group, and institutional choices in situations of conflict. To the extent that such choices reflect underlying values, these narratives implicitly are likely to embrace some values and ignore others. In so doing, they presumably activate schemata of values, beliefs, and attitudes, which are hierarchically associated with those perspectives.
>
> *(p. 240)*

Through messaging, viewers make sense of films, and normative ideologies are reinforced and (re)produced. As Stuart Hall (2009) explains, the communication process is a "complex structure in dominance and is sustained through the articulation of connected practices, each of which . . . retains its distinctiveness and has its own specific modality, its own forms and conditions of existence," (p. 163). The "objects" of such connected practices are meanings and messages delivered through "sign-vehicles" that operate through code (Hall, 2009). Thus, discourse is moved, messaged, and distributed to viewers through encoded signs in TV and film.

Hall reminds us that messaging is a dynamic "two-way street." In order for a message to be effective, it must also be decoded, understood, and transformed into social practice. It is these decoded meanings that "'have an effect,' influence, entertain, instruct or persuade, with very complex perceptual, cognitive, emotional, ideological or behavioural consequences," (Hall, 2009, p. 165). Thus, power and ideology act through signs in discourse that are encoded and decoded by messengers and receivers. Finally, if systems of coding and decoding are not aligned with one another, receivers may decode messages in varied and unintended ways. Thus, when exploring semiotically encoded messages in film, one cannot be certain as to how such messages are decoded, understood, and put into practice by viewers. Two different people may view the same death penalty film quite differently.

In addition to CDA, this study relies heavily upon three linguistics concepts—deixis, metaphor, and temporality—to analyze and frame the representation of execution within the context of death penalty films. While unique in their own right, examined together, these three concepts highlight the ways by which films provide viewers with a more or less intimate image of, and experience with, execution. Through the use of deixis, metaphor, and temporality, these films (re)produce messages about the acceptability of the death penalty. The following sections begin with a brief overview of deixis, metaphor, and temporality respectively, in order to explore the theory underlying subsequent analysis. It is worth noting that each film, along with its screenplay when available,[5] was individually examined for the presence of deixis and metaphor, as well as varying depictions of temporality; special attention was given to the scenes leading up to and portraying execution.

Deixis for Death

Deixis deals with the ways in which ideas, events, or objects are referred to without being directly named. Deixis can take a number of forms, including demonstratives, first and second person pronouns, tense, or specific time and place adverbs (Levinson, 1983, p. 54). Deictic "markers" are words in a speech fragment—such as *it, he, here*, or *now*—that indicate some content or meaning not explicitly mentioned in said fragment. Although the use of deixis can, at times, be subconscious, it can also reflect a deliberate choice speakers make in order to avoid saying something outright. For instance, Penelope (1990) asserts that deictics are often a tactic of avoiding things that speakers consider "too personal, too unpleasant or 'nasty' to mention out loud" (p. 136).

The question regarding any given text that shows signs of deixis is twofold. First, does the appearance of deictic markers coincide with specific topics, and second, what might be the source of such patterning? Execution scenes[6] were examined for the presence of deixis. Table 6.1 presents meaningful examples of deictic markers found throughout the execution scenes of all five films. Most notably,

Table 6.1 Examples of Death Penalty-Related Deixis

Film	Quote
Manhattan Melodrama (1934)	• "I came because I wanted you to understand, *before*. I wanted you to know why I *couldn't do anything*." • "But I can't *do it* to you, Blackie!" "You've *got to!*"
A Place in the Sun (1951)	• "You'll have *to go now*, son . . . . *Come on*, son."
I Want to Live! (1958)	• "One more thing, the gas chamber is—" "Now there's no use *dwelling on that*. Just hope for the best." "*It's around here someplace, isn't it?*" • "When you hear the pellets drop, count ten. Take a deep breath. *It's easier that way*."
In Cold Blood (1967)	• "Is he the—[no word spoken, glances at the executioner]." "Mmhmm."
Dead Man Walking (1995)	• "We can't remove the harness. There might not be time." "But *that's it*. When you hit the end of the rope your muscles lose control. I'm afraid I'll mess myself." "*It's nothing* to be ashamed of. *They all do it*."

Source: Author.

these markers are found in discussions about death, dying, and execution; in a number of films, deictic markers replace nearly all references to these subjects.

For example, in *Manhattan Melodrama*, while the scenes leading up to Blackie's execution follow him from the general prison population into isolation and deathwatch, his execution and impending death are not explicitly mentioned until just before he is taken to be executed. This is the case despite the fact that Blackie's execution is central to the film's dialogue. For instance, just before Blackie is to be executed, Jim comes to the prison to speak with him, explaining, "I came because I wanted you to understand, *before*—I wanted you to know why I *couldn't do anything*." Here, Jim is referring to Blackie's execution and the fact that he failed to give Blackie a stay; yet Jim never actually *says* this. Instead, Jim alludes to Blackie's execution and the role Jim has played in said execution.

Shortly after Jim and Blackie's exchange, the warden arrives, signaling that it is time for Blackie's execution. A deictic conversation ensues:

Jim: No! *I can't!* Blackie, I will commute you! *I can't stand it anymore!*
Blackie: You're out of your mind! You've made your decision—now *stick to it!* As far as I'm con-
          cerned you're the best friend I ever had, but above everything else you're the governor!
Jim: But *I can't do it to you*, Blackie!
Blackie: *You've got to!* You're right—get that—you're right!

Here, Blackie and Jim have a rather intense argument about the execution, which is just moments away, yet they refrain from using the word *execution* or mentioning death at all. Finally, Blackie explicitly reveals what the two have been discussing:

Blackie: Where do you come off commuting me? I deserve to die, see? I'm not afraid to spill it—I
          not only killed Snow—it was me got Mannie Arnold, too!
Jim: I don't care who you killed! I'm not going to let you die—*I can't!* Don't you see—*I can't do it!*

Despite openly acknowledging Blackie's death, the execution is still avoided. Thus while this scene is saturated with death, execution is never directly mentioned.

A similar pattern is revealed through analysis of the execution scene from *A Place in the Sun*. While visiting briefly with Angela just before his execution, a member of the execution team arrives to lead George to his death saying, "You'll have *to go now*, son." As he is walked down a corridor of prison cells one inmate calls out to George, "*So long*, kid." Here, we see explicit references made to George "leaving," but no one ever directly states where he is going—to be executed.

The deictic patterns explored above function to camouflage and de-personalize execution. By refraining from a direct discussion of execution, viewers are kept at a distance, the execution is kept at bay. Both *Manhattan Melodrama* and *A Place in the Sun* could be characterized as "law and order" or "rule of law" films. In both films, viewers know that the lead characters to be executed are guilty, or, at least in the case of George, not completely innocent. While viewers may be inclined to question the specific application of the death penalty presented in each film, execution as a sanctioned method of state punishment is never under scrutiny. This is, in part, achieved through the use of deixis. By avoiding an open discussion of execution, viewers are kept "in the dark" about just what it entails. Even death is couched in discrete references. Hence, while viewers are aware that characters are to be executed, execution remains disconnected from the happenings and conversations on screen, intangible and hazy. Not surprisingly, neither *Manhattan Melodrama* or *A Place in the Sun* depict execution. Instead, both films merely imply execution through scenes that depict the condemned being led away by the execution team.

Patterns of deixis present in the film *I Want to Live!* stand in stark contrast to those witnessed in *Manhattan Melodrama* and *A Place in the Sun*. For example, when Barbara in *I Want to Live!* is transferred to a new cell and put on "deathwatch," she attempts to discuss her approaching execution with the warden only to be diverted to the topic of dinner:

Barbara: One more thing, the gas chamber is—
Warden: Now there's no use dwelling on *that. Just hope for the best.*
Barbara: *It's right around here someplace, isn't it?*
Warden: You can order anything you like for dinner.
Barbara: I don't feel like eating. If you'll excuse me, I think I'll retire.

Here Barbara opens the discussion by explicitly naming the gas chamber, the contraption that will be used to carry out her execution. The warden responds by brushing off her question with the deictic marker "that," and telling her to "hope for the best," which perhaps means to hope for a stay of execution or the "smoothest" and least painful execution experience possible. Switching to deictic speech, Barbara rephrases her question only to be met with a complete topic change. The avoidance is almost palpable as Barbara's execution is "swept away" by the warden as the two engage in a linguistic power struggle to define her present experience. In this instance, not only is execution overtly inserted into the scene, and thus the minds of viewers, but attempts to mask execution through deixis actually highlight execution, as opposed to hiding it.

A similar exchange takes place just before Barbara is executed. As the last execution team member prepares to leave the gas chamber, he places a hand on Barbara's shoulder—she is already strapped into the gas chamber's chair—and says, "When you hear the pellets drop, count ten. Take a deep breath. *It's easier that way.*" Without saying so explicitly, the execution team member is telling Barbara to count and take a deep breath before the gas chamber begins to fill with gas as this will make dying "easier." Encoded into this message is an acknowledgment that while death by gas chamber is inherently unpleasant, there are ways to make the experience more "humane." Barbara's responds with just four words: "How would you know?" Her comment is blunt. Not only do her words challenge the execution team member's advice, but with this statement Barbara also contests the notion that execution can ever be humane. This exchange is followed by a rather intense and prolonged execution scene during which Barbara's body pulses beneath the straps of the gas chamber chair, her hands tensing and finally relaxing. Barbara's graphic execution is the culmination of a narrative of innocence, as her guilt is consistently challenged thought the film. Given this analysis, *I Want to Live!* can be read not only as questioning the specific application of the death penalty to Barbara but also as casting doubt on the state-sanctioned practice of execution altogether.

The power of deixis is also noted in examining its absence from the execution scene in *Dead Man Walking.* After being strapped in and hooked up in the execution chamber, Poncelet is asked if he has any last words. He first apologizes to the families of his two victims, acknowledging the pain he has caused them, asking their forgiveness, and stating that he hopes his execution will bring them relief. Then he explicitly addresses execution and the death penalty: "I just want to say, *killing is wrong,* no matter *who does it.* Whether it's me or y'all or your government." Here, the impact of Poncelet's words is palpable. He is direct and concise, calling attention to his execution, but more importantly, equating execution with murder. This comparison is further explored in the moments that follow, during which the film cuts back and forth between Poncelet's execution and the rape and murder he committed. Such dialogue and imagery is rather suggestive, imploring the viewer to confront execution and, moreover, to imagine it, if only for a moment, as absolutely no different from any other form of killing.

Execution Through Metaphor

Metaphor is the application of a figure of speech to an object or action. Metaphor serves a number of purposes. Semino (2008) argues that metaphor functions strategically in political speech, including coercion, legitimization, and representation. As Semino (2008) explains, the interpretation of metaphorical expressions involves "the projection of material from source to target domains, including . . . patterns of inference" (p. 86). Through such representation, messages are instantiated into a given text and have the power to persuade receivers about the legitimacy of people, acts, events, and decisions. While metaphors are not uncommon in the English language context, uncovering the reoccurrence of similar types of metaphor, as well as finding patterns of coincidence between the use of metaphor and specific topics, can be telling.

Table 6.2 provides examples of metaphor from the five films studied. Examinations of execution scene dialogue not only reveal a substantial amount of metaphor usage, but the presence of metaphor often coincides with discussions pertaining to execution and death.[7] This suggests that metaphor is yet another tactic employed to avoid mentioning execution outright.

In many instances, metaphor is used to indirectly reference the locale of an impending execution. When *Manhattan Melodrama*'s Blackie arrives at prison's death row he exclaims, "So this is the *dance hall*. Nice place you got here." The term "dance hall" is not unique to this film—Sing Sing prison referred to its death row as the "dance hall" for years. This reference likely originates in early euphemisms for being sent to the gallows and hung, such as "dancing with a stranger" or "to dance upon nothing." Blackie's comment also uses metaphor to juxtapose a dance hall, a "nice place," with the much starker reality he is experiencing—a prison cell that is down the hall from the electric chair. Similarly, when delivered to a new holding cell and placed on deathwatch, Barbara in *I Want to Live!* says wryly, "Let's skip the introductions—*this isn't a garden party*." Without directly exposing what occurs in this area of the prison (executions), Barbara manages to artfully criticize execution by comparing it to a garden party, something light and enjoyable.

In other instances, metaphor is suggestive of execution and the execution process more specifically. A number of such metaphors involve cooking, such as the exclamation, "They're goin' *to cook him*—like a steak!" made by one of Blackie's fellow inmates. Even more execution metaphors imply leaving or going somewhere. In *Manhattan Melodrama*, Jim says he's "*sending* Blackie *to the chair*."[8] Later in the film, Father Pat, the priest who took in the orphaned Jim and Blackie as children, points out that "we all have to be *given back* again sooner or later." Just what we are all "given back" *to* is unclear; however, it is clear that Father Pat is referring to death.

Similar metaphors are found in *A Place in the Sun*. For example, just before George's execution the warden tells him that "[he'll] have *to go* now," which while meaning he must be escorted to the

Table 6.2 Examples of Death Penalty Metaphors

Film	Quote
Manhattan Melodrama (1934)	• "So this is the *dance hall*. Nice place you got here." • "I was too busy getting to be Governor—so I could *send you to the chair!*" • "We all have to be *given back again* sooner or later, Blackie." • "They're goin' *to cook him*—like a steak!"
A Place in the Sun (1951)	• "*Death is a little thing*, George. You mustn't be afraid of it." • "You'll have *to go now*, son."
I Want to Live! (1958)	• "As I watch Barbara enter *the car that will feed her to the death cell* . . . ." • "Let's skip the introductions—*this isn't a garden party*."
In Cold Blood (1967)	• "You're *sending me to a better world* than this ever was."
Dead Man Walking (1995)	• "I'm *looking death in the eyes*. I mean, I'm *getting ready to go*." • "The *lungs go first*—like a fast choke." • "Guess if I had an allergic reaction to *the shot that knocks you out*—it gets messy." • "*Dead man walking!*"

Source: Author.

117

execution chamber could also be interpreted as implying that it is time to die. In *I Want to Live!*, the news anchor narrating Barbara's transfer to a male prison, which housed the execution chamber, asserts that this "may be *her last trip*, anywhere." While he does not come right out and say it, he implies that her last trip is going to end at the gas chamber. When Dick is asked for his last words in *In Cold Blood*, he replies, "You're *sending me* to a better world than this ever was." Similarly, just before his execution, *Dead Man Walking*'s Poncelet tells Sister Helen, "I'm looking death in the eyes. I mean, *I'm getting ready to go.*"

Taken literally, such words might lead individuals to believe that the condemned character is simply taking a trip, however, within the context of these films, viewers are aware that this is not the case. Leaving questions of the afterlife aside, viewers can be certain that whether framed as being "sent," "going," or taking a "trip," the condemned will soon experience a planned and scheduled state-sanctioned death. As with deixis, the use of metaphor in death penalty films can be used both to showcase and amplify the uncomfortable aspects of execution, as is the case in *I Want to Live!*, or to shroud such aspects in painless expressions of travel, as in *Manhattan Melodrama, A Place in the Sun, In Cold Blood*, and *Dead Man Walking*.

Metaphor and deixis are not mutually exclusive and often co-occur in death penalty films, as exemplified by the deictic metaphor "*I'm getting ready to go*," which is another way of saying getting ready "to die" or "to be executed." The existence of layered, co-occurring patterns of distinction and avoidance does not dilute the importance of such patterns, but instead highlights their linguistic complexity and impacts on film messaging. Temporality adds yet another layer of complexity to the linguistic messaging present in the films under study. Through temporality, the multidimensional linguistic processes that influence textual meaning-making are exposed, allowing an even more nuanced examination of the production of messages that reaffirm or contest the death penalty.

Death Time

Temporality refers to discourses of time. One of the most obvious incarnations of temporality is that of chronological time—minutes, days, and years all progressing forward into the future. Temporality, however, is not singular. Numerous ways of relating to and interpreting time can exist simultaneously. Moreover, temporal relations can be expressed using notions of movement, change, transition, progress, and ritual. In connection with assumption, ideology, and power, such temporal representations often serve to normalize certain places, people, and things while pathologizing others (Halberstam, 2005). Temporality can also function as a space of agency, resistance, and contestation. Hence, through an awareness of various temporal discourses, it becomes possible to expose underlying, taken-for-granted motivations and ideologies that reinforce the status quo. Temporality is especially well-suited to understanding the narratives created by film. Thus, while temporality is just one lens of many that could be applied to understanding the expression of execution in film, it is quite powerful. In the films explored here, execution can be understood as occurring during what I refer to as "death time."

"Death time" drastically alters the perception of time, transporting viewers closer to or farther from impending executions. As seen in Figure 6.1, death time is comprised of three distinct temporalities that are unevenly layered upon one another, interjecting into the present moment and interrupting a forward-moving, chronologically based film narrative: "routine time" (or the present), "hope time" (or the future), and "nostalgia/flashback time" (or the past). This is manifested through explicit and implicit references to time, as explored in Table 6.3. Death time varies from film to film. Films that question the death penalty are characterized by a heavy reliance upon routine time, while those that do not are characterized by nostalgia/flashback time; hope time is found in both types of films.

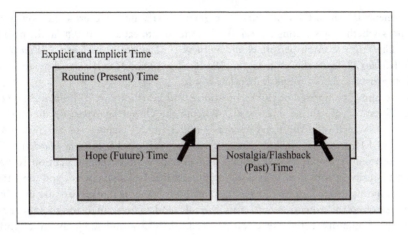

Figure 6.1 Death time; visual representation of "death time."
Source: Author

Table 6.3 Examples of Explicit and Implicit References to Time

Film	Quote
Manhattan Melodrama (1934)	• ". . . kind of *a going away present*, black, you know, for me, and lace *for the next guy*." • "Jim, if I can't live the way I want, at least lemme die *when* I want!"
A Place in the Sun (1951)	• "Love me for *the time I have left, then* forget me."
I Want to Live! (1958)	• "It's *time*." • "What a lovely *going away present*."
In Cold Blood (1967)	• "Is his heart *still* beating? *What time is it?*
Dead Man Walking (1995)	• "The *time's clicking away*." • "I just told them *if* I get a chance, I'd call *right before I go*." • "Oh the *time. It's been flying*." • "*Time to go*, Poncelet."

Source: Author.

Routine Time (Present)

Routine time begins when the condemned inmate is placed on "deathwatch" and is transferred to a special holding cell located near the execution chamber. Routine time is expressed in three primary ways in the films explored here: ritual, "lasts," and "counts." Ritual entails leading the viewer through execution scenes by following the ritual procedural work that is part of every execution and center upon the execution team. For instance, *I Want to Live!*, *In Cold Blood*, and *Dead Man Walking* all depict at least some aspects of execution preparation, including shaving of the head and/or body, changing of clothes, pre-harnessing, and placement into the execution apparatus (e.g., noose, electric chair, gas chamber, lethal injection gurney). Processions are another manifestation of ritual, as condemned inmates are led to the execution chamber by the execution team in strikingly similar ways—one team member linked into each arm of the inmate, often with another one or two team members following behind. Processions are found in all five films.

"Lasts" are another manifestation of ritual, but center upon the condemned. Leading up to an execution, a prisoner is moved through a series of "lasts"—last meal, last walk, last words. These are specific moments in which the condemned are granted the ability to exert some agency over their circumstances, whether by selecting a meal (or choosing not to eat a meal), setting the pace of movement, or addressing execution personnel and witnesses. *Manhattan Melodrama, I Want to Live!*, and *Dead Man Walking* all depict the last meal. *In Cold Blood* and *Dead Man Walking* show the condemned inmates being given a chance to speak their last words.

Finally, "counts," comprised of clocks, breathing, and heartbeats are prominent in several films. These manifestations of routine time exist only from the viewers' perspective; they are aspects of the narrative of which only the film's viewers—not the film's characters—are aware. *Manhattan Melodrama* and *I Want to Live!* include shots of watches and clocks. *In Cold Blood* and *Dead Man Walking* incorporate the sound of breathing and heartbeats into their execution scenes. These sounds are typically distorted in unrealistic ways, amplified or dramatized, and are often introduced in the moments leading up to execution as the prisoner is hooked up, strapped in, or otherwise connected to the execution apparatus. Sounds tend to grow increasingly louder and speed up to a point of intensity as the execution proceeds, then slow and suddenly halt, signifying the inmate's death. This sound-play is especially poignant during Perry's execution scene in the film *In Cold Blood*, wherein Perry's heartbeat is the most prominent noise in the scene. Perry dangles from a noose, bouncing back and forth slightly, until the heartbeat sound stops and the scene abruptly cuts to black, ending the film.

Hope Time (Future)

Hope time is future-oriented, signified by moments in a film narrative that thrust the condemned, along with those around them and the viewer, into a projected and unknown future. It is optimistic in that it often suggests the possibility of avoiding or overcoming death. For instance, the scene in which Barbara is transferred to San Quentin Prison for her execution in the film *I Want to Live!* is presented as if it were a news clip, with a news anchor narrating as follows:

> Today marks the beginning of the end for Barbara Graham. Our newsreel man captures her leaving Corona on what may be her last trip, anywhere . . . . *But even now, hope eternal rides with her. At any time before her scheduled appointment at the gas chamber at 10AM tomorrow, the court, or the governor himself, may yet decide to halt the execution.*

Here, the audience is told that "hope," personified, is riding with Barbara, along with the possibility that she will receive a stay before her execution takes place.

Later in the film, Barbara's execution is postponed, at which point Barbara eagerly asks, "Does, this mean that *I, might get to live?*" With the words still suspended on the tip of her tongue, Barbara has thrust herself into hope time. Unfortunately for Barbara, the prison warden brings her back to the present moment responding, "No, it's just a delay to give your lawyer time to argue in court this morning. *We wouldn't want you to think that.*" Rebuffed, Barbara corrects the warden, "That I'm not going to be executed. I like that word much better than gassed, don't you?" forcing the warden, and the viewer, to explicitly acknowledge her approaching execution.

Dick's last words from *In Cold Blood* provide another example of hope time. When asked if he has anything to say, Dick calmly replies, "You're *sending me* to a better world than this ever was." With these few words, we see Dick attempt to transcend his execution, to project himself beyond our earthly world and into some variant of "heaven." Interestingly, Dick then immediately addresses the police officers responsible for arresting him with "Nice to see you." By acknowledging the officers, Dick brings the characters, and the viewer, back to the present—the moment of Dick's execution. Thus in the case of both *I Want to Live!* and *In Cold Blood*, moments of hope time, a temporality that moves characters and viewer away from the present, are followed by abrupt returns to the present, in which a scheduled death is about to occur. Through this strategy, escapism is attempted but cast aside, and both the characters and the viewer must confront execution.

Nostalgia/Flashback Time (Past)

Nostalgia/flashback time also operates prior to and during an execution. Like hope time, it serves to transport the characters and viewer to a different time and place. While not optimistic, it often entails reminiscing for something that was. In *Manhattan Melodrama*, for example, we find Jim, Blackie, and Father Pat recounting Jim and Blackie's shared childhood in the death house cell. The three men smile and laugh, remembering the time Blackie hit a baseball through Father Pat's stained glass window. Just as a member of the execution team approaches, Blackie quips, "And to think, this is the first time the three of us have been together since the East Side. Funny kind of reunion. Anyway, this is once I wasn't late."

Moments of memory and flashback also appear in *A Place in the Sun*. While awaiting his execution, Angela visits George and the two discuss their romance:

Angela: All the same, I'll go on loving you, for as long as I live.
George: Love me for the time I have left, then forget me.
Angela: Goodbye, George. Seems like we always spend the best part of our time just saying goodbye.

As Angela exits the cell, George is led to his execution. Instead of following George to witness the execution, the camera returns to an image of Angela and George kissing—a time before George's conviction. The kissing pair is cast in a soft filter, as if glowing. The film ends with this image, the viewer and George, having escaped death—at least for the moment. Thus, not only do *Manhattan Melodrama* and *A Place in the Sun* fail to contest the death penalty, they use temporality to shield the viewer from it almost entirely.

As can be seen in the two aforementioned films, the presence of nostalgia/flashback time removes the execution from the narrative, thus removing the viewer from the scene of the execution. The opposite, however, is the case in the film *Dead Man Walking*, which includes a rather prolonged, dramatized flashback spliced with the central character's execution. Having seen Matthew Poncelet strapped to the gurney and hooked up to the IVs pending lethal injection, the scene abruptly cuts back and forth between shots of Poncelet's execution and Poncelet's crimes. The audience is pulled back into the past to witness, for the first time in the film, Poncelet and his accomplice brutally drag a teenage couple through the woods and violently attack them, raping the female and then killing her and her partner. The audience is then thrust forward into the present to watch as Poncelet's body is pumped with chemicals that stop his lungs and heart—another, albeit more sterile, depiction of violence. The scene ends with a bird's eye view of two dead teenagers in the woods and a cut to Poncelet, dead, still strapped to the gurney, arms wide like Jesus on the cross. Here, flashback is used to remind the viewer why Poncelet, a character who is somewhat sympathetic throughout the film, is being executed. At the same time, cutting between the crime and the execution also calls forth an implicit comparison, juxtaposing Poncelet's violence with that of the state and contesting, or at least questioning, the death penalty.

Explicit and Implicit Time

Within death time, there are also numerous references to explicit or implicit time that highlight or mask the execution. As previously noted, Table 6.3 provides examples of both explicit and implicit references to time. Explicit references to time remind the viewer of impending executions. Sometimes these references are quite literal, like the repeated visuals of a clock in *I Want to Live!* in the hours leading up to Barbara's execution, or questions about time like *In Cold Blood*'s Perry asking, "What *time* is it?" in reference to Dick's execution. In other instances, a time or date of execution is mentioned, bringing it to the forefront.

Implicit references to time are more complex and contextual. In some cases they obscure or camouflage execution. For example, in *Manhattan Melodrama*, when transferred to the death house cell and motioned in by a prison guard, Blackie playfully says, *"What's the hurry? I ain't goin' anywheres."* Although Blackie's statement could be interpreted in a number of ways, one interpretation is that he is referring to his upcoming execution—in other words, he is not going anywhere because he is to be executed, so what does it matter how long he takes to walk into his cell? Later, when asked if he has any special requests, Blackie states that he would like to send a black lace nightgown to his girlfriend, explaining it is "kind of *a going away present*, black, you know, for me, and lace *for the next guy*." Here we find an implicit reference to time that incorporates metaphor. The nightgown is a "going away present," signifying Blackie's approaching death. This is also suggested by the color black, to symbolize mourning. Similarly, in *I Want to Live!*, Barbara receives a necklace from the priest on duty, to which she says, "What a lovely *going away present*." Again, we find the use of a time metaphor to discuss the impending execution.

Implicit deictic and metaphoric time references are also used to highlight the grim reality of execution. The last words in the film *I Want to Live!* (1958) provide the one such example of highlighting through deictic time metaphor. *"It's over,"* uttered by Barbara's lawyer to her close friend just after the execution, is both an example of deixis and a temporal metaphor for death. "It's over" is quite similar to other deictic temporal metaphors that signify death, such as "it's all over for her" and "she's reached the end."

Applying varying understandings of temporality to execution scenes uncovers a variety of temporal strategies used to create film narratives. These strategies allow for the emphasis, highlighting, or camouflaging of certain aspects of capital punishment and result in the production of metamessages about execution. More specifically, through death time and the strategic use of explicit and implicit references to time, films become social products that contest or reinforce capital punishment as practiced in the United States.

Conclusion

This chapter explores the relationship between media and capital punishment through a critical analysis of the construction of death penalty discourses in popular film. It also demonstrates the usefulness of linguistic methodologies in analyzing death penalty films. As evidenced in execution scenes from *Manhattan Melodrama*, *A Place in the Sun*, *I Want to Live!*, *In Cold Blood*, and *Dead Man Walking*, movies do more than simply provide audiences with narratives—they actively engage in the creation, translation, and (re)production of discourse. Broadly speaking, this chapter explores several micro-instances of message construction and delivery as manifestations of societal discourse on the death penalty and execution through the use of media projects. In these instances, the strategic use of deixis, metaphor, and "death time" serve to highlight or mask execution, affirming, questioning, or contesting the death penalty.

This analysis not only details some of the processes through which discourse and ideology work in the context of execution films but also explores the ways in which deixis, metaphor, and temporality encode messages about capital punishment more broadly. Deixis and metaphor allow for the discussion of execution without the explicit mention of execution or death. Such avoidance can distract from or call attention to execution.[9] Similarly, through the interplay of shifting and overlapping temporalities, films are able to project narratives—and viewers—into the future or sweep them into the past, shielding them from the present moment of execution.

While it is likely that such messaging about the death penalty will influence viewers in *some* way, it is difficult to predict how viewers interpret and make sense of such messages. Discursive "conversations" between film, viewers, and society at large are dynamic and involve message encoding in film, decoding by viewers, and transformation into social practices in order to have any tangible influence on capital punishment practices. As Slater et al. (2006) stress, prior ideological stance—or one's prior political and social opinions—impacts this process of decoding and transformation:

> After all, if a story portrays situations and outcomes that a viewer finds ideologically problematic, the viewer may tend to become less engaged with the characters and the storyline. Conversely, of course, the more ideologically sympathetic the viewer finds the narrative, the greater this engagement is likely to be.
>
> *(p. 238)*

Thus, the more open a viewer is to a given narrative, the greater potential it holds to impact on a viewer's attitude toward capital punishment (see also Dardis et al., 2008). Thus, despite whatever death penalty messages actors, filmmakers, or the film industry may intend to "distribute" through film, viewers may decode and interpret such messages in rather divergent and unintended ways. As such, future research should examine the ways in which viewers perceive, analyze, and react to the discourse in death penalty films, as well as how these reactions are put into practice; individual surveys and interviews would likely prove most fruitful in this case. Questions of decoding aside, the analysis offered here not only provides illustration of execution discourse in American film, but also reminds us of the dynamic omnipresent nature of discourse in mainstream media.*

Appendix A

The "universe" of American death penalty films—films in which the capital punishment serves as a central plot point—compiled for this project was created using various internet search engines and terms, as well as film websites. The initial list of study contained 42 films from 1932 to 1999. This list began with a general Google search for "death penalty films," excluding documentaries. Once all relevant Google search sites were exhausted, signified by the same films appearing repeatedly and the list becoming saturated, the list was cross-referenced the master list with IMDB (Internet Movie Database) searches for "death penalty" and "death penalty films." It was next cross-checked using TCM.com (Turner Classic Movies) and Wikipedia. Films were then categorized by decade, genre, whether they were based upon true stories, whether they were made for television, opening weekend box office revenue, awards and nominations, and, finally, whether they contained at least one "notable" actor as defined using a subjective composite measure of awards and career notoriety.

Of the 42 films initially screened for study, four were fantasy, three were comedies, and three were science fiction; the remaining 33 films were dramas. Recall that documentary films were excluded from the initial list. However, fictionalized retellings of true stories, of which there were seven, were not excluded. Films belonging to the genres of comedy, horror, science fiction, and fantasy were eventually excluded from the study due to their sensationalized and unrealistic handling of capital punishment. Included among these is the Oscar-nominated 1999 film, *The Green Mile*, which blends historical fiction and magical surrealism. As stated, it was excluded from the study because it is considered a "fantasy" film.

While opening weekend box office revenue was initially included as an indicator of film popularity, it proved problematic as data were unavailable for any of the films produced prior to 1990 and was only available for 12 of the 19 films produced after 1990. Of these, only seven films grossed over

$5 million in ticket sales on opening weekend. However, some of the most popular death penalty films during this time period—based upon ultimate ticket sales and award nominations—had relatively small opening weekend box office grosses. For example, *Dead Man Walking* (1995) had opening weekend revenues of just $118,000, but grossed $39.3 million dollars overall.

Of the 42 films initially examined, 15 were either nominated for or won various awards from the film industry. Of these, there were seven Oscar nominees and five winners. Overall, 32 of the 42 films contained at least one notable actor, including all of the Oscar nominees and winners. This suggests that using the casting of notable actors as a measure of film popularity is likely misguided. The desire to examine "popular" or "notable" films led me to exclude films that never won an Oscar; I disregarded information pertaining to film revenues and casting.

Monster's Ball (2001), although not included in the initial list, was later analyzed and found to be consistent with the overall argument of this chapter. The film was excluded from the final analysis due to its release date and because it does not add any additional insight to the study but merely replicates findings exemplified by other films. Similarly, while not included in the final analysis, a preliminary systematic analysis of *The Green Mile* was also carried out. Findings from this analysis were consistent with those presented in this chapter. A total of three "made for television" movies were also excluded from this study because this is a study of film—not television. This resulted in the exclusion of another notable movie, *The Executioner's Song* (1982), which won two Primetime Emmy's.

Notes

1 For scholarly work on death penalty practices in the United States see Bohm (2013); Johnson (1989, 2005); Paternoster, Brame, & Bacon (2008); and Sarat (2001).

2 For an examination of death penalty discourse more generally, see Garland (2010).

3 The problems of (1) duration of effect after exposure to death penalty discourse and (2) the inability to control for repeat exposure vs. one-time exposure, as well as exposure to other capital punishment and criminal justice-related media, have been noted in studies of media impact on support for the death penalty (see Britto & Noga-Styron, 2014; Dardis et al., 2008; Holbert et al., 2008; Howells et al., 1995; Mutz & Nir, 2010; Slater et al., 2006; Till & Vitouch, 2012).

4 It is worth noting that the ultimate group of films explored here coincidentally provides a relatively evenly spaced smattering of films from the last century.

5 The screenplays from *Manhattan Melodrama*, *Dead Man Walking*, and *The Green Mile* were available online.

6 For the purposes of this study exception scenes were defined as the scenes leading up to, including, and just after characters' executions.

7 Garland (2010) argues that metaphor and associations function to "anchor [the death penalty] in familiar cultural scripts and established forms of authority," noting that the repetition of death penalty discourse(s) influence attitudes and opinions toward capital punishment, prompting people to "think of the death penalty in this way rather than that, to adopt one perspective rather than another, to make particular associations and inferences rather than others that would be equally possible" (p. 61). He highlights five basic metaphors that comprise death penalty discourse in the mainstream media and the political process, including the metaphor of rules, of war, of order and balance, of healing, and of the people's will, all of which are presented in support of capital punishment (Garland, 2010).

8 This quote is paraphrased. Jim actually said, "so I could send you to the chair!"

9 For a discussion of capital punishment discourse characterized by avoidance in Japanese news media, see Kita and Johnson (2014).

* I would like to acknowledge Dr. Robert Johnson for his valuable input during the preliminary analytical stages of this study.

References

Bohm, R. (2013). *Capital punishment's collateral damage.* Durham, NC: Carolina Academic Press.

Britto, S., & Noga-Styron, K. (2014). Media consumption and support for capital punishment. *Criminal Justice Review, 39*(1), 81–100.

Brooks, R. (1967). *In cold blood.* United States: Columbia Pictures Corporation.

Caldwell, R. (2009). Less human than human: American crime dramas' influence on capital punishment. *Interactions: Ege Journal of British and American Studies,* Fall 2009, 25–32.

Dardis, F., Baumgartner, F., Boydstun, A., & De Boef, S. (2008). Media framing of capital punishment and its impact on individuals' cognitive responses. *Mass Communication & Society, 11,* 115–140.

Fairclough, N. (2011). Critical discourse analysis. In J. P. Gee & M. Handford (Eds.), *The Routledge handbook of discourse analysis* (pp. 9–20). New York: Routledge.

Forster, M. (2001). *Monster's ball.* United States: Lee Daniels Entertainment, Lions Gate Films.

Garland, D. (2010). *Peculiar institution: America's death penalty in an age of abolition.* Cambridge, MA: The Belknap Press of Harvard University Press.

George, D., & Shoos, D. (2005). Deflecting the political in the visual images of execution and the death penalty debate. *College English, 67*(6), 587–609.

Halberstam, J. (2005). *In a queer place and time: Transgender bodies, subcultural lives.* New York: New York University Press.

Hall, S. (2009). Encoding/decoding. In M. G. Durham & D. M. Kellner (Eds.), *Media and cultural studies key works* (pp. 163–173). Hoboken, NJ: Wiley & Sons.

Harding, R. M. (1995–1996). Celluloid death: Cinematic depictions of capital punishment. *University of San Francisco Law Review, 30,* 1167–1179.

Holbert, L., Shah, D., & Kwak, N. (2008). Fear, authority, and justice: Crime-related TV viewing and endorsements of capital punishment and gun ownership. *Journalism and Mass Communication Quarterly, 81*(2), 343–363.

Howells, G., Flanagan, K., & Hagan, V. (1995). Does viewing a televised execution affect attitudes toward capital punishment? *Criminal Justice and Behavior, 22*(4), 411–424.

Johnson, R. (1989). "This man has expired": Witness to an execution. *Commonweal, 116*(1), 9–15.

Johnson, R. (2005). *Death work: A study of the modern execution process* (2nd ed.). Boston, MA: CENGAGE Learning.

Kita, M., & Johnson, D. (2014). Framing capital punishment in Japan: Avoidance, ambivalence, and atonement. *Asian Criminology, 9,* 221–240.

Lang, F. (1957). *Beyond a reasonable doubt.* United States: Bert E. Friedlob Productions.

Levinson, S. (1983). *Pragmatics.* Cambridge, United Kingdom: Cambridge University Press.

Mutz, D., & Nir, L. (2010). Not necessarily the news: Does fictional television influence real-world policy preferences? *Mass Communication and Society, 13,* 196–217.

Nielsen, L., Patel, N., & Rosner, J. (2013). "Ahead of the lawmen": Law and morality in Disney animated films 1960–1998. *Law, Culture and the Humanities.* Retrieved from https://doi.org/10.1177/1743872113480868

Önder, Ö., & Öner-Özkan, B. (2003). Visual perspective in causal attribution, empathy, and attitude change. *Psychological Reports, 93,* 1035–1046.

O'Sullivan, S. (2003). Representing "the killing state": The death penalty in nineties Hollywood cinema. *The Howard Journal of Criminal Justice, 42*(5), 485–503.

Paternoster, R., Brame, R., & Bacon, S. (2008). *The death penalty: America's experience with capital punishment.* New York: Oxford University Press.

Penelope, J. (1990). *Speaking freely: Unlearning the lies of fathers' tongues.* Oxford, United Kingdom: Pergamon Press.

Peterson, R., & Thurston, L. (1933). The effect of single pictures. In *Motion pictures and the social attitudes of children: A Payne Fund study.* New York City, New York: Macmillan & Company.

Robbins, T. (1995). *Dead man walking.* United States: Havoc, Polygram Filmed Entertainment, Working Title Films.

Russell, C. (1995). *Narrative mortality: Death, closure, and new wave cinemas.* Minneapolis, MN: University of Minnesota Press.

Sarat, A. (1999). The cultural life of capital punishment: Responsibility and representation in *Dead Man Walking* and *Last Dance. Yale Journal of Law & the Humanities, 11*(153), 153–190.

Sarat, A. (2001). *When the state kills: Capital punishment and the American condition.* Princeton, NJ: Princeton University Press.

Sarat, A., Chan, M., Cole, M., Lang, M., Schcolnik, M., Sidhu, J., & Sigel, N. (2014). Scenes of execution: Spectatorship, political responsibility, and state killing in American film. *Law & Social Inquiry, 39*(3), 690–719.

Schiller, L. (1982). *The executioner's song.* United States: Film Communications Inc.

Selznick, D. O., & Van Dyke, W. S. (1934). *Manhattan melodrama.* United States: Cosmopolitan Productions, Metro-Goldwyn-Mayer Studios.

Semino, E. (2008). *Metaphor in discourse.* Cambridge, United Kingdom: Cambridge University Press.

Slater, M., Rouner, D., & Long, M. (2006). Television dramas and support for controversial public policies: Effects and mechanisms. *Journal of Communication, 56,* 235–252.

Stevens, G. (1951). *A place in the sun.* United States: Paramount Pictures.

Surette, R. (2011). *Media, crime, and criminal justice: Images, realities, and policies* (4th ed.). Boston, MA: Wadsworth CENGAGE Learning.

Till, B., & Vitouch, P. (2012). Capital punishment in films: The impact of death penalty portrayals on viewers' mood and attitude toward capital punishment. *International Journal of Public Opinion Research, 24*(3), 387–399.

Wanger, W., & Wise, R. (1958). *I want to live!* United States: Figaro.

Zimring, F. (2003). *The contradictions of American capital punishment.* New York: Oxford University Press.

7

WHY WE NEED THE DEATH PENALTY

And What We Need to Do to Keep It

Andrew Fulkerson

Introduction

"I support the death penalty, warts and all." This could be the refrain for many death penalty supporters. However, such a view may be argued to amount to tacit approval, not only of capital punishment, but approval of the warts as well. I support the death penalty for certain aggravated murders, but I do not support the warts, which must be addressed, at least in large measure, for this ultimate penalty to remain viable. This chapter will be a discussion of why we need the death penalty and what we must do in order to remove the warts, including geographical and racial disparity, cost, quality of capital legal defense, and the continuing controversies and litigation over methods of execution.

First, some disclosure is in order. Before beginning any discussion or explanation in support of this position I will point out that I am a former judge and prosecuting attorney who has prosecuted a capital murder trial to a sentence of death for a man who killed a police officer during a routine traffic stop. The defendant was wanted on an arrest warrant for the alleged rape of one of his children. Aggravating factors included killing to avoid arrest (the man had told witnesses that he was aware of the warrant and would not be taken alive) and killing in a cruel or depraved manner (taunting the officer as he begged for his life). Does this professional experience color my opinion and create a cognitive bias in favor of the death penalty? That may be possible, but this chapter will attempt to be an objective discussion of why the death penalty should remain as a punishment for aggravated murders and with appropriate procedural protections and safeguards.

Constitutional Issues

One cannot dispute that the Constitution of the United States authorizes the use of capital punishment. The Fifth Amendment provides that a person cannot "be deprived of life, liberty or property, without due process of law." The Bill of Rights was not originally interpreted to apply to state actions, but the Fourteenth Amendment included, among other protections, an identical due process clause that obligated the states to provide the same protections as the Fifth Amendment due process clause required of federal action. Chief Justice Burger, in his dissent in *Furman v. Georgia* (1972) pointed out this constitutional recognition of the death penalty, stating that the framers had "no thought whatever of the elimination of capital punishment" (p. 380). Majority rulings of the Supreme Court of the United States (SCOTUS) have since held that capital punishment is constitutional and does not violate the Eighth Amendment prohibition against cruel and unusual punishment (*Gregg v. Georgia*, 1976;

Baze v. Rees, 2008). More recently, Justice Alito, writing for the majority, asserted that "it is settled that capital punishment is constitutional" (*Glossip v. Gross*, 2015, p. 2732).

The more recent constitutional challenges to the death penalty itself center on the Eighth Amendment prohibition against cruel and unusual punishment. In *Furman*, Justice Douglas pointed out that a prior SCOTUS decision, *In re Kemmler* (1890), held that "punishment by death is not cruel, unless the manner of execution can be said to be inhuman and barbarous" (Furman, 1972, p. 241). But Douglas cautioned that what is considered to be cruel and unusual under the Eighth Amendment "is not fastened to the obsolete, but may acquire meaning as public opinion becomes enlightened by a humane justice" (*Furman*, p. 242, citing *Weems v. United States*, 1910, p. 378). He further pointed out that the prohibition against cruel and unusual punishment "must draw its meaning from the evolving standards of decency that mark the progress of a maturing society" (*Furman*, p. 242 citing *Trop v. Dulles*, 1958, p. 101). But, even with our "evolving standards of decency" in our "maturing society," the Supreme Court, in a continuous line of cases from *Gregg v. Georgia* (1976) to *Glossip v. Gross* (2015), repeatedly asserts that the death penalty itself is constitutional. We thus begin this discussion with the assumption that the death penalty is constitutional. We have seen seven states abandon the option of the death penalty in the last decade (Death Penalty Information Center, n.d.a). So, while the government can constitutionally retain the practice of putting to death those killers whom we deem deserving of this most serious of all punishments, the public and policymakers can have a reasonable discussion of whether society should continue the use of the death penalty.

So, why do we need the death penalty? This chapter will first consider the theoretical underpinnings of arguments in favor of the death penalty.

Theory

Deterrence

The literature suggests mixed results with some studies supporting the death penalty as a deterrent (Ehrlich, 1975; Mocan & Gettings, 2003; Dezhbakhsh & Shepherd, 2006). Others suggest that there is no general deterrent impact from the use of the death penalty (Bailey & Peterson, 1997; Bedau, 2004). It appears that many of the studies claiming a deterrent effect are econometric studies utilizing methodologies that have been sharply criticized by sociologists (Bohm, 2017). Others report that the literature on deterrence from the death penalty is inconclusive (Chalfin, Haviland, & Raphael, 2013). Still others suggest that the conflicting research as to deterrence is further clouded by the "suspicion that researchers tend to find what they set out to find, or what they would prefer to find" (Schwarzschild, 2002, p. 10).

The fact that condemned killers nearly always fight their death sentence to the end is offered as support for deterrence.

> The fact that those who are condemned to death do everything in their power to get their sentences postponed or reduced to long-term prison sentences, in the way lifers do not, shows that they fear death more than life in prison.
>
> *(Pojman, 2004, p. 61)*

However, this argument fails to consider that fear of death while sitting on death row is not comparable to the suggested fear of death experienced by a person contemplating taking the life of another in real time. The condemned prisoner on death row has more than enough time to dwell on the state ordered end of his life. This is in sharp contrast to the much more constricted time frame within which the decision to kill the victim typically takes place.

Donohue and Wolfers (2006) compared the U.S. and Canada because of the geographical proximity and contrasting policies on the death penalty (the U.S. had it except for 1972–1976, and Canada had it but did not use it after 1962 and abolished it in 1976) and found that the homicide rates of the two nations moved in the same patterns. These patterns were the same even through the years between *Furman* and *Gregg* when the U.S. had no death penalty and the subsequent years when the U.S. restored the death penalty and Canada abolished capital punishment. They also compared the states that had the death penalty with those that did not for the period from 1960–2000 and found the same patterns of homicides in both groups, even for the *Furman-Gregg* years. Thus, it is suggested that the suspension of the death penalty by *Furman* or its reinstatement by *Gregg* had no impact on homicide rates.

While deterrence is a valid and important issue for consideration, the difficulty in assessing actual deterrence renders this argument problematic and unconvincing for either side. The conflicting research and controversy over deterrence and capital punishment should lead both abolitionists and retentionists to offer other more compelling arguments in favor of their respective positions regarding continued use of the death penalty.

Incapacitation

While there may be little or no generally deterrent effect from the use of the death penalty, the executed murderer is certainly incapacitated from the ability to kill again. In *Gregg v. Georgia* (1976, p. 183) SCOTUS pointed out that the two primary purposes of the death penalty are retribution and deterrence. But the court also noted the existence of incapacitation as an additional punitive purpose in a footnote to the decision (*Gregg v. Georgia*, 1976, p. 183, fn 28). The risk of future dangerousness is specifically listed as either a statutory aggravating circumstance or a specific sentencing element in only six states (Bohm, 2017). But one can be sure that the issue of future dangerousness of the convicted killer will be a source of argument by the prosecution in the punishment phase of any capital trial. Jurors are concerned with this risk, and prosecutors offer strong arguments to touch that nerve. Policymakers, too, should consider the impact of incapacitation on future killings.

Cassell (2004) argues that incapacitation is the most straightforward argument and the simplest justification to grasp because it saves innocent lives by preventing convicted murders from killing again. If someone's life is taken away, he no longer poses a risk to society and cannot commit serious crimes again in the future. This justification hinges on the concept of recidivism, which is the relapse of criminal behavior once punishment for past crime has been administered.

There are ample cases to illustrate the need for incapacitation by the use of capital punishment. Kenneth Allen McDuff was a serial killer who was sentenced to death in Texas for the 1991 kidnapping, rape, and murder of Colleen Reed. Not satisfied with merely repeatedly raping his victim, he inserted burning cigarettes into her vagina before finally killing her as she begged for her life. The horror endured by Colleen Reed is even more noteworthy because McDuff had previously been sentenced to death for the 1966 killing of two teenaged boys and another torturous rape and killing of a teenaged girl. McDuff escaped death by virtue of the temporary suspension of the death penalty in *Furman v. Georgia* in 1972. McDuff, the previously condemned killer, was released from custody in 1989, setting the stage for his kidnapping-rape-torture-murder of Colleen Reed (Cassell, 2004).

The option of life without parole (LWOP) carries no assurance that the prisoner will not be returned to the community. Executive clemency gives governors and presidents the power to pardon a prisoner or commute a sentence of LWOP to a term of years (van den Haag, 2014). A release by executive clemency is not possible if the prisoner has been executed. There is also the risk of escape. The notorious 2015 case in which a New York prison staff member aided two convicted murderers in their escape from custody is illustrative of this risk (CNN, July 29, 2015). While these two men were not convicted of capital murder, they were convicted killers.

While rare, it is not impossible for a prisoner in isolation, or even death row, to escape. Troy Leon Gregg, who was sentenced to death via the case that reinstated capital punishment, escaped from Georgia's death row with three other inmates in 1980. The escape was short-lived, with three of the men being captured within a day and Gregg being found dead after being beaten to death (Bohm, 2017). While this fact indicates that even a death sentence does not preclude any chance of escape, it does support the argument that only a *completed* death sentence avoids any chance of escape and repeating acts of violence against free citizens. An LWOP sentence presents the opportunity for the murderer to kill again, with prison staff or other inmates as potential future victims. A prisoner serving life without parole who kills other inmates or a guard will face no punishment other than what he has already earned—another LWOP sentence (Marquis, 2004, p. 127). As is seen from these examples, "some innocent people will die if we abolish the death penalty" (Cassell, 2004, p. 188).

Retribution

Even if there is little, or no deterrent value, there are those who support capital punishment based upon retribution. The term "retribution" itself may be entangled in a pervasive misuse of the word, as thoroughly discussed by George F. Kain and Dale Recinella in Chapter 8. It has also been suggested that the notion of retribution is so inexact as a theory of punishment that it should alert the reader to "a mental red light flashing" (Cottingham, 1979, p. 246). But, as found in the current literature, the term retribution appears to be the dominant justification offered by proponents for capital punishment (Bohm, 2017). Cottingham (1979) discusses multiple purposes of punishment that have been viewed as retributive in nature and opines that "it perhaps does no great harm to regard them as planets revolving around a single sun" (p. 245). For the purposes of this chapter, the term "retribution" will be that sun.

Some killings are so egregious that it seems nothing else will do. The killer has forfeited his right to life. In such cases a punishment of life imprisonment, even without the possibility of parole, lacks proportionality. Where deterrence, rehabilitation and incapacitation are forward looking and seek to prevent future criminal conduct, retribution is backward looking, with little concern for crime prevention (van den Haag, 2014). "The paramount moral purpose of punishment is retributive justice" (van den Haag, 2014, p. 233). It has also been suggested that the greater the punishment, the greater the use of retribution as the justification for the punishment (Radelet, 2016). Kantian philosophy proposes that death is the appropriate punishment for murder because there is no equivalence with any other form of punishment (Potter, 2002). In modern jurisprudence, the killer has wrongfully taken the life of another under aggravated circumstances that outweigh any mitigating factors. The United States Supreme Court held that "the primary justification for the death penalty is retribution" (*Spaziano v. Florida*, 1984, p. 461).

Retribution is not revenge. Retribution is a function of the government to mete out justice to those who have violated the codified criminal law of the state. This is in contrast to vengeance, which is a personal and private human response to crime by individuals (Robinson, 2008). Some may conflate retribution with revenge, suggesting that revenge is an improper justification for the death penalty. Such a position ignores the purpose of retribution as a reasonable state response to criminal conduct and "is aimed at rebalancing the scales of justice that were unfairly tipped in the favor of the offender when he or she committed a crime" (Robinson, 2008, p. 115).

Justice Potter Stewart stated in his concurring opinion in *Furman* that retribution cannot be ignored as a justification for punishment.

> I cannot agree that retribution is a constitutionally impermissible ingredient in the imposition of punishment. The instinct for retribution is part of the nature of man, and channeling that instinct in the administration of criminal justice serves an important purpose in

promoting the stability of a society governed by law. When people begin to believe that organized society is unwilling or unable to impose upon criminal offenders the punishment they 'deserve,' then there are sown the seeds of anarchy-of self-help, vigilante justice, and lynch law.

(Furman v. Georgia, 1972, p. 308)

The death penalty thus operates to satisfy the demand for punishment by society and victims. The application of retributive justice to crime and punishment may defuse and limit the demand for vigilante justice by some victims and families of victims. Cassell (2004, p. 197) opines: "[c]apital punishment's retributive function vindicates the fundamental moral principles that a criminal should receive his just deserts. Even if capital punishment had no incapacitative or deterrent utility, its use would be justified on this basis alone" (p. 197).

"Some People Just Need Killin'" (To Use a Crude Colloquialism): Desert Justice

In a similar vein to retributive justice is the notion of desert justice. It has been suggested that retributive justice includes two distinct facets: retribution as revenge and retribution as just deserts (Gerber & Jackson, 2013). In desert justice the offender deserves the punishment. Andrew von Hirsch (2007) opines that:

[f]airness . . . requires that penalties be allocated consistently with their blaming implications. The severity of the punishment (and thereby its degree of implied censure) should comport with the blameworthiness (that is, the seriousness) of the defendant's criminal conduct.

(p. 414)

A sentence of death is certainly proportional to an aggravated murder.

The relationships between retribution and desert justice have been described as dichotomous purposes of punishment. Retribution as revenge is seen as satisfying a societal need to even the score with the offender, and more directed at the relationship between the victim and the offender. Retribution as just deserts is a resetting of the scales of justice by meting out a punishment that is commensurate with the crime and more focused on the relationship between the offender and the community at large (Gerber & Jackson, 2013). Quite simply, this killer deserves to die. There is an elegant proportionality to death as the penalty for an aggravated murder. The death penalty is also necessary to distinguish the more egregious of aggravated murders from those that are less horrific. If the death penalty were not an option, then the only way to distinguish more aggravated murders is to lessen the punishment for less, but still aggravated, murders (Davis, 2002).

It could be argued that a consideration of desert-based justice demands a more fact-based analysis. The facts of some cases are so disturbing as to cry out for a sentence of death. Yet the facts proven in death penalty cases are often omitted from the arguments offered by opponents of the death penalty. "In some ways, these discussions are a bit like playing Hamlet without the ghost, reviewing the merits of capital punishment without revealing just what a capital crime is really like and how the victims have been brutalized" (Cassell, 2004, p. 183). Take the case of Juan Carlos Chavez, who kidnapped a 9-year-old boy at gunpoint. Chavez forced the boy into his truck and took him to his trailer, had him remove his clothes, had him lay face down on the bed and proceeded to anally rape the sobbing little boy. When Chavez discovered that police were searching for the boy and getting closer to them, he shot the boy as he tried to run away. Chavez hid the body for three days until he devised his plan to dispose of the body, which he dismembered and placed the parts in three planters and covered them with cement (*Chavez v. State*, 2002). Timothy McVeigh has been called the "most hated man in America" for his role in the horrific bombing of the Oklahoma City federal building that killed

131

168 and injured over 500 more on April 29, 1995 (Jones & Gideon, 1998, p. 621). McVeigh and his co-conspirator, Terry Nichols, created a 3,000–6,000 pound bomb with the intent of killing government employees in the Murrah Federal Building as retaliation against the federal government for its action in the deaths that resulted from the 1993 Branch Davidian siege in Waco, Texas (*United States v. McVeigh*, 1998). The blast destroyed the federal building and caused carnage so horrific that victims testified of escaping by "following a trail of blood out of the building" (p. 1202). Testimony included descriptions of

> a survivor who had lost an eye but who had not yet realized it and helping hold parents back as rescue workers brought out dead children from the day care center; Garrett's frantic search to find her son and her description of the dead children lined up on the street covered with glass combined with her pleas to "please don't lay our babies on this glass" because she did not realize that the babies were "already dead."
>
> *(p. 1202)*

The blast ignited by McVeigh killed 168 persons, including 19 children, and injured 674 others (Madeira, 2008). Can such deliberate, premeditated and indiscriminate carnage be adequately punished by anything except the forfeiture of the life of the killer? These descriptions from published court opinions can have a powerful effect, yet they pale in comparison to the suffering of the victims. As reported by Judge Alex Kozinski (2004), early in his legal career "[w]hatever qualms I had about the efficacy or morality of the death penalty were drowned out by the pitiful cries of the victims screaming from between the lines of dry legal prose" (p. 2).

Limits Imposed by Gregg and Its Progeny

As noted earlier, there is an elegant, albeit brutal, simplicity to the proportionality of the death penalty as a sanction for an aggravated murder. Yet, while elegant in the context of retributive or desert justice, the death penalty is far from elegant or simple in application. After the United States Supreme Court in *Furman v. Georgia* (1972) found in five different opinions that the death penalty was unconstitutional as practiced, based upon arbitrariness and lack of reasonable guidance and direction to juries, states made substantial reforms to procedures in capital litigation, leading to its reinstatement as a criminal punishment with *Gregg v. Georgia* (1976). Capital punishment has grown increasingly complex in practice since its return in *Gregg*. This complexity results from efforts to ensure due process and to guard against wrongful conviction or execution. The *Gregg* decision approved guided discretion by juries, including bifurcated trials in which issues of guilt or innocence and punishment are decided in separate proceedings. *Gregg* also upheld the Georgia requirement of finding that aggravating circumstances outweigh any mitigating factors and automatic appellate review.

The Supreme Court has also constricted the scope of the death penalty by excluding from eligibility for the death penalty those who were under age 18 at the time of the murder (*Roper v. Simmons*, 2005), those who suffer from intellectual disability (*Atkins v. Virginia*, 2002), rapists who did not kill the victim (*Coker v. Georgia*, 1977), and even those who rape young children (*Kennedy v. Louisiana*, 2008). By limiting the type of offense and type of offender that is eligible for capital punishment the court has done much to limit the almost random manner in which the pre-*Furman* death penalty operated.

Public Opinion and the Death Penalty

Public opinion has produced a significant influence on death penalty policymakers and court decisions in the modern (post-Gregg) era (Vollum, Longmire, & Buffington-Vollum, 2004; Bohm, Clark, & Aveni, 1991). Yet public opinion as a source of power and influence may be problematic due to the so-called "Marshall hypotheses" (Sarat & Vidmar, 1976; Bohm & Vogel, 1991; Lee, Bohm, & Pazzani, 2014). Justice Marshall, along with Justice Brennan, were the only justices in the five-judge plurality in *Furman v. Georgia* (1972) who ruled that the death penalty was *per se* unconstitutional. His concurring opinion was, in part, based upon his assertion that the death penalty "violates the Eighth Amendment because it is morally unacceptable to the people of the United States at this time in their history" (*Furman v. Georgia*, 1972, p. 360). But to support this claim, Marshall had to resort to socio-legal speculation, because the Gallup poll then reported that the March 3–5, 1972 poll indicated that 50% of the respondents supported the death penalty compared to 41% who opposed the punishment. The *Furman* decision was handed down on June 29, 1972. The next Gallup poll after *Furman* was from November 10–13, 1972, when 57% expressed support for the death penalty compared to 32% who opposed (Gallup, n.d.a.).

So, how does Justice Marshall overcome this apparent evidence of public support for capital punishment? In his opinion, Justice Marshall suggested that the public was sorely uninformed as to details of the administration of capital punishment and that if the public were properly educated on the subject, that a majority would oppose the continued use of the death penalty (*Furman v. Georgia*, 1972, p. 362). The "Marshall hypotheses" are that the public is uninformed about the manner in which the death penalty is administered; if better informed the public would oppose the death penalty; but those who support the death penalty on the basis of retribution are less likely to change their opinion even with more information (Lee et al., 2014).

A recent study suggests support for the first hypothesis, that the public is ill-informed; partial support for the second hypothesis, in that education on issues did not significantly reduce support for the death penalty but more information did increase the support for LWOP. The study also supported the third hypothesis, that those who support the death penalty based upon retributive justice theory did not report significant changes in level of support even after receiving more information (Lee et al., 2014).

The Supreme Court often refers to public opinion and legislative action in the various states as barometers of public opinion in its decisions. It has been said that "[n]o matter whether th' constitution follows th' flag or not, th' supreme coort follows th' iliction returns," in a quote by Finley Peter Dunne via a fictional turn of the twentieth-century literary character (Calabresi, 2006, p. 478). Studies suggest that while the Supreme Court does not bend to the public will as a direct influence, the members of the court are subjected to the same social and other factors that impact the general public and will issue opinions that are more or less liberal or conservative as society moves in those directions (Epstein & Martin, 2010). Current support for the continued use of capital punishment for murder stands at 60% in favor and 37% opposed as of October 5–9, 2016 (Gallup, n.d.a.). This is a sharp decline from the high of 80% support in 1994, but stable over the last five years of Gallup polling. It is, however, the lowest level of support since 1972 (Gallup, n.d.b.)

While a majority of respondents report support of the death penalty, the top reason for this support is the Biblical "eye for an eye" justification at 35%, followed by "they deserve it" and "save taxpayers money/cost associated with prison," tied at 14% each (Gallup, n.d.c.). The "eye for an eye" and "they deserve it" appear to be grounded in retributive or desert justice, while the "save taxpayers money" seems to fall into the Marshall hypothesis that the public is misinformed on at least some death penalty issues. That group of 49% of death penalty supporters also would be the last to have a change of heart as suggested by the empirical studies of the Marshall hypothesis due to their retributive justice perspective (Lee et al., 2014).

While public support of the death penalty is still strong, but declining, it has been stable over the last decade. But actions of state legislatures over the last ten years have shown a more marked decline of state support for capital punishment. Since 2007, seven states (Nebraska (2015), Maryland (2013), Connecticut (2012), Illinois (2011), New Mexico (2009), New Jersey (2007), and New York (2007)) have abolished the death penalty either through legislative or state court action (Death Penalty Information Center, n.d.a).

Election Results

This recent legislative and judicial support for eliminating the death penalty is in contrast to electoral outcomes in the 2016 general election. So, if it is true that the Supreme Court follows the election returns, abolitionists may lose some ground following the 2016 general election as California, Oklahoma and Nebraska all voted in favor of ballot initiatives supporting capital punishment (Herskovitz, 2016). Nebraska voters brought back the death penalty by a 60.64% to 39.36% margin after the state legislature abolished it in 2015 (Ballotpedia, n.d.) Oklahoma voters chose to retain the death penalty by nearly two to one (Herskovitz, 2016).

California had two separate initiated acts regarding the death penalty. Proposition 62 proposed the repeal of the death penalty and was defeated by a vote of 46% in favor of repeal of the death penalty and 53.2% opposed to repeal (California Secretary of State, n.d.). Proposition 66 proposed to retain the death penalty and took steps to speed it up the process of appeals and postconviction review. It also provides work and restitution requirements for condemned prisoners and allows the state to house condemned prisoners in any institution instead of the existing male and female "death row" units. Proposition 66 passed with 51.1% of the vote (California Secretary of State, n.d.). The provision for housing those under death sentence brings California in line with the State of Missouri that houses condemned prisoners in the general population of a prison instead of the isolated confinement practice of other death penalty states (Cunningham, Reidy, & Sorensen, 2005).

Warts

Arbitrariness

Who gets the death penalty? National data report 13,455 murder victims and 15,326 murder offenders in the FBI Uniform Crime Reports for 2015 (U.S. Department of Justice, n.d.). The Death Penalty Information Center (n.d.b) reports 49 death sentences were rendered in 2015 (down from 295 in 1998), and 28 condemned prisoners were put to death (down from a post-Gregg high of 98 in 1999). These data suggest that the death penalty has become a rarity in modern criminal justice.

A study of application of the death penalty in federal cases reviewed 2,975 murders that were determined to be eligible for the death penalty. The U.S. Attorney General authorized 463 cases for prosecution as capital offenses between 1989 and 2009. By year-end 2009, 262 of those approved as death eligible had been tried, and 68 of these defendants were sentenced to death (Gould & Greenman, 2010). Because of the timing of this report, there must be unresolved cases in the system that may eventually have resulted, or will, result in a death sentence. Even so, these data suggest a marked winnowing of the death-eligible cases to a tiny fraction of the total. Justice William Brennan noted in his concurring opinion in *Furman v. Georgia* (1972), "the rate of infliction [of the death penalty] is characterized as 'freakishly' or 'spectacularly' rare" (p. 293). Similarly, Justice Potter Stewart, in his *Furman* concurring opinion, stated "[t]hese death sentences are cruel and unusual in the same way that being struck by lightning is cruel and unusual" (p. 309). Does the contraction of the use of the death penalty portend a renewed look at Furman on the issue of arbitrariness? Or is this an artifact of the narrowing of the scope of the death penalty in the modern era of the death penalty?

The United States Supreme Court has steadily narrowed the scope of death-eligible offenses in the modern era following *Gregg v. Georgia* (1976). The following offenses and offenders were removed from consideration for the death penalty:

(1) rape of an adult victim (*Coker v. Georgia*, 1977);
(2) felony murder unless the defendant was the killer or played major role in the offense (*Enmund v. Florida*, 1982; *Tison v. Arizona*, 1987);

(3) intellectually disabled (*Atkins v. Virginia*, 2002);

(4) juveniles (*Roper v. Simmons*, 2005);

(5) rape a young child (*Kennedy v. Louisiana*, 2008).

Yet, even with these reforms, the machinery of death may still be applied to more than the "worst of the worst."

Gregg v. Georgia (1976) permitted the reinstatement of the death penalty, at least in part, on the basis of jury consideration of aggravating and mitigating factors as a remedy to the unfettered discretion that the court found unconstitutional in *Furman* (1972). The states and the federal courts utilize a system of statutory aggravating factors and require that the jury find the existence of at least one of these aggravators. It has been suggested that many of these factors are overly vague and promote an unreasonably broad application of the death penalty (Kirchmeier, 1998).

Further narrowing of death-eligible offenders may be made by revisions to statutory aggravating factors. The U.S. Supreme Court has held that the purpose of statutory aggravating factors is to limit the scope of death-eligible offenses (*Zant v. Stephens*, 1983). Critics state that some states use the overly broad aggravating factor of a murder that is committed during the course of a robbery (Blecker, 2001). The remedy is to replace one overly broad aggravating factor with three more focused aggravators: the killing of an unresisting victim, killing for economic gain, or killing an innocent witness to the crime (Blecker, 2001). It could be argued that most robberies that result in a death could fall within the scope of these suggested more narrow aggravating factors, but this suggestion appears to be a reasonable narrowing of capital offenses (Kirchmeier, 1998). Another proposal that may have some merit is from the Constitution Project and would limit capital punishment to the following situations: (1) the murder of a police officer acting in the line of duty; (2) a murder committed in a correctional institution; (3) murder of more than one victim; (4) murder involving torture; and (5) murder of persons involved in judicial processes such as judges, prosecutors, investigators, or witnesses (Bohm, 2017). Bohm (2017) suggests that such revisions to statutory aggravators will have the effect of reducing the total number of death sentences and thus lessening the risk of convicting and executing an innocent person.

Geographical Disparity—Prosecutorial Discretion

The narrowing of death-eligible offenses and offenders is one factor in the reduction in the use of capital punishment. Another significant factor is that of prosecutorial discretion. In most jurisdictions, the decision to charge as capital murder and to proceed to trial as a potential death case rests solely with the prosecuting attorney (Horowitz, 1997). The decision may turn on specific facts of the case, local funding for capital trials, political considerations, or the personal view of the prosecutor as to capital punishment. An elected prosecutor who appoints assistant or deputy prosecutors typically heads state court prosecutors' offices. The political nature of the elected prosecutor provides some degree of local control over the functions of the office, including the decision to seek the death penalty. However, this local influence can also result in geographical disparity within states (Horowitz, 1997).

Geographical disparity is starkly illustrated by the fact that 2% of the counties in the United States are responsible for more than half of the death sentences in the country. One state, Texas, has produced 38% of executions in the post-Gregg era. The Southern states are responsible for 82% of executions, compared to only 1% for the northeast (Dieter, 2013). Even within the state of Texas, the national leader in executions, Harris County (Houston), Texas, is clearly "the capital of capital punishment" (Phillips, 2008, p. 809). Between 1976 and 2008, Harris County, Texas, produced 104 executions. This number amounted to more than the other major urban areas in Texas combined and more than one-fourth of the executions in the state of Texas. Harris County alone produced more executions than the number two ranking execution state of Virginia (Phillips, 2008).

A study of geographical and racial disparity in Maryland by Paternoster, Brame, Bacon, and Ditchfield (2004) found significant differences between jurisdictions. A Baltimore County case was found to have an unconditional probability of a death sentence that was 23 times greater than in Baltimore City even after considering individual case characteristics. This geographical disparity across the state was found to be consistent comparing multiple jurisdictions, with some counties aggressively pursuing the death penalty and others being much less likely to do so.

The geographical disparity in the use of capital punishment is compounded by the fact that the decision to seek the death penalty rests with the local elected prosecuting attorney, whose discretion is largely uncontrolled by other government officials. New York and a few other states have a statutory procedure whereby the governor can supersede prosecutorial discretion and transfer control over a case to the state attorney general (Horowitz, 1997). The courts have generally refused to interfere with prosecutorial discretion. The Fifth Circuit Court of Appeals upheld the decision of the United States Attorney to not prosecute a person despite a grand jury decision recommending indictment (*United States v. Cox*, 1965). In *McCleskey v. Kemp* (1987) the U.S. Supreme Court noted without disapproval the broad discretion afforded prosecutors in charging and other decisions. More central control of capital punishment also exists at the federal level. Decisions to seek the death penalty, or enter plea agreements of capital cases must be approved by the U.S. Attorney General (Gould & Greenman, 2010).

A suggestion to minimize the geographical disparity that exists in the death penalty is to utilize committees to make the decision to seek the death penalty (Horowitz, 1997). This specific recommendation is that the legislature create committees consisting of seven persons, including three appointed by the governor, three appointed by the prosecuting attorney, and one appointed by the other six members. The proposal would leave all prosecutorial powers in place with the exception of whether to seek the death penalty (Horowitz, 1997). The prosecuting attorney would still make the decision to charge the defendant with first-degree murder, but the decision to seek death would reside with the committee. The prosecutor in this regime would still have the authority to enter into a plea agreement that avoids death, leaving open some continued risk of disparate treatment. The appointment of committee members by elected officials recognizes the politicization of the death penalty but was argued to lessen the influence of politics on the actual decision to seek death (Horowitz, 1997).

Another possible recommendation is to move capital litigation to a statewide prosecutors' office in the same vein as those utilized in centralized state public defender offices that control capital defense. Most states employ systems in which the decision to seek death and the costs of the prosecution fall on the county. Some counties are reluctant to incur the expense of a capital trial, which may result in underutilization of the death penalty. Other counties may be more aggressive and try more marginal cases, resulting in over-utilization, which may produce acquittals and reversals on appeal (Gershowitz, 2010). Intrastate geographical disparity caused by local financial constraints may be one explanation for the arbitrary application of the death penalty (Rupp, 2003). Statewide control and funding of the death penalty process is argued to be a means to eliminate the intrastate geographical disparity that is seen throughout the country.

Experience of prosecutors is also an issue. Counties that rarely seek the death penalty may have prosecutors with little or no experience in the highly technical arena of capital litigation. Lack of experience may lead to errors in motions and trial and produce reversible errors. It is suggested that use of specialized teams of prosecutors as well as defense counsel and judges would reduce reversals and retrials, which in turn would ultimately produce cost savings for the government (Gershowitz, 2010). Such a system eliminates the financial concerns for many counties as well as the arbitrariness that can result from individual beliefs and perspectives of different prosecutors.

The geographical disparity in capital trials and sentencing is unquestionable. This raises the issue of unconstitutional arbitrariness, as was found in *Furman v. Georgia* (1972), where Justice White observed, "there is no meaningful basis for distinguishing the few cases in which it is imposed from the many cases in which it is not" (p. 313). One could make a strong argument that a system in which cases with similar facts are treated in a dissimilar manner simply because of location is no better than a lottery system for deciding which defendant faces death and which does not. The result is nothing if not arbitrary.

A solution is moving to a state-controlled, or state-influenced, and state-financed system of capital punishment. Reform could be accomplished by either of the previously discussed systems: (1) the committee system for decisions to seek death with other prosecutorial power and functions reserved in the local prosecutor, which would require state financing in order to be complete, or (2) complete transfer to state control and operation, including the use of specialized state prosecutorial and defense teams and judges. The advantage of a state-operated system is the capital litigation expertise that would be present for both prosecution and defense. The least politically difficult system is the committee for determining whether to seek death. This process leaves enough local control to minimize resistance from local prosecutors to loss of influence. It also retains the benefit that comes from knowledge of local prosecutors of social norms that may sway juries. Additional state support for capital litigation resources should also be available as needed and requested by local prosecutors. State financing is also a key component to reducing the geographical disparity that is present with the current system.

Either system would certainly be effective in reducing the geographical disparity that now exists in capital punishment. It may also reduce the racial disparity that will be discussed later in the chapter It is posited that some prosecutors may welcome passing the responsibility for capital decisions to another entity (Horowitz, 1997). This may be true for some prosecutors, but the political reality is that many would probably resist such a transfer of power. Opposition or no, a solution must be found in order to address this obvious disparate treatment of similarly situated cases that exists for no reason other than the related variables of location and the discretion of the local prosecuting attorney.

The Death Penalty as Leverage

If there were no threat of capital punishment, would courts face more trials of aggravated murders? A study of plea bargaining in capital cases in New York State following its reinstatement of capital punishment in 1995 examined the impact of the death penalty as an inducement to accept a plea rather than risk the consequences of a trial (Kuziemko, 2006). The study suggested that defendants in capital cases were no more willing to plead guilty and forego a trial when the death penalty was an option, but they were willing to accept plea agreements that included harsher sentences when a plea agreement was reached. A Georgia study of the death penalty as leverage reached a contrary conclusion. The Georgia study found that the threat of a death sentence is a powerful motivation for a capital defendant to enter a plea agreement and is the causal factor in encouraging approximately 20% of capital defendants to enter into a plea agreement rather than going to trial (Thaxton, 2013). The receipt of notification by the prosecuting attorney that the state would seek the death penalty made it significantly more likely that the defendant would enter a plea agreement rather than go to trial (Thaxton, 2013). But capital defendants are not without bargaining power due to the fact that only one-third of capital trials conclude with a sentence of death (Dieter, 2009).

However, the Georgia study concluded that any cost savings resulting from avoiding trials by encouraging pleas appears to be offset by the greater costs associated with capital trials (Thaxton, 2013). This study, then, suggests the financial benefits derived from the leverage afforded by the risk of the death penalty are illusory.

Racial Disparity

The Fourteenth Amendment to the United States Constitution guarantees that all persons shall have equal protection of the law and prohibits purposeful discrimination by government officials. Racial disparity in capital punishment is well recognized and much discussed. Blacks made up 13.6 % of the population in 2010 (U.S. Census Bureau, n.d.), but constituted 41.9% of prisoners on death row at year-end 2013 and 34% of all executions from 1977–2013 (Snell, 2014). This is an obvious disparity based upon race. However, there is a difference between disparity and unlawful discrimination. It does not necessarily follow that disparate outcomes are the result of unwarranted and unconstitutional discrimination if there are relevant legal factors that explain the disparity.

In considering the disparate treatment of blacks in the application of the death penalty, the question is whether similarly situated black defendants are treated differently than white defendants (Baldus, Woodworth, Zuckerman, & Weiner, 1998). There is an abundant literature of studies of racial disparity and capital punishment. The U.S. General Accounting Office (1990) conducted a review of the relevant empirical literature of race and the death penalty for a report to the United States Senate Judiciary Committee. The report concluded that the studies indicate "racial disparities in the charging, sentencing and imposition of the death penalty after the Furman decision" (p. 5). The report states that race of victim disparity was found in 82% of the studies, with those who murder white victims being much more likely to receive the death penalty than those who murder blacks. The study notes that the aggravating factors are relevant legal variables and explain some of the disparity. However, even when the studies control for these variables, the race of victim disparity remains. The findings were equivocal when considering race of defendant. The report concludes by stating "the synthesis supports a strong race of victim influence. The race of offender influence is not as clear cut and varies across a number of dimensions" (U.S. General Accounting Office, 1990, p. 6).

More recent studies continue to suggest similar race of victim disparity, particularly when the victim is white and the offender is black (Grosso, O'Brien, Taylor, & Woodworth, 2014). Critics argue that many of these studies fail to account for legal variables such as the specific circumstances of cases and aggravating factors (Scheidegger, 2012). However, the greater weight of empirical evidence supports the existence of disparity based upon the race of victims (Bohm, 2017).

Such studies have not been persuasive to courts in considering equal protection challenges based upon empirical research. The U.S. Supreme Court held that even if the studies were valid, it would be insufficient to establish purposeful discrimination in violation of the Fourteenth Amendment (*McCleskey v. Kemp*, 1987). It is also recognized that proving purposeful discrimination is very difficult (Bohm, 2017).

Courts have taken steps to reduce the effect of race on death penalty outcomes. *Batson v. Kentucky* (1986) is a landmark case that deals with the process of jury selection and challenges to potential jurors for racial purposes. The jury selection process allows potential jurors to be removed from the pool for cause, such as bias or relationships with parties or witnesses. These challenges are unlimited and within the discretion of the trial judge. Each side is also allowed a limited number of peremptory challenges that require no cause or justification by the attorney making the challenge. Batson limited the use of peremptory challenges of potential jurors by prosecutors, requiring them to show a non-racially motivated reason for the strike. This change in procedure is intended to prevent prosecutors from removing jurors of the same race as the defendant from the jury pool solely based upon race. The prosecutor must provide the judge with a reasonable and nonracially motivated explanation for the strike (*Batson v. Kentucky*, 1986).

The *Batson* jury selection reform is limited in scope and does not reach another explanation for disparate death penalty outcomes that may exist due to different views of the death penalty by whites and blacks. Juries are "death qualified," and persons who cannot consider the death penalty as a punishment will be excluded from the jury pool (*Witherspoon v. Illinois*, 1967). It should also be noted that following *Wainwright v. Witt* (1985) jurors must also be "life qualified" and fairly consider life and death as punishments (Blume, Johnson, & Threlkheld, 2001). Excluding more blacks than whites from capital juries because more blacks cannot consider death as a punishment may explain some of the racial disparity in outcomes of capital cases (Bowers & Foglia, 2003). *Batson* also fails to address the greater risk of disparate treatment that has been reported in prosecutorial decisions in charging and whether to seek death (Baldus, Woodworth, & Pulaski, 1990).

Even if there was no evidence of intentional discrimination that produces the overrepresentation of blacks on death row, there are ethical issues to be considered in a system that continues to subject minorities to the death penalty in greater numbers (Baldus et al., 1998). States should take steps to reduce any influence of race on the death penalty and other criminal procedure and punishment. Such steps should include meaningful proportionality reviews of death eligible cases by appellate courts that could consider race (Blume & Vann, 2016). Other steps could include the proposal to limit local control over the decision to seek the death penalty as discussed in the previous section. This could reduce discriminatory charging decisions by prosecutors, as reported by some studies (O'Brien, Grosso, Woodworth, & Taylor, 2016; Baldus et al., 1990).

Quality of Defense Representation

Strickland v. Washington (1984) held that the Sixth Amendment requires not only assistance of counsel in criminal trial but effective assistance of counsel. In *Strickland*, SCOTUS established the two-pronged test of effectiveness requiring proof that: (1) defense counsel was deficient in performance; and (2) that this deficient performance resulted in prejudice to the defendant. The prejudice prong of Strickland is often difficult for the capital defendant to prove in a postconviction challenge based upon a claim of ineffective counsel (White, 2006). Horror stories abound of inexperienced, unprepared, drug- and alcohol-impaired, and even sleeping attorneys representing indigent defendants in capital trials that resulted in death sentences (White, 2006; Bright, 1994).

Some states have taken steps to remedy the problems related to effective assistance of counsel for those who lack the financial means to retain quality counsel and mount an effective defense. Many states now have public defender systems that include highly qualified and well-financed capital litigation teams. A 2010 report to the American Bar Association indicated that two-thirds of the states have a statewide commission that provides some level of supervision and standards for indigent defense (Stevens, Sheppard, Spangenberg, Wickman, & Gould, 2010). The report also found that 23 states provide 100% of the funding for indigent defense, with another eight states providing one-half or more of the funding. Eighteen states have indigent defense systems that are more than 50% funded by counties, and one state, Pennsylvania, leaves the full burden on the counties. Funding for indigent capital defense is a patchwork of methods that includes full state funding, reimbursement to counties in varying amounts, and county funding (Stevens et al., 2010).

In 2000, the state of North Carolina created a statewide office to oversee indigent defense, including all capital cases. The agency established rigorous standards for defense counsel in capital trials and appeals. Following these reforms, the state of North Carolina saw the number of annual death sentences imposed drop from an average of 12 per year to 5 (Woodward, 2007). This illustrates the importance of state commitment to capital indigent defense.

While some states have seriously addressed the task of providing effective assistance of counsel in capital cases, others still demonstrate only minimal concern for this important issue. As recently as 2010, it was reported that Texas and Alabama lacked public defender systems, leaving local judges to appoint counsel for indigent defendants at the sole discretion of the judge without regard to qualification or experience (Bright, 2010). This practice has led to questions of attorney loyalty to clients, including anecdotal reports of attorneys refusing to ask for needed continuances for fear of alienating the judge upon whom the attorney relies for appointment to cases (Bright, 2010). States that have public defender systems must also appropriate adequate funding in order to ensure effective representation. Critics have complained of woefully inadequate funding of public defender services in Georgia, even for capital cases (Bright, 2010).

The American Bar Association (ABA) has developed standards for defense counsel in capital cases that have been described as "the single most authoritative summary of the prevailing professional norms in the realm of capital defense practice" (Stetler & Wendel, 2014, p. 635). The ABA standards include requiring at least two defense attorneys for any capital case who meet practice experience in criminal and capital litigation, investigation practices, plea negotiations, motions practice, and sentencing (White, 2001). The ABA Guidelines (2003) also require an investigator and a mitigation specialist for the defense team. While the ABA Guidelines do not have the force of law, they have been recognized as "well defined norms" of capital litigation (*Wiggins v. Smith*, 2003, p. 524). Even if the United States Supreme Court does not recognize the ABA Guidelines as law, all states should adopt these guidelines for capital cases. Other reforms to the methods of providing effective defense counsel may include establishment of a registry of defense counsel who meet experience and training standards, equivalent funding and other resources for defense and prosecution, and peer review of defense lawyers and defense systems (Liebman, 2002).

Such actions could also address the oft-ignored issue of quality representation provided by retained counsel for those defendants who are not eligible for appointed counsel but not wealthy enough to put on a truly effective defense. In *Furman v. Georgia* (1972), Justice Douglas astutely pointed out that the rich and the poor may have good representation. Douglas noted that the poor often have the best lawyers appointed to represent them and the rich have the means to hire the best. The middle class can usually hire a lawyer, "but not a very good one" (p. 256). This is very true today, as many states have special teams of highly qualified and well-trained and financed teams of capital litigators to represent the poor. The middle class will not be eligible for a public financed defense but will be hard pressed to have the resources to hire an experienced capital defense counsel, mitigation specialists and expensive experts that are necessary to mount an effective defense.

To ensure access to effective assistance of counsel, all states should adopt the ABA standards for capital defense that are applicable to indigent and retained defense. States should establish specialized units of defense counsel for indigent capital cases and provide adequate funding for investigation, expert witnesses, and mitigation. Provisions should also be made for additional resources and support for privately retained counsel in appropriate cases.

Delay

It has been reported that in many states more condemned prisoners die of natural causes on death row than by execution (Christopher, 2014). The Bureau of Justice Statistics reported that in 2013 a total of 115 prisoners were removed from death row nationally. Of this number 39 were executed, 31 died of other causes and 45 had sentences or convictions reversed (Snell, 2014). In colonial America, death sentences were typically carried out in a matter of weeks (Banner, 2002). Recent Department of Justice statistics indicate that the time from sentence to execution had reached nearly 16 years by 2013 (Snell, 2014). What is the cost of these delays? Delay is a part of almost any legal process. A prisoner sentenced to a term of years will be given credit for any time served, mitigating any harm to the prisoner if there is a delay in transfer from one facility to another. But there is no credit for time served toward a death sentence that may be delayed for years or even decades (Christopher, 2014).

Delayed executions impact the prisoner and his or her family, the family of the murder victim, and others involved in the process. Delayed executions also frustrate any deterrent or retributive purpose of the intended punishment. Prisoners have claimed that these delays amount to an unconstitutional form of cruel and unusual punishment (Christopher, 2014). A compelling Eighth Amendment argument is the following:

> [e]xecuting an inmate after prolonged confinement on death row subjects him to two punishments: prolonged solitary confinement under sentence of death, and execution. Society's

desire for retribution could be met by imposing either execution or a prolonged period of solitary confinement. The combination of the two, however, is gratuitous and unnecessary.

(Simmons, 2009, p. 1256)

These so-called Lackey claims were the subject of *Lackey v. Texas* (1995), where the U.S. Supreme Court denied *certiorari*. The argument has found favor with Justice Breyer in his dissenting opinion in *Glossip v. Gross* (2015), at least in part due to the isolated conditions of confinement used in the death row of most states and the impact on the prisoner. The counterargument is that much of the delay experienced by the prisoner is a direct result of the use of procedural challenges raised by the prisoner in the quest for due process (Christopher, 2014). More specifically, litigation delays in recent years may also be said to be the result of controversies over lethal injection methods and procedures.

Methods of Execution—Lethal Injection

One of the greatest challenges in states that retain the death penalty is the ability to carry out an execution. The causes of this challenge are the controversies surrounding current methods of execution. In the years following the reinstatement of the death penalty in *Gregg v. Georgia* (1976), all death penalty jurisdictions adopted the use of lethal injection as the method of execution (Death Penalty Information Center, n.d.d). Challenges to the use of lethal injection based upon risk of unnecessary pain and suffering from the three-drug protocol of sodium thiopental (sedative), pancuronium bromide (paralytic) and potassium chloride (to induce cardiac arrest) were turned away by the U.S. Supreme Court in *Baze v. Rees* (2008). The petitioners alleged that, unknown to the execution team, there was a risk that the first drug administered (the sedative) could wear off because of the paralytic effects of the second drug, resulting in extreme pain from the second and third drugs before death. The court held that the petitioners had not established a "substantial risk of serious harm" that was considered to be an "objectively intolerable risk of harm" (p. 50). In his opinion, Chief Justice Roberts pointed out that states have been seeking better and more humane methods of execution for over a century and that he expected that to continue without any mandate from the court. Roberts was correct in his assessment, and between 2009 and 2013, 11 states changed from the three-drug process to one drug (Denno, 2014).

Due to shortages of chemicals needed for the manufacture of sodium thiopental, fear from being drawn into lawsuits, and adverse publicity, pharmaceutical companies withdrew from the lethal injection drug market. As a result, states were forced to find and use other drugs. In *Glossip v. Gross* (2015) the U.S. Supreme Court affirmed the use of Midazolam as the sedative drug in executions. The drug seems to have been chosen more because of availability than proven efficacy and has been involved in a number of problematic executions (Denno, 2016). The resulting drug shortages and availability problems have forced states to seek other sources of lethal injection drugs such as compounding pharmacies that are not regulated by the United States Food & Drug Administration (Denno, 2016; Fulkerson & Kinnison, 2016; Fan, 2015).

To ease concerns of potential drug suppliers, several states have enacted statutes that protect the identity of drug suppliers. These secrecy statutes have produced more legal woes for death penalty states and have been called "the newest front in death penalty litigation" (Jones, 2014). The U.S. Supreme Court has not taken up the issue of secrecy related to lethal injection, but the Fifth Circuit, Eighth Circuit, and Eleventh Circuit U.S. Courts of Appeal have all held there is no due process violation in state secrecy statutes related to lethal injection (*Sepulveda, v. Jindal*, 5th Cir. 2013; *Zink v. Lombardi*, 8th Cir. 2015; *Jones v. Commissioner, Georgia Dept. of Corrections*, 11th Cir. 2016). The secrecy legislation in most states does not prevent testing of drugs, only the identity of the supplier, but it does provide avenues for seeking new legal challenges and the resulting delay of intended executions (Fan, 2015). State statutes differ as to the information that is available to prisoners and the public, leaving variations as to what has been approved by the federal circuit courts of appeal that have considered the issue. The U.S. Supreme Court should grant certiorari in an execution secrecy case and set minimum standards for disclosure of relevant information that still provides for confidentiality of identity of participants and drug providers.

Drug availability and secrecy both combined to bring the state of Arkansas into the national and international spotlight in April 2017 in what one news media account referred to as a "frenzied battle over the death penalty" (Berman, 2017). The state had eight prisoners on death row whose appeals and postconviction challenges had all run their full course and were now eligible to be put to death. The Arkansas Department of Corrections also had a supply of Midazolam with a "use-by" date of April 30, 2017. Governor Asa Hutchinson signed death warrants for all eight men to be executed between April 17 and April 27, 2017. The schedule was for two executions per day on four separate days (Berman, 2017; Death Penalty Information Center, n.d.c). Arkansas law provides for confidentiality of the identities of those who participate in executions, including the manufacturers and suppliers of lethal drugs (Ark. Code Ann. § 5-4-617). The prisoners' legal teams filed new lawsuits challenging the compressed execution schedule and the use of Midazolam as part of the execution protocols. Additionally, the distributor of the drugs also filed suit claiming that the state used deception to obtain the drugs (*McKesson Medical-Surgical, Inc. v. State*, 2017). While a Pulaski County circuit judge granted a temporary restraining order based upon the McKesson claims, the Supreme Court of Arkansas set aside the restraining order, allowing executions to proceed (*State of Arkansas v. Gray and McKesson*, 2017).

The courts rejected the challenges related to execution drugs and secrecy issues (*McGehee v. Hutchinson*, 2017) and four of the prisoners were executed. The other four executions were stayed for reasons unrelated to the method of execution or secrecy issues. One prisoner obtained a stay because the Arkansas Parole Board recommended clemency, and the governor must wait for the statutory 30-day public comment period before acting on the recommendation (*Lee, McGehee et al. v. Hutchinson*, 2017). Another prisoner received a stay in order to obtain new DNA testing. The other two prisoners were granted stays pending a decision by the United States Supreme Court in *McWilliams v. Dunn* (2016) regarding mental health issues (*Davis v. State*, 2017; *Ward v. State*, 2017). Regardless of the outcome of those four cases, the state of Arkansas now has a supply of Midazolam that has exceeded it use-by date. While the execution secrecy issues did not prevent any of the four April 2017 executions, the issue was aggressively litigated in state and federal courts and even involved direct action by the pharmaceutical manufacturers and distributors. This problem does not appear to be going away.

The seemingly endless litigation over lethal injection methods and secrecy has done more to cause delays between sentencing and execution than other issues such as racial disparity, mental condition, and innocence (Denno, 2016; Denno, 2014; Dieter, 2008). The increase in elapsed time of death row for executed prisoners discussed in a previous section has increased from 146 months in 2006, when courts began entering stays of execution over lethal injection issues leading up to the decision in *Baze v. Rees* (2008), to 186 months in 2013 (Snell, 2014).

Lethal injection as the primary method of execution has also resulted in a number of so-called "botched executions" (Radelet, 2016). Many of these executions have received substantial media attention and include prolonged and painfully intrusive procedures to find suitable veins in condemned prisoners (Dieter, 2008). As stated earlier, many of these "botched" executions involved the use of the drug Midazolam (Denno, 2016). Justice Sotomayor described the Oklahoma execution of Clayton Lockett in her dissent in *Glossip* (2015):

> Oklahoma used midazolam for the first time in its execution of Clayton Lockett. That execution did not go smoothly. Ten minutes after an intravenous (IV) line was set in Lockett's groin area and 100 milligrams of midazolam were administered, an attending physician declared Lockett unconscious. When the paralytic and potassium chloride were administered,

however, Lockett awoke. Various witnesses reported that Lockett began to writhe against his restraints, saying, "[t]his s*** is f***ing with my mind," "something is wrong," and "[t]he drugs aren't working." State officials ordered the blinds lowered, then halted the execution. But ten minutes later—approximately 40 minutes after the execution began—Lockett was pronounced dead.

(p. 2782)

One solution that has been offered to solve the morass of legal, practical, and efficacy problems that are present with the use of lethal injection is that of nitrogen-induced hypoxia as the method of execution (Fulkerson & Kinnison, 2016). The State of Oklahoma recently adopted nitrogen-induced hypoxia as an alternate method of execution (H.B., 1879, Oklahoma Regular Session, 2015). There are numerous studies of inert gas, such as nitrogen, hypoxia related to high altitude aviation (Smith, 2005), SCUBA diving (Hobbs, 2008; Monteiro, Hernandez, Figlie, Takahashi, & Korukian (1996), euthanasia and suicide (Austin, Winskog, van den Heuvel, & Byard, 2011; Ogden, Hamilton, & Whitcher, 2010), and animal euthanasia (Quine, 1980; Raj & Gregory, 1995). This literature suggests that inert gas hypoxia may be a viable and humane method of execution (Fulkerson & Kinnison, 2016). Hypoxia supporter and former British Member of Parliament Michael Portillo asserts that this method is preferable to all others for the reason that if the state is to punish by death, then it should employ the method "that least resembles murder" (Petterle, 2008).This method has been criticized as a "gas chamber" (Christiansen, 2015), but the real criticism appears to be the lack of scientific study that went into the decision to adopt this method. Oklahoma appears to have been just as hasty in being the first to adopt nitrogen-induced hypoxia as it was in being the first to adopt lethal injection as methods of execution. States should seriously consider this method but should do so thoroughly and with the advice and counsel of medical, biomedical engineering, and legal authorities (Fulkerson & Kinnison, 2016).

Another discussed solution is a return to the firing squad as being better than the other available methods if performed properly (Denno, 2016). The firing squad has been observed by the U.S. Supreme Court to not be cruel and unusual punishment (*Wilkerson v. Utah*, 1878). However, it has been pointed out that the court had not yet made the Eighth Amendment applicable to the states at the time *of Wilkerson*, making that part of the decision *dicta* (Denno, 2016). The court, in *Glossip* (2015), pointed out that "the petitioners failed to identify a known and available alternative method of execution that entails a lesser risk of pain" (p. 2731). Justice Sotomayor's dissent in *Glossip* opined that a prisoner may prefer the firing squad to lethal injection. Chief Judge Alex Kozinski of the Ninth Circuit Court of appeals offered the following argument in favor of the firing squad as a method of execution:

> The firing squad strikes me as the most promising. Eight or ten large caliber bullets fired at close range can inflict massive damage, causing instant death every time. There are plenty of people employed by the state who can pull the trigger and have the training to aim true. The weapons and ammunition are bought by the state in massive quantities for law enforcement purposes, so it would be impossible to interdict the supply. And nobody can argue that the weapons are put to a purpose for which they are not intended: firearms have no purpose *other* than destroying their targets.
>
> *(Wood v. Ryan, 2014, p. 1103, dissenting opinion)*

The firing squad has a long history as a method of execution in the United States. There are currently two states (Oklahoma and Utah) that employ this method as an alternative to lethal injection. Utah has the most extensive recent history with the method, having completed three executions by firing squad between 1976 and 2010 (Denno, 2016). The best evidence is that the firing squad causes a death that is "swift and pain free" (Denno, 2016, p. 792).

It is clear that states are increasingly unable to carry out executions by use of lethal injection, and consideration of other means is essential if death sentences are to be performed. The problem of litigation and drug availability that was present in lethal injection executions at the time of *Baze* (2008) has only become worse (Denno, 2016). In order for the death penalty to remain viable, states must abandon lethal injection and move to another method that is known, available, and less likely to cause unnecessary pain. However, states must act with caution and deliberation in collecting and acting on relevant information in the process of considering new methods.

Cost

A frequent criticism of capital punishment is the cost of capital litigation compared with noncapital litigation. The earlier discussion of delay and methods of litigation over methods of execution are related to the issue of costs. Additionally, a capital trial is going to cost more than a noncapital trial primarily due to the recognition that the stakes are so much higher. The U.S Supreme Court has long recognized that "death is different" (*Woodson v. North Carolina*, 1976, p. 305). This recognition that "death is different" is at the heart of the so-called "super due process" that is followed in capital trials (Radin, 1980, p. 1143). This means that there will be more of everything. A capital trial will involve more pretrial motions, more investigation, more attention to jury selection, more witnesses, more expert testimony, and longer and more impassioned arguments by counsel (Thaxton, 2013).

A study of the costs associated with the death penalty in the state of Washington compared 39 cases in which the death penalty was sought and 108 aggravated murder cases in which the death penalty was not sought from 1997 to 2014. Data included trial reports, petitions for reimbursement of extraordinary criminal justice costs allowed by law, presentence detention costs, department of corrections costs, prosecution data, defense data, court data, state level appeals and postconviction review, and federal habeas corpus actions. The study concluded that the average increase for an aggravated murder case in which the death penalty is sought over one in which the death penalty is not sought is $1,058,885 in adjusted 2010 dollars (Collins, Boruchowitz, Hickman, & Larranga, 2016). This study also noted that in 75% of the cases in which a death sentence was imposed, either the conviction or sentence was reversed.

On a personal level, there is also a greater toll on the individuals involved in the process. This phenomenon is known as vicarious trauma and effects judges, jurors, and attorneys (Mattison, 2012). The physical and emotional strain on lawyers (Sheffer, 2013), judges, and jurors (Antonio, 2006) is substantial. These examples of "more" also mean that the trial will consume much more time than would a noncapital first-degree murder trial. The extra attention to the process observed at the trial level continues at the appellate and postconviction review levels as well. All of this "super due process" is necessary to ensure accuracy in the fact-finding and dispositional processes of capital litigation (Radin, 1980, p. 1143). As a result, it could be said that the associated costs are hardwired into the system. The additional costs of capital litigation and review are just something that must be absorbed if society is to retain the death penalty.

There are, however, very tangible savings to be had by reforms in the manner in which the government houses condemned prisoners while the appellate and postconviction review processes play out. Most states house those sentenced to death in isolation units until the time of execution (Lombardi, Sluder, & Wallace, 1996). Isolated confinement is far more expensive than is housing inmates in the general population of a maximum-security facility, with California spending $49,000 per prisoners the general population and over $70,000 for "supermax" confinement (Reiter, 2013). The state of Missouri has departed from this practice and since 1991 has housed the so-called "death row" prisoners in the general population of the Potosi Unit of the Missouri Department of Corrections. The prisoners are eligible for participation in all programs at the facility. A study of this practice suggests that the condemned prisoners in the general population are not more prone to disciplinary action than noncapital offenders serving life sentences. In fact, the death sentenced and LWOP prisoners had lower rates of misconduct than did the parole-eligible prisoners (Cunningham et al., 2005). The condemned prisoners are moved into protective custody at such time as the Supreme Court of Missouri enters a warrant setting the date of execution. The prisoner will be moved to a "holding cell" 48–72 hours before the execution (Cunningham et al., 2005). The savings to the state are estimated to be approximately 50% by housing condemned prisoners in the general population as compared with isolation (Cunningham et al., 2005).

Where trial, appellate and postconviction review costs are not amenable to reduction without sacrificing essential due process protections, significant savings can be had by adopting the Missouri practice of mainstreaming condemned prisoners until the time of execution. Further cost savings may be had from resolving the delays resulting from litigation over methods of execution.

Innocence

The Death Penalty Information Center (n.d.e) reports that 156 persons have been exonerated and released from sentences of death since 1973. All but seven of those were prior to 2000. Improvements in forensic science and the already extensive process of appeals and postconviction review have done much to lessen the risk of wrongful conviction and execution. Accordingly, this chapter will not address this issue other than to support the position that courts should accept freestanding claims of innocence upon a showing of clear and convincing evidence that the prisoner is factually not guilty. The United States Supreme Court has been reluctant to take up claims of innocence absent a corresponding constitutional violation "because of the very disruptive effect that entertaining claims of actual innocence would have on the need for finality in capital cases" (*Herrera v. Collins*, 1993, p. 417).

While disruptive, the extreme nature of the capital punishment makes it unconscionable to put to death an innocent person. Finality should yield to fairness. It is manifestly unfair for the state to kill an innocent person. The practice of allowing freestanding claims of actual innocence would further reduce any risk of wrongful executions. The United States Supreme Court should clearly rule that execution of an innocent person is a violation of the Eighth Amendment prohibition against cruel and unusual punishment and that such a claim may be the basis for federal habeas relief (Mourer, 2010).

Conclusion

There are killings so disturbing and killers so dangerous that some states and the federal government may wish to retain the death penalty as an option for those few crimes. Capital punishment has value as a symbol of official response to the most egregious of crimes. It has value to the families of some murder victims as a measure of retributive (with this term used based upon current nomenclature) and desert justice that rebalances the scales that were so violently tipped by the murder. While needed in appropriate and limited cases, capital punishment has serious problems that must be addressed in order to be able to fulfill its purposes.

Governments may be hard pressed to resolve the issues of arbitrary geographical and racial disparity, costs, and extreme delays in executions that in recent years are produced largely by endless litigation and drug availability related to lethal injection as the method of execution. The fact that seven states have legislatively abolished the death penalty, or refused to override judicial mandate, since 2007 is indicative of that sentiment. However, the fact that an election in one of those recent abolition states (Nebraska) brought it back in 2016 is evidence that voters want the death penalty as an option.

If the most problematic issues can be addressed, the death penalty can again be viable. Just as *Gregg v. Georgia* (1976) revived a previously deeply flawed system of the ultimate punishment, new reforms can also correct the flaws that remained or have developed in post-*Gregg* capital litigation. This chapter has offered solutions to geographical and racial disparity, defense, delays, methods of execution, and cost. The reforms that may face the most serious political challenges are those related to local prosecutorial control of certain death penalty decision making. These challenges are serious and may be difficult to address and resolve. But all of these challenges to the continued use of the death penalty as an option must be faced by any states that wish to retain the death penalty as a viable punishment for the most egregious of murders. States that cannot, or will not, address these issues may be better off to conclude that the death penalty is more trouble than it is worth.

References

American Bar Association. (2003). ABA guidelines for the appointment and performance of counsel in death penalty cases. Revised Edition, 2003. Retrieved September 16, 2017, from https://www.americanbar.org/content/dam/aba/migrated/2011_build/death_penalty_representation/2003guidelines.authcheckdam.pdf

Antonio, M. E. (2006). Jurors' emotional reactions to serving on a capital trial. *Judicature, 89*(5), 282–288.

Ark. Code Ann. § 5-4-617.

Austin, A., Winskog, C., van den Heuvel, C., & Byard, R. W. (2011). Recent trends in suicides utilizing helium. *Journal of Forensic Science, 56*(3), 649–651.

Bailey, W. C., & Peterson, R. D. (1997). Murder, capital punishment, and deterrence: A review of the literature. *The Death Penalty in America: Current Controversies, 135,* 152–155.

Baldus, D. C., Woodworth, G., & Pulaski, C. A., Jr. (1990). *Equal justice and the death penalty: A legal and empirical analysis.* Boston, MA: Northeastern University Press.

Baldus, D. C., Woodworth, G., Zuckerman, D., & Weiner, N. A. (1998). Racial discrimination and the death penalty in the post-Furman era: An empirical and legal overview with recent findings from Philadelphia. *Cornell Law Review, 83*(6), 1638–1770.

Ballotpedia. (n.d.). *Nebraska death penalty repeal, referendum 426.* Retrieved December 26, 2016 from https://ballotpedia.org/Nebraska_Death_Penalty_Repeal,_Referendum_426_(2016)

Banner, S. (2002). *The death penalty: An American history.* Cambridge, MA: Harvard University Press.

Bedau, H. A. (2004). An abolitionist's survey of the death penalty in America today. In H. Bedau & P. Cassell (Eds.), *Debating the death penalty: Should American have capital punishment?* (pp. 183–217). New York, NY: Oxford University Press.

Berman, M. (2017, April 21). Arkansas executed one death-row inmate: Three more executions are planned this month. *The Washington Post.* Retrieved May 14, 2017 from www.washingtonpost.com/news/post-nation/wp/2017/04/21/arkansas-executed-one-death-row-inmate-three-more-executions-are-planned-this-month/?utm_term=.d764dea48262

Blecker, R. (2001, January 7). The U.S. needs to rethink how it applies the death penalty. *The Orlando Sentinel* (from *The Washington Post*), p. G1.

Blume, J. H., Johnson, S. L., & Threlkheld, A. B. (2001). Probing "life qualification" through expanded *voir dire. Hofstra Law Review, 29*(4), 1209–1264.

Blume, J. H., & Vann, L. S. (2016). Forty years of death: The past, present, and future of the death penalty in South Carolina (still arbitrary after all these years). *Duke Journal of Constitutional Law & Public Policy, 11*(1/2), 183–254.

Bohm, R. M. (2017). *Deathquest: An introduction to the theory and practice of capital punishment in the United States* (5th ed.). New York, NY: Routledge.

Bohm, R. M., Clark, L. J., & Aveni, A. A. F. (1991). Knowledge and death penalty opinion: A test of the Marshall hypothesis. *Journal of Research in Crime and Delinquency, 28,* 360–387.

Bohm, R. M., & Vogel, R. E. (1991). Educational experiences and death penalty opinions: Stimuli that produce changes. *Journal of Criminal Justice Education, 2*(1), 69–80.

Bowers, W. J., & Foglia, W. D. (2003). Still singularly agonizing: Law's failure to purge arbitrariness from capital sentencing. *Criminal Law Bulletin, 39,* 51–86.

Bright, S. (1994). Counsel for the poor: The death sentence not for the worst crime, but for the worst lawyer. *Yale Law Journal, 103,* 1835–1883.

Bright, S. (2010). Legal representation for the poor: Can society afford this much injustice. *Missouri Law Review, 75*(3), 683–714.

Calabresi, S. G. (2006). The president, the Supreme Court, and the Founding Fathers: A reply to Professor Ackerman. *The University of Chicago Law Review, 73,* 469–485.

California Secretary of State. (n.d.). *Statement of vote summary pages (2016).* Retrieved December 26, 2016 from http://elections.cdn.sos.ca.gov/sov/2016-general/sov/06-sov-summary.pdf

Cassell, P. G. (2004). In defense of the death penalty. In H. Bedau & P. Cassell (Eds.), *Debating the death penalty: Should America have capital punishment?* (pp. 183–217). New York, NY: Oxford University Press.

Chalfin, A., Haviland, A. M., & Raphael, S. (2013). What do panel studies tell us about a deterrence effect of capital punishment? A critique of the literature. *Journal of Quantitative Criminology, 29*(1), 5–43.

Christiansen, S. (2015, June 24). How Oklahoma came to embrace the gas chamber. *New Yorker.* Retrieved from www.newyorker.com/news/news-desk/how-oklahoma-came-to-embrace-the-gas-chamber

Christopher, R. (2014). Death delayed is retribution denied. *Minnesota Law Review, 99,* 421–466.

Collins, P. A., Boruchowitz, R. C., Hickman, M. J., & Larranga, M. A. (2016). An analysis of the economic costs of seeking the death penalty in Washington State. *Seattle Journal for Social Justice, 14*(3), 727–779.

Cottingham, J. (1979). Varieties of retribution. *The Philosophical Quarterly, 29,* 238–246.

Cunningham, M. D., Reidy, T. J., & Sorensen, J. R. (2005). Is death row obsolete? A decade of mainstreaming death-sentenced inmates in Missouri. *Behavioral Sciences and the Law, 23,* 307–320.

Davis, M. (2002). A sound retributive argument for the death penalty. *Criminal Justice Ethics, 21*(2), 22–26.

Death Penalty Information Center. (n.d.a). States with and without the death penalty. *As of July 1, 2015.* Retrieved August 10, 2016, from www.deathpenaltyinfo.org/states-and-without-death-penalty

Death Penalty Information Center. (n.d.b). The death penalty in 2015: Year end report. Retrieved September 16, 2017, from https://deathpenaltyinfo.org/documents/2015YrEnd.pdf

Death Penalty Information Center. (n.d.c). *Background of Arkansas April 2017 executions.* Retrieved May 14, 2017 from https://deathpenaltyinfo.org/node/6722

Death Penalty Information Center (n.d.d). *Authorized methods.* Retrieved December 30, 2016 from www.deathpenaltyinfo.org/methods-execution?scid=8&did=245#state

Death Penalty Information Center (n.d.e). *Fact sheet: Innocence and the death penalty.* Retrieved September 16, 2017, from https://deathpenaltyinfo.org/innocence-and-death-penalty

Denno, D. W. (2014). Lethal injection chaos post-Baze. *Georgetown Law Journal, 102,* 1331–1382.

Denno, D. W. (2016). The firing squad as a "known and available alternative method of execution" post-Glossip. *University of Michigan Journal of Law Reform, 49*(4), 749–793.

Dieter, R. C. (2008). Methods of execution and their effect on the use of the death penalty in the United States. *Fordham Urban Law Journal, 35,* 789–816.

Dieter, R. C. (2009). *Smart on crime: Reconsidering the death penalty in a time of economic crisis.* Washington, DC: Death Penalty Information Center.

Dieter, R. C. (2013). *The 2% death penalty: How a minority of counties produce most death cases at enormous costs to all.* Washington, DC: Death Penalty Information Center.

Dezhbakhsh, H., & Shepherd, J. M. (2006). The deterrent effect of capital punishment: Evidence from a "judicial experiment". *Economic Inquiry, 44,* 512–535. doi: 10.1093/ei/cbj032

Donohue, J. J., & Wolfers, J. (2006). Uses and abuses of empirical evidence in the death penalty debate. *Stanford Law Review, 58,* 791–846.

Ehrlich, I. (1975). The deterrent effect of capital punishment: A question of life and death. *American Economic Review, 65,* 397–417.

Epstein, L., & Martin, A. D. (2010). Does public opinion influence the Supreme Court? Possibly yes (but we're not sure why). *Journal of Constitutional Law, 13*(2), 263–281.

Fan, M. D. (2015). The supply-side attack on lethal injection and the rise of execution secrecy. *Boston University Law Review, 95,* 427–460.

Fulkerson, A., & Kinnison, C. (2016). Lethal injection: Where do we go after Glossip v. Gross (2015)? *Criminal Law Bulletin, 52*(4), 923–960.

Gallup. (n.d.a). *Topics A to Z.* Retrieved August 10, 2016, from www.gallup.com/poll/1606/Death-Penalty.aspx

Gallup. (n.d.b). U.S. death penalty support at 60%. Retrieved September 16, 2017, from http://news.gallup.com/poll/196676/death-penalty-support.aspx?g_source=death%20penalty&g_medium=search&g_campaign=tiles

Gallup. (n.d.c). *Americans: "Eye for an eye" top reason for death penalty.* Retrieved September 16, 2017, from http://news.gallup.com/poll/178799/americans-eye-eye-top-reason-death-penalty.aspx?g source=position1&g_medium=related&g_campaign=tiles

Gerber, M. M., & Jackson, J. (2013). Retribution as revenge and retribution as just deserts. *Social Justice Research, 26,* 61–80.

Gershowitz, A. M. (2010). Statewide capital punishment: The case for eliminating counties' role in the death penalty. *Vanderbilt Law Review, 63,* 307.

Gould, J. B., & Greenman, L. (2010). Report to the Committee on Defender Services, Judicial Conference of the United States: Update of the cost and quality of defense representation in federal death penalty cases. Judicial Conference of the United States.

Grosso, C., O'Brien, B., Taylor, A., & Woodworth, G. (2014). Race discrimination and the death penalty: An empirical and legal overview. In J. R. Acker, R. M. Bohm, & C. S. Lanier (Eds.), *America's experiment with capital punishment: Reflections on the past, present and future of the ultimate penal sanction* (3rd ed., pp. 525–577). Durham: Carolina Academic Press.

H.B. 1879, Reg. Sess. (Okla. 2015) (signed by Governor Mary Fallin on April 17, 2015, with an effective date of November 1, 2015.

Herskovitz, J. (2016, November 9). Death penalty gains new support from voters in several U.S. states. *Reuters.* Retrieved November, 11, 2016 from www.reuters.com/article/us-usa-election-executionidUSKBN1343C7?feedType=RSS&feedName=topNews&utm_source=twitter&utm_medium=Social

Hobbs, M. (2008). Subjective and behavioral responses to nitrogen narcosis and alcohol. *Undersea Hyperbaric Medicine, 35*(3), 175–184.

Horowitz, J. A. (1997). Prosecutorial discretion and the death penalty: Creating a committee to decide whether to seek the death penalty. *Fordham Law Review, 65*(6), 2571–2610.

Jones, A. (2014, July 27). Secrecy over executions faces challenges: Trend not to divulge details such as provenance of lethal-injection drugs has triggered lawsuits by condemned. *Wall Street Journal.* Retrieved from http://search.proquest.com/docview/1548588406?accountid=14576

Jones, S., & Gideon, J. (1998). United States v. McVeigh: Defending the "most hated man in America." *Oklahoma Law Review, 51,* 617–657.

Joyce Mitchell pleads guilty to helping New York inmates escape. (n.d.). *CNN,* July 29, 2015. Retrieved August 15, 2016 from www.cnn.com/2015/07/28/us/new-york-prison-break-mitchell/

Kirchmeier, J. L. (1998). Aggravating and mitigating factors: The paradox of today's arbitrary and mandatory capital punishment scheme. *William & Mary Bill of Rights Journal, 6*(2/3), 345–459.

Kozinski, A. (2004). Tinkering with death. In H. Bedau & P. Cassell (Eds.), *Debating the death penalty: Should American have capital punishment?* (pp. 1–14). New York, NY: Oxford University Press.

Kuziemko, I. (2006). Does the threat of the death penalty affect plea bargaining in murder cases? Evidence from New York's 1995 reinstatement of capital punishment. *American Law and Economics Review, 8*(1), 116–142. doi: 10.1093/aler/ahj005

Lee, G., Bohm, R. M., & Pazzani, L. M. (2014). Knowledge and death penalty opinion: The Marshall hypotheses revisited. *American Journal of Criminal Justice, 39,* 642–659.

Liebman, J. S. (2002). Opting for real death penalty reform. *Ohio State Law Journal, 63,* 315.

Lombardi, G., Sluder, R. D., & Wallace, D. (1996). *The management of death-sentenced inmates: Issues, realities, and innovative strategies.* Paper presented at the Annual Meeting of the Academy of Criminal Justice Sciences, Las Vegas, Nevada, 1996.

Madeira, J. L. (2008). Blood relations: Collective memory, cultural trauma, & the prosecution & execution of Timothy McVeigh. *Studies in Law, Politics, and Society, 45,* 75–138.

Marquis, J. K. (2004). Truth and consequences: The death penalty. In H. Bedau & P. Cassell (Eds.), *Debating the death penalty: Should America have capital punishment? The experts on both sides make their best case.* New York, NY: Oxford University Press.

Mattison, T. M. (2012). *Vicarious trauma: The silent stressor.* Institute for Court Management, ICM Fellows Program.

Mocan, N. H., & Gettings, R. K. (2003). Getting off death row: The deterrent effect of capital punishment. *Journal of Law & Economics, 46,* 453, 453–478.

Monteiro, M. G., Hernandez, W., Figlie, N. B., Takahashi, E., & Korukian, M. (1996). Comparison between subjective feelings to alcohol and nitrogen narcosis: A pilot study. *Alcohol, 13*(1), 75–78.

Mourer, S. A. (2010). Gateway to justice: Constitutional claims to actual innocence. *University of Miami Law Review, 61*(4/6), 1279–1316.

O'Brien, B., Grosso, C. M., Woodworth, G., & Taylor, A. (2016). Untangling the role of race in capital charging and sentencing in North Carolina, 1990–2009. *North Carolina Law Review, 94*(6), 1997–2050.

Ogden, R. D., Hamilton, W. K., & Whitcher, C. (2010). Assisted suicide by oxygen deprivation with helium at a Swiss right-to-die organisation. *Journal of Medical Ethics, 36*(3), 174–179.

Paternoster, R., Brame, R., Bacon, S., & Ditchfield, A. (2004). The administration of the death penalty in Maryland, 1978–1999. *University of Maryland Law Journal of Race, Religion, Gender and Class, 4*(1), 1–97.

Petterle, D. (Director). (2008, January 15). How to kill a human being [Television series episode]. In P. Furlong (Producer), *Horizon, BBC Two.* London, England: British Broadcasting Corporation.

Phillips, S. (2008). Racial disparities in the capital of capital punishment. *Houston Law Review, 45,* 807–840.

Pojman, L. P. (2004). Why the death penalty is morally permissible. In H. A. Bedau & P. G. Cassell (Eds.), *Debating the death penalty: Should America have capital punishment? The experts on both sides make their best case.* (pp. 51–75). New York, NY: Oxford University Press.

Potter, N. T. (2002). Kant and capital punishment today. *The Journal of Value Inquiry, 36,* 267–282.

Quine, J. P. (1980). Euthanasia by hypoxia using nitrogen: A review after four years of operation involving 20,500 animals. *The Canadian Veterinary Journal*, *21*(11), 320.

Radelet, M. (2016). Examples of post-Furman botched executions. *Death Penalty Information Center*. Retrieved December 31, 2016 from www.deathpenaltyinfo.org/some-examples-post-furman-botched-executions

Radin, C. P. (1980). Respect for persons: Super due process for death. *California Law Review*, *53*, 1143–1155.

Raj, A. B. M., & Gregory, N. G. (1995). Welfare implications of gas stunning of pigs 1: Determination of aversion to the initial inhalation of carbon dioxide or argon. *Animal Welfare*, *4*(4), 273–280.

Reiter, K. (2013). The origins of and need to control supermax prisons. *California Journal of Politics Policy*, *5*(2), 146–167.

Robinson, M. (2008). Assessing scholarly opinion of capital punishment: The experts speak. In R. M. Bohm (Ed.), *The death penalty today* (pp. 113–157). Boca Raton, FL: CRC Press, Taylor & Francis Group.

Rupp, A. (2003). Death penalty prosecutorial charging decisions and county budgetary restrictions: Is the death penalty arbitrarily applied based on county funding? *Fordham Law Review*, *71*(6), 2735–2780.

Sarat, A., & Vidmar, N. (1976). Public opinion, the death penalty, and the Eighth Amendment: Testing the Marshall hypothesis. *Wisconsin Law Review*, *17*, 171–206.

Scheidegger, K. (2012). Rebutting the myths about race and the death penalty. *Ohio State Journal of Criminal Law*, *10*(1), 147–165.

Schwarzschild, M. (2002). Retribution, deterrence, and the death penalty: A response to Hugo Bedau. *Criminal Justice Ethics*, *21*(2), 9–11.

Sheffer, S. (2013). *Fighting for their lives: Inside the experience of capital defense attorneys*. Nashville, TN: Vanderbilt University Press.

Simmons, E. (2009). Challenging an execution after prolonged confinement on death row [*Lackey* revisited]. *Case Western Reserve Law Review*, *59*(4), 1249–1270.

Smith, A. (2005). Hypoxia symptoms reported during helicopter operations below 10,000 ft: A retrospective survey. *Aviation Space & Environmental Medicine*, *76*(8), 794–798.

Snell, T. L. (2014). Capital punishment in the United States, 2013, Statistical Tables. Bureau of Justice Statistics, U.S. Department of Justice.

Stetler, R., & Wendel, W. B. (2014). The ABA guidelines and the norms of capital defense representation. *Hofstra Law Review*, *41*(3), 635–696.

Stevens, H. R., Sheppard, C. E., Spangenberg, R., Wickman, A., & Gould, J. B. (2010). *State, county and local expenditures for indigent defense services fiscal year 2008*. Fairfax, Virginia: The Spangenberg Project, The Center for Justice, Law and Society at George Mason University.

Thaxton, S. (2013). Leveraging death. *The Journal of Criminal Law & Criminology*, *103*(2), 475–552.

U.S. Census Bureau. (n.d.). *2010 Census Briefs. The black population: 2010*. Retrieved December 30, 2016 from www.census.gov/prod/cen2010/briefs/c2010br-06.pdf

U.S. General Accounting Office. (1990). *Death penalty sentencing: Research indicates pattern of racial disparities*. Washington, DC: U.S. Government Printing Office.

van den Haag, E. (2014). Justice, deterrence and the death penalty. In J. R. Acker, R. M. Bohm, & C. S. Lanier (Eds.), *America's experiment with capital punishment: Reflections on the past, present, and future of the ultimate sanction* (3rd ed., pp. 229–242). Durham, NC: Carolina Academic Press.

Vollum, S., Longmire, D. R., & Buffington-Vollum, J. (2004). Confidence in the death penalty and support for its use: Exploring the value-expressive dimension of death penalty attitudes. *Justice Quarterly*, *21*(3), 521–546.

Von Hirsch, A. (2007). The "desert" model for sentencing: Its influence, prospects, and alternatives. *Social Research*, *74*(2), 413–434.

White, J. P. (2001). Establishing a capital defense unit in Virginia: A proposal to increase the quality of representation for indigent capital defendants. *Capital Defense Journal*, *13*, 323–358.

White, W. S. (2006). *Litigating in the shadow of death: Defense attorneys in capital cases*. Ann Arbor, MI: University of Michigan Press.

Woodward, A. (2007). It takes a village to save a life: A statewide model for indigent defense. *New York City Law Review*, *11*, 159–177.

Cases Cited

Atkins v. Virginia, 536 U.S. 304 (2002).

Batson v. Kentucky, 476 U.S. 79 (1986).

Baze v. Rees, 553 U.S. 35 (2008).

Chavez v. State, 832 So.2d 730 (Florida, 2002).

Coker v. Georgia, 433 U.S. 584 (1977).

Davis v. State, Arkansas Supreme Court Case No. CR-92-1385 and CR-00-528.

Enmund v. Florida, 458 U.S. 782 (1982).

Furman v. Georgia, 498 U.S. 238 (1972).

Glossip v. Gross, 576 U.S. ___, 135 S.Ct. 2726 (2015).

Gregg v. Georgia, 428 U.S. 153 (1976).

Herrera v. Collins, 506 U.S. 390 (1993).

In re Kemmler, 136 U.S. 436 (1890).

Jones v. Commissioner, Georgia Dept. of Corrections, 811 F.3d 1288 (11th Cir. 2016).

Kennedy v. Louisiana, 554 U.S. 407 (2008).

Lackey v. Texas, 514 U.S. 1045 (1995).

Lee, McGehee et al. v. Hutchinson, CV 195-DPM, Order entered (April 6, 2017).

McCleskey v. Kemp, 481 U.S. 279 (1987).

McGehee v. Hutchinson, 854 F.3d 488 (8th Cir. 2017).

McKesson Medical-Surgical, Inc. v. State, 60 CV-17-1921 (2017).

McWilliams v. Dunn, Supreme Court of the United States, No. 16-5294 (2016).

Roper v. Simmons, 543 U.S. 551 (2005).

Sepulveda, v. Jindal, 729 F.3d 413 (5th Cir. 2013).

Spaziano v. Florida, 468 U.S. 447 (1984).

State of Arkansas v. Gray and McKesson, Supreme Court Case No. CV-17-317 (2017).

Strickland v. Washington, 466 U.S. 668 (1984).

Tison v. Arizona, 481 U.S. 137 (1987).

Trop v. Dulles, 356 U.S. 86 (1958).

United States v. Cox, 342 F.2d 167 (5th Cir.), *cert denied*, 381 U.S. 935 (1965).

United States v. McVeigh, 153 F.3d 1166 (10th Cir. 1998).

Wainwright v. Witt, 469 U.S. 412 (1985).

Ward v. State, Arkansas Supreme Court Case No. CR-98-657 (2017).

Weems v. United States, 217 U.S. 349 (1910).

Wiggins v. Smith, 539 U.S. 510 (2003).

Wilkerson v. Utah, 99 U.S. 130 (1878).

Witherspoon v. Illinois, 391 U.S. 510 (1967).

Wood v. Ryan, 759 F.3d 1076 (9th Cir. 2014).

Woodson v. North Carolina, 428 U.S. 280 (1976).

Zant v. Stephens, 462 U.S. 862 (1983).

Zink v. Lombardi, 783 F.3d 1089 (8th Cir. 2015).

PART 2

Capital Punishment: Rationales and Religious Views

A. Rationales

8

RETRIBUTION AND CAPITAL PUNISHMENT

"It's in the Bible, Isn't It?"

George F. Kain and Dale Recinella

Introduction

Retributive theory is based on the correlation between the gravity of the crime and the severity of the punishment. Retribution is often cited as justification for the use of capital punishment and appears to be the primary basis of support for the death penalty in the United States (Bohm, 2017). Numerous authors have written on the many meanings of retribution, and for some authors, the concept of retribution is imprecise. Retribution is frequently referenced as having developed from the concept of *lex talionis*, and later from the biblical quotation "an eye for an eye." In this chapter, we explain what retribution actually *is*, in large part by illustrating in detail what it *is not*. Our research reveals that modern-day biblical support for retributive capital punishment is not at all dictated by biblical quotations often cited to justify its use, and, in fact, those phrases have an entirely different meaning—counter to the very words often used to justify a vengeance-based theory. The implications of our findings should have a significant impact in reframing the justification of retribution and, ultimately, our analysis leads us to the conclusion that the American death penalty cannot be justified by references claiming to be biblically retributive.

Retribution

In the United States, retribution, deterrence, incapacitation, and social order are the four major reasons provided by proponents for their death penalty support (Bohm, 1987; Lambert, Clarke, & Lambert, 2004). The retributive perspective can mean different things to different people. For some, retribution is an emotional rationale that represents a desire for vengeance or revenge (Bohm, 1992; Ellsworth & Gross, 1994; Radelet & Borg, 2000). For others, retributive justice is a theory of justice, which considers that punishment is a morally acceptable response to crime, with an eye to satisfaction and the psychological benefit bestowed to the aggrieved party and society. This can be seen as the most ancient justification of reaction to crime (Gobert & Dine, 1993). Retributionists see punishment as a reward for a crime committed. Once a person commits a crime, then he or she should be made to face whatever the consequence that has been prescribed for that offense (Banks, 2009; Greenawalt, 1983).

As one of its main characteristics, retributive justice focuses on establishing guilt for the past behavior of the wrongdoer, and the offender deserves to suffer due to the wrongful behavior. In this regard, retributive justice is a process of backward-looking punishment that is warranted as a response to a past event of injustice or wrongdoing. In effect, it acts to balance the scales of justice. Therefore, the main purpose of this retributive justice is that the offender is to be punished simply due to the commission of a crime. The rationale behind retributive justice is that criminal acts should be met with a painful reaction, without considering the consequences of that reaction. An offender's suffering should be of the same magnitude as that which his or her victim suffered (Murphy, 1994; Siddique, 1997; Moberly, 1996). Another feature of retributive justice emphasizes the adversarial relationship between the accused and the state, and the victims of crime are peripheral to the justice process and merely represented abstractly by the state. The criminal justice system focuses only on the offender to be punished, and the victim is regarded as a bystander in the battle between the state and the offender (Barrett, 2001).

It is important here to focus some attention on the concept of "just deserts," a variation of the retributive theory of punishment, which was developed by Kant (2005) and amplified by Von Hirsh (1987). This theory has been touted in the United States since the 1970s. In what some describe as a compromise of the other major theories/justifications of punishment, just deserts is a form of punishment designed to meet the general principles of justice and fairness by indicating the extent to which an offender deserves to suffer punishment. It is concerned with the techniques for identifying, classifying, and managing groups of offenses and offenders by levels of culpability of the offender and the depravity of the act. In other words, a penalty must be scaled to the gravity of the offense, and the punishment imposed on the offender should closely approximate the severity of his or her criminal act. Equally blameworthy individuals, therefore, should receive nearly similar sentences (proportionality). We note this here primarily to point out that, practically speaking, the theory of just deserts cannot be significantly distinguished from the principal of retributive vengeance or from the notion that "two wrongs somehow make a right." The revenge part of just deserts is therefore based on the principal of *lex talionis* and, in this view, holds that the death penalty is a morally just, deserved punishment (Bohm, 1992).

Lex talionis (Latin for "law of retaliation") is based on the principle of proportionate punishment, often expressed under the motto "Let the punishment fit the crime," which particularly applies to mirror punishments, but which may or may not be proportional. Davis (2005) notes that some may think of this law's goal as a core element of early biblical justice. *Lex talionis*, however, goes back to about the twentieth century BCE, found in the Code of Hammurabi. The Code of Hammurabi, regarded as the oldest and perhaps the harshest written ancient penal laws, accepted that punishment should be equal to the weight of the crime as literally as possible (Dyneley, 2010; Packer, 1968). At the root of the nonbiblical form of this principle is the belief that one of the purposes of the law is to provide equitable retaliation for an offended party. It defined and restricted the extent of retaliation. Biblical scholar Lawrence Boadt (2012) notes that the 282 laws engraved on a stone pillar attributed to Hammurabi cover many legal questions, but do not include every kind of case. The code "tries to keep revenge within limits by the 'law of retaliation' or proportional retribution" (p. 156). But biblical retribution is important to understand as well, and will be discussed shortly. Here, comparing Israelite/biblical law to the Code of Hammurabi (as well as to many other ancient law codes), Boadt concludes that Israelite law "is humane compared to the even more drastic penalties commonly found in the Assyrian laws of the twelfth century BC. And as a measure to end escalating blood feuds between families and the power of the wealthy to force tenfold repayment of loans from the weak, it was a step forward" (p. 157).

This understanding will become more relevant as we develop the theme of this chapter further. The Old Testament prescription of "an eye for an eye" has often been misinterpreted, notably in American justice, to signal retributive punishment as in just deserts, or to "let the punishment fit the crime." In other cultures, notably Islam, the code has been taken more literally; a thief may lose his left hand in punishment. Still, retribution has been subjected to various criticisms. Some would challenge the power of the state to punish criminals on behalf of the victim, arguing "if individuals have no moral right to exact retribution, how can a group of individuals in the society acquire such a moral right?" (Siddique, 1997). Retribution has also been criticized as a barbaric principle that serves as an excuse to unleash savage passion: "the community would be relegated to a primitive condition where the determination of the law to exact an eye for an eye and a tooth for tooth would cause immeasurable and intolerable cruelty in the name of evenhanded justice" (Rao, 1999).

All of these variations on retributive punishment and how they specifically relate to capital punishment are important to understand. However, what is perhaps more important relates to our original premise for this chapter, namely to focus on what retribution *is not*. In order to complete this task, we must now turn to biblical law and to attempt to understand its literal and figurative meaning.

Biblical Retribution

The first five books of the Bible are crucial to any discussion of the Bible and the American death penalty. The Hebrew Bible calls these books *Torah*. The Christian terminology for the first five books is *Pentateuch*. Consequently, the term *Torah* or *Pentateuch* is used to designate the combined books: Genesis, Exodus, Leviticus, Numbers, and Deuteronomy. Also, the record of the actual death penalty practices necessary to satisfy the requirements of *Torah* or *Pentateuch* is contained in the voluminous writings of *Talmud*. The Talmudic references are a record, a compilation over time, of the practices employed under the Biblical death penalty in order to ensure compliance with the restrictions on the death penalty set forth in the Scriptures. In order to comprehend the full impact of the severe Scriptural limitations imposed on the death penalty, we must deal with the Biblical truth in its practice, not just in theory.

Many modern readers tend to distinguish between the authority of what has been handed down in Scripture, the written law, versus that contained in the written record of the oral tradition. This is not the case with the ancient Hebrew law. In the eyes of Christians and Jews, the source of *Torah* is God. *Torah* means law. This is considered to be the Written Law given by God to the Hebrews. Yet there is more to the story. Orthodox Judaism holds that Moses received more than just the Written Law on Mount Sinai. It holds that when Moses came down the mountain, the Ten Commandments were in his hands, and the Oral Law, equally given to him by God, was in his head. Consequently, the "Written Law and Oral Law must be read together" (Rosenberg & Rosenberg, 1998).

The primary purpose of Oral Law was to maintain the understanding of Scripture across the generations. As values and customs changed over the ages, it was the Oral Law that maintained the meaning of Scriptural words, described activities that had fallen out of common usage, and determined the scope of critical commands. Even now we can observe that Scripture acknowledges the existence of Oral Law by referring briefly to matters that are assumed to exist outside of Scripture.[1]

We need not delve into the issues of whether or not the Oral Law meets a Christian understanding of divine revelation. That is not our concern here. Our focus is to answer the claimed divine support for the modern American death penalty by holding it up against the substance and procedures of the Biblical death penalty. Most of the substance and procedures are contained right in the Scripture verses of *Torah* or *Pentateuch*. The rest have been transmitted as part of the Oral Law, which has been written down and is called *Talmud*. The relevant provisions in *Talmud* have to do with the substance and procedures necessary to comply with the very strict limitations on the death penalty contained in the Scriptures of *Torah* or *Pentateuch*. Consequently, those procedures are a potent barometer of Biblical truth in measuring our own American death penalty system.

In *The Biblical Truth About America's Death Penalty*, Recinella (2004), co-author of this chapter, goes into extensive detail about the history of the transmission of both the Written Law and the Oral Law from Moses to successive generations. Ultimately, in order to preserve the Oral Law for future generations, it became necessary to compile it in written form. Some authors believe that the destruction of Jerusalem and the Temple by the Romans in the First Century AD played a significant role in this development. The written collection of the nuts and bolts of the Oral Law given to Moses on Mount

Sinai was completed about 200 AD. It is called the *Mishnah*. This compilation is what lawyers would refer to as "black letter law."

The second phase of this multi-century work was the compilation in written form of the commentary and debates of the sages concerning the black letter law. This commentary and reflection, similar in some ways to a Bible commentary on Scripture, took another 300 years to complete. It is called the *Gemara*. The *Mishnah* and *Gemara* together make up the *Talmud*, which literally means "teaching" (Berman & Grossman, 2011).

In the twelfth century, a Jewish scholar, Moses Maimonides, produced a comprehensive work that sorted and codified the entire Oral Law. This compilation is known as the *Mishneh Torah*. We will focus on the substantive and procedural laws concerning the Biblical death penalty found in *Torah* and *Talmud*. In cases where such laws are also reflected in the *Mishneh Torah*, quotes from the *Mishneh Torah* may be provided as well. All *Talmud* references are to *Mishnah*, the black letter law, unless otherwise indicated.

Christians have incorporated the Decalogue (the Ten Commandments) of the *Torah* into our consciousness. In some quarters, we even continue to quote the "eye for an eye" of *Torah* as support for certain substantive laws, e.g., the death penalty. Yet our selections have been arbitrary compared to the whole of the Written Law, as Crusemann (1996, p. 5) notes, "We have not adopted . . . into our legal system the reconciliation and restorative justice principles of *Torah*. We have certainly not employed the severe restrictions in *Torah* as to application and procedures of the Biblical death penalty." As sporadic as our use of *Torah* has been, we have virtually ignored the *Talmud*, leaving much of the relevant criminal procedures of the *Mishnah* far afield from our modern criminal procedures. This is especially true in the case of the death penalty.

Criminal procedural law for the Biblical death penalty contained numerous restrictions that are set forth in the Scriptures of *Torah* or *Pentateuch* and in *Talmud*; e.g., there must be at least two witnesses whose testimony agrees on virtually every detail in all material respects,[2] confessions of the accused are of no validity or effect, circumstantial evidence is not allowed, premeditation has to be proven by establishing that the accused was warned right before the act that he was about to commit a capital crime, and conviction requires a majority of two votes by the judges but release requires only a majority of one (Steinsaltz, 2006).

Furthermore, those subject to capital punishment under the Biblical death penalty were evaluated by the strict standards of criminal intent: "Thus, there were categories of people who were exempt from criminal punishment: minors, the mentally unstable, and the mentally retarded; so too, certain actions committed under duress were exempt" (Berman & Grossman, 2011).

Moreover, the substantive law of the Biblical death penalty excluded many factual situations from consideration as a capital crime. Some of these same factual situations are significant factors in the burgeoning of America's death rows today, e.g., the practice of felony murder. Put simply, under the American doctrine of felony murder, any person who willingly participates in the commission of a felony is liable for the murder of anyone killed during the commission of that felony. These include liability for persons shot by a co-defendant, persons killed by accident, and even persons shot by law enforcement officers responding to the crime. It also means that any accomplice to the commission of the crime has the same level of liability as the person who actually pulled the trigger or did the stabbing. Even if we can understand the rationale behind the felony murder rule, we might be shocked at the bizarre results when triggermen are out walking free because they cut a deal to turn state's evidence against their own accomplices, not infrequently less mentally acute accomplices who were recruited to drive or serve as lookouts and are now on death row.

In addressing the claimed biblical support for the modern American death penalty, the critical question is not whether the death penalty as punishment for felony murder is reasonable or even effective. The question is whether it is biblical. How does the doctrine of felony murder in America's death penalty measure up under the scrutiny of biblical truth? The answer to this question is not even ambiguous. The concept of felony murder in the American death penalty cannot be supported based upon biblical truth. Sprinkle (2006) elaborates further on this concept, speaking about God's biblical justice: "He distinguishes the guilt of intentional murder from that of unintentional manslaughter."

The Scriptures in *Torah* or *Pentateuch* and the provisions of *Talmud* also exclude from the death penalty the intentional killing of an unintended person, the intentional killing by indirect means, reckless homicide, and the liability of any accomplice (Steinsaltz, 2006). There may still be punishment, but under the standards of the Biblical death penalty, the punishment is not death. Needless to say, with all the restrictions we have already mentioned, it was very difficult for the biblical courts to impose the biblical death penalty. This problem was being faced as early as the Second Temple period.[3] For our purposes of assessing whether the Bible can properly be used to support the modern American death penalty, the Scriptures of the *Torah* or *Pentateuch* and the procedures in *Talmud* required to satisfy those Scriptures are our sources for the Biblical truth about the death penalty.

"An Eye for an Eye": Exodus 21:22–25.
Literal or Figurative? Mandated or Limited?

We now return to one of the most frequently quoted biblical phrases used to support capital punishment, namely "an eye for an eye, tooth for a tooth, life for a life" found in three books of *Torah*. Here we will present an interpretive translation of the passage found in Exodus 21:22–25 provided by Sprinkle (2006):

> (22) if men are in struggle with one another and butt a pregnant woman so that the product of her womb comes forth in fatal miscarriage, but there is no further serious injury to the woman, then someone (the guilty party or a representative of the guilty parties) will be charged tort in accordance with what the woman's husband requires of him, paying the amount for which he is culpable.
>
> (23) but if there is further serious injury to the woman, then you O Israelite will pay out as the guilty party according to the formula: "the *monetary value* of a life in exchange for the life lost,
>
> (24) the *value* of an eye in exchange for the eye lost, the *value* of a tooth in exchange for the tooth lost, the *value* of a hand in exchange for the hand lost, the *value* of a foot in exchange for the foot lost,
>
> (25) the *value* of an injury caused by burning in exchange for the burning inflicted, the *value* of a wound in exchange for the wound inflicted, the *value* of a stripe in exchange for the stripe inflicted.
>
> (p. 70)

The question posed by Sprinkle (2006) here is whether the *lex talionis* is literal or figurative.

> According to the figurative view, the *lex talionis* has to do with "composition" in the legal sense of the satisfaction of a wrong or injury by monetary payment. This is an old rabbinic interpretation. Modern scholars, however, frequently understand it to refer solely to literal retaliation involving execution and maiming. There are a number of arguments that favor the figurative interpretation. The literal application of the so-called *lex talionis* is inconsistent with the principles and legal outcomes of other laws elsewhere in the literary unit of Exodus. The penalty is not to strike the offender and injure him in exactly the same way in which he injured the other man as one would expect on the literal understanding of *lex talionis*—which, by the way, would be absurdly impractical—but for the offender to pay money, i.e., to pay for the medical costs and for the lost time of the man he injured . . . . The

system of ransom, even in "life for life," means that though the *lex talionis* could in principle be applied literally, normally it was not. Rather, monetary compensation usually substituted for literal *talion*.

(p. 74)

Other writers have debated this interpretation of *lex talionis*. Westbrook (1986) argues that the system of ransom seen in the Bible is also assumed in the ancient near Eastern laws, so that laws that seem to imply literal mutilation allowed monetary substitution for literal *talion*:

> It may therefore be concluded that the phrase "pay a life" refers to the payment of a fixed sum representing the value of a person. That value may be fixed by treaty or statute, but often appears to be a matter of traditional law. The term does not assume that the penalty in question must necessarily be the mirror-image of the loss caused. Payment of the penalty can thus take the form of the same type of item, a multiple of similar items, or an abstract legal act. The passage therefore provides no information as to the existence of a talionic principle for physical injuries in biblical law.
>
> *(p. 64)*

Isser (1990) confirms this perspective and adds:

> There is no neat correlation among all these (monetary) figures, but it is clear that ancient near Eastern societies for various purposes placed monetary values on human lives. The talionic formula, "a life for life" is better rendered "a person for a person." The principle is equivalent compensation, whether it involves the estimate of the fetus's value, the turning over of a slave or a household member, or the monetary value of a person. Some assumed "a life for life" meant the death penalty, but this is not explicit in the reading, and probably arose more from an ancient legal tradition.
>
> *(p. 44)*

Otto (1994) argues that similar laws under the code of Hammurabi reflect a legal reform taking into consideration the class structure of society in which *talion* was applied to upper classes, but monetary compensation continued to apply to lower classes and slaves. Sprinkle (2006) concludes that the argument for literal *talion* from comparative ancient near Eastern law is not as conclusive as the biblical evidence against it. Referring to similar "eye for an eye" phrases found in the books of Leviticus and Deuteronomy, he concludes:

> The *talionic* formula "life for life, eye for eye, tooth for tooth, hand for hand, foot for foot" is not applied literally, but merely means that the punishment varies with the severity of the accusation. On the basis of these arguments, a strong case can be made that the *lex talionis* did not have to be carried out literally but could have been applied figuratively through payment of ransom to achieve composition. The *lex talionis* was never meant to justify personal revenge . . . but it was meant to express the legal principle that the (monetary) penalty one can demand for an injury must be proportional to the degree of injury involved so that the less the injury, the less should be the penalty. It thus limits the penalty to the monetary equivalent of the injury caused . . . "life for life" does not imply capital punishment, but rather alludes to a system where composition is achieved through ransom where money substitutes for literal *talion*.
>
> *(pp. 78–79)*

Our central theme here, what retribution *is not*, can thus be summarized by what biblical scholar Christopher Wright (2004) has written:

> The notorious principle of the so-called *lex talionis*—"eye for eye, tooth for tooth"—was not to foster violent vengeance, but precisely the opposite, to limit vengeance. Punishment must be strictly proportionate to the offence. That it was a principal of *proportionality*, not a command to be taken *literally*, is shown here, and that the *actual* penalty for damaging an eye or knocking out a tooth is not the infliction of the same disfigurement on the offender, but rather granting freedom to the victim.
>
> *(p. 335)*

This theme is carried even further by an interesting study of the death penalty and the various forms of law included in the *Torah* offered by Gerstenberger (1995). He points out the irony that an explicit reason for imposing divine death threats is actually the preservation of life, rather like the warning posted at electrical installations—"Warning: Danger of Death." Divine threats of death against potential trespassers are counteracting likely catastrophes. Death injunctions or death threats alert us to the gravity of transgressions; they are intended to preserve the basis of human life, but they must not be understood in legal terms. They are not "law" in the accepted sense of the term but rather an anticipatory deterrent.

A law of limitation is every bit as much a law as one that mandates an activity. It is simply a law that is understood as providing a limit to the legality of an action. Let us look at some examples in modern terms. An instance of a law that mandates an activity would be the statutes that require me to obtain a registration and license plate for my vehicle. I must do this. No matter how many vehicles I own, I must do it for every single one. This is a law requiring specific behavior. The speed limit on a road is a law of limitation. It sets the maximum speed that I am legally allowed to travel. Any speed up to that limit is allowed and is legal.

When we apply this distinction between laws of mandate and laws of limitation to the "eye for an eye" statutes of the Mosaic Law, an amazing consistency between the words of Jesus in Matthew 5:17, 38–40 and the Mosaic Law of the Hebrew Scriptures comes into relief.

If the setting immediately preceding the handing down of the Mosaic Law was a blank slate, in other words, nobody was taking anybody's life as vengeance for killing someone, we might argue vigorously that the legal statutes of "eye for an eye, life for a life" must be mandates. God must have been ordering proportional retaliatory violence as God's revealed will. From our earlier analysis, we know that just the opposite was the case. God did not need to mandate killing in order for people to kill as punishment for murder. The Bible reveals that the Law of the Clan, escalating retaliatory violence by man, was already firmly rooted in the world as early as Lamech (Genesis 4:23–24).

Those living at the time of Moses were well aware of the Law of the Clan. Leviticus 24:17–20 would be understood as a law of limitation, paraphrased as follows:

> If anyone kills any human being, he alone shall be put to death . . . . If anyone maims his fellow, as he has done so shall it be the limit of what is done to him: not more than a fracture for fracture, not more than an eye for eye, not more than a tooth for tooth. The injury he inflicted on another shall be inflicted on him and not more.

We are surrounded by modern and historical examples of human retaliatory violence. In modern America, this Law of the Clan is referred to as "The Law of the Streets." The relevant question for us is whether the Bible reveals a God who desires human vengeance or, instead, a God who reserves vengeance unto himself. The Scriptures, as we explain here, support the latter.

In the limitations of the Mosaic Law, Moses undoes the legacy of Lamech and brings the people closer to where God started by limiting human vengeance to one life for one life. That may have been the best Moses could do in the face of the people's "hardness of heart," even though God wanted and revealed something different.[4]

The biblical record establishes that, in the beginning, God proclaimed that His vengeance protected Cain. God opposed human vengeance. After Lamech's legacy of human retaliatory violence, Moses had to allow the people at least one life in human vengeance for murder. Finally, it is reported in the Christian Scriptures that Jesus takes humanity back to where God started (Matthew 5:38–40) and reminds us to return good for evil because vengeance is only the Lord's (Romans 12:19, 21).

When the "eye for an eye, life for a life" of the Mosaic Law is properly understood, we see that in its Biblical-historical context, capital punishment may not have been God's ideal. Rather, the death penalty may have been allowed in limited form in the Mosaic Law because of the people's "hardness of heart." Furthermore, this "law of limitation" in the Mosaic Law would drastically reduce the violence described by Lamech, requiring both similarity in kind and proportionality of the violence in amount.

In summary, the "eye for an eye, life for a life" of the Mosaic Law introduces a drastic change in human affairs. The change, however, is by way of a law of limitation on human retaliatory violence. The progression in the Biblical record can be presented graphically as follows:

In the *Hebrew Scriptures*

- God Shows His Approach by How God Deals With Cain: God Prohibits Retaliatory Violence by Man (Genesis 4:15).
- Lamech's Legacy is the *Law of The Clan*: Escalating Retaliatory Violence by Man (Genesis 4:23–24).
- Moses Moves the People Back Toward Where God Started: Moses Allows Only Limited Retaliatory Violence by Man (Exodus 21:23–25; Leviticus. 24:17, 19–21; Deuteronomy. 19:21).
- Hosea Announces to the People that God Desires Mercy and Obedience: Not Sacrifices (Like Capital Punishment) (Hosea 6:6).

In the *Christian Scriptures*

- Jesus Christ Returns Humanity to the Place Where God Started: Jesus Prohibits Retaliatory Violence By Man (Matthew 5:17, 38–40).
- Jesus Christ Warns Pilate About the Sinfulness of Executing the Innocent (John 19:10–11).
- Paul Exhorts the People to Stay on Track (Lest They Fall Back into the Error of Lamech): Vengeance Belongs to God Alone (Romans 12:19, 21).

The Rule of Blood: Genesis 9:6

A test of this progression in the biblical record is to determine if the Bible reports that God has acted consistently with it. God did not slay Cain for killing Abel; rather God allowed Cain to go into exile. Some of biblical faith attempt to justify the American death penalty by the Noahide Law verse in Genesis 9:6, the so-called *Rule of Blood*: "Whoever shed the blood of man, by man shall his blood be shed; for in the image of God has God made man." (New International Version). The Bible records this verse in God's blessing of Noah and his family (Genesis 9:1–7).

Some death penalty proponents assert that the *Rule of Blood* is God's command that the entire world must use the death penalty. There are some major problems with that attempt, to wit:

- First, such attempts are limited to first-degree murder. There is no basis for this limitation in the text itself which, if read as a command, seems to cover all taking of human life: accidents, negligent homicide, even self-defense.

- Second, such attempts have not explained why other portions of the blessing do not also continue to be binding as God's law: e.g., the prohibition on consumption of rare meat, or the statement that any animal that kills a human must be executed.
- Finally, if the *Rule of Blood* is indeed God's command, God's perfect will, then the biblical record is establishing God's desire that anyone who kills another human being must be executed. Surely, God would apply this uniformly because that same biblical record also proclaims that God is infinitely just. Consequently, a prominent first-degree, premeditated murderer after the blessing of Noah's family but before the handing down of the Mosaic Law would have to be executed. What does the Bible report as God's punishment for the most significant and prominent first-degree murderer during that period, under the *Rule of Blood*?

The first prominent figure that commits premeditated, first-degree murder in the biblical record after Genesis 9:6 is none other than Moses. And God deals with Moses the same way God dealt with Cain: banishment from society. Our modern term for such punishment is prison. Think about that.

> Some time after that, when Moses had grown up, he went out to his kinsfolk and witnessed their labors. He saw an Egyptian beating a Hebrew, one of his kinsmen. He turned this way and that and, seeing no one about, he struck down the Egyptian and hid him in the sand
> *(Exodus 2: 11–12 TNK).*[5]

These Scriptures tell us quite clearly that Moses looked "this way and that" to make sure nobody was watching. To qualify for first-degree, premeditated murder under most states' laws, e.g., Florida's, one only needs the briefest amount of time for reflection—that is, the time it takes to put a bullet in a gun.[6] Looking this way and that to make sure no one saw the murder qualifies for premeditated, first-degree murder.

Under most states' laws (we will use Florida's for our illustration), Moses has committed premeditated, first-degree murder. He is eligible for the death penalty if there is at least one aggravating circumstance. In fact there are several.

- First, under the laws of Egypt, there was no legal or moral justification for Moses' act of freeing the Hebrew slave and killing the Egyptian slave master. That is enough to merit death row.[7]
- Second, the Egyptian that Moses has killed appears to have been acting in his official capacity as a slave master. That would also put Moses on death row.[8] Or Moses may have intended to allow the Hebrew slave to go free. That means the killing also occurred in the commission of a felony (felony murder). Either one of those factors is enough for Moses to qualify for death row.[9]
- Third, the biblical record reports that Moses took affirmative steps to hide the evidence of his crime. Moses not only freed the slave from his lawful employment, and then killed the Egyptian overseer to escape punishment, but he also hid the body in the sand.[10]

Depending how they are counted, that totals at least three or four aggravators. Only one is needed. Moses likely would be on Florida's death row.

If Genesis 9:6 is reporting that God's perfect will is for everyone in the world who intentionally kills a human being to be killed by a human being, Moses is finished. Pharaoh certainly wants Moses to be executed (when Pharaoh learned of the matter, he sought to kill Moses) (Exodus 2:15). The execution of Moses would have been the Rule of Blood in action. The governing authority of the country where the crime occurred was even willing to carry out the execution on God's behalf. Yet, according to the biblical record, that is not what happens. Instead, God allows Moses to go into exile and live in Midian. God is totally consistent here. He allows the same consequence to Moses that he allowed to Cain: exile, or in modern parlance: prison.

Based upon the biblical record, the conclusion is clear: the killing of those who have taken human life, human retaliatory violence, is not God's perfect will. The Rule of Blood Scripture verse in the Noahide Law describes human retaliatory violence. Yet, this passage does not describe God's perfect will because it does not describe what God does with Cain or with Moses. Rather, this may be another example where God's permissive will is in contrast to His divine will. It only temporarily allows for man's stubborn adherence to vengeance. In this respect, the Rule of Blood under the Noahide Law Genesis 9:6 is similar to the Mosaic Law seen in Exodus 21:23–25; Leviticus 24:17, 19–21; Deuteronomy 19:21.

The books of the *Torah* or *Pentateuch* are referred to by both Christians and Jews as "God's law" because they contain the Mosaic Law, the keystone of Jewish faith and a cornerstone of Judeo-Christian ethics and morality. The concept of "law" is crucial to our search. First and foremost, the issue of the death penalty involves law.

What is law? The answer is not simple. In Webster's Dictionary (1990), the definition of the word "law" is one of the longest entries in the dictionary. A portion of it reads as follows:

> A binding custom or practice of a community; a rule of conduct or action prescribed or formally recognized as binding or enforced by a controlling authority . . . the revelation of the will of God set forth in the Old Testament . . . the first part of the Hebrew Scriptures: Pentateuch.

(p. 678)

All law must have two essential components. One part of the law describes the "whats": identifying what is forbidden, what is allowed, what is required, and what is the punishment for breaking the law. Lawyers refer to this part of the law as the *substantive law.* The other aspect of law identifies the "*hows*": specifying how one is to be arrested, how one is to be determined guilty or innocent, and how the prescribed punishment is to be carried out. This portion of the law is called *procedural law.*

Our American death penalty system is primarily a regimen of procedural laws governing the process by which one is found to be deserving of death. This system of procedures is built on the foundation of a legal premise in substantive law. That premise is that certain crimes deserve death. One cannot claim the biblical record as support for the American death penalty without first comparing our substantive and procedural laws to the requirements of those Scriptures and the actual practices necessary to fulfill their limitations.

The Bible, the Law, and the Death Penalty

The Hebrew Scriptures

As we have already outlined, the Mosaic Law is describing a retributive system of punishment directly proportional to the harm caused. Many authors, as cited earlier, understand this to require proportional composition. If one is seeking to support a death penalty based on interpreting this Biblical standard as requiring retributive violence, as many death penalty proponents do, does not consistency require the parallel retaliatory violence for lesser offenses as well?

In other words, if we exact time in prison for the crimes of blinding someone, maiming someone, burning someone, or punching someone in the mouth, how can we then claim the endorsement of a Biblical mandate for applying proportional violence in kind to only the most grievous offense: killing? Is this an inconsistency that we can explain or justify based upon Scripture? Or is our failure to insist upon reciprocal maiming based upon the fact that it seems barbaric to have our government maim its citizens in the name of criminal justice? Is it any less barbaric for a government to kill its own citizens?

In the biblical record reported in Genesis, God deals with Cain by exile and not by vengeance. In fact, God prohibits vengeance against Cain. Cain is banished and ultimately settles in the land of Nod. Cain fears that he will be a fugitive and a vagabond, meaning essentially that he would be left to move from place to place without a fixed home, residing in places for only a short duration.

Cain's lament over his banishment sounds very similar to the attributes of modern imprisonment. One could hardly pick better words than "fugitive" and "vagabond" to describe the itinerant, rootless life of prison where men are constantly moving from one facility to another, never at home, never carrying more than a small box of property. Some of them must even work hard to conceal the nature of their crimes out of fear of violence from fellow inmates. Cast in modern terms, Cain's lot easily parallel's life in prison without possibility of parole. The major difference is that Cain will be allowed to marry, father children, and raise and support a family.

The biblical account continues to unfold with the descendants of Cain. By the fifth generation after Cain, Lamech appears and contributes the next major piece to our understanding from Scripture. The world has changed in the five generations elapsed since Cain. A new system, the Law of the Clan, has taken hold, as described previously (Genesis 4:23–24).

The Christian Scriptures

In understanding the biblical record from the Christian Scriptures, it is critical to know that for Paul and other Roman citizens, capital punishment involved death by the sword, the most dignified and least horrible form of capital punishment. For Jews and slaves, however, capital punishment at the hands of Rome meant crucifixion.

Paul is also a well-educated Jew, and he knows that of the four types of capital punishment allowed under the biblical death penalty, beheading by the sword is the only one allowed to the state. Danby (1919) translated the original writings and laws of the Jewish Sanhedrin: "Four modes of execution were given over to the court, but to the civil regime was given over only death by the sword alone" (pp. 10–11). Against this backdrop we read the following Scripture verse from the King James Version (KJV) in Romans 13:3–4:

> For rulers are not a terror to good works, but to the evil. Wilt thou then not be afraid of the power? Do that which is good, and thou shalt have praise of the same: For he is the minister of God to thee for good. But if thou do that which is evil, be afraid; for he beareth not the sword in vain: for he is the minister of God, a revenger to execute wrath upon him that doeth evil.

The two most significant words in this passage, vis-à-vis claimed scriptural support for the death penalty, are *sword* and *execute*. If government bears the *sword* as God's minister to *execute* offenders, it certainly sounds like we have a scriptural endorsement for secular capital punishment outside the context of the biblical death penalty.

We begin by looking at the meaning of the word *sword*. In fact there are distinctly different Greek words that we translate into English as *sword*. In a culture that is familiar with different metal slashing instruments, the words in Greek convey realities as different as *pistol* or *rifle*. For us moderns of the ammo age, they are all just *swords*. That was not the case in Paul's time.

A Concise Dictionary of the Words in the Greek New Testament: With Their Renderings in the Authorized English Language Version (Strong, 1992) reveals that *MACHAIRA* means a short sword worn on the belt; in King James English we would say a *dirk*; in modern English, a *dagger*. This is not the instrument used for decapitation, the form of capital punishment by sword in Paul's day (Hanks, 1997). This word is used as a symbol or metaphor for the authority of the courts to inflict punishment. We know that such punishments could include fines, flogging, etc. *RHOMPHAIA*, on the other hand, means a saber, a long and broad cutlass. This is the instrument used for decapitation, the form of capital punishment by sword in Paul's day. The word that is used in the original Greek Scriptures of Romans 13:4 is *MACHAIRA*. That does not seem to make any sense standing in a sentence with the word *execute*. Why would Paul use the word for *dagger* if he were talking about capital punishment? Should he not have used the word for a *broad sword*?

In *The Complete Word Study New Testament With Greek Parallel* (King James Version), we find verse 4 of Chapter 13 of Romans (Zodhiates, 1992, p. 532). The word *execute* is in italics, just like it is in the text of the King James Version of the Bible. This means that the word *execute* is not in the original Greek Scriptures. The word *execute* has been inserted by the translator to fill in a verb that is required for the sentence to make sense in English. The Greek original does not have this verb. The English translation does. Other Christian translations of the Bible have also filled in a verb. For example, the New International Version inserts the word *bring*. The New American Bible uses the word *inflict*. We can see that the usage of the word *execute* in the KJV does not mean capital punishment. It means *to carry out, to perform, to apply*. This is the same usage in modern English when we talk about *executing a football play*. The announcer on *Monday Night Football* may shake his head and say "sloppy execution" when the running back stumbles and fumbles; or "brilliant execution" when a timing pass hits the outstretched hands of a wide receiver one foot into the end zone. No one has been decapitated. No one has been killed. *Execute* can simply mean the act of getting something done, completing a task, fulfilling a duty. Now the verse in Romans 13:4 makes complete sense. A paraphrase would be: But if thou do that which is evil, be afraid; for he beareth not the power of judicial punishment in vain: for he is the minister of God, a revenger to *carry out* wrath upon him that doeth evil (italics added). When we properly understand Romans 13:4, based on the usage of the actual Greek words in the original Scriptures, it is clear that the verse contains no mandate for capital punishment. The verse simply supports the power of judicial authority to impose punishment for malefactors. There is no need to impose capital punishment to be faithful to the proper understanding of Romans 13:4.

But we must answer the claim by some death penalty proponents that the following passage from the Gospel of John is biblical proof that Jesus supports the death penalty. The scene is the trial of Jesus before Pilate:

> So Pilate said to him, "Do you not speak to me? Do you not know that I have power to release you and I have power to crucify you?" Jesus answered, "You would have no power over me if it had not been given to you from above. "

Death penalty supporters using this passage to establish divine mandate for state killing stop there and fail to quote the rest of what Jesus said. The entire exchange reads as follows:

> So Pilate said to him, "Do you not speak to me? Do you not know that I have power to release you and I have power to crucify you?" Jesus answered, "You would have no power over me if it had not been given to you from above. For this reason the one who handed me over to you has the greater sin."

> *(John 19:10–11, NIV)*

This full text can hardly be claimed as Jesus' support for capital punishment. In fact, the Scriptures tell us that Pilate's reaction to this exchange was just the opposite: "Consequently, Pilate tried to release him" (John 19:12 NIV).

Some biblical scholars tell us that:

> Jesus probably does not single out any specific individual, but by 'the one' he means anyone of the Jewish leadership that had handed him over to the Romans. They are all the more

guilty because, possessing the authority that has been committed to them by God, they have used this authority to encompass the death of an innocent person.

(Brown, Fitzmyer, & Murphy, 1968, p. 460)

That would make sense, especially in light of divine commandment reported in the Hebrew Scriptures about executing the innocent. As we approach the question of evidence to be permitted in a capital case, it is helpful to remember that the primary concern of the Biblical death penalty is the fear of executing the innocent. This is rooted in the Bible itself: "Keep far from false charge; do not bring death on those who are innocent and in the right" (Exodus 23:7 TNK). St. Thomas Aquinas (1947, Part 2–2, 64: a2) went so far as to call the killing of an innocent man "intrinsically evil."

The American death penalty is inherently defective in that it creates the risk of executing the innocent. Two of the most pro-death penalty U.S. Supreme Court Justices, Clarence Thomas and recently deceased Antonin Scalia, both acknowledged in *Kansas v. Marsh*[11] that because our human criminal justice system makes mistakes, the only way to guarantee innocent people will not be executed is to repeal the death penalty.

The Bible in the Courtroom

It is not unusual for prosecutors to quote the Hebrew Scriptures to juries in their arguments for death sentences in capital cases. In the last 15 years, almost 100 reported appeals of court decisions in death penalty cases have involved legal challenges by the defendant based on the grounds that the prosecutor used religious remarks to support imposing a death sentence (Blume & Johnson, 2002). There is no indication that the instances of this practice are decreasing. The most popular Scripture quotes to be used by prosecutors are those involving vengeance as justice. Eight reported appellate cases involved quotations of "eye for an eye." The verse from Exodus 21:12, "He that smiteth a man, so that he die, shall surely be put to death," appears in nine such cases. The Rule of Blood in Genesis 9:6, "[who] so sheddeth a man's blood, by man shall his blood be shed," was used by prosecutors in eight other appealed decisions. Finally, six appealed cases involved a quotation from Numbers 35:16, "the murderer shall [surely] be put to death." Other arguments usually involve statements that support the government's right to take life, either by analogy to Noahide Law or based on an interpretation of Romans 13.

Zgonjanin (2006) reported that while citations to the King James Version of the Bible are numerous, courts rarely use other relevant religious authoritative writings to support stated claims. For example, her Westlaw search for the word *Talmud* returned only three results in the Supreme Court cases, and *Torah* appears only five times. According to Zgonjanin:

> One needs go no farther than statistical data to conclude that the Bible is by far the most bellowed religious authority that judges use in their decision-making process and their written opinions. The continuous use of the Bible by judges to support their arguments in written opinions is unjustified and should be barred. The Bible contains many passages, but the scope of their impact on decision-making is impermissibly broad, including such decisions as life or death in capital cases. The use of religious references in judicial decision-making is not rare and cannot be underestimated. Since there is no bright line between a common expression such as "eye for an eye, tooth for tooth," and the biblical mandate "if anyone takes the life of a human being, he must be put to death," courts should never use either text especially not during the sentencing phase.
>
> *(p. 66)*

Those familiar with American death penalty practice know that religion and interpretation of Scripture are surprisingly common issues in the courtroom. One prominent American academic and theological commentator on the death penalty has written that his interest in applying his knowledge to the death penalty arose when a North Carolina public defender asked him to be an expert witness, to testify before the jury in a capital case as to whether or not the Bible mandates capital punishment (Megivern, 1997). This is just the tip of the iceberg. As Duffy (1997) relates:

> Religious arguments, however, are particularly powerful and are likely to resonate with most jurors. Prosecutors often draw support from the Bible for imposing the death penalty. The average juror, and even the legal system, holds the Bible sacrosanct and accords it great weight in influencing behavior. Yet, because they cannot ascertain the arguments' actual influence on jurors, judges often justify excusing biblical references by characterizing the references as innocuous . . . . Religions generally, and Christianity and Judaism in particular, provide moral principles to guide their adherents' actions, and the jurors in a capital sentencing face "the ultimate moral decision." Furthermore, the propriety of death as a form of punishment engenders a debate fraught with religious arguments, with principles and beliefs coming from authoritative religious texts.

"It's So Old It's New": Restorative Justice vs. Retribution

We now return to the discussion we began earlier in this chapter, continuing with a more informed description of retribution. As we previously noted, if we are to understand retribution, we must be able to carefully discern what it *is* and what it *is not*. We have attempted to separate retribution from revenge and, biblically speaking, we have made the case that "an eye for an eye and a tooth for a tooth" is not an informed description of biblical retribution and, in fact, means something entirely different.

Succinctly stated, the biblical "an eye for an eye, a tooth for a tooth" concept is restorative justice. This seemingly severe phrase, found in three books of *Torah*, was written to emphasize the seriousness of crime, and to impose the obligation of restitution in the strongest possible terms to ensure that victims were compensated commensurate with the degree of harm they experienced. Restorative justice, therefore, is not as new a concept as one might think and is the reason why we captioned this section, "it's so old it's new." Certainly, today's concept of restorative justice involves more than simply an "an eye for an eye," but the origin of restoration and compensation for victims is clearly rooted in biblical law.

Retribution must therefore be characterized as something far more meaningful than simply "an eye for an eye." In fact, a biblical view of retribution emphasizes the severity of the crime and the offender's responsibility for the restoration of the victims and their families. McCarthy (2016) states:

> God's saving work of reconciliation and the restoration of human life is the proper context for the injunction "an eye for an eye, a tooth for a tooth." The purpose is to point to the gravity of injuring or killing another person. The purpose is to require rigorous account- ability and to reinforce the obligation of restitution to the victims and their families. It means that no recompense—no sacrifice of restitution on the part of the offender—is too great. Compensation must be given, but the offender is called also to seek forgiveness and atone for the wrongs done. "A life for life" indicates that someone who kills another must give all of his or her life over to the restitution and care of the victims.
>
> *(p. 17)*

Some may still want to maintain the American death penalty; however, we have no choice but to admit that doing so is a function of our will, not God's, and a matter of our desire for revenge. Our examination of the facts allows for no other conclusion.

Notes

1 For example, the Scriptures require a man to grant his wife a "bill of divorce" when he divorces her. What is a bill of divorce? What can it say? What can it not say? All these matters are assumed by Scripture to be elaborated outside the Written Law. In fact, they are well covered by the Oral Law.

2 Numbers 35:30; Deuteronomy 17:6; 19:15.

3 The development of exigency courts and post-Talmudic Jewish courts, especially those of the Middle Ages in Europe, to achieve politically valued executions is beyond our scope. Those interested may find a detailed exposition of this subject in *The Biblical Truth About America's Death Penalty* (Recinella 2004).

4 This portion of the Mosaic Law may not have been God's perfect will. Rather, this may be another example where God's permissive will is in contrast to His divine will. Such was surely the case with polygamy and with the appointment of kings. God's will is monogamy, and he warned his people against the treacheries and burdens of appointing kings over themselves. Yet, polygamy, which first appears in the Bible through Lamech Gen. 4:23, persisted in Biblical times with such critical Biblical heroes as Abraham, Jacob, David and Solomon. And God's people appointed kings to rule over them. 1 Samuel 8:6–27.

5 TANAKH: The Holy Scriptures. © 1985 by the Jewish Publication Society (signified by TNK).

6 The law does not prescribe the precise period of time that must elapse between the formation of and the execution of the intent to take human life in order to render the [killing] a premeditated one; it may exist only a few moments and yet be premeditated. *McCutchen v. State*, 96 So. 2nd 152, 153 (Fla. 1957).

7 Florida Statutes §921.141, *Sentence of Death or Life Imprisonment for Capital Felonies*, provides in relevant part:

(5) AGGRAVATING CIRCUMSTANCES. . . .

(i) The capital felony was a homicide and was committed in a cold, calculated, and premeditated manner without any pretense of moral or legal justification.

Florida Statutes §921.141(5) (j).

8 Florida Statutes §921.141, *Sentence of Death or Life Imprisonment for Capital Felonies*, provides in relevant part:

(5) AGGRAVATING CIRCUMSTANCES. . . .

(k) The victim of the capital felony was an elected or appointed public official engaged in the performance of his or her official duties if the motive for the capital felony was related, in whole or in part, to the victim's official capacity.

Florida Statutes §921.141(5) (k).

9 Florida Statutes §921.141, *Sentence of Death or Life Imprisonment for Capital Felonies*, provides in relevant part:

(5) AGGRAVATING CIRCUMSTANCES. . . .

(d) The capital felony was committed while the defendant was engaged . . . in the commission of . . . or flight after committing . . . any robbery . . . [Note: under the laws of slavery, stealing a slave from the possession of its master or supervisor is the robbery of property]. . . .

(g) The capital felony was committed to disrupt or hinder the lawful exercise of any governmental function or the enforcement of laws.

Florida Statutes §921.141(5) (d) and (g). (Bracketed language mine).

10 Florida Statutes §921.141, *Sentence of Death or Life Imprisonment for Capital Felonies*, provides in relevant part:

(5) AGGRAVATING CIRCUMSTANCES. . . .

(e) The capital felony was committed for the purpose of avoiding or preventing a lawful arrest or effecting an escape from custody.

Florida Statutes §921.141(5) (e).

11 Kansas v. Marsh, 548 U.S. 163 (2006).

References

Aquinas, T. (1947). *Summa theologica*. London: Burns, Oates and Washburn.

Banks, C. (2009). *Criminal justice ethics: Theory and practice*. London: Sage.

Barrett, J. (2001). *Balancing charter interests: Victims' rights and third party remedies*. Toronto, ON: Carswell.

Berman, A. B., & Grossman, M. (Eds.). (2011). *The Oxford dictionary of the Jewish religion*. Oxford: Oxford University Press.

Blume, J. H., & Johnson, S. L. (2002). *Limiting religious arguments in capital cases, a call for reckoning: A conference reader on religion & the death penalty, pew forum on religious & public life.* Chicago: The University of Chicago Divinity School.

Boadt, L. (2012). *Reading the old testament.* Mahwah, NJ: Paulist Press.

Bohm, R. M. (1987). American death penalty attitudes: A critical examination of recent evidence. *Criminal Justice and Behavior, 14,* 380–396.

Bohm, R. M. (1992). Retribution and capital punishment: Toward a better understanding of death penalty opinion. *Journal of Criminal Justice, 20,* 227–236.

Bohm, R. M. (2017). *DeathQuest: An introduction to the theory and practice of capital punishment in the United States.* New York: Routledge.

Brown, R. E., Fitzmyer, A., & Murphy, R. E. (1968). *The Jerome biblical commentary.* Upper Saddle River, NJ: Prentice-Hall.

Crusemann, F. (1996). *The Torah: Theology and social history of old testament law.* Minneapolis: Fortress Press.

Danby, H. (1919). *Tractate Sanhedrin: Mishnah and Tosefta.* New York: Macmillan.

Davis, J. F. (2005). *Lex talionis in early Judaism and the exhortation of Jesus in Matthew 5.38–42.* London: T & T Clark International.

Duffy, B. C. (1997). Barring foul blows: An argument for a per se reversible-error rule for prosecutors' use of religious arguments in the sentencing phase of capital cases. *Vanderbilt Law Review, 50,* 1357–1359.

Dyneley, P. (2010). Review: The Code of Hammurabi, (1904). *American Journal of Theology, 8*(3).

Ellsworth, P., & Gross, S. (1994). Hardening of the attitudes: Americans' views on the death penalty. *Journal of Social Issues, 50,* 19–52.

Gerstenberger, E. (1995). *". . . He/they shall be put to death": Life preserving divine threats in old testament law: Ex Auditu, 11, 43.* Allison Park, PA: Pickwick Publications.

Gobert, J., & Dine, J. (1993). *Cases and materials on criminal law.* London: Blackstone Press Ltd.

Greenawalt, K. (1983). Punishment. *The Journal of Criminal Law and Criminology, 74,* 343–362.

Hanks, G. (1997). *Against the death penalty: Christian and secular arguments against capital punishment.* Scottsdale, PA: Herald Publishers.

Holy Bible, New International Version, ©1973, 1978, 1984. International Bible Society, Used by permission of Zondervan Bible Publishers.

Isser, S. (1990). Two traditions: The law of exodus 21:22–23 revisited. *The Catholic Bible Quarterly, 52,* 30–45.

Kant, I. (2005). *Groundwork for the metaphysics of morals* (Lara Denis, Ed.). New York: Broadview Press.

Lambert, E., Clarke, A., & Lambert, J. (2004). Reasons for supporting and opposing capital punishment: A preliminary study. *Internet Journal of Criminology,* 1–34. Retrieved December 4, 2007, from http://www.internetjournalofcriminology.com/

McCarthy, D. M. (2016). *Death penalty and discipleship.* Collegeville, MN: Liturgical Press.

McCutchen v. State, 96 So. 2nd 152, 153 (Fla. 1957).

Megivern, J. J. (1997). *The death penalty: An historical and theological survey.* Mahwah, NJ: Paulist Press.

Moberly, W. (1996). The ethics of punishment (1968). In N. V. Paranjape (Ed.), *Criminology and penology* (p. 144). Allahabad: Central Law Publications.

Murphy, J. G. (1994). Marxism and retribution. In A. Duff & D. Garland (Eds.), *A reader on punishment* (pp. 44–77). New York: Oxford University Press.

Otto, E. (1994). Aspects of legal reforms and reformations in ancient cuneiform and Israelite law. In B. M. Levinson (Ed.), *Theory and method in biblical and cuneiform law.* Sheffield: Sheffield Academic Press.

Packer, H. (1968). *The limits of the criminal sanction.* Stanford, CA: Stanford University Press.

Radelet, M., & Borg, M. (2000). The changing nature of death penalty debates. *Annual Review of Sociology, 26,* 43–61.

Rao, S. (1999). *Current issues in criminal justice and medical law.* New Delhi: Eastern Law House.

Recinella, D. S. (2004). *The biblical truth about America's death penalty.* Boston: Northeastern University Press.

Rosenberg, I. M., & Rosenberg, Y. L. (1998). Lone star liberal musings: "Eye for Eye" and the death penalty. *Utah Law Review, 505,* 510.

Siddique, A. (1997). *Criminology: Problems and perspectives.* Lucknow: Eastern Book.

Sprinkle, J. M. (2006). *Biblical law and its relevance.* Lanham, MD: University Press of America.

Steinsaltz, A. (2006). *The essential Talmud.* New York: Basic Books.

Strong, J. (1992). *A concise dictionary of the words in the Greek new testament: With their renderings in the authorized English language version.* Iowa Falls: World Bible Publishers.

Von Hirsh, A. (1987). *Past or future crimes: Deservedness and dangerousness in the sentencing of criminals.* New Jersey: Rutgers University Press.

Webster, G. and C. & Merriam, N. *Webster's Ninth new collegiate dictionary.* (1990). Springfield, MA: Merriam-Webster, Inc.

Westbrook, R. (1986). Lex talionis and exodus 21, 22–25. In J. Gabalda (Ed.), *Revue biblique* (pp. 52–69). Paris: Librairie Lecoffre.

Wright, C. J. (2004). *Old testament ethics for the people of god.* Downers, IL: InterVarsity Press.

Zgonjanin, S. (2006). Quoting the Bible: The use of religious references in judicial decision-making. *New York City Law Review, 9,* 31–91.

Zodhiates, S. (Ed.). (1992). *The complete word study new testament with Greek parallel.* (King James Version). Iowa Falls, IA: World Bible Publishers, Inc.

9

GENERAL DETERRENCE AND BRUTALIZATION

Anthony G. Vito and Gennaro F. Vito

Deterrence and the Death Penalty

The criminal justice system is intended to follow the wants and needs of society. The issue that may arise when invoking the death penalty is "What constitutes justice?" Is society by using the death penalty fulfilling the needs of society, so that citizens know what types of punishment will be carried out? Is it trying to fulfill the needs of the victim's family? To carry out justice, considerations should include the severity of the crime and the blameworthiness of the offender. Yet it is important that society makes certain, when handing out punishments such as the death penalty, that it is more than viewing the crime as a tort, where the victim's needs and retribution are the sole considerations.

Societies have long shown a desire to use the death penalty. The issue though is that as society continues to evolve, we have moved past the *lex talionis* (i.e., an eye for an eye) mindset. Issues such as a retaliation or compensation should not be the focuses for execution. Capital punishment cases must consider more issues than the harmfulness of the offense and punishing the offender. If society is concerned with following due process and serving justice, then seeking retribution is not a good justification for using the death penalty.

Levying a death sentence can also serve as a deterrent for future offenders, but it should not be the main point of justice. Imposing the death penalty on any offender for any kind of crime would be unjust. Yet the use of giving the offender the death penalty for a crime such as murder could help restore order, because the offender would pay back his or her "debt to society."

There are several justifications offered executing convicted murderers. For example, retribution emphasizes that criminals deserve to be punished because they have violated a legal system from which everyone benefits (Young, 1983). Thus, offenders have taken unfair advantage of the law-abiding citizens in society. Punishing them restores the social balance and reaffirms social bonds, sending the message that crime is unacceptable. As stated by van den Haag (1975, p. 15): "Retribution must be paid because it is owed, because it has been threatened, and a threat is a (negative) promise." It calls for execution when death is a deserved punishment—"it does not tolerate killing as a means to some greater social good" (Lempert, 1981, p. 1182). Since the state administers executions as a retributive punishment, it is a "controlled alternative to vengeance" (Mazerac, 2014–2015, p. 8). The concern of punishment is to right a wrong, not its effect on preventing future crimes. Retribution requires that offenders deserve (just desert) punishment (such as execution) proportional to their offense (in this case, homicide).

From a public policy perspective, one of the main justifications for the death penalty is deterrence. Deterrence theory suggests that swift, certain, and severe punishment reduces crime. The rational choice perspective holds that human beings calculate both the costs and benefits of criminal behavior before they decide whether to engage in crime. The threat of execution will prevent others from considering homicide. The goal of punishment is sentencing commensurate with the seriousness of the crime, the extent to which it adversely affects society, and the culpability of the offender. Deterrence provides a moral basis for capital punishment. The major premise is that executing murderers will save more lives than are taken. Executing killers provides a moral example—teaching people it is wrong to kill (Lempert, 1981, pp. 1187–1190).

Classical school theorists such as Beccaria and Bentham portrayed humans as rational, pleasure-seeking, pain-avoiding creatures. They assumed people would engage in criminal behavior when it brings them pleasure (generates rewards) and carries little risk of pain. From this perspective, the deterrent aspect of executions has the potential to reduce homicides in two ways.

First, executing murderers will prevent or discourage any other persons from committing a homicide. Such prevention justifies the death penalty as a crime prevention tool as a threat to potential offenders (Ball, 1955). As a general deterrent, executions should cause a decline in the homicide rate. Executing convicted murderers will deter other motivated offenders and serve as a general deterrent. The execution broadcasts to society what happens to murderers.

Second, execution will prevent future crimes by the convicted offender. This impact is specific deterrence—execution incapacitates the offender and future threats to society are eliminated (Andenaes, 1974; Bohm, 2012, p. 177). For example, several studies have traced the recidivism rates of former death row inmates who had their sentences commuted because of the *Furman* decision (see Vito & Wilson, 1988; Marquart & Sorensen, 1989). Because many of these offenders were eventually paroled, these studies test the argument that the death penalty, through incapacitation, prevents future murders. A study that followed the entire cohort (Marquart & Sorensen, 1989, p. 478) learned that only one committed murder following release from prison (Marquart & Sorensen, 1989). Both methods serve as moral justification for execution—to prevent future homicides and to protect the public.

For the proposed punishment to have the maximum deterrent effect, two aspects are relevant. First is certainty of apprehension and punishment. If offenders are caught and sanctioned, they may alter their behavior. Second, the offender must be aware of the existence of the punishment. This knowledge can also influence the decision making of the offender (Ball, 1955, pp. 350–351). However, from the deterrence perspective, the crucial issue is "What is the marginal deterrent effect of capital punishment? What deterrent benefit does execution provide over a life sentence?" (Lempert, 1981, p. 1192).

Philosophical Arguments and the Death Penalty

Regardless of the social scientific evidence, there exist certain philosophical arguments in supporting and negating the death penalty as a deterrent. Ernest van den Haag (1982, p. 326) argues, "Our penal system rests on the proposition that more severe penalties are more deterrent than less severe penalties." His statement lends credence to the view that society needs punishment to serve as a deterrent to would-be offenders. The question is what offenses should be eligible for capital punishment. Historically, society has had a wide, all-encompassing view of what offenses are worthy of the death penalty, covering some 50 to 200 different offenses. Yet the scientific evidence available to date fails to support van den Haag's (1982) arguments on the deterrent effect of the death penalty.

The philosopher Cesare Beccaria (1975) believed giving a person a life sentence better serves the needs of society. The view of life imprisonment, according to Beccaria (1975), was a concept known as perpetual servitude. Even today, when the average death penalty case takes 15 years, Beccaria (1975) would still argue that life imprisonment is a better deterrent.

Another philosophical issue with capital punishment is trying to determine what murder is and what capital punishment is. Beccaria (1975) argues that if society has laws to punish murder, it would not make sense to use execution to deter violence. Yet van den Haag (1982) argues that capital punishment is not the legal equivalent of murder because capital punishment is a lawful act. Some will make the argument that capital punishment is appropriate for heinous crimes. However, Amsterdam (1982) states there are two issues with this argument. First, everyday citizens do not typically commit heinous crimes. Second, using capital punishment to deter murder contradicts the logic that "two wrongs do not make a right."

A Brief of History of Capital Punishment and Deterrence

Historical accounts provide vivid examples of how capital punishment is not a deterrent. English history has shown the disdain that society had for pickpocketers. When a public hanging would take place for someone who committed pickpocketing, it has been well documented that pickpocketing took place during the hanging (Cassell, 2004). In eighteenth and nineteenth century in Virginia, the most common crime was horse stealing, which was also a capital offense. Since the late 1940s in the United States, executions have been banned from public view—a fact that supports the brutalization hypothesis (Bowers, 1988). If society thought deterrence worked and there was not a brutalization effect, then executions would be open to the public and be broadcast live on the television and the internet.

A brief history of capital punishment in the U.S. provides the background for the deterrent effect of the death penalty. From 1930 through 1967, 3,859 convicted offenders were executed in the United States (Culver, 1999). In 1972, the United States Supreme Court issued a landmark case— *Furman v. Georgia*. Here, the Supreme Court ruled that the "arbitrary and capricious" procedures leading to execution violate the Eighth Amendment—the defendant's right to due process of law. As a result, all death sentences at the time (over 600 death row inmates in 30 states) were commuted to a sentence of life imprisonment (Marquart & Sorensen, 1988).

In *Furman v. Georgia* (1972), Justice William Brennan made the argument that the sentence of the death penalty was inconsistent with "the sanctity of life." It is important to understand Brennan's view based on trying to protect the needs of society. When trying to hold offenders accountable for their actions, it is crucial to comprehend that people can tell right from wrong. However, that does not mean that all offenders are acting rationally when committing their offense. Based on this understanding that humans are not vicious animals, Brennan stated, "The deliberate extinguishment of human life by the state is uniquely degrading to human dignity." What he is articulating is that society is continuing to evolve and has new standards of decency, and that by using the death penalty this only moves society backward. It is demeaning not only for society as a whole but also the key players in the process of handling an execution—including the criminal and the executioner.

However, legislatures quickly took the stance that executions could be constitutionally acceptable if due process safeguards guided the capital sentencing process. In *Gregg v. Georgia* (1976), the court approved Georgia's "guided discretion" statute, outlining several procedures designed to prevent due process violations and exclude "extra-legal" factors, such as race, from capital sentencing. Guided discretion would ensure due process in capital sentencing.

Under the Georgia statute, prosecutors could seek the death penalty in homicide cases where "aggravating circumstances" were present—such as homicide plus a concurrent first-degree felony. In death penalty cases, the criminal justice system requires a bifurcated trial. What this means is that there will be two separate trials. The first trial establishes whether the defendant is guilty or not. If the defendant is found guilty, then a second trial takes place to determine if the defendant should receive the death penalty, based on mitigating and aggravating circumstances. The Supreme Court upheld this implementation, stating: "the punishment of death does not invariably violate the Constitution, objective standards to guide, regularize, and make rationally reviewable the process for imposing the sentence of death" could provide due process in capital sentencing.

Arguments for Deterrence

Those who argue for using the death penalty most often focus on its deterrent capabilities and that it provides retributive justice. Their focus is on making the offender an "example" for those in society thinking about committing similar acts but also making sure that retribution serves not only the victim's family but also greater society. On face value, one would assume that making sure that punishment is certain and severe would result in less crime and also deter crime more than less certain or severe punishments. Yet the overall research does not support this viewpoint. In fact, abolitionists argue that giving offenders life in prison without the opportunity for parole is just as much a deterrent as giving a person the death penalty.

The administration of the death penalty always contains the possibility of executing an innocent person. If an innocent person were executed, this would bring harm to society that would be beyond repair and be a major injustice. In this event, death penalty supporters who believe in deterrence would focus on the fact of whether more lives were saved even if an innocent person was executed—there could be a net gain as opposed to a net loss. If one innocent person was executed, but 50 people were saved as a result, death penalty supporters could accept it as a positive outcome because of the death penalty's deterrent capabilities.

Research Findings on the Deterrent Effect of Executions

General Deterrence

It is important for both society and criminal justice officials to be aware of information on the death penalty and deterrence. Scientific studies were cited as reasons U.S. Supreme Court Justice Antonin Scalia supported the deterrent effect of the death penalty as recently as *Glossip v. Gross*.

Certain flaws exist with applying deterrence theory to the death penalty. The main assumption of deterrence theory is that the offender is acting rationally and considering various factors such as certain and severity when committing a crime such as murder. Specifically, capital sentencing and deterrence theory assume that the offender knows what offenses are eligible for the death penalty (Bowers, 1988). Deterrence theory does not account for unexpected circumstances that could result in murder when the offender did not originally intend to do so, such as armed robbery, crimes committed under the influence of drugs or alcohol, and crimes of passion (Bowers, 1988).

Again, general deterrence is the proposition that increases in the certainty, severity, or swiftness of punishment produce decreases in criminal behavior for the population as a whole. Most researchers test either the certainty or severity of punishment. The severity of punishment is easy to measure. One could look, for example, at the average prison sentence for crimes in different jurisdictions. Studies on capital punishment (the ultimate in severity), though, are by far the most common tests of this aspect of deterrence theory (Cochran, Chamlin, & Seth, 1994). The executed offenders will never commit another crime (this is incapacitation rather than deterrence).

The issue is whether the death penalty serves as a general deterrent against homicide. Paternoster (2009, p. 240) offers a deterrence hypothesis for the death penalty:

> Because capital punishment is a more severe punishment than life imprisonment, then states that have the death penalty as a possible punishment for murder should have lower murder rates than states that punish murder with life imprisonment.

Concerning the death penalty, the most common research strategies focus on a comparison of homicide rates (1) between states that have the death penalty and those that do not and (2) executions and homicide over time within the same jurisdiction.

The scientific evidence on the deterrent effect of the death penalty can be broken down into two categories. First are studies that were conducted before 1975, the most famous of which was conducted by Thorsten Sellin (1959, 1967), which examined the deterrent effect of the capital punishment in states from 1920 to 1963. His major finding (Sellin, 1959, 1967) was the absence of conclusive evidence supporting the deterrent effect of the death penalty on the homicide rates. One of his studies used a matching technique to compare the murder rates of death penalty states with non–death penalty states for the years 1920 to 1955 and 1920–1962 (Sellin, 1980). The research discovered no difference between the two; executions did not affect homicide rates. A constant theme in this kind of research is the difficulty of untangling cause and effect and of controlling for differences among states. Replication of Sellin's work has led to the same conclusion—the death penalty fails to deter homicides (Bailey & Peterson, 1997; Zimring & Hawkins, 1986).

The second category is studies conducted after 1975. The first study to find a deterrent effect with the death penalty was by Ehrlich (1975). The study looked at multiple risk factors with a key variable being execution risk. The overall findings found that "an additional execution per year over the period in question may have resulted, on average, in seven or eight fewer murders." Ehrlich's work played a key role in such death penalty cases as *Fowler v. North Carolina* (1976) and *Gregg v. Georgia* (*1976*) as scientific evidence that was used to show support in the majority's opinion in each court case. However, Ehrlich's study has drawn strong criticism from multiple researchers, expressing concerns with the methodology that was used. In 1975, the National Academy of Sciences expressed the harshest criticism by stating that "research on this topic is not likely to produce findings that will or should have much influence on policy makers" (cited in Zimring & Hawkins, 1986 pg. 180).

However, some researchers have built off Ehrlich's (1975) piece by applying complex "econometrics" examining national execution/homicide data that report finding deterrent effects. However, several criminologists reexamined Ehrlich's methods and questioned his conclusion, stating it provided "no useful evidence on the deterrent effect of capital punishment" (National Research Council, 1978, p. 9; see also Baldus & Cole, 1975; Bowers & Pierce, 1975; Klein, Forst, & Filatov, 1982). Lempert (1981, p. 1215) asserts that Ehrlich's (1975) "conceptually and methodologically flawed" research deserves "no place in the debate on capital punishment" and that his conclusions were unsupported by replications of his work.

A key criticism of studies on the deterrent effect of the death penalty when it comes to econometric studies are based on but not limited to the following arguments. First, the studies do not account for different types of murder (Fagan, 2005; Fagan, Zimring, & Geller, 2006; Shephard, 2005). Second, time-series analysis is not used in any of the studies that would allow the researcher to able to account for any influence over the different years used in the study (Fagan, 2005). Third, none of the studies directly examined the deterrence hypothesis (Fagan, 2005). The final argument is that the studies do not account for other variations in the murder rate that is examined (Fagan, 2005).

Other regression-based studies produced mixed results on the deterrent effect of the death penalty. Lester (1979a) used states as the unit of analysis when studying the deterrent effect of the death penalty. The period that was examined was 1930–1965. The overall findings were that there was a greater likelihood of the homicide decreasing from one year to the next if the state executed one or more people.

Lester (1979b) builds off his previous work, using the proportion of executions to examine the deterrent effect of the death penalty. The study found significant results supporting the deterrent effect. If a state held between 1 and 8 executions, the number of homicides dropped by 51.8%; if there were 9 to 16 executions the number of homicides dropped by 69.2%; and if there were between 17 and 23 executions there was a 61.0% drop in the number of homicides. These results show that as the number of executions increases there is a greater deterrent effect on the number of homicides in a given state for the years 1930–1964.

Yet, in a later study, Lester (2000) reported results that conflict with his previous studies. Using data from 1977–1992 from the continental United States, the study did not support the deterrent effect. In states that had one or more executions the number of homicides decreased by 34.2%, but in states with no executions the number of homicides decreased by 46.4%.

Archer, Gartner, and Beittel (1983) conducted a national level study across several different countries using a "before-and-after" methodology on the effect of the death penalty on the homicide rate. Regardless of the country, the results of the study found no conclusive evidence to support the deterrent effect. In fact, any fluctuation in the homicide rate was a result of factors not related to the death penalty.

Yet Dezhbakhsh, Rubin, and Shepherd (2003) analyzed county-level, panel data for the post-*Gregg* era. Dezhbakhsh et al. (2003) looked at the deterrent effect of the death penalty for murder using county-level data for the years 1977 to 1996. The study found support for the deterrent effect that executions had on murder. Specifically, the authors found that one execution deterred on average 18 murders.

Kovandzic, Vieraitis, and Boots (2009) used the same data to produce econometric models. The overall results found no support that the death penalty will deter offenders from committing a homicide. Kovandzic et al. (2009) do offer reasons for why they found different results from previous economic studies. First, previous studies either omitted certain variables or failed to include state-specific trends and or dummy years in the model. Second, other studies may not have used valid and reliable instruments to examine the potential for bias between homicide and execution risk. The final issue is that previous studies may not have adjusted standard errors to account for serial correlation. Another issue that is mentioned is that economic studies on the death penalty tend to follow Becker's (1967) rational choice theory, which follows a cost-benefit model, while it would be more appropriate to use Cornish and Clarke's (1986) rational choice theory, where criminals rationally calculatie their decision based on bounded or limited rationality.

Shepherd (2005) looked at the issue of whether capital punishment deters different types of murder and, if there is a deterrent effect, on how long the offender waits on death row. The death penalty decreased the likelihood for murder involving crimes of passion, intimates, and acquaintances, and murders of Caucasians and African Americans. For every one execution, there is one less intimate murder, two fewer acquaintance murders, three fewer crimes of passions, three fewer murders of a Caucasian person, and 1.5 fewer murders of an African American (Shepherd, 2005). The results on the length of wait on death row were found to be significant. Specifically, there is one less murder for every 2.75 fewer years spent on death row (Shepherd, 2005).

Using state-level data for the years, 1978–1997 Zimmerman (2004) examined the effect that executions had on the number of murders. The results of Zimmerman's (2004) work found that one execution deterred 14 murders. In 2006, Zimmerman built on his previous study and looked at the impact of certain types of executions. The study found that the deterrent effect of the death penalty was largely based on using electrocution (i.e., the electric chair) in comparison to lethal injection or the gas chamber.

However, many of the studies looking at the same jurisdiction over time failed to find a relationship between executions and homicide rates. These studies took advantage of the moratorium on capital punishment that resulted from the 1972 *Furman* decision. McFarland (1983) examined the impact that news media coverage had on four executions to see if it affected the homicide rate. The data used were both news coverage and the weekly health statistics for homicide. The overall results showed no significant effect on increasing or decreasing the homicide rate. Any impact in places where it may have been affected was found to be due to severe weather conditions (i.e., snowstorm) rather than a celebrated news story resulting in execution.

Cloninger and Marchesini (2001) used death penalty data from the state of Texas to look at the issue of deterrence. The findings of the study support the notion that more executions result in fewer homicides. However, these results are often short lived based on how often executions occur or do not occur. This study lends support to the deterrence argument similar to other economic studies, but it cannot prove whether deterrence works.

In (2006), Cloninger and Marchesini built on their previous work by examining death penalty data in the state of Illinois. The study looked at pre (i.e., death penalty was allowed) and post (death penalty was placed on a moratorium) and the deterrent effect on homicide. The results of the study found that the four years postmoratorium saw an increase of 150 additional homicides. This would show support for the deterrence argument that not having the death penalty put Illinois citizens at a greater risk of being a victim of homicide.

Liu (2004) found support for the theoretical basis of deterrence from the economist viewpoint. The data used are state-level data from 1940 to 1950. The use of the death penalty serves a valuable deterrent to murder. Yet how effective it is as a deterrent is based on the certainty that the death penalty is utilized in a given state.

Shepherd (2005) would later find mixed results in an examination of counties during 1977–1996. Results indicated that of the 27 states that executed, 6 states saw a decrease in murder, 13 saw an increase in murder, and 8 states saw no change in the murder rate. Hence, only 22% of the states saw a deterrent effect of executions on murder (Shepherd, 2005).

Fagan et al. (2006) contributed to the knowledge about deterrence in their examination of two homicide groups in Texas, those who committed a crime that made them eligible for the death penalty and those whose crimes did not. Their conclusions revealed that although a decrease in homicide occurred, this decrease involved homicides that were not eligible for the death penalty. Consequently, the execution rates did not influence death eligible homicides, therefore invalidating the deterrence theory.

Utilizing panel data from 1977 to 2006, Kovandzic et al. (2009) concluded that the death penalty failed to deter crime. They argue that previous studies were unable to find similar conclusions due to the omission of variable bias, failing to adjust standard errors, and the exclusion of reliable and valid instruments to address simultaneity bias between execution risk and homicide (Kovandzic et al., 2009).

In two studies utilizing Texas, Land, Teske, and Zheng (2009, 2012) found support for deterrence. Their first study reported a range of effect from about .5 homicides to about 2.5 homicides depending upon the model (Land et al., 2009). The second study reported a deterrent effect for both nonfelony homicides when utilizing an autoregressive model (−1.96 per execution) and a nonautoregressive model (−1.4 per execution). However, nonfelony homicides are less likely to result in a conviction for first-degree murder that is required for the death penalty under Texas statutes (Radelet, 2012). Their findings are results from an exploratory study, and the objectives identified do not relate to public policy (Radelet, 2012).

Land et al. (2009), consistent with Zimmerman (2004), concluded that the actual announcement of the impending execution provides the deterrent effect. However, this contradicts studies conducted by criminologists and economists that have found little support for a relationship between homicide and the media announcement of an impending execution or a completed execution (Bailey, 1990, 1998; Hjalmarsson, 2009; King, 1978; Peterson & Bailey, 1991; Phillips, 1980; Stolzenberg & D'Alessio, 2004).

In assessing risk, Apel (2013) found that although individuals may have knowledge of criminal penalties, they are typically unable to estimate the probability and magnitude of the penalties accurately. Risk changes as individuals have personal experiences with crime and punishment. As they commit crimes and avoid punishment, offenders may become doubtful of sanctions and consider them improbable (Apel, 2013).

In their research, Manski and Pepper (2013) found that depending on the conditions imposed, executions both increased and decreased homicide. This ambiguity allows the community to draw its own conclusions, which often are determined by consensus. Manski and Pepper (2013) caution against seeking an all-or-nothing answer to the death penalty. A summary of deterrence research showed that the majority of capital punishment studies (70%) failed to support a deterrent effect for the death penalty (Dolling, Entorf, Hermann, & Rupp, 2009).

Reviews of general deterrence death penalty studies question the positive findings for executions. Critical reviewers conclude that the findings are so fragile that the deterrent effect of executions is difficult to determine. Donohue and Wolfers (2005) questioned the sensitivity of previous studies that have found a deterrent effect for the death penalty. The issues presented that researchers have not or cannot adequately deal with are based on not using theory to guide the research, measurement, and the model that is used. Donohue and Wolfers (2005) found that even in their models the deterrent effect of the death penalty is highly sensitive. They even go so far as to say, "econometric pyrotechnics . . . have yielded heat rather than light" (Donohue & Wolfers, 2005, pg. 842).

Yang and Lester (2008) conducted a meta-analysis of 104 deterrence studies of executions. They found that 60 of the studies reported a deterrent effect for executions, but 35 reported a significant brutalization effect. The meta-analysis findings of Yang and Lester (2008) overall showed that deterrence and brutalization were not statistically significant.

Berk (2005) scrutinized previous studies that showed a deterrent effect with the death penalty. Berk (2005) notes that there are multiple issues with these studies. First, is that it is extremely rare for a state to execute more than five people in a given year. In most years, there are less than five executions per year, and this represents 99% of death penalty data. Given this fact, there is no evidence to support the theory of deterrence and the death penalty when it comes to the number of executions and either the number of homicides or the homicide rate in a given year. Second, the state of Texas is an extreme outlier for the death penalty. When including Texas in death penalty research across all states it gives a false impression that deterrence is significant. Given these two key limitations, the vast majority of years and the vast majority of states do not support deterrence.

Berk (2009) makes a compelling argument about the issues present in the current econometric literature involving the death penalty and deterrence. What has taken place to date between those in favor and against the death penalty is an endless cycle of articles trying to argue that "my-model-is-better-than-your-model." Based on the previous studies by economists there are inherent limitations with the data. First, the use of observational data increases the risk of a weak research design (Berk, 2009). It would be much better to use a randomized experiment or even a strong quasi-experiment when the main goal is causal inference. Second, by using a causal model, it allows for better variables and covariates that can result in a clearer understanding of the death penalty and deterrence relationship than previous research (Berk, 2009). Understanding these issue is also important for matters of public policy because: (1) no credible evidence shows support for deterrence, (2) no credible evidence rules out deterrence, and (3) people need to know of what qualifies good evidence (Berk, 2009).

Going back to Berk's (2005) piece, he makes a great argument that sums up the issue with the current econometric work on the death penalty and deterrence:

> [My] analyses reported here are hardly exhaustive and are perhaps affected by [my] misunderstandings about the data provided, or by errors in the data themselves. Nevertheless, the results raise serious questions about whether anything useful about the deterrent value of the death penalty can ever be learned from an observational study with the data that are likely to be available.

Finally, the National Research Council (2012, p. 2) concluded that research to date on the effect of capital punishment on homicide is not informative about whether capital punishment decreases, increases, or has no effect on homicide rates. Therefore, the committee recommends that these studies not be used to inform deliberations requiring judgments about the effect of the death penalty on homicide. Consequently, claims research demonstrates that capital punishment decreases or increases the homicide rate by a specified amount or has no effect on the homicide rate and should not influence policy judgments about capital punishment.

The Brutalization Effect

Executions may have a different and negative effect beyond deterrence. Research has shown that the death penalty can have a brutalization effect on society (Bowers, 1988), meaning that using the death penalty would increase the likelihood of more murders taking place. Two such variants of the brutalization effect lend credence to view. One is the "suicide-murder syndrome"; this is based on several different cases that show that the offenders committed murder because they wanted to commit suicide but for whatever reason had failed to attempt suicide and wanted the government to kill them (Amsterdam, 1982). The other is the "executioner syndrome" (Bedau, 1982). Committing murder serves society and creates greater public good by killing the person (the victim deserves it for some reason) or the offender is doing so to become famous and have the spotlight.

Scholars suggest that the state's use of execution legitimizes violence, showing it is appropriate to kill people who have gravely offended them. Bowers and Pierce (1980) examined the impact of executions in New York state (1906–1963) and estimated that each execution led to two to three homicides that would otherwise not have occurred—a brutalization effect that was strongest during the first month following an execution.

Two pieces of research examined the results of Oklahoma's 1990 return to the use of capital punishment after a 25-year moratorium (Bailey, 1998; Cochran et al., 1994). Each study tracked weekly homicide figures for one year before and after the execution. Little or no evidence of deterrence emerged from these studies. Both studies, however, found that certain types of homicides increased following the execution—a brutalization effect. Extending the research of Cochran et al. (1994), Bailey (1998) conducted a multivariate autoregressive analysis and found support for the brutalization theory for total homicides and homicides involving both strangers and nonstrangers.

Research conducted by Cochran and Chamlin (2000) continued to show the lack of relationship between the death penalty and deterrence, with some concluding the brutalization effect existed in which executions produced a higher rate of homicides. The authors categorized homicides as stranger/nonstranger and felony/nonfelony. Felony murders occur when an offender commits homicide to further another felony (e.g., an aggravating circumstance). The death penalty may deter offenders because they planned to commit the underlying felony. The analysis revealed a small but significant deterrent effect for felony murder when it involved nonstrangers. However, this result overshadowed a much larger brutalization effect for homicides resulting from arguments among strangers.

Muddying the waters, researchers studying homicides in Texas between 1994 and 2007 got results that were the reverse of those found in California. In Texas, a short-term (lasting one month) modest deterrent effect emerged for nonfelony homicides, while felony homicides resulted in a smaller brutalization effect (Land et al., 2012).

Conclusion

What are the conclusions after decades of death penalty research? First, readers should remember most studies of the death penalty find it has no effect on homicides. Second, the brutalization and deterrent effects discovered in recent studies are small and sensitive to changes in calculation methods. The conservative conclusion is that there is no strong empirical evidence that the death penalty deters homicides.

There are those who will still try to provide a rebuttal to scientific studies that show that the death penalty has no deterrent effect. Typically, the arguments against these studies take the following forms. First, the deterrent ability of the death penalty has been greatly diminished because the punishment is not certain and severe. If the punishment were to be certain and severe, it would greatly affect the deterrent value. Second, the studies that have been conducted did not use the best statistical analysis, which resulted in greater unreliability (Committee on the Judiciary, U.S. Senate, 1982). The issue here is that citizens who are deterred by the threat of having the death penalty imposed on them will not show up in any data that are used. The final argument is that studies conducted using data from the 1960s and 1970s saw the homicide rate increase as the number of executions in those same states or counties decreased.

Many reasons exist that may explain why punishment does not deter crime. First, the offender may not be rational—a primary assumption of deterrence theory. Irrationality among offenders may be a product of their upbringing. Their failure to learn higher cognitive skills (moral reasoning, empathy, problem solving), neurotransmitter imbalances, ingestion of illegal drugs and/or alcohol, head injuries, personality characteristics (impulsivity, insensitivity, anxiety, impulsivity, and risk taking), and a tendency to think in terms of short-term rather than long-term consequences, as well as association with criminal peers (Bernard, Snipes, & Gerould, 2010, p. 353). For example, Steve Nunn, a former Kentucky representative, was convicted of the murder of Amanda Ross in 2011. While serving as a legislator, Nunn co-sponsored a bill that mandated the violation of a protection order as an aggravating circumstance in homicide cases under Kentucky criminal law. Nunn pled guilty to avoid the death penalty created by his own legislation in exchange for a sentence of life without parole (Fisher, 2016).

Second, individuals typically have no notion of the certainty and severity of punishment, altering their perceptions about deterrence (Kleck, Sever, Li, & Gertz, 2005; Nagin, 1998). The risk of execution is far from great. Up to 2012, only 15% of offenders sentenced to death since *Gregg* have been executed, and a large fraction of death sentences was subsequently reversed (National Research Council, 2012, p. 5).

Crime experts have rejected the use of the death penalty as an effective crime control measure. A survey of presidents of American criminological societies determined that the majority (88%) of these crime scholars reject the conclusion that the death penalty has a deterrent impact upon homicide rates (Radelet & Lacock, 2009). A national survey of police chiefs determined that only 1% of the respondents identify "expanded use of the death penalty" as a primary focus for reducing violent crime (Dieter, 1995).

In addition, several moral questions surround the use of the death penalty. First, the potential for the execution of the innocent is a major limitation on the morality of capital punishment. Through October 12, 2015, 156 death row defendants have either been: (1) acquitted of all charges related to the crime that placed them on death row, (2) had all charges related to the crime that placed them on death row dismissed by the prosecution, or (3) been granted a pardon based on evidence of innocence (Death Penalty Information Center, 2017b). In addition, it has been estimated that 13 death row inmates executed since 1976 may have in fact been innocent (Death Penalty Information Center, 2017a; see also Radelet, 2008–2009).

Second, racial disparities in capital sentencing, especially the failure to sanction killers of blacks, are evidence of bias (whether conscious or unconscious) on the part of actors in the criminal justice system. There is a plethora of research studies documenting bias in capital sentencing since the *Gregg* decision (see Baldus & Woodworth, 2003).

Finally, Steiker (2005, pp. 771–778) argues that capital punishment violates human dignity in the following ways:

1. It is excessive in relation to its purpose. Incapacitation can be accomplished via a sentence of life without parole.
2. It destroys the distinctively human capacities of the punished.
3. It destroys the distinctively human capacities of the society in whose name they are publically inflicted.

In this fashion, capital punishment is not a guarantor of greater personal security but a correlate of greater human degradation.

There is some experimentally based evidence that people are more likely to inflict punishment for vengeful aims rather than deterrence-based ones. Crockett, Ozdemir, and Fehr (2014, p. 2284) reported that people valued retribution-based punishment to reduce payoffs even in the absence of any future deterrence-based promise to prevent harm. Naturally, retribution is a less socially desirable motive for punishment than deterrence.

A scenario-based study of sentencing determined that individuals follow a just deserts (moral proportionality and deservedness) perspective rather than a deterrence-based one to sanction offenders (Karlsmith, Darley, & Robinson, 2002, pp. 295–297). Significantly, a review of 11 studies on capital jury decision making found that death penalty supporters, those who believed it is a deterrent and those who believed offenders sentenced to LWOP (life without parole) would still be released were more likely to sentence a defendant to death regardless of findings concerning aggravating and mitigating factors (O'Neil, Patry, & Penrod, 2004, p. 463).

In sum, the research evidence and moral arguments fail to support deterrence as a legitimate punishment for homicide. There is no credible evidence for execution as a deterrent to homicide, and the flawed implementation of capital sentencing fails to justify the continued use of execution as a method of punishment.

References

Amsterdam, A. G. (1982). Capital punishment. In H. A. Bedau (Ed.), *The death penalty in America* (3rd ed., pp. 346–358). New York: Oxford University Press.

Andenaes, J. (1974). *Punishment and deterrence.* Ann Arbor: University of Michigan Press.

Apel, R. (2013). Sanctions, perceptions, and crime: Implications for criminal deterrence. *Journal of Quantitative Criminology, 29*(1), 67–101.

Archer, D., Gartner, R., & Beittel, M. (1983). Homicide and the death penalty: A cross-national test of a deterrence hypothesis. *Journal of Criminal Law and Criminology, 74*(3), 991–1013.

Bailey, W. (1990). Murder, capital punishment, and television: Execution publicity and homicide rates. *American Sociological Review, 55*(5), 628–633.

Bailey, W. (1998). Deterrence, brutalization, and the death penalty: Another examination of Oklahoma's return to capital punishment. *Criminology, 36*(4), 711–733.

Bailey, W., & Peterson, R. (1997). Murder, capital punishment, and deterrence: A review of the literature. In H. Bedau (Ed.), *The death penalty in America: Current controversies* (pp. 135–175). New York: Oxford University Press.

Baldus, D., & Cole, J. (1975). A comparison of the work of Thorsten Sellin and Issac Ehrlich on the deterrent effect of capital punishment. *Yale Law Journal, 85*(2), 170–186.

Baldus, D., & Woodworth, G. (2003). Race discrimination and the death penalty: An empirical and legal overview. In J. Acker, R. Bohm, & C. Lanier (Eds.), *America's experiment with capital punishment: Reflections on past, present, and future of the ultimate penal sanction* (pp. 501–552). Durham, NC: Carolina Academic Press.

Ball, J. (1955). The deterrence concept in criminology and the law. *Journal of Criminal Law, Criminology & Police Science, 46,* 347–354.

Beccaria, C. (1975). *On crimes and punishment* (H. Paolucci, Trans.). Indianapolis, IN: Bobbs-Merrill.

Becker, G. S. (1967). Crime and punishment: An economic approach. *Journal of Political Economy, 76,* 169–217.

Bedau, H. A. (1982). *The death penalty in America* (3rd ed.). New York: Oxford University Press.

Berk, R. (2005). New claims about executions and general deterrence: Deja vu all over again? *Journal of Empirical Legal Studies, 2*(2), 303–330.

Berk, R. (2009). Can't tell: Comments on "Does the death penalty save lives?". *Criminology & Public Policy, 8*(4), 845–851.

Bernard, T., Snipes, J., & Gerould, A. (2010). *Vold's theorectical criminology.* New York: Oxford University Press.

Bohm, R. (2012). *DeathQuest: An introduction to the theory and practice of capital punishment in the United States.* Waltham, MA: Elsevier.

Bowers, W. J. (1988). The effect of executions is brutalization, not deterrence. In K. C. Haas & J. A. Inciardi (Eds.), *Challenging capital punishment: Legal and social science approaches* (pp. 49–89). Newsbury Park, CA: Sage.

Bowers, W. J., & Pierce, G. (1975). The illusion of deterrence in Isaac Ehrlich's research on capital punishment. *Yale Law Journal, 85*(2), 187–208.

Bowers, W. J., & Pierce, G. (1980). Deterrence or brutalization: What is the effect of executions? *Crime & Delinquency, 26*(4), 453–484.

Cassell, P. G. (2004). In defense of the death penalty. In H. A. Bedau & P. G. Cassell (Eds.), *Debating the death penalty: Should America have capital punishment?* (pp. 183–217). New York: Oxford University Press.

Cloninger, D., & Marchesini, R. (2001). Execution and deterrence: A quasi-controlled group experience. *Applied Economics, 33*(5), 569–576.

Cloninger, D., & Marchesini, R. (2006). Execution moratoriums, commutations, and deterrence: The case of Illinois. *Applied Economics, 38,* 967–973.

Cochran, J., & Chamlin, M. (2000). Deterrence and brutalization: The dual effects of executions. *Justice Quarterly, 17*(4), 685–706.

Cochran, J., Chamlin, M., & Seth, M. (1994). Deterrence or brutalization? An impact assessment of Oklahoma's return to capital punishment. *Criminology, 32*(1), 107–134.

Committee on the Judiciary, U.S. Senate. (1982). Capital punishment as a matter of a legislative policy. In H. A. Bedau (Ed.), *The death penalty in America* (3rd ed., pp. 311–318). New York: Oxford University Press.

Cornish, D. B., & Clarke, R. V. (1986). *The reasoning criminal: Rational choice perspectives on offending*. New York: Springer.

Crockett, M., Ozdemir, Y., & Fehr, E. (2014). The value of vengeance and the demand for deterrence. *Journal of Experimental Psychology—General, 143*(6), 2279–2286.

Culver, J. (1999). Twenty years after Gilmore: Who is being executed? *American Journal of Criminal Justice, 24*(1), 1–14.

Death Penalty Information Center. (2017a, January 7). *Executed but possibly innocent*. Death Penalty Information Center. Retrieved from www.deathpenaltyinfo.org/executed-possibly-innocent

Death Penalty Information Center. (2017b, January 7). *The innocence list*. Death Penalty Information Center. Retrieved from www.deathpenaltyinfo.org/innocence-list-those-freed-death-row

Dezhbakhsh, H., & Shepherd, J. (2006). The deterrent effect of capital punishment: Evidence from a "judicial experiment". *Economic Inquiry, 44*(3), 512–535.

Dieter, R. (1995). *On the front line: Law enforcement views on the death penalty*. Washington, DC: Death Penalty Information Center.

Dolling, D., Entorf, H., Hermann, D., & Rupp, T. (2009). Is deterrence effective? Results of a meta-analysis of punishment. *European Journal on Crime Policy and Research, 15*(2), 201–224.

Donohue, J., & Wolfers, J. (2005). Uses and abuses of empirical evidence in the death penalty debate. *Stanford Law Review, 58*, 791–845.

Ehrlich, I. (1975). The deterrent effect of capital punishment: A question of life and death. *American Economic Review, 65*, 397–417.

Fagan, J. (2005). *Deterrence and the death penalty: A critical review of new evidence*. Washington, DC: Death Penalty Information Center. Retrieved from www.deathpenaltyinfo.org/files/pdf/FaganTestimony.pdf

Fagan, J., Zimring, F., & Geller, A. (2006). Capital punishment and capital murder: Market share and the deterrent effects of the death penalty. *Texas Law Review, 84*(7), 1803–1868.

Fisher, J. (2016, December 26). *The Steve Nunn murder case*. Jim Fisher's True Crime. Retrieved from http://jimfishertruecrime.blogspot.com/2012/03/politician-from-hell-steve-nunn-murder.html

Hjalmarsson, R. (2009). Does capital punishment have a "local" deterrent effect on homicides? *American Law & Economics Review, 11*(2), 310–334.

Karlsmith, K., Darley, J., & Robinson, P. (2002). Why do we punish? Deterrence and just deserts as motives for punishment. *Journal of Personality & Social Psychology, 83*(2), 284–299.

King, D. (1978). The brutalization effect: Execution publicity and the incidence of homicide in South Carolina. *Social Forces, 5*, 683–687.

Kleck, G., Sever, B., Li, S., & Gertz, M. (2005). The missing link in general deterrence research. *Criminology, 43*(3), 623–660.

Klein, L., Forst, B., & Filatov, V. (1982). The deterrent effect of capital punishment: An assessment of the evidence. In H. Bedau (Ed.), *The death penalty in America* (pp. 138–159). New York: Oxford University Press.

Kovandzic, T., Vieraitis, L., & Boots, D. (2009). Does the death penalty save lives? New evidence from state panel data, 1977 to 2006. *Criminology & Public Policy, 8*(4), 803–843.

Land, K. C., Teske, R. H., Jr., & Zheng, H. (2009). The short-term effects of executions on homicides: Deterrence, displacement, or both? *Criminology, 47*(4), 1009–1043.

Land, K. C., Teske, R. H., & Zheng, H. (2012). The differential short-term impacts of executions on felony and non-felony homicides. *Criminology & Public Policy, 11*(4), 541–563.

Lempert, R. (1981). Desert and deterrence: An assessment of the moral bases of the case for capital punishment. *Michigan Law Review, 79*(6), 1177–1231.

Lester, D. (1979a). Executions as a deterrent to homicides. *Psychological Reports, 44*, 562.

Lester, D. (1979b). Deterring effect of executions on murder as a function of number and proportion of executions. *Psychological Reports, 45*, 598.

Lester, D. (2000). Executions as a deterrent to homicide. *Perceptual and Motor Skills, 91*(2), 696.

Liu, Z. (2004). Capital punishment and the deterrence hypothesis: Some new insights and empirical evidence. *Eastern Economic Journal, 30*(2), 237–258.

Manski, C., & Pepper, J. (2013). Deterrence and the death penalty: Partial identification analysis using repeated cross sections. *Journal of Quantitative Criminolog, 29*(1), 123–141.

Marquart, J., & Sorensen, J. (1988). Institutional and post-release behavior of Furman-commuted inmates in Texas. *Criminology, 26*(4), 677–694.

Marquart, J., & Sorensen, J. (1989). National study of the Furman-commuted inmates: Assessing the threat to society from capital offenders. *Loyola of Los Angeles Law Review, 23*(5), 5–28.

Mazerac, A. (2014–5). A stay at confinement lodge—How comfortable is too comfortable? How the enforcement of the eigtth amendment's cruel and unusual punishment clause is destroying the retributive and deterrent puroposes of punishment. *The Journal of Race, Gender & Poverty, 6*(1), 1–24.

McFarland, S. (1983). Is capital punishment a short-term deterrent to homicide? A study of the effects of four recent American executions. *Journal of Criminal Law & Criminology, 74*(3), 1013–1032.

Nagin, D. (1998). Criminal deterrence research at the outset of the twenty-first century. *Crime & Justice, 23*, 1–42.

National Research Council. (1978). *Deterrence and incapacitation: Estimating the effects of criminal sanctions on crime rates* (A. Blumstein, J. Cohen, & D. Nagin, Eds.). Washington, DC: National Academy of Sciences.

National Research Council. (2012). *Deterrence and the death penalty* (D. Nagin & J. Pepper, Eds.). Washington, DC: The National Academies Press.

O'Neil, K., Patry, M., & Penrod, S. (2004). Exploring the effects of attitudes toward the death penalty on capital sentencing verdicts. *Psychology, Public Policy, & Law, 10*(4), 443–470.

Paternoster, R. (2009). Deterrence and rational choice theories. In J. Miller (Ed.), *21st criminology—a reference handbook* (Vol. 1, pp. 236–244). Thousand Oaks, CA: Sage Publications.

Peterson, R., & Bailey, W. (1991). Felony murder and capital punishment: An examination of the deterrence question. *Criminology, 29*(3), 367–395.

Phillips, D. (1980). The deterrent effect of capital punishment: New evidence on an old controversy. *American Journal of Sociology, 86*(1), 139–148.

Radelet, M. (2008–2009). The role of innocence argument in contemporary death penalty debates. *Texas Tech Law Review, 41*, 199–220.

Radelet, M. (2012). The death penalty in Texas. *Criminology & Public Policy, 11*(3), 573–578.

Radelet, M., & Lacock, T. (2009). Do executions lower homicide rates? The views of leading criminologists. *Journal of Criminal Law & Criminology, 99*(2), 489–508.

Sellin, T. (1959). *The death penalty*. Philadelphia: The American Law Institute.

Sellin, T. (1967). *Capital punishment*. New York: Harper & Row.

Sellin, T. (1980). *The penalty of death*. Beverly Hills, CA: Sage.

Shepherd, J. (2005). Deterrence vs. brutalization: Capital punishment's differing impacts among states. *Michigan Law Review, 104*, 203–255.

Steiker, C. (2005). No, capital punishment is not morally required: Deterrence, deontology, and the death penalty. *Stanford Law Review, 58*, 751–790.

Stolzenberg, L., & D'Alessio, S. (2004). Capital punishment, execution publicity, and murder in Houston, Texas. *Journal of Criminal Law & Criminology, 94*(2), 351–380.

van den Haag, E. (1975). *Punishing criminals*. New York: Basic Books.

van den Haag, E. (1982). "In Defense of the Death Penalty: A Practical and Moral Analysis," pp. 323-341 in H.A. Bedau (ed.) The Death Penalty in America, Third Ed. New York: Oxford University Press.

Vito, G., & Wilson, D. (1988). Back from the dead: Tracking the progress of Kentucky's Furman-commuted death row population. *Justice Quarterly, 5*(1), 101–112.

Yang, B., & Lester, D. (2008). The deterrent effect of executions: A meta-analysis thiry years after Ehrlich. *Journal of Criminal Justice, 36*(5), 207–239.

Young, D. (1983). Let us content ourselves with praising the work while drawing a veil over its principles: Eighteenth century reactions to Beccaria's On crimes and punishments. *Justice Quarterly, 1*(1), 155–170.

Zimmerman, P. (2004). State executions, deterrence, and the incidence of murder. *Journal of Applied Economics, 7*, 163–193.

Zimring, F., & Hawkins, G. (1986). *Capital punishment and the American agenda*. Cambridge, UK: Cambridge University Press.

Cases Cited

Fowler v. North Carolina, 428 U.S. 904 (1976).

Furman v. Georgia, 408 U.S. 238 (1972).

Gregg v. Georgia, 428 U.S. 153 (1976).

10

INCAPACITATION AND LIFE WITHOUT PAROLE

Jonathan R. Sorensen and Thomas J. Reidy

The death penalty has been touted for its ability to permanently incapacitate offenders. The U.S. Supreme Court, in its Eighth Amendment analysis of the constitutionality of the death penalty, confirmed incapacitation as a legitimate penological justification (*Jurek v. Texas*, 1976). Some state death penalty schemes are explicitly predicated on the ability of the ultimate sanction to prevent capital defendants from committing "criminal acts of violence that constitute a continuing threat to society" (see Longmire, infra.). Most other states and the federal government allow evidence of a defendant's potential for violent conduct in the future as a statutory or nonstatutory aggravating circumstance (Shapiro, 2009).

Despite the importance placed on a defendant's potential to commit additional bad acts in the future during capital murder trials, the sentence of life without the possibility of parole (LWOP) is being relied on increasingly as an alternative to the death penalty in the United States (see Bohm, infra.). With the exception of Alaska, all states and the federal government have LWOP as an available sentencing option for capital murder. In Texas, one of the most recent states to adopt LWOP as an alternative to the death penalty, an assistant district attorney argued against passage of the law in testimony before a senate judicial committee,

> I think that life sentences without parole do create a segment of the prison population who have no hope. They know that they are going to be there for life, and they have nothing to lose. And I think it does create a terrific security problem for prison officials and for the staffs that work in prisons
>
> *(McInnis, 2003, pp. A-19)*

Similar arguments are made on a regular basis to juries in capital murder cases. In a recent federal case, for instance, after much expert testimony regarding the prevalence of violence in the Federal Bureau of Prisons, a U.S. attorney argued in closing that with a sentence of LWOP, "the defendant knows he is never getting out. He knows he has nothing to lose . . . . Do you really believe when he has nothing to lose, he will stop the fight . . .?" (*U.S. v. Savage*, 2013). Interviews with former jurors have shown that these arguments generally resonate and that the question of how a capital defendant may behave if allowed to live plays a central role in jury deliberations (Sandys, Pruss, & Walsh, 2009; Vartkessian, Sorensen, & Kelly, 2017). Despite such rhetoric, the question arises as to what level of additional protection the death penalty provides in terms of incapacitation relative to a sentence of LWOP. This chapter explores research related to incapacitation and the sentence of LWOP as well as issues stemming from housing this growing segment of the U.S. prison population.

Research on Incapacitation and LWOP

LWOP Versus Death

In terms of risk to the community, LWOP and a death sentence should have similar effects (barring escape) in precluding the possibility of harm to members of the community. However, LWOP prisoners may have a greater opportunity than death-sentenced inmates to continue to harm members of the community who work in prison as staff members, teachers, mental health professionals, chaplains, and visitors in addition to other inmates. This greater level of opportunity, however, is predicated on greater security precautions on death row and the eventual execution of a death-sentenced inmate. Although death-sentenced inmates are generally held under more secure conditions of confinement than LWOP inmates, studies have uncovered incidents of serious assaults and even murders (however rare) among those confined on death row (Edens, Buffington-Vollum, Keilen, Roskamp, & Anthony, 2005; Reidy, Sorensen, & Cunningham, 2013). The presumption of greater security on death row also fails to consider time spent in local facilities by death-sentenced inmates, most of whom are retried or resentenced at some point during their stays on death row. Further, the provision of extensive mandated appeals in death-sentenced cases has also resulted in more reversals/commutations to life sentences than executions, so most eventually exit death row to serve time in the general prison population (Snell, 2014).

Evidence for the effectiveness of a life sentence in incapacitating capital murderers was first gauged by examining the behavior of those who had been released from death row through commutation, retrial, or other remedy. One early study looked at the commutation of death-sentenced inmates after the abolition of the death penalty in Canada (Akman, 1966). During a two-year period, 1964–65, none of the 69 former death-sentenced inmates were involved in any serious assaults in prison. A survey of the behavior of U.S. inmates released from death row as a result of *Furman v. Georgia* (1972) found a cumulative prevalence of serious assaults of 3% over a 15-year follow up period (Marquart & Sorensen, 1989). Studies examining the behavior of former death row inmates released in the early to mid-twentieth century found similarly low rates of assault in Texas (Wagner, 1988) and New Jersey (Bedau, 1965).

These studies, however, were completed prior to the advent of LWOP in most jurisdictions. Thus, the carrot of parole was available and may have served as an incentive for former death row inmates to behave. Relatedly, the management and culture of prisons have changed in recent years, although these changes are likely to result in greater control and less violence in the institution. Prison homicide, for instance, decreased from a rate of 55 per 100,000 in 1980 to around 5 per 100,000 since 2000 (Noonan & Ginder, 2014). This figure is consistent with rates of homicide in the community, remarkable considering the demographic characteristics (age, gender, and race) of the prison population.

More recent studies have found similarly low rates of serious prison assaults and violence among former death row inmates in Arizona (Sorensen & Cunningham, 2009), Indiana (Reidy, Cunningham, & Sorensen, 2001), Oregon (Reidy et al., 2013), and Texas (Cunningham, Sorensen, Vigen, & Woods, 2011; Edens et al., 2005; Marquart, Ekland-Olson, & Sorensen, 1989). Interestingly, the issue of incapacitation is directly raised by the statutes in Oregon and Texas, which require that jurors determine whether there is a probability that capital defendants will commit criminal acts of violence in the future. Absent an affirmative response to the "future dangerousness" inquiry by jurors, capital defendants in those jurisdictions automatically receive life sentences. In the Texas and Oregon studies, then, all former death-sentences inmates had been found to be likely to commit acts of violence in the future, implying that the death sentence was necessary to protect society (prison or the general community) from capital defendants in those states. Nonetheless, "violence-predicted" studies of these former death-sentenced inmates found them to have cumulative rates of serious assault below 10% over the course of several years (Cunningham et al., 2011; Edens et al., 2005; Marquart et al., 1989, Reidy et al., 2013).

Statutes requiring a future dangerousness determination also raise the question of how successful juries are in their decision making, spawning comparisons of the behavior of inmates based on determinations made by jurors. Granted such comparisons are complicated by the fact that *most* violence-predicted inmates receive a sentence of death, and hence conditions of confinement are not typically equivalent to the group of "violence-rejected" inmates who *must* receive life sentences. This problem of nonequivalent conditions of confinement is partially resolved when comparisons are restricted to inmates who have received life sentences from a jury in spite of jury determinations that future violence is probable. Studies in Oregon (Reidy et al., 2013) and Texas (Marquart et al., 1989) found that when jury determinations concerning the future dangerousness of life-sentenced defendants were compared to behavioral outcomes in prison, juries performed no better than chance in the accuracy of their predictions. Given the low base rates of serious violent behavior, affirmative predictions (violence likely) were *incorrect* greater than 90% of the time, while negative predictions (no violence likely) were *correct* greater than 90% of the time.

Two studies have examined the prison behavior of defendants in federal capital murder trials whose cases included nonstatutory aggravating factors worded similarly to the "probability of criminal acts of violence" (PCAV) of the Texas and Oregon statutes. One study of the federal system examined 72 capital cases wherein jurors were asked to make a prediction about the future likelihood of criminal acts of violence when sentencing defendants. The results were similar to those noted in the state studies, with violence-predicted inmates committing acts of violence at very low rates (Cunningham, Sorensen, & Reidy, 2009). The study, however, was confounded by the fact that most of the violence-predicted inmates were sentenced to death and typically served time under more restrictive conditions than life-sentenced inmates. The other federal study examined the behavior of 145 federal inmates sentenced to LWOP (mostly through plea bargains), 104 of whom had the PCAV nonstatutory aggravating factor initially alleged by prosecutors compared to 41 cases in which the PCAV nonstatutory aggravator was not alleged (Cunningham, Reidy, & Sorensen, 2008). The violence-predicted LWOP inmates did not have significantly higher rates of assaultive infractions involving various levels of injury than the violence-rejected LWOP inmates. In fact, none of the LWOP inmates, regardless of prosecutorial assertion, were involved in an assault resulting in life-threatening or fatal injuries over an average time of 6.2 years served on their sentences. Regression models controlling for case characteristics and defendant attributes confirmed that the assertion of PCAV by prosecutors was not significantly related to assaults or other rule infractions.

Perhaps the strongest evidence to date that LWOP could safely be employed as an alternative to the death penalty comes from Missouri, the only jurisdiction to have fully "mainstreamed" its death-sentenced population (Lombardi, Sluder, & Wallace, 1997). As a result of a consent decree, Missouri Department of Corrections (MDOC) began modifying conditions of death row confinement in 1987. Progressive reforms were accelerated once death row was moved to the newly opened Potosi Correctional Center (PCC) in 1989, and by January 1991 capital punishment (CP) inmates were fully integrated into the general inmate population of PCC, which initially included all of the system's LWOP inmates. Since then all CP inmates and LWOP inmates in PCC have been eligible for the same programming, activities, and housing as the general population inmates. They share cells, meals, recreation, and work details and are subject to the same incentives and sanctions. Other than their sentence, CP and LWOP in Missouri are subjected to equivalent conditions of confinement, allowing for one of the best "natural" experiments to test the possible influence of their sentences on behavior while incarcerated.

Two studies have specifically examined the behavior of LWOP inmates relative to CP inmates housed in PCC. The first study focused on rates of violent institutional misconduct among 149 CP inmates in comparison to 1,054 LWOP inmates housed in PCC during January 1991 to January 2002 (Cunningham, Reidy, & Sorensen, 2005). Results showed that the annual rate of violent institutional misconduct among LWOP inmates was similar to CP inmates (9.6 and 7.6 per 100 annually), and significantly lower than other term-sentenced prisoners housed in PCC, whose rate of violent infractions was 42.5 per 100 annually. The second study compared the behavior of 85 CP inmates to 702 LWOP inmates housed in PCC during August 2006 through February 2015 (Cunningham, Reidy, & Sorensen, 2016). While the rates of violent misconduct appeared to be slightly higher among LWOP inmates relative to CP inmates (6.0 versus 3.5 per 100 annually), results from a regression model showed that initial differences were accounted for by other demographic variables, such as age, race, and mental health status.

Results from the studies described here have consistently shown that capital murderers sentenced to LWOP either after a death sentence or in lieu of a death sentence did not present a disproportionate threat to other inmates or staff while confined in prison under a life sentence. Another line of questioning concerns whether a sentence of LWOP is related to an increase in the likelihood that inmates will commit acts of violence in prison relative to inmates serving the more traditional life with parole (LWP) sentence.

LWOP versus LWP

Does LWOP achieve a greater incapacitation effect beyond that served by a traditional LWP sentence? The view of lifers by correctional administrators and staff historically has been that they are generally among the most manageable prisoners (Flanagan, 1980, 1995; Wardlaw & Biles, 1980). Perhaps their relative docility is owed to an acceptance of their fate, the effect of aging, the process of adjusting to the prison environment that comes with a lengthy incarceration, becoming accustomed to minor privileges accorded for good behavior, or the hope of eventual release (Johnson & Dobrzanska, 2005). Hope of eventual release from incarceration has always been the "light at the end of the tunnel" for those serving life sentences; and one of the primary ways to convince a parole board that a long-term inmate had been rehabilitated would be to use one's time productively and to behave well during his or her confinement. With the advent of LWOP sentences, fears surfaced about this group of inmates who, arguably having nothing to lose, would become a "new breed of super-inmates prone to violence and uncontrollable behavior" (Stewart & Lieberman, 1982, p. 16).

While some have suggested that capital murderers sentenced to LWOP be housed under austere and extremely restrictive conditions of confinement, barring misbehavior they are generally housed alongside parole-eligible inmates under conditions ranging from medium to maximum security confinement (Blecker, 2013). Several studies have compared the behavior of LWOP inmates to LWP inmates in an effort to determine the degree of similarity or dissimilarity that could potentially be linked to the missing incentive of parole. These studies addressed the extent to which LWOP inmates' behavior mirrors that of traditional lifers and other long-term inmates. They attempt to answer the question of whether LWOP inmates, like their LWP and long-term counterparts, are generally among the most manageable prisoners, or whether LWOP inmates represent a new breed of prisoners having nothing to lose and prone to violence in the institution.

One means of determining whether the level of rule violations committed LWOP exceeds that of other inmates involves simply comparing their levels of misconduct and violence to group rates of misconduct among a broader cohort of inmates serving time under similar conditions of confinement. One such examination including 145 LWOP inmates in the federal system (Cunningham et al., 2008) relied on high-security inmates serving sentences in U.S. penitentiaries during the same time period, 2001 through 2005 ($n = 18,561$) for comparison. The comparison relied on a variety of disciplinary outcomes that ranged from an omnibus category including any disciplinary violation to assaults resulting in varying levels of injuries. Not surprisingly, as seriousness of rule violations increased, the prevalence of involvement decreased. During an average observation period exceeding 6 years, and ranging from 6 months to 15 years, the proportion of LWOP inmates involved in incrementally more serious/harmful levels of rule violations was as follows: any disciplinary violation, 71.0%; potentially violent misconduct, 40.0%, serious misconduct, 32.4%, assaultive infractions, 20.7%; serious assaults, 9.0%; assaults resulting in moderate injuries, 0.7%; and, assaults resulting major injuries, 0.0%. Most importantly, LWOP inmates were found to commit various levels of rule violations at a rate similar to the broader pool of high-security inmates, with no significant differences between them.

The largest-scale study of LWOP inmates conducted to date relied on a similar methodology, restricting the comparison group to other high-security inmates but including control variables for the controls (Cunningham & Sorensen, 2006). The study examined institutional misconduct among a cohort of 9,044 inmates entering the Florida prison system during 1998 through 2002 who were sentenced to a term of 10 years or more serving their time in close-custody confinement. Included among the cohort were 1,897 LWOP inmates. The frequency and prevalence of various levels of institutional rule violations was examined through 2003, with follow-up periods ranging from 1 to 6 years and averaging 3.3 years (3.4 for LWOP inmates). The prevalence of rule infractions among LWOP inmates was as follows: total violations, 75.0%; potentially violent misconduct, 23.4%; assaults, 7.4%; assaults with injuries, 1.6%; and assaults with serious injuries, 0.6%. The frequency of violent rule misconduct among LWOP inmates was generally higher than inmates sentenced to 20 years or more in prison but lower than those sentenced to less than 20 years. Results from a survival analysis showed that LWOP inmates' time to commission of an infraction involving violence or having a high violence potential was longer than those serving less than 20 years, similar to those serving 20 to 29 years, and shorter than those serving 30 years or more. Specifically, the Cox regression model showed a reduction of 26.6% in the hazard rate for LWOP inmates over those sentenced to less than 20 years in prison.

Other studies have attempted to isolate the effect of parole by comparing the behavior among LWOP inmates specifically to lifers who were eligible for parole. The first study to examine misconduct among LWOP inmates in this manner was completed in Louisiana, one of the earliest states to implement a "natural-life term" in 1977 (Williamson, 1985). Inmates sentenced to life prior to that date could establish parole eligibility after serving 10.5 years. The study compared the rate of rule violations among three groups of inmates: 50 inmates with a life sentence (lifers) who would become eligible for parole, a group of 100 nonlifers (short-termers) who were also eligible for parole, and a group of 50 lifers who were not eligible for parole (natural-life group). The findings were somewhat mixed in that the natural-life group was more disruptive in terms of its rate of rule violations than the parole-eligible lifers, by a factor of two; and yet the natural-life group averaged fewer violations per month than the short-termers. The comparison of rates, however, between natural lifers and traditional lifers was confounded by the amount of time served during the observation period, with lifers having served more than 10 years on average in comparison to natural lifers who were still in the early stages of their sentence (the highest-risk period for inmate violations), with an average time served of less than 3 years at the point of data collection.

A study utilizing a similar methodology examined the effect of differential parole eligibility on inmates' level of institutional misconduct in Texas (Morris, Longmire, Buffington-Vollum, & Vollum, 2010). In September 1991, parole eligibility changed from 15 years (noncapital life) to 35 years (capital life), and two years later to 40 years, for inmates sentenced to life imprisonment for capital murder. While technically not life-without-parole, the newer statute severely limited capital lifers' chances of being released from prison. The study examined the behavior of 400 inmates sentenced during September 1987 through August 1994, three years before and after the implementation of the more restrictive parole eligibility standards on capital murderers. Relying on three multivariate modeling techniques to analyze eight groupings of misconduct outcomes, the authors found that capital lifers were no more likely than pre-capital lifers to commit rule infractions during their first three years of confinement in any of the models, and were significantly less likely to commit various types of rule violations in nearly half of the models. Most pertinent, analyses revealed that capital lifers were found to be less than half as likely to commit *violent* rule infractions in logistic regression models, and event history models showed that time to failure (commission of a *violent* act) for capital lifers was less than half that for noncapital life inmates at any given point during the three-year observation period. One limitation of the study, however, was the potential for cohort effects. While follow-up periods overlapped to an extent, the observation period for the noncapital lifers dated from the late 1980s into the early 1990s and the observation period for the capital lifers stretched through the mid-1990s, which, in itself, could have influenced inmates' level of offending and/or the level of reporting during either period.

Four studies have included information about the misconduct of LWOP inmates in Missouri. Two studies described earlier compare the behavior of mainstreamed CP inmates and LWOP inmates to a group of all "term-sentenced" inmates in PCC. The earlier study included 2,199 parole-eligible inmates in its comparison group during 1991 to 2002 (Cunningham et al., 2005). Controlling for other relevant variables in a logistic regression model, LWOP inmates and CP inmates were shown to be about half as likely to commit a violent rule violation in comparison to term-sentenced inmates. The second study contrasted the behavior of CP and LWOP inmates with the behavior of 3,000 parole-eligible inmates serving time in PCC during 2006 through 2015 (Cunningham et al., 2016). The results showed that those serving sentences for LWOP and CP inmates engaged in equivalent or lower rates of serious and violent misconduct in comparison to parole-eligible inmates. Such findings continue to illustrate that neither a capital or first-degree murder conviction nor associated sentences of LWOP or CP are indicative of elevated rates of violent maladjustment warranting special classification or housing considerations.

The remaining two Missouri studies specifically examined the behavior of LWOP and LWP inmates. The earlier study compared rule infractions among 323 LWOP inmates convicted of capital murder to those committed by 93 death-sentenced capital murderers and a sample of 232 LWP inmates convicted of second-degree murder during 1977 through 1992 (Sorensen & Wrinkle, 1996). All three groups committed violent rule infractions at an identical rate of 6 per 100 inmates annually. The second study compared the commission of general rule infractions among all 176 LWOP inmates entering prison during August 2006 through February 2014 to 172 randomly selected LWP meeting the same criteria (Sorensen & Reidy, in press). Negative binomial regression and proportional hazards models showed no significant differences between LWOP and LWP inmates in terms of their overall count of violations nor the number of months to the first violation.

Issues Related to the Incarceration of LWOP Inmates

Inmates serving LWOP represent a relatively small but singular class of inmates within federal and state prisons that pose unprecedented challenges to prison administrators and policymakers. Most LWOP inmates received this sentence for capital murder, but others face this sentence in some states for specific violent crimes or the accumulation of such crimes (e.g., the California Three Strikes Law), and others by receiving consecutive lengthy sentences resulting in a virtual LWOP sentence (Couzens & Bigelow, 2017). The concern that these inmates have been permanently incarcerated for violent crimes has led to an erroneous expectation of undisciplined behavior and unfettered violence toward staff and other inmates because they have no incentive to behave. Studies cited in this chapter clearly refute the image of an LWOP inmate as a disproportional risk to the safety and security of the prison environment. Nevertheless, permanent incapacitation of these inmates necessarily contributes to other adjustment difficulties involving psychological, social, physical, and institutional pains of imprisonment that make their incarceration experience different from younger inmates and those serving shorter terms of confinement. These considerations have a number of implications for institutional policy, inmate management, and research. Prison officials and researchers need to consider the broader context for understanding this population, including the ways these inmates cope with the unique strains associated with their permanent conditions of confinement and specialized programming needs as they age toward inevitable death in custody.

Legal and Political Landscape

Given the legal landscape and political will in the United States toward retribution, law and order, and the need for politicians to be viewed as "tough on crime," the number of inmates receiving undeviating life sentences will continue to increase, meaning that the population of elderly inmates will also rise. The Bureau of Justice Statistics (Carson & Sabol, 2016) reported the imprisonment rate for inmate's age 55 and older more than tripled from 1993–2013, and nearly a third of the oldest offenders were serving life or death sentences. Prisons will need to find creative solutions to manage the array of complications posed by this population incapacitated for a lifetime, especially as they become elderly with all the associated infirmities of aging. Leigey (2015), and others (e.g., Appleton & Grover, 2007), including the international community (e.g., European Court of Human Rights in *Vinter and Others v. The United Kingdom*, 2013), make strong penological, humanitarian, and financial arguments for altering a sentence of life with no chance of release to life with the potential for release after a lengthy term of years. The reality of such a politically charged decision in the United States is obvious. Arguments reinforcing harsh punishment, deterrence, and public protection will continue to dominate the conversation for retaining LWOP sentences for years to come, even long after these inmates continue to be a realistic threat to anyone due to age or medically related immobility. Rehabilitation of these inmates is not a goal. Rather, these LWOP inmates have permanently lost their liberty and will serve their sentences under austere living conditions, will experience a plethora of deprivations without the hope of release, and will die in prison.

Surprisingly little empirical evidence other than that related to violence risk is available about the broader implications of an LWOP sentence. Correctional administrators and policymakers must address this gap in knowledge in order to develop an affirmative and long-range strategy for managing this diverse population. The social, emotional, and health needs of these inmates are not uniform and will change over time as inmates age across decades of incarceration. No single solution to managing LWOP inmates will work, so the challenge for correctional administrators will be to develop creative and flexible approaches to management that take into account the variability within the LWOP population. Research can play a critical role in providing evidence-based constructive solutions to decision makers as they struggle with adapting to the specialized needs of LWOP inmates that promote inmate wellness and social order.

Security Factors Associated With LWOP

Elected officials, prosecutors, jurors, and lawmakers are more disposed to view LWOP inmates as being at high risk for prison violence because they "have nothing to lose" (McInnis, 2003; Cunningham & Sorensen, 2007; *U.S. v. Savage*, 2013). A mounting body of scientific evidence provided in this chapter contradicts the argument that these inmates pose a risk to public safety within the institution (Cunningham et al., 2005, 2016; Morris et al., 2010; Cunningham & Sorensen, 2006). LWOP inmates, after initial adjustment tribulations, settle into a relatively stable pattern of adjustment and are disproportionally less likely to engage in serious acts of violence as they progress through their sentence (Cunningham et al., 2005, 2008, 2016; Flanagan, 1995). In fact, studies across multiple states (Texas, Missouri, Florida, Indiana, Arizona, and Oregon) demonstrate that as a group LWOP inmates behave similarly or in many instances are better behaved than general population inmates in maximum-security prisons (see Cunningham, 2010). Inmates facing life without possibility of release, like other long-term inmates, can be safely controlled using current correctional policies and strategies (see Cunningham et al., 2016; Sorensen & Reidy, in press). However, institutions wishing to avoid simply "warehousing" these inmates face a wide array of management challenges such as the need for age appropriate programming, cost-effective health care, specialized housing, and avoidance of victimization.

Sentence length exerts a differential effect on LWOP inmates compared to those serving shorter sentences (Cunningham & Sorensen, 2007; Morris et al., 2010; Toman, Cochran, Cochran, & Bales, 2015). Some commentators equate the severity of an LWOP sentence to "America's other death penalty" (Johnson & McGunnigal-Smith, 2008), and the "penultimate penalty" (see Appleton & Grover, 2007). When LWOP inmates first enter prison and realize that no release is possible, some manifest their distress related to these circumstances through disciplinary infractions (Sorensen & Reidy, in press) as a reaction to unfairness in the criminal justice system (Toman et al., 2015) and also exhibit mental health symptoms (Leigey, 2015) early in their sentence. From a policy standpoint, prison officials should recognize these differences in adjustment patterns and consider focusing limited resources to design strategies and programs to foster adaptation early in an LWOP inmate's incarceration. Utilizing early interventions based on results from scientific inquiries about adaptation of LWOP inmates can be designed to educate the inmate about what to expect in the way of behavioral, social, and emotional changes and what resources can be brought to bear to reduce stress, resulting in less potential for behavioral maladjustment.

The overwhelming body of evidence suggests these LWOP inmates can be housed safely in a general population and do not require segregated or restrictive confinement to reduce violence because they "have nothing to lose" (Cunningham et al., 2016; Cunningham & Sorensen, 2006). As a group these inmates want to be left alone to control their lives as much as possible. Engaging in violence and serious disciplinary infractions come with a cost (e.g., isolation cell placement, restricted privileges, loss of social comforts and interactions) that most LWOP inmates are not willing to tolerate. These inmates are seen as a stabilizing force in prisons, with many earning "honor dorm" status or a reduced security level. Prison administrators must identify and establish management strategies for these permanently incapacitated inmates that may differ from short-term inmates to more selectively address their individual needs across a range of domains. By reducing the benign neglect associated with the "pains of permanent imprisonment" for LWOP inmates (Leigey, 2015) through affirmative actions, the safety and security of the institution will actually be enhanced as inmates experience less environmental strain and improved behavioral and psychological adaptation.

Sentence planning for LWOP inmates means creating more incentives through realistic and meaningful educational, vocational, and social programming specific to these inmates, which will not only benefit the inmate but will also foster more favorable relations between staff and inmates who are feeling less stressed and not as likely to lash out verbally or physically. A popular and creative example of self-improvement available to inmates is the "Puppies for Parole" program at Missouri's maximum-security prison. This program allows dogs from the local animal shelter to live in the prison and train with well-behaved inmate handlers, including LWOP inmates, who socialize the dogs for later adoption. Many other prisons across the country have implemented similar programs that benefit the community and inmates alike. Another example of creative thinking is seen at the Idaho State Correctional Center, where artistically talented inmates are engaged to paint murals on interior hallways. Such programs not only reduce inmate stress but also provide LWOP inmates with meaning, purpose, and a sense of accomplishment alien to their otherwise emotionally barren, empty, and monotonous life.

Coping and Adaptation of LWOP Inmates

Separation From Family

One of the most devastating pains of imprisonment reported by LWOP inmates is "unremitting loneliness" from being permanently separated from family, children, grandchildren, and other loved ones, resulting in a "profound sense of loss" (Johnson & McGunigall-Smith, 2008). These inmates will miss birthdays, kissing a child goodnight, ballgames, dance recitals, graduations, marriages, and various family interactions that make up the fabric of daily life in the community. As a policy recommendation, Leigey (2015) urges prisons to reinforce family ties for these inmates permanently separated from loved ones by allowing LWOP inmates expanded telephone privileges, computer video connection, and access to email to reduce the sense of isolation many of these inmates feel when family members cannot visit often, if at all, due to geographic constraints. In fact, some institutions have already implemented inmate email systems such as the Federal Bureau of Prisons TRULINCS system (Program Statement Number 4500.11). Efforts to house LWOP inmates as close as possible to family support systems in the community will certainly improve opportunities for maintaining quality connections with family, ease the financial burden of travel expenses, and reduce the sense of loneliness experienced by these inmates. As an example of aiding with maintenance of family relationships, Missouri's maximum security prison at Potosi introduced a creative solution by allowing quarterly picnics with homemade food brought in by family members for inmates that remained free of disciplinary infractions for extended periods of time (Cunningham et al., 2005, 2016). Some prisons have instituted parenting programs for inmates who wish to stay involved with their children in a meaningful way. For example, the Correctional Education Association (Bednarowski, 2013) has produced a resource guide for prison parenting instructors and programs across the nation.

Physical and Emotional Well-Being of Aging Inmates

Permanently incapacitating inmates by an LWOP sentence until death necessarily requires a discussion about the health needs of this ever-growing population of inmates as they age across a life term. According to the Bureau of Justice Statistics (Carson & Sabol, 2016), the number of state and federal prisoners age 55 or over has doubled each decade from 1993–2013, whereas the prison population grew by only 46%, and the growth rate for prisoners age 65 and older has been even more expansive. Consequently prison officials are faced with an increasing number of elderly and infirm prisoners that cannot be housed in general population units and require specialized care for life in the case of LWOP inmates.

Compared with the general population prison inmates, older prisoners have higher rates of mental illness, chronic medical conditions, and infectious diseases (Chari, Simon, DeFrances, & Maruschak, 2016). Physical illness (88%) is the most common cause of death in prison (Noonan & Ginder, 2014) among inmates age 55 and older, constituting more than half of prison deaths. A BJS Special Report on the Aging of the State Prison Population (Carson & Sabol, 2016) identifies 6,300 state prisoners age 65 or older who were sentenced to life imprisonment for violent crimes (Carson & Sabol, 2016) and will ultimately require some form of intervention and palliative care related to the disorders and disabilities of aging. For example, close to 50% of state and federal inmates age 50 and older experienced a physical disability, with nearly a third related to ambulatory impairment, followed closely by cognitive disorders (Bronson, Maruschak, & Berzofsky, 2015). Consistent with Leigey's (2015) call for formalized prison policies designed to improve or stabilize the physical and mental health and well-being of older LWOP inmates, a National Survey of Prison Health Care (Chari et al., 2016) was recently undertaken to identify the gaps in knowledge concerning the provision and delivery of medical and mental health services in U.S. prisons. Results from respondents in the 45 participating states revealed a wide disparity in the delivery of health and mental health services depending on the condition studied. For example, 100% of the respondents were screened for mental health conditions at intake, but less than half were screened for traumatic brain injury. Screening for infectious diseases also varied widely depending on the disease, with rates varying from 77% to 100%. All but one of the states provided outpatient mental health care, but services and placements for the seriously mentally ill varied considerably, with nearly two-thirds providing on-site inpatient care, whereas others used off-site facilities. Some states had dedicated facilities for the care of chronic illnesses, but others were either limited or did not provide such care. Similarly, a portion of the participating states provided hospice or nursing home care, with most respondents indicating off-site care was rarely used. Results such as these demonstrate a need for a more unifying policy regarding the provision of consistently applied comprehensive medical and mental health services across prison systems in the U.S.

Availability and quality of medical and psychiatric treatment in prison has been the subject considerable litigation forcing prison officials to improve institutional health care. For example, the U.S. Supreme Court in *Estelle v. Gamble* (1976) ruled that ignoring proper medical care equates to cruel and unusual punishment. Inadequate psychiatric treatment or failure to protect vulnerable or older LWOP inmates from victimization has also been the subject of considerable discussion and civil lawsuits (e.g., Haney, 2006; Leigey, 2015; Steiner, Ellison, Butler, & Cain, 2017; *Harold Cunningham v. Federal Bureau of Prisons*, 2012). On the other hand, numerous state initiatives have developed programs to address the myriad needs of aging or medically incapacitated inmates (McCarthy, 2013). California, for example, recently opened a new prison designed specifically for medically infirm prisoners, as well as those with dementia and mental illnesses. Other states and the federal system have similarly built or transformed prison units to care for elderly inmates, the chronically ill, those with complex medical conditions, dementia, and severe psychiatric disorders. The challenge for prison administrators will be to identify and use multidimensional and evidence-based interventions to improve geriatric programs (Maschi, Kwak, Ko, & Morrissey, 2012) to address the needs of the aging prison population, including a large number of LWOP inmates. Priorities should include staff training related to geriatric inmates, enhancement of palliative care services, and, of particularly necessity, screening for dementia and depression in older prisoners that will help identify those at risk and allow for earlier intervention to guide decisions about treatment and housing. Improving the well-being of elderly LWOP inmates can also be accomplished by use of senior sports teams, gym times separate from younger inmates, and preventive care and wellness education.

Some prison systems offer limited compassionate release or medical parole for severely debilitated inmates using narrowly defined criteria but not typically available for inmates convicted of violent crimes or those serving an LWOP term. A 2010 report by the Vera Institute of Justice described politics and public opinion as shaping the response to early release of geriatric inmates with a violent history, regardless of their degree of infirmity or any cost savings, with the expressed view that such inmates continue to represent a threat and that a life sentence indeed means no release under any circumstances, which trumps other considerations. A different view was espoused by a group of national experts representing a wide range of prison health care providers and administrators, who called for policy reforms regarding medically appropriate release policies and criteria related to a revised threat assessment commensurate with the degree of medical disability (Williams, Stern, Mellow, Safer, & Greifinger, 2012). Correctional decision makers should, however, reconsider the actual use of geriatric release policies while at the same time balancing risk with the need to protect the public.

As LWOP inmates age, attitudes toward self and others change for many of them. Greater emphasis is placed on self-control and tolerance, with increased empathy and willingness to assist others (Johnson & Dobrzanska, 2005; Leigey, 2015). Some develop insight about their crimes and empathy for their victims and the families of their victims. Programs such as Restorative Justice & First Steps to Healing or Victim-Offender Education Groups that foster constructive meetings between inmates and the families of their victims with the goal of healing, to the degree possible, should be embraced by policymakers. Some prisons have developed supportive programs such as "lifer" clubs that provide peer support and encourage socialization, activities, and a sense of belonging.

Many inmates struggle with the mental pains of lifetime incarceration and related deprivations (Haney, 2006), yet the mental health of the LWOP population has not been the subject of much research. Contrary to expectation, some studies and interviews show that the mental health of LWOP inmates generally improved after an initial period of adjustment and was not found to be a strong force over the length of their incarceration (Johnson & Dobrzanska, 2005; Leigey, 2010, 2015; Zamble & Porporino, 1988). Inmates serving LWOP eventually establish personal routines, mature coping styles, and relationships with a few trusted "lifers" to minimize stress and avoid conflict or victimization by predatory younger inmates (Zamble, 1992; Flanagan, 1995; Johnson & Dobrzanska, 2005; Leigey, 2010, 2015; Toch, 1995). Ultimately, however, LWOP inmates become subject to age-related decline in physical functioning, health, mental health, and cognitive abilities that disrupt their established coping methods and daily routines. Prisons should take a more proactive approach to screening for early identification of potentially disabling cognitive and mental health conditions to provide timely decisions about treatment, housing assignments, and programming.

Institutional Factors

Changes in long-term inmate adaptation, including those serving LWOP, have been largely due to self-generated improvement in emotional states, health, behavior, and social interactions rather than specifically fostered by the prison environment that provides limited support for such widespread change (Flanagan, 1995; Leigey, 2015; Toch & Adams, 1989; Zamble, 1992; Zamble & Porporino, 1988). Haney (2006) laments the absence of an organized, theoretically sound public policy for prison reform. Penal institutions are hampered in instituting major reforms by political considerations, institutional culture, overcrowding, and inertia from large and constantly shifting prison populations, a lack of creativity, economic constraints, and staffing levels. The unique environmental/situational factors, custody levels, and managerial styles of prison administrators and their policies have also been proffered as factors contributing to the extreme strains of prison life, especially in maximum security prisons where the majority of LWOP inmates reside (Blevins, Listwan, Cullen, & Jonson, 2010; Colvin, 1992; DiIulio, 1987; Haney, 2006; Morris, Carriaga, Diamond, Piquero, & Piquero, 2012; Morris et al., 2010). Of particular relevance is the study by Morris et al. (2012) applying "general strain theory" to demonstrate that inmates react differentially to institutional strains identified as adverse prison-level characteristics related to such factors as deprived conditions of confinement, gang influences, and population size. These findings mirror other studies showing the influence of prison-level conditions on inmate behavior that are equally applicable to the LWOP population. Some prisons are far better than others in managing conditions of confinement that are known to be critical to the adjustment of long-term inmates and the reduction of misconduct, particularly for those incapacitated for a lifetime. Before reforms can be instituted, prison officials and policy makers will need a better comprehension of the prison-level strains associated with lifetime confinement as exemplified by interviews of LWOP inmates (Johnson & McGunigall-Smith, 2008; Leigey, 2010, 2015) and others who have studied the psychology of prisonization (e.g., Haney, 2006). Policy administrators need to understand that inmates are significantly affected by prison conditions of confinement and should consider identifying and modifying unfavorable factors to reduce the strains associated with the LWOP population in particular. The recent settlement of a class action lawsuit (*Harold Cunningham v. Federal Bureau of Prisons*, 2012) filed on behalf of inmates (including many LWOP inmates) housed in solitary confinement in the federal "supermax" prison in Colorado highlighted their inadequate mental health care and conditions of confinement, resulting in a new system-wide mental health policy and construction of mental health units for seriously mentally ill inmates.

Interviews with LWOP inmates concerning deprivation of privacy, loss of liberty, the ability to make choices in their daily lives, the monotonous repetition of daily routines, and the feeling that life is over are concerns that most inmates are ill equipped to handle (Crawley & Sparks, 2006; Leigey, 2015). How do LWOP inmates learn to adjust to the empty, meaningless existence within a violent world that sometimes is unstable and unpredictable and always oppressive? Rather than deteriorating, research and interviews with LWOP inmates demonstrate many are self-motivated to improve their living situation and make the most of a very circumscribed and heavily monitored life. Higher levels of educational attainment have been also been shown to lead to a more positive adjustment to incarceration, including lower levels of misconduct (Cunningham et al., 2005; Steiner, Butler, & Ellison, 2014). However, after years of confinement, many inmates do not participate in educational programming for various reasons, including completion of all the classes/training offered, or ineligibility or lack of access to college programs, or staff or institutional bias against older inmates and LWOP inmates being given program opportunities. Others felt there was little practical to gain by participating in vocational programs or higher education that had no useful purpose in their lives. Institutional and vocational programming often is geared toward inmates preparing for release rather than to meet the needs of inmates that will never be released. Institutions may wish to rethink the range of programming available to LWOP inmates and develop creative programs of interest or practical significance geared toward more productive prison employment rather than menial duties. For example, Idaho, in partnership with Boise State University, offers a debate club that teaches inmates research and debate skills leading to actual debates. These Idaho inmates, including those sentenced to LWOP, are employed in meaningful jobs such as making facility repairs and working in prison industries, where they are considered steady and reliable workers. Inmates often help other inmates in a variety of ways, as exemplified by a California program that trains and utilizes convicted murderers to serve as aides for inmates suffering dementia. A similarly creative program in Idaho uses inmates trained to serve as companions for suicidal inmates. Other meaningful activities might include legal education for inmates wanting to appeal their case or assist other inmates with their legal matters.

Housing

Inmates serving an LWOP sentence have demonstrated their ability to avoid violence and adjust to a general prison population. Their adjustment is best exemplified by the study of Cunningham et al. (2016) representing the longest follow-up period to date for inmates sentenced to LWOP. Over a 25-year period these inmates consistently maintained a level of nonviolent behavior that was superior to that of other maximum-security inmates housed in the same facility. This study also reinforced a large body of work demonstrating an inverse relationship between age and prison misconduct. Such findings reinforce other empirical studies showing LWOP inmates are anything but a predatory and disruptive force in prisons. Administrators and policymakers may wish to reconsider or expand policies about the judicious dispersal of LWOP inmates to lower security levels and modify classification methods that heavily weigh sentence length in determining security requirements for some of these inmates. In the Oregon State Penitentiary, for example, a large proportion of the over 200 inmates housed in the honor unit with expanded privileges are LWOP inmates (Long, Premo, Van Valkenburg, personal communication, September 10, 2009).

The management of LWOP inmates growing old in prison necessarily includes a discussion of their housing assignments. Some institutions have opened specialty units for older inmates (see OLR Research Report, 2013), including the federal Administrative Maximum facility better known as super-max in Colorado. However, not all LWOP inmates share the same views toward specialized housing for the elderly, with some being in favor and others rejecting this form of segregated housing. Leigey's (2015) interviews with LWOP inmates frame the debate about specialty housing assignments for the elderly in terms of reducing institutional strain, victimization, and providing a quieter and more easily managed environment for staff. Alternatively, some inmates prefer mainstreaming and do not wish to be housed in specialty units that may be limited to certain institutions and thereby increase the geographical distance from family. Other LWOP inmates prefer interaction with younger prisoners and relish the role as mentor and being a positive influence on these inmates. Correctional administrators and policymakers will need to make individualized determinations related to LWOP inmate placement in units or prisons established for elderly inmates and give these inmates a voice in the decision.

Future Research

Studies of individual level predictors of prison behavior and violence for LWOP inmates have emerged over the last decade. However, many population and facility variables affecting the LWOP group and that have the potential for influencing inmate adjustment have not been explored to any great extent;

for example, population demographics, racial diversity, prison routines, proportion of gang infiltration, staffing ratios, unit assignments, levels of victimization, security levels, use of punitive administrative controls, and allocation of jobs and program resources. The implications from the LWOP scientific literature described in this chapter require closer scrutiny of prison management practices as applied to this population to meet their unique behavioral, social, emotional, and medical challenges that set them apart from inmates serving shorter prison terms.

Studies to date with LWOP inmates have focused largely on correlates of misconduct as the primary way to measure adjustment (e.g., Cunningham et al., 2016; Cunningham & Sorensen, 2006). However, broader conceptualizations of inmate adaptation other than misconduct should be considered such as inmate participation in programming and gathering surveys of inmate experiences (Toman et al., 2015). Institutional variables have also been shown to influence inmate misconduct and vary across and even within prisons (Steiner & Wooldredge, 2008). Future studies should begin to focus on macro-level perspectives (Wooldredge & Steiner, 2015) utilizing such factors as population composition, differences in violence across units and facilities, use of segregation and program resources, degree of gang infiltration, and inmate participation in jobs and other programming. Schenk and Fremouw (2012) concluded that it would be "incomplete to only consider the inmate and not contextual variables" (p. 441) when studying correlates of prison violence. Included in such contextual variables is an array of institutional incentives potentially available to inmates to reinforce satisfactory behavior. The successful development and utilization of creative incentives for LWOP inmates (e.g., dog training, family picnics) provides researchers with an opportunity to evaluate inmate adjustment across a range of behavioral and psychological variables to provide penal institutions with evidence-based data supporting the efficacy of such programs and the impact on LWOP inmates.

Inmates serving an LWOP sentence are not a homogeneous group and include subpopulations of capital murderers, habitually violent offenders, sex offenders and others whose consecutive sentences amount to de facto LWOP sentences. Comparative studies of individual and institutional variables among such inmate groups may have policy and management implications since the incarceration experiences of these groups may differ considerably, especially compared to general population inmates (see Cunningham et al., 2016).

Variations in the adaptation of LWOP inmates may vary based on inmate traits, and experiences imported to prison interacting with the strains of imprisonment over time need further theoretical and empirical exploration. For example, Morris et al. (2012) applied general strain theory (GST) to demonstrate variations in inmate behavior based upon environmental strain and the features of the prison environment. Fully testing GST and other theoretical perspectives among LWOP inmates by including an array of inmate and institutional factors may inform policymakers about more effective ways to manage this group.

Little research has been conducted on the aging aspect of the LWOP population. Available literature clearly demonstrates that the vast majority of these inmates in their 50s and older desist from disciplinary infractions, particularly violence (see Cunningham et al., 2005, 2016). However, the research also shows that an extremely small number of LWOP inmates continue their maladaptive and violent behavior even into old age. No studies to date have investigated this small but little understood sample of LWOP inmates to determine correlates and risk factors that set them apart from other well-adjusted LWOP inmates. Once this group is better understood, prison officials can then determine the most effective institutional response to achieve more satisfactory conduct. At a broader institutional level, future researchers might guide policy and aid decision makers by developing evidence-based information about the health and mental health needs of older LWOP inmates. For example, Chiu (2010) suggests studying the actual impact of geriatric release policies for infirm inmates through cost savings and the application of risk management procedures to determine the true risk these inmates pose to public safety.

References

Akman, D. D. (1966). Homicides and assaults in Canadian penitentiaries. *Canadian Journal of Corrections, 8,* 284–299.

Appleton, C., & Grover, B. (2007). The pros and cons of life without parole. *British Journal of Criminology, 47,* 597–615.

Bedau, H. A. (1965). Capital punishment in Oregon, 1903–1964. *Oregon Law Review, 45,* 1–39.

Bednarowski, J. (March 2013). Prison parenting programs: Resources for parenting instructors in prisons and jails. *Correctional Education Association.* Retrieved from www.ceanational.org/PDFs/parentingresources.pdf

Blecker, R. (2013). *The death of punishment: Searching for justice among the worst of the worst.* New York: Palgrave Macmillan.

Blevins, K. R., Listwan, S. J., Cullen, F. T., & Jonson, C. L. (2010). A general strain theory of prison violence and misconduct: An integrated model of inmate behavior. *Journal of Contemporary Criminal Justice, 26,* 148–166. doi: 10.1177/1043986209359369

Bohm, infra.

Bronson, J., Maruschak, L. M., & Berzofsky, M. (2015). Disabilities among prison and jail inmates, 2011–12, Washington DC: U.S. Department of Justice: Office of Justice Programs: Special Report, Bureau of Justice Statistics, NCJ249151.

Carson, E., & Sabol, W. J. (2016). Aging of the state prison population, 1993–2013, Washington DC: U.S. Department of Justice: Office of Justice Programs: Bureau of Justice Statistics, NCJ248766.

Chari, K. A., Simon, A. E., DeFrances, C. J., & Maruschak, L. (2016). National survey of prison health care: Selected findings. Washington DC: U.S. Department of Health and Human Services: Centers for Disease Control and Prevention, National Center for Health Statistics.

Chiu, T. (2010). *It's about time: Aging prisoners, increasing costs, and geriatric release.* New York: Vera Institute of Justice.

Colvin, M. (1992). *The penitentiary in crisis: From accommodation to riot in New Mexico.* Albany: SUNY Press.

Couzens, J. R. & Bigelow, T. A. (2017). The Amendment of the Three Strikes Sentencing Law. Echo Lake, CA: Barrister Press.

Crawley, E., & Sparks, R. (2006). Is there life after imprisonment? How elderly men talk about imprisonment and release. *Criminology & Criminal Justice, 6,* 63–82. doi: 10.1177/1748895806060667

Cunningham, M. D. (2010). *Evaluation for capital sentencing: A volume in the Oxford best practices in forensic mental health assessment series* (A. Goldstein, T. Grisso, & K. Heilbrun, Series Eds.). New York: Oxford University Press.

Cunningham, M. D., Reidy, T. J., & Sorensen, J. R. (2005). Is death row obsolete? A decade of mainstreaming capital punishment inmates in Missouri. *Behavioral Sciences and the Law, 23,* 307–320. doi: 10.1002/bsl.608

Cunningham, M. D., Reidy, T. J., & Sorensen, J. R. (2008). Assertions of "future dangerousness" at federal capital sentencing: Rates and correlates of subsequent prison misconduct and violence. *Law and Human Behavior, 32,* 46–63. doi: 10.1007/s10979-007-9107-7

Cunningham, M. D., Reidy, T. J., & Sorensen, J. R. (2016). Wasted resources and gratuitous suffering: The failure of a security rationale for death row. *Psychology, Public Policy and Law, 22,* 185–199. doi: 10.1037/law0000072

Cunningham, M. D., & Sorensen, J. R. (2006). Nothing to lose? A comparative examination of prison misconduct rates among life-without-parole and other long-term high-security inmates. *Criminal Justice and Behavior, 33,* 1–23. doi: 10.1177/0093854806288273

Cunningham, M. D., & Sorensen, J. R. (2007). Capital offenders in Texas prisons: Rates, correlates, and an actuarial analysis of violent misconduct. *Law and Human Behavior, 31,* 553–571. doi: 10.1007/s10979-006-9079-z

Cunningham, M; Sorensen, J.; & Reidy, T. (2009). Capital jury decision-making: The limitations of predictions of future violence. *Psychology, Public Policy, and Law, 15,* 223–256.

Cunningham, M. D., Sorensen, J. R., Vigen, M. P., & Woods, S. O. (2011). Correlates and actuarial models of assaultive prison misconduct among violence-predicted capital offenders. *Criminal Justice and Behavior, 38,* 5–25. doi: 10.1177/0093854810384830

Dilulio, J. (1987). *Governing prisons: A comparative study of correctional management.* New York: The Free Press.

Edens, J. F., Buffington-Vollum, J. K., Keilen, A., Roskamp, P., & Anthony, C. (2005). Predictions of future dangerousness in capital murder trials: Is it time to "disinvent the wheel?". *Law and Human Behavior, 29,* 55–86.

Flanagan, T. J. (1980). Time served and institutional misconduct: Patterns of involvement in disciplinary infractions among long-term and short-term inmates. *Journal of Criminal Justice, 8,* 357–367.

Flanagan, T. J. (Ed.). (1995). *Long term imprisonment: Policy, science, and correctional practice.* Thousand Oaks, CA: Sage Publications.

Haney, C. (2006). *Reforming punishment: Psychological limits to the pains of imprisonment.* Washington, DC: American Psychological Association.

Johnson, R., & Dobrzanska, A. (2005). Mature coping among life-sentenced inmates: An exploratory study of adjustment dynamics. *Corrections Compendium, 30*(6), 8–38.

Johnson, R., & McGunnigal-Smith, S. (2008). Life without parole, America's other death penalty: Notes of life under sentence of death by incarceration. *The Prison Journal, 88*, 328–346. doi: 10.1177/0032885508319256

Leigey, M. E. (2010). For the longest time: The adjustment of inmates to a sentence of life without parole. *The Prison Journal, 90*, 247–268. doi: 10.1177/0032885510373490

Leigey, M. E. (2015). *Serving a life without parole sentence: The forgotten men.* New Jersey: Rutgers University Press.

Lombardi, G., Sluder, R., & Wallace, D. (1997). Mainstreaming capital punishment inmates: The Missouri experience and its legal significance. *Federal Probation, 61*, 3–11.

Long, E., Premo, J., & Van Valkenburg, J. (2009, September 10). Personal interview with T. Reidy.

Longmire, infra.

Marquart, J. W., Ekland-Olson, S., & Sorensen, J. R. (1989). Gazing into the crystal ball: Can jurors accurately predict dangerousness in capital cases? *Law & Society Review, 23*, 449–468.

Marquart, J.W., & Sorensen, J.R. (1989). A national study of the Furman-commuted inmates: Assessing the threat to society from capital offenders. *Loyola of Los Angeles Law Review, 23*, 5–28.

Maschi, T., Kwak, J., Ko, E., & Morrissey, M. B. (2012). Forget me not: Dementia in prison. *The Gerontologist, 52*, 441–451. doi: 10.1093/geront/gnr131

McCarthy, K. (2013). State initiatives to address aging prisoners. Sacramento: California Office of Legislative Research. OLR Research Report, 2013-R-0166.

McInnis, J. (2003, April 2). Senate panel pushes no-parole sentencing option. *Houston Chronicle*, p. A-19.

Morris, R. G., Carriaga, M. L., Diamond, B., Piquero, N. L., & Piquero, A. R. (2012). Does prison strain lead to prison misbehavior? An application of general strain theory to inmate misconduct. *Journal of Criminal Justice, 40*, 194–201. doi: 10.1016/j.jcrimjus.2011.12.001

Morris, R. G., Longmire, D. R., Buffington-Vollum, J., & Vollum, S. (2010). Institutional misconduct and differential parole eligibility among capital inmates. *Criminal Justice and Behavior, 37*, 417–438. doi: 10.1177/0093854810361672

Noonan, M. E., & Ginder, S. (2014). Mortality in local jails and state prisons, 2000–2012, Statistical Tables. Washington, DC: U.S. Department of Justice: Office of Justice Programs: Bureau of Justice Statistics, NCJ247448.

Reidy, T. J., Cunningham, M. D., & Sorensen, J. R. (2001). From death to life: Prison behavior of former death row inmates in Indiana. *Criminal Justice and Behavior, 28*, 62–82.

Reidy, T. J., Sorensen, J. R., & Cunningham, M. D. (2013). Probability of acts of future violence: A test of jury accuracy in Oregon. *Behavioral Sciences and the Law, 32*, 286–305. doi: 10.1002/bsl.2064

Sandys, M., Pruss, H. C., & Walsh, S. M. (2009). Aggravation and mitigation: Findings and implications. *Journal of Psychiatry and Law, 37*(1–2), 189–235.

Schenk, A. M., & Fremouw, W. J. (2012). Individual characteristics related to prison violence: A critical review of the literature. *Aggression and Violent Behavior, 17*, 430–442. doi: 10/1016/j.jcrimjus.2014.08.001

Shapiro, M. (2009). An overdose of dangerousness: How "future dangerousness" catches the least culpable capital defendants and undermines the rationale for the executions it supports. *American Journal of Criminal Law, 35*, 101–156.

Snell, T. L. (2014). Capital punishment, 2013-statistical tables. Washington, DC: U.S. Department of Justice. Bureau of Justice Statistics, NCJ 24848.

Sorensen, J. R. & Cunningham, M. D. (2009). Once a killer, always a killer? Prison misconduct of former capital punishment inmates in Arizona. *Journal of Psychiatry & Law, 37*, 237–267.

Sorensen, J. R., & Reidy, T. J. (in press). Nothing to lose? An examination of prison misconduct among life-without-parole inmates. *Prison Journal.*

Sorensen, J. R., & Wrinkle, R. D. (1996). No hope for parole: Disciplinary infractions among capital punishment and life-without-parole inmates. *Criminal Justice and Behavior, 23*, 542–552. doi: 10.1177/0093854896023004002

Steiner, B., Butler, H. D., & Ellison, J. M. (2014). Causes and correlates of prison inmate misconduct: A systematic review of the evidence. *Journal of Criminal Justice, 42*, 462–470. doi: 10.1016/j.jcrimjus.2014.08.001

Steiner, B., Ellison, J. M., Butler, H. D., & Cain, C. M. (2017). The impact of inmate and prison characteristics on prisoner victimization. *Trauma, Violence, & Abuse, 18*, 17–36. doi: 10.1177/1524838015588503

Steiner, B., & Wooldredge, J. (2008). Inmate versus environmental effects on prison rule violations. *Criminal Justice and Behavior, 3*, 438–456. doi: 10.1177/0093854807312787

Stewart, J., & Lieberman, P. (1982). What is this new sentence that takes away parole? *Student Lawyer, 11*, 14–17.

Toch, H. (1995). The long-term inmate as a long-term problem. In T. J. Flanagan (Ed.), *Long term imprisonment: Policy, science, and correctional practice* (pp. 245–248). Thousand Oaks, CA: Sage Publications.

Toch, H., & Adams, K. (1989). *Coping: Maladaptation in prisons.* New Brunswick, NJ: Transaction Books.

Toman, E. L., Cochran, J. C., Cochran, J. K., & Bales, W. D. (2015). The implications of sentence length to prison life. *Journal of Criminal Justice, 43*, 510–521. doi: 10.1016/j.jcrimjus.2015.11.002

U.S. Dept. of Justice, Federal Bureau of Prisons, Program Statement Number 4500.11, April 9, 2015.

Vartkessian, E. S., Sorensen, J. R., & Kelly, C. E. (2017). Tinkering with the machinery of death: An analysis of juror decision-making in Texas death penalty trials during two statutory eras. *Justice Quarterly, 34*, 1–24. doi: 10.1080/07418825.2014.958188

Wagner, A. (1988). *A commutation study of ex-capital offenders in Texas, 1924–1971.* Unpublished dissertation, Sam Houston State University, Huntsville, TX.

Wardlaw, G., & Biles, D. (1980). *The management of long term prisoners in Australia.* Canberra, Australia: Australian Institute of Criminology.

Williams, B. A., Stern, M. F., Mellow, J., Safer, M., & Greifinger, R. B. (2012). Aging in correctional custody: Setting a policy agenda for older prisoner health care. *American Journal of Public Health, 102*, 1475–1481.

Williamson, H. (1985). Rule violations: Will lifers play by the rules? *Corrections Today, 47*(2), 138–140.

Wooldredge, J., & Steiner, B. (2015). A macro-level perspective on prison inmate deviance. *Punishment & Society, 17*, 230–257. doi: 10.1177/1462474515577151

Zamble, E. (1992). Behavior and adaptation in long-term inmates: Descriptive longitudinal results. *Criminal Justice and Behavior, 19*, 409–425.

Zamble, E., & Porporino, F. J. (1988). Coping, imprisonment, and rehabilitation: Some data and their implications. *Criminal Justice and Behavior, 17*, 53–70.

Cases Cited

Estelle v. Gamble, 429 U.S. 97 (1976).

Furman v. Georgia, 408 U.S. 238 (1972).

Harold Cunningham v. Federal Bureau of Prisons. (2012). The District Court of Colorado, Civil Action No. 12-cv-01570-RPM.

Jurek v. Texas, 428 U.S. 153 (1976). U.S. v. Savage, E. Dist. PA, No. 07–00550 (2013).

Vinter and Others v. The United Kingdom, Application Nos. 66069/09, 130/10, Eur. Ct. H.R. (July 9, 2013).

B. Religious Views

11

CHRISTIANITY AND
THE DEATH PENALTY

Tobias Winright

Newspaper headlines such as the following occasionally appear in the United States: "Death penalty overturned because of Bible quotes" (Davis, 2015). This particular article reports about a U.S. district judge's overruling of a death sentence because the prosecutor's closing statements included selected quotes from the Bible, without any objection from the defendant's defense attorneys, encouraging jurors to vote for capital punishment as in accordance with God's will. Not only is this case an example of inappropriate conduct by the prosecutor, it is also a misconception about both how most Christians in the twenty-first century understand the Bible and how they discern where to stand on controversial moral issues such as the death penalty.

Most Christian denominations draw on four authoritative sources to formulate their position on the morality of capital punishment: the Bible, the Christian tradition, human reason, and experience. Those Christians who appeal to "Scripture alone" tend to be Protestants who subscribe to fundamentalism and view the Bible as literally God's inerrant words that are unchanging and perennially true for all times and places. In contrast, most Christian churches—including Roman Catholicism and many other mainline Protestant churches—understand that the Bible, while inspired by God, was written by human persons during particular times and in specific places that are "at least somewhat different from the conditions and times in which we live" (Curran, 1993, p. 31). That is, although biblical passages may contain truths about God and the human condition, they also reflect cultural and historical perspectives with regard to some issues such as, for example, the legitimacy of slavery and women's subordination. Hence, Scripture may be the primary source for moral guidance, but it must be interpreted through methods that consider the original languages, such as Hebrew and Greek, with attention to different genres (e.g., poems, laws, letters, etc.) and historical-cultural contexts and circumstances.

Moreover, the Christian Bible consists of two testaments—the Hebrew Scriptures (also called the Old Testament) and the New Testament—and, for most Christians, the Hebrew Scriptures are to be read in light of the New Testament. Or, as evangelical Protestant ethicist Dennis P. Hollinger has put it, "We must also understand that the relationship of the Old Testament to the New Testament is linked to progressive revelation, the continual unfolding of God's plan and designs that reach their apex in the death and resurrection of Christ" (Hollinger, 2002, pp. 157–158). When passages in the Bible appear to contradict each other on a moral issue, most Christians go with what the New Testament passage instructs. Likewise, if there are passages in the New Testament that appear to be in tension, or problematic (again, wherever slavery or women's subordination, for instance, seem accepted or even approved), most Christians try to interpret them with an eye toward what Jesus Christ taught or did, since the Gospel of John refers to him as "the Word" of God (John 1:1). In other words, Christians regard Jesus Christ as the ultimate revelation of God—who God is, how God acts, and what God wills to "be done on earth, as it is in heaven" (Matthew 6:10)—and therefore he is the supreme norm for Christian character and behavior. Jesus is the *norma normans non normata* ("norming norm not normed by something else"), so that "every other norm, judgment, and conclusion has to be subordinated to our understanding of Jesus Christ and his gospel message" (Bretzke, 2004, p. 34). Another related way to deal with conflicting or problematic Bible passages is to view them in light of the overarching major themes of Scripture, such as mercy and forgiveness, which are also consonant with Jesus' life and work. Thus, for most Christians, instead of providing direct and explicit answers to issues, the Bible is helpful mainly as means "to illuminate their moral questions" (Farley, 2006, p. 183) and identifying their basic "orientation, dispositions, and values" that frame how to "deal with the moral issues facing our society today" (Curran, 1993, p. 32).

In addition to the Bible, most Christian denominations draw from tradition. While Christian tradition includes authoritative statements and documents from popes, bishops, and councils (for Roman Catholics this teaching authority is called the *magisterium*), it also includes more widely the writings of past theologians, the lives and examples of saints, creedal doctrines, the rubrics and practices of the liturgy, and the "sense of the faithful" (Farley, 2006, p. 186). The tradition is a living one. It is not static, and it continues to develop. Christians believe that the God's Holy Spirit inspires and animates the Christian tradition, guiding it in its application in different times and places "to ensure that the church will always be faithful to the basic gospel message" (Curran, 1993, p. 35). As with the Bible, there are tensions and differing views within the tradition. Also, not everything in tradition, such as past church positions on the acceptability of slavery, is still usable or valid. As with Scripture, the Christian tradition needs to be understood in connection with history, culture, circumstances (Farley, 2006, p. 186). Teachings from the tradition, too, have to be adjudicated by the norm of Jesus Christ. Accordingly, many theologians today highlight the importance of the revelation of Jesus as experienced in worship and, in particular, the Eucharist (also known as the Lord's Supper or Holy Communion).

The third font of moral wisdom, experience, includes a number of considerations. Basically, experience refers to "more intuitive and more completely human ways of knowing" (Curran, 1993, 38). It encompasses personal experiences in daily life, such as what one learns from a personal relationship with another person. It also includes, for many theologians and churches, giving special attention to voices on the margins, such as the poor and the oppressed (McCormick & Connors, 2002, p. 20). Moreover, experience is often understood as referring to secular disciplines as sources of human knowledge and wisdom, such as philosophy, psychology, sociology, criminology, literature, political science, biology, history, etc. (Curran, 1993, p. 39).

The fourth source of moral wisdom is reason, which often refers to philosophy and natural law theory. "Reason is often conceived in a somewhat intellectual perspective" (Curran, 1993, p. 38). Moreover, it is the practice of rational thinking—i.e., from the "light of reason"—about what is learned from the sources. "Reason, after all, is involved in addressing all of the sources" (Farley, 2006, p. 188). In other words, reason considers the three previous sources and arrives at a logical, consistent stance that can be persuasively justified and applied. We "use our reason to formulate some sort of specifically Christian moral response to the question or issue at hand . . . gained from the conversation among the three voices of experience, Scripture and tradition" (McCormick & Connors, 2002, p. 22).

Although throughout much of Christian history, capital punishment was regarded as morally justified, today most Christian denominations, including the Roman Catholic Church, drawing from these four fonts for ethical guidance, hold that it is not, and many mainline denominations have called for its abolition. Of course, the death penalty is an issue about which many Christians in the pews continue to disagree; however, more and more Christians—and especially Christian denominations, church leaders, and theologians, as well as a growing number of the laity—are against capital punishment.

Scripture

The Old Testament

The Bible is frequently invoked by Christians on opposing sides of the debate about capital punishment. Those who argue that the death penalty is morally justified refer to many passages in Scripture where executions are supposedly prescribed, while those who think that the death penalty is morally unjustified highlight passages apparently opposed to this lethal practice. The question, therefore, is how to adjudicate between these antithetical positions and arrive at a stance that is theologically coherent. The Bible passages that are typically mentioned by either side in this debate must be examined in view of their historical and literary contexts, the great themes of Scripture, and Jesus Christ's teaching and example.

Both supporters and opponents of capital punishment highlight passages from the Old Testament where this practice is mentioned, especially in the first five of its 39 books (or 46 in Roman Catholic editions that include deutero-canonical texts, which some Protestants include as the Apocrypha) of the Old Testament. The death penalty is rarely mentioned beyond these first five books, known collectively as the Pentateuch, or Torah (Law); neither the books of the Prophets nor those in the Writings refer much, if at all, to capital punishment.

In the Pentateuch, murder was not the only crime or sin (the two were not differentiated at the time) that warranted capital punishment. Many sins were offenses for which death was prescribed. Death was the penalty over 40 times and for more than 20 offenses in the Pentateuch (Brugger, 2014, p. 60). Among the acts that merited execution were: profaning the Sabbath (Exodus 31:14); striking or cursing either of one's parents (Exodus 21:15, 17; Leviticus 20:9); kidnapping a person (Exodus 21:16; Deuteronomy 24:7); mortally striking someone (Genesis 9:6; Exodus 21:12; Leviticus 24:17; Numbers 35:16); sorcery (Exodus 22:18; Leviticus 20:27); performing sacrifices to foreign gods (Exodus 22:20); bestiality (Exodus 22:19; Leviticus 20:15); adultery (Leviticus 20:10; Deuteronomy 22:22); sacrificing one's child to Molech (Leviticus 20:1–2); prostitution by a priest's daughter (Leviticus 21:9); false prophecy (Deuteronomy 13:5, 10); trespass upon sacred ground (Exodus 19:12–13; Numbers 1:51, 18:7); incest (Leviticus 20:11–12); blasphemy (Leviticus 24:16); coitus between males (Leviticus 18:22, 20:13); and neglecting to restrain a dangerous ox that causes the death of a person (Exodus 21:19).

Perhaps the most frequently recited saying used by supporters of the death penalty is the *lex talionis*, or "law of retaliation," which appears three times in the Hebrew Bible: "If any harm follows, then you shall give life for life, eye for eye, tooth for tooth, hand for hand, foot for foot, burn for burn, wound for wound, stripe for stripe" (Exodus 21:24–27; Leviticus 24:14–23; Deuteronomy 19:19–21). This refrain does not surface only in the Bible, for it was commonly known elsewhere, as evident in the Code of Hammurabi in ancient Mesopotamia. The phrase poetically conveys oral folk wisdom offering a memorable rule of thumb—namely, that there should be proportionality between punishment and crime. In other words, the punishment should fit the crime. Rather than vengeance, there should be retributive justice. The perpetrator must "pay back" or compensate for their crime, usually, in practice, through financial restitution (Buck, 2013, p. 88). The *lex talionis* did not require vengeance but aimed at establishing a limit on it and preventing the escalation of a blood feud, such as when Lamech boasted about making perpetrators pay seventy-fold (Genesis 4:23), a disproportionate response, indeed.

Moreover, these three passages do not actually apply a literal or exact retribution when examples are given to illustrate the *lex talionis* in practice. For instance, in Exodus 21:22–25, if two men brawl and hit a pregnant woman, different penalties result depending on whether the woman dies or if she is injured but has a miscarriage: a life for a life in the first case, a monetary fine in the second. It should be noted, however, that in this example the death penalty is imposed for the killing of the pregnant woman, without any consideration of whether it was accidental or maliciously intended—or something, such as manslaughter, in between these two possibilities. Moreover, in the verses immediately following, a slave who loses an eye or tooth from a beating by the master is to be freed, but neither is the master's eye to be gouged out nor is his tooth to be extracted as a punishment (Exodus 21:26–27). Likewise, in the Leviticus text, those who curse God are to be stoned, not cursed in return (Leviticus 24:14), and in the Deuteronomy text, the punishment for false testimony is not to have lies told about the liar but for the false witness to be put to death (Deuteronomy 19:19). Christians today do not call literally for removing someone's eye if she or he blinds someone else; nor do they propose burning arsonists, raping rapists, or stealing from thieves. The only crime that seems to have entailed a punishment that is exactly the same is when someone takes another person's life, whether maliciously or not; in that case, then the killer's life is forfeited. Again, the basic point in all of these illustrations of the *lex talionis* is that the punishment should fit the crime. In none of these specific examples, though, does murder—the intentional killing of an innocent person—explicitly appear.

Most, if not all, Christians today who regard the death penalty as morally justifiable do not seek to reintroduce this punitive practice for all or even most of the capital offenses from the Pentateuch. Some Christian theologians divide these laws of the Torah into civil, ceremonial, and moral laws, leaving only the moral laws as applying perennially. Doing so enables them to hold, for instance, that murder remains a moral offense warranting the execution of the perpetrator, whereas trespassing on sacred ground, for instance, is a ceremonial offense that no longer deserves the death penalty. Such classification is theologically anachronistic, however, for in their original historical and cultural context these offenses were viewed holistically as "moral, ceremonial, and civil all at once" (Yoder, 2011, p. 43). During the time that these passages were orally and then in written form circulating, criminal justice, politics, and religion were not separate institutions.

Nevertheless, some capital punishment retentionists focus on the offense of murder as being "in a different category from these other provisions of the Pentateuch in which putting to death was required for many other offenses" (Murray, 1996, p. 459). An Old Testament passage often cited in support of this view is in the Noahic covenant: "Whoever sheds the blood of a human, by a human shall that person's blood be shed; for in his own image God made humankind" (Genesis 9:6). John Murray interprets this passage as establishing murder to be perennially a capital offense because the deceased victim is a human being made in God's image. No other crime, Murray claims, warrants death for this specific reason. As image of God, human life is sacred, which is why murder is prohibited. Murray adds that humans, because they are made in God's image, are also the ones authorized by God to execute a murderer. That is, God is the author of life and death, but God authorizes humans, who are made in God's image, to execute murderers (Murray, 1996, p. 458). The Hebrew wording of Genesis 9:6, however, is unclear, as Murray himself acknowledges (Murray, p. 457). It cannot be determined definitively whether it is simply *descriptively* saying what tends to happen to violent people, or instead, as commonly assumed, *prescriptively* commanding capital punishment. In contrast to passages elsewhere that list laws, this passage is a poetically written proverb (McCormick & Connors, 2002, p. 104), akin to that spoken by Jesus in the New Testament when he tells his disciple to put away his sword, "for all who take the sword will perish by the sword" (Matthew 26:52). Jesus is not expressing support for capital punishment; he simply states what tends to happen to those who lead violent lives.

Of course, Genesis 9:6 also simply refers to the shedding of a person's blood without any reference to malicious motive or aggravating (or mitigating) circumstances, although most Christians today interpret it as referring to murder. Similarly, Leviticus 21:17 and 21:21 merely stipulate that anyone "who kills a human being shall be put to death." Elsewhere, however, nuance is added: "If [the killing] was not premeditated, but came about by an act of God," then the killer may flee for safety at God's altar; yet, if it was done "willfully" or "by treachery" then the killer shall be taken from that "altar for execution" (Exodus 21:13–14; see 1 Kings 2:28–34). Likewise, Numbers 35:16–19 highlights killings that are regarded as murder (e.g., using an iron object, a stone, or a wooden weapon to hit and cause the death of someone), with verses 20–21 mentioning hatred or enmity as motives. Someone who kills a person unintentionally, without these motives, may flee to one of six cities of refuge (Numbers 35:13–15, 22–28; Joshua 20:7–8). Nevertheless, most Bible passages do not provide detailed attention to motive and aggravating or mitigating circumstances as are taken into account today in order to distinguish between different degrees of murder for appropriate punishment.

Notably, passages like Genesis 9:6 reflect how the Hebrew people regarded blood as the source of all life, both human and animal. This belief in blood's sanctity was the basis for the Hebrew prohibition against eating animal blood as well as shedding human blood. In the Noahic covenant, humans are given permission to eat meat, but they "shall not eat flesh with its life, that is, its blood" (Genesis 9:4; also, Deuteronomy 12:23). The blood of every animal and human is sacred and belongs to God, which "means, in the case of animals, that the blood shall not be consumed; for humans it means there shall be no killing" (Yoder, 2011, p. 44). Killing a person, therefore, was not merely a moral or civil offense but a religious offense that demanded ceremonial compensation, a ritual in which the killer is executed by a *go'el* (which is the same Hebrew word for "redeemer") in expiation. Indeed, anthropologist René Girard argues that capital punishment in passages like Genesis 9:6 was a "mimetic reflex" or a form of sacrificial expiation to placate a God who was believed to have required such practices in order for there to be atonement between the people and God (Yoder, 2011, p. 98; Girard, 1977).

Giving further attention to the words that are used in connection with capital punishment in the Old Testament, this association with a ceremonial ritual of compensation comes to the fore. Deuteronomy 19 contains, for example, a significant word, "purge": "So you shall purge the evil from your midst" (19:19). Likewise, in Leviticus 20:1–5, the death penalty is required for sacrificing one's child to the god Molech, an offense violating "my [God's] sanctuary and profaning my [God's] holy name." In Deuteronomy 17:8–13, the consequence for contempt about decisions of Israel's court is capital punishment, because they should "purge the evil." Similarly, a daughter of a priest committing prostitution is said to "profane herself" (Leviticus 21:9). In many instances in the Hebrew Bible (e.g., Numbers 35:33), offenses are understood as profaning not only the offender but also as polluting the community. At the time, people had a corporate mentality, and it was believed that a serious offense committed by one person could result in God's punishment upon the entire community; therefore, some form of ritual cleansing or expiation was required—namely, capital punishment—to "purge" the offender and restore the purity or holiness of Israel (Westmoreland-White & Stassen, 2004, p. 125). Execution by stoning (e.g., 1 Samuel 30:6; 1 Kings 12:18), which was the standard method at the time, was thus "an action conveying a corporate obligation for removing sin from the community" (Gaertner, 2000, p. 1253). It was a ritualistic act of expiation, much like how ancient Israel's holy wars included the ban (*herem*)—the slaughter of all men, women, and children—and thus were somewhat akin to human sacrifices. Accordingly, after the Israelites' defeat at Ai, God told Joshua that the loss was because "Israel has sinned" (Joshua 7:11). Although it was actually one Israelite, Achan, who disobeyed the *herem* by keeping some plunder earlier from the battle at Jericho, all of the people of Israel were regarded as transgressors. Thus, in order to remove this sin, they stoned Achan and burned his family, livestock, tent, "and all that he had" (Joshua 7:24–25).

Christian supporters of capital punishment today do not call for reintroducing this method of execution—stoning by the men of the community. After all, these laws were originally promulgated in a time when prisons did not exist, therefore requiring quick and effective punishment of offenders who were viewed as a threat to the moral, ceremonial, and civil life of the community. The two options actually available back then for addressing grave threats were either execution or exile. Likewise, Christian proponents of the death penalty do not share the theological view of the ancient Israelites about corporate sin and the need to execute one guilty person (and their kin) in order to purge the evil that has polluted them all and to placate God. Yet even if supporters of capital punishment today do not explicitly employ such language in exactly the same way, the modern assumption that the execution of a murderer is required in order to balance some cosmic scale of justice echoes that ancient Hebrew expiatory worldview.

Christians who oppose capital punishment today draw, too, from the Old Testament. For there are also passages in the Hebrew Scriptures that lean against the death penalty. Indeed, God shows mercy to the Bible's first murderer, Cain, by sending him into exile and protecting him there (after Cain expresses fear that anyone who meets him might kill him), instead of having him executed (Genesis 4:14–15). On this primordial story, Pope John Paul II emphasizes the way that God shows mercy even when punishing the murderous Cain. God's protection of Cain, putting a "mark" on him in case anyone attempts to kill him, shows, "*Not even a murderer loses his personal dignity*" as image of God (John Paul II, 1995, no. 9; original emphasis). The pope thereby extends what Murray says about both the murdered human and the executioner as image of God to include also the murderer as image of God.

In addition, neither Moses nor David were executed for their capital offenses: Moses killed an Egyptian (Exodus 2:1–12) and David committed adultery with Bathsheba and arranged for the death of her husband Uriah (2 Samuel 11–12:25). Likewise, Tamar, who was accused of adultery, was allowed to live, and her adulterous act produced an ancestor of both David and Jesus (Genesis 38; Matthew 1:3; Luke 3:33). Similarly, the prophet Hosea's wife Gomer repeatedly committed adultery, but he forgave her and sought reconciliation with her (Hosea 3:1–5). In Ezekiel 33:11, moreover, God tells the prophet, "I have no pleasure in the death of the wicked, but that the wicked should turn from their ways and live." These passages reflect overarching themes in the Hebrew Scriptures, including mercy, steadfast love, peace, forgiveness, and a justice that is restorative rather than retributive (Skotnicki, 2012, p. 24).

Christian against capital punishment also commonly quote the Decalogue's sixth commandment (fifth in Catholic and Lutheran numbering), often from the King James Version, as "Thou shalt not kill" (Exodus 20:13; Deuteronomy 5:17). The Hebrew term, *rtsh*, may be translated either as "kill" or as "murder" (Bailey, 2005), so some Christians interpret it in a pacifistic way as prohibiting all forms of homicide, including killing in war, in self-defense, or in policing. After all, the word was used at least once for capital punishment (Numbers 35:30) and twice even for accidental manslaughter (Deuteronomy 4:41–43; Joshua 20:3). Yet, most theologians and Christian churches translate this commandment as forbidding the intentional killing of an innocent person, which is murder, and not necessarily as ruling out forms of justifiable homicide. As such, the sixth commandment does not proscribe capital punishment definitively.

Christian critics of capital punishment note, as well, that it is unclear whether the ancient Israelites actually always executed offenders, since "one cannot simply assume that these law codes literally reflect the general practice or that they served as more than symbolic reminders of the demands implicit in living according to the Covenant" (Megivern, 1997, p. 11). Besides, the Torah required at least two eye witnesses whose testimonies had to be in complete agreement (Deuteronomy 19:15–20; Numbers 35:30; Deuteronomy 17:2–7). Close relatives, women, slaves, or people with bad reputations were prohibited from serving as witnesses. If a witness were to be judged as giving false testimony with malicious intent, then he would instead receive the punishment that would have been administered to the defendant (Deuteronomy 10:16). Indeed, the practice of capital punishment was rare in post-exilic Jewish society, with the Mishnah, which is the record of authoritative oral interpretation of the written law of the Torah by Jewish religious leaders from about 200 BCE to about 200 CE, requiring 23 judges for a capital case. During that period, "there was strong Jewish sentiment against the death penalty" (Megivern, 1997, p. 11). By the time of Jesus, capital punishment by Jews was nearly impossible to implement, and most penalties could instead be addressed by monetary payments (Stassen, 1998, p. 121). As one Christian writer concludes, "significant safeguards and roadblocks are put in place to render the penalty of death practically nonexistent" (Buck, 2013, p. 91).

The New Testament

Given this overarching trajectory emphasizing the importance of human life—hence homicide is generally prohibited—while limiting the death penalty in the Hebrew Scriptures and within Judaism, the New Testament seems to be "a continuation or further development of the tradition" (Stassen,

1998, p. 122). The New Testament does not say much directly about capital punishment, either for or against it; nor does it explicitly come right out and condemn the practice. Indeed, New Testament authors probably assumed it as a given practice at the time, much like slavery, by governing authorities such as the Roman Empire (Brugger, 2014, p. 63). Nevertheless, a few texts from the New Testament are commonly cited by Christians who believe capital punishment is morally justified.

Saint Paul's warning to Christians in Rome is often quoted: "But if you do what is wrong, you should be afraid, for the authority does not bear the sword in vain! It is the servant of God to execute wrath on the wrongdoer" (Romans 13:4). Their assumption is that this passage, especially with its words translated as "the sword" and "to execute," directly refers to and endorses capital punishment. "Execute" here, however, merely refers to "carry out" or "implement." The passage's historical and literary context, though, is important. Immediately prior to this passage Paul identifies duties that Christians owe to their fellow Christians in the fledgling church in Rome, and he exhorts them to "live peaceably with all" others (Romans 12:18). He instructs them, "Do not repay anyone evil for evil" (Romans 12:17), and he adds: "Beloved, never avenge yourselves, but leave it to the wrath of God; for it is written, 'Vengeance is mine, I will repay, says the Lord'" (Romans 12:19). Such Christian behavior applies also toward governing authorities.

To be sure, Paul was not writing to Christians who wielded political authority, for at that time, between 54 CE and 59 CE, Christians were a minority group, not in positions of power (Brugger, 2014, p. 67). He was addressing a small band of Christians who lived in the shadow of the very capital of the Roman Empire. A few years earlier, in 49 CE, a tax revolt had led to the forceful expulsion of Jews, including Christians like Priscilla and Aquila (Acts 18:2–3), by Emperor Claudius from Rome. After Claudius' death in 54 CE, the edict expelling Jews lapsed, with Jews and Christians returning to Rome during the reign of his successor, Emperor Nero. Paul then was discouraging the small Christian community, which was already under some scrutiny for being subversive, from participating in another similar insurrection against Nero's latest tax, which might provoke soldiers who accompanied toll and tax collectors to use their swords against them (Stassen, 1998, p. 126; Yoder, 2011, p. 73). Accordingly, what Paul "had in mind was not individual malfeasance but 'rebellion' such as that which had led Emperor Claudius to expel the Jews from Rome a short time before" (Megivern, 1997, p. 18). As E. Christian Brugger observes, "[W]e may infer that the Apostle, who was instructing the young church on its dealings with the existing authorities and who wished to obviate potentially harsh reprisals against imprudent Christian decisions, adapted his instruction with a view to commending those attitudes which were most appropriate given the historical situation, namely, respect for and docility toward earthly rulers" (Brugger, 2014, p. 68).

Furthermore, some scholars note that the Greek word for "sword" (*machairan*) does not name the instrument used in capital punishment (Yoder, 2011, p. 46; Stassen, 1998, p. 126), but instead refers to a short sword typically carried by soldiers on police duty rather than in combat or when executing someone. Although the same *machairan* is mentioned in Acts 12:2 when Herod Agrippa has James killed with the sword, the "sword" in Romans 13:4 merely symbolized government's overarching authority to maintain law and order, which included executions that were a standard practice at the time. In his letter to the Romans, Paul was not necessarily offering a political theology for government or making a moral argument justifying capital punishment (Brugger, 2014, p. 70). Rather, he simply "acknowledges the validity and propriety, even the necessity, of the punitive function of the state" in order to maintain law and order (Megivern, 1997, p. 17).

A few other New Testament passages are invoked by supporters of capital punishment. Some claim Paul recognized that certain crimes existed that warrant the death penalty when he says in his defense before Festus, "If therefore I do wrong and have committed anything worthy of death, I refuse not to die" (Acts 25:11; Murray, 1996, p. 461). Similarly, some refer to the penitent malefactor who says about his and the other criminal's crucifixions, in contrast to Jesus': "And we indeed [are crucified] justly, for we receive the due reward for our deeds: but this man hath done nothing amiss"

(Luke 23:41). However, again, at that time, these persons likely assumed that the practice of capital punishment by the Romans was a given. Indeed, no governments or political authorities at the time abolished capital punishment, nor would doing so have even occurred to them. Also, when Paul said that he is willing to die, he was confessing that he was not afraid to die as a martyr (Stassen, 1998, p. 125). These passages, Christian opponents of the death penalty counter, are simply describing the situation rather than offering a theological justification for what ought to happen, so they do not necessarily provide a moral argument for capital punishment.

Turning to New Testament passages that critics of the death penalty tend to rely on, Jesus' teachings and example, as found especially in the Gospels, are especially emphasized. Again, Jesus Christ is the *norma normans non normata*. Core New Testament themes of mercy, forgiveness, love, reconciliation, and peace were taught and practiced by Jesus toward all sinners, and he railed against the sins of self-righteousness and vengeance. In his Sermon on the Mount, Jesus instructs his followers to forgive those who have wronged them and to love and pray for their enemies (Matthew 5:44; 6:14–15). Here Jesus explicitly mentions the *lex talionis*, and he says, "You have heard that it was said, 'An eye for an eye and a tooth for a tooth.' But I say to you, Do not resist the evildoer" (Matthew 5:38–39). According to Glen H. Stassen, "If 'life for life' is understood as a limiting of revenge by killing only the killer and not also the killer's family, then Jesus is here taking a further leap in the same direction, limiting it all the way down to zero" (Stassen,1998, p. 123). In this way, Jesus does not abolish the law of the Torah but fulfills it by redirecting his followers toward its ultimate end or goal (Matt 5:17). If the Hebrew Scriptures held life as sacred, Jesus "closed the loophole" by teaching that the lifeblood of every person, including evildoers, belongs to God and is sacred (Yoder, 2011, p. 40).

Christians against capital punishment also refer to the gospel story of the adulterous woman (John 7:53–8:11). Although these verses are absent in the oldest manuscripts of John's gospel, scholars view them as consonant with Jesus' life and teachings. Jesus was confronted by the religious leaders with a test that they hoped would trap him; they probably assumed that Jesus would not approve of executing her, so if he publicly spoke against her execution they would claim that he rejected the Torah (Stassen, 1998, p. 123). Instead of giving such a direct response, Jesus replies, "Let anyone among you who is without sin throw the first stone," and he tells the woman after her accusers departed the scene, "Neither do I condemn you. Go your way, and from now on do not sin again" (John 8:7, 11). If only the sinless are qualified to execute others, even Jesus, though Christians believe he "knew no sin" himself (2 Corinthians 5:21), refuses to do so. Of course, supporters of capital punishment might note that Jesus here was dealing with an adulterer, not a murderer, to whom it may not be prudent simply to say "go and sin no more."

Some death penalty supporters further assert that Jesus must have believed capital punishment to be morally legitimate because of his acceptance of his crucifixion on the cross; however, critics of capital punishment counter that the crucifixion should remind Christians that we all need mercy and should not be so eager to impose the death penalty on others (Stassen, 1998, p. 124). Indeed, while dying Jesus forgives his enemies who were crucifying him (Luke 23:34). In doing so, Jesus embodies and enacts the justice of God that ultimately is restorative rather than retributive (Yoder, 2011, p. 70). On this basis, Glen H. Stassen concludes, "Central to the biblical story is the emphasis on redemption, even of one's enemies . . ., [and the] death penalty terminates the chance for repentance" (Stassen, 1998, p. 127).

Moreover, drawing on the New Testament letter to the Hebrews, in which Jesus "offered for all time a single sacrifice for sins" (Hebrews 10:12) that "abolishes" the sacrificial sin offerings of the "first covenant" (Hebrews 10:9), the Mennonite pacifist John Howard Yoder argues that Jesus' execution on the cross "puts an end to the entire expiatory system, whether it be enforced by priests in Jerusalem or by executioners anywhere else" (Yoder, 2011, p. 103). If Christians believe that animal and grain sacrifices should no longer be performed to placate God, so too criminals ought not to be executed to satisfy some retributive notion of justice being served. Or, as Protestant theologian Karl Barth asks, "Now that Jesus Christ has been nailed to the cross for the sins of the world, how can we still use the thought of expiation to establish the death penalty?" (Barth, 1961, pp. 442–443). This very point leads Brugger, who is Roman Catholic, to suggest, "The re-presentation in the Eucharist of that timeless sacrifice is an august reminder of the fact that blood (human or otherwise) need no longer be spilt for the expiation of sins" (Brugger, 2014, 73).

The liturgy of the Eucharist underscores for many Christians this last point and reinforces how the overarching themes of the Bible converge in opposition to capital punishment (Berkman, 2004; Stassen, 1998, p. 126). Because worship is the original and primary place where Scripture is read and heard by Christians, the Bible should be interpreted through what transpires during the liturgy (Fodor, 2004, p. 141). Even the simple fact that Christians stand during the Gospel reading indicates an interpretive lens for adjudicating passages in the Hebrew Bible on the *lex talionis* with what Jesus says about it in the Sermon on the Mount. Repeatedly reading and hearing Scripture during Eucharistic worship "serves to accentuate the central motifs of faith, reinforce its principal themes, and rehearse its characteristic movements" (Fodor, 2004, p. 146). Accordingly, Catholic liturgical scholar Kevin Irwin suggests that Eucharistic worship offers an experience and understanding of justice that "should be the measure of the world's and the church's expectations" and runs counter to the "eye for an eye" retributive justice emphasized in society (Irwin, 1999, p. 180).

Nevertheless, while the New Testament passages emphasizing forgiveness, mercy, and reconciliation, according to Brugger, "exercised considerable influence on the conduct and beliefs of early Christians" (Brugger, 2014, p. 64), they did not necessarily lead these Christians to question the practice of the death penalty or to become activists for its abolition. Such opposition will become more pronounced within the Christian tradition after many more centuries have passed. Attempting to defend one's stance for or against capital punishment by relying on Scripture alone, therefore, is somewhat inconclusive. Exploring what the Bible says about the death penalty, while necessary for Christians, is insufficient, which is why most churches and denominations devote attention also to the other fonts of moral wisdom.

The Tradition

The turn to the liturgy indicates a transition into the source of moral wisdom known as tradition. According to Benedictine liturgical theologian Aidan Kavanagh, "liturgical tradition is not merely one theological source among others such as various biblical theologies. . . . Rather . . . liturgical tradition, in whatever Christian idiom, [is] the dynamic condition within which theological reflection is done, within which the Word of God is appropriately understood" (Kavanaugh, 1984, pp. 7–8). In addition to liturgy, tradition includes the history of Christian writings, teachings, and practices. As Brugger observes, the tradition can be divided into three historical periods, each with respective stances toward capital punishment (Brugger, 2013a, p. 116). First, during the initial three centuries of Christianity, Christians rejected the death penalty. Second, from the fourth to the nineteenth centuries, Christians accepted or approved of capital punishment. Third, during the twentieth and early twenty-first centuries, opposition to the death penalty gained traction among Christian churches and denominations.

During the first period, the earliest Christians were pacifists who opposed all forms of lethal force. They refused to use violence for self-defense, and they were forbidden from being soldiers and magistrates. Indeed, they were excommunicated if they, in such a capacity, killed anyone. The Apostolic Tradition (c. 235 CE), like other documents about baptism and communion from that time period, highlighted trades and professions that were ruled out since they involved both idolatry and bloodshed: "A soldier in command must be told not to kill people; if he is ordered to do so, he shall not carry it out. Nor should he take the oath. If he will not agree, he should be rejected [not allowed to be baptized]. Anyone who has the power of the sword, or who is a civil magistrate wearing the purple, should desist, or he should be rejected [excommunicated]. If a catechumen or a believer wishes to become a soldier they should be rejected for they have despised God" (Long, 2011, p. 30). Accordingly, one early Christian martyr, Maximilian, refused to enlist under the Roman proconsul Dion in

Numidia in 295 CE. "It is not right for me to serve in the army," he confessed, "since I am a Christian" (Long, 2011, p. 31). As he was led away to be put to death, Maximilian instructed his parents to give his clothes, which they had provided to him for military service, to his executioner.

Even so, the early Christians, similar to Saint Paul, did not deny that civil authorities had power, ultimately granted by God, over life and death. These Christians assumed that governments practice capital punishment. The earliest Christian writers, such as Justin Martyr (died c. 165) and Athenagoras (second century CE), were critical of unjust executions of Christians who had done no wrong. However, they allowed that the authorities could execute Christians if proven to be guilty of a truly capital offense. As Athenagoras put it, "If, indeed, anyone can convict us of a crime, be it small or great, we do not ask to be excused from punishment, but are prepared to undergo the sharpest and most merciless inflictions" (Brugger, 2014, p. 76). However, he also noted that Christians, themselves, can neither watch an execution nor kill anyone. Likewise, Tertullian (died c. 220) prohibited Christians from any profession that involved killing, for the "Gospel is one and the same for the Christian at all times whatever his occupation in life" (Brugger, 2014, p. 77). Referring to Jesus' teachings in the Sermon on the Mount, Tertullian asked, "Will a Christian, taught to turn the other cheek when struck unjustly, guard prisoners in chains, and administer torture and capital punishment?" During this first period of the Christian tradition, the answer was no. Christians may not execute others, although non-Christian authorities may legitimately do so as long as it is done to truly guilty criminals who deserve it.

The more systematic treatments of capital punishment by Clement of Alexandria (died c. 215), Origen (died c. 254), and Cyprian of Carthage (died c. 258) acknowledged that governments, though not Christian, are divinely authorized to protect the community and to punish malfeasants, including with death; nevertheless, these writers forbade Christians from participating in and administering the death penalty. The last major Christian writer from this earliest period, Lactantius (c. 250–c. 325), rejected capital punishment along with any forms of "the act of putting to death itself," without exception (Long, 2011, p. 37). He called on Christians to be merciful, patient, and kind to others, including enemies, because these qualities reflect our true nature as human beings whom God has created. Lactantius even urged Christians to refuse to accuse anyone of a capital offense, since doing so would lead to the perpetrator's execution. Still, he continued to acknowledge the non-Christian political rulers' authority to administer capital punishment.

The second period begins with Constantine's Edict of Milan (313), which made Christianity a tolerated rather than persecuted religion within the Roman Empire, and Theodosius' Edict of Thessalonica (380), which declared it the official state religion. Now the governing authorities were Christians, including the emperor, magistrates, soldiers, and even executioners. The previous bifurcation between what was expected of Christians and of non-Christian authorities collapsed, although the sense of an incongruity between being a Christian and participating in capital punishment remained. Saint Ambrose (d. 397), who was bishop of Milan, began what would come to be known as just war theory, which permitted Christians to be soldiers and to kill, as long as doing so was only to protect the innocent from grave harm. His protégé, Saint Augustine (d. 430), further developed this framework that both justified and limited the use of lethal force on behalf of society. However, they were comparably less sanguine about the death penalty.

Indeed, both of these theologian-bishops called for clemency for condemned criminals, and they strongly urged Christian authorities not to practice capital punishment. "Their advice to Christian magistrates was consistent: *restrain malefactors, but do not kill them*" (Brugger, 2013a, p. 118; original italics). Drawing on the biblical story of Cain and Abel, Ambrose wrote, "The person, therefore, who has not spared the life of a sinner has begrudged him the opportunity for the remission of his sins and at the same time deprived him of all hopes of remission" (Brugger, 2014, p. 88). Instead, Christian magistrates should show magnanimity and patience, and should be reluctant to kill. Likewise, in two letters to Christian magistrates, *Letter 133* and *Letter 134* (412 CE), Augustine wrote that if he "were making [his] plea to a non-Christian judge," he would "deal differently with him" even while still advocating mercy, but since he was corresponding with a Christian, he added, "Since the matter is being brought before you, I follow another method, another argument. We see in you a governor of exalted power, but we also recognize you as a son with a Christian idea of duty" to try to amend the perpetrator, and "spare them, now that you have arrested, summoned, and convicted them" (Brugger, 2014, p. 93). So, while theoretically accepting governing authorities'—including Christian authorities'—power to practice the death penalty, Ambrose and Augustine still hoped that Christian magistrates would instead show mercy and not execute criminals.

Subsequent writers during the Middle Ages, however, demonstrated less hesitancy about capital punishment, instead identifying parameters for its lawful use. Although clergy continue to be forbidden from shedding blood, including the death penalty, a confluence of factors—such as decentralization of authority in Europe, the rise of feudalism, and the increasing sense of lawlessness in society—contributed to a change in attitude among Christians toward capital punishment. The rule of law became a dominant concern, as reflected in treatises on political authority by jurists such as Gratian and John of Salisbury. Moral theology resembled legal thought and texts, and with regard to the death penalty, "the dominant concern of lawyers and theologians from the eleventh to the thirteenth centuries was not so much to limit the exercise of bloody punishment as to articulate clear foundations for its lawful infliction" (Brugger, 2013a, p. 119).

The most influential treatment of the topic was by the theologian Saint Thomas Aquinas (1225–1274), although his account is actually more philosophical, anchored in the work of the ancient Greek philosopher Aristotle. Accordingly, in a section of his *Summa Theologica* addressing the question "whether it is lawful to kill sinners?" Aquinas wrote that "it may be justifiable to kill a sinner just as it is to kill a beast, for as Aristotle points out, an evil man is worse than a beast, and more harmful" (Aquinas, 1948, ST, II-II, q. 64, art. 2, ad. 2). For Aquinas, as for Aristotle, the good of the whole is greater than that of the parts, so that the parts are subordinate to the whole. Analogously, if the health of one part of a person's body is sick and threatens the wellness of the whole body, then it is right to remove or amputate that limb. A criminal, according to Aquinas, "departs from the order of reason, and therefore falls away from human dignity," which means that "although it be evil in itself to kill a man who preserves his human dignity, nevertheless to kill a man who is a sinner can be good" (Aquinas, 1948, ST, II-II, q. 64, art. 2, ad. 2). A murderer, therefore, forfeits his humanity and rightly ought to be put to death.

Aquinas' "enormous influence" on subsequent Christian writers, especially Catholics, continued through the Council of Trent in the sixteenth century to the Second Vatican Council (1963–1965). A few Christians opposed the death penalty, though, as apparent when Pope Innocent III in 1210 required a heretical group known as the Waldensians to take an oath that included: "We declare that the secular power can without mortal sin impose a judgment of blood provided the punishment is carried out not in hatred but with good judgment, not inconsiderately but after mature deliberation" (Brugger, 2013a, p. 122). Evidently, up to then, the Waldensians had held the opposite view that, along with other beliefs, required correction according to the pope. In addition, major Protestants such as Martin Luther (1483–1546) and John Calvin (1509–1564), although calling for many reforms, "had no objection to the death penalty as such" (Megivern, 1997, p. 141). Indeed, as James J. Megivern notes: "By Luther's time the reigning mythology included the axiom that the death penalty was essential to the social order. It was a given that few doubted, a veritable cornerstone of the prevailing system" (Megivern, 1997, p. 142). Luther's two-swords teaching, whereby God rules church and society, and with regard to the latter, the "temporal sword [that] should and must be red and bloodstained, for the world is wicked and is bound to be so," influenced much of subsequent Protestant thinking about capital punishment, just as Aquinas' did for Catholics (Megivern, 1997, p. 142).

From the sixteenth century through the mid-twentieth century, Christian thinking about the death penalty stayed fairly consistent. Catholics relied philosophically on Aquinas' "part-to-whole and putrid limb analogues" to justify capital punishment for the sake of the common good (Brugger, 2013b, p. 128). Like their Protestant counterparts, they also claimed that the authority to conduct executions is granted by God to rulers, and they appealed to relevant supporting texts from Scripture. Of course, at the time of these writers, they did not have access to the level of biblical scholarship extant today, which may qualify and nuance one's interpretation of scriptural passages. In addition, during the "wars of religion" in the sixteenth and seventeenth centuries, Christians on all sides employed the death penalty as a weapon against alleged heretics.

However, there were individual theologians, religious orders, and other Christian groups, such as the historic peace churches from the radical reformation (e.g., pacifist Christian communities such as the Quakers and Mennonites), who continued to oppose its use. Also, an echo of the earlier discomfort with capital punishment was evident in the Catholic requirement that executioners had to do penance after putting someone to death, even though that act of executing someone was regarded as morally justified. During the eighteenth century, opposition to capital punishment percolated in Europe, but mostly from philosophical and political critics of Christianity. For this reason, the Catholic Church initially opposed the call for abolition of the death penalty. Cesare Beccaria (1738–1794) stands out, with his critical work of 1764, *On Crimes and Punishments*, which employed nonreligious reasons, such as social-contract theory, and questioned the authority of anyone to kill others deliberately (Megivern, 1997, pp. 217–218). Beccaria compared the death penalty to war and concluded that capital punishment cannot be justified as necessary or as a last resort, unless a person poses a serious and imminent threat to the security of a nation. More outright Christian abolitionists during the nineteenth century tended to be Protestants, including Lucretia Mott (1793–1880), William Lloyd Garrison (1805–1879), and Adin Ballou (1803–1890). On the question of whether a Christian can be an executioner, among other governmental professions, Ballou wrote,

> He cannot be an officer, elector, agent, legal prosecutor, passive constituent or approver of any government, as a sworn or otherwise pledged supporter thereof, whose civil constitution and fundamental laws, require, authorize or tolerate war, slavery, capital punishment, or the infliction of any absolute injury.
>
> *(Long, 2011, p. 121)*

Similarly, the Russian novelist Leo Tolstoy (1828–1910) also rejected the death penalty for Christian theological reasons, especially Jesus' teachings in the Gospels and the Sermon on the Mount.

During the first half of the twentieth century, most Christian denominations, including Catholicism, basically reiterated the earlier biblical and traditional rationales in support of the death penalty. Yet beginning in the 1960s, a growing emphasis on the inherent dignity and worth of individual human life led to increased opposition to capital punishment. In 1967, Donald Campion, S.J., provided the entry on the death penalty for the *New Catholic Encyclopedia*, wherein he considered the ambivalent passages of Scripture and the thinking of Aquinas, but also the observations from the social sciences that ancient people used the death penalty, as he put it, "not only to retaliate for murder or treason, but also to appease spirits offended by sorcery, incest, or sacrilege" (Megivern, 1997, p. 330). Campion went on to suggest, "Any further Catholic thought on the topic will undoubtedly reflect a new emphasis on the notion of the inalienable rights of the human person as set forth in recent authoritative documents" such as Pope John XXIII's 1963 encyclical on world peace, *Pacem in Terris* (Megivern, 1997, p. 332). Furthermore, Campion appreciatively drew from Beccaria and from the social sciences, respectively, to question the right of the state to employ capital punishment as normal rather than exceptional policy and its effectiveness as a deterrent or a means to protect society.

In 1968, in the United States, the National Council of Churches adopted a joint statement, with 103 Protestant church bodies in favor and none opposed, which identified ten reasons to oppose capital punishment. While some of the reasons are explicitly Christian or theological ones, most reflect insights from modern studies in the social sciences, including psychology, sociology, and criminology. The first and the final reasons are the most explicitly theological: first, "[b]elief in the worth of human life and the dignity of human personality as gifts of God" and, second, "[o]ur Christian commitment to seek the redemption and reconciliation of the wrong-doer, which are frustrated by his execution" (Megivern, 1997, p. 333–334). Today, most Protestant denominations morally oppose capital punishment and are calling for its abolition. These include: Episcopal Church, Evangelical Lutheran Church in America, Presbyterian Church USA, United Church of Christ, United Methodist Church, American Baptist Churches in the USA, Unitarian Universalist Association, American Friends Service Committee (Quakers), Mennonite Church, Church of the Brethren, Christian Church (Disciples of Christ), Christian Reformed Church in North America, and the Moravian Church. This statement from the United Methodist Church, which first expressed its opposition to the death penalty in 1956, is representative of most:

> We believe the death penalty denies the power of Christ to redeem, restore and transform all human beings. The United Methodist Church is deeply concerned about crime throughout the world and the value of any life taken by a murder or homicide. We believe all human life is sacred and created by God and therefore, we must see all human life as significant and valuable. When governments implement the death penalty (capital punishment), then the life of the convicted person is devalued and all possibility of change in that person's life ends. We believe in the resurrection of Jesus Christ and that the possibility of reconciliation with Christ comes through repentance. This gift of reconciliation is offered to all individuals without exception and gives all life new dignity and sacredness. For this reason, we oppose the death penalty (capital punishment) and urge its elimination from all criminal codes.
>
> *(United Methodist Church, 2016).*

Likewise, the World Council of Churches, which from around the globe includes most Protestant denominations and the Orthodox church, morally opposes the death penalty, as reflected in statements in 1990 and 1998.

The United States Catholic bishops went on record in opposition to the death penalty for the first time in 1974. A lengthier statement was issued in 1980, in which the bishops concluded that "in the conditions of contemporary American society, the legitimate purposes of punishment do not justify the imposition of the death penalty" (Brugger, 2013b, p. 131). Today the current stance of the Catholic Church on the issue of capital punishment is primarily anchored in Saint Pope John Paul II's encyclical *Evangelium Vitae*, which was issued in 1995. He especially highlights human dignity and the sanctity of life as bases for opposing not only capital punishment but also abortion and euthanasia. During his papacy, a new *Catechism of the Catholic Church* was published in 1992 and revised in 1997, with a significant change on the death penalty—indeed, a more principled opposition to it—reflected in the latter edition.

The topic of capital punishment is considered in the *Catechism*'s section dealing with the fifth commandment, "You shall not kill," and in a subsection (nos. 2263–2267) on "legitimate defense" (*defensio legitima*). The *Catechism* does not discuss state-sanctioned executions in a subsection titled "punishment," though the topic of punishment is also treated here within this "legitimate defense" subsection. That the *Catechism* deals with the death penalty under the heading of "legitimate defense" is significant, since that phrase is also used for other forms of lethal force in recent Catholic teaching, including just war, humanitarian intervention, and personal self-defense. On punishment itself, as part of the state's "requirement of safeguarding the common good" from criminal activity, civil authorities have "the right and duty to inflict punishment proportionate to the gravity of the offense" (no. 2266). Retributive justice, or "redressing the disorder introduced by the offense," is what the *Catechism* says is the "primary aim" of punishment (no. 2266). In addition, when an offender owns up to his crime and accepts the proportionate punishment, it becomes expiatory and thereby medicinally puts the prisoner on the path to correction—a point that appears to be a nod in the direction of regarding punishment as concerned not only with retributive but also with *restorative* justice.

In the 1992 edition, the *Catechism* referred to capital punishment in number 2266, which read: "Preserving the common good of society requires rendering the aggressor unable to inflict harm. For this reason the traditional teaching of the Church has acknowledged as well-founded the right and duty of legitimate public authority to punish malefactors by means of penalties commensurate with the gravity of the crime, not excluding, in cases of extreme gravity, the death penalty." However, these last ten words were omitted when the *Catechism* was revised in 1997—partly due to the influence of Sister Helen Prejean, author of the acclaimed book *Dead Man Walking* (Prejean, 1993), about which a movie was also made, whose letter about precisely this matter was delivered to Pope John Paul II on January 22, 1997, seven days before Cardinal Josef Ratzinger announced that a change would be made in the *Catechism* to reflect recent "progress in doctrine" about the death penalty (Prejean, 2005, pp. 123–136).

The 1997 *Catechism*'s Latin *editio typica* (i.e., the normative and definitive text) therefore refers to the death penalty only in number 2267, which consists of three paragraphs:

> Assuming that the guilty party's identity and responsibility have been fully determined, the traditional teaching of the Church does not exclude recourse to the death penalty, if this is the only possible way of effectively defending human lives against the unjust aggressor.
>
> If, however, nonlethal means are sufficient to defend and protect people's safety from the aggressor, authority will limit itself to such means, as these are more in keeping with the concrete conditions of the common good and more in conformity to the dignity of the human person.
>
> Today, in fact, as a consequence of the possibilities which the state has for effectively preventing crime, by rendering one who has committed an offense incapable of doing harm—without definitely taking away from him the possibility of redeeming himself—the cases in which the execution of the offender is an absolute necessity "are very rare, if not practically nonexistent."
>
> *(no. 2257, quoting John Paul II, Evangelium Vitae, no. 56)*

Accordingly, the only justification for killing a prisoner (as long as it is certain that he or she is truly guilty) is if there is no other way to protect others from a grave and imminent threat—conditions that the *Catechism*, echoing Pope John Paul II in *Evangelium Vitae*, says are extremely rare if at all possible today.

As John Berkman notes, when Pope John Paul II "acknowledges the possibility of emergency situations or settings in which it might be necessary to kill unjust aggressors as the only means of defending innocent persons, such judicial killings would not be retributive" or capital *punishment* (Berkman, 2004, p. 106; Winright, 2013). Put differently, it might be argued that the Catholic Church theoretically permits an execution as legitimate defense, but no longer theologically supports it as a punishment or a penalty. Fr. Raniero Cantalamessa, who is the Preacher to the Papal Household (under Pope John Paul II, Pope Benedict XVI, and Pope Francis), in some of his Lenten homilies in 2004 and 2005, provides a possible reason for this shift.

In his third Lenten sermon from 2005, Fr. Cantalamessa suggests, "The believer has another reason—Eucharistic—to oppose the death penalty. How can Christians, in certain countries, approve and rejoice over the news that a criminal has been condemned to death, when we read in the Bible: 'Do I indeed derive any pleasure from the death of the wicked? says the Lord God. Do I not rather rejoice when he turns from his evil way that he may live?' (Ezekiel 18:23)" (Cantalamessa, 2005). In his view, the practice of capital punishment is a system that sacralizes violence. It employs violence to punish violent criminals. Fr. Cantalamessa writes, "Something of the mechanism of the scapegoat is under way in every capital execution, including in those endorsed by the law" (Cantalamessa, 2005). A similar viewpoint is provided by Presbyterian theologian Mark Lewis Taylor, who describes capital punishment as a counter-liturgy:

The state, with its dramatic and awe-inspiring spectacles of execution, with its carefully orchestrated ritualized killings, takes on a kind of religious function . . . . The practice and protocol of execution, we might say, is a kind of human sacrifice, like that maintained in religio-imperial systems of the past

(Taylor, 2001, p. 41)

Like Fr. Cantalamessa, Taylor suggests that Christian liturgy offers a dramatic performance that should counter and oppose this state-sanctioned ritual of violence. According to Fr. Cantalamessa,

Jesus unmasks and tears apart the mechanism of the scapegoat that canonizes violence, making himself innocent, the victim of all violence . . . . Christ defeated violence, not by opposing it with greater violence, but suffering it and laying bare its injustice and uselessness.

(Cantalamessa, 2005)

It is noteworthy that Pope Benedict XVI wrote something very similar:

This is God's new way of conquering: He does not oppose violence with stronger violence. He opposes violence precisely with the contrary: with love to the end, his cross. This is God's humble way of overcoming: With his love—and only thus is it possible—he puts a limit to violence.

(Benedict XVI, 2005)

For these core theological reasons, it now appears that the Catholic Church rejects capital punishment in principle and permits, in practice and rarely if at all, only executions that are absolutely necessary to protect society. Accordingly, recent popes—John Paul II, Benedict XVI, and Francis—as well as conferences of bishops throughout the world call for the abolition of the death penalty. As Pope Francis most recently has stated, referring to how slavery was considered justified in the past but is now rejected as "mortal sin": "The same goes for the death penalty; for a time, it was normal. Today, we say that the death penalty is inadmissible" (Esteves, 2017).

Experience

In addition to giving attention to the Bible and tradition, most Christian churches and theologians consider experience as a font for moral guidance on the death penalty. This source already surfaced in recent tradition, where insights provided by the social sciences informed church statements. Research and studies in the fields of criminology, sociology, jurisprudence, and psychology in particular have received significant weight. In addition, economics has gained attention in recent years with regard to this issue. Hence, support for capital punishment among American Christians, like any others of their fellow citizens, has waned in recent years for a number of reasons: concern that wrongfully convicted persons may be executed; doubts that the death penalty acts as a deterrent; worries about economic and racial biases in capital cases; concerns about the financial costs involved; and revulsion at recent botched methods of execution. Even where these studies may appear inconclusive, it seems that a growing number of Christians prefer to err on the side of opposing the death penalty. Also, many Christians, because of what is revealed in these studies, now seek to address the root causes of crime, including homicides, such as culture, poverty, illiteracy, despair, and addictions (Stassen, 1998, pp. 127–129).

Moreover, the actual stories of personal experiences with the death penalty appear to have made a large impact on many Christians. Sister Helen Prejean's testimonial accounts—in books, film, lectures, and theater—are just one example. So, too, the examples of families of murder victims, who stand against the death penalty, have influenced many Christians to reconsider their stance on this topic (Penn, 1998; Blaugher, 2013). These, too, are encouraging Christians to give more attention to the needs of those most affected by the horrific crimes committed against them and their loved ones, even as they oppose the death penalty for perpetrators.

Reason

Due to the insights derived from the aforementioned fonts of moral wisdom, most Christians and denominations today reason that the death penalty is no longer morally justified. Indeed, support for the death penalty among Christians is waning in recent years in the United States, like other parts of the world. Until recently, polling data showed little difference between non-Catholic and Catholic support, hovering around 65–70%, for capital punishment. However, according to a poll conducted by Zogby International in 2004, American Catholic support for the death penalty decreased from 68 to 48%, with a third of those who formerly supported it now opposing it. Other recent polls (Gallup, Pew) have reflected similar a similar downward trajectory of support for capital punishment among American Catholics and other Christians. A 2016 Pew study found that white evangelical Protestants continue to back the use of the death penalty by a wide margin (69% favor, 26% oppose); white main-line Protestants also are more likely to support (60%) than oppose (31%) it; and Catholics are less likely to support it (43%) than oppose (46%) it (Oliphant, 2016). Those Christians who are most likely to support the death penalty morally tend to rely primarily or solely upon Scripture, understood in a literal or fundamentalist way. In contrast, those Christians who draw from the four sources of moral wisdom are more likely to oppose the death penalty today.

References

Aquinas, T. (1948). *Summa theologica: Vol. III* (Fathers of the English Dominican Province, Trans.). New York: Benziger Bros.

Bailey, W. A. (2005). *"You shall not kill" or "you shall not murder"? The assault on a biblical text*. Collegeville, MN: Liturgical Press.

Barth, K. (1961). *Church dogmatics: Vol. 3/4*. Edinburgh: T&T Clark.

Benedict XVI. (2005). *Our Lord has conquered with a love capable of going to death*. Retrieved May 15, 2017 from https://zenit.org/articles/benedict-xvi-s-reflection-on-peace/

Berkman, J. (2004). Being reconciled: Penitence, punishment, and worship. In S. Hauerwas & S. Wells (Eds.), *The Blackwell companion to Christian ethics* (pp. 95–109). Oxford, UK: Blackwell Publishing.

Blaugher, K. (2013). The power of stories stirring hearts and minds. In V. Schieber, T. D. Conway, & D. M. McCarthy (Eds.), *Where justice and mercy meet: Catholic opposition to the death penalty* (pp. 46–56). Collegeville, MN: Liturgical Press.

Bretzke, J. T. (2004). *A morally complex world: Engaging contemporary moral theology* (2nd ed.). Collegeville, MN: Liturgical Press.

Brugger, E. C. (2013a). The Catholic moral tradition: The ancient, medieval, and early modern views. In V. Schieber, T. D. Conway, & D. M. McCarthy (Eds.), *Where justice and mercy meet: Catholic opposition to the death penalty* (pp. 113–125). Collegeville, MN: Liturgical Press.

Brugger, E. C. (2013b). The church today: The church and capital punishment in the modern period. In V. Schieber, T. D. Conway, & D. M. McCarthy (Eds.), *Where justice and mercy meet: Catholic opposition to the death penalty* (pp. 126–136). Collegeville, MN: Liturgical Press.

Brugger, E. C. (2014). *Capital punishment and Roman Catholic moral tradition*. Notre Dame, IN: University of Notre Dame Press.

Buck, R. (2013). Hebrew scriptures—"an eye for an eye". In V. Schieber, T. D. Conway, & D. M. McCarthy (Eds.), *Where justice and mercy meet: Catholic opposition to the death penalty* (pp. 84–96). Collegeville, MN: Liturgical Press.

Cantalamessa, R. (2005). *Eucharist is god's absolute "no" to violence*. Retrieved May 15, 2017 from https://zenit.org/articles/eucharist-is-god-s-absolute-no-to-violence/

Curran, C. E. (1993). *The church and morality: An ecumenical and catholic approach*. Minneapolis: Fortress Press.

Davis, K. (2015, December 8). Death penalty overturned because of Bible quotes. *The San Diego Union-Tribune*. Retrieved May 2, 2017 from http://sandiegouniontribune.com/sdut-death-penalty-reversed-roybal-2015dec08-story.html

Esteves, J. A. (2017). *Pope Francis: The death penalty is a "mortal sin" and "inadmissible"*. Retrieved May 15, 2017 from www.americamagazine.org/faith/2017/05/11/pope-francis-death-penalty-mortal-sin-and-inadmissible

Farley, M. A. (2006). *Just love: A framework for Christian sexual ethics*. New York: Continuum.

Fodor, J. (2004). Reading the scriptures: Rehearsing identity, practicing character. In S. Hauerwas & S. Wells (Eds.), *The Blackwell companion to Christian ethics* (pp. 141–155). Malden, MA and Oxford, UK: Blackwell Publishing.

Gaertner, D. (2000). Stoning. In D. N. Freedman (Eds.), *Eerdmans dictionary of the Bible* (p. 1253). Grand Rapids, MI: Eerdmans.

Girard, R. (1977). *Violence and the sacred* (P. Gregory, Trans.). Baltimore, MD: Johns Hopkins University Press.

Hollinger, D. P. (2002). *Choosing the good: Christian ethics in a complex world*. Grand Rapids, MI: Baker Academic.

Irwin, K. (1999). *Responses to 101 questions on the Mass*. Mahwah, NJ: Paulist Press.

John Paul II. (1995). *The gospel of life [Evangelium vitae]*. New York: Random House.

Kavanaugh, A. (1984). *On liturgical theology*. Collegeville, MN: Liturgical Press.

Long, M. G. (Ed.). (2011). *Christian peace and nonviolence: A documentary history*. Maryknoll, NY: Orbis Books.

McCormick, P. T., & Connors, R. B. (2002). *Facing ethical issues: Dimensions of character, choices and community*. Mahwah, NJ: Paulist Press.

Megivern, J. J. (1997). *The death penalty: An historical and theological survey*. Mahwah, NJ: Paulist Press.

Murray, J. (1996). The sanctity of life. In D. K. Clark & R. V. Rakestraw (Eds.), *Readings in Christian ethics* (Vol. 2, pp. 457–462). Grand Rapids, MI: Baker Books. (Reprinted from J. Murray, *Principles of conduct*, 1957]).

Ofiphant, B. (2016). *Support for death penalty lowest in forty years*. Pew Research Center. Retrieved May 15, 2017 from www.pewresearch.org/fact-tank/2016/09/29/support-for-death-penalty-lowest-in-more-than-four-decades/

Penn, M. S. (1998). Leaven of forgiveness: Murder victims' families stand against the death penalty. In G. H. Stassen (Ed.), *Capital punishment: A reader* (pp. 9–13). Cleveland, OH: The Pilgrim Press.

Prejean, H. (1993). *Dead man walking: An eyewitness account of the death penalty in the United States*. New York: Vintage Books.

Prejean, H. (2005). *The death of innocents: An eyewitness account of wrongful executions*. New York: Random House.

Skotnicki, A. (2012). *The last judgment: Christian ethics in a legal culture*. Surrey, UK and Burlington, VT: Ashgate Publishing.

Stassen, G. H. (1998). Biblical teaching on capital punishment. In G. H. Stassen (Ed.), *Capital punishment: A reader* (pp. 119–130). Cleveland, OH: The Pilgrim Press.

Taylor, M. L. (2001). *The executed God: The way of the cross in lockdown America*. Minneapolis, MN: Augsburg Fortress.

United Methodist Church. (2016). *Book of discipline*. Retrieved May 15, 2017 from www.umc.org/what-we-believe/political-community#death-penalty

Vatican. (1997). *Catechism of the Catholic church*. Retrieved May 15, 2017 from www.vatican.va/archive/ccc_css/archive/catechism/p3s2c2a5.htm

Westmoreland-White, M. L., & Stassen, G. H. (2004). Biblical perspectives on the death penalty. In E. C. Owens, J. D. Carlson, & E. P. Elshtain (Eds.), *Religion and the death penalty: A call for reckoning* (pp. 123–138). Grand Rapids, MI: Eerdmans.

Winright, T. (2013). Liturgy and (God's) justice for all: The Eucharist as theological basis for translating recent Catholic teaching on capital punishment. In A. Houck & M. Doak (Eds.), *Translating religion* (pp. 118–136). Maryknoll, NY: Orbis Books.

Yoder, J. H. (2011). *The end of sacrifice: The capital punishment writings of John Howard Yoder* (J. C. Nugent, Ed.). Harrisonburg, VA: Herald Press.

12

CAPITAL PUNISHMENT IN JEWISH LAW[1]

Edna Erez and Kathy Laster

Introduction

The Torah (also referred to as the Five Books of Moses, the Scripture, or, in the Christian world, the Old Testament) provides a comprehensive account of law and punishment, including the use of the death penalty for a wide variety of offences. Before the destruction of the Second Temple in Jerusalem in 1 AD, the death penalty was imposed by the Jewish courts in line with biblical authority. But since those ancient times, Jewish law has been anti-capital punishment in orientation and practice.

Yet populist demands for the imposition of the death sentence nowadays are, more often than not, grounded in the biblical authority of the Old Testament. At pro-death penalty rallies, for instance, television cameras zoom in on placards quoting biblical verses, often inappropriately co-opted without a proper understanding of the context and the rich jurisprudence which underscores Jewish law's disavowal of the death penalty.[2]

The consensus of Jewish law scholarship, representing the full spectrum of religious observance,[3] is that claiming biblical support for capital punishment distorts the attitude of Jewish law to capital punishment, which, in principle, and certainly in practice, relatively quickly turned its back on the death penalty. There are various rationales for this position, but the core consideration is that Judaism is opposed to the taking of human life. This stricture even extends to preserving the life of someone who has committed a serious crime for which the death penalty is theoretically a sentencing option.

We argue that Jewish law's stance on capital punishment demonstrates the reluctance, even the abhorrence, of Jewish courts and judges to the death penalty. In Jewish law, capital punishment remains the symbolic representation of power forgone rather than exercised. There is humility in the Jewish position on capital punishment: an awareness that human institutions are imperfect and so cannot be trusted to inflict the ultimate sanction, which should be left to God.

In this chapter, we begin by outlining the scope of the death penalty in the Torah, noting the crimes deemed punishable by death and the forms of execution advanced in the sacred text. We go on, however, to explain that, as with the common law system, Jewish law is an oral tradition in which successive authoritative interpretations and commentaries have 'codified' the law as a living legal, moral, and spiritual system. We then review the acknowledged position of Jewish law on the death penalty, demonstrating that quite quickly a raft of procedural and substantive prerequisites for conviction in capital cases rendered the imposition of the death penalty difficult, if not impossible. We conclude with a discussion of the place of capital punishment in contemporary Israeli society, highlighting the symbolic significance of forbearance and restraint in the politics of punishment.

Biblical Capital Offences and Modes of Execution

According to biblical law, capital punishment applies to a wide range of offences that can be loosely grouped into three categories.

The first category is 'religious offences', such as desecration of the Sabbath (Exodus 31:15), for which the death penalty constitutes a marker of the severity of the sin. The penalty, however, was progressively not imposed by courts because this and other religious offences are fundamentally a sin against God, and so it is for God, rather than man, to exact punishment. To do otherwise would be to usurp the rights of God (Rudolph, 1996).

The second category of capital offences is crimes against the laws of decency and family integrity. These offences included, for instance, the crimes of incest (Leviticus 18) and adultery (Deuteronomy 22:22).

The final category of crime are those which simultaneously breach divine law and seriously disrupt social order, such as premeditated or deliberate murder. By contrast, accidental murder, or what we term manslaughter, was punishable by exile rather than death (Numbers 35:9ff; Deuteronomy 9:1ff).

The gravity of the offence also gave rise to different modes of execution, partly to signify the requisite degree of opprobrium for particular crimes. A system for categorizing capital crimes was developed by the renowned twelfth-century Jewish scholar Maimonides (1135–1204 AD), who lists 36 crimes that attract the death penalty in the Bible and classifies these offences according to the four modes of execution nominated in the Bible: stoning, burning, strangulation, and beheading (or 'slaying') (Maimonides, Mishneh Torah, Hilchot Sanhedrin 15).

Stoning (*Sekila*), according to Maimonides' classification, was the punishment for religious offences such as desecration of the Sabbath, idol worship, incitement to idolatry, blasphemy, sorcery, sodomy, bestiality, and child sacrifice. Cursing one's own parents and the crime of 'being a stubborn and rebellious son' also, in theory, rendered the offending offspring liable to stoning.

Stoning was probably the standard form of judicial execution in biblical times and is often expressly prescribed as the mode of execution (e.g., Leviticus 24: 14, 16, 23). As a survival of *vindicta publica* (Cohn, 1961), it was characterized in the early Judean period by the active participation of the wider community.

The offences punishable by burning (*Serefah*) were confined to adultery in specified categories of family relationship, such as between a man and his wife's daughter and adultery by the daughter of a priest (Leviticus 20:14, 21:9). Burning was an independent method of execution, but was also used to aggravate the punishment of stoning by burning the corpse after execution (e.g., Joshua 7:25).[4]

Punishment by strangulation (*Chenek*) applied to kidnapping of a fellow Israelite, false prophesying and prophesying in the name of another deity, adultery not captured in the family relationship specified in the *Serefah* category, wounding one's own parents, and insubordination before the grand court by a sage.

Beheading or slaying (*Hereg*) applied to only two categories, according to Maimonides: unlawful premeditated murder and 'being a member of a city that has gone astray'.[5]

In addition to Maimonides classification, hanging is also mentioned in the Bible as a method of execution (e.g., Genesis 40:22), and certainly it figures as an extra-legal or extra-judicial measure in parts of the Bible (e.g., Joshua 8:29).

The apparently long list of capital offences described in the Torah is still not as extensive as the crimes which constituted the so-called 'Bloody Code' of eighteenth-century English law, which included even relatively minor theft offences (Douglas & Laster, 1991).[6]

The biblical methods of execution appear, from a modern perspective, cruel. However, in practice, these modes of execution were progressively moderated by approaches that effectively minimized the pain to the offender as well as the defilement of his body. For example, while hanging the deceased after execution on a stake was used as a form of general deterrence (Deuteronomy 21:22), the body was kept on public display only until nightfall, at which time it had to be buried, "for a hanged person is an affront to God" (Deuteronomy 21:23).

Successive modifications to the mode of capital punishment were grounded in two biblical injunctions. The first was the requirement "to love thy neighbor as thyself" (Leviticus 19: 17), which was held to extend to criminals. To "love" the convicted felon in practice meant giving him the most humane ("beautiful") death possible (see Sanhedrin 45a for stoning and 52a for burning). The second rationale was that that judicial death should, as far as possible, resemble the taking of life by God. That is, the body should remain externally unchanged, as in the case of a natural death, and should not be mutilated or destroyed.

Such modifications are evident in the replacement of public stoning by a closed 'house of stoning', a two-story building from the top of which the convicted was pushed by one of the witnesses at his trial. It was expected that the fall would result in the felon's immediate death (Mishnah, Tractate Sanhedrin 6).[7]

If the fall failed to cause the condemned man's death, then the second witness at the trial against him was required to cast one stone directly at his heart (Sanhedrin 45a). As well as completing the execution, it was believed that this requirement—that witnesses cast the stone themselves—would deter witnesses from giving false evidence by imposing direct responsibility for the death on their shoulders. Only if both the fall and the 'single hit' efforts failed would the whole community participate in the stoning (as it is said, "the hand of the witnesses shall be first upon him to put him to death" [Sanhedrin 45a extrapolating from Deuteronomy 17:7]).

Similarly, over time, burning was transformed into a punishment that was more akin to strangulation than burning: "they will immerse [the offender] in mud . . . and wrap a cloth around his neck and each one [of the executioners] pulls until he opens his mouth, and then a wick is to be lighted and thrown into his mouth" (Mishnah, Tractate Sanhedrin 7:1). The rationale for the substitute method was, again, the need to preserve the body intact. Both opinions expressed in the Talmud (Rabbi Matna & Rabbi Elazar in Sanhedrin 52a) analogize the punishment with instances in the Bible where burning was carried out from heaven—the stories of Korach (Numbers 16:35) and Aaron's sons (Leviticus 10:2) both ended with the offenders being burned by God in a way which, the Talmud states, left their bodies intact.

Whether strangulation by cloth is easier, or involves less suffering than hanging, is a moot point. The salient issue is that despite the requirement to impose prescribed forms of capital punishment, the most humane form of death continued to preoccupy Jewish scholars, who sought to protect the dignity of the convicted while complying with the spirit of the law (see also Cohn, 1961).

Such sensibilities were a feature of Jewish punishment practice millennia before Foucault's disturbing account of the gruesome public spectacle of the execution and the infliction of pain on the body of the accused in eighteenth-century France (Foucault, 1995, p. 3).[8]

With the passage of time, changing social structures and political and economic needs also brought changes to the way in which capital punishment was administered and implemented. But any change to the dictates of God's law—as appearing in the Torah—could be regarded as a challenge to their perfection and timelessness. This dilemma was solved by the recognition of the 'Oral' Torah, which amplified and explained the Written Torah.

To appreciate the position of Jewish law and jurisprudence on capital punishment thus requires going beyond the blunt statements in the Scriptures. It requires an understanding of the capacity of Jewish theology to reconcile the Scriptures with their authoritative interpretation by scholars over time as well as with the practical administration of justice.

Sources of Jewish Law

Jews recognize that that Divine Law consists of two complementary parts: Torah, or the Scripture, which is the Written Law handed down by God to Moses on Mount Sinai, and the Oral Law of the Talmud that explains and amplifies the Torah (see generally, Rosenberg & Rosenberg, 1998, p. 510). Talmudic law was not immediately written down but initially passed down from generation to generation as a living tradition before it was eventually codified in written form.

According to Jewish belief, from the time of the giving of the Torah to Moses and throughout the centuries of its interpretation (the Midrash), the Written Torah has always been recognized as the primary source of Jewish law (Elon, 1978, p. 834). Its laws are deemed to be complete and perfect and so did not need, nor suffer, expansion or detraction (Cohn, 1971a, p. VIII). However, alongside this scripture, a rich body of interpretations were developed over time that constitute the Talmud.

The Mishnah, the first part of the Talmud developed by scholars (referred to as the Tanaim) from the beginning of the Christian era until 200 AD, eventually came to be written down and then edited and sealed by Rabbi Yehuda Hanasi (170–200 AD). The Mishnah in turn laid the foundations for the later development of the Talmud—the Gemara—developed by scholars (the Amoraim) from 200–500 AD. For these scholars, the finality of the content of the Mishnah and its authority was equivalent in status to the Written Torah.

Thus a substantial part of the Oral Law has grown out of interpretation of Scripture, according to elaborate rules of construction.

It was inevitable, however, that scriptural words and phrases would lend themselves to a number of possible interpretations. Therefore, there are several competing opinions for almost all issues and problems raised. The defining characteristic of the Talmud is a model of formal 'disputation' as the method for achieving greater understanding and problem solving.

These arguments or case-study disputes cover various historical periods in different parts of the world. But taken as a whole, the body of accepted interpretation has come to be treated as a continuous body of declarative and binding scholarly opinion about Jewish law, which is deemed, in its own right, to be a timeless reflection of God's word and law.

As a matter of practical legislation, whenever opinions differed on a given legal problem, one opinion was chosen as the binding authority and elevated to the status of positive law, or 'Halakha'. Designating the Halakha as the binding authority resolved the practical dilemma that it is not possible to observe two or more contradictory rules at the same time.

But a key element of Jewish Law is that it comprises not only the binding and enforceable Halakha but also includes divergent legal opinions that are considered to be persuasive authority on a particular point. Dissenting opinions were recorded in this way so that a later generation that might be greater in number and in wisdom will be able to reconsider views which did not find favour in the earlier period (Mishnah, Tractate Eduyot 1:4–6).

The rabbis who developed the Halakha understood both the need for certainty but also the need to revitalize a 'living legal system' to take account of future exigencies (Cohn, 1971a: XV). Lawyers in the common law tradition will find such an approach very familiar.

The Talmud itself, though a codification of oral law,[9] is not confined to the various rules of law, nor even to the processes of interpretation and reasoning. It also contains the more general teachings of many schools in different places and historical periods discussing law and rituals, manners and morals, history, philosophy, and the natural sciences. This is augmented by a rich scholarship of dialogue and debate, or 'responses', to questions posed at various times, as well as commentaries on key issues.[10]

Finally, the Talmud contains customary laws and 'rules' (*Takkanot*) developed by various communities that provide the rationale and the ethical principles underlying these laws.

Taken as a whole, all these sources reflect the abhorrence of Jewish law to the taking of a human life generally in any circumstance, including through the imposition of the death penalty.

The Demise of Capital Punishment

Capital cases induced a sense of awe, anxiety, and fear in Jewish judges because a life was at stake (Maimon-Fishman, 1938–9, p. 146). Jewish law has an overriding belief in the sanctity of human life because "man was created in the image of God" (Genesis 1:27). The sanctity of life is the most cherished value in Jewish law, and adherence to this fundamental value distinguished it very early on from the laws of other ancient nations (e.g., Greenberg, 1976; Johnson, 1988). The conviction that there is not any "nation so great that hath statutes and judgments so righteous as all this law" (Deuteronomy 4:8) was asserted in the Torah itself.

The sanctity of life is so central to Jewish law that it justifies even the desecration of the Sabbath or Yom Kippur (the holiest day in the Jewish religion) to treat a 100-year-old person, whose death is imminent, even if that treatment will only prolong his life by a single hour (Tractate Yoma 85a; Shulchan Aruch 329:4; Biur Halacha 329:4). The value of life has no measure or gradation; the life of the very old or the very young, the happy or miserable life, are all equally worthy (Tickutzinski, 1963, p. 36). The primacy of this value means that it required enormous confidence and wisdom for a court to determine to deprive a man of his life.[11]

The Talmud tells us that the imposition of the death penalty ceased with the destruction of the Second Temple in Jerusalem in 1 AD, the event that marked the beginning of the exile of the Jewish people and the loss of their political independence. Effectively, the courts lost, or rather surrendered, their criminal jurisdiction.[12] The reason advanced in the Midrash is that when the Sanhedrin (the Hebrew 'High Court') could no longer hold its sessions in its regular location (in a precinct of the Temple called Lishkat Hagazit), it was deprived of the benefit of the sense of justice and righteousness which the Temple inspired (Sanhedrin 41a; Ben-Zimra, 1962, p. 12).

This jurisdictional abrogation derives from the verse in the Torah: "if man come presumptuously upon his neighbor to slay him with guile, thou shalt take him from mine altar, that he may die" (Exodus 21:14). This verse is interpreted to mean that capital punishment can only be imposed under the auspice of the altar; that is, it was only valid while the Temple existed (Mechilta D'rashbi 21:15). The second, related, rationale for the abrogation of jurisdiction once the Temple was destroyed derives from the biblical verse, "and thou shalt come unto the priests and Levites, and unto the judge" (Deuteronomy 17:9), interpreted to mean that only when there is a priest can there be judgment in capital cases (Sanhedrin 52b).

Thus, a general proscription on the imposition of the death penalty already prevailed in the first century AD. Some scholars go further and argue that the Sanhedrin chose to go into exile 40 years before the destruction of the Temple in order to avoid adjudicating capital cases (Sabbath 16a).[13] The voluntary surrender of criminal jurisdiction is said to have been based on the fact that in those troubled times lawlessness had increased, and this would have required the court to impose the death penalty in a greater number of cases (Avodah Zarah 8b).

However, even before this period of voluntary surrender of jurisdiction, the rabbinical courts were so loathe to impose the death penalty that they progressively introduced a host of procedural and substantive requirements which effectively made conviction in capital cases difficult, if not impossible (Jacobs, 1995; Douglas, 2000).

Procedural and Evidentiary
Constraints on the Death Penalty

> A Sanhedrin that puts a man to death once in seven years is called a murderous one. Rabbi Eliezer ben Azariah says "Or even once in 70 years." Rabbi Tarfon and Rabbi Akiba said, "If we had been in the Sanhedrin no death sentence would ever have been passed"; Rabban Simeon ben Gamaliel said: "If so, they would have multiplied murderers in Israel."
>
> (Mishnah, Tractate Makkoth 1:10)

This scholarly discussion took place around 170 AD, when the Sanhedrin had been defunct for about 150 years. It is considered to be the most significant rabbinical statement on the issue and well captures the largely abolitionist stance of Jewish law. In this oft-quoted passage, the learned rabbis try to outdo each other in expressing their abhorrence at a judicial process that could end a life.

By this time, though, it was already rare for criminals to be executed. But Rabbi Eleazar Ben Azariah exhorts even more sparing use, "once every 70 years." Rabbi Tarfon and Rabbi Akiba go further still, advocating complete abolition.

Rabban Shimeon Ben Gamaliel, who was charged with administering the modest degree of self-rule accorded to the Jewish community under the Roman conquest, is the lone dissenting voice. His position echoes the perennial argument of the pro-capital punishment lobby, that capital punishment is the most effective deterrent to crime and its abolition would lead to an increase in crimes of violence and murder. The deterrence argument is supported by the biblical exhortation, "and all those who remain shall listen and fear, and they shall no longer continue to commit any such evil thing among you" (Deuteronomy 19:20).[14]

Probably for this reason, capital punishment formally remained a legitimate sentencing option. However, the countervailing biblical injunction, "for judgment is God's" (Deuteronomy 1:17), stayed the judicial hand and supported the development of the Halakha to curtail the application of the death penalty in practice. Effectively, the whole weight of Talmudic scholarship was devoted to radically changing the biblical forms of execution and humanizing them, for they were viewed as obsolete and inappropriate (Cohn, 1972).

Amelioration of the harshness of the law was achieved through procedural means as well as a strict interpretation of the substantive and evidentiary requirements for conviction in capital cases.

Procedural Hurdles

The adjudication of capital cases required a court of 23 judges, compared with a bench of just three to hear civil (monetary) matters (Mishnah, Tractate Sanhedrin 4). The authority for this requirement rested on the strict interpretation of the biblical exhortation "do not kill a truly innocent person" (Exodus 23:7).

Deliberation in capital cases had to commence and be completed during daylight hours (Sanhedrin 32a). According to the Mishnah (Sanhedrin 32a), the case could be determined in one day if the result was an acquittal. Judgment, though, had to be postponed to the next day if the verdict was for conviction. Judges (and witnesses) had to 'sleep on it'. The delay allowed a breathing space but also the possibility that last-minute evidence favorable to the accused might come to light.

Only one capital case could be heard on any given day because adequate time needed to be devoted to fully consider the defense case for each defendant (Sanhedrin 45b, Rashi commentary).

The adversarial system was not a feature of Jewish court process. However, adjudication in capital cases did resemble robust defense advocacy. The court itself was required to argue the defense case. If the defendant himself was unable to properly articulate arguments in his own defense, the court was obliged to put these on his behalf. If, on the other hand, the accused wished to effectively incriminate himself, the court had to admonish him (Tosaftah, Sanhedrin 9b).

The judges who argued in favour of the defendant opened the hearing. The Talmud maintains that the judges who argued against the defendant were allowed to change their minds in favour of acquittal, but not vice versa (Mishnah, Tractate Sanhedrin 4:1).

Anyone in court had standing to argue for the defense but not to argue against the accused. Rabbinical students sitting in court, for instance, were encouraged to put the case in favour of the accused but would not be heard otherwise. There was an incentive for rabbinical students to shine as defense advocates—the student who argued the most vigorously on behalf of the defendant was selected to join the bench for the adjudication (Mishnah, Tractate Sanhedrin 5:4).

Any member of the Sanhedrin who had witnessed the murder was barred from sitting on the case because he would not be in a position to effectively argue the defense case (Tractate Makot 22a).[15] Other classes of people were also disqualified from serving as members of the Sanhedrin, including the very old, the impotent, the castrated, and the childless. Such people were thought to be more inclined to cruelty, or perhaps to show less compassion (Sanhedrin, 36b; Maimonides, Mishneh Torah 2:3).[16]

If the Sanhedrin voted unanimously to convict the defendant, he had to be acquitted, because rather than this being regarded as a sign of overwhelming guilt, it was treated as an indication that the court had not adequately engaged itself in the consideration of the defense case. The assumption was that it should always be possible to find a convincing argument against conviction, or rather, to find an argument against the imposition of the death penalty (Sanhedrin 17a; Maimonides, Mishneh Torah 9:2).

At the end of the day, a majority of two was required for conviction but only a majority of one was needed for an acquittal (Maimonides, Mishneh Torah 9:2).

These layers of procedural protection all weighted court process heavily in favour of acquittal. The measures promoted caution, generous deliberation, and compassion. Just to be sure, these procedural protections were augmented by even more onerous substantive and evidentiary requirements, which rendered conviction in capital cases virtually impossible.

Substantive and Evidentiary Hurdles

Ignorance of the law constituted a valid defense in capital crimes. The Talmudic doctrine that "there is no punishment without warning" was stretched beyond all reasonable bounds. A full warning (*Hatra'a*), for instance, had to be given to the offender at the scene of the crime and just prior to the commission of the offense (Sanhedrin 8b; see also Bulz, 1977). Some commentators go further and suggest that the offender had to be told which mode of death he would suffer if he went on to commit the felony (Opinion of Rabbi Yehuda in Sanhedrin 8b).

Effectively, the warning requirements transformed the mental element or *mens rea* for capital offences by adding a new subjective requirement of conscious disregard of the consequences of committing the offence. In effect, only an offender who recklessly "permits himself to die" as a form of punishment (Sanhedrin 41a) could be sentenced to death.[17]

Transferred intent or transferred malice, well established in modern Western jurisprudence,[18] was explicitly excluded from the ambit of capital offences because such actions lacked the requisite mental element, "the one who intends to kill this, but kills another is exempted from capital punishment" (Maimonides, Rotzeach 4:1), although this position was at odds with biblical law (Bulz, 1977, pp. 43–45).

Conviction in criminal cases could not be based on a confession because, according to Talmudic law, "a person cannot represent himself as wicked" (Sanhedrin 9b).[19] Circumstantial evidence too was unacceptable (Maimonides, Sefer Hamitzvot, Mitzva 290). Rather, conviction for a capital offence was entirely dependent on the evidence given by two independent eyewitnesses.

These two witnesses had to be free adults of sound mind and body and of unimpeachable integrity, without any family connection to the defendant or personal interest in the case. The two witnesses also had to give entirely consistent accounts and satisfy a nearly impossible threshold—to be present together, at the same time, at the scene of the crime, with both observing the crime from the same vantage point. In effect, if one witness observed the crime from a window while the other witness watched on from a doorway, the testimony was deemed unreliable and so inadmissible (Tickutzinski, 1963, p. 39). The requirements are graphically captured in the Talmudic illustration:

> Where a man pursues another with a sabre in hand to slay, and the pursuer is warned, but the witnesses turn their eyes momentarily aside, and then they find the pursued in the throes of death and the pursuer holding the sabre dripping with blood, surely one might well consider the pursuer guilty. Therefore it is said 'and the innocent and the righteous slay them not'.
>
> *(Mechilta D'Rabbi Yishmael, Exodus 23:7)*

Any discrepancy in the details provided by the witnesses would invalidate the whole of their testimony. Proof thus had to be absolute, clear and incontrovertible—a near impossibility.

Even where the two witnesses met such stringent requirements, they were still repeatedly reminded by the court that their evidence concerned a matter of life and death and that their responsibilities were very weighty. The biblical incantation, "your brother's blood cries out to me from the earth" (Genesis 4:10) was interpreted by the rabbis to mean that a death sentence was to be regarded as not merely the loss of a single life but rather the end of a whole lineage—including that of unborn generations (Sanhedrin 37a). Witnesses were saddled with an overwhelming religious and social burden, as the court cautioned them that the destruction of one man through false evidence is tantamount to the destruction of the whole world (see Rabinowitz-Teomin, 1952).

Witnesses were effectively harangued by the court. They were questioned and vigorously cross-examined. Misleading questions were welcomed, including about trivial details that were expected to be recalled; for example, about the stems of the figs growing on the tree under which the murder was committed (Sanhedrin 40a). Witnesses were fair game, and tactics designed to confuse and perplex them were de rigeur (Sanhedrin 32b). It was a brave witness indeed who could withstand this level of pressure. And of course, bearing false witness was itself a capital offence!

Long before the development of the common law's injunction that it is "better that ten guilty persons escape, than one innocent person suffer" (Blackstone, 1853, p. 289), Jewish law set the bar much higher: "it is better to acquit a thousand guilty ones than one day to cause the killing of one innocent" (Maimonides, Sefer Hamitzvot, No. 290).

Where the complex warning regime was not complied with, the death penalty could not be imposed. But offenders were not let off scot free—the consequences of a crime were the first and primary criterion in determining the severity of the punishment, and murder was treated as having the most serious of consequences (Maimonides, Moreh Nevuchim 3:41). Instead, the offender was put in the *Kippa* (a cell or prison) with his hands and feet bound, and he was fed meagre rations of bread and water (Maimonides, Rotzeach 4:8). Although the origins of this practice was to distinguish between accidental and intentional murder (Sanhedrin 81b), it quickly became a substitute punishment for the death penalty.

For some offences, where the death penalty seemed too harsh relative to the gravity of the offense—as, for example, capital punishment for a 'stubborn and rebellious son' and for witnesses giving false testimony—the Midrashim also developed a system of monetary compensation to the victim (Baba Kama 3b).

The net effect of the technical legal obstacle course was that the death penalty relatively quickly died an unnatural death in the precepts of Jewish law and juridical practice.

The Death Penalty in Modern Israel

The only judicially sanctioned execution in modern Israel was that of Adolf Eichmann in 1962 for 'war crimes' and 'crimes against humanity' committed while he was a leader in the Nazi regime during World War II. Despite appeals for clemency by Eichmann and his family, the execution was carried out at midnight on May 31 (Kershner, 2016). This sole execution, albeit for an exceptional and grave crime involving genocide of the Jewish people, seemingly defies the anti-capital punishment precepts of Jewish law and the generally abolitionist position of Israeli law. How do we account for such exceptions?

In 1954, the fledgling Israeli Parliament, the Knesset, quickly moved to abolish capital punishment for all crimes other than for treason during war, genocide, and murder under Nazi rule by Nazis or their collaborators (see generally, Sangero, 2002). One reason for the swift move to abolition was that Jews had been executed by the British under the British Mandate, and rejecting this aspect of British rule was an import symbolic assertion of new and hard-won independence.

Introducing the bill, the Minister of Justice, Pinchas Rosen, justified the general abolitionist position of the government on rehabilitative grounds, paraphrasing Ezekiel (18:32): "We do not want the death of a sinner, but that he should repent of his ways and live." The minister went on to argue that society shares the guilt for the criminal activities of its members. It cannot therefore assert the moral high ground by imposing the ultimate sanction on an individual offender. The government also referenced the well-rehearsed arguments of rabbinical (and abolitionist) scholars, including that the risk of judicial error resulting in the death of an innocent person is irrevocable and thus unconscionable.

But the exceptions to full abolition under the Israeli legislation are nonetheless also consistent with the only two circumstances under which Jewish law countenances extra-judicial use of the death penalty—firstly, in times of emergency (*Hora'at Hasha'a*), and as a prerogative of kingship (*Din Malchut*).

The first exception, the 'Emergency rule', envisages situations where there is a genuine threat to the physical existence or the well-being of Israel, such as when the nation suffers intolerable levels of crime. In such circumstances, the courts are entitled to impose the death penalty even without a Sanhedrin. The exception is based on the biblical 'rule of the pursued' (*Din Rodef*), where the obligation is to save the life of the pursued preemptively, even if that action costs the life of the pursuer. However, once the pursued victim is killed, the pursuer may not then be harmed or executed, as "one is not killed for the past, but only for the future, for saving the pursued from injury or death" (Sh"ut [Responsa-Literature] Rule 17, 1).

In times of emergency, the state of Israel is understood to be in the position of the 'pursued', and thus the public interest can override the rights of the (offending) individual or individuals. Defense of the social order is deemed not to violate the precepts of Jewish law but rather to "build a fence around" the Torah (Sanhedrin 41) to both deter and protect the population from crime and misadventure.[20]

The second exception is a dimension of the prerogatives afforded to kingship. Wide-ranging powers were bestowed on leaders to promote the maintenance of social order by authorizing (only) a devoutly religious king, ruler, or community leaders more generally to impose the death penalty. The only time this prerogative is known to have been exercised by leaders of the Jewish community is contained in a reference in the writing of a fourteenth-century Spanish commentator, Haro"sh (Rabbi Asher Ben Yehiel). The application of the death penalty in this case was justified by contemporaries on the grounds that if the official (Spanish) authorities were permitted to adjudicate cases involving members of the Jewish community, then many more Jews would have been executed. Nevertheless, Haro"sh remains highly critical of the practice (Sh"ut Haro"sh Rule 17).

In biblical times, though, Halakha invested sovereign rulers with the power to administer "the king's justice" (*mishpat hamelech*). This pragmatic doctrine allowed Jewish kings to take a life if it was necessary in the interests of good government. The famous story about the wisdom of King Solomon, evidenced by his determination of which of the two women who claimed to be the mother of the same child was his mother, is, in part, an illustration of the right of the king to adjudicate on matters of life and death. Solomon threatened to cut the baby in two in order to elicit the protective instincts of the true mother (1 Kings 3:16–28). The forensic trick worked precisely because both women had no doubt that Solomon could inflict death on the child if he so chose.

In theory, both these traditional exceptions could provide the rational for Israel's military courts to impose the death penalty in the occupied territories of the West Bank and Gaza, which they have been empowered to do since their annexation in 1967. However, despite significant and provocative terrorist activity that has resulted in the death of women, children, and other civilians, the military courts have never resorted to the death penalty. This is so despite vociferous periodic agitation by some religious Zionists to execute terrorists.[21]

Ron Dudai (2017) argues that it has been useful for the state to keep the formal option of capital punishment 'on the books' because this gives pro-capital punishment rhetoric a symbolic airing while simultaneously acting as a symbol of self-restraint and moral self-legitimation by Israel in refusing to comply with hot-headed demands.

The anti-capital punishment sentiments of Jewish law run deep in the Israeli psyche.

Conclusion

An examination of the Jewish position on the death penalty could, at one level, be regarded as religious ethnic parochialism. An account of the death penalty under Jewish law documents how, progressively, the harshness of this form of biblical punishment came to be viewed as cruel, inappropriate, and ineffective. Over time, biblical sanctions were treated more as a solemn warning about the seriousness of particular crimes rather than a legitimate sentencing option.

At the very least, a review of the Jewish position on the death penalty calls into question reliance on biblical precepts still regularly invoked to legitimize the imposition of the death penalty.

But Jewish thought and practice on this subject is worthy of more serious study. An ancient culture, Jewish theology and jurisprudence is a sophisticated repository of every conceivable argument about the death penalty. Jewish scholarship has comprehensively debated the key issues of contemporary death penalty literature—human rights, social obligations, deterrence and intentionality, as well as the substantive and procedural considerations underscoring the operation of the death penalty in practice.

Finally, a review of the Jewish position on the death penalty also presents some lessons about the politics of punishment. In particular, the self-imposed restraint of Jewish law and contemporary Israeli practice on the death penalty demonstrates that 'self-image' can be as strong a determinant of change and reform as rational argument (Kornhauser & Laster, 2014). Perceiving oneself or one's social beliefs as 'better' or more enlightened—whether an accurate characterization or not—serves as a powerful motivator for restraint in the overheated arena in which the politics of punishment usually play out.

More often than not, appeals to a tribal, national, or social identity are used to justify vengeance and retaliation through punishment (Garland, 2010). But as Jewish law and the Israeli position illustrate, tradition can just as easily encourage control and restraint (Dudai, 2017).

Being well versed in the religious precepts and cultural values that underscore attitudes to crime and punishment are indispensable to those who seek to change hearts and minds about the use of the death penalty.

Notes

1 This chapter is a revised and expanded version of an earlier article by Erez (1981). We wish to thank Eli Solomon for his research assistance on aspects of Jewish law, and Ryan Kornhauser for other research assistance. Matthew Schwartz provided helpful comments and suggestions. Names of co-authors appear alphabetically.

2 Take the apparently self-evident often-cited biblical verse, "an eye for an eye, a tooth for a tooth" (Exodus 21:24; Leviticus 24:20). The oral tradition explains this verse as a reference to monetary compensation (Talmud, Tractate Bava Kama 83b), and the Rabbis of the Talmud are convinced that a literal interpretation is beyond the pale of Jewish jurisprudence (Talmud, Tractate Bava Kama 84a). Another interpretation of this phrase is that both the victim and offender should be treated alike, without regard to their social status (Rudolph, 1996).

3 Conservative Judaism's Committee on Jewish Law and Standards has declared "that existing death penalty laws should be abolished and no new ones be enacted" (Kalmanofsky, 2013, p. 2); the American Union for Reform Judaism believes that "there is no crime for which the taking of human life by society is justified" (Union for Reform Judaism, 2017); the Central Conference of American Rabbis "oppose[s] capital punishment under all circumstances" (Central Conference of American Rabbis, 2015); and the Orthodox Union "supports efforts to place a moratorium on executions in the United States and the creation of a commission to review the death penalty procedures within the American judicial system" (Orthodox Union, 2014; see also Diament, 2004).

4 However, this was not common practice and is not prescribed by Jewish law.

5 A *nidach* is a member of an *ir hanidachat*, a city that has gone astray. In Deuteronomy 13:13–19, the Torah dictates the collective punishment for an entire city that goes astray by committing idol worship. The punishment is particularly harsh, destruction of the entire city. However, it is important to note that "there never was and never will be" such a city (Tosefta, Tractate Sanhedrin 14(a)).

6 There were, at one point, more than 200 capital offences on the statute books, including many nonviolent offences such as theft, robbery, and forgery. On one estimate, approximately 35,000 people were sentenced to

death in England and Wales between 1770 and 1830; approximately 7,000 of those were executed, mostly for property crimes (Gatrell, 1996, p. 7).

7 Maimonides (Commentaries to Sanhedrin 6:4) considers this Talmudic method of execution to be consistent with the biblical dictate, because throwing stones *at* a felon is deemed to be equivalent to a stone being thrown *on* the offender, or the offender falling onto stone.

8 Foucault (1995, p. 3) graphically describes the 1757 execution in France of a regicide, who was condemned to be erected upon a scaffold, and have "the flesh . . . torn from his breasts, arms, thighs and calves with red-hot pincers, his right hand . . . burnt with sulphur, and, on those places where the flesh will be torn away, poured molten lead, boiling oil, burning resin, wax and sulphur melted together and then his body drawn and quartered by four horses and his limbs and body consumed by fire, reduced to ashes and his ashes thrown to the winds."

9 The most significant of the codifiers is considered to be Maimonides, who, among other things, divided the Talmud into subject areas. Other important codifiers were Alfasi (1013–1103 AD), Yaakov Ben Asher (c. 1269–1340 AD), known as 'Tur', and Yosef Karo (1488–1575 AD), author of the Shulchan Aruch. With the general acceptance of these codes as statements of the binding law, the metamorphosis of the Oral tradition into written authority was accomplished.

The codes of Alfasi, Karo, Tur, and Maimonides were also commented upon, and these commentaries are also considered legally binding.

10 The development of Jewish law was continued by the Savoraim (500–540 AD) and Geonim (500–1048 AD), the heads of religious academies (*Yeshivot*), and Rishonim (1050–1500 AD) through questions posed to them by members of their communities, as well as commentaries on the Talmud and Torah. The most celebrated and authoritative commentators are Shlomo Yitzhaki (1040–1105 AD), known as 'Rashi', and the Tosafists, so named because they developed the addenda (*Tosafot*) of the Talmud.

11 The designation of some cities as sanctuaries is another reflection of the sanctity of life in Jewish law. In an attempt to prevent situations in which a person who killed unintentionally would be killed by a *goeal hadam* ("redeemer of the blood")—a family relative who has the duty to pursue revenge—sanctuary cities (*ir miklat*) were established to protect these killers until the absence of intent to kill has been proven at trial (Joshua 20).

12 Jewish law is divided, like most modern legal systems, into monetary (civil) matters (*Diney Mamonot*) and capital or criminal matters (*Diney Nefashot*). The civil law is by far the largest jurisdiction and was not affected by the destruction of the Temple.

13 Cohn (1971b, pp. 346–349) submits that capital jurisdiction was suspended with the destruction of the Temple (in 70 AD) and that the Talmudic claim that capital jurisdiction was suspended 40 years before the destruction of the Temple (that is, in the year 30 AD) was established for the purpose of disassociating the Sanhedrin from any connection with the crucifixion of Jesus. The crucifixion had taken place that very year. If the Sanhedrin no longer exercised capital jurisdiction, then it could not have tried or executed Jesus. At that time, the Christians started to propagate their faith, and the Gospels, which blamed the Jews for the death of Jesus, were given wide publicity. The Jews, who had no knowledge of any Sanhedrial trial of Jesus, felt that they had to defend themselves. It was not enough to dismiss the Gospel stories as lies. The Jews believed that a suspension of capital jurisdiction might be a reasonable and acceptable argument in their defense, particularly in view of the fact that the Roman governors had in several cases deprived local provincial courts of capital jurisdiction. Ironically, the claim of the suspended capital jurisdiction aided the protagonists of Jewish guilt by relying on it to explain the delivery of Jesus by the Sanhedrin into the hands of the Roman governor, instead of executing him themselves.

14 Jewish law rates good governance very highly, including the role of deterrence. The Mishna (Tractate Avot 3:2) cites the opinion of Rabbi Hanina Segan Hakohanim—"Pray for the peace of the government for were it not for its authority, people would eat each other alive." Jewish law encourages creative thought but abhors chaos—the idea that "each person shall do what is right in his own eyes" (Judges 17:6). And yet the deterrence argument did not carry the day in the case of capital offences. Another aspect of the role of government in deterrence is the symbolic practice of *eglah arufa* (breaking a heifer's neck). If a body is found but the killer is unknown, the closest nearby town had to practice this ritual, which symbolizes a recognition that a crime has been committed against the deceased and God, and that the community has done all it can to prevent such crimes in its midst. Should the killer be found, he will be tried for the killing (Numbers 35.9f, Deuteronomy 9.1.f.)

15 Tickutzinski (1963, p. 46) cites the debates concerning this issue and brings opposing opinions.

16 For the impact the concern for compassion has on procedural aspects of capital cases, see Maimon-Fishman (1938–9, pp. 148–149).

17 Reiness (1956, p. 163) views this requirement as envisioning the argument raised four centuries later by Beccaria (1764), namely, that capital punishment conflicts with the idea of social contract, because the individual would not agree to having his life taken by the state.

18 Under the doctrine of transferred malice, where a "defendant does an act with the intention of causing a particular kind of harm to X, and unintentionally does that kind of harm to Y, then the intent to harm X may be added to the harm actually done to Y in deciding whether the defendant has committed a crime towards Y" (*Attorney General's Reference No 3 of 1994* [1997] 3 All ER 936, 941). Thus, for example, if a defendant puts poison into a pot of wine with the intention of poisoning X, but Y drinks the poison and dies, the defendant can be guilty of murder notwithstanding no intention to harm Y (*Agnes Gore's Case* (1611) 9 Co Rep 81a; 77 ER 853).

19 This rule is considered as one of the origins of the right against self-incrimination (Levy, 1968). For the status of confession in Jewish law in general, see Kirchenbaum (1970).

20 Din rodef served as the justification for the assassination of Israeli prime minister Yizhak Rabin by Yidgal Amir in November 1995. Rabin was perceived by some rabbinical circles as rodef because of his peace plan to return land for peace with the Palestinians. For discussion of deterrence *(Midgar Milta)* as an exception, see Ben-Zimra (1962) and Bazak (1972).

21 As Rabbenu Nissim (fourteenth century, Spain) explained, this mandate authorizes the king to serve as the head of the army and to administer penal laws necessary to maintain the social fabric (Derashot Haran 11). Following this logic, many religious Zionist jurists contend that it empowers Israel's penal laws with halachic sanction.

References

Bazak, J. (1972). Harigat nefashot besifrut hashut [Acts of murder in Responsa Literature]. In P. Eli (Ed.), *Proceedings of the fifth world congress of Jewish studies* (pp. 37–49). Jerusalem: Academic Press.

Beccaria, C. (1764). *Dei Delitti e Delle Pene [On Crimes and Punishment]*. Livorno: Coltellini.

Ben-Zimra, E. (1962). Din mavet shelo bifney habayit [Capital law when the temple does not exist]. *De'ot, 19*(Spring), 12–18.

Blackstone, W. (1853). *Commentaries on the Laws of England*. New York: William E. Dean.

Bulz, E. (1977). Hahatra'a bamishpat haivri [Warning in Jewish law]. In A. Shin'an (Ed.), *Proceedings of the sixth world congress of Jewish studies* (pp. 41–47). Jerusalem: R. H. Hacohen Press.

Central Conference of American Rabbis. (2015). *Resolution adopted by the CCAR: Capital punishment*. Retrieved from https://ccarnet.org/rabbis-speak/resolutions/all/capital-punishment-1979/

Cohn, H. H. (1961). *Al Onesh Haskilah [On the punishment of stoning]*. Ramat Gan: Bar Ilan University Press.

Cohn, H. H. (Ed.). (1971a). *Jewish law in ancient and modern Israel*. New York: Ktav Publishing House.

Cohn, H. H. (1971b). *The trial and death of Jesus*. New York: Harper & Row.

Cohn, H. H. (1972). Yesod lepenologia ivrit [Elements of Hebrew penology]. In P. Eli (Ed.), *Proceedings of the fifth world congress of Jewish studies* (pp. 191–202). Jerusalem: Academic Press.

Diament, N. J. (2004). Judaism and the death penalty; of two minds but one heart. *Tradition, 38*(1), 76–82.

Douglas, D. M. (2000). God and the executioner: The influence of Western religion on the death penalty. *William and Mary Bill of Rights Journal, 9*(1), 137–170.

Douglas, R., & Laster, K. (1991). A matter of life and death: The Victorian executive and the decision to execute 1842–1967. *Australian and New Zealand Journal of Criminology, 24*(2), 144–160.

Dudai, R. (2017). Restraint, reaction, and penal fantasies: Notes on the death penalty in Israel, 1967–2016. *Law and Social Inquiry*. Advance online publication. Retrieved from http://onlinelibrary.wiley.com/doi/10.1111/lsi.12293/full

Elon, M. (1978). *Mishpat Ivri [Jewish law]*. Jerusalem: Magness Press.

Erez, E. (1981). Thou shalt not execute: Hebrew law perspective on capital punishment. *Criminology, 19*(1), 25–43.

Foucault, M (1995). *Discipline and punish: The birth of the prison*. New York: Vintage Books.

Garland, D. (2010). *Peculiar institution: America's death penalty in an age of abolition*. Oxford: Oxford University Press.

Gatrell, V. A. C. (1996). *The hanging tree: Execution and the English people 1770–1868*. Oxford: Oxford University Press.

Greenberg, M. (1976). Some postulates of biblical criminal law. In J. Goldin (Ed.), *The Jewish expression* (pp. 18–37). New Haven: Yale University Press.

Jacobs, L. (1995). *The Jewish religion: A companion*. Oxford: Oxford University Press.

Johnson, P. (1988). *A History of the Jews*. New York: Harper & Row.

Kalmanofsky, J. (2013). *Participating in the American death penalty*. Retrieved from www.rabbinicalassembly.org/sites/default/files/assets/public/halakhah/teshuvot/2011-2020/cjls-onesh-mavet.pdf

Kershner, I. (2016, January 27). Pardon plea by Adolf Eichmann, Nazi war criminal, is made public. *The New York Times*. Retrieved from www.nytimes.com

Kirchenbaum, A. (1970). *Self-incrimination in Jewish law*. New York: Burning Bush Press.

Kornhauser, R., & Laster, K. (2014). Punitiveness in Australia: Electronic monitoring vs the prison. *Crime, Law and Social Change, 62*(4), 445–474.

Levy, L. W. (1968). *Origins of the first amendment*. New York: Oxford University Press.

Maimon-Fishman, Y. L. (1938–9). Diney nefashot bemishpatei yisrael [Capital laws in the laws of Israel]. *Sinai*, *3*, 1045–1049.

Orthodox Union (2014). *116th anniversary convention: Resolutions* (26 December 2014, New York).

Rabinowitz-Teomin, B. (1952). Mishpatei nefashot bedin hasanhedrin u'bedin malchut [Capital cases in the law of Sanhedrin and the law of the kingdom]. *Hatorah Vehamedinah*, *4*, 45–81.

Reiness, H. Z. (1956). Mishpat mavet bahalakha [Capital law in the Halakha]. *Sinai*, *29*, 1062–1068.

Rosenberg, I. M., & Rosenberg, Y. L. (1998). Lone star liberal musings on eye for eye and the death penalty. *Utah Law Review*, *1*(4), 505–542.

Rudolph, D. A. (1996). The misguided reliance in American jurisprudence on Jewish law to support the moral legitimacy of capital punishment. *American Criminal Law Review*, *33*(2), 437–462.

Sangero, B. (2002). On capital punishment in general and on the death penalty for murder committed during a terrorist act in particular. *Alei Mishpat*, *2*(1–2), 127–206.

Tickutzinski, Y. M. (1963). Mishpat hamavet alpi Hatorah beavar ubehoveh [Capital law according to the Torah in the past and in the present]. *Hatorah Vehamedinah*, *4*, 33–43.

Union for Reform Judaism. (2017). *Opposing capital punishment*. Retrieved from www.urj.org/what-we-believe/resolutions/opposing-capital-punishment

Cases Cited

Agnes Gore's Case, 9 Co Rep 81a; 77 ER 853 (1611)

13

DEATH PENALTY
IN *SHARIA* LAW

Sanaz Alasti[1] and Eric Bronson[2]

"Avoid [sentences of] death and flogging involving Muslims to the extent possible."

Ibn Abi Shayba[3]

Introduction

This chapter is intended to introduce a comparative study of death penalty in *sharia* law. The primary goal is to use a comparative approach by illustrating the similarities and differences in the practice of capital punishment over time and place in Islamic countries. We will review the current practice of death penalty in both Islamic states and secular Islamic countries. The second goal is to find out why capital punishment is less in practice in some Islamic countries.

The death penalty in Islamic countries is familiar to most readers because capital punishment exists in the domestic law of most Islamic nations, but the ways by which these states employ capital punishment are varied and inconsistent. With the advent of Islamic fundamentalism in the 1970s, more and more Islamic states began objecting to international norms for human rights and abolition of the death penalty, as being contrary to *sharia*, the historically formulated traditional law of Islam.

The question is why contemporary Islamic penal systems are so cruel and short on mercy when in secular criminal justice systems efforts are made to guarantee that prisoners are treated humanely. This comparative study reaches back to classical Islam and contemporary use of *sharia* law in Islamic countries to trace how and why punishments in Islamic nations came to diverge.

This research is organized into six sections. In section one we attempt to describe the contemporary status of the death penalty in Islamic countries. Section two argues about the crimes for which death is prescribed in *sharia* law. The third section reviews the harsh execution methods in Islamic law, and section four argues against the juvenile death penalty in *sharia* law. Section five is the study of the evidentiary process, procedures, and avoidance of death penalty in case of doubt. Finally the sixth section describes how, without challenging the death penalty per se as punishment in religious textual resources, evidentiary and procedural, barriers may lead to the moratorium.

The Contemporary Status of Death Penalty in Islamic Countries

More than two-thirds of the countries in the world have now abolished the death penalty in law or practice. From 55 retentionist countries, 27 of them are Islamic countries. In 11 Islamic countries abolition is in practice. In eight countries Islamic laws do not provide for the death penalty for any crime (abolitionist for all crimes) and in one Islamic countries laws provide for the death penalty only for exceptional crimes such as crimes under military law or crimes committed in exceptional circumstances (*de facto* abolition). Geographically the majority of these Islamic countries are located in the Middle East (see Figure 13.1).

It is estimated that there are over 900 million Muslims today. Many live in the Arab world, but many more live in countries such as Iran, Pakistan, Bangladesh, Indonesia, Malaysia, Nigeria, and Sudan (Bassiouni, 1988). Although all Islamic countries are not retentionist, practice varies considerably from one to another. For instance, some Islamic countries, like Iran and Saudi Arabia, are enthusiastic practitioners (please refer to Figure 13.2), with thousands of executions, while others, such as Kazakhstan (Kazakhstan is *de facto* abolitionist), conduct executions in only the rarest of cases; Islamic countries such as Albania, Azerbaijan, and Turkey have abolished capital punishment. The diversity of practice would suggest there is little consensus among Islamic countries. For example, Sudan recently banned the juvenile death penalty and amended its laws in January 2010 to set 18 years as the firm age of majority nationwide, but still it is not clear whether the new 2010 law extends to Islamic offenses (retaliation and prescribed crimes). *Qisas* (retaliation) concerns intentional crimes against the person. Its fundamental premise is the *lex talionis*, "eye for eye, tooth for tooth." *Lex talionis* is set out in the *Quran*, verse 5.32 (further developed by verse 17.33). Under *Hadd* or *Hudud* (prescribed crimes), important crimes deemed to threaten the existence of Islam are punishable by penalties set by the *Quran*, or by the *Sunna* or *Sunnah*. Islamic jurists consider that these sanctions immutable. They conclude that the judge is left with no discretion.

Countries that practice *sharia* law as the source of their criminal justice system are associated with the use of capital punishment as retribution for the largest variety of crimes. Therefore, among Islamic

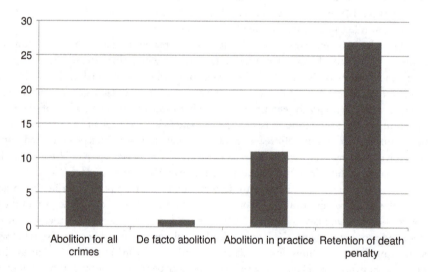

Figure 13.1 Status of the death penalty in 47 Islamic jurisdictions as of March 2017.

Abolition for all crimes: *Albania (2007), Azerbaijan (1998), Djibouti (1995), Kyrgyzstan (2007), Senegal (2004), Turkey (2004), Turkmenistan (1999), Uzbekistan (2008).*

De facto abolition: *Kazakhstan (2007).*

Abolition in practice: *Algeria, Brunei, Burkina Faso, Sierra Leone, Maldives, Mali, Mauritania, Morocco, Niger, Tajikistan, Tunisia.*

Retention: *Afghanistan, Bahrain, Bangladesh, Chad, Comoros, Egypt, Gambia, Guinea, Indonesia, Iran, Iraq, Jordan, Kuwait, Lebanon, Libya, Malaysia, Nigeria, Oman, Pakistan, Qatar, Saudi Arabia, Somalia, Sudan, Syria, United Arab Emirates, Yemen.*

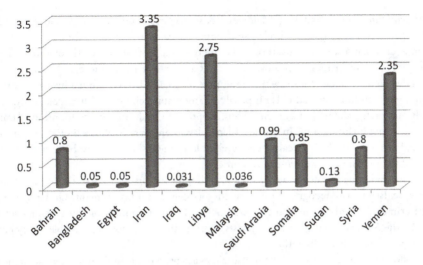

Figure 13.2 Execution rates in Islamic countries per million population—2010.
Source: www.deathpenaltyworldwide.org

nations we should distinguish Islamic states with Islamic criminal justice systems in which *sharia* law or Islamic law is a form of legislation (e.g., Iran) with a state religion, in which Islam as the official religion of a country, where Islamic courts may be used (e.g., Malaysia), and secular criminal justice systems in which government institutions are separated from the role of religion (e.g., Turkey).

Although William Schabas believes capital punishment is a mandatory penalty under the *sharia* for only a small category of crimes (Schabas, 2000), the death penalty in some Islamic countries is applicable to an overly broad range of crimes in addition to murder: incest, rape, sex between a non-Muslim and a Muslim female; adultery, sodomy; other homosexual acts after fourth conviction, drinking liquor after three convictions, drawing arms to create fear, defamation to sanctities, drug trafficking in a specified amount, corruption on Earth, fornication (fourth conviction), false accusation of unlawful intercourse (fourth conviction), and *Had* Theft (fourth conviction).

Degradation in death penalty is related to some complex patterns in history and social development. If we want to maintain why some Islamic countries have abolished the death penalty, we need to examine how different social traditions have emerged. A major difficulty is how to distinguish cruel and unusual punishments in religious and secular criminal justice systems. The most dramatic differences are related to the proportionality doctrine. Penal proportionality based on religious proportionality in Islam is completely different from the secular proportionality in the Western countries. For example, fornication between a non-Muslim man and a Muslim woman would not pass the secular proportionality doctrine. In the secular countries criminalizing sexual conduct is related to harm caused for the society rather than virtue of Muslims.

Capital Crimes in *Sharia* Law

When discussing punishments in Islamic criminal justice systems, keep in mind the relationship between the state and the concept of justice is derived from the religious principle of Islam. The *sharia*, the general and particular rules of Islamic *corpus juris*, is not just a code of law but a code of conduct of behavior and ethics, a combination of law and morality, inseparable. Evidence of this relationship can be seen in the penal code and punishments of the following Islamic countries: Mauritania, Somalia,

Sudan, Afghanistan, Brunei, Iran, Iraq, Maldives, Pakistan, Qatar, Saudi Arabia, Yemen, Aceh in Indonesia, and *sharia* states in Nigeria. All of these countries have death penalty statutes.

In Islamic criminal justice systems those who are deemed 'Corrupt on earth' or those who committed major economic crimes with subversive intent are often sentenced to die. Also, corporal punishment and other inhumane punishments are in practice in all Islamic criminal justice systems.

According to Muslim jurists, the death penalty is imposable only if God has specifically, precisely, and clearly authorized such a punishment. Thus, support of the death penalty found in Islamic texts should be clear and unambiguous. In classical Islamic law, there were five capital offenses, four known as the *hudud* crimes. The *hudud* death penalty eligible crimes were adultery, banditry, sodomy, and apostasy, and the fourth capital offense was murder.

Islamic law traditionally categorizes crimes according to the provenance of the authority to punish the offense. Islamic law recognizes four systems or category for punishment. Under *had* or *hudud*, important crimes deemed to threaten the existence of Islam are punishable by penalties set by the *Quran*, or by the *Sunna* or *Sunnah*. Islamic jurists consider these sanctions immutable. They conclude that the judge is left with no discretion.

The second system, *qisas*, concerns intentional crimes against the person. Its fundamental premise is the *lex talionis*, "eye for eye, tooth for tooth." *Lex talionis* is set out in the Quran, verse 5.32 (further developed by verse 17.33). The *lex talionis* appeared first in the Code of Hammurabi. It was a progressive penal reform, at that time aimed at enhancing the principle of proportionality. It is now seen as a basis for retribution. According to the *Quran*, the victim or his or her heirs are to inflict the punishment under the supervision of public authorities; the victims of such crimes may pardon the offender, in which case the death penalty set by *qisas* will not be imposed. In case the offender is pardoned by victims, two other systems of crime and punishment come into play. These are the *diyat* (prescribes restitution or compensation for the victim) and the *taazir* (public authorities set their own punishment, and the judge has wide discretion). Under the *taazir*, public authorities may provide for capital punishment, but no religious text requires them to do so.

In Islamic criminal justice systems the legislature has approved capital punishment in three different categories:

(1)-Prescribed Punishments (Hudud)

- **Sodomy** is punishable by death if both the active and passive persons are mature, of sound mind, and have free will. If an adult male of legal capacity commits sexual intercourse with an immature person, the doer will be killed and the passive one will be subject to *taazir* (discretionary punishment determined by the judge.)
- **Adultery**: The *Quran* (24:2 *Surah a Nur*) only stipulates 100 lashes for adultery. When, Prophet Mohammad stoned a number of men and women, and so this punishment is *sharia*, Islamic law. But there is no historical evidence that this ever happened; there are two specific stories that are repeated, and in each the prophet required not only confession, but the culprits actually asked for their punishments (Ebrahimi, 1333 Solar Hejira).
- **Banditry (Moharebeh or resorting to arms to frighten people)** is defined as an act of robbery by a group of armed men within the territory of the Islamic state that creates anarchy under which the property, privacy, safety, dignity, and religious values of the people would be violated. The crime is regarded as a war against God and his messenger. There are several alternative punishments for banditry, for instance execution, crucifixion, amputation of hand and foot and exile (5:33, *Surah Ma'ideh*).
- **Apostasy** has an ambiguous basis in Islamic law. There is no reliable evidence that Prophet Mohammad executed anyone for this crime. However, the penalty for apostasy was common during the caliphate of Abu Bakr, and there was a specific historical context that elicited the emergence of the law of apostasy (Ownes, 2004).
- Capital punishment based on the prescribed punishments is also imposed for **incest** and **rape.**

In some circumstances recidivism will lead to a death sentence in Islamic criminal justice systems or the death penalty has been prescribed, mainly in the *Shiite* school of Islam:

- The punishment of *fornication* after the fourth conviction is death, and the fornication of a non-Muslim with a Muslim female is capital punishment, as stated in the Holy *Quran*.
- *Lesbianism* (*Mosaheqeh*) is female homosexuality. Punishment for lesbianism is one hundred (100) lashes for each party. Punishment for lesbianism is established vis-à-vis someone who is mature and of sound mind and has free will and intention. In *sharia* law punishment for lesbianism there is no distinction between the doer and the subject, as well as a Muslim or non-Muslim. If lesbianism is repeated three times and punishment is enforced each time, death sentence will be issued on the fourth conviction. Article 131 of the former Islamic Penal Code of Iran provides that "if the act of lesbianism is repeated three times and punishment is enforced each time, death sentence will be issued the fourth time." The death penalty for lesbianism has been eliminated from the current Islamic Penal Code of Iran.
- *False accusation of unlawful intercourse* (**qadhf**) is prohibited under *sharia* law. Punishment for the fourth conviction is the death penalty. The rationale behind the Law of *qadhf* is here:
  (a) It serves as a protection for the generality of the Muslims. The law of the *qadhf* bans publishing people's unlawful connections and illicit relationships to the society.
  (b) To serve as a deterrent for the accuser and his like. When a person makes an allegation of adultery or fornication against someone and cannot prove his case, he should be punished for slander so that he might not slander in future.
- Punishment for the fourth conviction of **had theft** is the death penalty. Theft is defined in *sharia* as the act of taking other people's property without any lawful claim to it. Theft deprives a man of property. It is an encroachment upon the property of man without any justifiable society and is looked upon with terror. Therefore, strict measures have been ordered by the Islamic criminal justice systems against thieves. The punishment for theft is in the Holy *Quran*: "As to the thief, male or female, cut of his or her hands as punishment by way of example from Allah for their crime. And Allah is exalted in power." According to a tradition of Prophet Mohammad, this punishment does not apply to petty larceny. However, the classical Islamic jurists differ as to the definition of petty larceny in terms of value of the stolen item. For instance, the Islamic Penal Code of Iran regulates 16 different thefts, and just punishment of one category of theft is amputation. Punishment for nine categories of theft involves imprisonment and flogging.
- Punishment for **wine drinking** during the time of the Holy Prophet was beating with shoes, sticks, and hands without specifying the number of lashes. In contemporary Islamic criminal justice systems, punishment of wine drinking is 80 lashes, and for the third conviction the death penalty will be imposed.

(2)-*Retaliation* (**qisas**) is imposed for **murder:** The *Quranic* verses do not seem to require a nuanced inquiry into the circumstances of the murder before permitting the imposition of *qisas*. Classical Islamic law limited the death penalty. It required a specific intent of the murderer and granted certain family the right to override *qisas* by accepting *diyat* (blood-money) or other compensation in lieu of the murderer's death; also, classical Islamic law took into account the status of the victim and murderer (Anderson, 1951).

(3)-*Discretionary punishments* (**taazir**)

Discretionary punishments are the third category of punishments that provide for capital punishment. Islamic penal codes use capital punishment for offenses such as: **defamation to sanctities, drug trafficking** in a specified amount and for the **corruption on earth crimes.** Corruption on earth crimes have a vague definition. In Islamic criminal justice systems, corruption on the earth is not a crime; its definition can be attributed to crimes that include waging war against prophet and God, setting ablaze a mosque, destroying state property during internal rebellious, and any criticism of state.

Although the application of *hudud* is the right of God, and this made series of capital crimes an unalterable and unpardonable component of the Islamic criminal justice systems, the Muslim jurists have differed in their approach to the *hudud*. Disagreements are numerous, deep and recurring. The first approach to be noted demands the immediate and strict application of *hudud*, assessing this as essential prerequisite to truly defining a "Muslim majority society" as "Islamic" (Montazeri, 1998). According to a prominent Islamic scholar Mirza Ghomi (1992), while accepting the fact that the *hudud* is found in the textual references (the *Quran* and the tradition), considering the application of *hudud* to be based on the moves of the society must be just and, for some, has to be "ideal" before these injunctions could be applied. Thus, the priority is the promotion of social justice, fighting against poverty and illiteracy. Finally, there are others, also a minority, who consider the texts relating to *hudud* as obsolete and argue that these references have no place in contemporary Muslim societies (Ramadan, 2009).

Despite the presence of the death penalty in Jewish and Islamic law sources, religion continues to be a powerful and variable resource for people of faith as they wrestle with the morality of capital punishment. For instance, among those who opposed the death penalty for murders, 42% cited religion as their most important influence, while only 15% of those who favored the death penalty said the same (Owenes, 2004).

Harsh Execution Methods in *Sharia* Law

Methods of execution in Islamic countries vary and can include hanging, shooting, beheading, stoning, and dropping the convict from a high wall. In some Islamic countries public executions are carried out to heighten the deterrent effect of punishment. Jewish law prescribes harsh execution methods as well. For instance, the *Mishnah* (the first major written redaction of the Jewish oral traditions) mentions four methods of execution for a capital crime: stoning, burning, strangulation, and beheading. Short drop hanging or hanging by crane as an execution method is not in practice in the Western countries; however, some Islamic countries routinely hang capital offenders. This profound clash of attitudes was not the result of some difference in degree of civilization. It was the result of differences in traditions of status.

The common method of execution in classical Islam was beheading by the sword, but in certain cases different methods are prescribed. For instance, in the *Shiite* school, sodomy is punishable by beheading, stoning, burning, or dropping the convict from a high wall (Peters, 2006). In some Muslim countries governed by *sharia* law, stoning is still practiced. Stoning as a form of punishment is provided in the criminal codes of the following Muslim countries: Iran, one province in Indonesia (Aceh), two federal states of Malaysia (Terengganu, Kelantan), 12 federal states in northern Nigeria (Bauchi, Borno, Gombe, Jigawa, Kaduna, Kano, Katsina, Kebbi, Niger, Sokoto, Yobe, and Zamfara), Pakistan, Saudi Arabia, Sudan and the United Arab Emirates.

The *Quran* (24:2) only stipulates 100 lashes for this offence. However, Prophet Muhammad stoned a number of men and women (*Sahih Muslim* Chapters 623, 680, 682, and *hadith* Malik (493:1520)) and so this punishment is *sharia*, Islamic law. The man is to be buried up to his waist and a woman to above her breast. The stones are not to be too small, as death will not ensue; nor must they be too large, as death may come too soon.

By the way, the *Quran* does not even have that kind of punishment for adultery: The *Quran* speaks of 100 lashes and that is that, though cruel enough (see *Surah* 24:2 and 24:3), but based on the *hadith* (sayings and actions of Prophet Muhammad or tradition), stoning is the punishment for adultery. Some of the *hadith* no doubt have a claim to authenticity, but many, perhaps most, do not.

After Muhammad's death, the first generation of Muslim legal scholars included adultery as one of the six major offenses (*hudud*) in Islamic law for which the penalty is fixed by God in the *Quran* and whose application is the right of God (*haqq Allah*). This made adultery an unalterable and unpardonable component of the Islamic criminal justice systems. However, unlike the other five major offenses (*hadd*) clearly laid out in the *Quran*, both the application and the definition of adultery have been sources of confusion and controversy in the Islamic legal tradition for centuries. The inconsistencies between the *Quran* and the *hadith* with regard to the punishment for adultery were ultimately explained by the Caliph 'Umar (Caliph 'Umar is the second caliph, based on the *Sunnah* school of Islam; therefore his indication is not a source for *Shiite* school).

Although tradition declares Muhammad as occasionally ordering stoning, even the most reliable *hadiths* are not free from controversy. Because tradition demonstrates that while Muhammad may have confirmed stoning and not lashes for adulterers, there was a great deal of confusion as to whether he had done so before or after *Surah an Nur*, which unmistakably prescribes 100 lashes for adultery (Alasti, 2007).

For the preparation of stoning the convicted person is wrapped in a shroud and placed into a pit and buried either to the waist (if a man) or the chest (if a woman). If the individual is sentenced to flogging and stoning, flogging is carried out first and stoning is carried out consequently. If the adultery was proven in court by confession, the judge has the responsibility of throwing the first stone. But if the case was proven through witnesses, they start first, followed by the judge and then by any others who are present, the number of which cannot be less than three. The lack of presence of the religious judge or not throwing the first stones by the religious leader or the witnesses would not prevent the sentence from being carried out; it should be carried out under any circumstances (Alasti, 2007). The stones are then hurled one by one until the accused is killed. The former Islamic Penal Code of Iran was explicit regarding the proper stones to use. Article 104 states, with reference to the penalty for adultery: "the stones should not be too large so that the person dies on being hit by one or two of them; they should not be so small either that they could not be defined as stones." Under the law, the stones must be big enough to injure but not kill with just a few blows.

Victims who can dig themselves out are acquitted. In case the guilty escapes from the hole in which he is put during the stoning and if his guilt is proved by his own confession, it will result in pardon, because if the crime has been proved by confession his escape indicates his withdrawal. Men who are stoned to death are buried to the waist, while women are buried deeper, to stop the stones from hitting their breasts; as for women, the possibility of escaping is much smaller than for men. That is why in Islamic countries fewer men have been stoned than women. This apparent regard actually has a negative impact for women: if a prisoner manages to pull free during a stoning, he or she can be acquitted. In addition, the escape of a witness, denial after confession, and repentance of sin will also result in avoiding the punishment (Alasti, 2007).

In the Old Testament of the Bible, stoning is prescribed as the method of execution for crimes such as murder, blasphemy, or apostasy. The punishment of stoning to death (*rajm*) has a long tradition in Islam. When it comes to the practice of stoning adulterers, however, the traditions indicate that *Talmudic* law primarily influenced Mohammad. The *hadith* present Mohammad as initially prescribing stoning explicitly for Jews who had been found guilty of adultery, then later referring to the Jewish law whenever passing similar sentences on members of his own community. Mohammad even criticized the Jews for relaxing their adultery laws when Jewish people replaced stoning with smearing of coal on the face. A hadith recorded by al-Bukhari, on the authority of Ibn Umar, states: A Jew and a Jewess were brought to Allah's Apostle (S) on a charge of committing illegal sexual intercourse. The Prophet asked them: "What is the legal punishment (for this sin) in your Book (Torah)?" They replied: "Our priests have innovated the blackening of faces with charcoal and Tajbiya" (being mounted on a donkey, with their faces in opposite directions, then mortified in public). Abdullah bin Salaam said: "O Allah's Apostle, tell them to bring the Torah." The Torah was brought, and then one of the Jews put his hand over the Divine Verse of the *rajm* (stoning to death) and started reading what preceded and what followed it. On that, Ibn Salaam said to the Jew: "Lift up your hand." The Divine Verse of the *rajm* was under his hand. So Allah's Apostle (S) ordered that the two (sinners) be stoned to death, and so they were stoned.

Execution method seems to be harsh in religious sources, but the punishment, the harshest in Jewish law, was intended to be as quick and painless as possible given the nature of the punishment. Harsh Biblical penalties were carried out to the letter at one time, but certainly by *Mishnaic* times (the early first through early third centuries) courts favored a lenient interpretation of the law. Considering the stones' size and execution conditions, the Rabbis' ultimate concern was that the execution be as quick and as painless as possible, with minimal disfigurement. When one Rabbi suggested that the height of the platform should be increased so death by falling would be certain, another Rabbi responded that raising the platform is unacceptable, a fall from too high would result in disfigurement (Alasti, 2006). The death penalty debate in the *Talmud*, therefore, can be viewed as not so much about justice as about mercy. In the classic Jewish tradition, mercy occupies a central role (Ledewitz, 1993).

Juvenile Death Penalty in *Sharia* Law

Eighteen years is the internationally accepted minimum age for the imposition of capital punishment. According to Amnesty International, since 1990, only nine countries in the world are known to have executed juvenile offenders: China, Congo, Pakistan, Iran, Saudi Arabia, Yemen, Sudan, and the United States. Of those nine countries, five are Muslim. In a geopolitical sense, these countries are often considered to form the Muslim world.

Between 1990 and 2009, at least 82 executions against juvenile offenders have been carried out around in the world. China (2 children), Democratic Republic of Congo (1 child), Iran (46 children), Nigeria (1 child), Pakistan (4 children), Saudi Arabia (5 children), Yemen (2 children), Sudan (2 children), and the USA (19 children).

Although the number of juvenile offenders affected by the death penalty is small, the practice is in direct conflict with international law, violates the right to life, and is the ultimate cruel, inhuman, and degrading punishment. The execution of juvenile offenders continues in two Islamic countries: Iran and Saudi Arabia. Juvenile offenders remain on death row in several other Islamic countries around the world.

The patterns in most Islamic nations over the last two decades are consistent with the longer term declines in prevalence of juvenile executions, and many places now have a zero execution rate for juveniles, including Nigeria, Pakistan, and Sudan. In 2010, Sudan amended its laws to set 18 years as the firm age of majority, and in Nigeria a 13-year period without juvenile execution is widely viewed as a stage in the transition toward abolition. One exception is Iran; from 2004 to 2010 the rate of juvenile executions is 11 times higher than previous years. Another is Saudi Arabia, where there were four executions since 2003.

From 1990 to 2012, 60 children were executed in Islamic countries: 28 (46.7%) for *qisas* crimes, 9 (15%) for *hudud* crimes, and just a small portion of them for *ta'zir* crimes. The preceding indicates that, despite the abolition of the juvenile death penalty in a majority of Islamic countries, this punishment is still widely applied for *hudud* and *qisas* crimes in the major regions of the Muslim community where the Islamic law was elaborated.

Muslim scholars maintain that the criminal capacity of a child and consequently his criminal responsibility increase in accordance with his age (Sanad, 1991). The stages of human growth, from birth to the age of completing maturity, can be divided into three stages: (1) During the first stage, a child has no conscience and is indiscriminative. In this stage, a child is not responsible for actions committed in violation of the law; therefore, he or she is neither criminally liable nor responsible from a disciplinary aspect. Jurists have fixed the age of 7 for this stage. (2) This stage begins at 7 years of age and extends to the age of puberty. Through this stage, the child is not criminally liable for his acts, but he can meet with disciplinary action. (3) The third stage begins, for boys and girls, when they reach the age of puberty. A person in this stage shall be completely responsible for his actions (Elashhab, 1994).

The basis for jurists stipulating puberty age in criminal liability is a tradition by Prophet Moham-mad, who said: "No liability in three cases: a child till it reaches puberty, a sleeping person till he awakes, and a demented person till he regains his mental health."

Puberty in Islam is determined either by age (some scholars say it occurs at 11 years old, and some say at 12; others differentiate between males and females), or by the signs of puberty, or by both. Islamic jurists are not agreed over fixation of the age of puberty, at which the discrimination stage ends (Ibn Edris Shafi'I, 1980). There are five major schools of thought within Islamic law, and they hold diverse viewpoints even on some questions of responsibility and puberty. Among these five some *Shiites* say it is 15 years for boys and 9 years for girls. Some *Hanafi* and *Maliki* say it is 19 years for men, and 17 years for women, but for most jurists it is 15 years of age (Elashhab, 1994).

In almost all Islamic schools, girls—due to the earlier onset of puberty—potentially bear criminal responsibility several years before their male cohorts for *hudud* crimes (Cipriani, 2009).

Among the 47 Islamic nations that are part of the Islam world, only ten clearly base their minimum age of criminal responsibility provisions to some extent upon Islamic law. The *Quran* does not provide explicit age guidelines regarding the puberty age; therefore, Islamic jurists interpret relevant ages as objec-tive criteria for it. Several Islamic jurists relied on the standard version that criminal liability is determined by puberty, but the practice of juvenile death penalty has not been mentioned in any authoritative *hadith*.

Also, even after the onset of puberty, juveniles should not be automatically held criminally respon-sible for their illegal acts. For such responsibility to follow, children must have reached puberty and be of sound mind (Fathi Bahnassi, 1982). Indeed, in the case of the minimum criminal responsibility age, one may even argue that classic Islamic criminal law doctrine lies closer to international standards than to some countries' contradictory provisions (Cipriani, 2009).

Despite the abolition or moratorium of capital punishment for juveniles in Islamic countries, chil-dren are still being executed. It demonstrates simple attempts to outlaw the juvenile death penalty will not solve the problem because the moratorium was not proclaimed for genuine attempts to humanize the society but rather to please the international community. More execution of juveniles is possible, especially in the case of a change of political power.

Avoidance of Harsh Punishments in Case of Doubt

Although the death penalty has been prescribed in other religious sources, such as Jewish law, the *Talmud* seriously limits the use of the death penalty to criminals who were warned not to commit the crime in the presence of two witnesses and persisted in committing the crime, also in front of two witnesses. In Jewish law a court of at least 23 judges would have to be satisfied, to a legal certainty, that the capital offense had been committed by the accused before the court could impose a death sentence. Since the testimony of two eyewitnesses was required in *Mishnah*, and the witnesses were subjected to searching and detailed interrogation by the court, there was rarely an instance when the evidence met the prescribed legal standard.

Despite the scriptural mandate for capital punishment in Jewish law, two of the most influential sages of the second century of the first millennium, Rabbi Tarfon and Rabbi Akiva, stated in *Mishnah* that had they been in the *Sanhedrin* (the Supreme Court of ancient Israel) when Jews did have the political power to administer capital punishment in their community, no one would have ever been executed. The *Gemara* explains how they would preclude the death penalty without denying its divine legitimacy. The rabbis would ask improbable and obscure questions of the witnesses—such as whether it were not possible that the victim had been suffering from some fatal disease, which actually killed him. A lack of certainty by the witnesses on any material point would bar formal execution (Ledewitz, 1993).

The death penalty does exist in Islamic textual references, and almost all Islamic countries with an Islamic criminal justice system have not abolished the death penalty, but it is possible to consider various evidentiary, procedural, and barriers against the death penalty. These include the lack of a just and ideal religious criminal justice system for prosecution of *hudud* crimes (Mirza Ghomi, 1992). The Islamic legal maxim of **avoidance of hudud crimes in case of doubt** says that judges are to avoid imposing *hudud* punishments when beset by doubts as to the scope of the law or the sufficiency of the evidence. Moreover, **avoidance of hudud crimes in case of doubt**, more stringent evidentiary requirements, and pressures for twenty-first-century norms of jurisprudence make implementation of the death penalty increasingly rare.

In Islamic criminal law there is a principle that punishments are to be avoided whenever there is ambiguity or doubt as to the textual basis, evidence, or criminal culpability of the accused. In Islam, "*hudud* punishments are to be prevented in case of doubt." This is based on the prophetic tradition: "Prevent the application of *hadd* punishment as much as you can whenever any doubt exists." Shaykh Mufid (Abu 'Abd Allah Muhammad ibn Muhammad ibn al-Nu'man al-'Ukbari al-Baghdadi, known as Shaykh Mufid for his expertise in philosophical theology [c. 948–1022 CE] was an eminent Twelver *Shi'a* theologian) notes that defective contracts give rise to *hudud* avoidance if entered into in the presence of doubt or ambiguity (Muqni'ah, 1990). Also, Allameh Hilli (1999), who was an eminent Twelver theologian who flourished under the Mongols in Iraq and learned knowledge and philosophy from a famous Iranian scientist of the seventh century, "Khajeh Nasireddin-e Tousi," notes several types of *hadd*-averting doubt in one of his treatises.

The standard of proof in *hudud* punishment is very high and difficult to attain. It is even recommended by the *sharia* that a judge suggest the possibility of withdrawal of confession to an accused who has confessed to the commission of crime (Alasti, 2006).

Obviously, if these rules were followed in Islamic criminal justice systems, there would be almost no convictions in capital cases. Unlike the contemporary practice of capital punishment in Islamic countries, classical Islamic law has regarded wrongful execution as totally unacceptable. The extreme procedural and evidentiary hurdles employed in the classical death penalty systems can be understood as in part stemming from an abhorrence of convicting and executing the innocent.

A Lesson Learned

Even if the religious sources such as the *Quran* and *hadith* justify the death penalty in theory, that gives us no answer about whether the death penalty is justified as applied in Islamic nations today. Islamic criminal justice systems apply laws of 14 centuries ago equally today because they are of divine origin. The fact is many Islamic punishments were pre-Islamic and, indeed, were promulgated by the Prophet Muhammad (e.g., stoning, retaliation laws.)

As a general rule, the Islamic punishments to some extent belongs to the Arabs' tribal system of punishment, in addition; Imam Bukhari narrates a *hadith* (tradition) on the authority of Ibn Abbas that the law of retaliation was originally prescribed to the Israelites. It shows these punishments belong to many ancient cultures. The most significant difference between secular criminal justice systems and modern Islamic nations is the level of violence and existence of authoritarian regimes. The death penalty in the secular criminal justice systems differs from that of the *sharia* law in that it is part of a religious criminal justice system. In contemporary Islamic criminal justice systems, we would move to summary procedures, more courts, and a weakening of procedural and evidentiary restrictions.

Although scriptural mandates in Islamic sources may never be repealed because the law of God cannot be revised by humans, one could argue that the death penalty statutes in religious criminal justice systems are more symbolic than real. In contemporary secular criminal justice systems it is not permissible to execute a condemned man or woman by methods that cause unnecessary pain, delay, or disfigurement. Even in the rare case when the state has determined that the accused must be put to death because a heinous offense was committed, the condemned is legally entitled to consideration and dignity (Alasti, 2006). Thus, contemporary Jewish law considers the standard of decency; for this reason, they do not impose stoning, and it is possible for Muslim jurists to adopt the same approach. Most Muslim policymakers in offending countries want to make changes in certain aspects of their strict penal codes, and they are looking for the language and justifications that would make it palatable to do so.

The more the situation of the Muslim community changed, the more the revelation altered to match the community's needs. To coordinate with the contemporary standards of Islamic societies, Islamic scholars developed a vital exegetical tool called *naskh*, which can best be understood as the purposeful abrogation (not cancellation) of one verse with another. For the vast majority of Muslims in the world, *naskh* signifies that the *Quran* is a living, evolving scripture developed alongside the Muslim community. More than anything else, however, *naskh* demonstrates the importance of historical context in *Quranic* interpretation. And while it is true that, with the Prophet Mohammad's death, the Revelation ceased evolving, it would be counterfactual to argue that the Muslim community has also ceased evolving over the past fifteen hundred years. Quite the contrary; the fact is there can be no question that the *sharia* was developed within a clear historical context. Like the *Quran*, the tradition, the second most important source of Islamic law, is also a response to specific historical circumstances. Indeed, countless traditions strive to explain the historical context in which a certain revelation was revealed.

The question of whether to leave the death penalty in the statutes of Islamic countries, prolong the moratorium on it, or abolish it is one that I think embodies the larger realities of political, legal, and social developments in the Islamic countries. Must abolition of the death penalty await the decline of Islamic authoritarian governments, or will hardline regimes abolish the state killings to coordinate with the contemporary standards of Islamic societies? Several Muslim nations with large Islamic populations have recently gone long periods without executions. Most of the Islamic countries that are low-execution nations have secular criminal justice system rather than a religious criminal justice system. But the tiny nation of Brunei Darussalam combined an Islamic theocratic regime with no execution for the past half-century (Zimring, 2009). Although in 2014 Brunei's new Islamic Penal Code prescribed the death penalty for a variety of crimes, the enforcement of capital sentences has been postponed to 2018. The experience of death penalty in abolitionist Islamic countries demonstrates the death penalty is not a question of religion but of political dynamics and political will.

While the abolition of the death penalty for *hudud* and *qisas* crimes seems to be a very positive aspect of the law, the majority of executions of offenders in Islamic countries are cases of *taazir*, where the individual has been found guilty of nonreligious crimes, and mainly drug-related crimes. At the least, legislation in Islamic countries is urgently required to ensure that no person is sentenced to death for any nonreligious crime, including drug trafficking. The majority of Muslim jurists, historically and today, recognize the existence of scriptural sources that refer to such punishments, but some Islamic scholars believe the conditions under which they should be implemented are nearly impossible to reestablish. Mirza Ghomi, the author of *Jama al-Shetat*, and Mohammad Ali Abtahi, the author of *Tozihol al-Masayel*, believe before the reappearance of al-Mahdi (an ultimate savior of humankind and the final Imam of the Twelve *Shi'a* Muslims who would, in accordance with God's command, bring justice and peace to the world) these penalties, therefore, are almost never applicable.

Also, there are many examples from Islamic history of how these punishments have been suspended in practice. For example Umar Ibn al-Khatab (the second *Khalifa* of *Sunni* Muslims after Muhammad's death) suspended the *hadd* punishment in a time of war, because the required conditions for its application were impossible to meet. The *hudud* would, therefore, serve as a 'deterrent', the objective of which would be to stir the conscience of the believer to the gravity of an action warranting such a punishment. The penalties are Islamic, but conditions are not appropriate for their implementation.

The more the situation of the Muslim community changed, the more the revelation altered to match the community's needs and to coordinate with the contemporary standards of societies (Aslan, 2004). Thus, personal dignity and humanity are highly valued in current societies. Muslim jurists should continue adapting the tools to prohibit punishments that violate these values and that would have to be deemed problematic and in contrast to the idealism embodied in the ban on cruel and unusual punishment. Furthermore, in contrast to punishment in accord with norms of human rights, particular countries may treat people in arbitrary ways and severely curtail their freedom. This is in spite of, rather than in keeping with, religious law, because religions have the ability to adapt themselves with ideas. Therefore, Islamic law needs to be updated and meet the demands of modern times. The better course is to steer clear of such obstacles and focus on the purpose of the ride: that is, providing a humane and civilized criminal justice system the way religions originally intended.

Notes

1 Sanaz Alasti is Associate Professor of Criminal Justice and Director of the Center for Death Penalty Studies at Lamar University: Texas State University. Alasti has completed her postdoctoral research at Harvard law school, and she is the author of seven books.
2 Eric Bronson is Professor of Criminal Justice and the Dean of School of Justice at Roger Williams University, specializing in Corrections.
3 Ibn Abi Shayba, (d. 235/849 H.) was one of the peers of Ahmad ibn Hanbal, Ishaq ibn Rahuyah, and Ali ibn al-Madini in age, place of birth, and *hadith* memorization.

References

Abtahi, M. A. (1998). *Tozihol al-Masayel.* Qom, Iran: Abneh al-seyyede Mohammad [In Farsi].

Alasti, S. (2006). Comparative study of cruel & unusual punishment for engaging in consensual homosexual acts (In international conventions, the United States and Iran). *Ann. Surv. Int'l & Comp. L., 12,* 149–269.

Alasti, S. (2007). Comparative study of stoning punishment in the religions of Islam and Judaism. *Justice Policy Journal, 4*(1), 1–38.

Alasti, S. (2009). *Cruel and unusual punishment.* FL, US: Vandeplas Publishing.

Alasti, S. (2016). Juvenile death penalty in Islamic countries: The road to abolition is paved with paradox. *Capital Punishment: New Perspectives,* 63–84.

Anderson, J. N. D. (1951). Homicide in Islamic law. *Bulletin of the School of Oriental and African Studies, 13,* 811–828.

Arafah Dasuqi, M. A. (19-). *Hashiyat al-Dasuqi alá al-Sharh al-Kabir* (Vol. 3). Cairo, Egypt: al-Maktabah al-Tijariyah [In Arabic].

Aslan, R. (2003–2004). The problem of stoning in the Islamic penal code: An argument for reform. *UCLA J. Islamic & Near E. L.,* 91.

Bahaie Ameli, S. (19-). *al-Jame al-Abbasi.* Tehran, Iran: Farahani Publication [In Farsi].

Bahnassi, A. F. (1982). Criminal responsibility in Islamic law. In M. C. Bassiouni (Ed.), *The Islamic criminal justice system.* London: Oceana Publications.

Bassiouni, M. C. (1988). *Introduction to Islam.* Chicago, IL: Rand McNally & Company.

Cipriani, D. (2009). *Children's rights and the minimum age of criminal responsibility: A global perspective.* Surrey, England: Ashgate Publishing.

Elashhab, A. (1994). *The criminal liability in law and Islamic law.* Benghazi, Libya: National Publishing House.

Ibn Qudamah, A. A. (19-). *Al-Mughni* (Vol. 10). Beirut, Lebanon: Dar al-Ketab Arabi [In Arabic].

Ledewitz, B. (1993). Reflections on the Talmudic and American death penalty, *University of Florida Journal of Law and Public Policy, 6,* 33.

Mirza Ghomi. (1992). *Jama al-Shetat* (Vol. 1). Tehran, Iran: Keyhan Publication [In Farsi].

Montazeri, H. A. (1998). *Tozihol al-Masayel.* Tehran, Iran: Fekr Publication [In Farsi].

Ownes, E. (2004). *Religion and the death penalty.* Michigan: William Eerdmans Publishing Company.

Ramadan, T. (2009). *New directions in Islamic thought: Exploring reform and Muslim tradition* (K. Vogt & L. Larsen, Eds.). I.B. Tauris & Co Ltd.

Sabiq, S. (19-). *Fiqh Al-Sunnah* (Vol. 2). Beirut, Lebanon: Dar al-Ketab Arabi [In Arabic].

Sanad, N. (1991). *The theory of crime and criminal responsibility in Islamic law: Sharia.* Chicago: The University of Illinois, The Office of International Criminal Justice.

Sarakhsi, M. A. (19-). *Al-Mabsut.* Beirut, Lebanon: Dar al-Marefa [In Arabic].

Schabas, W. A. (2000). Symposium: Religion's role in the administration of the death penalty: Islam and the death penalty. *William & Mary Bill of Rights Journal, 9*, 223.

Shafi'i, M. E. (1980). *Ketab al-Omm* (Vol. 3). Beirut, Lebanon: Dar al-Fekr [In Arabic].

Tusi, M. H. (19-). *Al-Mabsut* (Vol. 7). Tehran, Iran: al-Maktabah al-Murtadawiyah [In Arabic].

Zimring, F., & Johnson, D. (2009). *The next frontier: National development, political change, and the death penalty in Asia.* Oxford: Oxford University Press.

PART 3

Capital Punishment and Constitutional Issues

14

THE U.S. SUPREME COURT AND THE DEATH PENALTY

Katherine J. Bennett and H. Chris Tecklenburg

In 1972, the United States Supreme Court ruled in *Furman v. Georgia* that the death penalty as imposed under existing laws was unconstitutional, amounting to cruel and unusual punishment. The primary concern expressed in the 5–4 *Furman* decision was that the death penalty was being administered in an arbitrary or capricious manner, and over 600 capital punishment sentences in death penalty states were vacated. Four years later, the Court ruled that state death penalty statutes that show that the punishment can be administered reliably and not arbitrarily are constitutional (*Gregg v. Georgia*, 1976). Accordingly, states have attempted to construct statutes that pass judicial scrutiny and to apply the death penalty to offenders in an equitable fashion; however, by 2015, at least one justice, Justice Breyer, concluded that the past 40 years have shown anything but reliability and consistency (dissenting opinion in *Glossip et al. v. Gross et al.* [2015]). This chapter reviews the past 40 years and the various death penalty issues that have come before the Supreme Court. Well over 140 death penalty cases have been decided in this time span, with the Court overruling itself in several decisions.

First Post-*Furman* Cases

By 1976, 33 states had revised their death penalty statutes, but *Gregg v. Georgia* was the first to be tested by the Supreme Court since it had declared capital punishment unconstitutional in *Furman*. Thus, the starting point of this chapter begins with *Gregg*. To address the concerns of arbitrariness and capriciousness expressed by the *Furman* court, Georgia had taken several precautions, which first included creating a bifurcated trial, in which guilt or innocence was determined, and upon a finding of guilt, then was followed by a sentencing phase. Next, at least one out of ten aggravating factors had to be found beyond a reasonable doubt during the penalty phase before the death sentence could be imposed. Finally, the state supreme court automatically reviewed the death penalty.

Following these procedures, Troy Gregg received the death penalty after being convicted of armed robbery and two counts of murder. The judge had instructed the jury that it could sentence Gregg to life or death on either murder count and that they could consider mitigating or aggravating circumstances as presented during the trial. However, the judge instructed the jury that it would only be authorized to impose the death penalty if it found beyond a reasonable doubt one of three factors.[1] The jury found the first two aggravating circumstances and sentenced Gregg to death. Gregg challenged the sentence as cruel and unusual punishment, but the U.S. Supreme Court approved of the death sentence and of Georgia's revised statutory scheme, releasing its decision on July 2, 1976.

On that same day, the Supreme Court ruled on the constitutionality of four other death penalty statutes from Florida, Texas, North Carolina, and Louisiana. The first, *Proffitt v. Florida* (1976), involved the constitutionality of Florida's revised sentencing statute. Under Florida's statute, the trial judge was required to weigh eight aggravating circumstances against seven mitigating factors in determining whether to impose the death penalty. Similar to Georgia's statute in *Gregg*, the Florida statute required the judge to consider the circumstances of the crime and the character of the defendant, with the sentence subject to review by the state supreme court. However, unlike *Gregg*, the judge determined the sentence, with the jury's role being primarily advisory. The Court held in *Proffitt* that the death penalty was not automatically cruel and unusual and that the Florida statute provided clear and precise guidance to both the judge and jury with regard to weighing and applying aggravating and mitigating circumstances.

The third case decided was *Jurek v. Texas* (1976) and involved Texas' attempt to create a statute that would avoid the problems identified in *Furman*. The statute identified capital offenses as those involving intentional and knowing murders that were committed in five situations. In determining whether to impose the death penalty, the jury was required after the verdict phase to answer three questions.[2] If the jury answered affirmatively to each, then the death penalty was imposed; however, if the answer were negative to any of the questions, then the sentence would be life imprisonment.

The primary issue in *Jurek* was whether the statute was constitutional since it did not specifically address mitigating circumstances, thus giving concern that the jury was not properly considering the character of the defendant. The lower court interpreted the second of the three questions that involved whether the defendant was a "continuing threat to society" as permitting the jury to consider mitigating factors. The Supreme Court agreed and held that while the Texas statute did not specifically mention mitigating circumstances, the jury was free to consider such evidence as it answered the previously noted questions.

The final two cases decided on the same day as *Gregg*, *Proffitt*, and *Jurek* addressed mandatory language in states' new death penalty statutes. In *Woodson v. North Carolina* (1976), the Court considered the constitutionality of North Carolina's revised statute. The provision at issue required the imposition of the death penalty for individuals convicted of first-degree murder. The Court held that mandatory sentences were unconstitutional, as the jury lacked any guiding standards with regard to sentencing. The Court reached a similar decision that same day in *Roberts v. Louisiana* (1976), involving Louisiana's statute mandating the death penalty for those who committed one of five categories of homicide, with the jury also finding "specific intent to kill or inflict great bodily harm."[3] If the jury rendered a guilty verdict of first-degree murder, then the death penalty was imposed automatically. Citing *Woodson*, the Court held that the mandatory death sentence violated the Eighth and Fourteenth Amendments, as the jury once again lacked standards and guidance in sentencing.

The rest of this chapter reviews the various issues in cases heard by the Supreme Court after these five. Most of the cases that have come before the Court involve the aforementioned issues, including mandatory/disproportionate sentencing and mitigating and aggravating circumstances, as well as vagueness challenges in statutes and jury instructions, jury selection, offender characteristics of race, age, insanity, mental retardation/intellectual disabilities, state's bifurcated sentencing procedures, and the constitutionality of different methods of capital punishment. To date, the Court has reversed its position with respect to at least four issues.

Mandatory/Disproportionate Sentencing/Violations of Due Process

Several cases heard shortly after *Roberts v. Louisiana* reinforced the prohibition against mandatory death penalty sentencing. Two such cases, *Washington v. Louisiana* (1976) and a per curiam case, *Roberts v. Louisiana* (1976), involving a different individual named Roberts, entailed mandatory imposition of the death penalty, per Louisiana law, for the murder of police officers. The Court ruled that a mandatory death penalty for first-degree murder of on-duty police violated the Eighth and Fourteenth

Amendments because mandatory sentencing did not allow for considering mitigating circumstances in individual cases.

Mandatory death sentences were unmistakably abolished in *Sumner v. Shuman* (1987). Shuman was given an automatic death sentence for the murder of a fellow prisoner pursuant to Nevada law. The Supreme Court held that it was a constitutional requirement that the sentencing authority consider aspects of the defendant's character or other circumstances as a mitigating factor. Due to the lack of such consideration in this case, the sentence violated the Eighth and Fourteenth Amendments.[4]

One year after the death penalty was reinstated in *Gregg*, the Court addressed disproportionate sentencing in *Coker v. Georgia* (1977). Coker had escaped prison and committed acts of armed robbery and rape. Coker was sentenced to death for rape of an adult woman, as two aggravating circumstances were found. The Supreme Court overturned the sentence, ruling that the Eighth Amendment barred excessive punishments in relation to the crime committed. The Court noted that punishment is excessive and unconstitutional if it "(1) makes no measurable contribution to acceptable goals of punishment, and hence is nothing more than the purposeless and needless imposition of pain and suffering; or (2) is grossly out of proportion to the severity of the crime."[5]

Another case involving disproportionate penalties, *Enmund v. Florida* (1982), involved accomplice liability. Enmund received the death penalty although he was in a car parked by the side of the road while a robbery and murder was taking place. Under Florida law, he was a constructive aider and abettor and thus a principal in the first-degree murder. However, the Supreme Court held that sentencing someone to death who did not kill, attempt to kill, or intend to kill violated the Eighth and Fourteenth Amendments. Two other cases before the Court during the 1980s involved similar circumstances, with the Court reaching different conclusions based on requisite intent.[6]

The Court also addressed proportionality of death sentences in *Pulley v. Harris* (1984). Harris claimed that the U.S. Constitution required California's capital punishment statute to compare his sentence with sentences imposed in similar capital cases. The Supreme Court rejected the argument that their prior cases required such comparative proportionality review, noting that the "Eighth Amendment does not require, as an invariable rule in every case, that a state appellate court, before it affirms a death sentence, compare the sentence in the case before it with the penalties imposed in similar cases if requested to do so but the prisoner."[7]

Returning to *Enmund* and *Tison v. Arizona* (1987) (see note 5), in (1991), the Court reversed the Idaho Supreme Court in a 5–4 decision in *Lankford v. Idaho*. Bryan Lankford was convicted of the first-degree murders of Robert and Cheryl Bravence in 1983. The prosecution was convinced that Lankford's brother was the killer, but Lankford was an accessory. Prior to sentencing, the state indicated that it would not be recommending the death penalty, and at the sentencing hearing, the prosecutor recommended an indeterminate life sentence. The defense offered mitigating evidence and argued against a life sentence, making no reference to the death penalty. At the conclusion, the trial judge noted the sentencing options available, which included death. Judging the two brothers equally culpable, he sentenced Lankford to death, with the Idaho Supreme Court upholding the sentence on appeal. However, the U.S. Supreme Court ruled that Lankford and his defense counsel were not given adequate notice that death was a possible sentence, thus violating Lankford's Fourteenth Amendment right to due process. Had the defense attorney known the death penalty was a possibility, she would have been able to address whether Lankford's role in the crime met the standard upheld in *Enmund* (1982) and *Tison* (1987).

Two early per curiam Georgia cases decided two years after the death penalty was reinstated were also unsuccessful before the Court for due process violations. In *Presnell v. Georgia* (1978), Presnell was convicted of rape, kidnapping with bodily injury, and murder with malice aforethought and given three death sentences. The Georgia Supreme Court overturned the first two death sentences, since they depended upon the defendant having committed forcible rape, and the jury had not properly convicted him of that offense. However, the Georgia Court upheld the third death sentence, holding that the evidence supported the conclusion that Presnell was guilty of forcible rape, even though the jury did not in fact find that. By holding that there was forcible rape, the element of bodily harm necessary for the death penalty was established. The Supreme Court overturned the death penalty, however, holding that Presnell's due process rights were violated. A few months later, in *Green v. Georgia* (1979), another per curiam opinion, Green attempted to introduce testimony of a third party, whose testimony at the earlier trial of Green's accomplice indicated that the accomplice had admitted to him that he had killed the victim. The trial court held that the statement was inadmissible hearsay, which was upheld by the Georgia Supreme Court. The U.S. Supreme Court reversed, holding instead that regardless of whether it was hearsay under Georgia law, excluding the testimony during the penalty phase constituted a violation of due process, as the testimony was highly relevant to a critical issue in the punishment phase.

With regard to the death penalty for nonhomicide crimes, the Court returned to *Coker* and *Enmund* again in (2008) in *Kennedy v. Louisiana*. Patrick Kennedy received the death penalty in 2003 for aggravated rape of a child. Beginning in 1995, Louisiana, as well as five other states, had reinstated the death penalty for child rape. *Coker* pertained to the unconstitutionality of capital punishment for the rape of an adult woman, and the instant case was the first opportunity for the Supreme Court to look at the issue of child rape. The court observed that deterrent or retributive purposes would not be advanced and that there was no national consensus for giving the death penalty to child rapists. The U.S. Supreme Court reversed the Louisiana Supreme Court and concluded that "imposing the death penalty for the rape of a child where the crime did not result, and was not intended to result in death of the victim"[8] was an Eighth Amendment violation.

The next sections pertain to the Supreme Court's review of the constitutionality of various state statutes. Early challenges centered on the opportunity for mitigating factors to be heard and several issues involving aggravating factors.

Mitigating Circumstances After 1976

Mitigating evidence and Ohio's death penalty statute came under review in *Lockett v. Ohio* (1978). The Ohio statute provided for the imposition of the death penalty if one of seven aggravating circumstances were found, unless the judge found at least one of three mitigating factors to be present.[9] Lockett challenged the constitutionality of the statute, claiming that it did not give the sentencing judge the opportunity to consider all relevant mitigating factors, as it was limited to only three. The Supreme Court agreed and held that the Ohio statute did not "permit the type of individualized consideration of mitigating factors required by the Eighth and Fourteenth Amendments."[10] Four years later in *Eddings v. Oklahoma* (1982), the death penalty was given to Eddings, a 16-year-old juvenile, who was tried as an adult for killing a police officer. While the Oklahoma statute permitted any mitigating factors to be introduced, the trial judge refused to consider the abusive upbringing and emotional disturbance of Eddings and only considered his youth at the time of the offense. The Supreme Court vacated the death sentence, noting that it was "imposed without 'the type of individualized consideration of mitigating factors . . . required by the Eighth and Fourteenth Amendments in capital cases.'"[11]

Similarly, the Court heard a dispute involving the exclusion of mitigating testimony in *Skipper v. South Carolina* (1986). Ronald Skipper, convicted of capital murder and rape, attempted to introduce testimony from two jailers and a regular visitor to the jail as mitigating evidence that showed he had "made a good adjustment" between the time of his arrest and his trial. The judge excluded the testimony as irrelevant and inadmissible and imposed the death sentence. The Supreme Court reversed and held that denying Skipper the ability to present the jailers' and visitor's testimony denied him the right to present all relevant mitigating evidence in front of the sentencing jury.[12]

The importance of presenting mitigating evidence was underscored in *Wiggins v. Smith* (2003). The Supreme Court ruled that failing to fully investigate and present mitigating factors violates a capital offender's Sixth Amendment right to effective assistance of counsel. The Court pointed to standards in the American Bar Association's Guidelines for the Appointment and Performance of Counsel in Death Penalty Cases as one source providing guidance and noted that effectiveness involves going beyond presentence investigation reports and social services records.

Aggravating Circumstances and Vagueness After 1976

The Supreme Court first addressed statutory aggravating circumstances alleged to be unconstitutionally vague in 1980. In *Godfrey v. Georgia* (1980), the Court examined that part of Georgia's statute that permitted imposing the death penalty if it was found beyond a reasonable doubt that the offense "was outrageously or wantonly vile, horrible or inhuman in that it involved torture, depravity of mind, or an aggravated battery to the victim."[13] The Court noted how the Georgia Supreme Court had applied this provision in the past and how it was inapplicable to Godfrey.[14] Thus, the Court held that administering the death penalty would violate the Eighth and Fourteenth Amendments.[15]

The Court would later uphold a death sentence from Georgia involving another aggravating circumstance in *Zant v. Stephens* (1983). Alpha Stephens challenged his sentence, which was based in part on the aggravating circumstance of "a substantial history of serious assaultive criminal convictions," which the Georgia Supreme Court had deemed unconstitutionally vague. However, in Stephens' case, two other aggravating circumstances applied, and hence the U.S. Supreme Court upheld his sentence. Likewise, the Court affirmed the sentence in *Barclay v. Florida* (1983), ruling that while the lower court should not have used Barclay's criminal record as an aggravating circumstance, doing so did not violate the Constitution, due to findings of additional aggravating circumstances.[16]

The issue of vagueness in Idaho's sentencing statute came under scrutiny in the case of *Arave v. Creech* (1993). Creech, in prison for multiple murders, was convicted for the beating and kicking death of a fellow inmate and sentenced to death, with the trial judge finding the statutory aggravating factor that Creech showed "utter disregard for human life."[17] Creech alleged that "utter disregard" was unconstitutionally vague, violating the Eighth and Fourteenth Amendments. However, the Court ruled that the "utter disregard" factor was constitutional given that Idaho in *State v. Osborn* (1981) had limited the construction of the language by supporting it in the context of other specific aggravating circumstances and clarifying it as "reflective of acts or circumstances surrounding the crime which exhibit the highest, the utmost, callous disregard for human life, i.e., the cold-blooded, pitiless slayer."[18]

California's statute was challenged for vagueness in *Tuilaepa v. California* (1994), consolidated with *Proctor v. California*. The U.S. Supreme Court affirmed the California Supreme Court's decision in both cases, upholding the death sentences given to Tuilaepa and Proctor. At the time, sentences of death in California required finding a defendant guilty of first-degree murder plus one or more aggravating circumstance listed in the penal code. Tuilaepa and Proctor challenged one of the circumstances as being unconstitutionally vague under the Eighth Amendment, with Tuilaepa challenging two more. The factor challenged by both offenders required "the sentencer to consider the 'circumstances of the crime' . . . 'and the existence of any special circumstances found to be true.'"[19] Tuilaepa also challenged a factor regarding "the presence or absence of criminal activity by the defendant which involved the use or attempted use of force or violence" and a consideration of the "age of the defendant at the time of the crime."[20] The Court found none of the factors challenged to be unconstitutionally vague, noting their relevance and that they were phrased in comprehensible terms.[21]

Challenges to Aggravating Circumstance of Future Dangerousness

In *Barefoot v. Estelle* (1983), the defendant was convicted of capital murder and sentenced to death. During the sentencing phase, one question submitted to the jury as required by state statute was "whether there was a probability that the petitioner would commit further criminal acts of violence and would constitute a continuing threat to society."[22] Two psychiatrists testified in the affirmative, and the Supreme Court upheld the sentence, seeing no merit to the argument that psychiatrists are incompetent to predict whether a criminal will commit crimes in the future and still represent a danger to the community. In addition, the Court held that "[p]sychiatric testimony need not be based on personal examination of the defendant but may properly be given in response to hypothetical questions."[23]

The Court addressed future dangerousness in subsequent cases such as *Ake v. Oklahoma* (1985) and *Tuggle v. Netherland, Warden* (1995), a per curiam opinion that was Lem Tuggle's second review by the Court.[24] Tuggle received the death penalty after a Virginia jury found two statutory aggravating circumstances of "future dangerousness" and "vileness." A psychiatrist attested to the future dangerousness, and the Virginia Supreme Court affirmed this sentence in 1984. However, in 1985, the Supreme Court had ruled in *Ake v. Oklahoma* that when a psychiatrist testifies for the prosecution on the possibility of an indigent defendant's future dangerousness, then the state must provide the defendant with an independent psychiatrist. The Court remanded this case in *Tuggle v. Virginia* (1985) so that Virginia could consider their earlier ruling in light of *Ake*. On remand, Virginia ruled that the future dangerousness aggravating circumstance was invalid, but the death sentence could still stand, based on the second aggravating factor, as per *Zant v. Stephens* (1983), discussed in the previous section of this chapter. The appellate court affirmed, reading *Zant* as mandating that the death penalty in a nonweighing state may still stand even when one aggravating factor has been invalidated, as long as another still exists. The Supreme Court vacated the lower court's judgment, remanding this case, ruling that the Fourth Circuit misinterpreted *Zant*, and noted that the *Ake* error was more serious than the invalidated factor in *Zant*. Also in *Zant*, two "unimpeachable" aggravating factors remained.[25] Because of the *Ake* error, Tuggle did not have the opportunity to present evidence from an independent psychiatrist, and the possibility existed that without that evidence, the jury was more persuaded to deliver the death penalty as opposed to life in prison.[26]

The Court reiterated its position in one recent case, *Lynch v. Arizona* (2016, per curiam), that when future dangerousness is considered at sentencing, due process means the defendant is entitled to have the jury informed that the only alternative sentence to death is life imprisonment with no parole. This case followed the Court's holding in *Simmons v. South Carolina* (1994). In *Simmons*, prosecution raised future dangerousness in closing arguments at the penalty phase, and the court refused the defense counsel's request to explain to the jury that Simmons was ineligible for parole and that life imprisonment meant life without parole. In reversing the South Carolina Supreme Court, the Majority stated "The State may not create a false dilemma by advancing generalized arguments regarding the defendant's future dangerousness while, at the same time, preventing the jury from learning that the defendant never will be released on parole."[27]

Weighing Mitigating and Aggravating Circumstances and Other Issues

The "weighing" of aggravating and mitigating circumstances has remained a complex issue, often involving other issues previously discussed such as mandatory language and issues of vagueness. In *Blystone v. Pennsylvania* (1990), Scott Blystone was sentenced to death for the murder of a hitchhiker, Dalton Smithburger, Jr., whom Blystone shot in the back of the head six times. Blystone challenged his sentence, alleging that Pennsylvania's death penalty statute violated the Eighth Amendment because it required the jury to impose the death penalty if there were at least one aggravating circumstance and no mitigating circumstances, or if there were one or more aggravating elements that outweighed mitigating elements.[28] Blystone killed Smithburger after robbing him, an aggravating factor, and the jury found no mitigating circumstances. The Supreme Court held that Pennsylvania's statute was constitutional, allowing a jury to consider all pertinent mitigating circumstances. Further, the mandatory nature of the statute was permissible. The Majority explicitly noted that this statute followed all requirements that the Court had upheld in *Lockett v. Ohio* and distinguished in cases such as *Woodson v. North Carolina* and *Roberts v. Louisiana*. As previously noted in this chapter, in 1976, North Carolina and Louisiana's statutes had been found unconstitutional in large part because of the mandatory imposition of a death sentence without allowing individualized consideration of defendants' characteristics and records. The Court stated that as long as statutes include the consideration of relevant mitigating circumstances such as the defendant's character, they avoid the arbitrariness and capriciousness defects found in *Furman*. The Court further emphasized that all states have independence to establish the type of punishment appropriate for murder and to legislate different forms of statutes, as long as they meet constitutional muster.[29]

One month later the Court revisited these issues in *Clemons v. Mississippi* (1990), holding that it is constitutional for an appellate court to reweigh aggravating and mitigating evidence when a jury-imposed death sentence was based in part on an invalid or improperly defined aggravating circumstance. Clemons was sentenced to death for the capital murder of Arthur Shorter, a pizza deliveryman killed by Clemons during the course of a robbery. The Mississippi State Supreme Court upheld the sentence even though the jury instruction regarding the aggravating factor that the murder was "especially heinous, atrocious, or cruel" was constitutionally invalidated in *Maynard v. Cartwright* (1988). In 1983, in *Zant v. Stephens*, the Court had held that in Georgia, because aggravating circumstances only make a defendant eligible for the death penalty, invalidating one of those factors does not require an appellate court to vacate the death sentence and remand the case to a jury. However, the Court did not address in *Zant* what would happen in "weighing" states like Mississippi, where juries or judges are required to weigh aggravating and mitigating factors in deciding on the sentence.

In *Clemons*, the Court ruled that there is no constitutional error with appellate courts deciding if the evidence supports the jury verdicts, including reweighing mitigating and aggravating factors in an individualized manner or by engaging in harmless error review. However, because the Court could not rule that the Mississippi state court engaged correctly in either method, they vacated and remanded this case. The lower court's opinion appeared to create a rule requiring affirming a death sentence "so long as there remains at least one valid aggravating circumstance."[30] An automatic rule affirming the death sentence would be invalid according to previous rulings in *Lockett* and *Eddings*, mandating individualized treatment.[31]

In a per curiam opinion in 1990, *Shell v. Mississippi*, the Court reversed the Mississippi Supreme Court, which had relied on the "especially heinous, atrocious, or cruel" aggravating factor in affirming Shell's death sentence. The Court followed precedent in *Maynard v. Cartwright* and *Godfrey v. Georgia*, ruling that using a limiting instruction is not constitutionally sufficient and remanding this case to be considered in light of the Court's decision in *Clemons*. The trial court judge had defined the three terms "heinous," "atrocious," and "cruel" to the sentencing jury, but the definitions themselves were seen as broad and vague and failed to give any limiting guidance to the sentencing jury.

The issue of weighing factors and the "especially heinous, cruel or depraved" aggravating circumstance" was also at issue in *Lewis v. Jeffers* (1990), an Arizona case. Jimmie Jeffers was convicted of first-degree murder for strangling Penelope Cheney to death after first attempting to kill her with an overdose of heroin. The trial court found two aggravating circumstances and no mitigating evidence at the sentencing hearing and sentenced Jeffers to death, following the Arizona statute. The Arizona Supreme Court vacated and remanded Jeffers' sentence after the court ruled in *Lockett* that nonstatutory mitigating factors must be considered. The trial court reached the same conclusion as before, finding two aggravating factors and no mitigating factors, and again gave Jeffers the death penalty. The Arizona Supreme Court affirmed this sentence after conducting its own analysis and weighing of the sentencing factors.

On habeas review in a federal district court, the federal court rejected Jeffers' allegation that the "especially heinous, cruel or depraved" aggravating circumstance was unconstitutionally broad and vague. However, in 1987, the Ninth Circuit vacated Jeffers' sentence, finding that this standard was unconstitutionally vague as it was applied to him. The Supreme Court reversed the Ninth Circuit, ruling that federal habeas review is limited to applying the "rational factfinder" determination of whether the state court had made an arbitrary or capricious decision, violating due process or the Eighth Amendment. When a state court, as the Arizona Supreme Court did in this case, applies a narrow definition to an aggravating circumstance that may be vague as written, then the constitutional requirement of limiting and guiding sentencing discretion is met.

The Court reversed the Florida Supreme Court the following year in *Parker v. Dugger* (1991). Robert Parker was convicted of the first-degree murders of Richard Padgett and Nancy Sheppard and the third-degree murder of Jody Dalton. At the advisory sentencing hearing, the jury found sufficient aggravating factors to warrant the death penalty for the two first-degree murders but also found that sufficient mitigating factors outweighed the aggravating ones and recommended life in prison to the trial judge. The trial judge overrode the jury's advisory recommendation and gave Parker the death penalty, reasoning that he could find no statutory mitigating factors but could find six aggravating factors. The sentence was affirmed by the Florida Supreme Court, although the state court ruled that there was insufficient evidence to support the "especially heinous, atrocious, and cruel" aggravating circumstance and the circumstance that the murder was committed during a robbery. A federal district court subsequently ruled that there were nonstatutory mitigating factors related to background, character, and the influence of alcohol and drugs, and by failing to consider these, the trial judge violated *Hitchcock v. Dugger* (1987) (see note 11). The Eleventh Circuit reversed and upheld the death sentence, interpreting the trial judge's silence as only indicating that the judge did not see these factors as outweighing aggravating factors. Similarly, the Supreme Court assumed the judge did in fact consider the nonstatutory mitigating factors but did not consider them to outweigh the aggravating circumstances. The evidence for this was in the sentencing order's statement by the judge that the court "has carefully studied and considered *all the evidence and testimony at trial and at advisory sentence proceedings*, the presentence Investigation Report, the applicable Florida Statutes, the case law, and all other factors touching upon this case."[32] However, the Florida Supreme Court erred by characterizing the trial judge's analysis as finding no mitigating factors at all, and there was no evidence that the Florida Supreme Court conducted a harmless error analysis. The Supreme Court reversed the circuit court's decision, remanding and mandating that the district court order the state court to review Parker's sentence in light of all of the evidence presented at the trial and sentencing hearing, reweigh the evidence, or conduct a harmless error analysis as established in *Clemons v. Mississippi.*

Two years after the Court looked at Arizona's death penalty statute in *Lewis v. Jeffers*, it again came under scrutiny in *Richmond v. Lewis* (1992). Richmond was convicted of first-degree murder and robbery and sentenced to death. The trial judge found two statutory aggravating factors, including the "especially heinous, cruel, or depraved manner" of the murder,[33] and no statutory mitigating factors. The Arizona Supreme Court affirmed the death sentence because of the existence of the one other aggravating factor and no statutory mitigating factors, but the sentence was eventually invalidated because the Arizona capital sentencing statute unconstitutionally limited defendants to statutory mitigating factors. Every pending death sentence in Arizona was vacated in 1978. At Richmond's resentencing in 1980, he was again sentenced to death based on three aggravating factors and no mitigating factors outweighing those. Although the Arizona Supreme Court affirmed the sentence again, there was some discrepancy over the "especially heinous, cruel, or depraved" factor, with two concurring justices not being able to find this factor but concluding there was enough evidence of the other two factors to sustain the death penalty.

On habeas review in 1990, the Ninth Circuit affirmed the sentence but issued an amended opinion in 1992 attempting to distinguish *Clemons* from the instant case because Arizona did not have a balancing or weighing statute as did Mississippi: "In *Clemons*, the invalidation of an aggravating circumstance necessarily renders any evidence of mitigation 'weightier' or more substantial in a relative sense; the same, however, cannot be said under the terms of the Arizona statute at issue here."[34] However, in reversing the Ninth Circuit, the Supreme Court looked at the relevant Arizona statute and concluded that Arizona was in fact a balancing state. Giving weight to the vague factor was an Eighth Amendment violation that was not corrected by the Arizona Supreme Court. The court reviewed their Eighth Amendment precedents in this area: under *Maynard v. Cartwright* (1988) and *Godfrey v. Georgia* (1980), if an aggravating factor in a statute does not provide guidance in choosing between the death penalty and a lesser sentence, then it is unconstitutionally vague. Under *Stringer v. Black* (1992) (see note 29) and *Clemons*, if a state is a "weighing" state, then constitutional error occurs when the sentencing judge or jury gives weight to an unconstitutionally vague aggravating factor even if there are other valid aggravating circumstances that are given weight. The error can be cured upon review if the appellate court applies "an adequate narrowing construction."[35]

Jury Instructions: Lesser-Included Offenses, "Briggs" Instructions, Previous Sentences

Several cases post-*Furman* have involved the issue of jury instructions toward lesser-included offenses. In the first of these, *Beck v. Alabama* (1980), a judge refused to give a jury instruction for felony murder, which was a lesser-included offense of the capital crime of robbery-intentional killing. The Alabama death penalty statute actually prohibited the judge from even giving the jury the option of convicting the defendant of the lesser-included offense. Thus, the jury's sole options were either to acquit or convict the defendant of the capital crime. The Supreme Court held that the death penalty could not be administered in these circumstances. The Court noted that giving the jury the third option of the lesser-included offense would ensure that the reasonable doubt standard would be fully applied.

Two years after *Beck*, the Court was again faced with this issue in *Hopper v. Evans* (1982). Hopper was convicted in Alabama of an intentional killing during a robbery and was given the death sentence. Since *Beck* was decided after Hopper's conviction, Hopper claimed he was entitled to a new trial since the jury did not receive instructions on lesser-included offenses in capital cases. The Court disagreed, finding that in Hopper's particular circumstance and considering the evidence, a jury instruction on lesser-included offenses would not have been warranted.[36]

Other cases involving jury instructions include *California v. Ramos* (1983), in which the defendant was sentenced to death after being found guilty of murder during a robbery. The jury was given a "Briggs" instruction, meaning an instruction that the governor may commute a life imprisonment sentence without parole to a sentence including the possibility of parole. The Supreme Court upheld the sentence and noted that the Constitution did not prohibit such instructions.

The Supreme Court reached a different conclusion in *Caldwell v. Mississippi* (1985), which involved comments made by a prosecutor to the jury indicating that a death sentence would be reviewed for correctness by the Supreme Court of Mississippi. The Court vacated the death sentence and held that it "is constitutionally impermissible to rest a death sentence on a determination made by a sentencer who has been led to believe, as the jury was in this case, that the responsibility for determining the appropriateness of the defendant's death rests elsewhere."[37]

In 1994, the Supreme Court addressed a novel question in *Romano v. Oklahoma*. Romano was convicted of murder, and the Oklahoma trial court allowed the prosecution to present information to the sentencing jury that Romano had already received the death penalty for another murder. The jury heard other aggravating and mitigating evidence, as required by Oklahoma's bifurcated capital murder trial process, and returned a sentence of death for the murder in this case. Romano appealed, but the Oklahoma Court of Criminal Appeals affirmed the death sentence. The Supreme Court granted certiorari to answer one question, "'Does admission of evidence that a capital defendant already has been sentenced to death in another case impermissibly undermine the sentencing jury's sense of responsibility for determining the appropriateness of the defendant's death, in violation of the Eighth and Fourteenth Amendments?'"[38] The Court affirmed the lower court's decision, finding no constitutional violations and writing that even though the evidence pertaining to the first murder and sentence was later deemed irrelevant because the prior sentence was overturned on appeal, it was accurate at the time the jury was deliberating. The Court cited precedent in *Lockett* and *Woodson*, noting that other aggravating factors outweighed mitigating ones and reasoned that instructions to the jury never implied that the jury's responsibility was any less in this case due to the previous sentence.[39]

Jury Instructions: Verdict Forms, Unanimity, Mitigating Factors

Challenges concerning jury instructions regarding verdict forms and unanimity have come before the Court in several cases. In *Mills v. Maryland* (1988), the Court held that jury instructions and verdict forms that lead reasonable jurors to believe that unanimity is required in finding mitigating factors is unconstitutional. Ralph Mills, a Maryland Correctional Institution inmate, was convicted of the first-degree murder of his cellmate and given the death penalty. During the sentencing hearing, the jury found one aggravating factor but could not unanimously agree on any mitigating factors offered by the defense. The Maryland capital punishment statute was alleged by Mills to be unconstitutionally mandatory as it was explained to the jury by the trial court judge and according to the verdict form instructions. The statute did not clearly specify what should happen if unanimity was not achieved in finding mitigating and aggravating circumstances, and it was possible that a jury could think that if they were unanimous in finding one or more aggravating factors but could not agree unanimously on any mitigating factors, then a sentence of death was required. The Court reversed the death sentence and remanded the case for resentencing, finding merit in the hypothetical situation created by Maryland's statute as presented by Mills' counsel: "'If eleven jurors agree that there are six mitigating circumstances, the result is that no mitigating circumstance is found. Consequently, there is nothing to weigh against any aggravating circumstance found, and the judgment is death, even though eleven jurors think the death penalty wholly inappropriate.'"[40] The Court emphasized that "[e]volving standards of societal decency have imposed a correspondingly high requirement of reliability on the determination that death is the appropriate penalty in a particular case."[41]

Two years later, the Court would visit a similar issue in *McKoy v. North Carolina* (1990), ruling that the unanimity requirement in North Carolina's death penalty statute violated the Eighth Amendment because it prevented juries from considering all mitigating evidence. Dock McKoy, Jr., was convicted of the first-degree murder of a deputy sheriff. Under North Carolina capital sentencing procedures, jurors were instructed by the trial court judge to answer both in writing and orally four questions. The first question asked whether there was evidence beyond a reasonable doubt of enumerated aggravating circumstances. After finding two aggravating circumstances, they were presented with the next question regarding the existence of one or more of eight mitigating factors by a preponderance of the evidence. The jury was instructed to have the jury foreman write "no" on the verdict form in the space beside each circumstance if there was not a unanimous finding of that circumstance. The instructions also required a "yes" if there was unanimity of the finding. The jury was unanimous with respect to two mitigating circumstances but was not unanimous in finding the six other circumstances. The third question asked whether there was a unanimous finding beyond reasonable doubt that mitigating circumstances or "circumstances found by you"[42] did not outweigh aggravating circumstances. The jury answered yes and moved to the last question which asked, "'Do you unanimously find beyond a reasonable doubt that the aggravating circumstance or circumstances found by you is, or are, sufficiently substantial to call for the imposition of the death penalty when considered with the mitigating circumstance or circumstances *found by you?*'"[43] The jury answered yes and recommended the death penalty. While this case was on direct appeal to the state supreme court, the U.S. Supreme Court ruled in *Mills* that death sentences cannot stand if they were arrived at by jury instructions and verdict forms that may have caused reasonable jurors to believe mitigating factors could not be considered unless they were found to exist by all 12 jurors. The Court noted that the unanimity requirement in North

Carolina's statute violated the Eighth Amendment because it prevented juries from considering all mitigating evidence. Further, requiring unanimity on mitigating factors is not constitutional merely because the State also requires unanimity on aggravating circumstances.

In a per curiam decision, *Delo v. Lashley* (1993), the Court examined mitigating factors and jury instructions, looking again at the 1978 case of *Lockett v. Ohio*, discussed in an earlier section. Lashley was convicted and sentenced to death by a Missouri jury for the beating and stabbing death in the course of a robbery of Janie Tracy. The defense requested that the sentencing jury be instructed that Lashley had no significant prior criminal history as a mitigating factor, but no evidence was offered by either the defense or prosecutor to support this, and the trial judge refused to give this instruction without evidence. Lashley appealed, claiming a due process violation, and the Eighth Circuit granted relief, relying on *Lockett* that the State is required to provide evidence or else the court has to instruct the jury of the mitigating factor. The Supreme Court reversed the Eighth Circuit, taking the opportunity to clarify *Lockett* and noting that the circuit court had misread *Lockett*. The Court unequivocally stated that *Lockett* and its progeny established that there is no Constitutional obligation for "state courts to give mitigating circumstance instructions when no evidence is offered to support them" nor is there a requirement that states have to produce the "evidence of the defendant's own criminal history."[44]

Texas' special instructions and allowance for mitigating factors was at issue the same year as the previous case. In *Johnson v. Texas* (1993), Johnson was convicted of capital murder during a store robbery. The jury sentenced Johnson to death after finding three special issues and being instructed that it could consider all aggravating and mitigating factors presented during the trial and the sentencing phase. Johnson claimed that two of the special issues did not allow the jury to consider fully the mitigating factors such as his youth. The Court affirmed the Texas Court of Criminal Appeals, ruling that the Texas procedures were constitutional and did allow adequate consideration of mitigating factors such as youth. The Court noted that four previous opinions since 1976 had addressed this particular statute, including *Jurek*, *Franklin v. Lynaugh* (1988, see note 12) and *Penry v. Lynaugh* (1989), discussed in a later section of this chapter. In *Jurek*, the Court held that the special issues provision was constitutional but later held in *Penry* that the jury instructions were too limited for full consideration of Penry's mental retardation and childhood abuse as mitigating factors and that a specific instruction to that effect was required. Unlike *Penry*, Johnson's mitigating factor was his youth, and the Court ruled that the special issue related to assessing future dangerousness allowed for consideration of youth.

Mandatory Nature of Jury Instructions

Whether instructions are mandatory has also reached the Supreme Court. In *Boyde v. California* (1990), the Court upheld California's statute. Boyde was convicted of the robbery, kidnapping, and murder of Dickie Gibson, shooting him in the back of the head and in his forehead. The jury found that Boyde committed the murder with "express malice aforethought and premeditation and deliberation."[45] At the sentencing phase, the instructions directed that the jury "shall impose" a sentence either of death or of life imprisonment depending on whether aggravating factors outweighed mitigating ones. Another instruction included the catchall category factor (k) allowing the jury to consider "any other circumstance which extenuates the gravity of the crime even though it is not a legal excuse for the crime."[46] Boyde claimed an Eighth Amendment violation with the instructions being impermissibly mandatory and preventing the jury from conducting an "individualized assessment of the appropriateness of the death penalty."[47] However, the Majority ruled that the two jury instructions were not unconstitutional, referring to the Court's decision in *Blystone* and the similar mandatory language upheld in the Pennsylvania statute. The California jury had freedom to consider mitigating factors, and there was no requirement, as Boyde maintained, to give a jury "freedom to decline to impose the death penalty even if the jury decides that the aggravating circumstances 'outweigh' the mitigating circumstances."[48]

Boyde also maintained that the California statute did not allow for consideration of non-crime-related potential mitigating factors regarding his character and background. The language in factor (k) related to other crime-related factors, and other factors specified were either on immediate circumstances of the crime or prior criminal history. However, the defense presented four days of testimony regarding Boyde's deprived childhood, school experiences, redeeming qualities, and other background and character factors, and the Court failed to believe that reasonable jurors would have thought that they could not consider any of this as mitigating evidence. The Court agreed that the jury instruction was unclear, but the jurors were also instructed to consider "*all of the evidence* which has been received during any part of the trial of this case."[49]

The first challenge to reach the Supreme Court that involved the Federal Death Penalty Act of 1994 concerned jury instructions, unanimity, deadlock, and vagueness in *Jones v. United States* (1999). Jones was convicted of the charge of kidnapping with death resulting to the victim. For the sentencing jury to find Jones to be death eligible, the prosecution had to prove at least one of 16 aggravating factors. The jury found two factors, as well as two additional nonstatutory factors, and, after weighing both aggravating and mitigating factors, sentenced Jones to death. The sentence was affirmed by the Fifth Circuit, and the Supreme Court granted certiorari to address three issues: "whether petitioner was entitled to an instruction as to the effect of jury deadlock; whether there is a reasonable likelihood that the jury was led to believe that petitioner would receive a court-imposed sentence less than life imprisonment in the event that they could not reach a unanimous sentence recommendation; and whether the submission to the jury of two allegedly duplicative, vague, and overbroad nonstatutory aggravating factors was harmless error."[50] The Court ruled that an instruction regarding deadlock is not required in every capital case, nor was there any proof that the jurors failed to apply instructions correctly or were confused about the consequences of a jury deadlock. With respect to the two non-statutory aggravating factors, the circuit court found them to be duplicative and vague. The Supreme Court disagreed but acknowledged that the nonstatutory aggravating factors may have been "loosely drafted,"[51] but any potential error was harmless.[52]

Juror confusion with whether or not instructions were mandatory was also at issue with respect to Virginia's capital sentencing statute in *Weeks v. Angelone* (2000). Weeks shot and killed a state trooper after the trooper pulled him and his uncle over for speeding. Weeks was the passenger in a car he had stolen during a burglary some weeks before. Weeks was convicted of capital murder. At the penalty hearing, the prosecutor alleged two aggravating factors, and the defense presented mitigating factors from ten witnesses. During sentencing deliberations, the jury asked the judge if a life sentence included "the possibility of parole and if so, under what conditions."[53] The judge instructed the jury to deliver the punishment that they felt was just and not to be concerned "with what may happen afterwards."[54] The jury later asked if they were required by law to return a death penalty sentence if they found one of the aggravating factors was present or did they have the option of deciding between the death penalty or life imprisonment, even given the existence of one of the factors. The judge responded by referring the jury to the written instructions, even though the defense asked the judge to explicitly explain that the jury could return a life imprisonment penalty or life imprisonment and a fine even if they found one or both of the aggravating factors to be proved beyond a reasonable doubt. The jury returned with a death penalty sentence. Part of Weeks' appeal concerned the judge's instructions as not adequately directing the jurors to also consider the mitigating evidence. The state supreme court held his claims on appeal were meritless and affirmed his conviction and sentence. The Supreme Court granted certiorari and affirmed the Fourth Circuit's holding.

The Court noted that the jury had been "adequately instructed," stating that "given that the trial judge responded to the jury's question by directing its attention to the precise paragraph of the constitutionally adequate instruction that answers its inquiry, the question becomes whether the Constitution requires anything more. We hold that it does not."[55] The Court referred to "several empirical factors"[56] supporting the presumption that the jury followed the jury instructions. These factors included the time spent in deliberation, including two hours after receiving the last instruction from the judge, and the fact that each juror affirmed in court that he or she had considered the mitigating evidence. Another "empirical factor" was the defense's closing statements noted that both of the aggravating factors could be found proved beyond a reasonable doubt and the jury could still return a life sentence.[57]

Jury Instructions and Standards of Proof for Mitigating Factors

Kansas jury instructions were considered recently in consolidated cases (*Kansas v. (Jonathan) Carr, Kansas v. (Reginald) Carr*, and *Kansas v. Gleason* (2016). Gleason was convicted of two counts of capital murder, one count of first-degree premeditated murder, aggravated kidnapping, aggravated robbery, and criminal possession of a firearm. The jury found four aggravating circumstances proved beyond a reasonable doubt and delivered a unanimous death sentence. The two Carr brothers were sentenced to death for what came to be known as the "Wichita Massacre," a horrific crime spree spanning December 7 through December 14, 2000.[58] The brothers were sentenced together, and the jury, after hearing two days of testimony from a sole survivor, found four aggravating circumstances beyond a reasonable doubt. The jury issued four death penalty verdicts against each brother separately after hearing mitigating evidence and finding that aggravating evidence outweighed mitigating evidence.

The Kansas Supreme Court vacated the death sentences in these cases because the juries were not informed that mitigating circumstances did not need to be proved beyond a reasonable doubt, thus violating the Eighth Amendment. All that is necessary is for mitigating circumstances to be proved to the satisfaction of each juror in a capital sentencing case. By not receiving that instruction, the lower court reasoned that jurors might not have considered some mitigating evidence because it had not been proven beyond a reasonable doubt. The state court also held that the Carr brothers had an Eighth Amendment right to individualized capital sentencing, which the trial court violated by holding a joint trial and sentencing.[59] While the jury was instructed to consider each brother separately, the Kansas Supreme Court deemed any assumption that it did so as illogical and that it was impossible to determine if either brother was entitled to mercy.

The U.S. Supreme Court reversed the Kansas Supreme Court and remanded these cases, holding that the Eighth Amendment does not require capital-sentencing courts to instruct juries that mitigating circumstances need not be proved beyond a reasonable doubt. The Court reasoned that it is probably impossible to even require applying a standard of proof to determining mitigating circumstances. One mitigating circumstance is "mercy," which the Court noted is not a fact that can be determined. Aggravating circumstances are factual elements that can be proven beyond a reasonable doubt, but "mitigation . . . is largely a judgment call."[60]

Further, joint capital sentencing proceedings do not violate the Eighth Amendment. Rather than an Eighth Amendment violation, the Majority stated that according to *Romano v. Oklahoma* (1994), the test for a constitutional violation due to "evidence improperly admitted at a capital-sentencing proceeding is whether the evidence 'so infected the sentencing proceeding with unfairness as to render the jury's imposition of the death penalty a denial of due process.'"[61] The jury received several different explicit instructions to consider each defendant separately in sentencing. The Court also observed that joint proceedings may be preferable when there is a single chain of events joining the defendants.[62]

Juror Exclusion

Several cases have involved the validity of excluding a juror and whether that action comported with *Witherspoon v. Illinois* (1968), which held that a state cannot execute an individual if he/she was convicted by a jury that was culled of those who revealed that they had conscientious scruples against or were otherwise opposed to capital punishment. In *Davis v. Georgia* (1976), a juror was excused for cause for "expressing scruples against the death penalty."[63] Unlike *Witherspoon*, while there was only one juror dismissed for cause in *Davis*, the Court deemed it sufficient, and still overturned the sentence. In *Adams v. Texas* (1980), the judge, pursuant to Texas statute, excluded several jurors who were "unwilling or unable to take an oath that the mandatory penalty of death or life imprisonment would 'not affect [their deliberations on any issue of fact.'"[64] The Supreme Court held that the statute contravened the Sixth and Fourteenth Amendments as construed and applied in *Witherspoon*.

Issues that involved jury exclusion appeared to be resolved by several cases during the 1980s.[65] However, some conflict among courts remained, and in 1992, the Supreme Court reversed the Illinois Supreme Court, ruling that during *voir dire* in a capital murder case, the defense counsel must be allowed to question potential jurors in depth about their views on the death penalty and their willingness to consider mitigating circumstances. In *Morgan v. Illinois* (1992), potential jurors were asked, "Would you automatically vote against the death penalty no matter what the facts of the case were?"[66] After several jurors had been questioned in this way, Morgan's counsel requested that the trial judge, who was conducting the *voir dire* according to state procedures, ask, "If you found Derrick Morgan guilty, would you automatically vote to impose the death penalty, no matter what the facts are?" The trial court responded that the way the question was being asked followed *Witherspoon v. Illinois* (1968) and was basically the same question as requested by defense counsel. The defense's requested statement was referred to as a "reverse-*Witherspoon* inquiry." The Supreme Court granted certiorari due to lower courts' conflicting rulings, with some, like Illinois in this case, stating that a "'reverse-Witherspoon' inquiry is unnecessary" when jurors have already sworn that they can be fair, impartial, and can follow the law.[67] The Court agreed that the trial judge should have allowed the defense's requested inquiry, noting the refusal to do so was a violation of due process.

In a more recent death penalty case, *Foster v. Chatman* (2016), the Supreme Court agreed with the petitioner, Timothy Foster, that the two Georgia prosecutors in his malice murder and burglary trial unconstitutionally culled the prospective jury of all African American potential jurors. The Court reversed the state habeas court and the Georgia Supreme Court, referring to evidence obtained through the Georgia Open Records Act such as the jury venire list showing that prosecutors focused on the race of black prospective jurors. Other written notes and evidence that reasons for striking prospective black jurors applied equally to jurors who were allowed to serve led the Supreme Court to rule that this was intentional discrimination and a violation of the Equal Protection Clause. This ruling followed two similar decisions in death penalty cases also within the past 12 years or so, a Texas case reversing the Fifth Circuit (*Miller-El v. Dretke*, 2005) and one reversing the Louisiana Supreme Court (*Snyder v. Louisiana*, 2008).[68]

Victims' Personal Characteristics and Victim Impact Statements

Another issue before the Court in death penalty litigation has focused on victim impact statements (VIS) and prosecutors' comments regarding victims. In *Booth v. Maryland* (1987), a jury sentenced the defendant to death after reviewing a presentence report. Pursuant to Maryland statute, the report included a VIS based on interviews with family and victims, providing information regarding the severe emotional impact of the crimes on the family and the family members' characterizations of the crimes and of the defendant. The trial court denied the defendant's motion to suppress the VIS, who claimed that the information was irrelevant and inflammatory. The Supreme Court reversed the sentence, holding that the Eighth Amendment was violated with the introduction of the VIS and that the Maryland statute was invalid to the extent that it required the inclusion of the VIS in the presentence report.

In *South Carolina v. Gathers* (1989), the prosecutor's closing argument during the sentencing phase included references to religious readings that the victim was carrying, as well as comments regarding personal qualities of the victim based on possession of such religious materials. The defendant received the death penalty, but the South Carolina Supreme Court reversed the sentence, and the U.S. Supreme Court affirmed, noting that punishment must be tailored specifically to the defendant's personal responsibility and guilt. The Court noted that

> the prosecutor's comments concerned the victim's personal characteristics, and [a]llowing the jury to rely on [this information] . . . could result in imposing the death sentence because of factors about which the defendant was unaware, and that were irrelevant to the decision to kill.[69]

Surprisingly, just two years after *Gathers*, *Payne v. Tennessee* (1991) overruled both of these decisions. Pervis Payne was convicted on two counts of first-degree murder and one count of assault with intent to commit murder in the first-degree. On appeal to the Tennessee Supreme Court, Payne argued that the emotional testimony of the adult victim's mother during the sentencing hearing and the prosecutor's closing statements were prejudicial under the Eighth Amendment, according to *Booth* and *Gathers*. The state court did not see the testimony as creating an unconstitutional risk of rendering the death sentence arbitrary and deemed her testimony harmless beyond a reasonable doubt. Further, the prosecutor's closing comments were relevant as they pertained to Payne's blameworthiness. The Supreme Court affirmed the Tennessee court. In overruling *Booth's* prohibition against considering victim impact statements at the sentencing phase of a death penalty case and *Gather's* extension to statements made by the prosecutor regarding a victim's characteristics, the Court stated that victim impact evidence shows each victim's "uniqueness as an individual human being."[70] The Majority emphasized the rights of states to structure procedures and remedies in death penalty cases and referred to victim impact evidence as another way of "informing the sentencing authority about the specific harm caused by the crime in question,"[71] better enabling the sentencing body to "assess meaningfully the defendant's moral culpability and blameworthiness."[72] However, one dissent characterized the decision as "a dramatic departure from the principles that have governed our capital sentencing jurisprudence for decades."[73]

Bifurcated Procedures, Vagueness, and Aggravating Factors as Elements of the Crime

A significant issue over the past 40 years has concerned bifurcated sentencing procedures authorizing the imposition of the death penalty in various states. Cases from Florida, Arizona, and Alabama have illuminated the constitutional complexities involved and the Supreme Court has undergone some shifting in opinion. This section reviews these cases in some detail.

Florida state law post-*Furman* required a separate sentencing procedure where a jury makes an advisory recommendation, but the court makes the final decision if it finds at least one aggravating factor and with the requirement that it must make written findings if its sentence was death. In *Gardner v. Florida* (1977), the jury returned a life imprisonment sentence after concluding that mitigating circumstances outweighed aggravating ones. However, the judge imposed the death penalty instead after viewing a presentencing report that he had ordered, of which portions were undisclosed to the attorneys. The Court held that Gardner was denied due process, as he did not have the ability to deny or explain the information contained in the presentencing report. Further clarifying the role of judge and jury in *Hildwin v. Florida* (1989, per curiam), Hildwin challenged the judge's agreement with the jury's unanimous decision recommending death, with the judge finding four aggravating circumstances. Hildwin challenged the sentence since the jury did not reach a specific finding regarding the aggravating factors, but the Court concluded that the Sixth Amendment did not require that the jury make such findings. The judge was free to make the findings, especially after a unanimous jury decision.

The Court addressed similar sentencing procedures in Arizona in *Walton v. Arizona* (1990), ruling that sentencing by judges and not juries was constitutional and Arizona's "especially heinous, cruel, or depraved" aggravating factor was not unconstitutionally vague. Walton was convicted of first-degree murder after robbing the victim and stealing his car before shooting him in the head. In the separate sentencing hearing where the prosecutor presented aggravating circumstances and the defense presented mitigating factors, the trial court judge followed Arizona's sentencing statute at the time and gave Walton the death penalty, finding two aggravating factors and no mitigating factors substantial enough to warrant mercy.[74]

Walton made four challenges already discussed in previous cases in this chapter. First, Walton alleged that Arizona's sentencing statute violated the Sixth Amendment because findings of fact regarding aggravating and mitigating factors rested with a judge and not a jury. The Court rejected this argument, referring back to *Clemons, Hildwin, Spaziano v. Florida* (1984) (see note 34), and *Proffitt*. The Court maintained that nothing in the Sixth Amendment requires that only a jury can make specific findings authorizing capital punishment. Rejecting the argument that aggravating circumstances are elements of the crime to be proved in front of a jury, the Court relied on precedent defining aggravating factors as "'standards to guide the making of [the] choice' between the alternative verdicts of death and life imprisonment."[75]

Walton also alleged constitutional violations in putting on defendants the burden of proving by a preponderance of the evidence substantial mitigating factors that call for leniency. Walton argued that the Court should have to consider all mitigating factors alleged by defendants unless the state could prove the negation of such mitigating factors by a preponderance of the evidence. The Court rejected this argument, referring back to two previous cases.[76]

Walton claimed that the use of "shall" language in Arizona's statute (the court "shall" impose the death penalty if one or more aggravating circumstances are found and mitigating circumstances are held insufficient to call for leniency) created the "presumption that death is the proper sentence."[77] The Court's recent decisions in *Blystone* and *Boyde* removed this challenge. For example, in *Blystone*, the Court observed that individualized sentencing is accomplished when jurors are allowed to consider all relevant mitigating factors. Further, the statutes at issue, such as Arizona's, were not "impermissibly mandatory," as the Court had decided in *Woodson* and *Roberts*, two of the four other cases decided on the same day as *Gregg v. Georgia*.

Walton's final claim referred to the aggravating factor that the murder was "especially heinous, cruel or depraved."[78] In 1980, the Court invalidated the "outrageously or wantonly vile, horrible or inhuman" aggravating factor in Georgia's statute (*Godfrey v. Georgia*), and in 1988, invalidated the "especially heinous, atrocious, or cruel aggravating circumstance" in Oklahoma's statute (*Maynard v. Cartwright*). However, these cases differed from *Walton* in that both involved jury instructions characterized as unconstitutionally vague, and the juries were not given any limiting definitions. Trial judges, as in Arizona, "are presumed to know the law."[79] In *Maynard*, the Court approved defining the "heinous, atrocious, or cruel" aggravating factor as murders involving torture or physical abuse, similar to the definition applied on appeal by the Arizona state court. The definition also was similar to Florida's "heinous, atrocious, or cruel" factor, approved by the Court in *Proffitt* and judged as giving sufficient guidance.

Writing the Majority opinion, Justice Scalia took the opportunity to write that over the past 15 years, the Court had applied two lines of (incompatible) reasoning in Eighth Amendment death penalty cases and that he would no longer support the second of those two lines. The first line, derived from *Furman*, is the rule that "a sentencer's discretion to return a death sentence must be constrained by specific standards, so that the death penalty is not inflicted in a random and capricious fashion."[80] The second line, now rejected by Justice Scalia, stemmed from *Woodson* and *Lockett* and mandated that the sentencer not be barred from considering any mitigating factor, thus running contrary to *Furman* and violating the Eighth Amendment.

Two years later, Florida's structure was again before the Court. *Sochor v. Florida* (1992) pertained to jury instructions and the "heinousness factor" but also took a close look yet again at weighing aggravating and mitigating factors in Florida's bifurcated structure. Sochor was convicted of first-degree murder and kidnapping. At the sentencing stage, the jury found four of a number of statutory aggravating circumstances for a death penalty recommendation, and the trial court accepted that recommendation. The sentence was upheld by the state supreme court on automatic review, in part finding no unconstitutional vagueness in the judge's jury instructions regarding the "heinousness factor."[81] The state supreme court did agree that another aggravating factor, the "coldness factor," showing that the crime was committed in a premeditated, calculated way, was not supported by the evidence but nonetheless found the sentence to fit the crime. The Supreme Court granted certiorari to address two of four questions raised by Sochor on appeal: whether or not the Eighth and Fourteenth Amendments are violated by the Florida statute's "heinousness factor" and by the state supreme court's failure to reweigh the death penalty sentence that Sochor received, absent the invalid aggravating "coldness factor." The Supreme Court vacated and remanded this case, upholding the heinousness factor but finding an Eighth Amendment violation with respect to the trial court judge's application of the "coldness factor." Once the coldness factor was invalidated by the state supreme court, that court would have been required to remedy the constitutional violation by conducting a harmless error analysis, which it failed to do.[82] Several concurring and dissenting opinions were written in this case, illustrating conflicting opinions regarding bifurcated procedures and judges as sentencers.[83]

Shortly after deciding *Sochor*, a per curiam opinion, *Espinosa v. Florida* (1992), reversed the Florida Supreme Court. Espinosa, convicted of first-degree murder, appealed his death sentence, arguing vagueness in the "wicked, evil, atrocious or cruel" jury instruction. The Florida Supreme Court disagreed and affirmed his sentence, maintaining that the jury recommends the sentence only and the trial judge conducts an independent analysis. However, the Supreme Court pointed to Florida's case law indicating that trial judges are required to "give 'great weight' to the jury's recommendation."[84] The instruction was impermissibly vague and presuming that the jury based its recommendation on that vague instruction invalidated their recommendation, so also presuming that the judge gave signification consideration to the jury's recommendation created the potential for unconstitutional arbitrariness, not unlike "direct weighing of an invalid aggravating factor,"[85] as was found in *Baldwin v. Alabama* (1985, see note 4). The Court continued to acknowledge that states can choose their procedures for delivering capital sentences and refrained from directly criticizing Florida's procedure but emphasized that "if a weighing State decides to place capital sentencing authority in two actors rather than one, neither actor must be permitted to weigh invalid aggravating circumstances."[86]

Three years later, the Court ruled in *Harris v. Alabama* (1995) that Alabama trial judges are required to only consider an advisory jury recommendation, as per Alabama's capital sentencing statute. Harris was convicted of capital murder of her husband. She planned the murder in order to gain his death benefits, sought assistance from her lover, and paid the persons who carried out the killing. Even though the trial jury recommended a life sentence for Harris, the trial judge, as allowed by Alabama law, sentenced her to death after finding that one statutory aggravating factor, committing murder for financial gain, outweighed all mitigating factors. Both the Alabama Court of Criminal Appeals and the state supreme court affirmed the sentence. The U.S. Supreme Court granted certiorari to address Harris' argument that the trial judge must give "great weight"[87] to the jury's recommendation. The Court agreed with the lower courts, holding that "the Eighth Amendment does not require the State to define the weight the sentencing judge must accord an advisory jury verdict."[88]

The Majority referred to statistics[89] showing that there had been 47 cases in Alabama where the judge imposed the death penalty when the jury had recommended life and only five cases where the judge rejected the jury's recommendation of the death penalty. What would make the picture of capital punishment in Alabama more complete, according to the Majority, would be knowing how many times a judge would have ruled differently if he or she had "not been required to consider the jury's advice"[90] in those cases where the judge did accept the jury's recommendation of life in prison. Determining whether or not Alabama's process is constitutional cannot be shown only by a "numerical tabulation of actual death sentences as compared to a hypothetical alternative."[91]

In 2002, the Court again returned to Arizona's statute in *Ring v. Arizona* but this time overruling itself and finding that Arizona's death penalty statute violated the Sixth Amendment to the extent that it allowed a judge rather than a jury to find the existence of an aggravating factor necessary for delivering a sentence of death. The Court overruled *Walton* in part, upholding *Apprendi v. New Jersey* (2000). Recall that the *Walton* Court decided that aggravating factors were "sentencing considerations" and not elements of the crime. However, the *Apprendi* Court appeared to reverse this perspective in holding in a noncapital case that additional facts not before a jury that enhance the maximum penalty violate the Sixth Amendment.

In the instant case, Ring was convicted of armed robbery and shooting to death a Wells Fargo armored van driver. The jury deadlocked on a premeditated murder charge but agreed on a felony murder conviction. Under Arizona's statute at the time, felony murder did not carry the death penalty unless the judge at sentencing found at least one statutory aggravating factor and no mitigating factor substantial enough to warrant a lesser sentence. At the sentencing hearing, the judge accepted testimony from an accomplice that Ring was the shooter as well as the leader of the planned robbery. Finding further that the shooting was committed in a heinous manner and the only mitigating factor was the absence of a serious criminal history, the judge sentenced Ring to death. Ring appealed, alleging a Sixth Amendment right to jury trial violation because the judge relied on his own fact-finding at sentencing in order to impose the death penalty. These were not facts submitted to the jury and proved beyond a reasonable doubt.

The Arizona Supreme Court observed that the *Apprendi* Court had actually maintained that *Walton* was still good law. The *Apprendi* Majority presented Arizona's capital sentencing scheme as carrying a maximum sentence of death for a first-degree murder conviction and thus not at odds with their ruling. Therefore, the Arizona Supreme Court ruled that under *Walton*, Arizona's procedures were constitutional. The state court agreed with one aggravating factor (murder for monetary gain) and agreed that the mitigating factor was not substantial enough to warrant leniency, upholding Ring's sentence.

The Arizona Supreme Court also described the capital sentencing scheme as it actually worked in Arizona and acknowledged Justice O'Connor's dissent in *Apprendi* as correctly presenting that statute. "A defendant convicted of first-degree murder in Arizona cannot receive a death sentence unless a judge makes the factual determination that a statutory aggravating factor exists. Without that critical finding, the maximum sentence to which the defendant is exposed is life imprisonment, and not the death penalty."[92] The Supreme Court granted certiorari in order to address the conflict between *Walton* and *Apprendi*, ruling that *Walton* could no longer be reconciled with *Apprendi* and deciding that a jury and not a sole sentencing judge must find Arizona's statutory aggravating factors necessary for the imposition of the death penalty.

Most recently, in 2016, the Supreme Court applied its decision in *Ring* to Florida's capital sentencing procedures in *Hurst v. Florida*. As noted before, under Florida's statute, an offender convicted of capital murder may be sentenced to death only through an additional sentencing hearing; otherwise, the maximum sentence is life in prison. Florida's hybrid proceedings required the sentencing judge to conduct an evidentiary hearing before a jury, followed by the jury rendering an "advisory sentence" without specifying the facts underlying its recommendation. The judge, weighing aggravating and mitigating circumstances, entered an independent sentence. Hurst was convicted of the first-degree murder, the jury recommended the death penalty, and the judge sentenced him to death. On appeal for other issues, a new sentencing hearing was granted with the same results. At the resentencing hearing, jury instructions included an explanation that aggravating circumstances constituted the murder being "especially 'heinous, atrocious, or cruel,'" or occurring during the commission of a robbery. If at least one circumstance was found beyond a reasonable doubt, the jury could recommend the death penalty, which it did. The sentencing judge independently found that the murder was heinous and committed during a robbery and delivered the sentence of death, noting that she was giving "'great weight' to her findings as well as to the jury's recommendation."[93]

Hurst appealed, arguing that the Sixth Amendment requires a judge, rather than a jury, to engage in the fact-finding process of weighing aggravating and mitigating circumstances and delivering the final sentence. Hurst claimed Florida's process violated the Court's ruling in *Ring*, but on appeal, the Florida Supreme Court affirmed this sentence, disagreeing with Hurst.

The Florida Supreme Court held that *Ring* did not apply to the instant case because the Supreme Court had upheld Florida's death penalty sentencing structure in two cases decided prior to *Ring*: *Hildwin* and *Spaziano*. The court expressly noted in *Hildwin* that the Sixth Amendment "does not require that the specific findings authorizing the imposition of the sentence of death be made by the jury."[94]

However, in January of 2016, the U.S. Supreme Court agreed with Hurst, reversing the state court and holding Florida's capital sentencing procedures unconstitutional under the Sixth Amendment as considered in *Ring*, based on *Apprendi*, where the Court held that facts increasing sanctions not authorized by a jury's guilty verdict must be submitted to juries as "elements" of the offense. Overruling *Hildwin* and *Spaziano* in relevant part, the Majority opinion clearly stated, "The Sixth Amendment requires a jury, not a judge, to find each fact necessary to impose a sentence of death. A jury's mere recommendation is not enough."[95]

Florida differed from Arizona's proceedings at the time of the *Ring* decision because it required an advisory jury verdict, but the Court noted this difference was immaterial. Jury advisory sentences were not binding on the sentencing judge, and juries were not required to make critical findings regarding aggravating or mitigating circumstances. Florida also pointed to the fact that the jury had found the existence of an aggravating circumstance when rendering its advisory sentence, but the Court still focused on the statutory requirement that the *trial court* independently find aggravating circumstances not outweighed by mitigating circumstances.

The Majority referred to "[t]ime and subsequent cases" as "wash[ing] away the logic of *Spaziano* and *Hildwin*."[96] In remanding the case, the Majority also noted that it would be left to lower courts to consider whether the trial judge's fact finding alone was harmless error.

Method of Execution

In a per curiam decision in 1992, the Court vacated a stay of execution of Robert Harris (*Gomez and Vasquez v. U.S. District Court for the Northern District of California*), who was contending that execution by lethal cyanide gas violated the Eighth Amendment's cruel and unusual punishment clause. Harris had failed to raise this claim in any of his four prior habeas petitions, and this was seen as another of Harris' "last-minute attempts to manipulate the judicial process,"[97] thus affecting the fairness of granting any relief on its merits.

In *Baze v. Rees* (2008) two inmates on death row alleged a substantial risk that Kentucky's three-drug injection protocol, particularly the sodium thiopental, would be improperly administered and likely to cause severe pain. The inmates also charged that Kentucky's refusal to adopt their alternative protocol was cruel and unusual punishment. The Supreme Court disagreed, affirming the Kentucky Supreme Court's ruling that the protocol did not create a "substantial risk of wanton and unnecessary infliction of pain, torture, or lingering death."[98] The Court noted that an Eighth Amendment violation on the part of a state refusing to adopt alternative procedures occurs only when "the alternative procedure is feasible, readily implemented, and in fact significantly reduces a substantial risk of severe pain."[99]

In 2015, the Court looked again at methods of execution. In *Glossip et al. v. Gross et al.*, the Court addressed whether Oklahoma's use of 500 milligrams of midazolam as the first drug in a three-drug protocol violated the Eighth Amendment.[100] Oklahoma had used the drug twice before in 2014 and 2015.[101] Per the protocol at the time, Oklahoma used 100 mg. of midazolam in the 2014 execution of Clayton Lockett, resulting in some serious effects.[102] A new protocol was developed which included 500 milligrams of midazolam and a number of safeguards including verification of the viability of the IV site.

After Lockett's execution, 21 death row inmates in Oklahoma filed a §1983 suit, alleging that the three-drug protocol was an Eighth Amendment violation and alleging that midazolam does not sufficiently sedate the person, thus causing severe risk of pain. Four of those plaintiffs moved for a preliminary injunction. The District Court denied the motion after hearing from a number of expert witnesses, basing their decision on the plaintiffs' failure to present an alternative method that would entail less risk of pain and finding that the plaintiffs also could not prove that the risk of the current (revised) protocol was "'sure or very likely to cause serious illness and needless suffering,' amounting to 'an objectively intolerable risk of harm.'"[103] The Tenth Circuit affirmed, also holding that the District Court's reliance on one expert witness testimony that was alleged to be erroneous did not make his testimony unreliable or render clear error in the District Court's decision.

Affirming the Tenth Circuit, the Court reasoned that the inmates did not offer an alternative, required by *Baze* in all Eighth Amendment claims challenging methods of execution. The Majority observed that while capital punishment is constitutional, the "Constitution does not require the avoidance of all risk of pain."[104] *Baze*, as the controlling opinion, established that a successful challenge must show that the method entails the "substantial risk of serious harm," or "needless suffering," or "severe pain." Challengers must also identify an alternative that is "feasible, readily implemented, and in fact significantly reduce[s] a substantial risk of severe pain."[105]

The Death Penalty and Characteristics of Offenders: Insanity, Race, Age, and Intellectual Disability

Insanity

The Supreme Court first addressed insanity and the death penalty in *Ford v. Wainwright* (1986). Ford was sentenced to death for first-degree murder and showed no signs of mental deficiencies during the murder, trial, and sentencing. While he was awaiting execution, signs of insanity began to appear. The court held that inflicting the death penalty upon an insane prisoner violates the Eighth Amendment as cruel and unusual punishment.

Race

One year later, the court heard *McCleskey v. Kemp* (1987), a case alleging that the imposition of the death penalty was administered in a racially discriminatory manner. Warren McCleskey, an African American male, was convicted for an armed robbery and killing of a white police officer. Following his conviction and death sentence, McCleskey filed an appeal in which he included a statistical study (the Baldus study)[106] showing that "black defendants who killed white victims have the greatest likelihood of receiving the death penalty."[107] The Supreme Court rejected McCleskey's claim and held that the study did not establish that the Georgia capital punishment system violated the Equal Protection Clause. In addition, the Court noted that to be successful, McCleskey would have had to prove that the jury in his specific case acted with discriminatory purpose.[108]

Age

The Supreme Court decided two disputes involving age in 1988 and 1989. In *Thompson v. Oklahoma* (1988), a 15-year-old was given the death sentence for his participation in a murder. Thompson was charged as an adult, since he was a child under Oklahoma law during the time of the offense. The Court vacated his sentence and held that executing anyone under the age of 16 constituted cruel and unusual punishment. However, in *Stanford v. Kentucky* (1989), the Court reached a different conclusion with regard to those over the age of 15. Two cases were consolidated, one concerning Kevin Stanford, who was 17 and four months when he committed murder, and a Missouri defendant who was 16 and six months at the time of his crime of murder. The Court held that it did not constitute cruel and unusual punishment to execute individuals who were 16 or 17 years old at the time of their crimes. In 2005, in *Roper v. Simmons*, the Court overruled *Stanford* and held that it was cruel and unusual punishment to execute those persons under 18 when they committed their crimes.

Part of the Court's reasoning in *Roper* had to do with the contention that juveniles lack maturity and have an underdeveloped sense of responsibility. Therefore, the retributive goal of punishment, holding an offender blameworthy, does not apply. Similarly, juveniles' impulsiveness and recklessness make them unlikely to consider deterrent effects of possible punishments. The Court referred to juveniles as "more vulnerable . . . to negative influences and outside pressures," lacking "control over their own environment," and unable to remove themselves from "horrific, crime-producing settings."[109] The Court also noted that a youth's "traits are less fixed" and are not incorrigible, referring to studies that showed only a small number of juveniles "develop entrenched patterns of problem behavior."[110]

Mental Retardation/Intellectual Disabilities

Three years after *Ford v. Wainwright*, the Supreme Court addressed the issue of intellectual disabilities, or mental retardation as it was referred to at the time, in *Penry v. Lynaugh* (1989). Penry was deemed competent to stand trial, although he had been found by a psychologist to be "mildly to moderately retarded"[111] and had the mental age of an approximately seven year old. In the case, the judge rejected Penry's request to have a jury instruction to consider his mental retardation and child abuse as a mitigating circumstance. The Court held that it was improper to reject the request but also said that the Eighth Amendment does not automatically prohibit the imposition of the death penalty for mentally retarded capital murderers.

Penry's case was reviewed again in *Penry v. Johnson* (2001). In 1989, the Court held that Penry's death sentence violated the Eighth Amendment because the jury had not adequately been instructed about mitigating evidence relating to childhood abuse and Penry's mental retardation. Penry was again found guilty of capital murder and sentenced to death when he was retried. In *Penry v. Johnson*, the Court considered whether the jury instructions complied with *Penry I* and whether allowing statements from a psychiatric report violated his Fifth Amendment rights. Penry contended that part of the report referring to his future dangerousness violated his Fifth Amendment privilege against self-incrimination because he was never warned that the statements he made to the doctor might later be used against him. On appeal, the Supreme Court rejected the alleged Fifth Amendment violation but reversed and remanded the part of the decision upholding jury instructions.[112]

One year later, the Court overruled *Penry I* in *Atkins v. Virginia* (2002), holding that executing mentally retarded defendants is cruel and unusual punishment under the Eighth Amendment. Atkins received the death penalty for capital murder in the course of an abduction and armed robbery in Virginia. He and his accomplice, Jones, accused each other of the actual murder, but Jones' testimony was deemed as more believable to Atkins' jury. Jones pled guilty to first-degree murder in exchange for his testimony, making him ineligible for a death sentence. Two aggravating factors were introduced at the sentencing phase: future dangerousness and the heinousness of the crime. A forensic psychologist testified for the defense that Atkins was "'mildly mentally retarded'"[113] with an IQ of 59, based on an intelligence test that the doctor had administered. The jury delivered the death penalty, but the state supreme court ordered a second penalty hearing because the wrong verdict form was used. The prosecution presented testimony at the second hearing that rebutted the defense's forensic psychologist's testimony regarding Atkins' mental ability. The prosecution's witness, Dr. Stanton Samenow, testified that Atkins was of average intelligence and instead possessed antisocial personality disorder. The jury returned a second death sentence. The state supreme court affirmed this sentence, despite Atkins' contention that he could not be given the death penalty because he was mentally retarded. The state court relied on the 1989 decision of *Penry v. Lynaugh*, which had ruled that execution of the mentally retarded was not unconstitutional. Two of the state court judges dissented, taking issue with Dr. Samenow's conclusions and writing strong concerns about Atkins' mental state, including the statement that "'the imposition of the sentence of death upon a criminal defendant who has the mental age of a child between the ages of 9 and 12 is excessive.'"[114] The Supreme Court granted certiorari, noting the "dramatic shift in the state legislative landscape that has occurred in the past 13 years"[115] since *Penry*. The Supreme Court reversed the Virginia state supreme court's decision, overturned *Penry*, and ruled that the death penalty applied to intellectually disabled offenders is excessive and unconstitutional, violating the Eighth Amendment. While reviewing the medical community's definitions of intellectual disability, the Court left it up to states to craft their own statutes defining such disabilities.

However, 12 years later, the Supreme Court reversed the Florida Supreme Court and ruled that Florida's threshold requirement for establishing intellectual disability was unconstitutional in *Hall v. Florida* (2014). Hall had been convicted and given the death penalty for the murders of Karol Hurst and Deputy Sheriff Lonnie Coburn, with the murder of Lonnie Coburn being reduced due to insufficient evidence showing premeditation. After the Court's ruling in *Hitchcock v. Dugger* (1987), Hall was allowed to present, as per that ruling, nonstatutory mitigating evidence. The evidence he presented pertained to his intellectual disability, or "mental retardation," as it was termed at the time. Evidence included school records, reports from teachers, a lawyer from another case, his counsel, medical professionals, and family members, placing him at the reasoning level of a toddler. Accounts of significant childhood abuse were also presented. Despite the testimony, the jury voted for the death penalty, and the sentencing judge agreed. The Florida Supreme Court affirmed this sentence, but in 2002, the Supreme Court delivered *Atkins*, holding execution of persons with intellectual disabilities to be unconstitutional. Hall had claimed that he had an intellectual disability in a 2004 motion and presented evidence of an IQ score of 71. He had been given nine IQ tests over 40 years that ranged from a low of 60 to 80, but the sentencing judge excluded the two tests below 70 as not meeting evidentiary standards and included the tests ranging from 71 to 80. The judge ruled that Hall thus did not meet Florida's statute mandating a threshold of 70 or below to substantiate intellectual disability. The Florida Supreme Court upheld the 70 cutoff score and denied Hall's appeal in 2012.

The Court noted that this case involved the issue of how to define an intellectual disability for purposes of *Atkins* and required a review of studies by the medical community, just as the Court had done prior to delivering the *Atkins* decision. The two criteria pertinent to defining intellectual disability in relation to capital sentencing issues have to do with deficits in intellectual and adaptive functioning and were addressed appropriately in Florida's statute. The statute also referred to an IQ test score that was two or more standard deviations below the average score of 100, or approximately 70 or below. However, the Court noted that nothing in the statute prevents courts from addressing measurement error. The state court's interpretation of the statute was more rigid in that it did not allow for a margin of error and barred additional evidence showing an intellectual disability.

Since *Atkins*, most states considered margins of errors in IQ tests in defining intellectually disabilities. Kentucky, Virginia, and Alabama employed strict cutoff scores like Florida, but others had cutoff scores of 75, and still others had abolished capital punishment altogether. "In 41 States an individual in Hall's position—an individual with an IQ score of 71—would not be deemed automatically eligible for the death penalty."[116] The Court concluded that a national public consensus, as well as a professional consensus, existed in terms of seeing a strict cutoff score of 70 as inhumane.

In *Brumfield v. Cain, Warden* (2015), the Court found a state court's denial of an *Atkins* hearing based on evidence of an IQ of 75 and no finding of impaired adaptive skills was "an unreasonable determination of the facts in light of the evidence presented in the State court proceeding"[117] within the meaning of AEDPA. Brumfield received the death penalty for the murder of an off-duty Baton Rouge, Louisiana, police officer. The *Atkins* ruling in standards for determining intellectual disabilities were left to the states, and Louisiana's standard consisted of three criteria: "(1) sub average intelligence, as measured by objective standardized IQ tests; (2) significant impairment in several areas of adaptive skills; and (3) manifestations of this neuro-psychological disorder in the developmental stage."[118] This diagnosis conformed to the American Association of Mental Retardation and the DSM-IV definitions. Brumfield raised an *Atkins* claim, offering mitigating evidence at his sentencing hearing presented by his mother, a social worker, and a clinical neuropsychologist. According to the neuropsychologist, IQ tests indicated Brumfield had an IQ of 75. He also had a fourth-grade reading level and had been diagnosed as learning disabled as a child and placed in special education. Brumfield requested funding for retaining the appropriate specialists to develop further his *Atkins* claim. The state trial court dismissed the petition, finding Brumfield had not demonstrated impaired adaptive skills, an IQ of 75 was not low enough, and another doctor who had examined Brumfield, but not testified, found an IQ a little bit higher than 75.

New evidence presented on appeal at the district court's hearing showed Brumfield to have an IQ between 65 and 70 and proof of subpar conceptual and adaptive skills, with the court finding that Brumfield met Louisiana's criteria for mental retardation and could not be executed. The Fifth Circuit reversed, but the Supreme Court vacated the Fifth Circuit's decision.

Louisiana's criteria for diagnosing intellectual disabilities included considering measurement error, and the Court observed that based on the test Brumfield was given, an IQ of 75 is "squarely in the range of potential intellectual disability."[119] The doctor who apparently found a higher IQ than 75 only administered a screening instrument and did not document an IQ score in his report, so the state court could not reasonably rely on this evidence. While there was also some contrary evidence, the Majority noted that Brumfield only needed "to raise a 'reasonable doubt' as to his intellectual disability to be entitled to an evidentiary hearing."[120]

Habeas Proceedings Involving Claims of Innocence

Over the past 40 years, the Court has also provided guidance on habeas corpus review of claims involving innocence. In *Sawyer v. Whitley* (1992) the Court ruled that federal habeas petitions involving claims of actual innocence must show that constitutional violations occurred during proceedings and, by the clear and convincing evidence standard, if those violations had not occurred, no reasonable jury would have found the defendant eligible for the death penalty. The constitutional violation claimed by Sawyer was the omission of mitigating psychological evidence at his sentencing hearing. However, the Court stated that this evidence did not relate to Sawyer's guilt or innocence, and even if it had been presented, it could not be shown that any reasonable jury would have seen this evidence as outweighing the aggravating factors. In *Herrera v. Collins* (1993), the Court held that claims of innocence based on newly discovered evidence are not grounds for federal habeas relief unless there are other constitutional violations that occurred in state criminal proceedings. The Court did note that Herrera could still petition for clemency under Texas law.

The Court looked again at *Sawyer* and *Herrera* in another habeas proceeding involving alleged innocence in *Schlup v. Delo* (1995). A Missouri prisoner was sentenced to death for the murder of another inmate. The lower court refused to hear this case because Schlup could not meet the showing of actual innocence as defined in *Sawyer*. The Court undertook this case to revisit the *Sawyer* standard and to assess whether it carried the risk of executing a person who is actually innocent. The Court rejected the rigorous *Sawyer* standard, moving instead to an earlier case, *Murray v. Carrier* (1986), which ruled that a habeas petitioner must show that "a constitutional violation has probably resulted in the conviction of one who is actually innocent."[121] The *Carrier* standard was determined to be the governing standard in habeas death penalty cases where petitioners alleged procedural constitutional violations prevented jurors from hearing evidence that would have proved actual innocence. *Schlup* was distinguished from *Herrera* in that *Herrera* was a substantive claim alleging innocence but no constitutional error during proceedings, and *Schlup* involved a procedural claim alleging ineffective assistance of counsel and withholding of evidence.

Conclusion

This chapter has presented a multitude of capital cases that have come before the Supreme Court over the past 40 years. These do not represent the full number of cases but do reflect major issues. The Court has reviewed numerous state capital sentencing statutes for such aspects as individual fairness and vagueness, jury instructions, bifurcated sentencing procedures, methods of execution, and offender characteristics, including insanity, race, intellectual disabilities, and age. Over 40 years, the Court has overruled itself in such issues as the constitutionality of allowing victim impact evidence at sentencing hearings and giving the death penalty to juveniles and those with intellectual disabilities. The standard of proof for aggravating circumstances has shifted, and states continue to experiment with crafting statutes that meet constitutional standards.

Notes

1 These three factors included: (1) that the murder was committed while the offender was engaged in the commission of other capital felonies; (2) that Gregg committed the murder for the purpose of receiving the victims' money and automobile; or (3) that the murder was "outrageously and wantonly vile, horrible and inhuman" in that it "involved the depravity of [the] mind of the defendant" (428 U.S. 153).

2 (1) Whether the conduct of the defendant causing the death was committed deliberately and with the reasonable expectation that the death would result; (2) whether it is probable that the defendant would commit criminal acts of violence constituting a continuing threat to society; and (3) if raised by the evidence, whether the defendant's conduct was an unreasonable response to the provocation, if any, by the deceased (428 U.S. 262).

3 428 U.S. 325.

4 The Court reached a similar conclusion in *Baldwin v. Alabama* (1985), where a jury was required to issue the death sentence if it found one of a number of aggravated crimes. The Supreme Court held that while the sentencing scheme would have been unconstitutional had the jury's determination been dispositive, the judge had the final say regarding sentencing. Thus, the death sentence was not truly automatic due to the discretion of the judge.

5 433 U.S. 584.

6 An accomplice to a murder was given the death penalty pursuant to a Mississippi statute that made accomplices equally responsible with the principal offender for the crime (*Cabana v. Bullock*, 1986). The Court cited *Enmund* and noted that the

> Eighth Amendment does more than require that a death sentenced Defendant be legally responsible for a killing as a matter of state law; it requires that he himself have actually killed, attempted to kill, or intended that a killing take place or that lethal force be used (474 U.S. 376).

The Court held that the district court should vacate the death sentence but could reimpose it if it determined that the defendant killed, attempted to kill, or intended that lethal force be used. This case differs from another accomplice liability case occurring in Arizona, *Tison v. Arizona* (1987), in which Tison took part in helping break his father out of prison and watched as the father kidnapped and killed a family of four. The state Supreme Court held that while Tison did not intend that the victims die, plan the homicides or fire the shots, he nonetheless had the requisite intent as he played an active role in the planning and helped execute the breakout that led to the murders. The U.S. Supreme Court noted

> [t]he Eighth Amendment does not prohibit the death penalty as disproportionate in the case of a defendant whose participation on a felony that results in murder is major and whose mental state is one of reckless indifference (481 U.S. 137).

However, the case was remanded since Arizona upheld the sentence based on a finding that the defendant "intended, contemplated, or anticipated that lethal force would or might be used, or that life would or might be taken."

7 465 U.S. 37.

8 554 U.S. 407. The Court acknowledged that this decision was limited to crimes against persons. "We do not address, for example, crimes defining and punishing treason, espionage, terrorism, and drug kingpin activity, which are offenses against the State" (*Id.* at 437).

9 The judge was required to consider "the nature and circumstances of the offense and the history, character, and condition of the offender," and determine whether the preponderance of the evidence established:

(1) the victim induced or facilitated the offense; (2) it is unlikely that the offense would have been committed but for the fact that the offender was under duress, coercion, or strong provocation; or (3) the offense was primarily the product of the offender's psychosis or mental deficiency.

10 The Court struck down the same statute on the same day in *Bell v. Ohio* (1978), deciding that

> A statute that prevents the sentence in capital cases from giving independent mitigating weight to aspects of the defendant's character and record and to the circumstances of the offense proffered in mitigation creates the risk that the death penalty will be imposed in spite of factors that may call for a less severe penalty, and when the choice is between life and death, such risk is unacceptable and incompatible with the commands of the Eighth and Fourteenth Amendments (438 U.S. 637).

11 455 U.S. 104.

12 Similar to *Skipper*, the Court decided *Hitchcock v. Dugger* (1987), a case in which the trial judge instructed the jury to not consider, and he himself did not consider, mitigating circumstances not stated in the Florida statute. The Supreme Court ultimately reversed the imposition of the death sentence, as it held that "Petitioner was sentenced to death in proceedings that did not comport with the requirement that the sentence may neither refuse to consider not be precluded from considering any relevant mitigating evidence" (481 U.S. 393). However, in *Franklin v. Lynaugh* (1988), the Court held that a defendant was not entitled to have his mitigating circumstance instructed to the jury. The judge had the jury decide two special issues during the sentencing phase, of which if it responded 'Yes' to both, then the death penalty would be imposed. The defendant had requested that the jury consider the mitigating circumstances while specifically answering those questions. The Supreme Court held that "Neither the instructions actually given nor the Texas Special Issues precluded jury consideration of any relevant mitigating circumstances, or otherwise unconstitutionally limited the jury's discretion" (487 U.S. 164).

13 446 U.S. 420.

14 In the past, the Georgia Supreme Court "Concluded (i) the evidence that the offense was 'outrageously or wantonly vile, horrible or inhuman,' must demonstrate 'torture, depravity of mind, or an aggravated battery to the victim,' (ii) the phrase 'depravity of mind' comprehended only the kind of mental state that led the murderer to torture or to commit an aggravated battery before killing his victim, and (iii) the word 'torture' must be construed in pari materia with 'aggravated battery' so as to require evidence of serious physical abuse of the victim before death" (446 U.S. 420). The Court noted that the "Georgia courts did not so limit the statute in the present case. Petitioner did not torture or commit an aggravated battery upon his victims or cause either of them to suffer any physical injury preceding their deaths. Nor can the death sentences be upheld on the ground that the murders were 'outrageously or wantonly vile, horrible or inhuman in that [they] involved . . . depravity of mind.' Petitioner's crimes cannot be said to have reflected a consciousness materially more 'depraved' than that of any person guilty of murder" (*Id.*)

15 The Court reached a similar decision in determining that a death penalty statute was vague in *Maynard v. Cartwright* (1988), which involved an Oklahoma statute that used "especially heinous, atrocious or cruel," as aggravating factors.

16 The Court reached a similar outcome as *Barclay* in *Wainwright v. Goode* (1983). *Wainwright* also involved a situation in which the judge considered an aggravating factor not in the statute (future dangerousness). The Florida Supreme Court had upheld the decision but was overturned by the U.S. Court of Appeals. Ultimately the Supreme Court reversed and held that the Eighth Amendment was not violated.

17 507 U.S. 463 at 465.

18 *Id.* at 468.

19 512 U.S. 967 at 975–6.

20 *Id.* at 976.

21 In dissent, Justice Blackmun explained in great detail how these factors were broad, open-ended, and provided no guidance or limiting discretion to sentencing juries. He noted that the first factor regarding consideration of the circumstances of the crime was unclear and lacked objectivity, and thus "poses an unacceptable risk that a sentencer will succumb to either overt or subtle racial impulses or appeals" (at 992). To support this contention, Justice Blackmun referenced a 1990 General Accounting Office Report, "Death Penalty Sentencing Research Indicates Pattern of Racial Disparities," that was presented to both Senate and House judiciary committees and concluded that a survey and synthesis of studies found "a 'remarkably consistent' conclusion that the race of the victim influenced the likelihood of being charged with capital murder or receiving the death penalty in 82% of cases, reprinted at 136 Cong. Rec. 12267–12268 (1990)" (at 992).

22 463 U.S. 880.

23 *Id.*

24 On September 1, 1995, in a 5–4 per curiam opinion, the Court vacated the stay of execution granted to Lem Davis Tuggle (*Netherland, Warden v. Tuggle*) but ordered the stay to remain in effect until September 20 to allow time for Tuggle's attorney to seek another stay. The Court noted that the Fourth Circuit erred in its belief that a habeas petitioner sentenced to death is entitled to a stay to allow the petitioner time to file a writ of certiorari. The lower court failed to apply the three-part inquiry required by *Barefoot v. Estelle* (1983), and the belief that the petitioner was entitled to the stay was rejected in *Autry v. Estelle* (1983) (per curiam), as well as addressed in *Maggio v. Williams* (1983) (per curiam).

25 516 U.S. 10 at 13.

26 Another issue has involved aggravating circumstances found during the sentencing phase but subsequently nullified in another proceeding. In *Johnson v. Mississippi* (1988), one of the aggravating circumstances found was a previous felony conviction. This circumstance was based on a 1963 felony conviction in another state, which was later overturned after the Mississippi Supreme Court had affirmed the defendant's death sentence. The Supreme Court held that "[b]y allowing petitioner's death sentence to stand despite the fact that it was based in part on the vacated New York conviction, the Mississippi Supreme Court violated the Eighth Amendment's prohibition against cruel and unusual punishment" 486 U.S. 578 (1988).

27 512 U.S. 154 at 171.

28 The statute stated that

> [t]he verdict must be a sentence of death if the jury unanimously finds at least one aggravating circumstance . . . and no mitigating circumstance or if the jury unanimously finds one or more aggravating circumstances which outweigh any mitigating circumstances 9711(c)(1)(iv).

29 However, the four-member dissent written by Justice Brennan argued that the Pennsylvania statute was impermissibly mandatory, giving the state legislature and not a jury the power to judge the appropriateness of a death sentence after finding no mitigating factors. Justice Brennan noted that certiorari was granted in order to consider whether a state might *mandate* such a sentence when a jury finds no mitigating factors.

30 494 U.S. 738 at 751.

31 In a habeas case decided on March 9, 1992, *Stringer v. Black* (1992), the Supreme Court reversed and remanded the Fifth Circuit and ruled that a petitioner who was given the death penalty before *Maynard* and *Clemons* were decided was not barred by *Teague v. Lane* (1989) in relying on those cases for postconviction relief. *Teague* prohibits petitioners in habeas proceedings from attempting to apply a new rule of law if that rule was announced before the individual's conviction was final or from trying to create a new rule or apply precedent in a way that would create a new rule. (See, e.g., *Graham v. Collins* (1993).

32 498 U.S. 315.

33 506 U.S. 40 at 42.

34 *Id.* at 46.

35 *Id.* at 48.

36 A similar outcome was reached in *Spaziano v. Florida* (1984), in which a Florida judge informed a defendant that he would instruct the jury on lesser included, noncapital offenses if he would waive the statute of limitations, which had expired on several of those offenses. The defendant refused and was sentenced to death, without receiving the jury instructions with the lesser included offenses. The Court held that Spaziano was not entitled to the lesser included instruction, since no lesser included offense actually existed. The Supreme Court stated that "a lesser included offense instruction detracts from, rather than enhances the rationality of the process" (468 U.S. 447) in such circumstances.

37 A similar case, *Lowenfield v. Phelps* (1988) involved the use of jury polling. More specifically, the judge polled the jury twice as to whether further deliberations would be helpful, and then reiterated his prior instructions, noting that he would impose a life sentence if the jurors could not reach a unanimous verdict, and asked them to consult with each other. The jury returned a death sentence. The Court held the jury polls and the supplemental charge did not impermissibly coerce the jury to return a death sentence.

38 512 U.S. 1 at 6.

39 The dissent returned to the *Caldwell* decision previously discussed, with Justice Ginsburg disagreeing that the jury's responsibility had been lessened and noted that "[u]nder *Caldwell's* . . . reasoning, diminution of jurors' sense of responsibility violates the Eighth Amendment's reliability requirement, whether or not a defendant can demonstrate empirically that the effect of this diminution was to bias the jurors' judgment toward death." *Id.* at 21.

40 486 U.S. 367 at 373–4.

41 *Id.* at 383–4.

42 494 U.S. 433 at 437.

43 *Id.* at 437.

44 507 U.S. 272 at 277.

45 494 U.S. 370.

46 Instructions 8.84.1 and 8.84.2 of the 1979 California Criminal Jury Instructions.

47 Citing *Penry v. Lynaugh*, 492 U.S. 302 at 319 (1989).

48 494 U.S. 370 at 377.

49 *Id.* at 383.

50 527 U.S. 373 at 375–6.

51 *Id.* at 402.

52 The district court had informed the jury that the sentencing choices were life without release, death, or "some other lesser sentence." However, under the FDPA, the "lesser sentence" was not an option for the crime for which Jones was convicted. The dissent saw this misinformation as making the sentence of death unreliable and would have remanded the case for a new sentencing trial. *Id.* at 405.

53 *Id.*

54 *Id.*

55 *Id.* at 234.

56 *Id.*

57 In dissent, Justice Stevens observed that "argument of counsel generally carry less weight with a jury than do instructions from the court", citing case precedent (*Boyde v. California* [1990]). *Id.*, dissent, fn. 3 at 242.

58 Reginald, the older brother, was convicted of one count of kidnapping, five counts of aggravated kidnapping, 10 counts of aggravated robbery, aggravated battery, criminal damage to property, one count of first-degree felony murder, four counts of capital murder, one count of attempted first-degree murder, 20 counts of rape or attempted rape, three counts of aggravated criminal sodomy, one count each of aggravated burglary and burglary, theft, and cruelty to animals, and three counts of unlawful possession of a firearm. Jonathan was convicted of first-degree murder, four counts of capital murder, one count of attempted first-degree murder, five counts of aggravated kidnapping, nine counts of aggravated robbery, 20 counts of rape or attempted rape, three counts of aggravated criminal sodomy, and one count each of aggravated burglary and burglary, theft, and cruelty to animals.

59 The older brother's visible handcuffs prejudiced the younger brother, according to the court, and the state court suggested that the joint trial hampered consideration of the younger brother as an individual. The state court also maintained that the older brother was prejudiced by the younger brother's cross-examination of their sister, who testified that the older brother told her he was the shooter but later recanted, and the depiction of the older brother corrupting the younger.

60 577 U.S. ___ at 10–13. At the sentencing phase of both cases, jurors were instructed that "The State has the burden to prove beyond a reasonable doubt that there are one or more aggravating circumstances and that they are not outweighed by any mitigating circumstances found to exist" (*Id.* at 12). The defendants maintained that this instruction would lead the jury to think that mitigating evidence had the same standard of proof as aggravating circumstances. The majority opinion maintained the instruction was clear and that mitigating circumstances just must be "found to exist" (Id.). Justice Scalia reviewed the Court's previous decisions that have already held that jurors do not have to be instructed that mitigating circumstances do not have to be proved beyond a reasonable doubt: "In any event, our case law does not require capital sentencing courts 'to affirmatively inform the jury that mitigating circumstances need not be proved beyond a reasonable doubt.' *Id.* In *Buchanan v. Angelone* (1998), we upheld a death sentence even though the trial court 'failed to provide the jury with express guidance on the concept of mitigation.' *Id.*, at 275. Likewise in *Weeks v. Angelone* (2000), we reaffirmed that the Court has 'never held that the State must structure in a particular way the manner in which juries consider mitigating evidence' and rejected the contention that it was constitutionally deficient to instruct jurors to 'consider a mitigating circumstance if you find there is evidence to support it,' without additional guidance. *Id.*, at 232–233."

61 *Id.* at 12.

62 The single dissenter, Justice Sotomayor, would not have granted certiorari in these cases, believing that the decision of the Kansas Supreme Court did not violate any federal constitutional right and that it should be left to the states to serve "as necessary laboratories for experimenting with how best to guarantee defendants a fair trial." *Id.*, dissent at 1; 5. She observed that the Court's holding in this case that the Eighth Amendment does not require that mitigating circumstances be proved beyond a reasonable doubt now calls into question the number of state statutes that do require a standard of proof for mitigating circumstances. Others such as Idaho and Oklahoma recommend an instruction specifying that mitigation does not need to be proved beyond a reasonable doubt.

63 429 U.S. 122.

64 448 U.S. 38.

65 For instance, in *Wainwright v. Witt* (1985), the defendant claimed that several jurors had been excluded from his trial due to their opposition to capital punishment. The Court of Appeals reversed the sentence, holding that one of the jurors was improperly excused for cause under *Witherspoon*. The Supreme Court reversed the Court of Appeals, holding that the juror was properly excused for cause and that there were adequate findings in the record to support the conclusion reached by the trial judge in dismissing the juror. *Lockhart v. McCree* (1986), held that "[t]he Constitution does not prohibit the removal for cause prior to the guilt phase of a bifurcated capital trial, of prospective jurors whose opposition to the death penalty is so strong that it would prevent or substantially impair the performance of their duties as jurors at the sentencing phase of the trial." For additional cases involving this issue, see *Darden v. Wainwright* (1986) (the Supreme Court held that it was proper to exclude a juror when they responded affirmatively to the question: "Do you have any moral or religious, conscientious moral or religious principles in opposition to the death penalty so strong that you would be unable without violating your own principles to vote to recommend a death penalty regardless of the facts?"); *Gray v. Mississippi* (1987) (the judge made the prosecutor use all of his preemptory challenges on jurors that expressed doubts on the death penalty, instead of excusing for cause. The judge then excused a juror for cause since later the prosecutor was out of preemptory challenges. The Court held that the juror was qualified to be seated under *Witherspoon*); and *Ross v. Oklahoma* (1988)(defense was forced to use preemptory challenge for juror who stated he would automatically vote to impose the death penalty if defendant was found guilty; the Supreme Court held that while it was error in failing to remove the juror for cause, such failure did not violate the defendant's Sixth and Fourteenth Amendment rights, since the prospective juror did not actually sit on the jury).

66 504 U.S. 719.

67 *Id.*, fn. 4 at 725.

68 All three cases applied the three-step *Batson* analysis (*Batson v. Kentucky*, 476 U.S. 79) as the controlling procedure for challenges to prospective juror strikes alleging racial animus.

First, a defendant must make a prima facie showing that a peremptory challenge has been exercised on the basis of race; second, if that showing has been made, the prosecution must offer a race-neutral basis for striking the juror in question; and third, . . . the trial court must determine whether the defendant has shown purposeful discrimination (*Snyder v Louisiana*, 552 U.S. 472 at 476–7).

69 490 U.S. 805.

70 501 U.S. 808 at 823.

71 *Id.* at 825.

72 *Id.*

73 *Id.* at 856.

74 The two aggravating factors were the commission of a murder "in an especially heinous, cruel or depraved manner" and committing a murder "for pecuniary gain" 497 U.S. 639.

75 *Poland v Arizona*, 476 U.S. 147 at 156 (1986).

76 *Martin v. Ohio* (1987) upheld Ohio's practice of imposing on a capital defendant the burden of proving by a preponderance of the evidence that she was acting in self-defense when she allegedly committed the murder. The Court's decision also did not violate the principle established in *Mullaney v. Wilbur* (1975), which struck down a state statute requiring convicted murder defendants to negate elements of the offense of murder in order to be entitled to a sentence for voluntary manslaughter.

77 497 U.S. 639 at 651.

78 *Id.* at 653.

79 *Id.*

80 *Id.* at 641.

81 504 U.S. 527 at 530–1, citing Fla. Stat. § 921.141(5)(h) (1991).

82 This was a 5–4 decision but various parts of the majority decision showed the conflicting opinions of several justices. Part I of the majority opinion was a unanimous decision written by Justice Souter; Part II was joined by six justices; Part III-A was joined by five justices; Part III-B-1 was joined by seven justices; Parts III-B-2 and IV were joined by four justices. Justice O'Connor wrote a concurring opinion. Three justices wrote opinions that were concurring in part and dissenting in part: Chief Justice Rehnquist was joined by Justices White and Thomas; Justice Stevens was joined by Justice Blackmun, and Justice Scalia filed the third such concurring/dissenting opinion.

83 One dissenting opinion objected to Florida's argument that a jury plays only an advisory role in sentencing recommendations, while the trial judge is the actual sentencer, an argument made partly to minimize the import of erroneous jury instructions. By 1992, some data existed looking at Florida's capital cases and the role of the jury. Data on 469 death penalty cases reviewed by the Florida Supreme Court on direct appeal between 1980 and 1992 and representing all or most of the capital cases reviewed showed that trial judges

never imposed lesser sentences when juries recommended the death penalty, and that when the trial judge did override a jury's sentence of life imprisonment, the state supreme court "normally" upheld the jury's life sentence.

84 505 U.S. 1079 at 1082.

85 *Id.*

86 *Id.* at 1083.

87 513 U.S. 504 at 510.

88 *Id.* at 512.

89 *Id.,* citing Alabama Prison Project, November 29, 1994.

90 *Id.*

91 *Id.* at 514. The lone dissenter, Justice Stevens, observed that judges are "far more likely than juries to impose the death penalty" because of the "political pressures they face" (at 521). Justice Stevens repeated the statistic cited in the majority opinion regarding Alabama judges overriding juries' life sentences in 47 cases and juries' death sentences in only five cases, as well as noting in a footnote the similar patterns in Florida and Indiana, although not as extreme. He then suggested that a correct comparison should be made between Alabama's procedures and sentencing formats relying solely on jury recommendations, which is the practice in the majority of states with death penalty statutes. In a strong rebuke, he pointed out that when judges override jury recommendations and impose the death penalty, then they not only break "the critical 'link between contemporary community values and the penal system'" (at 522, citing *Witherspoon,* 391 U.S., at 519, n. 15) but also "express contempt" for the community's judgment (at 522).

92 530 U.S. 466 at 538.

93 577 U.S. ___ at 3.

94 490 U.S. 638 at 640–1.

95 577 U.S. ___ at 1.

96 *Id.* at 9.

97 503 U.S. 653.

98 553 U.S. 35.

99 *Id.* at 36.

100 In 2013, states began using midazolam, a benzodiazepine tranquilizer, to induce unconsciousness as the first of a three-drug protocol in lethal injections.

101 In 1977, Oklahoma's lethal injection protocol involved three drugs: sodium thiopental (to induce unconsciousness); a paralytic to stop respiration, and potassium chloride to induce cardiac arrest. By 2008, 30 of the 36 states employing lethal injection used these drugs, and *Baze v. Rees* (2008) ruled that this method was not an Eighth Amendment violation. However, American production of sodium thiopental ceased in 2009 in response to opposition by anti-death penalty activists. Production moved to Italy but stopped entirely by 2011. In 2010, Oklahoma used pentobarbital for the first time when its supplies of sodium thiopental ran out, and other states followed suit. Pentobarbital was upheld constitutionally as similar to sodium thiopental and reliably putting the inmate in a "coma like state" "insensate to pain." The drug was manufactured in Denmark by death-penalty opponents, and, similar to what happened with sodium thiopental, the manufacturer was pressured by activists to halt shipment to the United States for use in executions.

102 The inmate, Clayton Lockett, began moving and talking about half an hour into the execution before the third drug was finished being administered. The execution was stopped, and Lockett died about ten minutes later. The main problem was the fact that Lockett had cut himself twice that morning in his arm where the IV would normally have been run. It took an hour and 12 attempts to find another site, with the right femoral vein finally being used. Some of the IV fluid leaked into tissue instead of the blood stream, and an investigation determined that this was most likely why the midazolam did not render Lockett unconscious for the whole procedure.

103 576 U.S. ___.

104 *Id.* at 4.

105 553 U.S. 35 at 52. The petitioners suggested that sodium thiopental or pentobarbital could be used instead of midazolam, but Oklahoma had not been able to obtain those drugs. (Although the dissent noted that Texas and Missouri still used pentobarbital in executions.) The inmates had argued that midazolam was too weak to maintain unconsciousness and insensitivity to pain when the other drugs were administered, and they argued that midazolam has a ceiling effect. The Majority saw both arguments as meritless and sided with the expert witness for the respondents who testified that there would be a "virtual certainty" that 500 milligrams of midazolam administered properly would make any individual sufficiently unconscious and insensitive to the pain of the other two drugs. The two expert witnesses for the petitioners had no scientific evidence available that could disprove this statement. The rest of the inmates' objections to the expert

witness testimony relied upon in the District Court's decision revolved around what the Majority described as "little more than a quibble about the wording," two of his references (drugs.com and a material safety data sheet), and a mathematical error. These criticisms were seen as irrelevant to his specific testimony regarding midazolam. Only four states have used midazolam, another point argued by petitioners because that indicates lack of consensus about the drug's efficacy. This argument was unpersuasive because it suggested that any new, improved drugs would automatically be disqualified.

106 Baldus, David C.; Pulaski, Charles; Woodworth, George (1983). "Comparative Review of Death Sentences: An Empirical Study of the Georgia Experience," *Journal of Criminal Law and Criminology*, 74(3): 661–753.

107 481 U.S. 279.

108 In 1991, the Court released its second opinion pertaining to the death sentence given to Warren McCleskey. Four years after *McCleskey v. Kemp*, the Court heard *McCleskey v. Zant* (1991). McCleskey received the death penalty for shooting an off-duty police officer during a robbery. In his second habeas petition, he alleged that incriminating statements he made in jail to another inmate and subsequently used in court were made without the assistance of counsel and thus in violation of *Massiah v. United States* (1964). The district court granted McCleskey relief under *Massiah,* but the Eleventh Circuit Court of Appeals reversed the lower court as an abuse of the writ because he had not raised the alleged *Massiah* violation in his first petition. The Supreme Court affirmed the Circuit Court and also observed that McCleskey could not demonstrate that the alleged violation caused an innocent person to be convicted.

109 543 U.S. 551 at 571.

110 *Id.* at 570, quoting Steinberg & Scott, Less guilty by reason of adolescence: Developmental immaturity, diminished responsibility, and the juvenile death penalty, 58 *Am. Psychologist* 1009.

111 492 U.S. 302.

112 The three special issues submitted to the jury were identical to the ones we found constitutionally inadequate as applied in *Penry I.* Although the supplemental instruction made mention of mitigating evidence, the mechanism it purported to create for the jurors to give effect to that evidence was ineffective and illogical. . . . Any realistic assessment of the manner in which the supplemental instruction operated would therefore lead to the same conclusion we reached in *Penry I:* "'[A] reasonable juror could well have believed that there was no vehicle for expressing the view that Penry did not deserve to be sentenced to death based upon his mitigating evidence'" 532 U.S. 782 at 804.

113 536 U.S. 304 at 308.

114 *Id.* at 311, citing 260 Va. at 394, 395–396, 534 S. E. 2d, at 323–324.

115 *Id.*

116 572 U.S. ___.

117 576 U.S. ___ .

118 *Id.* at 2.

119 *Id.* at 9. The *Atkins* Court acknowledged that "an IQ between 70 and 75 or lower . . . is typically considered the cutoff IQ score . . ." (536 U.S. 304 at 309, n. 5) and in 2014, the Court ruled in *Hall v. Florida*, 572 U.S. ___ "that it is unconstitutional to foreclose 'all further exploration of intellectual disability' simply because a capital defendant is deemed to have an IQ above 70."

120 *Id.* at 15.

121 477 U.S. 478 at 496.

References: Cases

Adams v. Texas, 448 U.S. 38 (1980).

Ake v. Oklahoma, 470 U.S. 68 (1985).

Apprendi v. New Jersey, 530 U.S. 466 (2000).

Arave v. Creech, 507 U.S. 463 (1993).

Atkins v. Virginia, 536 U.S. 304 (2002).

Autry v. Estelle, 464 U.S. 1 (1983) (per curiam).

Baldwin v. Alabama, 472 U.S. 372 (1985).

Barclay v. Florida, 463 U.S. 939 (1983).

Barefoot v. Estelle, 463 U.S. 880 (1983).

Batson v. Kentucky, 476 U.S. 79 (1986).

Baze v. Rees, 553 U.S. 35 (2008).

Beck v. Alabama, 447 U.S. 625 (1980).

Bell v. Ohio, 438 U.S. 637 (1978).

Blystone v. Pennsylvania, 494 U.S. 299 (1990).

Booth v. Maryland, 482 U.S. 496 (1987).
Boyde v. California, 494 U.S. 370 (1990).
Brumfield v. Cain, 576 U.S. ___ (2015).
Buchanan v. Angelone, 522 U.S. 269 (1998).
Cabana v. Bullock, 474 U.S. 376 (1986).
Caldwell v. Mississippi, 472 U.S. 320 (1985).
California v. Ramos, 463 U.S. 992 (1983).
Clemons v. Mississippi, 494 U.S. 738 (1990).
Coker v. Georgia, 433 U.S. 584 (1977).
Darden v. Wainwright, 477 U.S. 168 (1986).
Davis v. Georgia, 429 U.S. 122 (1976).
Delo v. Lashley, 507 U.S. 272 (1993) (per curiam).
Eddings v. Oklahoma, 455 U.S. 104 (1982).
Enmund v. Florida, 458 U.S. 782 (1982).
Espinosa v. Florida, 505 U.S. 1079 (1992) (per curiam).
Ford v. Wainwright, 477 U.S. 399 (1986).
Foster v. Chatman, 578 U.S. ___ (2016).
Franklin v. Lynaugh, 487 U.S. 164 (1988).
Furman v. Georgia, 408 U.S. 238 (1972).
Gardner v. Florida, 430 U.S. 349 (1977).
Glossip et al., v. Gross et al., 576 U.S. ___ (2015).
Godfrey v. Georgia, 446 U.S. 420 (1980).
Gomez et al. v. U.S. District Court for the Northern District of California, 503 U.S. 653 (1992) (per curiam).
Graham v. Collins, 506 U.S. 461 (1993).
Gray v. Mississippi, 481 U.S. 648 (1987).
Green v. Georgia, 442 U.S. 95 (1979) (per curiam).
Gregg v. Georgia, 428 U.S. 153 (1976).
Hall v. Florida, 572 U.S. ___ (2014).
Harris v. Alabama, 513 U.S. 504 (1995).
Herrera v. Collins, 506 U.S. 390 (1993).
Hildwin v. Florida, 490 U.S. 638 (1989).
Hitchcock v. Dugger, 481 U.S. 393 (1987).
Hopper v. Evans, 456 U.S. 605 (1982).
Hurst v. Florida, 577 U.S. ___ (2016).
Johnson v. Mississippi, 486 U.S. 578 (1988).
Johnson v. Texas, 509 U.S. 350 (1993).
Jones v. United States, 527 U.S. 373 (1999).
Jurek v. Texas, 428 U.S. 262 (1976).
Kansas v. Carr, 577 U.S. ___ (2016).
Kansas v. Carr, No. 14-450.
Kansas v. Gleason, No. 14-452.
Kennedy v. Louisiana, 554 U.S. 407 (2008).
Lankford v. Idaho, 500 U.S. 110 (1991).
Lewis v. Jeffers, 497 U.S. 764 (1990).
Lockett v. Ohio, 438 U.S. 586 (1978).
Lockhart v. McCree, 476 U.S. 162 (1986).
Lowenfield v. Phelps, 484 U.S. 231 (1988).
Lynch v. Arizona, 578 U.S. ___ (2016) (per curiam).
Maggio v. Williams, 464 U.S. 46, 48 (1983) (per curiam).
Martin v. Ohio, 480 U.S. 228 (1987).
Massiah v. United States, 377 U.S. 201 (1964).
Maynard v. Cartwright, 486 U.S. 356 (1988).
McCleskey v. Kemp, 481 U.S. 279 (1987).
McCleskey v. Zant, 499 U.S. 467 (1991).
McKoy v. North Carolina, 494 U.S. 433 (1990).
Miller-El v. Dretke, 545 U.S. 231 (2005).
Mills v. Maryland, 486 U.S. 367 (1988).
Morgan v. Illinois, 504 U.S. 719 (1992).

Mullaney v. Wilbur, 421 U.S. 684 (1975).
Murray v. Carrier, 477 U.S. 478 (1986).
Netherland, Warden v. Tuggle, 515 U.S. 951.
Parker v. Dugger, 498 U.S. 308 (1991).
Payne v. Tennessee, 501 U.S. 808 (1991).
Penry v. Johnson, 532 U.S. 782 (2001).
Penry v. Lynaugh, 492 U.S. 302 (1989).
Poland v. Arizona, 476 U.S. 147 (1986).
Presnell v. Georgia, 439 U.S. 14 (1978) (per curiam).
Proffitt v. Florida, 428 U.S. 242 (1976).
Pulley v. Harris, 465 U.S. 37 (1984).
Richmond v. Lewis, 506 U.S. 40 (1992).
Ring v. Arizona, 536 U.S. 584 (2002).
Roberts v. Louisiana, 428 U.S. 325 (1976).
Romano v. Oklahoma, 512 U.S. 1 (1994).
Roper v. Simmons, 543 U.S. 551 (2005).
Ross v. Oklahoma, 487 U.S. 81 (1988).
Sawyer v. Whitley, 505 U.S. 333 (1992).
Schlup v. Delo, 513 U.S. 298 (1995).
Shell v. Mississippi, 498 U.S. 1 (1990).
Simmons v. South Carolina, 512 U.S. 154 (1994).
Skipper v. South Carolina, 476 U.S. 1 (1986).
Snyder v. Louisiana, 552 U.S. 472 (2008).
Sochor v. Florida 504 U.S. 527 (1992).
South Carolina v. Gathers, 490 U.S. 805 (1989).
Spaziano v. Florida, 468 U.S. 447 (1984).
Stanford v. Kentucky, 492 U.S. 361 (1989).
State v. Osborn, 102 Idaho 405, 631 P. 2d 187 (1981).
Stringer v. Black, 503 U.S. 222 (1992).
Sumner v. Shuman, 483 U.S. 66 (1987).
Teague v. Lane, 489 U.S. 288 (1989).
Thompson v. Oklahoma, 487 U.S. 815 (1988).
Tison v. Arizona, 481 U.S. 137 (1987).
Tuggle v. Netherland, Warden, 516 U.S. 10 (1995) (per curiam).
Tuggle v. Virginia, 471 U.S. 1096 (1985).
Tuilaepa v. California, 512 U.S. 967 (1994).
Wainwright v. Goode, 464 U.S. 78 (1983).
Wainwright v. Witt, 469 U.S. 412 (1985).
Walton v. Arizona, 497 U.S. 639 (1990).
Washington v. Louisiana, 428 U.S. 906 (1976).
Weeks v. Angelone, 528 U.S. 225 (2000).
Wiggins v. Smith, 539 U.S. 510 (2003).
Witherspoon v. Illinois, 391 U.S. 510 (1968).
Woodson v. North Carolina, 428 U.S. 280 (1976).
Zant v. Stephens, 462 U.S. 862 (1983).

15

AGGRAVATING AND MITIGATING EVIDENCE

Carol S. Steiker* and Jordan M. Steiker**

By the late 1960s, the American death penalty was in significant decline. Prevailing capital statutes were notoriously rudimentary. They allowed (but did not require) the imposition of the death penalty for murder (and in some states for lesser offenses such as robbery, kidnapping, or rape). The decision whether to impose death was left entirely to the jury. Ohio's sentencing instructions were typical in this regard, advising the jury that "the punishment is death unless you recommend mercy, in which event the punishment is imprisonment in the penitentiary during life" (*McGautha v. California*, 1971, p. 194). In the vast majority of jurisdictions, juries were asked to decide guilt and punishment at the same time, with most evidence and attention focused on whether the defendant had committed the offense rather than the appropriate punishment to be imposed.

In 1972, in *Furman v. Georgia*, the U.S. Supreme Court invalidated prevailing capital statutes as unconstitutional under the Eighth Amendment. Although the various opinions supporting the court's judgment offered numerous grounds for the result, a uniting theme of the opinions condemned the arbitrariness produced by the "unguided discretion" of the state schemes. State officials condemned the court's intervention and swiftly sought to refashion their statutes to rectify constitutional defects. Unsurprisingly, given the prestige and influence of the American Law Institute, many states looked to the death penalty provisions of the Model Penal Code. The MPC, unlike many of the ALI Restatement projects, was less a codification of prevailing state criminal practices than a normative reshaping of substantive criminal law, offered to modernize and standardize state criminal laws. Adopted in 1962, the MPC capital provisions represented a stark departure from existing state capital statutes, and no state had embraced them prior to *Furman*. The MPC limited the death penalty to the crime of murder, categorically exempted juveniles, afforded trial judges the discretion to exempt defendants where "the defendant's physical or mental condition" called for leniency, and withheld the death penalty where the evidence, though sufficient to convict the defendant of the underlying charge, did not "foreclose all doubt respecting the defendant's guilt" (American Law Institute, 1980, MPC §210.6(1), p. 107). The most dramatic aspect of the MPC's new approach was its enumeration of aggravating and mitigating factors. The MPC no longer allowed the death penalty to be imposed simply on conviction of murder; it insisted that the jury additionally find the presence of at least one of eight enumerated aggravating factors at a separate sentencing phase. Moreover, the MPC enumerated eight mitigating factors and precluded the imposition of the death penalty unless the sentencer determined that "there are no mitigating circumstances sufficiently substantial to call for leniency" (American Law Institute, 1980, MPC §210.6(2), p. 109).

In 1976, the Supreme Court upheld three newly enacted state capital statutes, two of which borrowed substantially from the MPC approach. Over the ensuing 40 years, the use of aggravating and mitigating factors to guide the capital sentencing decision at a separate punishment phase has become the hallmark of the modern American death penalty. Aggravating factors have established essentially a new offense of "capital murder," and the focus on mitigation as a significant part of the death penalty decision completely transformed capital practice. This chapter explores the law and practice surrounding aggravating and mitigating evidence.

Aggravating Factors

In the decades following 1976, the Supreme Court developed a complex constitutional jurisprudence delineating the role of aggravating factors in the modern era of reformed capital statutes and ongoing judicial oversight. The court's continuing constitutional regulation of capital punishment was in large part a product of the provisional nature of its 1976 decisions, which approved three different reformed death penalty schemes without identifying which features of those schemes were necessary or sufficient to pass constitutional muster under the Eighth Amendment. But the need for continued constitutional elaboration of the role of aggravating factors was also the product of a mismatch between the goals of the drafters of the model death penalty provisions of the MPC and the Supreme Court's vision of the constitutional function of aggravating factors.

The drafters of the MPC, working in the late 1950s and early 1960s, were not trying to fix any perceived constitutional defect in state death penalty schemes. The constitutional litigation campaign that eventually produced *Furman v. Georgia* did not even commence until a year after the MPC was officially promulgated by the ALI.[1] Rather, the drafters of the MPC were dissatisfied with the definition of first-degree murder as codified in most American jurisdictions, which made "deliberate and premeditated" killing the highest grade of murder, eligible for capital punishment in the states that retained the death penalty. In the view of the MPC drafters, the "deliberate and premeditated" requirement "did not achieve a rational or intelligible limitation of capital murder" (American Law Institute, 1980, MPC §210.6 Commentary, p. 128). The concepts of deliberation and premeditation were defined differently in different jurisdictions, and even in their most sensible definition, they embodied the questionable judgment that a person who plans ahead is always worse than one who acts on sudden impulse. In creating a model death penalty statute, the MPC drafters were seeking to describe the worst murders and murderers in a way that better fit the penological goals of the criminal law.

In contrast, the Supreme Court was concerned that the absence of any standards to guide capital sentencing juries in the pre-*Furman* era led to arbitrary results that were not susceptible to review by appellate courts. When the court approved three reformed capital statutes in 1976 (from Georgia, Florida, and Texas), it noted that aggravating factors worked "to narrow the class of murderers subject to capital punishment" (*Gregg v. Georgia*, 1976, p. 196). The court explained that these factors "provide guidance to the sentencing authority, and thereby reduce the likelihood that it will impose a sentence that fairly can be called capricious or arbitrary" (pp. 194–95). Moreover, the court observed,

> Where the sentencing authority is required to specify the factors it relied upon in reaching its decision, the further safeguard of meaningful appellate review is available to ensure that death sentences are not imposed capriciously or in a freakish manner.

> (p. 195)

The court's focus on narrowing, guidance, and clarity was an attempt above all to constrain sentencing discretion. While the MPC drafters shared the view that there should be "tighter controls on [] discretionary judgment," they primarily crafted aggravating factors in order to include within the death penalty's ambit those murders that needed "a special deterrent" or that were "especially indicative of depravity and dangerousness" (American Law Institute (1980), MPC §210.6 Commentary, pp. 135–46).

This divergence in goals between the MPC drafters and the Supreme Court helps to explain much of the convoluted litigation around aggravating factors that followed the court's 1976 resurrection of the American death penalty. The remainder of this section tracks three strands of constitutional jurisprudence regarding aggravating factors, noting where the court diverges both from the MPC and from the court's own original commitments, and identifying issues that remain to be resolved.

Vague Aggravating Factors

In creating a list of aggravating factors for capital sentencers to consult, the drafters of the MPC sought to change the criteria for death-eligible murder from ones focused solely on the murderer's mental state (whether the offender killed with premeditation and deliberation, in the traditional first-degree murder formulation) to ones that tried to identify a broader range of considerations that make some murders worse than others. In particular, the MPC drafters sought to promote the penological goals of deterrence, incapacitation, and retribution. Thus, the drafters included as an aggravating factor that "the murder was committed by a convict under sentence of imprisonment" in recognition of "the need for a special deterrent to homicide by convicts under sentence of imprisonment" (American Law Institute, 1980, MPC §210.6 Commentary, p. 136). The drafters also included aggravating factors that addressed the defendant's past history of violence and the scope of the defendant's violent conduct in the case at issue (whether the defendant killed or created a risk of death to more than one person) as indicative that "the defendant is likely to prove dangerous to life on some future occasion" (pp. 136–37).

The drafters had the most difficulty, however, in addressing the penological goal of retribution, which seeks to punish most severely those offenders who are most blameworthy for their actions. The drafters had little trouble identifying those offenders who are *less* than ordinarily blameworthy for their actions. The MPC categorically exempted juvenile offenders from the death penalty decades before the Supreme Court required such exemption as a matter of constitutional law (*Roper v. Simmons*, 2005). The MPC also gave judges discretion to exempt those whose "physical or mental condition calls for leniency" (American Law Institute, 1980, MPC §210.6(1)(e)). But the drafters struggled to identify those offenders who are *more* than ordinarily blameworthy for their actions. The drafters recognized that the aggravating factors involving multiple murders and risk of harm to many people indicated not merely dangerousness, but also "depravity" (American Law Institute, 1980, MPC §210.6 Commentary, p. 136). But the drafters felt compelled to include a "residual category of murder," defined as those that are "especially heinous, atrocious or cruel, manifesting exceptional depravity" (p. 137). The drafters recognized that this catch-all aggravator was broad and fuzzy, noting, "Of course, virtually every murder is heinous" (p. 137). But the drafters felt that the "heinous, atrocious or cruel" formulation was appropriate in order to encompass "a style of killing so indicative of utter depravity that imposition of the ultimate sanction should be considered" (p. 137).

Many states included a catch-all aggravator similar to the MPC's in their post-*Furman* reformed capital statutes. Several states, including Florida, Mississippi, and Oklahoma, included aggravating factors that asked whether the killing was "heinous, atrocious, or cruel," though without the MPC's mention of "exceptional depravity" (*Maynard v. Cartwright*, 1988, p. 359). Georgia included an aggravating factor that asked whether the offense "was outrageously or wantonly vile, horrible or inhuman in that it involved torture, depravity of mind, or an aggravated battery to the victim" (*Godfrey v. Georgia*, 1980, p. 423). Idaho included an aggravating factor that asked whether "[b]y the murder, or circumstances surrounding its commission, the defendant exhibited utter disregard for human life" (*Arave v. Creech*, 1993, p. 465).

Despite having upheld Georgia's reformed capital statute against facial challenge in 1976, the Supreme Court quickly realized that the use of the catch-all aggravating factor posed a threat to the court's stated goals of reducing arbitrariness in capital sentencing and enhancing appellate review of the grounds for capital verdicts. In 1980, the court reversed a Georgia defendant's death sentence when the sentencing jury found only a single aggravating factor—that the defendant's murder was "outrageously or wantonly vile, horrible and inhuman." (Godfrey v. Georgia, p. 428). The court observed that "[t]here is nothing in these few words, standing alone, that implies any inherent restraint on the arbitrary and capricious infliction of the death sentence" (p. 428). The court concluded that the sentencing jury's reliance on Georgia's catch-all aggravating factor failed the criteria that the court had identified in 1976: a constitutionally valid capital sentencing scheme "must channel the sentencer's discretion by 'clear and objective standards' that provide 'specific and detailed guidance' and that 'make rationally reviewable the process for imposing a sentence of death'" (p. 428, citing *Gregg v. Georgia*, 1976). In later cases, the court went on to find that similar catch-all aggravating factors in other post-*Furman* statutes also failed constitutional muster (*Maynard v. Cartwright*, 1988; *Clemons v. Mississippi*, 1990).

The court did, however, offer Georgia and other states a potential fix for their unconstitutionally vague catch-all aggravating factors. State courts could provide a narrowed construction of overly broad statutory language so as to appropriately cabin its reach to a constitutionally acceptable objective core. At first, the court was fairly demanding of states with regard to this potential fix. For example, it held that the Georgia had failed to show "serious physical abuse of the victim before death" (part of the Georgia Supreme Court's narrowed construction of the "outrageously vile" aggravating factor), despite the defendant's commission of an extremely gory and terrifying multiple murder by shotgun (*Godfrey v. Georgia*, 1980, pp. 431–432). But the court later appeared to relax its vigilance in monitoring narrowed constructions offered by states in defense of catch-all aggravating factors. In 1993, the court declined to rule on whether Idaho's catch-all aggravating factor, which asked whether the defendant exhibited "utter disregard for human life," was overly broad on its face. Rather, the court upheld the Idaho Supreme Court's purportedly narrowed construction of the "utter disregard" factor, which asked instead whether the defendant was a "cold-blooded, pitiless slayer" (Arave v. Creech, p. 471). The court could not muster great enthusiasm for the narrowness of this latter construction, describing it merely as "not without content" (p. 471). But despite its acknowledgment that the narrowed construction was not as objective as some other, more clear-cut aggravating factors and that the question was a close one, the court nonetheless upheld the "utter disregard" construction. This 1993 holding signaled a growing impatience with vagueness challenges to aggravating factors, and defendants have had no further victories in the Supreme Court since then.

Because the drafters of the MPC were primarily concerned with giving capital sentencers the tools to promote the penological goals of punishment rather than with reducing discretion in the capital sentencing process, the post-*Furman* reliance on the MPC template for aggravating factors set the reformed capital statutes on a collision course with constitutional goals. However, this collision might have had a much greater impact had the court not dialed back its commitment to the goals it announced in 1976.

Channeling vs. Narrowing

The court's acceptance of the almost laughably broad "utter disregard" formulation as a sufficiently narrowed construction of a catch-all aggravating factor was not the only way in which the court backtracked on its 1976 principles. Having held that vague statutory aggravators without narrowed constructions were constitutionally invalid, the court then needed to address whether every capital sentence imposed on the basis of such vague aggravators necessarily had to be reversed. The short answer—the product of quite long and involved litigation over decades—is no.

In some states, like Georgia, capital sentencers were required to find at least one aggravating factor from a list in order for the defendant to be eligible for the death penalty. But after having found at least one eligibility factor, the sentencer was then instructed to consider all evidence in aggravation of the crime—not only statutory aggravating factors, but anything at all that might call for a sentence of death—and weigh it against all mitigating evidence. The court concluded that under such statutes (which the court confusingly called "non-weighing" statutes, because sentencers did not weigh *only* statutory aggravating factors), if the sentencer found a vague (or otherwise invalid) aggravating factor, its capital verdict could still stand as long as it found at least one *other* valid statutory aggravating factor. In the court's view, the existence of one valid aggravating factor was sufficient to make the defendant constitutionally death eligible; once the eligibility determination was made, evidence considered in aggravation no longer needed to be clear-cut, as the sentencer was free at that point to consider all evidence, statutory or not, vague or not, in aggravation or mitigation (*Zant v. Stephens*, 1983).

In some other states, like Florida, capital sentencers were similarly required to find at least one aggravating factor from a list, but at the weighing stage, the sentencer was instructed to weigh only *statutory* aggravating factors against all mitigating evidence (statutory or nonstatutory). In such states (which the court deemed "weighing states"), if the sentencer found a vague (or otherwise invalid) aggravating factor, the capital verdict could *not* be saved by the existence of at least one other valid aggravating factor. The court explained that in these "weighing" states, the invalid aggravating factor should not have been put on the scale to be weighed, as only valid statutory aggravating factors could be put on the aggravating side of the scale. Nonetheless, the court held that capital verdicts based on the weighing of an invalid aggravating factor in a "weighing state" could be saved *on appeal* if the appellate court concluded that a death verdict was appropriate after it reweighed the aggravating and mitigating evidence itself without considering the invalid statutory aggravating factor, or by conducting harmless-error review of the jury's verdict (e.g., concluding that the jury would have voted for death even if it had not weighed the invalid statutory aggravating factor) (*Clemons v. Mississippi*, 1990).[2]

Both of these decisions shared a common repudiation of the idea that aggravating factors must play a crucial role in channeling sentencing discretion by structuring the sentencer's deliberative process. In "non-weighing" states, the court held that statutory aggravating factors need play only a more-confined role in rendering a defendant death eligible; once the eligibility threshold is crossed, it is not essential for aggravating factors to further guide the deliberative process in the crucial phase of determining whether or not to actually impose a sentence of death. In "weighing" states, a sentencer's decision that is not properly guided by constitutionally valid aggravators can be saved by an appellate court's decision, far removed from the live evidence and deliberative process of the jury. In both contexts, the failure of aggravating factors to channel sentencer discretion to the conclusion of the sentencing process is not necessarily a constitutional failure.

If channeling capital sentencing discretion is not the crucial constitutional function of aggravating factors, then what is? The court gave its clearest answer to this question when it addressed the reformed capital statutes of yet another sub-category of states, in which aggravating factors appear in the definition of capital murder. Under these statutes, juries must find the existence of at least one of these factors at the guilt phase of the trial. The court upheld one such statute (from Texas) against facial challenge in 1976. Under the Texas scheme, aggravating factors were part of the definition of capital murder; at the sentencing phase, the jury was asked to answer three additional "special issues" (yes or no questions) that required a capital sentence if all three were answered "yes" (*Jurek v. Texas*, 1976). Louisiana has another permutation of such a statute, in which aggravating factors are part of the definition of capital murder and *also* have to be found by the jury at the sentencing phase. A Louisiana defendant challenged his death sentence when the only factor found at his sentencing phase was one that had already been found at the guilt phase of his capital trial (*Lowenfield v. Phelps*, 1988). Lowenfield argued that the jury, having already found at the guilt phase that Lowenfield "knowingly created a risk of harm to more than one person," had nothing left to do in the sentencing phase and thus could not be channeled or guided in its sentencing decision by aggravating factors that did nothing more than repeat an element of the offense.

The court held that Lowenfield's challenge rested "on a mistaken premise as to the necessary role of aggravating circumstances" (p. 244). Aggravating factors, ruled the court, need not play any role in guiding the sentencing body in the exercise of its discretion; rather, it is enough that it provides "a means of genuinely narrowing the class of death-eligible persons" (p. 244). The court held that the narrowing function can be performed either at the guilt phase or the sentencing phase and thus that aggravating factors have no distinctive constitutional role in shaping the sentencers' deliberative process: "There is no question but that the Louisiana scheme narrows the class of death-eligible murderers and then at the sentencing phase allows for the consideration of mitigating circumstances and the exercise of discretion. The Constitution requires no more" (p. 246).

The recasting of the constitutional role of aggravating factors from robust channeling to formal narrowing has diminished the significance and functionality of aggravating factors as a tool to constrain capital sentencing discretion. At the same time, however, the court's recasting of the core of the role of aggravating factors as a "narrowing" function raises the possibility of a different kind of challenge to current capital statutes. At no point has the court ever addressed in quantitative terms how much "narrowing" must occur for capital statutes to be deemed constitutional. Central to the court's rejection of prevailing capital statutes in *Furman v. Georgia* in 1972 was the sense that death eligibility was far too broad (in many jurisdictions, eligibility extended well beyond murder). But at no point in the post-*Furman* era, in which the ambit of the death penalty has been restricted largely to murder (*Kennedy v. Louisiana*, 2008), has the court addressed the permissible scope of the death penalty for murder. If aggravating factors must narrow the class of death-eligible murderers, is it sufficient for the class to be narrowed to almost-but-not-quite all murderers? This is no rhetorical question, as scholars have demonstrated the tendency of legislators to consistently expand the ranks of aggravating factors (Simon & Spaulding, 1999). Even before such expansion, the scope of aggravating factors was already quite broad. One study of the Georgia statute upheld in 1976 as a model of guided discretion found that 86% of all persons convicted of murder in Georgia over a five-year period after the adoption of Georgia's reformed statute were death eligible under that scheme and that over 90% of persons sentenced to death before *Furman* would also be deemed death eligible under the post-*Furman* Georgia statute (Baldus, Woodworth, & Pulaski, 1990, pp. 268 n.3, 102).

The broad reach of aggravating factors is especially troubling in the current moment, when death sentencing and executions rates have plummeted. In 2016, only 30 new death sentences were returned nationwide, and only 20 people were executed. Given that there are roughly 15,000 murders annually in the United States, the gap between authorization of the death penalty and its actual use reflects a breadth of statutory eligibility that is troublingly out of sync with prevailing practice on the ground. Although the days of challenging individual statutory aggravating factors as overly broad are probably over, challenges based on the failure of aggravating factors to perform their narrowing function *in the aggregate* are just beginning. Such a claim was made (unsuccessfully) in the James Holmes litigation in Colorado (*People v. Holmes*, 2014). Because the Holmes trial yielded a life verdict, the ruling will not be appealed. But further litigation along these lines is likely to continue and represents an as-yet undeveloped challenge to the diminished function of aggravating factors in contemporary capital sentencing schemes.

Judges vs. Juries

One final important line of doctrine regarding aggravating factors flows from the Sixth Amendment right to trial by jury rather than from the Eighth Amendment prohibition of cruel and unusual punishments. The ALI could not agree on whether judges or juries or both working in tandem should conduct capital sentencing, so the MPC authorized two different schemes for states to choose between—sentencing by jury, with possible override in favor of life (but not death) by the trial judge; and sentencing by judge alone. Most states in the post-*Furman* era gave capital sentencing authority entirely to juries, as had been the common-law tradition. A small minority gave the authority either to the trial judge alone, or to the trial judge after an advisory verdict by a jury (with override in the direction or either life *or* death). These various statutes permitting capital sentencing by trial judges foundered on the shoals of the Supreme Court's Sixth Amendment jurisprudence and as of 2017 have completely disappeared from the landscape of American capital punishment.

In 2000, the court rejected a noncapital sentencing scheme that allowed a trial judge to enhance a sentence for assault beyond the statutory maximum term if the judge determined that the assault was a hate crime (*Apprendi v. New Jersey*, 2000). The court reasoned that a factual finding that raised the statutory maximum sentence was in essence an element of a new crime and thus must be found beyond a reasonable doubt by a jury under the Sixth Amendment. This holding produced a seismic shift in noncapital sentencing practices, as the court later held that any finding that is essential for an increased sentence even *within* a statutory maximum term (e.g., in a sentencing guidelines regime) must be found by jury (*Blakely v. Washington*, 2004; *United States v. Booker*, 2005). *Apprendi* also had important consequences, eventually, for all forms of judge sentencing. Because most capital sentencing schemes require that an aggravating factor be found before a defendant could be eligible for the death penalty, the court held that such a finding is in essence an element of capital murder and must be found by a jury, not by a judge alone (*Ring v. Arizona*, 2002). The states that had authorized judges alone to conduct capital sentencings switched to jury sentencing in the wake of *Ring*. But the three states (Alabama, Delaware, and Florida) that had advisory jury/judicial override schemes did not change their practices for more than a decade, when the Supreme Court revisited the issue and belatedly declared that Florida's judicial override system violated *Ring*, because Florida law required capital sentencing judges to make their own independent determination of aggravating factors in order to sentence a defendant to death (*Hurst v. Florida*, 2016). Shortly thereafter, the Delaware Supreme Court held that its state's statute was sufficiently like Florida's to require its constitutional invalidation as well (*Rauf v. State*, 2016). Although the Alabama Supreme Court declined to invalidate the Alabama judicial override scheme, the Alabama Legislature voted in 2017 to end the practice and to rely instead on jury sentencing in capital cases.

The life and death of judge-sentencing in capital cases reflects a slow reconceptualization of the constitutional role of aggravating factors. In this context, the reconceptualization was not a move from channeling to narrowing under the Eighth Amendment but rather a move from sentencing factor to element of the crime of capital murder under the Sixth Amendment—even if the element is not found until the sentencing phase of the process.

Mitigating Evidence

Perhaps no area of American death penalty practice has changed more markedly over the past 40 years than the strategic approach to capital trial representation, with its new-found emphasis on uncovering and presenting mitigating evidence. Prior to the Supreme Court's intervention in the early 1970s, capital trials were not notably different from other cases involving serious felonies. Defense lawyers tended to focus on avoiding conviction on a charge that could produce the death penalty (generally first-degree murder). In many jurisdictions, the presentation of evidence was limited by law to facts relating to the circumstances of the offense, disallowing the introduction of evidence relevant to a broader assessment of the defendant's character, limitations, or potentially redeeming qualities. Most states made no mention of "mitigating evidence" in their instructions to the jury, instead inviting juries to decide between life and death based on their "absolute" or "unrestricted" discretion. In most states, capital trials were "unitary" events, with decisions on guilt and punishment made at the same time after a single proceeding; such proceedings made clear that the circumstances of the offense, rather than the character and background of the offender, provided the paramount grounds for the sentencing decision.

Today, all states employ bifurcated proceedings in capital cases, with a separate sentencing phase focused on the appropriate punishment. Most states enumerate "mitigating factors" supporting a sentence less than death, and every state permits jurors to consider unenumerated factors apart from those listed in their capital statutes. Supreme Court decisions require states to allow the introduction of mitigating evidence, broadly construed, and insist that state statutory schemes facilitate the consideration of such evidence in the ultimate sentencing decision. Professional norms, as well as federal constitutional doctrine, require capital trial attorneys to investigate potential mitigating evidence. Trial lawyers often enlist "mitigation specialists" to design and implement a mitigation investigation plan, designed to uncover and weave together various aspects of a defendant's life; such specialists—who did not exist 40 years ago—bring clinical and information-gathering expertise to evaluate, among other things, congenital, environmental, and experiential influences on a defendant's decision making and behavior. These aspects of modern capital practice reflect the extraordinary new role of mitigation in the American death penalty system.

Enumeration of Mitigating Factors

The MPC, which was highly influential in the design of many post-*Furman* state capital statutes, included eight enumerated mitigating circumstances. Only two circumstances, the defendant's lack of significant criminal history and the defendant's youth, were not directly related to the circumstances of the offense. The remaining six focused on circumstances reducing a defendant's culpability for the offense, including the influence of extreme mental or emotional disturbance, the victim's participation in the defendant's homicidal conduct or consent to the homicidal act, the defendant's belief in moral justification for his conduct, the fact that an accomplice committed the murder and the defendant's participation was relatively minor, the presence of duress or domination by another, and the defendant's impaired capacity to appreciate the wrongfulness of his or her conduct as a result of mental disease, defect, or intoxication. The MPC also permitted the introduction of any evidence the court deemed relevant to sentence, including (but not limited to) evidence of the nature and circumstances of the crime and the defendant's character, background, history, and mental and physical condition.

Of the 31 states in which the death penalty is currently available, all but five (Georgia, Idaho, Oklahoma, South Dakota and Texas) enumerate mitigating circumstances. All enumerating states follow the MPC's lead by asking in some way whether the defendant was impaired in his capacity to appreciate the wrongfulness of his or her conduct; many states ask this question directly, while others focus specifically on the presence of mental disease or defect, intoxication or drug abuse, duress or domination, or extreme mental or emotional disturbance. Most enumerating states also ask whether the defendant's participation in the offense was relatively minor. The most striking departure from the MPC is the refusal of enumerating states to embrace the mitigating factor concerning a defendant's belief in the moral justification for his conduct (which the MPC commentary suggested would encompass not only a perceived mercy killing of a "helpless invalid" but also an assassin's killing for political reasons, though the commentary predicted that the latter argument might well be "discounted by the extravagance of its departure from societal norms") (American Law Institute, 1980, MPC §210.6 Commentary, pp. 141–42).

States' enumerated mitigating circumstances overwhelmingly center on a defendant's reduced culpability as distinct from other grounds supporting a life sentence, such as positive or redeeming character traits, past contributions to society, connections to family members or other loved ones, remorse, or lack of dangerousness. In this respect, most enumerated mitigating circumstances are genuinely about *mitigating culpability*, even though the term "mitigation evidence" has come to mean both in law and in practice any and all grounds for *mitigating punishment*.

The Constitutional Status of Mitigating Evidence

When *Furman* condemned standardless discretion as unconstitutionally arbitrary, most states looked to the MPC approach of bifurcation coupled with the enumeration of aggravating and mitigating factors. Others, though, chose to revive the discarded practice of mandatory capital sentencing. Under this approach, conviction of a capital crime, such as murder or rape, would require imposition of death. Chief Justice Burger had warned in his *Furman* dissent that the move to mandatory sentencing might be worse than the prevailing system of unguided discretion, insisting that he "could more easily be persuaded that mandatory sentences of death without the intervening and ameliorating impact of lay jurors, are so arbitrary and doctrinaire that they violate the Constitution" (*Furman v. Georgia*, 1972, p. 402). When the court confronted mandatory schemes in *Woodson v. North Carolina* and *Roberts v. Louisiana* in 1976, it vindicated Burger's assessment, striking down the statutes and announcing that the Eighth Amendment requires "individualized" sentencing in capital cases. The *Woodson* plurality reasoned that mandatory schemes might encourage jury nullification, introducing a new form of arbitrariness—whether a particular jury was willing to act lawlessly to prevent the imposition of what it regarded as an unjust punishment. The plurality also insisted that the permissibility of mandatory sentencing in noncapital cases should not extend to the capital sphere because of the uniqueness of the death penalty. Because of the difference of death, "consideration of the character and record of the individual offender and the circumstances of the particular offense [is] a constitutionally indispensable part of the process of inflicting" capital punishment (*Woodson v. North Carolina*, 1976, p. 304). So was borne the longstanding tension in capital punishment law, which condemned the pre-*Furman* schemes for their excessive discretion and the post-*Furman* mandatory schemes because they eliminated discretion altogether.

The invalidation of mandatory schemes left many unanswered (and unanticipated) questions about the scope of the individualized sentencing guarantee. When the court confronted MPC-modeled schemes (Ohio and Florida) that limited sentencer consideration to enumerated mitigating factors, the court invalidated death sentences where the defendant presented mitigating evidence outside the scope of those factors. *Woodson* and *Roberts* rejected schemes that had permitted *no* consideration of mitigating evidence. In *Lockett v. Ohio*, the plurality declared that the sentencer should "not be precluded from considering, *as a mitigating factor*, any aspect of a defendant's character or record and any of the circumstances of the offense that the defendant proffers as a basis for a sentence less than death" (p. 604). Because Ohio's enumerated factors did not permit consideration of the defendant's evidence of her minimal participation in the offense or her youth (even though they *did* permit consideration of duress, coercion, strong provocation, and mental illness short of insanity), the plurality concluded she had been denied her right to individualized sentencing because of "the risk that the death penalty [would] be imposed in spite of factors which may call for a less severe penalty" (p. 605).

After *Lockett*, the court held that the individualization right extended to evidence unconnected to reduced culpability, invalidating a sentence where the trial court disallowed the introduction of evidence of the defendant's postcrime good behavior while awaiting trial. The court acknowledged that the defendant's evidence of his postcrime adjustment to jail "would not relate specifically to petitioner's culpability for the crime he committed," but concluded that the evidence was nonetheless constitutionally "'mitigating' in the sense that [it] might serve 'as a basis for a sentence less than death'" (*Skipper v. South Carolina*, 1986, p. 4).

The most problematic state scheme for the consideration of mitigating evidence (apart from the mandatory statutes) was the "special issue" approach embraced by Texas and Oregon. Like the MPC schemes, Texas and Oregon bifurcated guilt and punishment and allowed the introduction of mitigating evidence. But instead of asking the jury whether death was the appropriate punishment in light of aggravating and mitigating evidence, Texas and Oregon simply asked the jury to answer three questions: whether the crime was committed deliberately, whether the defendant would constitute a danger in the future, and whether the defendant had responded unreasonably to provocation. If the jury answered the questions affirmatively, a death sentence was required. Although the court sustained the Texas statute against a facial challenge (*Jurek v. Texas*, 1976), the court later recognized the tension between the special issue approach and the broad right of individualized sentencing recognized in *Lockett* and subsequent cases. The problem, as highlighted by Justice O'Connor in 1988, was that a defendant might present mitigating evidence that could not be given adequate consideration within the three narrow issues of deliberateness, dangerousness, and provocation (*Franklin v. Lynaugh*, 1988, p. 185). One year later, in *Penry v. Lynaugh*, the court invalidated the death sentence of a Texas inmate who had introduced evidence of his childhood abuse and intellectual disability. Justice O'Connor, writing for the court, held that the jury was unable to express a "reasoned moral response" to such evidence because Penry's intellectual disability and abusive background had relevance to his moral culpability beyond his capacity to act deliberately (p. 322); if the jury concluded his actions were deliberate, they would have to answer the special issue affirmatively even if they believed he was less deserving of death because of his experiences and impairments. Worse still, Penry's mitigating evidence might be treated as *aggravating* under the future dangerousness question, because his mitigating evidence suggested he was less capable of controlling his impulses.

In the wake of *Penry*, Texas and Oregon revised their capital statutes to permit the jury to consider directly whether mitigating evidence justifies a sentence less than death. Oregon also vacated the death sentences of those who had been sentenced under its original special issue scheme. But Texas continued to litigate whether death-sentenced inmates had been deprived of an adequate opportunity to avoid death based on the mitigation they proffered at trial. In the decade following *Penry*, virtually no Texas inmates received relief. The Supreme Court held that evidence of youth could be adequately addressed through the special issues because jurors could conclude that a defendant would become less dangerous as he matured. In so doing, the court suggested that state capital schemes could "structure" the consideration of mitigating evidence as long as the evidence could be given "some" consideration—even if the evidence could not be considered fully in its most important respect, as diminishing the defendant's culpability for the offense (*Johnson v. Texas*, 1993, p. 369). The Texas courts, as well as the lower federal courts addressing *Penry* claims, found innovative ways to sustain death sentences obtained under the old statute. They approved "nullification" instructions, which had been improvised by trial courts during the period between the *Penry* decision and the enactment of the new Texas statute, which had allowed juries to answer the special issues falsely if they believed a death sentence should not be imposed. These courts also created new tests for constitutional relevance, holding that *Penry* relief should be unavailable unless a defendant's mitigating evidence amounted to a uniquely severe condition and the defendant established a causal nexus between the condition and the offense. Applying these tests, lower courts routinely denied relief to defendants who had offered evidence of reduced culpability (including evidence of childhood deprivation or abuse, intellectual impairment, addiction, or mental illness) that could not be given significant mitigating effect under the former special issues.

Between 2001 and 2007, the Supreme Court decided six *Penry* cases and embraced a much more robust view of the individualization requirement.[3] The court rejected the notion that the inadequacy of the special issues could be cured by instructing jurors to nullify their answers to the special issues if they thought a life sentence was the appropriate punishment (*Penry v. Johnson*, 2001). In doing so, the court insisted that capital schemes must afford "full consideration" and give "full effect" to a defendant's mitigating evidence (p. 782). The court also emphatically rejected the test for constitutional relevance that had been used by the Texas courts to deny Penry relief. According to the court, a defendant need not demonstrate that his evidence establishes a uniquely severe condition or that has crime is attributable to that condition in order for the evidence to fall within the individualization requirement (*Tennard v. Dretke*, 2004, pp. 286–287). Instead, the court adopted its broadest formulation of the individualization right, holding that the only test for constitutional relevance is "whether the evidence is of such a character that it might serve as a basis for a sentence less than death" (p. 287).

Once that "low threshold for relevance is met, the Eighth Amendment requires that the jury be able to consider and give effect to a capital defendant's mitigating evidence" (p. 285). Illustrating the breadth of constitutionally relevant evidence, the court's sole example of evidence that fell outside of the broad scope of the individualization requirement was evidence of how frequently a defendant showers (p. 286).

Ultimately, the Texas litigation confirms that states must allow the introduction of evidence supporting a sentence less than death and must provide a vehicle for its full consideration. Occasionally trial courts restrict the introduction of potentially mitigating evidence on the ground that it does not relate to the defendant's character or background, such as evidence that a more culpable co-defendant received a life sentence (*Saldano v. State*, 2007), evidence that the victim's family opposes death, or evidence that the execution of the defendant will cause harm to the defendant's family (*Stenson v. Lambert*, 2007). The relative infrequency of these outlier cases reflects the consensus that defendants enjoy considerable leeway in presenting evidence plausibly supporting a life sentence.

The court also has rejected state rules preventing individual jurors from considering particular mitigating evidence unless the jury as a whole agrees about its existence. In the Maryland case rejecting the unanimity rule, the court highlighted the troubling possibility that all twelve jurors might have thought the death penalty inappropriate based on mitigating factors, but the jury as a whole could not produce a life verdict because they disagreed about which mitigating factors justified a non-death sentence (*Mills v. Maryland*, 1988). As a practical matter, individual jurors are now empowered to decide whether particular mitigating factors, or mitigating factors taken collectively, justify the imposition of a sentence less than death.

The Role of Mitigation in Contemporary Capital Practice

The revamping of capital statutes in the early 1970s slowly but decisively transformed capital practices. The widespread adoption of bifurcated proceedings—hastened by the court's approval of such schemes and its rejection of mandatory ones—made clear that the question of punishment was distinctly important in capital cases. The enumeration of mitigating factors also reinforced the idea that capital defense lawyers should investigate grounds for leniency apart from whether the state could establish the elements of the underlying offense. But in the early post-*Furman* years, trial lawyers appointed to represent capital defendants generally lacked the training, resources, and commitment to do competent punishment-phase investigation. Many such lawyers were appointed despite their lack of any significant capital experience. In some jurisdictions, predominantly in the South, lawyers were barely compensated for their out-of-courtroom time, or they were given paltry fee caps for their entire investigation or representation in the case. South Carolina, for example, paid $10 an hour for out-of-court time in capital cases and imposed a $5,000 fee cap for the total representation of a capitally charged defendant. Mississippi limited payment to $1,000 above actual attorney costs (Bright, 1994, p. 1867). As a result, many capital defendants went to trial with virtually no meaningful investigation (guilt or punishment phase) in their cases. Despite the sudden change in state capital statutes and emerging constitutional doctrines demanding heightened reliability in capital cases, many capital trials looked very similar to their older counterparts—rudimentary, truncated, and nonadversarial, with only the prosecution doing much investigation or preparation in advance of trial.

But the constitutional intervention by the court in *Furman* and subsequent cases also brought new energy and thought to capital punishment defense. Federally funded "resource centers" were established in several jurisdictions, housing full-time death penalty attorneys who would litigate directly on behalf of death-sentenced inmates and provide training and advice to other lawyers working on such cases at all stages—trial, direct appeal, state postconviction, and federal habeas. Nonprofits devoted to capital defense also emerged, and, together with the resource centers, these organizations marked the establishment of the new profession of "capital defense lawyer." Prior to *Furman*, lawyers who worked on capital cases were generalists who typically had no special expertise in capital litigation. Some states created their own offices for death penalty representation, and this public-defender model of capital defense predictably improved the quality and zealousness of representation. By the late 1980s and through the 1990s, capital defense became highly specialized, with experts emerging in trial, appellate, and postconviction advocacy; within capital trial representation, sub-specialties emerged in jury-selection techniques and mitigation investigation. Capital trial lawyers began to enlist "mitigation specialists" who would undertake comprehensive investigation of a defendant's background, family history, mental health, and intellectual limitations.

The changes in practice on the ground led the American Bar Association to promulgate in 1989 its *Guidelines for the Appointment and Performance of Counsel in Death Penalty Cases*.[4] The *Guidelines* underscored the importance of institutional mechanisms to effective capital representation, exhorting states to develop policies for the appointment of competent counsel in capital cases (two attorneys at trial) and to adhere to workload, training, and resource requirements. The *Guidelines* also emphasized that capital lawyers should understand "that the sentencing phase of a death penalty trial is constitutionally different from proceedings in other criminal cases" (Guideline 11.8.1, 1989). The *Guidelines* called upon counsel to uncover evidence relating to the defendant's "life and development, from birth to the time of sentencing" and to explore possible "medical, psychological, sociological or other explanations" for the commission of the offense (Guideline 11.8.3, 1989). At the time they were issued, the *Guidelines* reflected best practices in capital cases, but the commentary acknowledged that such practices often went unobserved. When the ABA issued updated *Guidelines* in 2003, the ABA emphasized that "these Guidelines are not aspirational" but rather "they embody the current consensus about what is required to provide effective defense representation in capital cases" (*Guidelines*, 2003, p. 920). The updated *Guidelines* call for the creation of a "defense team" including two attorneys, at least one mitigation specialist, one fact investigator, and at least one member qualified to screen for the presence of mental or psychological disorders or impairments (pp. 999–1000). Together with the accompanying commentary, the updated *Guidelines* provide a much more detailed account of the responsibilities regarding mitigation investigation, indicating that counsel should explore a client's medical history, family and social history, educational history, military service, employment and training history, and prior juvenile and adult correctional history. Within each of these categories, additional guidance is offered: "family and social history" encompasses, among other things, investigation regarding physical, sexual, or emotional abuse; family history of mental illness, cognitive impairments, substance abuse, or domestic violence; poverty, familial instability; traumatic events including criminal victimization, the death of loved ones, experiences of racism or other forms of bias, and inadequate government or social interventions (p. 1022).

The two versions of the *Guidelines* articulate a much more sophisticated practice of capital defense than existed in the pre-*Furman* or early post-*Furman* worlds. Apart from the extraordinary detail regarding potentially mitigating factors contained in the 2003 revised edition, the *Guidelines* also provide insight about the critical obligations of counsel in their efforts to wield such information effectively. For example, the *Guidelines* offer explicit directions regarding client contact, both to facilitate the discovery of potential mitigating evidence and to make it possible to negotiate a plea for a life sentence; without extensive client contact, the defense team might not earn the trust of the client that is typically crucial to avoid the imposition of a death sentence.

The *Guidelines* offer an approach to capital defense in which the overriding obligation of the defense team is to avoid a death sentence by humanizing the defendant. That task requires extensive exploration of the causes contributing to the offense and the utilization of experts to comprehend fully the medical, psychological, and social limitations of capital defendants. It also requires careful attention to strategy in linking the guilt phase defense to the mitigating case at punishment. When the court rejected mandatory death sentencing in 1976, it could not have imagined how radically the conception of best capital practices would change. The restoration of discretion in capital sentencing did not return capital defense to its pre-*Furman* form; together with bifurcation and the enumeration of mitigating factors, the court's recognition of constitutionally required individualized sentencing reoriented capital defense toward a comprehensive account of the bases for withholding death, even in highly aggravated cases.

Judicial Insistence on Mitigation Efforts

Changes in capital defense practice are reflected in the court's more recent decisions enforcing the Sixth Amendment right to effective assistance of counsel. In the first two decades post-*Furman*, the court developed a highly deferential test for assessing whether trial counsel's failure to investigate or present mitigating evidence necessitated reversal of a death sentence. The court insisted that no special representational requirements should be applied to capital cases, emphasizing that reviewing courts should defer to plausible strategic decisions made by capital trial counsel (*Strickland v. Washington*, 1984). The court rejected the notion that effective advocacy could be captured through concrete rules as opposed to a general standard of competent representation. Beginning in 2000, the court refashioned its approach, issuing a trio of cases finding ineffectiveness in punishment-phase capital investigation. In the first case, trial counsel had not begun preparation for the punishment phase until the week before trial (*Williams v. Taylor*, 2000). In the latter two cases, the court referenced the ABA *Guidelines* in holding that the failure of trial lawyers to uncover significant mitigating evidence amounted to Sixth Amendment violations requiring reversal of the death sentences imposed (*Wiggins v. Smith*, 2003; *Rompilla v. Beard*, 2005). Although the court remains divided about the status of the *Guidelines* in gauging Sixth Amendment violations in capital cases, the court seems clearly more inclined to find the failure to undertake basic investigatory efforts as presumptively ineffective when a defendant's life is on the line.

Conclusion

The breadth of the right to individualized sentencing is an unexpected by-product of the Supreme Court's decision to regulate American capital practices via the Eighth Amendment. The court's original impetus for subjecting state capital schemes to constitutional regulation was the widespread perception that death penalty decision making was arbitrary and discriminatory; only a minuscule number of offenders who committed death-eligible crimes were sentenced to death, and the absence of standards virtually assured that those selected to die would be arbitrarily or invidiously chosen. The observable influence of race in capital prosecutions for rape, in which African-American defendants with white victims were far more likely to receive capital sentences, underscored the risk of arbitrariness and discrimination. *Furman*'s insistence on guidance led a minority of states to return to mandatory death sentences, which in turn led the court to announce and then to expand a constitutional guarantee of individualized sentencing. The expansion of the individualization right—to encompass a defendant's right to present any and all considerations supporting a sentence less than death—appeared to undermine whatever guidance states achieved through their enumeration of aggravating factors. Even if states managed to successfully limit the pool of death-eligible defendants through such factors (a task that has proven quite elusive), the robust right to individualized sentencing would ensure that sentencers retain an unaccountable and unguided veto of the death penalty.

The fear that unbridled consideration of mitigating evidence undermines the effort to guide capital decision making led different members of the court to denounce the individualization line of case as incompatible with *Furman*'s insistence on guidance and standards. Justice Scalia, who described the "tension" between guidance and individualization as comparable to the "tension" between the Allied and Axis powers, announced in 1990 that he would no longer vote to grant relief on the ground that a defendant's right to individualized sentencing had been compromised (Walton v. Arizona, p. 664).

Justice Blackmun, agreeing that *Furman's* insistence on guidance cannot be reconciled with *Woodson's* demand for individualization, concluded that the death penalty cannot be administered in a constitutional fashion; unlike Justice Scalia, he regarded both principles as essential to the fair administration of capital punishment (*Callins v. Collins*, 1994). On that basis, Justice Blackmun indicated he would vote to reverse all capital sentences coming to the court, vowing no longer to "tinker with the machinery of death" (p. 1145). Whereas the enumeration of aggravating and mitigating factors appeared to be the salvation of the American death penalty in the wake of *Furman's* condemnation of standardless discretion, the tension between the commands of guidance and discretion has become a substantial destabilizing force.

The court's robust approach to mitigation has destabilized the American death penalty in another important respect. The increased expectations of capital defense teams in investigating and presenting mitigating evidence has markedly increased the cost of seeking and imposing the death penalty. The average capital trial costs hundreds of thousands of dollars more than its noncapital counterparts, with some capital trials costing in the millions. The costs include not simply the money spent in mitigation investigation and experts (which are significant in competently litigated cases); the newly important role of mitigation also extends the time of jury selection, sometimes for many months, as lawyers seek to identify jurors willing to consider mitigating evidence. Additional costs follow in postconviction litigation assessing the adequacy of trial-level representation. The Supreme Court recently held that if state postconviction lawyers ineffectively fail to pursue claims of trial-level ineffectiveness, federal habeas courts can provide a forum for litigating the trial-level claims de novo (*Martinez v. Ryan*, 2012).

The sky-rocketing costs of capital cases have shifted the issue of cost from the pro-death penalty to the anti-death penalty side of the ledger, as capital litigation costs now vastly exceed the cost of housing an inmate sentenced to life imprisonment. Cost considerations have undoubtedly contributed to the extraordinary drop in capital sentencing over the past two decades, from an average of around 310 per year nationwide in the mid-1990s to fewer than 50 per year in the most recent two years—amounting to more than an 80% decline. Part of the decline is likely attributable to the increasingly effective use of mitigation in some of the cases that go to trial: Terry Nichols, convicted for his role in the Oklahoma City bombing, and James Holmes, who killed 12 and injured 70 others in his Aurora, Colorado, movie-theater attack, were both spared the death penalty after extensive mitigation efforts prevented prosecutors from obtaining unanimous death verdicts in their cases. The decline in death sentencing undermines the death penalty by making a relatively marginal practice even more marginal; plunging death sentences also increase the vulnerability of capital punishment to constitutional attack. When fewer than 50 death sentences are produced nationwide in response to thousands of homicides, it becomes increasingly difficult to maintain that capital punishment meaningfully serves a deterrence or retributive function. And if the death penalty fails credibly to serve any purposes of punishment, it is almost by definition excessive and therefore unconstitutional under the Eighth Amendment. Robust mitigation practice, by raising costs and limiting death sentences, thus represents perhaps the greatest existential threat to the continued retention of the American death penalty.

Notes

* Henry J. Friendly Professor of Law, Harvard Law School.

** Judge Robert M. Parker Endowed Chair in Law, University of Texas School of Law.

1 The constitutional litigation campaign that produced *Furman's* temporary abolition in 1972 was inspired by a dissent from denial of certiorari penned by Justice Arthur Goldberg in 1963, in which he was joined by two other justices in calling for the Supreme Court to consider the constitutionality of the death penalty for the crime of rape. Rudolph v. Alabama, 375 U.S. 889 (1963) (Goldberg, J., dissenting).

2 The Court later abandoned its "weighing/non-weighing" distinction in Brown v. Sanders, 546 U.S. 212 (2006), but the new "test" that the Court announced in *Brown* is functionally identical to its earlier decisions in terms of the role of aggravating factors in constitutional analysis of capital sentencing schemes.

3 The six cases post-*Penry* cases in which the Court developed a more robust view of the individualization requirement were *Penry v. Johnson*, 532 U.S. 782 (2001); *Tennard v. Dretke*, 542 U.S. 274 (2004); *Smith v. Texas*, 543 U.S. 37 (2004); *Abdul-Kabir v. Quarterman*, 550 U.S. 233 (2007); *Brewer v. Quarterman*, 550 U.S. 286 (2007); and *Smith v. Texas*, 550 U.S. 297 (2007).

4 The 1989 ABA Guidelines are available at www.americanbar.org/content/dam/aba/migrated/2011_build/death_penalty_representation/1989guidelines.authcheckdam.pdf.

References

American Bar Association Guidelines for the Appointment and Performance of Counsel in Death Penalty Cases (1989). Retrieved from www.americanbar.org/content/dam/aba/migrated/2011_build/death_penalty_representation/1989guidelines.authcheckdam.pdf

American Bar Association (2003). Guidelines for the Appointment and Performance of Counsel in Death Penalty Cases (revised) (2003). *Hofstra Law Review, 31*, 913–1090.

American Law Institute. (1980). *Model penal code and commentaries.* Philadelphia, PA: American Law Institute.

Baldus, D. C., Woodworth, G., & Pulaski, C. A., Jr. (1990). *Equal justice and the death penalty: A legal and empirical analysis.* Boston, MA: Northeastern University Press.

Bright, S. (1994). Counsel for the poor: The death sentence not for the worst crime but for the worst lawyer. *Yale Law Journal, 103*, 1835–1883.

Simon, J., & Spaulding, C. (1999). Tokens of our esteem: Aggravating factors in the era of deregulated death penalties. In A. Sarat (Ed.), *The killing state: Capital punishment in law, politics, and culture* (pp. 81–113). New York, NY: Oxford University Press.

Cases Cited

Abdul-Kabir v. Quarterman, 550 U.S. 233 (2007).
Apprendi v. New Jersey, 530 U.S. 466 (2000).
Arave v. Creech, 507 U.S. 463 (1993).
Blakely v. Washington, 542 U.S. 296 (2004).
Brewer v. Quarterman, 550 U.S. 286 (2007).
Brown v. Sanders, 546 U.S. 212 (2006).
Callins v. Collins, 510 U.S. 1141 (1994).
Clemons v. Mississippi, 494 U.S. 738 (1990).
Furman v. Georgia, 408 U.S. 238 (1972).
Godfrey v. Georgia, 446 U.S. 420 (1980).
Gregg v. Georgia, 428 U.S. 153 (1976).
Hurst v. Florida, 136 S. Ct. 616 (2016).
Johnson v. Texas, 509 U.S. 350 (1993).
Jurek v. Texas, 428 U.S. 262 (1976).
Kennedy v. Louisiana, 554 U.S. 407 (2008).
Lockett v. Ohio, 438 U.S. 586 (1978).
Lowenfield v. Phelps, 484 U.S. 231 (1988).
Martinez v. Ryan, 566 U.S. 1 (2012).
Maynard v. Cartwright, 486 U.S. 356 (1988).
McGautha v. California, 402 U.S. 183 (1971).
Mills v. Maryland, 486 U.S. 367 (1988).
Penry v. Johnson, 532 U.S. 782 (2001).
Penry v. Lynaugh, 492 U.S. 303 (1989).
People v. Holmes, 2014 Colo. Dist. LEXIS 1775.
Rauf v. State, 145 A.3d 430 (Delaware 2016).
Ring v. Arizona, 536 U.S. 584 (2002).
Roberts v. North Carolina, 428 U.S. 325 (1976).
Rompilla v. Beard, 545 U.S. 374 (2005).
Roper v. Simmons, 543 U.S. 551 (2005).
Rudolph v. Alabama, 375 U.S. 889 (1963).
Saldano v. State, 232 S.W. 2d 77 (Tex. Crim. App. 2007).
Skipper v. South Carolina, 476 U.S. 1 (1986).
Smith v. Texas, 543 U.S. 37 (2004).

Smith v. Texas, 550 U.S. 297 (2007).
Stenson v. Lambert, 504 F.3d 873, 892 (9th Cir. 2007).
Strickland v. Washington, 466 U.S. 668 (1984).
Tennard v. Dretke, 542 U.S. 274 (2004).
United States v. Booker, 543 U.S. 220 (2005).
Walton v. Arizona, 497 U.S. 639 (1990).
Wiggins v. Smith, 539 U.S. 510 (2003).
Williams v. Taylor, 529 U.S. 362 (2000).
Woodson v. North Carolina, 428 U.S. 280 (1976).
Zant v. Stephens, 462 U.S. 862 (1983).

16

CAPITAL OFFENDERS' INTELLECTUAL DISABILITY AND "INSANITY"

Excluding and Delaying the Death Penalty

Peggy M. Tobolowsky

It is estimated that over 4% of the American adult population has a serious mental illness and that 1–3% of the general population is intellectually disabled (American Psychiatric Association (APA), 2013; National Institute of Mental Health, 2016; Tobolowsky, 2014). Traditionally, the estimates of seriously mentally ill and intellectually disabled death-sentenced offenders have exceeded those of the general population (Hensl, 2004; Tobolowsky, 2014; White, 1993). In *Ford v. Wainwright* (1986), the United States Supreme Court (the Court) ruled that the *carrying out* of a death sentence on a capital offender who is "insane" is unconstitutional cruel and unusual punishment under the Eighth Amendment. In *Atkins v. Virginia* (2002), the Court concluded that the *imposition* of a death sentence on an intellectually disabled offender is also unconstitutional under the Eighth Amendment. This chapter reviews the Court's rulings that established the categorical exclusion from the death penalty for intellectually disabled offenders and the constitutional basis to delay the carrying out of a death sentence on "insane" offenders, as well as their implementation by this country's capital punishment jurisdictions.

Intellectual Disability as a Categorical Exclusion From the Death Penalty

Treatment of Intellectual Disability Prior to Atkins

At common law, an extreme form of intellectual disability was characterized as "idiocy" (Ellis & Luckasson, 1985). Prior to the adoption of the current clinical designation of intellectual disability, the terms "mental deficiency" and "mental retardation" had been used to describe this mental disability. Regardless of the term used, contemporary clinical definitions of intellectual disability have included three essential elements: significant intellectual and accompanying adaptive functioning limitations that manifest during the developmental period of life (AAIDD Ad Hoc Committee on Terminology and Classification (AAIDD), 2010; APA, 2013; Tobolowsky, 2014).

Although the more extreme form of "idiocy" was recognized as a defense to prosecution at common law, no such defense has been recognized for the broader concept of intellectual disability (Ellis & Luckasson, 1985). To the contrary, characteristics often associated with intellectual disability, such as incomplete concepts of blameworthiness, limited communication skills, and vulnerability to suggestion, sometimes increased the difficulty of defending against accusations of crime. Consequently, despite the fact that criminal behavior by intellectually disabled persons is not believed to be higher than the general population, estimates of the portion of this country's incarcerated population that is intellectually disabled range from 2–25%. Prior to *Atkins*, estimates of the intellectually disabled death-sentenced population ranged from 4–20% (Tobolowsky, 2014).

Although there has been no attempt to establish an intellectual disability defense to criminal conduct itself, in the late 1980s, legislatures began to adopt a categorical exclusion from the most extreme criminal sanction—the death penalty—for intellectually disabled capital offenders. Moreover, in 1989, in *Penry v. Lynaugh*, the Court considered a claim that the execution of "mentally retarded" offenders was cruel and unusual punishment prohibited by the Eighth Amendment.

In *Penry*, the Court addressed the case of an intellectually disabled offender with an intelligence quotient (IQ) between 50 and 63 who had been found criminally competent and *not* criminally insane and was subsequently sentenced to death. In examining whether the imposition of the death penalty on intellectually disabled offenders such as Penry would violate the Eighth Amendment's prohibition of cruel and unusual punishment, a five-Justice majority determined that it would *not* be deemed unconstitutionally cruel and unusual either as that term was understood at the time of the adoption of the Bill or Rights or under the concept of the "evolving standards of decency" used by the Court to interpret this provision in its contemporary context (*Penry v. Lynaugh*, 1989; *Trop v. Dulles*, 1958, p. 101).

In terms of the concept's common law application, the *Penry* Court found that the common law exclusion from punishment for "idiots" and "lunatics" referred to individuals with more severe mental impairments than Penry, whose circumstances were addressed by the criminal competency and insanity procedures in contemporary practice (*Penry v. Lynaugh*, 1989). The Court further found that the evidence that a national consensus against the execution of "mentally retarded" offenders had emerged in contemporary times was insufficient, including the fact that Congress and two capital punishment states prohibited this punishment (as well as the 14 noncapital punishment states) (*Penry v. Lynaugh*, 1989).

The Atkins Decision

The Court revisited this constitutional claim over a decade later in *Atkins v. Virginia* (2002), concerning an intellectually disabled offender with an IQ of 59. A six-Justice majority concluded that the execution of "mentally retarded" capital offenders *does* violate the Eighth Amendment (*Atkins v. Virginia*, 2002). Although the basic legal issues raised in *Penry* and *Atkins* were largely the same, legislative action by capital punishment states and capital punishment practice in the intervening years convinced the Court that a national consensus against the execution of intellectually disabled offenders had emerged (*Atkins v. Virginia*, 2002).

As of the *Atkins* decision, Congress and 18 capital punishment states prohibited the execution of "mentally retarded" offenders (as well as the 12 noncapital punishment states) and few of the remaining 20 capital punishment states had executed an intellectually disabled offender since *Penry*. The Court further determined that the national consensus it had found against the execution of "mentally retarded" offenders reflected a judgment about the diminished personal culpability of these offenders, the limited relationship between intellectual disability and the retribution and deterrence punishment purposes served by the death penalty, and the potential for the characteristics of intellectual disability to undermine the procedural protections required in capital cases. In agreement with the national consensus it had found, the Court concluded that the execution of "mentally retarded" offenders is a constitutionally excessive punishment barred by the Eighth Amendment (*Atkins v. Virginia*, 2002).

When the *Atkins* Court barred the execution of "mentally retarded" offenders, it entrusted to capital punishment jurisdictions the responsibility to develop "appropriate ways" to identify these offenders and enforce the constitutional ban on their execution (*Atkins v. Virginia*, 2002, p. 317, quoting *Ford v. Wainwright*, 1986, p. 416). Thus, the 20 capital punishment jurisdictions without pre-*Atkins* bans had to develop a definition of "mental retardation" for these purposes and procedures to exclude such offenders from execution. Those capital punishment jurisdictions with pre-*Atkins* execution bans had to ensure that they were constitutionally adequate under *Atkins* (Tobolowsky, 2003).

As of 2016, 34 of the 38 states that authorized capital punishment as of the *Atkins* decision have legislatively and/or judicially established, to varying degrees, intellectual disability definitions and procedures for raising *Atkins* claims at trial or on collateral review, or both. Since *Atkins*, five of these states have abolished capital punishment, and two additional states have not enacted legislation to remedy a finding of unconstitutionality regarding their capital punishment statutes (*Rauf v. State*, 2016; Tobolowsky, 2014).[1] Nevertheless, these states' *Atkins* provisions are included in the following overview of *Atkins* implementation for illustrative purposes. As previously indicated, there is also a legislative ban on the execution of intellectually disabled federal offenders (18 U.S.C.A. § 3596, 2015; Tobolowsky, 2014).

The Definition of Intellectual Disability for Purposes of the Atkins Execution Ban

In its intellectual disability rulings regarding capital offenders, the Court has provided both general and specific guidance regarding the intellectual disability definition for *Atkins* purposes. In *Penry* and *Atkins*, the Court referred to the clinical definitions of "mental retardation" adopted by the American Association on Mental Retardation (now American Association on Intellectual and Developmental Disabilities (AAIDD)) and the American Psychiatric Association (APA) in describing the category of capital offenders it was addressing in its constitutional rulings. The *Atkins* Court also noted that the existing state intellectual disability definitions "generally conform[ed] to" the clinical definitions. These nationally recognized clinical definitions of intellectual disability required (1) significantly sub-average intellectual functioning, (2) limitations in adaptive functioning, and (3) manifestation of both types of limitations before age 18 (*Atkins v. Virginia*, 2002; *Penry v. Lynaugh*, 1989).

Although in a post-*Atkins* case, the Court stated that its *Atkins* "opinion did not provide definitive . . . substantive guides" defining intellectual disability for *Atkins* purposes, it nevertheless continued to refer to the clinical definition for making *Atkins* determinations (*Bobby v. Bies*, 2009, p. 831). In *Hall v. Florida* (2014), the Court subsequently addressed a case that raised the question of "how intellectual disability must be defined" in order to implement the Court's *Atkins* holding. The five-Justice *Hall* Court confirmed that the "clinical definitions of intellectual disability . . . were a fundamental premise of *Atkins*"; that *Atkins* provided "substantial guidance on the definition of intellectual disability"; and that "*Atkins* did not give the States unfettered discretion to define the full scope of the constitutional protection" (*Hall v. Florida*, 2014, pp. 1993, 1998–1999).

In *Hall*, after reviewing the clinical definitions, relevant medical practice, and objective evidence concerning other states' *Atkins* definitions, the Court found that Florida's use of a fixed IQ cut-off score of 70—without consideration of the test's standard error of measurement (SEM)—to preclude consideration of other evidence of intellectual disability in *Atkins* determinations "create[d] an unacceptable risk that persons with intellectual disability will be executed, and thus is unconstitutional." Instead, "an individual with an IQ test score "between 70 and 75 or lower," may show intellectual disability by presenting additional evidence regarding difficulties in adaptive functioning" (*Hall v. Florida*, 2014, pp. 1990, 2000).

In *Brumfield v. Cain* (2015), the Court found that a state trial court had improperly denied an offender an *Atkins* hearing based on erroneous factual determinations concerning the offender's intellectual and adaptive functioning. In this connection, the Court found that the offender's IQ score of 75 was "squarely in the range of potential intellectual disability" accounting for the SEM, and that there was "sufficient evidence to raise a question" regarding his adaptive functioning limitations (*Brumfield v. Cain*, 2015, pp. 2278–2279). In 2016, the Court accepted for resolution a claim that it is unconstitutional, under the Eighth Amendment and *Atkins* and *Hall*, to "prohibit the use of current medical standards on intellectual disability, and require the use of outdated medical standards" in determining an *Atkins* claim (*Moore v. Texas*, 2016; *Moore v. Texas*, Petition, 2015, p. i).

As previously indicated, the federal government and 18 capital punishment states had pre-*Atkins* execution bans regarding intellectually disabled capital offenders, and 16 capital punishment states have adopted post-*Atkins* bans. All 34 states have adopted legislative and/or judicial intellectual disability definitions for *Atkins* purposes. Most states adopted some variation of the nationally recognized clinical definitions of intellectual disability, but the level of detail of the definitional provisions varies considerably. The statutory ban on the execution of intellectually disabled *federal* offenders does not include any statutory definition of the term. Federal courts, however, have typically applied the three-part clinical definitions of the term in their consideration of federal offenders' *Atkins* claims (Duvall & Morris, 2006; Tobolowsky, 2014).

Although there has been a slight evolution of the clinical description of the *intellectual functioning element* of the intellectual disability definition, the post-*Penry* AAIDD and APA definitions have consistently included assessment of this element through IQ testing and test results at least as high as 75, including consideration of the SEM (AAIDD, 2010; APA, 2013; Tobolowsky, 2014). All 34 states with *Atkins* intellectual disability definitions include an intellectual functioning criterion. Although four states have not further defined this criterion, the remaining states are almost equally divided between the use of an IQ benchmark for this criterion of either 70 or 75 and below—either as a fixed benchmark, as the measure for a rebuttable presumption, or through calculations using standard deviations below the IQ instrument mean. Some states expressly permit non-IQ evidence regarding this criterion. California is the only state that does not reference an IQ benchmark at all but authorizes a case-by-case determination of intellectual functioning based on all relevant evidence. On the other hand, Arkansas' definition only includes a rebuttable presumption regarding this criterion based on an IQ of 65 or below (Blume, Johnson, & Seeds, 2009; Ellis, 2014; Everington, 2014; Fabian, Thompson, & Lazarus, 2011; Polloway, 2015; Tobolowsky, 2014).

As described in *Hall*, in addition to Florida, nine other states using an IQ of 70 benchmark could be interpreted to consider an IQ of 70—without consideration of the SEM—as an outcome determinative cutoff score that precluded consideration of evidence of the other prongs of intellectual disability (*Hall v. Florida*, 2014). The Court's finding that Florida's use of this approach was unconstitutional would apply equally to these additional states. In addition, while some states expressly required consideration of the SEM prior to *Hall*, other states had not specifically addressed this issue. The *Hall* Court made clear that "clinical definitions of intellectual disability, which take into account that IQ scores represent a range, not a fixed number, were a fundamental premise of *Atkins*. And those clinical definitions have long included the SEM" (*Hall v. Florida*, 2014, p. 1999; Tobolowsky, 2014).

Another factor that could potentially impact the interpretation of IQ scores is the "Flynn effect," addressing the increase in IQ scores over time and the need to make a downward adjustment of IQ scores if based on assessment instruments with norms that do not reflect this increase. Although the AAIDD and APA have referenced the "Flynn effect," most states have either not addressed or not resolved its use in *Atkins* proceedings (Flynn, 2006; Tobolowsky, 2014).

The clinical definition of the *adaptive functioning criterion* of intellectual disability has evolved somewhat since *Atkins*. Prior to *Atkins*, both the AAIDD and the APA assessed this criterion based on limitations in 2 of 10 (or 11 for the APA) specific adaptive skill areas (e.g., self-care, communication, self-direction, and work), and the Court referenced this aspect of the clinical definitions in its *Atkins* opinion (*Atkins v. Virginia*, 2002; *Bobby v. Bies*, 2009). Both of these professional organizations subsequently consolidated these specific skill areas into three broader categories (i.e., conceptual, social, and practical adaptive skills or domains), and they require assessed limitations in at least one of these adaptive skill categories (AAIDD, 2010; APA, 2013; Tobolowsky, 2014).

All 34 states with *Atkins* intellectual disability definitions include an adaptive functioning criterion. However, ten of these states have not legislatively or judicially defined this criterion. Eleven states have specifically adopted the clinical adaptive functioning criterion referenced in *Atkins* involving deficits in 2 of the 10 (or 11) specific skill areas, and four states have specifically or generally adopted the subsequent consolidated adaptive functioning categories. Four states adopted a more general pre-*Penry* clinical adaptive functioning definition. Five states adopted a more generalized or nonclinical definition of adaptive functioning or combined a pre-*Atkins* general clinical definition with a nonclinical set of criteria (Blume et al., 2009; Ellis, 2014; Everington, 2014; Fabian et al., 2011; Polloway, 2015; Tobolowsky, 2014).

In light of the importance the *Hall* Court attached to the intellectual disability clinical definitions, jurisdictions' failure to define the adaptive functioning criterion or their adoption of outdated or nonclinical definitions subjects them to potential challenge. Such potential challenges are reflected in the Court's 2016 acceptance for resolution of a claim contending that Texas has unconstitutionally "prohibit[ed] the use of current medical standards on intellectual disability, and require[ed] the use of outdated medical standards" in determining both intellectual and adaptive functioning for *Atkins* purposes (*Moore v. Texas*, 2016; *Moore v. Texas*, Petition, 2015, p. i).

Contemporary clinical definitions of intellectual disability have consistently required that an individual's intellectual and adaptive functioning limitations originate during the *developmental period* of life. At the time of *Atkins*, both the AAIDD and the APA quantified this developmental period onset as occurring prior to 18 years of age (AAIDD, 2010; APA, 2013; *Atkins v. Virginia*, 2002; *Bobby v. Bies*, 2009). The APA has subsequently maintained the developmental period onset criterion, but has deleted the specific age benchmark (APA, 2013; *Hall v. Florida*, 2014).

Thirty-two of the 34 states with *Atkins* procedures include a developmental period onset criterion in their intellectual disability definitions. Twenty-five of these states use the 18-years-of-age benchmark to define this criterion. Three states use a 22-years-of-age benchmark. Four states do not further define the developmental period onset criterion. Although intellectual disability is generally a "lifelong" condition, some states additionally require that it be established at the time of the crime and/or at the time of the *Atkins* proceeding (Blume et al., 2009; Ellis, 2014; Everington, 2014; Fabian et al., 2011; Polloway, 2015; Tobolowsky, 2014).

Thus, 34 of the 38 capital punishment states (as of *Atkins*) have adopted some variation of the clinical intellectual disability definitions for *Atkins* purposes. In *Hall*, the Court made explicitly clear that the "clinical definitions of intellectual disability . . . were a fundamental premise of *Atkins*" (*Hall v. Florida*, 2014, p. 1999). To the extent that any of these states have not adopted and implemented a full clinical intellectual disability definition for *Atkins* purposes, they risk constitutional challenge, as in *Hall* (*Moore v. Texas*, 2016; Polloway, 2015; Tobolowsky, 2014).

Procedures to Address Atkins Claims

The *Atkins* Court's entrustment to the states of the "task of developing appropriate ways to enforce the constitutional restriction upon [their] execution of sentences" (*Atkins v. Virginia*, 2002, p. 317, quoting *Ford v. Wainwright*, 1986, pp. 416–417) included not only the adoption of constitutionally appropriate definitions of intellectual disability but also constitutionally appropriate procedures to identify intellectually disabled offenders and exclude them from execution (*Schriro v. Smith*, 2005). The intellectual disability exclusion from execution issue can be raised during original trial proceedings, on direct appeal, and on collateral review. However, the Court has provided only limited explicit guidance in *Atkins* and subsequent cases regarding key elements of *Atkins* procedures, i.e., the burden and standard of proof and the timing of and fact-finder regarding the intellectual disability determination (Tobolowsky, 2014).

Although the Court has previously found constitutional a state's assignment of the burden of proof to the defendant regarding affirmative defenses (*Patterson v. New York*, 1977) and criminal competency (*Medina v. California*, 1992), the Court has not addressed this issue concerning intellectual disability. The federal statute does not contain any procedural provisions regarding *Atkins* determinations, but the federal courts have uniformly assigned federal defendants the burden of proof regarding their

Atkins claims. All of the states with *Atkins* procedures have assigned the defendant the burden of proof to establish intellectual disability during *Atkins* proceedings (Blume, Johnson, & Seeds, 2010; Tobolowsky, 2014).

Although the Court found that a state requirement that a defendant establish his criminal incompetency by a clear and convincing evidence standard of proof was unconstitutional (*Cooper v. Oklahoma*, 1996), it has not made a standard of proof ruling regarding intellectual disability. The federal courts have applied a preponderance of the evidence proof standard regarding federal defendants. Regarding trial-related proceedings, 26 states use a preponderance of the evidence standard of proof; four states use clear and convincing evidence; two states use both of these standards depending on the fact-finder and timing of the determination; one state uses a beyond a reasonable doubt standard; and one state has not adopted an *Atkins* standard of proof (Blume et al., 2010; Tobolowsky, 2014).

By vacating a federal collateral review court's "preemptive" requirement of a state jury determination of an *Atkins* claim (unless waived), the Court has at least suggested that a jury determination of intellectual disability is not constitutionally required (*Schriro v. Smith*, 2005). Virtually all federal courts have adopted a judicial determination of *Atkins* claims for federal defendants. In all 34 states with *Atkins* trial-related procedures, the trial judge is authorized, under certain circumstances, to determine *Atkins* claims. In 19 states, the trial judge is the exclusive fact-finder. All states that have considered the issue have determined that there is no defendant right to a jury determination of the *Atkins* issue, but there is a potential for a jury determination, under certain circumstances, in 15 states (Blume et al., 2010; Tobolowsky, 2014).

The Court has not addressed the timing of the *Atkins* determination in trial-related proceedings. Virtually all of the federal courts have adopted a pretrial determination for federal defendants. In 13 states, a pretrial determination by the judge is required, authorized, or generally preferred. In five states, the trial judge makes the *Atkins* determination at various points after the guilt determination. In six states, the defendant has the opportunity for both a judicial pretrial and, if adverse, a subsequent jury sentencing phase resolution of the *Atkins* issue. Four states permit the court to make the *Atkins* determination pretrial *or* the jury to make it during sentencing (or before sentencing in one state). One state authorizes the guilt fact-finder (judge or jury) to make the *Atkins* determination during the guilt phase and one state during the sentencing phase. Two states require the sentencing fact-finder to determine the *Atkins* issue during sentencing. Two states have not addressed the timing of the *Atkins* determination. In states that authorize an *Atkins* jury determination, the degree of required unanimity varies (Blume et al., 2010; Tobolowsky, 2014).

In their direct appellate review of *Atkins* trial-related determinations, state and federal appellate courts have considered challenges to jurisdictions' *Atkins* definitions and procedures, as well as application issues and factual determinations concerning intellectual disability. Federal and state capital offenders can also raise *Atkins*-related claims in their respective postconviction collateral review proceedings. Moreover, because of the constitutional nature of the *Atkins* claim, state offenders can also seek federal habeas corpus relief regarding these claims. Finally, due to the Court's retroactive application of its *Atkins* constitutional holding, offenders convicted prior to *Atkins* have been able to seek collateral relief regarding their intellectual disability. Although the prescribed federal and state collateral review procedures generally apply to *Atkins* claims, some jurisdictions have adopted additional procedures regarding *Atkins* claims. On collateral review of *Atkins* claims, offenders must prove their intellectual disability using the same definition as in trial-related proceedings; and, in most jurisdictions, they must prove their claim to the trial court by a preponderance of the evidence (Tobolowsky, 2014).

Thus, although the Court has not yet addressed the constitutionality of any specific *Atkins* procedure, there is a high degree of consistency in the *Atkins* collateral review procedures. Although there are more procedural variations in trial-related *Atkins* proceedings, the federal courts typically permit and the majority of states with *Atkins* procedures require or permit the trial court to make a pretrial determination of intellectual disability. In these trial-related proceedings, the defendant typically bears the burden of proof, and, in most jurisdictions, the standard of proof is preponderance of the evidence (Blume et al., 2010; Tobolowsky, 2014).

Implementation of the Atkins Execution Exclusion

Since *Atkins*, hundreds of state and federal capital offenders have sought to establish their intellectual disability for *Atkins* purposes. In addition to the varying *Atkins* intellectual disability definitions and procedures previously described, implementing courts have demonstrated significant variations in the evidence considered and approaches to the ultimate assessment of intellectual disability, often departing from clinical guidance. These differences include varying consideration of intellectual and adaptive functioning assessment instruments and their administration and interpretation, expert testimony and evidence, and lay evidence concerning intellectual disability. The manner in which capital punishment jurisdictions have implemented *Atkins* has been the subject of significant legal and intellectual disability professional scholarship, including the departure from clinical intellectual disability principles by some jurisdictions (Blume et al., 2009; Ellis, 2014; Everington, 2014; Fabian et al., 2011; Polloway, 2015; Tobolowsky, 2014). Some national studies have also been conducted regarding the outcomes of *Atkins* litigation (Blume, Johnson, Marcus, & Paavola, 2014; Tobolowsky, 2014).

One study involved a search of a leading legal data base, using relevant search terms, from the date of the *Atkins* decision through January 1, 2014. During this period, 21 federal offenders raised *Atkins* claims in connection with trial proceedings or on collateral review. The federal courts resolved the *Atkins* claims of 15 of these offenders during the study period and found six offenders intellectually disabled and ineligible for a death sentence (Tobolowsky, 2014).

In this study, over 400 state offenders raised *Atkins* claims in state courts in connection with trial proceedings or on collateral review. Of the over 300 resolved *Atkins* claims, 60 offenders were found intellectually disabled. State offenders seeking federal collateral relief on *Atkins* claims face strict limitations regarding the filing of such claims and restrictive standards regarding the granting of relief. During the study period, over 150 state offenders initiated federal collateral review of their *Atkins* claims. Of the over 130 resolved *Atkins* claims, federal courts granted the *Atkins* claims of 13 state capital offenders (Tobolowsky, 2014).

Another national study, using a data base search and other sources, identified 371 death-eligible or death-sentenced offenders who raised *Atkins* claims as of the end of 2013. These researchers found that the *Atkins* claim success rate was 55% overall. With regard to the unsuccessful *Atkins* claims, approximately 52% were unsuccessful on all three elements of the intellectual disability definition; 31% on the intellectual functioning criterion only; 12% on the adaptive functioning element; and 2% on the developmental onset factor (Blume et al., 2014).

In this study, regarding the intellectual functioning criterion, the average IQ score for successful *Atkins* claimants was 68, and the average for those who were unsuccessful solely on this element was 78. However, there was considerable variation in how courts considered evidence regarding IQ scores and related evidence. These researchers identified major contributing factors to unsuccessful claims based on adaptive functioning limitations: (1) courts' consideration of the facts of the crime or behavior in the highly structured prison setting as reflective of adaptive functioning; (2) assertions of alleged false claims of intellectual disability to avoid execution; and (3) articulated stereotypes regarding the possible level of adaptive functioning by intellectually disabled individuals (Blume et al., 2014).

These researchers also observed meaningful differences in *Atkins* outcomes among the states— often associated with the degree to which states deviated from clinical definitions and principles of intellectual disability. For example, during the study period, 0 of the 24 resolved *Atkins* claims were successful in Florida, the state regarding which the *Hall* Court found its IQ assessment approach was unconstitutional. Eight of the 45 resolved claims (18%) were successful in Texas, a state that used a more general pre-*Atkins* clinical adaptive functioning definition and nonclinical adaptive functioning criteria (the *Briseno* factors). Finally, these researchers found a diminished likelihood of success regarding *Atkins* claims resolved by juries rather than judges: 22 unsuccessful claims out of 23 *Atkins* jury determinations (Blume et al., 2014; *Ex parte Briseno*, 2004).

Thus, approximately 15 years since the *Atkins* Court held that the imposition of a death sentence on an intellectually disabled offender is unconstitutional under the Eighth Amendment, most capital punishment jurisdictions have developed definitions and procedures to determine *Atkins* claims. During this period, hundreds of state and federal capital offenders have sought *Atkins* death penalty exclusions, with varying degrees of success depending, in part, on the jurisdiction and its intellectual disability definitions and procedures (Blume et al., 2014; Polloway, 2015; Tobolowsky, 2014). As the Court's *Hall* decision reflects, the task is ongoing to ensure that capital punishment jurisdictions have developed and implemented constitutionally "appropriate ways" to identify intellectually disabled offenders and exclude them from execution (*Atkins v. Virginia*, 2002, p. 317; *Hall v. Florida*, 2014).

The Execution Prohibition Regarding "Insane" Offenders: The Requirement of Competency for Execution

The Ford Decision

Execution of "insane" offenders was prohibited at common law based on rationales including its limited retribution and deterrence purposes and insanity's negative impact on the offender's ability to defend himself against execution. However, neither the definition of insanity in this context nor the procedures for determining it were clearly articulated. American capital punishment states widely adopted the common law prohibition of the execution of "insane" offenders, but, prior to the Court's decision in *Ford v. Wainwright* (1986), few states defined insanity in this context, and procedures for determining insanity varied widely (Tobolowsky, 2007). Prior to *Ford*, the Court rejected due process and other challenges to Georgia and California post-capital sentencing insanity procedures and proceedings (*Caritativo v. California*, 1958; *Nobles v. Georgia*, 1897; *Solesbee v. Balkcom*, 1950).

In *Ford*, the Court addressed a federal collateral review proceeding involving a Florida offender who began to manifest delusional behavior several years after his capital proceeding. He had sought a determination of his sanity for execution purposes pursuant to the Florida procedure that defined sanity in this context as "the mental capacity to understand the nature of the death penalty and the reasons why it was imposed upon him" (*Ford v. Wainwright*, 1986, pp. 403–404). Under Florida procedure, following a joint offender interview by three psychiatrists appointed by the governor, the sanity determination was made solely by the governor. After the psychiatrists' unanimous determination that Ford had some type of disorder, but was "sane" for execution purposes, the governor, without any accompanying explanation, signed a death warrant for Ford's execution. Ford unsuccessfully sought both state court and federal collateral review hearings regarding his pre-execution sanity (*Ford v. Wainwright*, 1986).

In *Ford*, the Court addressed "whether the Eighth Amendment prohibits the execution of the insane" (*Ford v. Wainwright*, 1986, p. 405) and, if so, whether the federal trial court should have held a hearing on Ford's sanity claim. With regard to the primary constitutional claim, a five-Justice majority noted the substantial evolution of the Court's due process and capital punishment jurisprudence since it last reviewed a case involving execution sanity decades previously. The *Ford* Court referenced the long-standing prohibition of the execution of the "insane"—recognized at common law and universally adopted in this country, as reflected by the fact that no American capital punishment jurisdiction permitted it. The Court also recognized the continuing application of several of the common law rationales for this execution prohibition, including the limited "retributive value," offense to humanity, and "natural abhorrence" associated with executing "insane" individuals. Against this backdrop of historical and contemporary condemnation, and citing its rationale as to "protect the condemned from fear and pain without comfort of understanding, or to protect the dignity of society itself from the barbarity of exacting mindless vengeance," the Court concluded that the "Eighth Amendment prohibits a State from carrying out a sentence of death upon a prisoner who is insane" (*Ford v. Wainwright*, 1986, pp. 409–410).

By constitutionally prohibiting the "carrying out" of a death sentence on an "insane" offender, the *Ford* Court's ruling addressed an offender's competency for the execution of an imposed death sentence rather than any diminished culpability that would avoid the imposition of a death sentence itself (as subsequently established in *Atkins* for intellectually disabled offenders). Thus, through a finding of "insanity" in this context, i.e., execution competency, a capital offender could delay an imposed death sentence rather than avoid its imposition (Tobolowsky, 2007).

As discussed in subsequent sections, in addition to the *Ford* constitutional ruling, one Justice articulated a potential definition of "insanity" in the context of execution competency. The five Justices in the *Ford* majority, and two additional Justices, also found that the Florida procedures used to determine Ford's execution competency were constitutionally inadequate, but they had varying views on the required elements for a constitutionally adequate procedure (*Ford v. Wainwright*, 1986). As it later did in *Atkins*, the Court entrusted the capital punishment states with the "task of developing appropriate ways to enforce the constitutional restriction upon [their] execution of sentences" (*Atkins v. Virginia*, 2002, p. 317, quoting *Ford v. Wainwright*, 1986, pp. 416–417)—including definitions for "insanity" or execution competency and procedures to determine it. Over 20 years after *Ford*, the Court revisited the constitutional adequacy of "insanity" definitions and procedures in *Panetti v. Quarterman* (2007), as described in the subsequent sections.

As of 2016, 36 of the 38 states that authorized capital punishment as of the *Panetti* decision have legislatively and/or judicially established, to varying degrees, execution competency definitions and/or procedures (Tobolowsky, 2007).[2] Although, as noted previously, several of these states have subsequently either abolished capital punishment or had their capital systems deemed unconstitutional, these states' *Ford* provisions are included in the following overview of *Ford* implementation for illustrative purposes. There is also a legislative ban on the carrying out of a death sentence regarding federal offenders who lack execution competency (18 U.S.C.A. § 3596, 2015).

Execution Competency Definitions

It is estimated that 5–10% of death-sentenced offenders are seriously mentally ill (Blume, Johnson, & Ensler, 2013; Tobolowsky, 2007). However, insanity for *Ford* execution competency purposes involves a narrower concept than a mental illness diagnosis. Prior to *Ford*, American capital punishment jurisdictions that had adopted a definition of execution competency used one or both prongs of a definition that included an offender's awareness or understanding of his imminent execution and its reason or purpose (a "cognitive" prong) and/or his ability to convey relevant information to counsel or the court (an "assistance" prong). In his concurring opinion in *Ford*, Justice Powell was the only Justice who offered a potential minimum constitutional definition of "insanity" for execution competency purposes, and his definition reflected the cognitive prong only: "those who are unaware of the punishment they are about to suffer and why they are to suffer it" (*Ford v. Wainwright*, 1986, p. 422).

In *Panetti v. Quarterman* (2007), the Court reviewed a federal de novo collateral review execution competency determination involving a Texas offender whose delusional disorder caused him to believe that he was going to be executed for "preaching the Gospel" rather than the government's stated reason for his execution. Under a controlling federal appellate interpretation of *Ford*, the federal trial court found that Panetti's knowledge of the fact of his impending execution and its factual predicate rendered his delusional beliefs irrelevant for *Ford* purposes. The federal appellate court confirmed its view that the "awareness" required by Justice Powell in *Ford* was "not necessarily synonymous with 'rational understanding'" (*Panetti v. Dretke*, 2006, p. 821; *Panetti v. Dretke*, 2004, pp. 707–709; *Panetti v. Quarterman*, 2007).

The five-Justice *Panetti* Court addressed the question "whether the Eighth Amendment permits the execution of a prisoner whose mental illness deprives him of 'the mental capacity to understand that [he] is being executed as a punishment for a crime'" (*Panetti v. Quarterman*, 2007, p. 954). Contrary to the appellate court's "flawed interpretation" of *Ford* (*Panetti v. Quarterman*, 2007, p. 956), the Court stated that evidence of Panetti's "severe" delusions was not irrelevant to the determination of execution competency. The Court noted that a majority of the *Ford* Justices had described insanity for execution purposes as encompassing a lack of comprehension or awareness of the reasons for the punishment. Nothing in *Ford* indicated (1) that delusions that prevented an offender from reaching a rational understanding of the reasons for his punishment were irrelevant to a determination of execution competency; (2) that they were relevant only with regard to the government's stated reason for the execution; or (3) that execution competency is limited to an offender's identification of the stated reason for his execution (*Panetti v. Quarterman*, 2007).

To the contrary, the *Panetti* Court stated that "[a] prisoner's awareness of the State's rationale for an execution is not the same as a rational understanding of it. *Ford* does not foreclose inquiry into the latter" (*Panetti v. Quarterman*, 2007, p. 959). The Court found that it "is therefore error to derive from *Ford*, and the substantive standard for incompetency its opinions broadly identify, a strict test for competency that treats delusional beliefs as irrelevant once the prisoner is aware the State has identified the link between his crime and the punishment to be inflicted" (*Panetti v. Quarterman*, 2007, p. 960). Although the *Panetti* Court reversed the flawed execution competency determination, it declined to establish a uniform standard for all execution competency determinations (*Panetti v. Quarterman*, 2007).

As of 2016, the majority of the 38 capital punishment states as of *Panetti* have legislatively or judicially adopted a definition of *Ford* execution competency. Twenty states use some variation of the cognitive prong, identified by Justice Powell in *Ford*, regarding an offender's awareness or understanding of his imminent execution and its reason or purpose. Eleven states use both a cognitive prong and an assistance prong involving an offender's ability to convey relevant information to counsel or the court or assist in his representation. Seven states have not expressly established a *Ford* execution competency definition. The federal statute incorporates the cognitive prong in its definition (Ackerson, Brodsky, & Zapf, 2005; Kirchmeier, 2010; Seeds, 2009; Tobolowsky, 2007).

To the extent that it was unclear prior to *Panetti*, the *Panetti* Court clarified that an assessment of an offender's awareness or understanding of his imminent execution and its reason or purpose encompasses a rational understanding, including consideration of the offender's delusions (Blume et al., 2013; Greenberg, 2012; Kirchmeier, 2010; Tobolowsky, 2007). Post-*Panetti* courts considering offenders' execution competency have generally acknowledged this clarification of *Ford*'s requirements (*Commonwealth v. Banks*, 2011; *Ferguson v. Secretary, Florida Department of Corrections*, 2013; *Green v. State*, 2012; *Overstreet v. State*, 2013; *State ex rel. Cole v. Griffith*, 2015; *State v. Irick*, 2010). Any jurisdiction that does not incorporate this clarified cognitive standard in its execution competency determinations risks constitutional challenge.

Execution Competency Procedures

In addition to establishing the constitutional ban on the execution of "insane" individuals, the five *Ford* Court majority Justices, and two additional Justices, found that the Florida execution competency proceedings had not met basic due process standards (*Ford v. Wainwright*, 1986). The *Panetti* Court found that the Texas execution competency proceedings failed to provide the minimum due process required by *Ford* (*Panetti v. Quarterman*, 2007).

The seven *Ford* Court Justices raised several criticisms of the Florida execution competency procedure that made the governor the sole decision maker in an exclusively executive branch inquiry that did not require consideration of any evidence from the offender. The Justices shared the concern that the Florida procedure did not incorporate an opportunity for the offender to be heard (*Ford v. Wainwright*, 1986). In his concurring opinion, Justice Powell identified the elements of a minimum constitutional execution competency procedure that could include a "substantial threshold showing" to initiate an execution competency review and a proceeding "far less formal than a trial," but that should at least incorporate a "fair hearing" by an "impartial officer or board that can receive evidence and argument" from the defense, including defense psychiatric evidence (*Ford v. Wainwright*, 1986, pp. 426–427). Because it found that the Florida proceedings had not met basic due process standards, the *Ford* Court determined that they were not entitled to deference on federal collateral review and that Ford's execution competency was subject to a hearing and determination in the federal proceedings (*Ford v. Wainwright*, 1986).

In *Panetti*, the Court addressed a Texas execution competency proceeding in which the state court had initially concluded that Panetti had failed to meet the required threshold "substantial showing" of execution incompetency and had denied his motion without a hearing (*Panetti v. Dretke*, 2004, p. 703). Following a federal collateral review court's execution stay, the state court subsequently appointed two mental health experts and, based on their report, denied Panetti's competency motion without an evidentiary hearing or ruling on defense objections to the report or its motions for an independent expert and a hearing (*Panetti v. Quarterman*, 2007).

The *Panetti* Court concluded that Justice Powell's opinion in *Ford* established minimum constitutional procedures that a state must provide following an offender's satisfaction of the prescribed threshold showing regarding execution competency (which the Court found was satisfied in this case). The Court identified the following minimum essential elements of such a constitutional procedure: a fair hearing, with an opportunity to be heard and to present evidence and argument, including defense psychiatric evidence. Finding that the Texas execution competency proceeding lacked these essential elements, the *Panetti* Court found that it failed to provide the minimum due process required by *Ford* and was not entitled to deference on federal collateral review (*Panetti v. Quarterman*, 2007).

As of 2016, 35 of the 38 capital punishment states as of *Panetti* have some type of statutory or judicially established execution competency procedure. However, these state procedures vary considerably in detail and scope regarding how and when the issue can be raised, the fact-finding procedure and the prescribed fact-finder, the standard of proof, and the ultimate short- and long-term effect of a finding of incompetency for execution. The federal execution competency statute does not include a procedure, and there is no federal judicially established procedure beyond the constitutional minimum requirements identified in *Ford* and *Panetti* (Tobolowsky, 2007).

Approximately 20 states directly or indirectly permit multiple parties, such as defense and prosecuting attorneys or prison authorities, to initiate an inquiry regarding an offender's execution competency. Of the remaining states, about half entrust this responsibility solely to the offender or his attorney and about half to correctional authorities. Most states require some general threshold showing of execution incompetency, such as "good reason" or "reasonable cause," to initiate a competency inquiry. Although most states generally establish that their competency procedures apply to the post-capital-sentencing phase, some states authorize a competency inquiry only after an offender's execution date has been set (Tobolowsky, 2007).

In 28 states, a judge is required or permitted to determine execution competency, with one of these states permitting an alternative jury determination. In four states, mental health professionals are the primary decision makers. In two states, a jury determines execution competency, and in one state, the governor makes the determination. Most states require or authorize the decision maker's appointment of one or more mental health professionals to examine the offender, but only approximately ten states expressly authorize the appointment of an independent mental health expert for the offender (Tobolowsky, 2007).

Most, but not all, states expressly require or permit either an execution competency hearing before the decision maker or some alternative mechanism to present defense information to the decision maker. Other aspects of the decision making process have not been expressly prescribed by a substantial number of the states. Less than 15 states expressly assign a burden of proof regarding execution competency. All, but one, of these states place the burden on the offender to establish his execution incompetency. Less than 20 states identify a standard of proof regarding execution incompetency. All but four of these states apply the preponderance of the evidence standard and the remaining four states use the clear and convincing evidence standard. Fifteen states or less expressly (1) provide the offender's right to appointed counsel regarding competency proceedings, to cross-examine witnesses, or to appeal adverse determinations; or (2) require the decision maker to make factual findings or provide a statement of reasons for the competency determination (Tobolowsky, 2007).

Following a finding of execution incompetency, states typically transfer the offender to a state or prison mental health facility. Although the Court has addressed the involuntary administration of medication in other contexts (*Riggins v. Nevada*, 1992; *Sell v. United States*, 2003; *Washington v. Harper*, 1990), it has not addressed the issue of the involuntary administration of medication for the sole purpose of restoring or maintaining execution competency (*Singleton v. Norris*, 2003). A few states expressly prohibit such use of medication (*Singleton v. State*, 1993; *State v. Perry*, 1992; Utah Code Ann. § 77–19–205, 2012). One state potentially permits it (Ariz. Rev. Stat. Ann. § 13–4022, 2010). Most states have not expressly addressed the issue (Entzeroth, 2009; Shannon & Scarano, 2013; Tobolowsky, 2007).

Over ten states provide for some type of periodic review of an incompetent offender's execution competency. However, almost 20 states require no further action after the incompetency determination until the mental health facility indicates some change in the offender's competency status, or the court sua sponte or some other designated party initiates further action. An indication of the restoration of the offender's competency typically results in a repetition of the initial competency procedures or some alternative type of review by the initial decision maker. In a few states, the burden of proof shifts to the government in these subsequent proceedings. On the other hand, in one state, an initial finding of execution incompetency would result in a sentence modification to life imprisonment without parole. In four states, a period of prolonged or repeated incompetency for execution could result in an indefinite or permanent suspension of execution. In situations in which an offender has been found competent for execution in his initial proceedings, approximately ten states expressly permit subsequent competency proceedings, but typically require a threshold showing of changed circumstances (Tobolowsky, 2007).

Thus, the prescribed execution competency procedures vary significantly in detail and scope. Of course, the minimum constitutional procedures identified in *Ford* and *Panetti* establish the constitutional "floor" for execution competency determinations. Even prior to *Ford* and *Panetti*, a number of states adopted express execution competency procedures that satisfy these minimum constitutional requirements. A few states expressly modified or clarified their procedures to comply with these constitutional mandates (*Commonwealth v. Banks*, 2011; Fla. R. Crim. P. 3.811, 3.812; *State ex rel. Clayton v. Griffith*, 2015). The express execution competency procedures in some of the other states do not fully comply with the constitutional requirements. Any state whose express procedure or actual practice does not satisfy the *Ford* and *Panetti* requirements risks constitutional challenge (Tobolowsky, 2007).

Implementation of Ford's Execution Competency Requirement

In the over 30 years since *Ford*, capital offenders have been able to raise a constitutional claim regarding their execution competency. Using legal data bases and other sources, researchers gathered information on capital offenders who had raised *Ford* claims from 1986, when *Ford* was decided, to mid-2013. During this period, they found that, of the 1,307 "*Ford*-eligible" capital offenders,[3] 140 asserted *Ford* claims. Of these claims, 120 were unsuccessful, with 71 of the unsuccessful claims actually decided on the merits. Twenty of the *Ford* claims were successful, resulting in a finding of execution incompetency (Blume et al., 2013).

These researchers found significant variations among the states, both regarding the number of *Ford* claims resolved on the merits and their outcomes. Of the total 91 *Ford* claims resolved on the merits, 15 of the 38 capital punishment states as of *Panetti* and the federal criminal justice system resolved zero *Ford* claims. Fifteen states resolved one to three *Ford* claims during the study period, and seven states resolved four or five *Ford* claims. Texas resolved 32 *Ford* claims on the merits. Of course, the *Ford* outcomes in most states were based on a very small number of resolved claims, but they ranged from 0% findings of execution incompetency in 12 states to 100% success in one state, with an overall state success rate of 22% of *Ford* claims resolved on the merits. The Texas *Ford* success rate, representing the outcomes of over one-third of the 91 claims resolved on the merits, was 22% (Blume et al., 2013).

These researchers also examined the *Ford* claimants' mental health and competency litigation histories, and variations based on claimants' race or ethnicity. In 57 of the 91 cases resolved on the merits, offenders had documented delusions, schizophrenia, or both. In 55 of the 91 cases, there were documented challenges regarding the offender's competency previously in the criminal proceedings. Although the *Ford* claim filing rates generally matched the racial and ethnic composition of the death row population, 60% of the successful *Ford* claims involved African American claimants (Blume et al., 2013).

Thus, over 30 years ago, the *Ford* Court held that execution of the "insane" is unconstitutional under the Eighth Amendment. As first articulated by Justice Powell in *Ford*, and confirmed in *Panetti*, the Court has identified a minimum constitutional definition of execution competency and accompanying procedures to determine it (*Ford v. Wainwright*, 1986; *Panetti v. Quarterman*, 2007). The federal criminal justice system and the capital punishment states have adopted execution competency definitions and procedures that vary significantly in detail and scope, but all are required to adhere to the constitutional minimum standards set by the Court or face constitutional challenge (Tobolowsky, 2007). Researchers have documented the relatively small proportion of "*Ford*-eligible" capital offenders who have pursued *Ford* claims and the relatively modest level of success regarding these claims and have raised related issues concerning the implementation of *Ford* (Blume et al., 2013). As the Court's *Panetti* decision reflects, the task is ongoing to ensure that capital punishment jurisdictions have developed and implemented constitutionally "appropriate ways" to identify capital offenders who are not competent to be executed (*Ford v. Wainwright*, 1986, p. 416).

Conclusion

In *Ford*, the Court held that the execution of an "insane" capital offender who is incompetent for execution is unconstitutional (*Ford v. Wainwright*, 1986). In *Atkins*, the Court held that the imposition of a death sentence on an intellectually disabled offender is unconstitutional (*Atkins v. Virginia*, 2002). Capital punishment jurisdictions have implemented these constitutional mandates in varying ways and to varying degrees. As the *Panetti* and *Hall* decisions reflect, the task is ongoing to ensure that jurisdictions adopt constitutionally "appropriate ways" to implement these constitutional requirements (*Atkins v. Virginia*, 2002, p. 317, quoting *Ford v. Wainwright*, 1986, p. 416; *Hall v. Florida*, 2014; *Panetti v. Quarterman*, 2007).

Notes

1 Since *Atkins*, Connecticut, Illinois, Maryland, New Jersey, and New Mexico have abolished the death penalty. New York's death penalty statute was found unconstitutional in 2004, as was Delaware's statute in 2016. As of 2016, Montana, New Hampshire, Oregon, and Wyoming have not yet adopted *Atkins*-specific definitions or procedures (*Rauf v. State*, 2016; Tobolowsky, 2014). While not adopting specific *Atkins* definitions or procedures for statewide use, the Oregon Supreme Court, in ruling on an *Atkins* claim, found that a trial court had applied a clinical definition of intellectual disability that was no longer current (after the *Atkins* hearing) and remanded the matter for a new hearing based on the current clinical definition. The appellate court also found that a jury determination of intellectual disability was not constitutionally required (*State v. Agee*, 2015).

2 Prior to its abolition of capital punishment, Illinois did not adopt *Ford* definitions or procedures. As of 2016, Virginia has not yet done so.

3 The "*Ford*-eligibility" of 1,280 of these capital offenders was based on the fact that they were executed during the study period (Blume et al., 2013).

References

AAIDD Ad Hoc Committee on Terminology and Classification. (2010). *Intellectual disability: Definition, classification, and systems of supports* (11th ed.). Washington, DC: American Association on Intellectual and Developmental Disabilities.

Ackerson, K. S., Brodsky, S. L., & Zapf, P. A. (2005). Judges' and psychologists' assessments of legal and clinical factors in competence for execution. *Psychology, Public Policy and Law, 11,* 164–193.

American Psychiatric Association. (2013). *Diagnostic and statistical manual of mental disorders* (5th ed.). Washington, DC: American Psychiatric Publishing.

Blume, J. H., Johnson, S. L., & Ensler, K. E. (2013). Killing the oblivious: An empirical study of competency to be executed litigation. *UMKC Law Review, 79,* 1–24.

Blume, J. H., Johnson, S. L., Marcus, P., & Paavola, E. (2014). A tale of two (and possibly three) *Atkins*: Intellectual disability and capital punishment twelve years after the Supreme Court's creation of a categorical bar. *William & Mary Bill of Rights Journal, 23,* 393–414.

Blume, J. H., Johnson, S. L., & Seeds, C. (2009). Of *Atkins* and men: Deviations from clinical definitions of mental retardation in death penalty cases. *Cornell Journal of Law and Public Policy, 18,* 689–733.

Blume, J. H., Johnson, S. L., & Seeds, C. (2010, September). Implementing (or nullifying) *Atkins*?: The impact of state procedural choices on outcome in capital cases where intellectual disability is at issue. *Cornell Law School Legal Studies Research Paper Series*. Retrieved July 31, 2016 from http://ssrn.com/abstract=1670108

Duvall, J. C., & Morris, R. J. (2006). Assessing mental retardation in death penalty cases: Critical issues for psychology and psychological practice. *Professional Psychology: Research and Practice, 37,* 658–665.

Ellis, J. W. (2014). *Hall v. Florida*: The Supreme Court's guidance in implementing *Atkins*. *William & Mary Bill of Rights Journal, 23,* 383–391.

Ellis, J. W., & Luckasson, R. A. (1985). Mentally retarded criminal defendants. *George Washington Law Review, 53,* 414–493.

Entzeroth, L. S. (2009). The illusion of sanity: The constitutional and moral danger of medicating condemned prisoners in order to execute them. *Tennessee Law Review, 76,* 641–659.

Everington, C. (2014). Challenges of conveying intellectual disabilities to judge and jury. *William & Mary Bill of Rights Journal, 23,* 467–485.

Fabian, J. M., Thompson, W. W., & Lazarus, J. B. (2011). Life, death, and IQ: It's much more than just a score: Understanding and utilizing forensic psychological and neuropsychological evaluations in *Atkins* intellectual disability/mental retardation cases. *Cleveland State Law Review, 59,* 399–430.

Flynn, J. R. (2006). Tethering the elephant: Capital cases, IQ, and the Flynn effect. *Psychology, Public Policy, and Law, 12*(2), 170–189.

Greenberg, J. (2012). Note: For every action there is a reaction: The procedural pushback against *Panetti v. Quarterman*. *American Criminal Law Review, 49,* 227–268.

Hensl, K. B. (2004). Restored to health to be put to death: Reconciling the legal and ethical dilemmas of medicating to execute in *Singleton v. Norris*. *Villanova Law Review, 49,* 291–328.

Kirchmeier, J. L. (2010). The undiscovered country: Execution competency & comprehending death. *Kentucky Law Journal, 98,* 263–299.

National Institute of Mental Health. (2016). *National institute of mental health*. Retrieved July 25, 2016 from www. nnimh.nih.gov

Polloway, E. A. (Ed.). (2015). *The death penalty and intellectual disability*. Washington, DC: American Association on Intellectual and Developmental Disabilities.

Seeds, C. (2009). The afterlife of *Ford* and *Panetti*: Execution competence and the capacity to assist counsel. *Saint Louis University Law Journal, 53,* 309–348.

Shannon, B. D., & Scarano, V. R. (2013). Incompetency to be executed: Continuing ethical challenges & time for a change in Texas. *Texas Tech Law Review, 45,* 419–451.

Tobolowsky, P. M. (2003). *Atkins* aftermath: Identifying mentally retarded offenders and excluding them from execution. *Journal of Legislation, 30,* 77–141.

Tobolowsky, P. M. (2007). To *Panetti* and beyond—Defining and identifying capital offenders who are too "insane" to be executed. *American Journal of Criminal Law, 34,* 369–431.

Tobolowsky, P. M. (2014). *Excluding intellectually disabled offenders from execution: The continuing journey to implement Atkins*. Durham, NC: Carolina Academic Press.

White, W. S. (1993). Effective assistance of counsel in capital cases: The evolving standard of care. *University of Illinois Law Review, 1993*, 323–378.

Cases and Laws Cited

18 U.S.C.A. § 3596 (West 2015).

Ariz. Rev. Stat. Ann. § 13–4022 (2010).

Atkins v. Virginia, 536 U.S. 304 (2002).

Bobby v. Bies, 556 U.S. 825 (2009).

Brumfield v. Cain, 135 S. Ct. 2269 (2015).

Caritativo v. California, 357 U.S. 549 (1958).

Commonwealth v. Banks, 29 A. 3d 1129 (Pa. 2011).

Cooper v. Oklahoma, 517 U.S. 348 (1996).

Ex parte Briseno, 135 S.W. 3d 1 (Tex. Crim. App. 2004).

Ferguson v. Secretary, Florida Department of Corrections, 716 F. 3d 1315 (11th Cir. 2013).

Fla. R. Crim. P. 3.811, 3.812.

Ford v. Wainwright, 477 U.S. 399 (1986).

Green v. State, 364 S.W. 3d 434 (Tex. Crim. App. 2012).

Hall v. Florida, 134 S. Ct. 1986 (2014).

Medina v. California, 505 U.S. 437 (1992).

Moore v. Texas, 136 S. Ct. 2407 (2016).

Moore v. Texas, Petition for a Writ of Certiorari, No. 15–797 (U.S. Dec. 15, 2015).

Nobles v. Georgia, 168 U.S. 398 (1897).

Overstreet v. State, 993 N.E. 2d 179 (Ind. 2013).

Panetti v. Dretke, 401 F. Supp. 2d 702 (W.D. Tex. 2004), *aff'd*, 448 F. 3d 815 (5th Cir. 2006), *rev'd, Panetti v. Quarterman*, 551 U.S. 930 (2007).

Panetti v. Quarterman, 551 U.S. 930 (2007).

Patterson v. New York, 432 U.S. 197 (1977).

Penry v. Lynaugh, 492 U.S. 302 (1989).

Rauf v. State, 145 A. 3d 430 (Del. 2016).

Riggins v. Nevada, 504 U.S. 127 (1992).

Schriro v. Smith, 546 U.S. 6 (2005).

Sell v. United States, 539 U.S. 166 (2003).

Singleton v. Norris, 319 F. 3d 1018 (8th Cir.) (en banc), *cert. denied*, 540 U.S. 832 (2003).

Singleton v. State, 437 S.E. 2d 53 (S.C. 1993).

Solesbee v. Balkcom, 339 U.S. 9 (1950).

State v. Agee, 364 P. 3d 971 (Ore. 2015).

State ex rel. Clayton v. Griffith, 457 S.W. 3d 735 (Mo. 2015).

State ex rel. Cole v. Griffith, 460 S.W. 3d 349 (Mo. 2015).

State v. Irick, 320 S.W. 3d 284 (Tenn. 2010).

State v. Perry, 610 So. 2d 746 (La. 1992).

Trop v. Dulles, 356 U.S. 86 (1958).

Utah Code Ann. § 77–19–205 (LexisNexis 2012).

Washington v. Harper, 494 U.S. 210 (1990).

PART 4

The Death Penalty's Administration

17

THE FINANCIAL COST OF THE DEATH PENALTY

Examining the Evidence

Gordon P. Waldo

Introduction

From a moral perspective, cost as a rationale either for or against the death penalty may be problematic. Many might agree with the statement that: "Cost, as a determining factor in a death penalty case, should be viewed as a smokescreen for other arguments. . . . Letting cost enter the equation—on either side—does a disservice to the very basic moral precepts to which everyone desires to hold" (Walsh, 1996, p. 37). Others, however, would say: "this argument misses the very point of cost analysis—figuring cost is the first step towards weighing the benefits of the death penalty against its alternatives . . . if there existed an alternative to the death penalty that claimed all of the same benefits, then society should choose the less costly method of the two" (Leeman, 2004, p. 20). Mark Costanzo essentially makes the same case when he says: "Capital punishment as social program must be defended . . . on the basis of a cost-benefit analysis. In the absence of compelling evidence that the death penalty . . . makes our streets safer, wise policy-makers should choose the cheaper option of LWOP and spend the savings on crime prevention" (Costanzo, 2001, p. 69).

In the Gallup Poll, depending on the year being polled, between 10% and 20% of those who support the death penalty appear to do so because of the cost, and this has apparently changed very little in the past 25 years. In 1991, 13% said, "Save taxpayers money," in 2001 this response increased to 20%, in 2003 it dropped back to 11%, and in 2014 it was at 14% (Swift, October 23, 2014). The number one reason for favoring the death penalty in all four periods was retribution, but cost was the second reason. During the same period when people who opposed the death penalty were asked their reasons to favor abolition, 'cost' did not even appear in the 1991, 2001, or 2003 poll results. Cost did appear in the 2014 poll, but only 2% listed the financial cost as a reason they opposed the death penalty (Swift, October 23, 2014). Apparently the public is unaware of the studies reviewed in this chapter. There is a troubling concern about the 10–20% who think cost is an appropriate reason for using the death penalty. What if the judge is in that 10–20% category and uses the lower cost rationale in making the decision to apply the death penalty, or what if members of the sentencing trial jury used that rationale in making the decision to vote for death? This is not just a hypothetical question; apparently it has happened! "[S]ome capital jurors report that one of their reasons for imposing a death sentence is the higher cost of life imprisonment" (Costanzo & White, 1994, p. 9). Another way of measuring the increasing concern for the cost of the death penalty relative to its abolition is found in an article by Galliher, Koch, Keys, and Guess (2002). They studied the different arguments used by legislators when they were considering a bill to create a death penalty in Alaska. Similar bills were being debated in both 1973 and again in 1983. In 1973 only 9% of the arguments presented opposing the bill to establish an Alaskan death penalty related to the excessive costs. Only ten years later in 1983, however, the number had more than doubled and 20% of the arguments against the creation of a death penalty in Alaska related to the high costs involved (Galliher et al., 2002, p. 130).

Review of the Literature on the
Financial Cost of Capital Punishment

Numerous studies have been conducted on the cost of the death penalty. Some have studied specific components of the death penalty system, while others have attempted to be comprehensive. They have been conducted in different states, at different times, with varying differences in the death penalty systems. The studies have been conducted under different auspices and by people with different perspectives. They have been conducted by academicians, legislative commissions, and journalists. This chapter tries to include as many of these different contributions as space permits, but it does not pretend to be a meta-analysis of the material. A meta-analysis would be next to impossible with most of these disparate materials, and to call it such would make it sound much more rigorous and 'scientific' than is deserved. There is an attempt, however, to organize the various materials in a somewhat systematic fashion by looking at the earliest studies first because in general, with some significant exceptions, the studies have improved over time. The materials are presented chronologically, with the early articles briefly summarized and the later studies receiving more discussion.

Cost Studies 1978–1989

One of the earliest articles by Barry Nakell (1978) noted that capital cases require more money at every step in the process and made an important point that is repeated by others:

> Although it may cost less to execute a particular offender than to maintain the offender in prison for life, it costs far more to finance a system in which the decision is made to execute some people, all of whom are processed through the entire system, and some of whom must still be maintained for life. (Nakell, 1978, p. 68)

This is true even though the state bore the cost of a death sentence for all of the cases.

The New York State Defenders Association conducted a study in 1982 and estimated that the cost per case of the "first three stages . . . would total no less than $1,828,100" (New York State Defenders Association, Inc., 1982, p. 1). They then projected that if the death penalty cases continued in their current pattern of escalation by the year 2000 the death penalty would cost the state of New York $1,075,000,000 annually just for defense expenditures. In 1985 Margot Garey wrote one of the early articles from the perspective of a legal scholar. She notes that "In an effort to garner public support for the death penalty, some proponents . . . argue that the death penalty saves money because the cost of executing convicted murderers is less than the cost of imprisoning them" (Garey, 1985, p. 1222). Garey mailed out questionnaires to prosecutors and defense attorneys in states that had capital punishment statutes. Questions were asked concerning the difference between death penalty cases and non-death penalty cases in terms of pretrial activities, trial activities, and post-conviction activities. Garey made an important point: "The added costs of a death penalty system begin to accrue long before the trial" (Garey, 1985, p. 1246). She concludes, "The argument that the death penalty costs less to punish than does life imprisonment is erroneous" (Garey, 1985, p. 1270). Cook, Slawson, and Gries reference a study conducted in 1987 by the Kansas Legislative Research Department that estimated that extra death penalty cases would cost an additional $133,000 per case for a total cost of approximately $9,000,000 (Cook, Slawson, & Gries, 1993, p. 7).

A study in Florida by Dave Von Drehle in 1988 concluded that death penalty cases cost as much as $116,700 more at trial and sentencing, $160,000 more for mandatory state reviews, at least $1 million more for appeals, and $312,600 more for jail costs (Von Drehle, 1988, p. 12A). Von Drehle states that "Florida taxpayers have paid more than $57 million for the death penalty since 1973. This number is based on the most conservative figures available. The real cost could easily be twice that or more" (Von Drehle, 1988, p. 12A). This came to $3.2 million per execution or $3.8 million per year (Von Drehle, 1988, p. 1A).

An article by Spangenberg and Walsh in 1989 said the early studies are limited because they have only focused on separate parts of the process, and this does not come close to covering the entire cost. They said, "The only conclusion that can be drawn is that . . . capital punishment is simply more expensive than life imprisonment" (Spangenberg & Walsh, 1989, p. 58). Also in 1989, the Criminal Justice Section of the New York Bar Association passed a resolution opposing the reintroduction of the death penalty in New York because it would: devastate the already financially strained criminal justice system and overwhelm its ability to deliver proper prosecution, defense and judicial services . . ., (creating) a crisis of unprecedented dimension in the Criminal Justice System of this state and in every county thereof (Haines, 1996, p. 229).

Cost Studies 1990–2005

The quality of studies and the data available improved during the 1990s, but the studies still varied greatly in their sophistication. The study by Blakley in 1990 lamented the lack of research on the cost of the death penalty. "While many people talk about the costs, few have attempted to quantify them. It seems to be 'common knowledge' that the death penalty costs more than life imprisonment but few can say why" (Blakley, 1990, p. 61). He did a study of two cases in Kentucky that went through long appeals. The costs associated with one case were estimated to be as much as $7,354,000 and the other $3,221,000. One case was much farther along than the other, but the appeal process had not been completed in either case. In 1992 *The Dallas Morning News* reported that 25% of death penalty verdicts were overturned by higher courts increasing the cost of those executed. But "even when those verdicts are upheld, it's cheaper to lock someone up for life than to try to execute him" (Hoppe, March 8, 1992, p. 1). The study found that the trial process and postconviction appeals took 7.5 years and cost an average of $2.3 million per case. The study also said that "to imprison someone in a single cell at the highest security level for 40 years costs (only) $750,000" (Hoppe, March 8, 1992, p. 1).

In examining the overall quality of the various studies related to the cost of the death penalty, two studies in North Carolina, one by Cook, Slawson, and Gries (1993, and a later one by Cook (2009) stand out. Starting with the 1993 study, which was one of the first truly empirical studies of the cost of the death penalty, Cook, et al. examined the costs of the death penalty in North Carolina compared to the cost of noncapital murder cases. They collected data on the time spent by attorneys on death penalty and non-death penalty cases from the "offices of the district attorneys, public defenders, the Appellate Defenders, and the Attorney General" and the incarceration costs in prison (Cook, et al., 1993, pp. 2–3). They make an important distinction between the cost of a specific execution and the cost of maintaining a death penalty system. In a specific case a defendant is determined to be death eligible and is charged, tried, sentenced, and executed. This case is then compared to a non-death penalty case resulting in an LWOP sentence, and the difference in cost is the additional cost of the death penalty to the state. This shows that the death penalty costs more, but perhaps not a great amount more, particularly if the defense attorney in the death penalty case was poorly prepared. This approach, however, does not consider the cost of all the other cases that were originally charged as death penalty cases but for a variety of reasons never resulted in a death sentence. When these additional costs of having a death penalty system are considered the results are much more costly. This latter approach is used by Cook et al. (1993) as well as many of the other researchers that came after them because it is the cost of the entire death penalty system that is critical.

Throughout their analysis Cook et al. talk about the costs related to three groups: complete death penalty guilt and sentencing trials (DP), partial death penalty capital murder trials (PDP), and non-death penalty capital murder trials (NDP). At the trial level the average costs for DP cases were $84,099, for PDP cases $57,290, and for NDP cases $16,697. DP trials cost more than five times as much as NDP trials (Cook et al.,1993, p. 47). It is clear, however, that the total cost of the death penalty system must also include the cost of the PDP cases. The authors present some interesting data describing the cases in the different groups not directly related to the question of cost. In the NDP group 37% had private attorneys, in the PDP group 20% had private attorneys, but only 10% of those in the DP group had private attorneys. In the NDP group 42% were found guilty, 92% of those in the PDP group were found guilty, but, by definition, everyone in the DP group was found guilty (Cook et al.,1993, p. 46). (It would be interesting to know whether having a private attorney played a role in prosecutors' decisions determining which cases were in which group but that information was not available). They found that "The extra cost . . . of prosecuting a case capitally, as compared with a noncapital prosecution, is . . . $274 thousand" (Cook et al., 1993, p. 76). They conclude, "Combining all of these figures gives an overall extra cost . . . of $8 million, or an average of $4 million per year" for having a death penalty system (Cook et al., 1993, p. 79). They conclude, "The extra costs of adjudicating murder cases capitally outweigh the savings in imprisonment costs . . . the death penalty cannot be justified solely on the grounds of economy" (Cook et al., 1993, p. 2).

David Erickson conducted a study in 1993 of the cost of the death penalty in Los Angeles County, California. It is different from most of the other studies in that it is limited to only one county, but Erickson was able to collect data that were not available in most other studies. His primary measure is a count of the number of items or days involved in various activities. Death penalty (DP) cases had an average of 23.8 pretrial motions filed compared to non-death penalty (NDP) cases filing 6.6 motions; DP cases required 19.2 days to select a jury and NDP cases only 3.4 days; the average number of full court days needed to process DP cases was 129.9 and NDP cases needed only 19.5 days. Erickson says, "When all the quantifiable factors are added up, the total cost [of DP cases] . . . is $1,898,323 compared to . . . $627,322 [for NDP cases]" (Erickson, 1993, p. 25). Erickson summarizes the findings in terms perhaps more understandable to policy makers. "At this cost, the county of Los Angeles could write a check to the state department of corrections for the cost of 40 years of confinement in a maximum-security prison, pay for a full (NDP) murder trial . . . and still save nearly $1 million . . . by not pursuing a single death penalty trial" (Erickson, 1993, pp. 3–4).

The figure of $3.8 million per year reported for Florida in the previous section calculated by Von Drehle in 1988, or $8 million if converted into 2017 dollars, was eclipsed in magnitude by a study conducted in Florida 12 years later by S.V. Date. The costs reported in Date's study make Von Drehle's earlier statement, "And the cost is growing," appear prophetic. Date calculated that the death penalty was costing the state of Florida $51 million more per year than it would cost to give every death row inmate a life sentence without any possibility of parole (LWOP). This calculation was based on the average death row inmate being incarcerated in his early 20s and dying in his 70s, approximately 50 years of incarceration. Date says, "at the rate at which Florida is executing its killers . . . it's costing about $24 million per electrocuted murderer" (Date, 2000, p. 12A).

In Arizona the Attorney General's Capital Case Commission sponsored a study in 2001 on death penalty costs (Williams, 2001). The study examined both state and county costs of the Arizona death penalty. The median cost for cases that received a full death penalty trial (DP) was $163,897. For cases that were charged with the death penalty but ended in a plea to a lesser charge (PDP) the median cost was $128,454, and for non-death penalty cases (NDP) the median cost was $70,231. The difference between DP cases and NDP cases ($163,897 − $70,231 = $93,666) indicates that even using very incomplete data and rarely using mitigation specialists the death penalty is still more than twice as costly as LWOP.

In 2003 a study was conducted by the Kansas Legislative Division of Post Audit (KLDPA). The study was conducted by examining seven cases that received the death penalty (DP), seven cases that were tried as death penalty cases but received a lesser sentence, or a 'partial' death penalty case (PDP), and eight cases of capital murder where the death penalty was not sought (NDP) (KLDPA, 2003, p. 10). The average total cost for a DP case was $1,510,000, for a PDP case $900,000, and for an NDP case $790,000. Using these figures DP cases cost approximately twice as much as NDP cases. This is a very conservative estimate because the study assumed that the DP cases would all be executed relatively soon, and 14 years later none of the death penalty cases had been executed. Trials for DP cases cost 16 times as much as NDP cases ($508,000 vs. $32,000), and the difference in the cost of appeals was 21 times as much ($401,000 vs. $19,000) (KLDPA, 2003, p. 13).

Larranga and Mustard did a study in Washington State in 2004 examining only the trial costs, which is approximately one-third of the total cost of the death penalty. The study concluded that "On average, a death penalty trial costs more than double the amount spent on a non-death penalty trial . . . $432,000 compared to $153,000" (Larranaga & Mustard, 2004, p. 3). There had been 31 death sentences in Washington, and one volunteer had been executed at the time of this study. Not counting the costs associated with non-death penalty verdicts, the trial costs alone for that one execution would be $8,649,000.

In 2004 the Tennessee Office of Research did a study of death penalty costs but noted that "Because cost and time records were not maintained, the Office of Research was unable to determine the *total, comprehensive cost* of the death penalty in Tennessee" (Morgan, 2004, p. 12). In the study, there were 47 death penalty (DP) cases and 193 life (NDP) cases (Morgan, 2004, p. 14). The cost of county paid attorneys and experts in DP cases was $57,702 compared to the average cost for NDP cases of $15,493 (Morgan, 2004, p. 20). Postconviction defense costs for private appointed attorneys was $48,492 for DP cases and $1,193 for NDP cases (Morgan, 2004, p. 26). The average costs at the court of Criminal Appeals was $20,784 for DP cases compared to $1,577 for NDP cases (Morgan, 2004, p. 23). The study projected the average incarceration costs would be $491,202 for death penalty cases and $1,218,344 for the life cases (Morgan, 2004, p. 37). The study concluded that, "Overall, first-degree murder cases in which the prosecution has filed a notice to seek the death penalty cost more than life . . . cases" (Morgan, 2004, p. i).

In 2004 Baicker did an interesting study that is different from the other studies included in this review. The research was not primarily concerned with determining the cost of the death penalty, although that was necessary to address her concern. Baicker was interested in the impact on county budgets of having a death penalty trial. This essentially required her to examine the cost of the death penalty from a different perspective. The study is important for this review because it is virtually the only study that attempts to look across the entire United States at all counties in death penalty states examining the impact of a death penalty trial on the county budget. There are limitations in her data that would cause her figures to be underestimates of the cost, but she can include many other county level variables not available to most other studies. Baicker states that in a Jasper County, Texas, case, "the county raised property taxes by 8% to pay for the trial and delayed new computer purchases and construction" (Baicker, 2004, p. 1). She then talks about an impact in New Jersey in 1991 when the state spent $16 million "to impose the death penalty, and the next year the state laid off 500 police officers because they could not afford to pay them" (Baicker, 2004, p. 2). Baicker makes an interesting observation: "when one county raises tax rates, neighboring counties, apparently freed from competitive constraints, do so as well" (Baicker, 2004, p. 2). Baicker found that "these trials are quite costly relative to county budgets (with each trial causing an increase in county spending of more than 4.2 million)" (Baicker, 2004, abstract). She concludes by stating that the "analysis shows that counties bear the large and unexpected burden of capital convictions in part by raising taxes and in part by decreasing expenditures on police" (Baicker, 2004, p. 13). She goes on to say, "The estimated increase in [short-term]) taxes and expenditures is significant [for any county having a death penalty conviction], amounting to more than $5.5 billion over the 20-year period. This is true for large and small counties alike" (Baicker, 2004, p. 13). With numbers at the county level such as these it is no wonder that Acker, Bohm and Lanier noted that, "State, (county) and federal budgets are finite. Money used to . . . [fund[capital punishment systems must come from new revenues or from other previously-funded programs. Of course, no budget report will [list] funds previously allocated for education, medical research, or feeding and caring for the elderly as being reappropriated [to fund a death penalty system]" (Acker, Bohm, & Lanier, 2003, pp. 18–19).

In 2005 a study on the cost of the New Jersey death penalty was conducted by Mary Forsberg. New Jersey reinstated the death penalty in 1982 but had not carried out an execution. During this period, there had been 197 capital trials, 60 resulting in a death sentence. Of these 60 death sentences received, however, 50 were reversed by the higher courts and turned into LWOP sentences. Like other studies this report notes the difficulties in getting comprehensive cost data: "this effort was hampered by reluctance . . . of many state officials to supply . . . fairly basic information . . . . We have, however . . . what we feel is a credible analysis by going through the phases of death penalty cases" (Forsberg, 2005, p. 1). Forsberg found that the state had spent a minimum of $253.3 million on capital punishment since it had been reinstated. Forsberg stated that "The $253 million is a net cost . . . over and above the costs that would have been incurred had the 1982 statute required life without parole instead of death" (Forsberg, 2005, p. 15). The report described some of the factors involved in creating higher costs for death penalty cases. For example, (1) death penalty cases require two to five times more pretrial motions, (2) three to five times longer pretrial defense investigations, (3) 80 times longer for jury selection, (4) 30 more court days per trial, (5) $66,000 more per case in court fees, (6) ten times greater likelihood that a case will proceed to trial, (7) two defense lawyers instead of one, (8) a larger jury pool, (9) two additional clerks at the State Supreme Court, (10) longer and more complicated appeals, and (11) proportionality review by the State Supreme Court that is not required for non-death penalty cases (Forsberg, 2005, pp. 5–14). Forsberg made a final observation: "New Jersey taxpayers over the past 23 years have paid more than a quarter billion dollars on a capital punishment system that has executed no one" (Forsberg, 2005, p. 17).

Cost Studies 2006–2016

A study in 2006 by the Washington State Bar Association examined the additional cost of a death penalty (DP) case over a non-death penalty (NDP) case in terms of the prosecution and defense attorneys' involvement. They calculated that trial costs for prosecution and defense attorneys were $470,000 greater for DP trials than NDP trials, court personnel costs were $70,000 greater, direct appeals cost $100,000 more, and personal restraint petitions cost an additional $137,000. The sum of the cost figures that they provide is $777,000 more per case, and they note that these are very conservative calculations and the true numbers could be much greater (Washington State Bar Association, 2006, p. 32).

The New Jersey Death Penalty Study Commission issued a report in 2007 noting that the courts and the prosecutor's office could not provide any data on cost. The Office of the Public Defender calculated that "elimination of the death penalty would result in a cost savings of $1.46 million per year" for the Public Defender's Office (New Jersey Death Penalty Study Commission, 2007, p. 31). The Department of Corrections found that abolishing the death penalty would reduce corrections cost between $974,430 and $1,299,240 for each inmate over the inmate's lifetime. The Administrative Office of the courts reported that eliminating the death penalty would result in savings on proportionality reviews of $93,018 per review (New Jersey Death Penalty Study Commission, 2007, p. 32). The commission concluded that "the costs of the death penalty are greater than the costs of life in prison without parole. . . . There is no compelling evidence that the New Jersey death penalty rationally serves a legitimate penological intent" (New Jersey Death Penalty Study Commission, 2007, p. 23).

In 2008 Roman et al. did a comprehensive study of the cost of the death penalty in Maryland. "The final estimates cover the stages of pretrial, guilt/innocence, penalty, appellate, post-conviction and other post-sentencing" (Roman, Chalfin, Sundquist, Knight, & Darmenov, 2008, p. 17). They analyzed the data in terms of days of effort involved and the dollar cost to taxpayers. Not including attorney time spent on pretrial days, the average number of days spent on the different cases was: non-death notice (NDP) cases 6.8 days, death notice (PDP) cases 18 days, and death sentence (DP) cases 23.8 days (Roman et al., 2008, p. 24). DP cases required more than three times as much time as NDP cases. The NDP cases cost $1,103,000, PDP cases cost $1,793,000, and DP cases cost $3,017,000 (Roman et al., 2008, p. 25). In the regression analysis they found "a strong, positive association between both the filing of a death notice and a death sentence and the cost of processing the case" (Roman et al., 2008, pp. 29–30). They conclude, "We find there are substantial costs . . . associated with the death penalty . . . we estimate the total cost of the death penalty to Maryland taxpayers for cases that began between 1978 and 1999 to be at least $186 million . . . this estimate does not include some costs of the death penalty that could not be empirically tested" (Roman et al., 2008, p. 3).

The California Commission on the Fair Administration of Justice (CCFAJ) issued a report in 2008 on the death penalty, and the findings related to cost are staggering.

> With a dysfunctional death penalty law, the reality is that most California death sentences are actually sentences of lifetime incarceration . . . . The same result can be achieved at a savings of well over one hundred million dollars by sentencing the defendant to lifetime incarceration without possibility of parole.
>
> *(CCFAJ, 2008, pp. 75–76)*

The report states that, the annual cost of the Current System is $137.7 million, the cost of an Improved System that would be more fair and efficient is $232.7 million, and the Life Without Parole (LWOP) system is $11.5 million. The Current System is twelve times more expensive than an LWOP System and an Improved System would cost more than twenty times as much as an LWOP System (CCFAJ, 2008, p. 84). The cliché that 'everything costs more in California' apparently applies to the death penalty.

Cook did a second study in North Carolina in 2009. Although the numbers in the 1993 study by Cook, Slawson and Gries represented a sizable savings in state and county expenditures on the death penalty, in Cook's 2009 study the savings are even greater. This latter study is more extensive, precise, and updated compared to the 1993 study, which was one of the best studies that had been conducted at that time. Cook begins his 2009 article with the statement, "the death penalty has become quite rare in North Carolina. . . . Yet the cost of the death penalty to state government remains high"

(Cook, 2009, p. 498). Cook was acknowledging what has become obvious to many: the mere existence of the death penalty, whether it is used or not, incurs significant financial expenditures. The 2009 study examined the costs incurred during the trial phase and the appellate and resentencing phase at the state level. The study also included the incarceration costs for death row inmates. Cook found that the death penalty trial costs alone came to an extra $13.1 million in one fiscal year. Cook also makes a distinction between "cash" costs and "in-kind" costs. The "cash" costs are the extra dollars discussed earlier that the state diverts from other sources to pay additional attorneys hired by the prosecutor or defense, private investigators, expert witnesses, jury expenses, etc. The "in-kind" costs refer to the redistribution of personnel time counted in hours or days. These costs occur when attorneys in the prosecutor or defense attorney's offices are placed full-time on a death penalty case and other cases they would have worked on are temporarily shelved or reassigned to other overloaded attorneys. "If the death penalty were abolished, there would be cost savings of both types—cash and in-kind costs" (Cook, 2009, p. 516). The study reported that attorneys spent 63,526 extra hours on death penalty cases. They also estimated that death penalty cases increased courtroom time by 691 days. A reallocation of these in-kind costs away from death penalty cases could result in a higher conviction rate of guilty defendants for other crimes or for a lower number of innocent people being convicted for a crime they didn't commit. Cook concludes, "Thus abolition of the death penalty would have reduced state expenditures on murder cases by about $10.8 million per year" (Cook, 2009, p. 525). He continues saying that abolition of the death penalty would also provide in-kind cost savings by freeing up: . . . resources in the courts and district attorney's offices, as well as the Office of Appellate Defender and the North Carolina Supreme Court. These in-kind costs . . . (would be) the equivalent of nine assistant prosecutors each year, as well as 345 days of trial court time and . . . 10% of the resources of the Supreme Court and the Office of the Appellate Defender (Cook, 2009, p. 525).

Gould and Greenman in 2010 presented a report on the cost of the federal death penalty. The study only covers defense costs, not the total costs involved, but they broke these defense costs down better than most of the other studies. They found that the cost differential was even greater than found in earlier studies, and not just because of inflation (Gould & Greenman, 2010, p. viii). The median defense costs for death eligible but not tried as death penalty cases (NDP) was $44,809; the costs for death penalty (DP) trials was $465,602, more than ten times as much. For cases that started out as death penalty cases, the cost of 'partial' death cases (PDP) that resulted in a guilty plea, avoiding many of the costs involved in a full trial, was $200,933, still more than four times costlier than NDP cases and almost half the cost of DP cases (Gould & Greenman, 2010, p. x). The defense cost data that they report are broken down into sub-categories better than in most of the other studies. For example, the median cost of experts used in NDP cases is $5,275 compared to $101,592 in DP cases, a ratio of almost 20 to 1. The cost of a simple item such as transcribing the trial materials was surprising; for NDP cases it was $210, but for DP cases it was $10,269, almost 50 times as much (Gould & Greenman, 2010, p. x). In NDP cases the median number of attorney hours was 436; in DP cases 2,746 hours were required. For NDP cases the median number of in-court hours is only 34, compared to 353 for DP cases. A final quote from the study raises considerable concern, although the implications have been well known by criminologists for a long time. "There was a strong association between a lower cost defense representation and an increased likelihood of a death sentence; the lowest cost cases were more than twice as likely to yield sentences of death" (Gould & Greenman, 2010, p. x).

In 2010 the Legislative Services Agency in Indiana did a cost study that included the cost for defense attorneys, expert witnesses, appeals, and incarceration. Prosecutor costs, local law enforcement costs, etc., were not available. The death penalty (DP) cases cost an average of $523,298, partial death penalty cases (PDP) cost an average of $251,513, and non-death penalty cases (NDP) cost an average of

$133,487 (Legislative Services Agency, 2010, p. 2). The DP cases cost approximately four times as much as the NDP cases. If prosecutor charges had been included the ratio would have been much higher.

In 2012 Terance Meithe collected data from the Clark County, Nevada Courts electronic records system and surveyed defense attorneys to determine the time spent on death penalty (DP) and non-death penalty (NDP) murder cases. Meithe compared the median number of hours spent on the pretrial, trial, penalty, and postconviction stages. Adding all four phases together the DP cases averaged 2,298 hours and the NDP cases averaged 1,087 hours of defense attorney time (Meithe, 2012, pp. 2–6). Meithe concluded, "the overall cost saving differential for defense counsel would be about $15 million if these cases were prosecuted as noncapital murders" (Meithe, 2012, p. 7). The obvious limitations of the study are clearly stated by Meithe, indicating that if the time of judges, prosecutors, jurors, court personnel, expert witnesses, investigators, etc., had been counted the costs would have been several times as much (Meithe, 2012, p. 7).

In Florida the third study of costs related to the death penalty by Melissa Holsman was published in 2012, but it is not directly comparable to the previous studies (Von Drehle, 1988; Date, 2000) because of numerous data limitations. The article states, "the time it takes to present a capital case on appeal in both state and federal court is a major factor. The tab for taxpayers can exceed hundreds of thousands of dollars" (Holsman, 2012, p. 1). She acknowledges that her estimates represent a small portion of the true costs, but even with these limitations the average DP case costs at least $1 million more than a NDP case, and if all costs could be included the costs would be considerably more (Holsman, 2012, p. 2).

Similar to the Erickson study in 1993, Petersen and Lynch did a study in 2012 focusing only on Los Angeles County, using homicide cases from 1996 to 2008. The major focus of the study is on prosecutorial discretion, but they also examine the question of the 'hidden cost' of the death penalty. They measure the cost in terms of the amount of time allocated to cases, and they refer to this as a measure of 'time-cost'. They found that after controlling for a number of variables, the DP cases averaged 888 days from filing to resolution, PDP cases 550 days, and NDP cases averaged 398 days (Petersen & Lynch, 2012, p. 1260). They state that "the myth that death sentences are cheaper than LWOP sentences has been debunked" (Petersen & Lynch, 2012, pp. 1271–1272). In conclusion the researchers say, "Our findings suggest that the very existence of the death penalty . . . ensures significant costs. . . . It is difficult to imagine a justification for maintaining this 'broken system'" (Petersen & Lynch, 2012, p. 1274).

In a recent study Marceau and Whitson (2013) examined the cost of capital punishment in Colorado. They used data from only one agency, but probably the most important agency in dealing with the death penalty, the prosecutor's office, the one that makes the decision to seek the death penalty. As discussed earlier in this chapter many studies have been unable to obtain data from the prosecutor's office, and when it was available, the prosecutors frequently downplayed the cost on their agencies, saying that these staff members were already on the payroll and they would be getting paid anyway. Marceau and Whitson obtained reasonably accurate data on the number of prosecutorial days spent in court on each case. Records were maintained on the amount of time prosecutors spent in the courtroom on the pretrial activities, the jury selection process, the guilt phase trial, and the sentence phase, but the large number of days spent by attorneys and staff outside of court were not available. In total days, a death penalty (DP) case required an average of 148 prosecution days compared to 24 days for a non-death penalty (NDP) case. Marceau and Whitson raise another dimension; in DP cases, there are a greater number of days between the time a defendant is initially charged with a crime and when the sentence is finally announced. On average NDP cases take 526 days between the date the charges are filed by the prosecutor and the sentence is passed, approximately a year and a half. DP cases average 1,902 days between the date defendants are charged and the date they receive their sentence, more than five years. The authors state: "the per-case cost of a death penalty trial and sentencing compared to an (NDP) trial and sentencing is staggering" (Marceau & Whitson, 2013, p. 154). The authors conclude, "Colorado paid for twenty-two new death prosecutions but has to show for it only five death penalty sentencing procedures, two possible future executions. The cost of death prosecutions is high, and the execution yield is extraordinarily low" (Marceau & Whitson, 2013, p. 155).

The Kansas Judicial Council Death Penalty Advisory Committee (KJCDPAC) did a study in 2014 that examined the dollar cost and the number of work days in examining death penalty (DP) cases compared to death-eligible non-death penalty (NDP) cases. Data were collected on the average salary, and the hours spent on each case by prosecution and defense attorneys, judges and the cost of expert witnesses, psychiatric examinations, mitigation specialists, transcripts, travel, and jury expenses. All of the costs combined total $664,530 for DP cases and $217,302 for NDP. The report concludes that DP cases, "incur costs 3 to 4 times higher where the death penalty is sought than in cases where it is not" (KJCDPAC, 2014, p. 15). Data were not available for the costs for private attorneys, appeals, petitions, and new trials, and if these costs were included it would make the cost differential considerably greater.

The Idaho Office of Performance Evaluations did a study in 2014 examining the time required in capital and noncapital cases to complete parts of the guilt and penalty phase trials, plus some components of the appeal and postconviction phase of the death penalty system. They compared the number of offenders originally sentenced to death with the number of offenders currently serving a death sentence and the reasons for a new sentence (Office of Performance Evaluations Idaho Legislature, 2014, p. iii). Of the 40 offenders sentenced to death since 1977, only three have been executed, and the federal courts have determined that 21 of the 40 cases required a new sentencing hearing. "We found violations of the U.S. Constitution are the leading cause for Idaho to change a death sentence to a life sentence" (Office of Performance Evaluations Idaho Legislature, 2014, p. iv). The report complains throughout of the lack of financial data, but they had fairly good data from the Office of the Public Defender and from the Department of Correction (DOC). The Public Defender's Office provided data on the total number of billable hours spent on capital litigation in Idaho from 2001 to 2013. In that period, "staff accumulated 79,178 billable hours on capital litigation for 10 defendants sentenced to death—an average of 7,918 hours per defendant . . . (and) 16,980 billable hours of litigation for 95 defendants with a life sentence—an average of approximately 179 hours per defendant" (Office of Performance Evaluations Idaho Legislature, 2014, p. 31). Using this one crude measure, death penalty cases cost 44 times as much as non-death penalty cases. The Idaho DOC found that its "operational cost for two recent executions was $102,567" (Office of Performance Evaluations Idaho Legislature, 2014, p. 33). This is an area that is frequently ignored, and none of the previous studies provided as much detail relative to the actual cost of the execution process itself. The Idaho study also found "that for those who went to trial, reaching a judgment of guilty or not guilty took 7 months longer for capital cases than for noncapital cases" (Office of Performance Evaluations Idaho Legislature, 2014, p. iv). They concluded their report with an observation that is becoming increasingly more and more obvious: "death penalty cases are inherently more expensive" (Office of Performance Evaluations Idaho Legislature, 2014, p. vi).

A 2014 Nevada study examined the cost of death penalty (DP) and non-death penalty (NDP) murder cases in two Nevada counties. Only the in-court prosecution and courtroom costs were available. The appeal costs are greatly underestimated because "many of the sample cases are still being adjudicated" (Nevada Legislative Auditor, 2014, p. 11). Nevertheless, "Case costs, incorporating the trial and appeal phases, averaged about three times more for death penalty versus non-death penalty cases" (Nevada Legislative Auditor, 2014, p. 16). They conservatively concluded, "we estimate the death penalty . . . costs about $532,000 more than other murder cases where the death penalty is not sought" (Nevada Legislative Auditor, 2014, p. 10).

In 2016, Collins, et al., conducted a study in Washington state. The authors state that "The current study . . . utilize[d] quasi-experimental methods to estimate cost differences using a wide variety of data sources" (Collins, Boruchowitz, Hickman, & Larrañaga, 2016, p. 741–742). They obtained comparable costs for jails, trials (prosecution and defense), courts, law enforcement, postconviction petitions and appeals, and postconviction prison. They state that their research determined that "it costs more than one million dollars on average to seek the death penalty in a given case than to seek LWOP. . . . Additionally, 75 percent of the cases where the death sentence was imposed, either the conviction and/or the death sentence have been reversed" (Collins et al., 2016, p. 778). They note that there are limitations in their research, primarily the unavailability of various sources of data that other researchers have referenced. However, they state that "We are confident that the costs estimations that we provided in this study are as accurate as possible given the data and number of observations that were available" (Collins et al., 2016, p. 776). They conclude that "one thing is clear: the practice of seeking the death penalty, as it is currently used, creates economic and geographic disproportionality that raises significant legal, fiscal, and social concerns" (Collins et al., 2016, p. 779).

In 2016, Brambila and Migdail-Smith borrowed from the model that John Roman had used in his 2008 Maryland study to conduct a study in Pennsylvania. There had been 408 death sentences in Pennsylvania but only three executions, and those three were all volunteers that did not use the appeal process. The study concluded that the death penalty system in Pennsylvania had resulted in only three voluntary executions at the exorbitant cost of $272 million each, for a total of $816 million (Brambila & Migdail-Smith, 2016, para. 1). "But, this cost appraisal is also conservative. . . . It's in 2008 dollars and does not account for inflation; it doesn't include murderers who have had more than one capital trial and it excludes capital-eligible cases in which prosecutors unsuccessfully sought the death penalty" (Brambila & Migdail-Smith, 2016, para. 2 & 8). John Roman, who conducted the 2008 study in Maryland, referred to the Pennsylvania study, saying, "because of the paper's conservative calculations, the cost of having a death penalty in Pennsylvania could well be more than $1 billion" (Brambila & Migdail-Smith, 2016, para. 10). Roman went on to say, "We're spending tons of money—that can be spent for better purposes, whether that's education or crime prevention—on putting people on death row who are never going to be executed" (Brambila & Migdail-Smith, 2016, para. 11). Pennsylvania State Senator Stewart Greenleaf, the Republican chair of the Senate Judiciary Committee, said, "We're scratching for every dollar that we can right now, to continue to spend that kind of money is hard to justify" (Brambila & Migdail-Smith, 2016, para. 4).

A Nebraska study in 2016 examined the cost of the death penalty prior to the 2016 ballot referendum to reinstate the death penalty that had been abolished in 2015 (Goss, Strain, & Blalock, 2016). The report noted that in the period of 1973–2014 there were 1,842 murders in Nebraska; 281 resulted in first-degree murder convictions, the death penalty was sought in 119 cases, and 33 of these cases received the death penalty. Of the 33 cases that received the death penalty, 14 had their sentences commuted by the court, 6 died in prison, 10 still have appeals in process, and only 3 have been executed (Goss et al., 2016, p. 2). The study found "that Nebraska's . . . death penalty cost the state . . . approximately $14.6 million annually, and each additional death penalty arraignment costs the state almost $ 1.5 million" (Goss et al., 2016, p. 1). As part of this report they also reviewed many of the studies discussed in this chapter and concluded, "the average U.S. state with the death penalty would have saved $46,474,823 had the state eliminated the DP and replaced (it) with LWOP" (Goss et al., 2016, p. 2).

A still more recent study was conducted in Oregon, which currently has a moratorium on the death penalty that prevents executions but not death sentences (Kaplan, Collins, & Mayhew, Nov. 21, 2016). They studied aggravated murder cases in Oregon from 2000 to 2013. They once again discuss the problems in obtaining data: "no cost data were . . . provided by district attorneys or the courts" (Kaplan et al., p. iii). They obtained cost data from local jails, the Department of Corrections, Public Defense Services, and the Oregon Attorney General's Office. "We approached . . . cost estimations from a conservative standpoint, meaning the costs are intentionally underestimated" (Kaplan et al., 2016, p. iii). They compared murder cases that received the death penalty with similar cases that didn't and found that the average cost differential was between $800,000 and $1,000,000 more for death penalty cases. Note that these numbers do not include prosecutor or court expenditures, which would greatly increase the cost. This study also speaks to the tremendous increase over time in death penalty system costs in Oregon. In the 1980s the average death penalty case cost $274,209, in the 1990s it was $1,107,441, and in the 2000s it was $1,783,148 (Kaplan et al., 2016, p. vi). The report ended by saying, "we can conclude that Oregon's death penalty is intensely time-consuming, expensive, and draining on all those involved in the process" (Kaplan et al., 2016, p. 76).

Remaining Issues—Retribution, Deterrence, and Plea Bargaining

Given that all the research on the cost of the death penalty has found it to be much more expensive than an LWOP system, there are other arguments used by death penalty proponents essentially claiming that all of these cost studies should be ignored. The major pro-death penalty arguments used in this regard are retribution, deterrence, and the impact of abolition on plea bargaining in murder cases. The first two will be briefly discussed, and the third, plea bargaining, which has been raised more recently, will be examined in more detail.

The retribution argument essentially says that cost is irrelevant; some crimes require nothing less than the death penalty, and a price can't be placed on justice. For example, Florida Rep. Victor Crist "said he doesn't care how much it costs to speed up the death penalty process in Florida. . . . We should be executing more people a year than we send to death row, in order to catch up" (Date, 2000, p. 1A). Matt Powell, a prosecutor in Lubbock County, Texas, says he never takes cost into consideration in making a death penalty decision. He said "'I don't dispute that it's more expensive' but he doesn't believe that cost is a valid issue to consider" (Carver, 2009). However, not all prosecutors agree with this position. A Sierra County California District Attorney said, "If we didn't have to pay $500,000 a pop for Sacramento's murders, I'd have an investigator and the Sheriff would have a couple of extra deputies and we could do some lasting good for Sierra County law enforcement" (Erickson, 1993, p. 5). It is not easy to dissuade staunch retributivists from their positions. But what if the money spent to execute a murderer, someone who was going to eventually die in prison anyway, was spent instead to bring about some kind of positive change in the criminal justice system that would reduce the number of murders? Or, what if the money was used to fund an inner-city delinquency prevention program that prevented as few as ten youths a year from becoming criminals, thereby preventing thousands of crimes, and a significant number of murders every year? What if the millions saved could be used by homicide detectives and prosecutors to increase homicide convictions by 10% a year, providing justice and a feeling of closure to numerous family members and at the same time removing dangerous criminals from the streets, thereby preventing additional crimes, some that were murders?

Even some prosecutors have accepted the logic of this position. Norman Kinne, a district attorney in Dallas, Texas, said, "Even though I'm a firm believer in the death penalty, I also understand what the cost is. . . . I think we could use the money better for additional penitentiary space, rehabilitation efforts, drug rehabilitation, education, and especially devote a lot of attention to juveniles" (Mandery, 2012, p. 99). James Farren, the prosecutor in Randall County, Texas, said "The process has become so . . . time-draining and resource-draining that the local prosecutors who choose to seek the death penalty in most cases are going to opt not to. It's simply unfair to the taxpayers to bankrupt the county pursuing that result in a single case" (Davis, July 2, 2016). There are numerous other examples that could be given, and with rational consideration even hard-core retributivists might recognize that there are better ways to spend the money currently being used on maintaining a death penalty system.

The deterrence argument would require a long chapter or a book to discuss in any detail, and the common-sense logic that proponents use concerning deterrence is hard to overcome. Relative to cost considerations, death penalty proponents claim that the death penalty deters potential murderers, and if it is abolished there will be more murders committed, which will make the costs to the system even greater. For years, however, studies have shown that states without the death penalty have lower murder rates than states that have it (Waldo, 2016, p. 485). The best, simplest, and most academically defensible response to the deterrence argument, however, is provided by a recent report from the National Research Council of the National Academies of Science. This group of acknowledged experts reviewed the large body of research that has been conducted on deterrence and the death penalty. They concluded that all the numerous studies were flawed in major ways. The committee stated "that research to date . . . is not informative about whether capital punishment decreases, increases, or has no effect on homicide rates . . . (this research) should not influence policy judgments about capital punishment" (Nagin & Pepper, 2012, p. 2). They concluded that policy makers should make their decisions based on other issues related to the death penalty. This would obviously suggest that cost should be considered when policy makers make decisions about the death penalty. At the same time, the implication of this statement is that deterrence claims should be ignored and not enter into any decisions made about capital punishment.

The third argument concerning plea bargaining appears, on the surface, to have more merit. Some prosecutors have claimed that abolition of the death penalty will reduce their ability to plea bargain in homicide cases and will therefore increase the number of cases going to trial and thus erase any cost savings that might have occurred due to abolition. Other prosecutors, however, disagree completely with that logic. For example, two prosecutors from states that had abolished the death penalty did not see any changes in their prosecutorial systems because of abolition. Edward Defazio, a prosecutor in Hudson County, New Jersey, said, "We have not viewed [repeal of the death penalty] as an impediment in the disposition of murder cases . . ., we have really seen no difference in the way we conduct our business in prosecuting murder cases" (EJUSA, no date). Scott Harshbarger, a former district attorney and former attorney general of Massachusetts, stated, "Eliminating the death penalty . . . will not hinder the prosecutorial capacity to seek, or the court's ability to impose, 'life without parole' sentences for serious, heinous crimes and criminals" (EJUSA, no date).

It is also noteworthy that Thurgood Marshall had made a constitutional statement about this issue in the Furman v. Georgia decision in 1972. In this decision, Marshall stated, "If the death penalty is being used to encourage guilty pleas and thus to deter suspects from exercising their rights under the Sixth Amendment to jury trials, it is unconstitutional" (*Furman v. Georgia*, 1972). The legality of plea bargaining itself has been questioned (Kuziemko, 2006, pp. 117–118). Langbein stated in an article about plea bargaining, "If you turn to the American Constitution in search of authority for plea bargaining, you will look in vain. Instead, you will find . . . a guarantee of trial. The Sixth Amendment provides: 'In all criminal prosecutions, the accused shall enjoy the right to . . . trial . . . by an impartial jury'" (Langbein, 1978, p. 9).

Because of questions that had been raised about the impact of abolition on plea bargaining, and the cost of abolition, in 2008 Ehrhard conducted an exploratory study on the impact of abolition on plea bargaining. He stated, "One of the most troubling criticisms of plea bargaining is that it is coercive . . . as prosecutors may threaten the death penalty to encourage defendants to plead guilty. This issue raises ethical and legal concerns and carries significant implications regarding the human and financial costs of capital punishment" (Ehrhard, 2008, p. 313). Ehrhard used data from interviews with defense attorneys and prosecutors to obtain information about their experiences and views regarding the plea-bargaining process in relation to the death penalty: ". . . defense attorneys said the death penalty gives prosecutors great leverage and is a powerful tool at the prosecution's disposal. While few prosecutors said the death penalty was used as leverage in their own county, some speculated that it was used in this way in other counties" (Ehrhard, 2008, p. 316). Ehrhard concludes that "while the death penalty may act as a tool in processing cases efficiently and cost-effectively, there are ethical and potentially human costs to consider in using the death penalty as leverage" (Ehrhard, 2008, p. 323). It becomes apparent that while Ehrhard is concerned about the financial cost, the greater concern is with some of the human costs of using the death penalty as a bargaining tool, such as convicting an innocent person.

Regardless of Marshall's position on the constitutional issue, or Ehrhard's concerns about ethical and human costs, the impact of abolition of the death penalty on plea bargaining continues to be an important argument in favor of capital punishment because of the potential cost savings. In the study by Marceau and Whitson discussed earlier, they briefly spoke to this issue in their conclusion: "the facts also belie the claim that death prosecutions result in speedier justice. These results reveal no empirical support for the claim that the death penalty is cost-effective based on its ability to induce guilty pleas to first degree murder" (Marceau & Whitson, 2013, p. 158).

Scheidegger questions the assumption made by other studies that repeal of the death penalty would produce considerable savings in trial costs. He states that, "If a state repeals the death penalty but is unwilling to accept a greater number of murderers going free after relatively short sentences, then greater number of life-sentence cases will probably have to go to trial rather than being resolved by plea" (Scheidegger, 2009, p. 15). He used Bureau of Justice Statistics (BJS) data which included data on the 75 largest counties. He selected 33 of the 75 counties but does not explain why he did not use all the 75 counties available. Of those selected 27 were in death penalty states and six were in abolition states. Scheidegger states that "more likely than not there is a real difference in total plea bargain rates between states with the death penalty and those without it. Murder convictions with sentences of 20 years or more were obtained by plea in 18.9% of the cases in counties with the death penalty and 5.0% in those without" (Scheidegger, 2009, p. 10). He concludes, "Further research is needed before a reliable estimate of net costs or savings of a state having the death penalty as an available sanction can be made" (Scheidegger, 2009, p. 15).

Kuziemko was trying to determine whether the threat of the death penalty affects the plea-bargaining process, not the cost of the death penalty per se, although she speaks to this issue. She examined the impact of the death penalty on both the defendant's propensity to plead guilty and the charge to which the defendant entered a plea. She said it is possible that the death penalty would encourage plea bargains, but the question had never been empirically examined. Her study was a 'natural experiment' that studied the impact of the death penalty on plea bargaining. She used cases before and after the restoration of capital punishment in New York, (the 'natural experiment'). She examined the degree of the crime charged and the proportion of death sentences handed down in the prior year. Kuziemko concluded that ". . . the death penalty . . . does not seem to increase defendants' propensity to plea bargain . . . the death penalty does not seem to reduce the total number of cases that proceed to trial. Thus . . . the costs of capital trials do not appear to be offset by reducing total trial costs through plea bargains" (Kuziemko, 2006, p. 140).

In 2013 Thaxton conducted a very extensive and statistically sophisticated study concerning the use of the death penalty as leverage in plea negotiations in death eligible cases. He discusses Kuziemko's earlier study, praising it as a pioneering work, but at the same time saying, "Unfortunately the study suffers from several limitations that may have ultimately masked any true effect that the death penalty has on plea-bargaining rates" (Thaxton, 2013, p. 475). Thaxton used a data set of recent capital charging-and-sentencing decisions in Georgia that avoids many of the shortcomings of previous research. He collected data from multiple agencies and had detailed information on each murder case in Georgia. This permitted the inclusion of a much larger set of control variables. Prosecutors filed a notice of intent to seek the death penalty in 400 cases and the death penalty was given to 54 cases. He says that his study provided evidence that the threat of the death penalty did influence the likelihood of a plea agreement being reached. "Across all four models, defendants noticed for the death penalty were significantly . . . more likely to accept a plea" (Thaxton, 2013, p. 521). Thaxton concluded that although the death penalty did cause a small percentage of defendants to agree to a plea to a lesser sentence, it did not keep enough murder defendants from opting for a trial to offset the high costs associated with a capital trial, subsequent appeals, and death row incarceration (Thaxton, 2013, p. 476). "Based on the high costs associated with litigating a single capital trial and the rather modest ability of the death penalty to deter defendants from pursuing trial, capital punishment does not appear to be a cost-justified bargaining chip" (Thaxton, 2013, p. 484). Thaxton concludes by saying, "The government's use of the death penalty to obtain convictions quickly and cheaply appears to fail on both of these dimensions" (Thaxton, 2013, p. 549).

The major California study discussed earlier (CCFAJ, 2008) also discussed the plea-bargaining issue. The study acknowledged, consistent with Thaxton's later findings, that if the state abolished the death penalty in favor of an LWOP system the number of LWOP trials would probably increase slightly. But the authors went on to say, "California currently processes approximately 120 LWOP cases each year, but fewer than 5% of them are disposed of by a plea of guilty. Even if all cases formerly charged as death cases become LWOP cases and all of those cases go to trial that would add approximately $5 million to the cost of LWOP trials and $3 million to the cost of LWOP appeals. Both the trials and appeals would be considerably less expensive than death cases, because there would be no penalty phase, and no right to counsel for a habeas petition" (CCFAJ, 2008, p. 81). These increased costs of the LWOP system pale in comparison to the costs of the death penalty system in California discussed earlier in this chapter.

Goss et al. discuss how plea bargaining can increase rather than decrease the cost of the death penalty system. They discuss the case of the 'Beatrice Six,' who were wrongfully convicted in Nebraska and were later exonerated. "The state won convictions . . . under threats that the six would be given the death penalty if they did not admit guilt. In 2008 DNA evidence exonerated all six and in July 2016, a federal jury awarded the wrongfully convicted $28.1 million in damages" (Goss et al., 2016, p. 23). There are many other cases similar to this that make the plea-bargaining argument opposing abolition of the death penalty moot.

Conclusion

The conclusion is simple. Despite the claims of some prosecutors and strong death penalty advocates, these studies show that the cost of a death penalty system is much greater than an LWOP system. The studies have varied in many ways. Some have studied specific components while others have been more comprehensive. They have been conducted in different states, at different times, with varying differences in the state systems. They have been conducted under different auspices, for different purposes, and by people with different perspectives. Studies have been made by academicians, legislative commissions, journalists, and interested citizens. The studies clearly varied in quality, style, and type of publication. Most importantly, however, despite all of these differences, the studies all agree in one very important way—they all found that the death penalty system was much more expensive than an LWOP system. The costs vary greatly from state to state and study to study, but it would be safe to say that on average the death penalty system is probably at least two or three times as expensive as an LWOP system, considerably more in some states and perhaps a little less in others. Yes, there may be a few more LWOP trials required, but if so these trials will be much less expensive than death penalty trials and will greatly reduce the costs of the postconviction appeal process. It may also reduce another problem with plea bargaining, the risk that an innocent person would confess to a crime he did not commit to avoid the death penalty.

It is also clear that if the death penalty system is retained the total cost of the system will continue to increase exponentially even as the number of cases decrease. Fortunately, for a variety of reasons, the number of death sentences imposed has been declining at a very high rate. For example, in 1995 there were 310 death sentences in the United States, in 2005 there were 140, in 2015 there were 49, and in 2016 it was down to 30 (DPIC, 2017, Death Sentences by Year). The number of executions has also declined from 98 in 1999 to 20 in 2016 (DPIC, 2017, Executions by Year). Better defense teams, increasing costs, and concerns about executing an innocent person appear to be major factors in this decline. With fewer cases to defend at the trial level, more time and resources will go into the remaining new death penalty cases and the older cases still on death row, making each case more and more costly even as the number of death sentences and executions continue to decline.

H. L. Mencken is credited with having said "Explanations exist, they have existed for a long time, there is always a well-known solution to every human problem—neat, plausible, and wrong" (Mencken, 1920, p. 158). His statement is sometimes rephrased as "for every complex question there is a simple answer, and it is wrong." Yes, it is true, few complicated questions have a simple answer, but questions related to the cost of the death penalty and the best use of limited resources are exceptions. This, to use a colloquial phrase, is a 'no-brainer'—abolish capital punishment and use the money that is being wasted to prevent more crimes, solve more crimes, save more lives, eliminate the risk of executing the innocent, and make the United States a better, safer, and more humane country.

References

Acker, J. R., Bohm, R. M., & Lanier, C. S. (2003). *America's experiment with capital punishment: Reflections on the past, present, and future of the ultimate penal sanction.* Durham, NC: Carolina Academic Press.

Baicker, K. (2004). The budgetary repercussions of capital convictions. *Dartmouth College and the National Bureau of Economic Research, 4*(1), 1–26.

Blakley, A. F. (1990). The cost of killing killers. *Northern Kentucky Law Review, 18*, 61–79.

Brambila, N. C., & Migdail-Smith, L. (2016, June 19). Executing justice: A look at the cost of Pennsylvania's death penalty. *The Reading Eagle.* Retrieved July 5, 2016 from www.readingeagle.com/news/article/executing-justice-a-look-at-the-cost-of-pennsylvanias-death-penalty

Carver, L. (2009, December 13). Death penalty cases more expensive than lifetime imprisonment, but local CDA says cost never a consideration. *Lubbock Avalanche-Journal.* Retrieved July 11, 2016 from http://lubbockonline.com/stories/121309/loc_535156806.shtml#.V4PLOE-FOUl

(CCFAJ) California Commission on the Fair Administration of Justice (CCFAJ). (2008, June 30). *Report and recommendations on the administration of the death penalty in California.* Retrieved June 18, 2016 from http://deathpenalty.org/downloads/FINAL%20REPORT%20DEATH%20 PENALTY%20ccfaj%20June%2030.2008.pdf

Collins, P. A., Boruchowitz, R. C., Hickman, M. J., & Larrañaga, M. A. (2016). An analysis of the economic costs of seeking the death penalty in Washington state. *Seattle Journal for Social Justice. 14*, 727–779. Retrieved September 13, 2017, from http://digitalcommons.law.seattleu.edu/cgi/viewcontent.cgi?article=1832&context=sjsj

Cook, P. J. (2009). Potential cost savings from abolition of the death penalty in North Carolina. *American Law and Economics Review*, 498–529. Retrieved July 7, 2016 from www.unc.edu/~fbaum/teaching/articles/Cook-cost-study.pdf

Cook, P. J., Slawson, D. B., & Gries, L. A. (1993). *The costs of processing murder cases in North Carolina.* Durham, NC: Terry Sanford Institute of Public Policy, Duke University. Retrieved May 18, 2016 from www.deathpenaltyinfo.org/northcarolina.pdf

Costanzo, M. (2001). *Just revenge: Costs and consequences of the death penalty.* New York: St. Martin's Press.

Costanzo, M., & White, L. T. (1994). An overview of the death penalty and capital trials: History, current status, legal procedures and cost. *Journal of Social Issues, 50*, 1–18.

Date, S. V. (2000, January 4). The high price of killing killers. *Palm Beach Post.* A SECTION, p. 1A. Retrieved June 14, 2016 from www.deathpenaltyinfo.org/node/2289

Davis, A. (2016, July 2). Is death knell near for the death penalty in Texas? *Amarillo Globe News.* Retrieved July 11, 2016 from http://amarillo.com/news/latest-news/2016-07-02/death-knell-near-death-penalty

(DPIC) Death Penalty Information Center (1917). *Death sentences in the United States from 1977 by state and year.* Retrieved January 15, 2017 from www.deathpenaltyinfo.org/ death-sentences-united-states-1977-present

(DPIC) Death Penalty Information Center (2017). *Executions by year.* Retrieved January 7, 2016 from www.deathpenaltyinfo.org/executions-year

Ehrhard, S. (2008). Plea bargaining and the death penalty: An exploratory study. *Justice Systems Journal, 29*(3), 313–325. Retrieved June 17, 2016 from www.ncsc.org/~/media/Files/PDF/Publications/Justice%20System%20Journal/Plea%20Bargaining%20and%20the%20Death%20Penalty.ashx

EJUSA. (no date). "Plea Bargain". "The Plea Bargain Myth: Securing Life with Death". *Equal Justice USA.* Retrieved on June 16, 2016 from http://ejusa.org/learn/plea-bargains/

Erickson, D. (1993). *Capital punishment at what price: An analysis of the cost issue in a strategy to abolish the death penalty.* Master's Thesis, Graduate School of Public Policy, University of California at Berkeley. Retrieved July 7, 2016 from www.deathpenalty.org//downloads/Erickson1993COSTSTUDY.pdf

Forsberg, M. E. (2005, November). *Money for nothing: The financial cost of New Jersey's death penalty.* New Jersey Policy Perspective. Retrieved July 21, 2016 from www.njadp.org/forms/cost/MoneyforNothingNovember18.html

Furman v. Georgia, 408 U.S. 238 (1972).

Galliher, J. F., Koch, L. W., Keys, D. P., & Guess, T. J. (2002). *America without the death penalty: States leading the way.* Boston, MA: Northeastern University Press.

Garey, M. (1985). The cost of taking a life: Dollars and sense of the death penalty. *U.C. Davis Law Review,* *18*, 1221–1273. Retrieved June 4, 2016 from http://heinonline.org/HOL/Page?handle=hein.journals/davlr18&div=37&g_sent=1&collection=journals

Goss, E., Strain, S., & Blalock, J. (2016, August 15). *The economic impact of the death penalty on the state of Nebraska: A taxpayer burden?* Goss & Associates Economic Solutions. Retrieved August 17, 2016 from http://death penaltyinfo.org/files/pdf/The-Economic-Impact-of-the-Death-Penalty-on-the-State-of-Nebraska.pdf

Gould, J. B., & Greenman, L. (2010). *Update on the cost and quality of defense representation in federal death penalty cases.* Report to the Committee on Defender Services Judicial Conference of the United States. Retrieved July 26, 2016 from www.uscourts. gov/sites/default/files/fdpc2010.pdf

Haines, H. H. (1996). *Against capital punishment: The anti-death penalty movement in America, 1972–1994.* New York, NY: Oxford University Press.

Holsman, M. E. (2012, October 8). Cost of Florida's death row easily exceeds $1 million per inmate. *Scripps Treasure Coast Newspapers,* p. 1. Retrieved June 15, 2016 from www.tcpalm.com/news/special-report-cost-of-floridas-death-row-easily-exceeds-1m-per-inmate-ep-381918261–342957662.html

Hoppe, C. (1992, March 8) Executions cost Texas millions study finds it's cheaper to jail killers for life. *The Dallas Morning News.* Retrieved August 28, 2016 from http://standdown.typepad.com/DallasMorningNews-%20ExecutionsCostTexasMillions-1992–0308-Hoppe.pdf

Kaplan, A. B., Collins, P. A., & Mayhew, V. L. (2016, November 16). *Oregon's death penalty: A cost analysis.* Lewis & Clark Law School and Seattle University. Retrieved November 18, 2016 from www.deathpenaltyinfo.org/files/pdf/OregonDeathPenaltyCostAnalysis.pdf

(KJCDPAC) Kansas Judicial Council Death Penalty Advisory Committee (2014, February 13). *Report of the judicial council death penalty advisory committee.* Retrieved July 2, 2016 from www.deathpenaltyinfo.org/documents/KSCost2014.pdf

(KLDPA) Kansas Legislative Division of Post Audit (2003, December). *Performance audit report: Costs incurred for death penalty cases: A K-GOAL audit of the department of corrections.* A Report to the Legislative Post Audit Committee. Retrieved July 19, 2016 from www.kslpa.org/assets/files/reports/04pa03a.pdf

Kuziemko, I. (2006). Does the threat of the death penalty affect plea bargaining in murder cases? Evidence from New York's 1995 reinstatement of capital punishment. *American Law and Economics Review, 8,* 116–142. Retrieved May 10, 2016 from https://www0.gsb.columbia.edu/faculty/ikuziemko/papers/deathpenalty_aler.pdf

Langbein, J. H. (1978). Torture and plea bargaining. *University of Chicago Law Review, 46*(1), 2–22. Retrieved June 20, 2016 from http://chicagounbound.uchicago.edu/cgi/viewcontent.cgi?article=4154&context=uclrev

Larranga, M. A., & Mustard, D. (2004). *Washington's death penalty system: A review of the costs, length, and results of capital cases in Washington state.* Seattle, Washington: Washington Death Penalty Assistance Center. Retrieved July 7, 2016 from http://abolishdeathpenalty.org/wp-content/uploads/2013/08/WAStateDeathPenaltyCosts.pdf

Leeman, M. (2004, May 2). *The death penalty: A breakdown of cost.* Economics Research Paper, Rasmusen G492, pp. 1–26. Retrieved June 27, 2016 from www.rasmusen.org/zg492/paper_examples/Leeman.G492.doc

Legislative Services Agency (2010, January 6). *Fiscal impact statement: Murder sentencing and sentence enhancement.* Indiana Office of Fiscal and Management Analysis. Retrieved July 26, 2016 from www.deathpenaltyinfo.org/documents/INCostAssess.pdf

Mandery, E. J. (2012). *Capital punishment in America: A balanced examination* (2nd ed.). Sudbury, MA: Jones & Bartlett Learning.

Marceau, J. F., & Whitson, H. A. (2013). The cost of Colorado's death penalty. *University of Denver Criminal Law Review, 3,* 145–153. Retrieved July 2, 2016 from www.law.du.edu/documents/criminal-law-review/issues/v03-1/Cost-of-Death-Penalty.pdf

Meithe, T. (2012, February 21). *Estimates of time spent in capital and non-capital murder cases: A statistical analysis of survey data from Clark county defense attorneys.* Department of Criminal Justice, University of Nevada, Las Vegas, NV. Retrieved July 20, 2016 from www.deathpenaltyinfo.org/documents/ClarkNVCostReport.pdf

Mencken, H. L. (1920). *Prejudices: Second series.* New York: Alfred A. Knopf Publisher.

Morgan, J. G. (2004, July). *Tennessee's death penalty: Costs and consequences.* Tennessee Comptroller of the Treasury, Office of Research. Retrieved July 27, 2016 from www.deathpenaltyinfo.org/documents/deathpenalty.pdf

Nagin, D. S., & Peppers, J. V. (eds). (2012). *Deterrence and the death penalty*. Washington, DC: The National Academies Press.

Nakell, B. (1978). The cost of the death penalty. *Criminal Law Bulletin, 14*, 69–80. Retrieved June 22, 2016 from www.ncjrs.gov/App/Publications/abstract. aspx?ID=43994

Nevada Legislative Auditor. (2014). *Performance audit: Fiscal costs of the death penalty 2014*. Carson City, Nevada. Retrieved June 28, 2016 from www.deathpenaltyinfo.org/documents/NevadaCosts.pdf

New Jersey Death Penalty Study Commission. (2007, January). *New Jersey death penalty study commission report*. Retrieved July 7, 2016 from www.njleg.state.nj.us/committees/dpsc_final.pdf

New York State Defenders Association, Inc. (1982). *Capital losses: The price of the death penalty for New York state*. Albany, NY. Retrieved June 22, 2016 from www.ncjrs. gov/app/abstractdb/AbstractDBDetails. aspx?id=88172

Office of Performance Evaluations Idaho Legislature (2014, March). *Financial costs of the death penalty*. Retrieved June 29, 2016 from https://legislature.idaho.gov/ope/publications/reports/r1402.pdf

Petersen, N., & Lynch, M. (2012, Fall). Prosecutorial discretion, hidden costs, and the death penalty: The case of Los Angeles county. *Journal of Criminal Law and Criminology, 102*(4), 1232–1274. Retrieved June 6, 2016 from http://scholarlycommons.law.northwestern.edu/cgi/viewcontent.cgi?article=7444&context=jclc

Roman, J., Chalfin, A., Sundquist, A., Knight, C., & Darmenov, A. (2008, March). *The cost of the death penalty in Maryland*. Research Report, Urban Institute Justice Policy Center. Retrieved May 10, 2016 from www. deathpenaltyinfo.org/CostsDPMaryland.pdf

Scheidegger, K. S. (2009, February). The death penalty and plea bargaining to life sentences. *Criminal Justice Legal Foundation*. Working Paper 09–01, pp. 1–17. Retrieved on May 10, 2016 from www.cjlf.org/publications/papers/wpaper09-01.pdf

Spangenberg, R. L., & Walsh, E. R. (1989). Capital punishment or life in prison: Some cost considerations. *Loyola of Los Angeles Law Review, 23*, 45–58. Retrieved June 6, 2016 from http://digitalcommons.lmu.edu/cgi/viewcontent.cgi?article=1614&context=llr

Swift, A. (2014, October 23). *Americans: "Eye for an eye" top reason for death penalty*. Gallup. Retrieved August 3, 2016 from www.gallup.com/poll/178799/americans-eye-eye-top-reason-death-penalty.aspx

Thaxton, S. (2013). Leveraging death. *Journal of Criminal Law and Criminology, 103*(2), 474–552. Retrieved June 17, 2016 from http://scholarlycommons.law.northwestern.edu/cgi/viewcontent.cgi?article=7449&context=jclc

Von Drehle, D. (1988, July 10). Capital punishment in paralysis: Huge caseload bloats lethargic costly system in Florida, U.S. *The Miami Herald*, p. 12A.

Waldo, G. P. (2016). Chapter 13: Capital punishment: Basics and concerns. In W. G. Doerner (Ed.), *Criminal justice: Basics and concerns* (pp. 467–510). Durham, NC: The Carolina Academic Press.

Walsh, T. J. (1996). On the abolition of man: A discussion of the moral and legal issues surrounding the death penalty. *Cleveland State Law Review, 44*, 23–45. Retrieved August 3, 2016 from http://engagedscholarship.csuohio.edu/cgi/viewcontentcgi?article=1574&context=clevstlrev

Washington State Bar Association (2006, December). *Final report of the death penalty subcommittee of the committee on public defense*. Retrieved July 7, 2016 from www.wsba.org/~/media/Files/WSBA-wide%20Documents/wsba%20death%20penalty%20report.ashx

Williams, L. M. (2001, July). *Case study on state and county costs associated with capital adjudication in Arizona: Data set III research report to Arizona capital case commission*. The Williams Institute. Retrieved June 21, 2016 from www.azag.gov/sites/default /files/sites/all/docs/Criminal/ccc/Attachment%20D%20-%20Data%20Set%20III.pdf

18

PROSECUTORS AND THE DEATH PENALTY

Stacy K. Parker

Introduction

Prosecutors are arguably the most important people in the criminal justice system when it comes to the death penalty: no one can face a possible death sentence unless a prosecutor decides to seek it. A mysterious question is how prosecutors make decisions in death-eligible cases, that is, cases in which the death penalty may legally be sought. While some prosecutors may announce why they have chosen to seek or not to seek the death penalty in certain cases, they are under no obligation to do so. Furthermore, the reasons they might give could be pretextual. Although a definite answer to the question of how prosecutors make decisions in death penalty cases cannot be obtained, there is still a lot of information to shine some light on prosecutors' decision making. This chapter is divided into two sections. The first section addresses prosecutorial discretion, including who makes decisions and factors that affect them. The second section discusses legal issues that can be particularly challenging for prosecutors in death penalty cases.

Prosecutorial Discretion

Generally speaking, state prosecutors have complete discretion to decide whether or not to seek the death penalty in any case that is death eligible; however, the federal system has a more complex, yet centralized decision-making process.

Death Penalty Decisions at the Federal Level

The United States Attorney General is the chief lawyer for the United States government, the chief law enforcement officer in the country, and the head of the Department of Justice. The Federal Death Penalty Act of 1994 makes the U.S. Attorney General the gatekeeper of the death penalty in the federal system (Bohm, 2012). Each federal district in the United States has a United States Attorney who is selected by the president of the United States and confirmed by the Senate. The U.S. attorneys in every district generally have the authority to use their discretion in making decisions regarding criminal cases in their district. This authority is somewhat limited, however, by the Federal Death Penalty Act of 1994, which requires the U.S. Attorney General to make the ultimate decision regarding whether or not the death penalty may be sought in any given case (Bohm, 2012). According to the United States Attorneys' Manual, the purposes of this requirement are to limit the possibility that arbitrary factors such as race, religion, or ethnicity do not affect the death penalty decision; to ensure that decisions are made based on individualized consideration of the facts of each case; and to strive for consistent, fair application of the death penalty across the nation. The U.S. attorneys have authority to seek the death penalty in every state—whether or not the state itself permits capital punishment.

Death Penalty Decisions at the State Level

Thirty-one states have laws permitting the death penalty as of June 2017. Not only do decision processes vary among the states, most charging decisions are made at the county level. Because there are more than 3,000 counties in the United States, there is very little consistency is the application of death penalty laws throughout the country. This portion of the chapter will discuss factors that affect individual use of discretion at the county and state levels, the concept of superseding authority, and the proposal that committees be used to make death penalty decisions.

Most state-level prosecutors are elected at the county, or its equivalent, level. Variously called state's attorneys, district attorneys, and prosecuting attorneys, most of these officials are elected by voters in each jurisdiction. (This chapter uses the terms prosecutors and prosecuting attorneys to describe the government officials charged with handling criminal matters at the state level and the term county to describe local court jurisdiction.) Prosecutors are the chief lawyer and law enforcement officer of the counties throughout the United States. These officials generally have the authority to use their discretion as they see appropriate; that is, they are free to make charging, sentencing, and plea-bargaining decisions based on their professional judgment. This authority gives prosecutors the most power of any participant in the criminal justice system regarding the death penalty: these are the people who decide if the death penalty is going to be sought or not in every death-eligible case. Some prosecutors use their discretion to actively use death penalty laws while others never or rarely seek to use them. Before exploring the factors that affect prosecutorial discretion, though, it is important to discuss the importance of discretion in the death penalty system.

Unfettered jury discretion led the United States Supreme Court to strike down capital punishment laws in the 1972 *Furman v. Georgia* decision. The court was concerned that juries had too much discretion to make life and death decisions and held that the death penalty laws were therefore arbitrary and the system of capital punishment used at the time was unconstitutional. New death penalty laws that provided guided discretion to juries were upheld in 1976 in the case of *Gregg v. Georgia*. Guided discretion laws enumerated factors that jurors should consider deciding if defendants should be sentenced to death. The laws did nothing to guide or limit the use of discretion by prosecutors. In fact, the court affirmed the prosecutors' use of discretion to select cases where the death penalty would be sought. The court refused to presume that prosecutors would be motivated by reasons other than legal factors, such as likelihood of a death verdict or strength of the evidence, when deciding whether or not to seek the death penalty. Research studies since the reinstatement of the death penalty have actually shown that geography and race are more important factors when prosecutors seek the death penalty (Dieter, 2013). This will be discussed in detail later in the chapter.

The *Gregg* decision also ratified the use of proportionality reviews that required courts to compare cases that did and did not result in death sentences. Ideally, such a system could operate as a check on prosecutors' use of discretion. Proportionality reviews were not required by the United States Constitution, however, according to the court's decision in *Pulley v. Harris* in 1984. Accordingly, the court has upheld unfettered discretion for prosecutors in death penalty cases.

There are a few dangers to justice when prosecutors have unrestricted discretion regarding the death penalty. First, prosecutors can decide whether or not to enforce laws that were passed by the legislature (Horowitz, 1997). This can result in criminal behavior being ignored or prosecutors refusing to seek the death penalty (Horowitz, 1997). Horowitz was concerned that such a refusal to seek the death penalty can result in supersedure of authority by other members of government (1997).

Supersedure will be discussed in detail later in the chapter. Horowitz also suggested that giving complete death penalty discretion to one person could permit individual characteristics of prosecutors to override legal considerations (1997). He argued that this subjective system left defendants at the mercy of prosecutors' whims, which is unfair (1997).

The second danger to justice when prosecutors have unrestricted discretion in death penalty cases is that laws may not be uniformly applied throughout a state (Horowitz, 1997). The varying amounts of crime and resources among counties, as well as the political nature of capital punishment, can result in disproportionate application of death penalty laws within a state (Horowitz, 1997). Horowitz explained that counties that support the death penalty would expect death penalty laws to be used while counties that oppose the death penalty would expect their will to be done (1997). This does not always happen, though, because in some states there is the possibility that the county prosecutors' decision not to seek the death penalty can be overruled by other authorities (Horowitz, 1997). This leads to the third danger to justice—that the threat of supersedure may affect prosecutors' decision making (Horowitz, 1997).

Some state constitutions and other laws permit governors, courts, or legislatures to remove prosecutorial authority from the local prosecutor under certain circumstances (Horowitz, 1997). This supersedure of authority can usurp the prosecutors' use of discretion, and it can also restrict prosecutors' abilities to be open and honest with voters. Horowitz stated that prosecutors who oppose the death penalty face three options related to death penalty laws: (1) they can be forthright about their opposition to the death penalty and face the possibility of supersedure; (2) they can violate their own beliefs and seek the death penalty on occasion; or (3) they can deny that they never intend to seek the death penalty but refuse to seek the death penalty anyway (1997). According to Horowitz, death-opposing prosecutors being subjected to such choices is offensive to democracy (1997). He argued that allowing those running for prosecutor to announce their opposition to the death penalty would not be a problem—voters would know the candidates' views and vote accordingly; however, a problem would exist if another government official decides to usurp the authority of those elected (1997). When a prosecutor who opposes the death penalty is confronted by a governor with supersedure power, the resulting power struggle can be costly and harmful (Horowitz, 1997). Horowitz explained that this is what happened when Bronx District Attorney Robert Johnson, who opposed the death penalty, faced New York Governor George Pataki, who supported it, and a supersedure battle began (1997).

After the New York State Legislature authorized the death penalty for first-degree murder and provided absolute discretion for individual prosecutors to decide whether or not to seek the death penalty in 1995, Bronx District Attorney Johnson announced that he would use his discretion to seek life without parole rather than death sentences for reasons that included his concerns that innocent people could be executed, the death penalty system was unfair, and the cases would be expensive (Horowitz, 1997). Johnson was overwhelming reelected less than a year after making this announcement (Horowitz, 1997). Nevertheless, Governor Pataki later questioned this position in 1995 after a man was arrested for killing five people (Horowitz, 1997). According to Horowitz, the governor let the matter go, but Pataki took definitive action in 1996 after a New York City police officer was murdered and Angel Diaz was charged (1997). This time, the governor issued an executive order, pursuant to New York's supersedure statute, usurping Johnson's authority and replacing him with the New York attorney general (Horowitz, 1997). This was not the first time supersedure had occurred: New York governors had invoked supersedure power previously, but, Horowitz explained, most of those cases involved cases in which the elected prosecutor was potentially involved in crime and corruption of public officials (1997). Pataki's executive order resulted in a lawsuit in which Johnson challenged the governor's action as unprecedented because no other governor had ever used his power of supersedure because there was a disagreement over possible sentencing (Horowitz, 1997). The case ultimately made its way to the New York Court of Appeals, the state's highest court.

In the Matter of Johnson v. Pataki was decided by the New York Court of Appeals in 1997. This court upheld the lower courts' rulings that the governor was within his authority to issue executive orders superseding authority over the Angel Diaz criminal case. The court reasoned that the prosecutor's assertion that he would not seek the death penalty amounted to a blanket policy that could serve to preclude the death penalty in the case involving the murder of the police officer. According to the court, the governor acted within his authority as granted by the state constitution and statutes, though the court also acknowledged that executive orders are largely beyond the review of courts. The court rejected Johnson's arguments that, as an elected official with exclusive authority to prosecute crimes in Bronx County, he was insulated from supersedure. Additionally, the court disagreed with Johnson's contention that supersedure was limited to subordinates in the executive branch or to cases where the prosecutor has a conflict of interest. Finally, the court held that the governor's executive order expressed more than just a disagreement about sentencing; rather, the executive orders expressed a threat to the execution of death penalty law.

Horowitz (1997) discussed how other states such as California and Colorado, which had supersedure and death penalty laws similar to New York's, could find themselves in a similar supersedure battle. He argued that Pataki's actions did not curtail discretion; it merely transferred it from one individual to another (1997). Horowitz warned that as long as the decision to seek death or not rested with only one person, decisions will be subject to the whims of individuals with their own personalities, beliefs, and agendas (1997). His recommendation to establish committees to make death penalty decisions will be discussed later in this chapter.

The issue of supersedure arose again in 2017 after Florida Governor Rick Scott removed State Attorney Aramis Ayala from 23 death-eligible cases after the prosecutor publicly announced that she would not seek the death penalty in any case (Rohrer, Stutzsman, & Lotan, 2017). Ayala stated that she would not use death penalty statutes because the Florida death penalty system was chaotic, expensive, and harmed victims' family members by extending the time before cases conclude (Mettler, 2017). The first death-eligible case to arise under her jurisdiction, like in New York, involved the killing of a police officer (Mettler, 2017). In the Florida case, however, the suspect was also accused of killing his pregnant ex-girlfriend (Mettler, 2017). Governor Scott requested that the state attorney, whose jurisdiction included Orange and Osceola counties, recuse herself from the cases (Mettler, 2017). After Ayala refused, the governor appointed a special prosecutor for these two cases and did not rule out trying to remove the prosecutor from office (Mettler, 2017). In April 2017, the governor signed 21 additional orders that removed the elected prosecutor from 21 other first-degree murder cases and assigned them all to State Attorney Brad King, a pro-death penalty prosecutor from a nearby jurisdiction (Rohrer et al., 2017).

Pro- and anti-death penalty advocates immediately chose sides, and State Attorney Ayala filed legal proceedings to prevent her removal from the cases (Mettler, 2017; Rohrer et al., 2017). Death penalty supporters, including many local Republican leaders, believed that Ayala was neglecting her duties by failing to follow the law (Hannan, 2017). Governor Scott's decisions cited a law that allows supersedure in cases where the prosecutor is unfit or has a conflict of interest (Rohrer et al., 2017). Members of the Florida Legislature threatened to cut funding to Ayala's office (Hannan, 2017), and one local official posted on Facebook that Ayala, the first African American state attorney, "should be tarred and feathered if not hung from a tree" for her refusal to seek the death penalty (Mettler, 2017). On the other side of the case, more than 130 prosecutors, law professors, and former judges argued in a letter to the governor that his decisions interfered with the prosecutor's authority to use discretion (Hannan, 2017). They argued that the governor should not have the ability to undermine the local prosecutor and residents by selectively choosing cases he disagrees with to supersede (Mettler, 2017). An ACLU official in Florida stated that Scott's orders were an overreach of his power that could promote politically motivated decisions in criminal cases (Hannan, 2017). The family members of Sade Dixon, the defendant's pregnant ex-girlfriend he is accused of murdering, agreed with State Attorney Ayala

(Mettler, 2017). Sade Dixon's mother stated that closure would be delayed if the defendant received the death penalty because the case would be in the court systems for numerous years (Mettler, 2017). She would prefer a sentence of life in prison (Mettler, 2017).

The first round of legal battles ended with Circuit Judge Frederick Lauten denying Ayala's request to delay criminal proceedings against the defendant, Markeith Loyd, until after her lawsuits were to be heard by the Florida Supreme Court (Harris, 2017). Stating that the governor has "broad authority to assign another state attorney," Judge Lauten refused to stop the criminal proceedings, but Ayala's cases could still proceed to the Florida Supreme Court (Harris, 2017). In fact, the Florida Supreme Court declined to issue an emergency order as requested by Ayala; instead, it intends to make a decision after both sides have the opportunity to fully argue their cases (Associated Press, 2017). Multiple petitions, responses, and friend of the court briefs had been filed, and a date for oral arguments was set for June 28, 2017, in this supersedure case at the time this chapter was written (Florida Supreme Court Case Docket, 2017). Curiously, although prosecutors and former judges from across the country filed briefs in support of the state attorney, the Florida Prosecuting Attorney's Association and the Florida Attorney General filed briefs opposing the state attorney (Florida Supreme Court Case Docket, 2017). The case is certainly full of political issues, if not legal ones, as the Democratic state attorney and allies including civil rights organizations, families of homicide victims, and former prosecutors, state supreme court judges, and United States solicitors general, face off against the Republican governor, attorney general, and legislature (Kam, 2017).

Despite their significance, supersedure cases are anomalies. Nearly every death penalty-related decision rests with one person—the elected prosecutor of the jurisdiction. Although, as previously mentioned, the United States Supreme Court refused to assign improper motivations to prosecutors making such decisions, the fact is that geography, race, and individual characteristics of the prosecutors themselves have been shown to most significantly affect decisions related to the death penalty (Dieter, 2011; Dieter, 2013; Fair Punishment Project, 2016). To complicate matters, these factors are often intertwined.

Geography

The effect that geography has on the death penalty and prosecutorial discretion is most obvious when looking at its use by state and by region. Since the death penalty was reinstated in 1976, 82% of executions occurred in states in the South while less than 1% occurred in the Northeast (Dieter, 2013). The states of Texas, Oklahoma, Virginia, and Florida have carried out 60% of executions since 1976 (Dieter, 2013). Obviously, prosecutors in those states choose to use death penalty laws more than those in other states.

There are also tremendous differences in the use of the death penalty within states. In Texas, the country's most active death penalty state, four counties alone (Harris, Dallas, Tarrant, and Bexar) have been responsible for almost 50% of executions even though those counties comprise only 34% of the state's population (Dieter, 2013). In fact, most counties have not had a single case result in an execution (Dieter, 2013). A similar pattern is revealed in California, which is home to the country's largest death row. Los Angeles, Riverside, and Orange counties make up less than 40% of the state's population, but they are responsible for more than half of the death row population. In Ohio, Cuyahoga County is responsible for almost 40% of a death penalty indictments while it represents just over 11% of the state's population (Ohioans to Stop Executions, 2014). Many studies reveal inconsistencies by county in several other states, including Florida, Indiana, Maryland, Missouri, and North Carolina (Dieter, 2013). These county level differences have a tremendous cumulative effect. The majority of executions throughout the country have occurred in only 2% of the nation's counties, and only 2% of counties account for the majority of those on death row (Dieter, 2013). Most counties have not used death penalty laws at all (Dieter, 2013). Since it is generally the county prosecutor who decides whether or not to seek the death penalty, these statistics reveal that few prosecutors use their discretion to seek the death penalty, while those who use their discretion to seek the death penalty do so often.

Race

While numerous studies have revealed disparities in the use of the death penalty based on the race of the victim and the race of the offender, a few looked specifically at the effects of race on the use of prosecutorial discretion in death eligible cases. Perhaps the best-known study was the major focus of the case of *McCleskey v. Kemp* in 1987. This case extensively discussed what has become known as the "Baldus study," which was used to challenge the constitutionality of the death penalty. The Supreme Court ultimately held that statistical analyses that show disparate treatment between the races did not cause the death sentence in McCleskey's case to be unconstitutional; however, the study still provided important information regarding race and the death penalty. Although the court focused much of its attention to the study's findings that defendants in Georgia charged with killing white victims were more likely to receive the death penalty than those charged with killing black victims, some of the other findings are more relevant to this chapter. According to the authors of the Baldus study, the Georgia statute stated that penalty hearings *shall* be conducted when a defendant was convicted of murder with an aggravating factor; however, prosecutors chose not to proceed to a penalty hearing in 60% of such cases (Baldus, Pulaski, & Woodworth, 1983). In other words, prosecutors used their discretion to actually seek the death penalty in 40% of death-eligible cases. The researchers also found that race and severity of the crime affected prosecutors' decisions to seek a penalty hearing (Baldus et al., 1983). Specifically, prosecutors sought the death penalty in 70% of eligible cases when the victim was white and the offender was black (Baldus et al., 1983). Conversely, prosecutors sought the death penalty in only 19% of death-eligible cases when the victim was black and the offender was white (Baldus et al., 1983). Prosecutors were least likely to seek the death penalty cases when both the victim and offender were black: only 15% of eligible cases (Baldus et al., 1983). Baldus, Pulaski, and Woodworth also found that although the decision to seek the death penalty was affected by the seriousness of the case, the race of the victim affected how severe the case was considered to be:

> Georgia juries appear to tolerate greater levels of aggravation without imposing the death penalty in black victim cases; and, as compared to white victim cases, the level of aggravation in black victim cases must be substantially greater before the prosecutor will even seek a death sentence.
>
> *(p. 710)*

Radalet and Pierce examined the effects of race and prosecutorial discretion in Florida and found that race was related to how seriously prosecutors classified cases (1985). In their study, Radalet and Pierce compared homicide classification levels (that is, felony, possible felony, or nonfelony murder) as determined by police versus those determined by prosecutors (1985). If prosecutors classified the cases at a more serious level, they were considered to be "upgraded," while cases were considered to be "downgraded" if prosecutors classified the cases at a less serious level (Radalet & Pierce, 1985). The researchers found that race did not play much of a role when both the victims and offenders were black; prosecutors were more likely to upgrade cases involving white victims than black victims; and cases involving white victims were most likely to be upgraded and least likely to be downgraded when the offenders were black (1985).

In another study of prosecutorial discretion and the death penalty, Paternoster (1983) found that the race of the victim was a statistically significant factor in the prosecutors' decisions to seek the death penalty in South Carolina. After controlling for multiple factors such as number of victims and victim/offender relationship, Paternoster found that the race of the victim was the most important factor affecting the prosecutors' decisions (1983).

Racial differences in the use of the death penalty do not necessarily signal that the system is rife with discrimination; in fact, many studies that found racial disparities also found geographic disparities. For example, Paternoster (1983) found that rural counties in South Carolina were much more likely to seek the death penalty than urban counties unless both the offenders and victims were white. Further, he found that prosecutors in rural counties were 11 times more likely to seek the death penalty when there were black offenders and white victims than prosecutors in urban counties were when there were black offenders and black victims (Paternoster, 1983). Paternoster and colleagues published a study of the Maryland death penalty system in 2003. Like previous studies, they found statistically significant differences in the likelihood that prosecutors would seek the death penalty based on the race of the victim and that prosecutors in Baltimore County were significantly more likely to seek the death penalty than those in Baltimore City (Paternoster et al., 2003). Specifically, even after controlling for case characteristics, prosecutors in Baltimore County were more than 13 times more likely to seek the death penalty than those in Baltimore City (Paternoster et al., 2003). The City of Baltimore's population is predominately black while the County of Baltimore's population is predominantly white.

That both race and geography significantly affect prosecutorial decision making does not necessarily mean that the system is racially discriminatory. Race and geography are terribly difficult to untangle, and even prosecutors with no apparent discriminatory intent may consider race when making strategic decisions. Rural counties may take a tougher stance on crime, and cities may accept crime as a part of life. Resources could vary drastically and affect prosecutors' decision making. Public opinion could play a factor. According to a 2007 Gallup Opinion Poll, African Americans are more likely to oppose the death penalty, while whites are more likely to support it (Saad, 2007). Prosecutors may believe that communities with largely black populations may be opposed to them seeking the death penalty (Dieter, 2011). Likewise, prosecutors may prefer white members of the jury because they believe whites are more likely to vote for the death sentence (Dieter, 2011). The issue of race, prosecutors, and jury selection will be discussed later in this chapter.

Individual Characteristics

That 2% of counties across the United States account for the majority of executions and inmates on death row, combined with the fact that the busiest counties use death penalty laws at rates that are disproportionate to their populations, may cause one to suspect that perhaps the personalities of the chief prosecutors affect how their offices proceed with death-eligible cases. The Fair Punishment Project analyzed the personalities and practices of who it deemed to be "America's Top Five Deadliest Prosecutors" (2016). This study concluded that the "personalities and predilections" (p. 25) of prosecutors play a more important role in the use of prosecutorial discretion than the seriousness of the offenses or the characteristics of the offenders (Fair Punishment Project, 2016). This section of the chapter is going to discuss the individuals featured in the Fair Punishment Project study.

The list of "deadliest" prosecutors included three chief prosecutors who personally obtained more than 35 death sentences each and two who oversaw the offices that obtained a combined 309 death sentences (Fair Punishment Project, 2016). At the time of the report, only one of those prosecutors remained in office, but he had announced plans to retire at the end of the year (2016). In the years after these prosecutors and their chief assistants left office, death sentences dropped precipitously in their jurisdictions (Fair Punishment Project, 2016).

Joe Freeman Britt of Robeson County, North Carolina, personally obtained 38 death sentences during his 14-year term—the most of any prosecutor in state history (Fair Punishment Project, 2016). This is particularly notable because the death penalty was not legal in North Carolina until

June 1, 1977, which was three years into his term (NCDPS, 2013). Before Britt took office, the last execution from Robeson County occurred in 1949 (NCDPS, n.d.). No death sentences were handed down in the 27 years before Britt took office, and only two have been imposed since his departure in 1988 (Fair Punishment Project, 2016). Britt was accused of misconduct in more than 80% of the capital cases he handled, and misconduct was actually found in nearly 37% of the cases (Fair Punishment Project, 2016). Even after two intellectually challenged brothers he sent to death row were exonerated by DNA evidence after serving 30 years in prison, Britt maintained their guilt (Fair Punishment Project, 2016). When the current prosecutor criticized Britt for his handling of that case, Britt retorted by calling the new prosecutor a vulgar slang term for female genitalia (Fair Punishment Project, 2016).

Robert H. Macy served as the prosecutor for Oklahoma County, Oklahoma, for 21 years and personally attained 54 death sentences (Fair Punishment Project, 2016). Nicknamed "Cowboy," Macy actually reached for his gun after a jury found six defendants he was prosecuting not guilty (Fair Punishment Project, 2016). He bragged about being responsible for the execution of a 16-year-old offender; made fun of mental illness; and had an antagonistic disposition (Fair Punishment Project, 2016). He was alleged to have engaged in prosecutorial misconduct in more than 94% of his death penalty cases, and misconduct was actually found in approximately 33% of cases (Fair Punishment Project, 2016). Almost half of the death sentences he obtained were overturned by courts, and three of those sentenced to death were later exonerated (Fair Punishment Project, 2016). Like Britt, the use of capital punishment dramatically spiked when Macy was elected and dropped significantly after his departure (Fair Punishment Project, 2016).

Donald V. Myers, chief prosecutor of the 11th Judicial Circuit in South Carolina, also had an interesting nickname: "Dr. Death" (Fair Punishment Project, 2016). During his more than 38 years in office, Myers personally attained 39 death sentences; was accused of misconduct in nearly 62% of the cases; and misconduct was actually found in more than 46% of cases, which resulted in the reversal of six of the death sentences he obtained (Fair Punishment Project, 2016). Myers was known to be passionate about the death penalty, even keeping a paperweight on his desk modeled after the South Carolina electric chair (Fair Punishment Project, 2016). People he sent to death row included those with cognitive impairments and two juveniles (Fair Punishment Project, 2016). He was theatrical in the courtroom—once staging a pretend funeral for an infant victim by presenting a crib covered with a shroud to the jury (Fair Punishment Project, 2016). Myers had one case involving an African American defendant that he called various derogatory names overturned *twice* for engaging in racist jury selection (Fair Punishment Project, 2016).

Lynne Abraham, the only female on the list of deadliest prosecutors, did not personally try most of the cases, but she is credited with 108 death sentences during her 19-year tenure as Philadelphia County District Attorney (Fair Punishment Project, 2016). Since her departure from office in 2010, only three cases resulted in sentences of death (Fair Punishment Project, 2016). One of her top assistants was reprimanded by the courts on several occasions for prosecutorial misconduct and was known to keep pictures of the defendants he obtained death sentences for, which he would annotate after executions (Fair Punishment Project, 2016).

Johnny Holmes of Harris County, Texas, also oversaw an office that extensively achieved death sentences—201 during the course of his 21-year term (Fair Punishment Project, 2016). He also relied on assistant prosecutors who often engaged in questionable behavior or prosecutorial misconduct (Fair Punishment Project, 2016). There was one exoneration during his tenure (Fair Punishment Project, 2016). Holmes left office in 2000, and Harris County now averages one death sentence per year (Fair Punishment Project, 2016).

Together, the five deadliest prosecutors accounted for 440 people being sentenced to death. Compare this to current death row populations. The entire state of Texas has 254; the entire state of Florida has 395 (DPIC, 2016). The total death row population as of October 2016 was 2,902 (DPIC, 2016).

If all of the individuals sentenced to death as a result of these five prosecutors/jurisdictions were still on death row, they would make up more than 15% of it today.

The deadliest prosecutors shared similar personality characteristics. They were enthusiastic about the death penalty—many to the point that achieving a death sentence was more important than achieving justice (Fair Punishment Project, 2016). Most engaged in or oversaw assistants who were frequently accused of misconduct (Fair Punishment Project, 2016). Two had nicknames that appear related to their affection for dead or masculinity. Every jurisdiction saw a dramatic decrease in the use of death penalty laws after these officials left office (Fair Punishment Project, 2016). According to the Fair Punishment Project, "[t]his overzealous, personality-driven, win-at-all-costs pursuit of capital punishment seriously undermines the legitimacy of the death penalty today" (2016, pp. 25–26)

Death Penalty Teams and Committees

Some have suggested or even implemented the use of teams or committees to make charging and sentencing recommendations in death penalty cases to minimize or limit disparities between jurisdictions. This section of the chapter will discuss the use of teams or committees.

Gershowitz proposed a team approach to address the problem of geographic disparities; specifically, he proposed creating a separate, state-level system of prosecution for death penalty cases (2010). He argued that the entire team of elite prosecutors, defense lawyers, and judges from throughout the state should be selected after extensive review of their profession backgrounds, including reversal rates and ethics (Gershowitz, 2010). This team would be paid by the state and would handle all aspects of a death penalty case from the charging decision through the appeal (Gershowitz, 2010). Gershowitz acknowledged that such a system would be quite expensive but argued that there would be substantial monetary savings over time (2010). According to Gershowitz, the team of elite lawyers and judges would decrease the likelihood of wrongful convictions and reversals of convictions because they would provide better trials and be more likely to abide by the law (2010). He suggested that this system would decrease geographic disparity because state-wide funding would permit wealthy and poor counties to have equal access to the death penalty system (Gershowitz, 2010). Additionally, Gershowitz argued that the system he proposed would "restore confidence in both the overall system and individual verdicts" (2010, p. 311).

Horowitz recommended that state legislatures create committees to decide whether or not the death penalty would be sought in death-eligible cases (1997). He proposed that the committee would be comprised of three members appointed by the governor, three appointed by the prosecutor, and one chosen by the already-appointed six (Horowitz, 1997). According to Horowitz, this seventh position would serve to ensure that the committee would operate neutrally and engage in true case-by-case decision making (1997). Horowitz argued that the prosecutors' roles would only be diminished slightly because every decision other than whether or not to seek death would still be made by the prosecutor of each jurisdiction (1997). He cited the Federal Election Commission and state civil rights commissions as establishing the precedents for legislatures creating committees for executive branches (Horowitz, 1997).

Horowitz argued that moving the decision of whether or not to seek the death penalty from an elected official to a multiple-member committee would improve the entire death penalty process for several reasons (1997). First, Horowitz argued, committees would allow politicians to have open discussion of the death penalty (1997). Candidates for governor or prosecutor would be able to share their death penalty views while campaigning and, if elected, feel empowered to appoint committee members that share the same view (Horowitz, 1997). He argued that candidates for office must be free to state their opinions in a functioning democracy (Horowitz, 1997). Otherwise, as discussed earlier, those running for prosecutor may feel unable to express their anti-death penalty stance for fear of future supersedure actions by the governor (Horowitz, 1997).

Horowitz stated that the second advantage of committees would be the increased legitimacy of the process by which the discretionary decision of what sentence to seek is made (1997). According to Horowitz, committees would simultaneously politicize and depoliticize death penalty decision making (1997). Although the members of the committees would be appointed, the public is more supportive of decisions made by groups as opposed to individuals (Horowitz, 1997). Committees could mitigate the influence of prosecutors' individual proclivities and ensure that decisions are made based on case factors (Horowitz, 1997).

The third advantage of committees is that they would increase the accountability of those making decisions (Horowitz, 1997). According to Horowitz, the use of committees would increase accountability while reducing secrecy (1997). He argued that committees' decisions should be written and published, which would help to ensure consistency of decisions (Horowitz, 1997).

Horowitz wrote that the fourth advantage of using committees would be the diminished possibility of discrimination in the application of the death penalty (1997). He argued that there would be pressure on both governors and prosecutors to appoint committee members that would represent the counties' diverse populations (Horowitz, 1997).

No state has adopted Horowitz's recommendation that legislatures establish death penalty committees by statute; however, the Joint Task Force to Review the Administration of Ohio's Death Penalty (hereinafter "Joint Task Force") did recommend a change in state law to establish a death penalty charging committee (Final Report and Recommendations, 2014). The Joint Task Force was comprised of judges, prosecutors (including county and state attorney general's offices), defense attorneys, law professors, office holders, and others (Final Report and Recommendations, 2014). The Joint Task Force met regularly for more than two years, and this author attended many of the open meetings, including the one in which the possibility of a statewide death penalty committee was discussed. This was potentially the most contested and debated proposal made by any of the Joint Task Force's committees. Although many proposed recommendations resulted in votes with few dissenters, the committee recommendation passed in a vote of eight in favor and six opposed—only one proposal passed by a smaller margin (Final Report and Recommendations, 2014).

Recommendation 34 of the Joint Task Force:

> To address cross jurisdictional racial disparity, it is recommended that Ohio create a death penalty charging committee at the Ohio Attorney General's Office. It is recommended that the committee be made up of former county prosecutors, appointed by the Governor, and members of the Ohio Attorney General's staff. County prosecutors would submit cases they want to charge with death as a potential punishment. The Attorney General's office would approve or disapprove of the charges paying particular attention to the race of the victim(s) and defendant(s).
>
> *(p. 14)*

The committee structure recommended was based on part on the Illinois state-wide review committee that was recommended by the Illinois Commission on Capital Punishment (Final Report and Recommendations, 2014). Despite the fact that the committee as recommended would be comprised of former county prosecutors selected by the governor and members of the Ohio Attorney General's Office and would be housed on that office, these are the very members of the Joint Task Force that most vehemently objected. In fact, the two county prosecutors and representative from the Attorney General's Offices (hereinafter referred to as "the prosecutors") on the Joint Task Force were so dissatisfied with this and other recommendations that they filed a Dissenting Report (2014). The prosecutors objected to 25 of the Joint Task Force's 56 recommendations (Dissenting Report, 2014). The longest argument opposing a recommendation related to the formation of a statewide charging committee (Dissenting Report, 2014).

The prosecutors had four categories of concern with Recommendation 34: faulty premise, no proper standards, needless delays, and constitutional concerns (Dissenting Report, 2014). Each will be discussed here in turn. The prosecutors first argued that the Joint Task Force began with an incorrect belief that county prosecutors discriminate against African Americans, either intentionally or unintentionally (Dissenting Report, 2014). They argued that there was no evidence that the death penalty was being used disproportionately against African Americans by county prosecutors in Ohio (Dissenting Report, 2014). Accordingly, the prosecutors argued that there was no evidence that they were abusing their discretion in death penalty cases (Dissenting Report, 2014). The prosecutors then argued that Recommendation 34 provided no standards that would apply to guide the committee; rather, the decisions of the committee would be based on the individual members' subjective standards (Dissenting Report, 2014). The prosecutors maintained that local prosecutors were in the best position to evaluate legal factors in cases as well as factors such as availability of resources (Dissenting Report, 2014). The prosecutors called "offensive" (p. 17) the portion of the recommendation that instructs the committee to direct specific attention to the offenders' and victims' race (Dissenting Report, 2014). The prosecutors then claimed that a charging committee would cause needless delays because "[e]very death-penalty defendant will argue that the charging committee failed to pay 'particular attention to the race of the victim(s) and defendant(s)'" (Dissenting Report, 2014, p. 19). Finally, the prosecutors stated that the committee would create constitutional concerns, including the powers granted to county prosecutors and the separation of powers among the branches of government (Dissenting Report, 2014).

Most of the recommendations of the Joint Task were to *change* the laws and rules that would require action by the legislative or judicial branches. No action has been taken on Recommendation 34; however, one Ohio county voluntarily created a type of charging committee. After a new prosecutor was elected, the Cuyahoga County Prosecutors Office created an internal review committee to assess whether the death penalty be sought in death-eligible cases (Caniglia, 2015). Another new prosecutor has been elected for Cuyahoga County, but the review committee remains in place (Capital Case Charging Protocol, n.d.). Although the review team is to make a recommendation in every case that is death eligible, there is a provision for the county prosecutor to overrule the committee (Capital Case Charging Protocol, n.d.).

Legal Issues Affecting Prosecutors in Death Penalty Cases

There are many legal issues that affect prosecutors in all cases, but two of the most important legal issues are of particular significance in death penalty cases. Prosecutors are required to provide the defense with exculpatory evidence. That is, they must provide the defense with evidence that could be helpful to the defendants' cases. Additionally, prosecutors are not permitted to remove potential jurors from the pool based on their race. The United States Supreme Court has issued landmark cases addressing disclosure of evidence and race-based jury selection. This section of the chapter will discuss those cases and how they affect prosecutors in death penalty cases.

Disclosure of Exculpatory Evidence

The landmark case involving exculpatory evidence was actually a case that involved the death penalty. Before the defendant's trial, the defense had requested to examine copies of statements given by the co-defendant. The prosecution shared several statements with the defense but withheld the one in which the co-defendant admitted to actually killing the victim. The defendant admitted to participating in the crime during the trial, but he denied killing the victim. He claimed that his co-defendant, who had not had a trial yet, actually caused the death of the victim. The defendant was found guilty of first-degree murder, sentenced to death, and his conviction and sentence were upheld by the Maryland Court of Appeals before he learned about the statement that had been withheld by the prosecution. He claimed that he was denied due process of law because the evidence had not been disclosed by the prosecution. When the case made its way to the United States Supreme Court as *Brady v. Maryland*, the court agreed that Brady's right to due process had been violated. In its decision, the court held that "suppression by the prosecution of evidence favorable to an accused upon request violates due process where the evidence is material either to guilt or to punishment, irrespective of the good faith or bad faith of the prosecution" (p. 87). According to the court, the prosecution had a duty to disclose all evidence that was important to the crime or the punishment. In a later case, *Strickler v. Greene* (527 U.S. 263), the court held that evidence is material when "there is a reasonable probability that his conviction or sentence would have been different had these materials been disclosed" (1999, p. 296). Because the withheld statement could have let the jury conclude that the defendant did not actually commit the murder, it was relevant to his sentence. The jury might not have chosen a death sentence if it heard evidence that the co-defendant actually killed the victim. The prosecution was, therefore, required to disclosed the co-defendant's statement.

The *Brady* decision did not stop prosecutors from failing to turn over exculpatory evidence. Prosecutors are the ones to determine what evidence is exculpatory and material, and *Brady* did not provide a remedy for when future violations occur. While prosecutors can fail to disclose evidence in any case, these failures have so much more meaning in death penalty cases because the stakes are so high. The case of *Connick v. Thompson* illustrates the problems with *Brady* violations and the lack of remedies.

John Thompson was charged with murder in 1985 in Orleans Parish, Louisiana, and he was later convicted and sentenced to death. After seeing news of his arrest, victims of an earlier robbery came forward to identify Thompson as the assailant. Robbery investigators recovered a piece of fabric that had the offender's blood on it. Before the robbery trial, prosecutors received a report from the crime lab indicating that the blood type on the tested fabric was B. This report was not given to Thompson's defense lawyer, and Thompson was convicted of the robbery. It was later discovered that the prosecutor intentionally withheld the blood evidence. Because he could have been questioned about this robbery at the subsequent murder trial, he chose not to testify on his own behalf at that trial. The jury found Thompson guilty of murder and he received the death penalty. Challenges to his convictions were unsuccessful, and Thompson received an execution date. Thompson was one month from this execution date when a private investigator going through the crime lab's files discovered the undisclosed blood analysis report. Thompson's blood was then drawn for comparison, and there was no match. With a blood type of O, Thompson could not have been guilty of the robbery. Had he not been convicted of robbery, Thompson would have testified in his defense at the murder trial. Additional *Brady* problems occurred before the murder trial. Prosecutors failed to disclose: (1) audiotapes of a statement that showed a witness knew about the possibility of receiving reward money; (2) a police report that was inconsistent with a prosecution witness' testimony; and (3) police reports in which an eyewitness described the assailant's hair as different from how the defendant's hair was styled. Both convictions were overturned, and a jury found him not guilty at his second murder trial after his defense showed evidence that a different man committed the crime. Thompson was released from prison after serving 18 years in prison, including 14 on death row.

Thompson filed a civil rights lawsuit against Harry Connick, the elected prosecutor of Orleans Parish, after he was released from prison (*Connick v. Thompson*, 2011). He won and the jury awarded him $14 million. The United States Supreme Court overturned this award even though the prosecution admitted that *Brady* was violated. In a 5–4 decision, the court held that a prosecutor's office was not liable for a civil rights action for failing to adequately train staff about the duty to avoid violating civil rights based on a single *Brady* violation. Rather, Thompson did not provide evidence that there was a pattern of behavior by untrained employees.

Race and Jury Selection

In *Batson v. Kentucky* (1986), the United State Supreme Court held that the Equal Protection Clause prohibits prosecutors from using peremptory challenges to exclude people from juries based on race (476 U.S. 79). To challenge the prosecutors' actions, the defense must establish a *prima facie* case of purposeful discrimination. This can be done based only on the prosecutors' use of peremptory challenges. The burden then shifts to the prosecution to provide a reason other than race for why potential jurors were struck. If the prosecutors cannot state a race-neutral reason for the strikes, the trial court can put the struck juries back in the jury venire.

Equal Justice Initiative published a study on the continuing use of racial discrimination in jury selection in 2010. The nonprofit organization studied jury selection in eight states, which resulted in 20 findings related to race and jury selection:

1. The 1875 Civil Rights Act outlawed race-based discrimination in jury service, but 135 years later illegal exclusion of racial minorities persists.
2. Racially biased use of peremptory strikes and illegal racial discrimination in jury selection remains widespread, particularly in serious criminal cases and capital cases.
3. The United States Supreme Court's 1986 decision in *Batson v. Kentucky* has limited racially discriminatory use of peremptory strikes in some jurisdictions, but the refusal to apply the decision retroactively has meant that scores of death row prisoners have been executed after convictions and death sentences by all-white juries, which were organized by excluding people of color on the basis of race. Moreover, dozens of condemned prisoners still face execution after being convicted and sentenced by juries selected in a racially discriminatory manner.
4. Most state appellate courts have reversed convictions where there is clear evidence of racially discriminatory jury selection. However, by frequently upholding convictions where dramatic evidence of racial bias has been presented, appellate courts have failed to consistently and effectively enforce anti-discrimination laws and adequately deter the practice of discriminatory jury selection.
5. EJI studied jury selection in eight states in the Southern United States: Alabama, Arkansas, Florida, Georgia, Louisiana, Mississippi, South Carolina, and Tennessee. State appellate courts in each of these states—except Tennessee, whose appellate courts have never granted *Batson* relief in a criminal case—have been forced to recognize continuing problems with racially biased jury selection. The Mississippi Supreme Court concluded in 2007 that "racially profiling jurors and [ ] racially motivated jury selection [are] still prevalent twenty years after Batson was handed down."
6. Alabama appellate courts have found illegal, racially discriminatory jury selection in 25 death penalty cases in recent years, and compelling evidence of racially biased jury selection has been presented in dozens of other death penalty cases, with no relief granted.
7. In some communities, the exclusion of African Americans from juries is extreme. For example, in Houston County, Alabama, 80% of African Americans qualified for jury service have been struck by prosecutors in death penalty cases.
8. The high rate of exclusion of racial minorities in Jefferson Parish, Louisiana, has meant that in 80% of criminal trials, there is no effective black representation on the jury.
9. There is evidence that some district attorney's offices explicitly train prosecutors to exclude racial minorities from jury service and teach them how to mask racial bias to avoid a finding that anti-discrimination laws have been violated.
10. Hundreds of people of color called for jury service have been illegally excluded from juries after prosecutors asserted pretextual reasons to justify their removal. Many of these assertions are false, humiliating, demeaning, and injurious. This practice continues in virtually all of the states studied for this report.

11. There is wide variation among states and counties concerning enforcement of anti-discrimination laws that protect racial minorities and women from illegal exclusion.
12. Procedural rules and defaults have shielded from remedy many meritorious claims of racial bias.
13. Many defense lawyers fail to adequately challenge racially discriminatory jury selection because they are uncomfortable, unwilling, unprepared, or not trained to assert claims of racial bias.
14. Even where courts have found that prosecutors have illegally excluded people of color from jury service, there have been no adverse consequences for state officials. Because prosecutors have been permitted to violate the law with impunity, insufficient disincentives have been created to eliminate bias in jury selection.
15. In some communities racial minorities continue to be underrepresented in the pools from which jurors are selected. When challenges are brought, courts use an inadequate and misleading measure of underrepresentation known as "absolute disparity," which has resulted in the avoidable exclusion of racial minorities in many communities.
16. Under current law and the absolute disparity standard, it is impossible for African Americans to effectively challenge underrepresentation in the jury pool in 75% of the counties in the United States. For Latinos and Asian Americans, challenges are effectively barred in 90% of counties.
17. The lack of racial diversity among jurors in many cases has seriously compromised the credibility, reliability, and integrity of the criminal justice system and frequently triggered social unrest, riots, and violence in response to verdicts that are deemed racially biased.
18. Research suggests that, compared to diverse juries, all-white juries tend to spend less time deliberating, make more errors, and consider fewer perspectives.
19. Miami; New York; Los Angeles; Hartford, Connecticut; Jena, Louisiana; Powhatan, Virginia; Milwaukee, Wisconsin; and the Florida Panhandle are among many communities that have seen unrest, violence, or destruction in response to non-diverse criminal jury verdicts.
20. The lack of racial diversity among prosecutors, state court judges, appellate judges, and law enforcement agencies in many communities has made jury diversity absolutely critical to preserving the credibility of the criminal justice system (Equal Justice Initiative, 2010, pp. 5–7).

A recent United States Supreme Court decision illustrates many of the findings by the Equal Justice Initiative study and shows that racially discriminatory use of peremptory challenges by prosecutors did not stop after *Batson v. Kentucky*. In 2016 the Supreme Court reversed a defendant's capital murder conviction and death sentence in a Georgia case (*Foster v. Chatman*, 578, U.S. __). According to the syllabus of the court:

> Foster, through the Georgia Open Records Act, obtained from the State copies of the file used by the prosecution during his trial. Among other documents, the file contained (1) copies of the jury venire list on which the names of each black prospective juror were highlighted in bright green, with a legend indicating that the highlighting "represents Blacks"; (2) a draft affidavit from an investigator comparing black prospective jurors and concluding, "If it comes down to having to pick one of the black jurors, [this one] might be okay"; (3) notes identifying black prospective jurors as "B#1," "B#2," and "B#3"; (4) notes with "N" (for "no") appearing next to the names of all black prospective jurors; (5) a list titled "[D]efinite NO's" containing six names, including the names of all of the qualified black prospective jurors; (6) a document with notes on the Church of Christ that was annotated "NO. No Black Church"; and (7) the questionnaires filled out by five prospective black jurors, on which each juror's response indicating his or her race had been circled.
>
> *(2016, para. 1)*

Pursuant to *Batson*, prosecutors provided what they considered to be race-neutral justifications for their peremptory jury strikes. Although lower courts accepted the prosecutors' justifications, the United States Supreme Court did not. According to the prosecution, potential African American juror Garrett was struck as a last-minute decision. The Supreme Court noted that Garrett's name was on the list of definite noes. Prosecutors justified striking some African American jurors based on characteristics like their ages or marital status, but the court listed white jurors who were accepted with the same or similar characteristics.

Conclusion

Prosecutors are powerful members of the criminal justice system. Thousands of prosecutors and assistants work hard to uphold laws and to achieve justice every day. Like any other profession, there are those who do not live up to the expectations of their position and cast a shadow over others. This chapter has discussed issues and studies that may not have shown prosecutors in the most positive light; however, prosecutors remain key participants in the death penalty system and need to be respected. Decisions in death penalty cases cannot be taken lightly. If there is to be a fair death penalty system, it must start with those who make the decision on whether or not to seek it and the factors that guide them. Whether the decisions are made by individual people, committees, teams, or other methods, race and geography cannot be factors influencing these decisions in a fair system. Likewise, if there is to be a fair death penalty system, those who participate in the system need to follow the rules. There cannot be a fair death penalty system if prosecutors do not diligently follow the law.

References

Associated Press. (2017, April 26). Florida court won't rule immediately in case of prosecutor. *WCTV*. Retrieved from www.wctv.tv/content/news/Florida-legislators-propose-cutting-budget-of-prosecutor-417251263.html

Baldus, D. C., Pulaski, C., & Woodworth, G. (1983). Comparative review of death sentences: An empirical study of the Georgia experience. *Journal of Criminal Law and Criminology, 74*(3), 661–753. Retrieved from http://scholarlycommons.law.northwestern.edu/cgi/viewcontent.cgi?article=6378&context=jclc

Bohm, R. M. (2012). *Deathquest: An introduction to the theory and practice of capital punishment in the United States* (4th ed.). New York: Routledge.

Caniglia, J. (2015, November 25). Eluding death: Ohio prosecutors charge far fewer capital murder cases. *The Plain Dealer*. Retrieved from http://connect.cleveland.com/staff/jcaniglia/posts.html

Capital Case Charging Protocol. (n.d.). *Cuyahoga county office of the prosecutor*. Retrieved from http://prosecutor.cuyahogacounty.us/en-US/capital-charging-protocol.aspx

Death Penalty Information Center. (2016). *United States attorney memorandum*. Retrieved from https://deathpenaltyinfo.org/documents/FedDPRules2011.pdf

Deters, J., O'Brien, R., & Schumaker, S. (2014). *Dissenting report form the joint task force to review the administration of Ohio's death penalty*. Retrieved from www.supremecourt.ohio.gov/Boards/deathPenalty/dissentingReport.pdf

Dieter, R. C. (2011). *Struck by lightning: The continuing arbitrariness of the death penalty thirty-five years after its re-instatement in 1976*. Death Penalty Information Center. Retrieved from https://deathpenaltyinfo.org/documents/StruckByLightning.pdf

Dieter, R. C. (2013). *The 2% death penalty: How a minority of counties produce most death cases at enormous costs to all*. Death Penalty Information Center. Retrieved from https://deathpenaltyinfo.org/documents/TwoPercentReport.pdf

Equal Justice Initiative. (2010). *Illegal racial discrimination in jury selection: A continuing legacy*. Retrieved from https://eji.org/sites/default/files/illegal-racial-discrimination-in-jury-selection.pdf

Fair Punishment Project. (2016). *America's top five deadliest prosecutors: How overzealous personalities drive the death penalty*. Retrieved from http://fairpunishment.org/wp-content/uploads/2016/06/FPP-Top5Report_FINAL.pdf

Florida Supreme Court Case Docket. (2017, June 2017). *Florida* Supreme Court. Retrieved from http://jweb.flcourts.org/pls/docket/ds_docket?p_caseyear=2017&p_casenumber=653

Gershowitz, A. M. (2010). Statewide capital punishment: The case for eliminating counties' role in the death penalty. *Vanderbilt Law Review, 63*(2), 307–335. Retrieved from http://vanderbiltlawreview.org/articles/2010/03/Gershowitz-Statewide-Capital-Punishment-63-Vand.-L.-Rev.-307-20101.pdf

Hannan, L. (2017, March 21). Agree with my politics or I'll take away your power. *Slate*. Retrieved from www.slate.com/articles/news_and_politics/trials_and_error/2017/03/rick_scott_s_decision_to_reassign_a_prosecutor_who_opposes_the_death_penalty.html

Harris, T. (2017, March 28). *Judge sides with Florida governor in removal of prosecutor*. Associated Press. Retrieved from https://apnews.com/adad04dae4aa4576a6f69e761da111d0/fight-between-florida-governor-prosecutor-back-court

Horowitz, J. A. (1997). Prosecutorial discretion and the death penalty: Creating a committee to decide whether to seek the death penalty. *Fordham Law Review, 65*(6), 2571–2610. Retrieved from www-lexisnexis-com.mu.opal-libraries.org/hottopics/lnacademic/?shr=t&csi=7364&sr=%20AUTHOR%28Horowitz%29+AND+DATE+IS+1996

Kam, D. (2017, April 24). State Attorney Aramis Ayala gets prominent backers in death penalty dispute. *Orlando Weekly*. Retrieved from www.orlandoweekly.com/Blogs/archives/2017/04/24/state-attorney-aramis-ayala-gets-prominent-backers-in-death-penalty-dispute

Mettler, K. (2017, March 21). Florida prosecutor refuses to seek death penalty for alleged cop killer, defies Gov. Rick Scott's order to step aside. *Washington Post*. Retrieved from www.washingtonpost.com/news/morning-mix/wp/2017/03/21/floridas-first-black-prosecutor-a-death-penalty-boycotter-defies-gov-rick-scott/?utm_term=.a267ec4c3c8d

North Carolina Department of Public Safety. (n.d.). *Persons executed in North Carolina 1941–1950*. Retrieved from www.ncdps.gov/Adult-Corrections/Prisons/Death-Penalty/List-of-persons-executed/Executions-1941-1950

North Carolina Department of Public Safety. (2013). *History of capital punishment in North Carolina*. Retrieved from www.ncdps.gov/Adult-Corrections/Prisons/Death-Penalty/History

Ohioans to Stop Executions. (2014). *The death lottery: How race and geography determine who goes to Ohio's death row*. Retrieved from www.otse.org/wp-content/uploads/2014/04/OTSE-Report-The-Death-Lottery.pdf

Ohio Joint Task Force. (2014). *Final report and recommendations*. Retrieved from www.supremecourtofohio.gov/Boards/deathPenalty/finalReport.pdf

Paternoster, R. (1983). Race of victim and location of crime: The decision to seek the death penalty in South Carolina. *Journal of Criminal Law & Criminology, 74*(3), 754–785. Retrieved from http://scholarlycommons.law.northwestern.edu/cgi/viewcontent.cgi?article=6379&context=jclc

Paternoster, R., Brame, R., Bacon, S., Ditchfield, A., Biere, D., Beckman, K., . . . Murphy, K. (2003). *An empirical analysis of Maryland's death sentencing system with respect to the influence of race and legal jurisdiction*. Retrieved from www.aclu-md.org/uploaded_files/0000/0377/md_death_penalty_race_study.pdf

Radalet, M. L., & Pierce, G. L. (1985). Race and prosecutorial discretion in homicide cases. *Law and Society Review, 19*(4), 587–621. Retrieved from http://eds.b.ebscohost.com.mu.opal-libraries.org/eds/pdfviewer/pdfviewer?vid=1&sid=4c9aee6c-6bc1-4ebd-b4f5-797bbb6197a9%40sessionmgr102&hid=121

Rohrer, G., Stutzman, R., & Lotan, G. T. (2017, April 3). Gov. Rick Scott reassigns 21 murder cases, citing Aramis Ayala's death penalty stance. *Orlando Sentinel*. Retrieved from www.orlandosentinel.com/news/politics/political-pulse/os-rick-scott-ayala-death-penalty-20170403-story.html

Saad, L. (2007). Racial disagreement over death penalty has varied historically. *Gallup*. Retrieved from www.gallup.com/poll/28243/racial-disagreement-over-death-penalty-has-varied-historically.aspx

Cases Cited

Batson v. Kentucky, 476 U.S. 79 (1986).
Brady v. Maryland, 373 U.S. 83 (1963).
Connick v. Thompson, 563 U.S. 51 (2011).
Foster v. Chatman, 578 U.S. ___ (2016).
Furman v. Georgia, 408 U.S. 238 (1972).
Gregg v. Georgia, 428 U.S. 153 (1976).
In the Matter of *Johnson v. Pataki*, 91 N.Y.2d 214 (1997).
McCleskey v. Kemp, 481 U.S. 279 (1987).
Pulley v. Harris, 465 U.S. 37 (1984).
Strickler v. Greene, 527 U.S. 263 (1999).
June 30, 2017 (Death Penalty Handbook)

19

COUNSEL FOR THE DESPISED AND THE CONDEMNED

Capital Defense Attorneys

Jeffrey L. Kirchmeier*

Introduction

United States Supreme Court Justice Thurgood Marshall once noted that a defense attorney's work "is a crucial component of the system of protections designed to ensure that capital punishment is administered with some degree of rationality" (*Strickland v. Washington*, 1984, p. 715 [Marshall, J., dissenting]). As the former capital defense lawyer Marshall knew, defense attorneys play an essential role in capital cases. In such cases, the quality of legal representation can literally make a difference between life and death (see, e.g., *Powell v. Alabama*, 1932, p. 69).

In a criminal case, an individual faces prosecution by the government, which has a substantial amount of resources. The defendant is protected against this overwhelming government power by a defense attorney. When a person is accused of a crime, and in particular where the person's life is at stake, it is important that the person has a qualified lawyer, knowledgeable in the law, who will stand beside the accused. As the Supreme Court recognizes, a criminal defendant "requires the guiding hand of counsel at every step in the proceedings" (*Powell v. Alabama*, 1932, pp. 68–69).

The right of a criminal defendant to have counsel is so important that the drafters of the Bill of Rights incorporated the right into the Sixth Amendment. That amendment guarantees that: "In all criminal prosecutions, the accused shall enjoy the right . . . to have the Assistance of Counsel for his defence" (U.S. Const. VI amend). That right is an essential element of our justice system, recognizing that a defense attorney is necessary for a fair trial (Amar, 1998, p. 116). The Sixth Amendment, which has been held to apply to the states through the Fourteenth Amendment, "stands as a constant admonition that if the constitutional safeguards it provides be lost, justice will not still be done" (*Johnson v. Zerbst*, 1938, p. 462).

Thus, the Supreme Court has held that a person accused of a crime has a right to have a trial court appoint counsel if the defendant cannot afford an attorney. "An accused is entitled to be assisted by an attorney, whether retained or appointed, who plays the role necessary to ensure that the trial is fair" (*Strickland v. Washington*, 1984, p. 685).

A defense attorney helps protect the innocent from being convicted by fighting on behalf of the accused in court. Capital defense lawyers challenge the evidence against a defendant, helping to ensure that an innocent person is not executed.

But guilty defendants are also entitled to attorneys. For one reason, only a small percentage of capital defendants are ultimately sentenced to death and executed, even if guilty. So a defense attorney still plays an important role in sentencing and other stages of legal proceedings, including appeals. Even

Figure 19.1 U.S. Supreme Court Justice Thurgood Marshall.
Source: Photograph by Robert S. Oakes, National Geographic, Courtesy the Supreme Court of the United States.

for guilty clients, then, a capital defense attorney, in theory, serves the systemic goal that only those most deserving of the death penalty are executed.

Further, whether an accused person is guilty or not guilty, it is the defense lawyer who strives to make sure that the government follows the rules and that the defendant is treated fairly. The defense attorney forces the government to comply with the constraints of the U.S. Constitution, protecting the rights of the client and the rights of everyone. As one professor and defense attorney asserted, "The zealous defense attorney is the last bastion of liberty—the final barrier between an overreaching government and its citizens" (Dershowitz, 1982, p. 415).

Considering the long history of racial discrimination and other types of discrimination in the United States, defense lawyers are necessary to battle against unfair prejudices in the court system and from individuals in the system. For example, it falls on defense attorneys to be vigilant against jury selection that excludes African Americans from juries (*Batson v. Kentucky*, 1986). Defense attorneys also have used sociological research to challenge the way the death penalty is applied unfairly based upon race (*McCleskey v. Kemp*, 1987). Similarly, in recent years, defense attorneys have worked to fight against practices such as a stop-and-frisk policy where police racially profiled individuals on the street (see, e.g., *Floyd et al. v. City of New York et al.*, 2013). Because the American criminal justice system has had a devastating impact on minorities and their communities, oftentimes if falls upon defense lawyers to fight back against police actions, discriminatory laws, biased government officials, and unfair procedures.

Many people form their concepts of defense attorneys—whether good or bad—from watching television and movies. There have been a number of great films with a focus on someone representing people accused of capital crimes. For example, in the 1957 film *Paths of Glory*, Kirk Douglas portrayed a colonel defending three soldiers at their court-martial, where they were sentenced to death. The most famous fictional death penalty lawyer probably is Atticus Finch. In the 1962 movie based on Harper Lee's book *To Kill a Mockingbird*, Finch, played by Gregory Peck, represented a man charged with rape, which was a capital offense in Alabama during the period where the movie was set.

The defense attorney's job, however, is not easy. Capital defense lawyers represent individuals accused of horrible crimes. So, as in *To Kill a Mockingbird*, some people in society may be critical of the work that defense attorneys do, mistakenly associating the attorney with the client's alleged crime. Further, capital defense attorneys generally have fewer resources than the government prosecutors they face. And the work does not pay as well as much other legal work (*McFarland v. Scott*, 1994, pp. 1257–58). Thus, these death penalty lawyers often face long odds at all stages, including a plea negotiation process that is more complex than in noncapital cases (Denno, 1992, p. 454).

Yet many attorneys do take on the challenge of representing someone charged with a capital crime or representing someone who already has been sentenced to death. Capital defense lawyers often accept cases where they know they face long odds because they know they are needed to represent the poor and the despised. And they recognize that our constitutional system only works with zealous advocates representing the accused.

As discussed in this chapter, in the modern death penalty era, there have been a number of issues connected to death penalty representation. For example, death penalty defendants almost always are poor and unable to pay for counsel, so they often must rely upon appointed counsel or volunteer lawyers to represent them in court.

Although many of these capital defense attorneys do an outstanding job representing their clients, sometimes the representation is inadequate. There are a number of instances where capital defendants have been sentenced to death and even executed due to mistakes made by their attorneys. Supreme Court Justice Ruth Bader Ginsburg, after nearly eight years on the court, explained, "I have yet to see a death case, among the dozens coming to the Supreme Court on eve of execution petitions, in which the defendant was well represented at trial" (Ginsburg, 2001).

The United States Constitution makes certain guarantees to those accused of capital crimes. Not only has the U.S. Supreme Court deemed that criminal defendants have a right to counsel, but it also has dictated that such representation must meet a basic level of competence. Cases in this area have created other issues for capital representation and the future of death penalty cases.

This chapter explains some of the responsibilities of capital defense attorneys and how their work differs from the work of most other lawyers. It also considers what happens when capital defense lawyers make mistakes and how difficult it is for appeal and postconviction attorneys to correct mistakes made by earlier attorneys in the process. Additionally, this chapter explains how the Supreme Court has dictated that the Constitution entitles defendants to competent defense attorneys. Finally, it briefly summarizes the important role that capital defense lawyers have played and continue to play in the history of the United States death penalty.

THE ROLE OF CAPITAL DEFENSE COUNSEL

Capital defense attorneys must be highly qualified and prepared to competently handle complicated legal cases. At every level, capital cases are among the most complex and time-consuming types of legal cases. Beginning with a high-stakes trial and a sentencing hearing unlike other types of criminal cases, death penalty defense lawyers face unique challenges. And after the trial and sentencing, appellate and collateral postconviction proceedings attorneys face numerous hurdles such as procedural rules in the labyrinthine area of habeas corpus law.

The Work of Capital Defense Attorneys

In all criminal cases, a defense attorney protects a person, and, by asserting an individual's rights, helps uphold the rights embedded in the U.S. Constitution. But the heightened stakes in capital cases significantly increase the responsibilities of a defendant's lawyer. In a long line of cases, the U.S. Supreme Court has stressed how capital cases differ from other criminal cases because "the penalty of death is qualitatively different from a sentence of imprisonment." Therefore, "[b]ecause of that qualitative difference, there is a corresponding difference in the need for reliability in the determination that death is the appropriate punishment in a specific case" (*Woodson v. North Carolina*, 1976, p. 305).

To understand the role of a capital defense attorney, it is important to understand the modern death penalty and its constitutional underpinnings. The modern era of death penalty litigation in the United States, which helped define the role of capital defense attorneys, began in 1972 with the Supreme Court's decision in *Furman v. Georgia*. In that case, a divided Supreme Court concluded that statutes that gave broad discretion to jurors about whether or not to sentence a defendant to death violated the constitution (*Furman v. Georgia*, 1972).

Following *Furman*, a large number of states rewrote their death penalty statutes to try to comply with the dictates of the Eighth and Fourteenth Amendments. In response to these new statutes, the Supreme Court held that states could not have a system where the death penalty was imposed automatically following a conviction (see *Woodson v. North Carolina*, 1976; *Roberts v. Louisiana*, 1976).

However, a majority of the Supreme Court Justices held that states may impose the death penalty if jurors are given guidelines in their sentencing decision. In *Gregg v. Georgia*, the court upheld Georgia's capital sentencing scheme, which required jurors to consider aggravating factors that weighed in favor of the death penalty against mitigating factors that weighed against the death penalty (*Gregg v. Georgia*, 1976). Not all constitutional sentencing schemes follow an identical structure (*Jurek v. Texas*, 1976). But they all do require that jurors have guidance in the sentencing process and that capital defendants have an opportunity to present a case for why they should not be sentenced to death.

Thus, after *Furman* and *Gregg*, a death penalty defense lawyer representing an individual accused of a capital crime must handle a trial that generally is bifurcated. In other words, the attorney faces what are essentially two trials. First, in the guilt phase, the trial determines whether or not the defendant is guilty of a capital crime. Second, in most cases if a defendant is found guilty, then another penalty "trial" takes place to determine whether the defendant should be sentenced to death or life in prison. At this penalty phase, the defense attorney may introduce helpful evidence about the defendant's background and the circumstances of the crime (*Lockett v. Ohio*, 1978).

The attorney should begin preparing for both phases of the trial from the moment the case is assigned or accepted. A homicide trial is often complex on its own. Murder cases often feature many different types of evidence, requiring a range of experts from pathologists to ballistics specialists to DNA experts (ABA Guidelines, 2003, p. 955).

At the same time as an attorney is preparing for trial, the attorney also must be preparing for the sentencing phase in the event the client is convicted of capital murder (White, 2005). For one thing, there generally is not enough time in between hearings for the type of extensive investigation that is required to prepare for sentencing. Additionally, the lawyer must understand and anticipate how choices one makes during the guilt-phase of trial may affect the sentencing (Streib, 2003/2004, p. 409). For example, plans for sentencing

> should shape the relationship with the client, prosecutor, court personnel, and jurors; it should determine how voir dire proceeds . . . ; and it should directly affect the nature of the defense presented during the guilt trial and the affirmative mitigating case put on at the penalty trial.
>
> (*Goodpaster, 1983, p. 320*)

In the sentencing phase of a capital trial, prosecutors present aggravating factors to argue that a defendant should be sentenced to death, while defense attorneys present mitigating factors, arguing why a defendant should not be sentenced to death. Mitigating factors may include evidence that the defendant played a lesser role in the crime, that the defendant is brain-damaged, that the defendant was abused as a child, and various mental health issues (Kirchmeier, 2004, p. 631). Such factors do not excuse a defendant's crime. But they might help explain experiences that have affected the defendant and might show why a defendant should be sentenced to life in prison instead of executed.

The U.S. Supreme Court has held that these mitigating factors may not be limited by statute, and therefore defense counsel must be knowledgeable of a range of possible arguments (*Lockett v. Ohio*, 1978, pp. 608–609; *Eddings v. Oklahoma*, 1982, pp. 115–116). The large number of possible mitigating factors may be categorized as including ones that show redeeming qualities of the defendant, factors that show the defendant had lesser involvement in the murder, factors that illustrate how the defendant's sentence may be affected by the legal proceedings, and factors that help explain why the defendant committed the crime (Kirchmeier, 2004, p. 658).

The sentencing phase generally requires attorneys to investigate a defendant's entire life, often using the perspective of psychiatric expertise. Thus, capital defense attorneys must complete a broad investigation as they prepare for capital trials. They also must work with investigators, mitigation specialists, mental health professionals, and other experts (Cooley, 2005, pp. 59–65).

Beyond the legal and procedural requirements for capital cases, many death penalty defense lawyers have to face other challenges that may make a case seem hopeless, such as working with a client who may have mental health issues that affect the case or the attorney-client relationship. Especially if attorneys are not adequately educated about psychiatric issues, sometimes it even can be a challenge for the attorney to communicate effectively and have a good relationship with the client (MacLean, 2009, p. 661). In extreme cases, a defense attorney may have to counsel a despairing client who wishes to give up on legal challenges and be executed (Blume, 2005, p. 939–940).

The importance of capital representation does not end at the trial or at the sentencing, once a defendant is convicted and sentenced to death. Defense attorneys represent condemned clients in appeals, state and collateral postconviction review proceedings, and clemency proceedings (Radelet & Zsembik, 1993, pp. 289–314).

Although procedures vary by jurisdiction, generally, after a defendant is sentenced to death, an appellate lawyer represents the defendant on appeal to the state's highest court or to a specialized court. There, the appellate attorney raises claims from the trial record regarding both the trial and the sentencing based both upon state law and federal constitutional law (*Orazio v. Dugger*, 1989).

Following the appeal, usually a new attorney represents the capital defendant in collateral postconviction review proceedings in state and federal courts. At this stage, the new lawyer generally must reinvestigate the guilt-phase evidence as well as evidence available for the sentencing phase of the trial (*Williams v. Taylor*, 2000, pp. 395–399). Attorneys at these stages also help check to make sure that state and federal laws were followed at the defendant's trial.

In collateral postconviction review proceedings, and in particular during federal habeas corpus proceedings, courts and Congress have imposed a complex layer of procedural requirements that an attorney must navigate. Failure to properly file claims or raise issues may result in those claims never being reviewed by state and federal courts. Attorneys must become familiar with doctrines such as procedural default, exhaustion, and abuse-of-the-writ. An attorney's failure to properly comply with procedural rules at trial and at other proceedings may ultimately affect whether or not a client is executed (*Wainwright v. Sykes*, 1977; Stevenson, 2002).

In addition to the court proceedings, defense attorneys represent capital defendants in clemency proceedings. Although the procedures vary from state to state, attorneys must put together arguments for why a defendant should not be executed and present the case to a governor and/or a clemency board (Acker & Lanier, 2000; Alfieri, 2004).

Court decisions provide some guidance to defense attorneys regarding what they must do in their cases to meet a standard of constitutional competency. But other resources, such as training sessions, experienced attorneys, and scholarship, also provide some guidance for attorneys. Similarly, as discussed in the next section, ethical rules and other work by experts explain how capital defense attorneys should do their job.

Ethical Commands and Standards for Capital Defense Lawyers

Because of problems that occur when lawyers do not competently represent death penalty defendants and because of the complexity of capital cases, experts have provided some guidelines for lawyers who handle death penalty cases. These guidelines take various forms and come from different sources, including cases, experts, and ethical rules.

All criminal defense attorneys have certain core responsibilities no matter the crime at issue in their cases. For example, a defense attorney serves a function of assisting a defendant through the legal hurdles presented at trial.

> From counsel's function as assistant to the defendant derive the overarching duty to advocate the defendant's cause and the more particular duties to consult with the defendant on important decisions and to keep the defendant informed of important developments in the course of the prosecution.
>
> *(Strickland v. Washington, 1984, p. 688)*

Additionally, "[c]ounsel also has a duty to bring to bear such skill and knowledge as will render the trial a reliable adversarial process" (*Strickland v. Washington*, 1984, p. 688).

Death penalty cases, by their nature, feature defendants who are accused of horrible crimes. Thus, some lawyers may be deterred from representing such defendants, especially in small communities, where attorneys may be worried that their representation of a murderer may affect their business.

Yet, because of the unpopularity of death penalty clients and because they are often poor, it is even more essential that attorneys represent such defendants (Vick, 1995, p. 329). The American Bar Association Model Rules of Professional Conduct encourages lawyers to provide legal services to clients who are poor and to accept court appointments to represent clients (ABA Model Rules of Professional Conduct 6.1, 6.2).

It is also important that attorneys represent their capital clients well. Ethical rules dictate that all attorneys have a responsibility to provide competent representation to clients (ABA Model Rules of Professional Conduct 1.1).[1] Generally, such competent representation "requires the legal knowledge, skill, thoroughness and preparation reasonably necessary for the representation" (ABA Model Rules of Professional Conduct 1.1).

In order to help guide lawyers who specifically represent capital clients, the American Bar Association has published "Guidelines for the Appointment and Performance of Defense Counsel in Death Penalty Cases" (American Bar Association [2003]). In the guidelines, the ABA provides "a national standard of practice for the defense of capital cases in order to ensure high quality legal representation for all persons facing the possible imposition or execution of a death sentence by any jurisdiction" (American Bar Association, 2003, Guideline 1.1, p. 919). Although these guidelines do not constitute binding constitutional requirements, they provide a road map for capital defense attorneys to follow in these complex cases (*Bobby v. Van Hook*, 2009).

Because of the complexity and because of the high stakes in capital cases, these guidelines reinforce that it is necessary for defense attorneys to provide high quality representation at every stage of capital proceedings, including pretrial hearings, jury selection, trial proceedings, sentencing proceedings, appeal, and collateral post-conviction proceedings. Attorneys also must fully and thoroughly investigate facts related to both guilt and sentencing.

For example, the ABA Guidelines state: "Counsel at every stage have an obligation to conduct thorough and independent investigations relating to the issues of both guilt and penalty." Further, Guideline 10.7 explains that investigation regarding guilt and penalty needs to be done regardless of the client's statements about such evidence (American Bar Association, 2003, ABA Guideline 10.7, pp. 1015–1016).

In researching the client's background, attorneys must obtain all relevant records regarding the client's history. Additionally, "[i]t is necessary to locate and interview the client's family members . . . and virtually everyone else who knew the client and his family, including neighbors, teachers, clergy, case workers, doctors, correctional, probation, or parole officers, and others" (American Bar Association, 2003, Commentary to ABA Guideline 10.7, p. 1024).

In addition to ethical rules and the ABA Guidelines, some jurisdictions have their own qualifications for appointed counsel. For example, some states like Virginia specifically require that appointed trial counsel have certain experiences before they are appointed to capital cases. Similarly, a jurisdiction also may require appointed counsel to have undergone specific training and may require that more than one attorney be appointed to death penalty cases (see, e.g., Virginia Code Annotated Section 19.2–163.8 (2013); Virginia Indigent Defense Commission Homepage).

Jurisdictions also may use the ABA Guidelines as a vehicle for improving capital representation. For example, Arizona's standards for appointment of lead counsel in capital cases require that the attorney is "familiar with and guided by the performance standards in the 2003 American Bar Association Guidelines for the Appointment and Performance of Defense Counsel in Death Penalty Cases." Other requirements for lead counsel in Arizona include that the attorney has been lead counsel in at least nine felony jury trials and was lead or co-counsel in at least one death penalty jury trial (Arizona Rules of Criminal Procedure 6.8(b)(iii) [West 2016]).

Legislators, judges, attorneys, and scholars drafted these standards and guidelines to improve the quality of capital representation. Many were written to help address existing problems within the legal system. Although these guidelines and standards have helped to improve capital representation, problems still persist.

Problems Resulting From Poor Representation

Despite the ethical commands, sometimes due to various reasons, defense lawyers have provided sub-par representation to clients accused of capital crimes. Because of the high stakes in capital cases, counsels' errors may significantly harm their clients. One lawyer has noted, "In the area of death penalty prosecutions, lawyer skill is the single most important factor in determining whether a defendant is sentenced to death rather than life" (Dow, 1996, p. 694).

A good defense attorney helps make sure that trials are fair and that procedures comply with the U.S. Constitution and other laws. Such attorneys also work to ensure that sentencing proceedings are fair.

But sometimes capital defendants receive poor representation. When the attorneys do not provide competent representation, the system breaks down.

When the system fails, innocent people may be convicted and sentenced to death. As one federal district court judge noted, "innocent people are sentenced to death with materially greater frequency than was previously supposed and . . . convincing proof of their innocence often does not emerge until long after their convictions" (*United States v. Quinones*, 2002, p. 257). And studies have shown that mistakes by defense lawyers have been a significant factor leading to wrongful convictions and innocent people being sentenced to death (Liebman, Fagan, & West, 2000).

The quality of representation by lawyers varies for a number of reasons. In the overwhelming majority of capital cases, capital defendants cannot afford attorneys and must rely upon appointed counsel (Millman, p. 284; Vick, 1995, p. 334). Some have estimated that "approximately ninety percent of those charged with capital murder are indigent when arrested, and virtually all are indigent by the time their cases reach appellate courts" (D. W. Vick, 1995, p. 334).

And, while many appointed counsel are outstanding lawyers, the system for appointing counsel and providing representation varies across jurisdictions (Armstrong, Nov. 16, 2014). In response to Supreme Court decisions in the 1960s, states developed new systems for providing criminal defense services to the poor. States may provide criminal defendants with attorneys through a public defender system, through appointing counsel on a case-by-case basis, or by contracting with individual attorneys. States continue to work on improving these services, although "[f]rom the moment of their creation, these systems have been constrained by severe underfunding" (Vick, 1995, pp. 377–80).

Some of those systems do not compensate attorneys adequately. And states may not provide adequate funding for attorneys to fully investigate a case. In some cases, attorneys may not be motivated to do a good job or unable to provide quality representation. Additionally, because of the nature of the crimes involved in capital cases, some qualified attorneys may not want to represent individuals accused of horrible crimes.

Similar issues may exist for appointing counsel to represent capital defendants on appeal and in collateral postconviction proceedings. For example, states take different approaches regarding whether and how they appoint and pay for attorneys to represent capital defendants seeking state collateral postconviction relief (Hammel, 2002, pp. 83–99).

In 1987, Congress attempted to improve the quality of capital representation by providing funding for postconviction defender organizations. For a period, "the lawyers at these programs made a substantial contribution to justice by building an expertise and working long hours to provide representation in cases when no volunteer lawyer stepped forward to represent the condemned inmate" (Bright, 2003, pp. 138–139). But in 1995, Congress eliminated federal funding for these programs.

Today, funding limitations and other demands can require attorneys to carry too many cases. And overworked attorneys generally cannot do a good job representing their clients. For example, one state comptroller concluded that its state's postconviction defender office was "on the verge of collapse because of its excessive caseload" (American Bar Association, March 2007, "Evaluating Fairness and Accuracy in State Death Penalty Systems," p. 151).

Thus, in a number of situations, capital defendants have been sentenced to death, lost appeals, and even executed partly because they received poor representation. For example, in December 2008, John Ramirez was sentenced to death in Texas. At the closing argument of his sentencing hearing, Ramirez's attorney followed Ramirez's request and merely read a sentence from the Bible.[2] Later, Ramirez's postconviction attorney failed to file a clemency petition after he could not find another attorney to represent Ramirez. In 2017, Ramirez came within two days of being executed before a federal judge stayed his scheduled execution (Tolan, Feb. 6, 2017).

Other capital defendants in similar situations have not received stays. For example, Texas executed Raphael Holliday in November 2015 after his lawyers asserted they would no longer represent him. When Holliday tried to get a court to assign new counsel, his appointed lawyers argued against Holliday's motion (Tolan, Feb. 6, 2017).

In some cases, trial lawyers have slept during the trial. Similarly, in other cases, attorneys have been intoxicated or on drugs during trial. For example, when Jerry White was being tried for capital murder in Florida, the judge had to have the state attorney check the defense attorney's breath for alcohol each morning. Later testimony indicated that the attorney was using cocaine and other drugs. White was convicted, sentenced to death, and executed (Kirchmeier, 1996, p. 426).

One 2014 report examined at least 80 death row inmates since 1996 represented by attorneys who had missed important filing deadlines. The report explained that through "missing the filing deadline, those inmates have usually lost access to habeas corpus, arguably the most critical safeguard in the

United States' system of capital punishment." Of the cases examined with missed deadlines, 16 of those inmates were executed (K. Armstrong (Nov. 15, 2014); Armstrong (Nov. 16, 2014).

In another case, an appointed capital defense lawyer mistakenly filed the client's initial state habeas petition in the wrong court. The attorney did not know that the Supreme Court of Virginia had exclusive jurisdiction in such capital cases. The attorney later filed the petition in the correct court, but that court found it was too late. Thus, state and federal courts refused to hear the capital defendant's claims on the merits (*Weeks v. Angelone*, 1999, p. 257).

One Georgia case involving two co-defendants illustrates the dire consequences of attorney error. In separate hearings, unconstitutionally composed juries sentenced co-defendants John E. Smith and Rebecca Machetti to death. Machetti's lawyers raised objections to the jury composition in the state courts, but Smith's attorneys did not. Machetti eventually won a new trial on the jury issue from the federal court of appeals. But federal courts refused to hear Smith's identical claim because his attorney did not properly raise the claim earlier. Thus, Smith was executed while Machetti was not, based upon the different actions of their lawyers (Bright, 1994, 1839–1840).

A study by the Texas Defender Service examined federal habeas capital cases between 1995 and 2001. The study found that people on death row "face a one-in-three chance of being executed without having the case properly investigated by a competent attorney and without having any claims of innocence or unfairness presented or heard" (Texas Defender Service, 2002, p. x).

Similar studies have found patterns of poor representation across the country. For example, a 2011 investigation by the *Philadelphia Inquirer* reviewed death-penalty appeals across three decades. The study found that nearly one-third of the capital convictions in the state since 1978 had been reversed or sent back for new hearings because of defense counsel mistakes. The study found that while some attorneys did a great job, others often spent "little time preparing their cases and put on only the barest defense." Many of the lawyers also were overworked and underpaid (Phillips, Oct. 23, 2011).

Other studies revealed that a significant number of capital defense attorneys have been disciplined by bar organizations. Nearly 13% of the people executed in Louisiana as of January 1990 had been represented by attorneys who had been disciplined. In several other states, capital defense attorneys were disciplined at a rate many times higher than the rate for other attorneys (Coyle et al., 1990, p. 44).

Despite such errors and other mistakes, courts apply a high standard for capital defendants to get their cases reversed based on incompetence of counsel, as discussed in the next section. Thus, although some cases are reversed due to an earlier attorney's incompetence, an even larger number of cases featured significant attorney errors that did not result in relief for defendants.

THE CONSTITUTIONAL RIGHT TO EFFECTIVE ASSISTANCE OF COUNSEL

The Sixth Amendment of the United States Constitution provides that criminal defendants have a right to counsel. The Constitution similarly guarantees this right to counsel in state courts under the Fourteenth Amendment. All felony and misdemeanor defendants who may lose life or liberty are entitled to this right (see *Alabama v. Shelton*, 2002; *Scott v. Illinois*, 1979).

The Supreme Court has interpreted the Constitution to require appointment of counsel for criminal defendants who cannot afford an attorney when they are being tried for a crime and when their case is appealed (*Douglas v. California*, 1963). A capital defendant, however, generally is not constitutionally entitled to the appointment of defense counsel at other important stages of review.[3]

Additionally, the Supreme Court has asserted that the Constitution requires that criminal defense counsel at trial and on direct appeal provide competent representation (*Evitts v. Lucey*, 1985). Yet, courts struggle with applying the standard for when defense counsel provides ineffective assistance under the Constitution.

The Right to Counsel and the Standard for Ineffective Assistance of Counsel

A landmark capital case about the right to counsel was the famous Scottsboro case that resulted in the Supreme Court's decision in *Powell v. Alabama*. In 1931, nine African-American youths aged 12 to 19 had been charged with raping two white women on a freight train. All but one of them were sentenced to death after a trial with little constitutional protections. Through years of litigation, their case established that the Due Process Clause of the United States Constitution requires in at least some cases that state courts provide indigent capital defendants with appointed counsel (*Powell v. Alabama*, 1932).

In *Powell*, the court reasoned, "Even the intelligent and educated layman has small and sometimes no skill in the science of the law." Thus, "[l]eft without the aid of counsel he may be put on trial without a proper charge, and convicted upon incompetent evidence, or evidence irrelevant to the issue or otherwise inadmissible" (*Powell v. Alabama*, 1932, p. 69). The court gave new trials to the Scottsboro defendants, who many believe were innocent.

Several decades later, the Supreme Court held that all criminal defendants have a right to counsel. In 1963 in *Gideon v. Wainwright*, the court concluded that the Sixth and Fourteenth Amendments of the U.S. Constitution require that states provide counsel to criminal defendants who could not afford attorneys (*Gideon v. Wainwright*, 1963).

But it is not sufficient that a warm body appear to represent a capital defendant. The Supreme Court has affirmed that "the right to counsel is the right to the effective assistance of counsel" (*McMann v. Richardson*, 1970, p. 771, n. 14). A capital defendant's attorney at trial and at sentencing must meet a certain standard. Otherwise, a defendant may later assert the constitutional claim that previous counsel was ineffective.

In 1984 in *Strickland v. Washington*, the Supreme Court adopted a standard for a defendant to prove that a trial or capital sentencing attorney provided ineffective assistance of counsel (*Strickland v. Washington*, 1984). In order to establish a Sixth Amendment violation, a defendant must show two things.

The first prong of the test requires that a defendant show the lawyer's representation was deficient. "This requires showing that counsel made errors so serious that counsel was not functioning as the 'counsel' guaranteed the defendant by the Sixth Amendment" (*Strickland v. Washington*, 1984, p. 686). The second prong requires that "the deficient performance prejudiced the defense. This requires showing that counsel's errors were so serious as to deprive the defendant of a fair trial, a trial whose result is unreliable" (*Strickland v. Washington*, 1984, p. 686).

In analyzing ineffective assistance of counsel claims, though, courts are highly deferential in analyzing an attorney's performance. Courts "indulge a strong presumption" that a trial attorney's decisions all fall "within the wide range of reasonable professional assistance" (*Strickland v. Washington*, 1984, p. 689).[4]

This presumption, along with the requirement that defendants show they were prejudiced by counsel's conduct, make it difficult to establish a successful Sixth Amendment claim (Hessick, 2009, p. 1077). For example, in various cases, "[l]awyers who show up at trial drunk, who have sexual affairs with the spouse of the defendant they represent, who go through entire trials without raising even a single objection, who file one-page appellate briefs from city drunk tanks have all been deemed constitutionally competent" (Dow, 1996, p. 695).

Although the *Strickland* standard makes it very difficult for defendants to prove ineffective assistance of counsel, in more recent years the court has found ineffective assistance in several cases (Kirchmeier, 2016, pp. 269–270). Still, many judges, lawyers, and commentators have noted that *Strickland* provides a high hurdle for collateral postconviction review attorneys arguing that prior counsel was ineffective. Thus, the standard not only fails to prevent miscarriages of justice, it does little to improve the quality of capital defense representation (Bernhard, 2002, p. 346).

For example, Justice Harry Blackmun of the U.S. Supreme Court wrote that a decade after the court established the *Strickland* standard, "practical experience establishes that the *Strickland* test, in application has failed to protect a defendant's right to be represented by something more than 'a person who happens to be a lawyer'" (*McFarland v. Scott*, 1994, p. 1259 (Blackmun, J., dissenting) (quoting *Strickland v. Washington*, 1984, p. 685). One commentator noted that the court's standard for establishing ineffective assistance of counsel "has been roundly and properly criticized for fostering tolerance of abysmal lawyering" (Geimer, 1995, p. 94).

Ineffective Counsel Standard for Other Stages of Legal Proceedings

Capital defendants' right to effective counsel is not limited to trial. Not only do they have a constitutional right to counsel at trial, they also have a right to effective counsel during capital sentencing proceedings, during plea bargains, and on direct appeal.

It is important that the constitutional right to counsel applies to capital sentencing hearings because there are a number of cases where counsel was unprepared for the complexity of death penalty sentencing procedures (see *Glover v. United States*, 2001, p. 203). In recent years in cases such as *Rompilla v. Beard* and *Wiggins v. Smith*, the Supreme Court has stressed the importance of competent counsel during capital sentencing proceedings. For example, an attorney's failure to prepare adequately for a capital sentencing hearing may be found to be constitutionally ineffective if the attorney's work was based on a failure to do an adequate investigation (see *Wiggins v. Smith*, 2003; *Rompilla v. Beard*, 2005). Cases such as these have led at least one commentator to note hopefully that even though

> the Sixth Amendment standard for competent representation in capital cases remains far below what research has shown is required to mount a successful 'case for life,' the Court finally appears to be patrolling at least the outermost parameters of ineffective representation.
>
> *(Sunby, 2006, p. 1946)*

Plea bargaining is also an important stage of a capital case. At that stage before trial, defense counsel negotiates with the prosecutor to try to come to an agreement about resolving the case and the sentence. In numerous cases, qualified defense attorneys have saved the lives of their clients through the process of plea bargaining.

In 2012, the court clarified that the right to effective assistance of counsel applied to an attorney's work during plea bargain negotiations. In *Lafler v. Cooper*, the court held that in a state habeas proceeding, a court may find constitutionally ineffective assistance of the trial attorney under the *Strickland* standard where the attorney provided bad advice in telling a client to reject a favorable plea bargain where the defendant was later convicted (*Lafler v. Cooper*, 2012). Similarly, in *Missouri v. Frye*, the court held that counsel may be deemed to be ineffective for not telling a client about a plea offer (*Missouri v. Frye*, 2012).

Most Supreme Court cases on the Sixth Amendment right to counsel have focused on the quality of work done by trial attorneys, sentencing attorneys, and appellate attorneys. But in some recent decisions, the court has shown a concern about the quality of representation by collateral postconviction review attorneys. For example, in the Alabama case of Cory Maples, his collateral review lawyers left their jobs at the large law firm where they worked. When a court ruling was sent to the firm, it was returned to the court because nobody had told the court or the law firm mailroom that the lawyers had left the firm. In *Maples v. Thomas*, the Supreme Court held that because the attorneys had abandoned the client without notice, "an attorney no longer acts, or fails to act, as the client's representative"[5] (*Maples v. Thomas*, 2012, p. 281).

Through the 1990s the Supreme Court appeared not to show constitutional concern regarding the adequacy of collateral postconviction review counsel (*Coleman v. Thompson*, 1991). But in 2012, the Supreme Court significantly stressed the importance of such attorneys. In *Martinez v. Ryan*, the court held that a defendant may show that a collateral review attorney was constitutionally ineffective as a means to allow federal courts to address habeas corpus claims (*Martinez v. Ryan*, 2012).

The Supreme Court and lower courts continue to evaluate the effectiveness of attorneys using the *Strickland* standard. While ineffective assistance of counsel claims have been successful for some defendants, it remains a difficult standard for defendants to meet. Because of that, commentators, scholars, attorneys, and others continue to criticize the standard.

Despite the laxity of the constitutional standard, jurisdictions and the bar continue to work to improve the quality of representation of poor people accused of capital crimes. In recent years, several states have worked to create systems that improve death penalty defense. And many in the legal system now recognize that capital defense lawyers must be specially trained, resulting in "the emergence of a

Figure 19.2 Defense attorney Clarence Darrow.

Source: Photo available at: https://commons.wikimedia.org/wiki/File:Clarence_Darrow_cph.3b31130.jpg Clarence Darrow October 1913, Public Domain

professional capital defense bar" (Sunby, 2006, p. 1947). As long as there is a death penalty, errors by counsel will still lead to death sentences. But hopefully states, attorneys, judges, legislators, and others will continue to work to minimize the frequency of such errors.

DEFENSE ATTORNEYS' ROLE IN THE HISTORY OF THE DEATH PENALTY

Death penalty lawyers not only fulfill an essential function in representing their clients, they also have played an important role in the history of the death penalty in the United States. For example, attorney Clarence Darrow obtained fame for his successful representation of capital defendants Nathan Leopold and Ricard Loeb in 1924, saving the two young men from the death penalty. But he also achieved fame as an outspoken critic of the use of capital punishment in any circumstance (Darrow, 1989).

Another well-known attorney who represented individuals charged with capital crimes was Thurgood Marshall. Marshall, who became famous as a civil rights lawyer, represented capital defendants at trial and on appeal as counsel for the NAACP Legal Defense and Education Fund (see *Lyons v. Oklahoma*, 1944; *Taylor v. Alabama*, 1948). After later serving as Solicitor General of the United States, Marshall served as an Associate Justice of the Supreme Court of the United States from 1967 until he retired in 1991 (Williams, 1998).

When the Supreme Court began addressing the constitutionality of the death penalty in the 1970s, Justice Marshall was a consistent voice against the use of capital punishment. In one case, he wrote, "[T]he taking of life 'because the wrongdoer deserves it' surely must fail, for such a punishment has as its very basis the total denial of the wrongdoer's dignity and worth" (*Gregg v. Georgia*, 1976, p. 241 [Marshall, J., dissenting]).

Remembering his days as a capital defense attorney, Justice Marshall sometimes would recount to other justices stories about his years as a defense lawyer. For example, he used a story about his trial experience while attempting to convince other justices that the death penalty was applied unfairly against poor people and minorities (O'Connor, 1992, p. 1218).

Although, as discussed earlier, errors by death penalty defense attorneys have affected the outcomes of a number of cases, many death penalty defense attorneys do outstanding work. One study found that capital defense attorneys "invest their heart and soul into their cases, and the work proves emotionally and personally exhausting" (Goodrum, Pogrebin, & Greife, 2015, p. 3). At the same time, these inspiring attorneys feel an obligation to represent the poor and to fight against economic and racial injustices.

Capital defense lawyers often make many sacrifices to represent their clients well. Many attorneys do capital defense work even though they could make more money doing other types of legal work. Further, some lawyers represent capital defendants in collateral review proceedings pro bono, that is, without pay. They believe all capital defendants are entitled to quality representation and are willing to donate a significant amount of time to the cause. As one defense attorney explained,

> I've always liked working for the underdog, [and] the criminal defendant certainly is an underdog in the system. I'm appalled at some of the racism and classism that continues to exist in America and this is one way to fight [against] that sort of thing.
> *(Goodrum, Pogrebin, & Greife, 2015, p. 3).*

In a number of cases, attorneys have worked long hours, sometimes without pay, on behalf of their clients. In some cases—like those of Earl Washington, Jr., Anthony Porter, and Ernest Willis—"heroic lawyering contributed to the defendant's exoneration" after the innocent men had been wrongfully convicted and sentenced to death (Alschuler, 2006, p. 226).

In addition to the outstanding work that many attorneys do for their clients, defense attorneys have played an important role in exposing inherent problems in the capital punishment and criminal justice system. For example, in the 1950s and 1960s, lawyers at the NAACP Legal Defense and Education Fund (LDF) organized constitutional challenges to capital punishment. They initially focused on the discriminatory nature of the way the death penalty was applied, but they expanded their attacks also to address a number of other constitutional problems with capital punishment (Mandery, 2013, pp. 60–62).

The work of LDF and lawyers such as Anthony G. Amsterdam eventually led to the United States Supreme Court striking down death penalty statutes in 1972, effectively ending capital punishment in the United States for a period (*Furman v. Georgia*, 1972). Although the court upheld the constitutionality of new death penalty statutes in 1976, attorneys continued to challenge the fairness of the U.S. death penalty (*Gregg v. Georgia*, 1976; Kirchmeier, 2016, p. 79).

In the 1980s, attorneys raised claims that highlighted racial disparities in the use of the death penalty. Working with social scientists, lawyers presented courts with evidence that defendants who killed white victims were significantly more likely to get the death penalty than those who killed African Americans. Ultimately, the Supreme Court rejected the challenge in 1987 (*McClesky v. Kemp*, 1987). But attorneys continued to work both within the courts and with legislators to expose and challenge racial disparities and other discriminatory bias in the legal system.

Today, capital defense attorneys—such as David Bruck, Judy Clarke, Bryan Stevenson, Christina Swarns, and numerous others—continue to expose problems with the U.S. capital punishment system. Lawyers may highlight problems through representing individual clients or by working with activists in other ways.

For example, attorneys have shown how errors are made in the legal system by proving there are innocent people on death rows across the country. More than 150 people who were sentenced to death have been exonerated since 1973, largely through the work of defense lawyers (*The Innocence List*, Death Penalty Information Center).

Attorneys have used the courtroom to expose other problems in the American capital punishment system. In recent years, they have attacked the way that the condemned are executed, illustrating several failings in the use of lethal injection. Capital defense attorneys continue to challenge the way that the condemned are killed, often acting as the main check on jurisdictions that continue to experiment with using different lethal injection drugs on humans (Denno, D. W., 2007).

Defense lawyers have been instrumental in educating judges, officials, and the public about the United States system of capital punishment. After years of losing capital cases representing intellectually disabled defendants and defendants under the age of 18, persistent capital defense lawyers eventually convinced the Supreme Court that the execution of such defendants violates the Eighth Amendment (*Atkins v. Virginia*, 2002; *Roper v. Simmons*, 2005).

Similarly, Supreme Court Justices—such as Justice Harry Blackmun, Justice Lewis Powell, and Justice John Paul Stevens—voted to uphold the constitutionality of the death penalty for many years. Eventually, though, after years of hearing the arguments of capital defense attorneys, they each became convinced that the death penalty was unconstitutional (Kirchmeier, 2016).

Further, along with the efforts of legislators, activists, and others, the work of capital defense attorneys has led to a number of states putting moratoria on executions and ending the use of the death penalty in recent years. For example, in 2004, the work of attorneys led the New York Court of Appeals to find that the state's death penalty violated the New York Constitution (*People v. LaValle*, 2004).

Similarly, in recent years, several state legislatures and courts have responded to the work of defense attorneys and others by abolishing the death penalty. Since 2004, the death penalty has been abolished by court decision or by legislative action in states such as New York (2004), New Jersey (2007), New Mexico (2009), Illinois (2011), Connecticut (2012), Maryland (2013), and Delaware (2016) (Death Penalty Information Center (2017). *States With and Without the Death Penalty*). In all of these states, capital defense lawyers were instrumental in exposing problems with the use of the death penalty in the United States.

Conclusion

As long as some states and the federal government continue to maintain a death penalty, capital defense attorneys will continue to represent the condemned and to battle against unfairness in the legal system. When the most-despised members of society are on trial, it is essential that a system of justice provide competent representation. Fortunately, there have been many such lawyers who have taken on the important role of representing clients in cases that are complex and challenging intellectually and emotionally.

As the Supreme Court stated many years ago, "From the very beginning, our state and national constitutions and laws have laid great emphasis on procedural and substantive safeguards designed to assure fair trials before impartial tribunals in which every defendant stands equal before the law." Yet, "this noble idea" of a fair and equal legal system cannot exist if poor persons charged with a crime must face their accusers without skilled and dedicated lawyers by their side (*Gideon v. Wainwright*, 1963, p. 344).

Notes

* Professor of Law, City University of New York School of Law. J.D., Case Western Reserve University School of Law, 1989; B.A., Case Western Reserve University, 1984.

1 "A lawyer shall provide competent representation to a client."

2 The Bible verse was: "For I know my transgressions and my sin is always before me. Amen." (Tolan, Feb. 6, 2017)

3 For example, the Supreme Court has stated that there generally is no constitutional right to a lawyer during state collateral review and during federal habeas corpus review. (*Pennsylvania v. Finley*, 1987) But in more recent decisions, the Supreme Court has held that if post-conviction counsel is constitutionally ineffective, such a finding may allow a capital defendant to bring claims that could not otherwise be raised in federal court (*Maples v. Thomas*, 2012; *Holland v. Florida*, 2010).

4 "Judicial scrutiny of counsel's performance must be highly deferential. It is all too tempting for a defendant to second-guess counsel's assistance after conviction or adverse sentence, and it is all too easy for a court, examining counsel's defense after it has proved unsuccessful, to conclude that a particular act or omission of counsel was unreasonable" (*Strickland v. Washington*, 1984, p. 689).

5 *Maples v. Thomas* more specifically addressed the issue of whether the attorney abandonment would satisfy one of the prongs that needed to be shown to overcome a procedural default of a habeas corpus claim (*Maples v. Thomas*, 565 U.S. 266 [2012]).

References

Acker, J. R., & Lanier, C. S. (2000). May God—or the governor—have mercy: Executive clemency and executions in modern death-penalty systems. *Criminal Law Bulletin*, *36*, 200–237.

Alfieri, A. V. (2004). Mercy lawyers. *North Carolina Law Review*, *82*, 1297–1318.

Alschuler, A. (2006). Celebrating great lawyering (reviewing Welsh S. White, *Litigating in the Shadow of Death: Defense Attorneys in Capital Cases*, by Welsh S. White), *Ohio State Journal of Criminal Law*, *4*, 223–236.

Amar, A. R. (1998). *The bill of rights*. New Haven and London: Yale University Press.

American Bar Association. (2003). American bar association guidelines for the appointment and performance of defense counsel in death penalty cases. *Hofstra Law Review*, *31*, 913–1090.

American Bar Association. (2007, March). *Evaluating fairness and accuracy in state death penalty systems: The Tennessee death penalty assessment report*. pp. 1–334. Retrieved from www.americanbar.org/content/dam/aba/migrated/moratorium/assessmentproject/tennessee/finalreport.authcheckdam.pdf

Arizona Rules of Criminal Procedure 6.8(b)(iii) (West 2016).

Armstrong, K. (2014, November 15). Lethal mix; lawyers' mistakes, unforgiving law. *The Washington Post*. Retrieved from http://www.washingtonpost.com/sf/national/2014/11/15/last-chance-pleas-from-death-row-often-tossed-over-late-filings/?utm_term=.8b0e5dda28e7

Armstrong, K. (2014, November 16). When lawyers stumble, only their clients fall. *The Washington Post*. Retrieved from www.washingtonpost.com/sf/national/2014/11/16/when-lawyers-stumble-only-their-clients-fall/

Bernhard, A. (2002). Take courage: What the courts can do to improve the delivery of criminal defense services. *University of Pittsburgh Law Review*, *63*, 293–346.

Blume, J. H. (2005). Killing the willing: "Volunteers," suicide and competency. *Michigan Law Review*, *103*, 939–1009.

Bright, S. B. (1994). Counsel for the poor: The death sentence not for the worst crime but for the worst lawyer. *Yale Law Journal, 103*, 1835, 1839–1840.

Bright, S. B. (2003). The politics of capital punishment: The sacrifice of fairness for executions. In J. R. Acker, R. M. Bohm, & C. S. Lanier (Eds.), *America's experiment with capital punishment*, 2nd ed. (pp. 127–146). Durham, NC: Carolina Academic Press.

Cooley, C. M. (2005). Mapping the monster's mental health and social history: Why capital defense attorneys and public defender death penalty units require the services of mitigation specialists. *Oklahoma City University Law Review, 30*, 23–119.

Coyle, M., Strasser, F., & Lavelle, M. (1990, June 11). Fatal defense: Trial and error in the nation's death belt. *The National Law Journal, 12*(40), 30–44.

Darrow, C. (1989). *Attorney for the damned: Clarence Darrow in the courtroom* (A. Weinberg, Ed.). Chicago: University of Chicago Press.

Death Penalty Information Center. (2017). *States with and without the death penalty*. Retrieved from www.deathpenaltyinfo.org/states-and-without-death-penalty

Denno, D. W. (1992). Death is different and other twists of fate. *Journal of Criminal Law and Criminology, 83*(2), 437–467.

Denno, D. W. (2007). The lethal injection quandary: How medicine has dismantled the death penalty. *Fordham Law Review, 76*, 49–124.

Dershowitz, A. M. (1982). *The best defense: The courtroom confrontations of America's most outspoken lawyer of last resort.* New York: Random House.

Dow, D. R. (1996). The state, the death penalty, and Carl Johnson. *Boston College Law Review, 37*, 691–711.

Geimer, W. S. (1995). A decade of Strickland's tin horn: Doctrinal and practical undermining of the right to counsel. *William & Mary Bill of Rights Journal, 4*, 91–178.

Ginsburg, R. B. (2001, April 9). *In pursuit of the public good: Lawyers who care, Joseph L. Rauh lecture at the David A. Clarke school of law of the university of the district of Columbia*. Retrieved from www.supremecourt.gov/publicinfo/speeches/viewspeech/sp_04-09-01a

Goodpaster, G. (1983). The trial for life: Effective assistance of counsel in death penalty cases. *New York University Law Review, 58*, 299–362.

Goodrum, S., Pogrebin, M., & Greife, M. W. (2015). Representing the underdog: The righteous development of death penalty defense attorneys. *Criminal Law Bulletin, 51*(2), 3–37.

Hammel, A. (2002). Diabolical federalism: A functional critique and proposed reconstruction of death penalty federal habeas. *American Criminal Law Review, 39*, 1–82.

Hessick, C. B. (2009). Ineffective assistance at sentencing. *Boston College Law Review, 50*, 1069–1122.

Innocence List, Death Penalty Information Center. Retrieved at www.deathpenaltyinfo.org/innocence-list-those-freed-death-row

Kirchmeier, J. L. (1996). Drinks, drugs, and drowsiness: The constitutional right to effective assistance of counsel and the Strickland prejudice requirement. *Nebraska Law Review, 75*, 425–475.

Kirchmeier, J. L. (2004). A tear in the eye of the law: Mitigating factors and the progression toward a disease theory of criminal justice. *Oregon Law Review, 83*, 631–730.

Kirchmeier, J. L. (2016). *Imprisoned by the past: Warren McCleskey, race, and the American death penalty.* New York: Oxford University Press.

Liebman, J. S., Fagan, J., & West, V. (2000). *A broken system: Error rates in capital cases, 1973–1995.* Retrieved from http://www2.law.columbia.edu/instructionalservices/liebman/

MacLean, B. A. (2009). Effective capital defense representation and the difficult client. *Tennessee Law Review, 76*, 661–676.

Mandery, E. J. (2013). *A wild justice: The death and resurrection of capital punishment in America.* New York: W. W. Norton.

O'Connor, S. D. (1992). Thurgood Marshall: The influence of a raconteur. *Stanford Law Review, 44*, 1217–1220.

Phillips, N. (2011, October 23). In life and death cases, costly mistakes. *The Philadelphia Inquirer.* Retrieved from www.deathpenaltyinfo.org/documents/philly_life_death.pdf

Radelet, M. L., & Zsembik, B. A. (1993). Executive clemency in post-Furman capital cases. *University of Richmond Law Review, 27*, 289–314.

Stevenson, B. A. (2002). The politics of fear and death: Successive problems in capital federal habeas corpus cases. *New York University Law Review, 77*, 699–795.

Streib, V. (2003/2004). Would you lie to save your client's life? Ethics and effectiveness in defending against death. *Brandeis Law Journal, 42*, 405–434.

Sunby, S. E. (2006). The death penalty's future: Charting the crosscurrents of declining death sentences and the McVeigh factor. *Texas Law Review, 84*, 1929–1972.

Texas Defender Service. (2002). *Lethal indifference: The fatal combination of incompetent attorneys and unaccountable courts in Texas death penalty appeals.* p. x. Retrieved from http://texasdefender.org/wp-content/uploads/Lethal-Indiff_web.pdf

Tolan, C. (2017, February 6). When your lawyer abandons you on death row. *Vice.* Retrieved from www.vice.com/en_us/article/when-your-lawyer-abandons-you-on-death-row

Vick, D. W. (1995). Poorhouse justice: Underfunded indigent defense services and arbitrary death sentences. *Buffalo Law Review, 43*, 329–460.

Virginia Code Annotated Section 19.2–163.8 (West 2013).

Virginia Indigent Defense Commission Homepage. Retrieved at www.indigentdefense.virginia.gov/index.htm

White, W. S. (2005). *Litigating in the shadow of death: Defense attorneys in capital cases.* Ann Arbor: University of Michigan Press.

Williams, J. (1998). *Thurgood Marshall: American revolutionary.* New York: Three Rivers Press.

Cases Cited

Alabama v. Shelton, 535 U.S. 654 (2002).
Atkins v. Virginia, 536 U.S. 304 (2002).
Batson v. Kentucky, 476 U.S. 79 (1986).
Bobby v. Van Hook, 558 U.S. 4 (2009).
Coleman v. Thompson, 501 U.S. 722 (1991).
Douglas v. California, 372 U.S. 353 (1963).
Eddings v. Oklahoma, 455 U.S. 104 (1982).
Evitts v. Lucey, 469 U.S. 387 (1985).
Floyd et al. v. City of New York et al., 959 F. Supp. 2d 540 (S.D.N.Y. 2013).
Franklin v. Lynaugh, 487 U.S. 164 (1988).
Furman v. Georgia, 408 U.S. 238 (1972).
Gideon v. Wainwright, 372 U.S. 335 (1963).
Glover v. United States, 531 U.S. 198 (2001).
Gregg v. Georgia, 428 U.S. 153 (1976).
Holland v. Florida, 560 U.S. 631 (2010).
Johnson v. Zerbst, 304 U.S. 458 (1938).
Jurek v. Texas, 428 U.S. 262 (1976).
Lafler v. Cooper, 566 U.S. 156 (2012).
Lockett v. Ohio, 438 U.S. 586, 608–09 (1978).
Lyons v. Oklahoma, 322 U.S. 596 (1944).
Maples v. Thomas, 565 U.S. 266 (2012).
Martinez v. Ryan, 566 U.S. 1 (2012).
McCleskey v. Kemp, 481 U.S. 279 (1987).
McFarland v. Scott, 512 U.S. 1256 (1994).
McMann v. Richardson, 397 U.S. 759 (1970).
Missouri v. Frye, 566 U.S. 133 (2012).
Orazio v. Dugger, 876 F.2d 1508 (11th Cir. 1989).
Pennsylvania v. Finley, 481 U.S. 551 (1987).
People v. LaValle, 817 N.E.2d 341 (N.Y. 2004).
Powell v. Alabama, 287 U.S. 45 (1932).
Roberts v. Louisiana, 428 U.S. 325 (1976).
Rompilla v. Beard, 545 U.S. 374 (2005).
Roper v. Simmons, 534 U.S. 551 (2005).
Scott v. Illinois, 440 U.S. 367 (1979).
Strickland v. Washington, 466 U.S. 668 (1984).
Taylor v. Alabama, 335 U.S. 252 (1948).
United States v. Quinones, 205 F. Supp. 2d 256 (S.D.N.Y. 2002).
Wainwright v. Sykes, 433 U.S. 72 (1977).
Weeks v. Angelone, 176 F.3d 249 (4th Cir. 1999).
Wiggins v. Smith, 539 U.S. 510 (2003).
Williams v. Taylor, 529 U.S. 362 (2000).
Woodson v. North Carolina, 428 U.S. 280 (1976).

20

THE CAPITAL JURY AND SENTENCING

Neither Guided Nor Individualized

Wanda D. Foglia and Marla Sandys[1]

The jury plays a pivotal role in the capital trial process. Beyond deciding guilt, as juries do routinely in criminal trials, the capital jury decides whether the defendant lives or dies. As Haney, Sontag, and Costanzo (1994) put it:

> Capital trials are unique in American jurisprudence and, indeed, in human experience. Under no other circumstances does a group of ordinary citizens calmly and rationally contemplate taking the life of another, all the while acting under color of law.
>
> *(p. 149)*

Deciding whether another person should live or die is obviously an important and difficult decision, but the United States Supreme Court has made it clear that the Sixth Amendment requires that ordinary citizens must make this decision (*Hurst v. Florida*, 2016). The Court recognizes what an "awesome" responsibility it is to decide the sentence in a capital case (*Caldwell v. Mississippi*, 1985, p. 329) and has established elaborate constitutional mandates for how the capital jury is to make this decision. The patchwork of constitutional requirements that has been layered onto the capital process requires the capital jury to decide whether to impose the death penalty in a way that many now believe is not humanly possible. This chapter presents a review of the empirical literature to determine whether those concerns are warranted.

The Role of the Jury

The jury was key to reviving the death penalty in 1976 when the United States Supreme Court decided *Gregg v. Georgia* and companion cases, holding that statutes that guided the jurors' discretion could cure the arbitrariness that led them to find the death penalty unconstitutional as applied four years earlier in *Furman v. Georgia* (1972). The Court emphasized the importance of the need for guidance when they stated "where discretion is afforded a sentencing body on a matter so grave as the determination of whether a human life should be taken or spared, that discretion must be suitably directed and limited so as to minimize the risk of wholly arbitrary and capricious action" (*Gregg v. Georgia*, 1976, p. 189). At the same time, they decided two cases holding that the death penalty could never be mandatory (*Roberts v. Louisiana*, 1976; *Woodson v. North Carolina*, 1976) because "death is different" from lesser penalties and "individualized sentencing" is required by the Eighth Amendment (*Woodson*, p. 303–05). Two years later the Court elaborated on this requirement by making it clear that the sentencer cannot be precluded from considering any relevant mitigating evidence (*Lockett v. Ohio*, 1978). From the outset of the modern era of capital punishment, therefore, the jury's role has been difficult because avoiding arbitrariness through guiding discretion, and allowing individualized sentencing by mandating unlimited consideration of mitigation, are difficult to reconcile.

Doubts About the Jury's Ability to Follow the Law

At least six different United States Supreme Court Justices have indicated that they do not believe it is possible to avoid the arbitrariness condemned in *Furman* and also have the individualized sentencing required by *Woodson* and *Lockett*. Justices Brennan and Marshall took the position in their concurrence in *Furman* that the death penalty always violates the Eighth Amendment's prohibition against cruel and unusual punishment because it is inherently arbitrary. A third of the five concurring justices in *Furman*, Justice Douglas, argued that unless the death penalty is mandatory, which the Court clearly rejected in *Woodson* and *Roberts*, it would be unconstitutional because it would be inherently subject to discrimination.

Since reinstituting the death penalty in *Gregg*, Justices Scalia, Thomas, and Blackman all argued that it is impossible to have both guided discretion and individualized sentencing, but reached different conclusions. Justices Scalia and Thomas decided to reject individualized sentencing (*Walton v. Arizona*, 1990). In contrast, Justice Blackman concluded that the death penalty could not be administered in accordance with the Constitution (*Callins v. Collins*, 1994).

In 2009, the American Law Institute (ALI), which formulated the Model Penal Code, also decided that one could not avoid arbitrariness with guided discretion and at the same time allow jurors to consider any relevant evidence they found mitigating (Death Penalty Information Center, 2017a). The ALI withdrew the section on capital punishment (§210.6) from their Model Penal Code, in part because of the tension between guided discretion and individualized sentencing (American Law Institute, 2009). Like Blackman, they concluded that it was not possible to have both; thus it was impossible to have a death penalty that meets constitutional standards.

In his dissent in *Glossip v. Gross* (2015), Justice Breyer, joined by Justice Ginsburg, also questioned the constitutionality of the death penalty. Justice Breyer relied on three rationales for concluding that it was "highly likely that the death penalty violates the Eighth Amendment" and, although they did not focus directly on the jury, the capital jury is implicated to some extent in each of the problems cited (p. 2776–2777). For instance, one of the three constitutional problems Justice Breyer sees in the current administration of the death penalty is its unreliability, as evidenced by the numerous exonerations and legal errors. He argues that the practice of death qualification of jurors may be one of the reasons the death penalty is not more reliable, citing a couple of examples of the plethora of scholarly research finding that death qualification "skews juries toward guilt and death" (2015, p. 2758, citing Rozelle, 2006, p. 807).

Each jurisdiction with the death penalty has its own statute, but many aspects of the process are the same in every state and in the federal system because the United States Supreme Court has held they are constitutionally required. This chapter will focus on the aspects of the jury's role that are uniform in all jurisdictions because they are mandated by the Sixth and Eighth Amendments to the United States Constitution. We concentrate on the legal standards governing the jury's sentencing decisions because its role in the sentencing process was key to the determination that the death penalty is constitutional. We include sections on capital juror qualifications, the timing of the sentencing decision, guiding juror discretion, fears of future dangerousness and early release, and the influence of race. Each section describes the applicable law and what the empirical evidence tells us about how the process actually works. We conclude by discussing what the evidence reveals about the constitutionality of capital punishment.

Capital Juror Qualifications

Requirements of Jurors Who Serve on Capital Cases

Jurors who serve on capital cases must meet qualifications beyond those required of jurors who serve on noncapital cases; these are referred to as death-qualification and life-qualification standards. At their core, these standards are designed to determine whether the prospective juror could consider voting for a sentence of death and life, respectively.

Death-Qualification

While the framing of the standard has changed over the years, a prospective juror who is death-qualified is someone who could consider voting for a sentence of death once he or she is convinced, beyond a reasonable doubt, that the defendant is guilty of a capital offense. Hence, death-qualification is designed to prevent jurors who could not consider voting for a sentence of death, and thus are unable to follow the law, from serving on a capital case. Historically, the focus was on discovering and excluding from serving those prospective jurors who indicated that they had conscientious or religious scruples against the death penalty, but the standard was modified in 1968 when the Court decided *Witherspoon v. Illinois* (1968). There the United States Supreme Court determined that only those who made it "unmistakably clear" (p. 522, footnote 21) that they would never consider voting for a sentence of death were not death-qualified; these jurors are known as *Witherspoon* excludables. The standard was clarified in *Wainwright v. Witt* (1985), wherein the United States Supreme Court explained that

> the proper standard for determining when a prospective juror may be excluded for cause because of his or her views on capital punishment . . . is whether the juror's views would prevent or substantially impair the performance of his duties as a juror in accordance with his instructions and his oath.
>
> *(p. 424, internal citation omitted)*

Life-Qualification

The *Witt* standard was the first indication that persons whose views were so in favor of capital punishment that they would not consider life might also be ineligible to serve on a capital jury. That specific determination, however, was not decided until *Morgan v. Illinois* (1992). In *Morgan*, the Court held that a person who, upon being convinced of a defendant's guilt, would not consider mitigation in support of a life sentence, is someone who could not follow the law and thus should be excused from serving on the jury; these jurors are known as mitigation impaired, a group of which are known as 'automatic death penalty' voters, or ADPs.

The goal of the qualification process, therefore, is to exclude prospective jurors at the extremes. Prospective jurors who say that they would not consider a sentence of death and those who say that they would not consider a sentence of life should both be excluded from serving due to an inability to follow the law. To the extent that the qualification process works as intended, the resultant jury should be comprised of jurors in between those two extremes, jurors who can consider voting for both death and life.

Research on the Qualification of Capital Jurors

Research on the qualification of capital jurors is directed at four broad questions. First is the process effect: does the process of selecting a capital jury do anything to impact the impartiality of the jurors selected to serve on the case? Second is the composition effect: do the qualification standards exclude specific groups of individuals? That is, are there systematic differences in the groups of people found qualified and disqualified from serving on a capital jury? Third, do the qualification standards operate as intended? Here, the issue is whether the qualification standards are successful in selecting jurors who are both death and life qualified. Finally, recent research has focused on how the selection process is affected by race. We now turn to a discussion of the research on each of these issues.

Process Effect

One of the many ways in which capital juries are unique is the procedure through which the jurors are selected. Given that capital jurors must be able to consider the entire range of sentencing options, much of the selection process is devoted to that determination. Hence, prospective jurors are asked, during jury selection, if they could consider voting for a sentence of death, a sentence of life, and any other sentencing options available in their state. They are thus required to talk about their views of sentencing before they have determined whether the defendant is guilty.

Haney (1984) conducted an experiment to assess the potential impact of the death qualification process using a videotape of jury selection. The only difference between the experimental and the control groups was that the video for the experimental group included a 30-minute segment on death qualification. Persons in the experimental group, who watched the segment on death qualification, were more likely than those in the control group to believe that the defendant was guilty and that he deserved a sentence of death. Thus, the mere exposure to the process of death qualification was associated with differences in the way in which people viewed the evidence and their stated voting preferences.

A meta-analysis by Allen, Mabry, and McKelton (1998) supports this process effect. Allen et al. reviewed 14 studies that looked at the relationship between attitudes toward the death penalty and the probability of favoring conviction. They not only found that those favoring the death penalty were more likely to convict but also found that the studies that used some sort of simulated *voir dire* resulted in a stronger impact on the likelihood of convicting than those that just questioned subjects about their attitudes toward the death penalty.

Some direct evidence of a process effect comes from the Capital Jury Project (CJP). The CJP conducted in-depth interviews with 1,198 former capital jurors, 42.9% of whom sat on cases resulting in life sentences and 57.1% on cases resulting in death sentences, from 14 states (Bowers, Foglia, Ehrhard-Dietzel, & Kelly, 2010). Each former juror was asked about the impact of questions about their attitude toward the death penalty, and 11.3% said that the questions made them think the defendant "must be" or "probably was" guilty and 9.2% said they made them think the "appropriate punishment must be . . . or probably was the death penalty" (Bowers & Foglia, 2003). Although these percentages are not large, they still reflect that about 1 out of 10 jurors were conscious of and willing to admit being biased by the jury selection process.

Composition Effect

A recent survey by the Pew Research Center (2016) found that while general support for capital punishment was at its lowest in decades (49%), demographics still matter. For instance, 55% of men compared to 43% of women were in favor of capital punishment. Further, 57% of whites and only 29% of blacks were in favor of capital punishment. Given that qualification standards relate to prospective jurors' attitudes toward capital punishment, it is not surprising that both women and blacks are less likely to be death-qualified than men or whites (Fitzgerald & Ellsworth, 1984; Summers, Hayward, & Miller, 2010).

Demographics are not the only characteristic that distinguishes between persons qualified and excluded from serving on a capital jury. Rather, persons found death-qualified are also more likely to trust prosecutors and to distrust defense attorneys, to infer guilt when a defendant does not take the stand (Fitzgerald & Ellsworth, 1984), and to hold more positive views of a prosecutor's witness (Cowan, Thompson, & Ellsworth, 1984). Research also suggests that people who are death qualified are less receptive to an insanity defense (Ellsworth, Bukaty, Cowan, & Thompson, 1984) and that they believe myths associated with the insanity defense (Butler & Wasserman, 2006). In contrast, those who are excluded by either *Witherspoon* or *Witt* standards are found to be less punitive, more due process oriented, more open to mitigation, and less receptive to aggravation (Haney, Hurtado, & Vega, 1994).

The differences between those qualified and those excluded from serving on a capital jury further manifest in likely votes as well. For instance, eligible jurors who watched a 2.5-hour-long videotaped reenactment of a homicide trial, followed by (12-member) group deliberation, revealed differences in votes for guilt as related to their qualification status (Cowan et al., 1984). Specifically, *Witherspoon* excludables were significantly less conviction prone (34.5% voted not guilty) than those found death qualified (13.7% who voted not guilty). The same pattern of findings holds for the *Witt* standard: those categorized as excluded by *Witt* are both less conviction prone and less likely to vote for death than their includable counterparts (Butler & Moran, 2007).

Jury Selection in Practice

Perhaps the best way to determine whether death and life qualification standards are operating as intended is to look at jurors who actually serve on capital cases. One would expect these jurors to remain open to both a sentence of death and a sentence of life. Data from the CJP reveal that, however, many jurors are inclined to see death as "the only acceptable punishment." For example, when asked if death is the only acceptable punishment, an unacceptable punishment, or sometimes acceptable as punishment, a full 71.5% said death was the only acceptable punishment for someone previously convicted of murder. Approximately half of the jurors said death was the only acceptable punishment for a planned, premeditated murder (57%), when more than one victim is killed (53.7%), the killing of a police officer or prison guard (48.8%), and murder by a drug dealer (46.1%); almost one-quarter of the jurors believed death was the only acceptable punishment for a killing that occurs during the course of another crime (24.3%) (Bowers, Kelly, Kleinstuber, Vartkessian, & Sandys, 2014). The CJP has data showing which jurors actually sat on killings of a police officer or prison guard, killings with multiple victims, and killings during another crime. Our review of those data reveals that the percentages saying death was the only acceptable punishment was nearly the same for the jurors actually hearing those types of cases as it was for the jurors who sat on other types of cases. Furthermore, a follow-up set of interviews conducted by CJP researchers from cases decided between 1999 and 2009 reveal remarkably similar percentages saying that death is the only acceptable punishment,[2] thus revealing that jury selection proceedings have not improved significantly since the original CJP data were collected (Bowers et al., 2014).

In contrast to the percentages that are not life qualified, very few CJP jurors ever responded that death was unacceptable for any of the murders in the question. The highest percentage, 6%, came in response to "killing occurs during the course of another crime." Hence, as Bowers et al. (2014) concluded: "With few exceptions jury selection appears to have succeeded in eliminating jurors unmistakably opposed to capital punishment, but failed to eliminate jurors who voiced a pro-death stand" (p. 436). It may be because prospective jurors are less likely to be asked directly about their ability to vote for a sentence of life than a sentence of death (Sandys, Walsh, Pruss, & Cunningham, 2014), or that some jurors are latent ADPs (Sandys & Trahan, 2008); they are unaware during jury selection that once they become convinced of guilt, they are unwilling to consider a sentence less than death.

The research findings regarding death and life qualification are consistent, revealing that those found qualified to serve on a capital jury differ from those excused, to the detriment of the defendant. Given the United States Supreme Court's deference to trial judges' determination of a prospective juror's impartiality (*Wainwright v. Witt*, at 425–426), however, the related research has changed focus. In particular, the most recent research on the qualification of capital jurors focuses on the role of race.

Race and Capital Jury Selection

To this point, our discussion of the qualifications of capital jurors has focused on reasons why a prospective juror might be excused from serving for cause. All jurors must meet the qualification standards, and thus there are unlimited challenges for cause. In addition to these cause challenges, each side has a limited number of peremptory challenges, the precise number of which varies by state. Technically, peremptory challenges allow each side to exclude prospective jurors without providing a reason to the court. There are, however, two limitations: jurors cannot be struck from serving due to either their race (*Batson v. Kentucky*, 1986) or their gender (*J.E.B. v. Alabama*, 1994).

The extent to which race permeates capital jury selection is evidenced by the fact that the United States Supreme Court has heard four cases (*Batson v. Kentucky*, 1986; *Foster v. Chatman*, 2016; *Miller-El v. Dretke*, 2005; *Snyder v. Louisiana*, 2008), that each address basically the same question: Can the state excuse (all) black prospective jurors by means of peremptory challenge, or does doing so violate the Equal Protection Clause of the Fourteenth Amendment? In each case, petitioner prevailed, new trials were granted, and the Court reiterated its finding that race can play no part in the selection of jurors: The "Constitution forbids striking even a single prospective juror for a discriminatory purpose" (*Foster v. Chatman*, 2016, citing *Snyder v. Louisiana*, 2008, internal quotation marks omitted).

Clearly, the *Batson* remedy, which requires a race-neutral reason for striking a qualified prospective juror, is ineffective (Stevenson & Friedman, 1994). Researchers in Pennsylvania (Baldus, Woodworth, Zuckerman, Weiner, & Broffitt, 2001), Caddo Parish, Louisiana (Noye, 2015), and North Carolina (Grosso & O'Brien, 2012) have all demonstrated that prosecutors use their peremptory challenges more often to strike black than white prospective jurors. It may be that prosecutors are relying on the long-established finding that in general, blacks are more opposed to capital punishment than whites (Pew Research Center, 2016). Findings from the CJP reveal further that black jurors are more likely than white jurors to have lingering doubt about guilt and more likely to think the defendant was sorry, regardless of the race of the defendant and victim (Bowers, Steiner, & Sandys, 2001). Black and Hispanic jurors also are less likely than whites to vote for death, even when controlling for the race of the defendant and victim, viciousness of the crime, and other juror demographic characteristics (Foglia, 2012). Hence, summarily dismissing black and Hispanic jurors by use of peremptory challenges, regardless of actual qualification status, deprives defendants of jurors who are constitutionally entitled to serve and whose views meaningfully contribute to the reasoned moral decision (*Penry v. Lynaugh*, 1989) required of capital jurors.

Capital jurors begin their task biased against the defendant. Research reveals that the mere exposure to capital *voir dire* is associated with a greater likelihood of conviction and votes for death. Similarly, those found qualified to serve as jurors are more conviction prone and death prone than those excluded from serving as capital jurors. Further, capital jurors are more likely to be death than life qualified, ADPs still make their way onto the jury, and blacks are still more likely to be kept off of capital juries. In the next section, we turn to a review of the timing of sentencing decisions and the implications thereof for capital jurors to abide by the constitutional requirement to wait until the sentencing phase to reach such a decision.

When the Jury Decides the Sentence

The Law on When Sentence Should be Decided

When the United States Supreme Court held that guided discretion could make the death penalty constitutional in *Gregg v. Georgia* (1976) and companion cases, it approved of statutes that separated the guilt and punishment portions of the trial. After the jurors are selected, they are presented with the guilt evidence and then deliberate to determine whether the defendant is guilty of capital murder, similar to how they decide guilt in any criminal jury trial. If they determine beyond a reasonable doubt that the defendant is guilty of capital murder, the same jury comes back to the courtroom and hears the aggravating and mitigating evidence they are supposed to consider and the guidance they are supposed to follow when deciding the sentence. Research shows that many jurors cannot be doing this because they decide the sentence before the sentencing phase even begins.

Research on When the Sentence Is Decided

In the CJP interviews, all jurors were asked the following question: "After the jury found [defendant's name] guilty of capital murder but before you heard any evidence or testimony about what the punishment should be, did you then think [defendant's name] should be given a death sentence, a sentence of life without the possibility of parole (or the alternative in that state), [or were you] undecided? Nearly half of the jurors nationwide had already decided what the punishment should be at the end of the guilt phase, before the sentencing phase had even begun. Regardless of jurisdiction, at the end of the guilt phase only approximately half of these jurors maintained that they were undecided, or still had an open mind as required by law, on what sentence to impose. Nationwide, nearly one-third (30.3%) had decided on death and 18.8% had decided on life prior to hearing sentencing evidence and instructions that were supposed to guide their sentencing decision (Bowers et al., 2014). Most of the jurors who prematurely decided the sentence said they were absolutely convinced (70.4% of those who chose death and 57.5% of those who chose life). Nearly all the remaining jurors said they were pretty sure, with only 2.6% of the pro-death jurors and 4.8% or the pro-life jurors saying they were not too sure what the sentence should be (Bowers et al., 2014).

Analysis also was conducted to see if early pro-death jurors were merely sitting on more aggravated cases and early pro-life jurors on less aggravated cases compared to those who managed to remain undecided until the sentencing phase as the law requires. Comparing responses to a wide range of questions about the nature of the crime, the number of victims, the number of perpetrators, the relationship between the defendant and the victim, and the type of guilt evidence presented revealed no sizable or consistent differences that could explain why some jurors took a premature stance for death or life (Bowers, Sandys, & Steiner, 1998, Appendix B).

Most of the evidence of premature decision making comes from the CJP interviews with former capital jurors, and different types of analysis by different researchers have found evidence of sizable proportions of jurors deciding the sentence before the sentencing phase begins (Bentle & Bowers, 2001; Bowers et al., 2014; Bowers, Fleury-Steiner, & Antonio, 2003; Bowers & Foglia, 2003; Bowers, Sandys, & Steiner, 1998; Bowers & Steiner, 1998; Foglia, 2003). Two other studies that interviewed former capital jurors but were not part of the CJP also found evidence of premature decision making (Constanzo & Constanzo, 1994; Geimer & Amsterdam, 1988). Costanzo and Costanzo interviewed former capital jurors from Oregon and found that 26% said they did not need to hear evidence at the penalty phase because they had already decided the defendant deserved to die after hearing about the crime. In their interviews of Florida jurors, Geimer and Amsterdam found that 39.3% of the jurors who recommended death explained their position in ways indicating that they believed that the law mandated death once someone was convicted of first-degree murder.

The strength, consistency, and impact of this premature decision making confirm what social psychology research and common experience tell us: that once people form an opinion they tend to interpret subsequent information to support their position (Nickerson, 1998). It is clear that the United States Supreme Court recognizes how important it is to keep an open mind when they repeatedly cite a line from *Reynolds v. United States* (1879, p. 155): "a juror who has formed an opinion cannot be impartial" (cited in *Irvin v. Dowd*, 1961, p. 722; *Morgan v. Illinois*, 1992, p. 727; *Turner v. Louisiana*, 1965, p. 471). Brewer provides empirical evidence to support this conclusion when he compares CJP jurors who prematurely decided death to the rest of the sample and found the early pro-death jurors were significantly less receptive to mitigation (2005).

Statutory standards are supposed to be guiding the jurors' sentencing discretion, and jurors are supposed to be providing individualized sentencing by giving meaningful consideration to the mitigating evidence; this cannot be happening for the half of the jurors who are deciding the sentence before they have even heard the sentencing instructions or the sentencing evidence.

Guiding Juror Discretion

As indicated previously, guiding juror discretion was key to the United States Supreme Court's determination that the death penalty could be constitutional. Since the modern era of capital punishment was ushered in with *Gregg v. Georgia* and companion cases in (1976), the Court has repeatedly wrestled with what form this guidance should take and whether jurors are in fact following the guidance. Here we summarize the case law on guiding juror discretion and then examine what the research reveals about how successful attempts to guide juror discretion have been.

The Law on Guiding Juror Discretion

When the United States Supreme Court decided that guiding sentencing discretion could make capital punishment constitutional, it approved three different types of statutes aimed at providing such guidance. All three types of statutes require jurors to find the existence of one aggravating circumstance listed in the statute beyond a reasonable doubt. *Gregg v. Georgia* (1976) approved what were called "threshold" statutes: Once the jury meets that threshold of finding a statutory aggravator beyond a reasonable doubt, jurors can then consider additional aggravating and mitigating circumstances, without additional guidance, to decide whether to sentence the defendant to death. The "balancing" statute approved in *Proffitt v. Florida* (1976) required jurors to find a statutory aggravator beyond a reasonable doubt and then to weigh aggravating and mitigating factors listed in the statute to determine whether to recommend a death sentence. At the time, trial judges in Florida could then independently find and weigh aggravation and mitigation and make their own determinations of the sentence, but the United States Supreme Court has since held that allowing the judge to decide violates the Sixth Amendment right to a jury trial and that the jury must make the findings and decide the sentence (*Hurst v. Florida*, 2016). The Court approved Texas' "directed" statute in *Jurek v. Texas* (1976). In 1976, the Texas statute required the jury to answer three questions about the defendant's future dangerousness, the defendant's intent to kill or level of responsibility, and the victim's provocation. However, *Penry v. Lynaugh* (1989) subsequently required that the statute explicitly instruct the jury to consider mitigation, so that the third question was changed. Now, if the jury finds beyond a reasonable doubt that the defendant will be dangerous in the future and the defendant actually killed the victim or intended to kill, it then determines whether there is sufficient mitigating evidence to warrant a life sentence. At the same time it approved the three guided discretion statutes, the Court rejected mandatory death penalty statutes (*Roberts v. Louisiana*, 1976; *Woodson v. North Carolina*, 1976), holding that the jurors always must have discretion to assess "the character and record of the individual offender and the circumstances of the particular offense" (*Woodson*, at 304).

Modifying Guidance on Mitigation

In the years since deciding *Gregg* and companion cases, the United States Supreme Court has decided additional cases modifying the type of guidance required by the Constitution beyond the tweaking described earlier of the three statutes they approved in 1976. Arguably the most significant decision was *Lockett v. Ohio* (1978) where the Court built on the *Woodson* requirement of individualized sentencing. A plurality of the Court in *Lockett* found that "(t)he sentencer . . . [cannot] be precluded from considering, *as a mitigating factor*, any aspect of a defendant's character or record and any of the circumstances of the offense that the defendant proffers as a basis for a sentence less than death" (p. 604; emphasis in original; footnotes omitted). The *Penry* case that led to the modification of the third question in Texas was an elaboration of this line of cases. In *Penry*, the Court reasoned that a full consideration of mitigation was required to insure that the death penalty was appropriate in a specific case because "defendants who commit criminal acts that are attributable to a disadvantaged background or to emotional and mental problems, may be less culpable than defendants who have no such excuse" (*Penry v. Lynaugh*, 1989, p. 319, quoting *California v. Brown*, 1987, p. 545). The Court revisited the role of mitigation to find that jurors must consider mitigation even if it does not "relate specifically to the culpability for the crime" (*Skipper v. South Carolina*, 1986, p. 4; also see *Tennard v. Dretke*, 2004) and even if it does not "excuse" the crime (*Eddings v. Oklahoma*, 1982, p. 113). Capital jurors are free to determine how much weight to give specific mitigating evidence, but "they may not give it no weight by excluding such evidence from their consideration" (*Eddings v. Oklahoma*, 1982, p. 115).

Not only is mitigation different from aggravation because it cannot be limited, but it also does not have to be found beyond a reasonable doubt and does not have to be found unanimously. The United States Supreme Court has not ruled on whether it would be unconstitutional to require mitigation be proven beyond a reasonable doubt, but no state applies that burden to mitigation (Palmer, 2001). Further, the Court assumed that requiring mitigation to be proved beyond a reasonable doubt would be unconstitutional without deciding the issue in *Kansas v. Carr* (2016). The Court has decided jurors do not have to be unanimous on findings of mitigation (*McKoy v. North Carolina*, 1990; *Mills v. Maryland*, 1988).

Modifying Guidance on Aggravation

The United States Supreme Court also has modified the guidance regarding statutory aggravating factors since 1976. *Zant v. Stephens* (1983) held that the Constitution required only that a single aggravator listed in the statute be found before the death penalty can be imposed. Although some states restrict jurors to only considering statutory aggravators (for example: 42 Pa.Cons. Stat. Section 9711, 2001), *Zant v. Stephens* held that such a restriction is not required by the Constitution. In *Ring v. Arizona*, the Court made it clear that the jury must find that the required aggravating factor has been proven beyond a reasonable doubt (2002). The Court also reversed prior case law in *Payne v. Tennessee* (1991) to allow victim impact statements, which include personal information about the victim and the impact of his or her death on family, friends, and the community. This is the kind of evidence that makes a death sentence more likely and thus acts like nonstatutory aggravating factors.

United States Supreme Court's Confidence in Jurors

The United States Supreme Court has been very willing to assume that jurors understand and follow sentencing instructions. In *Weeks v. Angelone* (2000), the Court held that it was not unconstitutional for a trial judge to refuse to provide clarification in response to a jury's question and merely refer them back to the sentencing instructions. Writing for the five-member majority, Justice Rehnquist acknowledged that there was a "slight possibility" that the jurors misunderstood the instructions (p. 236) but argued that there is a "presumption" that they do understand (p. 242).

More recently, the United States Supreme Court held that the failure to provide an instruction on the burden of proof for mitigation was not unconstitutional (*Kansas v. Carr*, 2016), even though the Kansas Supreme Court had previously mandated that the jury be told mitigation only needed to be proven to a juror's satisfaction, not beyond a reasonable doubt. Justice Scalia wrote the majority opinion, joined by every other Justice except Justice Sotomayor, and argued that since the instructions never told them mitigation has to be proven beyond a reasonable doubt we have no reason to think the jury would assume that. In her dissent in *Carr*, Justice Sotomayor points out that what the jury thinks is an empirical question and that the majority just presumed what the jury would think without any empirical evidence. The next section will summarize some of the many studies that provide empirical evidence of what jurors think and show that the majority opinion's confidence in the jury's understanding of the sentencing instructions was misplaced.

The Empirical Evidence on Juror Comprehension of Sentencing Guidance

The worst thing was that we weren't clear on those instruction[s] . . . we had to decide from them . . . pick them apart to understand what they meant, they weren't clear [. . .] and we were all very tired and . . . stressed out.

(Barner, 2014, p. 6)

This quote from a former capital juror from Missouri compels one to ask how jurors' discretion can be guided if they do not understand the guidance. Barner analyzed the transcripts of interviews with former capital jurors collected by the CJP and presents numerous quotes from the jurors themselves that either misstate the law, reflecting they did not understand the instructions, or directly complain about being confused by the instructions. The jurors confirmed in their own words the findings of numerous studies that demonstrate that many jurors do not understand the instructions that are supposed to be guiding their sentencing discretion.

Considering Aggravating and Mitigating Evidence

Research using different methodologies consistently finds widespread misunderstanding of the instructions regarding how aggravating and mitigating evidence is supposed to be used to decide the sentence in a capital case in accordance with constitutional requirements. Much of the research involves using mock jurors, which are typically college students or people summoned for jury duty but not picked for a jury, who are asked to assume the role of a juror in the study. This approach has the advantage of allowing the researcher to isolate and to control exactly what the subjects hear. Further, college students, by definition, have more formal education than the general public from which jurors are selected and as such should reveal higher levels of comprehension. On the other hand, one can argue that real jurors would take the process more seriously and pay closer attention to instructions, which is why other researchers have studied individuals who had actually served as capital jurors. The evidence shows that both approaches, with their different advantages and disadvantages, tell the same story: both mock and real jurors fail to understand sentencing instructions.

There is a long line of mock jury research, using different pattern instructions from different states, that shows misunderstandings of how to handle aggravating and mitigating evidence when deciding whether a defendant deserves death (Blankenship, Luginbuhl, Cullen, & Redick, 1997; Diamond & Levi, 1996; Frank & Applegate, 1998; Haney & Lynch, 1994, 1997; Luginbuhl, 1992; Lynch & Haney, 2000; Otto, Applegate, & Davis, 2007; Tiersma, 1995). These mock jurors often show greater misunderstanding of how to treat mitigation compared to aggravation, which is understandable considering aggravation is a more familiar term and the beyond a reasonable doubt standard that applies to aggravation is also more familiar and has just been used during the guilt phase. For example, after Haney and Lynch (1994) read the standard California capital sentencing instructions three times to upper division college students, only 8% could correctly define both terms and, while 64% provided partially correct definitions of aggravation, only 47% were able to provide partially correct definitions for mitigation.

Studies also have examined how comprehension can be improved. Haney and Lynch (1997) found that attorney closing arguments did not substantially improve comprehension. Some researchers have tried rewriting the instructions with the help of a linguist and giving subjects written copies of the instructions (Diamond & Levi, 1996) or added clarifying instructions that specifically debunked common misunderstandings (Otto et al., 2007). Although comprehension was improved with these techniques, some jurors still misunderstood the instructions. When Otto et al. (2007) gave subjects either Florida's pattern capital sentencing instructions or the same instructions with further clarification focused on common misunderstandings, the additional clarification improved overall comprehension from an average of 46.3% to 59.4%. This was a significant improvement, but many still failed to understand the instructions. Again, the results show that it is especially difficult to get jurors to understand how to consider mitigating evidence. Despite clarification that specifically told jurors that it was a common mistake to think that mitigation had to be proven beyond a reasonable doubt and that this was not the correct standard, comprehension only improved from 31% to 45%, leaving over half the jurors still failing to understand mitigation did not have be proven beyond a reasonable doubt. Research also has shown that the process of deliberation did not improve comprehension (Diamond, 1993).

Interviews with individuals who actually served as capital jurors and thus discussed and applied the instructions to decide a defendant's sentence demonstrate similar problems with understanding the statutory guidance. Interviews with former capital jurors from Florida, California, and Oregon, as well as the CJP's interviews with former capital jurors from 14 states, confirm that many actual jurors failed to understand the sentencing instructions. These states had very different types of statutory guidance, but in each state jurors were failing to understand the guidance in ways that made the jurors discount the importance of mitigation and made a death sentence more likely than it would be had the jurors been following the guidance.

Geimer and Amsterdam (1987–1988) interviewed 54 jurors from ten trials in Florida that were evenly split between recommendations for death and life. When asked to explain the reasons for their death or life decisions, nearly two-thirds (65%) said that the statutory guidance relating to aggravating and mitigating circumstances had "little or no influence" on their sentencing recommendation. One clear indication that the jurors did not understand how they were supposed to make their decision was that more than half the jurors voting for death said they believed that death was the presumed punishment unless they could be convinced otherwise. In interviews with 30 jurors from five death and five life cases in California, researchers found that jurors were confused about how to make the sentencing decision and tended to focus on the crime or other issues that had come up during the guilt phase. Haney, Sontag, and Costanzo report that one-third of these California jurors refocused the penalty phase entirely on the crime in a way that "amounted to a presumption in favor of death" (1994, p. 162). Interviews with 27 jurors from five death and four life cases in Oregon also revealed that jurors narrowed their focus in ways that undercut the importance of mitigation. Oregon's statute is similar to Texas' directed statute and makes the sentencing decision depend heavily on whether jurors think the defendant will be dangerous in the future. One juror explained: "We just had to stick to those . . . basic criteria. We couldn't deviate with this mitigating circumstance (sic), or testimony of people that had spoken on his behalf or against him" (Haney et al., 1994, pp. 165–166).

The most extensive exploration of how former capital jurors made their sentencing decisions comes from the interviews with former jurors collected by the CJP. The sample includes states from different parts of the country and states with threshold, balancing, and directed statutes. Results show widespread misunderstanding of instructions in every state, regardless of geographic location or type of statute. Although nuances of the process can vary, the constitutional requirements imposed by the United States Supreme Court must be met in every state. The *Lockett* line of cases make it clear that jurors cannot be restricted regarding what they can consider as mitigating evidence, but approaching half the jurors nationwide (44.6%) failed to understand that they could consider any relevant mitigating evidence (Bowers & Foglia, 2003). The percentages getting this wrong ranged from 24.2% in California to 58.7% in Pennsylvania, but substantial percentages got this wrong regardless of the statutory sentencing scheme. Although the Court has held that jurors need not be unanimous on mitigation (*McKoy v. North Carolina*, 1990; *Mills v. Maryland*, 1988), two-thirds nationwide (66.5%) either thought they had to be unanimous or said they did not know whether they had to be unanimous or not. Again, substantial percentages failed to understand this constitutional requirement in every state, ranging from a low of 36.8% in Florida to a high of 89.0% in Georgia (Bowers & Foglia, 2003). Because some states do not specify a burden of proof for mitigating evidence, jurors were only considered incorrect on the question about the burden of proof for mitigation if they indicated mitigation had to be proven beyond a reasonable doubt. Almost half the jurors (49.2%) incorrectly claimed that mitigation had to be proven beyond a reasonable doubt, ranging from a low of 32.0% in Pennsylvania to a high of 66.0% in Texas (Bowers & Foglia, 2003). This evidence counters the Court's presumption in *Carr* that jurors would not jump to that conclusion when the instructions were silent on the burden of proof for mitigation. It should be noted that some states, such as Pennsylvania, affirmatively tell jurors that mitigation only has to be proven by a preponderance of the evidence (42 Pa. Cons. Stat. Section 9711), but nearly a third of the jurors still get this wrong in Pennsylvania.

The United States Supreme Court has not imposed as many constitutional requirements on aggravating evidence as it has on mitigating evidence, but it has required that at least one statutory aggravator be proven beyond a reasonable doubt before a death penalty can be imposed (*Zant v. Stephens*, 1983). Even though this standard of proof should be familiar, as it is the standard for guilt in all criminal trials and the jury was supposed to have just used it to find the defendant guilty of a capital offense, the CJP found that, nationwide, 29.9% of the jurors failed to realize that aggravation had to be proven beyond a reasonable doubt. The percentage failing to understand the burden of proof for aggravation ranged from a low of 15.6% in Kentucky to 48.3% in Missouri (Bowers & Foglia, 2003).

The more recent interviews conducted by CJP researchers of former capital jurors from trials taking place from 1999 to 2009 in seven states demonstrate that these problems with juror understanding persist. Comparing the results from the original CJP with the more recent interviews shows that the proportion failing to realize mitigation does not need to be proven beyond a reasonable doubt increased from 49.2% to 57.4%, while the percentage failing to realize they did not need to be unanimous on findings of mitigation decreased slightly from 66.5% to 62.5% (Bowers et al., 2014). The percentages failing to understand how to handle mitigating evidence is considerable in both the original and the more recent CJP samples. The empirical evidence demonstrates that whether you are looking at capital jurors who decided cases in the late 1980s and early 1990s or cases from the first decade of the new millennium, substantial percentages are misunderstanding how to handle mitigating evidence in ways that make it harder to find mitigation than it would be if jurors were following the law.

Erroneously Believing the Law Requires Death

Another indication that jurors fail to understand the sentencing instructions is that a significant proportion of jurors think that the law requires the death penalty once certain facts are proven, even though the United States Supreme Court has made it clear that the death penalty can never be mandated under law (*Woodson v. North Carolina*, 1976). In their interviews with former capital jurors from Florida, Geimer and Amsterdam found that 39.2% of the jurors who voted for death believed that the law required the death penalty for convictions for first-degree murder (1988).

The CJP found that half (50.3%) the approximately 1,200 jurors from 14 different states thought that death was required by law if either of two commonly found aggravating circumstances was proven (Bowers & Foglia, 2003). The former capital jurors interviewed by the CJP were asked: "(a)fter hearing the judge's instructions, did you believe that the law required you to impose a death sentence if the evidence proved that . . ." the defendant's "conduct was heinous, vile or depraved" or the defendant "would be dangerous in the future." Nationwide, 43.9% thought the law required the death penalty if the defendant's conduct was heinous, vile, or depraved, ranging from a low of 29.5% in California to a high of 67.1% in North Carolina. If the evidence proved that the defendant would be dangerous in the future, 36.9% of the jurors thought the law required death, ranging from a low of 20.4% in California to a high of 68.4% in Texas (Bowers & Foglia, 2003). In some states heinous, vile, or depraved and/or future dangerousness are statutory aggravators but, regardless of whether they are mentioned in the statute, a substantial percentage of jurors in every state find that they not only weigh in favor of death but that they actually require death. These are extremely important factors, as 81.5% of the jurors thought the evidence did prove that the defendant's conduct was heinous, vile, or depraved, and 78.2% thought the evidence proved that the defendant would be dangerous in the future (Bowers & Foglia, 2003). All told, 45% thought the law required death in their case because they thought that one of these factors was proven and also erroneously thought it required death (Bowers & Foglia, 2003).

The more recent CJP interviews from jurors that decided cases from 1999 to 2009 shows virtually no change in the percentages thinking death is required under these two commonly found aggravating circumstances. In the more recent sample, 42.3% thought the law required death if the evidence proved the defendant's conduct was heinous, vile, or depraved, which is very close to the 43.9% found in the original sample. A slightly higher percentage (44.8%) thought death was required if the defendant would be dangerous in the future, but this was because the proportion of jurors from Texas was three times as high in the new sample compared to the original sample. Because the Texas statute requires jurors to answer a question about the defendant's future dangerousness to determine if the defendant is eligible for the death penalty, it focuses the jury on that issue, and over two-thirds of the jurors from Texas in both samples thought future dangerousness actually mandated death. Once jurors from Texas are omitted from each sample, the percentages in the original and more recent samples believing that future dangerousness mandates death were virtually identical (33.2% and 33.3%) (Bowers et al., 2014).

Evading Responsibility for the Punishment Decision

Yet another indication that jurors do not understand the sentencing instructions comes from jurors' responses about responsibility for the sentencing decision. The United States Supreme Court emphasized how important it is for the jury to recognize its responsibility for the defendant's sentence in *Caldwell v. Mississippi* (1985). In *Caldwell*, the prosecutor argued that jury members should not view themselves as deciding the defendant would die because an appellate court would review their decision to insure it was correct. The Court vacated the sentence, holding that a sentence of death is unreliable if it is imposed by a jury that believes that the ultimate responsibility for the sentence rests with others. They recognized that jurors would be reluctant to accept responsibility, as they are in a "very unfamiliar situation and called on to make a very difficult and uncomfortable choice," and the prosecutor's statement created an "intolerable danger that the jury will in fact choose to minimize the importance of its role" (1985, p. 333).

The erroneous beliefs about the law requiring death just discussed allow some jurors to shift responsibility away from themselves and onto the law. Haney et al. report that there was a tendency among the former capital jurors they interviewed from both California and Oregon "to shift or abdicate responsibility for the ultimate decision—to the law, to the judge, or to the legal instructions—rather than to grapple personally with the life and death consequences of the verdicts they were called upon to render" (1994, p. 160). The directed statute in Oregon seemed to make it especially easy to avoid feeling responsible, as evidenced by numerous quotes from former capital jurors like the following:

> We are not sentencing him to death—we are just answering these questions. We talked about it. We are just answering these questions—to get a clear mind so as not to feel guilty that I sentenced him to die. That's how the law has it—just answer these questions.
> *(Constanzo & Constanzo, 1994, p. 162)*

Direct questions about responsibility asked by the CJP provide additional evidence of jurors' reluctance to take responsibility for the sentence. CJP jurors were asked to rate from least to most responsible the

(1) law, (2) judge, (3) jury, (4) individual juror, and (5) defendant. Over 80% of the CJP jurors assigned primary responsibility to the defendant or the law, while only 5.5% said the individual juror and only 8.9% said the jury as a whole were most responsible. Another question about responsibility asked about the relative responsibility of the jury, judge, and appellate judges. In the ten CJP states where the jury decision was binding on the judge at the time, only 29.8% thought the jury was strictly responsible. Nearly 1 in 5 (17%) thought the appellate judge was mostly responsible, which was precisely the problem that led the Court to find the sentence unreliable in *Caldwell* (Bowers & Foglia, 2003). The more recent CJP interviews found that the percentages seeing the jury or individual juror as primarily responsible are even lower than they were in the original sample. Removing the Delaware jurors, for whom the sentence was nonbinding at the time,[3] only .9% thought the individual juror and 5.3% thought the jury as a group was primarily responsible in the more recent CJP sample (Bowers et al., 2014).

This widespread reluctance to take responsibility for the sentence, combined with misunderstandings about how to handle aggravating and mitigating evidence and erroneous beliefs about the death penalty being mandatory, demonstrate that the death penalty is not working in the way the Constitution requires. And while it is constitutional to consider future dangerousness in sentencing decisions when allowed by state statute, jurors' myopic concern with its potential prejudices the defendant in two different ways. Here we discussed how some jurors think the law mandates death if they believe the defendant will be dangerous in the future. Next we turn to a discussion of the second way concern with future dangerousness prejudices the defendant, namely how erroneous assumptions about the early release of defendants not given the death penalty combine with fears of future dangerousness to make the jury more likely to impose a death sentence.

Fears of Future Dangerousness and Erroneous Assumptions of Early Release

The Law on Concerns About Future Dangerousness

The United States Supreme Court recognized that jurors might be concerned about the defendant's future dangerousness and unclear about how long a defendant would spend in prison if not given death in *Simmons v. South Carolina* (1994; also see *Shafer v. South Carolina*, 2001). The Court cited some of the earlier CJP research in *Simmons* to support its assertion that there was a "reasonable likelihood of juror confusion about the meaning of the term 'life imprisonment'" (1994, pp. 169–170, footnote 9, citing Bowers, 1993; Eisenberg & Wells, 1993). Reasoning that jurors might be worried about a potentially dangerous defendant being released on parole if he or she was sentenced to life, they held that if the alternative to death was life without parole (LWOP) and the prosecution puts the defendant's future dangerousness "at issue," then the jury must be informed that the defendant cannot be paroled (1994, p. 156). The Court argued that jurors should not be forced to make what they called a "false choice" between death or an incorrect or false understanding of the alternative (1994, p. 161).

After hearing how the defendant committed a capital murder, it is not surprising that jurors are generally concerned about the defendant's future dangerousness. The two states with directed statutes, Texas and Oregon, explicitly focus the jurors' attention on this issue by requiring that the jury find that the defendant will be dangerous in the future before he or she is eligible for the death penalty. Some other states include future dangerousness as a statutory aggravator, others allow it to be considered as a nonstatutory aggravator (Vartkessian, 2012), while others technically preclude jurors from considering future dangerousness in their sentencing decision.[4] Interviews with former capital jurors conducted by the CJP indicate that it is a concern for nearly all capital jurors, and the only thing they discuss more than future dangerousness is the facts of the crime (Eisenberg & Wells, 1993; also see Blume, Garvey, & Johnson, 2000–2001; Bowers & Steiner, 1999; Foglia, 2003).

Research on Fears of Future Dangerousness

Requiring that the jury be told LWOP means no parole when the prosecutor puts future dangerousness at issue is a good first step. However, research showing future dangerousness is virtually "always 'at issue,'" as emphasized in the title of an article by Blume et al. (2000–2001, p. 397), suggests that jurors should always be told LWOP means no parole, regardless of what the prosecutor puts forth. Blume et al. analyzed responses from the sub-set of CJP jurors from South Carolina and, although these jurors claimed the prosecution had not put future dangerousness at issue, over half of them said that jury deliberations focused on future dangerousness "a great deal" or "a fair amount." In addition, nearly 70% said keeping the defendant from ever killing again was "very" important (43%) or "fairly" important (26%) when deciding the defendant's sentence. To make sure jurors were not expressing concern about the defendant's killing in prison, the researchers also looked at a question asking if they were concerned about the defendant getting back into society if not given the death penalty and found that 60% of these same jurors said they were "greatly" concerned (31%) or "somewhat" concerned (29%). Based on this evidence the authors argue that most jurors will be worried about future dangerousness whether or not it is made an issue, and the jury should always be told there will be no parole when the alternative to death is LWOP.

The preoccupation with future dangerousness is confirmed by interviews with former capital jurors from all 14 states in the CJP sample. Many volunteered that they felt they had to vote for death to make sure the defendant did not get back onto the street (Bowers & Foglia, 2003). Overall, 73% said penalty deliberations focused on the defendant's dangerousness if ever allowed back into society, and there was a statistically significant association between discussing dangerousness and a death sentence: The more jurors discussed future dangerousness, the more likely they were to vote for death (Bowers & Foglia, 2003).

These concerns about future dangerousness are especially troubling because many jurors also are erroneously underestimating how long someone not given the death penalty actually spends in prison, and these erroneous assumptions make them more likely to vote for the death penalty. There is an abundance of research, done by the CJP and others, showing that many capital jurors underestimate how long someone not sentenced to death usually spends in prison and, the lower their wrong estimates, the more likely they are to vote for death (Blume et al., 2000–2001; Bowers, 1995; Bowers & Foglia, 2003; Bowers & Steiner, 1999; Costanzo & Costanzo, 1994; Foglia, 2003; Haney, 1997; Steiner, Bowers, & Sarat, 1999).

A summary of the interviews with 1,198 CJP jurors from 14 states shows that in every state, most of the CJP jurors believed *most* defendants would be released before they were even eligible for parole, even in the states that had LWOP at the time of the interviews (Bowers & Foglia, 2003). The median estimate for when most defendants get released for the national sample was 15 years. In every state, the median estimate was well below the mandatory minimums all defendants had to serve before even being eligible for parole in each of these states.

Bowers and Steiner (1999) show that jurors who espouse extremely low estimates are more likely than those giving the more realistic estimate of 20+ years to choose death: the more jurors underestimate when defendants usually get released, the more likely they are to consistently take a stand for death and ultimately vote for death. As Bowers and Foglia note "[b]oth statistical analyses and jurors' narrative accounts of the decision process demonstrate that these unrealistically low estimates made jurors more likely to vote for death" (2003, p. 82). The difference in the percentage choosing death between those with low and high estimates of release actually gets more pronounced as the trial progresses, which is consistent with jurors' narrative reports that the dangerousness of the defendant if released is a dominant topic in sentencing deliberations.

All 31 states currently with the death penalty and the federal statute provide LWOP for at least some capital offenses (Death Penalty Information Center, 2017b), and most states have statutes requiring that the jury be told parole is not an option (*Simmons v. South Carolina*, 1994). However, the CJP data show that it is difficult to convince jurors that the defendant really will not be released on parole. As one typical juror in a death case said, he believed defendants usually get released in 15 years even though he observed that officially they say the sentence is:

> Life imprisonment, but even though now it says without possibility of parole, we were still concerned that someday he'd get out on parole. We didn't want him out again at all.

Another juror who ultimately voted for death said:

> I was undecided. I had a personal problem with the life sentence, but then the judge explained to me that if he gets a life sentence there was absolutely no chance that he would get out. I thought he might get out. I still don't trust anybody about it.
>
> *(Bowers & Steiner, 1999, p. 698)*

In Pennsylvania, 38.6% of the jurors who actually voted for death said they would have preferred life without parole if it had been an alternative, as indeed it was in the cases they decided (Bowers & Foglia, 2003).

The follow up interviews done by the CJP of jurors who decided cases between 1999 and 2009 reveal that this is the one area where there has been some improvement in jurors' perceptions. In the new sample the median estimate is 25 years as opposed to the 15 years found in the original sample, and actually 7 out of 10 former jurors estimate that defendants will spend 25 years or more in prison if not given the death penalty. The increase in the number of jurisdictions providing LWOP and the widespread use of instructions on the lack of parole eligibility probably explain this increase in the estimates of when someone not given death is likely to be released (Bowers et al., 2014). However, we still see that almost a third of the jurors erroneously believe that most defendants not given death will be out in less than 25 years and, as we have seen, this can make them more likely to impose death than they would be if they had more accurate perceptions of a LWOP sentence.

Race and the Capital Jury

The history of capital punishment in the United States is inextricably linked with racial disparities in sentencing (Banner, 2002). A review of that complicated relationship is beyond the scope of this chapter. However, a brief discussion of key findings, as they relate to jury decision making, is warranted and is presented next.

The most consistent finding in research on race and the death penalty is a race-of-victim effect. The United States General Accounting Office's (1990) review of prior research determined that 82% of the studies indicated that defendants were more likely to get the death penalty if the victim was white. This same race of victim effect has emerged in more recent studies conducted in jurisdictions as diverse as Connecticut (Donohue, 2011), Colorado (Hindson, Potter, & Radelet, 2006), North Carolina (Unah, 2009), and the Armed Forces (Baldus, Grosso, Woodworth, & Newell, 2012). These archival analyses focused on outcome by race, even when controlling for a multitude of variables, fail to separate the effect of prosecutorial decision making from jury decision making.

In order to look specifically at the impact of race on juror decision making, researchers have conducted experiments using mock jurors. For instance, Lynch and Haney (2011) determined the juror eligibility and death qualification status of nonstudent adults who were then assigned to view one of four videotapes of a simulated capital penalty trial that varied the race of the defendant and victim (black or white). The participants deliberated in groups of four to seven people for as long as 1.5 hours. Rather than a main effect of race-of-victim on sentence outcomes, Lynch and Haney found that white male participants differed from other race/gender groups. Specifically, white males were more likely to vote for death for the black defendant, but there were no differences between the groups in terms of sentence preferences for the white defendant.

The strong influence of white males on sentencing outcomes is supported by findings from the CJP, especially when the defendant is black and the victim is white. Bowers et al. (2001) found that the percentage of black defendant-white victim cases that resulted in death jumped from 23.1% with four white male jurors to 63.2% with five white males on the jury. In contrast, the percentage of these cases that resulted in death dropped from 71.9% to 42.9% when the number of black males on the jury went from zero to one.

A recent study of the relationship between racial bias and preferences for a sentence of death provides a possible explanation for both race-of-victim and race-of-defendant effects. Levinson, Smith, and Young (2014) administered measures of both implicit and explicit bias to jury-eligible citizens in six high-use death penalty states. Participants read a case summary on a computer and then viewed an evidence slideshow that included four photographs. One of the photographs included a tombstone that presented the name of the victim; the name was altered—Edward Walsh or Jamal Washington— depending on the race-of-victim condition. The authors did not obtain a main effect for either race of victim or race of defendant. Rather, the bias measures interacted with the race of defendant and victim. In particular, higher scores of explicit racial bias (as measured by the Modern Racism Scale) predicted a race-of-victim effect, with a greater likelihood of a preference for a sentence of death when the victim was white. In contrast, higher scores of implicit racial bias (as measured by the 'Value of Life' Implicit Association Test) predicted a race-of-defendant effect, with preferences for death higher in the black defendant condition.[5] If these cognitive biases are ignored in the context of an actual trial, "then race-of defendant effects might be attributable to an unintentional decrease in receptivity to mitigation evidence proffered by a Black defendant" (Levinson et al., 2014, p. 567). Research is needed to discover the ways in which these biases may impact receptivity to mitigation and, arguably even more importantly, the ways in which to combat the unconstitutional influence of race on capital juror decision making.

Conclusion

Because the jury plays such a pivotal role in making the death penalty constitutional, this chapter has concentrated on the constitutional requirements the jury must meet and the evidence of whether they meet those standards in practice. The evidence is consistent: many are biased by the jury selection process and yet still getting onto capital juries even though they are not open to a life sentence; are deciding the sentence before they have heard evidence they are supposed to consider and guidance they are supposed to follow; are not understanding the instructions that are supposed to be guiding their discretion once they hear them; and are influenced by impermissible considerations of race. Instead, capital jurors have unrealistic assumptions about early release, and those assumptions are associated with their primary concerns of a defendant's future dangerousness and ensuring that she or he never be released from prison.

The question then becomes, how much, if any, departure from constitutional requirements should be tolerated? The United States Supreme Court has adopted the reasonable likelihood standard of *Boyde v. California* (1990) in deciding on the constitutionality of how jurors applied the instructions, and more recently, understood the instructions (*Kansas v. Carr*, 2016). That standard requires more than a "possibility" but less than "more likely than not" that jurors are acting inconsistently with constitutional requirements. Research by Bowers et al. (2010) reveals that the chance that all 12 jurors on a single case committed zero errors in violation of constitutionally mandated requirements is nil. They examined how many jurors made mistakes in each of six areas and found that nearly half or more violated Constitutional mandates in the areas of premature decision making (49.1%), believing death penalty is mandatory (50.2%), underestimating the death penalty alternative (58.5%), having a pro-death predisposition (80.8%), evading punishment responsibility (82%), and misunderstanding sentencing instructions (83.1%). In fact, not one of the 1198 jurors interviewed got everything correct in all six areas. The mean, median, and modal number of errors per juror was 4. It seems clear that there is more than a meager possibility that the fate of capital defendants is being decided by jurors who are not abiding by constitutional requirements; it actually is more likely than not, which is more than what *Boyde* requires. Hence, it is not a matter of whether it is possible to balance guided discretion and individualized sentencing; the evidence suggests that we have neither, and thus the doubters are right: capital juries are not deciding sentences in the way the Constitution demands.

Notes

1 The late William J. Bowers was supposed to be a co-author on this chapter, but failing health and his passing made that impossible. He still contributed immensely through early discussions about the chapter and his work on the Capital Jury Project; we dedicate this chapter to him.
2 An extension of the CJP has interviewed 152 jurors in seven states (Bowers et al., 2014).
3 The Delaware Supreme Court has since found that allowing the judge to determine the sentence is unconstitutional (*Rauf v. Delaware*, 2016).
4 For example, Indiana provides for 18 statutory aggravators (IC 35–50–2–9, Death Penalty Sentencing Procedure), none of which is future dangerousness. Further, the pattern instruction regarding aggravators reads, in part:

> You are not permitted to consider any circumstances as weighing in favor of the sentence of [life imprisonment without parole] or [death or life imprisonment without parole] other than the aggravating circumstances specifically charged by the State in the Charging Information (Indiana Judges Association, 2014, Indiana Civil and Criminal Jury Instructions, No. 15.0440).

Hence, technically, Indiana jurors are precluded from considering future dangerousness in their sentencing decision.
5 Implicit bias as measured through the Black-White stereotype Implicit Association Test was not significantly associated with sentencing preferences.

References

Allen, M., Mabry, E., & McKelton, D. (1998). Impact of juror attitudes about the death penalty on juror evaluations of guilt and punishment: A meta-analysis. *Law and Human Behavior, 22* (6), 715–731. DOI: 10.1023/A:1025763008533

American Law Institute. (2009). *Report of the Council to the membership of the American Law Institute on the matter of the death penalty*. Philadelphia, PA: The Executive Office.

Baldus, D. C., Grosso, C. M., Woodworth, G., & Newell, R. (2012). Racial discrimination in the administration of the death penalty: The experience of the United States armed forces (1984–2005). *Journal of Criminal Law and Criminology, 101*, 1227–1335.

Baldus, D. C., Woodworth, G., Zuckerman, D., Weiner, N. A., & Broffitt, B. (2001). The use of peremptory challenges in capital murder trials: A legal and empirical analysis. *University of Pennsylvania Journal of Constitutional Law, 3*, 3–170.

Banner, S. (2002). *The death penalty: An American history*. Cambridge, MA: Harvard University Press.

Barner, J. R. (2014). Life or death decision making: Qualitative analysis of death penalty jurors. *Qualitative Social Work, 13*(6), 842–858.

Bentele, U., & Bowers, W. J. (2001). How jurors decide on death: Guilt is overwhelming, aggravation requires death, and mitigation is no excuse. *Brooklyn Law Review, 66*(4), 1013–1080.

Blankenship, M. B., Luginbuhl, J., Cullen, F. T., & Redick, W. (1997). Jurors' comprehension of sentencing instructions: A test of the death penalty process in Tennessee. *Justice Quarterly, 14*(2), 325–351.

Blume, J. H., Garvey, S. P., & Johnson, S. L. (2000–2001). Future dangerousness in capital cases: Always 'at issue'. *Cornell Law Review, 86*, 397–410.

Bowers, W. J. (1993). Capital punishment and contemporary values: People's misgivings and the court's misperceptions. *Law & Society Review, 27*(1), 157–175.

Bowers, W. J. (1995). The capital jury project: Rationale, design and preview of early findings. *Indiana Law Journal, 70*(4), 1043–1102.

Bowers, W. J., & Foglia, W. D. (2003). Still singularly agonizing: Law's failure to purge arbitrariness from capital sentencing. *Criminal Law Bulletin, 39*(1), 51–86.

Bowers, W. J., Foglia, W., Ehrhard-Dietzel, S., & Kelly, C. (2010). Jurors' failure to understand or comport with constitutional standards in capital sentencing: Strength of the evidence. *Criminal Law Bulletin, 46*(6), 1147–1240.

Bowers, W. J., Fluery-Steiner, B. D. & Antonio, M. E. (2003). The capital sentencing decision: Guided discretion, reasoned moral judgment, or legal fiction. In J. R. Acker, R. M. Bohm, & C. S. Lanier (Eds.), *America's experiment with capital punishment: Reflections on the past, present, and future of the ultimate penal sanction* (2nd ed., pp. 413–467). Durham, North Carolina: Carolina Academic Press.

Bowers, W. J., Kelly, C. E., Kleinstuber, R., Vartkessian, E. S., & Sandys, M. (2014). The life or death sentencing decision: It's at odds with constitutional standards; is it beyond human ability? In J. R. Acker, R. M. Bohm, & C. S. Lanier (Eds.), *America's experiment with capital punishment: Reflections on the past, present, and future of the ultimate penal sanction* (3rd ed., pp. 425–496). Durham, NC: Carolina Academic Press.

Bowers, W. J., Sandys, M. D., & Steiner, B. D. (1998). Foreclosed impartiality in capital sentencing: Jurors' predispositions, guilt-trail experience, and premature decision making. *Cornell Law Review, 83*(6), 1476–1556.

Bowers, W. J., & Steiner, B. D. (1998). Choosing life or death: Sentencing dynamics in capital cases. In J. R. Acker, R. M. Bohm, & C. S. Lanier (Eds.), *America's experiment with capital punishment: Reflections on the past, present, and future of the ultimate penal sanction* (pp. 309–349). Durham, NC: Carolina Academic Press.

Bowers, W. J., & Steiner, B. D. (1999). Death by default: An empirical demonstration of false and forced choices in capital sentencing. *Texas Law Review, 77*(3), 605–717.

Bowers, W. J., Steiner, B. D., & Sandys, M. D. (2001). Death sentencing in black and white: An empirical analysis of the role of juror's race and jury racial composition. *University of Pennsylvania Journal of Constitutional Law, 9*(1), 171–274.

Brewer, T.W. (2005). The attorney-client relationship in capital cases and its impact on juror receptivity to mitigation evidence. *Justice Quarterly, 22*(3), 340–363. http://dx.doi.org/10.1080/07418820500219169

Butler, B., & Moran, G. (2007). The role of death qualification and need for cognition in venirepersons' evaluations of expert scientific testimony in capital trials. *Behavioral Sciences & the Law, 25*(4), 561–571.

Butler, B., & Wasserman, A. W. (2006). The role of death qualification in venirepersons' attitudes toward the insanity defense. *Journal of Applied Social Psychology, 36*(7), 1744–1757.

Constanzo, S., & Constanzo, M. (1994). Life or death decisions: An analysis of capital jury decision making under the special issues sentencing framework. *Law and Human Behavior, 18*, 151–170.

Cowan, C. L., Thompson, W. C., & Ellsworth, P. C. (1984). The effects of death qualification on jurors' predisposition to convict and on the quality of deliberation. *Law and Human Behavior, 8*(1–2), 53–79.

Death Penalty Information Center. (2017a). *Leading law group withdraws model Death Penalty laws because system is unfixable*. Retrieved from www.deathpenaltyinfo.org/leading-law-group-withdraws-model-death-penalty-laws-because-system-unfixable

Death Penalty Information Center. (2017b). *Life without parole*. Retrieved from www.deathpenaltyinfo.org/life-without-parole#States

Diamond, S. S. (1993). Instructing on death: Psychologists, juries, and judges. *American Psychologist, 48*(4), 423–434.

Diamond, S. S., & Levi, J. N. (1996). Improving decisions on death by revising and testing jury instructions. *Judicature, 79*(5), 224–232.

Eisenberg, T., & Wells, M. T. (1993). Deadly confusion: Juror instructions in capital cases. *Cornell Law Review, 79*, 1–17.

Ellsworth, P. C. (1989). Are twelve heads better than one. *Law and Contemporary Problems, 52*(4), 205–224.

Ellsworth, P. C., Bukaty, R. M., Cowan, C. L., & Thompson, W. C. (1984). The death-qualified jury and the defense of insanity. *Law and Human Behavior, 8*(1–2), 81–93.

Fitzgerald, R., & Ellsworth, P. C. (1984). Due process vs. crime control: Death qualification and jury attitudes. *Law and Human Behavior, 8*(1–2), 31–51.

Foglia, W. D. (2003). They know not what they do: Unguided and misguided discretion in Pennsylvania capital cases. *Justice Quarterly, 20*(1), 187–211.

Foglia, W. D. (2012). *Racial differences among capital jurors: Empathy, trust in government, and retributive attitudes*. Presentation at the Annual Meeting of the American Society of Criminology in Chicago, IL.

Frank, J., & Applegate, B. K. (1998). Assessing juror understanding of capital-sentencing instructions. *Crime & Delinquency, 44*(3), 412–433.

Geimer, W. S., & Amsterdam, J. (1988). Why jurors vote life or death: Operative factors in ten Florida death penalty cases. *American Journal of Criminal Law, 15*(1), 1–54.

Grosso, C. M., & O'Brien, B. (2012). A stubborn legacy: The overwhelming importance of race in jury selection in 173 post-Batson North Carolina capital trials. *Iowa Law Review, 97*(5), 1531–1559.

Haney, C. (1984). On the selection of capital juries: The biasing effects of the death-qualification process. *Law and Human Behavior, 8*(1–2), 121–132.

Haney, C. (1997). Violence and the capital jury: Mechanisms of moral disengagement and the impulse to condemn to death. *Stanford Law Review, 49*(6), 1447–1486.

Haney, C., Hurtado, A., & Vega, L. (1994). "Modern" death qualification: New data on its biasing effects. *Law and Human Behavior, 18*(6), 619–633.

Haney, C., & Lynch, M. (1994). Comprehending life and death matters: A preliminary study of California's capital penalty instructions. *Law and Human Behavior, 18*(4), 411–436.

Haney, C., & Lynch, M. (1997). Clarifying life and death matters: An analysis of instructional comprehension and penalty phase closing arguments. *Law and Human Behavior, 21*(6), 575–595.

Haney, C., Sontag, L., & Costanzo, S. (1994). Deciding to take a life: Capital juries, sentencing instruction, and the jurisprudence of death. *Journal of Social Issues, 50*(2), 149–176.

Hindson, S., Potter, H., & Radelet, M. L. (2006). Race, gender, region and death sentencing in Colorado, 1980–1999. *University of Colorado Law Review, 77*(3), 549–594.

I.C. (2017) title 35 article 50. chapter 2 section 9. Retrieved from http://iga.in.gov/legislative/laws/2017/ic/titles/035/#35-50-2-9

Indiana Judges Association. (2014). *Indiana civil and criminal jury instructions.* No. 15.0440 Retrieved from www.indianajudgesassociation.org/jury_instructions.html

Levinson, J. D., Smith, R. J., & Young, D. M. (2014). Devaluing death: An empirical study of implicit racial bias on jury-eligible citizens in six death penalty states. *New York University Law Review, 89*(2), 513–581.

Luginbuhl, J. (1992). Comprehension of judges' instructions in the penalty phase of a capital trial: Focus on mitigating circumstances. *Law and Human Behavior, 16*(2), 203–218.

Lynch, M., & Haney, C. (2000). Discrimination and instructional comprehension: Guided discretion, racial bias, and the death penalty. *Law and Human Behavior, 24*(3), 337–358.

Lynch, M., & Haney, C. (2011). Mapping the racial bias of the white male capital juror: Jury composition and the "empathic divide". *Law & Society Review, 45*(1), 69–101.

Nickerson, R. S. (1998). Confirmation bias: A ubiquitous phenomenon in many guises. *Review of General Psychology, 2*(2), 175–220.

Noye, U. (2015). Blackstrikes: A study of the racially disparate use of peremptory challenges by the Caddo parish district attorney's office. *Reprieve Australia,* 1–11. Retrieved from https://blackstrikes.com/resources/Blackstrikes_Caddo_Parish_August_2015.pdf

Otto, C. W., Applegate, B. K., & Davis, R. K. (2007). Improving comprehension of capital sentencing instructions: Debunking juror misconceptions. *Crime & Delinquency, 53*(3), 502–517.

Palmer, L. J., Jr. (2001). *Encyclopedia of capital punishment in the United States.* Jefferson, NC: McFarland.

Pa.C.S. (2001) title 42 ch. 97. sec. 9711.

Pew Research Center. (2016). *Support for the death penalty lowest in more than four decades.* Retrieved from www.pewresearch.org/fact-tank/2016/09/29/support-for-death-penalty-lowest-in-more-than-four-decades/

Rozelle, S. D. (2006). The principled executioner: Capital juries' bias and the benefits of true bifurcation. *Arizona State Law Journal, 38*(3), 769–807.

Sandys, M., & Trahan, A. (2008). Life qualification, automatic death penalty voter status, and juror decision making in capital cases. *The Justice System Journal, 29*(3), 385–395.

Sandys, M., Walsh, S. M., Pruss, H., & Cunningham, D. (2014). Stacking the deck for guilt and death: The failure of death qualification to ensure impartiality. In J. R. Acker, R. M. Bohm, & C. S. Lanier (Eds.), *America's experiment with capital punishment: Reflections on the past, present, and future of the ultimate penal sanction* (3rd ed., pp. 393–423). Durham, NC: Carolina Academic Press.

Steiner, B. D., & Bowers, W. J., & Sarat, A. (1999). Folk knowledge as legal action: Death penalty judgements and the tenet of early release in a culture of mistrust and punitiveness. *Law and Society Review, 33*(2), 461–505.

Stevenson, B. A., & Friedman, R. E. (1994). Deliberate indifference: Judicial tolerance of racial bias in criminal justice. *Washington and Lee Law Review, 51*(2), 509–527.

Summers, A., Hayward, R. D., & Miller, M. K. (2010). Death qualification as systematic exclusion of jurors with certain religious and other characteristics. *Journal of Applied Social Psychology, 40*(12), 3218–3234.

Tiersma, P. M. (1995). Dictionaries and death: Do capital jurors understand mitigation? *Utah Law Review, 1995*(1), 1–49.

Unah, I. (2009). Choosing those who will die: The effect of race, gender, and law in prosecutorial decision to seek the death penalty in Durham county, North Carolina. *Michigan Journal of Race & Law, 15*(1), 135–179.

U.S. General Accounting Office. (1990). *Death penalty sentencing: Research indicates pattern of racial disparities.* Report to the subcommittees on civil and constitutional rights, house judiciary committee. Washington, DC: U.S. General Accounting Office.

Vartkessian, E. S. (2012). What one hand giveth, the other taketh away: How future dangerousness corrupts guilty verdicts and produces premature punishment decisions in capital cases. *Pace Law Review, 32*(2), 447–487.

Cases Cited

Batson v. Kentucky, 476 U.S. 79 (1986).
Boyde v. California, 494 U.S. 370 (1990).
Caldwell v. Mississippi, 472 U.S. 320 (1985).
California v. Brown, 479 U.S. 538 (1987).
Callins v. Collins, 510 U.S. 1141 (1994).
Eddings v. Oklahoma, 455 U.S. 104 (1982).
Foster v. Chatman, 578 U.S. _____ (2016).
Furman v. Georgia, 408 U.S. 238 (1972).
Glossip v. Gross, 576 U.S. _____ (2015).
Gregg v. Georgia, 428 U.S. 153 (1976).
Hurst v. Florida, 577 U.S. _____ (2016).
Irvin v. Dowd, 366 U.S. 717 (1961).
J. E. B. v. Alabama ex rel. T.B., 511 U.S. 127 (1994).
Jurek v. Texas, 428 U.S. 262 (1976).
Kansas v. Carr, 577 U.S. _____ (2016).
Lockett v. Ohio, 438 U.S. 586 (1978).
McKoy v. North Carolina, 494 U.S. 433 (1990).
Miller-El v. Dretke, 545 U.S. 231 (2005).
Mills v. Maryland, 486 U.S. 367 (1988).
Morgan v. Illinois, 504 U.S. 719 (1992).
Payne v. Tennessee, 501 U.S. 808 (1991).
Penry v. Lynaugh, 492 U.S. 302 (1989).
Proffitt v. Florida, 482 U.S. 242 (1976)
Rauf v. Delaware, 145 A.3rd 430 (2016).
Reynolds v. United States, 98 U.S. 145 (1879).
Ring v. Arizona, 536 U.S. 584 (2002).
Roberts v. Louisiana, 428 U.S. 325 (1976).
Shafer v. South Carolina, 532 U.S. 36 (2001).
Simmons v. South Carolina, 512 U.S. 154 (1994).
Skipper v. South Carolina, 476 U.S. 1 (1986).
Snyder v. Louisiana, 552 U.S. 472 (2008).
Tennard v. Dretke, 542 U.S. 274 (2004).
Turner v. Louisiana, 379 U.S. 466 (1965).
Walton v. Arizona, 497 U.S. 639 (1990).
Wainwright v. Witt, 469 U.S. 412 (1985).
Weeks v. Angelone, 528 U.S. 225 (2000).
Witherspoon v. Illinois, 391 U.S. 510, 523 (1968).
Woodson v. North Carolina, 428 U.S. 280 (1976).
Zant v. Stephens, 462 U.S. 862 (1983).

21

THE PENALTY PHASE OF THE CAPITAL MURDER TRIAL

A Social-Psychological Analysis

Mark Costanzo and Zoey Costanzo

Whether a defendant receives the most severe punishment available in the American legal system—the death penalty—is determined by a unique legal proceeding: the penalty phase of the capital murder trial. The penalty phase begins after the guilt phase ends. The defendant, who has now been found guilty of a capital crime, is tried by jury to answer a single question: should the defendant be sentenced to life in prison without the possibility of parole, or should he be sentenced to death by execution? This question cannot be answered merely by analyzing the facts of the case. Because the only question is whether or not the defendant deserves to be executed for this crime, testimony and arguments presented during the penalty phase focus on issues of morality, motivation, justice, free choice, and the psychological history of the defendant. Perhaps more than any other legal decision, the penalty phase decision relies on arguments grounded in human psychology.

A penalty phase is a rare event with many unusual features. The unusual components of this rare legal proceeding include the special selection process used to assemble a capital jury, the instructions used to guide the jury in making the life-or-death decision, the nature of evidence presented during the penalty phase, the arguments made by defenders and prosecutors at trial, and the decision making of jurors. This chapter will summarize research on the distinctive components of the penalty phase and use social-psychological theories to provide some insight into the process and content of the penalty phase trial.

The Creation of the Penalty Phase

The constitutionality of capital punishment has been challenged on the grounds that it violates the Eighth Amendment's prohibition against "cruel and unusual punishment" or the Fourteenth Amendment's guarantee of "equal protection" under the law. In the 1972 case of *Furman v. Georgia*, the Supreme Court held that because of the "uncontrolled discretion of judges or juries" the death penalty was being "wantonly and freakishly" applied. Capital punishment—as administered at the time—was ruled unconstitutional. But by 1976, the court had approved a series of reforms aimed at controlling the discretion of judges and jurors (*Gregg v. Georgia*, 1976). Perhaps the most important reform was the creation of bifurcated capital trials, where guilt is decided in the first phase and, if the defendant is found guilty, a second "penalty phase" is conducted to determine whether the person found guilty should be sentenced to death or life in prison. In states that authorize the death penalty, only "aggravated" murder or murder with "special circumstances" is eligible for the death penalty. State laws vary, but examples of capital crimes include murder for hire, murder during the commission of a robbery or rape, murder of a police officer, or kidnapping and murder. The federal crimes of espionage and treason can also result in a death sentence.

In later decisions, the Supreme Court further restricted imposition of the death penalty. The court has held that mentally retarded murderers cannot be put to death (*Atkins v. Virginia*, 2002), that only juries (not judges) can decide whether a convicted murderer should be sentenced to death (*Ring v. Arizona*, 2002), and that those who commit their crimes as juveniles cannot be sentenced to death (*Roper v. Simmons*, 2005).

Death Qualification and Its Biasing Effects on Juries

Only capital murder trials include the process of death qualification (DQ). This process occurs during jury selection. In capital cases potential jurors are asked whether they would be willing to consider imposing a sentence of death if the defendant is eventually found guilty. Until 1985, the process was based on the standard established in *Witherspoon v. Illinois* (1968). Under *Witherspoon*, prospective jurors could be excluded from capital juries if they were unwilling to impose the death penalty regardless of the facts and circumstances of the case. Later, in *Wainwright v. Witt* (1985), the legal standard was modified to exclude potential jurors whose attitudes toward the death penalty would "prevent or substantially impair" them from performing their duties as jurors in a capital case. This somewhat broader standard for excluding jurors expanded the ability of prosecutors to exclude jurors based on their attitudes toward the death penalty (Thompson, 1989). In an effort to counterbalance this rather one-sided process, most states began to allow for the exclusion of jurors who expressed the view that their support for the death penalty would prevent them from voting in favor of a life sentence. In 1992, in the case of *Morgan v. Illinois*, the Supreme Court ruled that persons who say they would automatically impose the death penalty should also be excluded from capital juries. Unfortunately, research indicates the number of people who would be unwilling to consider a sentence of LWOP is far smaller (roughly 12 times less) than the number of people who would be unwilling to consider a sentence of death (Luginbuhl & Middendorf, 1988; Miller & Hayward, 2008).

Research indicates that the process of death qualification systematically disadvantages defendants and tilts the scale toward a sentence of death. The biasing effects of death qualification are well established. One effect of death qualification is a change in the demographic composition of the jury. Because African Americans and women are significantly more likely to oppose capital punishment, they are significantly more likely to be excluded from capital jury service. African Americans are already underrepresented in most jury pools (Fukurai & Krooth, 2003), and the process of DQ reduces their numbers even further (Swafford, 2011). Democrats, low-income persons and people who oppose the death penalty on religious grounds are also more likely to be excluded (Yelderman, Miller, & Peoples, 2016).

Of course, demographic characteristics are significantly correlated with attitudes relevant to the criminal justice system. One early study found that, compared to excluded jurors, those jurors that survived the DQ process were significantly more punishment oriented, less worried about convicting the innocent, less likely to be concerned that capital punishment might be unfair to minorities, and more likely to judge penalty phase evidence as aggravating rather than mitigating (Haney, Hurtado, & Vega, 1994). A more recent series of studies by Butler and her colleagues found that death-qualified jurors are more likely to be white, middle class, politically conservative, more punitive in their orientation toward criminals, more affected by victim impact statements urging the death penalty, and more skeptical of defenses involving mental illness (Butler & Moran, 2007; Butler & Wasserman, 2006; Butler, 2007, 2008).

The skewing of demographic and attitudinal characteristics that occurs as a result of DQ, and the process of DQ itself, shape how jurors interpret and respond to evidence during the penalty phase. Although the focus of this chapter is the penalty phase, it is important to note that death-qualified juries are more likely find the defendant guilty than are non-death-qualified jurors. This "conviction-proneness" has been demonstrated in a large number of studies (Allen, Mabry, & McKelton, 1998).

There is also some research indicating that exposure to the process of DQ makes jurors more likely to vote for the death penalty and to believe that the legal system disapproves of people who are opposed to capital punishment. Discussion of a potential penalty prior to trial conveys the message that the defendant is probably guilty. Further, the qualified jurors' public statements of willingness to consider the death penalty tends to create a sense of commitment to that sentencing option (Haney, 1984; Paternoster & Brame, 2008). Later, during the penalty phase, the biases introduced by the DQ process increase the probability of a death sentence. Qualified jurors are likely to perceive the evidence presented during the penalty phase in ways that favor a sentence of death. Such jurors are more likely than excluded jurors to perceive themselves as similar to the victim, to see the defendant as being remorseless and incapable of rehabilitation, and to identify with the victim's family (who may offer victim impact statements during the penalty phase; Butler, 2008). Qualified jurors are also more likely to be receptive to aggravating circumstances that support a sentence of death and unreceptive to the mitigating circumstances that support a sentence of life (Haney, 2005; Stevenson, Bottoms, & Diamond, 2010). Those jurors who "pass" the DQ process tend to filter penalty phase evidence through beliefs and preconceptions that favor the prosecution.

Although the DQ process may be successful in excluding potential jurors who are unable to vote for death under any circumstances (and the small number of jurors who would vote for death under all circumstances), it corrupts the impartiality of the penalty decision. By systematically removing those jurors with scruples against the death penalty, the process of DQ degrades the impartiality of the capital trial.

The Structure and Content of the Penalty Phase

The jurors who hear testimony during the penalty phase have already completed the guilt phase of the trial. They have already heard all of the legally permissible evidence indicating that the defendant committed the crimes, and they have found him guilty beyond a reasonable doubt. Consequently, during the penalty phase, traditional forms of evidence proving that the defendant committed the crime (e.g., DNA, fingerprints, eyewitness identification, confessions) are no longer relevant. The only remaining question for jurors is whether the defendant deserves to die for his crimes. The content of the penalty phase—what information is provided to jurors—is determined by how the legal system frames the life-or-death decision. In most states, jurors are instructed to weigh or balance aggravating factors that support a sentence of death against mitigating factors that support a sentence of life. Unfortunately, research shows that jurors have difficulty understanding the concept of "aggravation" and have great difficulty understanding both the concept of "mitigation" and the concept of "weighing" (Costanzo, 1997). Forty years ago, in *Lockett v. Ohio* (1978), the U.S. Supreme court defined mitigation at capital sentencing expansively as including: "any aspect of a defendant's character or record, or any of the circumstances of the offense that the defendant proffered as a basis for a sentence less than death."

Just as death qualification creates a bias in favor the death penalty, the ambiguity of penalty phase instructions tends to increase the probability of a death sentence. That ambiguity appears to allow emotions and racial prejudice to influence the sentencing decision. Strong feelings of anger toward the defendant are aroused during the capital trial, and these feelings make jurors more likely to vote for death. Research shows that jurors who feel more anger toward the defendant rate aggravating circumstances as more important than jurors who feel less anger (Nunez, Schweitzer, Chai, & Myers, 2015).

Moral Disengagement Theory

The theory of moral disengagement developed by Albert Bandura (2016) provides a useful framework for understanding the motives and arguments of attorneys and jurors in the penalty phase. The theory attempts to explain how people justify and distance themselves from morally troubling behaviors. Generally, the job of prosecutors in the penalty phase is to promote moral disengagement, and the job of defenders is to prevent it.

Because the decision to send a defendant to the execution chamber may create moral distress, the mechanisms of disengagement described by Bandura are likely to be activated. There are several such mechanisms. First, there is some form of justification for the morally troubling act. In the case of the life or death decision, the justification may be that God demands a life for a life, or that execution is the only way to prevent the defendant from committing acts of violence in prison. Euphemistic language is also used to sanitize the act of sentencing someone to die. Indeed, jury instructions, with their legalistic emphasis on the vague concepts of aggravation, mitigation, and weighing serve to sanitize the act of deciding that a person should be killed for his crimes. Bandura discusses the use of "advantageous comparison," which involves comparing the morally troubling act with acts that are even more objectionable. This technique is employed when prosecutors argue that a jury's decision to execute the defendant is far more humane that what the killer did to his victims, and that modern forms of execution like lethal injections minimize the suffering of the person being killed.

Other mechanisms of disengagement involve displacing or obfuscating responsibility for the morally troubling act. Prosecutors and jurors themselves may attempt to minimize their responsibility for deciding that a defendant should be executed. During deliberations, jurors may argue that the penalty phase instructions essentially require that they choose death over life imprisonment. This argument minimizes their role in the decision. Further, because the penalty decision is a group decision, responsibility is diffused among 12 people. This spreading of responsibility across the group lessens the moral culpability of each individual juror. Finally, the mechanism of dehumanization enables jurors to shift blame for the penalty decision onto the defendant. If the defendant can be viewed as less than human, he can be more easily sentenced to death. Of course, given the horrible nature of capital crimes, the task of making the defendant seem like an animal is much easier than it is in other legal contexts.

If we look through the lens of moral disengagement theory, the task of the prosecutor during the penalty phase is to argue that the defendant is less than human, that only a sentence of death is just, and that, given the nature and heinousness of the crime, the law requires the ultimate penalty. Such arguments promote moral disengagement. In contrast, defenders must labor to prevent jurors from morally disengaging from the penalty decision. They must strive to humanize the defendant, to emphasize that the law allows for mercy, and to urge jurors to feel the full weight of personal responsibility for the penalty decision.

Although there has been no direct research on how moral disengagement affects the penalty phase, there has been an in-depth study of prison personnel who carry out the execution process (Osofsky, Bandura, & Zimbardo, 2005). Compared to prison guards who had no involvement in the process, guards who carried out executions showed substantially higher levels of moral disengagement. As they carried out executions, many found it helpful to think about the victims rather than the condemned man: "You really need to think about the victims, you have to think about what your client did to others" (p. 386). Most executioners felt that the death penalty was sanctioned by their religious beliefs, an effective deterrent, and that "the law says this and we should follow it." The study also found that the as prison personnel participated in more executions, their level of moral disengagement increased.

The Use of Psychological Expertise During the Penalty Phase

Social and clinical psychologists are often enlisted by defense teams to provide expertise during the penalty phase. These experts attempt to highlight how a defendant's environment, his formative experiences during childhood, and his cognitive and emotional state may help explain his horrifying crimes. By situating the origins of the defendant's violent behavior in his past experiences, psychological experts can expand jurors' focus beyond the crime itself. Broadly speaking, the goal of the psychological expert is to humanize the defendant and to help jurors find a reason to show compassion and spare the defendant's life. As one expert puts it,

> The range of factors that impact developmental trajectory and adult functioning are extraordinarily broad. Accordingly, a mental health expert addressing mitigation and moral culpability at capital sentencing faces the daunting task of identifying any factors that might adversely impact physical, neuropsychological, psychoeducational, personality, social/interpersonal, moral, and vocational development and capability.
>
> *(Cunningham, 2016, p. 211)*

To identify factors that might help to explain the defendant's criminal behavior or lessen his culpability, a forensic psychologist must conduct a thorough assessment of the defendant's past history as well as an assessment of his mental and emotional state. Because of the sweeping nature of such an assessment, the psychologist will typically rely on defense team investigators who have conducted interviews with important people in the defendant's life (e.g., parents, siblings, teachers, friends, coworkers). The purpose of this comprehensive psychological analysis is not to excuse or justify a murderer's actions. Instead, the purpose is to reveal those aspects of a defendant's life that may help to explain why the defendant resorted to violence and why he might be deserving of compassion (Garbarino, 2011).

Of course, the role of prosecutors in the penalty phase is to discount the importance of the defendant's history and to continually refocus the attention of jurors on the hideousness of the crime and the suffering of the victim(s). Prosecutors tend to emphasize that the defendant freely chose to kill and that any evidence offered in mitigation is far too weak to excuse or explain the evil choices freely made by the defendant (Costanzo & Peterson, 1994). Because of this prosecutorial emphasis on choice, part of the job of the defense psychological expert is contextualize the concept of choice. The expert must challenge the assumption of free, informed choice:

> Choice may be "informed" only if an individual is free from coercion and able and motivated to appreciate the consequences of an action. Unless these conditions are met, a person cannot give informed consent to do something, even if that person "chooses" to do so.
>
> *(Garbarino, 2011)*

This more nuanced conception of choice is difficult to convey to jurors. The expert might need to explain how choices are shaped by unconscious processes, how the environment restricts the number of *perceived* options, and why a particular defendant's mental state may have rendered him unable to consider alternative courses of action.

Prosecutors often portray the defendant as a psychopathic predator devoid of redeeming human qualities. In contrast, defenders must make a subtler, more complex argument that takes into account the biological, psychological, and social factors that lessen the culpability of the defendant. In addition, the defense argument must take into account both the cumulative effect of relevant risk factors (e.g., early exposure to violence and abuse, poverty) that predispose a person to criminal behavior, but also the absence of protective factors (e.g., a supportive adult caregiver, success at school) that might prevent a vulnerable person from becoming a violent criminal (Fabian, 2009; Hawkins, et al., 2000).

In cases where the defendant suffers from brain damage, serious mental illness, or very low IQ, the defense can make a simpler, more easily understood argument for mercy. For example, two major areas of the brain (the amygdala and the prefrontal cortex) are clearly implicated in free choice (Burns & Bechara, 2007). These areas of the brain interact to influence decision making and willpower. If one or both of these brain areas are clearly damaged or dysfunctional, it can be argued that the defendant did not choose his criminal behavior but, instead, was unable to control his actions. If the defendant does not suffer from brain damage or severe mental illness or mental disability, a more subtle mitigation argument is needed. For example, if the main explanatory factor is a defendant's history of abuse as a child, the prosecution is likely to argue that although child abuse is relatively common, only a tiny fraction of people who were abused as children grow up to be murderers. The response of the defense expert might be to point out that although most adults who were abused as children do not murder, those adults often display other serious problems such as substance abuse, criminal behavior, and some level of psychopathology. Further, the expert will need to explain how individual behavior is a product of a unique combination of risk factors that predispose someone to violent behavior as well as exposure to protective factors that reduce the likelihood of violent behavior. However, because no specific combination of exposure to risk and protective factors guarantees that a person will become violent or nonviolent, this complex argument is likely to be less satisfying to jurors than an argument based on brain damage or mental illness.

Defendants should undergo a thorough psychological assessment before trial, and the results of that assessment should be presented during the penalty phase (Berry & Knott, 2015). On appeal, the failure to present relevant information about a defendant's mental health or history of abuse may lead to a judgment of ineffective assistance of counsel and to a death sentence being reduced to a sentence of life in prison without parole (Chandra & Watson, 2016).

The Risk of Future Violence

One potent factor that pushes jurors toward a sentence of death is the perception that the defendant will continue to pose a risk of violence unless he is sentenced to death (Sandys, Pruss, & Walsh, 2010). In Texas and Oregon, whether or not the defendant is likely to present a continuing threat of violence is a "special issue" that the jury must consider in deciding to sentence a defendant to death (Krauss, McCabe, & McFadden, 2009). In most other jurisdictions, risk of future violence is considered as a potential aggravating factor. As a counterweight, the defense can present "positive prisoner evidence" that can be considered as a mitigating factor (*Skipper v. South Carolina*, 1986). Such evidence consists of factors indicating that the defendant will adjust positively to life in prison.

Assessing the probability of future violence is difficult and unreliable. However, in capital cases, where the only alternative to the death penalty is life in prison without parole, the research strongly indicates that capital murderers do not pose an elevated risk of violence (Cunningham, Sorensen, Vigen, & Woods, 2011; Otto & Douglas, 2010). For nearly all capital defendants who are sentenced to life, the violent behavior they exhibited outside prison does not continue once they are inside prison walls. For example, Sorensen and Cunningham (2010) examined the disciplinary records of 51,527 prison inmates and found that convicted murderers did not account for a disproportionate share of prison violence. Even characteristics that are predictive of violence outside prison (e.g., psychopathy) do not seem to be predictive of violence inside prison (Edens, Buffington-Vollum, Keilen, Roskamp, & Anthony, 2005). Perhaps the most important finding in this area is that capital juries are unable to predict future prison violence (Reidy, Sorensen, & Cunningham, 2013). Indeed, the violence predictions of capital juries are wrong about 90% of the time. Because only a small minority of capital offenders commit acts of serious violence in prison, juries vastly overpredict the likelihood that a capital defendant will be violent in prison. Although it seems intuitively obvious that someone who commits a murder in society at large will continue to be violent, prison is a vastly different environment that suppresses the violent tendencies of former murderers.

Victim and Execution Impact Statements

In *Payne v. Tennessee* (1991), the U.S. Supreme Court ruled that victim impact statements (VISs) were admissible in capital sentencing trials. The court decided it was fair to use VISs to emphasize the victim's "uniqueness as an individual human being." Part of the court's reasoning was that, although no information about victim's character or the impact of the victim's death on survivors was presented in capital trials, the defense was permitted to present information about the defendant (mental impairment, mental illness, child abuse or neglect, remorse) in the form of mitigating circumstances. The *Payne* decision was, in part, intended to rebalance a system that the court believed "unfairly weighted the scales in a capital trial" in favor of the defendant (Pitt, 2013).

Victim impact statements are made by the victim's surviving family members and friends and typically attempt to explain how the loss of a loved one damaged the lives of survivors (Mitchell, Myers, & Broszkiewicz, 2015). A VIS can be presented live, via video, or in a written document. In principle, such statements serve to inform the jury about the extensive and continuing suffering caused by the defendant's crimes. When the victim's loved ones plead for the jury to choose death, a VIS can have a powerful influence on the penalty decision (Paternoster & Deise, 2011). Some VISs not only humanize the victim but also dehumanize the defendant (e.g., by referring to the defendant as a monster or an animal). As predicted by moral disengagement theory, such dehumanization of the defendant may cause death-qualified jurors to lean toward a sentence of death (Myers & Greene, 2004).

Whether or not it is relevant or fair to allow VISs is a matter of continuing controversy. It has often been argued that VISs unfairly bias jurors toward harsher punishment for defendants. In addition, there is the issue of "victim quality." If a victim is portrayed as a valued and virtuous person by several survivors, that victim might elicit more sympathy than victims who don't have such advocates or whose lives were less virtuous. More sympathy for the victim (and greater anger toward the defendant) might translate to harsher punishment for the defendant. This difference in the perceived quality of the victims might result in unequal treatment of defendants convicted of the same crime.

Although it is probably true that most VISs urge jurors to vote for the sentence of death, not all survivors argue in favor of death. Here are a couple of examples:

> He is an evil creature, who I would condemn to many, many long years of anguish and despair. He doesn't deserve a quick, painless, humane death . . . a humane death penalty should be reserved for killers who are capable of honest remorse.
>
> He's an animal. I don't wish for him to die, I wish for him to have a long, suffering, cruel death. Hopefully terminal cancer.
>
> *(Szmania & Gracyalny, 2006, p. 238)*

The handful of studies that have examined the impact of VISs have all found that VISs shift the sentencing choice toward death. For example, Butler (2008) conducted an experimental study where participants were presented with identical capital trials except that one condition included a VIS statement while the other did not. Participants in the VIS condition were more sympathetic toward the prosecution case, more likely to feel compassion for the victim, identified more strongly with the victim, believed that the victim had endured worse treatment, and felt that the family suffered more as a result of the death. Those in the VIS condition were also more likely to sentence the defendant to death. The subjects exposed to a VIS also generally felt that this information was essential to communicate the magnitude of the crime's effect on the family, as well as essential to making a just conviction decision. Paternoster and Deise (2011) conducted an experiment using death-eligible potential jurors and a video recording of an actual penalty phase that included victim impact evidence. Participants who viewed testimony on victim impact felt greater anger toward the defendant, felt more empathy for the victim, were more likely to perceive the victim and victim's family positively, and to have unfavorable perceptions of the offender. These feelings led to a greater tendency to impose the death penalty.

Beginning in the 1990s, some courts began to allow execution impact statements (EISs) during the penalty phase (Wolff & Miller, 2009). Such statements are used to explain the severe negative impact that a death sentence would have on the family of the defendant. EISs serve as a counterweight to the perspective presented in VISs. An EIS may bolster the mitigating evidence presented during the penalty phase by including mention of defendant characteristics (e.g., mental impairment or mental illness) that may help to explain the defendant's crime. More directly, an EIS might encourage jurors to consider the possibility that a death sentence would increase the suffering of the defendant's family and friends (Wolff & Miller, 2009; Beck, Britto, & Andrews, 2007).

Just as VISs enable the families of victim's to play an expanded role in the justice system, EISs allow the families of the defendant to play an expanded role in the system. Many legal scholars argue that EISs restore some balance to the legal system by countering the highly emotional and often persuasive VISs (Thomas, 2000). Because the U.S. Supreme Court has not yet ruled on the admissibility of EISs in capital sentencing trials, the decision to allow EISs is made on a state-by-state basis.

Closing Arguments: How Attorneys Attempt to Sway Jurors

During the penalty phase, defense attorneys attempt to provide jurors with reasons why the defendant should not be executed for his crimes. Prosecuting attorneys attempt to provide jurors with reasons for sending the defendant to the execution chamber.

In the most thorough study of penalty phase closing arguments to date, Costanzo and Peterson (1994) analyzed the content of 40 penalty phase summations. They found that arguments could be grouped into seven broad categories: The attorney's feelings and judgments, the defendant's character and life history, the characteristics of the murder(s), the character and suffering of the victim and the victim's family, the obligations of the jurors, the nature of the two sentencing options, and arguments about morality and justice. The researchers explained attorney arguments using social-psychological theories of persuasion.

As expected, prosecutors and defenders offered starkly different perspectives on the defendant, the crime, and the life-or-death decision. For example, prosecutors tended to describe the defendant as uniquely deserving of the death penalty ("of all the cold-blooded murderers I have seen, heard about, read about or worked on their cases, this is the worst because it was the coldest"), while defenders argued that their case was not the kind of case that warrants a sentence of death ("cases like Charles Manson of Jeffrey Dahmer, you can all think of cases in which the horror of the acts . . . and the number of acts . . . comes down to the ultimate penalty"). Defenders spent far more time humanizing the defendant and describing how his past history—often a history of abuse and neglect—might explain or mitigate his crimes: "What John got was just about daily torture. How can you expect that he's going to come out of that situation and not be damaged in some way?" Prosecutors often countered by arguing that the defendant freely chose to commit murder ("He has made choices, that's what put him here. Don't relieve him of responsibility for the choices he has made"), and that many people have been abused but few commit murder ("his home life was terrible, yet he's the only one in that house that turns out to be a killer").

Prosecutors strive to shift jurors' attention from the past suffering or psychological impairments of the defendant to his heinous behavior. Whereas defenders focused on the destructive influences that shaped the defendant's behavior, prosecutors focused on the most salacious and disturbing details of the murder and the suffering of the victim. Here are a couple examples:

> Think about how this crime was committed. Think about the kind of person you would have to be to chop off a person's head. Think about that. Not because you are angry, not because you are in a blood frenzy, but so that you can destroy dental records.
>
> Put yourself in their shoes, into their place to know the terror and humiliation and the degradation that this man put them through before he ended their lives. . . . What mother of a dead victim should we tell that [the defendant's problems] outweigh the death of their daughter?

Closing arguments also attempted to frame the decision-making process for jurors and to characterize the two sentencing options. Defenders emphasized that a sentence of death would serve no useful purpose ("if the execution of the defendant would bring back the victim, your decision would be easy; unfortunately nothing any of us can do is going to bring back the victim"), and that a life sentence is sufficiently severe punishment ("you couldn't be lenient in this case if you wanted to be . . . the law will not allow it . . . think about spending the rest of your life in a five foot by eight foot cell with a toilet in the middle"). Prosecutors argue that only a sentence of death is morally sufficient: "it's therapeutic for those who have been wronged"; the victims "deserved to be avenged."

It is not uncommon for attorneys to make religious appeals to the jury. Miller and Bornstein (2005) have categorized the types of religious appeals found in penalty phase summations. Prosecutors generally rely on biblical quotes that support retribution, including "an eye for an eye" and "he that smiteth a man, so that he die, shall surely be put to death." Such quotes appear to provide religious authorization for the death penalty. Indeed, some prosecutors go further in their closing arguments, suggesting that the jury can be seen as an extension of God's authority. Relying on quotes such as, "whoever resists authority has opposed the ordinance of God; and they who have opposed will receive condemnation upon themselves," some prosecutors have argued that the jury is, "the tool of the Lord." Finally, prosecutors sometimes compare the character and crimes of the defendant to notorious Bible villains such as Judas, Cain, or even Satan.

In contrast, defense attorneys emphasize Bible quotes and stories that support mercy and condemn revenge (Miller & Bornstein, 2005). Such quotes include the story of Jesus intervening when a woman is about to be stoned to death, "Let whoever among you who is without sin cast the first stone." Another prominent example is the story of Jesus dying on the cross and asking God to show mercy to his tormentors ("forgive them, for they know not what they do"). Defense attorney may also argue that quotes like "do not judge, or you too will be judged" indicate that jurors should avoid playing God by deciding who should die. Going beyond the Christian Bible, defenders sometimes note that the leaders of most major religious groups have called for the abolition of capital punishment.

It would seem natural for attorneys to use their closing arguments to interpret and clarify the penalty phase instructions to jurors. Because in nearly all states jurors are instructed to weigh aggravating against mitigating factors to decide on a sentence, closing arguments might be extensively used to help jurors understand the meaning of these important technical terms. Based on the only study of this issue, summations do little to clarify instructions. Although the instructions were mentioned in 80% of summations,

> They typically were discussed in very superficial or cursory fashion, often in no more than a sentence or two. . . . Even when attorneys did comment on the weighing process, they sometimes omitted and were often oblique or confusing about the decision rule by which that process was supposed to produce a verdict."
>
> *(Haney & Lynch, 1997, p. 588)*

In addition, some factors (e.g., age of the defendant at the time of the crime) were argued to be both aggravating and mitigating.

How Jurors Decide Between Life and Death

Much of what we know about juror's use of the information presented during the penalty phase comes from the pioneering work of the Capital Jury Project (CJP) (see Chapter 20, this volume). The CJP researchers conducted in-depth posttrial interviews with 1,198 capital jurors from 14 states (Connell, 2009).

Most analyses of the CJP data set have yielded findings consistent with the results of simulation studies. A finding that consistently emerges from analyses of the CJP data set is that jurors have serious difficulty understanding and following the penalty phase jury instructions (Bentele & Bowers, 2001; Bowers, Sandys, & Steiner, 1998). Specifically, many jurors struggle with and misinterpret the meaning of aggravating and mitigating factors, and many jurors form a strong sentencing preference before the penalty phase even begins. As one juror put it,

> I don't think [an attorney] even knows what the heck this stuff is . . . and it wasn't explained to us and this was the most important thing. . . . The way this stuff is worded . . . is because that's how the law books told them they have to word it. But that wasn't told to us . . . and we're sitting here thinking that they [the court] tried to trick us.
>
> *(Barner, 2015, p. 847)*

Just as happens in the simulation studies, when instruction comprehension is poor, jurors in the CJP studies tend to vote for the death penalty (Bowers, Foglia, Ehrhard-Dietzel, & Kelly, 2010).

Another line of inquiry pursued by the CJP attempted to identify factors that predicted the sentencing preferences of individual jurors. After statistically sifting through an extensive set of potentially aggravating and mitigating factors, researchers found that one of the strongest predictors of a preference for a death sentence was a perceived lack of remorse by the defendant. Other factors that elicited a preference for death included a defendant with a history of violent crimes, child victims, and especially heinous or brutal murders (Bowers, Kelly, Kleinstuber, Vartkessian, & Sandys, 2014). As one juror from a different study put it, "there was nothing that could give him sympathy in this case because the crime itself was so awful" (Costanzo & Costanzo, 1994).

Another predictor of a death sentence is fear among jurors that the defendant will continue to be violent in the future (Bowers & Kelly, 2010). This last finding may be due the widespread belief among jurors that a sentence of life imprisonment means that someday the defendant will be released from prison on parole. Many jurors often wrongly assume that unless they vote for a death sentence, the defendant will be eligible for parole and may eventually be released from prison. In one study, only 18.4% of capital jurors believed that capital defendants sentenced to life without parole would actually spend the rest of their lives in prison (Bowers & Steiner, 1999). Here are quotes from two jurors who share this belief:

> If you give him life imprisonment, he's going to get out. We all knew that. We talked about that. . . . It's that simple. The only way I can guarantee that [he will stay in prison] is to vote the death penalty.
>
> *(Costanzo & Costanzo, 1994, p. 163)*

> Even if we vote for death, he would probably never be put to death. He was going to be on death row probably till he dies. But that was the only way to keep him in prison.
>
> *(p. 444)*

Using the CJP data, Devine and Kelly (2015) found that juror preferences for life or death prior to deliberation were strong predictors of the eventual penalty decision. Specifically, if two-thirds or more of penalty phase jurors prefer life or death as deliberations begin, that majority preference was very likely to prevail as the final verdict. This finding is consistent with research on noncapital trials (Devine, Clayton, Dunford, Seying, & Pryce, 2001).

As moral disengagement theory would suggest, jurors find ways of distancing themselves from a sentence of death. Data from the CJP indicate that, instead of claiming personal responsibility for the sentence, many jurors report that the law required that they vote for death (Bentele & Bowers, 2001). More than 80% of jurors assign primary responsibility to the defendant (49.3%) or to the law (32.8%). Only 14.4% believed that individual jurors or the jury collectively bore primary responsibility for the penalty decision (Bowers, Fleury-Steiner, & Antonio, 2003). Other researchers have found that jurors emphasized the importance of reaching consensus and tended to discuss the sentencing decision in terms of the group's interpersonal dynamics rather than in terms of individual responsibility. Jurors did not necessarily feel that they had chosen the most appropriate sentence, but they did feel that they had chosen the only possible sentence given the composition of their jury (Costanzo & Costanzo, 1994).

The abstruseness of the penalty phase instructions tends to amplify racial bias. In a high fidelity simulation study, Lynch and Haney (2009) studied the deliberations of mock juries assembled from 539 community residents. Juries watched a realistic video of a penalty trial and then received penalty phase jury instructions. The race of both the defendant and the victim were manipulated by changing the photographs and voices in the video trial. Findings revealed that juries were more likely to choose a death sentence when the defendant was black. The effect was strongest when the victim was white. If the defendant was black, the proportion of whites on the jury (especially white males) was a significant predictor of a death sentence. Other studies have found that bias against black defendants is greater for jurors who have a poor understanding of penalty phase instructions and that the use of simplified instructions written in clear language significantly reduces the bias against black jurors (Shaked-Schroer, Costanzo, & Marcus-Newhall, 2008).

Capital jurors are asked to interrupt their lives, to listen to the details of horrible crimes, and then to decide whether a defendant should be killed for his crimes. It would be surprising if this extraordinary experience did not have a lasting effect. Although research on this topic is limited, those who have looked at the after-effects of capital jury service have found evidence of negative effects, including nightmares, relationship problems, regret, depression, and physical distress (Antonio, 2008; Costanzo & Costanzo, 1994). The prevalence and duration of these problems among capital jurors is not yet known.

Conclusion

The outcome of the penalty phase—a sentence of life in prison or death by execution—is produced by an unusual and biased process. Several features of this process, including death qualification, vague jury instructions, victim impact statements, misunderstanding of mitigation, and the difficulty of humanizing the defendant, all tilt the outcome toward a sentence of death. The penalty phase is constructed to produce a judgment about the moral culpability of a defendant. But despite the best efforts of the courts, this qualitative, emotional judgment cannot be reduced to a series of calculations about the relative weights of aggravating and mitigating factors. Although ongoing tinkering with penalty phase procedures might make the process somewhat fairer, no amount of legal tinkering is likely to solve the problems inherent in the penalty phase. These problems will persist until we eliminate the need for a penalty phase by abolishing the death penalty.

References

Allen, M., Mabry, E., & McKelton, D. (1998). Impact of juror attitudes about the death penalty on juror evaluations of guilt and punishment: A meta-analysis. *Law and Human Behavior, 22,* 715–731.

Antonio, M. E. (2008). Stress and the capital jury: How male and female jurors react to serving on a murder trial. *Justice System Journal, 29,* 396–407.

Bandura, A. (2016). *Moral disengagement: How people do harm and live with themselves.* New York: Worth Publishers.

Barner, J. R. (2015). Life or death decision making: Qualitative analysis of death penalty jurors. *Qualitative Social Work, 13,* 842–858.

Beck, E., Britto, S., & Andrews, A. (2007). *In the shadow of death: Restorative justice and death row families.* New York: Oxford University Press.

Bentele, U., & Bowers, W. (2001). How jurors decide on death: Guilt is overwhelming, aggravation requires death, and mitigation is no excuse. *Brooklyn Law Review, 66,* 1011–1079.

Berry, W., & Knott, H. (2015). Ineffective counsel resulting from failure to explore history of brain injury in a capital case. *Legal Digest, 43,* 391–394.

Bowers, W. J., Fleury-Steiner, B., & Antonio, M. E. (2003). The capital sentencing decision: Guided discretion, reasoned moral judgment, or legal fiction. In J. Acker, R. M. Bohm, & C. S. Lanier (Eds.), *America's experiment with capital punishment* (2nd ed., pp. 413–468). Durham, NC: Carolina Academic Press.

Bowers, W. J., Foglia, W. D., Ehrhard-Dietzel, S., & Kelly, C. E. (2010). Jurors' failure to understand or comport with constitutional standards in capital sentencing: Strength of the evidence. *Criminal Law Bulletin, 46,* 1147–1229.

Bowers, W. J., & Kelly, C. E. (2010). *The jury vs. the juror: Individual and group influences on the death/life sentencing decision.* Presented at the Annual Meeting of the American Society of Criminology, San Francisco, CA.

Bowers, W. J., Kelly, C. E., Kleinstuber, R., Vartkessian, E., & Sandys, M. (2014). The life or death sentencing decision: It's at odds with constitutional standards, is it beyond human ability? In J. R. Acker, R. M. Bohm, & C. S. Lanier (Eds.), *America's experiment with capital punishment* (3rd ed., pp. 425–496). Durham, NC: Carolina Academic Press.

Bowers, W. J., Sandys, M., & Steiner, B. (1998). Foreclosed impartiality in capital sentencing: Jurors' predispositions, guilt-trial experiences, and premature decision making. *Cornell Law Review, 83,* 1476–1556.

Bowers, W. J., & Steiner, B. (1999). Death by default: An empirical demonstration of false and forced choices in capital sentencing. *Texas Law Review, 43,* 606–638.

Burns, K., & Bechara, A. (2007). Decision making and free will: A neuroscience perspective. *Behavioral Sciences and the Law, 25,* 153–162.

Butler, B. (2007). Death qualification and prejudice: The effect of implicit racism, sexism, and homophobia on capital defendants' right to due process. *Behavioral Sciences and the Law, 25,* 857–867.

Butler, B. (2008). The role of death qualification in venirepersons' susceptibility to victim impact statements. *Psychology, Crime & Law, 14*(2), 133–141.

Butler, B., & Moran, G. (2007). The impact of death qualification, belief in a just world, legal authoritarianism, and locus of control on venirepersons' evaluations of aggravating and mitigating circumstances in capital trials. *Behavioral Sciences and the Law, 25,* 57–68.

Butler, B., & Wasserman, A. (2006). The role of death qualification in venirepersons' attitudes toward the insanity defense. *Journal of Applied Social Psychology, 36,* 1744–1757.

Chandra, S., & Watson, C. (2016). Court overturns death sentence for failure to introduce defendant's mental health history for mitigation purposes. *Legal Digest, 44,* 263–265.

Connell, N. M. (2009). *Death by jury: Group dynamics and capital sentencing.* El Paso, TX: LFB Scholarly Publishing.

Costanzo, M. (1997). *Just revenge: Costs and consequences of the death penalty.* New York: St. Martin's Press.

Costanzo, M., & Peterson, J. (1994). Attorney persuasion in the capital penalty phase: A content analysis of closing arguments. *Journal of Social Issues, 50,* 125–147.

Costanzo, S., & Costanzo, M. (1994). Life or death decisions: An analysis of capital jury decision making under the special issues sentencing framework. *Law and Human Behavior, 18,* 151–170.

Cunningham, M. D. (2016). Forensic psychology evaluations at capital sentencing. In R. Jackson & R. Roesch (Eds.), *Learning forensic assessment research and practice* (pp. 202–228). New York: Routledge.

Cunningham, M. D., Sorensen, J. R., Vigen, M. P., & Woods, S. O. (2011). Correlates and actuarial models of assaultive prison misconduct among violence-predicted capital offenders. *Criminal Justice and Behavior, 38,* 5–25.

Devine, D. J., Clayton, L. D., Dunford, B. B., Seying, R., & Pryce, J. (2001). Jury decision making: 45 years of empirical research on deliberating groups. *Psychology, Public Policy, and Law, 7,* 622–727.

Devine, D. J., & Kelly, C. E. (2015). Life or death: An examination of jury sentencing with the capital jury project database psychology. *Public Policy, and Law, 21,* 393–406.

Edens, J. F., Buffington-Vollum, J. K., Keilen, A., Roskamp, P., & Anthony, C. (2005). Predictions of future dangerousness in capital murder trials: Is it time to "disinvent the wheel?". *Law and Human Behavior, 29,* 55–86.

Fabian, J. M. (2009). Mitigating murder at capital sentencing: An empirical and practical psycho-legal strategy. *Journal of Forensic Psychology Practice, 9*(1), 1–34. doi: 10.1080/15228930802425084

Fukurai, H., & Krooth, R. (2003). *Race in the jury box: Affirmative action in jury selection.* Albany: State University of New York Press.

Garbarino, J. (2011). Understanding criminal "choices" in context. *American Journal of Orthopsychiatry, 81,* 157–161.

Haney, C. (1984). Examining death qualification: Further analysis of the process effect. *Law and Human Behavior, 8,* 133–151.

Haney, C. (2005). *Death by design: Capital punishment as a social psychological system.* New York, NY: Oxford University Press.

Haney, C., Hurtado, A., & Vega, L. (1994). "Modern" death qualification. *Law and Human Behavior, 18,* 619–633.

Haney, C., & Lynch, M. (1997). Clarifying life and death matters: An analysis of instructional comprehension and penalty phase closing arguments. *Law and Human Behavior, 21,* 575–595.

Hawkins, J. D., Herrenkohl, T. I., Farrington, D. P., Brewer, D., Catalano, R. F., & Harachi, T. W. (2000). *Predictors of youth violence.* Washington, DC: U.S. Department of Justice.

Krauss, D. A., McCabe, J. G., & McFadden, S. (2009). Limited expertise and experts: Problems with the continued use of future dangerousness in capital sentencing. In R. F. Schopp, R. L. Weiner, B. H. Bornstein, & S. L. Willborn (Eds.), *Mental disorder and criminal law: Responsibility, punishment, and competence* (pp. 135–157). New York: Springer.

Luginbuhl, J., & Middendorf, K. (1988). Death penalty beliefs and jurors' responses to aggravating and mitigating circumstances in capital trials. *Law and Human Behavior, 12,* 263–281.

Lynch, M., & Haney, C. (2009). Capital jury deliberation: Effects on death sentencing, comprehension, and discrimination. *Law and Human Behavior, 33,* 481–496.

Miller, M. K., & Bornstein, B. (2005). Religious appeals in closing arguments: Impermissible input or benign banter. *Law and Psychology Review, 29,* 29–61.

Miller, M. K., & Hayward, R. (2008). Religious characteristics and the death penalty. *Law and Human Behavior, 32,* 113–123.

Mitchell, K., Myers, B., & Broszkiewicz, N. (2015). Good or essential? The effects of victim characteristics and family significance on sentencing judgments and perceptions of harm. *Psychiatry, Psychology and Law, 23,* 651–669.

Myers, B., Godwin, D., Latter, R., & Winstanley, S. (2004). Victim impact statements and mock juror sentencing: The impact of dehumanizing language on a death qualified sample. *American Journal of Forensic Psychology, 22,* 39–55.

Myers, B., & Greene, E. (2004). The prejudicial nature of victim impact statements: Implications for capital sentencing policy. *Psychology, Public Policy, and Law, 10,* 492–515.

Nunez, N., Schweitzer, K., Chai, C. A., & Myers, B. (2015). Negative emotions felt during trial: The effect of fear, anger, and sadness on juror decision making. *Applied Cognitive Psychology, 29,* 200–209.

Osofsky, M. J., Bandura, A., & Zimbardo, P. G. (2005). The role of moral disengagement in the execution process. *Law and Human Behavior, 29,* 371—393.

Otto, R. K., & Douglas, K. (Eds.). (2010). *Handbook of violent risk assessment.* New York: Routledge.

Paternoster, R., & Brame, R. (2008). Reassessing race disparities in Maryland capital cases. *Criminology, 46,* 971–1008.

Paternoster, R., & Deise, J. (2011). A heavy thumb on the scale: The effect of victim impact evidence on capital decision making. *Criminology, 49,* 129–161.

Pitt, D. (2013). No Payne, no gain? Revisiting victim impact statements after twenty years in effect. *Chapman Law Review, 16,* 475–499.

Reidy, T. J., Sorensen, J. R., & Cunningham, M. D. (2013). Probability of criminal acts of violence: A test of jury predictive accuracy. *Behavioral Sciences and the Law, 31,* 286–305.

Sandys, M., Pruss, H. C., & Walsh, S. M. (2010). Aggravation and mitigation: Findings and implications. *Journal of Psychiatry & Law, 37,* 189–236.

Shaked-Schroer, N., Costanzo, M., & Marcus-Newhall, A. (2008). Reducing racial bias in the penalty phase of capital trials. *Behavioral Sciences & the Law, 26,* 603–617.

Sorensen, J. R., & Cunningham, M. D. (2010). Conviction offense and prison violence: A comparative study of murderers and other offenders. *Crime & Delinquency, 56,* 103–125.

Stevenson, M. C., Bottoms, B. L., & Diamond, S. S. (2010). Jurors' discussions of a defendant's history in capital sentencing deliberations. *Psychology, Public Policy, and Law, 16,* 1–38.

Swafford, A. T. (2011). Qualified support: Death qualification, equal protection, and race. *American Journal of Criminal Law, 39,* 147–158.

Szmania, S. J., & Gracyalny, M. L. (2006). Addressing the court, the offender, and the community: A communication analysis of victim impact statements. *International Review of Victimology, 13,* 231–249.

Thomas, T. (2000). Execution impact evidence in Kentucky: It is time to return the scales to balance. *Northern Kentucky Law Review, 27*, 411–429.

Thompson, W. (1989). Death qualification after Wainwright v. Witt and Lockhart v. McCree. *Law and Human Behavior, 13*, 185–215.

Wolff, K. T., & Miller, M. K. (2009). Victim and execution impact statements: What judges should know about case law and psychological research. *Judicature, 92*, 148–157.

Yelderman, L. A., Miller, M. K., & Peoples, C. D. (2016). Capital-izing jurors: How death qualification relates to jury composition, jurors' perceptions, and trial outcomes. In B. H. Bornstein & M. K. Miller (Eds.), *Advances in psychology and law* (Vol. 2, pp. 27–54). New York: Springer.

Cases Cited

Atkins v. Virginia, 536 U.S. 304 (2002).
Furman v. Georgia, 404 U.S. 238 (1972).
Gregg v. Georgia, 428 U.S. 153 (1976).
Lockett v. Ohio, 438 U.S. 586 (1978).
Payne v. Tennessee, 501 U.S. 808 (1991).
Ring v. Arizona, 536 U.S. 584 (2002).
Roper v. Simmons, 543 U.S. 551 (2005).
Skipper v. South Carolina, 476 U.S. 1 (1986).
Wainwright v. Witt, 460 U.S. 412 (1985).
Witherspoon v. Illinois, 391 U.S. 510 (1968).

22

THE APPELLATE PROCESS IN CAPITAL CASES

Vanessa Woodward Griffin and O. Hayden Griffin, III

Introduction

In 1972, in *Furman v. Georgia*,[1] the United States Supreme Court ruled that the manner in which the death penalty was applied in the United States was unconstitutional. There was ample foreshadowing to the decision in *Furman*. The rate of executions had dwindled in the decade prior (Crocker, 2003), and no federal execution had occurred in the previous nine years. Further, there was an overabundance of challenges regarding the constitutionality of capital punishment, and support for the death penalty had waned (Golden, 2001).

The court's rationale for such a ruling was multifaceted—there was a need for evaluation of capital punishment regarding its use, methods, and procedures. Specifically, there was concern involving judges and juries' discretionary power in determining whether a defendant should be sentenced to death, resulting in what seemed to be capricious verdicts. Also among the reasons for the court's ruling was a need for rigorous review of sentencing procedures to ensure protection of the defendant, specifically, a bifurcated trial: one trial to establish guilt, another to establish the proper sentence. Most important, however, was the requisite of defendants' right to appeal.

The foundation of American jurisprudence lies within both equal protection and procedural fairness. As required by the Fifth and Fourteenth Amendments, American citizens are to receive due process of law. Due process is a judicial concept that mandates protection of individuals' rights. Specifically, the Constitution assures both substantive and procedural due process, meaning it prohibits states from depriving its individuals of their constitutional rights and guarantees a fair process in legal proceedings so that defendants' constitutional rights are protected.

While the appellate process is ostensibly embedded within due process, the right to a criminal appeal is neither a longstanding nor constitutional right.[2] In fact, the United States did not establish the right to appeal in capital cases until 1889[3] (Coleman Jr, 1983). The right to appeal in other criminal cases was introduced two years later, at which time the United States Court of Appeals was created[4] (Baker, 1985; Domecus, 1978).

Regardless of its legal history, the appeals process is a fundamental safeguard of constitutional rights. While the Constitution guarantees fairness in laws and procedural justice, it is certainly fallible—fairness does not warrant exactness. Thus, stringent review of legal and constitutional error is particularly exigent in cases involving defendants who have been sentenced to death.

The Appellate Process in Criminal Cases

Ideally, appeals provide a way to have the work of one judge verified by many (Leflar, 1976). Within the appellate process, the facts of the case and guilt or innocence of a defendant are generally immaterial—the appellate process focuses on procedural error(s) and then determines if that error(s) potentially changed the outcome of the case. If the appellate court determines that the error was consequential to the outcome, the appellate judge deems it reversible error (Vollum, Del Carmen, Frantzen, San Miguel, & Cheeseman, 2014).

Regardless of the type of case, the right to appeal is ingrained in American law—albeit not inherently constitutional law (Dalton, 1985). While appellate courts do not necessarily hear all of these cases, all people who have been convicted of a crime in the United States have the right to appeal their conviction to an appellate court.

The appellate process is contingent upon whether the case was tried in a state or federal court. If a defendant is in the federal court system, his or her appeal would be to whatever circuit court to which the state they were convicted of a crime belongs (for instance, the state of California is part of the Ninth Circuit Court of Appeals). However, as Friedman (1993) has noted, despite the growing number of federal crimes, criminal justice is still predominantly a state matter.

If a criminal defendant has been charged with a state crime, then his or her case will be appealed to one of two different types of courts. In ten states, the only appeals court is their court of last resort within the state—most often called a "supreme court" within that state. These states are mostly among the states with the smallest populations, and the numbers of appeals filed each year does not justify the creation of any intermediate appeals courts to alleviate the workload of courts of last resort. In 35 states, there are intermediate appellate courts to first hear appeals, and in five states, there are actually two intermediate appeals courts to hear appeals (Neubauer & Fradella, 2014). The American state court system stays very busy. In 2010, 103.5 million cases were filed in various state courts, and 272,975 appeals were filed in state appellate courts (LaFountain, Schauffler, Strickland, & Holt, 2012).

Types of Appeals

There are two types of appeals: appeals by right and appeals by permission. As the name implies, appeals by right are cases in which if a defendant is convicted, he or she is automatically allowed to appeal the trial court's decision. In appeals by permission, an appellate court need not do anything beyond acknowledge that the court received the appeal (Griffin, Woodward, & Sloan, 2016). Even in appeals by right, the amount of oversight or consideration an appellate court gives a case may be limited. Except in exceedingly rare cases, the purpose of an appellate court is not to review a trial transcript and determine if a jury ruled correctly. As Alschuler (1989) noted, despite the conventional wisdom among many attorneys that a criminal trial can be essentially a matter of luck or a "roll of the dice," once a jury renders a verdict, appellate courts seem to hold these decisions to a degree of reverence or sacredness that should rarely be cast aside.

Reexamination of Appeals in Capital Cases

Following the decision of *Furman v. Georgia*, the court identified a dearth of appellate protections within the death penalty process. Thus, the right to appeal became a predominant focus of capital punishment cases more so than other types of cases, considering that the final result of harmful error—death—cannot be undone.

Ostensibly, the court's invalidation of the death penalty was foreseeable. At the federal level, no one had been executed in nearly a decade; five years prior, a Senate bill had been introduced to abolish the death penalty (to no further avail) (Golden, 2001), and there had been a number of challenges to the constitutionality of the death penalty. Further, only ten years before *Furman*, the court decided that the Eighth Amendment clause on cruel and unusual punishment was to be applied to the states[5] (Klein, 2009).

In *Furman*, by a 5–4 decision, the court decided that the manner in which the death penalty was imposed was unconstitutional, as it was a violation of both the Eighth and Fourteenth Amendments (Herman, 2004), as its implementation was both arbitrary and capricious. What was particularly important about the majority decision was that it spoke to the process in which the death penalty was imposed—not necessarily the death penalty itself. Thus, within the decision, the court outlined a number of guidelines that, when followed, would ideally ensure that when the death penalty was imposed, it would pass constitutional muster. During the next four years, 35 states modified their capital punishment procedures in an effort to address both the arbitrariness and capriciousness of the death penalty. Specifically, states took one of two routes within their modified statutes: they either required fixed capital punishment (thus, the mandated sanction for certain crimes was the death penalty) or they outlined methods of "guided discretion" (Redlich et al., 1994, p. 242); specifically, they developed new rules to guide juries and judges on objectively determining which offenders were fitting of execution.

In 1976, the court reviewed five death penalty statutes cases; specifically, *Gregg v. Georgia*[6] and its accompanying cases: *Jurek v. Texas*,[7] *Proffitt v. Florida*,[8] *Roberts v. Louisiana*,[9] and *Woodson v. North Carolina*[10] (Crocker, 2003; Golden, 2001). In *Gregg*, *Proffitt*, and *Jurek*, the court ruled in favor of the states' statutes (Driggs, 2001). In *Woodson*, the court ruled that mandatory death sentences were unconstitutional. In the *Woodson* decision, Justice Stewart wrote that there was a distinction between death penalty and life imprisonment cases, citing a need for more intense judicial scrutiny in cases in which the offender had a sanction of death (Bird, 2003). Of the cases affirmed, the most notable was *Gregg* and the review of Georgia's modified statutes, which include "the bifurcation of trials into guilt and penalty phases, the application of aggravating and mitigating factors to determine just punishment, and the use of other favors permitting jury guidelines, jury discretion, and appellate review of death sentences" (Gee, 2011, p. 219).

In his opinion for the majority, Justice Brennan remarked that determining what was cruel and unusual punishment changed with the times. Borrowing from Chief Justice Warren's statement in the decision for *Trop v. Dulles*,[11] Brennan purported that there was no perpetual standard to be established; punishment must be assessed by examining the "evolving standards of decency" (Golden, 2001; Herman, 2004). The outcome of *Gregg* was the establishment of three main tests to determine the constitutionality of the death penalty. Golden (2001) described these guidelines:

> Three main tests exist, each ensuring that punishment is not excessive. First, the punishment must not involve unnecessary infliction of pain. Second, the punishment must not be grossly out of proportion to the crime. Third, the punishment must not be imposed under passion or prejudice. One way to ensure that the courts apply each of these tests is to require review of the sentence (p. 453).

Process of Appealing in Capital Cases

Super Due Process and Automatic Appeals

The decisions in both *Furman* and *Gregg* established the rights of capital offenders within both the trial and appeals process. While many of these rights are applicable to *all* offenders, those cases resulting in a death sentence were viewed as more exigent and in need of assiduous judicial review. Thus, offenders in capital cases would receive what is known as "super" due process (Radin, 1979; Zazzali,

2008), which essentially requires an additional level of judicial scrutiny. Theoretically, this line of thinking was prudent, considering that harmful error found after the fact would not be reversible. Further, it holds the courts accountable by reexamining procedure as well as "constitutional principles with the intensity and the depth that that has been occasioned by capital murder prosecutions" (Zazzali, p. 98).

One of the ways in which this is accomplished is through a direct and automatic appeal. This is reflected in all death penalty granting states, with the exception of South Carolina (Snell, 2005). Generally, the appeal is filed to the state court of last resort to review what occurred during the trial; however, two states, Alabama and Tennessee, require that the direct appeal is to the intermediate appeals court (Latzer & Cauthen, 2007). During the automatic appeal process, prosecutors and defense attorneys will file legal briefs with the applicable court, and in some cases, those attorneys will have oral arguments before the applicable court. In these proceedings, the court can affirm a defendant's conviction and/or sentence, reverse the conviction, or reverse the sentence of death (Mays & Fidelie, 2017). Within the states, the automatic appeal can generally not be waived, with some exception. For instance, Indiana and Kentucky allow the defendant to waive his/her right to an appeal. Further, in Mississippi, the issue has never been considered formally, and in Wyoming, there is no precedent or statute that prohibits a waiver. Lastly, some states distinguish between waivers for types of appeals. Some require automatic appeal only for sentencing, not trial error (South Dakota and Tennessee), or only allow for waiver of trial, not sentencing error (Virginia) (Snell, 2005).

While 37 of the 38 states that authorize the death penalty have automatic appeals, the federal system does not. The Federal Death Penalty Act, a part of the Violent Crime Control and Law Enforcement Act of 1994 (FDPA), expanded the number of capital crimes and also outlined the appellate process for federal death penalty cases (Connor, 2010). In fact, prior to its passing, there was no established procedure regarding the death penalty in federal courts (Herman, 2004). According to the FDPA, in a federal death penalty case the defendant must manually file an appeal. Further, s/he can later waive that appeal. In fact, the federal system only requires that the court of appeals hear the case if there is actual evidence of a constitutional violation that would constitute harmful error. When challenged, the court ruled that this adhered to the requirement of meaningful appellate review as established in *Gregg*. In fact, the constitutionality of the FDPA's lacking automatic appeal was not fully addressed until six years after its passing, in *United States v. Hammer*[12] (Golden, 2001; Herman, 2004).

The idea of voluntariness within waiving appeals is a bit of an oddity (Brisman, 2008); however, some offenders simply wish to avoid further harm to their victim's family and friends and are reluctant to engage in the "uncertainty of death row confinement" (Johnson, 1981, p. 575). For instance, at different stages, both Timothy McVeigh and Aileen Wuornos stated that they preferred execution to other forms of punishment (Brisman, 2008). Some have questioned why there are differing policies on voluntariness of waiver, considering that when one waives his or her appeals, s/he is saving the state both time and money. Yet, the appeal is not solely a review of an individual's case—it is to provide continual judicial scrutiny to the trial and sentencing procedure, to ensure that capital punishment is considered in context of societal changes, as capital punishment is to be examined within *evolving standards of decency*. In *Pulley v. Harris*,[13] the court argued for meaningful appellate review, as it "ensures that the death sentence will not be imposed arbitrarily or capriciously" (Golden, 2001). In *Commonwealth v. McKenna*,[14] the Pennsylvania Supreme Court opined that the intention of a waiver was never for defendants to determine their own sentence and that there is "societal interest in ensuring that death sentences be imposed fairly" (Golden, p. 455). Moreover, Justice Marshall[15] argued that permitting a defendant in a capital case to waive his or her appeal is simply state-assisted suicide (Brisman, 2008; Urofsky, 1984). While this has been an issue of debate, the court has not ruled as to whether volunteering to waive one's appeal/s is a constitutional right (Dama, 2006).

Traditional Appeals

If a defendant who has been sentenced to death is not successful in his or her direct appeal to a court of last resort, they will then have the opportunity to file a postconviction appeal (Latzer & Cauthen, 2007), which conforms to the traditional appellate process. Since trial issues were already considered in the automatic appeal, a subsequent appeal through the state courts should only focus upon procedural or legal claims that were not considered during the first appeal. To appeal a trial verdict, a defendant (or more commonly—his or her defense counsel) must file a notice of appeal with the trial court. If denied, then they must appeal to a higher court, which may be the intermediate appeals court or the state's court of last resort (Latzer & Cauthen, 2007).

One crucial aspect of appeals is that they must be filed in a timely manner. If the statute of limitations for an appeal has lapsed, a state appellate court will decline to hear the appeal. In addition to the notice of appeal, a defendant has to include a complete transcript of all court proceedings in which an error is alleged, in addition to a legal brief that must describe what these alleged errors are and why these errors warrant some corrective action(s) by an appellate court. Furthermore, the brief must include any legal precedent supporting such a decision. In many instances, an appeals court will do nothing beyond read the materials and affirm a trial court's conviction. If oral arguments are heard, the appellate court may come to the same conclusion. If errors are found that are not deemed harmless, an appellate court will order a new trial. Only in an exceedingly miniscule number of cases will an appeals court reverse a conviction without ordering additional legal proceedings by a lower court (Champion, Hartley, & Rabe, 2012). Such would almost be unimaginable for a case in which a defendant received a sentence of death. Additionally, although the right to counsel attaches to direct appeals, the court has not ruled the same for postconviction review; however, all capital punishment cases have written statutes to provide council for indigent defendants during the state's postconviction review (Bohm, 2014; Tabak, 2003).

Habeas Corpus Appeals

After appellants have exhausted their appeals in state courts, they are not out of legal options for challenging either their conviction or sentence. Within the Constitution and separate from the Bill of Rights is the right to file a *habeas corpus* petition. *Habeas corpus* is a Latin phrase with a literal translation of "you have the body." When an appellant who files a *habeas corpus* petition, which is to be filed with the federal courts, s/he is essentially arguing that his/her imprisonment is unconstitutional and thus is requesting that the state explain why it is detaining the appellant. Unlike a typical appeal, *habeas corpus* petitions are not limited to alleged legal errors during criminal proceedings, but if a federal court chooses, it can reconsider any portion of the criminal proceedings anew. Such a process may seem radical, but it was included by the framers of the Constitution as an added protection for due process (Williamson, 1973). This process was not designed by the framers but instead was an integral part of the common law. The great legal theorist Sir William Blackstone referred to *habeas corpus* as "the great writ." (Clinton, 1977).

For approximately the first one-hundred years, the United States legal system did not mirror its present day procedures, as common law systems are more informal. Thus, in the past, a *habeas corpus* petition was more often used to assert basic rights. However, as various states began to codify common law principles into evidentiary law, the necessity of *habeas corpus* petitions began to wane. That changed in 1867 with the passage of the Habeas Corpus Act. This law allowed the federal courts to review the convictions of prisoners who were convicted in state courts. Initially, the federal courts only reviewed whether a particular state court had the proper jurisdiction of a case. In time, however, federal courts began to greatly expand their scope of review and would even review cases using a de novo standard. One of the reasons some federal courts were willing to engage in such extensive reviews was that it would be a full year before the passage of the Fourteenth Amendment and roughly 80 years before the Supreme Court would begin to impose the selective incorporation doctrine that would hold that the states needed to guarantee their citizens the protections of the Bill of Rights (Clinton, 1977). Indeed, *habeas corpus* motions filed by prisoners would be instrumental in the due process revolution that occurred during the 1960s, which led to the great expansion of constitutional rights for defendants in state courts (Hoffman, 1989).

While *habeas corpus* petitions were certainly instrumental in Americans having increased access to their constitutional rights, some people have been concerned with the *habeas corpus* process. A common complaint is that multiple petitions will clog up the court system and waste time. Additionally, as former Supreme Court Associate Justice Sandra Day O'Connor (1981) would write while she was a judge for the Arizona Court of Appeals, habeas corpus petitions inevitably meddled in the business of state courts and the federal review of state court decisions drastically increased the amount of time required to litigate criminal cases. Indeed, during the due process revolution, Congress, in 1966, applied the abuse of the writ doctrine to federal *habeas corpus* rules so that an appellant can only file one single petition unless the appellant could allege new information that was unavailable to the appellant at the time he or she initially filed a first *habeas corpus* petition (Doyle, 2006). However, should a habeas petition be denied for technical reasons, that did not bar the appellant from resubmitting the same petition[16] (Alpert, 2011; Vollum et al., 2014).

As noted in *McCleskey v. Zant*,[17] the court established the abuse of writ doctrine (Redlich et al., 1994), which requires that a novel claim cannot be filed—the appellant must solely focus on the claims made within the state courts. An appellant could have reasonably known about that evidence at the time of the filing of the first petition. An additional requirement of *habeas* proceedings is that even once an appellant has successfully demonstrated constitutional error, the burden of proof remains on the appellant to show that there was harmful, not harmless, error (Redlich et al., 1994).

Habeas appeals are first heard in a United States District Court. Depending on the outcome, the appellant may wish to continue his/her appeals. If permitted by the U.S. District Court or Court of Appeals, the appellant can then appeal to the Court of Appeals; should his or her appeal be denied in the Court of Appeals, the appellant can petition for a writ of certiorari from the Supreme Court. If denied, the appellant has exhausted all his or her appeals (Vollum et al., 2014; Wells, 1989).

Policies and Restrictions Within the Appellate Process

Prisoners Litigation Reform Act

Considering the wide latitude of *habeas corpus* proceedings, it is questionable why prisoners in a state prison would bother filing appeals in state court if they could potentially receive better protections in federal court. After 1996—state inmates lost this ability. Spawned by the belief that bored prison and jail inmates were needlessly filing frivolous lawsuits that wasted the time of the court system, in 1995, Congress passed and then President Bill Clinton signed the Prisoners Litigation Reform Act (PLRA). Not only did the act seek to limit the number of lawsuits, but the act was also passed because the federal courts had taken over several state prison systems (in some cases for years) and ordered multiple expenditures that many people within state governments believed were not only costly but unwarranted. In a similar vein to Congress' rule changes in 1966, PLRA made it so that no state prisoner could file a *habeas corpus* petition until he or she had exhausted all claims in the prison grievance system and state courts. As Schlanger (2015) noted, the law seemed to have the desired effect of those who sought to clear court dockets. From 1996 to 2012, inmate lawsuits decreased by 60%.

Antiterrorism and Effective Death Penalty Act of 1996

In the same year that PLRA took effect, Congress passed and then President Bill Clinton signed the Antiterrorism and Effective Death Penalty Act of 1996 (AEDPA). The act was passed in the wake of several terrorist attacks that occurred during that time period, and among the primary legislative purposes was to provide federal prosecutors with the jurisdiction to prosecute alleged terrorists who committed crimes against the United States in which the crimes originated outside of U.S. borders (McGarvey, 1998). Further, the court applied the act in *Cooey v. Strickland*,[18] stating that an additional purpose of the policy was to "restore and maintain the proper balance between state criminal adjudications and federal collateral proceedings" (*Cooey*, as cited in Alpert, 2011). While the title of the legislation would seem to be targeted at terrorism, the legislation had several rules that directly targeted *habeas corpus* petitions (Goodwin, 2013). The first targeted change was an attempt to end de novo review of state court decisions. According to the legislation, a writ of habeas corpus should not be granted unless a state court acted either "contrary to" or represented "an unreasonable application" of federal law (Steinman, 2001). In *Williams v. Taylor*,[19] the Supreme Court interpreted these new regulations by creating a two-prong test to determine if state court decisions should receive review by the federal courts. The court ruled that for a *habeas corpus* petition to receive federal review a state court decision had to either rule contrarily to a previous Supreme Court ruling or a state court opinion unreasonably applied Supreme Court precedent. Furthermore, AEDPA established a one-year statute of limitations for the filing of habeas corpus petitions. That one-year time period begins after an appellant has exhausted his or her state legal remedies. The only exceptions to this are if the delay in filing was due to the state or due to the discovery of pertinent evidence not in the year limitation. Also reiterated by AEDPA was that a second *habeas corpus* petition could not be filed unless the Supreme Court makes a new retroactive ruling that is relevant to an appellant's case. If an appellant meets these criteria, the second petition can only be heard by an appellate court panel, and the decision of that panel cannot be reviewed by the Supreme Court (Zheng, 2002).

The AEDPA has placed more restrictions on procedures of habeas appeals than any other legislation (Vollum et al., 2014). There has been concern regarding how AEDPA impedes constitutional protections afforded to death row inmates. This limitation has certainly caused hindrance in certain cases. For example, in *Broom v. Strickland*,[20] Broom became the first survivor of a failed execution by lethal injection, after spending two hours being prodded by a needle. Ironically, Broom had previously filed a petition arguing against Ohio's method of lethal injection. Yet, because it was filed past the year limit, his case was never heard. Further, in the post-AEDPA case of *Cullen v. Pinholster*,[21] the court ruled that new evidence generally can have no impact on the federal court's review of a state's decision. According to Marceau (2012), it holds states' sovereignty at a higher standard than the Fourteenth Amendment. There is also the question of how AEDPA conforms to the *evolving standard of decency* clause cited in *Gregg*. However, in 1998, in *Penry v. Lynaugh*,[22] the court cited a "contemporary standards of decency" analysis, that, according to Oldenkamp (2007), "avoids Top's subjective factors and instead regards the aggregate legal or formal position of all state and federal execution statutes as the *sine qua non* of standards of decency" (p. 965). However, the court referred to "evolving standards of decency" once again within *Atkins v. Virginia*[23] and *Roper v. Simmons*[24] (Bird, 2003). In Atkins, the return to evolving standards did not clarify the court's role in defining evolving standards of decency; however, in *Roper*, "a rare exception to *Penry* analysis, [the court] has been chastised for its return to international law considerations and judicial discretion in noting substantial shifts in society" (Oldenkamp, p. 965).

Mixed Petitions and the AEDPA

Independent of AEDPA, in *Rose v. Lundy*,[25] the court ruled that mixed petitions to the court would result in an automatic dismissal. Mixed petitions are those that include appeals that have been exhausted as well as those that have not. Marceau (2012) purported that it was not the individual policies of

AEDPA and mixed petition dismissal that were so problematic—it was the combination of two: the requirement of federal courts to dismiss those petitions containing any claim that had not been exhausted by the state courts and the one-year limitation to file a habeas appeal. After AEDPA was passed, the court reevaluated the mixed petition ruling and affirmed it, purporting that filing a mixed petition could result in a dismissal that ran over the one-year limit (Vollum et al., 2014). Marceau contended that this would vastly diminish the number of petitions heard within the federal courts.

The Rule of Five and the Rule of Four

Governed by its own set of rules, the Supreme Court requires that four Justices must decide to grant a writ of certiorari. Conversely, in order to stay an execution, five of the nine justices must vote in favor of the stay (Freedman, 2015; Lax, 2003). In certain cases, these antithetical polices have collided, resulting in distressing outcomes.

The rule of four has been general knowledge for almost a century and was first cited during hearings for the Judiciary Act in an effort to assuage concern regarding judicial power of case review (Revesz & Karlan, 1988). The rule of four is itself problematic, considering that the majority could dismiss the grant after it has been heard, which would "undermine the whole philosophy of the 'rule of four'" (Bourguignon, 1979, p. 287).

The rule of five refers to the number of justices who must vote to stay an execution. Thus, there have been cases in which four justices vote to grant a writ of certiorari, and only those same four vote to stay the execution. Unless a justice changes his or her vote to create a "courtesy five" vote, then a case may be on the docket for an already executed appellant (Freedman, 2015).

Section 1983 Lawsuits

As previously mentioned, AEDPA prohibited appellants from filing a second habeas appeal. Two cases that exemplified these consequences were *Nelson v. Campbell*[26] and *Hill v. McDonough.*[27] Both cases challenged the constitutionality of lethal injection, arguing it constituted cruel and unusual punishment. However, prior to filing this petition, both appellants had already filed habeas petitions; thus, their second petitions were dismissed (Alpert, 2011; Vollum et al., 2014). Prior to these cases, petitions regarding method of execution were seen by the court predominantly as habeas challenges. However, this changed within these two cases, where the court decided that §1983 "is an appropriate vehicle for bringing method-of-execution challenges" (Alpert, 2011, p. 873). Section 1983, part of the Civil Rights Act of 1871, provides appellants to petition on the grounds of a violation of their civil rights. §1983 has been most popular for cases regarding the constitutionality of lethal injection; however, in 2008, the court upheld the constitutionality of the three-drug combination for lethal injection in *Baze v. Rees,*[28] making it difficult to challenge the constitutionality of the procedure of an execution involving lethal injection (Gee, 2011). In addition to methods of execution, §1983 has also been deemed an appropriate avenue to petition for the testing of DNA to challenge one's conviction (Freedman, 2015). §1983 is less restrictive than habeas appeals, as it does not have a statute of limitations but instead, is based upon the statute of limitations for personal injury within the applicable state (Marceau, 2012).

Protections Created by the Courts

Many people have decried so-called "judicial activism" whereby the courts make rulings that have the effect of law that is deemed contrary to legislative intent. American law often gives the courts such opportunities. Phrases such as "due process" are inherently vague and naturally subject to various interpretations. For instance, the "right to privacy" as established in *Griswold v. Connecticut*[29] later gave way to the trimester evaluation criteria of *Roe v. Wade*[30] through which the courts are supposed to analyze the various restrictions that states frequently make on abortion. Given that the courts have essentially ruled that death row inmates deserve "super due process," it is little wonder that not only have the courts have consistently reviewed death verdicts, but the court has also created rules through which various death penalty statutes and regulations are evaluated.

In addition to the procedural protections established by the Supreme Court in *Furman* and *Gregg*, which the court created to comply with due process, the Supreme Court has created many additional safeguards that might not come from every person's reading of the Constitution. In *Coker v. Georgia*,[31] the court ruled that the imposition of the death penalty for the crime of rape was disproportionate to the offense. In *Beck v. Alabama*,[32] the court ruled that a jury was to be allowed to consider a lesser punishment than the death penalty. To the court, giving a jury a choice of death or acquittal seemed like almost no choice at all. In *Ring v. Arizona*,[33] the court ruled that a jury, not a judge, should be the decider of whether a convicted defendant should receive the death penalty. In *Roper v. Simmons*,[34] the Supreme Court ruled that juveniles under the age of 18 could not receive the death penalty. In *Kennedy v. Louisiana*,[35] the court struck down a law which allowed for the death penalty for the rape of children under the age of 12. Clearly, this list of cases are only a select handful of the constitutional questions that the Supreme Court has considered involving capital punishment litigation, but it illustrates that the Supreme Court has not been afraid to strike down laws that Supreme Court justices believe violate notions of due process or evolving standards of decency—two completely subjective concepts. For instance, in *Kennedy v. Louisiana*, Justice Kennedy, who wrote the majority opinion, essentially did a census of the states and found only six states had such a law that allowed for the death penalty for those defendants found guilty of child rape. Thus, since there were so few states with the law, Justice Kennedy believed that this supported the notion that there was a societal consensus that such a punishment was not representative of evolving standards of decency. With this ruling, the court has essentially created an environment in which the court can strike a law (or laws) down as unconstitutional before a consensus or a movement is allowed to ever take place—not that such a thing would necessarily have ever occurred.

The appellate process in capital cases tends to be excessively lengthy. For instance, in their evaluation of 14 states' direct appeals process, Latzer and Cauthen (2007) found that the time from filing to completion of the direct appeal was almost three years (966 days). Virginia had the lowest median time of 295 days, while Kentucky had the highest: 1,388 days. In one extreme case in California, Uelmen (2009) wrote that in *People v. Burgener*,[36] the direct appeals process had been going on for almost 30 years.

> Burgener was sentenced to death in 1981 for a robbery murder committed in 1980. At the time, he was thirty years old. By the time of this opinion's writing, Burgener was fifty-eight years old, and his direct appeals had not yet been concluded. As the court noted, this was the fourth published opinion on appeal, —and it may not be the last. . . . Thus, after twenty-eight years, the direct appeal has yet to be determined. His confinement on death row for forty years will have cost the State of California $3,680,000 more than if he had been confined pursuant to a sentence of life without parole.

The exorbitant time is attributable to a number of factors, much of which is ingrained within the policies of "super" due process. For instance, the bifurcated trial certainly slows the process, and the use of a jury in sentencing increases the likelihood of appeals, with one study showing that the majority of reversals were attributable to harmful error during sentencing (Latzer & Cauthen, 2007).

In addition to a long, enduring process, the likelihood that a conviction and the sentence will be affirmed is high. For instance, in Florida from 1991–2000, 92% of the 343 direct appeals heard by the Supreme Court had their convictions affirmed, and 61% had their death sentence affirmed. Much of the remaining 39% relief was short-lived.

While the death penalty is a primary focus of the criminal justice system, it is imposed rather rarely. In fact, in 2010, only 390 cases heard by state courts involved appeals of death sentences (LaFountain et al., 2012). Moreover, Blume and Eisenberg (1998) found that in Alabama, only 3 of every 100 murders resulted in an affirmed penalty of death.

Conclusion

No area of American law has undergone such a dramatic transformation as much as capital punishment litigation The evolving appellate process has radically changed American jurisprudence in both added procedures in court systems and added constitutional protections for defendants. In earlier times in America (and perhaps still true of some other countries), once an individual was found guilty and sentenced to death, the execution took place shortly thereafter—sometimes on the same day as the sentence was issued. In present-day society, such focus on death row inmates' rights in the appellate process have resulted in such a complex and convoluted system of rules and regulations, which ironically, in some cases, has resulted in diminished rights of offenders, including some of whom have been lingering on death row decades after their initial sentence was imposed. Furthermore, in no area of law has the Supreme Court had such a dramatic impact, whereby not only have multiple statutes been struck down, but the court has used the concepts of due process and evolving standards of decency to widely mandate how the death penalty is imposed within the United States. Although different states and the federal government have passed many laws affecting the imposition of the death penalty in America, the Supreme Court holds a formidable position in this process as well.

Notes

1 *Furman v. Georgia*, 408 U.S. 238 (1972).
2 *McKane v. Durston*, 153 U.S. 684 (1894); *Carroll v. United States*, 354 US 394 (1957).
3 Act of February 6, 1889, ch. 113, 25 Stat. 655.
4 March 3, 1891, ch. 517, § 5; 26 Stat. 826, 827–28.
5 *Robinson v. California*, 370 US 660 (1962).
6 *Gregg v. Georgia*, 428 U.S. 153 (1976).
7 *Jurek v. Texas*, 428 U.S. 262 (1976).
8 *Proffitt v. Florida*, 428 U.S. 242 (1976).
9 *Roberts v. Louisiana*, 428 U.S. 325 (1976).
10 *Woodson and Waxton v. North Carolina*, 428 U.S. 28 (1976).
11 *Trop v. Dulles*, 356 U.S. 86 (1958).
12 *United States v. Hammer*, 121 F. Supp. 2d 794 (2000).
13 *Pulley v. Harris*, 465 U.S. 37 (1984).
14 *Commonwealth v. McKenna*, 383 A.2d 174, 181 (Pa. 1978).
15 *Lenhard v. Wolff*, 444 U.S. 807 (1979).
16 *Stewart v. Martinez-Villareal*, 523 U.S. 637 (1998).
17 *McCleskey v. Zant*, 499 U.S. 467 (1991).
18 *Cooey v. Strickland*, 479 F.3d 412 (2007).
19 *Williams v. Taylor*, 529 US 362 (2000).
20 *Broom v. Strickland*, 579 F.3d 553 (2009).
21 *Cullen v. Pinholster*, 131 S.Ct. 1388 (2011).
22 *Penry v. Lynaugh*, 492 US 302 (1989).
23 *Atkins v. Virginia*, 536 U.S. 304 (2002).
24 *Roper v. Simmons*, 543 U.S. 551 (2005).
25 *Rose v. Lundy*, 102 S. Ct. 1198 (1982).
26 *Nelson v. Campbell*, 541 U.S. 637 (2004).
27 *Hill v. McDonough*, 126 S. Ct. 1189 (2006).
28 *Baze v. Rees*, 553 U. S. 35 (2008).
29 *Griswold v. Connecticut*, 381 U.S. 479 (1965).
30 *Roe v. Wade*, 410 U.S. 113 (1973).

31 *Coker v. Georgia*, 433 U.S. 584 (1977).
32 *Beck v. Alabama*, 447 U.S. 625 (1980).
33 *Ring v. Arizona*, 536 U.S. 584 (2002).
34 *Roper v. Simmons*, 543 U.S. 551 (2005).
35 *Kennedy v. Louisiana*, 554 U.S. 407 (2008).
36 *People v. Burgener*, 46 Cal. 4th 231 (Cal. 2009).

References

Alpert, T. (2011). Blind dates: When should the statute of limitations begin to run on a method-of-execution challenge? *Duke Law Journal, 60*(4), 865–918.

Alschuler, A. W. (1989). The Supreme Court and the jury: Voir dire, peremptory challenges, and the review of jury verdicts. *The University of Chicago Law Review, 56*(1), 153–233.

Baker, T. E. (1985). Compendium of proposals to reform the United States Court of Appeals. *University Florida Law Review, 37*, 225–295.

Bird, D. G. (2003). Life on the line: Pondering the fate of a substantive due process challenge to the death penalty. *American Criminal Law Review, 40*, 1329.

Blume, J., & Eisenberg, T. (1998). Judicial politics, death penalty appeals, and case selection: An empirical study. *Southern California Law Review, 72*, 465–503.

Bohm, R. M. (2014). *Deathquest*. New York: Taylor & Francis.

Bourguignon, H. J. (1979). The second Mr. Justice Harlan: His principles of judicial decision making. *The Supreme Court Review, 1979*, 251–328.

Brisman, A. (2008). Docile bodies or rebellious spirits: Issues of time and power in the waiver and withdrawal of death penalty appeals. *Valparaiso University Law Review, 43*, 459–512.

Champion, D. J., Hartley, R. D., & Rabe, G. A. (2012). *Criminal courts: Structure, process, and issues* (3rd ed.). Boston: Pearson.

Clinton, R. N. (1977). Rule 9 of the federal habeas corpus rules: A case study on the need for reform of the rules enabling acts. *Iowa Law Review, 63*, 15–84.

Coleman Jr, W. T. (1983). Supreme Court of the United States: Managing its caseload to achieve its constitutional purposes. *Fordham Law Review, 52*, 1–36.

Connor, E. M. (2010). The undermining influence of the federal death penalty on capital policymaking and criminal justice administration in the states. *The Journal of Criminal Law and Criminology, 100*(1), 149–212.

Crocker, P. L. (2003). Not to decide is to decide: The U.S. Supreme Court's thirty-year struggle with one case about competency to waive death penalty appeals. *Wayne Law Review, 49*, 885–938.

Dalton, H. L. (1985). Taking the right to appeal (more or less) seriously. *The Yale Law Journal, 62*, 62–107.

Dama, K. M. (2006). Redefining a final act: The fourteenth amendment and states' obligation to prevent death row inmates from volunteering to be put to death. *University Pennsylvania Journal of Constitutional Law, 9*, 1083–1103.

Domecus, K. L. (1978). Congressional prerogatives, the constitution and a national court of appeals. *Hastings Constitutional Law Quarterly, 5*, 715–765.

Doyle, C. (2006). *Federal habeas corpus: A brief legal overview*. Washington, DC: Congressional Research Service.

Driggs, K. (2001). Regulating the five steps to death: A study of death penalty direct appeals in the florida Supreme Court, 1991–2000. *Thomas Law Review, 14*, 759.

Freedman, E. M. (2015). Idea: No execution if four justices object. *Hofstra Law Review, 43*, 639–666.

Friedman, L. M. (1993). *Crime and punishment in American history*. New York: Basic Books.

Gee, H. (2011). Eighth amendment challenges after Baze v. Rees: Lethal injection, civil rights lawsuits, and the death penalty. *Boston College Third World Law Journal, 31*(2), 217–244.

Golden, S. L. (2001). Constitutionality of the federal death penalty act: Is the lack of mandatory appeal really meaningful appeal. *Temple Law Review, 74*, 429.

Goodwin, D. (2013). An appealing choice: An analysis of and a proposal for certificates of appealability in "procedural" habeas appeals. *New York University Annual Survey of American Law, 68*(4), 791–842.

Griffin, O. H., Woodward, V. H., & Sloan, J. J. (2016). *The money and politics of criminal justice policy*. Durham, NC: Carolina Academic Press.

Herman, J. (2004). Death denies due process: Evaluating due process challenges to the federal death penalty act. *DePaul Law Review, 53*, 1777–1895.

Hoffman, J. L. (1989). The Supreme Court's new vision of federal habeas corpus for state prisoners. *The Supreme Court Review, 1989*, 165–193.

Johnson, K. L. (1981). Death row right to die—suicide or intimate decision? *Southern California Law Review, 54*, 575–631.

Klein, R. (2009). Twentieth annual Supreme Court review: An analysis of the death penalty jurisprudence of the October 2007 Supreme Court term. *Touro Law Review, 25*, 625–677.

LaFountain, R. C., Schauffler, R. Y., Strickland, S. M., & Holt, K. A. (2012). *Examining the work of state courts: An analysis of 2010 state court caseloads.* Washington, DC: National Center for State Courts.

Latzer, B. P. D., & Cauthen, J. N. G. P. D. (2007). *Justice delayed? Time consumption in capital appeals: A multistate study.* Retrieved from http://articles.westga.edu:2048/login?url=http://search.ebscohost.com/login.aspx?direct=true&db=ncj&AN=SM239209&site=eds-live&scope=site

Lax, J. R. (2003). Certiorari and compliance in the judicial hierarchy discretion, reputation and the rule of four. *Journal of Theoretical Politics, 15*(1), 61–86.

Leflar, R. A. (1976). *Internal operating procedures of appellate courts.* Chicago: American Bar Foundation.

Marceau, J. F. (2012). Challenging the habeas process rather than the result. *Washington & Lee Law Review, 69*(1), 85–206.

Mays, L. G., & Fidelie, L. W. (2017). *American courts and the judicial process* (2nd ed.). New York: Oxford University Press.

McGarvey, S. M. (1998). Missed opportuinty—the affirmation of the death penalty in the AEDPA: Extradition scenarios. *Journal of Legislation, 24*, 99–110.

Neubauer, D. W., & Fradella, H. F. (2014). *America's courts and the criminal justice system.* Belmont, CA: Sage.

O'Connor, S. D. (1981). Trends in the relationship between the federal and state courts from the perspective of a state court judge. *William & Mary Law Review, 22*(4), 801–819.

Oldenkamp, D. R. (2007). Civil rights in the execution chamber: Why death row inmates' section 1983 claims demand reassessment of legitimate penological objectives. *Valparaiso University Review, 42*, 955–1015.

Radin, M. J. (1979). Cruel punishment and respect for persons: Super due process for death. *Southern California Law Review, 53*, 1143.

Redlich, N., Coleman, Jr., J. E., Waglini, S. S., Preate Jr., E., Stevenson, B., Hentoff, N., . . . & Tabak, R. J. (1994). Politics and the death penalty: Can rational discourse and due process survive the perceived political pressure? *Fordham Urban Law Journal, 21*(2), 239–279.

Revesz, R. L., & Karlan, P. S. (1988). Nonmajority rules and the Supreme Court. *University of Pennsylvania Law Review, 136*(4), 1067–1133.

Schlanger, M. (2015). Trends in prisoner litigation, as the PLRA enters adulthood. *UC Irvine Law Review, 5*, 153–178.

Snell, T. L. (2005). *Bureau of justice statistics bulletin: "Capital punishment 2003".* Primary Source. Washington, DC: United States, CQ Press. Retrieved from http://articles.westga.edu:2048/login?url=http://search.ebscohost.com/login.aspx?direct=true&db=edspac&AN=hsdc04p.249.11110.722409&site=eds-live&scope=site

Steinman, A. N. (2001). Reconceptualizing federal habeas corpus for state prisoners: How should AEDPA's Standard of Review operate after *Williams v. Taylor. Wisconsin Law Review*, 1493, 1496-1539.

Tabak, R. J. (2003). The egregiously unfair implementation of capital punishment in the united states: "Super due process" or super lack of due process? *Proceedings of the American Philosophical Society, 147*(1) 13–23.

Uelmen, G. F. (2009). Death penalty appeals and habeas proceedings: The California experience. *Marqette Law Review, 93*, 495–514.

Urofsky, M. I. (1984). A right to die: Termination of appeal for condemned prisoners. *The Journal of Criminal Law and Criminology, 75*(3), 553–582.

Vollum, S., Del Carmen, R. V., Frantzen, D., San Miguel, C., & Cheeseman, K. (2014). *The death penalty: Constitutional issues, commentaries, and case briefs.* Abingdon: Routledge.

Wells, D. (1989). Federal habeas corpus and the death penalty: A need for a return to the principles of Furman. *The Journal of Criminal Law and Criminology, 80*(2), 427–490.

Williamson, R. A. (1973). Federal habeas corpus: Limitations on successive applications from the same prisoner. *William & Mary Law Review, 15*, 265–285.

Zazzali, H. J. R. (2008). The death penalty on appeal: Constitutionality, equality, and proportionality review. *Seton Hall Legislative Journal, 33*, 95–97.

Zheng, L. (2002). Actual innocence as a gateway through the statute-of-limitations bar on the filing of federal habeas corpus petitions. *California Law Review, 90*(6), 2101–2141.

23

CLEMENCY

Failsafe or Fantasy?

Cathleen Burnett

> The pardon process, of late, seems to have been drained of its moral force. Pardons have become infrequent. A people confident in its laws and institutions should not be ashamed of mercy.
> —statement by Supreme Court Justice Kennedy (Moylan & Carter, 2009, p. 89)

Introduction

The clemency appeal is the last hope for the condemned in the death penalty process. It is a petition that is generally made when the condemned has exhausted all other judicial appeals, after having been denied in the courts. Facing execution, the prisoner requests clemency, also known as commutation, of the death sentence. Granting clemency is an executive function and is a very broad power with little statutory limitation, thus enabling the decision maker complete discretion to consider anything in making a determination. A grant of clemency can be a stay of execution (which halts the execution timing, usually to permit additional consideration of some issue) or a reduced sentence (usually to life without parole) or a pardon (which has the effect of an exoneration). There is no appeal beyond this decision, and the decider is not required to give reasons for his or her determination. The courts have consistently upheld this authority as discretionary and unreviewable (Korengold, Noteboom, & Gurwitch, 1996, p. 350). This unfettered executive function means that clemency is not part of the judicial system per se.

Sarah Cooper and Daniel Gough (2014, pp. 58–73) provide a concise history of the evolution of the clemency power from ancient Egypt and continuing through the early colonial days of this nation, when the framers drew from their British common law experience to develop executive clemency within the federal and state constitutional rubrics for the separation of powers. They observe that the clemency power was most typically used for political expediency purposes as an act of mercy, given to those rightfully convicted of criminal wrongdoing (Cooper & Gough, p. 72). A grant of executive clemency could be useful to keep peace and political allegiance by blunting the harshness of criminal sentencing, famously advocated by Alexander Hamilton: "the ability to exercise clemency would ensure that citizens are treated fairly, as a rigid system of justice 'would wear a countenance too sanguinary and cruel,'" (Cooper & Gough, p. 64). In fact, "the early federal clemency power was most frequently used to mitigate the effects of punishing popular rebellions" (Cooper & Gough, p. 65). Then, in the beginning of the twentieth century, as the rehabilitative theory of justice gained favor, it was a "trend towards merciful punishment that originally transformed the clemency power from a political tool to a familiar feature of the criminal justice system" (Cooper & Gough, p. 71). Clemency could be more commonly used to benefit the reformed offender. In addition, executive clemency can also serve as a check on the integrity of the judiciary, since the executive is free to consider unlimited factors that may have been missed or rejected by the judicial system in determining guilt and/or punishment. This purpose of clemency has been identified as "justice-enhancing" (Kobil, 2003, p. 225), that is, correcting a wrongful conviction, one that is undeserved. Whether the grant of clemency is justice-enhancing or simply mercy awarded by an act of grace to a guilty person, a grant of clemency is never guaranteed nor required.

All 31 states with the death penalty have a clemency process, although there are several different models that states created to provide executive clemency (*Herrera v. Collins*, 1993, 506 U.S. 414; Strach, 1999, p. 892; Acker & Lanier, 2000, pp. 216–220; Ridolfi & Gordon, 2009, pp. 34–40; Cooper & Gough, 2014, p. 73; Giannini, 2015, pp. 107–110). The most common form of executive clemency is when the power is reserved to the governor alone. Governors are given exclusive authority in 20 states (Alabama, Arkansas, California, Colorado, Indiana, Kansas, Kentucky, Mississippi, Missouri, Montana, New Hampshire, North Carolina, Ohio, Oregon, South Carolina, South Dakota, Tennessee, Virginia, Washington, and Wyoming). Governors in seven states (Arizona, Florida, Idaho, Louisiana, Oklahoma, Pennsylvania, and Texas) have the power to commute a death sentence if and only if a board of pardons recommends clemency, but they are not required to follow the recommendation. A pardons board or similar agency makes the clemency decision in the remaining four states (Georgia, Nebraska, Nevada, and Utah), although governors generally have some role in determining the composition of those boards and in some instances serve on them (Acker & Lanier, 2000, pp. 216–220 and "States with and without the death penalty," 2017).

Sarah Cooper and Daniel Gough (2014, p. 109) have reviewed the state structures that provide for executive clemency and give a description of some of the procedures that operate in the states.

> State practices vary widely in how pardons are administered. For example, in a majority of states, even those in which the governor has the final authority to issue a pardon, some sort of review board oversees the investigation and data collection for pardon applications. State pardon hearing procedures also vary across the nation, including full board hearings, ex parte review use of the Federal Rules of Evidence, and partial due process rights for the applicant. Finally a majority of states require that victims receive notice of a pardon application.

These procedures, however do not illuminate *how* decision making occurs in these various states. Some research sheds light on executive clemency deliberations within states (for example: in California (Moylan & Carter, 2009; Brown and Adler, 1989); in Georgia (Clayton, 2013; Marlowe & Davis-Correia, 2013); in Illinois (Sarat, 2005a); in Missouri (Burnett, 2002); in New York (Freilich & Rivera, 1999; Acker, Harmon, & Rivera, 2010); in Texas (Woods, 2001; Sigler, 2007); and in Virginia (Crawford, 2012). Although these state-specific studies give a glimpse into the decision-making process, there is generally an extraordinary lack of transparency in all state clemency deliberations, hindering the public's understanding. In fact, secrecy is one of the included features in many state procedures (Burnett, p. 163). Other barriers to transparency such as no requirement to publish a statement giving reasons for the clemency decision and lack of record-keeping (Cooper & Gough, pp. 74–81, Korengold et al., 1996, p. 351) are common and seem designed to protect the decision maker from media and public scrutiny. As a result, there is more that is unknown about specific state administrations than is known even when individual cases may be highly publicized.

Clemency Trends in Death Penalty Cases

As of this writing, there have been 9,001 executions (U.S.A. executions by date, 2017; Number of executions since, 1976, 2017) and 1,398 grants of clemency since 1900. Austin Sarat (2005a) provided the complete documentation of 1,343 commutations of capital cases from 1900 through 2004. The Death Penalty Information Center reports that since 1976 there have been 282 capital cases receiving clemency (Clemency, 2017). Taking into account of the overlap in years, the total number of grants of clemency since 1900 is 1,398.

Scholars consistently agree that grants of clemency in capital cases were much more common before *Furman v. Georgia* (1972) than after *Furman*. According to Palacios (1996, p. 347) "(t)he heyday of commutations was the early and mid-1940s, during which twenty to twenty-five percent of death penalties were commuted." In contrast, clemencies have dramatically decreased in the post-*Furman* period, even as executions increased (Kobil, 2003, p. 223; Gershowitz, 2001, p. 675). Clemencies have "plummeted" (Barkow, 2008); are "virtually extinct" (Heise, 2015); and are a 'rare event' (Garvey, 2004, p. 1320). Documentation for these trends has been the subject of several studies.

Adam Ortiz (2002, p. 4) calculated the clemency rate in capital cases between 1992 and 2002 by creating a ratio of clemencies to executions by state. He reported that the national average in 2002 was 6.14%, or 1 clemency per 16 executions.

> Nine states have ratios above the national average: Illinois (8.33 percent), Florida (11.76 percent), Georgia (17.24 percent), North Carolina (23.81 percent), Montana (50 percent), Maryland (66.67 percent), Idaho (100 percent), Ohio (200 percent), and New Mexico (500 percent). However, twenty-three states have ratios below that national ratio. Texas has one of the lowest ratios in the United States, with 0.37 percent, or one clemency per 272 executions; Oklahoma's ratio is 2 percent, with one clemency per fifty executions; and Missouri's is 3.51 percent, with one clemency per twenty-eight executions. Sixteen of the twenty-three states with lower ratios have a ratio of 0 percent.

Michael Heise (2003, p. 309) has reviewed clemencies in capital cases from 1973–1999, finding that

> before 1985, the number of successful clemency petitions was slightly more than three times greater than the number of executions (105 to 32). After 1984, however, the ratio reversed: the number of executions (566) was seven times larger than the number of removals through clemency (73).

Austin Sarat and Nasser Hussain (2004, p. 1310) examined executive clemencies granted in the 1990s:

> During the 1990s, from one to three death row inmates were granted clemency every year in the entire nation—compared to approximately sixty to eighty executions each year. This is a dramatic shift from several decades ago, when governors granted clemency in 20% to 25% of the death penalty cases they reviewed. In Florida, one of the pillars of the 'death belt,' governors commuted 23% of death sentences between 1924 and 1966, yet no Florida death penalty sentences were commuted in the 1990s.

John Blume and Lindsey Vann (2016, p. 201) report on South Carolina that "(n)o other state has executed so many inmates in the modern era (post-*Furman*) without a single commutation." These numbers expose the current picture that executive clemency in death penalty cases is no longer *frequently* granted for reasons of innocence, or for any other reasons.

Despite this consensus in the direction of clemency grants, the explanations for these striking trends are diverse and more than likely encompass a combination of both specific circumstances with more general systemic legal trends. Individually, some governors may simply refuse to consider *any* clemency, for whatever reason. For example, Governor Frank Keating of Oklahoma said many times that he would not grant clemency for murderers (Dinsmore, 2002, p. 1845). Some governors defer to the courts' decisions, using the standard of whether or not the petitioner had "full and fair access to the courts" (Gershowitz, 2001, p. 677) before denying clemency. This yardstick is a narrow approach that does not take advantage of the executive's unfettered authority to consider anything in clemency decision making and is likely a means of avoiding responsibility and potential political fallout.

In considering systemic explanations, researchers posit that the declining trend in grants of executive clemency can be understood by (1) the societal shift from rehabilitation to retribution as the dominant theory for punishment, (2) the politicization of crime control policies, and (3) the enhanced judicial protections against convicting the innocent derived from the Fourth, Fifth, and Sixth Constitutional Amendments (Rapaport, 2003, pp. 364–365). In addition, James Acker et al. (2010) maintain that changing capital litigation expectations may also contribute to the declining trend in clemencies. Specifically, they suggest that the rejection of mandatory death sentences in *Woodson v. North Carolina* (428 U.S. 280, 1976) and the increasing use of mitigating factors in sentencing required in *Gregg v. Georgia* (428 U.S. 153, 1976) and *Wiggins v. Smith* (539 U.S. 510, 2003) has decreased the 'need' for clemency.

Political Influences on Executive Clemency

Since the late 1960s, the increasing political attention that crime and the death penalty receive in this 'tough on crime' era likely causes governors to be more reluctant to grant clemencies in order to avoid the appearance of being soft on crime. The concomitant rise of the victims' rights movement (Giannini, 2015, p. 112), which insists offenders receive their just punishment, also increases resistance to grants of mercy that reduce deserved punishment. In such an environment, administrations that grant clemency petitions run the risk of appearing to discount the suffering of victims (Sarat, 2005a, p. 121) as they are granting mercy to the condemned, actions that, in most situations, would generate negative publicity and public opinion. Referring to the presidential powers, Samuel Morison's statement (2005, p. 105) can apply equally to state executive clemency decisions: "Executive clemency is an inherently political act."

However, there is some disagreement concerning the *impact* of political pressures on the decision makers. A few authors minimize the political influence. In 1996, Michael Korengold, Todd Noteboom, and Sara Gurwitch recognized that while there might be some political consequence related to clemency decision making, there is no evidence that granting clemency is "political suicide." This conclusion was based primarily on the authors' assumption that voters are not single-issue voters. Confirming this judgment, a 2002 report published by the Criminal Justice Section of the American Bar Association revealed that "governors have not suffered any measurable political consequences for granting clemency to death row inmates" (Ortiz, 2002, p. 1). Because this research covered only a ten-year (1992–2002) period, there are other reports that contradict the generalizability of this conclusion.

The overwhelming body of research supports the impact of politics and political pressures on the granting of death row clemencies (Moylan & Carter, 2009, pp. 94–95). Taking a longer scrutiny than Adam Ortiz (2002), Mary Margaret Giannini (2015, p. 109) offers examples of governors who suffered negative political repercussions from granting clemency to death row prisoners. For example, former Ohio Governor Michael DiSalle partially attributed his 1962 reelection loss to his death sentence commutation of several individuals. Former California Governor Pat Brown also believed he lost his reelection bid to Ronald Reagan because of the appearance of indecision regarding a death row prisoner (Brown & Adler, 1989, p. 52). Elizabeth Rapaport (2003, p. 369) recounts another case when Governor Brown, who was personally opposed to the death penalty, was faced with blatant political pressures from legislators.

> He (Governor Brown) was presented with a clemency petition for capital prisoner Richard Lindsey, a brain damaged man who pleaded guilty to the murder of a child. Governor Brown was disposed to grant the petition; however, he was informed that the legislator possessing the swing vote on a bill giving farm laborers a living wage would vote against the bill if Governor Brown commuted Lindsey's death sentence. Governor Brown was fully committed to the bill. He allowed the execution to take place, and the farm labor legislation passed in due course. Brown reports that he has never made peace with his decision.

As evidenced in the narrative about Governor Brown, the role of political influence is typically hidden behind closed doors. Sister Helen Prejean (1993, p. 171) exposed how a board recommendation can protect a governor from responsibility for clemency decisions. Her account is about the Louisiana Pardon Board chairman, who told her he was conflicted many times about the morality of decision making being sacrificed to loyalty to the governor. He described the way such a shield for the governor is institutionally arranged.

> When we left the hearing and went behind closed doors to decide Baldwin's fate, I just couldn't convince myself that the man was really guilty and deserved to die, and right there from the room where we were meeting I called the governor's office. His chief legal counsel came to the phone and when I told him about the case—I was upset, I was crying—I said that if your job was to dispense mercy, that this seemed as clear a case for mercy that I had yet seen, but he told me that I know the governor did not like to be confronted with these cases and wanted us to handle it. . . . "Why do you think we appointed you? This is why you're chair of this committee. If you can't hack it, we'll just have to replace you with someone who can." He wasn't saying this in a mean or nasty way, he was just reminding me of the loyalty required of me when I took the job.

Taking responsibility for clemency decisions can be risky, whether the decider is a governor or a board. Because of the perceived or real risks to political careers, Austin Sarat (2008, p. 188) observed that "[t]oday governors reserve their clemency power largely for cases where there is indisputable proof that someone has been erroneously convicted and no other remedy is available." By the same token, governors are not likely to lose votes by permitting executions to take place. Jeffrey Kubik and John Moran (2003) found that states are approximately 25% more likely to conduct executions in gubernatorial election years than in other years, suggesting that governors tap into the support of public opinion for the death penalty in order to gain votes.

In contrast to those governors proceeding with executions, Figure 1 lists governors morally opposed to the death penalty who granted mass commutations. Sensitive to potential negative political consequences, these governors, no longer seeking political office, intentionally waited until the end of their term and took the opportunity to make blanket commutations clearing their state's death row (except for Ohio Governor Celeste).

Governor Celeste selected the eight for commutation based upon their unusual facts and life histories; four were women, leaving 101 inmates on death row (Radelet & Zsembik, 1993, p. 298). Only two of Governor Celeste's clemencies would be considered justice-enhancing, given because either guilt was doubtful or for equity reasons. Notice that Illinois Governor Ryan pardoned four persons for reasons of justice, while the other 167 blanket commutations to life without parole would be considered acts of mercy rather than decisions made on the basis of the merits of the individual cases. Significantly, Governor Ryan wrote a lengthy justification for his actions, couching his decisions in terms of both retributive theory by claiming the legal system is broken and of victims' rights (In Ryan's Words—I Must Act, 2017; Sarat, 2004, 2005a, 2005b, 2008). He accurately anticipated considerable criticism for his actions.

Punishment Theories Justifying the Role of Clemency

Criticisms of blanket commutations or any clemencies granted as a matter of grace (Markel, 2004, p. 416) come from the retributivist perspective, which maintains that promoting individual responsibility and accountability are the only purposes for punishment (Harris & Redmond, 2007, p. 2). Retributivist punishment theory assumes that punishment is imposed only to the extent that it is deserved, and therefore executive clemency is needed only to correct judicial errors (Markel, 2004; Kobil, 2012; Giannini, 2015), only appropriate as a corrective for wrongful convictions and/or

Table 23.1 Death Row Mass Commutations Since 1900

Year	State	Governor	Number of Commutations	Circumstances
2015	Maryland	O'Malley	4	All after repeal bill became law
2011	Illinois	Quinn	15	All before signing repeal bill
2007	New Jersey	Corzine	8	All before signing repeal bill
2003	Illinois	Ryan	171	All including 4 pardons at the end of his term
1991	Ohio	Celeste	8	Selected 8 on way out of office
1986	New Mexico	Anaya	5	All at the end of his term
1970	Arkansas	Rockefeller	15	All on way out of office
1965	Tennessee	Clement	5	All after repeal bill failed by one vote
1964	Oregon	Hatfield	3	After the state repealed the death penalty
1963–65	Massachusetts	Peabody	nd	All, refused to sign death warrants
1957–59	Oregon	Holmes	3	During his term, had blanket policy
1911–15	Oklahoma	Cruce	12	Refused to sign any death warrants during his term

Sources: Clemency (2017) and Sarat (2005a)

punishment when there are doubts about innocence, questions of the proportionality of the sentence to the crime, or questions of culpability (Clayton, 2013, p. 756). However, limiting executive clemency to situations in which the prisoner's conviction and death sentence is flawed or in some way in violation of the legal process essentially makes clemency an instrumental part of the judicial process. Such a role is not the traditional view of clemency as an act of grace, where broad discretion to consider the widest possible range of factors and information is given to the executive (Dinsmore, 2002, p. 1842; Harris & Redmond, 2007, p. 2; Dailo, 2014, p. 429).

As an act of grace (or mercy), executive clemency is defended by two groups of theories. Rehabilitation or redemptive theory justifies granting clemency as an act of mercy for the individual who is indeed guilty but who may be the focus of humanitarian sympathy (Dailo, 2014, p. 255; Ridolfi & Gordon, 2009; Clayton, 2013). The second set of theories that supports executive clemency as an act of grace are utilitarian. Within this perspective, grounds for clemency would be those that benefit the community, serve the "public good" (Clayton, p. 758) or public welfare (Dailo, p. 255) or serve a purpose of atonement, that is, preserving the possibility that victims can reconcile with the perpetrators with the goal of restoring community (Garvey, 2004). Sarah Cooper and Daniel Gough's (2014, p. 72) contention that the primary function for clemency is political expediency also fits within this utilitarian perspective.

Reasons Given for Executive Clemency

In most instances, the executive does not issue a statement of reasons for or against granting clemency. When clemency is granted, sometimes statements are provided as support for these decisions, as Governor Ryan provided when he cleared the Illinois death row. However, there is no consensus among states that any particular reason automatically triggers a clemency award. Michael Radelet and Barbara Zsembik (1993) examine the reasons given for clemency grants from 1973 to 1992. They classify the reasons as either judicial expediency (that is, saving the time and money of going through a new sentencing proceeding) or humanitarian. It could be argued that the judicial expediency cases (59%) were clemencies based on justice concerns grounded in the retributive rationale, because of recognized legal flaws in the cases. The remaining humanitarian clemency cases (41%) were split almost evenly (52%/48%) between reasons of mercy (mercy, mental problems, and other) and justice (guilt doubtful and equity), respectively. Other reasons that have been publicly given for granting clemency requests have been mostly in the category of mercy: appellate dissents indicate uncertainty, age, rehabilitation, veteran status, victim families' rejection of death penalty, or a request by Pope John Paul II (Burnett, 2002, p. 158). Given that the reasons that are published are not at all consistent across the states or even within states, the national picture of the clemency process might best be described as capricious.

Empirical Studies: Who Gets Executive Clemency?

Believing that the diminishment of executive clemencies in modern times is in part due to the influence of politics, it is logical to posit that the structure for decision making might make a difference in outcomes. If the decision maker is one person, there is nowhere for that person to hide from the responsibility and accountability for granting clemencies. Such exposure would likely depress the issuance of clemencies for prisoners condemned to death. Earlier empirical research either does not account for differences in structure of decision making or supports this hypothesis generally for issuing pardons (Pridemore, 2000; Heise, 2003; Argys & Mocan, 2004; Giannini, 2015, pp. 109–110). However, with more data available, recent empirical studies find no link between models of decision makers and commutations (Heise, 2013; Heise, 2015). Using data gathered by the Bureau of Justice Statistics on every person sentenced to death from 1973 through 2010, Michael Heise (2015) evaluated the impact of the defendant's characteristics, of political factors, and of structural factors to assess the likelihood that commutation would be granted. Of the defendant's characteristics, sex, race, and education showed positive relationships to commutations. Women and African Americans on death row were more likely to receive clemency. Those less educated were more likely to receive clemency. The political factors produced mixed results, with Democratic governors more likely than Republican governors to grant clemency and older governors more inclined toward clemency; however, election cycles were not a significant influence. Of the structural factors, the models for decision making did not perform differently, but a regional effect was shown, with Southern states more likely to deny clemency. Finally, if the clemency petition came up after 1984, it was less likely to receive clemency. Post-1984, having prior felonies did not have any significant relationship to the outcome.

The empirical research does not include data about the actual reasons for the outcomes. Michael Heise (2015) and John Kraemer (2008) do include a legal variable, prior felonies, to assess. Both found no relationship of prior felonies to the outcome. John Kraemer raised the retributive concern that commutations were more related to personal characteristics and nonlegal factors than to criminal culpability. Commutations appear to be acts of grace, not subject to appeal, even as they are increasingly rare.

Court Decisions and Clemency

After the United States Supreme Court reinstated the death penalty in 1976 (*Gregg v. Georgia*), it wasn't until 1993 that the court gave any attention to the executive clemency process as it relates to the death penalty process. In *Herrera v. Collins* the court relied on executive clemency as a justification for rejecting Herrera's innocence claim.

Herrera v. Collins (506 U.S. 390)

Herrera was convicted of capital murder and sentenced to death in Texas in January 1982. Ten years after his conviction, Herrera urged in a second federal habeas petition that he was "actually innocent" of the murder for which he was sentenced to death. He presented new evidence that the jury had not heard. Justice Rehnquist wrote the majority opinion in which the court not only rejected Herrera's request to be granted a District Court evidentiary hearing on the new evidence, but the court acted as a fact finder and directly rejected his new evidence, thereby ending his judicial process. In siding with the Court of Appeals in rejecting Mr. Herrera's petition and to offset the criticism that their decision would contravene "a principle of fundamental fairness 'rooted in the traditions and conscience of our people,'" the court (pp. 411–412) stated:

> This is not to say, however, that petitioner is left without a forum to raise his actual innocence claim. For under Texas law, petitioner may file a request for executive clemency. . . . Clemency is deeply rooted in our Anglo-American tradition of law, and is *the* (emphasis added) historic remedy for preventing miscarriages of justice where judicial process has been exhausted.

Notice that the court described clemency as *the* remedy for preventing wrongful convictions (p. 412). Later in the opinion, the court also describes a pardon as both an act of grace (p. 413), and as "the failsafe in our criminal justice system" (p. 415). Justice Rehnquist stated that there are many constitutional provisions to ensure against the risk of convicting an innocent person, and even as mistakes are likely to be made (which the dissent recognized), there is always the appeal to executive clemency that provides the "failsafe" in our criminal justice system. Interestingly, the court does not investigate the concept of pardon as an act of grace. Had they done so, the court would have had to observe that a pardon is both discretionary and unreliable as a failsafe. Instead, to support their contention that clemency is the failsafe, the court cited a 1932 study (Borchard) in which 47 out of 65 cases received clemency when it was determined that individuals had been wrongfully convicted of crimes. Then the court cited a 1992 study (Radelet, Bedau, & Putnam) to support the assertion that "clemency has been exercised *frequently* in capital cases in which demonstrations of 'actual innocence' have been made" (p. 415). With these two studies for documentation, the court stated that "history shows that the traditional remedy for claims of innocence based on new evidence, discovered too late in the day to file a new trial motion, has been executive clemency" (p. 416). But the research studies that the court cites conclude with proposals for reform of the legal system that created these fatal mistakes. Actually, the efficacy of executive clemency as the failsafe for miscarriages of justice is questioned, even contradicted, by the Radelet, Bedau, and Putnam study (1992), which makes the case that at least 23 innocents have been executed, despite the possibility of executive clemency considerations. The court, however, did not evaluate the efficacy of executive clemency as a failsafe for correcting wrongful convictions and ignored the fundamentally discretionary and politically sensitive nature of executive clemency as an act of grace. They declared executive clemency to be the failsafe without considering the inherent contradiction that it is capricious and not at all reliable.

In dissent, Justice Blackmun highlighted the uncertainty that characterizes executive clemency as a possibility, not a failsafe. He agreed with the majority that a pardon is an act of grace. But he disagreed with its role as a failsafe. Fundamentally, Justice Blackmun argued (p. 440), the

> vindication of constitutional rights guaranteed by the Constitution has never been made to turn on the unreviewable discretion of an executive official or administrative tribunal. . . . If the exercise of a legal right turns on "an act of grace," then we no longer live under a government of laws.

In popular culture, the term *failsafe* implies that a safety net exists such that no wrongfully convicted person, indeed no innocent person, will be executed because the clemency process will act if the courts don't. And yet it is clear that states have differing mechanisms for dealing with clemency. Governors give various reasons, but governors do not use the same criteria to reach their decisions, nor do they agree upon a set of standard reasons that warrant clemency grants. Thus one governor might grant clemency in a particular case, but another governor would not. Such variation is the definition of arbitrariness.

Herrera v. Collins is one of a long line of cases narrowing the court's review of innocence claims (Burnett, 2010). To do this, the court has developed a pinched definition of innocence (Burnett, 2010), one that permits the public to believe that a fair review is being done while disregarding the public sense of innocence. The court has limited the standard for relief for actual innocence claims from "clear and convincing" to "no reasonable juror would find proof of guilt beyond a reasonable doubt" to, in Mr. Herrera's case, "truly persuasive demonstration of actual innocence" (Burnett, p. 32). These restrictive legal standards combined with legislative limitations memorialized in the passage in 1996 of the Anti-Terrorism and Effective Death Penalty Act (AEDPA) sacrifice review on the merits of capital cases so as to reach procedural finality of the case. The AEDPA added stringent time limitations for filing federal habeas corpus petitions, such that serious reversible errors could go undetected (Clayton, 2013). Thus, the importance of executive clemency became truly a life or death matter, even though it was never conceived to be an integral part of the legal system (Cooper & Gough, 2014). The heightened need for a failsafe only increased the pressure on executive clemency as "the only possible relief for some inmates who have failed to file a federal habeas petition within the statute of limitations" (Ridolfi & Gordon, 2009, p. 33).

Even as the retributive rationale for executive clemency gains prominence in criminal justice practices, that does not mean that governors will accept this role to be a failsafe. That said, there certainly are no guidelines for governors (or boards) to rationally assist in weighing any new or mitigating evidence they might consider in a clemency request. Austin Sarat (2008, pp. 188–189) observes that

> governors are reluctant to substitute their judgment for those of state legislators and courts, and, in death cases, to use clemency much at all. . . . As a result, Chief Justice Rehnquist's description of clemency as a "failsafe" in the killing state may do more to help legitimate judicial dismantling of various procedural protections than to point toward an efficacious device for correcting law's failures in the killing state.

If clemency is a failsafe, then it becomes part of ensuring the legal system works as it should. If it is part of the judicial process, one would expect due process to be a feature of this decision making. Mary Margaret Giannini (2015, p. 110) says it well: "Using the pardon power as a means to ensure fairness in our criminal justice system suggests that the practice should be mandatory, subject to articulated reasons by the grantor, and reviewable by the courts." Five years after the *Herrera* decision, the Supreme Court took up the question of what due process could be expected in clemency decisions.

Ohio Adult Parole Authority v. Woodard (523 U.S. 272, 1998)

Woodard was sentenced to death for aggravated murder, and after his appeals were exhausted, he was notified that a mandatory clemency hearing had been scheduled for him and that he was eligible for a voluntary interview with one or more Ohio Adult Parole Authority members. Under Ohio law, however, he could not receive immunity for any incriminating statements he might make at the voluntary interview. Also, his request that his lawyer be allowed to participate in the hearing was denied. The court of appeals held that Woodard had failed to establish a life or liberty interest protected by due process arising out of the clemency proceeding itself. His argument taken to the Supreme Court invoked the Fifth Amendment's due process clause to apply to the state's clemency procedure when the life of the person is at stake. In an 8–1 decision, the Supreme Court held that Ohio's clemency procedures did not violate due process; however, the majority was not able to agree as to the extent of due process protections that should attach to the clemency proceedings. Justice Rehnquist wrote the opinion of the court giving the judgment, to which the other seven justices agreed; however, Justice O'Connor wrote a concurring opinion joined by three others that articulated the expectation for a "minimal life interest" claimed by the death row prisoner. With Justice Stevens writing in his dissent for due process, a majority of five justices could open the door to minimal due process for the condemned in clemency appeals.

Justice Rehnquist first affirmed that "pardon and commutation decisions have not traditionally been the business of courts; as such, they are rarely, if ever, appropriate subjects for judicial review" (p. 276). Compounding the hands-off approach to executive clemency, Part II of Rehnquist's opinion does not use the term *failsafe* at all. He states that

> [a] death row inmate's petition for clemency is also a "unilateral hope." The defendant in effect accepts the finality of the death sentence for purposes of adjudication, and appeals for clemency as a matter of grace (p. 282). . . . Clemency proceedings are not intended primarily to enhance the reliability of the trial process (p. 284) and are not an integral part of the . . . system for finally adjudicating the guilt or innocence of a defendant. . . . Respondent is already under a sentence of death, determined to have been lawfully imposed. If clemency is granted, he obtains a benefit; if it is denied, he is no worse off than he was before (p. 285).

Justice O'Connor, concurring in part, wrote that because a death row prisoner retains some life interest before execution, "some *minimal* procedural safeguards apply to clemency proceedings" (p. 289). Even though there might be a situation in which judicial intervention might be warranted, in this case Ohio's process did not violate the Fifth Amendment. Justice Stevens, in dissent, said

> it is "abundantly clear" that the respondent has a life interest protected by the Due Process Clause (p. 292) . . . because death is a different kind of punishment (p. 293). . . . Those considerations [that death sentences be and appear to be based on reason rather than caprice or emotion] apply with special force to the final stage of the decisional process that precedes an official deprivation of life (p. 295).

Through Justice O'Connor's opinion, the *Woodard* case offered an opening to the death row prisoner that the court might entertain petitions to define what minimal procedural safeguards might apply to executive clemency decisions. However, only one case, *Harbison v. Bell* (129 S. Ct. 1481, 2009) has reached the Supreme Court for argument since *Woodard*. Justice Stevens wrote for the court in *Harbison* ruling that federally appointed counsel can represent indigent capital clients in state clemency procedures. Justice Stevens said that "in authorizing federally funded counsel to represent their state clients in clemency proceedings, Congress ensured that no prisoner would be put to death without meaningful access to the 'failsafe' of our justice system" (p. 1491).

There have been other challenges in lower courts that have been unsuccessful in claiming any procedural due process elements. The result of these cases has been to affirm the status quo of *mere access* to executive clemency proceedings and the acceptability of virtually any procedure.

Lower Court Challenges

One of the few cases finding a constitutional claim, *Young v. Hayes* (218 F.3d 850), came from Missouri in 2000. In this case the U.S. Court of Appeals for the Eighth Circuit stayed an execution based on a potential denial of due process. A death row prisoner alleged that the circuit attorney had deliberately interfered with his efforts to present evidence to the governor by threatening to fire a subordinate if she provided truthful information that supported the inmate's petition for clemency. The Eighth Circuit remanded the case for further inquiry so as to find whether the allegation was true because "such conduct on the part of a state official is fundamentally unfair. It unconscionably interferes with a process that the State itself has created" (p. 853). The bottom line may be that if a state violates the very process it created, then the due process claim has merit. For a similar case see *Wilson v. U.S. Dist. Court for N. Dist. of California* (161 F.3d 1185, 1998).

However, most claims of due process violations under *Woodard* made by death sentenced prisoners facing execution have failed at the lower court level and have not been considered by the Supreme Court (Kobil, 2012). In each of these cases, the court applied *Woodard's* minimal due process expectations to leave the state's process unchanged.

In *Duvall v. Keating* (162 F.3d 1058, 1998), the death sentenced prisoner challenged the Oklahoma clemency process because of Governor Keating's many statements that he would not grant clemency to murderers. In this case, the Board of Pardons and Parole did not recommend clemency, which was a prerequisite for the governor to consider the matter. Therefore, the court ruled there was no due process violation.

A related question about the impartiality of the decision maker was raised in two cases in which the governor had served as that state's attorney general during earlier proceedings in the cases. In each instance the court rejected the claim. In *Buchanan v. Gilmore* (139 F.3d 982, 1998), the inmate alleged that because the governor served as attorney general of Virginia in prior proceedings concerning his case, he should be disqualified by a conflict of interest from considering his clemency application. In *Bacon v. Lee* (353 N.C. 696, 2001) the plaintiffs alleged that because Governor Easley was the attorney general of North Carolina throughout part, or all, of each and every plaintiff's appellate and postconviction review proceedings in state and/or federal court, and was also the local prosecutor in the initial trial proceedings of plaintiff McLaughlin, he had an inherent conflict of interest that precluded him from fairly considering any plaintiff's clemency request and so did not qualify as a neutral and impartial decision maker. The court ruled that the *Woodard* precedent of minimal due process expectation depends on having access and participation. Therefore, there was no constitutional violation with this clemency process. A similar situation of potential conflict of interest was not litigated in Missouri, a state ranked fifth in overall executions. Jay Nixon served as attorney general between 1993 and 2008, promoting 59 executions during that period. Then, serving between 2008 and 2016 as governor, he presided over 21 additional executions, granting just two clemency requests despite maintaining his belief in those prisoners' guilt. In a study of clemency petitions in the same state between 1989 and 2000, Cathleen Burnett (2002, p. 169) reports that at least 18 petitions (36%) unsuccessfully claimed actual innocence. These extreme numbers might very well raise questions about undue partiality in the clemency process.

How boards function also raised questions about procedural due process expectations. The Texas clemency system was tested in *Faulder v. Texas Bd. of Pardons & Parole* (178 F.3d 343, 1999). In this case, the petitioner argued that the board members did not meet together to decide, allowed the board to act in secrecy, and provided no reasons for its decisions, among other complaints. The appellate court decided the *Woodard* standard was not violated.

In *Gilreath v. State Bd. of Pardons & Paroles* (273 F. 3d 932, 2001) the petitioner claimed that the appearance of impropriety by board members was a violation of due process. The Eleventh Circuit Court rejected his contentions, saying that there was no evidence of impropriety with a board member missing the oral presentation part of the proceedings because he could read a summary of the proceedings and no evidence that the decisions of the two members who were under investigation would be influenced in any particular way.

In *Sepulvado v. La. Bd. of Pardons & Parole* (171 F. App'x. 470, 2006) the Fifth Circuit Court ruled that there are no specific requirements that clemency proceedings must occur in order to offer minimal due process. "Sepulvado had full access to the clemency process, and the Board considered his application before denying him a clemency hearing" (p. 473).

In *Mann v. Palmer* (713 F.3d 1306, 2013), the petitioner was sentenced to death in 1983 and, facing a death warrant, had a clemency hearing in which he had the opportunity to participate and have the representation of counsel in 1985. After appellate and collateral review, he was again sentenced to death in 1990. The governor signed his death warrant for April 2013 without an updated clemency investigation that gave Mann the opportunity to be heard and to have counsel present. He claimed a denial of due process. However, the court concluded that the first hearing was satisfactory, and Mann would not have succeeded even if Florida had given him access to the records of those proceedings.

In *Schad v. Brewer* (732 F.3d 946, 2013) the inmate claimed that the Clemency Board was biased, as the governor placed undue influence on board members. The evidence to support the allegation was provided by previous board members, not current members. The court rejected Schad's claim. The conclusion is inescapable: identifying clemency as a failsafe is a cruel deception, an illusion of justice or mercy, unlikely to materialize.

Since *Herrera* and *Woodard*, the Supreme Court has not found any state clemency process unconstitutional (Kobil, 2012). Instead, the court has affirmed executive clemency as a "unilateral hope" (*Woodard*, 280), tolerating its functioning as discretionary, unreviewable, capricious, and arbitrary. Executive clemency remains a matter of grace, clearly dependent upon the discretion of the executive decision maker and without guidelines. As a failsafe, executive clemency seems to fall short of being the historic remedy for correcting miscarriages of justice that the court declared it to be in *Herrera*. The status quo assumes that the governor (or decision makers) actually hears the new evidence of innocence and/or of mitigation and will take action in appropriate cases. While the court has not offered any clarifying guidelines to modify the executive clemency appeal process, others have made some suggestions.

Suggested Due Process Reforms for the Executive Clemency Process

The suggested reforms are based on the presumption that if executive clemency is to be a failsafe, it functions as part of the legal system, and then the life interests of the condemned prisoner must be considered subject to some due process.

Alyson Dinsmore (2002, p. 1827) argues for meaningful review in the executive clemency process. She states that in *Herrera* the court

> elevated clemency to the level of a critical component in the death penalty system, in which clemency serves as a safeguard against the execution of the innocent. However, the Court failed to recognize that there was no guarantee the evidence would be heard or looked at during the clemency proceeding.

Furthermore, she maintains that one way to provide meaningful review would be to require that all new evidence of innocence be considered at a clemency hearing (p. 1854). Molly Clayton (2013) suggests having public clemency hearings, perhaps modeling them along the lines of parole hearings. Not much is known about the public's formal role in influencing executive clemency decisions, although some cases reach national attention. Who is permitted to file a clemency appeal on behalf of the condemned? In many states, not only does the condemned submit a petition for clemency but the public and/or religious leaders also offer formal petitions. One wonders whether these petitions are merely pro forma applications or if they make a difference to the decision maker. Finally, Adam Gershowitz (2001, p. 711) further specifies what elements of minimal due process might be ensured:

the right of the petitioner to present evidence, to make a statement, to have the assistance of counsel, and to appear before the final decision maker(s).

These reform efforts consider political influences to work against failsafe considerations in clemency decisions (Burnett, 2003). Politics in many forms clearly influence the decision making, and rather than being a failsafe for the wrongly convicted, the use or non-use of clemency may serve more as a failsafe for the executive's career. Is it possible to limit political influences in executive clemency, and is that desirable? Beau Breslin and John Howley (2002) defended using political influences to benefit the condemned. This debate about the usefulness of political influences is not one that is on the public agenda; there is no political will to standardize the clemency system or to limit the decision maker's discretion in the clemency authority.

Conclusion

Rather than a failsafe, executive clemency is more like a "Hail Mary" pass to the end zone in a football game, where the only hope for winning is that someone on your team will make the catch. This chapter has examined executive clemency as it relates to death penalty cases. As an act of grace, executive clemency is never required nor obligatory. It is rarely granted—none were granted in 2015 (Clemency, 2017). It is discretionary and there is no appeal beyond the clemency decision. States set up their own procedures and implement them with little transparency. There are no standards or procedures to guide the decision makers; in fact, clemency is an unfettered power by intention. Most condemned turn to executive clemency as their only hope for justice because the legal system is so broken it cannot and will not address its own problems (Palacios, 1996). The national trend of fewer grants of mercy when the legal standards for relief are extraordinarily narrow raises the issue of how many miscarriages of justice are not prevented.

Court watchers have been critical of the Supreme Court's appearance of "abdicating" its responsibility to conscientiously review death penalty appeals (Palacios, 1996) or. worse, promoting the illusion of justice when there is no justice (Kobil, 2003). Nothing has significantly changed since Daniel Kobil wrote (2003, p. 239):

> It would be disturbingly cynical and morally indefensible for the Court to refuse to acknowledge the flaws that frequently render clemency an ineffective safeguard in capital cases. The Court essentially would be perpetuating a constitutional "bait and switch." On the one hand, the Court would be telling condemned individuals that they have no right to judicial review of claims of innocence because clemency serves that purpose. At the same time, the Court would be turning a blind eye to clemency processes that are fundamentally unfair.

The *Herrera* and *Woodard* cases have had the effect of diverting attention from the flaws in the legal system to promising relief without substance. These legal cases provide little support for the desperate environment within which the state clemency structures work. Given the ambiguous boundaries set by the court, the social and political arrangements for executive clemency decision making compound the difficulty of averting wrongful executions. Adam Gershowitz (2001) has written perceptively about the diffusion of responsibility in clemency decision making, which in reality permeates all legal stages of capital cases. When no one takes responsibility for safeguarding against miscarriages of justice, the purpose of the administration of justice is undermined. Governors and pardon boards fail to take responsibility, as well as do the courts.

The fundamental contradiction regarding executive clemency is whether it is *extralegal* or an *integral* part of the death penalty process. Based in the executive branch of government, it is not subject to the same due process expectations that characterize judicial decision making. As an act of grace, executive clemency is free of constraints; it is unmerited and undeserved. If, on the other hand, clemency is to serve the purpose of failsafe, ensuring the integrity of the legal system, then it acts as an integral part of the legal process. If the latter is true, the question becomes clear. To be the remedy for miscarriages of justice, should clemency have any due process requirements as befitting the legal system itself? The dilemma that confronts executive clemency provokes exasperation: how does one require due process when clemency has no requirements?

When there is no agreement about what executive clemency is, how it works in reality may be most enlightening. It would be helpful to have more ethnographic case studies of decision making in specific cases and states such that the veil behind which decision making occurs becomes transparent. This research should be a factor to add to public awareness and action, likely the only avenue for holding officials, either executive or judicial, accountable for their decision making.

At present, there is no failsafe for the wrongfully death sentenced, no failsafe for remedying miscarriages of justice. Neither is there very much mercy. Consequently, it is a fantasy, a long-shot hope, to rely on executive clemency when facing execution. The conclusion is inescapable: identifying clemency as a failsafe is a cruel deception, an illusion of justice or mercy, unlikely to materialize. Does the death penalty need a failsafe to reassure society that the system works as it should? If one is not available, as this chapter suggests, then continuing executions will undermine trust in the integrity of the entire criminal justice system. How can society keep executing?

References

Acker, J., Harmon, T., & Rivera, C. (2010). Merciful justice: Lessons from 50 years of New York death penalty commutations. *Criminal Justice Review, 35*(2), 183–199.

Acker, J., & Lanier, C. (2000). May god—or the governor—have mercy: Executive clemency and executions in modern death—penalty systems. *Criminal Law Bulletin, 36*(3), 200–237.

Anti-Terrorism and Effective Death Penalty Act. (1996). Pub. L. No. 104–132, 110 Stat. 1214.

Argys, L., & Mocan, N. (2004). Who shall live and who shall die? An analysis of prisoners on death row in the United States. *The Journal of Legal Studies, 33*(2), 255–282.

Barkow, R. (2008). The ascent of the administrative state and the demise of mercy. *Harvard Law Review, 121*, 1332–1365.

Blume, J., & Vann, L. (2016). Forty years of death: The past, present, and future of the death penalty in South Carolina (still arbitrary after all these years). *Duke Journal of Constitutional Law & Public Policy, 11*(1–2), 183–254.

Borchard, E. (1932). *Convicting the innocent.* New Haven, CT: Yale University Press.

Breslin, B., & Howley, J. (2002). Defending the politics of clemency. *Oregon Law Review, 81*(1), 231–254.

Brown, E., & Adler, D. (1989). *Public justice, private mercy: A governor's education on death row.* New York: Weidenfeld and Nicolson.

Burnett, C. (2002). *Clemency appeals.* Boston, MA: Northeastern University Press.

Burnett, C. (2003). The failed failsafe: The politics of executive clemency. *Texas Journal on Civil Liberties & Civil Rights, 8*, 191–205.

Burnett, C. (2010). *Wrongful death sentences: Rethinking justice in capital cases.* Boulder, CO: Lynne Rienner Publishers.

Clayton, M. (2013). Forgiving the unforgivable: Reinvigorating the use of executive clemency in capital cases. *Boston College Law Review, 54*, 751–788.

Clemency. (Accessed 2/5/2017). Retrieved from www.deathpenaltyinfo.org/clemency

Cooper, S., & Gough, D. (2014). The controversy of clemency and innocence in America. *California Western Law Review, 51*, 55–110.

Crawford, M. (2012). A losing battle with the "Machinery of Death": The flaws of Virginia's death penalty laws and clemency process highlighted by the fate of Teresa Lewis. *Widner Law Review, 18*, 71–98.

Dailo, N. (2014). Give me dignity by giving me death: Using balancing to uphold death row volunteers dignity interests amidst executive clemency. *Southern California Review Law and Social Justice, 23*, 249–294.

Dinsmore, A. (2002). Clemency in capital cases: The need to ensure meaningful review. *UCLA Law Review, 49*, 1825–1858.

Freilich, J., & Rivera, C. (1999). Mercy, death, and politics: An analysis of executions and commutations in New York State, 1935–1963. *American Journal of Criminal Justice, 24*(1), 15–29.

Garvey, S. (2004). Is it wrong to commute death row? Retribution, atonement, and mercy. *North Carolina Law Review, 82*, 1319–1343.

Gershowitz, A. (2001). Essay: The diffusion of responsibility in capital clemency. *Journal of Law & Politics, 17*(4), 669–711.

Giannini, M. (2015). Measured mercy: Managing the intersection of executive pardon power and victims' rights with procedural justice principles. *Ohio State Journal of Criminal Law, 13*, 89–137.

Harris, J., & Redmond, L. (2007). Executive clemency: The lethal absence of hope. *American University Criminal Law Brief, 3*(1), 2–15.

Heise, M. C. (2003). Mercy by the numbers: An empirical analysis of clemency and its structure. *Virginia Law Review, 89*, 239–310.

Heise, M. C. (2013). The geography of mercy: An empirical analysis of clemency for death row inmates. *Thurgood Marshall Law Review, 39*, 3–27.

Heise, M. C. (2015). The death of death row clemency and the evolving politics of unequal grace. *Alabama Law Review, 66*, 949–987.

In Ryan's Words—"I Must Act." (Accessed 2/1/2017). Retrieved from www.deathpenaltyinfo.org/ryans-words-i-must-act

Kobil, D. (2003). How to grant clemency in unforgiving times. *Capital University Law Review, 31*, 219–241.

Kobil, D. (2012). Compelling mercy: Judicial review and the clemency power. *University of St. Thomas Law Journal, 9*, 698–729.

Korengold, M., Noteboom, T., & Gurwitch, S. (1996). And justice for few: The collapse of the capital clemency system in the United States. *Hamline Law Review, 20*, 349–370.

Kraemer, J. (2008). An empirical examination of the factors associated with the commutation of state death row prisoners' sentences between 1986 and 2005. *American Criminal Law Review, 45*, 1389–1417.

Kubik, J., & Moran, J. (2003). Lethal elections: Gubernatorial politics and the timing of executions. *Journal of Law & Economics, 46*(1), 1–25.

Markel, D. (2004). Against mercy. *Minnesota Law Review, 88*, 1421–1480.

Marlowe, J., & Davis-Correia, M. (2013). *I am Troy Davis.* Chicago, IL: Haymarket Books.

Morison, S. (2005). The politics of grace: On the moral justification of executive clemency. *Buffalo Criminal Law Review, 9*, 101–238.

Moylan, M., & Carter, L. (2009). Clemency in California capital cases. *Berkeley Journal of Criminal Law, 14*, 37–104.

Number of executions since. (1976). (Accessed 2/5/2017). Retrieved from www.deathpenaltyinfo.org/executions-year

Ortiz, A. (2002). Clemency and consequences: State governors and the impact of granting clemency to death row inmates. *American Bar Association*, (July), 1–8.

Palacios, V. (1996). Faith in fantasy: The Supreme Court's reliance on commutation to ensure justice in death penalty cases. *Vanderbilt Law Review, 49*, 311–372.

Prejean, H. (1993). *Dead man walking.* New York, NY: Vintage Books.

Pridemore, W. A. (2000). An empirical examination of commutations and executions in post-*Furman* capital cases. *Justice Quarterly, 17*, 159–183.

Radelet, M., Bedau, H., & Putnam, C. (1992). *In spite of innocence.* Boston, MA: Northeastern University Press.

Radelet, M., & Zsembik, B. (1993). Executive clemency in post-*Furman* capital cases. *University of Richmond Law Review, 27*, 289–314.

Rapaport, E. (2003). Straight is the gate: Capital clemency in the United States from Gregg to Atkins. *New Mexico Law Review, 33*, 349–379.

Ridolfi, K., & Gordon, S. (2009). Gubernatorial clemency powers: Justice or mercy? *Santa Clara Law Digital Commons*, (Fall), 25–41, http://digitalcommons.law.scu.edu/ncipscholarship/3.

Sarat, A. (2004). Putting a square peg in a round hole: Victims, retribution, and George Ryan's clemency. *North Carolina Law Review, 82*(4), 1345–1376.

Sarat, A. (2005a). *Mercy on trial: What it means to stop an execution.* Princeton, NJ: Princeton University Press.

Sarat, A. (2005b). Mercy, clemency, and capital punishment: Two accounts. *Ohio State Journal of Criminal Law, 3*, 273–286.

Sarat, A. (2008). Memorializing miscarriages of justice: Clemency petitions in the killing state. *Law & Society Review, 42*, 183–224.

Sarat, A., & Hussain, N. (2004). On lawful lawlessness: George Ryan, executive clemency, and the rhetoric of sparing life. *Stanford Law Review, 56*(5), 1307–1344.

Sigler, M. (2007). Mercy, clemency, and the case of Karla Faye Tucker. *Ohio State Journal of Criminal Law, 4*, 455–486.

States with and without the death penalty. (Accessed 2/5/2017). Retrieved from www.deathpenaltyinfo.org/states-and-without-death-penalty

Strach, P. (1999). Ohio Adult Parole Authority v. Woodard: Breathing new life into an old fourteenth amendment controversy. *North Carolina Law Review*, 77(2), 891–929.

U.S.A. executions by date. (Accessed 2/5/2017). Retrieved from http://deathpenaltyusa.org/usa1/indexdate1.htm

Woods, S. (2001). A system under siege: Clemency and the Texas death penalty after the execution of Gary Graham. *Texas Tech Law Review, 32*, 1145–1190.

Woodson v. North Carolina, 428 U.S. 280 (1976).

Young v. Hayes, 218 F.3d 850 (2000).

Cases Cited

Bacon v. Lee, 353 N.C. 696 (2001).

Buchanan v. Gilmore, 139 F.3d 982 (1998).

Duvall v. Keating, 162 F.3d 1058 (1998).

Faulder v. Texas Bd. of Pardons & Parole, 178 F.3d 343 (1999).

Furman v. Georgia, 408 U.S. 238 (1972).

Gilreath v. State Bd. of Pardons & Paroles, 273 F. 3d 932 (2001).

Gregg v. Georgia, 428 U.S. 153 (1976).

Harbison v. Bell, 129 S. Ct. 1481 (2009).

Herrera v. Collins, 506 U.S. 390 (1993).

Mann v. Palmer, 713 F.3d 1306 (2013).

Ohio Adult Parole Authority v. Woodward, 523 U.S. 272 (1998).

Schad v. Brewer, 732 F.3d 946 (2013).

Sepulvado v. La. Bd. of Pardons & Parole, 171 F. App'x. 470 (2006).

Wiggins v. Smith, 539 U.S. 510 (2003).

Wilson v. U.S. Dist. Court for N. Dist. of California, 161 F.3d 1185 (1998).

Woodson v. North Carolina, 428 U.S. 280 (1976).

Young v. Hayes, 218 F.3d 850 (2000).

24

EXECUTION METHODS IN A NUTSHELL

Deborah W. Denno[1]

Introduction

As the current prevailing method of execution, lethal injection is being subjected to an unprecedented degree of scrutiny. At no other time in this country's history have doctors or medical organizations been so committed to evaluating a method of execution. Such examination has illuminated the ongoing finger-pointing between law and medicine concerning responsibility for lethal injection's flaws. Medical societies may have shunned involvement with lethal injection, perhaps at times inappropriately, but physicians contributed to the method's creation and continue to take part in its application. Both law and medicine turned a blind eye to a procedure about which warnings were blared repeatedly. The problem rests not only with "American society," but also with the legal and medical communities that are part of it (Denno, 2007, 2014a, b, 2016, 2017).

The Search for a Medically Humane Execution

This country's centuries-long search for a medically humane method of execution landed at the doorstep of lethal injection (see Table 24.1). Of the 32 existing death penalty states, lethal injection is the sole method of execution in 24 states and it is one of two methods of execution in 11 states (three states fall into both categories) (see Table 24.2) (Denno, 2017; Death Penalty Information Center, 2017).

Statistics demonstrating lethal injection's dominance, however, belie the rapidly changing impact of recent lethal injection challenges and other influences on the death penalty. Indeed, by the end of 2016—even after two United States Supreme Court cases had upheld separate lethal injection protocols—states had carried out the fewest number of executions the country had recorded in 25 years, and juries put forth the lowest number of death sentences in 45 years. Likewise, about 40% of the American public was against the death penalty, the largest such percentage in over four decades. Of course, there have been backlashes. But undeniable evidence shows the death penalty's slide, and lethal injection litigation is a crucial domino in the deck (Denno, 2017; Death Penalty Information Center, 2017).

Before Lethal Injection

This country's turn to lethal injection reflects states' growing reliance on medicine as a response to philosophical, financial, and political pressures to eliminate the death penalty. For example, New York State's increasing opposition to capital punishment in the early 1800s—a move prompted by a series of disastrous public hangings attended by crowds of thousands—led the state's governor to ask the legislature in 1885 "whether the science of the present day" could not find a less barbaric means to execute. The governor's appointed commission of three "well known citizens" ultimately selected the electric chair, following the commission's impressively detailed two-year study of every execution method ever used throughout history (Denno, 1994, 2007).

In 1890, the murderer William Kemmler became the first person in the country to be electrocuted. New York's decision to enact electrocution spurred intense legal and scientific battles, resolved only when the U.S. Supreme Court decided that the Eighth Amendment would not apply to the states. Kemmler was executed in a day of confusion and horror, suffering a slow demise of burning flesh and ashes. Such catastrophe did not dissuade states from adopting this new method of purported scientific advancement. Electrocution still was deemed superior to hanging or, at the very least, was far less visible (Denno, 1994, 2007).

The problems with electrocution only worsened with the passing decades, despite (or perhaps because of) the enhanced scrutiny of the method's application (Denno, 1997, 1998, 2003, 2009c). By the time Allen Lee Davis was executed in Florida in 1999, over a century after Kemmler, the tragedies of the method appeared insurmountable: Davis suffered deep burns and bleeding on his face and body, as well as partial asphyxiation from the mouth strap that belted him to the chair's headrest. Millions of people around the world viewed virtually the results of Davis' execution through the Florida Supreme Court's web site postings of Davis' postexecution color photographs—ultimately crashing and disabling the Florida court's computer system for months. While the botched Davis execution did not halt electrocutions, it did prompt the Florida Legislature to enable inmates to choose between electrocution and lethal injection (Denno, 2002, 2007).

In light of this troubling execution method's history, lethal injection's popularity is understandable. Modern hangings risked being too long and cruel, like their predecessors. Lethal gas was judged the worst of all. In 1992, for example, Donald Harding's 11-minute execution and suffocating pain were so disturbing for witnesses that one reporter cried continuously, "two other reporters 'were rendered walking "vegetables" for days,'" the attorney general ended up vomiting, and the prison warden claimed he would resign if forced to conduct another lethal gas execution. While the firing squad has not been systematically evaluated, and may even be the most humane of all methods, it always has carried with it the baggage of its brutal image and roots. The law turned to medicine to rescue the death penalty (Denno, 1994, 1997, 2007, 2016).

My publications provide a thorough account of this law-medicine partnership based on historical research as well as extensive interviews with the major parties involved in lethal injection's origin. The legal system relied on anesthesiology just enough to understand the concept of lethal injection but not to account sufficiently for its barbarity when misapplied on human beings (Denno, 1994, 1997, 2002, 2007, 2014a, b, 2016).

The Advent of Lethal Injection

Lethal injection was considered a potential execution method in the United States as early as 1888. The New York governor's appointed commission rejected it, in part because of the medical profession's belief that, with injection, the public would begin to link the practice of medicine with death (Denno, 1994, 2007, 2014a, b).

Six decades later, Great Britain's Royal Commission on Capital Punishment also dismissed lethal injection, concluding after a five-year study of Great Britain's entire death penalty process that injection was no better than hanging, the country's long-standing method. Critical to the Royal Commission's investigation of lethal injection, however, was the substantial weight the commission gave to medical opinions and expertise. The commission solicited input from members of two of the country's most established medical organizations—the British Medical Association and the Association of Anaesthetists—as well as prison medical officers (Denno, 1997, 2007).

The host of problems these medical experts detected with lethal injection still ring true today. For example, based on such medical contributions, the Royal Commission determined that a standard lethal injection could not be administered to individuals with certain "physical abnormalities" that make their veins impossible to locate; rather, it was likely that executioners would have to implement intramuscular (as opposed to intravenous) injection, even though the intramuscular method would be slower and more painful. Significantly, the commission emphasized that lethal injection requires medical skill. While the British medical societies made clear their opposition to participating in the process, the Royal Commission still believed that acceptable executioners could be located, even in the medical profession. Nonetheless, other obstacles to lethal injection proved determinative. In particular, the commission found a lack of "reasonable certainty" that lethal injections could be performed "quickly, painlessly and decently," at least at that time. Ultimately, in 1965, the British abandoned the death penalty, with only a few exceptions (Denno, 1997, 2007).

In the United States, the 1960s saw a number of American legal organizations and advocates express concern about the degree of discretion that existed in the application of the death penalty, particularly among sentencing juries, and the resulting risk of arbitrariness, such as race discrimination. Such groups made a strategic decision to halt all executions by way of strong and concerted legal challenges in all cases in which an execution seemed likely. The groups believed that a country that was execution free could finally start to understand why the death penalty was no longer necessary (Denno, 2016, 2017). As Michael Meltsner explains, "[i]t is not easy to trace the evolution of this change in policy, for it came about only after a number of complex, interrelated, tactical and moral considerations coalesced, but of its importance there can be no doubt" (Denno, 2016, p. 756).

This U.S. execution ban, which started in 1967, thereby prompted an unofficial "de facto" moratorium on the application of the death penalty. Such a hiatus would be perpetuated some years further by the court's 1972 decision in *Furman v. Georgia*. In *Furman* and related cases, the court held 5–4 that the imposition of the death penalty in the cases before it violated the Eighth and Fourteenth Amendments. Because *Furman* comprised a per curiam decision of just one paragraph along with nine separate opinions, however, the case had no singular message. That said, the opinions indicated that most of the justices were troubled by the degree of discretion given to sentencing juries along with the resulting arbitrariness in death-sentencing decisions. While *Furman* was aimed toward striking down the procedures in Georgia and Texas, it ended up having a broad effect, essentially invalidating nearly every death sentencing system of every jurisdiction in the country (Denno, 2016, 2017).

The Impact of *Gregg v. Georgia*

This stalemate, however, would quickly change four years later. In 1976, the court decided *Gregg v. Georgia*, holding that the death penalty is not per se a cruel and unusual punishment and that the guided discretion approach that many states had since adopted satisfied Eighth Amendment requirements. Within seven months of the court's decision, Utah executed Gary Gilmore by firing squad, thereby revitalizing this country's death penalty and ending a moratorium that had lasted nearly ten years (Denno, 2016, 2017).

With *Gregg* the United States immediately had to grapple with the problem of how states were going to execute their death row inmates. Such a quandary appeared to spur an interest in a new execution technique for three primary reasons. First, states had encountered highly publicized problems and botched executions with the prior procedures, most particularly electrocution and lethal gas, and there were concerns about going back to them. Second, a public interest developed in the potential for having executions televised, in which case states would need a method that could appear humane and palatable to a viewing audience. Third, legislatures were troubled by the cost of refurbishing the electric chair and gas chamber and searched for the possibility of a cheaper method. Thus, lethal injection seemed to be the solution to all three issues: the method was billed as humane and botch-free, and the drugs recommended for an injection were far cheaper than electrocution or lethal gas. As earlier noted, some form of injecting a deadly toxin into inmates had been considered as early as 1888 in this country and then decades later in Great Britain, but *Gregg* fueled a rising interest in finally applying such an injection method. Remarkably, this reexamination of the lethal injection issue did not include any acknowledgment by legislators of the medical opinion evidence gathered by the New York or the British Commissions. Seemingly oblivious to prior concerns, American lawmakers emphasized that lethal injection appeared more humane and visually palatable relative to other methods. It was also cheaper (Denno, 1997, 2002, 2007, 2016).

Oklahoma Roots

In May 1977, one year after *Gregg*, Oklahoma became the first state to adopt lethal injection. Contrary to the thorough and deliberative approaches taken by the New York and British commissions, however, accounts suggest that two doctors (at most) were the sole medical contributors to the method's creation. At each step in the political process, concerns about cost, speed, aesthetics, and legislative marketability trumped any medical interest that the procedure would ensure a humane execution (Denno, 2002, 2007).

The two key legal players in the development of Oklahoma's lethal injection statute were then-Oklahoma State Senator Bill Dawson and then-Oklahoma House Representative Bill Wiseman. Dawson claimed that he first thought of using drugs for human execution when he was a college student. Wiseman said he acquired the idea in 1976, when he visited his personal physician, the president of the Oklahoma Medical Association (OMA), and inquired about a more humane way to execute death row inmates. Strikingly, that physician later informed Wiseman that the OMA board did not want to become entrenched in the venture because licensed physicians could not participate in executions. In subsequent years, American medical societies continuously would echo the OMA's stance, balking at any official involvement in lethal injection. Yet lawmakers would proceed with their decision making, regardless (Denno, 2007).

With medical societies out of the picture, both Dawson and Wiseman turned elsewhere. Eventually, they consulted with A. Jay Chapman, then chief medical examiner for Oklahoma. From the start, Chapman was upfront about his glaring lack of expertise. Indeed, when I initially contacted him for an interview, his "first response was that [he] was an expert in dead bodies but not an expert in getting them that way" (Denno, 2007, p. 66). Wiseman also warned Chapman about OMA's position and the effect such views could have on Chapman's medical career. Chapman was not worried: "'To hell with them: let's do this'" (Denno, 2007, p. 66).

The two men pulled out a pad and quickly drafted a statute based on Chapman's dictation: "'An intravenous saline drip shall be started in the prisoner's arm, into which shall be introduced a lethal injection consisting of an ultra-short-acting barbiturate in combination with a chemical paralytic'" (Denno, 2007, pp. 66–67). Chapman assumed that the chemicals used would be sodium thiopental (what has in fact been used) and the paralytic would be chloral hydrate; yet both Wiseman and Chapman believed the statute should be vague. Neither of them was certain if or when lethal injection would be implemented or what drugs might then be available. Unfortunately, such stunning unknowns had no impact on Wiseman's confidence in the procedure's potential success. As Wiseman recounted, lethal injection (a name he said he created) had the following benefits in his mind: "No pain, no spasms, no smells or sounds—just sleep, then death" (Denno, 2007, p. 67). Such optimism is disturbing given Wiseman's complete lack of medical background and other circumstances—most particularly, the problems with injection that the Royal Commission had detected, critical commentary about the drugs Chapman and Wiseman were considering, and the in-hindsight difficulties that recent litigation has revealed (Denno, 2007).

Completely independent of Wiseman's or Chapman's input or knowledge, Dawson also sought the advice of Stanley Deutsch, who then was head of Oklahoma Medical School's anesthesiology department. Deutsch and Dawson never met, but simply talked once on the phone when Dawson called to ask Deutsch to recommend a method for executing prisoners through the intravenous administration of drugs. Deutsch responded with a two-page letter that recommended two types of drugs: "an ultra short acting barbiturate" (for example, sodium thiopental) in combination with a "nueormuscular [sic] blocking drug" (for example, pancuronium bromide) to create a "long duration of paralysis" (Denno, 2007, p. 68). But Deutsch's February 28, 1977, correspondence was probably sent too late to contribute to the Oklahoma State Senate's March 2, 1977, passage of the initial version of the statute, which contained language identical to the final statute (Denno, 2007).

By all accounts, then, Chapman was the major, if not the primary, creator of lethal injection. At the same time, he remains shocked by reports that lethal injection generally is not performed by doctors but rather by individuals with little to no familiarity with the procedure. From the start, Chapman stated that he thought there were "no ethical constraints to a doctor administering the drug to the condemned person" (Denno, 2007, p. 69). He also noted that he personally "would have no hesitation to participate in a judicial execution" because such an act "cannot reasonably be construed to be the practice of medicine" (Denno, 2007, p. 69). Rather, he expressed the belief that, during a lethal injection, "the sensations would be similar to being placed under anesthetic" and "'[t]here would be nothing unpleasant'" (Denno, 2007, pp. 69–70).

In theory, lethal injection might have held much appeal. Yet the lawyers and doctors so fervently advocating its use had a distorted concept of how the procedure would operate in reality. Two professions (law and medicine), blinded by resolve, plunged together into a dark legal and medical hole from which they have yet to emerge (Denno, 2007, 2014a, b, 2016, 2017).

No Medical or Scientific Study

A detailed investigation of lethal injection's creation and history shows that at no point was the procedure medically or scientifically studied on human beings. That the Oklahoma statute (and later, the more specifically designated protocol) did not have medical justification became clear during the legislative debate. At one point, the lethal injection bill stalled, in large part because of concern that lethal injection had not been tested sufficiently. Indeed, William Hughes, a physician and chairman of the OMA's legislative committee, who might have offered an informed perspective, had not even read the bill before it was submitted to the legislature. Nor did he want to. Once again, the OMA turned its back on the lethal injection process (Denno, 2007).

Nevertheless, on March 2, 1977, the Oklahoma State Senate voted 26–20 to change the state's execution method from electrocution to lethal injection. This vote followed a two-hour debate that focused on a range of issues—deterrence (with some senators saying that the electric chair was the better deterrent to murder), humaneness (with some senators saying that lethal injection was more humane), and retribution (with some senators arguing that lethal injection was "an easy way out") (Denno, 2007, p. 70). One particularly critical point discussed served as an eerie harbinger of events to come—the problems that lethal injection could potentially cause. Yet this subject was narrow and limited. For example, one senator warned that some drug-using inmates might be less affected by the injection and survive, rendering the inmate a "vegetable to take care of" (Denno, 2007, p. 71). Remarkably, however, such a comment laments the economic repercussions of the problem—the state's need to provide care for an inmate after a botched execution—not the Eighth Amendment issue of cruelty or the sheer inhumanity of causing such a horrifying and preventable mistake (Denno, 2007).

In fact, questions of cost caught the attention of legislators. Dawson had informed the state senate that, according to the Oklahoma Department of Corrections, $50,000 would be needed to renovate the electric chair because it had been damaged. Building a gas chamber would require $250,000. By contrast, "[w]hen he [Dawson] pointed out that the cost of execution by injection would be only about $10, the argument 'did seem to carry some weight' in the discussion" (Denno, 2007).

On April 20, 1977, the Oklahoma House of Representatives passed the bill with a 74–18 vote. Critically, however, that version of the bill dropped a key amendment requiring the state to continue using the electric chair until death by drugs had been ruled legal by the U.S. Supreme Court. The amendment's disappearance presents a disturbing irony: The method of execution that so dominates this country's death penalty system might never have been implemented in its state of origin without Supreme Court approval (Denno, 2007).

Immediately after the bill's passage Chapman expressed alarm about how lethal injection would be practiced. His statements in *The Daily Oklahoman* foreshadowed the problems to come, problems that have remained unresolved for 40 years (Denno, 2007):

> Dr. A. Jay Chapman, state medical examiner, said [in May 1977] that if the death-dealing drug is not administered properly, the convict may not die and could be subjected to severe muscle pain.
>
> The major hazard of using lethal drugs in the execution of criminals is missing the vein in establishing an intravenous "pathway" for the drugs, he warned.
>
> Dr. Chapman, an early proponent of the execution method, said it is not necessary that a physician administer the drug, but it should be someone knowledgeable in drug injection.
> . . .
> In describing what he perceives as the ideal process for administering the drug, Dr. Chapman said a "drip" should be started intravenously in the prisoner's arm. Direct shots into the vein would not be used.
>
> When the intravenous pathway was secured, "one big push of drugs" would be made.
>
> Dr. Chapman said the drug injection could take only several seconds and would feel like the sudden "loss of consciousness" felt by surgery patients who have anesthesia induced.
> . . .
> The barbiturate drug which could be used, Dr. Chapman said, is a hypnotic sedative named "thiopental." It simply would put the prisoner to sleep.
>
> The paralytic agent, which would cause respiratory muscles to cease functioning, may be a curare-type compound, he said.
>
> State Corrections Director Ned Benton said . . . his office will work throughout the summer with the medical examiner's office to find the best method of drug injection "which could be defended in court."
>
> Benton said it was his understanding that state laws do not restrict who gives shots.
>
> *(Denno, 2007, p. 72)*

Chapman's initial concerns all have played out continuously in executions across the country for the last quarter-century. For example, occurrences of "severe muscle pain" and "missing the vein," as well as fears that "the convict may not die," have been real and repeated problems. Likewise, the need to have available "someone knowledgeable in drug injection" raises one of the most significant issues of all. But such comments also prompt a key question: How could Chapman support a bill—indeed create a procedure—knowing all too well the dangerous complications associated with it? While Chapman offered blunt statements in 2006 that he "'never knew we would have complete idiots injecting these drugs . . . [w]hich we seem to have,'" from the beginning, he explicitly warned of that possibility (Denno, 2007, pp. 72–73).

News articles from the late 1970s make clear the tentative status of Oklahoma's protocol. A 1979 *Daily Oklahoman* article, for example, emphasized that "[o]fficials with the State Department of Corrections say it may be years—if ever—before they are required to carry out mandates of the 1977 Legislature, which approved the drug injection law." The article also noted that "[o]fficials feel that if and when they have to use the injection law, new and better drugs may be available" (Denno, 2007, p. 73). Such statements suggest officials had limited confidence in the effectiveness of the chemicals that Chapman introduced and even anticipated they might never be used. Likewise, while Oklahoma Department of Corrections officials adopted a protocol in 1978 outlining how an injection would occur, the department noted that the protocol might need "a few modifications or refinements" (Denno, 2007, p. 74).

Chapman provided those modifications in 1981 as one of his last responsibilities as state medical examiner. Perhaps Chapman's most crucial change was adding a third drug, potassium chloride, to the prior two-drug lethal injection mix. In doing so, Chapman effectively set the final drug framework for all future lethal injection executions. It is now this combination of all three chemicals that continues to make lethal injection so controversial (Denno, 2007), in addition to further and more recent developments that this chapter will discuss.

Overall, lethal injection's history shows how such a medically complex process became ensconced in both law and politics. This powerful dynamic surfaced in *The Daily Oklahoman*'s comment about viewing the injected inmate: "Officials do not plan to monitor the prisoner's life signs during the execution [in order to] avoid moral judgments about the procedure because of immense controversy over capital punishment" (Denno, 2007, p. 75). That very issue remains a source of contention today. From the beginning, then, the social and legislative push in favor of the death penalty permeated the lethal injection procedure—a troubling mix that continues full throttle (Denno, 2007).

Human Execution and Animal Euthanasia

The drive for the return of capital punishment also led other states to look at execution methods. Several states initially considered the use of lethal injection because of comparisons between human execution and animal euthanasia. In 1973, then-Governor Ronald Reagan of California recommended lethal injection when he analogized it to putting injured horses to sleep. Similarly, in 1977, Texas State Representative Ben Grant, who created the Texas lethal injection bill, stated that his experiences presiding over a hearing on the humane treatment of animals persuaded him of the method's benefits (Denno, 2007).

At the same time, the absence of deliberation about the best way to lethally inject a human resulted in a shocking inconsistency: the methods for euthanizing animals require substantially more medical consultation and concern for humaneness than the techniques used to execute human beings. According to the American Veterinary Medical Association (AVMA), it is not acceptable for veterinarians to administer potassium chloride—lethal injection's third drug—to an animal that is not anesthetized. The AVMA manual for the euthanasia of animals also specifies the association's rigorous training requirements, which exhibit far more thought than the procedures set forth in most lethal injection protocols. The contrasting procedures for humans and animals underscore the sheer disregard for injection's medical justification (Denno, 2007).

Not surprisingly, this issue found its way into lethal injection litigation even before the Supreme Court's initial involvement in 2008. For example, the Ninth Circuit in 2005 considered it "somewhat significant that at least nineteen states have enacted laws that either mandate the exclusive use of a sedative or expressly prohibit the use of a neuromuscular blocking agent in the euthanasia of animals" (*Beardslee v. Woodford*, 2005, p. 1073). The question becomes, then, whether states will continue to hold the standard for executing human beings below that used by veterinarians to euthanize animals. In this country, the euthanasia of animals is a highly regulated and evolving process, based on strict guidelines periodically revised and modernized by the AVMA. Lethal injection's history shows that the method was never subjected to medical and scientific study, much less held to the standards for animal euthanasia (Denno, 2007).

What Does 'Physician Participation' Mean?

Given the lack of medical justification for lethal injection, a focus on physician participation in the method's implementation is critical. States increasingly have looked to physician involvement in lethal injections in an attempt to prevent problems—ranging from California's option of including anesthesiologists, to Missouri's requirement of a physician's presence, to Georgia's enacted statute forbidding medical boards from reprimanding doctors who participate in executions, to Florida's inclusion of "a physician" among the possible execution team members for each aspect of the execution procedure in one of a number of the state's protocols. Although some physicians have indicated a willingness to engage in executions, a number of medical associations have protested (Denno, 2007, 2014a,b).

Attempting to determine whether medical associations appropriately are shunning involvement is a daunting task. What moral measure should be used? What legal compass? On some level, the process can be compared to a Rorschach inkblot test, which psychologists use to assess individuals' perceptions of a scene. Observers' differing responses reflect their varying values, motivations, and experiences. In this sense, medical associations will view the scene of a lethal injection far differently from a legislature pressing to perpetuate the death penalty. The legal system is concerned with retribution and deterrence; the medical system is centered on health and well-being (Denno, 2007).

When the inkblot's pool of observers includes the whole of society—ranging from the public to the courts to the supervising wardens—the vast array of interpretations of the lethal injection scene becomes increasingly intricate (Denno, 2007). Starting in 2008, the Supreme Court—the ultimate arbiter of such conundrums—also began taking the inkblot test. Regardless, as the following sections show, how the legal system handles lethal injection remains in disarray.

Copying Oklahoma

Concerns over the lack of medical testing initially were considered so pronounced that Oklahoma's lethal injection bill stalled prior to state senate approval. Legislative history indicates that lethal injection was not to be used so quickly and confidently, if at all. Also, at one point, the Oklahoma Legislature considered requiring that injection could not supplant electrocution without "being ruled legal by the U.S. Supreme Court" (Denno, 2007, p. 78).

Until 2009, evidence suggests that the protocols in lethal injection states that revealed their chemical information were modeled after Oklahoma's original three-drug combination: (1) sodium thiopental, a barbiturate anesthetic that brings about deep unconsciousness; (2) pancuronium bromide, a total muscle relaxant that paralyzes all voluntary muscles and causes suffocation; and (3) potassium chloride, a toxin that induces irreversible cardiac arrest (Denno, 2014a). Therefore, most states mirrored the legal and scientific choices that Oklahoma officials made 40 years ago. Lethal injection was not actually used, however, until 1982, when Texas botched the execution of Charles Brooks, Jr. Not even the substantial numbers of comparably botched executions that followed deterred states from switching to the method with relative confidence and speed (Denno, 2007, 2014a,b).

Despite the benefits of hindsight, states did not medically improve upon the method that consistently had resulted in documented debacles. As the trial court in *Baze v. Rees* (2005) concluded, "[T]here is

Table 24.1 States Adopting Lethal Injection by Year: 1977–2017★

1977	Oklahoma • Texas
1978	Idaho
1979	New Mexico
1981	Washington
1982	Massachusetts
1983	Arkansas • Illinois • Montana • Nevada • New Jersey • North Carolina • Utah
1984	Mississippi • Oregon • South Dakota • Wyoming
1986	Delaware • New Hampshire
1988	Colorado • Missouri
1990	Louisiana • Pennsylvania
1992	Arizona • California
1993	Ohio★★
1994	Kansas • Maryland • Virginia
1995	Connecticut • Indiana • New York • South Carolina
1998	Kentucky • Tennessee
2000	Florida • Georgia
2002	Alabama
2009	Nebraska

★Information for this chart comes from Denno (2014a, p. 1341) and Death Penalty Information Center (2017).

★★In 2001, Ohio changed from a choice state to a single-method state.

scant evidence that ensuing States' adoption of lethal injection was supported by any additional medical or scientific studies. . . . [Rather,] the various States simply fell in line relying solely on Oklahoma's protocol" (*Baze v. Rees*, 2005, p. ★2). Indeed, after Oklahoma adopted lethal injection on May 11, 1977, Texas followed suit the next day and Idaho and New Mexico soon after. State after state followed accordingly. As Table 24.1 shows, 39 states joined this movement between 1977 and 2009, switching to lethal injection like falling dominoes until every single death penalty state was included. Many of these states simply copied the language of Oklahoma's lethal injection statute (Denno, 2009b, 2014a, p. 1341; Death Penalty Information Center, 2017).

The 39-state figure alone is remarkable. Even more extraordinary is that six states, including Oklahoma, made the switch by 1982, the year this country's first lethal injection execution took place. Another seven states changed in 1983 alone. Therefore, within a year of the country's first lethal injection execution, 13 states—over one-third of all death-penalty states at that time—had decided to engage in executions with the new method. In addition, 12 states enacted lethal injection in the nine-year stretch from 1994, when Kansas, Maryland, and Virginia adopted the method, to 2002, when Alabama did. Nebraska was a lone wolf, switching to lethal injection in 2009, a year after the Nebraska Supreme Court finally declared electrocution unconstitutional. By 2009, then, all death-penalty states in this country had switched to lethal injection, either entirely or as an option, and nearly all states used a protocol consisting of the same three drugs (Denno, 2014a)

Table 24.2 Execution Methods by State: 2017★

Single-Method States (24)

Arizona • Arkansas • Colorado • Delaware • Georgia • Idaho • Indiana • Kansas • ★Kentucky • Louisiana • Mississippi • Montana • Nebraska • Nevada • North Carolina • Ohio • ★★Oklahoma • Oregon • Pennsylvania • South Dakota • ★Tennessee • Texas • ★Utah • Wyoming

---

Choice States (11)

Lethal injection or hanging (2): New Hampshire • Washington

Lethal injection or firing squad (1): ★Utah

Lethal injection or electrocution (6): Alabama • Florida • Kentucky • South Carolina • Tennessee • Virginia

Lethal injection or lethal gas (2): California • Missouri

States Without the Death Penalty (18)

Alaska • Connecticut • Hawaii • Illinois • Iowa • Maine • Maryland • Massachusetts • Michigan • Minnesota • New Jersey • New Mexico • New York • North Dakota • Rhode Island • Vermont • West Virginia • Wisconsin (Also—the District of Columbia)

★ Information for this chart comes from Denno (2014a, p. 1343) and Death Penalty Information Center (2017). Kentucky, Tennessee, and Utah have provisions that are not retroactive and therefore allow choices for some inmates. These three states are listed in both the Single-Method States and Choice States categories.

★★ Oklahoma now allows for the use of nitrogen gas only if the lethal injection is unavailable. Nitrogen gas is not a method that condemned prisoners in Oklahoma may elect (Okla. H.R. 1879, 2015 Leg., Reg. Sess. (Okla. 2015)). As of 2017, nitrogen gas has also been proposed in bills in Alabama and Mississippi, but not signed into law (Death Penalty Information Center, 2017).

Of the 32 death-penalty states that exist in mid-2017, lethal injection is the sole method of execution in 24 states, as shown in Table 24.2. Three states—Kentucky, Tennessee, and Utah—have also adopted lethal injection as their sole execution method but have done so with provisions that are not retroactive. Therefore, Table 24.2 also lists these three states as choice states. Thus, lethal injection is one of two possible methods of execution in 11 states, including Utah (which allows some inmates the choice of firing squad) as well as Kentucky and Tennessee (which allow some inmates the choice of electrocution). A growing number of states, 18 in total, no longer have the death penalty, a figure that includes New Mexico, New Jersey, and Maryland, the most recent state to join this list (Denno, 2014a; Death Penalty Information Center, 2017).

Statistics demonstrating lethal injection's dominance, however, ignore the effect that lethal injection challenges can have on capital punishment. Indeed, it was the dominance of lethal injection that imperiled the death penalty's longevity when lethal injection faced legal challenges. The events leading up to the Supreme Court's first lethal injection decision in *Baze v. Rees* (2008) illustrated this effect. In 2006, for example, executions plunged to about half their 1999 numbers, a trend that continued in 2007 and 2008. Numerous states and the federal government ceased executions entirely, often at least partly due to problems and legal challenges related to lethal injection (Denno, 2014a).

Beginning on September 26, 2007, the day the court granted certiorari in *Baze*, no additional executions were conducted until May 6, 2008. Although the court did not declare a general moratorium on executions during this seven-month period, a de facto moratorium evolved when the court granted stays of execution for individual cases that came before it. Historically, such a lengthy hiatus is rare. After *Baze* was decided, those stays ended when the justices denied the underlying appeals. Executions began again, but so did lethal injection litigation, and with a vengeance (Denno, 2014a).

Baze v. Rees

By 2007, the growing number of legal challenges to lethal injection and the variance among state responses resulted in a sufficient number of circuit splits for the Supreme Court to grant certiorari to review the issue. The court chose *Baze v. Rees* (2008), a Kentucky case, to determine the future direction of lethal injection (Denno, 2009b). In *Baze*, a 7–2 decision with a plurality opinion, the court upheld the constitutionality of Kentucky's lethal injection protocol under the Eighth Amendment's Cruel and Unusual Punishment Clause. The court found that the defendants had failed to show that Kentucky's three-drug combination posed a "substantial" or "objectively intolerable" risk of "serious harm" compared to "known and available alternatives" (*Baze v. Rees*, 2008, p. 61). The typical formula, which Kentucky was then using, consisted of a serial sequence of the three previously mentioned drugs: sodium thiopental, pancuronium bromide, and potassium chloride (Denno, 2014a).

A primary concern in *Baze*, and lethal injection challenges generally, rested with the second drug, pancuronium bromide. Without adequate anesthesia, pancuronium can cause an inmate excruciating pain and suffering because the inmate slowly suffocates from the drug's effects while paralyzed and unable to cry out. The inmate's agony increases dramatically when executioners inject the third drug, potassium chloride, which creates an intense and unbearable burning. The *Baze* Court agreed that if the sodium thiopental is ineffective, it would be reprehensible to inject the second and third drugs into a conscious person. A key issue in litigation was whether prison officials and executioners can determine if an inmate is aware and in torment because pancuronium is such a powerful mask of emotions. Starting in 2006, this litigation so successfully prompted death-penalty moratoria and execution stalemates across the country that a Supreme Court case like *Baze* appeared inevitable (Denno, 2014a).

Yet in many ways, *Baze* was a puzzling choice. Kentucky had conducted only one execution by lethal injection and thus offered an extremely limited record on which to base a lethal injection challenge. Other states had far better evidentiary and execution data. Moreover, the suit that petitioners brought had not been scrutinized by the federal hearings being carried out in similar kinds of cases. Rather, Kentucky's hearings took place only in state court and concerned only Kentucky's procedures and short execution history. Some death penalty opponents came to believe that the justices who voted to hear *Baze* did so only because they "regarded the challenge as insubstantial and wanted to dispose of it before many more state and federal courts could be tied up with similar cases" (Denno, 2014a, p. 1334).

However, the *Baze* opinion had quite the opposite effect. Limits to the *Baze* Court's analysis suggest that the decision is by no means a definitive response to the issue of lethal injection's constitutionality. In fact, *Baze* was so splintered that none of its seven opinions garnered more than three votes, and the justices offered a wide range of explanations and qualifications in their reasoning. In addition, the decision was confined to Kentucky and its particular protocol. Voices on both sides of the death-penalty debate have emphasized that *Baze* left doors open for future lethal injection challenges. Even members of the *Baze* Court itself anticipated the repercussions of the opinion's shortcomings: in separate concurrences, Justices Stevens, Thomas, and Alito expressed concern that the *Baze* decision would only lead to additional debate and litigation. Until now, however, criticisms and concerns regarding developments in lethal injection protocols after *Baze* have been largely predictive (Denno, 2014a).

When the Supreme Court affirmed Kentucky's three-drug protocol in *Baze*, some commentators predicted that there would be a surge of executions because the de facto moratorium had created a backlog of death-row inmates. That forecast was never realized; apart from a slight rise in 2009, executions have continued their downward trend (Denno, 2014a). One reason for this decline may be that the death penalty's popularity has weakened in recent years. Whether because of discoveries of innocence among death-row inmates, a reduction in the number of individuals eligible for execution, racial disparities, botched executions, or other reasons, the courts and the public have shown more skepticism of the capital punishment process in the twenty-first century than they have since the early

1970s (Denno, 2017, Death Penalty Information Center, 2017; Denno, 2014b). Yet lethal injection challenges may have contributed to this skepticism. According to one death-penalty commentator, lethal injection challenges "have already held up more executions, and for a longer time than appeals involving such . . . issues as race, innocence, and mental competency" (Denno, 2014a, pp. 1345–1346).

Baze as Precedent

Given the narrowness and ineffectiveness of the *Baze* opinion, the court's decision has had minimal impact. Rather than offering guidance on the future direction of lethal injection, the legal issues and procedures evaluated by the *Baze* Court have been overshadowed by far more pragmatic threats to the continuation of executions by lethal injection—most particularly the complete unavailability of sodium thiopental that started after *Baze* was decided and rampant shortages of other lethal injection drugs that states had begun to use as substitutes. In addition there began to be a range of botched executions seemingly connected to some states' uses of some of these substitute drugs (Denno, 2014a, 2014b, 2016, 2017; Death Penalty Information Center, 2017). Considered together with the ongoing mass of lethal injection challenges and protocol changes that have occurred since 2008, it can be argued that *Baze* has rendered itself moot. Strikingly, even Kentucky itself—the "model" state at the heart of *Baze*—has switched to a single-drug protocol, such that it is no longer "substantially similar" to the procedure the *Baze* Court hailed as the standard for other states to follow (Denno 2014a, b).

Yet this is a remarkable conclusion to reach regarding a Supreme Court opinion less than a decade after its issuance, particularly in a case that marks the court's first foray into the constitutionality of an execution method in over six decades. I base this assertion on two grounds. First, although *Baze* has not been entirely void of precedential force, my analysis of all cases from 2008–2013 that have cited *Baze* indicates that the case's value as precedent has been limited. Second, citations to *Baze* decreased substantially in the years immediately following the decision. This decline is most likely because the nature of lethal injection challenges now bear on issues that have only remote or nonexistent parallels to those that prompted *Baze* in the first place (Denno, 2014a, 2014b). In addition, recent developments have shown that some of the purposes for which *Baze* may have been used in the past are no longer viable, the reliance on foreign-sourced drugs being a particularly striking example. Indeed, lethal injection litigation after *Baze* is so prolific and variable that it seemingly dwarfs the extent to which *Baze* has been applied to dismiss challenges. In sum, the *Baze* opinion's already constrained precedential force is barely relevant to recent litigation spurred by this country's unanticipated drug shortages (Denno, 2014a, 2016).

Glossip v. Gross

Merely seven years after *Baze*, the Supreme Court attempted to review yet another lethal injection protocol, this time involving the drug "midazolam," which some states had substituted for the missing sodium thiopental. In *Glossip v. Gross* (2015), the court held 5–4 that three death row inmates failed to establish that midazolam created "a substantial risk of severe pain" when used as the first of three drugs in Oklahoma's lethal injection procedure (*Glossip*, 2015, p. 2731). Writing for the majority, Justice Samuel Alito explained that the evidence presented from both sides supported the district court's view: "midazolam can render a person insensate to pain" and petitioners had failed to demonstrate midazolam's inadequacy under the Eighth Amendment's Cruel and Unusual Punishments Clause (*Glossip*, 2015, p. 2731). In addition, the court provided "two independent reasons" to affirm the district court's determination: first, petitioners could not "identify a known and available alternative method of execution that entails a lesser risk of pain, a requirement of all Eighth Amendment method-of-execution claims," and second, they were unable to show that the district court committed clear error in rejecting petitioners' arguments (Denno, 2016, p. 2731).

The court's rationale concerning alternative methods of execution potentially represents *Glossip*'s broadest impact. The case's striking dissents captured much of the legal and media commentary, but this chapter focuses on how *Glossip* may serve as Eighth Amendment precedent. Such an objective is particularly timely given states' ongoing frustrations in finding lethal injection drugs, despite the *Glossip* court's approval of midazolam (Denno, 2016; Death Penalty Information Center, 2017).

Glossip's credibility rests on the belief that *Baze* "cleared any legal obstacle to the use of [this] three-drug protocol" (*Glossip*, 2015, p. 2733). Yet there is no basis for that belief; quite the contrary. The three-drug protocol at issue in *Baze* is no longer viable due to ongoing and unpredictable shortages of lethal injection drugs during the years following the court's decision. Indeed, these shortages have created far more litigation and upheaval than the wide range of lethal injection challenges that preceded *Baze*. The litigation has also targeted two developments: first, the continual efforts by departments of corrections to seek never-tried lethal injection drugs and protocols and, second, a series of widely publicized botched executions, a disproportionate number of which have involved the use of midazolam. Overall, then, states have adopted wholly inappropriate drug substitutes to keep executions going despite risky and chaotic results (Denno, 2016; Death Penalty Information Center, 2017).

Glossip follows *Baze* as the court's most recent decision on execution methods, yet the *Glossip* Court's analysis is extraordinarily scant. Two primary examples of this deficiency are the way the court examines the history of changes in execution methods over time, and the court's explanation of why and how Oklahoma adopted lethal injection. Equally problematic is the court's focus on "anti-death-penalty advocates" as the basis for states' current problems with lethal injection because the argument ignores the reasons behind the extensive litigation that led to *Glossip* (Denno, 2016).

Glossip's Misuse of History

For a topic as vast, historic, and significant as how this country executes its death row inmates, the *Glossip* Court spends remarkably little time explaining the past. In less than two pages, the court reviews changes in the United States' five execution methods over the nineteenth and twentieth centuries, from hanging to electrocution to lethal gas to the firing squad and, finally, to lethal injection. Yet at no time during this brisk review does the court explain why states switched their methods of execution, except to say that each new method was "the most humane" (or words along those lines) relative to the method it replaced. In addition, the court mentions that each state's introduction of a new method rendered that new method constitutional (Denno, 2016).

As this chapter noted at the start, however, the complete history of execution method transitions is far more extensive than the *Glossip* Court suggests. That history is replete with detailed accounts at the legislative, judicial, and correctional levels that explain why each new method failed so profoundly in its goal to be more humane than the method it replaced. Hanging, lethal gas, and electrocution were adopted and initially used with great fanfare only to be criticized and replaced after decades of technical failures and botched executions. As a result, lethal injection, the latest method, is now used almost exclusively. But this record of exclusivity is no victory for lethal injection. Regardless of the outcome in *Glossip*, lethal injection's dominance demonstrates only that other methods have failed. States seem to have exhausted alternative methods of execution, apart from changing the drugs and procedures of lethal injection itself (Denno, 2016).

The court's brevity is not confined to recounting this country's changes in execution methods. For example, the court explains that lethal injection was first enacted following a nine-year hiatus in capital punishment in the United States, spanning from 1967 to 1976; yet the Court neither mentions why the hiatus occurred nor why the United States turned to a new method of execution in 1976 over what had been the most popular method pre-*Gregg*—electrocution. The *Glossip* Court mentions that Oklahoma "eventually settled" on the types of drugs that would be included in the protocol: sodium thiopental, pancuronium bromide, and potassium chloride. But the court does not explain the process behind the method's adoption, which—as earlier noted—was exceptionally quick and slapdash. The *Glossip* Court wholly ignores this critical backdrop, as it matter-of-factly describes Oklahoma's creation and adoption of lethal injection in just one paragraph (Denno, 2016).

The *Glossip* Court also states that the court "has never invalidated a State's chosen procedure for carrying out a sentence of death as the infliction of cruel and unusual punishment" (Glossip, 2015, p. 2732). That characterization is technically correct. But it is only part of a much longer story that the court does not tell. Until 2008, in *Baze v. Rees* (2008), the court had never reviewed evidence concerning whether any method of execution violates the Eighth Amendment's Cruel and Unusual Punishments Clause. Legislative changes in execution methods during the nineteenth and twentieth centuries, however, demonstrate that states typically change their method of execution when they perceive that their current method is vulnerable to a constitutional challenge. The *Glossip* Court therefore skirts any discussion involving states' efforts to avoid the constitutional scrutiny of their execution methods. The court also mischaracterizes prior cases that appear to constitutionally endorse the firing squad or electrocution under the Eighth Amendment, and wrongfully implies that the court "rejected a challenge to the use of the electric chair" in two cases. Furthermore, the *Glossip* Court never mentions that two states, Nebraska and Georgia, have both held electrocution unconstitutional under their respective state statutes. In addition, the court does not acknowledge that all former electrocution states now use lethal injection as either the sole method or a choice method because of the problems associated with electrocution (Denno, 2016).

Glossip as Precedent

This backdrop is critical for examining the *Glossip* Court's viability as precedent for two reasons. First, the court mischaracterizes the history of the constitutionality of execution methods, implying through omission or indirect assertion that the history is unproblematic, when it has long been plagued by botched executions and gross ineptitude on the part of legislatures, courts, and departments of corrections. As a result of these problems, starting in the nineteenth century, states continuously switched from one method of execution to the next to search for the "more" or "most" humane method of execution as well as to avoid potential constitutional challenges to the method they sought to replace. Second, the court's veneer of acceptance of midazolam provides fuel for the court's requirement that petitioners demonstrate "a known and available alternative method of execution" as a possible replacement to lethal injection. After all, if the court has "never invalidated" any of the prior execution methods, including the three-drug procedure in *Baze*, such a track record spotlights the status quo's success. Any effort to change an accepted execution method should require petitioners to overcome steep obstacles. Yet the brief and one-sided story that the *Glossip* Court tells defies the long-documented case law and scholarship that offer a substantially different perspective. This contrast, among others, puts *Glossip* on shaky ground as precedent (Denno, 2016).

Glossip's Focus on "Anti-Death-Penalty Advocates"

The *Glossip* Court's distorted history raises another concern. If this country's experiences with execution methods have been primarily inconsequential, and the problems with lethal injection's three-drug protocol seemingly quelled by *Baze*, it is unclear how the issues in *Glossip* evolved. The court's answer, in a nutshell, is "anti-death-penalty advocates" (Denno, 2016). After *Baze* had presumably fostered states' abilities to successfully carry out executions quickly and humanely—a fictional representation in and of itself—"anti-death-penalty advocates" introduced yet another vehicle of obstruction by "pressur[ing] pharmaceutical companies to refuse to supply the drugs used to carry out death sentences" (Denno, 2016, p. 764).

The court never identifies, however, who these "anti-death-penalty advocates" are. Nor does the court explicate how these anti-death penalty advocates possessed such extraordinary power to create the drug shortages that dismantled the original three-drug protocol validated in *Baze*. The court also fails to explain how or why such shortages forced states like Oklahoma to acquire inappropriate drugs, such as midazolam, when these states could have chosen other types of drugs for their protocol. While the court focuses on the "anti-death-penalty advocate" explanation as it recounts all the factors driving lethal injection's troubles, the court never mentions that three of the most highly influential factors had nothing to do with anti-death penalty advocacy (Denno, 2016).

The first factor, for example, reveals that post-*Baze* efforts to reignite the execution process were problematic from the start, even before the issues with drug shortages came about. Rather than eliminating obstacles, the same sorts of impediments that have always accompanied lethal injection executions followed *Baze*—namely, inexperienced or incompetent prison personnel, and vague protocols and constraints on execution witnesses. A continuing wave of troubles also followed the *Baze* decision concerning the selection, training, preparation, and qualifications of the lethal injection team. The types and sources of drugs used in lethal injection executions are just a small part of the problem, since the entire process can be riddled with disorganization and preparatory mayhem irrespective of whatever is injected into the inmate. Lethal injection botches and ineptitude on all levels post-*Baze* have far exceeded the difficulties that existed pre-*Baze* (Denno, 2016).

A second influential factor was that, at least initially, the depletion of sodium thiopental had nothing to do with the death penalty. In 2014, a report published by the Government Accountability Office documented a variety of drug shortages occurring throughout the country from January 2007, a year-and-a-half before *Baze* was decided, to June 2013. The report included a review of the shortages associated with the chemicals used to create sodium thiopental. Thus, the start of the scarcity of sodium thiopental in the United States was wholly divorced from the so-called anti-death penalty "movement." Rather, the lethal injection process was affected by a pharmaceutical fact of life: drugs can often become unavailable, at times unpredictably. These shortages can impact citizens' health and, in the case of lethal injection, their death (Denno, 2016).

The third, and perhaps most significant, factor concerns the District of Columbia Circuit Court's decision in *Cook v. FDA* (2013). In 2013, *Cook* held that the Food and Drug Administration ("FDA") must approve all drugs imported into the country, including the drugs used in lethal injection protocols. This decision extinguished efforts by departments of corrections to purchase lethal injection drugs outside of the country because those drugs did not meet FDA standards, a matter that is still the subject of dispute. For example, in 2015, the FDA informed Nebraska that it could not import sodium thiopental from India to use in the state's lethal injection executions even though the Nebraska Department of Corrections had paid $54,400 for the drug. Also in 2015, the FDA stopped Texas and Arizona from importing sodium thiopental from India, and investigative reporters revealed that Harris Pharma had sold to all three states. Investigators discovered that Chris Harris, the head of Harris Pharma, had no pharmaceutical training whatsoever, as well as a flawed record he could better hide in India, away from FDA scrutiny. Once again, departments of corrections in key death penalty states were willing to buy and illegally use a death penalty drug from a grossly disreputable source, all the while knowing that faulty drugs heighten the likelihood of a botched execution. Yet Nebraska, Texas, and Arizona are still trying to get around the FDA ruling so that they can continue their executions using Harris Pharma's drugs, despite their very low likelihood of success (Denno, 2016).

Who Are the "Anti-Death-Penalty Advocates"?

Overall, then, departments of corrections were not impacted directly by anti-death penalty advocates when they purchased substitute drugs for lethal injection purposes. This circumstance prompts two questions: who are the anti-death penalty advocates that the court references, and what exactly did they do to the lethal injection process? One of the great frustrations of *Glossip* is that the court never fully addresses nor answers these questions. Instead, the court explains the troubles that these "anti-death-penalty advocates" created, even though scholars and the news media documented both the continued quest by departments of corrections to seek drugs and the resulting protocol changes (Denno, 2016).

One reason why the court may have evaded answering these questions is because providing an explanation would require a detailed account of all the problems facing legislatures, courts, and departments of corrections during the time between *Baze* and the grant of certiorari to *Glossip*. These troubles include a host of terribly botched lethal injection executions documented by petitioners' briefs, academics, and the media, and the highly problematic efforts by departments of corrections to acquire the drugs necessary for execution. Instead, the court resolves this dilemma—in just a few pages—by scapegoating the "anti-death-penalty advocates" who supposedly created the shortages and, therefore, all of the problems with lethal injection that *Baze* had presumably cleared (Denno, 2016).

The *Glossip* Court first points to the "activists" who "pressured" not only the company that made sodium thiopental (Hospira) in both the United States and Italy, but also the Italian government, in order to get both sources to stop selling sodium thiopental in the United States. Later, activists also extended such pressure to Lundbeck, the Danish manufacturer of pentobarbital, the drug prisons used when sodium thiopental was no longer available. These drug-blocking efforts came as no surprise to those who know that almost all European countries prohibit the death penalty and that the European Union encourages banning the death penalty in all countries. Anti-death penalty advocacy groups in Europe, such as Reprieve, are particularly focused on eliminating the death penalty by way of stopping lethal injection. Yet these groups, as effective as they are, could not possibly have the degree of impact that the court presumably attributed to them. There are additional forces at play (Denno, 2016).

It appears the *Glossip* Court would include European countries and the European Union under its "anti-death-penalty advocates" umbrella, given the extent of the court's discussion of European blocks on lethal injection drugs. But targeting European countries as disrupting the U.S. death penalty ignores the reality that each country has a right to refuse to sell drugs created for health to the United States, where they will be injected to cause death. Even if part of the pressure stems from a particularly influential anti-death penalty advocacy group, such as Reprieve, these groups are often simply informational messengers to European drug companies and pharmacies. Frequently, drug companies are unaware of how their drugs are being used and are disturbed and concerned when anti-death penalty advocacy groups inform them. In this sense, the court's use of the term "pressure" is misleading: providing information is not pressure (Denno, 2016).

Of course a company's association with the death penalty also can have financially detrimental effects that can deter its willingness to sell lethal injection drugs to departments of corrections. Consumers may not want to purchase drugs that are linked to executions. Regardless, even if the court believed that European countries constituted some of the "anti-death-penalty advocates" the court derides, *Cook v. FDA* (2013) would still require the FDA to ban importation of these drugs from all countries, not just Europe (Denno, 2016).

Apart from Italy, England, Denmark, and other countries, what other sources might be included among the "anti-death-penalty advocates" the court mentions? Ironically, the FDA has most likely contributed the most to the lethal injection drug shortages by way of *Cook*; yet, the court would hardly include the FDA as an "anti-death-penalty advocacy" group nor as an institution that has been pressured by such groups. The FDA operates by its own standards, irrespective of what is happening to the death penalty (Denno, 2016).

The Role of Medical Professionals

The same reasoning that applies to the FDA could also apply to other groups that may not be traditionally considered anti-death penalty advocates nor as organizations necessarily influenced by them. There is a broad net of potential sources. That net could encompass a range of medical professionals such as physicians, nurses, and pharmacists, because all three groups have been involved in lethal injection executions, either directly or indirectly. Doctors and other medical professionals have long participated in carrying out all execution methods, most particularly lethal injection. Doctors not only created the original three-drug protocol but also advised legislatures, courts, and prisons about the types and amounts of lethal injection drugs that should be used. In a number of executions, doctors have directly engaged in the actual implementation of the injection procedure. During Oklahoma's horribly botched lethal injection of Clayton Lockett in 2014, for example—the execution that prompted *Glossip* and now a blistering grand jury report—records show that both a doctor and an emergency medical technician tried to inject Lockett with drugs under circumstances involving gross incompetence (Denno, 2016).

The role of such medical professionals has long been controversial, however, and medical organizations and drug manufacturers have increasingly discouraged such participation on the basis that doctors and drugs should promote health rather than death. The International Academy of Compounding Pharmacists has similarly discouraged its members from providing lethal injection drugs, the group's first official stance on the issue. The most sweeping demonstration of this posture, however, is Pfizer Inc.'s 2016 announcement that it had enforced restrictions on where its drugs are distributed so that they could not be used in lethal injection executions. Thus, the decision by Pfizer—one of the largest pharmaceutical manufacturers in the world—along with similar types of controls adopted by over 20 other drug companies, substantially hinders departments of corrections' efforts to get drugs. While such companies provide "either moral or business reasons" for their decisions, it would be a gross mischaracterization to say that they were buckling to pressure only by anti-death-penalty advocacy groups (Denno, 2016). According to Pfizer, for example, "medical principles and business concerns have guided their policies," not anti-death penalty campaigns or Europe's block on exporting drugs (Denno, 2016, p. 771). Likewise, pressure from shareholders concerned about harm to the company's reputation for health has shown far more influence. In essence, then, medical professionals and pharmaceutical companies do not need anti-death penalty advocacy groups to tell them to avoid involvement in the death penalty process—they already know (Denno, 2016).

"Anti-death-penalty advocates" could also include the public itself. After all, drug companies seem to fear negative public perception above all else. If the public links a company and its drugs to the death penalty process, the financial repercussions could be severe for the company even in the United States, where a majority of individuals still support the death penalty. Because a company's association with the death penalty may not be a good business model, a substantial number of states have enacted secrecy provisions that shield the identity of medical professionals, pharmaceutical companies, and pharmacies involved with the execution process. Yet Pfizer's decision may make it so that all these entities, especially compounding pharmacies, want to buck contributing to the process altogether, irrespective of the guarantee of secrecy. Regardless, states continue to have problems finding drug sources, a circumstance suggesting that anonymity is not enough to keep these groups involved in the lethal injection process (Denno, 2016).

Conclusion

Midazolam, the drug at issue in *Glossip*, was developed in the 1970s by the Swiss pharmaceutical company Hoffmann-La Roche. The drug's recent significance in lethal injection debates has come as an unwelcome surprise to the company, which insists "that it 'did not supply midazolam for death penalty use and would not knowingly provide any of [its] medicines for this purpose'" (Blinder, 2017). Dr. Armin Walser, a retired chemist and one of the drug's inventors, has expressed similar dismay at the drug's appropriation for lethal injections. "'I didn't make it for the purpose . . . I am not a friend of the death penalty or execution'" (Blinder, 2017). Indeed, midazolam's journey from pharmaceutical lab to state execution chambers has been "filled with secrecy [and] political pressure," and

Walser only learned of the connection between his work and lethal injection in 2015 (Blinder, 2017). His amazement and discomfort indirectly parallel that of lethal injection's creator, A. J. Chapman, upon learning of the procedure's haphazard administration. Both scenarios about these medical professionals—Walser and Chapman—strikingly illustrate the divide between the personal and professional expectations of the scientific and medical communities that develop these drugs and procedures and the reality of how and why they are used by the criminal justice system.

If members of the public and selected medical and pharmacy groups can be considered anti-death penalty advocates, at some point the court may have to face a growing reality: "anti-death-penalty advocates" may simply represent the general American public. With such a development, the Supreme Court may, yet again, be accused of being out of touch with mainstream America. Because departments of corrections could be boxed into an execution methods corner if lethal injection becomes unworkable, they may ultimately need a drug-free alternative method of execution to help them escape. Finding a method that is also "a known and available alternative" may simply be a matter of states reverting to their more simplistic execution pasts (Denno, 2016). Regardless, the crystal ball is always murky when it comes to predicting the future of execution methods (Denno, 2009a): neither time nor the Supreme Court's involvement makes such predictions any clearer.

Note

1 I am most grateful to Marianna Gebhardt for her contributions to this chapter and to Fordham Law School for research funding.

References

Chart 1.

Chart 2.

Blinder, A. (2017). When a common sedative becomes an execution drug. *New York Times*. Retrieved from www. nytimes.com/2017/03/13/us/midazolam-death-penalty-arkansas.html

Death Penalty Information Center. (2017). Retrieved from https://deathpenaltyinfo.org/

Denno, D. W. (1994). Is electrocution an unconstitutional method of execution? The engineering of death over the century. *William and Mary Law Review, 35*, 551–692.

Denno, D. W. (1997). Getting to death: Are executions constitutional? *Iowa Law Review, 82*, 319–464.

Denno, D. W. (1998). Execution and the forgotten eighth amendment. In J. R. Acker, R. M. Bohm, & C. S. Lanier (Eds.), *America's experiment with capital punishment: Reflections on the past, present, and future of the ultimate penal sanction* (pp. 547–577). Durham: Carolina Academic Press.

Denno, D. W. (2002). When legislatures delegate death: The troubling paradox behind state uses of electrocution and lethal injection and what it says about us. *Ohio State Law Journal, 63*, 63–260.

Denno, D. W. (2003). Lethally humane? The evolution of execution methods in the United States. In J. R. Acker, R. M. Bohm, & C. S. Lanier (Eds.), *America's experiment with capital punishment: Reflections on the past, present, and future of the ultimate penal sanction* (2nd ed., pp. 693–761). Durham: Carolina Academic Press.

Denno, D. W. (2007). The lethal injection quandary: How medicine has dismantled the death penalty. *Fordham Law Review, 76*, 49–128.

Denno, D. W. (2009a). The future of execution methods. In C. S. Lanier, W. J. Bowers, & J. R. Acker (Eds.), *The future of America's death penalty* (pp. 483–497). Durham: Carolina Academic Press.

Denno, D. W. (2009b). For execution methods challenges, the road to abolition is paved with paradox. In C. J. Ogletree, Jr. & A. Sarat (Eds.), *The road to abolition? The future of capital punishment in the United States* (pp. 183–214). New York: New York University Press.

Denno, D. W. (2009c). When Willie Francis died: The 'disturbing' story behind one of the eighth amendment's most enduring standards of risk. In J. H. Blume & J. M. Steiker (Eds.), *Death penalty stories* (pp. 17–94). New York: Foundation Press.

Denno, D. W. (2014a). Lethal injection chaos post-*Baze*. *Georgetown Law Journal, 102*, 1331–1382 (excerpts reprinted with permission).

Denno, D. W. (2014b). America's experiment with execution methods. In J. R. Acker, R. M. Bohm, & C. S. Lanier (Eds.), *America's experiment with capital punishment: Reflections on the past, resent, and future of the ultimate penal sanction* (3rd ed., pp. 707–725). Durham: Carolina Academic Press.

Denno, D. W. (2016). The firing squad as "a known and available alternative method of execution" post-Glossip. *University of Michigan Journal of Law Reform, 49,* 749–793.

Denno, D. W. (2017). Courting abolition. *Harvard Law Review, 130,* 1827–1876 (book review).

Okla. H.R. 1879, 2015 Leg., Reg. Sess. (Okla. 2015).

Cases Cited

Baze v. Rees, No. 04-CI-01094, 2005 WL 5797977 (Ky. Cir. Ct. July 8) (2005), *aff'd* 217 S.W. 3d 207 (Ky.) (2006), *aff'd,* 553 U.S. 35 (2008).

Baze v. Rees, 553 U.S. 35 (2008).

Beardslee v. Woodford, 395 F.3d 1061 (9th Cir.) (2005).

Cook v. Food & Drug Admin, 733 F.3d 1 (D.C. Cir.) (2013).

Furman v. Georgia, 408 U.S. 238 (1972).

Glossip v. Gross, 135 S. Ct. 2726 (2015).

Gregg v. Georgia, 428 U.S. 153 (1976).

25

CALIFORNIA'S CHAOTIC DEATH PENALTY

Stacy L. Mallicoat, Brenda L. Vogel, and David Crawford

California is home to the largest death row population in the nation (Death Penalty Focus, 2017). In fact, it is the largest death row population in the Western Hemisphere (Nichols, 2016). As of January 6, 2017, there were 750 people on death row in California; 2.8% (21) of the condemned were women and 97.2% (729) were men (CDCR, 2017, January 20). California's condemned men are housed at San Quentin State Prison north of San Francisco, and the 21 condemned women are confined at the Central California Women's Facility near Chowchilla. With respect to race, 36% are black, 34% are white, 24% are Hispanic, and 6% are identified as "other" (CDCR, 2017, January 20). They range in age from 24 to 86 years (CDCR, 2017, January 20). Nearly two dozen require wheelchairs or walkers, and at least one is confined to bed in diapers (St. John, 2015).

While the state has been very active in sentencing people to death, it has done little to carry out these punishments. Since the reinstatement of the death penalty in California in 1978, the state has executed only 13 individuals (with an additional two who were extradited to other states and executed). Many of these individuals spent a significant amount of time on death row prior to being executed. The state's last execution was over a decade ago when, on January 12, 2006, Clarence Ray Allen died by lethal injection. The average length of time from sentence of death to execution in California is over two decades (California Commission on the Fair Administration of Justice, 2008). One inmate, Douglas Stankewitz, has been on death row since October 1978, or nearly 39 years.

While only 13 men have been executed in California since 1978, 120 death row inmates have died. Seventy-one of them died of natural causes, 25 died by their own hand, eight others are listed as dying by "other" means, and one death is "pending" classification (CDCR, 2017, January 20). Notably, it is more common to die of natural causes or suicide on death row than it is to be executed (Dickerson, 2016; Reese, 2015). Suicide rates on death row are roughly ten times greater than in general society and several times greater than in the general prison population (Stryker, 2016).

This chapter provides a broad overview of California's death penalty and is organized into three sections. First, we highlight how the death penalty in California continues in an arbitrary and discriminatory fashion due to issues in prosecutorial discretion and juror decision making. Second, we describe how the current de-facto abolition came into being through legislative review, legal challenges, shifts in public opinion, and myriad voter-initiated propositions and constitutional amendment efforts. Finally, we conclude this chapter with a review of the current challenges facing California's use of the death penalty.

The Failure of *Furman* and *Gregg*: The Effect of Prosecutorial and Jury Discretion on Death Sentences

In 1972, the U.S. Supreme Court held that the practice of sentencing offenders to death was unconstitutional. In a 5–4 decision where each of the nine justices were compelled to author their own concurring or dissenting opinions, the majority opinion held that while the current policies across the nation were problematic, reform was possible. The *Furman* court held that since juries had complete discretion in determining who would be sentenced to death, that the penalty nationwide was "imposed arbitrarily, infrequently and often selectively against minorities" (Bohm, 2012, p. 52). Prior to the decision in *Furman*, California's Supreme Court invalidated the state's death penalty scheme in *California v. Anderson* (1972). What was particularly unique about California's state constitution at the time was that it forbade punishments that were cruel OR unusual (whereas the Eighth Amendment of the U.S. Constitution protects against punishments that are cruel AND unusual). This is a distinction that remains in the California State Constitution today.

In an effort to reform death penalty practices both within California and nationwide, legislators returned to create new laws that would limit the unregulated discretionary power of juries. While the court struck down laws that provided for mandatory death sentences for offenders convicted of capital crimes (*Woodson v. North Carolina*, 1976), they did approve procedural reforms that included guided discretion statutes, bifurcated trials and automatic appellate review of death sentences (*Gregg v. Georgia*, 1976). While the intent was to create a death sentencing process that eliminated the arbitrary and discriminatory practices of the past, we question whether such practices continue to exist today. To answer this question, we look at the effect of prosecutorial and jury decision making in death cases.

Prosecutorial Decision Making and Geographic Disparities

According to California state law, the decision to seek the death penalty comes with three provisions that are not mandated in other criminal cases. First, both aggravating and mitigating evidence must be allowed into evidence. The presence of both aggravating and mitigating evidence is presumed to reduce the sentencing discretion highlighted by *Furman*. Second, death penalty cases must be bifurcated, or separated into two separate trials, a guilt phase and a sentencing phase. The jury first decides if the defendant is guilty, and if he or she is found guilty, the same jury weighs the aggravating and mitigating circumstances in the sentencing phase. Finally, all death penalty cases must receive an automatic appeal to the State Supreme Court, where the court determines if any legal errors were made (Mallicoat, 2014).

The decision to pursue the death penalty for a death-eligible defendant is the responsibility of the elected district attorney in each county (California Commission on the Fair Administration of Justice, 2008). As long as the case is a homicide deemed "death-eligible" or "capital," then the prosecutor may choose to seek either the death penalty or life in prison without the possibility of parole (LWOP). According to section 190.2 of the California Penal Code, for a case to be considered death eligible, the prosecutor must show, at the guilt phase, that the case included "special circumstances." Some of these 33 special circumstances include: the murder was carried out for financial gain; the offender was lying in wait; the murder was especially heinous, atrocious, or cruel; or the victim was a peace officer, firefighter, prosecutor, federal law officer, or judge.

The rate at which prosecutors seek the death penalty, however, varies a great deal across California's 58 counties. Prosecutors in Los Angeles County, by far, have sent more people to death row (234) than any other county in the state (CDCR, 2017, January 11). Taken together, Los Angeles, Riverside, and Orange counties account for 389 (or 52%) the 750 people on death row (CDCR, 2017, January 11). In some years, Los Angeles county has sentenced more offenders to death than the entire state of Texas. On the other hand, 20 counties have not added a single person to the current list of condemned inmates (CDCR, 2017, January 11). These geographic disparities mean that specific regions through-out the state are responsible for a majority of the state's death sentences (Segura, 2016), and this has garnered the attention of scholars.

In 2000, the governor of Illinois placed a moratorium on the death penalty in his state based on the recommendations of the Illinois Commission. In his 2003 study, Sanger examined the California death penalty system in light of the Illinois Commission's 85 recommendations. With respect to prosecutorial discretion, Sanger concluded that "the imposition of the death penalty in California varies depending on the court's geographical location. Indisputably, prosecutorial discretion is a major factor" (2003, p. 148). The Illinois Commission had three specific recommendations regarding the manner in which prosecutors should select cases for death. Specifically, they urged the state (1) to require a statewide protocol, including statewide recommendations to guide the local prosecutors; (2) to create a statewide committee to review death penalty charging decisions; and (3) to mandate that prosecutors notify the defendant within 120 days of his/her intention to seek the death penalty. Sanger's analysis revealed that "California leaves local prosecutors the discretion to decide whether or not to allege special circumstances and, if so, whether to seek the death penalty" (p. 164). Further, California has no requirement for statewide review. Finally, there is no mandate that prosecutors notify defendants of their intention to seek the death penalty in a timely manner. In fact, "defense counsel in California may not know until almost the day of trial whether the prosecution intends to seek the death penalty" (p. 149).

A limitation to the Sanger (2003) study, however, is that there was no statistical analysis to examine if the rate of death penalty charges was reflective of the number of homicides in a given county. Pierce and Radelet (2005) addressed this issue when they examined all homicides that occurred in California between January 1, 1990, and December 31, 1999. They calculated the ratio of homicides to death sentences across all 58 counties and compared it to the state average of .89 death sentences per 100 homicides. They uncovered tremendous sentence variation; individual county averages varied from .45 per 100 to 10 per 100. Notably, while 910 homicides took place in San Francisco County dur-ing the study period, there were no death sentences handed down because the district attorney, now U.S. Senator Kamala Harris, and her predecessor vowed not to seek a death penalty sentence (Pierce & Radelet, 2005).

In addition to geographic disparities, Pierce and Radelet also found that "death sentencing in Cali-fornia is highest in counties with a low population density and a high proportion of non-Hispanic white residents. The more white and more sparsely populated the county, the higher the death sen-tencing rate" (2005, p. 31). The connection between sentencing and race is not new; considerable research suggests that charging, conviction, and sentencing decisions in death penalty cases are also affected by the race of both the victim and the defendant (Baldus, Woodworth, & Pulaski, 1990; Ditchfield, 2007; Lee, 2007; Pierce & Radelet, 2005).

Most of this research, however, focuses on disparities between white and African American defen-dants. In order to address this deficiency in the literature, Lee (2007) examined death-eligible charging in all homicide cases, between 1977 and 1986, in San Joaquin County, California, a county where nearly 20% of the residents were Hispanic and 6% were African American. The findings indicated a pattern of racial and gender discrimination in death-eligible charging practices. Specifically, defen-dants in cases where the victim was white faced greater odds of being charged with capital homicide than defendants in cases where the victim was Hispanic. Additionally, defendants in cases with a female victim versus a male victim had higher odds of facing a capital homicide charge. These find-ings remained present while controlling for a number of legally relevant factors like heinousness of the crime and relationship between the victim and the defendant.

Since district attorneys are locally elected and presumably reflect the wishes of their constituents, prosecutors may suggest that geographical variation in pursuing the death penalty is not a problem. However, according to the California Commission on the Fair Administration of Justice (2008), "the California Supreme Court has consistently rejected claims that the discretion conferred on the district attorney of each county to seek the death penalty results in a county-by-county disparity in capital prosecutions, causing arbitrariness forbidden by the federal Constitution" (p. 151). Given the geographical and racial variation in death penalty sentencing, the California Commission concluded that the disparities

> should be subjected to further study and analysis in California. Evidence of disparities in the administration of the death penalty undermines public confidence in our criminal justice system generally. California is the most diverse state in the country. It is our duty to ensure that every aspect of the criminal justice system is administered fairly and evenly, and that all residents of the state are accorded equal treatment under the law. This is especially true when the state chooses to take a life in the name of the people.
>
> *(p. 152)*

Juror Decision Making

While the charging decisions of prosecutors varies considerably across the state, there is also evidence of arbitrariness within the jury box. The intention of the *Gregg* decision was to eliminate the arbitrariness ruled unconstitutional in *Furman*. In *Gregg* and similar cases, the USSC affirmed several types of statutes that provided guided discretion to juries in order to reduce arbitrary decisions. Some states mandate that juries find at least one aggravating factor, other states require that jurors weigh aggravating and mitigating factors (Bowers, 1995). In California, state law simply states that jurors should sentence an offender to death if they conclude that the aggravating factors outweigh the mitigating factors (California Penal Code Section 190.3)

Research suggests that jurors in capital cases rely not only on the evidence presented during the trial but that the physical characteristics of the defendant and his/her demeanor during the trial can influence juror decision making (Antonio, 2006; Bowers, 1995; Eberhardt, Davies, Purdie-Vaughns, & Johnson, 2006; Espinoza, 2009; Haney, Sontag, & Costanzo, 1994).

Much of this research incorporates data from the Capital Jury Project (CJP), a study that examined how actual jurors in capital cases from 14 states (including California) made life and death decisions (Bowers, 1995). The study had three primary objectives: to examine and describe jurors' exercise of discretion; to identify the sources of arbitrariness; and to assess the efficacy of different capital statutes in controlling arbitrariness (Bowers, 1995). The study was conducted against the legal backdrop that found the actions of pre-*Furman* capital juries as capricious and arbitrary. Capital jurors were interviewed to "identify the points at which various influences (including aspects of arbitrariness) may come into play, and to reveal the ways in which jurors reach their sentencing decisions" (Bowers, 1995, p. 1082).

Using data from the CJP, Antonio (2006) examined the effect of defendant demeanor on juror decision making while controlling for aggravating circumstances. Results suggest that a defendant's appearance during the trial was a significant factor influencing jurors' punishment decision. When the defendant appeared sorry or remorseful, jurors favored life over death; when the defendant appeared "emotionally uninvolved," jurors favored death over life in prison (Antonio, 2006, p. 232).

Also based on data from the CJP, Haney et al. (1994) compared how 57 capital jurors in Oregon and California (states with very different penalty phase instructions) reach their verdicts. In California, jurors are provided relatively little guidance at the penalty phase; jurors are instructed to "weigh" both aggravating and mitigating factors, yet the state does not specify what those factors are. Haney et al. (1994) found that the structure of the penalty instructions had a significant impact on the way in which deliberations proceeded. Specifically, compared to the Oregon jurors in their sample, the California jurors deliberated longer, "with much broader, more irregular, and less coherent agendas"

(p. 160). They were "more confused and less accurate about the instructions that were to guide their decision-making task (including several serious mistakes about the basic meaning of aggravation and, especially, mitigation)" (p. 160). In fact, "Many of the [California] jurors who were interviewed simply dismissed mitigating evidence that had been presented during the penalty phase because they did not believe it 'fit in' with the sentencing formula" (p. 167). Finally, in line with Antonio's (2006) results discussed earlier, California jurors in the Haney et al. (1994) study were more likely to consider whether or not the defendant expressed remorse (as based on in-court observations of the defendant) as part of their deliberations.

Interviewing capital jurors, like what was done for the CJP, is only one methodology that has been used to understand juror decision making. Some researchers have used a "mock juror" methodology; subjects are provided with a capital trial transcript and asked to render a verdict and/or penalty in the case. In a series of studies conducted in California, Espinoza and his colleagues have used this method to examine how ethnicity, socioeconomic status (SES), mitigating circumstances, and aggravating circumstances influence decisions of capital jurors (Espinoza, 2009; Espinoza & Willis-Esqueda, 2008, 2014). In all three studies, respondents were provided with a trial transcript in which certain factors (i.e., defendant ethnicity [Hispanic or white], defendant SES, aggravating circumstances, or mitigating circumstances) were varied. Respondents were asked to act as jurors and render a decision in the guilt and the penalty phase of the case.

Results of the 2009 study indicate that the subjects "gave the low SES, Mexican-American defendant who committed a crime with extenuating aggravating circumstances the death penalty significantly more often than all other conditions" (Espinoza, 2009, p. 40). These results are consistent with those of the 2008 study demonstrating that bias against Mexican American defendants occurred most when the Mexican American defendant was of low SES and represented by a Mexican American defense attorney. (Espinoza & Willis-Esqueda, 2008).

In their most recent study, Espinoza and Willis-Esqueda (2014) examined the effect of mitigating factors on juror decision making. Using a sample of death-eligible venire persons, the authors found that European American respondents "gave the low SES Latino defendant in the weak mitigation evidence condition the death penalty significantly more often than all other conditions. In addition, European American jurors found the low SES Latino defendant more responsible, more to blame, believed this defendant acted with more intent, and believed the viciousness of the crime was higher compared with all other conditions" (p. 294). Interestingly, however, the authors found that Latino respondents were less influenced by the extralegal factors of defendant ethnicity and SES.

Taken collectively, the inconsistent application of the death penalty by district attorneys across the state and the findings on juror decision making call into question the assumption of a fair and unbiased capital punishment system purportedly put into place by *Furman*.

The Current State of De-Facto Abolition

In this section, we examine how legislative efforts to reform the system have failed, while legal challenges have led to a de facto abolition in the state, where executions have been halted for over a decade. We also review how changes in public opinion led to two voter initiatives to abolish the death penalty.

Legislative Review of California's Death Penalty

In 2000, a Field Poll found that 73% of Californians would favor Governor Davis halting all executions to study the fairness of the state's death penalty (DiCamillo & Field, 2000). While an official moratorium was never enacted, in 2004 the California State Senate created a bi-partisan commission to review the state's criminal justice system and the issue of wrongful convictions. The commission was chaired by California Attorney General John K. Van de Kamp. Members included district attorneys, public defenders, judges, legal scholars, police chiefs, and community activists. The duties of the commission included the following:

1. To study and review the administration of criminal justice in California to determine the extent to which that process has failed in the past, resulting in wrongful executions or the wrongful conviction of innocent persons.
2. To examine ways of providing safeguards and making improvements in the way the criminal justice system functions.
3. To make any recommendations and proposals designed to further ensure that the application and administration of criminal justice in California is just, fair, and accurate.

While the commission reviewed many facets of the criminal justice system and their relationship to issues of wrongful conviction (such as the use of eyewitness testimony, interrogations, jailhouse snitches, etc.), the primary intent of the commission was to investigate the efficacy of the state's capital punishment system.

The countless hours of review, public hearings, and discussions over a four-year period led to 60 recommendations for reforms in seven different areas to the California State Legislature. These recommendations led to the passage of five bills by the Senate. For example, SB 171 was introduced by Senator Alquist as part of the 2005–06 legislative session and was designed to reform the system under which interrogation would be recorded. The existing law stated that "under specified condition, the statements of witnesses, victims, or perpetrators of specified crimes may be recorded and preserved by means of videotape." SB 171 would have required that any custodial interrogation of an individual suspected of a serious felony (including homicide) be recorded electronically (SB 171, 2006). Another example was SB 1544, which would have required the development of statewide guidelines regarding eyewitness identifications (SB 1544, 2006). Unfortunately, all five bills were vetoed by then-Governor Schwarzenegger. While these attempts failed, there have been small efforts to close the gap in some areas of concern. One of the few reforms that passed requires the recording of interrogations for juveniles who are suspects in murder cases (SB 569, 2013). Another partial reform requires corroborating evidence in cases where a jailhouse informant is used (SB 687, 2011). However, there are still dozens of areas where pervasive issues persist. Ultimately, the state legislature has been unable to capitalize on the efforts of the California Commission to overhaul the criminal justice system or our practice of the death penalty (Sanger, 2016).

Legal Challenges and California's Moratorium

Prior to the decision in *Furman v. Georgia* (1972), California was actively engaged in carrying out executions. Between 1878 (the date of California's first execution) and 1972, California had the seventh highest number of executions nationwide ($n = 709$). With 13 executions in the past four decades, California is now a state with one of the fewest number of executions in the post-*Furman* era. The current moratorium in the state is largely the result of legal challenges raised by death row inmates.

The first case to halt executions involved Michael Morales. Morales was convicted of the rape and murder of Terri Winchell in 1981. After spending over two decades on death row, his execution date was set for February, 21, 2006. Prior to the execution, the two court appointed anesthesiologists who were hired to minimize Morales' pain during the execution withdrew their participation. The doctors expressed concern at a court request that they intervene if the sedative failed. At the same time, professional organizations such as the American Medical Association and the American Society of Anesthesiologists were opposed to the involvement of doctors in lethal injections (Grace, 2006). As a result, Michael Morales' execution was stayed. In hopes of being able to carry out the execution, the state proposed an alternative option of carrying out the execution using a one-drug protocol of a lethal dose of a barbiturate. In response, U.S. District Court Judge Jeremy Fogel imposed additional requirements on the state, including mandates that the drugs would have to be administered directly into the vein, which in turn would require the person administering the drug to be in the execution chamber with Morales. The state refused these additional requirements, and the execution was stayed until a hearing on the state's execution protocol could be heard (Finz, Egelko, & Fagan, 2006).

On December 15, 2006, the U.S. District Court held in the case of *Morales v. Tilton* that California's lethal injection protocol "created an undue and unnecessary risk that an inmate will suffer pain so extreme that it violates the Eighth Amendment." While Judge Fogel felt that the current practice was unconstitutional, he left the door open for the state to revise its protocol. The decision identified five specific deficiencies in the state's lethal injection protocol:

1. ***Inconsistent and unreliable screening of execution team members.*** During previous executions, members of the execution team had questionable moral violations or had struggled with stress disorders that could affect their ability to perform their job effectively.
2. ***A lack of meaningful training, supervision, and oversight of the execution team.*** The execution team had no prior training or education on the procedures and chemicals that are used in executions. Furthermore, the execution team was not adequately prepared to address potential complications.
3. ***Inconsistent and unreliable recordkeeping.*** A review of records from prior executions revealed several areas where important information was missing or incomplete. Examples include a lack of documentation on the heart rates of the condemned and missing data on how much sodium thiopental was left over following the execution.
4. ***Improper mixing, preparation, and administration of sodium thiopental by the execution team.*** A review of previous executions noted that execution team members did not follow the directions provided by the manufacturer of the sedative (sodium thiopental). This raises the question of whether previous executions were carried out properly.
5. ***Inadequate lighting, overcrowded conditions, and poorly designed facilities in which the execution team must work.*** The facility at San Quentin where executions were held was not designed to carry out lethal injections. The current facility restricted the viewing opportunities of both the members of the execution team and the witnesses to the execution (*Morales v. Tilton*, 2006).

As a result of the court's decision in *Morales v. Tilton*, the California Department of Corrections and Rehabilitation was charged with amending the state's lethal injection protocol. State executions were halted, and California has remained in a de facto moratorium for the past decade (Mallicoat, 2014).

Voter Initiatives and California's Death Penalty

Over the past eight years, Californians have seen three initiatives presented to voters that would either reform or end the use of the death penalty in the state. Following the failed attempts to reform the system at the legislative level, coupled with legal challenges that halted executions, both supporters and opponents of the policy believed that reform to the policy could be achieved through the use of direct democracy. While several other states nationwide had abolished the death penalty through legislative action and gubernatorial approval, this is not an option in California due to the passage of the 1978 Briggs Initiative, which expanded the death penalty's special circumstances—only subsequent voter initiatives or the courts can overturn previous ballot measures. As part of these efforts, abolitionists pointed to both statewide and nationwide trends in public opinion that showed a decrease in support for the practice.

Over the past four decades, residents of California have expressed strong support for the death penalty. While the Gallup Poll measures national trends, the Field Poll has measured support for the death penalty amongst Californians since 1956. During this time, support for the death penalty has been as low as 49% in 1956, and as high as 83% in 1985 and 1986. In addition, public opinion has been more decisive over the years. In 1956, 22% of Californian adults had no opinion about the practice. By the late 1990s, this had changed to only 6% with no opinion, with 74% in favor of the practice and 20% opposed (DiCamillo & Field, 1997). During the 2000s, support remained high, ranging from 63% to 72%, and scholars have suggested that public sentiment played a significant role in the continued legal and legislative support for the death penalty (Bohm, 1991; Boots, Cochran, & Heide, 2003).

In recent years, concerns about the high costs of maintaining a system of death, the increased risk of executing an innocent individual, and concerns about the fair administration of capital punishment have all contributed to decreases in public support. At the same time, support for alternatives to the death penalty, such as life without the possibility of parole (LWOP) have increased. In 2010, 7 in 10 state voters were in support of the death penalty (compared to general opposition). Yet when asked whether they would advocate for a death sentence over life without the possibility of parole, 41% stated that they would choose the death penalty in cases of first-degree murder, while 42% indicated that they would support LWOP (DiCamillo & Field, 2010).

Proposition 34 (2012)

In 2012, California voters were presented with the option of abolishing the death penalty through the initiative process. As part of this process, proponents of the measure collected 504,760 valid signatures from California voters and spent $1,418,122 to place the initiative on the ballot. Proposition 34 would have eliminated the death penalty for people convicted of murder and would have replaced it with the punishment of LWOP. If approved by the voters, the law would be retroactive and would have replaced the death sentences of 725 people on death row at the time with an LWOP sentence. The measure would have also required inmates to work, and 50% of their wages would have gone to satisfy any fines or restitution orders that the court had issued against them. Cost savings from the elimination of the death penalty would be used to create a $100-million dollar fund to support law enforcement efforts related to unsolved murder and rape cases (Proposition 34, 2012).

One of the major messages of the campaign was that eliminating the death penalty would result in significant cost savings to the state. Research by Judge Arthur Alarcón and Paula Mitchell (2011) noted that the state had spent over $4 billion between 1978 and 2010 while only carrying out 13 executions. This sum includes $1.94 billion dollars on the pretrial and trial costs for approximately 1,940 death penalty trials, $925 million on automatic appeals and habeas corpus petitions at the state level, $775 million on federal habeas corpus petitions, and $1 billion on the costs of incarceration. In addition, a fiscal impact statement prepared by the California Legislative Analyst noted that the cost savings to individual counties from the costs of murder trials, and the costs to the state from death penalty appeals, and the housing of offenders on death row would save approximately $100 million dollars within the first few years of abolishing capital punishment (Proposition 34).

General statewide polls prior to the election noted a general reduction in the levels of support for the death penalty in California and an increased willingness to support life without the possibility of parole. For example, a survey by the Public Policy Institute of California in September 2012 asked what should the penalty be for first-degree murder. Fifty percent of likely voters stated that the punishment for this crime should be LWOP and 42% of respondents expressed support for the death penalty (Baldassare, Bonner, Petek, & Shrestha, 2012). Yet specific polling data on Proposition 34 found that most voters were opposed to eliminating the option. For example, a September 2012 USC Dornsife/*Los Angeles Times* poll found that only 38% of those polled were in support of abolishing the death penalty, while 51% were opposed. However, as more voters learned about the status of the death penalty in California and the financial burdens of the system, later polls found an increase in the number of those in favor of Prop 34 (Leonard & Dolan, 2012). A subsequent poll by USC Dornsife/*Los Angeles Times* in October noted that support for Prop 34 had increased to 42% while opposition fell to 45%. However, voters continued to be undecided (USC Dornsife, 2012). Such trends continued up to the election. A Field Poll completed just prior to the election found that 45% of voters were likely to vote yes, while 38% noted that they were voting no (DiCamillo & Field, 2012).

Trends in the polling data appeared to be moving in a favorable direction in the final days up to the election. However, no poll noted that a majority of respondents were in favor of the proposition. Indeed, the large number of undecided voters on the issue meant that the outcome of the election would likely be close. In the end Proposition 34 was narrowly defeated, with 52% of voters opposing abolition (6,460,264 votes) and 48% of voters in favor of abolition (5,974,243 votes) (Proposition 34).

The Death Penalty Reform and Savings Act of 2014

Shortly after Proposition 34 failed, supporters of California's beleaguered death penalty system countered by launching their own effort to prevent repeal and revive executions. Proposition 34 had surprised many observers by coming so close to eliminating death sentences and death row altogether. Falling short by only a few hundred thousand votes, the ballot initiative likely garnered support from people who were not ardent abolitionists but understood that the system was very expensive to maintain for such a negligible public safety impact. As death penalty opponents gathered at the finish line, supporters acknowledged that they had to act in order to save the system. As San Bernardino County District Attorney Mike Ramos put it, "We need to fix the death penalty, or it's going to go away. It's that simple" (Chammah, 2015). Death penalty supporters therefore took a two-pronged approach: to offer an alternative to repeal by marshaling the same arguments that resonated for Prop 34 and to undermine those same arguments by resuming executions after such a long hiatus.

Just over a year after Prop 34's defeat, death penalty supporters filed their own ballot initiative called The Death Penalty Reform and Savings Act of 2014 (Office of the Attorney General, 2013). It was drafted as a constitutional amendment with new restrictions on the California Supreme Court and directions to send postconviction appeals back to their original trial courts, among other changes to judicial procedures in capital cases. It also included provisions designed to limit the time that an appeal can take and to change the regulations governing how and where condemned prisoners may be housed. Instead of focusing on the complicated legal maneuverings proposed in the initiative, The Death Penalty Reform and Savings Act of 2014 was presented to the public as a simple "fix" for California's "broken" death penalty system. As former Governor Gray Davis put it in a press conference announcing the campaign, "This initiative will bring commons sense reforms to a broken system" (Mintz, 2014). Although the initiative failed to gather enough signatures to qualify—perhaps because it was drafted as a constitutional amendment[1]—it's sponsors quietly announced that it would shift its focus to 2016 (Nirappil, 2014).

Proposition 62 and 66 (2016)

California's November 2016 ballot saw two competing initiatives related to the death penalty. Proposition 62 was in many ways similar in its intent to Proposition 34 in that it aimed to abolish the death penalty and replace it with LWOP; if passed, it would also require inmates to work and for their wages to be applied to fines and restitution orders. While Proposition 34 mandated that 50% of these wages would be used for this purpose (similar to any other inmate), Proposition 62 increased this share to 60% for the formerly condemned and for future individuals sentenced to LWOP. Another difference was that Proposition 62 did not mandate where the cost savings would be allocated. The Legislative

Analyst Office found that the cost savings by abolishing the death penalty and replacing it with LWOP would save the state over $150 million dollars annually (Legislative Analyst's Office, 2016a).

At the same time, those who had opposed Prop 34 and sponsored the aborted reform initiative presented their own ballot language for voters to consider. Proposition 66 posited that the state's system of capital punishment could be reformed and allow executions to resume by changing the procedures that govern the appellate process related to death sentences. One of these changes included shifting habeas corpus petitions from the state Supreme Court to the Superior Court (trial court). In addition, the measure limited the state appeals process to five years and would have expanded the pool of eligible attorneys to serve as appellate counsel (Proposition 66). While proponents of the measure suggested that these reforms would save the state $30 million dollars annually, the Legislative Analyst's Office was unable to determine the cost savings from these reforms. In fact, the LAO noted that while there could be potential savings for the state correctional budget, costs to the state courts to manage any legal challenges by those sentenced to death were unknown (Legislative Analyst's Office, 2016b).

In the months prior to the election, polling data about the success of Prop 62 and 66 were mixed. A poll by USC Dornsife/*Los Angeles Times* in October 2016 asked 1,500 likely voters how they would vote on these initiatives. Forty-four percent of respondents stated that they would likely favor of Prop 62, with 46% opposed (8% unknown). The same poll found that 35% would likely support Proposition 66, while 42% would likely oppose it, with a significant number of respondents (19%) noting that they were undecided (USC/LA Times Poll, 2016). Similar polls noted large numbers of undecided voters on Proposition 66 (Hoover Golden State Poll, 2016).

While each of these polls included language that spoke generally about these two competing propositions, only the Field Poll included the actual language from the ballot label that voters would see on Election Day. In a September 2016 Field Poll, neither proposition registered a majority of support. Forty-eight percent of voters stated that they were likely to vote yes on Proposition 62. Thirty-two percent stated they were likely to vote no on the measure, and 15% were undecided. Meanwhile, 35% of likely voters stated that they would vote yes on Proposition 66, while 23% were likely to vote no. What was particularly noteworthy was that 40% of those polled stated that they were undecided about Proposition 66, a likely indication that the ballot language was confusing to voters (DiCamillo, September 2016). In the days prior to the election, Proposition 62 was polling higher than Proposition 66, with 51% of likely voters in support of Prop 62 and 48% in favor of Prop 66 (DiCamillo, November 2016).

With two competing measures on the ballot, it was possible that both measures would pass. Under California state law, if both measures would have received a majority share of the voters, the initiative that received the largest number of "yes" votes would be declared the winner. In the case of these two initiatives, only one measure passed with more than 50% of the votes cast. Proposition 62 received 6,361,788 of "yes" votes, totaling 46.85% of the votes cast. In contrast, proposition 66 received 6,626,159 votes, or 51.13% of votes cast. While "No on 66" received roughly the same number of votes as "Yes on 62" (6,333,731 compared to 6,361,788), there were far fewer people who voted no on 62 compared to those who voted yes on 66 (California Secretary of State, 2016).

An analysis of the votes cast for Proposition 62 indicates that the majority of counties throughout the state voted no on the measure. Of the 58 counties throughout the state, only 15 voted in favor of the measure. In many of these counties, this majority was a narrow victory. Support for Proposition 62 was primarily focused in the northern region of the state, with the exception of Santa Barbara and Los Angeles County. In addition, support was almost exclusively limited to coastal counties. Figure 25.1 highlights the results of Proposition 62 by county.

In contrast, there were 38 counties that voted in favor of Proposition 66 and 20 counties that were opposed. Support for the measure was much more evenly distributed between the northern and

Figure 25.1 Proposition 62 (2016) Results by County.
Source: http://elections.cdn.sos.ca.gov/sov/2016-general/sov/06-sov-summary.pdf

southern regions of the state. Figure 25.2 presents the results of Proposition 66 by county. While most of the counties that voted in favor of Proposition 66 were against Proposition 62 (and vice versa), it is interesting to note that there were six counties (Fresno, Inyo, Mono, Napa, Sierra, and Trinity) where a majority of the votes cast were against both measures.

The Future of California's Death Penalty

Over the last ten years, several attempts have been made through legislative action, legal challenges, public opinion, and the initiative process to end the use of capital punishment in California. In this section, we review how some of these current challenges may impact the future of the death penalty in California.

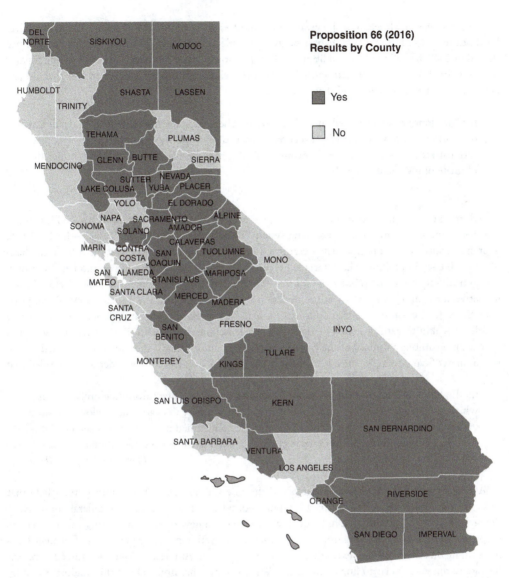

Figure 25.2   Proposition 66 (2016) Results by County.

Source: http://elections.cdn.sos.ca.gov/sov/2016-general/sov/06-sov-summary.pdf

The Case of Ernest Dewayne Jones

In 2014, Federal District Court Judge Cormac J. Carney held that California's death penalty violated the Eighth Amendment's ban against cruel and unusual punishment as a result of the lengthy delays in carrying out the punishment. In this case, the defendant, Ernest Dewayne Jones, was sentenced to death in 1995. Yet almost two decades later, his case was still moving through the appeals process.

One of the central arguments in the case was that these delays are a direct consequence of the structure of the state's system, including the lengthy period of time that it takes to appoint counsel to a defendant for the postconviction process as well as the time that it takes for cases to be heard by the courts at various levels. For Jones, it took almost eight years for the Supreme Court to affirm his death sentence. His first state habeas petition was filed in October 2002. While this petition was denied in 2009, he had filed two additional habeas petitions during this time, the last of which formed the basis for this case. Judge Carney held that such delays result in a system that fails to hold any deterrent or retributive value and that

> for Mr. Jones to be executed in such a system, where so many are sentenced to death but only a random few are actually executed, would offend the most fundamental of constitutional protections—that the government shall not be permitted to arbitrarily inflict the ultimate punishment of death.
>
> *(Jones v. Chappell, 2014)*

Arbitrariness was the crux of the *Jones* ruling, especially as it was compounded by the long delays featured in the California death sentencing system. Drawing from *Furman v Georgia*—the 1972 U.S. Supreme Court case that temporarily overturned every death penalty statute nationwide on the basis of their arbitrary imposition (characterized by Justice Stevens in his concurring opinion as "wantonly and so freakishly imposed" [*Furman v. Georgia*, 408 U.S. 238, 310])—Carney noted the glaring disparity between the more than 900 death sentences issued since 1978 and the 13 executions during that same time. Justices on the *Furman* court had posited that receiving a death sentence for committing murder was akin to getting struck by lightning when walking in the rain. For Carney, the selection for execution among this pool of the condemned had no rational basis, and rather it depended on the randomness of circumstances outside of the inmates' control, over the course of decades. He ruled that

> the Eighth Amendment simply cannot be read to proscribe a state from randomly selecting which few members of its criminal population it will sentence to death, but to allow that same state to randomly select which trivial few of those condemned it will actually execute. Arbitrariness in execution is still arbitrary, regardless of when in the process the arbitrariness arises.
>
> *(Jones v. Chappell, 2014)*

As a result, Jones' sentence was vacated and the case was appealed. The Ninth Circuit held that previous case law under *Teague v. Lane* prohibited consideration of this claim in federal court. Here, the precedent of *Teague* states that individuals cannot establish new rules of law during a federal habeas corpus case, and, despite drawing from the arbitrariness in death sentencing precedent of *Furman*, Carney's ruling on arbitrariness in executions was a new approach. As a result, Jones was forced to return his case to the state courts to litigate his claim. What is somewhat ironic about this holding is that by returning it to the lower courts, it will add even additional time to his appeals process, the claim that is at the heart of his legal challenge (*Jones v. Davis*, 2015).

Legal Challenges to California's Lethal Injection Protocol

In November 2014, death penalty proponents filed a lawsuit against the CDCR aimed at procuring a workable lethal injection protocol. It had been nearly a decade since the last execution in California at that point, and two years since the CDCR had last attempted to develop a method of lethal injection that could pass muster with regulators and the courts, and for which necessary drugs could be obtained. Represented by the same attorney who drafted The Death Penalty Reform and Savings Act of 2014, plaintiffs Kermit Alexander and Bradley Winchell—whose close relatives had been murdered by people now on death row—alleged that the department had deliberately delayed creating a viable execution method and listed a series of demands (*Winchell v. Beard*, 2015). First among them, the suit sought to compel the state to promulgate a new set of regulations according to a process outlined in the Administrative Procedures Act. This would mean that the draft execution protocol—and justifications for any changes from previous incarnations—had to be filed with the Office of Administrative Law, and subsequently, the department had to make all relevant documents available to the public and accept and respond to subsequent critiques thereof. However, the suit also demanded, because of the CDCR's alleged dereliction, the regulations should take effect concurrent with the vetting process by invoking emergency provisions of the APA. In other words, executions should resume without first completing a legislatively required and court-mandated oversight process. Perhaps the most unexpected demand in the suit was that the state should not search for a new single-drug "cocktail" in order to perform lethal injections since the department likely had access to expired sodium thiopental left over from its previous three-drug executions. It could be that these more drastic demands were intended to be bargaining chips, or perhaps they were sincere, if pitiless, attempts to resume executions as quickly as possible. In either case, the state reached a settlement in early June 2015 and agreed to develop and promulgate a new set of execution regulations within 120 days of a ruling in an unrelated case at the U.S. Supreme Court, *Glossip v. Gross* (2015).

The ruling in *Glossip* came on June 29, 2015, and, after a small extension, the CDCR announced new regulations for conducting executions on October 27. The proposal was the first nationwide to offer executioners a choice among four different drugs—sodium thiopental, pentobarbital, amobarbital, and secobarbital (CDCR, 2015). Sodium thiopental is a barbiturate that was often used for surgeries in previous decades before more reliable drugs replaced it.[2] In the original three-drug "cocktail" that California and other states used for executions, sodium thiopental was used to sedate a condemned person and would be followed by a paralytic agent and then a final drug used to induce cardiac arrest. Sodium thiopental has since become increasingly difficult for corrections departments to obtain because its manufacturer ceased production in order to prevent its use in lethal injection. Pentobarbital, the second option, has been used by other states as a substitute for sodium thiopental and on its own as a single-drug execution method. It too has become increasingly difficult for corrections departments to track down, leading them to turn to gray and black market sources or to compounding pharmacies. Meanwhile, amobarbital and secobarbital, the final options, have never been used in the history of the death penalty.

In addition to these four drugs, other drugs were considered by the CDCR for use in carrying out lethal injections. Much of this debate was a reflection of the difficulties by other states in securing these drugs for the purposes of lethal injection. For example, the difficulty over obtaining pentobarbital was a direct contributor to the rise of using midazolam in three-drug methods, the central concern in *Glossip v. Gross*. Similarly, Propofol was actually floated by some corrections departments as a potential substitute for the outdated sodium thiopental, but the medical community protested quickly and forcefully enough that such plans were quickly dropped. Upon notice that Propofol was under consideration for use in executions, its manufacturer stated that:

> Fresenius Kabi is doing its utmost to help ensure the safety and availability of Propofol for patients and those who care for them. In line with its mission "caring for life" Fresenius Kabi, as the largest provider of Propofol in the U.S., is committed to ensuring Propofol is only used for its intended and clinically approved medical purposes. Clearly the use of Propofol for lethal injections is contrary to our mission and not in line with FDA approved indications for Propofol. Therefore, Fresenius Kabi and other manufacturers have imposed distribution controls to protect the U.S. supply of this medically necessary drug.
>
> *(Fresenius Kabi, 2017)*

Notably, the proposed execution protocol does not offer any insight about which of the four drugs would be preferable, or what kind of factors are involved with the decision over which to use. In fact, despite different strengths and pharmacology, the regulations proposed using the same dosage and rate of administration regardless of the drug selected.

To gather feedback on its proposed execution regulations, the CDCR held a public hearing in the Capitol on January 22, 2016. Kent Scheidegger, of the Criminal Justice Legal Foundation, who brought the lawsuit on behalf of Winchell and Alexander and authored the Death Penalty Reform and Savings Act, urged the CDCR to dismiss any possible objections, whether they might come from moral, medical, or good-governance perspectives. The overwhelming majority of comments came from people who either opposed executions outright or raised concerns about specific aspects of the CDCR's proposal. A representative from the American Civil Liberties Union, for example, raised concerns about the decision making that went into choosing these four options and urged regulators to allow more time for to review documentation. Others questioned whether it was appropriate to use amobarbital and secobarbital without any evidence of their efficacy, and questioned why the regulations did not specify how the drugs would be obtained.

At the start of 2017, the future of the lethal injection in California remains uncertain. After several extensions, the public comment period finally culminated in the April 2016. The CDCR was then tasked with reviewing and responding to the critiques raised by the public, either by amending its proposal or justifying the initial provisions in spite of challenges raised by commenters. However, this process is somewhat unclear at this point. With the passage of Prop 66, it would seem that the oversight process no longer applies. Yet the constitutionality of Prop 66 has already been challenged in court, resulting in a stay in the implementation of this new law. Meanwhile, the Office of Administrative Law rejected the CDCR's first final draft of the regulations near the end of December 2016 and has given the department four months to amend and correct protocol (Office of Administrative Law, 2016).

Legal Challenges to Proposition 66

In the days following the passage of Proposition 66, Ron Briggs (the author of California's death penalty law in 1978) and John Van de Kamp (former Attorney General to the State of California) filed a legal challenge against the implementation of Prop 66 (*Ron Briggs and John Van de Kamp v. Jerry Brown*, 2016). Their argument focuses on three issues: (1) the law eliminates the system of checks and balances within the court system by forcing the first appeal to be heard by the original judge in the case, versus a higher court with more independence; (2) the law also sets a time limit on appeals; and (3) the law is invalid because the measure includes more than one subject. As a result of this legal challenge, the implementation of Proposition 66 has been stayed until the court hears the case sometime in 2017 (*Ron Briggs and John Van de Kamp v. Jerry Brown*, 2016). However, this hearing will go on without Chief Justice Tani Cantil-Sakauye and Justice Ming W. Chin, as they both serve on the Judicial Council who is listed as a defendant in the lawsuit. While both justices are often viewed as two of the more conservative members of the court, Chief Justice Cantil-Sakauye has spoken publically in the past about the failures of the state's death penalty and the need to create structural changes, which would likely be cost prohibitive (Dolan, 2011). At this point, it is unknown who from the Court of Appeals will be called on to replace these justices for this case.

Conclusion

What does the future hold for the death penalty nationwide and how will this impact California? On one hand, the number of new death sentences annually has fallen dramatically in recent years. For example, in 2010, there were 109 death sentences nationwide. Just five years later, the number of death sentences handed down was fewer than half, with 49 sentences. This is even more of a dramatic reduction given that in 1996, there were 315 death sentences nationwide (Death Penalty Information Center, 2017). Meanwhile, California has continued to sentence people to death, a somewhat contrary approach to punishment given the national trends.

In addition, the state continues to struggle with issues such as long delays in the appellate process and challenges in developing a lethal injection protocol. While Proposition 66 and other legal challenges have aimed to address these issues, it is possible that these efforts will only increase the delays and costs associated with carrying out the death penalty. Like California, many other states have struggled with the problems in their lethal injection protocols. To date, the U.S. Supreme Court has upheld the use of lethal injection. In *Baze v. Rees* (2008) the court stated that Kentucky's use of a three-drug protocol does not constitute cruel and unusual punishment. Similarly, the case of *Glossip v. Gross* in 2015 held that Oklahoma's three-drug protocol involving midazolam did not violate the Eighth Amendment. However, the shortage of drugs, coupled with several recent controversial executions, has led several states to develop new protocols for their lethal injection process.

In addition to reviewing the lethal injection process, several U.S. Supreme Court cases during the twenty-first century have effectively chipped away at the death penalty against certain populations, including the intellectually disabled (*Atkins v. Virginia*, 2002, and *Hall v. Florida*, 2014), and juveniles (*Roper v. Simmons*, 2005). Some scholars have questioned whether it was just a matter of time before the court considered the overall constitutionality of the death penalty.

The death of Justice Antonin Scalia created a vacancy on the court that could have been filled by a justice who was more likely to question the justification of the death penalty. President Obama nominated Merrick Garland, a moderate jurist from the U.S. Court of Appeals for the D.C. Circuit, to fill the vacancy left by Scalia. While he would have been far more centrist than his predecessor, he may not have been supportive of abolishing the death penalty. As a former prosecutor, he oversaw the case against Oklahoma City bomber Timothy McVeigh. However, the Republican-led Senate refused to hold hearings on the nomination and the seat went unfilled for the remainder of President Obama's time in office. In fewer than two weeks following his inauguration, President Trump announced Neil Gorsuch as his nominee. Gorsuch has served on the Tenth Circuit Court of Appeals for the past decade. His judicial philosophy is similar to that of Justice Scalia, and it is likely that Gorsuch will not likely be receptive to cases from death row inmates (Koh, 2017).

Given that a judicial abolition of the death penalty is unlikely in the near future, will we see more states abolish the death penalty? Seven states have abolished the death penalty in the past decade through legislative actions, and four other states have called for gubernatorial moratoria, which means that no executions will be carried out while these governors are in office.[3] However, no state has recently been successful at abolishing the death penalty via the popular vote. Indeed the failure of California's Prop 34 and 62 and the success of Proposition 66 is not an isolated phenomena. In 2016, voters in Nebraska overturned the state's 2015 ban on the death penalty and reinstated the practice (Referendum 426, 2016). In Oklahoma, voters approved a law that not only allows the state legislature to adopt any execution methods, but it also prevents the state courts from declaring capital punishment as unconstitutional (State Question 776, 2016). Indeed, it appears that California's stance on capital punishment will remain "chaotic" for at least the near future.

Notes

1 For an initiative to qualify for the ballot, its campaign must gather signatures from registered voters at a level equivalent or greater than a certain percentage of the votes cast in the previous gubernatorial election. Initiative statutes, which simply add or modify existing states, require signature equivalent to 5% of the votes in the previous election—to amend the state constitution, the threshold is 8%.

2 See, for example, that propofol is a preferred anesthetic in the World Health Organization's list of essential medicines, and that sodium thiopental could be substituted based on "local availability and cost." World Health Organization, *19th Model List of Essential Medicines*, 8 May 2015, available at www.who.int/medicines/publications/essentialmedicines/EML2015_8-May-15.pdf.

3 States that have abolished the death penalty in the past decade include New York (2007), New Jersey (2007), New Mexico (2009), Illinois (2011), Connecticut (2012), Maryland (2013), and Delaware (2016). States with

gubernatorial moratoria include Oregon (2011), Colorado (2013), Washington (2014), and Pennsylvania (2015). See www.deathpenaltyinfo.org for current information on states with the death penalty.

References

Alarcón, A., & Mitchell, P. (2011). Executing the will of the voters? A roadmap to mend or end the California legislature's multi—billion—dollar death penalty debacle, 44 Loy. L.A. L.Rev. S41, S61.

Antonio, M. E. (2006). Arbitrariness and the death penalty: How the defendant's appearance during trial influences capital jurors' punishment decision. *Behavioral Sciences and the Law, 24*, 215–234. doi: 10.1002/bsl.673

Baldassare, M., Bonner, D., Petek, S., & Shrestha, J. (September 2012). *PPIC statewide survey: Californians & their government.* Retrieved from www.ppic.org/content/pubs/survey/S_912MBS.pdf

Baldus, D. C., Woodworth, G., & Pulaski, C. A. (1990). *Equal justice and the death penalty: A legal and empirical analysis.* Boston: Northeastern University Press.

Bohm, R. M. (1991). American death penalty opinion 1936–1986: A critical examination of the Gallup polls. In R. Bohm (Ed.), *The death penalty in America: Current research* (pp. 113–145). Cincinnati, OH: Anderson.

Bohm, R.M. (2012). Deathquest: An introduction to the theory and practice of punishment in the United States. 4th Edition. New York: Routledge

Boots, D. P., Cochran, J. K., & Heide, K. M. (2003). Capital punishment preferences for special offenders populations. *Journal of Criminal Justice, 31*, 553–565.

Bowers, W. J. (1995). The capital jury project: Rationale, design, and a preview of early findings. *Indiana Law Journal, 70*, 1043–1102.

California Commission on the Fair Administration of Justice. (2008). *Final report.* Retrieved from http://digitalcommons.law.scu.edu/cgi/viewcontent.cgi?article=1000&context=ncippubs

California Department of Corrections and Rehabilitation. (2015, November 6). *Notice of change to regulations, title 15, sections: 3349, 3349.1, 3349.2, 3349.3, 3349.4, 3349.5, 3349.6, 3349.7, 3349.8, and 3349.9,* Retrieved from www.cdcr.ca.gov/Regulations/Adult_Operations/docs/NCDR/2015NCR/15-10/NCR%2015-10%20Notice%20of%20Proposed%20Regulations.pdf

California Department of Corrections and Rehabilitation (CDCR). (2017, January 11). Retrieved from www.cdcr.ca.gov/Capital_Punishment/docs/CondemnedInmateSummary.pdf?pdf=Condemned-Inmates

California Department of Correction and Rehabilitation (CDCR). (2017, January 20). Retrieved from www.cdcr.ca.gov/Capital_Punishment/history_of_capital_punishment.html

California Secretary of State. (2016). *Statement of votes.* Retrieved from http://elections.cdn.sos.ca.gov/sov/2016-general/sov/2016-complete-sov.pdf

California Senate Bills 171, and 1544 (2005–06 Session) and Senate Bills 756, 511 and 609 (2006–07 Session).

Chammah, M. (2015). *The unfolding campaign to save the death penalty.* The Marshall Project. Retrieved from www.themarshallproject.org/2015/11/19/the-unfolding-campaign-to-save-the-death-penalty#.Ozix6ICP6

Civil Rights Litigation Clearinghouse: University of Michigan Law School. Lopez v. Brown. (2017, January 31). Retrieved from www.clearinghouse.net/detail.php?id=14816

Death Penalty Focus. (2017, January 3). Retrieved from http://deathpenalty.org/facts/death-penalty-is-broken-beyond-repair-costly-failure/

Death Penalty Information Center. (2017). *States with and without the death penalty.* Retrieved from www.deathpenaltyinfo.org/states-and-without-death-penalty

DiCamillo, M. (2016, September 22). *Death penalty repeal (Prop. 62) holds narrow lead, but is receiving less than 50% support.* Most voters aren't sure about Prop. 66, a competing initiative to speed implementation of death sentences. Retrieved from www.field.com/fieldpollonline/subscribers/Rls2547.pdf

DiCamillo, M. (2016, November 4). *Voters inclined to support many of this year's statewide ballot propositions.* Field Poll. Retrieved from www.field.com/fieldpollonline/subscribers/Rls2555.pdf

DiCamillo, M., & Field, M. (1997, March 14). *Slight ebbing in support for capital punishment but 74% still favor it.* Field Poll. Retrieved from www.field.com/fieldpollonline/subscribers/Release1837.pdf

DiCamillo, M., & Field, M. (2000, June 22). *Significant decline in once overwhelming majority support for capital punishment: Three out of four favor Governor Davis declaring a death penalty moratorium.* Field Poll. Retrieved from www.field.com/fieldpollonline/subscribers/Release1965.pdf

DiCamillo, M., & Field, M. (2010, July 22). *Seven in ten Californians continue to support capital punishment.* Field Poll. Retrieved from www.field.com/fieldpollonline/subscribers/Rls2351.pdf

DiCamillo, M., & Field, M. (2012, November 2). *More voters now favor death penalty's repeal (Propo. 34), but yes vote less than a majority.* Retrieved from www.field.com/fieldpollonline/subscribers/Rls2432.pdf

Dickerson, K. (2016, September 14). A Look Inside San Quentin, Home of Death Row. Retrieved from http://fox40.com/2016/09/14/a-look-inside-san-quentin-home-of-death-row/

Ditchfield, A. (2007). Intrastate disparities in capital punishment. *The Georgetown Law Journal*, *95*, 801–830.

Dolan, M. (2011, December 24). California chief justice urges reevaluating death penalty. *LA Times*. Retrieved from http://articles.latimes.com/2011/dec/24/local/la-me-1222-chief-justice-20111221

Eberhardt, J.L., Davies, P.G., Purdie-Vaughns, V.J., & Johnson, S.L. (2006) Looking deathworthy: Perceived stereotypicality of Black defendants predicts capital-sentencing outcomes. *Psychological Science*, *17*, 383–386.

Espinoza, R. K. E. (2009). Juror bias and the death penalty: Deleterious effects of ethnicity and SES. *The American Association of Behavioral and Social Sciences Journal*, (Fall), 33–41.

Espinoza, R. K. E., & Willis-Esqueda, C. (2008). Defendant and defense attorney characteristics and their effects on juror decision making and prejudice against Mexican Americans. *Cultural Diversity and Ethnic Minority Psychology*, *14*, 364–371. doi: 10.1037/a0012767

Espinoza, R. K. E., & Willis-Esqueda, C. (2014). The influence of mitigation evidence, ethnicity, and SES on death penalty decisions by European American and Latino venire persons. *Cultural Diversity and Ethnic Minority Psychology*, *21*, 288–299.

Finz, S., Egelko, B., & Fagan, K. (2006, February 22). *State postpones Morales execution/Judge's new order: Officials refuse to revise method of lethal injection.* SF Gate. Retrieved from www.sfgate.com/news/article/STATE-POSTPONES-MORALES-EXECUTION-Judge-s-new-2503523.php

Fresenius Kabi. (2017). How the use of propofol in executions would impact patient safety in the U.S. Retrieved from www.propofol-info.com

Grace, F. (2006, February 21). *Execution delayed when docs withdraw.* CBS News. Retrieved from www.cbsnews.com/news/execution-dela5yed-when-docs-withdraw/

Haney, C., Sontag, L., & Costanzo, S. (1994). Deciding to take a life: Capital juries, sentencing instructions, and the jurisprudence of death. *Journal of Social Issues*, *50*(2), 149–176.

Hoover Golden State Poll. (2016, October 4–14). Retrieved from www.politico.com/states/f/?id=00000158-2013-dfca-a97b-b43f579c0001

Koh, C. (2017, January 31). Here are Trump Supreme Court nominee Neil Gorsuch's most interesting decisions. Miami Herald. Retrieved at http://www.miamiherald.com/news/politics-government/article129927159.htm

Lee, C. (2006). Hispanics and the death penalty: Discriminatory charging practices in San Juaquin County, California. *Journal of Criminal Justice*, *35*, 17–27

Legislative Analyst's Office. (2016a). Proposition 62. Retrieved from www.lao.ca.gov/BallotAnalysis/Proposition?number=62&year=2016

Legislative Analyst's Office. (2016b). Proposition 66. Retrieved from www.lao.ca.gov/BallotAnalysis/Proposition?number=66&year=2016

Leonard, J., & Dolan, M. (2012, September 30). Californians back change on three strikes but not on death penalty. *Los Angeles Times*. Retrieved from http://articles.latimes.com/2012/sep/30/local/la-me-poll-three-strikes-20120930

Mallicoat, S. (2014). California's experience with the death penalty. In C. Gardiner & P. Fiber-Ostrow (Eds.), *California's criminal justice system* (2nd ed., pp. 213–236). Durham, NC: Carolina Academic Press.

Mintz, H. (2014, February 13). *California executions: Three former governors back ballot measure to hasten executions.* Mercury News, Bay Area New Group. Retrieved from www.mercurynews.com/2014/02/13/california-executions-three-former-governors-back-ballot-measure-to-hasten-executions/

Nichols, C. (2016, September 21). Did California spend $56 billion to execute 13 people? *Politifact California*. Retrieved from www.politifact.com/california/statements/2016/sep/21/tom-steyer/did-california-spend-5-billion-execute-13-people/

Nirappil, F. (2014, May 10). *Death-penalty reform initiative pushed to 2016.* San Diego Union Tribune. Retrieved from www.sandiegouniontribune.com/sdut-death-penalty-reform-initiative-pushed-to-2016-2014may10-story.html

Office of Administrative Law. (2016). *Decision of disapproval of regulatory action.* Retrieved from https://oal.blogs.ca.gov/files/2016/12/Decision-of_Disapproval_2016-1104-02S_CDCR.pdf

Office of the Attorney General. (2013). *The Death Penalty Reform and Savings Act of 2014.* Office of the Attorney General of California. Retrieved from https://oag.ca.gov/system/files/initiatives/pdfs/13-0055%20%2813-0055%20%28Death%20Penalty%29%29.pdf

Pierce, G. L., & Radelet, M. L. (2005). The impact of legally inappropriate factors on death sentencing for California homicides, 1990–1999. *Santa Clara Law Review*, *46*, 1–47.

Proposition 34. (2012). *Death penalty initiative statute.* Retrieved from https://ballotpedia.org/California_Proposition_34,_the_End_the_Death_Penalty_Initiative_(2012)

Proposition 62. (2016). *Repeal of the death penalty initiative.* Retrieved from https://ballotpedia.org/California_Proposition_62,_Repeal_of_the_Death_Penalty_(2016)

Proposition 66. (2016). *Death penalty initiative.* Retrieved from https://ballotpedia.org/California_Proposition_66,_Death_Penalty_Procedures_(2016)

Reese, P. (2015, September 21). How California death row inmates die. *The Sacramento Bee*. Retrieved from www. sacbee.com/site-services/databases/article35995422.html

Referendum 426. (2016). *Nebraska death penalty repeal*. Retrieved from https://ballotpedia.org/Nebraska_Death_Penalty_Repeal,_Referendum_426_(2016)

Sanger, R. M. (2003). Comparison of the Illinois commission report on capital punishment with the capital punishment system in California. *Santa Clara Law Review, 44*, 101–234.

Sanger, R. M. (2016). Fourteen years later: The capital punishment system in California. Santa Barbara and Ventura Colleges of Law. Available at SSRN: https://ssrn.com/abstract=2830677 or http://dx.doi.org/10.2139/ssrn.2830677

Segura, L. (2016, January 17). Ten years after last execution, California's death row continues to grow. *The Intercept*. Retrieved from https://theintercept.com/2016/01/17/ten-years-after-last-execution-californias-death-row-continues-to-grow/

Senate Bill 171. (2006). Retrieved from www.leginfo.ca.gov/pub/05-06/bill/sen/sb_0151-0200/sb_171_vt_20060930.html

Senate Bill 569. (2013). Retrieved from www.leginfo.ca.gov/pub/13- 14/bill/sen/sb_0551-0600/sb_569_bill_20131013_history.html

Senate Bill 687. (2011). Retrieved from www.leginfo.ca.gov/pub/11-12/bill/sen/sb_0651-0700/sb_687_cfa_20110404_112922_sen_comm.html

Senate Bill 1544. (2006). Retrieved from www.leginfo.ca.gov/pub/05-06/bill/sen/sb_1501-1550/sb_1544_vt_20060930.html

Senate Resolution (SR) 44 of the 2003–04 Legislation Session. Retrieved at http://leginfo.legislature.ca.gov/faces/billNavClient.xhtml?bill_id=200320040SR44

State Question 776. (2016). *Oklahoma death penalty*. Retrieved from https://ballotpedia.org/Oklahoma_Death_Penalty,_State_Question_776_(2016)

Stryker, A. (2016, April 13). In California Death Row's "adjustment center," condemned men wait in solitary confinement. Retrieved from http://solitarywatch.com/2016/04/13/in-californias-death-rows-adjustment-center-condemned-men-wait-in-solitary-confinement/

St. John, P. (2015, March 30). California's death row, with no executions in sight, runs out of room. *Los Angeles Times*. Retrieved from www.latimes.com/local/crime/la-me-ff-death-row-20150330-story.html

USC Dornsife College of Letters, Arts and Sciences. (2012). *California voters closely divided on death penalty*. Retrieved from https://dornsife.usc.edu/usc-dornsife-latimes-poll-proposition-34-36-oct-2012/

USC Dornsife College of Letters, Arts and Sciences/Los Angeles Times Poll. (2016, October 22–30). Retrieved from https://gqrr.app.box.com/s/a9b4isapqwvrsozul1wt1ebdmxn5zn78

Cases Cited

Atkins v. Virginia, 536 U.S. 304 (2002).

Baze v. Rees, 535 U.S. 35 (2008).

Furman v. Georgia, 408 U.S. 238 (1972).

Gregg v. Georgia 428 U.S. 153 (1976)

Glossip v. Gross, 576 U.S. ___ (2015).

Hall v. Florida, 572 U.S. ___ (2014).

Jones v. Chappell, 31 F. Supp. 3d 1050 (2014).

Jones v. Davis, 806 F. 3d 538 (2015).

Morales v. Tilton, 465 F. Supp. 2d 972 (2006).

Ron Briggs and John Van de Kamp v. Jerry Brown, 2016.

Ron Briggs and John Van de Kamp v. Jerry Brown, Petition for Writ of Mandate, California Supreme Court, S238309, filed (2016, November 9).

Roper v. Simmons, 543 U.S. 551 (2005).

The People of the State of California v. Robert Page Anderson, 493 P.2d 880, 6 Cal. 3d 628

Winchell v. Beard, Superior Court the State of California, County of Sacramento, Case No. 34–2014, 80001968 (2015).

Woodson v. North Carolina, 428 US 280 (1976)

26

REFLECTIONS ON
THE ABBATOIR

Dennis R. Longmire and Alexander H. Updegrove

Within the death penalty literature, Texas is infamous for its long and troubled history with executions. From the suspicious linkage between racially motivated mob lynchings and the rise of state-sanctioned killing in the early 1920s (Marguart, Ekland-Olsen, & Sorensen, 1994) to the almost weekly killings in 2000 under then Governor George W. Bush's purview (Texas Department of Criminal Justice, 2016), Texas has appeared unapologetically infatuated with death. And yet it remains unclear whether this commitment to capital punishment truly resides in Texans' DNA, as popular narratives would suggest, or if it is a perception largely driven by a relative few decision makers and an incomplete presentation of the facts. This chapter will explore the mythos of the Texas capital punishment system and examine the underlying assumptions contributing to this image before ultimately focusing on the critical role the Texas Legislature has played in the evolution of capital punishment practices within the State.

A Texas-Sized Reputation

Without a doubt, when it comes to its capital punishment system Texas appears to live up to its unofficial motto, 'everything is bigger in Texas.' As Phillips (2009, p. 753) aptly stated, "Understanding capital punishment in Texas is a prerequisite for understanding capital punishment in America." A quick look at the empirical evidence demonstrates just how accurate this statement is. Texas executed 534 (37.4%) of the total 1,428 inmates executed in the post-*Furman* era—a number 4.77 times as high as the number of inmates executed by Oklahoma, the state with the second highest number of executions (112) (Death Penalty Information Center, 2016a). On average, Texas executes 13.35 inmates per year, or more than one per month. In 2015, 13 of the 28 executions nationwide occurred in Texas (Death Penalty Information Center, 2016b). Historically, Texas employed lethal injection before other states (Reinhold, 1982), was one of three states to usher in post-*Furman* death-sentencing procedures (*Jurek v. Texas*, 1976), and has violated the Vienna Convention by executing eight Mexican nationals without providing consulate access (Mexico v. United States of America, 2004; Warren, 2015).

These factors have all contributed to a Texas-sized reputation for the Lone Star State as being devoted to capital punishment. As one legislator put it, "In Texas, a lot of people feel like it's a settled issue" (Weber, 2014, para. 10). This sentiment appears frequently in publications discussing the death penalty and Texas. For example, an editorial in the *Houston Chronicle* drew attention to a popular Texas stereotype suggesting it is "a violent, lawless, backward state, a hang-'em high kind of place that relishes the death penalty, that's obsessed with guns, that's anti-education, anti-science, anti-immigrant, anti-environment" ("Myths die hard," 2015, para. 2). Additionally, Texas has been labeled "ground zero for capital punishment" (Walpin, n.d., para. 1), the "execution capital" of the U.S. (Bryce, 1998), and "the nation's busiest execution chamber" (Dow, 2014, para. 1). Former Governor Rick Perry (2010, p. 12) famously wrote, "if you don't support the death penalty and citizens packing a pistol, don't come to Texas." Perhaps no one better described the Texas experience of capital punishment than Dow (2014, para. 3), who remarked, "If killing people were like playing the violin, Texas would have been selling out Carnegie Hall years ago."

Challenging the Popular Narrative

The problem with romanticizing Texas as the last state truly committed to doling out frontier justice is the image does not hold up under close inspection. In reality, Texas' capital punishment legacy is more nuanced than many accounts allow for. What follows is a brief attempt to put the statistics cited above in their proper context. To begin with, although two recent public opinion surveys estimate three out of every four Texans support capital punishment (Longmire & Cavanaugh, 2007; Ramsey, 2012), the latter demonstrates only half of Texans (53%) support the death penalty when contrasted with life imprisonment without parole (LWOP). Until recently, Texan jurors were forced to choose between sentencing a capital defendant to death or life in prison. Capital inmates sentenced to life in prison automatically became parole eligible after serving 40 years. Life imprisonment without parole (LWOP) standards enacted in 2005, in contrast to life in prison, prevented capital inmates from becoming parole eligible. In 2016, a survey of Harris county residents found only 1 out of every 4 (27%) Texans supported capital punishment over LWOP (Klineberg, 2016). Such tepid support for capital punishment over LWOP explains why, after adopting a true LWOP sentence for capital murderers, Texan jurors only sentenced two defendants to death in 2015 (Death Penalty Information Center, 2016c). Additionally, Texas inmates executed since 1976 have only hailed from 92 of the state's 254 counties. Of these 92 counties, the number of executed inmates sentenced in a particular county has only reached double digits for 11. Six of these 11 counties—Bexar (San Antonio), Dallas, Harris (Houston), and Tarrant (Fort Worth)—account for 260 (48.7%) of Texas' 534 post-*Furman* executions.

Historically, Harris County alone has contributed 125 (23.4%) of the total number of offenders executed in Texas (Southern Methodist University, 2016). More recently, however, Dallas has replaced Harris County as the primary provider of new death row inmates. From 2008 to 2013, Dallas County sentenced 11 defendants to death, while Harris County sentenced only six ("Dallas county's dubious death penalty distinctions," 2013). Clearly, county-level disparities exist concerning the willingness (and ability) to hold capital trials. Focusing exclusively on the total number of inmates Texas executes each year, when the majority of death sentences originate from a mere handful of large counties, inaccurately suggests state-wide use of a practice that is, in reality, principally concentrated in large urban counties.

The Abbatoir: An Alternative Narrative

Lifton and Mitchell (2000) make an interesting observation in their work. Rather than serving separate functions in a capital punishment system, these authors argue the public, legislators, prosecutors, jurors, appeals courts, wardens, and correctional staff all have a single unified purpose: to guarantee an execution takes place. By conceptualizing death as the end product of an assembly line, Lifton and Mitchell (2000) assert the blame for an inmate's death is divided among so many individual actors that it overcomes the human aversion to killing. Diluting the responsibility for killing another person has a curious effect. Many decision makers are uneasy with their role in the killing process but still carry out their duties in a manner that passes the condemned inmate further down the assembly line while denying their personal responsibility in his death (Cabana, 1996; Lane, 1993; Updegrove & Longmire, in press). According to Lifton and Mitchell (2000), the system itself isolates death penalty actors so that they perceive insurmountable obstacles to interrupting death, when in fact, the momentum toward death can be stopped at any point in the process. Elected legislators, prosecutors, appellate judges, and governors fear contradicting public opinion; jurors assume prosecutors only seek the death penalty in cases that warrant it; wardens feel they are following the orders of the state; and dissenting members of the public despair of overcoming a practice so institutionalized and therefore protest by quiet abstinence rather than boisterous calls for abolition.

In short, Lifton and Mitchell's (2000) insight suggests the death penalty persists in Texas not because there is a particularly high demand for it but because the fragmented design of its capital punishment system has duped decision makers into *thinking* there is a high demand for it among their fellow decision makers. To the extent this observation is true, Texas' continued reliance on capital punishment is most accurately described as a high-stakes staring contest where each death penalty actor is afraid to be the first to blink. Comparisons to Hans Christian Andersen's short story, *The Emperor's New Clothes*, are also appropriate. From this perspective, many Texas death penalty actors may privately support vital reforms, but each is afraid to be the first to propose them. In cases where reforms *are* proposed, many more death penalty actors may refuse to endorse these reforms until they are confident the proposals enjoy enough support to make a difference. In this manner, the system itself functions to suppress threats against its continued existence and efficient functioning (Updegrove & Longmire, in press). This system will continue to persist until death penalty actors collectively find the courage to assert their agency, recount their victimization by the system, and add their voice to the opposition. As death penalty actors begin to publically reject their role in the assembly line, this will provide the impetus for more death penalty actors to follow suit.

The Pre-*Furman* Texas Legislature

Although research abounds on public attitudes toward the death penalty (Dugan, 2015; Zorn, 2007), prosecutorial decision making (Petersen & Lynch, 2012; Sorensen & Marguart, 1991), capital jurors (Levinson, Smith, & Young, 2014; Lynch & Haney, 2011), and to a lesser extent those who carry out death sentences (Cabana, 1996; Osofsky, Bandura, & Zimbardo, 2005), few scholars appear to have examined the role legislatures play in the evolution of capital punishment systems within states. This is an unfortunate oversight because, as the Texas Civil Rights Project (2000, p. 2) recognized, "the forum for changes in Texas and the rest of the country now rests in the hands of the state legislatures and state courts." More importantly, state legislatures can introduce legislation tomorrow advocating for desperately needed reforms, whereas state courts must wait until a capital case reaches them and even then are guided by precedents that have typically found capital punishment acceptable. For these reasons, it is important to understand the development of legislative attitudes toward the death penalty as well as the legislature's current climate.

According to best estimates, 755 inmates were executed in Texas from 1608 until 1964, when a nationwide moratorium on executions was imposed due to the impending *Furman v. Georgia* decision eventually delivered in 1972 (Bragg & Shephard, 2000; Death Penalty Information Center, 2016d). During much of this time, arson, kidnapping, robbery, and rape could be punished with death in addition to murder (Texas State Library and Archives Commission, 2016). Marguart et al. (1994) report African Americans composed 76% of the capital defendants sentenced to death for rape between 1924 and 1972. The same authors note a similarly situated white defendant was five to ten times less likely to be sentenced to death. Even worse, for every African American defendant sentenced to prison for raping a white female, 35 more received death sentences. By the time of *Gregg v. Georgia* (1976), Texas Penal Code §19.03 specified the death penalty could only be applied to murderers who: (1) knowingly killed an on-duty police officer or fireman; (2) killed in the process of a "kidnapping, burglary, robbery, aggravated rape, or arson"; (3) were a hitman or hired the services of a hitman; (4) killed in the process trying to escape prison; or (5) killed a correctional officer while imprisoned.

As Carson (2016) records, Texas has employed various methods of execution over the years. Before the state assumed the mantle of killing in 1923, each county acted of its own accord, executing a total of 394 inmates from 1819–1923 (Texas State Library and Archives Commission, 2016). Then, starting in 1923, "the Walls" unit (formally known as the "Huntsville Unit") in Huntsville consolidated all executions under one roof while simultaneously replacing the hangman's noose with the electric chair known as "Old Sparky" (Carson, 2016; Texas Civil Rights Project, 2000). Texas would go on to electrocute 361 inmates over a 40-year span. When the moratorium took effect in 1964, the governor pardoned the 52 inmates then on death row. Death row itself moved the following year from "the Walls" unit to the newly constructed Ellis unit nearby. After a multiple inmate breakout in 1998, death row moved about 60 miles east of Huntsville to its current location at the Polunsky Unit, formerly known as the Terrell unit, in Livingston, Texas. Old Sparky transitioned to storage during the interim, and has served as the centerpiece for the execution exhibit at Huntsville's Texas Prison Museum beginning in 1989 (Grissom, 2011).

The Post-*Furman* Texas Legislature

1977

Although the Supreme Court reinstated the death penalty for Texas in *Jurek v. Texas* (1976), the first post-*Furman* execution of a Texan did not take place until December 7, 1982 (Reinhold, 1982). This also constituted the first execution in the nation using lethal injection. The Texas Legislature proposed 16 bills addressing aspects of capital punishment during the 65th (1977) legislative session. Of these, only one was passed—House Bill 945 outlawed the electric chair and introduced lethal injection as the lawful means to execute capital offenders. House Joint Resolution 71 called for the outright abolition if the death penalty, while HB 1613 requested a moratorium on executions until the next legislative session. Two more bills—SCR 83 and HCR 115—proposed studies of Texas' capital punishment system. The rationale driving these bills was:

> All previous studies relating to the deterrent value, legality, and humaneness of capital punishment have been wholly inconclusive, offering no coherent guidance to the legislatures throughout the nation which, in some instances, have contorted this most solemn of issues into an abstract political plaything.
>
> *(para. 2)*

House Concurrent Resolution 2071 would have introduced LWOP while retaining life in prison and the death penalty. According to HB 568, the court of Criminal Appeals would have been required to unanimously affirm a conviction and death sentence rather than the current threshold of a simple majority. In contrast to these protections, HB 913 and HB 904 sought to expand the number of death-eligible offenses to include police and correctional officers who killed an individual under their care, except in cases of attempted escape. Senate Bill 153 and HB 562 sought to require the court to instruct jurors that capital defendants not sentenced to death could be eligible for parole in as few as 20 years even though their sentence was recorded as "life in prison." Finally, SCR 22 and HCR 91 praised Texan television networks for refusing to broadcast executions to their viewers.

1979

Although 13 death penalty-related bills were proposed during the 67th legislative session, only HB 2118 passed. This bill allowed death row inmates greater access to a spiritual adviser. The bills that did not pass included HB 330, which sought to replace the death penalty with LWOP while retaining life in prison as an alternative sentence; HB 105, which called for restricting the punishment for a capital crime to life in prison; and HB 247, which requested a moratorium on executions until the next legislative session. House Concurrent Resolution 85 called for a study of capital punishment within the state. Historically, Texas can seek the death penalty for defendants who had neither directly killed the victim nor hired a hitman to do the job. This practice is known as the "law of parties." Senate Bill 453 would have protected these defendants by repealing the law of parties. In contrast, six bills called for expanding the number of death-eligible crimes. House Bill 2193 targeted the murder of a minor, HB 1997 targeted the murder of a child 13 years or younger if the defendant represented a parental figure to the child, HB 1745 addressed murder while attempting aggravated sexual abuse, HB 1578 focused on the murder of a government employee for the purpose of interfering with their official duties, HB 1185 targeted the murder of three people within a year if they were all connected to the same enterprise, and HB 390 addressed the murder of a school teacher or college professor. Finally, HB 982 would have allowed juveniles aged 15–16 to be tried for capital crimes, and their cases would have been automatically transferred to the adult court system (at that time the current threshold was 17).

1981

The 68th Legislature passed two out of 18 death penalty bills proposed. House Bill 1164 set life in prison as the default sentence if jurors lacked the necessary information to determine if an aggravating circumstance was present in capital cases. Court actors were, however, forbidden from informing jurors of this rule. The second successful bill, HB 1167, provided for two alternate jurors to replace any of the 12 initial jurors who might get sick or die during the course of a capital trial. Previously, judges were obligated to declare a mistrial if one of the jurors was unable to continue in his or her duties. Among the bills that failed to pass, SB 640 and HB 1132 would have required the Texas Court of Criminal Appeals to overturn any death sentence where it was unclear if an aggravating circumstance was present. House Bill 164 would have replaced death with LWOP while retaining life in prison as an alternative sentence for noncapital murderers, HB 160 would have abolished the death penalty, and HB 157 would have imposed a moratorium on executions until the next legislative session. On the other end of the spectrum, HB 33 called for lowering the minimum age an individual could be charged with a capital crime from 17 to 15. Juveniles charged with a capital crime would have been automatically transferred to the adult court system. Eight bills sought to increase the number of death-eligible crimes. Senate Bill 1079 and HB 1919 targeted the murder of a prosecutor; HB 1923 addressed the murder of a known minor; HB 1124 proposed making involuntary manslaughter a first-degree felony, which would have rendered it death eligible under certain circumstances; HB 1920 focused on the murder of a legislator by anyone other than a spouse; HB 1086 would have qualified the murder of a child under 17 as death eligible; HB 745 targeted murder during attempted aggravated sexual abuse; and HB 575 singled out murder at a location primarily reserved for conducting religious services.

1983

The 68th Legislature proposed 13 death penalty-related bills, but ultimately passed none. House Bill 184 attempted replacing death with LWOP, HB 183 would have abolished the death penalty, and HB 146 would have imposed a moratorium on executions until the next legislative session. Senate Bill 1413 and HB 1234 would have introduced LWOP while retaining life in prison and death. These bills would have separated the sentencing phase into two stages. In the first stage, jurors would have indicated whether any aggravating circumstances were present. If none were present the defendant would have been sentenced to life in prison. If aggravating circumstances were deemed present, jurors then would have weighed the mitigating circumstances against the aggravating circumstances in the second stage. Finding that the mitigating circumstances outweighed the aggravating evidence would have resulted in

LWOP instead of death. Similarly, HB 1235 introduced LWOP while retaining life in prison and death. Perhaps as a follow-up to HB 2118 (1979), HB 1022 would have allowed the condemned's family, friends, and spiritual advisers to be present at the execution if requested by the condemned, while HB 573 would have allowed family to visit the condemned in the 24 hours immediately prior to execution. House Bill 678 prevented death from being automatically available in capital crimes by requiring the state to indicate which cases they intended to seek the death penalty for. The same bill specified a capital defendant sentenced to life in prison must serve a minimum of 30 years before becoming eligible for parole. Finally, four bills would have increased the number of death-eligible offenses. Senate Bill 814 targeted murder while attempting aggravated sexual abuse; HB 70 more narrowly targeted murder while attempting aggravated sexual abuse against a victim under 17; SB 19 addressed the murder of a child under 7; and HB 83 would have made two murders within a year a capital crime.

1985

The 69th Legislature proposed 21 bills and passed two. House Bill 8 made the murder of two people in pursuit of the same criminal objective a capital crime, while HB 667 allowed the Texas Department of Corrections to hold executions at other locations besides "the Walls" unit in Huntsville if they preferred. Despite passing this law over 30 years ago, all post-*Furman* executions to date have taken place at "the Walls" unit. In keeping with previous sessions, HB 2356 proposed imposing a moratorium on all executions until the next legislative session. House Bill 1544 would have made unplanned, provoked murders of passion a noncapital offense, HB 631 would have mandated LWOP for murder and capital murders where the defendant was not sentenced to death, and HB 150 and HB 91 would have introduced LWOP while retaining life in prison and death. Whereas current law required a defendant to automatically be sentenced to death if jurors found aggravating circumstances present, HB 150 would have additionally prescribed LWOP in cases where fewer than six jurors supported a death sentence. House Bill 2144 proposed holding a hearing to determine whether the defendant was primarily responsible for the capital murder. This would have protected against death sentences under the law of parties. Senate Bill 939 attempted to clarify language in one of the aggravating circumstances presented to jurors. In contrast, six bills proposed expanding the number of death-eligible offenses. Senate Bill 987 and HB 1710 targeted the murder of a child under 14 or over 64, SB 193 and HB 1022 addressed murder of a child under six, HB 1245 focused on the murder of a child known to be under 4, and HB 638 targeted the murder of another inmate while incarcerated. Two bills, SB 1221 and HB 1678, sought to exempt medical professionals from all execution procedures except certifying death. Finally, HB 1079 would have moved the site of execution from "the Walls" unit to the local county jail in the jurisdiction where the crime had occurred.

1987

None of the 15 death penalty-related bills proposed during by the 70th Legislature became law. House Bill 727 sought to replace death with LWOP while still retaining life in prison. Six bills called for introducing LWOP in addition to life in prison or death. Senate Bill 210 and HB 431, in addition to introducing LWOP, would have also forbidden capital defendants from accepting a plea bargain unless they accepted a LWOP sentence. Senate Bill 15, HB 726, and HB 52 were almost identical, with the exception that capital defendants could also accept plea bargains to life in prison instead of just LWOP, and only six jurors would need to vote for LWOP at trial to avoid a death sentence. House Bill 553 was also similar to SB 210 and HB 431, although it would have also permitted inmates sentenced to LWOP to receive parole if they had served a minimum of 25 years and were at least 65 years old after serving their minimum time. House Bill 13 sought to protect against the law of parties by requiring jurors to find whether the defendant's actions were the ultimate cause of the victim's death. Only defendants directly responsible for the killing would be eligible to receive a death sentence. House Bill 205 relaxed the language of an aggravating circumstance to increase the likelihood jurors could find it present. Finally, seven bills proposed increasing the number of death-eligible offenses. Senate Bill 863 and HB 69 targeted the murder of another while incarcerated, HB 1048 addressed the murder of a child known to be under 4, HB 466 focused on the murder of an individual under 13 or over 64, HB 57 concentrated on the murder of an individual under 15 or over 64, HB 264 targeted the murder of an off-duty police officer, and HB 264 would have made drug dealing a capital crime if the customer died as a result of the drugs.

1989: Regular Session

During the 71st regular session, the legislature proposed 31 death penalty-related bills but failed to pass a single one. Five bills would have introduced LWOP in some fashion (SB 1471, SB 775, HB 210, HB 207, and HB 119). SB 775 would have also permitted furloughs and HB 119 would have also allowed elderly inmates to become parole eligible after serving a minimum sentence. House Bill 210 would have completely replaced death with LWOP, thereby abolishing the death penalty. Senate Bill 1764 would have required jurors to weigh the aggravating circumstances against the mitigating evidence to determine if death was a proportionally appropriate punishment. Similarly, HB 55 proposed requiring jurors to determine if the defendant was intellectually disabled, and an affirmative finding would have prevented issuing a death sentence. This marks the first time the Texas Legislature acknowledged the role intellectual disability can play in the commission of capital crimes and pre-dated the U.S. Supreme Court's concerns about this issue raised in *Atkins v. Virginia* in 2002 . House Bill 3017 sought to create the Death Penalty Review Court to advise the Court of Criminal Appeals on the quality of errors alleged on appeal. Because members of the review court would be appointed by the Court of Criminal Appeals, however, it is unlikely the new court would have provided any additional protections against executions. Both SB 348 and HB 1374 proposed clarifying language in the description of aggravating circumstances presented to jurors.

Almost half of the bills introduced during this legislative session sought to increase the number of death-eligible offenses (14 of 31). Senate Bill 1296 targeted the murder of a public or private school student or employee; SB 377 and HB 1170 addressed the murder of emergency medical responders; SB 348, HB 242, and HB 10 focused on making some drug-related offenses a capital crime; SB 56, HB 2866, and HB 380 concentrated on the murder of a child under 15; HB 745 targeted the murder of a court actor performing his or her duties; HB 227 addressed the murder of a prisoner, while HB 36 more narrowly addressed the murder of an inmate by an employee; HB 184 singled out "sexual molestation" of the murder victim's body; and HB 42 targeted the murder of an individual by someone under a restraining order.

An additional two bills sought to give Texas jurisdiction over murders of Texas residents regardless of whether the crime occurred in state (HB 3120 and HB 3119). House Bill 224 proposed cutting the amount of time the Court of Criminal Appeals had to review death decisions in half, as well as cutting the time allotted for an extension in the CCA's review in half. Instead of ordering an entirely new trial upon discovery of error, SB 915 and HB 123 would have required the Court of Criminal Appeals to uphold a conviction and only issue a new sentencing review if the alleged error occurred during the original sentencing phase. Finally, HB 1107 proposed preventing prosecutors and defense attorneys from individually and privately questioning capital jurors in capital cases unless the state was seeking the death penalty.

1989–1990: Called Sessions

Because the Texas Legislature only meets every other year during regular sessions, pressing concerns that arise in the interim between regular sessions are addressed in as many special 'called sessions' as necessary to resolve the issue. Fifteen death penalty-related bills were proposed during six separate called sessions between 1989 and 1990, none of which passed. During the first session, HB 21 sought to replace life in prison with LWOP, HB 121 called for jurors to weigh all mitigating evidence against aggravating circumstances when reaching a sentence, and HB 89 would have required jurors to assess the intellectual ability of the defendant, with a finding in favor of intellectual disability producing a life sentence. In contrast, three bills proposed increasing the number of death-eligible offenses. House Bill 51 targeted murder of a child under 15, SB 12 addressed murder of an individual under 7 or over 64, and SB 17 focused on making some drug-related crimes a capital offense. Two bills, after failing to gain traction during the first called session, were repeatedly proposed during the subsequent four additional sessions (called sessions two through five). The first would have made murdering a victim while under community supervision a capital offense (HB 16, HB 23, HB 34, and HB 90). The second, also proposed during the sixth and final called session, would have made murdering a child under 6 years of age a capital offense (SB 3, SB 7, SB 13, SB 14, and SB 30).

1991: Regular Session

Two of the 24 death penalty-related bills proposed by the 72nd Legislature became law. House Bill 9 allowed a defendant to plead guilty to a capital crime in return for a life sentence, and increased the minimum time to be served for a life sentence before becoming parole eligible from 15 years to 35 years. While current law required a defendant to be sentenced to death if jurors found all three aggravating circumstances present, SB 880 allowed jurors to sentence the defendant to life in prison by a vote of ten or more even if all three aggravating circumstances were present. Additionally, this bill modified language in the definition of what constitutes an aggravating circumstance in an attempt to avoid issuing death sentences to defendants tried according to the law of parties. Senate Bill 880 also required the Court of Criminal Appeals to uphold a conviction and only issue a new sentencing phase in the case of an alleged error solely affecting the original sentencing phase. Among bills that failed to pass, SB 1479 sought to introduce LWOP while retaining life in prison (with parole eligibility becoming available after the passage of 15 years) and death, HB 129 would have made even attempted capital felonies, then considered noncapital offenses, capital offenses, and SB 1598 would have required offenders whose death sentences were commuted to life in prison to have served 30 years before becoming parole eligible. Eleven bills proposed increasing the number of death-eligible offenses. House Bill 62 targeted the murder of a minor, SB 415 addressed murder of a child under the age of 11 or an adult over the age of 64, SB 10 and HB 775 focused on murder of a child under the age of 10, SB 556 and SB 497 concentrated on murder of a child under the age of 6, and HB 1612 addressed murder of a child under the age of 4. Similarly, HB 2422 targeted murder associated with organized crime, HB 332 focused on murder while under correctional supervision, HB 137 would have made it a capital crime for police or correctional officers to murder someone in their custody, and HB 23 would have made any murder eligible for capital punishment if the defendant had been previously convicted of an unrelated murder. House Bill 2771 would have required jurors to determine whether, after sentencing a defendant to death, the execution should occur as close to the county where the crime was committed as possible. House Bill 390, on the other hand, would have required executions to take place at noon on the courtroom steps in the county where the crime had occurred. Finally, HB 2679 would have prevented capital defendants from obtaining pretrial release.

1991: Called Sessions

Five death penalty-related bills were proposed during two called sessions in 1991, none of which passed. The first bill would have required jurors to determine if sufficient mitigating evidence was present to outweigh the aggravating circumstances. If at least ten jurors agreed, the defendant would be sentenced to life in prison rather than death (HB 226 and HB 36). In a second bill, any errors identified by the Court of Criminal Appeals as solely affecting the sentencing phase of the original capital trial would result in only granting the defendant a new sentencing phase rather than an entirely new trial (HB 227 and HB 35). The final bill, SB 68, would have made the murder of a child known to be under 6 years of age a capital crime.

1993

The 73rd Legislature passed four of the 18 death penalty-related bills proposed. House Bill 537 required two-thirds of the entire Board of Pardons and Paroles to endorse parole for a capital defender serving a life sentence rather than a majority vote from a three-person panel. Senate Bill 13 made the murder of a child under 6 years of age a capital crime, while SB 818 made the murder of another person while incarcerated for the purposes of organized crime a capital crime. This bill also made the murder of another person while serving a life sentence for murder, indecency with a child, aggravated kidnapping, aggravated sexual assault, or aggravated robbery a capital crime. House Bill 798 clarified that SB 880, which was passed in 1991, applied retroactively. Of those bills that failed to pass, SB 1190 introduced LWOP as a sentencing option in addition to life in prison and death, while HB 92 proposed replacing the existing life in prison which allowed capital inmates to be considered for parole after 40 years with pure LWOP. House Bill 2735 would have required jurors to determine whether a capital defendant was intellectually disabled or demonstrating mental illness. If jurors answered in the affirmative, the defendant would be sentenced to life in prison rather than death. Similarly, HB 1784 would have required jurors to determine if a capital defendant was intellectually disabled and sentence such individuals to life in prison. On the other hand, HB 1640 and HB 25 sought to make the murder of a court witness or informant a capital crime. House Bill 1578 would have lowered the minimum threshold for seeking the death penalty from age 17 to 13, and automatically transferred these juveniles to the adult court system. Finally, SB 984 and HB 1562 proposed streamlining the appeals process in capital cases to shorten the time between convictions and executions.

1995

Of the 16 bills proposed by the 74th legislature, only SB 440 went on to become law. This bill specified the procedures for appointing attorneys to capital offenders who wished to make appeals, in addition to changing the appeals process to decrease the length of time between conviction and execution. Proposed House Bills 573 and HB 527 would have prevented the execution of intellectually disabled defendants. After the Oklahoma City bombing, the Texas Legislature drafted a concurrent resolution asking prosecutors to seek the death penalty in any future case involving terrorism (SCR 137). Five bills proposed increasing the number of death-eligible offenses. Senate Bill 1390 and HB 1667 targeted some drug-related crimes, SB 891 addressed racially motivated murders, HB 182 concentrated on murder of a chaplain associated with a police or fire department, as well as known emergency medical responders, and HB 65 targeted murder of an inmate by a correctional officer. House Bill 3 would have streamlined the appeals process to hasten executions, and SB 143 would have allowed capital defendants to forgo their right to automatic appellate review altogether. House Bill 611 proposed allowing prosecutors to seek the removal of any juror they perceived to have imposed an unduly high threshold for establishing aggravating circumstances to have been present. For the first time, SB 38 and HB 285 advocated for victim rights to permit close relatives to witness executions. Finally, HB 2817 and HB 1805 would have made HB 537, passed in 1993, apply retroactively.

1997

The 75th Legislature passed two of nine death penalty-related bills proposed. Senate Bill 1728 clarified SB 440, passed in 1995, by adding a hard deadline for filing certain appellate documents, while

HB 806 made the murder of a known police officer acting on official business a capital crime even if she or he was off duty at the time of death. Among bills that failed to pass, HB 1655 would have prevented the execution of intellectually disabled defendants. Four bills sought to increase the number of death-eligible offenses. Senate Bill 1844 targeted aggravated sexual assault of a victim under 14 years of age, SB 493 addressed racially, sexually, and religiously motivated murders, HB 151 focused on murder of an inmate by a correctional officer, and HB 93 targeted murder caused by an explosive—likely in response to the Oklahoma City bombing.

1999

The 76th Legislature passed three of 30 death penalty-related bills. Senate Bill 39 required the court, upon the defense attorney's request, to inform jurors a capital defendant sentenced to life in prison would not become parole eligible until serving at least 40 years. House Bill 1516 established procedures for appointing attorneys to capital habeas corpus cases, increased the length of several deadlines, and required the state to reimburse counties up to $25,000 in attorney fees in capital cases. In addition to prohibiting the execution of intellectually disabled defendants, HB 245 recognized a defendant's intellectual disability as a legitimate justification for submitting a habeas corpus petition after the deadline had passed. Seven of the proposed bills would have replaced life in prison with LWOP (SB 38, HB 1619, HB 425, HB 172, HB 151, HB 135, and HB 77). House Bill 892 would have allowed the defense to request a hearing determining whether the state was seeking the death penalty based on the race of the defendant or victim. An affirmative finding would result in trying the defendant for a noncapital offense. Three bills proposed changes to how the Board of Pardons and Paroles reviewed capital cases. The first, SB 1698, would have required the board to meet as a body in capital clemency cases. House Bill 398 would have required the board to consider a greater variety of questions before denying clemency, while HB 397 proposed mandating the board hold a public hearing and record its rationale for clemency decisions.

Nine bills proposed during this legislative session involved efforts to increase the number of death-eligible offenses. Senate Bill 49 and HB 2738 targeted murder motivated by hate for a particular people group; HB 1025 addressed murder involving torture; HB 887 focused on murder of a child under 13 years of age if the defendant had previously been convicted of criminal abuse or neglect toward the child; HB 796 concentrated on murder while under correctional supervision; HB 684 and HB 663 targeted murder by the subject of a restraining order against the protected person; HB 222 focused on murder of parole officers while performing their duties; and HB 388, in acknowledgement of the deadly Columbine shooting, targeted murder committed on school property or property where a school event was taking place. Similarly, HB 41 would have lowered the threshold for charging an individual with a capital crime from age 17 to 16. Finally, HB 657 called for reimbursing victims' relatives for travel expenses related to witnessing an execution.

2001

The 77th Legislature passed two of 30 death penalty-related bills, but only one became law. Governor Rick Perry vetoed HB 236, which would have prevented the execution of intellectually disabled defendants. House Bill 1925, which became law, prohibited protestors and bystanders from bearing firearms within 1,000 feet of "the Walls" unit or any other execution site the state might select. This bill was motivated by the highly contentious activities of protestors surrounding the execution of Gary Graham (AKA Shaka Sankofa) on June 22, 2000. During one protest in Houston, several members of the New Black Panthers Party openly carried rifles and waved them in the air in protest of the pending execution.

Among legislation that ultimately failed to pass during this session, HJR 59 would have allowed the governor to establish a moratorium on executions until repealed by a later governor; SJR 25 and HJR 56 would have imposed a moratorium on executions until the next legislative session and require the completion of a study of Texas' capital punishment system; SB 680 would have created a Capital Punishment Commission to study issues of DNA, race, and appellate review in capital cases; and HB 720 would have created a Texas Capital Punishment Commission to study issues of innocence and appellate review. House Bill 2048 proposed raising the threshold for charging a defendant with a capital crime from 17 to 18 years of age, while HB 1860 proposed requiring courts to hold pretrial hearings to determine if a defendant charged with committing a capital crime before the age of 18 had been cognitively developed enough to appreciate the consequences of his or her actions.

Six bills supported introducing LWOP. Senate Bill 85, HB 30, HB 365, and HB 632 called for retaining life in prison and death, while HB 869 and HB 685 would have replaced life in prison with LWOP while retaining death as an option. Senate Bill 793 would have required the Board of Pardons and Paroles to meet as a body to make capital clemency decisions. In contrast, HJR 21 and HB 260 would have allowed the governor to commute death sentences to LWOP without input from the Board of Pardons and Paroles. House Bill 3246 proposed expanding the options available for the defense in capital cases when arguing their defendant was incompetent to be executed. According to HB 2515, jurors could have submitted written questions to be asked of witnesses in capital cases. House Bill 1416 would have required jurors to assess a defendant's future dangerousness in light of the fact that he would be spending at least the next 40 years in prison. In the first bill of its kind, HB 520 introduced a maximum sum of $200,000 to be awarded to wrongfully convicted capital defendants. Two bills sought to increase the number of death-eligible offenses. Senate Bill 1249 targeted arson if a firefighter died, while HB 322 addressed murder on school property or property where a school event was taking place. House Bill 1962 would have changed the cause of death on condemned inmate's death certificates from "homicide" to "legal execution." Similar to previous bills, HB 1328 attempted to streamline the appeals process to hasten death. House Bill 1247 would have prevented the execution of intellectually disabled inmates but defined intellectual disability as an IQ below 65 rather than the accepted two standard deviations below the mean in psychology, which uses an IQ of 70 as a soft cut-off. Finally, HB 347 would have reimbursed victims' relatives for travel expenses related to witnessing an execution

2003: Regular Session

The 78th Legislature passed three of 52 bills related to the death penalty. House Bill 11 made the murder of an individual the defendant had threatened to terrorize a capital crime, HB 562 required all inmates incarcerated for a capital crime to provide DNA samples for inclusion in a database, and HB 1011 clarified that requesting postconviction DNA analysis only constituted a direct appeal to the Court of Criminal Appeals if the defendant had been sentenced to death. Of those bills that ultimately failed to pass, HR 559 would have set March 25, 2003 aside as a "Day of Innocence" recognizing wrongfully convicted capital offenders. Senate Joint Resolution 12 and HJR 22 proposed allowing the governor to enact a moratorium on executions until repealed by a later governor. Senate Joint Resolution 28 and SB 601 called for allowing the governor to grant more than one 30-day reprieve for a single inmate facing execution. Six bills sought to implement LWOP in some fashion (HB 210, HB 366, HB 614, and SB 332), with two replacing death with LWOP (HB 343 and HB 345). Four bills introduced mechanisms for preventing the execution of intellectually disabled defendants (HB 614, SB 163, SB 332, and SB 389). House Bill 360 would have only permitted entering a capital confession into evidence if it was recorded on video, while HB 351 would have prevented entering informants' testimony into evidence in all cases except a cellmate's testimony corroborated by audio or video.

House Joint Resolution 6 proposed prohibiting the execution of any inmate whose trial had included DNA evidence analyzed by the Houston Police Department. Similarly, HB 3255 would have ordered the retesting of all DNA evidence tested at a forensic laboratory known to have conducted flawed work in the past. Four bills called for raising the threshold age for charging a defendant with a capital crime from 17 to 18 years of age (HB 127, HB 372, HB 1048, and SB 218). Two bills proposed a study of Texas' capital punishment system accompanied by a moratorium on executions until the next legislative session (HB 357 and SB 444), while two more bills would have examined all post-*Furman* capital convictions to determine if jurors convicted defendants based on their race or gender or the victim's race or gender (HB 353 and HB 370). House Bill 1740 would have required prosecutors to use standardized guidelines for seeking the death penalty and employ different guidelines for seeking the death penalty for defendants aged 17–21 relative to adults over 21 years old. Senate Bill 219 would have required the Board of Pardons and Paroles to meet as a body for capital clemency reviews in capital cases. Four bills addressed the standards for appointing capital attorneys (HB 615, HB 665, HB 1734, and SB 1224), and SB 1224 and SB 727 would have increased the amount of money a county could be reimbursed for capital expenses from $25,000 to $50,000. Senate Bill 1854 and HB 3397 would have allowed counties to dispose of evidence used in capital cases five years after the trial unless the state or defense objected.

Two bills proposed increasing the number of death-eligible offenses. Senate Bill 320 called for prosecutors to seek the death penalty in any case where a police officer had been killed, whereas HB 563 targeted murder of a known security guard while performing his or her duties. House Bill 2166 would have modified the type of evidence considered to be 'mitigating' or 'aggravating', while HB 2165 would have modified the language of aggravating circumstances and prescribed a sentence of life in prison if even a single juror failed to find an aggravating circumstance present. The existing law required 10 of the 12 jurors in capital cases to agree that an aggravating circumstance was absent before issuing a life sentence. House Bill 2090 would have changed the cause of death on condemned inmates' death certificates from "homicide" to "judicial execution," HB 540 proposed lowering the burden of proof required to demonstrate that a juror was biased in favor of the prosecution, and HB 520 would have increased the minimum length of time to be served for a life sentence by five years for each 12-month period the defendant had eluded capture after committing the offense. Finally, HB 170 would have reimbursed victims' relatives for travel expenses related to witnessing an execution.

2003: Called Session

Eleven death penalty-related bills were proposed during the called session, but none passed. Senate Joint Resolution 4 and SB 15 would have allowed the governor to grant multiple 30-day reprieves to the same inmate. Senate Bill 33 and HB 17 introduced LWOP while retaining life in prison with eventual eligibility for parole and death. Senate Bill 17 and HB 29 would have raised the threshold age for charging a defendant with a capital crime from 17 to 18 years of age. Four bills proposed introducing mechanisms to prevent executing intellectually disabled defendants (HB 18, SB 13, SB 14, and SB 57). Finally, HB 19 would have improved the standards for appointing defense attorneys in capital cases.

2005: Regular Session

The 79th Legislature passed four of 42 death penalty-related bills. Senate Bill 1791 made the murder of any judge in Texas a capital crime, SB 60 replaced life in prison with LWOP while retaining death, HB 93 changed the cause of death on condemned inmates' death certificate from "homicide" to "judicial execution," and SB 1507 allowed the defense to request whether the prosecution intended to introduce evidence of previous criminal wrongdoing for which the defendant had not been convicted during the sentencing phase of a trial. Among failed bills, HB 452 would have abolished the death penalty, while HJR 73 would have imposed a moratorium on executions until the next legislative session.

Senate Joint Resolution 11 would have allowed the governor to issue multiple 30-day reprieves for the same inmate. Similarly, HJR 14 proposed allowing the governor to issue a moratorium on executions until repealed by a later governor. House Joint Resolution 24 sought to prevent the execution of any defendant convicted based on DNA evidence analyzed by Houston's police department. Senate Bill 741 would have overturned death sentences issued based on the testimony of a single eyewitness or accomplice. Four bills proposed raising the threshold age for charging a defendant with a capital crime from 17 to 18 (HB 61, HB 333, HB 434, & SB 226). Senate Bill 548 would have required the Board of Pardons and Paroles to meet as a body for capital clemency decisions, HB 2125 would have required the board to hold a public hearing and then record the rationale for capital clemency decisions, and HB 2123 would have required the board to take a variety of new factors into consideration during capital clemency decisions. Four bills sought to introduce mechanisms for preventing the execution of intellectually disabled defendants (HB 419, SB 65, SB 85, and SB 231).

Senate Bill 1200 would have required police officers and prosecutors to provide the defense with DNA evidence their agencies had collected in capital cases where the defendant had been sentenced to death. The bill also allowed judges from the original trial court to request DNA retesting. Two bills would have created a Texas Innocence Commission to study factors that contributed to wrongful convictions (HB 618 and SB 1033), while three would have created a Texas Capital Punishment Commission to study Texas' capital punishment system in general (HB 432, HB 458, and SB 544). Senate Bill 925 would have permitted the defense team to appeal a determination that their client was competent to be executed. House Bill 450 would have only allowed confessions into evidence if they were accompanied by a video demonstrating the defendant had knowingly waived his or her Miranda rights. Similarly, HB 431 sought to prevent entering informants' testimony into evidence in all cases except a cellmate's testimony corroborated by audio or video recordings. House Bill 3396 would have prohibited using pancuronium bromide for lethal injections, HB 2165 would have modified what could be considered mitigating and aggravating circumstances—most notably discounting future dangerousness as justification for a death sentence, and HB 408 would have required using different juries for the guilt and sentencing phases of capital trials. House Bill 48 proposed allowing for the destruction of evidence five years after a capital trial unless the prosecution or defense objected. Finally, HB 966 would have made murder of security guards while performing their duties a capital crime.

2005: Called Session

There was only one death penalty-related bill introduced during this session. House Bill 19 sought to improve the requirements for serving as a capital defense attorney but failed to become law.

2007

The 80th Legislature passed three of 32 death penalty-related bills. Senate Bill 705 required the Office of Court Administration of the Texas Judicial System to keep records of all jury instructions issued and the sentences associated with capital cases. This report would be published annually. House Bill 1545 streamlined the appeals process to hasten the death of the condemned, and HB 8 made the second conviction for a sexually violent offense against a child under 14 a capital crime. This law was quickly invalidated by *Kennedy v. Louisiana* the following year, however, when the Supreme Court prohibited sentencing a defendant to death in cases where the victim had not died. Among bills that failed to pass, HB 745 and HB 3740 would have abolished the death penalty. Two bills would have allowed the governor to issue a moratorium on executions until repealed by a later governor (HJR 23 and SJR 21), and two bills proposed allowing the governor to issue multiple 30-day reprieves to the same inmate (B 301 and SJR 12). Four bills called for studying Texas' capital punishment system (HB 3996, SB 263, and SB 1947), one of which also proposed a moratorium on executions until the next legislative session (HB 809). Senate Bill 249 would have prevented the execution of intellectually disabled defendants, while HB 3816 would have allowed district judges to identify wrongful convictions retroactively and inform the governor and attorney general of their existence. Senate Bill 1823 sought to increase the funds allotted to a county for capital representation from $25,000 to $100,000 and dedicate $150,000 to *habeas corpus* proceedings instead of the current $25,000. Senate Bill 1655 would have established the Capital Writs Committee, which would have provided representation for capital defendants wishing to appeal their sentence.

House Bill 1160 proposed prohibiting the use of pancuronium bromide in lethal injections. House Bill 810 sought to prevent entering informants' testimony into evidence in all cases except a cellmate's testimony corroborated by audio or video, HB 806 would have made identifications produced by poorly conducted police lineups inadmissible in court, and HB 802 would have only allowed confessions into evidence if they were accompanied by a video demonstrating the defendant had knowingly waived his or her Miranda rights. Senate Bill 306 sought to save the state money by only assigning a second lawyer to a capital defendant after the prosecution indicated it intended to seek the death penalty. Senate Bill 498 proposed streamlining the appeals process to hasten death. Senate Bill 208 would have allowed capital defendants and victims' relatives to speak before the Board of Pardons and Paroles on relevant clemency issues, while HB 3416 would have provided counseling to capital jurors struggling to process traumatic evidence presented during trial. Two bills proposed allowing some attorneys previously found to have provided inadequate capital representation to represent capital defendants again (HB 1266 & SB 528). House Bill 1107 sought to make the accidental death of a police officer by a drunken driver a capital crime. Finally, HB 804 would have lowered the burden of proof required to demonstrate a prospective capital juror was biased in favor of the prosecution, and HB 339 would have required taking DNA samples from all defendants charged with a capital crime even if they were later acquitted at trial.

2009

The 81st Legislature passed three of 34 bills. Senate Bill 1091 established the Capital Writs Committee to represent capital defendants in habeas corpus proceedings, while SB 839 prescribed life in prison for juveniles in capital cases where the state was not seeking the death penalty. These juveniles become parole eligible after serving 40 years. In 2007, a judge on the Court of Criminal Appeals refused a 20-minute extension past the court's closing time that would have allowed the defense attorney to fix a computer malfunction and print the required documents to file an appeal. The offender was executed mere hours later. House Bill 4314 allows for submitting documents electronically or in print. Among failed bills, HB 682 and HB 297 would have abolished the death penalty. Four bills proposed allowing the governor to grant multiple 30-day reprieves (HB 1148, HJR 58, SB 169, and SJR 7), while HJR 24 proposed allowing the governor to enact a moratorium until repealed by a later governor. House Bill 304 sought to prevent prosecutors from seeking the death penalty based on the law of parties, while HB 111 sought to prevent prosecutors from trying two or more defendants jointly in the same capital trial. House Bill 2267 would have prevented both. Five bills proposed studying various aspects of Texas' capital punishment system (HB 788, HB 913, SB 115, and SB 1655), with HB 877 citing the nine inmates exonerated in the post-*Furman* era as justification for the study. Senate Bill 1581 would have saved the state money by only appointing a second attorney after the prosecution has indicated it intends to seek the death penalty, while SB 1173 would have required courts to inform the defense when an execution had been scheduled.

Four bills proposed making Texas' treatment of capital defendants with intellectual disabilities comply with *Atkins v. Virginia* (HB 1152, HB 4466, SB 167, and SB 1139). House Resolution 480 called for impeaching Sharon Keller, the judge who exhibited "willful disregard for human life" by refusing to keep her office open long enough for the defense to file an appeal after missing the deadline due to computer problems. Similarly, HB 2189 proposed requiring all appeals-related offices to stay open on execution days until the execution had occurred. House Bill 938 would have only allowed confessions into evidence if they were accompanied by a video demonstrating the defendant had knowingly waived his or her Miranda rights, while HB 298 sought to prevent entering informants' testimony into evidence in all cases except a cellmate's testimony corroborated by audio or video. House Bill 921 would have allowed the defense to request separate juries for the guilt and sentencing phases of a capital trial, HB 2115 would have increased the penalty for failing to appear at trial if charged with capital murder, and HB 916 would have lowered the burden of proof to find a juror was biased in favor of the prosecution. Finally, HB 825 sought to prevent judges from deferring adjudication in cases where juveniles were charged with capital murder.

2011

The 82nd Legislature passed three of 28 bills. Senate Bill 1308 allowed some attorneys who had previously provided inadequate capital representation to still represent capital defendants. Although attorneys are compensated for initial habeas corpus proceedings, a few rare defendants are permitted to submit a second subsequent habeas appeal, and House Bill 1646 allowed for the payment of attorneys for these seconds appeals. Senate Bill 377 made the murder of a child under 10 a capital crime.

Among failed bills during this session, both HB 852 and HB 819 called for abolishing the death penalty for adults and LWOP for juveniles. Two bills proposed allowing the governor to grant multiple 30-day reprieves to the same inmate (SB 1688 and SJR 44), while HJR 97 would have allowed the governor to enact a moratorium on executions until repealed by a later governor. An additional two bills would have created studies of Texas' capital punishment system (SB 1835), with HB 1641 also calling for a moratorium until the next legislative session. Senate Bill 1079 and HB 1670 would have prohibited the execution of intellectually disabled defendants and defined intellectual disability as an IQ score of 75 or below. Senate Bill 1832 and HB 3762 sought to require the defense to be notified of the drugs to be used for lethal injection a month before the execution, SB 1028 and HB 1918 would have saved the state money by only assigning a second attorney after the prosecution indicated it was seeking the death penalty, and SB 973 would have retroactively commuted juveniles LWOP sentences to life in prison with the possibility of parole after 40 years.

House Bill 3400 would have allowed a single juror to prevent a death sentence by finding an absence of aggravating circumstances rather than the ten jurors currently required to agree. Additionally, it would have required a unanimous finding that the defendant was intellectually sound enough for jurors to issue a death sentence rather than the current ten votes required. House Bill 2200 would have prevented jointly trying two defendants in the same capital trial, HB 855 would have prevented seeking the death penalty based on the law of parties, and HB 2511 would have prevented both. House Bill 543 proposed only allowing confessions into evidence if they were accompanied by a video demonstrating the defendant had knowingly waived his or her Miranda rights, while HB 689 sought to prevent entering informants' testimony into evidence in all cases except a cellmate's testimony corroborated by audio or video records. House Bill 488 would have lowered the burden of proof for establishing a juror was biased in favor of the prosecution. Finally, HB 566 would have made murder of a person who had filed a restraining order against the defendant a capital crime.

2013: Regular Session

The 83d Legislature passed three of 28 death penalty-related bills. House Bill 577 clarified language allowing public defenders not on the list of capital-qualified attorneys to represent defendants in non-capital habeas corpus proceedings, SB 1044 saved the state money by allowing the defense to access criminal history records for free, and SB 1292 required DNA testing of all DNA evidence before the start of a trial to avoid wrongful convictions and costly capital trial expenses.

Among failed bills during this session, SJR 7 and SB 88 would have allowed the governor to issue multiple 30-day reprieves to the same inmate, while HJR 80 would have allowed the governor to enact a moratorium until repealed by a later governor. Three bills proposed allowing the defense to request a hearing to determine whether the prosecution was seeking the death penalty for primarily racial reasons or raise this concern on appeal (HB 2458, HB 2614, and SB 1270). Senate Bill 750 would have defined intellectual disability as an IQ of 75 or below. Five bills would have mandated life in prison for juveniles rather than allowing the possibility of LWOP (HB 901, HB 924, and SB 187), two of which would have also mandated LWOP for adult capital offenders (HB 164 and HB 1703). Similarly, HB 3617 would have made a capital felony committed by a juvenile a first-degree felony. Senate Bill 89 proposed studying Texas' capital punishment system, while HB 166 would have established the Timothy Cole Exoneration Review Commission to study wrongful convictions. House Joint Resolution 36 called for abolishing the Court of Criminal Appeals and creating 'the Supreme Court' to solely handle capital appeals. Two bills would have made murder of a prosecutor a capital crime (HB 1845 and HB 3134). House Bill 1337 would have allowed victims' relatives to provide input into clemency proceedings overseen by the Board of Pardons and Paroles. House Bill 261 would have prevented jointly trying two defendants in the same capital trial, while HB 319 would have prevented seeking the death penalty based on the law of parties. Finally, HB 320 proposed only allowing confessions into evidence if they were accompanied by a video demonstrating the defendant had knowingly waived his or her Miranda rights, and HB 189 sought to prevent entering informants' testimony into evidence in all cases except a cellmate's testimony corroborated by audio or video.

2013: Called Sessions

Eleven bills were proposed during two called sessions. Senate Bill 2 was the only bill to pass, and mandated life in prison for juvenile capital offenders with the possibility of parole after 40 years rather than allowing for the possibility of LWOP. House Bill 45 would have prevented passing laws to restrict abortion until the death penalty was abolished, while HB 59 called for studying capital exonerations. The remaining bills addressed the same issue resolved by SB 2.

2015

The 84th Legislature passed four of 22 death penalty-related bills. House Bill 48 established the Timothy Cole Exoneration Review Commission to study factors contributing to wrongful convictions. House Bill 1914 increased the maximum time for the Board of Pardons and Paroles to reconsider previously denied decisions in capital cases to ten years. Prior to this law, all denied cases were reconsidered in one to five years. Senate Bill 1071 required notifying the defense when an execution date had been set, while SB 1697 prohibited disclosing information related to the names or addresses of entities providing lethal injection drugs, as well as the personnel administering them. In contrast, HB 1587, which did not pass, would have required the Texas Department of Corrections (TDC) to post the name, quantity, expiration date, and supplier of lethal injection drugs to its website at least 45 days ahead of scheduled executions. If TDC acquired the drug closer to the scheduled execution, it would have been required to post the information at least two weeks before the execution.

Four additional bills that did not pass proposed abolishing the death penalty (HB 1032, HB 1527, SB 1661, and SJR 54). Senate Bill 180 sought to allow the governor to issue multiple 30-day reprieves to the same inmate. Instead of mandating life in prison for juveniles charged with a capital crime as currently required, SB 1083 would have allowed for sentencing juveniles to life in prison or a prison term of 5–99 years. House Bill 2110 would have required notifying the nearest consulate when an execution date had been set for a foreign national, SB 226 proposed defining intellectual disability as an IQ of 75 or below, and HB 564 sought to prohibit entering informants' testimony into evidence in all cases except a cellmate's testimony corroborated by audio or video. House Bill 341 would have prevented seeking the death penalty based on the law of parties, while HB 267 would have prevented jointly trying two or more defendants in the same capital trial. House Bill 2673 proposed lifelong exclusion from the federal Supplemental Nutrition Assistance Program (SNAP), which provides food stamps, for individuals convicted of a variety of criminal offenses, including capital crimes. Currently, adults convicted of a capital crime can only be released if found innocent, while individuals convicted of committing a capital crime before 18 are sentenced to life in prison or LWOP. This bill is likely a response to the court's *Miller v. Alabama* (2012) decision prohibiting mandatory LWOP for juveniles. Under this ruling, juveniles can still be sentenced to LWOP, but only on an individual basis and after mitigating evidence supporting a more lenient sentence (life in prison) has been presented.

Finally, HB 277 sought to make murder of a prosecutor because of his or her job a capital crime, and HB 112 called for making murder while engaging in human trafficking a death-eligible offense.

Conclusion

Overall, it appears the Texas Legislature has become progressively less supportive of capital punishment in recent years. Whereas the legislature's early efforts often concentrated on increasing the number of death-eligible offenses, its modern efforts have more frequently proposed vital capital punishment reforms. Of course, proposing reforms should not be confused for passing them. Almost every session has included a bill calling for the abolition of the death penalty since 1976, and yet it has struggled to gain traction. Other proposed reforms eventually become law, but only after a decade or more had passed. The four bills which appear most ripe for passage during the next legislative session are: (1) repealing the law of parties; (2) prohibiting jointly trying two defendants together in the same capital trial; (3) rendering informants' testimony inadmissible in court except in cases of a cellmate's testimony corroborated by audio or video; and (4) only allowing confessions into evidence if accompanied by a video demonstrating the defendant knowingly waived Miranda rights. Perhaps the most hotly contested current topic is the struggle between calls for transparency of lethal injection procedures—particularly regarding the identity of the drug supplier—and the state's attempt to operate in secrecy. Unsurprisingly, the legislature sided with the state on this issue at the expense of capital defendants in the most recent session. Ultimately, this review of the Texas Legislature's evolution on the issue of capital punishment demonstrates its larger-than-life reputation is not entirely warranted but does have merit when considering its continued reluctance to enact desperately needed reforms.

The death penalty in Texas continues to be a source of concern to Texas' legislators and citizens alike. This chapter is being written as the Texas Legislature begins its 85th regular legislative session, and there have already been several bills introduced that focus on the death penalty. Until this punishment option is taken off of the list of possible sanctions in this state, it appears that Texas and its legislators will continue to fall prey to the troubled actions that U.S. Supreme Court Justice Harry Blackman so aptly referred to as "tinker[ing] with the machinery of death" when articulating the reasons for his dissent in the Texas-based case of *Callins v. Collins* (1994).

References

Bragg, S. N., & Shephard, A. (2000, April 5). *Statistics of murders and executions in Texas and Connecticut.* Retrieved May 11, 2016, from www.cga.ct.gov/2000/rpt/2000-R-0337.htm

Bryce, R. (1998, December 14). Why Texas is execution capital: Explanations range from the history of slavery to the state's budget for legal defense. *The Christian Science Monitor.* Retrieved from http://www.csmonitor.com/1998/1214/121498.us.us.5.html.

Cabana, D. A. (1996). *Death at midnight: The confession of an executioner.* Boston, MA: Northeastern University Press.

Carson, D. (2016). *History of the death penalty in Texas.* Texas Execution Information Center. Retrieved May 11, 2016 from www.txexecutions.org/history.asp

"Dallas county's dubious death penalty distinction" [Editorial]. (2013, December 27). *The Dallas Morning News*. Retrieved from http://www.dallasnews.com/opinion/editorials/20131227-editorial-dallas-countys-dubious-death-penalty-distinction.ece.

Death Penalty Information Center. (2016a). *Number of executions by state and region since 1976*. Retrieved February 17, 2016 from www.deathpenaltyinfo.org/number-executions-state-and-region-1976

Death Penalty Information Center. (2016b). *Execution list 2015*. Retrieved February 12, 2016 from www.death-penaltyinfo.org/execution-list-2015

Death Penalty Information Center. (2016c). *The death penalty in 2015: Year end report*. Retrieved February 17, 2016 from http://deathpenaltyinfo.org/documents/2015YrEnd.pdf

Death Penalty Information Center. (2016d). *Executions in the U.S. 1608–2002: The Espy file*. Retrieved May 11, 2016 from www.deathpenaltyinfo.org/executions-us-1608-2002-espy-file

Dow, D. R. (2014, May 15). Why Texas is so good at the death penalty. *Politico*. Retrieved February 17, 2016, from http://www.politico.com/magazine/story/2014/05/texas-death-penalty-106736?o=2.

Dugan, A. (2015, October 15). Solid majority continue to support death penalty. *Gallup Poll*. Retrieved from www.gallup.com/poll/186218/solid-majority-continue-support-death-penalty.aspx

Grissom, B. (2011, February 5). Texplainer: Could Texas fire up old sparky? *The Texas Tribune*. Retrieved May 12, 2016 from www.texastribune.org/2011/02/05/texplainer-could-texas-fire-up-old-sparky/

Klineberg, S. L. (2015, July 1). The disconnect between Texans and their elected officials. *TribTalk*. Retrieved from www.tribtalk.org/2015/07/01/the-disconnect-between-texans-and-their-elected-officials/Legislative

Klineberg, S. L. (2016). Thirty-five years of the Kinder Houston Area Survey: Tracking responses to a changing America. Kinder Institute for Urban Research. Retrieved from https://kinder.rice.edu/uploadedFiles/Center_for_the_Study_of_Houston/53067_Rice_HoustonAreaSurvey2016_Lowres.pdf.

Lane, J. M. (1993). "Is there life without parole?": A capital defendant's right to a meaningful alternative sentence. *Loyola of Los Angeles Law Review, 26*(2), 327–394.

Levinson, J. D., Smith, R. J., & Young, D. M. (2014). Devaluing death: An empirical study of implicit racial bias on jury-eligible citizens in six death penalty states. *New York University Law Review, 89*(2), 513–581.

Lifton, R. J., & Mitchell, G. (2000). *Who owns death?: Capital punishment, the American conscience, and the end of executions*. New York, NY: Harper Perennial.

Longmire, D. R., & Cavanaugh, M. (2007). *2007 Texas crime poll*. Huntsville, TX: College of Criminal Justice, Sam Houston State University.

Lynch, M., & Haney, C. (2011). Looking across the empathic divide: Racialized decision making on the capital jury. *Michigan State Law Review, 2011*(3), 573–607.

Marguart, J. W., Ekland-Olson, S., & Sorensen, J. R. (1994). *The rope, the chair, & the needle: Capital punishment in Texas, 1923–1990*. Austin, TX: University of Texas Press.

Mexico v. United States of America. (2004). *International Court of Justice*. Retrieved February 17, 2016 from www.icj-cij.org/docket/files/128/8188.pdf"Myths die hard" [Editorial]. (2015, May 22). *Houston Chronicle*. Retrieved from http://www.chron.com/opinion/editorials/article/Myths-die-hard-6282036.php.

Osofsky, M. J., Bandura, A., & Zimbardo, P. G. (2005). The role of moral disengagement in the execution process. *Law and Human Behavior, 29*(4), 371–393.

Perry, R. (2010). *Fed up!: Our fight to save American from Washington*. Boston, MA: Little, Brown and Company.

Petersen, N., & Lynch, M. (2012). Prosecutorial discretion, hidden costs, and the death penalty: The case of Los Angeles County. *The Journal of Criminal Law & Criminology, 102*(4), 1234–1274.

Phillips, S. (2009). Legal disparities in the capital of capital punishment. *The Journal of Criminal Law & Criminology, 99*(3), 717–756.

Ramsey, R. (2012, May 24). UT/TT poll: Texans stand behind death penalty. *The Texas Tribune*. Retrieved from www.texastribune.org/2012/05/24/uttt-poll-life-and-death/

Reinhold, R. (1982, December 7). Technician executes murderer in Texas by lethal injection. *New York Times*. Retrieved from www.nytimes.com/1982/12/07/us/technician-executes-murderer-in-texas-by-lethal-injection.html

Sorensen, J. R., & Marquart, J. W. (1991). Prosecutorial and jury decision-making in post-Furman Texas capital cases. *New York University Review of Law & Social Change, 18*(3), 743–776.

Southern Methodist University. (2016). *Texas execution statistics*. Retrieved February 18, 2016 from http://people.smu.edu/rhalperi/texascounty.html

Tex. H.B. 3, 74th Leg., R.S. (1995).

Tex. H.B. 8, 69th Leg., R.S. (1985).

Tex. H.B. 8, 80th Leg., R.S. (2007).

Tex. H.B. 8, 84th Leg., R.S. (2015).

Tex. H.B. 9, 72d Leg., R.S. (1991).

Tex. H.B. 10, 71st Leg., R.S. (1989).
Tex. H.B. 11, 78th Leg., R.S. (2003).
Tex. H.B. 13, 70th Leg., R.S. (1987).
Tex. H.B. 16, 71st Leg., 2d C.S. (1989).
Tex. H.B. 25, 73d Leg., R.S. (1993).
Tex. H.B. 29, 78th Leg., 1st C.S. (2003).
Tex. H.B. 31, 70th Leg., R.S. (1987).
Tex. H.B. 33, 67th Leg., R.S. (1981).
Tex. H.B. 34, 71st Leg., 4th C.S. (1989).
Tex. H.B. 35, 72d Leg., 2d C.S. (1991).
Tex. H.B. 36, 72d Leg., 2d C.S. (1991).
Tex. H.B. 42, 71st Leg., R.S. (1989).
Tex. H.B. 45, 83d Leg., 2d C.S. (2013).
Tex. H.B. 48, 79th Leg., R.S. (2005).
Tex. H.B. 51, 71st Leg., 1st C.S. (1989).
Tex. H.B. 55, 71st Leg., R.S. (1989).
Tex. H.B. 57, 70th Leg., R.S. (1987).
Tex. H.B. 59, 83d Leg., 1st C.S. (2013).
Tex. H.B. 62, 72d Leg., R.S. (1991).
Tex. H.B. 65, 74th Leg., R.S. (1995).
Tex. H.B. 69, 70th Leg., R.S. (1987).
Tex. H.B. 70, 68th Leg., R.S. (1983).
Tex. H.B. 77, 76th Leg., R.S. (1999).
Tex. H.B. 83, 68th Leg., R.S. (1983).
Tex. H.B. 85, 66th Leg., R.S. (1979).
Tex. H.B. 89, 71st Leg., 1st C.S. (1989).
Tex. H.B. 92, 73d Leg., R.S. (1993).
Tex. H.B. 93, 75th Leg., R.S. (1997).
Tex. H.B. 93, 79th Leg., R.S. (2005).
Tex. H.B. 123, 71st Leg., R.S. (1989).
Tex. H.B. 227, 71st Leg., R.S. (1989).
Tex. H.B. 236, 77th Leg., R.S. (2001).
Tex. H.B. 1545, 80th Leg., R.S. (2007).
Tex. H.B. 1562, 73d Leg., R.S. (1993).
Tex. H.B. 1578, 66th Leg., R.S. (1979).
Tex. H.B. 1612, 72d Leg., R.S. (1991).
Tex. H.B. 1640, 73d Leg., R.S. (1993).
Tex. H.B. 1667, 74th Leg., R.S. (1995).
Tex. H.B. 1678, 69th Leg., R.S. (1985).
Tex. H.B. 1710, 69th Leg., R.S. (1985).
Tex. H.B. 1784, 73d Leg., R.S. (1993).
Tex. H.B. 1920, 67th Leg., R.S. (1981).
Tex. H.B. 1923, 67th Leg., R.S. (1981).
Tex. H.R.J. Res. 36, 83d Leg., R.S. (2013).
Tex. S.B. 12, 71st Leg., 1st C.S. (1989).
Tex. S.B. 13, 78th Leg., 1st C.S. (2003).
Tex. S.B. 15, 78th Leg., 1st C.S. (2003).
Tex. S.B. 30, 71st Leg., 6th C.S. (1989).
Tex. S.B. 38, 76th Leg., R.S. (1999).
Tex. S.B. 49, 76th Leg., R.S. (1999).
Tex. S.B. 56, 71st Leg., R.S. (1989).
Tex. S.B. 57, 78th Leg., 1st C.S. (2003).
Tex. S.B. 65, 79th Leg., R.S. (2005).
Tex. S.B. 69, 72d Leg., 1st C.S. (1991).
Tex. S.B. 1598, 72d Leg., R.S. (1991).
Tex. S.B. 1728, 75th Leg., R.S. (1997).
Texas Civil Rights Project. (2000). *The death penalty in Texas: The seventh annual report on the state of human rights in Texas*. Retrieved May 11, 2016 from www.texascivilrightsproject.org/wp-content/uploads/2009/01/2000-the-death-penalty-in-texas.pdf

Texas Department of Criminal Justice. (2016). *Executed offenders.* Retrieved May 11, 2016 from www.tdcj.state. tx.us/death_row/dr_executed_offenders.html

Texas State Library and Archives Commission. (2016). *The death penalty.* Retrieved May 12, 2016 from www.tsl. texas.gov/exhibits/prisons/inquiry/deathpenalty.html

Updegrove, A. H., & Longmire, D. R. (in press). Systems thinking, system justification, and the death penalty: Thirty-eight years of capital punishment legislation in Texas. *Corrections: Policy, Practice and Research.*

Walpin, N. (n.d.). Why is Texas #1 in executions? PBS. Retrieved February 17, 2016, from http://www.pbs.org/ wgbh/pages/frontline/shows/execution/readings/texas.html. Warren, M. (2015, October 2). Foreign nationals, part II. *Death Penalty Information Center.* Retrieved February 17, 2016 from www.deathpenaltyinfo.org/ foreign-nationals-part-ii#executed

Weber, P. J. (2014, April 16). Texas gubernatorial candidate faces thorny death penalty choice. *Public Broadcasting Service.* Retrieved from www.pbs.org/newshour/rundown/texas-death-penalty/

Zorn, E. (2007, May 18). Public opinion on the death penalty teeters on the "if only" wedge. *Chicago Tribune.* Retrieved from http://blogs.chicagotribune.com/news_columnists_ezorn/2007/05/public_support_.html

Cases Cited

Atkins v. Virginia, 536 U.S. 304 (2002).
Callins v. Collins, 510 U.S. 1141 (1994).
Furman v. Georgia, 408 U.S. 238 (1972).
Gregg v. Georgia, 428 U.S. 153 (1976).
Jurek v. Texas, 428 U.S. 262 (1976).
Kennedy v. Louisiana, 554 U.S. 407 (2008).
Miller v. Alabama, 567 U.S. ___ (2012).

27

THE FEDERAL DEATH PENALTY

Stephanie Mizrahi

Introduction

This chapter covers the prosecution of capital cases by the federal government. It covers the application of the death penalty by the United States Department of Justice (DOJ) to cases involving violations of certain federal criminal laws. As such, it does not cover the myriad of U.S. Supreme Court cases dealing with constitutional issues regarding the death penalty that apply to both state and federal capital prosecutions, although there is considerable overlap. Instead, after a brief overview of the history of the federal death penalty, this entry will look at the structure and institutions governing the use of the federal death penalty, the key statutes establishing the modern-day federal death penalty regime, how the federal government decides to seek the death penalty and for what cases, and some of the critiques of current federal death penalty law and policy.

The History of the Federal Death Penalty

The use of the federal death penalty dates to the earliest years of the United States. The first execution took place three years after the formation of the federal government under the U.S. Constitution, when Thomas Bird was hanged for murder after beating a shipmate to death.

According to the Death Penalty Information Center (DPIC), between 1790 and 2016, the federal government has executed under its authority 336 men and four women. The racial make-up of these executions were: 39% Caucasian, 35% African-American, 25% Hispanic, and 19% Native American (DPIC, 2016).

Little (2000) divides the history of the federal death penalty into four eras (p. 538). The era of mandatory death sentences (1790–1897), the era of unguided discretion given to juries (1897–1972), the suspension of the death penalty after the case of *Furman v. Georgia* (1972–1988), and the era of guided discretion (1988–present). In the era during which Thomas Bird was executed, the death penalty was mandatory for a number of crimes including treason, murder, piracy, forgery, and aiding the escape of a federal capital defendant (Little, 2000, p. 538). In 1897, based on concerns that juries were nullifying entire cases because of the reluctance to impose the death penalty, Congress passed an act to reduce the cases in which the penalty of death may be inflicted (Little, 2000). The 1897 act gave juries discretion to qualify their verdict by adding "without capital punishment" to certain crimes involving murder and rape. In addition, the act abolished the death penalty with regard to a number of offenses and reduced the penalty of death to life at hard labor for others.

In 1972, the United States Supreme Court, in the case of *Furman v. Georgia* (1972), invalidated the death penalty for all states and the federal government, holding that the death penalty as then applied violated the Eighth and Fourteenth Amendments because its application was often arbitrary and discriminatory and that there was "no meaningful basis for distinguishing the few cases in which [the death penalty] is imposed from the many cases in which it is not" (p. 248, n. 11). Most state legislatures moved quickly to create death penalty systems that would meet the Court's concerns, including instituting bifurcated trials (guilt phase and a sentencing phase) and the consideration of statutorily mandated aggravating and mitigating factors. In just four short years after the *Furman* case, the new schemes were before the Court in *Gregg v. Georgia* (1976) and the death penalty—at least at the state level—was back on the table. However, the federal government did not reinstate its death penalty until the passage of the Anti-Drug Abuse Act of 1988, which reinstated the death penalty for homicides in the course of drug trafficking. The act also addressed the concerns of the Court by adopting a death penalty process similar to that adopted by most states and approved by the Court in *Gregg*.

Despite its 1988 reinstatement, the federal government has only executed three people. In June 2001, Timothy McVeigh was executed for the bombing of the Murrah Federal Building in Oklahoma City in April of 1995—at the time, the most deadly act of terrorism carried out on U.S. soil. The execution of McVeigh was followed a week later with that of Juan Raul Garza, the first person executed under the provisions of the 1988 act. In March of 2003, Louis Jones, Jr., was executed for the kidnapping and murder of a female member of the U.S. military on a U.S. Air Force Base (DPIC, 2016; Hatch & Walsh, 2016). As of this writing, the most recent defendant sentenced to death under federal law is Dzhokhar Tsarnaev for the terrorist attack on the Boston Marathon on April 15, 2013. Tsarnaev was charged with 17 capital offenses, many of which were related to the use of a weapon of mass destruction (Hatch & Walsh, 2016).

Until McVeigh's execution in 2001, federal executions took place in the state in which the crime was committed. In 1999, the United States built a federal death row facility at its prison at Terra Haute, Indiana. The executions of McVeigh, Garza, and Jones all took place at Terra Haute, although McVeigh's was also televised by close-circuit television to a gathering of victims and witnesses in Oklahoma City (Bohm, 2012). Although most future executions of federal death row inmates will likely take place at Terra Haute, in some cases, federal executions can still take place in the state where the crime was committed (Bohm, 2012).

Key Federal Death Penalty Statutes, 1988–2016

Since the passage of the Anti-Drug Abuse Act of 1988, several additional statutes have shaped (or tried to shape) the modern federal death penalty in a variety of ways. In addition to the 1988 Act, these include the Federal Death Penalty Act of 1994 (part of the Violent Crime Control and Law Enforcement Act), the Racial Justice Act of 1994; the Antiterrorism and Effective Death Penalty Act of 1996; and the Innocence Protection Act of 2004. While a brief description of each of these is presented here, a more detailed discussion of the 1994 and 1996 acts are part of the relevant sections here (see also DPIC, 2016).

Federal Death Penalty Act of 1994 (FDPA)

Passed as part of a 1994 Omnibus Crime Bill, the Federal Death Penalty Act created a myriad of death-eligible offenses in the federal criminal code—almost all involving some type of homicide. The act also established more detailed procedures for imposing the death penalty based on constitutional and U.S. Supreme Court requirements (Hatch & Walsh, 2016). The federal offenses eligible for the death penalty are discussed in more detail later.

Racial Justice Act of 1994 (RJA)

What did not make it into the 1994 crime bill was a proposal to allow inmates to use statistics on the racial disposition of the death penalty to challenge their own sentences as discriminatory based on race. If the defendant could show that statistically the death penalty was being applied in a racially discriminatory manner, the state would then have the burden to show a nonracial basis for applying the death penalty in the defendant's case. Failure to do so would preclude the use of the death penalty in that case. The statistical analysis used by the defendant would need to show a pattern of racial discrimination in the relevant jurisdiction and compare cases "similar in level of aggression to the case being challenged" (Chemerinsky, 1995, p. 530; see also Racial Justice Act, H.R. 4017).

In part, the RJA was passed in response to the case of *McCleskey v. Kemp* (1987), which denied the defendant an opportunity to use statistical evidence of racial bias in the use of the death penalty in the state of Georgia to challenge his own sentence (Chemerinsky, 1995; Lungren & Krotoski, 1995). A controversial provision, the RJA was dropped as part of the effort to reconcile House and Senate versions of the crime bill and out of fear that its inclusion would doom passage of the entire bill (Chemerinsky, 1995; Lungren & Krotoski, 1995; New York Times, 1994).

Those in favor of the bill argued that it was a vital and long-needed protection against the clearly discriminatory application of the death penalty against minorities—mostly African Americans. As eloquently argued by law professor Erwin Chemerinsky (1995) of the University of Southern California:

> In almost every important area—employment, housing, public benefits, peremptory challenges—proof of racially disparate impact can be used to require the government to prove a nonracial explanation for its actions. Not, however, with regard to the one area where the government determines who lives and who dies.
>
> *(p. 520)*

Those opposed to the RJA argued that it would move death penalty cases away from the characteristics of individualized justice—such as the facts of the crime and the character and record of the defendant—and toward a focus on quotas and statistical claims wholly unrelated to the case at hand (Lungren & Krotoski, 1995). In addition, introducing statistical evidence under the RJA in death penalty cases would greatly increase the cost and time it takes to litigate a death penalty case (Lungren & Krotoski, 1995). Others argued that the RJA would have the effect of blocking the imposition of the death penalty altogether. Instead, protections against racial discrimination should be established at the front end during charging decisions and at trial (Lungren & Krotoski, 1995; Mccollum, 1995).

Antiterrorism and Effective Death Penalty Act of 1996 (AEDPA)

Partly passed in response to the 1995 Oklahoma City bombing, a significant portion of this act was also designed to address perceived abuses of the writ of habeas corpus by death row inmates—an issue that had been festering for a number of years. The writ of habeas corpus and the effects of the AEDPA are discussed in more detail later.

Innocence Protection Act of 2004

Part of the 2004 Justice for All Act signed by President George W. Bush, the bill was designed to address the number of death row inmates that had been found innocent—mostly based on DNA evidence—and released since the reinstatement of the death penalty in 1976 (Bohm, 2012). At the time the bill was introduced, 85 defendants had been released based on the discovery of their actual innocence (Bohm, 2012). The act (1) provides rules and procedures for DNA testing for federal inmates and prohibits the destruction of DNA evidence while a defendant remains incarcerated; (2) provides funding to states for the costs of postconviction testing; (3) includes grants to states for improving the quality of defense and prosecution counsel assigned to capital cases; and (4) increases the cap on compensation for wrongfully imprisoned death row inmates to $100,000 per year of imprisonment (Bohm, 2012, pp. 109–110; see also 118 Stat. 2279). Interestingly, earlier versions of the act introduced in 2000 included provisions prohibiting the federal government from seeking the death penalty for federal crimes committed in states that did not have the death penalty (with some exceptions) and allowing life without parole sentences for drug kingpin offenses under the 1988 act (mentioned earlier) (Little, 2000). Neither of these provisions made it into the final bill (see discussions of the federalization of the death penalty and the use of the Death Penalty Protocol later).

The Federal Death Penalty in Operation

Of the 58 nations that retained the death penalty as of 2014, the United States is the only Western democracy among the group (Hatch & Walsh, 2016). Still, the fact remains that since the reinstatement of the federal death penalty in 1988, the United States has only executed three people. There are, however, a number of federal inmates under sentence of death. According to the DPIC (2016), between 1988 and 2016, the U.S. Attorney General has authorized the federal government to seek the death penalty against 503 defendants. Of those, 295 were taken to trial (15 of those are currently on or awaiting trial). Fourteen of these defendants were found not guilty of the capital charges. "Two were declared innocent by the government and charges were dismissed against a third when grave questions were raised about his guilt" (DPIC, 2016, n.p.). One defendant was granted clemency. Of the remaining cases that went to trial, there were 151 life sentences and 81 death sentences imposed by the juries. "Of these 81 sentences of death, three defendants received a death sentence twice. Three additional defendants received death verdicts, but new trials were granted and life sentences resulted" (DPIC, 2016, n.p.). Of the 503 defendants for whom the death penalty was authorized, 50% were African-American, 27% Caucasian, 18% Hispanic, 4% Asian/Indian/Pacific Islander/Native American, and 1% Arab. Sixty-two percent of the defendants "on death row under active death sentences" are nonwhite (DPIC, 2016, n.p.).

Death Eligible Crimes Under Federal Law

Over 40 sections of the United States criminal code set forth crimes that are eligible for the federal death penalty. Most of these were established with the passage of the Federal Death Penalty Act of 1994. A consequence of this varied list of offenses is that "the federal government provides the death penalty for murder under a wider array of circumstances than any of the states" (Hatch & Walsh, 2016, p. 300). Almost every federal death penalty offense is also prosecutable under state criminal statutes (Connor, 2010; Little, 2000).

Table 27.1 shows a U.S. Department of Justice list of the federal capital offenses as of 2012, along with their corresponding criminal code sections (DOJ, 2014, p. 7). Of the 41 sections listed, only four do not involve a death or homicide: (1) espionage (18 U.S.C. 794); (2) mailing of injurious articles with intent to kill or resulting in death (18 U.S.C. 1716); (3) bank-robbery related murder or kidnapping (18 U.S.C. 2113); and (4) treason (18 U.S.C. 2381).

With the exception of first-degree murder (18 U.S.C. 1111), the remaining sections generally involve three categories: murder or death in the commission of a specific type of act or crime, murder or death at a specific type of location or involving a specific type of property, or murder or death involving a specific type of victim. For example, a murder is a capital offense when it involves the death of a law enforcement officer (or a retaliatory murder of an officer or a family member), important government officials, federal judges, foreign officials, a state correctional officer, a state

Table 27.1 Federal Capital Offenses, 2012

Statute	Description
8 U.S.C. 1342	Murder related to the smuggling of aliens.
18 U.S.C. 32–34	Destruction of aircraft, motor vehicles, or related facilities resulting in death.
18 U.S.C. 36	Murder committed during a drug-related drive-by shooting.
18 U.S.C. 37	Murder committed at an airport serving international civil aviation.
18 U.S.C. 115(b)(3) [by cross-reference to 18 U.S.C. 1111]	Retaliatory murder of a member of the immediate family of law enforcement officials.
18 U.S.C. 241, 242, 245, 247	Civil rights offenses resulting in death.
18 U.S.C. 351 [by cross-reference to 18 U.S.C. 1111]	Murder of a member of Congress, an important executive official, or a Supreme Court justice.
18 U.S.C. 794	Espionage.
18 U.S.C. 844(d), (f), (i)	Death resulting from offenses involving transportation of explosives, destruction of government property, or destruction of property related to foreign or interstate commerce.
18 U.S.C. 924(i)	Murder committed by the use of a firearm during a crime of violence or a drug-trafficking crime.
18 U.S.C. 930	Murder committed in a federal government facility.
18 U.S.C. 1091	Genocide.
18 U.S.C. 1111	First-degree murder.
18 U.S.C. 1114	Murder of a federal judge or law enforcement official.
18 U.S.C. 1116	Murder of a foreign official.
18 U.S.C. 1118	Murder by a federal prisoner.
18 U.S.C. 1119	Murder of a U.S. national in a foreign country.
18 U.S.C. 1120	Murder by an escaped federal prisoner already sentenced to life imprisonment.
18 U.S.C. 1121	Murder of a state or local law enforcement official or other person aiding in a federal investigation; murder of a state correctional officer.
18 U.S.C. 1201	Murder during a kidnapping.
18 U.S.C. 1203	Murder during a hostage taking.
18 U.S.C. 1503	Murder of a court officer or juror.
18 U.S.C. 1512	Murder with the intent of preventing testimony by a witness, victim, or informant.
18 U.S.C. 1513	Retaliatory murder of a witness, victim, or informant.
18 U.S.C. 1716	Mailing of injurious articles with intent to kill or resulting in death.
18 U.S.C. 1751 [by cross-reference to 18 U.S.C. 1111]	Assassination or kidnapping resulting in the death of the president or vice president.
18 U.S.C. 1958	Murder for hire.

(Continued)

Table 27.1 (Continued)

Statute	Description
18 U.S.C. 1959	Murder involved in a racketeering offense.
18 U.S.C. 1992	Wilful wrecking of a train resulting in death.
18 U.S.C. 2113	Bank robbery-related murder or kidnapping.
18 U.S.C. 2119	Murder related to a carjacking.
18 U.S.C. 2245	Murder related to rape or child molestation
18 U.S.C. 2251	Murder related to sexual exploitation of children.
18 U.S.C. 2280	Murder committed during an offense against maritime navigation.
18 U.S.C. 2281	Murder committed during an offense against a maritime fixed platform.
18 U.S.C. 2332	Terrorist murder of a U.S. national in another country.
18 U.S.C. 2332a	Murder by the use of a weapon of mass destruction.
18 U.S.C. 2340	Murder involving torture.
18 U.S.C. 2381	Treason.
21 U.S.C. 848(e)	Murder related to a continuing criminal enterprise or related murder of a federal, state, or local law enforcement officer.
49 U.S.C. 1472–1473	Death resulting from aircraft hijacking.

Source: (Bureau of Justice Statistics, National Prisoner Statistics Program (NPS-8), 20142).

official assisting in a federal investigation, a court officer or juror, a witness, victim, or informant, and a U.S. national in a foreign country. A murder or death can also result in a capital offense when it takes place on or involves certain types of property such as certain transportation facilities—particularly airports—federal government facilities, maritime facilities, and deaths resulting from carjackings, wrecking of trains, or aircraft hijackings. In addition, deaths resulting from certain types of crimes—such as certain drug-related offenses, kidnappings, hostage-takings, smuggling of aliens, civil rights offenses, transportation of explosives, sexual assault or exploitation of children, racketeering and criminal enterprise offenses, murder for hire, and the use of weapons of mass destruction—are eligible for the federal death penalty.

The wide range of homicides eligible for the death penalty has not escaped scholarly criticism. Connor (2010) notes that prior to the late twentieth century, federal criminal law focused on crimes that were truly national in nature; ones that for lack of statutory authority or resources states could not reasonably enforce or prosecute. Today, Connor argues, "it cannot be said that the majority of these crimes reach conduct directed against the U.S. as an entity, nor can it be said that the substantive crimes describe behavior that is not proscribed by the criminal codes of each of the fifty states" (2010, p. 156).

Little refers to the increase of death eligible crimes under the FDPA as the 'federalization' of death penalty law and notes that of the 26 defendants sentenced to death between 1988 and 2000, "all were convicted of criminal conduct duplicative of capital murder conduct as defined by the states in which the murders occurred" (Little, 2000, p. 533). He also argues that the trend toward federalization brings together unusual bedfellows, as those who are most avidly anti-federalization and would likely argue for the repeal of the federal death penalty are also often pro-death penalty by the states (Little, 2000).

The Federal Death Penalty in Practice

Federal death penalty cases, like all federal cases, are prosecuted in the United States District Court located in the state or district (in states that have more than one federal district) in which the crime took place. The federal government may seek the federal death penalty for violations of federal law even in states or jurisdictions that have no death penalty of their own (Connor, 2010; DPIC, 2016; Mysliwiec, 2010; *U.S. v. Gabion*, 2013). The prosecution of federal death penalty cases is conducted by the U.S. attorney for the relevant district, but the decision as to whether or not to seek the death penalty in the first place rests with the Capital Review Committee and the Attorney General. Trials and motions are conducted in similar fashion to capital cases at the state level, with a separate trial for the guilt phase and the sentencing phase conducted by the same jury, the consideration of statutorily required mitigating and aggravating factors during the death penalty phase, and a unanimous jury verdict needed for a recommendation of the death sentence. The conduct of federal capital proceedings is subject to the Federal Rules of Criminal Procedure, the Federal Rules of Evidence, the Rules of Appellate Procedure, and special rules governing the conduct of Section 2254 cases (habeas corpus petitions) (see www.uscourts.gov/rules).

While there are many similarities between state and federal death penalty prosecutions, there are some differences found in the Federal Death Penalty Act (1994) worth noting. Robert Bohm, in his iconic book *Death Quest*, highlights some of the features unique to federal death penalty law (2012, pp. 104–105). First, as noted earlier, the local prosecuting attorney (the U.S. attorney) must seek authorization from the U.S. Attorney General before filing notice of intent to seek the death penalty. Rarely, if ever, is a local county prosecutor required to get authorization from a state's attorney general or governor before doing so. Second, before appointing defense counsel in a federal capital case, the Court must consider the recommendation of the federal public defender as to which defense counsel are qualified for such an appointment. Third, the statutory aggravating factors to be considered by the jury differ depending on whether the crime involves a homicide, a nonhomicide drug offense, or espionage or treason. Fourth, judges in federal capital cases must specifically instruct the jury that "in considering whether a sentence of death is justified, it shall not consider the race, color, religious beliefs, national origin, or sex of the defendant or of any victim" (Bohm, 2012, p. 105; 108 Stat. at 1966). Fifth, if a jury recommends a death sentence, each juror must sign a certificate swearing that the decision was not discriminatory based on any of the listed factors. Finally, the federal government is limited as to when the death penalty can be imposed on Native Americans.

The Federal Death Penalty on Appeal

Federal defendants convicted and sentenced to death have an automatic right to appeal both the conviction and the sentence to the U.S. Circuit Court of Appeals for the circuit in which the case was tried—much as state defendants have an automatic right to appeal to the state's appellate courts. As well as matters of law and procedure, defendants may also have any facts overlooked or unavailable at trial reviewed by the appellate court. Other than that, all reviews are discretionary and can only be requested once except in very rare circumstances. The U.S. Supreme Court will only review a case if all other avenues have been exhausted and a substantial federal question is involved, particularly if review by the Supreme Court is needed to resolve a conflict among circuits on the same question. Review by the Supreme Court is exceedingly hard to get and requires a vote by at least four of the justices. Once all avenues of appeal have been exhausted, the president of the United States has the sole authority to pardon federal death row inmates.

The AEDPA and the Great Writ of Habeas Corpus

Habeas corpus is Latin for "you have the body." The writ of habeas corpus—sometimes referred to as the Great Writ—"is a judicial order directed at those detaining any person to bring the detainee to court and explain the reasons for the detention" (del Carmen, Vollum, Dial, Frantzen, & San Miguel, 2008). In the world of civil versus criminal law the writ is an odd hybrid. A motion for a writ of habeas corpus is a criminal matter in that the detention being challenged is the result of a criminal conviction. It can only be used by a defendant who is in custody. Yet, technically, it is viewed as a civil suit, with the claim being made against the warden of the institution in which the detainee is being held. Thus some of the most significant criminal procedure cases in U.S. law have civil case names— *Gideon v. Wainwright* (1963) for example (the famous case that held that states must provide counsel for all defendants in any felony matter if they cannot afford it). A successful writ of habeas corpus is a rarity, in part because "it must be filed with the court that originally tried the offender" (del Carmen et al., 2008, p. 302).

The writ originated in England in the eleventh century and later became key to the ability of those voicing displeasure at the monarchy to challenge their imprisonment (del Carmen et al., 2008). It became a formal legal right in 1679. Its history as a tool for challenging the state (in the form of king or governor) also made it important to the original colonists in their struggle against the crown and later in addressing their concern about an overly powerful central government. Such views of the writ led it to be enshrined in the first article of the U.S. Constitution:

> The privilege of the Writ of Habeas Corpus shall not be suspended, unless when in Cases of Rebellion or Invasion the public Safety may require it.
>
> *(U.S. Const. art. I, § 9)*

Since the Civil War, the power to suspend the writ in these very rare cases has rested with both the legislative and executive branches (del Carmen et al., 2008). Originally a federal right, the Federal Habeas Corpus Act of 1867 extended the right to state defendants challenging their detention under the provisions of the federal constitution. However, before state inmates can file a federal habeas corpus petition, they must have exhausted all state criminal and habeas corpus proceedings.

Until the early twentieth century, the writ remained mostly unaltered. Inmates "were allowed to file successive petitions even for claims or issues already litigated . . . as well as for claims not previously litigated" (del Carmen et al., 2008, p. 306). That started to change in 1924 with two cases, *Salinger v. Loisel* and *Wong Doo v. U.S.* In both those cases, the Court took steps to allow judges to dismiss successive petitions if they believed inmates were filing the petitions in bad faith—such as solely to avoid imposition of sentence (see also del Carmen et al., 2008).

Congress codified these restrictions in the Judiciary Act of 1948, which allowed federal courts to deny successive habeas corpus petitions if:

> it appears that the legality of such detention has been determined by a judge or court of the United States on a prior application for a writ of habeas corpus and the petition presents no new ground not theretofore presented and determined, and the judge or court is satisfied that the ends of justice will not be served by such inquiry.
>
> *(28 U.S.C. 2244, 62 Stat. at 966)*[1]

A number of court cases and amendments through the 1990s made adjustments to habeas corpus and death penalty procedures, but the most significant came with the passage of the AEDPA in 1996. Passed in the wake of the 1995 Oklahoma City bombing (a number of the provisions of the act address terrorist crimes and prosecutions), Congress took the opportunity to address concerns that the habeas corpus petitions were being abused and that death sentences that represented the will of the community were taking too long to be carried out as a result. "The AEDPA represents the most restrictive piece of legislation that affects the ability of inmates to use the Great Writ" (del Carmen et al., 2008, p. 309). As of this writing, the U.S. Supreme Court has upheld the act and narrowly interpreted its provisions in light of the legislative intent to limit the use of the habeas corpus petition to delay death sentences. The concept of habeas corpus is not solely a federal one, nor is the writ available only to death penalty inmates. Nevertheless, it is included in this entry in some detail because it is one of the most important protections federal death penalty defendants have to challenge their sentence

Under the AEDPA, an initial habeas corpus petition must be filed within one year of one of the following: (1) the date on which conviction became final; (2) the date on which any obstacles to making the motion either by the state or the federal government was removed (if the obstacle was created by state or government action); (3) the date of a new U.S. Supreme Court decision that has been made retroactive; or (4) "the date on which the facts supporting the claim or claims presented could have been discovered through the exercise of due diligence" (28 U.S.C. 2244, 2255). A rule or new law is only retroactive if the U.S. Supreme Court specifically and explicitly deems the law to apply retroactively. In a 2016 paper, Vladeck notes that this does not provide a lot of time for potential petitioners to see if an appeal arguing that a rule should be made retroactive finds its way to the Court and the needed ruling handed down.

For state death penalty inmates, a petition can only be filed if they have exhausted all state remedies, there is no state corrective process available, or circumstances are such that any state processes that are available are ineffective to protect the rights of the petitioner (28 U.S.C. 2254(b)). In addition, a petition can be denied on the merits even if the petitioner has failed to exhaust all state remedies, meaning they would not be able to reappeal. In addition, a state conviction can only be reviewed by the federal court if the conviction was contrary to or involved an unreasonable application of federal law or was based on an unreasonable determination of the facts in light of the evidence presented in state court (28 U.S.C. 2254(d)). The state determination of the facts is presumed correct, and the burden is on the petitioner to rebut the presumption by clear and convincing evidence (28 U.S.C. 2254(e)). Even where a state court decision was incorrect but reasonable, the petitioner would be unlikely to meet this burden (del Carmen et al., 2008, citing *Williams v. Taylor*, 529 U.S. 362 [2000]).

In addition, if a defendant failed to make a claim in state court proceedings, the federal courts cannot hear the claim in a habeas corpus proceeding unless the claim relies on a new retroactive law or on a "factual predicate that could not have been previously discovered through the exercise of due diligence" (28 U.S.C. 2254(d)). The petitioner also must show by clear and convincing evidence that, but for the error, the petitioner would not have been convicted.

Probably the most significant impact of the AEDPA has been in the area of successive petitions. Instead of allowing federal courts to dismiss successive petitions if they believe them to be filed in bad-faith, the AEDPA amended section 2244 to prohibit all successive petitions if the claim was already presented in a prior petition. In other words, successive same-claim petitions are no longer allowed (Bohm, 2012). Second or successive petitions based on claims not present in a prior petition are allowed if the claim is based on a new rule of constitutional law made retroactive on collateral review by the Supreme Court or is based on new evidence unavailable through the exercise of due diligence at the time of trial. Successive petitions must also be granted a certificate of eligibility from the Court of Appeals authorizing the district court to consider the claim (28 U.S.C. 2244; see also Bohm, 2012).

The AEDPA and the Issue of Retroactivity

As noted earlier, the AEDPA has imposed probably the most stringent restrictions on the habeas writ in its history. One of the many issues that has drawn criticism is the AEDPA's retroactivity requirement. Under the AEDPA, a death penalty inmate can file a second or successive petition litigating a new claim under a new constitutional rule only if the U.S. Supreme Court has specifically made that claim retroactive and only with advanced permission of the Court of Appeals (certificate of eligibility). In addition, the inmate has only one year from the date of the decision articulating the new rule, not the date of any later decision making the new rule retroactive. Thus, argues Vladeck in his 2016 critique, inmates relying on a new constitutional rule that was not explicitly made retroactive in the opinion that established the new rule could have a problem.

> Taken together, these roadblocks make it exceedingly difficult even for a prisoner with a patently meritorious claim for postconviction relief based upon a new rule of constitutional law (including a claim that might require his immediate release) to obtain such relief through a second or successive petition.
>
> *(Vladeck, 2016, p. 225)*

To begin with, under *Teague v. Lane* (1989), rules handed down by the U.S. Supreme Court can be applied retroactively if the ruling establishes a "watershed" rule of criminal procedure or establishes a new "substantive" rule. Vladeck argues that this leaves inmates filing a second or successive petition under a new rule that was not explicitly made retroactive one of three options. First, the lower courts could decide that prior Supreme Court decisions have made clear that the law is retroactive (for example, a rule that is clearly substantive and thus always retroactively enforceable). However, there is no guarantee that the lower courts will do so and that all lower courts will agree—necessitating a review by the Supreme Court to resolve the conflict. If the Court of Appeals does not grant the inmate permission to appeal (since the rule has not been "made" retroactive), the inmate is out of luck (denials of permission to appeal cannot be appealed). Second, the inmate can wait for a first-time petitioner (who does not need permission) to appeal the retroactivity of the rule. However, the problem here is similar. There is no guarantee that the question will reach the Supreme Court—thereby making any ruling applicable to all circuits—in time to help the petitioner in need of the ruling (Vladeck, 2016, p. 225). Finally, Vladeck argues that the best option is for a petitioner in this situation is to file an petition asking the Supreme Court to file an original writ of habeas corpus. This approach may actually be the "cleanest vehicle through which the Justices can make a new rule retroactive since it does not require either the creative statutory interpretation or the fortuitous circumstances necessary to the other two avenues for review" (Vladeck, 2016, p. 226). However, as Vladeck points out, the United States Supreme Court has not exercised its original habeas jurisdiction since 1925.

When Does the Federal Government Seek the Death Penalty? The Death Penalty Protocol

The decision as to whether or not to seek the death penalty on a death eligible case rests entirely with the attorney general of the United States based on the recommendations of the Department of Justice's (DOJ) Capital Review Committee (CRC). The recommendation of the CRC is in turn governed by the procedures set out in the U.S. Attorney's Manual (USAM) known as the Death Penalty Protocol (DPP) (see U.S. Department of Justice, n.d., hereinafter USAM). The institution of the death penalty review process within the DOJ (as opposed to local federal prosecutors) began in 1995 under Attorney General Janet Reno, and a Capital Case Unit within the Criminal Division was formed in 1998 (Little, 2000).

Several authors have argued that one reason the United States has retained the death penalty longer than any other democracy is a result of its federal system, where each of the 50 states can decide whether to allow the death penalty as part of its criminal justice system or not (Hatch & Walsh, 2016; Little, 2000). The fact that the federal government can hold concurrent jurisdiction with states that do not have the death penalty creates certain issues as to when the Department of Justice should authorize the death penalty. Section 90–10.110 of the USAM states that when concurrent jurisdiction over a crime exists with a state or local government, "a federal indictment for an offense subject to the death penalty should be obtained only when the Federal interest in the prosecution is more substantial than the interests of the state or local authorities." In addition, as part of determining whether or not to initiate charges when the defendant is subject to prosecution in another jurisdiction (most often by state or local authorities), federal prosecutors must weigh all relevant considerations including the "ability and willingness to prosecute effectively" and the "probable sentence upon conviction" (USAM § 9–27.240). Critics of the DPP argue that this leads federal prosecutors to step in when a state prosecution would only result in life without parole (Connor, 2010). Other scholars have argued

> that the federal death penalty is used as a "safety valve" for states that do not have the death penalty—obviating their need to establish (or reestablish) one.
>
> *(Mysliwiec, 2010)*

In July 2011, Attorney General Eric Holder—as a result of the recommendations of the Capital Issue Team of the Sentencing and Corrections Working Group—issued revisions to the DPP. The following summary of the DPP is based on Attorney General Holder's July 2011 and April 2014 memoranda to all prosecutors (United States Department of Justice, 2011, hereinafter Memo, 2011, United States Department of Justice, 2014, hereinafter Memo, 2014) as well as the provisions of the USAM (as of February 12, 2017).

The heart of the DPP lies in the Standards of Determination set forth in Section 9–10.140 of the USAM. Holder's 2011 revisions codified in the standards a number of factors that were commonly considered in decisions on whether or not to seek the death penalty, including "the strength of the evidence, the role of the defendant in the capital offense, and the defendant's willingness to plead guilty to a life or near-life term of imprisonment" (Memo, 2011, p. 1). The standards are divided into four categories: fairness, national consistency, adherence to statutory requirements (specifically the consideration and weight given to aggravating and mitigating factors), and law enforcement objectives (USAM § 9–10.140).

Section 9–10.140 (A) of the USAM requires "all reviewers to evaluate each case on its own merits and on its own terms." In addition, federal prosecutors are prohibited from using considerations of characteristics such as race or ethnic origin in any recommendation or decision as to whether to seek the death penalty (USAM § 9–10.140(A)). The national consistency standard requires prosecutors to treat "similar cases similarly, when the only material difference is the location of the crime" (USAM, § 9–10.140(B)).

In Section 9–10.140(C), the standards address the consideration of statutory aggravating and mitigating factors, including how they should be weighed and analyzed:

> Reviewers are to resolve ambiguity as to the presence or strength of aggravating or mitigating factors in favor of the defendant. The analysis employed in weighing the aggravating and mitigating factors should be qualitative, not quantitative; a sufficiently strong aggravating factor may outweigh several mitigating factors, and a sufficiently strong mitigating factor may outweigh several aggravating factors.

In a separate section of the USAM and in his 2011 memo, Holder made clear that "the death penalty may not be sought, and no attorney for the Government may threaten to seek it, solely for the purpose of obtaining a more desirable negotiating position" (Memo, 2011, p. 2; USAM § 9–10.120). In addition, the USAM requires consultation with the family of the victim or victims on whether to seek the death penalty, and the views of the family should be included in any submission made to the department (USAM, § 9–10.100). Finally, "no final decision to seek the death penalty shall be made if defense counsel has not been afforded an opportunity to present evidence and argument in mitigation" (USAM § 90–10.130).

In a 2010 report on defense counsel for federal capital cases (Gould & Greenman, 2010), federal judges raised concerns about the length of time it took for the attorney general's office to decide whether or not to seek the death penalty. Holder addressed this issue in his 2011 memo, where he made clear a preference for pre-indictment determinations whenever possible on whether or not to seek the death penalty. Further revisions in 2014 made submission of all capital eligible cases for pre-indictment review mandatory absent extenuating circumstances (Memo, 2014, p. 1). Noting that in the vast majority of times, the death penalty is not sought in death-eligible cases, Holder went on to state that a "pre-indictment decision not to seek the death penalty provides early certainty about the death penalty question, and saves enormous resources, including substantial savings of time and money by courts, prosecutors and defense attorneys" (Memo, 2014, p. 1).

While sole authority to decide to seek the death penalty rests with the Attorney General, local U.S. attorneys can ask to have the decision reconsidered. Under the 2011 revisions to the DPP, the CRC also reviews these reconsideration requests (USAM § 90–10.160).

This revised procedure ensures that when a United States Attorney or an Assistant Attorney General asks the Attorney General to alter the initial decision based on changed circumstances, the request will be accorded review consistent with the process used for the original submission (Memo, 2011, p.3).Critiques of the Death Penalty Protocol

Death penalty observers have noted that in practice, the use of the death penalty in federal cases is limited, as the majority of capital cases take place in state criminal justice systems (Connor, 2010; Mysliwiec, 2010). As Mysliwiec points out, if the Department of Justice was trying to use the DPP to substitute the federal government's preference for the death penalty over the judgments of states that do not have one, the federal capital prosecutions in the minority of states that do not have the death penalty "would be far higher, to attempt to match state capital prosecutions in the . . . states that do have a state death penalty" (2010, p. 275). Yet as two useful critiques of the application of the death penalty protocol argue, it is the potential for how it's applied that raises constitutional and policy concerns.

After discussing the centralized review process represented by the DPP, Connor argues that while uniformity and consistency across federal districts in determinations regarding when to seek the death penalty is a useful goal (especially given that the modern death penalty structure in the U.S. was put in place largely to address concerns about arbitrary and discriminatory application), the values underlying the standards of determination leave too much discretion (Connor, 2010; see also *Furman v. Georgia*, 1972). As a result, argues Connor,

> the federal death penalty obstructs the ability of, and obscures the incentives for individual states to set criminal justice policy within their respective territorial jurisdictions, and furthermore . . . this tendency is manifestly out of step with constitutional norms surrounding the death penalty.
>
> *(2010, p. 152)*

Both Connor and Mysilwiec raise particular concerns over the issue of a lack of 'appropriate punishment' as a criterion for instituting federal capital prosecutions in non-death penalty states, arguing that the concept of 'appropriate punishment' means punishment that is not harsh enough.[2] Mysilwiec notes that states cannot prevent the federal government from prosecuting federal offenders in their state—even if the crime is not an offense under state law (2010, citing *Gonzales v. Reich*, 2005) and that the effect of national consistency efforts tend to be unidirectional toward harsher sentences—including the death penalty. Connor, in her critique, notes a number of examples of federal death penalty prosecutions where the state did not, or could not, apply the death penalty, including:

- prosecutions initiated in federal court where the death penalty is unavailable in the state;
- simultaneous state and federal prosecutions;

- federal prosecutions following a reversal of state convictions;
- federal prosecutions following state acquittals; and
- federal prosecutions where new evidence emerges after state convictions.

In sum, argues Connor, "a fair inference is that the federal interest is deemed more substantial than the state interest when a federal prosecution is more likely to produce a death sentence" (2010, p. 167).

Connor goes on to argue that in some instances, such federal prosecutions, especially when they follow state prosecutions, are unfair and violate constitutional norms such as equal protection and double jeopardy (which was originally meant to provide certainty and finality to criminal prosecutions and force government officials to either make their case or move on).

Furthermore, those and other constitutional doctrines—such as the Commerce Clause and the Sixth Amendment—have proven insufficient to deal with the reality of concurrent state and federal jurisdiction.

In addition to constitutional issues, both Connor and Mysilwiec criticize federal death penalty prosecutions in concurrent jurisdictions on policy grounds: that it interferes with the ability of the states to experiment with their governments and policies, which is an important aspect of American federalism. Connor lists three areas where the ability of federal prosecutors to override state level death penalty decisions negatively impacts the accountability and policymaking ability of state criminal justice actors by:

- decreasing state legislative accountability and displacing local preferences;
- decreasing the accountability of local prosecutors; and
- interfering with the ability of juries to reflect local factors and values by basing capital juries on the federal district with different population demographics.

Both Connor and Mysilwiec argue for stronger protections to ensure a balance between the need for national consistency in federal prosecution decisions and respect for the legislative will of the states. Connor recommends congressional action to prohibit the federal government from taking on any federal prosecutions once a state prosecution arising out of the same act has been initiated.

> By situating the instigation of a state prosecution as the triggering point of this federal law, the focus is drawn away from the results of the state proceeding, and the question of whether a state sentence is sufficiently punitive to vindicate federal interests is avoided (Connor, 2010, p. 208).

By contrast, Mysilwiec argues for a revision to the DPP to reflect language similar to that once in place under Attorney General Janet Reno but removed under Attorney General John Ashcroft. The language was lodged in the USAM provisions defining "substantial federal interest" and read: "In states where the imposition of the death penalty is not authorized by law, the fact that the maximum federal penalty is death is insufficient standing alone, to show a more substantial interest in federal prosecution" (Mysliwiec, 2010, pp. 270–271).

Role of Defense Counsel: An Update to the Spencer Report

In 1998, the Federal Death Penalty Cases Subcommittee of the Committee on Defender Services of the United States Judicial Conference published the Spencer Report on federal defense representation in death penalty cases (Spencer, Cauthron, & Edmunds, 1998). Its recommendations "aimed at containing costs while ensuring high quality defense services in capital cases were approved by the Judicial Conference in September of 1998" (Gould & Greenman, 2010).

Impact Since the Federal Death Penalty Act of 1994

- While the impact of the Federal Death Penalty Act of 1994 was only partially felt by the time of the Spencer Report, the subcommittee found that the number of capital cases requiring capital defense services has had an even greater impact in the years since (p. viii).
- The process of deciding in which cases the United States will seek the death penalty has been increasingly centralized within the Department of Justice leading to more defendants being authorized for death penalty prosecution absent requests by local prosecutors (p. viii).
- A higher portion of authorized cases have gone to trial rather than being settled in a plea agreement (p. ix).

Costs of Capital Defense

- Authorized cases cost more than eight times (based on median cost) than cases that were eligible for the death penalty but where the penalty was not authorized (p. ix).
- Costs of defending cases between 1998 and 2010 have increased substantially. Factors include: inflation, increased case complexity, legal developments resulting in increased obligations on counsel, advances in forensic science, and geographical location (p. ix).
- There was a strong association between a lower cost defense representation and an increased likelihood of a death sentence at trial (p. x).
- Expert services, including expert witnesses, investigators, and all other services other than counsel, are a significant component of capital defense costs (p. xi).

Perspectives of Judges and Attorneys

- The perception of quality and availability of defense counsel was higher among judges than lawyers (p. xi).
- Lawyers highlighted concerns about the lack of deference to the wishes of local U.S. Attorneys, particularly when the prosecution and defense had arrived at a mutually acceptable plea agreement (p. xi).

National Uniformity and Consistency

- There was a strong association between the state in which a prosecution was brought and the likelihood of a death sentence (p. xi).

Taken from the 2010 Executive Summary. For more detail see Gould & Greenman (2010) and Spencer, Cauthon, & Edmunds (1998).

Figure 27.1 Findings and Recommendations from the 2010 update to the Spencer Report on Defense Counsel Service in Federal Death Penalty Cases.

In September 2010, a follow-up report was completed (Gould & Greenman, 2010). A number of important findings were presented in the 2010 report and are set out in Figure 27.1.

As seen in Figure 27.1, the subcommittee found concerns that since the FDPA of 1994 and the centralizing of death penalty determinations in the Department of Justice's CRC, there has been an increase in cases seeking the federal death penalty (although as discussed earlier, only three federal executions have been carried out) and a concurrent rise in the need for, and cost of, quality capital defense counsel. Interestingly, but not surprisingly, the perception of how well the federal government is doing in this area differs between judiciary and counsel. In addition, as new technologies continue to push the boundaries of forensic science, capital cases will continue to increase in complexity and costs will likely continue to increase beyond the 2010 findings.

Updating the commentaries to the Spencer Report recommendations, the 2010 subcommittee noted such things as the benefits of appointing new counsel on appeal and the benefits of relying on federal public defender organizations to provide capital defense services wherever possible (Gould & Greenman, 2010, p. xii).

Conclusion

In his 2000 overview of the federal death penalty, Little presented some thoughtful predictions about its future:

> First, it is likely to go forward, with an actual execution occurring in the next twelve months [that turns out be Timothy McVeigh's execution in June 2001]. Second, concerns about it could well combine with 'anti-federalization' forces to produce a reduction of federal criminal jurisdiction. Third, it will continue to be bound up with concerns about statistical race disparities and geographic non-uniformity, which will not disappear no matter how many procedural protections we erect. Fourth, it is certain to be the continued object of federal judicial, as well as legislative, attention. Fifth, it will continue to leave the United States isolated from the international community.
>
> *(p. 579)*

With the exception of his second prediction, Little's speculations have been quite accurate. Almost every year the U.S. Supreme Court hears cases on some aspect of the death penalty or another affecting federal and state prosecutions. The death penalty has been disallowed for juveniles and mentally disabled defendants. Sentences of death based on nonunanimous jury determinations have been overturned. The racial disparities in the application of the death penalty at the federal and state levels has been shown again and again. Yet the United States retains the federal death penalty in all its glory and remains just as isolated from all other Western democracies

Little goes on to conclude his overview with the following:

> Absent an unexpectedly sweeping change in popular sentiment, the federal death penalty is not going to be repealed or suspended. When the first federal execution occurs, . . . some victims may be cheered and some prosecutors will feel vindicated. But others of us will find it a significant occasion to pause and consider the justness and ability of the path we currently tread.
>
> *(2000, p. 580)*

At the time of this writing, the U.S. political system is facing its greatest challenge, and its citizenry is more polarized than ever. At first glance, it appears unlikely that the new White House administration will have any interest in abolishing or reducing the use of the federal death penalty. At the same time, these recent events may just cause people to start down Little's path of pause and consideration, on many issues, including the death penalty. Where that path will lead as we close in on the third decade of the twenty-first century remains to be seen.

Notes

1 This provision—among many others—would be amended by the AEDPA in 1996. (For an excellent summary of the history of the Great Writ, see also del Carmen et al., 2008.)

2 Although the term 'appropriate punishment' is no longer included in the definition of substantial federal interest under Section 90-10.110 of the USAM, prosecutors are expected to consider "the ability and willingness [of the state] to prosecute effectively" and the "probable sentence upon conviction" under Section 9-27.240. Connor's and Mysilwiec's arguments are still worth considering under the current language, as the federal government has not shown a tendency to step in when a state's penalties are more severe and would not be able to prevent a state from imposing a more severe sentence based on a state prosecution in any case.

References

Anti-Drug Abuse Act of 1988, PL 100–690, 102 Stat. 4181.

Antiterrorism and Effective Death Penalty Act of 1996, PL 104–132, 110 Stat. 1214.

Bohm, R. M. (2012). *Death quest: An introduction to the theory and practice of capital punishment in the United States.* Waltham, MA: Anderson Publishing.

Chemerinsky, E. (1995). Eliminating discrimination in administering the death penalty: The need for the Racial Justice Act. *Santa Clara Law Review, 35*, 519–533.

Connor, E. M. (2010). The undermining influence of the federal death penalty on capital policymaking and criminal justice in the United States. *Journal of Criminal Law and Criminology, 100*(1), 149–211.

Death Penalty Information Center. (2016). *Federal death penalty.* Retrieved January 5, 2017 from www.deathpenaltyinfo.org/federal-death-penalty

del Carmen, R. V., Vollum, S., Dial, K. C., Frantzen, D., & San Miguel, C. (2008). *The death penalty: Constitutional issues, commentaries, and case briefs.* Newark, NJ: Matthew Bender & Company, Inc.

Federal Death Penalty Act, PL 103–322, 108 Stat. 1796 (Title VI of the Violent Crime Control and Law Enforcement Act of 1994).

Gould, J. B., & Greenman, L. (2010). *Update on the cost and quality of defense representation in federal death penalty cases.* Report to the Committee on Defender Services. Judicial Conference of the United States. Retrieved from www.uscourts.gov/file/fdpc2010pdf

Hatch, V. L., & Walsh, A. (2016). *Capital punishment: Theory and practice of the ultimate penalty.* Oxford: Oxford University Press.

Innocence Protection Act of 2004. PL 108–405, 118 Stat. 2279 (Title IV of the Justice For All Act of 2004).

Little, R. K. (2000). The future of the federal death penalty. *Ohio Northern University Law Review, 26*, 529–580.

Lungren, D. E., & Krotoski, M. L. (1995). The Racial Justice Act of 1994: Undermining enforcement of the death penalty without promoting racial justice. *University of Dayton Law Review, 20*, 655–697.

Mccollum, B. (1995). The struggle for effective anti-crime legislation: An analysis of the Violent Crime Control and Law Enforcement Act of 1994. *University of Dayton Law Review, 20*, 561–565.

Mysliwiec, P. (2010). The federal death penalty as a safety valve. *Virginia Journal of Social Policy and Law, 17*, 257–280.

New York Times. (1994, July 22). Pull the plug on this crime bill. *New York Times.* Retrieved from www.nytimes.com

Racial Justice Act of 1994, H.R. 4017. Introduced March 11, 1994.

Spencer, J. R., Cauthron, R. J., & Edmunds, N. G. (1998). *Federal death penalty cases: Recommendations concerning the cost and quality of defense representation.* Report to the Committee on Defender Services. Washington, DC: Judicial Conference of the United States.

United States Department of Justice. (n.d.). United States Attorney's Manual. Title 9, Chapter 9–10.000. Retrieved February 12, 2017 from www.justice.gov/usam/united-states-attorneys-manual

United States Department of Justice, Office of Attorney General. (2011, July 27). *Memorandum from Attorney General Eric H. Holder to all federal prosecutors: Changes to death penalty protocol.* Washington, DC: Author. Retrieved from www.justice.gov/oip/foia-library/death_penalty_protocol/download. (Memo, 2011).

United States Department of Justice, Office of Attorney General. (2014, April 7). Memorandum from Attorney General Eric H. Holder to all federal prosecutors: Revisions to death penalty protocol. Washington, DC: Author. Retrieved from www.justice.gov/oip/foia-librarydeath_penalty_protocol/download. (Memo, 2014)

United States Department of Justice, Office of Justice Programs, Bureau of Justice Statistics. (2014). *Capital punishment, 2012-statistical tables.* Washington, DC: Bureau of Justice Statistics. Report No. NCJ245789.

U.S. Const. art. I, § 9.

Vladeck, S. L. (2016). Special topic: Johnson v. United States: Using the Supreme Court's original habeas jurisdiction to make new rules retroactive. *Federal Sentencing Reporter, 28* (February), 225.

Cases Cited

Furman v. Georgia, 408 U.S. 238 (1972).
Gideon v. Wainwright, 372 U.S. 335 (1963).
Gonzales v. Reich, 545 U.S. 1 (2005).
Gregg v. Georgia, 428 U.S. 153 (1976).
McCleskey v. Kemp, 481 U.S. 279 (1987).
Salinger v. Loisel, 265 U.S. 224 (1924).
Teague v. Lane, 489 U.S. 288 (1989).
United States v. Gabion, 719 F.3d 511 (6th Cir.) (2013).

28

THE DEATH PENALTY AND THE UNITED STATES ARMED FORCES

Catherine M. Grosso[1]

Introduction

Before focusing on the death penalty in the military, it is useful to remember how the military prosecutes crimes. This military justice system is similar to but not the same as the state or federal criminal justice systems. Congress created the military justice system under authority provided in Article I of the Constitution. As such, military courts are Article I rather than Article III courts. The Uniform Code of Military Justice (UCMJ) defines the crimes and procedures for the military. The Manual for Courts Martial (MCM) provides the rules for courts martial.

Courts martial are temporary tribunals, convened by a "convening authority," normally a general or an admiral in the accused's command, for the purpose of determining the guilt and punishment of members of the armed forces (UCMJ, Art. 822). Courts martial were not established along the same guidelines or, really, for the same purpose as civilian courts. Courts martial are an extension of the executive power to aid the president in maintaining discipline in the armed forces. They serve the dual purposes of providing discipline and justice (Schlueter, 2008).

The convening authority refers charges to a court martial, decides what kind of court martial to convene, and selects the people who will serve as jurors for the court-martial ("the members"). Types of court martial follow the level of crime. All capital cases would be referred to a general court martial (MCM 201(f)). A general court martial deciding a capital case must be composed of at least 12 members and a military judge (UCMJ Art. 825).

The decision of a court martial is appealed first to the convening authority. The convening authority has discretion to reduce both the crime of conviction and its punishment (UCMJ, Art. 60). Once the convening authority has approved the case, appeals lie to a service court of criminal appeals. Each branch of the military has a court of criminal appeals: the Air Force Court of Criminal Appeals, the Army Court of Criminal Appeals, the Navy-Marine Criminal Appeals, and the Coast Guard Court of Criminal Appeals (UCMJ, Art. 66). The Court of Appeals for the Armed Forces reviews all capital cases as affirmed by any of the courts of criminal appeals (UCMJ, Art. 67). As with state supreme courts, the United States Supreme Court has discretion to review the decisions of the Court of Appeals for the Armed Forces (UCMJ, Art. 67a).

What Crimes Are Death Eligible Under the Uniform Code of Military Justice

Capital punishment has long been available as a penalty in the United States armed forces. There are currently 14 death-eligible offences in the Uniform Code of Military Justice. This contrasts with civilian law, where only intentional or felony murder can lead to a death sentence (*Kennedy v. Louisiana*, 2008). All but one of these offenses reflects unique military or national security implications. For example, consider mutiny, sedition, or espionage (Sec. 894 & 906A). These crimes relate uniquely to national security concerns. Eight additional death eligible offenses in the UCMJ apply only "in time of war" or during combat operations against a foreign power. The remaining two offenses with important military implications have no express "time of war" requirement (Sec. 902 & 910). These two offenses, forcing a safeguard and willfully hazarding a vessel, however, appear not to have been applied since the Korean War.

The fourteenth death-eligible offense punishes murder committed by U.S. military personnel during peacetime anywhere in the world. Section 118 makes both premeditated and felony murder death eligible. The UCMJ established murder and rape as death eligible military offenses in 1950.[2] The UCMJ authorized the death penalty for rape until 2012. The United States Supreme Court held the death penalty unconstitutional as excessive punishment for rape of an adult woman in *Coker v. Georgia* (1977) and then in *Kennedy v. Louisiana* (2008) for rape of a child. The only service member executed for rape since 1950 was Pvt. John Bennett. His execution, in 1961, is also the most recent military execution.

Unlike the first 13 death-eligible offenses discussed earlier, death eligibility for murder requires no connection between the murder and military interests or functions. Courts martial were first granted jurisdiction to try murder and rape cases during the Civil War when these acts were "committed by persons who are in the military service of the United States" during times of "war, insurrection, or rebellion" (Articles of War, 1863, p. 736). In 1916, an amendment to the Articles of War added that "no person shall be tried by court martial for murder or rape committed within the geographical limits of the States . . . and the District of Columbia in time of peace" (Article of War, 1916, p. 664).

These provisions, which denied courts martial jurisdiction to try murder and rape offenses when committed within the geographical limits of the United States during times of peace, survived many revisions to the Articles of War, including the Elston Act in 1948. Congress finally granted courts martial the jurisdiction to try crimes of murder and rape committed in the United States during peacetime with the adoption of the UCMJ in 1950.

The UCMJ applies to all military personnel and gives military courts martial jurisdiction.[3] A murder conviction is the basis of all of the military death sentences imposed since 1960. The UCMJ defined capital murder in language precisely tracking the provisions of typical 1950s civilian death penalty statutes that defined first-degree and felony murder as capital offenses.[4] While the statute defined the behavior that makes a crime eligible for a death sentence, it provided no guidance to the decision maker deciding between a death sentence and imprisonment for life.

Furman v. Georgia (1972) held that providing that kind of unguided discretion to sentencing authorities in civilian jurisdictions violated the cruel and unusual punishments provision of the Eighth Amendment of the United States Constitution. *Furman* invalidated state death penalty statutes across the United States, but the majority opinions did not address its applicability to military courts. As noted earlier, military courts martial are Article I rather than Article III courts, and the Bill of Rights does not always apply to military courts in the same manner as to Article III courts (*United States v. Easton*, 2012). The *Furman* Court's concerns about the risks of unbridled discretion of sentencing authorities, however, appeared to apply with equal force to the military system.

Justice Powell, writing for the four dissenting justices, suggested that the case voided military capital punishment law (*Furman*, 1972, pp. 417–418). Justice Blackmun also emphasized this point in his separate dissent (412). Two years later, Justice Marshall echoed that concern in his dissent in the case of *Schick v. Reed* (1974, p. 271). However, neither Congress nor the president made any effort to reform military law or procedures.

Shortly thereafter, the United States Supreme Court ruled in *Gregg v. Georgia* (1976) and *Proffitt v. Florida* (1976) that guiding sentencing decisions with statutory lists of aggravating circumstances comparable to those found in Section 210.6 of the Model Penal Code and bifurcating guilt and penalty trials satisfied the requirements of the Eighth Amendment because they materially reduced the breadth of capital charging and sentencing discretion. In the court's view, these reforms limited death sentences to the most aggravated cases, thereby eliminating the risk of arbitrariness and discrimination in the administration of capital punishment.

In 1981, the Navy-Marine Corps Court of Military Review denied the applicability of *Furman* to the military (*United States v. Rojas*). The court found that military law, while not notably distinguishable from the unconstitutional civilian capital punishment laws struck down by *Furman*, had to be understood in the context of the unique military justice system. The court rejected a "comparison of literal statute provisions" to determine whether *Furman* required changes because "[t]he death penalty is imposed and administered in the military justice system under procedures established by Congress and the President in the UCMJ and [Manual for Courts Martial], respectively" (928–29). The court concluded that the military justice system itself mitigated any risk of arbitrary decision making. Finally, the court reasoned that the procedures in place arose from the needs of commanders "to establish and maintain the armed forces" and should be seen as part of "the peculiar requirements which flow from a disciplined, ever-ready and effective military community" (929).

A June 1983 Air Force Court of Military Review rejected the reasoning by the Navy-Marine Corps court, holding that *Furman*'s requirements applied to courts martial and that the court martial system was not in compliance with those requirements (*United States v. Gay* 1983). The Court of Military Appeals settled the conflict between the lower military courts, ruling that *Furman* applied to courts martial in *United States v. Matthews* (1983) and then affirming the decision in *Gay* (1984).

President Ronald Reagan asked his legal advisors to bring military law into conformity with the requirements of the Eighth Amendment. His 1984 executive order limited death eligibility to capital cases in which the fact finder found one or more statutory aggravating circumstance present in the case and found that "any extenuating or mitigating circumstances are substantially out-weighed by any aggravating circumstances." The executive order was codified in the Manual for Courts Martial, Rule 1004.

Recall that the UCMJ defines 14 death-eligible offenses, many of which relate uniquely to national security matters. Perhaps because of this, the executive order limits the application of certain aggravators to offenses *other than* premeditated or felony murder.[5] Other factors facially apply to all death-eligible offenses, but in practice they have no applicability to non-security-related premeditated and felony murders. One such aggravating circumstance has clear relevance to murder cases. This factor identifies a crime as aggravated when "the lives of persons other than the victim, if any, were unlawfully and substantially endangered" (Rule 1004(c)(4).

Civilian-style premeditated and felony murders constitute the vast majority of death eligible murders committed by military personnel in peacetime. Rule 1004 treats premeditated and felony murders separately. The rule assigned premeditated murder cases (Art. 118(1)) an extensive list of distinctly civilian-style aggravating circumstances. Section (c)(7) defines the following aggravating circumstances for premeditated murder cases: (i) accused under confinement for 30-plus years, (ii) felony murder, (iii) evidence of a pecuniary motive, (iv) compulsion or contract murder, (v) murder to facilitate escape or avoid apprehension, (vi) murder of an important federal official, (vii) murder of a commissioned or noncommissioned officer knowingly killed "in the execution of office," (viii) murder for obstruction of justice, (ix) infliction of substantial pain and suffering, and (x) murder of multiple victims. The order also defines one additional aggravating circumstance limited to felony murder alone—"the accused was the actual perpetrator of the killing" (Sec. (c)(8)). These factors comprise the majority of the rule. The executive order's focus on civilian aggravating circumstances for premeditated murder was understandable given that six of the seven murder cases from the military in which a death sentence had been imposed between 1979 and 1984 involved typical civilian murders with no special military implications. The Model Penal Code clearly inspired these aggravating circumstances, as it did almost every state death penalty statute after *Furman*.

One part of one of the premeditated murder aggravating circumstances is tailored to military circumstances. This aggravator classifies as death eligible the premeditated murder of a "commissioned, warrant, noncommissioned, or petty officer of the armed services of the United States" killed "in the execution of office" when the accused had knowledge of the victim's status (codified in Rule 1004(c) (7)(G)). The remainder of that aggravating factor reflects an effort to provide special protection for law enforcement and corrections officers that is found in most civilian jurisdictions.

The executive order does not list specific mitigating circumstances. Again this mirrors the approach in a civilian system like the Georgia system approved by the Supreme Court in *Gregg v. Georgia* (1976). The executive order allowed military lawyers to advise their commanders that the military system now available for the capital prosecution of premeditated and felony murder was in full compliance with *Furman*.

Decision Making in Death-Eligible Murder Cases

The following section presents an overview of decision making in the U.S. military capital punishment system. Under military law and practice, the death penalty statute is applied in a three-stage process by two decision makers—the convening authority and the court martial members. This section reviews both law and practice. The applied data draw on a study examining the role of race in the administrative death penalty in the United States Armed Forces between 1984 and 2005 (Baldus, Grosso, Woodworth, & Newell, 2011) (the Baldus study). That study sought to identify and document the procedural history of every death-eligible murder during the time period.

A capital prosecution in a death-eligible case is commenced by the convening authority. The convening authority has total discretion to seek a death sentence in a death-eligible case. A decision to seek a death sentence is known as a "capital referral," a decision that is heavily influenced by the Article 34 "advice" letter of the commander's staff judge advocate (his chief legal advisor).

Article 34 advice letters take a variety of forms. Some provide an explicit recommendation about whether the convening authority should seek a death sentence in the letter or in the accompanying charge sheet. The letter other times tells the convening authority what must exist factually to justify a capital referral without suggesting whether or not to make a capital referral.

If a case is capitally charged and the capital referral is not withdrawn by the convening authority, the case advances to a capital court martial with the government seeking a death sentence. As would be the case in civilian jurisdictions, the decision of the convening authority not to bring capital charges is often based on a pretrial agreement in which the accused pleads guilty in exchange for the convening authority's waiver of the death penalty. Likewise in capitally charged cases, the convening authority often withdraws the capital charge in exchange for a guilty plea to the crime charged or a less serious offense. In contrast to civilian courts, a military accused's case may not advance to a capital sentencing hearing on the basis of a guilty plea. Nor may the accused waive a jury trial and have a military judge decide the guilt and penalty. Military judges may not impose death sentences. If the government seeks a death sentence, the case must be tried and sentenced by members (jurors).

The role of convening authorities in the military death penalty distinguishes it from its civilian counterparts with respect to plea bargains. Military prosecutors may on their own motion initiate plea negotiations leading to a waiver of the death penalty and may propose such an agreement to the convening authority, but no plea bargain involving a waiver of the death penalty can go forward without the personal consent of the senior officer who convened the court martial. The convening authority has absolute discretion to accept or reject the proposed course of action.

The capital referral and plea bargaining decisions of the convening authority took death off the table in 58% of the 97 death-eligible cases in the Baldus study. The remaining 42% advanced to a capital court martial with the government seeking a death sentence. This rate is comparable to the 39% rate in the eight civilian jurisdictions on which post-*Furman* data are available from the 1970s and 1980s (Baldus, Woodworth, & Pulaski, 1990, p. 233), but it is higher than the civilian rates in most jurisdictions since 1990.[6]

Since 1990, the military capital charging rate has declined sharply, as it has in many civilian jurisdictions. Since November 18, 1997, the military life sentence option has included a life sentence without possibility of parole (LWOP). The availability of LWOP may contribute to an increase in the frequency with which convening authorities waive the death penalty in death-eligible cases by declining to charge them capitally or withdrawing a capital charge as part of a plea bargain.

The UCMJ permits a jury to find guilt based on two-thirds of the members present, but death eligibility requires unanimity (UCMJ Art. 52). Likewise, Rule 1004(a)(2) makes a condition precedent for the imposition of a death sentence the accused's conviction of capital murder "by the concurrence of all the members of the court martial." The risk of receiving a death sentence dropped out for 27% of those found guilty of premeditated or felony murder in the Baldus study because of a nonunanimous finding of guilt.

A unanimous finding of liability for capital murder by the court martial members advances the case to a capital sentencing hearing. Court martial members consider the aggravating factors and mitigating circumstances during the penalty trial to decide whether to impose a life or death sentence. At this stage, members in the Baldus study cases sentenced 50% of the accused to death. This rate is comparable to the 53% penalty trial death sentencing rate in the 12 civilian jurisdictions on which data are available from the 1970s and 1980s (Baldus, Woodworth, & Pulaski, 1990, p. 233), but it is higher than the average civilian penalty trial rate since 1990.

Overall, the death sentencing rate among all 97 death-eligible cases in the Baldus study was 15% (15/97). This rate is higher than comparable figures in most states on which we have data both before and after 1990.

The appellate review process following the imposition of a military death sentence commences with the accused's request for clemency by the convening authority. The convening authority has complete discretion to reduce both the crime of conviction and its punishment. Convening authorities disallowed the death sentence in two of the 15 death sentenced cases in the Baldus study.

If a death sentence is approved by the convening authority, as noted earlier, appeals lie to the branch-specific courts of military review, the Court of Appeals of the Armed Forces (CAAF), and the United States Supreme Court. Death was taken off the table for eight defendants by an appellate military court decision, a decision on remand by the convening authority, or court members in a second capital sentencing hearing.

Five defendants, including two sentenced after the Baldus study, remain under a death sentence. One of these defendants Ronald Gray, appears to have exhausted his military and civilian appeals. President George W. Bush approved Ronald Gray's death penalty on July 28, 2008, as required under the UCMJ Section 871(a) (Myers, 2008). This decision exhausted Gray's direct appeals and allowed him to initiate habeas corpus proceedings in federal courts. Gray then sought and obtained a stay of his execution in federal court with leave to file his first habeas petition, which he subsequently did (Execution of ex-soldier, 2008). The federal district court dismissed his petition without relief in September 2015 and lifted the stay of execution (Brooks, 2016). Gray, however, remains on death row. The military has not executed any prisoners since 1961, when it hanged John A. Bennett for raping an 11-year-old girl (Serrano, 1994).

Racial Discrimination and the Military Death Penalty

Concerns about race disparities in the administration of capital punishment in the U.S. armed forces have deep roots. Robert Lilly's studies of military executions in Europe during World War II suggested that black soldiers accused of rape and murder of white victims were disproportionately executed for their crimes (Lilly & Thomson, 1997). Other examples outside the context of the death penalty also show pervasive race discrimination. For example, during World War II the armed forces stationed in England segregated black soldiers from European white women after white soldiers objected to black soldiers appearing socially with white women (282–83). Decades later in 1972, a Pentagon-sponsored study of the military justice system concluded that "the military system does discriminate against its members on the basis of race and ethnic background" (Department of Defense, 1972, p. 17). The report continued, "The discrimination is sometimes purposive; more often it is not."

Another concern is that the military justice system lacks even the transparency present in civilian systems. Concerns about lack of transparency came to light in recent years in the context of sexual assault. The Invisible War, a widely acclaimed investigative documentary, presented compelling evidence of both the prevalence and invisibility of sexual assault in the military (Ziering & Barklow, 2012). It showed the ways that the military justice system can focus inward and insulate behavior from review. The decisions of commanders and courts martial members typically receive little scrutiny either within or outside the military.

The sexual assault reform movement proved an exception to this general rule (Murphy, 2014). Highly aggravated murders that implicate the authority and effectiveness of the military command have provided a second exception. For example, capital prosecutions of soldiers for the murder of their officers in combat situations attract substantial attention in the civilian media. Extensive press coverage attended the prosecution of Hassan Akbar, who murdered two officers in Kuwait in 2003 and was sentenced to death (MSNBC, 2005). This is not typical of the prosecution of murder in the military. Much happens out of the public eye, in the context of a particular command and in a place anywhere in the world.

Both the history and the practice suggested that looking more closely at the influence of race might be helpful. David Baldus and colleagues undertook an extensive research project seeking to understand the role of race in the administration of justice in the armed forces ("the Baldus study"). The project took more than five years to complete. The scholars started by searching for the names of every person in any branch of the military who was prosecuted for homicide and whose case may have been factually death eligible. They then compiled an extensive file on each case in order to verify death eligibility for inclusion in the study. Death eligibility required strong evidence that (1) a case that was not capitally charged would, if it had been so charged, have supported a conviction of capital murder and a finding of one or more aggravating factors in the case and (2) both of these findings would have been sustained on appeal if the sufficiency of the evidence supporting the death eligibility of the case had been challenged.

The final sample for analysis included 97 death-eligible cases, a sample understood to include all death-eligible cases prosecuted by the U.S. armed forces during the research period. Figure 28.1 shows the overall decision making and outcomes for the cases in the study. Forty-one of the 97 cases were charged capitally and faced a capital court martial. Thirty of the 41 cases advanced from a capital court martial to a capital sentencing hearing; of these, 15 resulted in a death sentence. Eighty of the 97 death-eligible cases involved one or more white victims. Forty cases involved a minority accused. Twenty-five involved a minority accused and one or more white victims.[7]

The Baldus study examined the influence of race both in (1) the decision making overall, i.e., looking only at which cases receive a death sentence, and (2) each decision point present in a given capital charging and sentencing system (charging, guilt verdict, and sentencing verdict). Figure 28.1 shows both the overall death sentencing rate, on the far right side, and the decision making for each decision point, in columns B-D.

The Baldus study also reported both unadjusted and adjusted results. Unadjusted disparities do not take into account case characteristics, other than race, that may affect charging and sentencing decisions. These disparities can provide an important base line understanding of the risk of discrimination in a system. Adjusted results, however, consider and control for the rich factual information about each case and each defendant. Adjusted disparities seek to identify and control for those facts that bear

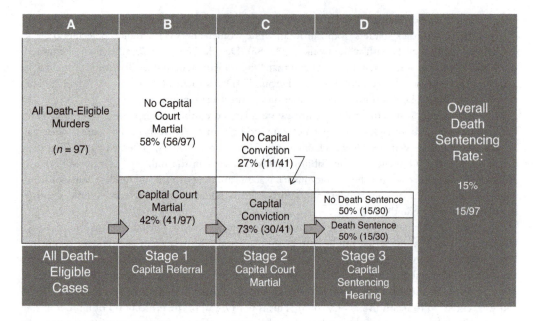

Figure 28.1 Overview of Decision Making and Outcomes.

on the comparative deathworthiness of all of the offenders in the analysis. Baldus and colleagues used multiple techniques for controlled analysis in this study.

In summary, the study reports evidence of systematic racial disparities in the charging and sentencing decisions of convening authorities and court-martial members that nonracial characteristics do not explain. As explained in more detail later, the study presented race effects in three areas. Minority defendants faced odds of receiving a death sentence that were 5.2 times higher than the odds faced by similarly situated white defendants. Cases involving at least one white victim faced odds of receiving a death sentence that were 12.5 times higher than the odds faced by similarly situated cases with no white victims. Finally, minority defendants who killed at least one white victim faced odds of receiving a death sentence that were 6.6 times higher than the odds faced by all other cases.

The first question of interest is whether certain subgroups of cases were more likely to receive a death sentence compared to all other cases in the study. The outcome of interest in these analyses is the fact of receiving a death sentence. Is race a significant factor in the receipt of a death sentence? The Baldus study documented white-victim and minority-accused/white-victim disparities in the imposition of death sentences among all death-eligible cases (see Figure 28.2).

Figure 28.2 depicts the differential rates that different groups of offenders are sentenced to death. Column A reports death sentencing rates separately for the minority and white accused. The left bar embraces 40 minority accused, ten of whom were sentenced to death for a rate of 25%. For the 57 white offenders represented by the right bar, five received a death sentence for a rate of 9%. Column A documents a 16-percentage point disparity. The risk faced by minorities is 2.8 times higher than the risk faced by nonblack offenders. In spite of the small sample of death sentences imposed, this quite large disparity is statistically significant at the .05 level.

Columns B and C present similar information for two other subgroups groups of interest. Column B presents the disparities in outcomes for cases with at least one white victim, in the left bar, compared to cases with no white victims in the right bar, showing an 11-point unadjusted white-victim disparity and a relative risk of 2.8 that is not statistically significant. Column C presents a 28-point

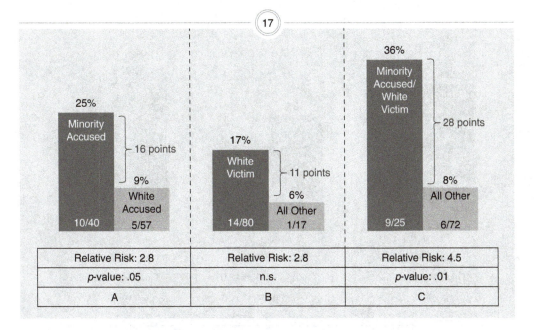

Figure 28.2   Racial Disparities in the Imposition of Death Sentences Among All Death-Eligible Cases.

increased risk of a death sentence for minority accused/white victim cases, a relative risk of 4.5, that is statistically significant at the .01 level.

The 11-point unadjusted white-victim disparity and the 28-point minority-accused/white-victim disparity are consistent with the findings of many studies of civilian death penalty systems. However, the 16-percentage point independent minority-accused disparity reported in Column A distinguishes the military system from the typical civilian system.

No known comparable post-*Furman* study from a state system reveals an independent minority- or black-defendant disparity of this magnitude among all death-eligible cases. Typically, in every civilian system on which comparable data exist, the unadjusted analysis of death sentencing among all death-eligible cases reports a lower death sentencing rate for the minority or black defendant cases than it does for the white defendant cases.

The next step in analysis of this type is to introduce controls reflecting rich factual information about each case and each defendant. Figure 28.3 reports the adjusted linear effect, the relative risk based on the disparity in adjusted linear effects, the odds multiplier, and the level of statistical significance for each racial subgroup—minority accused, white victim, and minority accused/white victim cases. An adjusted linear effect is a standardized measure of impact derived from the logistic regression. It allows a comparison of the unadjusted disparities to adjusted disparities using similar language.

As you can see, the race effects for death sentencing among all death eligible cases—i.e., for the system overall—persist even after the introduction of controls. Column A reports that, on average, minority accused were 12-percentage points more likely to be sentenced to death than white accused. In terms of the odds-based disparity, the full regression model reports that minority accused faced odds of being sentenced to death that were 5.2 times higher than similarly situated white accused (Baldus et al., 2011, tbl. 4).

Column B reports that accused in white-victim cases are 12-percentage points more likely to be sentenced to death than are similarly situated accused in cases with no white victims present, an

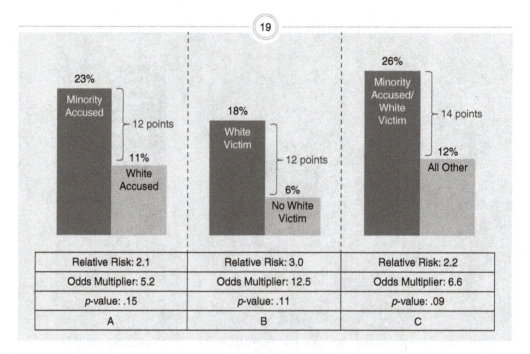

Figure 28.3 Racial Disparities in the Imposition of Death Sentences Among All Death-Eligible Cases, Fully Controlled.

estimate that approaches significance with a *p*-value of .11. Stated in terms of odds, defendants in white-victim cases face odds of receiving a death sentence that are 12.5 times higher than the odds faced by similarly situated defendants with no white victims. As a point of comparison, in the Georgia research presented to the United States Supreme Court in *McCleskey v. Kemp* (1987), the odds multiplier for the white-victim variable was 4.3.

The combined effect of both accused and victim race is reported in Column C. It documents that minority-accused/white-victim cases are 14-percentage points more likely to be sentenced to death among all death-eligible cases than accused in all other cases with different accused/victim racial combinations, with an odds multiplier of 6.6, significant at the .09 level.

The racial disparities documented in the imposition of death sentences among all death-eligible cases—in both uncontrolled and controlled analyses—provide important evidence about the role of race in this system.

Because of the small sample of 97 death-eligible cases in which only 15 death sentences were imposed, few of the racial disparities estimated overall and at three different decision points are statistically significant beyond the .05 level.[8] Nevertheless, because of their magnitude and consistency, Baldus and colleagues concluded that these findings support an inference of real race effects in the system.

The researchers concluded that the principal source of the white-victim disparities in the system was the combined effect of convening authority charging decisions and court-martial members' guilt trial decisions that advance cases to capital sentencing hearings. Specifically, after adjustment for nonracial case characteristics, on average, the probability that a white-victim case will advance to a capital sentencing hearing is 27-percentage points higher (*p* = .03) than the probability that a similarly situated minority-victim case will advance that far in the process. When the racial disparity is stated in terms of odds enhancement, the adjusted odds multiplier for the white-victim cases was 28.1. This

Table 28.1 Minority-Accused Disparities in the Outcomes of Capital Sentencing Hearings

A	B	C	D	E	F
		Unadjusted Disparities	Adjusted Disparities(applying alternate measures of culpability)		
			Nonracial Case Characteristics in a Logistic Regression Analysis[1]	Five-Level Race-Purged Regression Based Culpability Scale	Six-Level Salient Factors Based Culpability Scale
a.	Minority Accused	71% (10/14)	44%	59%	56%
b.	White Accused	31% (5/16)	26%	42%	35%
c.	Disparity (*Row a.* − *Row b.*)	40 pts.*	18 pts.	17 pts.	21 pts.
d.	Relative Risk (*Row a. / Row b.*)	2.3	1.4	1.4	1.6

Level of significance of disparity: * = .10

[1] When this analysis is limited to the three nonracial variables in the Column D analysis that had a relationship to the death sentencing outcomes that was statistically significant beyond the .10 level, the minority-accused effect is 14-points, with a 3.0 odds multiplier, significant at the .39 level.

is the strongest race effect documented in the system and it is consistent after adjustment for three different measures of offender culpability.

When the convening authority and member decisions that jointly advance cases to a capital sentencing hearing are analyzed separately, the white-victim effect is substantial in each analysis, but in neither is it statistically significant. With respect to race-of-accused disparities, the research documented no such effects in convening authority decisions advancing cases to a capital guilt trial.

In contrast, they identified effects for race of the accused in two sets of members' decisions. First, when panel members decide on guilt in capital trials, there is a moderate, though not statistically significant, minority-accused effect in their unanimous guilt decisions. Second, as shown in Table 28.1, the minority-accused effect is much more substantial in the members' death-sentencing decisions. Specifically, there is an unadjusted 40-percentage point minority-accused disparity in members' death-sentencing rates (71% for minority accused versus 31% for white accused) that is statistically significant at the .10 level. Upon adjustment with a variety of culpability measures, the minority-accused disparities decline to 17- from 21-percentage points (depending on the measure of accused culpability used in the analysis) and were not significant because of the small sample sizes. These independent race-of-accused disparities are substantially larger than the race-of-defendant effects documented in any comparable study of jury death sentencing of which we are aware.

The data reveal no white-victim effects in the members' capital sentencing decisions because only one black-victim case advanced this far in the system.

The 16 multiple-victim cases are a major source of racial disparities in the system, particularly minority-accused/white-victim disparities. Among these 16 cases, after adjustment for offender culpability, the minority-accused/white-victim disparity is between 75 and 88 percentage points, with a relative risk ranging from 4.9 to 10.8; two of three disparities are significant beyond the .10 level.

The Baldus study found compelling evidence that the race of the accused and of the victim influenced charging and sentencing decisions in the processing of death-eligible murder cases during the study period.

Civilian Crimes in a Military Death Penalty System

A different concern about the administration of capital punishment in the military relates to the extent to which the dual and dueling roles of discipline and justice play out in charging and sentencing decisions. As noted earlier, the military law on capital punishment combines military and civilian concerns in many respects, but when it comes to premeditated and felony murder the statute closely resembles civilian state law. The question here is whether the administration of the military death penalty follows the civilian model contemplated by military law or whether practice has, in fact, imposed a gloss on the law that nullifies the apparent civilizing influence.

The limitation of jurisdiction to military crimes followed naturally from the perception that the main function of courts martial jurisdiction, including its most severe punishments, was to maintain military discipline, control, and authority. This rationale was hard to defend when in 1950, military courts martial jurisdiction, including the use of the death penalty, was expanded to cover both military and civilian murders committed anywhere in the world during both war and peace. Consequently the vast bulk of murders committed by military personnel and adjudicated in military courts have no military implications and little relevance to the courts martial goal of maintaining military discipline, control, and authority. Highly aggravated homicides with significant military implications comprise only a small proportion of death-eligible military murders that have been committed since 1950 and more specifically since 1984.

The Slow Civilianization of Courts Martial

There is a history of resistance by some military leaders to efforts to "civilianize" the military criminal justice system.[9] This resistance appeared most famously during the 1920s in the office of the Judge Advocate General of the Army over the availability of appeal from certain court martial cases (Lindley, 1990). Commanders resisting such change perceive the military criminal justice system principally as a means of promoting discipline to protect the authority and effectiveness of the military command and view efforts to civilianize the military system as a threat to those goals. For example, William Winthrop, "the greatest departmental authority upon Military Law," stated in 1886 that "Courts-martial are not courts, but are, in fact, simply instrumentalities of the executive power provided by Congress for the President as Commander-in-Chief to aid him in properly commanding the army and enforcing discipline therein" (Winthrop, 1886, p. 54). This tension pits the "demands of discipline" against "the requirements of justice" (Barry, 2002, p. 67).

Courts martial are Article I rather than Article III courts (Duke & Vogel, 1960). As such, courts martial were not established along the same guidelines or, really, for the same purpose as civilian courts. Courts martial are an extension of the executive power (provided by Congress) to aid the President in maintaining discipline in the armed forces. "Despite periodic reforms, the military justice system, like the military system as a whole, has long been viewed as an extension of the Executive Branch to serve its military needs" (Turley, 2002, p. 665). One aspect of this is that courts-martial "need not provide a military accused with the same procedural rights available to a civilian defendant in a criminal trial conducted under Article III" (*Willenbring v. Neurauter*, 1998, p. 157). Courts martial form an essential part of a commander's tools for maintaining effective command and control.

Accordingly, courts martial historically have not been held to the same due-process standards as civilian courts. While many of the protections of the Bill of Rights have been applied to the military through statute, civilianizing changes typically have been resisted by military personnel (Wiener, 1958b, pp. 294–296). As early as 1912, the Judge Advocate General of the Army stated in a Congressional committee hearing that "the introduction of fundamental principles of civil jurisprudence into the administration of military justice is to be discouraged" (Ansell, 1919, p. 7). In subsequent testimony, the Judge Advocate General of the Army emphasized again that a court martial must be—first and foremost—the tool by which a commander maintains discipline and control (Lindley, 1990, pp. 66–68). A thorough history of the courts martial system and efforts to "civilianize" the system over the past century, by Kevin J. Barry (Captain, U.S. Coast Guard Ret.) (2002), casts these efforts as long, hard-fought battles met with great resistance by the military.

Resistance in the Noncapital Context

In the noncapital context, military leaders resisted a number of civilianizing reforms. The same leaders perceived the adoption of the Uniform Code of Military Justice (UCMJ) in 1950 as unnecessarily imposing civilian procedures on military courts for the "primary purpose" of "creat[ing] a system that would be regarded with favor by the public, which would earn and hold the public's confidence" (Prugh, 2000, p. 25). Officers raised concerns that adopting the UCMJ "made the effective [and efficient] administration of military discipline within the Armed Forces more difficult" (29–30). Colonel Frederick Wiener, who was at one time a strong voice for those opposing civilianizing changes, argued that the requirement that the accused in a military trial be represented by qualified lawyers (as imposed by the UCMJ in 1950) was unnecessary and impractical (Barry, 2002, p. 72).[10] At least one officer argued, "The pendulum has swung . . . from too much emphasis on the 'military' aspect of military justice to too much emphasis on the civilian procedural aspects of law" (Prugh, 2000, p. 30).

While acceptance of the UCMJ grew over time, the resistance to imposing civilian procedures and protections on military justice continues until today. This is reflected in resistance to suggestions by the 2001 Commission on the 50th Anniversary of the Uniform Code of Military Justice (the "Cox Commission") that the convening authority, a senior officer who functions as the prosecutor in military cases, relinquish control over the selection of the members who serve in courts martial (Cox, 2001). The Cox Commission recommended limiting the role of the convening authority, commenting that "the far-reaching role of commanding officers in the court martial process remains the greatest barrier to operating a fair system of criminal justice within the armed forces" (7–8). This recommendation reflects the concern that members may feel the need to vote to convict the accused to curry favor with their commanding officer who, in fact, prosecutes the case.

The Cox Commission report anticipated that this recommendation would engender controversy, and it did. Scholars argued that limiting the role of the convening authority would be inconsistent with the needs of military command (e.g., Essex & Pickle, 2002; Behan, 2003). No action has been taken to implement this recommendation. Similar concerns appeared in the face of parallel reforms with respect to sexual assault (Murphy, 2014).

The Capital Context

Grosso, Baldus, and Woodworth (2010) used the same data used in the race study to examine this issue in the capital context. Their analysis turns on the treatment of "military murders." A military murder is not "a murder committed by a member of the U.S. armed forces." Every murder in the study was committed by U.S. military personnel. "Military murder" concerns the nature of the murder rather than the perpetrator. A "military crime" in this context is a crime that has a "reasonably direct and palpable" impact on "good order and military discipline" (Winthrop, 1920, p. 723; see also Duke & Vogel, 1960). This might include some crimes that could also be recognized in civilian courts, but if the circumstances in which they occurred "directly affect military relations and prejudice military discipline" they may be considered military crimes (Winthrop, 1920, p. 724). As applied in this study, two characteristics led to coding a case as "military murder": an attack on an officer or a race motive. We coded all other cases as "civilian cases."

Grosso and colleagues found an abrupt distinction between the charging and sentencing practices in the first six years after the 1984 order and the charging and sentencing practices after 1990. Until

1990, the military administered the death penalty as required by the written law. In contrast, after 1990 charging and sentencing practices turned many of the civilizing aspects of the 1984 order into dead letter. In the cases between 1990 and 2005, the death penalty was reserved for a distinct subset of "militarily implicated" cases.

Table 28.2 updates their research by including the two death sentences imposed since 2005 and illustrates their findings among the death sentenced defendants. All of the cases in the table arose under Section 118 (murder). Table 28.2 presents a list of these cases with a few details of the crime and the year the sentence was imposed. Table 28.2 also characterizes the status of the murder as typical of "civilian" murders or somehow uniquely "militarily implicated."

Table 28.2 Death Sentenced Accused, 1984–2017 (by year of sentence)

A	B		C	D
	Defendant Name	*Brief Factual Summary*	*Year of Sentence*	*Crime Type*[1]
1.	Dock, Todd A.	Dock robbed a cab driver and then murdered him with multiple stab wounds.	1984	C
2.	Turner, Melvin	Turner murdered his 11-month-old daughter with a razor blade.	1985	C
3.	Curtis, Ronnie A.	Two victims. Curtis robbed and stabbed to death his commanding officer and the officer's wife to avenge perceived racial slights.	1987	M
4.	Murphy, James T.	Three victims. Murphy bludgeoned his wife with a hammer and then drowned her in the bathtub. He then drowned his 5-year-old stepson and his own 21-month-old son.	1987	C
5.	Gray, Ronald A.	Gray abducted, raped, sodomized, beat and fatally shot an Army private four times. Two and a half weeks later, Gray raped, sodomized, bound, gagged, beat, and fatally stabbed a cab driver. He also raped and attempted to kill an Army private, stabbing her in the neck and side multiple times after tying her hands behind her back.	1988	C
6.	Thomas, Joseph L.	Thomas killed his wife with a tire iron to collect insurance proceeds.	1988	C
7.	Loving, Dwight J.	Loving robbed and fatally shot two cab drivers in the head in one evening and later attempted to kill a third.	1989	C
8.	Gibbs, Curtis A.	Gibbs killed and nearly decapitated a female drinking companion with a sword.	1990	C
9.	Simoy, Jose F.	The accused and four co-perpetrators robbed individuals delivering proceeds to a bank on an airbase and in the process killed a police officer with pipe blows to the head and nearly killed another person. Simoy was not the person who wielded the pipe.	1992	M

A	B		C	D
	Defendant Name	Brief Factual Summary	Year of Sentence	Crime Type[1]
10.	Parker, Kenneth G.	Two victims. Motivated by a perceived racial attack on a black Marine by white Marines, six co-perpetrators kidnapped, robbed and killed with a shot to the heart the first white Marine they encountered. Accused was the shooter. Second victim was the male spouse of Walker's paramour.	1993	M
11.	Walker, Wade L.	Two victims. The accused was a co-perpetrator of Kenneth Parker (line 10) in both of his murders. Walker was not the shooter.	1993	M
12.	Kreutzer, William J.	Kreutzer fired a rifle on his unit while it was in an outdoor drill formation on an Army post. Killed one soldier. The ambush wounded several others, including at least one officer.	1996	M
13.	Quintanilla, Jessie A.	In retaliation for perceived discriminatory treatment, the accused killed his executive officer with a shot in the back. The accused also attempted to kill his commanding officer.	1996	M
14.	Akbar, Hassan K.	Two victims. At night in wartime, the accused feigned an attack on the unit by rolling live hand grenades into three tents with sleeping officers and opened fire as the occupants fled their tents. Shot one officer. A second officer died of 87 shrapnel wounds. The accused injured 14 other nondecedent military victims.	2005	M
15.	Witt, Andrew	Two victims. Witt stabbed to death an airman and the airman's wife after they repeatedly phoned him, alleging sexual misconduct. Witt stabbed another nondecedent airman.	2005	C
16.	Hennis, Timothy	Three victims. Hennis stabbed one adult and two children to death in their home in 1985. Hennis was convicted in state court in 1986, found not guilty in 1989, and found guilty in a court martial and sentence to death based on new DNA evidence in 2006.	2010	C
17.	Hasan, Nidal	Thirteen victims. Hassan opened fire on soldiers at Fort Hood for approximately ten minutes. He injured more than 30 nondecedent victims.	2013	M

[1] "C" indicates a civilian murder. "M" indicates a military murder.

Cases in Table 28.2 illustrate the coding in the study. Looking first at those coded "M" in Column D, a number of the cases involve attacks on troops or commissioned officers. Akbar, Hasan, and Kreutzer involved attacks on U.S. troops on duty. Curtis and Kreutzer involved commissioned officer victims. Other militarily implicated cases include those where race or a response to perceived racism motivated the murder. Parker, Quintanilla, and Walker explicitly involved race.

In contrast, civilian-style murders involve family and acquaintance victims. Gibbs, Murphy, Turner, Witt, and Thomas exemplify this type of civilian-style murder. Likewise, stranger victims in felony murders pose comparatively little threat to military discipline and control and the effectiveness of the military mission. In Table 28.2, Dock and Loving exemplify this type of civilian-style murder.

Sixty percent (9/17) of the cases in Table 28.2 involve civilian-style murders that are reminiscent of the civilian-style death sentenced cases that immediately antedated the adoption of the 1984 executive order. Contrast the cases between 1984 and 1990 with those after 1990. In the first set, seven of eight (88%) are civilian cases. The cases since 1990 form a mirror opposite. Since 1990, seven of the nine death sentences have been imposed in cases with clear military implications (78%).

The two civilian-style cases that resulted in a death sentence since 1990 present factors that reasonably would overcome a presumption against seeking death for civilian-style crimes. The first defendant in Line 15 of Table 28.2, *Witt* (2005), is a brutal two-victim case with five aggravating factors. The second defendant in Line 16 of Table 28.2, *Hennis* (2010), involved a military prosecution for a triple murder following an improper state court acquittal. The military recalled Hennis to active duty and sought jurisdiction of this case in order to work around the double jeopardy bar facing the state court and seek a death sentence.[11]

The nearly complete absence of death sentencing for civilian-style murder since 1990 other than these two is not explained by the absence of highly aggravated civilian murders since then. What seems to explain the decline is a substantial shift by convening authorities and members away from death sentencing in civilian-style murders.

Convening authorities may lack incentives to seek death in run-of-the-mill civilian murders, especially those with a single victim. Officers and commanding generals likely see little professional advantage from such prosecutions. In contrast, when the authority and effectiveness of the military mission is threatened, convening authorities experience pressure to maintain discipline.

Similarly, one can imagine how commanders, particularly in the combat units from which the majority of the death eligible cases arise, can identify with the commissioned officer victim cases, while having much less concern with death-eligible cases whose Rule 1004 aggravating factors do not implicate military discipline. When troops are engaged in active combat, commanders focus on things that really matter to the military, which include civilian murders to a much lesser extent.

Opposition to capital punishment in Western Europe may also have had an impact on commanders. Before 1990, commanders in Western Europe capitally referred 59% (10/17) of the civilian murder cases prosecuted in Western Europe, but from 1990 through 2005, none (0/7) of the civilian cases from Western Europe were capitally referred. This explanation could not, however, explain fully the discrepancies documented earlier. Even after the European cases are removed from consideration, a 39-point civilian versus military disparity, significant at the .005 level, persisted in the decision to seek a capital court martial, and a 20-point disparity, significant at the .07 level, persisted in death sentencing among all death-eligible cases.

Commanders may also hesitate to commit the time and expense of a capital prosecution given apparent diminishing likelihood that members will return a death verdict or that a death sentence actually imposed will ever be executed. In contrast to civilian jurors for whom capital defendants are normally complete strangers, members in a capital court martial are also members of the accused's military organization. Enlisted members may be more able to understand the circumstances of the accused's situation that resulted in the murder than their counterparts on a civilian jury. On the likelihood of an execution, no one has been executed in the military since 1961. Most recently, President

Barack Obama commuted the death sentence of Dwight Loving, 28 years after his death sentence was imposed.

Overall, the military approach to civilian murder resembles the approach of civilian prosecutors in large urban communities. With resources scarce and the prospects of a death sentence and execution uncertain, capital prosecutions are limited to highly aggravated, highly publicized cases that clearly implicate the interests of justice in civilian eyes. For the military convening authorities, the calculus appears quite comparable with the overriding concern being the maintenance of discipline and the protection of the authority and effectiveness of the military command.

Conclusion

This chapter presents a brief overview of the administration of capital punishment by the U.S. armed forces. The findings presented here also suggest that narrowing the reach of capital murder into civilian-style death eligible murders may be an advisable course of action. These kinds of amendments would bring law into line with practice and may also eliminate some of the race effects document by the Baldus study.

Notes

1 The chapter combines and revises, rather than rewrites, two articles published with the late Professor David C. Baldus of the University of Iowa College of Law. He remains my silent and missed co-author. I am grateful to the *Journal of Criminal Law and Criminology* and my co-authors for graciously granting permission to reprint and edit the following article: David C. Baldus, Catherine M. Grosso, George Woodworth, and Richard Newell, "Racial Discrimination in the Administration of the Death Penalty: The Experience of the United States Armed Forces (1984–2005)," *Journal of Criminal Law and Criminology*, vol. 101 (2011), p. 1227 and to the *University of Michigan Journal of Law Reform* and my co-author a for the following article: Catherine M. Grosso, David C. Baldus, and George Woodworth, "The Impact of Civilian Aggravating Factors on the Military Death Penalty (1984–2005): Another Chapter in the Resistance of Armed Forces to the Civilianization of Military Justice," *University of Michigan Journal of Law Reform*, vol. 43 (2010), p. 569.

2 There appears to be one capital crime—espionage—that was added since 1950. It was created by the Department of Defense Authorization Act for Fiscal Year (1986).

3 During the 1960s, the Supreme Court found that courts martial had jurisdiction to try servicemen only when the crime had a "service connection" (*O'Callahan v. Parker*, 1969, p. 272). However, in 1987 the Court abandoned the "service connection" requirement, holding that court martial jurisdiction was established by one factor—the military status of the accused (*Solorio v. United States*, 1987, p. 439).

4 The death penalty sections of Article 118 of the UCMJ as adopted in 1950 read as follows: "Any person subject to this code who, without justification or excuse, unlawfully kills a human being, when he (1) has a premeditated design to kill; . . . or (4) is engaged in the perpetration or attempted perpetration of burglary, sodomy, rape, robbery, or aggravated arson; is guilty of murder, and . . . shall suffer death or imprisonment for life as a court martial may direct."

5 See for example Rule 1004(c)(3) (accused had intent (i) to "cause substantial damage to the national security of the United States"), Section (c)(2)(B) (ii) (accused "knowingly created a grave risk of substantial damage to a mission, system, or function of the United States" if such damage "would have resulted had the intended damage been effected"), or Section (c)(5)("the accused committed the offense with the intent to avoid hazardous duty").

6 For example, a study in Maryland found that prosecutors advanced to trial seeking a death sentence in 27% of the death-eligible cases (353/1311) (Paternoster, Brame, Bacon, & Ditchfield, 2004, p. 24). Similarly, a Virginia study of cases prosecuted between 1995 and 1999 found the state sought a death penalty 30% of the time during that period (Joint Legislative Audit, 2002, p. 51 tbl. 17).

7 The cases of eight additional accused who were charged capitally but acquitted of capital murder by members are included only in the analysis of convening authority charging decisions.

8 The three different decision points were capital charging decisions by convening authorities, guilt trial decisions by courts-martial members, and death-sentencing decisions by members in a capital sentencing hearing.

9 Here, "civilianize" refers to the procedural protections imported from the civilian courts in an effort to reform the military system.

10 Wiener later argued that the Sixth Amendment right to counsel does not apply to the military justice system (Wiener, 1958a, p. 49). At the same time, in a second 1958 paper, Wiener wrote with favor about the rights accorded members of the military by Congress and seemed to approve of the reforms (Wiener, 1958b, pp. 303–304).

11 Hennis was convicted of murder and sentenced to death in 1986 for raping and murdering a woman (by stabbing) and then killing her two young daughters by slitting their throats. Following a retrial after appeal, a new jury acquitted him in April 1989. The military opened a case against him in 2006 after DNA evidence implicated him more clearly and civilian authorities were barred by the constitutional protection against double jeopardy.

References

Ansell, S. T. (1919). Military justice. *Cornell Law Quarterly, 5*, 1.

Baldus, D. C., Grosso, C. M., Woodworth, G., & Newell, R. (2011). Racial discrimination in the administration of the death penalty: The experience of the United States Armed Forces (1984–2005). *Journal of Criminal Law & Criminology, 101*, 1227.

Baldus, D. C., Woodworth, G., & Pulaski, C. A., Jr. (1990). *Equal justice and the death penalty.* Boston: Northeastern University Press.

Barry, K. J. (2002). A face lift (and much more) for an aging beauty: The Cox Commission recommendations to rejuvenate the Uniform Code of Military Justice. *Law Review of Michigan State University-Detroit College of Law, 2002*, 57.

Behan, C. W. (2003). Don't tug on superman's cape: In defense of convening authority selection and appointment of court-martial panel members. *Military Law Review, 176*, 190.

Brooks, D. (2016, December 22). Military to execute murderer and rapist Ronald Gray, a former soldier, after 8-year delay. *Fayetteville Observer*. Retrieved from http://www.fayobserver.com/af4d3fd2-67d8-50f2-b794-eecc9f703c7c.html.

Cox III, W. T. (chair). (2001). *Report of the commission on the 50th anniversary of the Uniform Code of Military Justice* (May). Retrieved from www.loc.gov/rr/frd/Military_Law/pdf/Cox-Commission-Report-2001.pdf

Duke, R. D., & Vogel, H. S. (1960). The constitution and the standing army: Another problem of court-martial jurisdiction. *Vanderbilt Law Review, 13*, 435.

Essex, T., & Pickle, L. T. (2002). A reply to the report of the commission on the 50th anniversary of the Uniform Code of Military Justice (May 2001): "The Cox Commission." *Air Force Law Review, 52*, 233.

Grosso, C. M., Baldus, D. C., & Woodworth, G. (2010). The impact of civilian aggravating factors on the military death penalty (1984–2005): Another chapter in the resistance of armed forces to the civilianization of military justice. *University of Michigan Journal of Law Reform, 43*, 569.

Joint legislative audit and review commission of the Virginia General Assembly, review of Virginia's system of capital punishment (2002, January). Retrieved from http://jlarc.state.va.us/reports/rpt274.pdf

Lilly, J. R., & Thomson, M. (1997). Executing U.S. soldiers in England, World War II: Command influence and sexual racism. *British Journal of Criminology, 37*, 262.

Lindley, J. M. (1990). *"A soldier is also a citizen": The controversy over military justice, 1917–1920.* New York and London: Garland Publishing.

MSNBC. (2005, April 29). Soldier gets death penalty for killing officers in Kuwait. *MSNBC*. Retrieved from http://msnbc.msn.com/id/7667169

Murphy, E. (2014). The military justice divide: Why only crimes and lawyers belong in the court-martial process. *Military Law Review, 220*, 129.

Myers, S. L. (2008, July 29). Execution by military is approved by president. *New York Times*, A13.

Paternoster, R., Brame, R., Bacon, S., & Ditchfield, A. (2004). Justice by geography and race: The administration of the death penalty in Maryland, 1978–1999. *Margins: University of Maryland Law, Journal of Race, Religion, Gender & Class, 4*, 1.

Prugh, G. S., Jr. (Maj.). (2000). Observations on the Uniform Code of Military Justice: 1954 and 2000. *Military Law Review, 165*, 21.

Schlueter, D. A. (2008). *Military criminal justice: Practice and procedure* (7th ed.). New York: Matthew Bender.

Serrano, R. A. (1994, July 12). Last soldier to die at Leavenworth hanged in an April storm. *Los Angeles Times*, 14.

Turley, J. (2002). Tribunals and tribulations: The antithetical elements of military governance in a Madisonian democracy. *George Washington Law Review, 70*, 649.

United States. (1972). Report of the Task Force on the Administration of Military Justice in the Armed Forces. Washington, D.C.: U.S. G.P.O.

Wiener, F. B. (1958a). Courts-martial and the bill of rights: The original practice (pt. 1). *Harvard Law Review*, 72, 1.

Wiener, F. B. (1958b). Courts-martial and the bill of rights: The original practice (pt. 2). *Harvard Law Review*, 72, 266.

Execution of ex-soldier is stayed. (2008, Dec. 3). *Wall Street Journal*. A13.

Winthrop, W. (1886). *Military Law, Vol. 1*. Boston: W.H. Morrison.

Winthrop, W. (1920). *Military Law and Precedents* (2nd. ed.) Washington, D.C.: Government Printing Office.

Ziering, A., Barklow, T. K. (Prod.), & Kick, K. (Dir.). (2012). *The Invisible War* [Motion picture] (U.S.A: 2012).

Cases Cited

Coker v. Georgia, 433 U.S. 584 (1977).
Furman v. Georgia, 408 U.S. 238 (1972).
Gregg v. Georgia, 42 U.S. 153 (1976).
Kennedy v. Louisiana, 370 U.S. 660 (2008).
McCleskey v. Kemp, 481 U.S. 279 (1987).
O'Callahan v. Parker, 395 U.S. 258 (1969).
Proffitt v. Florida, 428 U.S. 242 (1976).
Schick v. Reed, 419 U.S. 256 (1974).
Solorio v. United States, 483 U.S. 435 (1987).
United States v. Easton, 71 M.J. 168 (C.A.A.F. 2012).
United States v. Gay, 16 M.J. 586, 596 (en banc) (A.F.C.M.R. 1983).
United States v. Gay, 18 M.J. 104 (C.M.A. 1984).
United States v. Matthews, 16 M.J. 354 (C.M.A. 1983).
United States v. Rojas, 15 M.J. 902 (N.M.C.M.R. 1981).
Willenbring v. Neurauter, 48 M.J. 152 (C.A.A.F. 1998).

Statutes & Executive Order

Articles of War (1863). 12 Stat. 731.

Articles of War (1916). 39 Stat. 619.

Department of Defense Authorization Act for Fiscal Year 1986, Pub. L. No. 99-145; 99 Stat. 583 (1985).

Elston Act (Selective Service Act), ch. 625, § 235, 62 Stat. 604 (1948).

Elston Act in 1948. Pub. L. No. 759, § 235, 62 Stat. 604 (1948).

Executive Order, Amendments to the Manual for Courts Martial, United States, 1969 (Revised Edition) (1984, January 24).

Model Penal Code, Section 210 (withdrawn 2009).

Uniform Code for Military Justice (UCMJ), 10 U.S.C.A. Subt. A, Pt. II, Ch. 47 (2017).

PART 5

The Death Penalty's Consequences

29

THE TOPOGRAPHY OF CAPITAL PUNISHMENT

Geographic Variations in Seeking, Achieving, and Carrying Out the Death Penalty

Adam Trahan, Kaleigh B. Laird, and Douglas N. Evans

It is tempting to think about the death penalty in broad generalizations. Perhaps the most common generalization we encounter is that America is a "death penalty country." Much is made about the fact that the United States is one of the last remaining developed nations to execute its citizens. It's a true statement, of course. In terms of confirmed executions in any given year, we typically find ourselves around fifth in the world after countries such as China, Iran, Saudi Arabia, and Pakistan (Amnesty International, 2015). However, characterizing the United States as a "death penalty country" is a generalization that, when explored more closely, starts to lose some accuracy.

It is arguably more accurate to describe the United States as a country with a foot in both camps. Nearly 40% of states are true abolitionist locales. Laws in these states do not allow the death penalty as a punishment for any crime. The remaining states are often labeled as "death penalty states" due to the fact that their laws do allow the death penalty as a punishment for capital murder. Here, however, we encounter another less-than-accurate generalization. Many of the states that do allow capital punishment have not carried out an execution in decades. The last executions in Kansas and New Hampshire occurred before 1976. Colorado, Oregon, Pennsylvania, and Wyoming have not had an execution since the 1990s (Death Penalty Information Center [DPIC], 2016a). These states allow the death penalty but can be considered abolitionist in practice. Even in high usage states like Texas, Florida, and Oklahoma, most of the executions that are carried out each year are administered by prosecutors and juries from just a few counties around the state. Of course, it is important not to be reductive about the issue. Some of the county and state governments that regularly administer the death penalty have executed a rather astonishing number of people.

To complicate matters even further, the administration of capital punishment not only varies across space; it also varies across time. That is, the geography of capital punishment is always changing. For example, as we will describe in greater detail shortly, a total of seven states have repealed their capital punishment laws and effectively abolished capital punishment over the past ten years. That number had reached eight total states when the Nebraska state legislature repealed the death penalty in May 2015 (Young, 2015). However, the citizens of Nebraska passed a ballot initiative to reinstate the death penalty about one month prior to our writing this chapter in 2016 (Hammel, 2016). Before 2005, we might have discussed here the geographic differences in charging, sentencing, and executing juveniles in the United States. However, the Supreme Court has since exempted juveniles from capital punishment (*Roper v. Simmons*, 2005).

In short, the geography of capital punishment in the United States is a complicated thing to make sense of. We will attempt in this chapter to provide a portrait of "where" we charge defendants with capital murder, sentence them to death, and ultimately carry out executions that both respects the complexity of the issue but is easy to follow. What we provide here is a portrait of the geography of capital punishment through the end of 2016. We started this introduction by stating that it is tempting to think about capital punishment in broad generalizations. As we explore the differences across space in how we administer the death penalty, it may be helpful to instead think about America's practice of capital punishment as if it were displayed on a topographic map. That is, our experiences with capital punishment vary considerably across geographic space, with hills and valleys separating a few small locations with very high peaks.

Capital Punishment Laws Across States

We will start with the most basic geography of capital punishment—states with and states without capital punishment. A total of 31 states have laws that permit the death penalty as a punishment for capital murder and 19 do not. The federal government and U.S. military also maintain capital punishment systems, although they rarely administer the death penalty. The federal government and military have executed three and zero people since 1976, respectively (DPIC, 2016a). Table 29.1 provides a reference for states with and without capital punishment laws.

The content of capital punishment laws in the 31 states that allow the practice vary somewhat. The Supreme Court has laid out rather ambiguous guidelines for how states must go about administering capital punishment. In *Gregg v. Georgia* (1976) and accompanying cases, the Supreme Court established the framework for the so-called "modern era" of capital punishment. This framework contained two main criteria that state laws must meet in order to pass constitutional muster. First, the court required that capital punishment laws effectively narrow the class of death-eligible crimes to aggravated murder. This led states to pass death penalty statutes that specified aggravating factors that would render a

Table 29.1 States With and Without Capital Punishment Laws.

Death Penalty States (31)		Non-Death Penalty States (19)
Alabama	Ohio	Alaska
Arizona	Oklahoma	Connecticut
Arkansas	Oregon	Delaware
California	Pennsylvania	Hawaii
Colorado	South Carolina	Illinois
Florida	South Dakota	Iowa
Georgia	Tennessee	Maine
Idaho	Texas	Maryland
Indiana	Utah	Massachusetts
Kansas	Virginia	Michigan
Kentucky	Washington	Minnesota
Louisiana	Wyoming	New Jersey
Mississippi		New Mexico
Missouri		New York
Montana		North Dakota
Nebraska		Rhode Island
Nevada		Vermont
New Hampshire		West Virginia
North Carolina		Wisconsin

Source: DPIC (2016b)

defendant eligible for capital punishment. Second, the court required that states provide capital jurors with guidance on how to go about making sentencing decisions. Prior to the modern era, jurors were not offered guidance and were consequently administering death sentences arbitrarily (*Furman v. Georgia*, 1972). Thus, states enacted sentencing guidelines that articulate what factors jurors must consider and how they must consider them when deciding whether to sentence defendants to death.

The court has historically been quite lenient in determining whether the laws in any given state meet these two criteria (Mandery, 2014). The Justices have not compelled a particular statute or set of statutes. Instead, the court has permitted states to enact and enforce a variety of laws so long as they seemingly narrow the applicability of capital punishment and provide some guidance for jurors' sentencing decisions. This approach has created geographic variation in the content of states' capital punishment laws. Thus, whether states proscribe the death penalty is not the only geographic distinction among capital punishment laws. Even among states that do permit the death penalty, there are differences—some subtle and some quite broad—in the legal framework used to apply the death penalty. The following sections describe the geography of guided discretion statutes in states' capital punishment laws.

Variations in Guided Discretion Statutes

Guided discretion statutes ostensibly govern how jurors are to go about making sentencing decisions in capital cases. Understanding how they are used from state to state will require us to at least briefly address several landmark U.S. Supreme Court cases on the subject. Other chapters will discuss these cases and their effects in much greater detail. Here we will cover only the aspects of the rulings most pertinent to understanding the different frameworks states use to apply capital punishment.

In *Furman v. Georgia* (1972), The Supreme Court ruled in a 5–4 decision that the death penalty was being applied in ways that conflicted with the Eighth Amendment's prohibition against cruel and unusual punishment. Although each of the nine justices wrote their own opinion, the general implication that came out of decision was that the death penalty *could* be applied in a constitutional way provided that there were guidelines that would ensure some consistency regarding which capital offenders (and offenses) would be sentenced to death. Political leaders in many states around the country were displeased with the court's ruling and quickly began devising strategies to get their death penalty systems back. State legislators wrote new capital statutes that essentially created entirely new methods for applying the death penalty. Ultimately, five different state frameworks were put before the Supreme Court to determine which, if any, would remedy the constitutional deficiencies identified in *Furman*. The new capital punishment systems created in North Carolina and Louisiana were rejected by the court because they mandated death sentences for all convicted capital murders (*Woodson v. North Carolina*, 1976; *Roberts v. Louisiana*, 1976). The frameworks created in Georgia, Texas, and Florida were confirmed and would go on to shape capital sentencing statutes throughout the country (*Gregg v. Georgia*, 1976; *Jurek v. Texas*, 1976; *Proffitt v. Florida*, 1976).

The capital sentencing scheme created in Florida has been adopted by a majority of death penalty states. In this scheme, the jury is presented with evidence of aggravating and mitigating factors. Aggravating factors are presented by the prosecution and are designed to act as evidence in support of the death penalty. Common aggravating factors include murder committed during the course of another felony, murder of multiple people, murder of young children, and especially heinous, vile, or depraved murder (DPIC, 2016j). Mitigating factors are presented by the defense and are designed to act as evidence in support of a life sentence. Mitigating factors are more varied than aggravators as they can include potentially any characteristic of the offender, victim, or offense that might make the defendant less deserving of the death penalty (*Lockett v. Ohio*, 1978). Common mitigating factors include evidence that the offender is, or was at the time of the crime, mentally ill, that the victim provoked the offender, and that the offense was committed under duress. After the defense and prosecution present their cases, the jury is instructed that they must "weigh" aggravating factors against mitigating factors to arrive at their sentencing decision. Although the death penalty is never required, the implication of the weighing scheme is that if aggravating factors "outweigh" mitigating factors, the appropriate penalty may be death. As such, the states that retain this sentencing scheme first developed in Florida are commonly referred to as "weighing states."

By also affirming the capital sentencing statutes created during the same time in Texas (*Jurek v. Texas*, 1976) and Georgia (*Gregg v. Georgia*, 1976), the court tacitly acknowledged that other mechanisms can achieve the same constitutionally required goals of legitimacy and consistency in the application of the death penalty. These alternative schemes also rely on mitigating and aggravating factors, much like the Florida model. The main distinction is how juries take them into account in making sentencing decisions. In Georgia, for example, jurors must find that one or more aggravating factors was proven beyond a reasonable doubt. If not, the defendant is not guilty of *capital* murder and is thus not eligible for the death penalty. In cases where the jury does find the defendant guilty of capital murder, jurors may then consider mitigating factors and any other aggravating factors they encountered at the sentencing phase and decide whether to return a death sentence. States that have adopted this sentencing scheme are referred to as "non-weighing states" because the sentencing guidelines do not explicitly require jurors to counterweigh aggravating and mitigating factors (see *Zant v. Stephens*, 1983).

Texas is considered a non-weighing state, yet its scheme is somewhat different than Georgia's. Capital jurors in Texas are presented with two "special issues" at sentencing. First, jurors must consider whether there is a probability that the defendant would commit "criminal acts of violence that would constitute a continuing threat to society." This question is designed to tap whether jurors, after hearing the evidence, feel that the defendant would be dangerous in the future. If they answer is in the affirmative, they are tasked with considering mitigating evidence that might reduce the defendant's moral blameworthiness (Texas Code of Code of Criminal Procedure § 37.071).

Non-weighing states are not specific to any particular region in the United States but include California, Kentucky, Louisiana, Missouri, Oregon, South Carolina, South Dakota, Virginia, Washington, and, of course, Georgia and Texas. A third generalized model has emerged in that it is essentially a combination of the other two models. This hybrid model involves first a finding of fact that one or more aggravating factors has been proven beyond a reasonable doubt, similar to the Georgia/non-weighing model. If this criterion is met, the jurors are then tasked with a weighing-type analysis of aggravating and mitigating factors (Winchester, 2016). The only "hybrid states" in the U.S. currently are Utah and Colorado. Weighing states include the remaining 18 states.

Changes in State Geography

Even this basic state-to-state geography of capital punishment is in flux. Over the past ten years, seven states have abolished their capital punishment systems. This shift is historically unprecedented both in the number of states that have moved away from capital punishment and the rate of change. From the time the Supreme Court reinstated capital punishment in *Gregg v. Georgia* (1976) until 2007, the number of death penalty states remained quite stable. During most of this 30 years, 38 states maintained death penalty systems. The remaining 12 states either eradicated the death penalty before the modern era or never reinstated it after the *Gregg* decision allowed states to reestablish the death penalty. Massachusetts and Rhode Island are exceptions in that they both officially repealed the death penalty in 1984 (DPIC, 2016c, 2016d). However, they did not execute a single person in the modern era (DPIC, 2016e).

The seven states that have abolished capital punishment over the past decade, along with the year of their abolition, are as follows: New Jersey (2007), New York (2007), New Mexico (2009), Illinois (2011), Connecticut (2012), Maryland (2013), and Delaware (2016). Regarding the geography of this shift, the trend toward abolition has occurred outside the Southern United States. It's not surprising that the American South has been absent from this group, given that Southern states consistently lead the nation in executions. Furthermore, except for Illinois and New Mexico, the states that have recently pivoted away from capital punishment are in the Northeastern United States.

At least one other implication can be drawn from this experience that is pertinent to the geography of capital punishment. There are several themes in the reasons cited by policy makers for why they abolished capital punishment. A variety of interest groups, including politicians, activists, and scholars, work to understand how trends may shape the future of capital punishment in the United States. Capital punishment is always changing, and being able to identify what drives this change and where the next change might be occurring is of significant inherent and practical importance. In press releases, conferences, and other media, governors and state legislative leaders have, in most instances, been quite transparent about why they passed legislation to abolish their capital punishment systems. In this transparency, two longstanding topics of interest in capital punishment policy and scholarship emerged across states as reasons why government officials decided to wash their hands of capital punishment.

Cost

First, political leaders in several states explicitly cited the high cost of capital punishment as a primary impetus for repeal. In 2007, New Jersey became the first of these states to abolish capital punishment. After appointing a state commission to study the death penalty, legislators in New Jersey passed a bill to repeal the death penalty and replace it with life in prison. Then-Governor Jon Corzine signed the bill on December 17, 2007 (Peters, 2007). The report by the study commission cited a variety of reasons for repealing the death penalty, including that it was not consistent with evolving standards of decency. However, the finding that was perhaps most compelling to lawmakers did not relate to justice, per se, but the economic cost of maintaining their system of capital punishment. The commission found that the state of New Jersey spent an average of $72,602 annually on each inmate on death row. The average cost incurred by the state for each inmate in general population was $40,121 (State of New Jersey, 2007). Such differences in spending between death row and general population are not uncommon, but one particular fact made New Jersey's experience somewhat unique—they never executed anyone. The last execution in the state of New Jersey was carried out in 1963 (DPIC, 2016a). Thus, sentencing someone to death in New Jersey essentially amounted to a de facto life sentence but at almost twice the cost. The New Jersey Department of Corrections estimated that the repeal would save the state $1.3 million per inmate over his lifetime (Richburg, 2007).

Then-Governor Martin O'Malley signed legislation to repeal Maryland's death penalty on May 2, 2013, following a seven-year lobbying effort led in part by O'Malley himself. This lobbying effort was built around two primary tenets. First, proponents of the repeal argued that the death penalty was not producing a deterrent effect. Second, they showed the high cost of maintaining the death penalty in Maryland and articulated ways in which that money could be more effectively spent (O'Malley, 2015; Wagner, 2013; Wagner & Davis, 2013). Connecticut also repealed the death penalty in 2012 in part because of its high cost. Representative Auden Grogins explained "the law is costly . . . it is not unusual for the legal process, from the beginning to the end, to take 20 years" (Dixon, 2012).

Innocence

One of the most troubling aspects of the administration of capital punishment in the United States is the rate at which we sentence people to death for crimes they did not commit. Thanks in large part to DNA technology, a total of 156 people have been exonerated and released from death row because they were found to be factually innocent (DPIC, 2016f). What may be even more troubling than the sheer number of innocent people who have been convicted of capital murder and sentenced to death is the rate at which we sentenced innocent people to death. A study by Gross, O'Brien, Hu, and Kennedy (2014) found that as many as 1 in every 25 people sentenced to death are factually innocent. Leaders in several of these recent abolitionist states cited the risk of sentencing innocent people to death and potentially executing the innocent as major reasons why they supported repeal. Legislators in Connecticut and Maryland discussed "mistakes" and the irreversibility of execution in explaining why they voted to abolish the death penalty in their states (Vigdor, 2012; Wagner, 2013). The most compelling cases of innocence leading to repeal were in Illinois and New Mexico. In remarks after he signed legislation to repeal the death penalty, then-governor of New Mexico Bill Richardson stated:

> I do not have confidence in the criminal justice system as it currently operates to be the final arbiter when it comes to who lives and who dies for their crime. If the State is going to undertake this awesome responsibility, the system to impost this ultimate penalty must be perfect and can never be wrong. But the reality is the system is not perfect—far from it. The system is inherently defective. DNA testing has proven that. Innocent people have been put on death row all across the country . . . including four New Mexicans.
>
> *(DPIC, 2016g)*

No state has had more troubling experiences with wrongful capital convictions than Illinois. In January of 2000, then-Governor George Ryan garnered national attention by issuing a moratorium on the death penalty in Illinois. From the time when Illinois reinstated the death penalty in 1977 until the moratorium, a total of 13 men had been exonerated and freed from the state's death row due to innocence. Illinois actually executed fewer people (12) during this same period of time. The state would issue seven additional exonerations before ultimately repealing the death penalty via legislation in 2011 (DPIC, 2016h). Five of these exonerees were part of what became known as the "death row ten" (Nicodemus, 1999). This was a group of ten death row inmates in Illinois who claimed they were innocent and that their convictions were the result of false confessions they made while being tortured by the now infamous Chicago Police Commander John Burge and the detectives under his command. Tactics that Burge and his detectives allegedly used to obtain confessions included shocking suspects in the genitals, suffocating them by placing a plastic bag over their heads, and staging mock executions of suspects during interrogations (Conroy, 2005; Mills, 1999).

Three years after the moratorium, Governor Ryan emptied out the state's death row by commuting the sentences of the 167 people awaiting execution in Illinois at the time. The moratorium would ultimately come to an end on March 9, 2011, when then-Governor of Illinois Pat Quinn signed legislation repealing the death penalty (Wills, 2011). In a statement issued after signing the bill, Governor Quinn stated "since our experience has shown that there is no way to design a perfect death penalty system, free from the numerous flaws that can lead to wrongful convictions or discriminatory treatment, I have decided to abolish it" (De Vogue, 2011).

No state seems to have been led to abolition based on one factor alone. Often several factors, sometimes in combination, played a role in the ultimate abolition of the death penalty in each of these states. For instance, press releases following Connecticut's repeal cited lawmakers' concerns over racial and socioeconomic discrimination, wrongful convictions, and costs as well as various moralistic apprehensions (see DPIC, 2016i). Arguing in support of Maryland's abolition bill, Governor O'Malley pointed out that the cost of the death penalty combined with its inability to produce any significant deterrent effect equated to investing in policy that fails to provide a return (Wagner & Davis, 2013). It will be interesting to observe whether these issues lead other states to repeal their death penalty systems and/or prompt a national debate regarding the utility of capital punishment in the coming years. Indeed, several states have come quite close to repeal in recent history only to fall short by a small number of votes or executive vetoes (Acker, Bohm, & Lanier, 2014). It seems then that some states have been on the cusp of abolition, and any of the already cited factors might push them over the edge at any time.

Charging and Sentencing

In most all jurisdictions around the United States, the decision to charge defendants with capital murder and seek the death penalty lies with local prosecutors. As noted, what makes any homicide defendant eligible for the death penalty is the presence of at least one aggravating factor. However, prosecutors are never required to file capital murder charges regardless of the number of aggravators they find during investigation or the strength of the evidence. Seeking the death penalty is an entirely discretionary act. When prosecutors do decide to charge defendants with capital murder, this marks the beginning of the capital punishment system. It may not go far, however. Jurors in capital cases ultimately decide whether to sentence people convicted of capital murder to death (*Ring v. Arizona*, 2002). And, much like prosecutors, jurors are never required by law to administer death sentences (*Roberts v. Louisiana*, 1976; *Woodson v. North Carolina*, 1976). No matter the number of aggravating factors jurors agree upon nor their gravity, whether a defendant is deserving of death is left up to the (guided) discretion of capital jurors.

All of this discretion gives way to some significant geographic variation in filing capital murder charges by prosecutors and returning death sentences by jurors. In the sections that follow we will explore this geographic variation and identify the places that most commonly seek and administer death sentences. It is important to note, however, that the geography of charging and sentencing is different than the geography of other aspects of capital punishment in at least two respects. First, capital charging and sentencing are the only features of the death penalty system that occur at the county level. After sentencing, state governments take over, to house death row inmates, see to their appeals, and ultimately carry out executions. Second, the places that most commonly charge defendants with capital murder and sentence them to death are not always the same places that most commonly execute people. For instance, over 90% of all executions carried out since 1976 occurred in just nine Southern states collectively referred to as the "death belt" (Ogletree, 2002). The initial stages in the sequence of capital punishment—charging and sentencing—have a somewhat different topography.

Filing Capital Charges

Simple counts of how many capital murder charges have been filed in certain places is not necessarily the most meaningful way to measure geographic disparities in seeking the death penalty. The frequency of capital charges in any given county can be confounded by factors such as population size or the prevalence of capital murder. It's arguably much more telling to explore the geography of charging and sentencing relative to capital murder rates, which capture the prevalence of capital murder as a function of population size. Doing this presents a challenge, though. It requires coherently differentiating which homicides occurred with the presence of at least one aggravating factor (capital murder) from those that had no aggravating factor (noncapital homicide). Here we will review two meticulous studies of capital charging practices in South Carolina conducted at two different periods of the state's capital punishment history. These studies show how arbitrary capital charging can be from one county to another even in a geographically small state.

Songer and Unah (2006) explored prosecutors' decisions to seek the death penalty in homicide cases that occurred in South Carolina from 1993 to 1997. The state of South Carolina is separated into 16 judicial districts, with each judicial district encompassing two to five counties. They first calculated the rate of filing capital charges among all homicides. Their findings showed considerable geographic variation within the state in regard to seeking the death penalty. The percent of all homicides in each district that were charged as capital murder ranged from a low of 1.9% to a high of 14.9%. That is, the most active district sought the death penalty in over 1 in 10 cases; the least active saw capital charges filed in fewer than 2 in 100. What is more, this disparity is not the result of some outlier on either end of the range. Four of South Carolina's 16 judicial districts sought the death penalty in at least 12.9% of homicides; six districts sought the death penalty in fewer than 3.9% of homicides.

To measure for the prevalence of filing capital charges among capital murder cases specifically, Songer and Unah (2006) classified each homicide based on the presence or lack thereof of common statutory aggravating factors. It is not necessarily a true disparity if a greater proportion of homicides are charged with capital murder in one county, or judicial district, than another. It very well could be that a greater proportion—of homicides in the more active districts actually are capital murder—i.e., murder with the presence of at least one aggravating circumstance. Songer and Unah's findings suggest this is not the case, however. They found no relationship between the rates of aggravated murder and capital murder charging. For instance, Judicial District 9 showed the lowest percent (1.9) of homicides charged as capital murder but had the third highest percent of aggravated murder (28.9) of all 16 of South Carolina's judicial districts.

Paternoster (1983) explored all 1,686 homicides that occurred from June 8, 1977, to December 31, 1981, in which the offender was known. The stated purpose of his research was to study arbitrariness and discrimination in the administration of capital punishment, one form of which is geographic variation in the likelihood prosecutors seek the death penalty. His findings showed considerable variation across South Carolina's 16 judicial districts in the likelihood of prosecutors seeking the death penalty. The percentage of all homicides in which prosecutors sought the death penalty ranged from 2.1% to 27.9%.

Using data from original police incident reports and indictment and disposition records kept by the State Office of the Attorney General, Paternoster was able to determine which cases met the statutory criteria for capital murder. This showed that 321 (19%) of the 1,686 homicides included in his sample occurred with the presence of at least one aggravating factor and were therefore eligible for the death penalty. Among this subset of capital murders, the geographic variation in seeking the death penalty was even more pronounced. The percentage of all capital murders in which prosecutors sought the death penalty ranged from 86.7% to 16.7% across South Carolina's 16 judicial districts.

These findings show that the geographic distribution of (capital) murder cannot explain "where" and "why" we seek the death penalty. The places and people that most directly experience aggravated murder are not necessarily the same as those that pursue executions. Of course, filing capital murder charges represents seeking the death penalty but not its achievement. The effort of prosecuting defendants for capital murder can arguably be for naught if the jury decides not to return a death sentence. This next section reviews the geographic distribution of capital sentencing.

Sentencing Defendants to Death

In the event that a defendant is found guilty of capital murder, the trial proceeds to a second phase wherein lawyers for both sides present mitigating and aggravating factors and jurors ultimately decide whether to sentence the defendant to death. As mentioned, jurors are never compelled to return a death sentence. Instead, they use discretion in making what the court has referred to as a "reasoned moral choice" (*Penry v. Lynaugh*, 1989). Much like every other aspect related to the administration of capital punishment, there is considerable geographic variation in the death sentences handed down each year in the U.S.

Capital sentencing figures again show a topography were there are few but considerably high peaks surrounded by hills and valleys. The most comprehensive research on this topic is Smith's (2012) analysis of county sentencing patterns across the United States from 2004 to 2009. His findings showed 90% of all U.S. counties did not sentence a single person to death during this time. Furthermore, there was considerable variation even among the 10% of counties that returned at least one death sentence. Only 4% (121) of counties in the U.S. sentenced more than one person to death. These 121 counties accounted for approximately 76% of all death sentences handed down from 2004 to 2009. Fewer than 1% (29) of U.S. counties returned death sentences at a rate of at least one per year. These counties accounted for roughly 44% of all death sentences. A total of 14 counties sentenced 10 or more people from 2004 to 2009 for a rate of almost 2 per year. These 14 counties accounted for roughly one-third of all death sentences in the United States. Moreover, the counties that actively sentence defendants to death tend to be clustered within a handful of states. In 2009 alone, two-thirds of all death sentences were administered in just 5 states. These states include Alabama, Arizona, California, Florida, and Texas.

Much like prosecutors' decisions to seek the death penalty, the most pertinent geographic variation is arguably not the differences we observe *across* states but *within* states. It is arguably not that surprising that death sentences vary across states given that most states either do not have the death penalty or seldom, if ever, actually use it. Intrastate variation at the county level is arguably a better way to explore potential arbitrariness. Variation within states essentially amounts to jurors operating under the same capital statutes but differently applying those statutes. Texas and Florida, given that they are among the most active death penalty locales, provide telling examples.

From 2004 to 2009, nearly half of all counties in the state of Florida did not sentence a single person to death. Approximately three-fourths of all Florida counties sentenced two or fewer people to death. Only three counties—Doval (13), Broward (10), and Polk (8)—returned more than six death sentences for an average of at least one per year (Smith, 2012). Bowers and Pierce (1980) analyzed sentencing data in Florida from 1973–77 and found that death sentences were 2.5 times more likely in the Panhandle than the southern region of the state. Similar geographic concentrations of death sentences have been observed in Texas. From 2004 to 2009, 222 of Texas' 254 counties, or 87%, did not sentence a single person to death. Of the remaining 34 counties, 17 sentenced only one person to die during these six years. Only four counties—Bexar (10), Dallas (8), Harris (21), and Tarrant (10)—returned an average of more than one death sentence per year (Smith, 2012).

Similar to capital charging patterns, the county-level variation in death sentences cannot be explained by homicide rates or population size. To be sure, many of the counties around the U.S. that seldom, if ever, sentence anyone to death also seldom, if ever, experience murder, much less aggravated murder. It is not necessarily the case, however, that the most active death penalty jurisdictions are those that experience the most lethal violence (Lewin, 1995). In fact, some research suggests suburban counties tend to sentence more people to death than urban counties despite having lower murder rates in general (Bowers & Pierce, 1980; Lewin, 1995; Paternoster, 1983). For example, at the end of 1999, San Mateo County, which is a suburb of San Francisco, was responsible for 17 people on California's death row at the time. Neighboring San Francisco county, despite having a population 20% larger with twice as many murders as San Mateo County, was responsible for only four death row inmates (Willing & Fields, 1999).

Before we move to the next stage of the geography of capital punishment, it is important to be explicit about one very important fact—the "places" that most commonly file capital charges and secure the death penalty are not necessarily the same places that most commonly carry out executions. Some states operate similar to New Jersey, which had sentenced people to death but had not carried out an execution for over 30 years prior to abolition. This can even further complicate the topography of capital punishment because states that seldom carry out executions can have relatively large death row populations.

The most telling example comes via the state of California. Most people do not associate California with the death penalty primarily because the state seldom executes people. Only 13 people have been executed by the state of California since 1976. That ranks them seventeenth on the list of total executions during that time (DPIC, 2016b). They do, however, sentence people to death quite regularly. From 2004 to 2009, California led the nation with a total of 110 new death sentences. Florida and Texas were next with 100 and 97 death sentences, respectively. Death sentences in California were highly concentrated in a couple counties. A full 64% of California counties sentenced no one to death from 2004 to 2009. A full 90% of counties returned no more than one death sentence in those six years. Only six counties returned more than one death sentence. A total of three counties—Los Angeles (33), Riverside (15), and Orange (14)—collectively accounted for more than half of all the death sentences handed down in California from 2004 to 2009. In the year 2009 alone, the same number of people were sentenced to death in Los Angeles County (13) as the entire state of Texas (Smith, 2012).

The result of California sentencing a lot of defendants to death but rarely executing them is a gigantic death row population. The total number of people on death row in California stands at is 741, which gives them the largest death row population in the United States. California's death row population is larger than the next two largest state death row populations—Florida (396) and Texas (254)—combined (DPIC, 2016b). Pennsylvania has a similar albeit less dramatic disjuncture between sentencing and executing offenders. A total of three people have been executed in the state of Pennsylvania since 1976, which ranks them near the bottom of total executions during that time. Pennsylvania currently has the fifth-largest death row population (175) in the United States. Of course, some states quite regularly see death sentences through to execution.

Executions

Before we discuss the geography of executions, it is important to keep a few contextual points in mind. First, we must again be cautions of broad generalizations. In the first section of this chapter we discussed the basic state-to-state geography of capital punishment laws. Specifically, 31 states in the country have laws that allow for capital punishment and 19 states do not. There is, however, a very important distinction in the geography of capital punishment between states that *allow* for capital punishment and those that actually *practice* it.

A total of 34 states have carried out at least one execution since the Supreme Court reinstated capital punishment in 1976. However, the total number of executions carried out in each of these states varies considerably. Four states—Connecticut, Colorado, New Mexico, and Wyoming—have executed only one person in this 40-year history. A total of 11 states have carried out fewer than five executions. Almost half (15) of the states that have carried out at least one execution since 1976 have executed fewer than ten people (DPIC, 2016b).

From there, there is a rather gradual increase in the state execution totals. Nine states have carried out more than ten but fewer than 40 executions. What this tells us is that 70% (24 of 34) of the states that have executed at least one person have executed an average of less than one person per year. Of course, several of the remaining ten states have carried out a relatively large number of executions. Five of these states—Florida, Oklahoma, Missouri, Texas, and Virginia—have execution totals above 80 for an average of more than two per year since 1976. Virginia and Oklahoma are the first states on the slope to exceed 100 executions, with totals of 111 and 112, respectively. From there, we climb very steeply to Texas, which has carried out 538 executions over the past 40 years (DPIC, 2016b). This total amounts to more executions than the next six states combined. Table 29.2 shows the total number of executions by each state since 1976. It also provides execution totals for each state over the past two, five, and ten years, which we will subsequently discuss.

Recent Trends in Execution

Measuring execution over the life span of the "modern era" (i.e., 1976 to present) doesn't necessarily give us an accurate portrait of our more recent experiences with the geography of execution. Many of these 34 states' total execution figures are inflated by the past. That is, some states carried out executions somewhat routinely in the early part of the modern era but have been relatively inactive in recent history. For instance, Georgia, which ranks sixth in the total number of executions (69) since 1976, trails only Texas in the number of executions carried out over the past two years with 14. Thus, when

Table 29.2 Execution Totals by State in the Past 2, 5, 10, and 40 Years

State	1976–2016	2007–2016	2012–2016	2015 & 2016
Texas	538	159	61	20
Oklahoma	112	29	16	1
Virginia	111	13	2	1
Florida	92	28	21	3
Missouri	87	21	19	7
Georgia	69	30	17	14
Alabama	58	23	3	2
Ohio	53	29	7	0
North Carolina	43	0	0	0
South Carolina	43	7	0	0
Arizona	37	15	9	0
Louisiana	28	1	0	0
Arkansas	27	0	0	0
Mississippi	21	13	6	0
Indiana	20	3	0	0
Delaware	16	2	1	0
California	13	0	0	0
Illinois	12	0	0	0
Nevada	12	0	0	0
Utah	7	1	0	0
Tennessee	6	4	0	0
Maryland	5	0	0	0
Washington	5	1	0	0
Nebraska	3	0	0	0
Pennsylvania	3	0	0	0
Kentucky	3	1	0	0
Montana	3	0	0	0
Idaho	3	2	1	0
South Dakota	3	3	2	0
Oregon	2	0	0	0
New Mexico	1	0	0	0
Colorado	1	0	0	0
Wyoming	1	0	0	0
Connecticut	1	0	0	0

we start to pare down the time span of our analysis to more recent years, the landscape changes even further. We calculated execution totals for each state over the past ten, five, and two years using the execution databased created and monitored by the Death Penalty Information Center (DPIC, 2016e).

The figures in Table 29.1 show that over the past ten years (2007–2016) only ten states have carried out an average of at least one execution per year. These states include Texas, Oklahoma, Virginia, Florida, Missouri, Georgia, Alabama, Ohio, Arizona, and Mississippi. There is a rather consistent geographic trend in these figures. Seven of these ten states are in the Southern region of the United States. The three states not in the South include two states on the Southern border—Missouri and Ohio—as well as Arizona. Furthermore, we can start to see quite a significant degree of separation between these and the remaining states on the list. Many of these ten states have executed far more than one person per year since 2007. For instance, if we double the minimum number of executions to 20, for an average of at least two per year, only three of the ten states—Arizona, Mississippi, and Virginia—fall off the list.

When we shrink our window to the past five years, we find that the number of states that have kept pace in carrying out executions drops further. Over the past five years (2012–2016), a total of eight states have executed at least five people for an average of at least one execution per year. These states include the ten states listed above that executed an average of at least one person per year over the past decade except Virginia and Alabama. It is important to note, though, that five of these eight states far exceeded the minimum threshold of at least one per year. Florida, Georgia, Missouri, Oklahoma, and Texas each executed more than 15 people for a rate of more than three per year since 2012.

Over the past two years (2015–2016), the number of states that have kept pace in executions shrinks further from eight to only five. Alabama, Florida, Georgia, Missouri, and Texas each executed at least two people since 2015 for an average of at least one execution per year. However, two of these states—Florida and Alabama—barely eclipsed the mark. Florida has executed three people since 2015; Alabama carried out zero executions in 2015 but executed two people in 2016. The three remaining states of Texas, Missouri, and Georgia all exceeded the threshold quite comfortably.

Exploring execution rates over the past ten, five, and two years reveals two rather consistent geographic trends. First, only four states met the threshold of "an average of at least one execution per year" in each of the three time frames. Three of these states—Texas, Florida, and Georgia—are all firmly situated in the Southern region of the United States, and Missouri lies on the Southern border. Furthermore, almost all of these states far exceeded the minimum of one per year in every time frame. Second, fewer states met the threshold each time we narrowed the time frame to more recent years. That is, ten states executed an average of at least one person per year in the past decade. That number dropped to eight over the past five years and finally to five states over the past two years.

These figures lead to a rather simple yet potentially important conclusion—the United States has experienced a rather significant and consistent decline in executions. This decline, which began in earnest at the turn of the century, saw the total number of executions in 2016 recede to a 15-year low (DPIC, 2016b). Does this decline describe the United States as a whole, though? We've learned that executions are distributed very unevenly across geographic space, which calls into question the notion that the United States in general has experienced a decline in executions. To be sure, executions in many states across the U.S. "declined" far before the national figures began to drop in the year 2000. What is at issue here is whether the execution decline itself has been (un)evenly distributed across space.

On the one hand, it might be easy to conceive of just a few states declining and thus disproportionately driving down national execution totals since 1999. Texas could certainly drive down national execution figures all on its own. If, for instance, Texas experienced a precipitous decline in executions, the national total would drop given that Texas accounts for a sizable proportion of all executions in any given year. However, state execution trends over the past several years suggest that most all states, certainly those consistently responsible for most executions, have been in decline. Figure 29.1 shows execution trends from 1990 to 2016 for the U.S. as a whole as well as Texas and Oklahoma, which rank first and second on total executions in the modern era.

The handful of other states that, along with Texas and Oklahoma, form the pack of execution leaders in the U.S. have also declined during this time. Except for a few aberrant years in some of states, executions in Virginia, Florida, Missouri, Georgia, Alabama, and Ohio have all slowed to a trickle. In fact, we previously included Virginia and Florida in the figure above but ultimately removed them because the lines showing their execution trends were muddied at the bottom of the graph. What makes this particularly intriguing is that it suggests the national decline has not been driven by one or

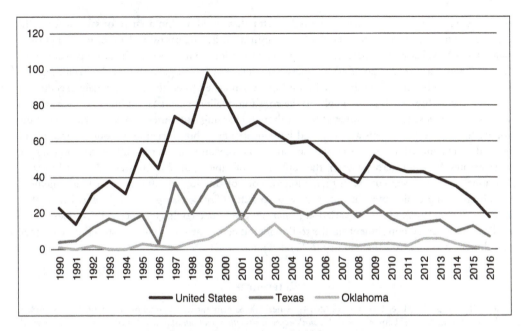

Figure 29.1   Execution trends in the United States, Texas, and Oklahoma, 1990–2016.

several states acting as outliers and dragging national totals down. Executions have waned in most all of the historical epicenters across the United States.

Conclusion

It can be easy to get lost in the facts and figures that describe the complex geography of capital punishment in the United States. In sum, a total of 31 states have capital punishment laws in place, but the content of those laws vary, primarily in how they attempt to guide jurors' sentencing discretion. Many of these laws are arguably symbolic, though, when you consider that most of these states seldom apply them. The capital punishment process begins when local prosecutors choose to file capital murder charges. Capital punishment is only secured when jurors plucked from the local community decide to return a death sentence. In these respects, the administration of capital punishment is a very local event. Different counties, oftentimes within the same state, have very different patterns of capital charging and sentencing. The likelihood that someone who committed aggravated homicide would be charged with capital murder and sentenced to death can be very different across county lines. What is more, variations in homicide rates and the proportion of homicides that are capital murder cannot explain the variations we observe in capital charging and sentencing. Even still, securing a death sentence does not actually assure an execution. That too depends largely on where we find ourselves.

Some states, such as Texas, characteristically progress through the capital punishment process to execution. To be sure, this progression can take a long time, and a host of factors can derail the process. But a convicted capital murder who is sentenced to death in Texas stands a considerably higher likelihood of being executed than a person in a similar situation who commits a similar crime in, say, California. This highly arched topography has some interesting implications for the constitutionality of capital punishment in the United States.

The Supreme Court suspended capital punishment in 1972 in large part because it was being applied arbitrarily. The court heard evidence that legally relevant criteria, such as extraordinary characteristics of offenses, offenders, or victims, could not explain why some people received death sentences while others were spared. The only factor that could, within a range of statistical signifi-cance, explain punishment outcomes was "the constitutionally impermissible basis of race" (*Furman v. Georgia*, 1972). What we find here in the geographic variations in how we use the death penalty in the United States is a certain type of arbitrariness—that place matters a great deal in the likelihood that a defendant will be charged with capital punishment, sentenced to death, and ultimately executed.

The greatest threat in this topography to the constitutionality of capital punishment is the variation we observe *within* states (Paternoster, 1983). Although charging and sentencing are carried out at the county level, these procedures are governed by state statutes. Thus, variation in county-level charg-ing and sentencing within any given state amounts to prosecutors and jurors differently applying the same statutes. Variation across states in the application of capital punishment is not necessarily a con-stitutional issue. The Supreme Court has a long history of sanctioning different models and methods for administering capital punishment from state to state (*Gregg v. Georgia*, 1976; *Jurek v. Texas*, 1976; *Proffitt v. Florida*, 1976). However, variation *within* any given state could amount to arbitrariness in the application of capital punishment similar to that identified by the court when it struck down capital punishment statutes across the country in *Furman v. Georgia* (1972).

References

Acker, J. R., Bohm, R. M., & Lanier, C. S. (2014). America's experiment with capital punishment. In J. R. Acker, R. M. Bohm, & C. S. Lanier (Eds.), *America's experiment with capital punishment: Reflections on the past, present, and future of the ultimate penal sanction* (pp. 3–15). Durham, NC: Carolina Academic Press.

Amnesty International. (2015). *Death sentences and executions 2014*. Retrieved from www.amnestyusa.org/research/reports/death-sentences-and-executions-2014

Bowers, W. J., & Pierce, G. L. (1980). Arbitrariness and discrimination under post-Furman capital statutes. *Crime and Delinquency, 26*, 563–632.

Conroy, J. (2005). The mysterious third device. *Chicago Reader*. Retrieved from www.chicagoreader.com/chicago/the-mysterious-third-device/Content?oid=917880

Death Penalty Information Center. (2016a). *Jurisdictions with no recent executions*. Retrieved from www.deathpenaltyinfo.org/jurisdictions-no-recent-executions

Death Penalty Information Center. (2016b). *Facts about the death penalty*. Retrieved from www.deathpenaltyinfo.org/documents/FactSheet.pdf

Death Penalty Information Center. (2016c). *Massachusetts*. Retrieved from www.deathpenaltyinfo.org/massachusetts-0

Death Penalty Information Center. (2016d). *Rhode Island*. Retrieved from www.deathpenaltyinfo.org/rhode-island-0

Death Penalty Information Center. (2016e). *Searchable execution database*. Retrieved from www.deathpenaltyinfo.org/views-executions

Death Penalty Information Center. (2016f). *Innocence database*. Retrieved from www.deathpenaltyinfo.org/innocence

Death Penalty Information Center. (2016g). *Governor Bill Richardson signs repeal of the death penalty*. Retrieved from www.deathpenaltyinfo.org/governor-bill-richardson-signs-repeal-death-penalty

Death Penalty Information Center. (2016h). *Illinois*. Retrieved from www.deathpenaltyinfo.org/illinois-1

Death Penalty Information Center. (2016i). *Connecticut*. Retrieved from www.deathpenaltyinfo.org/connecticut-1

Death Penalty Information Center. (2016j). *Aggravating factors for capital punishment by state*. Retrieved from www.deathpenaltyinfo.org/aggravating-factors-capital-punishment-state

De Vogue, A. (2011, March 9). Illinois abolishes death penalty, 16th state to end executions. *ABC News*. Retrieved from http://abcnews.go.com/Politics/illinois-16th-state-abolish-death-penalty/story?id=13095912

Dixon, K. (2012, April 12). State House votes to repeal death penalty. *The Connecticut Post*. Retrieved from www.ctpost.com/news/article/State-House-votes-to-repeal-death-penalty-3474483.php

Gross, S. R., O'Brien, B. O., Hu, C., & Kennedy, E. H. (2014). Rate of false conviction of criminal defendants who are sentenced to death. *Proceedings of the National Academy of Sciences of the United States of America, 111*(20), 7230–7235.

Hammel, P. (2016, November 9). Nebraskans vote overwhelmingly to restore death penalty, nullify historic 2015 vote by state legislature. *Omaha World-Herald*. Retrieved from www.omaha.com/news/politics/nebraskans-vote-overwhelmingly-to-restore-death-penalty-nullify-historic-vote/article_38823d54-a5df-11e6-9a5e-d7a71d75611a.html

Lewin, T. (1995, February 23). Who decides who will die? Even within states, it varies. *The New York Times*. Retrieved from www.nytimes.com/1995/02/23/us/who-decides-who-will-die-even-within-states-it-varies.html?pagewanted=all

Mandery, E. (2014). *A wild justice: The death and resurrection of capital punishment in America*. New York: W. W. Norton & Co.

Mills, S. (1999, July 20). Torture allegations lead to case review—man convicted in '84 based on confession. *Chicago Tribune*. Retrieved from www.archive-org-2013.com/org/j/2013-11-21_3204724/

Nicodemus, C. (1999, February 3). Lawyers urge review of 10 capital cases. *The Chicago Sun-Times*. Retrieved from www.highbeam.com/publications/chicago-sun-times-p392330/feb-3-1999

Ogletree, C. J. (2002). Black man's burden: Race and the death penalty in America. *Oregon Law Review, 81*(1), 15–38.

O'Malley, M. (2015, November 6). Why the death penalty needs to go. *CNN*. Retrieved from www.cnn.com/2015/11/06/opinions/omalley-capital-punishment/

Paternoster, R. (1983). Race of the victim and location of the crime: The decision to seek the death penalty in South Carolina. *The Journal of Criminal Law and Criminology, 74*(3), 754–785.

Peters, J. W. (2007, December 17). Death penalty repealed in New Jersey. *New York Times*. Retrieved from www.nytimes.com/2007/12/17/nyregion/17cnd-jersey.html

Richburg, K. B. (2007, December 14). N. J. approves abolition of the death penalty, Corzine to sign. *The Washington Post*. Retrieved from www.washingtonpost.com/wp-dyn/content/article/2007/12/13/AR2007121301302.html\

Smith, R. J. (2012). The geography of the death penalty and its ramifications. *Boston University Law Review, 92*, 227–289.

Songer, M. J., & Unah, I. (2006). The effect of race, gender, and location on prosecutorial decisions to seek the death penalty. *South Carolina Law Review, 58*, 161–210.

State of New Jersey. (2007). *New Jersey Death Penalty Study Commission Report*. Retrieved from www.njleg.state.nj.us/committees/dpsc_final.pdf

Vigdor, N. (2012, April 12). Republicans contribute to death penalty repeal. *The Greenwich Time*. Retrieved from www.greenwichtime.com/news/article/Republicans-contribute-to-death-penalty-repeal-3478534.php

Wagner, J. (2013, February 4). Maryland governor appeals to lawmakers to end death penalty. *The Washington Post*. Retrieved from www.washingtonpost.com/local/md-politics/maryland-gov-omalley-appeals-to-lawmakers-to-end-death-penalty/2013/02/14/ad731df6-76c5-11e2-8f84-3e4b513b1a13_story.html?utm_term=.931dced0eb41

Wagner, J., & Davis, A. C. (2013, May 2). O'Malley signs death penalty repeal, medical marijuana bill and other measures. *The Washington Post*. Retrieved from www.washingtonpost.com/local/md-politics/omalley-to-sign-death-penalty-repeal-and-scores-of-other-bills-thursday-morning/2013/05/02/b0f98bb4-b319-11e2-9a98-4be1688d7d84_story.html?utm_term=.dd5497b427df

Willing, R., & Fields, G. (1999, December 20). Geography of the death penalty. *USA Today*. Retrieved from www.crimelynx.com/geog.html

Wills, C. (2011, March 9). Illinois Governor Pat Quinn abolishes death penalty, clears death row. *Washington Post*. Retrieved from www.washingtonpost.com/wp-dyn/content/article/2011/03/09/AR2011030900319.html

Winchester, C. G. (2016). Weighing death: Is death penalty eligibility "especially heinous, cruel or depraved"? *Arizona Law Review, 58*, 511–539.

Young, J. (2015, May 28). Nebraska's death penalty is repealed. *Lincoln Journal Star*. Retrieved from http://journalstar.com/legislature/nebraska-s-death-penalty-is-repealed/article_e2ee72ab-cfe2-548c-b0f7-8a3ccf3b05fa.html

Cases and Statutes Cited

Furman v. Georgia, 408 U.S. 238 (1972).

Gregg v. Georgia, 428 U.S. 153 (1976).

Jurek v. Texas, 428 U.S. 262(1976).

Lockett v. Ohio, 438 U.S. 586 (1978).

Penry v. Lynaugh, 492 U.S. 302 (1989).

Proffitt v. Florida, 428 U.S. 242 (1976).

Ring v. Arizona, 536 U.S. 584, (2002).

Roberts v. Louisiana, 428 U.S. 325 (1976).

Roper v. Simmons, 543 U.S. 551 (2005).

Texas Code of Code of Criminal Procedure § 37.071, Section 3.

Woodson v. North Carolina, 428 U.S. 153 (1976).

Zant v. Stephens, 462 U.S. 862 (1983).

30

AGE, CLASS, AND SEX DISPARITIES IN CAPITAL PUNISHMENT

Etta F. Morgan

Capital punishment has always been the ultimate punishment in some societies. Methods of execution have changed from earlier barbaric forms such as stoning, beheading, and quartering to more "civilized" (used loosely) forms, most notably, hanging, shooting, lethal gas, electrocution, and lethal injection. Although these forms of death appear more humane, there have been many issues related to the carrying out of these methods. Historically, persons have been put to death for minor crimes in addition to heinous crimes. For example, in the past persons could be put to death for marrying members of certain ethnic groups, trading with Indians, or even stealing. It was also common for persons identified as witches to be put to death. As societies have evolved from their more primitive states, we have seen a shift in the types of crimes that are now punishable by death. Currently, crimes that are so heinous in nature and against the moral fiber of society are reserved for the death penalty.

Although the Supreme Court in *Furman v. Georgia* (1972) declared all death sentences unconstitutional, some states were quick to reform their death penalty statutes and had them enacted by the close of 1972. Still others reformed their death penalty statutes throughout the '70s, being sure to meet the guided discretion and consideration of mitigating factors as handed down in the guidelines by the Supreme Court in *Furman* and *Lockett v. Ohio* (1978). As states revised their death penalty statutes and enacted new laws during the '70s, Colorado added certain drug offenses as capital crimes, such as if a perpetrator tried to engage anyone under the age of 25 in any activity that included the use, sale, distribution or manufacture of narcotics (Cantwell, 1980). The '80s also offered several instances of fine-tuning death penalty statutes in hopes of eliminating issues that could cause a death sentence to be overturned. Alabama enacted a statute giving juries some latitude in conviction offense options. Specifically, the new statute allowed the jury to now consider lesser included offenses in addition to the capital offense. Perhaps most important during this period, Alabama and Arizona established the bifurcated trial for its capital cases (Schechter-Ryan, 1982; Cantwell, 1983). Bifurcated trials enhance due process and give the defense team an opportunity to focus on and to prepare for the sentencing phase of the trial. Throughout the '90s, states continued to make statutory changes to their death penalty statutes. While some of these changes dealt with adding aggravating and mitigating factors to existing statutes and automatic appeals/review of the conviction and sentence, several states also addressed the issue of age and transfers to adult court (Snell, 1999).

As one reviews the historical accounts of the death penalty, there is one aspect that stands out, and that is the place women occupy as recipients of the death penalty. Before examining women and the death penalty, it is important to put into context the position or status of women in society over time as we try to understand this obvious unbalanced scale of justice. We begin this journey to try and unravel what has led to such an unbalanced scale of justice by first examining ideologies that have created in some minds "the second sex," more commonly referred to as woman.

Social Institutions as Norms

There are several terms that will assist us in arriving at a rather crude definition of woman as it is used in today's society. While we use the terms sex (gender) and class quite often, do you ever stop to think about the meaning of the words? Probably not, but in some instances these meanings change over time, since they are socially constructed. For the purposes of this essay, these terms will be defined as follows. *Sex* is commonly referred to as one's biological designation based on his/her genitalia and reproductive functions. One can postulate that this is the beginning of sex/gender role assignments. Next, we turn our attention to the term *gender*, which is often used interchangeably with sex. Lorber (1994) and Denny (2011) note that gender is not only socially constructed but also socially reinforced. The reinforcements are so subtle that we often fail to notice. It is only when someone exhibits a behavior that does not fit the expected behavior that we take notice. When this occurs we try to place the individual in his/her societal assigned gender role. Because this action occurs, it creates the idea of oneness between the terms sex and gender, so therefore, we interchange the two. As sex is used herewithin, it will encompass all the attributes of gender as well.

Class for this chapter will be defined as a division of society based upon wealth, thereby creating social classes (i.e., upper class, middle class, and lower class) (Mantsios, 2013). Each class impacts and is impacted upon in society in different ways, as we will discuss in more detail later. Finally, *age* is merely defined as one's position on a chronological life span. Sex, class, and age are factors that influence many areas in our lives, such as family, socialization, education, careers, and the law. Sex, class, and age are also some extralegal factors that have a great impact on the administration of justice and most importantly in the application of the death penalty in America.

Age Disparities

Historically, juveniles have received a certain degree of protection from harsh sentences because it was believed that these youths were mainly wayward and in need of positive role models and supervision. In order to keep them from being treated as adults, reformers worked to establish a separate system for juveniles. With the passage of the Juvenile Court Act of 1899, the juvenile court was established, supposedly with the focus on the treatment of juveniles rather than punishment. Although at the time of its inception it was believed that juveniles would receive adequate protection of their basic rights, this was not the case, as evidenced in *Kent v. United States* (1966); *In re Gault* (1967); and *In re Winship* (1970). While *McKeiver v. Pennsylvania* (1971) requested a jury trial as part of his due process rights, the Supreme Court ruled that a jury was not needed specifically to ensure due process protections related to fact finding because judges could make that determination. In essence, the court found that a jury would not assist in any manner the issue of fact finding. It also noted that having a jury might change the protective nature of the process intended by juvenile court.

Over the years many methods have been devised to control, rehabilitate, educate, and provide positive role models for the youths of this country in hopes of deterring their criminal tendencies. However, it appears that instead of fostering respect for the laws of society and the criminal justice system, youths have become less respectful of authority figures and the laws which govern our society. As a result, we had an increase in juvenile delinquency and violent crimes committed by juveniles. Because of the increase in violent juvenile crime, society's attitude changed from one of tolerance to intolerance, and we moved toward a more punitive approach for violent juvenile offenders.

With the "get tough" policy on crime, those who oppose juvenile courts believed that as a separate court, juvenile court was too lenient on juvenile offenders and that these juveniles needed to be under the guidelines of a more punitive system such as the adult court system. For this reason, these advocates suggested that serious and violent juveniles be subject to certification to be tried as adults. The Supreme Court in *Kent* outlines specific factors to be addressed by judges in certification decisions. These factors include (1) an adherence to due process procedures and (2) a full investigation into the matter at hand as well as any information that may be used to assist in the decision-making process related to certification. Judicial waivers are the most common, although there are other types of waivers available.

Attitudinal changes toward juvenile behavior may have influenced the modifications of waiver statutes in the 1990s. A review of these modifications reveal that in relation to judicial waivers, (1) some states lowered the age of eligibility for transfer while others eliminated age requirements, (2) in some instances, new offenses were made eligible for judicial waiver, and (3) ages were raised and lowered based on the offense involved (Bilchik, 1997). Certification to adult court has some advantages, such as the right to a jury trial or plea bargaining, and some disadvantages; most notably, the juvenile begins his/her criminal record when certified to adult court. Once certified, juveniles were susceptible to any sentence that is applicable to adults, even the death penalty.

Death sentences for juveniles have been a part of United States history since the 1600s. There have been more than three hundred executions of juvenile offenders that have been documented in the United States, and 22 of these executions occurred during the modern era of the death penalty. A closer examination of death sentences for juveniles reveals that 38 death sentences were imposed for juveniles in the 1970s with 12 each year for 1975 and 1977. A breakdown of these 24 juveniles reveals that there were two 15-year-olds, nine 16-year-olds, and 13 17-year-olds, respectively. Thirty-two of the 38 death sentences were reversed (Streib, 2005).

During the '80s death sentences for juveniles rose to 65, with the most being imposed in 1982 (14). All but one of these juveniles was 17. Forty-seven of the 65 death sentences imposed in the '80s were reversed. A procedural issue was raised in *Eddings v. Oklahoma* (1982); Eddings was a juvenile but tried as an adult for his crime. Citing the refusal of the judge to review all of the mitigating evidence presented, the petitioner asked the court for relief. After review, the court ruled that the sentence must be vacated. In *Thompson v. Oklahoma* (1988), the petitioner sought relief from execution. The question presented to the court was whether or not the execution of an offender who was 15 years old at the time of the crime violated the Eight Amendment. The majority of the court, citing (1) evolving standards of decency, (2) legislation that had established a minimum age for the imposition of the death penalty, and (3) the minor's lack of culpability, ruled that the judgment is vacated and remanded. The next year, in *Stanford v. Kentucky* (1989), the court ruled that the Eighth Amendment does not protect minors 16 years old or 17 years old from the death penalty.

The most death sentences imposed on juveniles in one year occurred in 1994 (17). Overall, the '90s had the highest number of death sentences imposed on juveniles, with a total of 101. Most of those sentenced were 17 but there were 24 16-year-olds and two 15-year-olds also sentenced during this period. There was a noticeable decline in death sentences for juveniles in the early part of 2000s. The first four years only produced 22 death sentences, as it appears that public opinion toward juveniles and the death penalty was changing.

Indirectly, *Atkins v. Virginia* (2002) established a protected class—the mentally disabled—from the death penalty. *In re Stanford* (2002), the court decided not to address the issue of the death penalty for juveniles although at least four justices (Stevens, Ginsburg, Breyer, and Souter) wanted to do so. Continued challenges to the death penalty for juveniles was brought before the Missouri Supreme Court in *Simmons v. Roper* (2003). The Missouri Supreme Court, in its review of the case, noted that there appeared to be a national trend that viewed the death penalty for juveniles as a violation of the Eighth Amendment's protection against cruel and unusual punishment. This case was granted certiorari by the U.S. Supreme Court as *Roper v. Simmons* (2005). In its *Roper* ruling, the court held that under the Eight Amendment's evolving standard of decency, the death penalty for persons 17 years old is cruel and unusual punishment. In response to *Roper* several jurisdictions selected a minimum age of 18 years old in order for one to be death eligible. Prior to the *Roper* ruling, Streib (2005) noted that Texas housed the majority of juveniles sentenced to death. As with adults, the Southern region had the most death sentenced juveniles.

Class Disparities

America is a class-conscious society. It has been basically divided into three distinct socioeconomic classes, which not only provides social status but also identifies prestige status. Power relationships are closely related to socioeconomic classes (Vanneman & Cannon, 1987). Because we are a capitalist society, this economic foundation helps to confirm and maintain powerbrokers at various levels. It is no longer restricted to the owners of the companies because the power relationships have taken on new meanings, noting that the conflicts that were originally confined or existed between the owners and the workers have been recreated. There now exists a hierarchy that has conflicts between the company and workers as well as between the workers within their respective classes and the classes below them. Today, with the reassignment of power relationships, even the lowest worker along the socioeconomic (SES) scale has status and power over the nonemployed. This hierarchy serves to create and recreate social statuses as one's position in society changes (Vanneman & Cannon, 1987). Our social structure is impacted both socially and politically by the economic status of our citizens.

The laws in society are structured (1) to represent shared views of acceptable and unacceptable behaviors and (2) to ensure that the interests of those with power are maintained. Because norms and values are different based upon the various conditions that affect one's life, those norms may be in conflict with the established set of norms upon which the laws are based. Since laws normally reflect the values of the middle and upper classes, it stands to reason that those of the lower classes will be identified more often as criminal than their middle and upper class counterparts (Chambliss & Seidman, 1971). The legal system is comprised of many agencies that carry out various processes, and at every level there is a discretionary decision as to whether or not to fully employ the duties of the agency. This discretionary decision determines the future contact a citizen may have with the legal system based upon the perceived rewards for the agency and its personnel. In most situations, enforcement is geared toward those persons without political power and who are of the lower socioeconomic class.

The differential treatment of the poor in America has been a part of our society for an extended period. The question is, why has it persisted? One could argue that those in the criminal justice system continue to perpetuate the belief that crime is the work of the poor. Crimes committed by the middle and upper classes are not viewed the same as those of the poor. Society refuses to admit that it is partially responsible for the lack of opportunities afforded its poor, knowing that the poor still have the same aspirations as others in society (Reiman & Leighton, 2012). Unfortunately, the imposition of capital punishment is also impacted and administered based on economics. Due to the high costs associated with prosecuting a capital case, prosecutors must not only weigh the monetary costs but also the personal and political consequences that may occur as a result of prosecuting a capital case. An indigent offender is far easier to target for prosecution than someone with the resources to aggressively prepare a proper defense in a capital case, unlike the indigent offender, who would be assigned a public defender with limited resources with which to prepare a case.

Additionally, the SES of the victim also plays a role in the decision to prosecute. Individuals viewed as productive and valuable citizens with strong ties to the community tend to be revered, unlike those who are view as "needy" and looking for handouts (Phillips, 2009). This may be due to the pressures on the prosecutor from the community based upon the individual's level of activity within the community. Regardless of the socioeconomic status of the offender or victim, the administration of capital punishment should not rest on this factor (class). For too long, the rich get richer and the poor get prison (Reiman & Leighton, 2012), which has been substantiated by the research. It is time offenders are held accountable for their crimes and tried and sentenced in a fair and equitable manner that can withstand the Eighth and Fourteenth Amendments tests. Class is not the only factor that influences the administration of justice and, more specifically, capital punishment. We find that society also uses the sex of an offender as a factor to be considered in administering capital punishment.

Sex and the Death Penalty

Chivalry, Patriarchy, Women, and the Law

Historically, chivalry was most often associated with knights and men and their conduct within society. This conduct included gallantry, honor, and violence. Since violence was expected as a means of settling disputes, wives of knights were often abused according to today's societal standards. Women during this period were considered property of their men, as well as property that could be won through fighting. Knights earned honor through violence whether in war or defending the honor of a 'lady.' Defending the honor of a lady only applied to those women who were considered 'ladies' who adhered to the rules of womanhood and femininity. The idea of chivalry suggested that women were weak and needed men to take care of them (Carroll, 1997). While chivalry appeared to protect women, it also reinforced gender roles and a class system, because all women were not afforded the same protection of honor as those of the knightly class. Although knights killed many people in order to gain honor, they did not kill women because it was not honorable and it would show a lack of gallantry (Shatz & Shatz, 2012). Chivalry has been imbedded in American society for many years. The ideas of chivalry have even influenced several Supreme Court decisions. For example, in *Bradwell v. Illinois* (1872), the court noted that women should not practice law. Then in 1908 the court ruled in *Muller* that women could only work a prescribed number of hours in the workplace. The court's opinion in *Hoyt v. Florida* (1961) strongly stated that women should not maintain a presence outside of the home in the public sphere. Rulings such as these only served to reinforce the ideology of a woman's place is in the home.

While some societies have moved away from notions of chivalry, it remains a firm ideology in true Southern cultures. One ongoing Southern tradition and perhaps one of the most prevalent reminders of chivalrous attitudes toward women is the debutante ball. The essence of this ball tells society that the young girl is of impeccable character, possesses all the virtues of a lady, and knows her place in society. Therefore, she is to be honored and her reputation is to be defended at all times. The elements of chivalry are imbedded in patriarchy. The major difference in the two is the keeper of honor. In patriarchy it shifts the burden of maintaining honor from the knight, as in medieval times, to the father as ruler/head of the home, the husband, brother, or other male in the family.

Women in American society are subjected to the ideology of patriarchy, which emphasizes male domination and the oppression of women (Johnson, 2014). In this type of society women are considered second-class citizens. Gender roles and positions are established based upon male dominance, which creates a power hierarchy that places men at the top. Men are therefore the powerbrokers who control society through policymaking. To this end, men tend to determine cultural ideas that are identified as the "norms" in society while also maintaining a superior position over women and controlling a large portion of income and wealth in society. Characteristics in men such as strength, control, and the ability to think and be logical, though, are not valued in women. Instead, women are expected to be objects of beauty for men and their pleasures as well as objects to be controlled. When women step outside the realm of their established female identity and gain power, it is not viewed the same as a man gaining power in society, since in some instances, their work is not valued. The oppressive nature of patriarchy seeks to maintain women as second-class citizens even though not all women experience oppression the same (Johnson, 2014).

For example, fathers have always been viewed as the rulers of their homes, and sons occupied a position over their mothers because of their sex (gender). In the home, daughters were on the bottom of the hierarchy scale by virtue of their sex (gender). In the past, women were considered property of their fathers or husbands, and some males still believe this today (Morgan, 2012). Male dominance in society dictated and continues to dictate the laws of society in both the private and public sectors. Laws are created and passed by legislative bodies composed mainly of rich, white men and persons who share their interests. As a result, our laws reflect and protect their interests (Price & Sokoloff, 1995). Cases such as *Reed v. Reed* (1971); *Frontiero v. Richardson* (1973); *Craig v. Boren* (1976) provided small legal gains for women in regard to constitutional law issues. Research by Hoff (1991) suggests that the Supreme Court issued several gender-biased decisions that failed to provide equality for women.

Additionally, the court has ruled against gender-specific criteria in employment decisions that limited opportunities for women (*Dothard v. Rawlinson*, 1977; *International Union v. Johnson Controls*, 1991). These latter cases show a shift in the chivalrous protections that had been afforded women in previous rulings, instead, women have been given a minor voice in decisions that affect them. As we turn our attention to criminal law, we must note that there may be constitutional issues that arise as a result of criminal cases that can only be addressed if raised in criminal court. There is a conflict in values; chivalry says do not kill women—protect them, but they cannot be violent. Historically, women were not executed as a general rule. With liberation came accountability, so we now are more likely to sentence women to death, with a slight residual effect of second-class status in that women who kill their "owners" (the most serious offense) can be put to death.

Women Offenders

Criminal offending is basically a male-dominated phenomena; however, women do commit crimes, just not at the same rate as men. The extent of crimes committed by women appears to have increased over time, but is it due to more criminal activity or is it the result of a change in policy and practices within society today? The types of crimes committed by women and girls vary with age and duration. Women and girls quite often commit the crime of theft, which includes larceny, forgery, embezzlement, and fraud. Women and girls who engage in shoplifting tend to steal personal items that they believe are needed, such as jewelry, clothing, makeup, and food. Many of the women who engage in these activities are living in poverty but are still trying to maintain a societal image of a beautiful woman and, in some instances, merely to feed their families, while, on the other hand, women in the workforce focus on different types of crimes.

With increased roles in the workplace, the types of crimes committed by women began to change. For example, crimes of embezzlement and fraud rose among women as more women had access to large sums of money and bookkeeping accounts. Although these women had good-paying jobs, they were often paid less than men for the same positions. So when they experienced financial difficulties, they simply "advanced money" and/or paid false invoices in order to get money from the company, thinking that the company had plenty of money and would not miss it. Women also commit the crimes of robbery and burglary to a somewhat lesser degree than men. Women who commit these acts report that they most often work with others when committing burglary and that they were on drugs at the time of the burglary (Decker, Wright, Redfern, & Smith, 1993). Yet women robbers tend to work alone and, ironically, target female victims. However, women robbers will also lure men with the promise of sex or join with a male in order to rob other men (Belknap, 2015). Several robberies committed by women are drug related.

Having been introduced to drugs by male associates, girlfriends, and in some cases parents, women drug users struggled to support their habits. Many of these women exchanged sexual favors for drugs or the money to buy drugs. In some instances, women drug users allowed themselves to be prostituted by drug dealers as a means of supporting their drug addiction. Unfortunately, many drug-using women commit various crimes in order to support their addiction, and this may lead to incarceration. Seldom do we find women drug dealers, but there are some. Most women who tend to sell drugs gain entry into the selling market through a close male associate. Their time in the business is limited, since most users do not expect to buy drugs from women. It appears that female methamphetamine dealers whose lives more closely mirrored a normal lifestyle had a more positive experience than other women drug dealers, whether they were selling crack, cocaine, or methamphetamine. For these women dealers, selling was just a means by which they could achieve more in society and become more independent because of the extra income (Morgan & Joe, 1996). Other types of crimes committed by women include assault, child abuse, and homicide.

Normally, we do not associate aggressive behaviors with women. Instead, we tend to think of them as loving, caring, and nurturing. However, research (Sommers & Baskin, 1993) has found that women will respond to aggressive behaviors in kind and they will be aggressive as a means of retaliation to previous acts of aggression that they have experienced. Sommers and Baskin (1993) also found intoxication played a role in some aggressive behaviors exhibited by women. Perhaps one of the most difficult criminal acts to understand is the one in which a mother inflicts harm or permits harm to occur toward her child or children. Although both women and men tend to kill their child(ren), society pays more attention to the act when a woman kills her child(ren). In some high profile cases of women killing their children, it was noted that they suffered from a mental illness that had not been identified. Regardless of the reason, society is not sympathetic toward women who kill their child(ren). Other homicides committed by women in society draw attention to problems such as intimate partner violence and economic inequality. As with all violent crimes, violent crimes committed by women has been decreasing, and the apparent increase is due mainly as a result in policy changes instead of actual incidents over time (Belknap, 2015). While these criminal acts are not acceptable behaviors in our society, the quest for the American Dream tends to force some people into crime so as to appear to be "normal." Having briefly discussed the historical foundation of differential treatment of women and the types of crimes committed by women, we now focus our attention on the processing of women through the criminal justice system.

Criminal laws not only prescribe acceptable behaviors for its citizens but also maintain social control over them (Roberts, 1994). Women who do not adhere to prescribed gender roles and commit criminal offenses are viewed differently by our criminal justice system. Previous research (Farnworth & Teske, 1995; Erez, 1989; Kruttschnitt, 1982; Mann, 1984; Pollock, 2002; Spohn & Spears, 1997; Visher, 1983; Zingraff & Thompson, 1984) suggests that, as a group, women have been treated more leniently in the criminal justice system than men. These studies found that the preferential treatment of women may be positive or negative and is most often influenced by the women's perceived threat to the community. The processing of women through the criminal justice system also seems to differ for women when compared to their male counterparts. While the prosecution rates for men and women who committed violent felonies differed slightly, their rates of conviction were similar, with major differences appearing in sentencing (Spohn & Spears, 1997). Judges and sometimes juries tend to view violent women offenders differently and consider extra-legal factors when determining the appropriate punishment (Morgan, 2012). If this is true, then it may explain the disproportionate number of women sentenced to death and executed in relation to their male counterparts. Female violence is seen as a greater violation (gender bias) than male violence.

Gillespie (1986), in his study of women offenders, found that women received differential treatment in capital cases. Sentencing women to death is not a new phenomenon, but the number of women sentenced to death has never been near or equal to the number of men sentenced to death since the keeping of records. In a 1987 study of capital cases in Florida, Foley found that while sex (gender) did not influence the trial outcome, it did influence the conviction offense. This study also revealed that women were treated more leniently and were less likely than men to be convicted of first-degree murder, thereby removing the possibility of being sentenced to death (Foley, 1987). Steffensmeier and Demuth (2006) found that sex influenced sentencing, noting specifically that instead of a prison sentence, women receive some type of community corrections, and if they do get a prison sentence, it will be shorter that a similarly situated male. Prison sentences are normally given to women who exhibit masculine rather than feminine qualities. Additionally, Carroll (1997) noted that the influence of gender in capital cases makes one question whether the administration of the death penalty as it relates to women can maintain the standards set forth in *Furman*. Death sentences in the United States have been reserved mainly for men with serious criminal histories and women who commit heinous crimes and who do not conform to gender expectations.

Findings by Snell (2014) revealed that (1) the death penalty is more prevalent in the South, which is sometimes referred to as the "death belt" in criminal justice and the Bible belt in other circles; (2) more women are under death sentences in the South than any other region; and (3) more persons have been removed from their death sentences in the South than any other region. The application of death sentences was fairly rare during previous decades and continues to be for women in comparison to men in this country. Historical data on women sentenced to death are limited, so our discussion of death sentences will focus mainly on data from 1973–2013 and limited data for the years 2014–2015 (Streib, 2013; Cantwell, 1980; Schechter-Ryan, 1982; Snell, 1999, 2014; NAACP, 2000–2016). In the '70s, women received 22 death sentences compared to 1,171 males during the same period. A closer look reveals that there were 519 death sentences for men in 1975 and 1976 but only 11 for women the same years, with eight death sentences being given in 1975, the most death sentences for women during any one-year period during the '70s. Of the approximately 1,193 death sentences meted out in the '70s, women only received 22 death sentences. All but one of these 22 death sentences were reversed. Velma Barfield was executed and will be discussed during our discussion on the execution of women (Streib, 2013). At the close of the '70s epoch, it was clear that states had crafted death penalty statutes that were meeting the guidelines of the court and rapidly increasing the number of death row inmates to mirror pre-*Furman* numbers.

Death sentences were on a fast track in the '80s with a total of 2,587. In 1980, 173 men were sentenced to death. The fewest number of death sentences in one year during this era. While men received 2,536 death sentences, only 51 women were on the receiving end of death sentences during this same period. Eleven death sentences, the most in any year of the modern death penalty era, were handed down to women in 1989 (Snell, 2014). Of the 51 death sentences, 39 were reversed. Seven of the women were executed and will be discussed in more detail later. At least four of the women sentenced to death in the eighties had their sentences commuted and one, Priscilla Ford died of natural causes in 2005 (Death Penalty Information Center, 2015a; Schechter-Ryan, 1982; Cantwell, 1983; Streib, 2013). The modern era of the death penalty has created a society of death penalty inmates whose population is larger than some rural areas in America.

The number of new death sentences in the '90s almost reached 3,000 with approximately 2,866 new death sentences being imposed. A breakdown of the years reveal that, beginning in 1993, the number of death sentences begin to rise (290) and continued through 1994 (311), 1995 (310), and 1996 (315). The largest number of death sentences (10) imposed on women during this period occurred in 1992, followed by seven death sentences each year for the years 1991 and 1995. Six additional death sentences each year were also imposed on women in both 1990 and 1993. At the close of the '90s, a total of 56 more women found themselves under the sentence of death; however, over time, 25 of these death sentences were reversed, five were commuted, and one woman was executed, Aileen Wuornos. Wuornos will be discussed with other executed women. This was the first time in United States history that new death sentences reached this proportion (Death Penalty Information Center, 2015a; Snell, 2000; Streib, 2013).

Death sentences for the next era began with the imposition of 223 new death sentences, and women represented 3.6% (8) of that total. New death sentences took a downward turn the following year, with only 153 imposed (151 males and 2 women). During 2002, there was a slight increase in the number of new death sentences imposed 166 (161 males and 5 women), followed by a steady decline in 2003, with 151 (149 males and 2 women), and 2004, with 138 (133 males and 5 women). After rising in 2005 to 140 new death sentences (135 males and 5 women), overall death sentences have continued to decline each year thereafter reaching an all-time low of 73 in 2014 (Death Penalty Information Center, 2015b; Snell, 2014; Streib, 2013). Of the 49 women sentenced to death between January 2000 and December 2012, 11 of those sentences have been reversed. Since the beginning of the modern era of capital punishment, women have received approximately 178 new death sentences (without the breakdown of gender numbers from 2013-spring 2015). Reversals and commutations removed 122 women from death row while at least two women have been exonerated, Sabrina Butler and Debra Milke, but not before spending five and 15 years, respectively, on death row; however, currently, there are 54 women under the sentence of death awaiting execution in the United States (NAACP Legal Defense and Education Fund, 2000–2016).

The reasons cited most often for reversals of death sentences for women include (1) ineffective assistance of counsel, (2) the jury selection process, and (3) prosecutorial misconduct. A brief discussion of these reasons follows and will include some cases from men due to the nature of the conduct by prosecutors:

Ineffective Assistance of Counsel

In *Powell v. Alabama* (1932), the Supreme Court agreed that counsel should be provided for indigent defendants and noted that counsel should have reasonable time to prepare a defense as elements of the Fourteenth Amendment's due process clause dictate. While many thought that *Gideon v. Wainwright* (1963); *Douglas v. California* (1963) guaranteed the right to effective assistance of counsel, it was not until *Cuyler v. Sullivan* (1980) that the Supreme Court ruled on this issue. In *Cuyler v. Sullivan* (1980), the Supreme Court ruled that without counsel's ability "to invoke the procedural and substantive safeguards that distinguish our system of justice, a serious risk of injustice infects the trial itself" (p. 343). The right to effective assistance of counsel was extended beyond the trial to the defendant's first appeal in *Evitts v. Lucey* (1985).

Because of economic costs associated with death penalty cases, the best lawyers are systematically barred from them, since states are not going to adequately provide resources to investigate, prepare, and try these cases. Only a few capital offenders can afford the type of lawyer really needed because of the complexities of these cases. Yet most capital offenders are indigent and must be represented by a court appointed lawyer. Oftentimes these lawyers are of two types (1) pretty good—has experience trying death penalty cases but is not well-versed in death penalty law and (2) lawyer in name only—may be one who has passed the state bar but can barely pass muster. In some states in the "death belt," there are established standards for counsel in death penalty cases. For example, in Alabama a lawyer must have five years criminal law experience. Yet, even with standards such as these, some death row inmates receive ineffective assistance of counsel. For example, the attorney in *Alabama v. Thomas* (1981) had more than ten years criminal experience and had even tried death penalty cases, but under the old law. He made numerous mistakes that helped sentence his client to death, such as failing to establish a definite division of responsibilities for trial preparation, knowing that capital cases were bifurcated trials. During the defense attorney's disposition, the following exchange occurred regarding trial preparation:

Q. What, if you can recall, factors led you to believe this wasn't a death case?

A. From years of practice and being a shothouse killing and both people having knives and what used to be referred to around here as a n—cutting or a n—killing. And, unfortunately, that was an attitude that was changing, in the change, I suppose, maybe about that time. But it happened to be a black on black. But it still surprised me, because the black on black weren't dispensed equal and just either at that time.

(Burroughs, 1985, pp. 14–15)

In other death penalty cases an attorney was held in contempt of court and jailed for intoxication during the trial (*Alabama v. Haney*, 1988), and the court in *Young v. Zant* (1980) noted that the lead attorney in this case had no understanding of Georgia's bifurcated trial proceedings: even when they were explained to him, he still could not comprehend.

Jury Selection Process

The use of peremptory challenges to remove prospective jurors because of their race and views regarding the criminal justice system has been a practice for years. The belief was that black jurors were more sympathetic than white jurors. Perhaps the most notable case regarding the removal of potential jurors based due to race is *Batson v. Kentucky* (1986); although the issue had been raised in *Swain v. Alabama* (1965), the court ruled that there was no inference of discrimination. In *Batson*, however, the court ruled that the exclusion of potential jurors based on their race was a violation of the Equal Protection Clause of the Fourteenth Amendment. Arizona and Texas Courts also ruled against race-based peremptory challenges (*State v. Gardner*, 1988; *Seubert v. State*, 1988). The removal of potential jurors has also been the subject of several death penalty cases that have come under review by state and federal courts. The Supreme Court also addressed the issue of excluding women from jury service in *Glasser v. United States* (1942); *Ballard v. United States* (1946); *Hoyt v. Florida* (1961); and *Taylor v. Louisiana* (1975). In all these cases, except *Hoyt*, the court held that the exclusion of women from the jury panels was not acceptable. It also stated that women bring a distinct voice to the proceedings and that voice must be heard. In essence, without women on the jury, it is not truly representative of the community, as required by the Sixth Amendment. In *J.E.B. v. Alabama* (1994), the Supreme Court held that "gender, like race, is an unconstitutional proxy for juror competence and impartiality" (p. 158).

The use of race-based peremptory challenges appears often in the death belt but is not unique to the area. According to Hudson (1988), the idea was "shared with prosecutors, while I was a prosecutor, almost everywhere, at state conventions, at national conventions . . . I look to it as more of a social application" (p. 67). For example, in *Alabama v. Thomas* (1981), prosecutors would hold private meetings on Sundays to discuss prospective jurors. In this case, it was determined through depositions of former prosecutors that records of past jurors had been kept over a 20-year period with various information (i.e., race, previous cases, the type of verdicts rendered, where they worked, etc.) to help provide some insight about how this person might vote, whether for or against the state. The continued use of peremptory challenges to exclude black prospective jurors was argued November 2, 2015, before the Supreme Court in *Foster v. Chatman*, No. 14-8349, a case from the death belt (Georgia). The court found enough evidence to reverse and remand this case, although the Georgia Supreme Court ruled against the defendant in previous review. It appears that this is a practice that will continue and be challenged throughout our state and federal courts. There are other issues with the jury that are sometimes raised as a part of prosecutorial misconduct.

Prosecutorial Misconduct

Prosecutors, as elected officials, have the responsibility to uphold the law while at the same time trying to insure the public's safety. Unfortunately, in a rush to convict an offender, they sometimes do not follow the appropriate procedures. Instead of being ethical in their practice of the law, they in fact break the law just to win a case. These miscarriages of justice in death penalty cases have caused many innocence people to be executed and others to lose numerous years imprisoned for a crime they did not commit. Types of misconduct by prosecutors include improper comments during the trial, failure to provide a full and true discovery, failure to disclose mitigating evidence, withholding exculpatory evidence, making false statements to Superior Court, using perjured testimony, and exhibiting unprofessional conduct during the trial (*Mooney v. Holohan*, (1935); *Brady v. Maryland*, 1963; *Caldwell v. Mississippi*, 1985; Minsker, 2009; *R. David Favata*, 2015).

Sabrina Butler was sentenced to death in March 1990, convicted of killing her infant son, becoming the only woman on Mississippi's death row at 18 years old. During her trial she exercised her constitutional right not to testify. The prosecutor made derogatory comments regarding her unwillingness to testify in this case. The defense objected, and the comments became an issue in her appeal to the Mississippi Supreme Court. In reviewing the appeal, the Mississippi Supreme Court said that the comments made by the prosecutor were reversible error and were cause for her conviction to be reversed. The court further noted that the trial court judge should have declared a mistrial when the comments were made. Additionally, the court stated that there was no evidence that a murder had been committed *Butler v. State*, 608 So.2d.314 (1992). Sabrina Butler was exonerated in 1995, becoming the first woman to be exonerated from death row after serving five years for a crime that never happened.

The second woman to be exonerated from death row was Debra Milke. The Arizona Supreme Court upheld a lower court's ruling dismissing all charges against Milke due to police and prosecutorial misconduct. The Arizona Court of Appeals also barred any further prosecution of Milke. Unfortunately, these actions came after Milke spent 23 years on death row (Death Penalty Information Center, 2013). Luckily for her, women are seldom executed. Milke's case is not an isolated case. There have been allegations of prosecutorial misconduct in at least half of the death sentences imposed in Arizona since 2002. The Arizona Supreme Court has verified a substantial number of these allegations. A study by Harvard Law School's Fair Punishment Project (2016) found that five prosecutors in this country (three from the death belt) accounted for numerous allegations of misconduct. Of the alleged allegations in the death belt, two of the three prosecutors were found to have engaged in prosecutorial misconduct an average of 26.5% of the time.

Prosecutorial misconduct has been cited as the reason the Delaware Supreme Court has overturned three death sentences in recent years: Jermaine Wright (May 2014); Isaiah McCoy (January 2015); and Chauncey Starling (December 2015) (Death Penalty Information Center, 2015b). As a result of the *McCoy v. State of Delaware* (2012), the prosecutor, R. David Favata, was cited by the Board of Professional Responsibility as having violated the Delaware Lawyers' Rules of Professional Conduct. He was charged with seven violations, and the board recommended that his license be suspended for six months and one day. He will have to meet the conditions of readmission for the Delaware Bar Association (Favata, 2015). There have also been notable problems in Missouri, Pennsylvania, California, and Oklahoma as well in recent years, but none of these prosecutors have received any type of disciplinary action (Death Penalty Information Center, 2015b; Minsker, 2009). With issues such as ineffective assistance of counsel, improper jury selection processes and prosecutorial misconduct, it stands to reason that most states have enacted automatic appeals. Yet in spite of the safeguards in place, innocent people are still executed. The pathway to an execution requires the offender's status to change from a respectable citizen to criminal. This change in identity creates a stigma that degrades one's status in society.

Society has in place mechanisms that are used to degrade its members that do not conform to socially acceptable behaviors (Garfinkel, 1956). Our society uses labels to represent status, whether good or bad; however, it is the "bad" labels that promote degradation of identity, and once applied, the damage is permanent because some in society will always place the "criminal" label first. Even those who have been acquitted of crimes find themselves still having to contend with the label. While both sexes experience this issue, it is more difficult for women than men because men are afforded some leeway to be 'bad boys'. Women criminals are often identified as women who are disreputable and lack moral integrity. In essence, these women do not possess the qualities of 'real women'. Because this difference is not acceptable in society, it allows society to ostracize women offenders.

For those women charged with or convicted of a capital offense the degradation exacerbates. Previous noteworthy labels such as wife, mother, lover, and caregiver have now been replaced with the label of murderer, a label that identifies these women as different from ordinary women and no longer to be recognized as such. When women are sentenced to death, does that mean an execution is forthcoming? Unlikely. Women are seldom executed in the United States. Instead, in many instances, they are processed out of the system as they move through the capital punishment process (Streib, 2003). As noted earlier, many death sentences imposed on women have been reversed, commuted, and exonerated. For those women who are executed, research by Streib (2003); Gillespie (2009) failed to identify any real, distinct characteristics associated with the women and/or their cases. In determining which women will be executed, it is more like taking a chance on the lottery than an actual process in the system of justice.

The same cannot be said about men, since they are more likely to be executed. Since the modern era of the death penalty, more than 1,422 death sentences have been carried out. Of these, only 16 females have been executed, compared to 1,406 males. Based upon the number of death sentences imposed on women and the number of executed women in this country, it is apparent that the death penalty is reserved mainly for men and women who exhibit masculine traits or who fail to exhibit 'lady-like' behaviors. In the following sections, we take a brief look at some of the women executed since 1976.

Prior to the 1984 execution of Velma Barfield, no woman had been executed since Elizabeth Duncan in August 1962. Velma Barfield by most accounts was a God-fearing woman, but she had a sinister side and a criminal past. Addicted to prescription drugs, Velma had to find a way to support her addiction. According to the North Carolina Department of Public Safety Offender Public Information (2016), Velma Barfield had been arrested and convicted of presenting worthless checks, for revocation of probation, and for violation of a regulated controlled substance before she was convicted of murder and sentenced to death. It was later discovered that the murder of Stuart Taylor (her boyfriend) was not the first time Velma Barfield had murdered someone. In fact, she confessed to the murder of her mother and two others for whom she was the caregiver. Based upon this confession, authorities decided to exhume the body of her late husband and performed an autopsy. It was discovered that Velma had killed him with arsenic, like the others. Velma Margie Barfield for all intents and purposes was a female serial killer. For a more thorough review of this case read *State v. Barfield*, 259 S.E.2d510 (N.C., 1979). The next woman executed was Karla Faye Tucker in Texas.

Interestingly, the South, with its deep religious roots, fails to exercise forgiveness in relation to those who are convicted of any crime and most especially a capital crime. It is these same beliefs that those who support the death penalty cite as justification for the death penalty; however, they show no empathy for one who turns her life around while on death row. Karla Faye Tucker was the first women to be executed in Texas since the 1800s. As with many offenders, Tucker was said to have found Christ while on death row; however, it was hard for most people to get beyond the gruesomeness of the crime for which she was convicted (see *Tucker v. State*, 1988). Judias Buenoano was also executed in 1998, making her the first woman executed in Florida since the 1800s, for the murder of her husband, a son, and a boyfriend in Colorado. She also attempted to kill another boyfriend in Florida by bombing his car, but he survived. It was his discussion with authorities that led to the investigation into the other deaths and her subsequent convictions (see *Buenoano v. State*, 478 So.2d. 387 (FLA App., 1985); *Buenoano v. State*, 527 So.2d. 194 [FLA, 1988]).

There were two executions in 2000, Betty Lou Beets in Texas and Christina Riggs in Arkansas. Betty Lou Beets murdered two former husbands and involved her children in both of them. After each murder she solicited the aid of her children to dispose of the bodies. She also shot and wounded another husband, but she was only convicted of the murder of Jimmy Don Beets. Like Judias Buenoano, Betty Lou was called the "Black Widow" (see *Beets v. State*, 1987). Christina Riggs was not only a murderer but also the murderer of her children. Riggs carefully planned to kill her children. As a nurse, she had access to various drugs and used that access to steal Elavil, morphine, and potassium chloride. First, she drugged them with Elavil, an antidepressant, to put them to sleep. After waiting a period to ensure that they were sleep, she continued to carry out her plan. Using the potassium chloride (one of the ingredients used in lethal injection), she injected Justin, but he awoke to the pain. She then injected him with morphine, but he would not be quiet, so Riggs smothered him. Leaving him dead, she went to kill her daughter. Instead of trying the injection again, she just smothered her. Ironically, she laid them out as if it was for some type of death ceremony in her bed before attempting suicide (*Riggs v. State*, 1999). No one really knows why she decided to kill them. At her trial, Riggs asked to be sentenced to death and was not concerned with appealing the case. She merely wanted the state to put her to death. Riggs was one of those who have been identified as 'volunteers for execution'. Upon her execution, Christina Riggs became the first woman executed in Arkansas since before the Civil War.

Oklahoma has the distinction of being the only state that executed women in 2001. The executions of Wanda Jean Allen, Marilyn Plantz, and Lois Nadean Smith represented the most women executed in a single year since the modern era of the death penalty. Wanda Jean Allen was the first women executed in Oklahoma since it became a state and the first black woman put to death in the United States since the 1950s. The murder of Gloria Leathers was the second killing of a person with whom she (Wanda) was engaged in a lesbian relationship. Wanda Jean Allen met Gloria Jean Leathers while in prison for killing her first lover, Dedra Pettus. Based on family accounts, Wanda Jean Allen was mentally challenged, but this information was not shared with the defense until after her conviction. Perhaps knowing the circumstances of her illness might have assisted the defense in preparing a diminished capacity defense that would have persuaded the jury to sentence her to life without parole.

During 2002, two women were executed in the United States: Lynda Lyon Block (Alabama) and Aileen Wuornos (Florida). Lynda Lyon Block was different from most of the women on Alabama's death row. She was from a middle-class background, educated, and still considered herself a "lady in every sense of the word." As a Libertarian, she often stated that the government had no right to interfere in her life (Personal Communication, 1998). When questioned about the shooting of Officer Motley, she stated that the officer had no right to ask George (Block's co-defendant) for identification since he did not believe in government issued documents such as driver's licenses. Because she felt so strongly about the government's interference in the lives of citizens, she represented herself and failed to follow the procedures of the court, noting on several occasions that the court did not have jurisdiction over her (*Lynda Lyon Block*, 1996). Although she was very intelligent, Block would sometimes act as though she was illiterate. Aileen Wuornos has been the only woman sentenced to seven death sentences in the United States and has been identified as a serial killer. She started killing men in December 1989 and continued until November 1990. All of her victims that have been found were shot multiple times and robbed. The body of Peter Siems was never found. It is not clear as to why Wuornos continued to prostitute while maintaining a lesbian relationship with Tyria Moore. Both the state and defense experts noted that she (Wuornos) suffered from some mental deficiencies, but the state's expert contended that the severity of the defect was not to the point that she could not make the right decisions (*Wuornos v. State of Florida*, 1994). There was a break in the execution of women after the execution of Aileen Wuornos in 2002.

The next execution of a woman occurred in Texas in 2005. Frances Elaine Newton killed her entire family, a husband and two children, for pecuniary gain. All three victims had been shot to death. Five years later in 2010, Virginia executed Teresa Lewis, who hired two men to kill her husband and a stepson for the same reason, pecuniary gain. There was one execution of a woman in 2013 (Kimberly McCarthy in Texas); two in 2014 (Suzanne Basso and Lisa Coleman, both in Texas); and one in Georgia in 2015 (Kelly Gissendaner). As you can see, these executions follow the execution trend—most executions occur in the Southern region of the United States.

Of the executions that have occurred, three of the women, Allen, Wuornos, and Coleman, were in lesbian relationships. It is hard to determine if this extra-legal factor had any bearing on the convictions and sentences imposed given the heinousness of their crimes. Eight of the 16 women executed killed their spouses or significant other. Riggs and Newton killed their own children, while Lewis and Coleman killed someone else's child for whom their relationship could be identified as a stepparent

(Death Penalty Information Center Women and the Death Penalty, 2013). In recent years, we find a decline in the number of death sentences imposed for both men and women.

The death penalty in the United States started to decline during the period 1996–2005 and has continued losing support (Death Penalty Information Center, 2015a). Previous research by Rice/ Kinder Institute for Urban Research (2000, 2014) found that when residents were asked in 2000 which penalty they preferred for first-degree murder, a large number of the respondents/residents in the Houston area preferred the death penalty; however, by 2014 that number had fallen significantly. During the same period, respondents/residents noted that they preferred life without parole 31% of the time in 2000, but by 2014, respondents/residents' support for life without parole rose to 39.1%. Other polls conducted by Pew Research Center (April, 2015), also revealed that support for the death penalty is declining and varies based on race, gender, religion, and political identity. Specifically, more whites (63%) support the death penalty than minority groups.

For 2015, overall there were only 49 new death sentences imposed. "Nearly two-thirds of the new death sentences in the U.S. in 2015 were imposed in the same 2% of American counties that have disproportionately accounted for more than half of all death sentences in the past" (Death Penalty Information Center (2015b)/The Death Penalty in 2015: Year End Report). In 2016, death sentences were at an all-time low. The notable absence of death sentences in 2016 offers hope that the decline will continue.

Summary

As we began our discussion on juveniles, stating that we moved from tolerance to intolerance in relation to juveniles and their behavior, we have now come full circle returning to a period of tolerance or exercising the duty of society to protect its children. Court rulings have established that the safeguards of due process are necessary to protect anyone who experiences the criminal justice process. These sentencing (age, class, and sex) disparities are not the only disparities that exist in our criminal justice system. These sentencing disparities and differences within society force us to realize how fluid meanings and norms are as well as recognize the power of wealth and position as a means of change.

It appears that capital punishment has run its cycle in American history if year-end 2016 is an indicator. Given that the overall support for the death penalty has dropped in the United States for all offenders, we believe that trend will continue and there will be fewer death sentences imposed in the coming years. As a result of the decline in death sentences, we should move toward eliminating capital punishment for a more humane type of sentencing that serves the purpose of punishment.

References

Belknap, J. (2015). *The invisible woman: Gender, crime and justice* (4th ed.). Samford, CT: Cengage.

Bilchik, S. (1997). *Juvenile justice reform initiatives in the states (1994–1996)*. Washington, DC: Office of Juvenile Justice and Delinquency Prevention.

Burroughs, R. (1985). *Deposition (CC-81–865–60)*. Tuscaloosa, AL: Tuscaloosa Court Reporting.

Cantwell, M. (1980, December1). *Capital punishment 1979 national prisoner statistics.* Retrieved November 15, 2015 from www.bjs.gov/index.cfm?ty=pdetail&iid=3305

Cantwell, M. (1983, July 1). *Capital punishment 1982*. Retrieved November 15, 2015 from www.bjs.gov/index. cfm?ty=pdetail&iid=3410

Carroll, J. (1997). Images of women and capital sentencing among female offenders: Exploring the outer limits of the eighth amendment and articulated theories of justice. *Texas Law Review, 75*, 1413–1453.

Chambliss, W., & Seidman, R. (1971). *Law, order, and power*. Reading, MA: Addison-Wesley Publishing Company.

Death Penalty Information Center. (2013). *Women and the Death Penalty*. Washington, D.C. Retrieved November 21, 2015 from www.deathpenaltyinformationcenter.org/women-and-death-penalty#facts

Death Penalty Information Center. (2015a). *Facts about the Death Penalty*. Washington, DC: Death Penalty Information Center.

Death Penalty Information Center. (2015b). *The Death Penalty use in 2015: Year end report*. Washington, DC: Death Penalty Information Center.

Decker, S., Wright, R., Redfern, A., & Smith. D. (1993). A woman's place is in the home. *Justice Quarterly, 19,* 143–162.

Denny, K. (2011). Gender in context, content, and approach: Comparing gender messages in girl Scout and Boy Scout handbooks. *Gender and Society, 25*(1), 27–47.

Erez, E. (1989). Gender, rehabilitation, and probation decisions. *Criminology, 27*(2), 307–327.

Fair Punishment Project. (2016). *America's top five deadliest prosecutors: How overzealous personalities drive the Death Penalty.* Cambridge, MA: Harvard Law School.

Farnworth, M., & Teske, R., Jr. (1995). Gender differences in felony court processing: Three hypotheses of disparity. *Women and Criminal Justice, 6*(2), 23–44.

Foley, L. (1987). Florida after the Furman decision: The effect of extralegal factors on the processing of capital offense cases. *Behavioral Science and the Law, 5*(4), 457–465.

Garfinkel, H. (1956). Conditions of successful degradation ceremonies. *American Journal of Sociology, 61*(5), 420–424. University of Chicago Press.

Gillespie, L. (1986). *Differential death: Executed women.* Paper presented at the Western Society of Criminology Meeting. Newport beach, CA.

Gillespie, L. (2009). *Executed women in the 20th and 21st centuries.* Landham, MD: University Press of America.

Hoff, J. (1991). *Law, gender & injustice: A legal history of U.S. women.* New York: New York University Press.

Hudson, J. (1988). *Deposition (CV-87-C-2046-W).* Tuscaloosa, AL: Donna Skinner Court Reporting.

Johnson, A. (2014). *The gender knot: Unraveling our patriarchal legacy* (3rd ed.). Philadelphia, PA: Temple University Press.

Kruttschnitt, C. (1982). Respectable women and the law. *The Sociological Quarterly, 23*(2), 221–234.

Lorber, J. (1994). *Paradoxes of gender.* New Haven, CT: Yale University Press.

Mann, C. (1984). *Female crime and delinquency.* Tuscaloosa, AL: University of Alabama Press.

Mantsios, G. (2013). Media magic: Making class invisible. In T. Ore (Ed.), *The social construction of difference & inequality: Race, class, gender, and sexuality* (6th ed., pp. 91–100). New York, NY: McGraw-Hill.

Minsker, N. (2009). Prosecutorial misconduct in Death Penalty cases. *California Western Law Review, 45*(2), 373–404.

Morgan, E. (2012). Women on death row. In R. Murskain (Ed.), *Women and justice: It's a crime* (5th ed., pp. 468–484). New York, NY: Pearson.

Morgan, P., & Joe, K. (1996). Citizens and outlaws. *Journal of Drug Issues, 26,* 125–142.

NAACP Legal Defense and Educational Fund, INC. (2000–2016). *Death row U.S.A.* New York, NY: NAACP Legal Defense and Educational Fund.

North Carolina Department of Public Safety Offender Public Information. (2016). View Offender: Velma Barfield. Retrieved January 4, 2016 from http://webapps6.doc.state.nc.us/opi/viewoffender.do?method=view&offenderID=0019092&SENTENCEINFO=yes

Personal Communication. (1998). *Death row interviews by Etta F. Morgan at Tutwiler prison.* Montgomery, AL: Etta Morgan.

Pew Research Center. (April 2015). Less support for death penalty, especially among democrats: Supporters, opponents see risk of executing the innocent. Washington, D.C.: Pew Research Center.

Phillips, S. (2009). Status disparities in the capital of Capital Punishment. *Law & Society Review, 43*(4), 807–838.

Pollock, J. (2002). *Women, prison and crime* (2nd ed.). Independence, KY: Cengage.

Price, B., & Sokoloff, N. (1995). *The criminal justice system and women: Offenders, victims, and workers* (2nd ed.). New York: McGraw Hill.

Reiman, J., & Leighton, P. (2012). *The rich get richer and the poor get prison: Ideology, class, and criminal justice* (10th ed.). New York: Routledge.

Rice/Kinder Institute for Urban Research. (2000–2014). *Whichpen survey.* Houston, TX: Rice/Kinder Institute for Urban Research.

Roberts, D. (Summer, 1994). The meaning of gender equality in criminal law. *Journal of Criminal Law and Criminology, 85*(1), 1–14.

Schechter-Ryan, S. (1982, December 1). *Capital punishment 1981: National prisoner statistics.* Retrieved November 15, 2015 from www.bjs.gov/index.cfm?ty=pdetail&iid=3409

Snell, T. (1999, December 12). *Capital punishment 1998.* Retrieved November 15, 2015 from www.bjs.gov/index.cfm?ty=pdetail&iid=459

Snell, T. (2000, December). Capital punishment 1999. Retrieved November 15, 2015 from www.bjs.gov/content/pub/pdf/cp99.pdf.

Snell, T. (2014 December 9). *Capital punishment, 2013-statistical tables.* Retrieved November 15, 2015 from www.bjs.gov/index.cfm?ty=pdetail&iid=5156

Shatz, S., & Shatz, N. (2012). Chivalry is not dead: Murder, gender, and the Death Penalty. *Berkeley Journal of Gender, Law & Justice, 27*(1), 64–112.

Sommers, I., & Baskin, D. (1993). The situational context of violent female offending. *Journal of Research in Crime and Delinquency, 30*, 136–162.

Spohn, C., & Spears, J. (1997). Gender and case processing decisions: A comparison of case outcomes for male and female defendants charged with violent felonies. *Women & Criminal Justice, 8*(3), 29–59.

Steffensmeier, D., & Demuth, S. (2006). Does gender modify the effects of race-ethnicity on criminal sanctioning? Sentences for male and female white, black, and Hispanic defendants. *Journal of Quantitative Criminology, 22*, 241–261.

Streib, V. (2003). Executing women, juveniles, and the mentally retarded: Second class citizens in capital punishment. In J. Acker, R. Bohm, & C. Lanier (Eds.), *America's experiment with capital punishment: Reflections on the past, present, and future of the ultimate penal sanction* (2nd ed., pp. 301–323). Durham, NC: Carolina Academic Press.

Streib, V. (2005). *The juvenile Death Penalty today: Death sentences and executions for juvenile crimes*, January 1, 1973-February 28, 2005, Issue #77. Ada, Ohio: Author.

Streib, V. (2013). *Death Penalty for female offenders*, January 1, 1973, through December 31, 2012. Author.

Vanneman, R., & Cannon, L. (1987). Class divisions and status rankings: The social psychology of American stratification. In R. Vanneman & L. Cannon (Eds.) *The American perception of class* (pp.39–52). Philadelphia: Temple University Press

Visher, C. (1983). Chivalry in arrest decisions. *Criminology, 21*(1), 5–28.

Zingraff, M., & Thompson, R. (1984). Differential sentencing of men and women in the U.S.A. *International Journal of the Sociology of Law, 12*, 401–413.

Cases Cited

Alabama v. Haney, CC-87-559 (1988).

Alabama v. Thomas, CC-81-865 (1981).

Atkins v. Virginia, 536 U.S.304 (2002).

Ballard v. United States, 329 U.S. 187 (1946).

Batson v. Kentucky, 476 U.S. 79 (1986).

Beets v. State, 767 S.W. 2d. 711 (TX. Cr. App. 1987).

Bradwell v. Illinois, 83 U.S. 130 (1872).

Brady v. Maryland, 373 U.S. 83 (1963).

Buenoano v. State, 478 So.2d. 387 (FLA App. 1985).

Buenoano v. State, 527 So.2d. 194 (FLA 1988).

Butler v. State, 608 So.2d 314 (Miss 1992).

Caldwell v. Mississippi, 472 U.S. 320 (1985).

Craig v. Boren, 429 U.S. 190, (1976).

Cuyler v. Sullivan, 446 U.S. 335 (1980).

Dothard v. Rawlinson, 433 U.S. 321 (1977).

Douglas v. California, 372, U.S. 353 (1963).

Eddings v. Oklahoma, 455 U.S. 164 (1982).

Evitts v. Lucey, 469 U.S. 387 (1985).

Frontiero v. Richardson, 411 U.S. 677 (1973).

Foster v. Chatman, No. 14-8349, (October 2015).

Furman v. Georgia, 408 U.S. 238 (1972).

Gideon v. Wainwright, 372 U.S. 335 (1963).

Glasser v. United States, 315 U.S. 827 (1942).

Hoyt v. Florida, 368 U.S. 57 (1961).

In re Gault, 387 U.S. 1 (1967).

In re Stanford, 123 S. Ct. 472 (2002).

In re Winship, 397, U.S. (1970).

International Union v. Johnson Controls, 499 U.S. 187 (1991).

J.E.B. v. Alabama, 511 U.S. 127 (1994).

Kent v. United States, 383 U.S. 541, (1966).

Lockett v. Ohio, 438 U.S. 586 (1978).

Lynda Lyon Block, CR-94-0529 (1996).

McCoy v. State of Delaware, No. 558, 2012 and 595 (2012).

McKeiver v. Pennsylvania, 403 U.S. 528 (1971).

Mooney v. Holohan, 294 U.S. 103 (1935).

Muller v. Oregon, 208 U.S. 412 (1908).
Powell v. Alabama, 287 U.S. 45 (1932).
R. David Favata, Esquire, No. 303 (2015).
Reed v. Reed, 404 U.S. 71 (1971).
Riggs v. State, 339 Ark. 111, 3 S.W. 3d. 305 (Ark. 1999).
Roper v. Simmons, 125 S. Ct. 1183 (2005).
Stanford v. Kentucky, 492 U.S. 361 (1989).
State v. Barfield, 259 S.E.2d510 (N.C. 1979).
State v. Gardner, 157 Arizona 541, 760 P 2d 541 (1988).
Seubert v. State, 749 SW 2d 585 (Texas Criminal Appeals 1988).
Simmons v. Roper, 112 S.W. 3d. 397 (Mo. 2003).
Swain v. Alabama, 380 U.S. 202, 203, 205, (1965).
Taylor v. Louisiana, 419 U.S. 522 (1975).
Thompson v. Oklahoma, 487 U.S. 815 (1988).
Tucker v. State, 771 S.W. 2d. 523 (Tex. Cr. App. 1988).
Wuornos v. State, 644 So. 2d. 1000 (1994).
Young v. Zant, 506 F. Supp.274 (1980).

31

RACE AND THE DEATH PENALTY

Kristie R. Blevins and Kevin I. Minor

"Time for a tree and a rope."

(Facebook text posted in 2016 by a sitting judge in Burnet County,
Texas underneath a mug shot of Otis Tyrone McKane, a black man arrested for
killing a white San Antonio police officer; the judge was provided racial sensitivity training.)

Various types and levels of racial oppression have been pervasive in the United States since African slaves were introduced in the colony of Jamestown, Virginia, in 1619 (Sluiter, 1997). America's culture and social climate have undergone drastic changes throughout different eras in history. Until about a century and half ago, the majority of black individuals in the U.S. were considered to be property. After slavery was abolished, African Americans were seen as an inferior class and treated accordingly, as exemplified by practices like segregation and convict leasing in the South. It was only a bit over 50 years ago, with the 1964 Civil Rights Act, that all American citizens were legally guaranteed equal rights and privileges as provided by the Constitution. Nonetheless, there remains evidence of structural inequalities based on race in contemporary social institutions such as education, employment, housing, and the criminal justice system (Gaddis, 2015).

Discrimination based on race should be identified and remedied in all social establishments, but it is especially important to do so in the one system that can literally determine whether someone lives or dies—the death penalty process. The capital punishment system in America has been challenged on many grounds but is still an option for eligible murder cases in 31 states, the federal government, and the U.S. military. One of the most commonly cited and persistent problems with the death penalty in the U.S. is inequality of sentencing based on race of the defendant and/or the victim, and a multitude of empirical studies have presented solid evidence that racial disparities are present in the modern system, just as they were when the system was established.

This chapter provides an overview of what is known about race and the death penalty in the U.S., beginning with the early years through the *Furman* case in 1972. Next is a discussion of important death penalty challenges and the resulting changes that created the current capital punishment process, followed by a review of the Supreme Court case that challenged the death penalty based directly on race. A summary of research concerning racial disparities in the contemporary system is presented next, and some possible explanations about how and why racial disparities enter the system are offered afterward. The chapter ends with an overview of possible paths for recourse for cases in which there are racial biases and conclusions based on the information presented.

The Pre-*Furman* Death Penalty: Race and Capital Punishment in America Through 1972

Many early American political leaders and their constituents recognized the country should have a justice system of its own, a system that provided certain rights to citizens and was not based entirely on the British code. By the time the U.S. Constitution was ratified by the original 13 colonies in 1787 and the Bill of Rights was added in 1791, it contained some guaranteed freedoms and rights that were not present in the prior English system. When individuals were convicted of committing crimes, reformation was recognized as a primary underlying philosophy for the correctional system, but residents also desired elements of retribution (Tongue, 2015). This retributive philosophy carries the assumption that the punishment should fit the crime, that everyone convicted of a particular criminal offense should receive the same punishment regardless of individual characteristics or circumstances. Historically, though, retribution has been problematic in its application to sentencing for many types of crimes, even under sentencing guidelines, because individual characteristics such as gender, education, and race somehow manage to infiltrate the process and create disparities based on factors not related to the case (Mustard, 2001).

Evidence suggests that one particular individual characteristic, race, has resulted in disparities in the American capital punishment system from its inception until the present day. These disparities were not unexpected in the early years, as there were basically two sets of laws, one for whites and one for blacks. That is, many states, especially Southern states, implemented separate criminal codes for minorities. These codes served as a set of laws specifically for black individuals and included some offenses that were not considered crimes if committed by a white person. Further, many of these codes stipulated that a black person could be executed as punishment for *any* crime. These codes were amended during the first two decades of the 1800s but still allowed for vast inconsistencies based on race. For example, a black man could be executed for crimes such as rebellion, burglary, and assaulting a white female, while a white man would receive much less severe penalties for the same crimes (Allen & Clubb, 2008; Steiker & Steiker, 2015).

Separate criminal codes were abolished by the end of reconstruction in 1877 and, aside from Jim Crow laws authorizing racial segregation, criminal laws and prescribed punishments were supposed to be applied to everyone in a given jurisdiction. In other words, the laws and system theoretically would be equivalent for everyone. However, this egalitarian ideology was belied by widespread vigilante lynchings, most of which involved black victims in the South (Zimring, 2003). Lynchings occurred throughout the early period of capital punishment (i.e., before 1930) and were not exclusive to the South, but they became particularly frequent there between 1880 and 1930, when nearly 2,500 blacks are estimated to have been killed by mostly all white mobs (Paternoster, Brame, & Bacon, 2008). Similarly, Garland (2005) estimates that of some 4,000 documented lynchings across the nation between 1882 and 1940, 300–400 were public torture lynchings concentrated in Southern locales, in which victims were publically tortured and humiliated before being put to death. These aggravated murders were an assertion of white supremacy in attempt to preserve racial caste at a time when traditions were threatened by change in the wake of a breakdown of Reconstruction. Moreover, Garland observes that public torture lynchings were frequently condoned and sometimes participated in by local legal officials. Indeed, as Banner's (2006, p. 106) historiography reveals of lynching generally, "the line between a lynching and an official execution could be thin." Not surprisingly, lynching was especially common for black males thought to have violated sexual norms with white females. And modern era death sentences and executions have been concentrated disproportionately in states where lynching was historically most common (Zimring, 2003).

Many of the details of capital cases prior to 1972 were never recorded or have been lost, but there is some basic information concerning dates, race and age of defendant, and type of crime committed for most individuals legally executed in the U.S. Aggregate racial comparisons of those executed with the racial makeup of the population provide anecdotal evidence of the racial discrimination that existed. It should be noted that there are some limitations with early census records because they were based primarily on incorporated areas with populations of 100,000 or more, but they estimate that African Americans comprised 9.7 to 19.3% of the total population in the U.S. from 1790 to 1970. That means African Americans accounted for, on average, about 13% of those living in the U.S. during that time period. This average is skewed by the larger percentages of African Americans reported during the years when slavery was legal. African Americans constituted 17.53% of the people in the areas included in the 1790–1860 census, though 88.08% of them were considered to be the property of slave owners. The average percentage of African Americans in those same areas decreased to 11% for the period 1870 to 1970 (Gibson & Jung, 2005). Keep these general percentages in mind while viewing the racial breakdown of executions.

Examinations of existing information on rape cases prior to *Furman* have shown that black men convicted of raping a white woman were almost always executed (or lynched), while white men were rarely even prosecuted for raping a black female (Paternoster, 1991). Historical statistics indicate there were a total of 455 executions for rape from 1930 to 1972. Of these, 405 defendants were black, 48 were white, and two were from other racial groups. Put simply, about 90% of those executed for rape during the premodern period of capital punishment (1930–1972) were black (Bessler, 1997; Williamson, 1984), a number that is especially startling when considering that blacks made up only about 12% of the American population during that time (Mello, 1995) and that black males constituted around 6%. Furthermore, data from rape convictions during 1945 to 1965 reveal that blacks convicted of rape were almost seven times more likely than whites to receive a death sentence (Wolfgang & Riedel, 1973, 1975). It is also notable that there were no white men executed for the crime of rape from 1930 to 1950; only African American men were executed for rape during those two decades (Hartung, 1952).

It has been argued that racial breakdowns of these defendants alone are not very informative to the extent that people of a certain race are more prone to commit capital rape. The combined defendant-victim racial effect, however, is more informative. For instance, a Florida study showed that 5% of white males convicted of raping white females were sentenced to death from 1940 to 1964, while 54% of cases in which a black male raped a white female resulted in a capital sentence. Notably, not one of the eight white males convicted of raping a black female was sentenced to die for his crime (Bedau, 1982). Consistently, empirical research has shown that the race of both the offender and the victim is the only statistically significant variable that explains disproportionate death sentences for the crime of rape in this country (Archibald, 2015; Marquart, Ekland-Oison, & Sorensen, 1994).

Nationwide data for pre-*Furman* executions also show disproportionate percentages of black defendants were executed for murder and other crimes as well (Bohm, 1991; Schneider & Smykla, 1991). Of 11,528 recorded executions for murder, 5,103 (44.27%) were African Americans and 5,203 (45.13%) were white. For crimes other than rape and murder, such as burglary and theft, 54.82% of those executed were black and 32.86% were white. And of the 506 pre-*Furman* executions for unspecified felonies or unknown crimes, 294 (77.87%) were African Americans, while only 43 (8.50%) were white defendants (Blanco, 2016). Moreover, comparisons of those executed during this time period indicate that the average age of black men put to death was significantly lower than the mean age of white men (Bowers, 1984). In general, it appears as though the public was much quicker to execute African Americans than whites during the pre-*Furman* era. Although early data regarding race of victims are limited for crimes other than rape, it seems that this pattern was especially true for those who committed crimes with white victims.

These types of disparities and other inconsistencies based on factors such as race became an impetus for the significant challenges to the constitutionality of the death penalty that occurred in the 1960s and 1970s. Some of these challenges were unsuccessful, while others resulted in procedural changes intended to safeguard against racial discrimination and other injustices in the capital punishment process. But have these safeguards resulted in meaningful changes in the application of the death penalty? Have modern procedures created a more equal process?

Challenging Disparities Within the Changing Social Context

The American capital punishment process has been challenged on many grounds, though few cases make it to the U.S. Supreme Court. Prior to the 1970s, the court considered challenges based on issues such as the constitutionally of particular methods of execution (*In re Kemmler*, 1890; *Malloy v. South Carolina*, 1915; *Wilkerson v. Utah*, 1879), public versus private executions (*Rooney v. North Dakota*, 1905), legal representation of indigent defendants (*Powell v. Alabama*, 1932), failed execution attempts (*Francis v. Resweber*, 1947), and exclusion of potential jurors (*Witherspoon v. Illinois*, 1968). The overt issues of disparities and possible discrimination based on race or other individual characteristics of the defendant and/or the victim were not directly addressed by the court during this era. But inconsistencies in capital sentencing began to draw the attention of legal advocates and reformers.

Perceptible changes in the social context of American culture began to emerge in the wake of World War II. Activists called attention to the fact that African American soldiers had been engaged in a war to secure freedom for the oppressed while they were facing numerous types and sources of oppression themselves. In 1948, President Truman issued Executive Order 9981 to end racial segregation in the armed forces and mandate equal opportunities and treatment of military personnel regardless of race, religion, or national origin. Four years later, members of the Supreme Court agreed to hear five school desegregation cases simultaneously, as *Brown v. Board of Education* (1954), and eventually ruled that racially segregated schools were unequal and inferior for African American children and were therefore in violation of the Equal Protection Clause of the Fourteenth Amendment. These events accentuated the degree of existing racial prejudice and created conditions that fostered collective efforts to garner equal rights—all of the privileges and immunities guaranteed in the constitution—for all citizens. These cooperative endeavors, as part of the civil rights movement, gained momentum throughout the 1950s, peaked in the late 1960s, and advanced equality for many matters. For example, President Johnson signed the Civil Rights Act of 1964. This decree was intended to provide equal access to public places, employment, and schools, and it prohibited discrimination based on race, religion, sex, or national origin. The law made racial segregation unlawful and was later expanded with explicit statements to provide equality for housing and voting policies as well. The unrest and acts of violence brought about by civil rights antagonists should not be overlooked, but, ultimately, egalitarianism triumphed, at least as written in law and policy. But would this new equality actually come to fruition in the real world? Would everyone have similar opportunities to achieve the American dream? And, when society was wronged, would punishments for those wrongs be consistent based on characteristics of the crimes rather than attributes of the individuals responsible? Would the ultimate punishment be meted out in a more consistent manner? Answers to these questions would certainly require time and a review of evidence, but it was the ideal time for reformers to call attention to, challenge, and provide suggestions to improve systemic flaws—including shortcomings of the capital punishment system—that perpetuated disparities and discrimination based on race.

The procedures in death penalty jurisdictions were set up so that the life or death decision in eligible cases was based on decisions of two primary sets of actors in the process. First, prosecutors had discretion whether to seek a death sentence versus a prison sentence. If a death penalty was sought and guilt was established, the jury (and, in a few places, judges) made the final decision on the punishment to be administered (Baldus & Woodworth, 2003a). Activists voiced concerns about the nearly unrestricted amount of discretion in the process and how it could lead to inconsistent, or arbitrary and capricious, application of capital sentences based on factors such as race. During the 1960s, a recommended guide to state legislatures was released by the American Law Institute in the form of the Model Penal Code. The suggestions in this document were intended, in part, to constrain some of the discretion in death penalty cases. Specifically, there were recommendations that capital punishment should be an option to prosecutors for only certain types of cases and that jury members should have to make decisions about the presence of aggravating and mitigating factors in each case before making the sentencing decision (Baldus & Woodworth, 2003a). Some of the institute's recommendations were the center of a death penalty challenge ruled on by the Supreme Court in *McGautha v. California* (1971).

Attorneys for the petitioner in *McGautha* argued that capital juries should have structured guidance in death penalty cases and that there should be a distinct phase for determining guilt of a defendant before a second penalty phase reserved for the purpose of deliberating on the punishment. The court ruled that "[f]or a court to attempt to catalog the appropriate factors in this elusive area could inhibit rather than expand the scope of consideration, for no list of circumstances [for jury consideration] would ever be really complete" (p. 192). The court went on to rule that the Constitution only guarantees the rights of defendants be maintained throughout the process of a fair trial, and that a capital trial with separate guilt and punishment phases does not make the capital process a better one. Nonetheless, these same types of issues, as well as others, were viewed differently by the court just a year later in *Furman v. Georgia*.

1972 to 1976: The Moratorium Era

Executions ceased in the U.S. after June 1967 pending examination of legal issues by the Supreme Court. To build wider support for their attack on the constitutionality of capital punishment, the National Association for the Advancement of Colored People (NAACP) Legal Defense and Educational Fund (LDF) attorneys who argued *Furman v. Georgia* (1972) had broadened their focus from racial discrimination to arbitrariness more generally (Mandery, 2013). The *Furman* decision involved three black petitioners who had been sentenced to death; two were convicted of rape and the other of murder (a second murder case from California was initially part of the group, but that state's supreme court ruled its capital punishment law unconstitutional earlier in 1972). After reviewing the facts of the cases, the court ruled that the administration of capital punishment at the time violated the Eighth Amendment's provision against cruel and unusual punishment and the Fourteenth Amendment's provision of equal protection of the law. The court based its ruling on the fact that capital punishment was administered in an "arbitrary and capricious" manner at the time because "juries (or judges, as the case may be) have practically untrammeled discretion to let an accused live or insist that he die" (p. 250). Certain justices realized that those with less power (i.e., African Americans and other minorities) in society were given death sentences and executed while those with more power (i.e., whites) received prison sentences. Justice Douglas wrote that the capital process was "pregnant with discrimination" and cited a statement by former Attorney General Ramsey Clark, who said, "It is the poor, the sick, the ignorant, the powerless, and the hated who are executed" (p. 251). In fact, those with power in society "are given prison terms, not sentenced to death" (p. 252). Justice Stuart, who also concurred with the opinion, compared receiving a sentence of death to getting struck by lightning. He concluded that the current administration of capital punishment was in direct violation of the Eighth and Fourteenth Amendments because it was "so wantonly and freakishly imposed" (p. 310). Justice Brennan, who along with Justice Marshall thought capital sentences were constitutionally unacceptable as a form of punishment, agreed that death sentences were not fairly applied. Justice Brennan also suggested that there was no rational explanation for why such a small number of people were sentenced to death, while many who committed the same crimes went to prison. Therefore, there must be irrational reasons, such as racial biases, that explain why only a small percentage of those eligible actually receive the death penalty.

The *Furman* ruling brought about a temporary moratorium on capital sentencing in the United States, allowing the more than 550 inmates awaiting execution on death row at the time to have their sentences commuted to life in prison (Bedau, 1997). The backlash against the ruling motivated several state legislatures to amend and write new capital sentencing procedures that would meet the constitutional requirements of the Eighth and Fourteenth Amendments. Four years after *Furman*, the

U.S. Supreme Court elected to again consider the constitutionality of the death penalty as it reviewed revised capital sentencing laws in several states. The court examined two different approaches to improve capital sentencing procedures from five states. Some states implemented mandatory death sentences for particular crimes, which were challenged in *Roberts v. Louisiana* (1976) and *Woodson v. North Carolina* (1976). The court did not accept the mandatory sentencing legislation in these cases but did go on to accept the guided discretion models set forth in three other cases. The Supreme Court ruled that administration of capital sentences could meet the requirements of the Eighth and Fourteenth Amendments if the states would give capital jurors guided discretion as set forth in *Gregg v. Georgia* (1976); *Jurek v. Texas* (1976); and *Proffitt v. Florida* (1976). States could meet constitutional requirements if they created statutes that would give capital jurors information and instructions to guide them in deciding the appropriate punishment. States created lists of aggravating circumstances, described procedures that should be used in weighting aggravating and mitigating circumstances, and implemented bifurcated capital trials with comparative proportionality and appellate review (Poveda, 2009). These changes served to limit death eligibility to cases deemed most appropriate for capital punishment (Shatz & Dalton, 2013).

The next year, the class of eligible cases was restricted further when the court ruled that death was not an appropriate sentence for rape of an adult when the victim was not killed (*Coker v. Georgia*, 1977). This decision was not made on grounds of the tremendous racial disparities evident within the system but because "a sentence of death is grossly disproportionate and excessive punishment [when the victim did not die] and is therefore forbidden by the Eighth Amendment" (p. 592). As was true of the arbitrariness logic used in *Furman*, this reasoning permitted the court to continue circumventing the issue of racial discrimination in capital punishment and perpetuate an ideology that, instead of being intractably grounded in racist history, problems with the death penalty are rectifiable through legalistic decree (Steiker & Steiker, 2016). Nevertheless, once a case was deemed death eligible, jury members continued to have a great deal of discretion in their sentencing decisions as long as they followed the structured guidelines or jury instructions. And there is still the question of whether average jury members can comprehend legal guidelines and instructions and ultimately apply the death penalty in a consistent and unbiased manner from case to case (Baldus, Pulaski, & Woodworth, 1983; Baldus, Woodworth, and Pulaski, 1990; Bedau, 1997; Blankenship, Luginbuhl, Cullen, & Redick, 1997; Bowers, 1995; Bowers & Pierce, 1980; Diamond, 1993; Diamond & Levi, 1996; Luginbuhl, 1992; Luginbuhl & Howe, 1995).

There were other challenges to the death penalty after its reinstatement, beginning in 1976. Race was still a big issue for objectors, and the court still had not directly considered evidence concerning racial disparities and discrimination, or whether the post-*Furman* systems had resulted in a reduction in such inconsistencies (Baldus & Woodworth, 2003a). Perhaps part of the reluctance to challenge capital punishment with empirical findings based on race stemmed from the *Washington v. Davis* (1976) precedent. While this case was about employment procedures, not the death penalty, the court ruled that proof of disproportionate impact alone is not enough to establish unconstitutional discrimination.

The Case for Race: *McCleskey v. Kemp* (1987)

The case that some argue was the most profound challenge to the death penalty based on race, and indeed to capital punishment generally, was decided in 1987 (Kirchmeier, 2015; Shatz & Dalton, 2013). The attorney serving as director for the NAACP's LDF argued the case for the petitioner in *McCleskey v. Kemp* (1987). This case marked the first time that the U.S. Supreme Court considered a direct constitutional claim that capital punishment was administered in a racially discriminatory manner.

McCleskey, a black male who was sentenced to death for killing a white police officer during a robbery, petitioned the U.S. Supreme Court, claiming that Georgia's capital sentencing system violated the Eighth Amendment's provision against cruel and unusual punishment and the Fourteenth Amendment's guarantee of equal protection of the law because it was administered in a racially discriminatory manner. McCleskey claimed that those who were convicted of killing whites were more likely to receive a death sentence than all other defendants. He also maintained that black defendants were more likely to be sentenced to die than white defendants. McCleskey insisted that he was discriminated against because of his race and that of his victim and that the large amount of discretion involved in the process could have allowed racial prejudices to influence juror decisions (Flexon, 2012; Patterson, 1995).

In his appeal, McCleskey's lawyer presented statistical evidence of racial disparities that was offered by Baldus et al. (1990). The Baldus study was based on data from more than 2,000 Georgia homicides from the 1970s. The analyses of the homicide data revealed that 11% of defendants with white victims received a capital sentence, while only 1% of those convicted of killing blacks were sentenced to death. They also concluded that black defendants convicted of killing white victims, like McCleskey, were the most likely to receive a sentence of death. Additionally, after controlling for a myriad of variables related to case characteristics, defendants convicted of killing white victims were about 4.3 times more likely to receive a death sentence than those who killed black victims (Baldus et al., 1990; Baldus & Woodworth, 2003a); black defendants who killed white victims were most likely to be sentenced to death versus any other interracial victim and defendant combination (Baldus et al., 1990; Flexon, 2012).

The court recognized the Baldus Study as valid and agreed that it suggested racial disparities were evident within the Georgia capital system. Baldus, Woodworth, and Pulaski (1994) cited part of a memo written while the case was pending. In this memo, Justice Scalia wrote about his opinion that racial discrimination in capital punishment is "real, acknowledged in the decisions of this Court, and ineradicable" (p. 371). In the end, however, the court rejected both constitutional claims by a five to four vote and stated that the study was "insufficient to demonstrate discriminatory intent or unconstitutional discrimination in the Fourteenth Amendment context, [and] insufficient to show irrationality, arbitrariness and capriciousness under any kind of Eighth Amendment analysis" (*McCleskey v. Kemp*, 1987, p. 891). The court referred to the precedent set in previous cases that any defendant claiming a violation of the Fourteenth Amendment must prove that the jurors in his or her specific case purposefully discriminated against him or her, or that the statute in question was written with the purpose to create and maintain discrimination, which McCleskey was unable to do in his case (Flexon, 2012). Further, the court asserted that the discrepancies suggested by the Baldus study were not comparable to those revealed in *Furman v. Georgia* (1972) and that "apparent disparities in sentencing are an inevitable part of our criminal justice system" (p. 893). Some scholars believe that the *McCleskey* ruling created a burden of proof for claims of discrimination in death penalty cases that is far heavier than the standard used in more typical cases such as voting policies or employment discrimination (Cook & Kende, 1996).

While the court essentially blocked the discussion of discrimination based on race in death penalty cases within the courts, it ultimately shifted responsibility to Congress by advising McCleskey that his claims would better be handled by the legislative bodies. The court reasoned that it does not make the laws and punishments; rather, it determines if they are applied constitutionally in each case. In this case, the question was whether the law of Georgia was applied properly. Accordingly, the court suggested that legislative bodies are better equipped to address problems with the statutes themselves (Alexander, 2014; Baldus & Woodworth, 2003a; Ross, 1997). In the end, then, *McCleskey* did not result in any changes or other mandates for capital punishment systems. Instead, the ruling effectively signaled the court's refusal to outlaw capital punishment even though the institution is racially biased (Kirchmeier, 2015). Rather than diverting focus from race by emphasizing arbitrariness or type of crime, the *McCleskey* Court framed race in terms of individualistic procedures rather than aggregate outcomes (Steiker & Steiker, 2016).

Post-*Furman* Research: Data From the Modern Era, 1976 to 2016

Reformers were anxious to see if the post-*Furman* statutory improvements would reduce racial biases in the administration of the death penalty. The first execution under the post-*Furman* guidelines took place in Utah on January 17, 1977, and involved a white defendant convicted of killing a white male victim. The next four executions (two in 1979, one each in 1981 and 1982) also involved white defendants with white victims. The sixth execution, which occurred in Texas in December of 1982, was a black man convicted of killing a white man. The following three executions, all in 1983, were white defendants with white victims, and the tenth execution, in Louisiana during December of 1983, was a black defendant convicted of murdering a white man. In other words, eight of the first ten defendants executed under modern death penalty statutes were white. Perhaps more importantly, the victims were white in nine of the ten cases. That trend concerning race of defendant did not continue very long. Table 31.1 contains a racial breakdown of the 1,437 defendants executed in the U.S. from the time the death penalty was reinstated in 1976 until October 1, 2016, as well as the victims associated with these cases. Table 31.2 presents the combinations of the races of the defendants and victims for the 1,403 defendants who did not have multiple victims of different races (34 individuals executed since *Furman* did have multiple victims of different races). Data for both of these tables were retrieved from the most recent *Death Row U.S.A.* quarterly report sponsored by the LDF (Fins, 2016).

Raw numbers like the ones in Tables 31.1 and 31.2 have often been presented as evidence of racial disparities in the application of the death penalty in this country. For example, Table 31.1 shows that 34.52% of those executed were African American, while African Americans make up only 13.3% of the U.S. population (U.S. Census Bureau, 2016). More specifically, all but four executed blacks were men, and black males comprise 6 to 7% of the population. But, are such numbers enough to establish true racial disparities within the system? What if individuals of a certain race are more prone to

Table 31.1 Race of Defendants Executed Post-*Furman* Through October 1, 2016.

Race	Defendants (N = 1,437)		Victims (N = 2,106)	
	N	%	N	%
White	799	55.60	1,593	75.64
Black	496	34.52	323	15.34
Hispanic	119	8.28	145	6.89
Native American	16	1.11	5	0.24
Asian	7	0.49	40	1.90

Table 31.2 Defendant/Victim Racial Combinations (*n* = 1403).

Race of Defendants (N = 1403)	Race of Victims					
	White		Black		Other Race	
	N	%	N	%	N	%
White	740	52.74	20	1.43	23	1.64
Black	282	20.10	167	11.90	35	2.49
Other Race	67	4.78	3	0.21	66	4.70
Total:	1,089	77.62	190	13.54	124	8.84

committing death-eligible crimes? According to the Federal Bureau of Investigation (2016), African Americans (primarily men) have been arrested for about half of the murders and nonnegligent homicides reported to police annually. Is a comparison of that 50% to the 34.52% of executions enough to establish racial disparities in the other direction?

What about race of victims? A review of supplementary homicide reports shows that African Americans (again, mostly males) consistently account for about half the murder victims each year (Federal Bureau of Investigation, 2016); yet only about 15% of the victims of executed defendants were African American (see Table 31.1). Table 31.2 reveals that 282 blacks were executed for killing whites, compared with only 20 whites executed for killing blacks. Further, a study of executions from 1977–2013 reported that just ten whites were executed following conviction for killing a black male (Baumgartner, Grigg, & Mastro, 2015). Data maintained by the Death Penalty Information Center (DPIC) show that of 1,448 executions carried out from 1977 through mid-March 2017, 11 executions involved white males convicted of killing at least one black male victim, while 159 involved black males convicted of killing at least one white male. Likewise, of 1,436 executions between 1977 and mid-2016, 150 (10.4%) involved a black male convicted of killing a white female. This compares with 14 executions of a white male for killing a black female. Almost 85% of the executions of black males convicted of killing white females occurred in the South; a quarter of all modern era executions in Alabama fit this profile, as did 17% of those in Louisiana and Virginia, respectively. Is this evidence of racial discrimination within America's capital punishment system? The answer, to date, is probably no. At the very least, politicians and policy makers want to see comparisons of cases that are truly similarly situated from a legal perspective. That is, they want to see what happens regarding race of the defendant and/or victim when other factors related to the case are held constant—when such variables are used as controls as they were in the Baldus et al. (1990) study presented in *McCleskey v. Kemp* (1987).

A plethora of research has been conducted in many jurisdictions in an attempt to provide valid, reliable, replicable findings in regard to race and the death penalty after controlling for other issues relating to the cases. In addition to the data presented in *McCleskey*, a couple of early studies set the tone for the many studies to come. One of the early studies of post-*Furman* cases used information from homicide reports in Louisiana from 1976 until the end of 1982. Results revealed that defendants charged with murdering white victims were two times as likely to receive a sentence of death compared to defendants who had killed African Americans, regardless of the race of the defendant and while controlling for a number of mitigating circumstances (Smith, 1987).

Similarly, a series of studies of capital cases in Kentucky suggested that a black defendant convicted of killing a white individual was significantly more likely to receive a death sentence than others who had been convicted of murder. Aside from race, the only other significant predictor of a black defendant receiving a capital sentence was if the defendant was charged with killing more than one person. These results held true even after controlling for factors such as the level of seriousness of the offense, prior criminal record of the defendant, and prior relationship of the defendant and victim (Keil & Vito, 1989, 1990, 1995).

Some researchers have asserted that racial disparities in certain jurisdictions can be explained by prior relationships between the defendant and the victim. For instance, black murderers with white victims have been shown to be significantly less likely to know their victims. These stranger killings might be viewed as more dangerous to jury members than murders that involve a family member, friend, or other acquaintance (Gillespie, Loughran, Smith, Fogel, & Bjerregaard, 2014). Given that white defendants were more likely to know their victims, the racial bias might actually be against the white offenders who received death sentences, because they were generally considered by jurors to be less dangerous than black defendants who received the death penalty (Heilbrun, Foster, & Golden, 1989; Paternoster, 1983).

Thomson (1997) found that white offenders received a capital sentence one and a half times as often as did minority offenders in Arizona. However, when examining the race of the victims, he found that defendants who had murdered a white victim received a death sentence twice as often as offenders who had killed a minority victim when controlling for other demographics of the defendant and victim and characteristics of the crime. When looking at the races of both the defendant and the victim, he found that minority defendants convicted of killing a white individual received the death penalty more than three times the rate of minorities who murder minority victims. Also, he found that whites who killed minorities were sentenced to death half as often as whites who killed other whites.

Many studies have explored relationships between application of the modern death penalty and race of the defendant, victim, and/or the combined races of defendants and victims. The important point is that the findings from most of these studies are consistent, regardless of details such as jurisdiction, number of years studied, research methodology, control variables, and data analysis techniques. Although there have been a few exceptions with inconsistent or null findings based on race (Marquart et al., 1994; Klein & Rolph, 1991), the overall consensus is that disparities based on race of the victims are typically present in death penalty cases. While the impact of race of defendant is much less consistent (Phillips, 2012), there is almost always evidence of disparities based solely on race of the victims or the racial combinations of the defendants and victims (Baldus & Woodworth, 2003b; Bowers, Steiner, & Sandys, 2001; Robinson, 2008; U.S. General Accounting Office, 1990; Williams & Holcomb, 2001).

These consistencies are summarized nicely in reviews of studies. The U.S. General Accounting Office (1990) conducted an evaluation of 28 prior studies concerning any relation of race of the defendant and victim to capital sentencing. After examining the quality of the studies and rating about 60% of them to be medium or high quality, the authors concluded that the race of the victim was influential throughout the entire capital process. They found that the majority of the studies provided some evidence that death sentences were more likely to be given to black offenders and strong evidence that death sentences were significantly more likely to be given in cases with a white victim. Taken together, these studies provided strong support for the hypothesis that the race of the victim was indicative of receiving a death sentence, while the relationship of the race of the defendant and likelihood of receiving a sentence of death was not as clear. These findings were consistent across the several states studied and the different methodologies used. A more recent review of 18 studies published from 1990 to 2003 produced similar results: defendants with white victims were significantly more likely to be sentenced to death than defendants with victims of other races (Baldus & Woodworth, 2003b). These reviews, as well as the vast body of individual studies, have helped to confirm that there are disparities based on race of victims and/or the combination of victim/defendant races in more than half of the 31 states with the death penalty, as well as the U.S. military system. In each of these jurisdictions, capital punishment was significantly more likely to be the result in cases with white victims as compared to cases with victims of other races (Baldus et al., 1990, 1994; Baldus, Grosso, Woodworth, & Newell, 2012; Baldus, Woodworth, & Grosso, 2002; Beckett & Evans, 2016; Bowers & Pierce, 1980; Fleury-Steiner, Dunn, & Fleury-Steiner, 2009; Gross & Mauro, 1989; Goldfarb, 2016; Heilbrun et al., 1989; Hindson, Potter, & Radelet, 2006; Holcomb, Williams, & Demuth, 2004; Jennings, Richards, Smith, Bjerregaard, & Fogel, 2014; Keil & Vito, 1989, 1990, 1995; Paternoster, 1983; Paternoster & Brame, 2003, 2008; Pasternoster, Brame, Bacon, & Ditchfield, 2004; Phillips, 2012; Pierce & Radelet, 2002, 2005; Radelet & Pierce, 1991, 2011a, 2011b; Smith, 1987; Sorensen & Wallace, 1995; Thomson, 1997; Unah, 2011; Williams & Holcomb, 2001).

Why Are There Racial Disparities in the Capital Punishment System?

An abundance of empirical studies have established that there are racial disparities, at least based on race of victims, within America's death penalty process. These findings inevitably lead to the question of why such disparities exist. Is it outright racial discrimination, or is the relationship being driven by other factors such as motivation for the crime, geographic region, social class (and its relationship with income and quality of attorney), or murder being committed during the course of other serious crimes (see Bright, 1994; Jennings et al., 2014; Stauffer, Smith, Cochran, Fogel, & Bjerregaard, 2006; Thomson, 1997; Williams, 2016)? Unfortunately, there is currently no clear answer, only speculation, for this troublesome question.

Although it is not clear where racial disparities enter the process, it is possible that they begin when prosecutors, who are overwhelmingly white, implement their discretion in charging a defendant with a capital crime and continue until the actual execution occurs (Bedau,1997; Hood, 1996; Paternoster, 1983). There is evidence to suggest that racial biases may be an issue throughout the entire process. For example, in his study of homicides in South Carolina, Paternoster (1983) found that the racial combination of victim and defendant had a strong effect on the prosecutor's decision to seek death even when holding other predictors constant, and Keil and Vito (1995, p. 27) concluded that capital jurors in Kentucky "evaluated aggravating circumstances differently, depending on the race of the killer and the victim."

Prosecutors must consider many variables as they are deciding whether to seek a death sentence. A key factor for prosecutors, especially if they are facing reelection, is meeting public demands. Baldus and Woodworth (2003a) suggest that highly visible cases, such as interracial cases that frequently receive high levels of media attention, often result in community outrage and the public's desire to seek the maximum punishment. Additionally, family members of white victims might be more intent on seeking the death penalty for the defendant, as whites are more likely to support capital punishment than blacks (Bohm, 2003; Unnever, Cullen, & Jonson, 2008). If prosecutors respond to these types of dynamics as expected, the result is usually increased percentages of capital cases with white victims.

Racial biases may also enter the process at the jury level, and many problems have been identified with the selection and final composition of capital juries. First, research has shown that sentencing decisions of potential jurors are likely influenced by their personal beliefs and individual characteristics, including religion, sex, age, level of education, political affiliation, and race (Applegate, Cullen, Fisher, & Vander Ven, 2000; Bohm, 2003; Boots, Cochran, & Heide, 2003; Eisenburg, Garvey, & Wells, 2001; Flexon, 2012; Lynch & Haney, 2000, 2009). The race of potential jurors is important because blacks are less likely than whites to support the death penalty (Cochran & Chamlin, 2006; Peffley & Hurwitz, 2007). Yet blacks are significantly less likely to serve on capital juries than whites because of issues such as low representation on lists from which prospective jury members are drawn, exclusion by prosecutors during the selection process, or hardship releases excusing them from service (Baldus & Woodworth, 2003a; Robinson, 2008). The U.S. Supreme Court has barred prosecutors from striking potential jurors based on race, but racial discrimination in jury selection is next to impossible for defendants to demonstrate in any but the most blatant instances. Research shows that potential jurors who are black continue to be excluded from capital juries at disproportionately high rates (Eisenberg, in press; Pollitt & Warren, 2016). Low numbers of African Americans serving on capital juries is especially problematic when considering that a sentence of death is given in about 72% of cases when there are no black jurors and about 43% of cases when there is at least one black male on the jury (Bowers et al., 2001).

In addition, there is evidence that potential jurors, as well as other actors in the system, bring certain predispositions into the process (Dovidio, Smith, Donnella, & Gaertner, 1997). Research has shown that white jurors are not apt to relate to African American defendants or victims and that both white and black individuals tend to view young African American males as predisposed to violence, threats to the community, and more deserving of punishment (Baldus & Woodworth, 2003a). Furthermore, a study of 445 jury-eligible individuals (82.7% of subjects were white) in six death penalty states found that participants associated whites with the words "worth" or "value" and blacks with the words "worthless" or "expendable." The researchers also discovered substantial evidence of implicit and explicit racial biases that were more pronounced among death-qualified jurors than jurors who would be excluded from capital cases (Levinson, Smith, & Young, 2014).

Another factor to consider in terms of possible biases introduced by capital jurors is that many of them do not fully comprehend the legal terminology used in the procedural guidelines and sentencing instructions they are supposed to follow throughout the sentencing process (Blankenship et al., 1997; Severence & Loftus, 1982). The lack of understanding may result in jurors relying on what they have experienced or what they think they know. Given that most jurors have received information about crime, the criminal justice system, and other races primarily from indirect sources such as media or the experiences of others (Dixon, 2007; Flexon, 2012), their beliefs about race and crime may be biased based on how popular media or news outlets present information (Dixon & Linz, 2000). Consequently, such a reliance on personal beliefs and possibly inaccurate information about society, particular races, and/or elements of crime and the criminal justice system undermines the system of structured guidance and inevitably introduces personal, often racial, biases into the capital sentencing process.

Most jurors do not realize that they could be letting race of the defendant and/or the victim influence their decisions. While there are exceptions, most death-qualified jurors do not realize they harbor any type of racial prejudice or other preconceptions about defendants or victims based on individual characteristics. But there is some level of bias concerning certain individual characteristic within each juror—within every person (Culotta, 2012)—and cognitions related to biases or stereotypes are often unconscious and automatic (Andersen, Moskowitz, Blair, & Nosek, 2007; Gross & Mauro, 1984). As a result, jurors, prosecutors, judges, or other people in the system may not be aware that personal biases have influenced their decisions.

Evidence is also emerging that errors resulting in miscarriages of capital justice may be disproportionately high in cases involving black defendants. For example, a 2017 analysis by the Death Penalty Information Center (DPIC) revealed that most of the recent exonerated death row cases involved misconduct by police or prosecutors as the major cause and also that defendants exonerated from death row in misconduct-related cases were disproportionately black (DPIC, 2017). In part, these patterns might reflect minority defendants being disproportionately likely to have inadequate defense representation in their cases (Cole, 1999), such that misconduct and errors that ought to have been effectively challenged were in fact not.

Still, these facts do not answer the question of why racial discrepancies are so pervasive in the American death penalty system. While there is no definitive answer to this query, the explanations offered are usually rooted in either a consensus or conflict theoretical orientation. Consensus accounts emphasize the salience of variables presumed legally relevant, like offense seriousness and prior legal record, and use the disproportionate involvement of blacks in violent crime to explain race-of-defendant disparities. With regard to race of victim, they point out that the majority of capital homicides are intraracial, involving white offenders and white victims, and employ this to explain why more than half of modern era executions have involved white offenders and victims. Conflict analyses posit that various societal groups interact based more on conflict than accord and that the more powerful groups will use their authority and other means of control to retain power and oppress subordinate groups. Race is an important basis for group formation; whites have relatively more power, and whether by intent or by effect, laws are created and enforced, and punishments are administered, in a way to protect that social hierarchy and control less powerful groups such as African Americans (see Quinney, 1970). Less powerful groups are underrepresented in positions of authority and often form a large segment of socially disadvantaged citizens (Archibald, 2015). Members of less powerful groups are seen as less valuable, so crimes are seen as less serious and deserving of less punishment when they are the victims (Hawkins, 1987). Conversely, crimes against the powerful group are taken more seriously, and those who offend against this group's members (white victims) are construed to deserve severe punishments. Perhaps the most serious situations involve members of a subordinate group (African Americans) committing actions against those in power (white victims), which are defined as significant threats to the prevailing social order (e.g., killing of a police officer or rape and murder of a white woman). As such, these situations are strong candidates to be assigned the harshest punishments (Gross & Mauro, 1984).

Scholars should continue to explore these and other possible explanations for the observed racial discrepancies within the capital punishment system. Understanding the underlying sources of racial inequalities will be helpful in creating policies and procedures to help reduce flaws and create a more egalitarian process. Since it is unlikely that any large-scale changes in the process will be implemented in the immediate future, death row inmates will have to continue seeking corrective action for biases in their individual cases, as required by *McCleskey*.

Opportunities for Recourse: Are There Methods to Right the Wrongs?

As part of the ruling of the *McCleskey* case, members of the court acknowledged their responsibility to ensure that existing laws are applied in a way that is consistent with the Constitution and suggested that the petitioner's claims of unfair treatment were best addressed in the legislature where laws are created. This recommendation did not go unnoticed by lawmakers, and two federal bills were proposed in the 1988 and 1990. The two proposals were the Racial Justice Act and the Fairness in Death Sentencing Act. The purpose of these acts was to provide death row inmates with an outlet in which to challenge their sentences based on claims of racial discrimination in a process similar to those used by individuals claiming discrimination in regard to employment or housing (Baldus et al., 1994; Baldus & Woodworth, 2003a). The acts would create a process whereby inmates could present evidence of racial discrimination in their individual cases, and the state would have a chance to refute the claims. These proposals were strongly opposed by prosecutors, who offered contradictory arguments against the acts. Some prosecutors argued that the proposals were unnecessary because there was no racial discrimination in the death sentencing process, while others reasoned that the bills would essentially result in elimination of the death penalty as an option because some racial discrimination was going to be present within the capital punishment system regardless of any safeguards. Unfortunately, each of these proposals has been defeated in the Senate each year they were presented for a vote (Ross, 1997).

After the failure of the two federal proposals, two states, North Carolina and Kentucky, implemented their own versions of a Racial Justice Act. Although the intent of each act was similar, they were very different in practice. North Carolina's Racial Justice Act allowed a defendant sentenced to death to present statistical evidence to establish that his or her race, or the race of the victim(s), influenced the probability of receiving a capital sentence in a specific jurisdiction, or that race influenced the dismissal of potential jurors. This legislation was set up so that evidence of discrimination in the jurisdiction was enough; defendants did not have to prove discrimination in their own cases. If they were successful in meeting that standard, their sentences would be commuted to life without parole (Alexander, 2014; Phillips, 2012). This act was criticized for being too favorable to defendants, was amended in 2012, but was ultimately completely repealed in 2013.

Kentucky's Racial Justice Act is still active, though it is much more restrictive than North Carolina's legislation. The Kentucky statute only allows defendants to bring challenges against the prosecutor's decision to charge; it does not allow for challenges of jury discrimination or race impacts during any other part of the process. Kentucky's Act has not been used very often because it is difficult for defendants to present substantial evidence that race influenced the prosecutor's decision to seek the death penalty (Alexander, 2014).

The introduction of the federal proposals, followed by similar acts in two states, provided hope for legitimate opportunities to produce more equality in death sentences. While the original process would still be flawed, there would be room for adjustment on the back end. Regrettably, the remaining Racial Justice Act in Kentucky is so restrictive that it is unlikely to result in considerable changes.

In the wake of the failed legislative forums, defendants sentenced to death are once again forced to turn to the courts with claims of racial discrimination in their own cases. Although constitutional challenges based on race-related factors have not been very successful historically, some modern cases have offered room for more optimism. In 2005, a death row inmate challenged his death sentence by claiming that prosecutors were rejecting and selecting jury members based on race. The Supreme Court recognized that prosecutors had excluded 91% of black prospective jurors and ruled in his favor (*Miller-El v. Dretke*, 2005). More recently in *Foster v. Chatman* (2016), the Court struck down a capital conviction in Georgia based on documents showing that prosecutors had struck all prospective black jurors due to race.

Most recently still, the Court heard *Buck v. Davis* (2017), in which a black petitioner claimed that he was denied effective assistance of counsel during his Texas death penalty trial, which was a violation of the Sixth Amendment. His argument was based on his attorney calling an expert witness to provide evidence concerning the petitioner's likelihood of committing future violent acts. The attorney had reviewed the expert's report and knew its content, yet he allowed the expert to testify that the defendant's race—being black—increased the probability of violence in the future. The petitioner won his challenge based on the Sixth Amendment, but Chief Justice Roberts made a noteworthy statement in delivering the opinion of the court. When rejecting the lower court's statement that the mention of race in this case was minimal, Chief Justice Roberts wrote,

> when a jury hears expert testimony that expressly makes a defendant's race directly pertinent on the question of life or death, the impact of that evidence cannot be measured simply by how much air time it received at trial or how many pages it occupies in the record. Some toxins can be deadly in small doses. The State acknowledges, as it must, that introducing 'race or ethnicity as evidence of criminality' can in some cases prejudice a defendant.
>
> *(pp. 19–20)*

Perhaps this statement will be the first of many in an era in which legal and procedural improvements will be implemented within the capital punishment process. At the same time, though, the chief justice offered an observation of a quite different kind:

> In fact, the distinction could well cut the other way. A prosecutor is seeking a conviction. Jurors understand this and may reasonably be expected to evaluate the government's evidence and arguments in light of its motivations. When a defendant's own lawyer puts in the offending evidence, it is in the nature of an admission against interest, more likely to be taken at face value.
>
> *(p. 20)*

The tacit posture here seems to be one of permissibility toward letting prosecutors use race as evidence of future dangerousness, as jurors are assumed capable of fairly evaluating it. But it is hard indeed to envisage an expert witness for the prosecution in a capital case not relying, at base, on aggregate level prediction studies of violent recidivism to support the link of race to future dangerousness. Yet this is precisely the kind of reliance the court declined to allow when McCleskey offered aggregate evidence of race of victim bias. Hence, while *Buck v. Davis* can legitimately be read as a win for racial justice in capital cases, it can also be seen as an instance of something that is good for the goose not being good for the gander.

Conclusion

Among Americans, the top reason cited in support of the death penalty is retribution—punishment for the crime that was committed (Radelet & Borg, 2000; Whited, 2016). Retributive justice implies that offenders should face a proportionate punishment for their crime and that defendants convicted of the same crime should receive the same punishment. Accordingly, even for the ultimate sentence of death, the sanction should be based on the crime, not extralegal factors such as individual characteristics. However, there is little doubt that death sentences are applied inconsistently and that racial disparities exist throughout the American capital punishment process (Baldus et al., 1990, 1983; Bowers & Pierce, 1980; Dovidio et al., 1997; Givelber, 1994; Heilbrun et al., 1989; Hood, 1996; Keil & Vito, 1995, 1990, 1989; Radelet, 1989; Smith, 1987; Thomson, 1997; Zeisel, 1981). The question is no longer whether racial disparities exist; it is now the twofold query of if and how the disparities can be corrected. Clearly, the post-*Furman* improvements in statutory frameworks to restrict the types of death-eligible cases and provide guidance and instructions did not serve to completely eliminate racial biases from the capital punishment process (Beckett & Evans, 2016).

It has been suggested that human biases and prejudices, such as those based on race, are inherent within every individual, even in the presence of rules, guidelines, and instructions; such biases will affect any system that involves human input (Baldus et al., 1994; Beardsley, Kamin, Marceau, & Phillips, 2015; Mourer, 2014). Consequently, it is impossible to remove human biases from the death penalty process. Some capital punishment supporters maintain that those types of inconsistencies are secondary to retribution and justice on behalf of the victims and their families (van den Haag, 1985) and that abolishing the death penalty would do more harm than the racial inequalities within the system (see Baldus & Woodworth, 2003a). Other supporters, as well as those who oppose capital punishment, claim that the death penalty should not be used if it cannot be applied equally based on legal factors (Flexon, 2012).

Two Supreme Court Justices have made profound statements concerning the state of the modern capital punishment process in their dissenting opinions in two different capital cases. In *McCleskey v. Kemp* (1987, p. 367), Justice Stevens wrote, "The Court's decision appears to be based on a fear that the acceptance of McCleskey's claim would sound the death knell for capital punishment in Georgia. If society were indeed forced to choose between a racially discriminatory death penalty (one that provides heightened protection against murder 'for whites only') and no death penalty at all, the choice mandated by the Constitution would be plain." Later, in *Callins v. Collins*, 1994, p. 1152) Justice Blackmun stated,

> From this day forward, I no longer shall tinker with the machinery of death. For more than 20 years I have endeavored—indeed, I have struggled—along with a majority of this Court, to develop procedural and substantive rules that would lend more than the mere appearance of fairness to the death penalty endeavor. Rather than continue to coddle the Court's delusion that the desired level of fairness has been achieved and the need for regulation eviscerated, I feel morally and intellectually obligated simply to concede that the death penalty experiment has failed. It is virtually self-evident to me now that no combination of procedural rules or substantive regulations ever can save the death penalty from its inherent constitutional deficiencies.

Justice Powell, the author of the majority ruling in McCleskey, was more succinct. Upon being asked in retirement if he would change any of his votes, he pointed to *McCleskey v. Kemp* and added that he had come to regard the death penalty as nonviable and unconstitutional (Jeffries, 2001).

Perhaps these justices are correct in their implications that the system is broken and should be abandoned. It is possible, though, that additional research with as many legal and extra-legal measures as possible may shed more light on the source of racial disparities in capital punishment. Extant research has resulted in the ability to predict who is most likely to receive a death sentence, and future research may lead to a better understanding of why things are the way they are. Greater understanding could lead to more viable responses to create more equality (Flexon, 2012). In the meantime, jurisdictions that opt to retain the death penalty must continue reckoning with the conclusion of the Equal Justice Initiative (2015) in a recent analysis of lynching:

Lynching reinforced a legacy of racial inequality that has never been adequately addressed in America. The administration of criminal justice in particular is tangled with [that history] in profound and important ways that continue to contaminate the integrity and fairness of the justice system.

(p. 3)

It is no wonder, then (as Garland, 2010 put the matter), that capital jurisdictions invest so much energy and resources into carefully differentiating their modern death penalties from the nation's lynching past.

References

Alexander, R. (2014). A model state racial justice act: Fighting racial bias without killing the death penalty. *Civil Rights Law Journal, 24,* 113–157.

Allen, H. W., & Clubb, J. M. (2008). *Race, class, and the death penalty: Capital punishment in American history.* Albany, NY: SUNY Press.

Andersen, S. A., Moskowitz, G. B., Blair, I. V., & Nosek, B. A. (2007). Auto-Matic thought. In E. T. Higgins & A. Kruglanski (Eds.), *Social psychology: Handbook of basic principles* (pp. 138–174). New York: Guilford.

Applegate, B. K., Cullen, F. T., Fisher, B. S., & Vander Ven, T. (2000). Forgiveness and fundamentalism: Reconsidering the relationship between correctional attitudes and religion. *Criminology, 38,* 719–754.

Archibald, S. N. (2015). *Capital punishment in the U.S. states: Executing social inequality.* El Paso, TX: LFB Scholarly Publishing.

Baldus, D. C., Grosso, C. M., Woodworth, G., & Newell, R. (2012). Racial discrimination in the administration of the death penalty: The experience of the United States Armed Forces (1984–2005). *Journal of Criminal Law and Criminology, 101,* 1227–1335.

Baldus, D. C., Pulaski, C., & Woodworth, G. (1983). Comparative review of death sentences: An empirical study of the Georgia experience. *Journal of Criminal Law and Criminology, 74,* 661–753.

Baldus, D. C., & Woodworth, G. (2003a). Race discrimination and the death penalty: An empirical and legal overview. In J. R. Acker, R. M. Bohm, & C. S. Lanier (Eds.), *America's experiment with capital punishment: Reflections on the past, present, and future of the ultimate penal sanction* (2nd ed., pp. 501–552). Durham, NC: Carolina Academic Press.

Baldus, D. C., & Woodworth, G. (2003b). Race discrimination in the administration of the death penalty: An overview of the empirical evidence with special emphasis on the post-1990 research. *Criminal Law Bulletin, 39,* 194–226.

Baldus, D. C., Woodworth, G., & Grosso, C. M. (2002). Arbitrariness and discrimination in the administration of the death penalty: A legal and empirical analysis of the Nebraska experience (1973–1999). *Nebraska Law Review, 81,* 486–753.

Baldus, D. C., Woodworth, G., & Pulaski, C. (1990). *Equal justice and the death penalty.* Boston: Northeastern University Press.

Baldus, D. C., Woodworth, G., & Pulaski, C. (1994). Reflections on the "Inevitability" of racial discrimination in capital sentencing and the "impossibility" of its prevention, detection, and correction. *Washington and Lee Law Review, 51,* 359–430.

Banner, S. (2006). Traces of slavery: Race and the death penalty in historical perspective. In C. J. Ogletree, Jr. & A. Sarat (Eds.), *From lynch mobs to the killing state: Race and the death penalty in America* (pp. 96–113). New York: New York University Press.

Baumgartner, F. R., Grigg, A. J., & Mastro, A. (2015). Black lives don't matter: Race-of-victim effects in U.S. executions, 1976–2013. *Politics, Groups and Identities, 3,* 209–221.

Beardsley, M., Kamin, S., Marceau, J. F., & Phillips, S. (2015). Disquieting discretion: Race, geography, and the Colorado death penalty in the first decade of the twenty-first century. *Denver University Law Review, 92,* 431–452.

Beckett, K., & Evans, H. (2016). Race, death, and justice: Capital sentencing in Washington State, 1981–2014. *Columbia Journal of Race and Law, 6,* 77–114.

Bedau, H. A. (1982). *The death penalty in America.* New York: Oxford University Press.

Bedau, H. A. (1997). *The death penalty in America: Current controversies.* New York: Oxford University Press.

Bessler, J. D. (1997). *Death in the dark: Midnight executions in America.* Boston: Northeastern University Press.

Blanco, J. I. (2016). *Death penalty USA: The database of executions in the United States.* Retrieved May 27, 2017 from www.deathpenaltyusa.org/usa1/crimra.htm

Blankenship, M. B., Luginbuhl, J., Cullen, F. T., & Redick, W. (1997). Jurors' comprehension of sentencing instructions: A test of the death penalty process in Tennessee. *Justice Quarterly, 14,* 325–351.

Bohm, R. M. (1991). *The death penalty in America: Current research.* Cincinnati, OH: Anderson.

Bohm, R. M. (2003). American death penalty opinion: Past, present, and future. In J. R. Acker, R. M. Bohm, & C. S. Lanier (Eds.), *America's experiment with capital punishment: Reflections on the past, present and future of the ultimate penal sanction* (2nd ed., pp. 27–54). Durham, NC: Carolina Academic Press.

Boots, D. P., Cochran, J. K., & Heide, K. M. (2003). Capital punishment preferences for special offender populations. *Journal of Criminal Justice, 31,* 553–565.

Bowers, W. J. (1984). *Legal homicide: Death as punishment in America, 1864–1982.* Boston: Northeastern University Press.

Bowers, W. J. (1995). The capital jury project: Rationale, design, and early findings. *Indiana Law Journal, 70,* 1043–1102.

Bowers, W. J., & Pierce, G. L. (1980). Arbitrariness and discrimination under post-Furman capital statutes. *Crime and Delinquency, 26,* 563–635.

Bowers, W. J., Steiner, B. D., & Sandys, M. S. (2001). Death sentencing in black and white: An empirical analysis of the role of jurors' race and jury racial composition. *Journal of Constitutional Law, 3,* 171–271.

Bright, S. B. (1994). Counsel for the poor: The death sentence not for the worst crime but for the worst lawyer. *Yale Law Journal, 103,* 1835–1883.

Cochran, J. K., & Chamlin, M. B. (2006). The enduring racial divide in death penalty support. *Journal of Criminal Justice, 34,* 85–99.

Cole, D. (1999). *No equal justice: Race and class in the American criminal justice system.* New York: The New Press.

Cook, J. A., Jr., & Kende, M. (1996). Color-blindness in the Rehnquist court: Comparing the Court's treatment of discrimination claims by a Black death row inmate and White voting rights plaintiffs. *Thomas M. Cooley Law Review, 13,* 815–852.

Culotta, E. (2012). Roots of racism. *Science, 336,* 825–827.

Death Penalty Information Center. (2017). *Statement of Robert Dunham, executive director of the death penalty information center, on the release of the national registry of exonerations' reports exonerations in 2016 and race and wrongful convictions in the United States.* Retrieved June 5, 2017 from https://deathpenaltyinfo.org/documents/DPIC-StatementOnNationalRegistryReports.pdf

Diamond, S. S. (1993). Instructing on death. *American Psychologist, 48,* 423–434.

Diamond, S. S., & Levi, J. N. (1996). Improving decisions on death by revising and testing jury instructions. *Judicature, 79,* 224–232.

Dixon, T. (2007). Black criminals and White officers: The effects of racially misrepresenting law breakers and law defenders on television news. *Media Psychology, 10,* 270–291.

Dixon, T., & Linz, D. (2000). Overrepresentation and underrepresentation of African Americans and Latinos as lawbreakers on television news. *Journal of Communication, 50,* 131–154.

Dovidio, J. F., Smith, J. K., Donnella, A. G., & Gaertner, S. L. (1997). Racial attitudes and the death penalty. *Journal of Applied Social Psychology, 27,* 1468–1487.

Eisenberg, A. (in press). Removal of women and African-Americans in jury selection in South Carolina capital cases, 1997–2012. *Northwestern University Law Journal.* Available at SSRN: https://ssrn.com/abstract=2832370.

Eisenberg, T., Garvey, S. P., & Wells, M. T. (2001). Forecasting life and death: Juror race, religion, and attitude toward the death penalty. *Journal of Legal Studies, 30,* 277–311.

Equal Justice Initiative. (2015). *Lynching in America: Confronting the legacy of racial terror.* Montgomery, AL: Equal Justice Initiative.

Federal Bureau of Investigation. (2016). *Crime in the United States 2015.* Washington, DC: U.S. Department of Justice.

Fins, D. (2016). *Death row U.S.A.: A quarterly report by the Criminal Justice Project of the NAACP Legal Defense and Educational Fund, Inc.* New York: NAACP Legal Defense and Educational Fund, Inc.

Fleury-Steiner, B. D., Dunn, K., & Fleury-Steiner, R. (2009). Governing through crime as commonsense racism: Race, space, and death penalty 'reform' in Delaware. *Punishment and Society, 11,* 5–24.

Flexon, J. (2012). *Racial disparities in capital sentencing: Prejudice and discrimination in the jury room.* El Paso, TX: LFB Scholarly Publishing.

Gaddis, S. M. (2015). Discrimination in the credential society: An audit study of race and college selectivity in the labor market. *Social Forces, 93,* 1451–1479.

Garland, D. (2005). Penal excess and surplus meaning: Public torture lynching in twentieth-century America. *Law & Society Review, 39,* 793–833.

Garland, D. (2010). *Peculiar institution: America's death penalty in an age of abolition.* Cambridge, MA: Harvard University Press.

Gibson, C., & Jung, K. (2005). *Historical census statistics on population totals by race, 1790 to 1990, and by Hispanic origin, 1970 to 1990, for large cities and other urban places in the United States.* Washington, DC: U.S. Census Bureau, U.S. Department of Commerce.

Gillespie, L., Loughran, T. A., Smith, M. D., Fogel, S. J., & Bjerregaard, B. (2014). Exploring the role of victim sex, victim conduct, and victim-defendant relationship in capital punishment sentencing. *Homicide Studies, 18*, 175–195.

Givelber, D. (1994). The new law of murder. *Indiana Law Journal, 69*, 375–423.

Goldfarb, P. (2016). Matters of strata: Race, gender, and class structures in capital cases. *Washington and Lee Law Review, 73*, 1395–1443.

Gross, S. R., & Mauro, R. (1984). Patterns of death: An analysis of racial disparities in capital sentencing and homicide victimizing. *Stanford Law Review, 37*, 28–110.

Gross, S., & Mauro, R. (1989). *Death and discrimination: Racial disparities in capital sentencing.* Boston, MA: Northeastern University Press.

Hartung, F. E. (1952). Trends in the use of capital punishment. *Annals of the American Academy of Political and Social Sciences, 284*, 8–19.

Hawkins, D. F. (1987). Beyond anomalies: Rethinking the conflict perspective on race and criminal punishment. *Social Forces, 65*, 719–745.

Heilbrun, A. B., Jr., Foster, A., & Golden, J. (1989). The death sentence in Georgia, 1974–1987: Criminal justice or racial injustice? *Criminal Justice and Behavior, 16*, 139–154.

Hindson, S., Potter, H., & Radelet, M. (2006). Race, gender, region and death sentencing in Colorado, 1980–1999. *University of Colorado Law Review, 77*, 549–594.

Holcomb, J. E., Williams, M. R., & Demuth, S. (2004). White female victims and death penalty disparity research. *Justice Quarterly, 21*, 877–902.

Hood, R. (1996). *The death penalty: A world-wide perspective.* New York: Oxford University Press.

Jeffries, J. (2001). *Justice Lewis F. Powell: A biography.* New York: Fordham University Press.

Jennings, W. G., Richards, T. N., Smith, M. D., Bjerregaard, B., & Fogel, S. J. (2014). A critical examination of the "white victim effect" and death penalty decision-making from a propensity score matching approach: The North Carolina experience. *Journal of Criminal Justice, 42*, 384–398.

Keil, T. J., & Vito, G. F. (1989). Race, homicide severity, and applications of the death penalty: A consideration if the Barnett Scale. *Criminology, 27*, 511–531.

Keil, T. J., & Vito, G. F. (1990). Race and the death penalty in Kentucky murder trials: An analysis of post-Gregg outcomes. *Justice Quarterly, 7*, 189–207.

Keil, T. J., & Vito, G. F. (1995). Race and the death penalty in Kentucky murder trials: 1976–1991. *American Journal of Criminal Justice, 20*, 17–36.

Kirchmeier, J. L. (2015). *Imprisoned by the past: Warren McCleskey and the American death penalty.* New York: Oxford University Press.

Klein, S., & Rolph, J. (1991). Relationship of offender and victim race to death penalty sentences in California. *Jurimetrics, 32*, 33–48.

Levinson, J. D., Smith, R. J., & Young, D. M. (2014). Devaluing death: An empirical study of implicit bias on jury-eligible citizens in six death penalty states. *New York University Law Review, 89*, 513–581.

Luginbuhl, J. (1992). Comprehension of judges' instructions in the penalty phase of a capital trial: Focus on mitigating circumstances. *Law and Human Behavior, 16*, 203–218.

Luginbuhl, J., & Howe, J. (1995). Discretion in capital sentencing instructions: Guided or misguided? *Indiana Law Journal, 70*, 1161–1182.

Lynch, M., & Haney, C. (2000). Discrimination and instructional comprehension: Guided discretion, racial bias, and the death penalty. *Law and Human Behavior, 24*, 337–358.

Lynch, M., & Haney, C. (2009). Capital jury deliberation: Effects on death sentencing, comprehension, and discrimination. *Law and Human Behavior, 33*, 481–496.

Mandery, E. J. (2013). *A wild justice: The death and resurrection of capital punishment in America.* New York: W. W. Norton.

Marquart, J. W., Ekland-Oison, S., & Sorensen, J. R. (1994). *The rope, the chair, and the needle: Capital punishment in Texas, 1923–1990.* Austin: University of Texas Press.

Mello, M. A. (1995). *Dead wrong: A death row lawyer speaks out against capital punishment.* Madison, Wisconsin: The University of Wisconsin Press.

Mourer, S. A. (2014). Forgetting Furman Arbitrary death penalty sentencing schemes across the nation. *William and Mary Bill of Rights Journal, 22*, 1183–1220.

Mustard, D. B. (2001). Racial, ethnic, and gender disparities in sentencing: Evidence from the U.S. Federal Courts. *Journal of Law and Economics, 44*, 285–314.

Paternoster, R. (1983). Race of victim and location of crime: The decision to seek the death penalty in South Carolina. *The Journal of Criminal Law and Criminology, 74*, 754–785.

Paternoster, R. (1991). *Capital punishment in America.* New York: Lexington Books/Macmillan.

Paternoster, R., & Brame, R. (2003). *An empirical analysis of Maryland's death sentencing system with respect to the influence of race and legal jurisdiction.* College Park, MD: University of Maryland.

Paternoster, R., & Brame, R. (2008). Reassessing race disparities in Maryland capital cases. *Criminology, 46*, 971–1008.

Paternoster, R., Brame, R., & Bacon, S. (2008). *The death penalty: America's experience with capital punishment.* New York: Oxford University Press.

Pasternoster, R., Brame, R., Bacon, S., & Ditchfield, A. (2004). Justice by geography and race: The administration of the death penalty in Maryland, 1978–1999. *Margins, 4*, 1–98.

Patterson, C. M. (1995). Race and the death penalty: The tension between individualized justice and racially neutral standards. *Texas Wesleyan Law Review, 2*, 80–95.

Peffley, M., & Hurwitz, J. (2007). Persuasion and resistance: Race and the death penalty in America. *American Journal of Political Science, 51*, 996–1012.

Phillips, S. (2012). Continued racial disparities in the capital of capital punishment: The Rosenthal era. *Houston Law Review, 50*, 131–155.

Pierce, G. L., & Radelet, M. L. (2002). Race, region and death sentencing in Illinois, 1988–1997. *Oregon Law Review, 81*, 39–96.

Pierce, G. L., & Radelet, M. L. (2005). The impact of legally inappropriate factors on death sentencing for California homicides. *Santa Clara Law Review, 46*, 1–47.

Pollitt, D., & Warren, B. (2016). Thirty years of disappointment: North Carolina's remarkable appellate Batson record. *North Carolina Law Review, 94*, 1956–1996.

Poveda, T. G. (2009). The death penalty in the post-*Furman* era: A review of the issues and the debate. *Sociology Compass, 3/4*, 559–574.

Quinney, R. (1970). *The problem of crime.* New York: Dodd, Mead.

Radelet, M. L. (1989). Executions of whites for crimes against blacks: Exceptions to the rule? *The Sociological Quarterly, 30*(4), 529–544.

Radelet, M. L., & Borg, M. J. (2000). The changing nature of death penalty debates. *Annual Review of Sociology, 26*, 43–61.

Radelet, M. L., & Pierce, G. L. (1991). Choosing those who will die: Race and the death penalty in Florida. *Florida Law Review, 43*, 1–34.

Radelet, M. L., & Pierce, G. L. (2011a). Death sentencing in East Baton Rouge Parish, 1990–2008. *Louisiana Law Review, 71*, 647–673.

Radelet, M. L., & Pierce, G. L. (2011b). Race and death sentencing in North Carolina, 1980–2007. *North Carolina Law Review, 89*, 2119–2160.

Robinson, M. B. (2008). *Death nation: The experts explain American capital punishment.* Upper Saddle River, NJ: Pearson/Prentice Hall.

Ross, M. (1997). The death penalty is applied unfairly to blacks. In D. Bender & B. Leone (Eds.), *The death penalty: Opposing viewpoints* (pp. 65–72). San Diego, CA: Greenhaven Press.

Schneider, V., & Smykla, J. O. (1991). A summary of executions in the United States, 1608–1987: The espy file. In R. M. Bohm (Ed.), *The death penalty in America: Current research* (pp. 1–19). Cincinnati, OH: Anderson.

Severence, L. J., & Loftus, E. F. (1982). Improving the ability of jurors to comprehend and apply criminal jury instructions. *Law and Society Review, 17*, 153–197.

Shatz, S. F., & Dalton, T. (2013). Challenging the death penalty with statistics: *Furman, McCleskey*, and a single county case study. *Cardozo Law Review, 34*, 1227–1282.

Sluiter, E. (1997). New light on the "20 and odd Negroes" arriving in Virginia, August 1619. *The William and Mary Quarterly, 54*, 395–398.

Smith, M. D. (1987). Patterns of discrimination in assessments of the death penalty: The case of Louisiana. *Journal of Criminal Justice, 15*, 279–286.

Sorensen, J. R., & Wallace, D. H. (1995). Capital punishment in Missouri: Examining the issue of racial disparity. *Behavioral Sciences and the Law, 13*, 61–80.

Stauffer, A. R., Smith, M. D., Cochran, J. K., Fogel, S. J., & Bjerregaard, B. (2006). The interaction between victim race and gender on sentencing outcomes in capital murder trials. *Homicide Studies, 10*, 98–117.

Steiker, C. S., & Steiker, J. M. (2015). The American death penalty and the (in)visibility of race. *The University of Chicago Law Review, 82*, 243–294.

Steiker, C. S., & Steiker, J. M. (2016). *Courting death: The Supreme Court and capital punishment.* Cambridge, MA: Harvard University Press.

Thomson, E. (1997). Research note: Discrimination and the death penalty in Arizona. *Criminal Justice Review, 22,* 65–76.

Tongue, M. E. (2015). Does the punishment fit the crime? A comparative note on sentencing laws for murder in England and Wales vs. the United States of America. *Missouri Law Review, 80,* 1257–1278.

Unah, I. (2011). Empirical analysis of race and the process of capital punishment in North Carolina. *Michigan State Law Review, 2011,* 610–658.

Unnever, J. D., Cullen, F. T., & Jonson, C. N. (2008). Race, racism, and support for capital punishment. In M. Tonry (Ed.), *Crime and justice: A review of research* (pp. 45–96). Chicago, IL: University of Chicago Press.

U.S. Census Bureau. (2016). *Quick facts, United States: Race and Hispanic origin, July 1, 2015.* Washington, DC: U.S. Department of Commerce.

U.S. General Accounting Office. (1990). *Death penalty sentencing: Research indicates pattern of racial disparities: GGD-90-57.* Washington, DC: U.S. General Accounting Office.

van den Haag, E. (1985). Refuting Reiman and Nathanson. *Philosophy and Public Affairs, 14,* 165–176.

Whited, W. H. (2016). *"Eye for an eye" or "turn the other cheek?" Exploring the moderating roles of revenge and forgiveness when examining death penalty support and religious fundamentalism* (doctoral dissertation). Hattiesburg, MS: University of Southern Mississippi.

Williams, K. (2016). *Most deserving of death? An analysis of the Supreme Court's death penalty jurisprudence.* Abingdon, UK: Routledge.

Williams, M. R., & Holcomb, J. E. (2001). Racial disparity and death sentences in Ohio. *Journal of Criminal Justice, 29,* 207–218.

Williamson, J. (1984). *The crucible of race: Black-white relations in the American South since emancipation.* New York: Oxford University Press.

Wolfgang, M. E., & Riedel, M. (1973). Race, judicial discretion, and the death penalty. *Annals of the American Academy of Political and Social Science, 407,* 119–133.

Wolfgang, M. E., & Riedel, M. (1975). Rape, race, and the death penalty in Georgia. *American Journal of Orthopsychiatry, 45,* 658–668.

Zeisel, H. (1981). Race bias in the administration of the death penalty: The Florida experiment. *Harvard Law Review, 456,* 456–468.

Zimring, F. E. (2003). *The contradictions of American capital punishment.* New York: Oxford University Press.

Cases Cited

Brown v. Board of Education, 347 U.S. 483 (1954).
Buck v. Davis, 580 U.S. ___ (2017).
Callins v. Collins, 510 U.S. 1141 (1994).
Coker v. Georgia, 433 U.S. 584 (1977).
Foster v. Chatman, 578 U.S. ___ (2016).
Francis v. Resweber, 329 U.S. 459 (1947).
Furman v. Georgia, 408 U.S. 238 (1972).
Gregg v. Georgia, 428 U.S. 153 (1976).
In re Kemmler, 136 U.S. 436 (1890).
Jurek v. Texas, 428 U.S. 262 (1976).
Malloy v. South Carolina, 237 U.S. 180 (1915).
McCleskey v. Kemp, 481 U.S. 279 (1987).
McGautha v. California, 402 U.S. 183 (1971).
Miller-El v. Dretke, 545 U.S. 660 (2005).
Powell v. Alabama, 287 U.S. 45 (1932).
Proffitt v. Florida, 428 U.S. 242 (1976).
Roberts v. Louisiana, 428 U.S. 325 (1976).
Rooney v. North Dakota, 196 U.S. 319 (1905).
Washington v. Davis, 426 U.S. 229 (1976).
Wilkerson v. Utah, 99 U.S. 130 (1879).
Witherspoon v. Illinois, 391 U.S. 510 (1968).
Woodson v. North Carolina, 428 U.S. 280 (1976).

32

WRONGFUL CAPITAL CONVICTIONS

Talia Roitberg Harmon and Diana Falco

The execution of an innocent person may be one of the most compelling issues surrounding capital punishment. Since the Supreme Court ruled that "death is different" and irreversible (Woodson v. NC, 1976, p. 305), research and discussions on wrongful capital convictions has become a very timely and extremely important topic. Since 2000, the number of people who have been released from death row due to innocence has grown. This growth has been significant over the last few decades. In fact, the most recent average suggests that there have been approximately 4.29 exonerations nationwide per year (www. deathpenaltyinfo.org, 1/3/17). Recent Gallup polls suggest that 60% of Americans currently support the death penalty (Gallup, 2017). This support has significantly declined by around 20% from the high of 80% in the mid-1990s (Kirchmeier, 2002). Scholars have posited that much of this decline may be attributable to the issue of wrongful capital convictions (Baumgartner, De Boef, & Boydstun, 2008; Unnever & Cullen, 2005; Harmon, Besch, Amendola, & Pehrson, 2016). The media has taken notice of the issue and has publicized exoneration cases, especially the exceptionally dramatic cases involving DNA evidence (Aronson & Cole, 2009; Scheck, Neufeld, & Dwyer, 2000; Garrett, 2008). This chapter will begin with a discussion of the various definitions of wrongful convictions. Next, evidence will be presented regarding the extent of the problem in the context of exonerations and wrongful executions. Third, the main causes of wrongful convictions and factors that led to the discovery of errors will be presented. Finally, the impact the innocence issue has had on overall death penalty public opinion will be discussed.

Definitions of Wrongful Convictions

In their seminal research, Bedau and Radelet brought the innocence issue to light and sparked intense debate on the extent of the problem of wrongful capital convictions (Bedau & Radelet, 1987). According to Radelet and Bedau, the most compelling definition of innocence involves the "factually innocent," which are cases where the defendant was completely uninvolved in the crime or no crime actually occurred. Bedau and Radelet also included the legally innocent in their innocence definition. The legally innocent group included a relatively small number of cases where the defendant was later found to be NGRI (not guilty by reason of insanity) or to have acted in self-defense (Radelet & Bedau, 2014). Another larger group of innocence cases would include defendants who were guilty of murder but who were guilty of a lesser degree of murder and thus were not the "worst of the worst": those who were convicted of capital murder but who really should have been convicted of a lesser degree of murder and not sentenced to death. Finally, Radelet and Bedau (2014) identify these various definitions and also include the innocent victims in the death row inmate's family among 'the innocent'.

Exonerations Research

Since Bedau and Radelet's study was published in 1987 and it received so much attention, including a critique directed at the 23 wrongful executions that they identified, much of the research post-1987 has been dominated by exonerations of convictions that are less controversial and more objectively supported as "wrongful" by official acknowledgment of a reversal or not guilty verdict by the criminal justice system.

A fairly large number of articles, reports, and books, as well as documentaries, focusing on specific exonerations or on larger populations of cases have been produced. These studies tend to utilize a narrative methodology and are largely journalistic in orientation (Gardner, 1952; Yant, 1991; Frank & Frank, 1957). Much of this research has most commonly focused on single exonerated individuals. Examples include examinations of the cases of Randall Dale Adams (Adams, Hoffer, & Hoffer, 1991), Walter MacMillian (Earley, 1995), John Henry Knapp (Parloff, 1996), Clarence Lee Brandley (Davies, 1993), Anthony Porter (Armbrust, 2002), Joe Spaziano (Mello, 2001), Earl Washington (Edds, 2003), and the Ford Heights Four (Warden & Protess, 1998). As previously mentioned, the first compilation of cases was conducted by Bedau and Radelet (1987); however, their pool of cases also included 23 wrongful executions. In an effort to be less controversial, in their updated book in 1992, they limited their cases to the exonerated. Moreover, in 1996, they presented brief vignettes of the 68 exoneration cases nationwide since 1972. The standard used by Radelet, Lofquist, and Bedau (1996, p. 914) to identify these cases involved "deferring to the decision made by the final court or jury that evaluated the evidence in the case." In their study, Radelet and his colleagues found that erroneously convicted defendants spent an average of approximately seven years on death row prior to release (Radelet, Lofquist, & Bedau (1996, 1996). Additionally, they noted that a majority of those released from death row were African Americans or other minorities. The Death Penalty Information Center (DPIC) has subsequently taken over the list of the exonerated and continually provides a short summary of each case on its website. At the end of 2016, the list contained 156 exonerations to date (DPIC, 12.12.16).

One of the first studies to attempt to identify predictors of wrongful convictions was conducted by Harmon (2001a). Previous research on wrongful convictions in capital cases had focused primarily on qualitative methods designed to provide in-depth descriptive analyses of these cases (Borchard, 1932; Gardner, 1952; Radin, 1964; Bedau & Radelet, 1987). In contrast, Harmon (2001a) utilized a quantitative comparison between the 76 documented cases from 1970–1998 in which prisoners were released from death row because of "doubts about their guilt" (identified by Radelet et al. [1996]) and a matched group of inmates who were executed. Through the utilization of a logistic regression model, significant predictors of cases that resulted in a release from death row as opposed to an execution were identified. These significant factors included the following factors: allegations of perjury of witnesses, the discovery of new evidence postconviction, type of attorney on appeal, and strength of the evidence.

Numerous scholars have continued to utilize a comparison group approach to study and advance knowledge in this area (see Leo & Gould, 2009, Gould & Leo, 2010). In their 2009 study, Leo and Gould argued that social scientific methods would allow for more accurate and exact depictions of the multifactorial and complex nature of causation in wrongful conviction cases. The authors discussed and illustrated several social science approaches to the study of wrongful conviction: aggregated case studies, matched comparison samples, and path analysis. They argue that utilizing all of these methods would assist criminal law and procedure scholars to better advance and understand the causes, characteristics, and consequences of wrongful convictions.

In their recent study of wrongful convictions that were not limited to capital cases, Gould, Carrano, and Young (2013) utilized a comparison methodology to determine significant factors that were present in cases that led the system to rightfully acquit or dismiss charges against innocent defendants (so-called "near misses") that were not present in cases that led the system to erroneously convict the innocent. The results indicated that ten factors—the age and criminal history of the defendant, the punitiveness of the state, *Brady* violations, forensic error, a weak case, a family defense witness, inadvertent misidentification, and lying by a noneyewitness (perjury)—help explain why an innocent defendant, once indicted, ends up erroneously convicted rather than released. Moreover, they found that other factors traditionally suggested as sources of erroneous convictions, including false confessions, criminal justice official error, and race effects, appear in statistically similar rates in both sets of cases; thus, they likely increase the chance that an innocent suspect will be indicted but not the likelihood that the indictment will result in a conviction. Additionally, the qualitative review of the cases revealed how the statistically significant factors are connected and exacerbated by tunnel vision, which prevents the system from self-correcting once an error is made.

Executions Research

In more recent years, as the study of wrongful convictions has advanced, attention has turned to establishing lists of compelling claims of executions of the innocent (see Grassroots Investigative Project, 2000; Lofquist & Harmon, 2008), which is a smaller and more controversial subset of cases lacking the type of official recognition and verification provided by legal exoneration.

While fewer in number than works detailing exonerations, there are also some analyses of cases that assert the innocence of executed individuals. One of the best known is the detailed case analysis of Roger Coleman (Tucker, 1997). Other key case analyses include Dennis Stockton (Jackson, Burke, & Stockton, 1999), Gary Graham (Welch & Burr, 2002), Odell Barnes (Burtman, 2002), Timothy Baldwin (Ingle, 1990), Anthony Darden (Ingle, 1990), Larry Griffin (Burnett, 2002), Billy Conn Gardner (Wiseman, 1996), and David Wayne Spence (Berlow, 2000). One of the first studies to attempt to identify compelling claims of innocence that resulted in an execution rather than exoneration was undertaken by Lofquist and Harmon (2008). This research identified 16 compelling claims of factually innocent executions post-*Furman* and provided brief vignettes describing each case. Moreover, in a companion study, Harmon and Lofquist (2005) identified predictors of case outcomes among capital defendants with strong claims of factual innocence by comparing two groups of factually innocent capital defendants: those who were exonerated and those who were executed. Through the use of a logistic regression model, the following variables were significant predictors of case outcome (exoneration v. execution): allegations of perjury, multiple types of evidence, prior felony record, type of attorney at trial, and the race of the defendant.

The next section will focus on those factors that have been traditionally identified by prior research as causal factors that are related to wrongful convictions. These include perjury of witnesses, prosecutorial misconduct, ineffective assistance of counsel, racial bias, faulty forensic evidence, mistaken eyewitness identification, and false confessions.

Traditional Causes/Factors Associated With Wrongful Capital Convictions

In their summary of the research on wrongful convictions over the past century, Gould and Leo (2010) analyze the causes and consequences of wrongful convictions. They suggest that the traditional sources of error are all contributing sources of error, not exclusive causes. The factors they describe overlap with the following factors we discuss here:

Perjury of Witnesses

Perjury of witnesses refers to perjury by experts, eyewitnesses, jailhouse informants, accomplices, and others. Based on prior research on wrongful capital convictions, this factor is generally recognized as one of the most important factors leading to wrongful convictions (Bedau & Radelet, 1987; Radelet,

Bedau, & Putnam, 1992, Harmon, 2001a). This category includes both the knowing and unknowing use of perjury by the prosecutor. Most prevalent among wrongful capital convictions includes perjury among jailhouse informants (Harmon, 2001b).

When looking more closely at this specific problem, Natapoff (2006) analyzed the role that criminal informants play in the conviction of capital murder cases. She argues that criminal informants play a prominent role in creating wrongful convictions. Her research reviews some of the data on criminal informant-generated wrongful convictions, describing the institutional relationship among the informant, police, and prosecutors that make the falsehoods so pervasive and difficult to discern using the traditional tools of the adversarial process. The article concludes with a suggestion to decrease the false testimony of criminal informants by requiring a pretrial reliability hearing. She suggests a process that would resemble the reasoning in *Daubert v. Merrell Dow Pharms* (1993), in which the Supreme Court ruled that it was necessary for reliability hearings for expert witnesses. The hearing would evaluate the credibility and trustworthiness of jailhouse informants prior to allowing them to testify at trial. This would permit fuller disclosure of the deals that informants make with the state, allow more thorough testing of the truthfulness of informants, and reduce opportunities for abuse. This process would decrease the reliance on criminal informant testimony as the main evidence against a defendant and prevent wrongful convictions based on informant testimony.

Prosecutorial Misconduct

Prosecutorial misconduct typically includes the suppression of exculpatory evidence (*Brady*), utilization by the prosecution (knowingly) of perjured testimony at trial, and inappropriate comments at the sentencing phase by the prosecutor (Harmon, 2001b). Harmon (2001b) and Bedau and Radelet (1987) found this factor as the leading and most prevalent reason leading to wrongful capital convictions. In a recent piece, Joy (2006) suggests that prosecutorial misconduct is the result of three institutional conditions: vague ethics rules that provide ambiguous guidance to prosecutors; considerable discretionary authority with little to no transparency; and inadequate remedies for prosecutorial misconduct that create perverse incentives for prosecutors to engage in misconduct. Joy (2006) suggests modest proposals to reduce incidence of prosecutorial misconduct, including the identification by the American Bar Association of clearer, more specific rules that can provide better guidance; the increase of transparency and setting of clearer limits on prosecutorial discretion; the enforcement by each office of its own internal norms for the exercise of discretion; public access of these norms, notwithstanding interference by the public; and more accountability and effective remedies for prosecutorial misconduct.

Ineffective Assistance of Counsel

The issue of ineffective counsel in capital cases has been well-documented (Bright, 1992, 1994). Additionally, much of the previously discussed research identifies this factor as a primary cause of erroneous capital convictions (Bedau & Radelet, 1987; Gross, 1996; Yant, 1991; Huff, Rattner, & Sagarin, 1996). One reasonable explanation for the prevalence of ineffective counsel claims could be the extreme cost of litigating capital cases. As suggested by Bright (1994), individuals charged with capital murder usually cannot afford the fees associated with an adequate legal defense. Nor do most states provide the experts and resources necessary to present the best defense in a capital trial.

In general, there is reason to believe that capital defense representation has probably improved significantly since 2000, when the United States Supreme Court raised the bar for effective assistance of counsel in capital cases by requiring a more effective investigation into mitigation evidence. More specifically, even though the court did not change the actual standard for ineffective assistance of counsel, they interpreted the standard differently over the years. The standard that was established in *Strickland v. Washington* (1984), where the court ruled that it was not ineffective assistance for the defense lawyer to fail to investigate possible mitigation evidence, changed when, 16 years later in *Williams v. Taylor*, the court ruled that a strikingly similar case fell below the standard of "reasonably effective assistance" (see 529 U.S. 362, 395–96 [2000]). The court then reaffirmed this more rigorous standard to investigate mitigation evidence in *Wiggins v. Smith*, 539 U.S. 510, 524 (2003), which held that defense counsel must make attempts to obtain all reasonably available mitigating evidence.

Racial Bias

The issue of racial discrimination has long played an essential component in the debate over the death penalty. For instance, "nearly 90 percent of those executed for rape since 1930 were black" (Wolfgang & Riedel, 1976, p. 105). More recent studies have continued to indicate that racial discrimination continues in the application of the death penalty (Baldus, Woodworth, & Pulaski, 1990; Baldus, Woodworth, Zuckerman, Weiner, & Broffitt, 1998; Keil & Vito, 1995; Radelet & Pierce, 1991).

Much of the prior research on the relationship between racial discrimination and innocence has focused on the role of the race of the defendant in contributing to a wrongful conviction. Studies on wrongful convictions have reached the conclusion that the race of the offender is a significant factor leading to errors (Bedau & Radelet, 1987; Huff, Rattner & Sagarin, 1996; Radelet, Lofquist & Bedau, 1996; Dwyer, Neufeld, & Scheck, Neufeld, & Dwyer, 2000). Numerous exoneration cases establish the link between racism and wrongful convictions (see Clarence Brandley & Walter McMillian (cases summarized in Harmon, 2004). Moreover, quantitative studies suggest that the combination of the race of the defendant and victim are important predictors of wrongful capital convictions (Harmon, 2001a, 2004). These innocence studies support the conclusion that cases involving minority defendants and white victims are more likely to result in a death sentence than any other racial combination, thus supporting the persistence of racial bias in the application of the death penalty as a leading factor in contributing to wrongful capital convictions.

Forensic Evidence

Fabricant and Carrington (2016) deconstruct the jurisprudence of two forensic disciplines that have been implicated in a number of wrongful convictions. They examined forensic odontology (bite mark evidence) and forensic hair microscopy and describe in detail the many flaws in the specifics of the two aforementioned forensic sciences. In regard to odontology, a number of overturned cases have found that scientifically invalid evidence and erroneous jurisprudence led to those convictions. The courts precluded legitimate claims of innocence in dozens of cases, including capital convictions. Fabricant and Carrington suggest that forensic science attributed to bite marks is not as sound as was once believed, and there are many convictions that were based on bite mark evidence, yet the science has not been empirical validated in its entirety. The authors argue for the requirement of a pretrial reliability screening prior to allowing bite mark evidence at trial.

Garrett and Neufeld (2009) explored forensic science testimony by prosecution experts in the trial of wrongful felony convictions that were exonerated by postconviction DNA testing. This study found that in the bulk of the trials, 82 cases, or 60%, of forensic analysts called by the prosecution provided invalid testimony at trial. This was discovered by examining trial transcripts of previously exonerated individuals who had forensic analysts testimony used at their trials. The study found the testimony wrought with errors. The research found the outcome cannot be attributed to a small percentage of analysts. In fact, these cases were widespread and included invalid testimony by 72 forensic analysts called by the prosecution and employed by 52 laboratories, practices, or hospitals from 25 states.

Giannelli (2007) examined the failures of crime labs in a number of different states and the FBI lab. He argued that if all the forensics sciences applied the same level of scrutiny and standards as DNA lab analysis, wrongful convictions would be less likely to occur. Currently, faulty/misinformed forensic science has accounted for a significant number of wrongful convictions. A recent study of 200 DNA exonerations found that forensic evidence (prevalent in 57% of the cases) was the second leading type of evidence (after eyewitness identifications at 79%) used in wrongful noncapital conviction cases. While less prevalent in capital cases, DNA was a catalyst in 20 out of the 156 post-Furman capital exonerations (www.deathpenaltyinfo.org, retrieved on 12/24/2016). The research suggests the following policy implications: the accreditation of crime labs; ensuring components are maintained and enforced; the standardization of technical procedures to address problem issues; the certification of examiners; and the creation of forensic science commissions.

Mistaken Eyewitness Identification

Loftus has documented the significant problems of eyewitness misidentification and false memory (Loftus, 1996, 2003). However, the research on causes of wrongful capital convictions suggest that this factor, while important, may be less prevalent in capital as opposed to noncapital cases (Bedau & Radelet, 1987; Radelet et al., 1992; Harmon, 2001a).

False Confessions

Leo and his colleagues' extensive research on interrogation techniques and false confessions is significant (Davis, Leo, & Follette, 2010; Drizin & Leo, 2004; Leo, 2001; Leo & Ofshe, 1998). In a recent article, Leo and Davis (2010) examined the processes through which false confessions, once obtained by police, may lead to wrongful convictions. They examined the psychological processes linking false confession to wrongful conviction and failures of postconviction relief. Moreover, the authors discussed the reciprocal influences of the mechanisms and their biasing impact on the perceptions and behaviors of suspects, investigators, prosecution and defense attorneys, juries, and trial and appellate judges. Additionally, Leo & Liu (2009) conducted a study of potential jurors to determine their perceptions of psychological interrogation techniques and their impact on the risk of false confessions. Their results suggest that potential jurors greatly underestimate the likelihood of false confessions and the risk that psychologically coercive interrogation techniques may have on eliciting false confessions.

Typical Factors That Lead to the Discovery of Wrongful Convictions

Prior research suggests the discovery of wrongful convictions tends to surface for numerous reasons. A primary factor in capital cases is the appointment of new counsel and the continued investigation that counsel conducts. In her research, Harmon (2001b) found that the appointment of new counsel is very likely the main reason for capital exonerations (Harmon, 2001b). The discovery of errors and new evidence that resulted in exoneration are usually the result of the hard work and dogged investigation by defense attorneys whose dedication goes above and beyond the normal standards and requirements of appellate attorneys; frequently, this work and investigation continue long after the defendant has been convicted. In many exoneration capital cases, the attorneys worked pro bono for many years before seeing their clients exonerated. In these situations, the system provided no financial support to assist the defense attorneys. It was also customary for these attorneys to hire investigators, using their own money, to conduct complete reinvestigations of the cases in order to discover new exculpatory evidence. In many, if not most, cases, the system had nothing to do with the new evidence coming to light. An investigation unrelated to the actual judicial process, conducted by a filmmaker, journalist, reporter, law class, or family member, often led to the discovery of new exculpatory evidence. The fact that some of these defendants were fortunate to have attorneys represent them pro bono for many years fighting for their cause, or were "lucky" to have a third party become involved, cannot be considered a part of the official criminal justice process (see Radelet & Bedau, 2014 for a complete discussion of "the role of lady luck").

Other prevalent reasons for the discovery of errors include recantations due to religious conversion or feelings of guilt, the accidental discovery of physical evidence, a confession from the 'true culprit', and the continued investigation by a journalist, filmmaker, or a newspaper reporter. These factors were also found by Bedau & Radelet (1987) and Radelet et al. (1992).

Innocence, Media, and Public Opinion

Public support for capital punishment is arguably the primary factor supporting its continued use in the United States. Although public support for the death penalty has decreased significantly since the 1990s, general national support for the sanction remains, and more than half of Americans support its use (Gallup, 2017). Opponents of the death penalty have spent decades trying to inform the public about a range of issues associated with its use (e.g., costs, failure to deter, botched executions, wrongful convictions/innocence, racial disparities, etc.). Those arguments, along with a declining violent crime rate since the 1990s, may have contributed to the decrease in support for the most punitive sanction in our justice system. More recently the discussion of wrongful convictions and the execution of innocent people has come to the forefront of public debate and discussions.

The innocence argument has been gaining ground, and we are seeing the topic more frequently discussed by policy makers (politicians and advocacy groups—both abolitionists and retentionists), journalists and media, and academics and researchers. In their discussion of the changing death penalty arguments, Radelet and Borg (2000) suggest that death penalty retentionists are now willing to accept that innocent defendants may be executed. They argued that

> [u]ntil a decade ago, the pro-death penalty literature took the position that such blunders were historical oddities and could never be committed in modern times. Today the argument is not over the existence or even the inevitability of such errors, but whether the alleged benefits of the death penalty outweigh these uncontested liabilities.
>
> *(p. 50)*

Americans who support capital punishment may become more knowledgeable about the possibility and frequency of wrongful convictions in capital cases and pause to consider how this new information shapes their views on the subject.

Sarat (2005) similarly suggests that innocence is a primary factor in changing the debate on the death penalty and that the issue of innocence has helped to inform what he refers to as the "new abolitionism." Correspondingly, Young (2004) suggests that "the high level of support for the death penalty that has characterized this nation for decades has shown signs of erosion, primarily as a result of mounting evidence that erroneous convictions may be more common than previously thought" (p. 152). Concern over the execution of the innocent continues to grow, and the public has more access to information about this issue than ever before.

One of the shifts in focus to innocence and the death penalty occurred after reports of Northwestern University journalism students uncovering evidence that helped to free numerous death row inmates in the state of Illinois. Public concern over the number of people wrongfully convicted began to grow. Fan, Keltner, and Wyatt (2002) noted that media reports included "the growing DNA evidence leading states like Illinois to release more wrongly convicted inmates than the number that the state has executed" (p. 441). Based off of the knowledge of 13 exonerated death row inmates in Illinois, then-Governor George Ryan undertook one of the most significant efforts by any politician to reduce the possibility of executing innocent defendants in the future by declaring a moratorium on the death penalty in his state in February 2000 (Fan et al., 2002). Then, on January 11, 2003,

Governor Ryan used his clemency powers to pardon four and to commute 167 inmates sentenced to death (Sarat, 2005). Governor Ryan's actions garnered significant media attention. The popular documentary film, *Deadline* (2004), later told the story of the Northwestern University students and Governor Ryan's efforts to draw attention to the potentially irreversible acts of injustice in the criminal justice system. What happened in Illinois is often thought to have influenced the changing tide in how the media now covers stories on the death penalty in America.

Media and Innocence

It's hard not to notice the increase in media coverage on the wrongfully convicted over the last two decades. The decrease in support for the death penalty seen in public opinion polls may be largely due to public and media attention on exonerations (Harmon & Lofquist, 2005). In one study, Fan et al. (2002) examined the influence of news reports on support for capital punishment. The researchers compared a sample of 39,472 *Washington Post* and Associated Press news stories (scored for favorability toward the death penalty) to corresponding time trends in a series of public opinion polls from 1977 to 2001. They found that the media progressively increased their coverage on innocence over time and that there was a corresponding decrease in support for the death penalty. The researchers stated that their study had "shown that press coverage is a plausible driving force for opinion about the death penalty and that a major contributor to the recent movement of public opinion against the death penalty has been increased coverage of the innocence frame" (p. 449–450). They further suggested that the "innocence frame, in fact, had over ten times the impact of general press discussion unfavorable to the death penalty" (p. 450).

According to Fan et al. (2002), "since the early 1990s, mass media have increasingly framed capital punishment in terms of the execution of innocent individuals, while in earlier years the frames concentrated on moral or utilitarian arguments for the death penalty" (p 441). A number of television shows, documentaries, and feature films have highlighted the issue of wrongful convictions within the American criminal justice system. A recent documentary, *The Fear of 13* (2015), told the story of Nick Yarris, a 2004 exoneree from Pennsylvania's death row who served 21 years after being wrongfully convicted of murder. Frontline's *Death by Fire* (2010) presented the story of Todd Willingham, who was executed in 2004 for the arson-murder of his three children even after serious doubts about his guilt. After a reexamination of his case, forensic experts suggest that that the fire was accidental and not arson and concluded that Willingham was not responsible for the deaths of his children. Similarly, the 2005 TV movie, *The Exonerated*, shared the stories of six death row exonerees whose stories were told by highly regarded television and film stars, including Susan Sarandon, Brian Dennehy, and Danny Glover.

Although they did not all involve capital cases, PBS' Frontline series has continued to highlight a number of cases and issues involving innocence and wrongful convictions since 2000 (*Burden of Innocence*, 2003; *Requiem for Frank Lee Smith*, 2002; *The Child Cases*, 2011; *The Confessions*, 2010). Relatedly, a number of documentary filmmakers have taken on projects to highlight the wrongful convictions of crimes involving multiple defendants. Ken Burns, David McMahon, and Sarah Burn's 2012 documentary, *The Central Park Five*, tells the story of five black and Latino teenagers who were wrongfully convicted for the rape of a white woman in New York City's Central Park in 1989. Other documentaries have similarly highlighted the cases of the "West Memphis Three," who were teenage boys wrongfully convicted of the murders of three 8-year-old children in 1993 (*Paradise Lost: The Child Murders at Robin Hood Hills*, 1996; *Paradise Lost 2: Revelations*, 2000; *Paradise Lost 3: Purgatory*, 2011; *West of Memphis*, 2012). More recently, the documentary *Southwest of Salem: The Story of the San Antonio Four* (2016), chronicles the story of four Latina lesbians who were exonerated in 2016 after their wrongful convictions for gang-raping two young girls in San Antonio, Texas, in 1994.

It is hard not to notice the media's shift in focus on the wrongfully accused and convicted in both capital and noncapital offenses. Examples of this new media frame continue and appear to grow in popularity. An excellent example of public interest in wrongful convictions can be seen with the incredibly popular Netflix series *Making a Murderer* (2015), which tells the story of Steven Avery, a man who was exonerated after serving almost two decades in prison. As the documentary filmmakers were working to tell the story of his wrongful conviction and release, they found themselves in the midst of a new story when Steven Avery was accused and convicted of murder in another case. The filmmakers, through interviews with Steven, his family, and his two attorneys, suggested that there was a significant amount of evidence to cast doubt about Avery's guilt (although much of this is disputed by the prosecutors in Wisconsin involved in his case) as well as the guilt of his co-conspirator and teenage nephew, Brendan Dassey. This documentary television series was extremely popular, and within months after its release it had over 19 million viewers (Nededog, 2016). The series is expected to return with a second season to update the viewers on both Steven and Brendan's efforts to appeal their cases. Although this series did not involve a capital defendant, its popularity demonstrates that the public is interested in hearing the stories of the wrongfully accused.

A number of recent books on wrongful convictions have become very popular and were #1 New York Times Bestsellers. In his first attempt at nonfiction, popular legal thriller and crime author John Grisham wrote *The Innocent Man: Murder and Injustice in a Small Town* (2006). His book told the story of Ron Williamson, who was sentenced to death and released 11 years later for a crime he didn't commit. More recently, in *Just Mercy: A Story of Justice and Redemption,* Bryan Stevenson shares the deeply moving work he has done to help free the wrongfully accused, particularly for those defendants sentenced to death. Although Stevenson discusses various issues within the American criminal justice system throughout his book, he focuses the book around the case of Walter McMillian, a black man who was sentenced to death for a murder in Alabama that he didn't commit. Both of these incredibly popular and bestselling books suggest that the American public is interested in this topic and wish to learn more about injustices within our justice system.

The increase in the use of social media as a platform to disseminate information on issues of crime and justice may also impact public opinion. Advocacy groups such as *The Innocence Project* (both the national organization as well as numerous regional affiliates) have hundreds of thousands of followers on Facebook who are both viewing and sharing their posted stories with others. There is also the emergence and growing popularity of internet podcasts. Along with the growth of this type of media, there are now a number of popular podcasts that focus on the topics of wrongful convictions and innocence in the criminal justice system. Numerous new podcasts on the topic arose, including "Actual Innocence" and "Wrongful Conviction." The host of "Wrongful Conviction," Jason Flom, a founding member of the Innocence Project, interviews men and women who were wrongfully convicted of crimes they did not commit (of which many were sentenced to death). In the podcasts, Flom allows these victims of injustice to share their stories, many of whom seek to educate the public on wrongful convictions and the impact it has on the wrongfully accused, their families, and society. Likewise the popularity of the podcast "Serial," which told the story of Adnan Sayand, a teenager convicted of murdering his girlfriend in Maryland, is arguably one of the most popular podcasts to date, with each episode being downloaded more than 3 million times (Roberts, 2014). "Serial" and the related podcasts "Undisclosed" and "Truth & Justice" all lend evidence to suggest that the public is extremely intrigued by information suggesting that people are being wrongfully convicted in our justice system.

Overall, these examples serve to support the idea that the media framework on innocence and wrongful convictions has changed. There is no doubt that there is more media coverage on this issue and that the public is interested in reading, viewing, and listening to more information about innocence and wrongful convictions. Researchers, however, are only in the beginning stages of examining the influence that information on innocence has on public opinion and support for capital punishment.

Public Opinion and Innocence

Social science research on the death penalty has impacted the way in which the American public now discusses and debates policies on capital punishment (Radelet & Borg, 2000). Academics and researchers are now specifically examining how the innocence argument is related to public opinion and support for the death penalty. In an effort to gain a better understanding of these beliefs, Unnever and Cullen (2005) empirically evaluated the relationship between the two constructs. Using data collected by the Gallup Organization in 2003 (n = 899), the researchers first explored general support for the death penalty and found that 54% of respondents favored the death penalty over life imprisonment without the possibility of parole for those convicted of murder. They also evaluated respondents' beliefs that innocent people have been executed and whether the death penalty is applied unfairly. The findings indicate that 74% of respondents thought an innocent person had been executed in the past five years and 36% of respondents believed the death penalty is applied unfairly. Respondents who believed that innocent people have been executed were significantly less likely to support capital punishment. Similarly, respondents who believed that the death penalty is applied unfairly were also significantly less likely to support the sanction.

Unnever and Cullen further examined the relationship between race of respondent and views toward capital punishment, innocence, and fairness. Similar to previous research, they found that African Americans were significantly less likely to support capital punishment than whites. To examine this relationship in terms of innocence and fairness, the results of their research showed that 29% of the difference in support for capital punishment between African Americans and whites could be attributed to differences in beliefs about innocence and fairness. They also found that beliefs about innocent people being put to death had more of an impact on African American support (or lack of support) for the death penalty than whites. The authors suggest that among African Americans, news of death row exonerations may be "experienced as vicarious victimizations" and that "it is easier to imagine that they, someone they know, or a member of their racial group would find themselves wrongly accused and convicted of a capital crime" (p. 30).

Using data from the General Social Survey, Young (2004) also found a connection between race, innocence, and support for the death penalty. The researcher examined the relationship between racially prejudiced beliefs and views toward convicting innocent defendants as well as overall death penalty support. The analysis of the data found that those who held racially prejudiced beliefs toward African Americans were more likely to prefer convicting innocent defendants over acquitting guilty defendants. Young also found that those who prefer convicting the innocent over acquitting the guilty were more likely to support the death penalty. This was similarly found in Young's (2000) study suggesting that those who believed convicting the innocent was not as serious of a judicial mistake as letting the guilty go free were more likely to support the death penalty.

Lambert, Camp, Clarke, and Jiang (2011) reexamined and conducted additional analyses from a study testing the Marshall hypotheses suggesting that additional information about the death penalty would lead to a reduction in support for its use (see also Lambert & Clark, 2001). Using a sample of undergraduate university students (n = 730) at one public university in Michigan, the researchers surveyed students about their views toward the death penalty and their knowledge about capital punishment and collected general demographic characteristics of participants. During the second part of their survey they randomly assigned short essays (one on deterrence, one on innocence, and one control essay). Following the essay, students were asked about any changes in their views about deterrence, innocence, and overall support for capital punishment. Of particular interest to this discussion is whether information about the possibility and frequency of innocent people being put to death was found to change one's views toward the death penalty. The researchers found that 38% of those who read the innocence essay reported a reduction in support for capital punishment. In fact, students who read the essay on innocence were 483% more likely to report a reduction in death penalty support than students who read the control essay. Their final model showed that race and type of essay read were the only significant predictors of a decrease in support for capital punishment. White students were found to be significantly less likely to report a change in views than nonwhite students. Previous research has often found that whites are more likely to support the death penalty than nonwhites. This appears to suggest that race also plays a role in the ability of information about innocence to change levels of support for capital punishment.

As mentioned earlier, researchers are only beginning to examine the influence of information about innocence on support for the death penalty. It is clear that additional research needs to be done before any definitive conclusions can be made. However, it is clear that media reports and outlets for discussions on wrongful convictions has grown significantly, and public interest seems to be gaining. As we continue to read, see, and hear more about innocent defendants being exonerated from death row, researchers will continue to be called upon to further investigate the relationship.

References

Adams, R. D., Hoffer, W., & Hoffer, M. M. (1991). *Adams v. Texas*. New York, NY: St. Martin's Press.

Armbrust, S. (2002). Chance and the exoneration of Anthony Porter. In D. Dow & M. Dow (Eds.), *The machinery of death: The reality of America's death penalty regime* (pp. 157–166). New York, NY: Routledge.

Aronson, J. D., & Cole, S. A. (2009). Science and the death penalty: DNA, innocence, and the debate over capital punishment in the United States. *Law & Social Inquiry, 34*(3), 603–633.

Balaban, B. (Director). (2005, January 27). *The exonerated* [TV Movie]. USA: Court TV & Radical Media.

Baldus, D. C., Woodworth, G., & Pulaski, C. A. (1990). *Equal justice and the death penalty: A legal and empirical analysis*. Boston: Northeastern University Press.

Baldus, D. C., Woodworth, G., Zuckerman, D., Weiner, N. A., & Broffitt, B. (1998). Race discrimination and the death penalty in the post-Furman era: An empirical and legal analysis with recent findings from Philadelphia. *Cornell Law Review, 83*, 1638–1770.

Baumgartner, F. R., De Boef, S. L., & Boydstun, A. E. (2008). *The decline of the death penalty and the discovery of innocence*. New York, NY: Cambridge University Press.

Bedau, H. A., & Radelet, M. L. (1987). Miscarriages of justice in potentially capital cases. *Stanford Law Review, 40*, 21–179.

Berg, A. (Director). (2012). *West of Memphis* [Documentary]. New Zealand: Disarming Films & WingNut Films.

Berlinger, J., & Sinofsky, B. (Directors). (1996). *Paradise lost: The child murders at Robin Hood Hills* [Documentary]. USA: Home Box Office (HBO) & Creative Thinking International Ltd.

Berlinger, J., & Sinofsky, B. (Directors). (2000). *Paradise lost 2: Revelations* [Documentary]. USA: Home Box Office (HBO), Creative Thinking International Ltd., & Hand to Mouth Productions.

Berlinger, J., & Sinofsky, B. (Directors). (2011). *Paradise lost 3: Revelations* [Documentary]. USA: Home Box Office (HBO) & Radical Media.

Berlow, A. (2000, May 11). The hanging governor. *Salon.com*. Retrieved from www.salon.com/2000/05/11/bush_56/

Bikel, O. (Director). (2002, April 11). *Requiem for Frank Lee Smith* [Documentary, TV Episode]. USA: Frontline.

Bikel, O. (Director). (2003, May 1). *Burden of Innocence* [Documentary, TV Episode]. USA: Frontline.

Bikel, O. (Director). (2010, November 9). *The confessions* [Documentary, TV Episode]. USA: Frontline.

Borchard, E. M. (1932). *Convicting the innocent: Errors of criminal justice*. New Haven, CT: Yale University Press.

Bright, S. B. (1992). In defense of life: Enforcing the Bill of Rights on behalf of poor, minority and disadvantaged persons facing the death penalty. *Missouri Law Review, 57*, 849–870.

Bright, S. B. (1994). Counsel for the poor: The death sentence not for the worst crime but for the worst lawyer. *Yale Law Journal, 103*, 1835–1883.

Burnett, C. (2002). *Justice denied: Clemency appeals in death penalty cases*. Boston, MA: Northeastern University Press.

Burns, K., McMahon, D., & Burns, S. (Directors). (2012). *The Central Park Five* [Documentary]. USA: Florentine Films & WETA.

Burtman, B. (2002). Innocence lost. In D. Dow & M. Dow (Eds.), *The machinery of death: The reality of America's death penalty regime* (pp. 144–156). New York, NY: Routledge.

Chaudry, R., Miller, C., & Simpson, S. (2015). *Undisclosed podcast*. Retrieved from www.undisclosed-podcast.com

Chevigny, K., & Johnson, K. (Directors). (2004). *Deadline* [Documentary]. USA: Big Mouth Productions.

Davies, N. (1993). *White lies: Rape, murder, and justice Texas Style*. New York, NY: Pantheon.

Davis, D., Leo, R., & Follette, W. C. (2010). Selling confession: Setting the stage with the "sympathetic detective with a time-limited offer". *Journal of Contemporary Criminal Justice, 26*(4), 441–457.

Deeter, J. (Director). (2010, October 19). *Death by fire* [Documentary, TV Episode]. USA: Frontline.

Demos, M., & Ricciardi, L. (Directors). (2015). *Making a murderer* [Documentary TV Series]. USA: Synthesis Films & Netflix.

Drizin, S. A., & Leo, R. A. (2004). The problem of false confessions in the post-DNA world. *North Carolina Law Review, 82*(3), 891–1007.

Earley, P. (1995). *Circumstantial evidence: Death, life, and justice in a Southern Town.* New York, NY: Bantam.

Edds, M. (2003). *An expendable man: The near-execution of Earl Washington, Jr.* New York, NY: New York University Press.

Esquenazi, D. S. (Director). (2016). *Southwest of Salem: The story of the San Antonio Four* [Documentary]. USA: Motto Pictures & Naked Edge Films.

Fabricant, M. C., & Carrington, W. T. (2016). The shifted paradigm: Forensic sciences' overdue evolution from magic to law. *Virginia Journal of Criminal Law, 4* 1–115. Retrieved from http://dx.doi.org/10.2139/ssrn.2572480

Fan, D., Keltner, K., & Wyatt, R. (2002). A matter of guilt or innocence: How news reports affect support for the death penalty. *International Journal of Public Opinion Research, 14,* 439–451.

Flom, J. (2016). *Wrongful convictions podcast* (reVolver). Retrieved from www.wrongfulconvictionpodcast.com

Frank, J., & Frank, B. (1957). *Not guilty.* Garden City, NY: Doubleday.

Gallup Poll. (2017). Retrieved January 8, 2017 from www.gallup.com/poll/1606/death-penalty.aspx

Gardner, E. S. (1952). *The court of last resort.* New York, NY: William Sloane Associates.

Garrett, B. L. (2008). Judging innocence. *Columbia Law Review, 108,* 55–142.

Garrett, B. L., & Neufeld, P. J. (2009). Invalid forensic science testimony and wrongful convictions. *Virginia Law Review, 95*(1), 101–190. Retrieved from http://ssrn.com/abstract=1354604

Giannelli, P. C. (2007). Wrongful convictions and forensic science: The need to regulate crime labs. *North Carolina Law Review, 86,* 162–236. Retrieved from http://ssrn.com/abstract=1083735

Gould, J., & Leo, R. (2010). One hundred years later: Wrongful convictions after a century of research. *The Journal of Criminal Law and Criminology (1973–), 100*(3), 825–868. http://www.jstor.org/stable/25766110?seq=1#page_scan_tab_contents.

Gould, J. B., Carrano, J., Leo, R. A., & Young, J. K. (2013). Predicting erroneous convictions: A social science approach to miscarriages of justice. https://papers.ssrn.com/sol3/papers.cfm?abstract_id=2231777.

GrassRoots Investigative Project. (2000). *Reasonable doubts: Is the U.S. executing innocent people?* Hyattsville, MD: Quixote Center.

Grisham, J. (2006). *The innocent man: Murder and injustice in a small town.* New York, NY: Doubleday.

Gross, S. R. (1996). The risks of death: Why erroneous convictions are common in capital cases. *Buffalo Law Review, 44,* 469–500.

Harmon, T. R. (2001a). Predictors of miscarriages of justice in capital cases. *Justice Quarterly, 18*(4), 949–968.

Harmon, T. R. (2001b). Guilty until proven innocent: An analysis of post-Furman capital errors. *Criminal Justice Policy Review, 12*(2), 113–139.

Harmon, T. R. (2004). Race for your life: An analysis of the role of race in erroneous capital convictions. *Criminal Justice Review, 29*(1), 76–96.

Harmon, T. R., Besch, R., Amendola, A., & Pehrson, N. (2016). Post-Furman death row exonerations and publicity in the news. *Criminal Law Bulletin, 52*(6), 1590–1619.

Harmon, T. R., & Lofquist, W. (2005). Too late for luck: A comparison of post-Furman exonerations and executions of the innocent. *Crime and Delinquency, 51,* 498–520.

Huff, R. C., Rattner, A., & Sagarin, E. (1996). *Convicted but innocent: Wrongful conviction and public policy.* Thousand Oaks, CA: Sage Publications.

Ingle, J. B. (1990). *Last rights: 13 fatal encounters with the state's justice.* Nashville, TN: Abingdon Press.

Innocence and the Death Penalty | Death Penalty Information Center. (2017). Retrieved January, 2017 from www.deathpenaltyinfo.org/innocence-and-death-penalty

Jackson, J., Burke, W. F., Jr., & Stockton, D. W. (1999). *Dead run: The untold story of Dennis Stockton and America's only mass escape from death row.* New York, NY: Times Books.

Joy, P. A. (2006). The relationship between prosecutorial misconduct and wrongful convictions: Shaping remedies for a broken system. *Wisconsin Law Review, 2006,* 399–431. Retrieved from http://ssrn.com/abstract=948307

Keil, T. J., & Vito, G. (1995). Race and the death penalty in Kentucky murder trials: 1976–1991. *American Journal of Criminal Justice, 20,* 17–36.

Kirchmeier, J. L. (2002). Another place beyond here: The death penalty moratorium movement in the United States. *University of Colorado Law Review, 73,* 1–116.

Koenig, S. (Executive Producer). (2014). *Serial podcast.* Retrieved from www.serialpodcast.org

Lambert, E., Camp, S., Clarke, A., & Jiang, S. (2011). The impact of information on death penalty support, revisited. *Crime & Delinquency, 57*(4), 572–599.

Lambert, E., & Clark, A. (2001). Individual's support for the death penalty: A partial test of the Marshall hypothesis. *Criminal Justice Policy Review, 12*, 215–234.

Leo, R. (2001). False confessions: Causes, consequences, and solutions. In S. Westervelt & J. Humphrey (Eds.), *Wrongly convicted: Perspectives on failed justice* (pp. 36–54). New Brunswick, NJ: Rutgers University Press.

Leo, R. A., & Davis, D. (2010). From false confession to wrongful conviction: Seven psychological processes. *Journal of Psychiatry and Law, 38*, 9–57. Retrieved from http://ssrn.com/abstract=1328622

Leo, R. A., & Gould, J. B. (2009). Studying wrongful convictions: Learning from social science. *Ohio State Journal of Criminal Law, 7*(1), 7–30.

Leo, R. A., & Liu, B. (2009). What do potential jurors know about police interrogation techniques and false confessions. *Behavioral Sciences and the Law, 27*, 381–399.

Leo, R., & Ofshe, R. (1998). The consequences of false confessions: Deprivations of liberty and miscarriages of justice in the age of psychological interrogation. *The Journal of Criminal Law and Criminology, 88*, 429–496.

Lofquist, W. S., & Harmon, T. R. (2008). Fatal errors: Compelling claims of executions of the innocent in the post-Furman era. In R. C. Huff & M. Killias (Eds.), *Wrongful conviction: International perspectives on miscarriages of justice* (pp. 93–115). Philadelphia, PA: Temple University Press.

Loftus, E. F. (1996). *Eyewitness testimony.* Cambridge, MA: Harvard University Press.

Loftus, E. F. (2003, November). Make believe memories. *American Psychologist, 58*(11), 867–873.

Mello, M. (2001). *The wrong man: A true story of innocence on death row.* Minneapolis, MN: University of Minnesota Press.

Natapoff, A. (2006). Beyond unreliable: How snitches contribute to wrongful convictions. *Golden Gate University Law Review*, 2006; Loyola-LA Legal Studies Paper No. 2006–17. Retrieved from SSRN http://ssrn.com/abstract=905864

Nededog, J. (2016, February 12). Here's how popular Netflix's "making a murderer" really was according to a research company. *Business Insider.* Retrieved from www.businessinsider.com/netflix-making-a-murderer-ratings-2016-2

Parloff, R. (1996). *Triple jeopardy: A story of law at its best—and worst.* Boston, MA: Little, Brown.

Radelet, M. L., & Bedau, H. A. (2014). The execution of the innocent. In J. R. Acker, R. B. Bohm, & C. S. Lanier (Eds.), *America's experiment with capital punishment* (3rd ed., pp. 357–372). Durham, North Carolina: Carolina Academic Press.

Radelet, M. L., Bedau, H. A., & Putnam, C. E. (1992). *In spite of innocence: Erroneous convictions in capital cases.* Boston, MA: Northeastern University Press.

Radelet, M. L., & Borg, M. (2000). The changing nature of death penalty debates. *Annual Review of Sociology, 26*, 43–61.

Radelet, M. L., Lofquist, W. S., & Bedau, H. A. (1996). Prisoners released from death rows since 1970 because of doubts about their guilt. *Thomas M. Cooley Law Review, 13*, 907–966.

Radelet, M. L., & Pierce, G. L. (1991). Choosing those who will die: Race and the death penalty in Florida. *Florida Law Review, 43*, 1–34.

Radin, E. D. (1964). *The innocents.* New York, NY: William Morrow.

Riley, C. (Producer), & Sington, D. (Director). (2015). *The fear of 13* [Documentary]. UK: Dogwoof Pictures.

Roberts, A. (2014, December 23). The "Serial" podcast: By the numbers. *CNN.* Retrieved from www.cnn.com/2014/12/18/showbiz/feat-serial-podcast-btn/

Robinson, D. (Producer). (2016). *Actual innocence podcast.* Retrieved from www.actualinpod.com

Ruff, B. (2016). *Truth & justice podcast.* Retrieved from www.truthandjusticepod.com

Sarat, A. (2005). Innocence, error, and the "new abolitionism": A commentary. *Criminology & Public Policy, 4*(1), 45–54.

Scheck, B., Neufeld, P., & Dwyer, J. (2000). *Actual innocence: Five days to execution and other dispatches from the wrongly convicted.* New York, NY: Doubleday.

Stevenson, B. (2015). *Just mercy: A story of justice and redemption.* New York, NY: Spiegel & Grau.

Tucker, J. C. (1997). *May god have mercy: A true story of crime and punishment.* New York, NY: Norton.

Unnever, J. D., & Cullen, F. T. (2005). Executing the innocent and support for capital punishment: Implications for public policy. *Criminology & Public Policy, 4*(1), 3–38.

Upin, C. (Director). (2011, June 28). *The Child Cases* [Documentary, TV Episode]. USA: Frontline.

Warden, R. & Protess, D. (1998). *A promise of justice: The eighteen year fight to save four innocent men.* New York: Hyperion.

Welch, M., & Burr, R. (2002). The politics of finality and the execution of the innocent: The case of Gary Graham. In D. Dow & M. Dow (Eds.), *The machinery of death: The reality of America's death penalty regime* (pp. 127–143). New York, NY: Routledge.

Wiseman, C. M. (1996). Representing the condemned: A critique of capital punishment. *Marquette Law Review, 79*, 731–758.

Wolfgang, M. E., & Riedel, M. (1976). Rape, racial discrimination and the death penalty. In H. A. Bedau & C. M. Pierce (Eds.), *Capital punishment in the United States* (pp. 99–121). New York: AMS Press.

Yant, M. (1991). *Presumed guilty: When innocent people are wrongly convicted.* Buffalo, NY: Prometheus Books.

Young, R. L. (2000). Punishment at all costs: On religion, convicting the innocent, and supporting the death penalty. *William & Mary Bill of Rights Journal, 9,* 237–246.

Young, R. L. (2004). Guilty until proven innocent: Conviction orientation, racial attitudes, and support for capital punishment. *Deviant Behavior, 25,* 151–167.

Cases Cited

Daubert v. Merrell Dow Pharms, 509 U.S. 579 (1993).
Strickland v. Washington, 466 U.S. 668 (1984).
Wiggins v. Smith, 539 U.S. 510 (2003).
Williams v. Taylor, 529 U.S. 362 (2000).
Woodson v. North Carolina, 428 U.S. 280 (1976).

33

LIVING AND WORKING ON DEATH ROW

Robert Johnson

There are over 2,900 prisoners living under sentence of death in 34 states and the federal prison system.[1] The vast majority of death row prisoners live under conditions of solitary confinement.[2] Conditions of solitary confinement vary across a limited spectrum. In states in which executions occur with regularity, conditions of solitary confinement tend to be more repressive, with prisoners spending virtually all of their time alone in their cells and heavily restrained when out of their cells for limited periods of solitary recreation, individual showers, or noncontact visits. In states where executions are rare, conditions tend to be more relaxed, with prisoners allowed out of their cells for longer periods, sometimes including small-group recreation and even contact visits.[3] In this article, the focus is on the more restrictive solitary confinement death row regimes, since these are the regimes more closely associated with the death penalty in action.

As in all prisons, and particularly all restricted housing units, a category that includes death rows, the roots of the experience of living on death row are firmly planted in the cell, the involuntary home base and monastic domicile of the prisoner. The day on death row begins and ends in the cell and can be characterized as a barren routine embodied in a barren cage. Cush, in his essay "Death Row Days," covers the elements of a typical day on death row, starting with awakening in the cell:

> At approximately 5:50AM the doors on the wing slam shut and I know that the Restricted Housing Unit guards on the 10–6 shift are leaving and the 6–2 shift will be coming on duty. I'm in a single person cell. The cell is literally all concrete and steel. The bed I was sleeping on is a concrete slab with a thin mattress on it. The walls are cinderblocks three-quarters of the way around, but the front of the cell is a wall of steel bars from left to right. Imagine the old style western cells with the whole front open to look right into the cell with no privacy and that is exactly what this cell looks like today. The toilet is right next to the bed and built into the back wall. The toilet and sink are a single unit of brushed steel. I must wash and drink water from the same sink-bowl above the toilet. There is a metal cabinet affixed to the wall at the front of the cell for personal property to be put into, and there is a cement table right beside it for me to put my food tray on. A plastic chair completes the furnishings of the cell.[4]

On typical death rows, such as that described by Cush, all meals are taken in the cell. The food is bland, unappetizing, and unhealthy. "The food menu has been the same for many years without improvement or a break in the monotony. The food quality is so bad that the majority of men here have high blood pressure and/or diabetes." Writing with a bitter sense of irony, and perhaps mindful of the high death rate on death row, Cush observes that "[t]he restricted movement and poor food is in itself a death sentence."[5]

Death rows have an ambiance all their own, at least as experienced by the prisoners themselves, who report distinctive odors (the smell of death and rot)[6] and an architecture and social climate that converge to make death rows feel like zoos:

> The way the cells are situated I can speak to another prisoner but I cannot see the person I am speaking to. The cells and cell-wing is set up in such a way that you hear and smell everything in your immediate area. It is truly like a zoo.[7]

The stresses of living under sentence of death in zoo-like solitary cages have been well documented.[8] Many prisoners deteriorate, and some experience recurring bouts of mental illness. Cush described the tragedy of such experiences in these words:

> I am in an area now where one of the men is seriously mentally ill. He talks to himself all day and late into the night. Often he screams that he is being raped and acts out the drama over and over again.[9]

This behavior borders on the normal on death row and other restricted housing units.[10] "Over the years," Cush continues, "I have been in this situation and worse. There have been times when the man next door would be smearing himself with his own feces and shouting all day and night."[11]

Condemned prisoners leave their cells for three main reasons: recreation, showers, and visits. Recreation is typically limited to brief stints in solitary cages described as akin to dog kennels.

> When the shift changes at 6AM, a guard comes around to take a list of those who want to go out to the dog kennel-run like exercise yards that I can go to five days a week for two hours a day. The two days a week that I do not get an opportunity to go to the yard I am confined to the cell for twenty-four hours. There is no shelter from the weather elements when there is inclement weather so on rainy or snow days I am confined to the cell for many days straight without even a brief relief.[12]

When out of the cell en route to exercise areas, prisoners are shackled and under heavy guard. Cush reports that prisoners feel vulnerable to attack as they pass the cells of other prisoners or when they are alone in the presence of officers. "Going to the exercise yard is a risk at times because then a person can be subjected to attacks from guards or prisoners." This danger reflects, in part, the fact that "many people are damaged mentally from their long-term stays in the RHU," including "guards and prisoners."[13]

Be that as it may, attacks occur with some regularity. Cush reports that

> there has been a number of savage attacks of prisoners throwing feces and urine on each other. I was in a cage that was right next to two men throwing feces and urine on each other with wild abandon. Over the years I've been attacked by guards and prisoners at different times when going to the yard.

Cush values the exercise enough to brave the risks involved, but "many, many others" do not and instead "refuse to go out because they fear being attacked." Cush reports that "[t]here are men who have not been out in the exercise yard for ten or more years."[14]

All departures from the cell, for recreation, showers, or visits, occur under heavy guard and are experienced as invasive and degrading. Again, quoting Cush:

> When I get to go to the shower I am handcuffed and escorted by guards down the wing and put into a glass shower. We are allowed only three showers a week and the showers are timed. Even in the shower there is no privacy. There is a window that runs the full length of the shower room so that I am always under observation from the guards in the security bubble. The cuffs are removed once I'm in the shower, but the cuffs are put back on and I'm escorted back to my cell.[15]
>
> When I get to go to a visit with my family or friends it is a noncontact visit. There is a Plexiglass window between us and we must speak through a telephone to communicate. The visits are under a time restraint and there is never enough time. We are under constant and complete observation by the guard(s) during the visit.[16]

Tragically, some prisoners forgo all departures from the cell, instead living in their cloistered cells, battling mental illness or suffocating with fear:

> I sit in that cell, you know, and it seems like I'm just ready to scream or go crazy or something. And you know, the pressure, it builds up, and it feels like everything is—you're sitting there and things start, you know, not hearing things, things start to coming in your mind. You start to remember certain events that happened, bad things. It just gets to a person. I sit up at night, you know. You just sit there, and it seems like you're going to go crazy. You've got three walls around you and bars in front of you, and you start looking around, you know, and it seems like things are closing in on you. Like last night, when I sit in there and everything's real quiet, things, just a buzzing noise gets to going in my ears. And I sit there, and I consciously think, "Am I going to go crazy?" And the buzzing gets louder; and you sit there and you want to scream and tell somebody to stop it. And most of the time you get up—if I start making some noise in my cell, it will slack off. And it sounds stupid, I know, but it happens. . . . Sometimes I wonder if I don't get it stopped, I'm going crazy or something. And you know, maybe tonight when I lay down it's not going to break when I get up and try to make some noise.[17]

The isolation of death row, in concert with the isolation of the condemned within death row, is seen by prisoners to invite abuse by staff. From the point of view of condemned prisoners, death row is a world of its own and a law unto itself. "They can do anything they want to you," noted one prisoner. "Who's going to stop them?"[18]

It is troubling to realize that many condemned prisoners believe that their guards—with or without cause—would resort to violence. In extreme cases, fear of officer violence may merge with fear of execution. One death row prisoner, visibly afraid when speaking with me, put the matter this way:

> When you're on death row and you're laying down in your cell and you hear a door cracking, you'll think of where it comes from. When you hear it crack. And when you hear the keys and everything, when something like this happens, the keys come through here: I'm up. I'm up because you don't know when it's going to take place. The courts give you an execution date, that's true. But you don't know what's going to take place between then and your execution date. You don't know when you're going to be moved around to the silent cell over here. That's right down the hall, what they call a waiting cell. You don't know when you're going to be moved down there. And this keeps you jumpy, and it keeps you nervous, and it keeps you scared.[19]

Such fear, which borders at times on raw panic, is a reflection of the vulnerability many of these prisoners feel, as well as the distrust they have for their keepers.

Death row prisoners describe death row as a human pressure cooker marked by tension so palpable that it can be disabling.[20] "The main thing," one condemned prisoner informed me, describing his emotional deterioration,

> is the mental pressure: you're always depressed. But I think another main thing is the physical deterioration of the body. You sit up there and you just feel yourself getting weaker, you know? Your back hurts, you know? You're sick a lot—cold and low blood. You lose your energy.[21]

The risk of deterioration on death row is real, likely affecting all death row prisoners to some degree.[22] Fear of deterioration can be a source of anxiety, leading prisoners to question their sanity. "I'm already walking on a hairline of being sane and insane," one prisoner informed me. "I could fall either way at any time."[23]

The experience of correctional officers working on death row offers parallels that of prisoners living on death row. For officers as well as inmates, the setting has a distinctive ambiance; officers use terms like "eerie" and "scary." The setting is described as "controlled" and "regimented," requiring officers to be "very security conscious" and under pressure to "do the job right" and avoid all mistakes. Officers believe that the prisoners, facing death, have nothing to lose; proper security is the wall that keeps inmates at bay and officers safe. But like all human systems, security is imperfect. Hence the threat of error lurks in the background, creating a distinctive anxiety about one's safety. "The officers are very aware of the reasons that the offenders are on death row and feel that there was nothing to stop the offender from causing harm to officers if given the opportunity."[24]

The structure and routine of the job on death row make it in some respects an easier assignment than a normal housing block, where prisoners have a fair amount of freedom of movement and there are many unstructured interactions between inmates and officers. But structure and routine must be actively sought and preserved. Thus, most death row officers, much like the inmates they guard, report being suspicious, vigilant, and fearful; in their view, danger encroaches on their daily work lives, potentially compromising their safety and, in fact, the overall security of death row. These officers typically cite the dangers posed by the prisoners as justification for custodial repression that is the trademark of death row, including long stints for prisoners in their cells and elaborate security procedures that are called into play whenever prisoners are removed from their cells. Nevertheless, it is widely believed by staff that prisoners, given the slightest chance, would feel free to attack or even kill guards. "What more can we do to them?" worried officers ask. The guards thus come to fear the potential violence of their captives just as the prisoners fear the potential violence of their keepers. Too often, shared fears give way to mutual hate, making life on death row a trial for officer and inmate alike.[25]

For some death row officers I interviewed, an insidious fear lurked in the background of their daily work lives. Said one officer, "You know in the back of your mind who you're dealing with, *what* they are, but still you don't bring it to the surface." Other officers spoke of conscious fears very much in the forefront of their thinking. The prisoners, they believe, are violent men bent on escape. These officers work under constant pressure. As one said, "They will hurt you to get away. You've got to watch them all the time. You know if these guys get a chance, you're gone. They'll kill you. They've all killed before." In the words of another officer, "There was always that thought in my mind, 'If they ever get out of here, I'm as good as dead.' I feel they don't have anything to lose. If we get in their way, they just get rid of us quick." Security procedures are in place to restrain the prisoners and protect the officers, but they fail to reassure many officers. Assessed against a backdrop of fear, regulations appear flawed. "If they want to escape, they can," said one officer with an air of futility. "Somebody's going to slip up somewhere along the line."[26]

A troubling and pervasive sign of fear, also revealed in my interviews, is that some officers see themselves as potential hostages. This is particularly true on the few death rows that operate as congregate solitary confinement death rows—those with prisoners out of their individual cells in small groups much of the day, but strictly isolated from the rest of the prison within the confines of death row. "The inmates constantly threaten to take hostages," said one officer.[27] That fearful eventuality preoccupies a number of officers, who envision scenarios that would result in their being taken hostage. A common fear is that a harried, and thus distracted, control officer will open the wrong door at the wrong time, unleashing one or more inmates on a defenseless fellow officer. The officers respond to such intimidating contingencies with a grim fatalism, taking the attitude that they should do what they can to control their own lives and let other matters sort themselves out. "Anybody can get attacked or taken hostage at any time. But I just have a job to do, and I just go ahead and do it and hope that nothing will happen. I just try to do my job, be alert and observant, and nothing should go wrong. If it does, I'll just have to deal with it."[28] As another officer put it, "You have to deal with it as it comes. You do what you have to do in the line of your duties, your job. You focus on what you're doing."[29]

Given these fears, officers may be tempted to be distant and harsh as a sort of preemptive strategy to maintain control or, instead, to placate death row prisoners, trying to appease them to gain their cooperation. Officers note that the job requires strict scrutiny and control of the prisoners, so what outsiders would consider harsh and impersonal treatment is simply the norm for officers. Appeasement, in contrast, is a more troubling response. One officer stated the premise underlying appeasement quite baldly: "Anybody facing death, they gotta be dangerous. If he calls and he needs something, you got to try to get it for him." The problem for the staff—and for the weaker inmates they must protect—is that appeasement corrodes the officers' authority and undermines control, ultimately lowering the general level of security and making everyone unsafe. "We're supposed to be a team," complained one officer, "and what happens to [fellow officers] happens to me." If colleagues are visibly fearful, they are a liability: their presence emboldens the more predatory prisoners, which in the long run spells trouble for officers and inmates alike.[30]

The officers' fears are sufficiently widespread that they are visible to at least some death row prisoners, who see the fears of officers generating both abuse and neglect, with consequences that are troubling for officers as well as inmates:

> There seems to be too much security. There seems to be an abnormal amount of fear in the guards simply because we have a death sentence and that makes it hard for us to have the same courtesies that we should—that other inmates have. For example, the guards are so afraid of us where they won't get close to us or they won't come up and talk to us when we need something done seriously. It could be a medical problem or something. And because of this fear in the guards, we don't get the assistance we need like other inmates do. . . . You can easily tell it's fear in the officers and other employees of the institution. Just because we have this death sentence, people are so afraid of us that they don't want to get close to us and because of this very thing we just don't get what I would say [is] the compassion that we need or the assistance that we need. Sometimes it's hard to find the right word, but I know that it is something that we don't get that every man, regardless of his condition, should have.[31]

The main casualty of fear, in my assessment, is simple human compassion. The limited compassion found on death row contributes to the distinctively cold interpersonal climate found in these settings, leaving officers and inmates alike feeling isolated, vulnerable, and alone.

Notes

1 Death Penalty Information Center. www.deathpenaltyinfo.org/death-row-inmates-state-and-size-death-row-year?scid=9&did=188#state.
2 Robert Johnson, "Solitary Confinement Until Death by State-Sponsored Homicide: An Eighth Amendment Assessment of the Modern Execution Process," *Washington & Lee Law Review*, vol. 73, pp. 1213–1242.

3 Robert Johnson & Harmony Davies, "Life Under Sentence of Death: Historical and Contemporary Perspectives," in J. R. Acker, R. M. Bohm, & C. S. Lanier, eds., *America's Experiment with Capital Punishment: Reflections on the Past, Present, and Future of the Ultimate Penal Sanction* (Durham, NC: Carolina Academic Press, 3rd ed., 2014), pp. 661–686.

4 Qahhar Ali Cush, "Death Row Days," *Tacenda Literary Magazine*, 2013, pp. 2–4, 2.

5 Ibid., p. 3.

6 See Robert Johnson & Gabe Whitbread, "Lessons in Living and Dying in the Shadow of the Death House: A Review of Ethnographic Research on Death Row Confinement," Hans Toch, James R. Acker & Vincent Bonventre, eds., *Living on Death Row* (Washington, DC: APA Books, 2018). [forthcoming]

7 Cush, "Death Row Days," p. 3.

8 See generally, Johnson, 1981; Johnson, 1990. Robert Johnson, *Condemned To Die: Life Under Sentence of Death* (Elsevier, 1981); Robert Johnson, *Death Work: A Study of the Modern Execution Process* (Wadsworth, 1990)

9 Cush, "Death Row Days," p. 3.

10 Craig W. Haney, "Mental Health Issues in Long-Term Solitary and 'Supermax' Prison Confinement," *Crime & Delinquency*, vol. 49, no. 1 (2003), pp. 124–156.

11 Cush, "Death Row Days," p. 3.

12 Ibid., p. 2.

13 Ibid., pp. 2–3.

14 Ibid., p. 3.

15 Ibid., p. 4.

16 Ibid., p. 4.

17 Johnson, 1981, p. 49.

18 Johnson, 1990, p. 101.

19 Ibid., p. 104.

20 See, generally, Johnson, 1981.

21 Johnson, 1990, p. 104.

22 Professor Stanley Brodsky and I independently found that 70% of Alabama's condemned prisoners exhibited signs of deterioration. My finding, based on content analysis of interviews, was that "7 of every 10 prisoners diagnosed themselves as suffering physical, mental or emotional deterioration in what was typically portrayed as the interpersonal vacuum constituting the human environment of death row." See Robert Johnson, "Life Under Sentence of Death," in R. Johnson & H. Toch, eds., *The Pains of Imprisonment* (Prospect Heights, Illinois: Waveland Press, 1988), p. 132. Brodsky found a 70% deterioration rate for this same population using objective personality tests. Brodsky's results are reported in depositions pertaining to *Jacobs v. Britton*, No. 78-309H et al. (S.D. Ala., 1979). See Johnson, 2005, p. 116. Anecdotal evidence from interviews on Texas' death row suggests that deterioration is widespread. See Dave Mann, "Solitary Men," *Texas Observer*, November 10, 2010, www.texasobserver.org/solitary-men. For a general discussion of the threats to mental health posed by solitary confinement in general, see Craig W. Haney, "Mental Health Issues in Long-Term Solitary and 'Supermax' Prison Confinement," *Crime & Delinquency*, vol. 49, no. 1 (2003), pp. 124–156.

23 Johnson, 1990, p. 104.

24 Kelly L. Brown & Melissa Benningfield, "Death Row Correctional Officers: Experiences, Perspectives, and Attitudes," *Criminal Justice Review*, vol. 33, no. 4 (December 2008), pp. 524–540, 536–537.

25 Johnson, 1990, p. 110.

26 All quotations in this paragraph are drawn from Johnson, 1990, p. 110.

27 Ibid.

28 Ibid., p. 111.

29 Ibid.

30 All quotations in this paragraph drawn from Johnson, 1990, p. 111.

31 Johnson, 1981, p. 60.

34

CAPITAL PUNISHMENT AND VICTIMS' AND OFFENDERS' FAMILIES

Lynn Pazzani

Introduction

This chapter examines how capital punishment affects two seemingly different groups of people: capital murder victims' families and the family members of offenders who commit capital crimes. For victims' families, there is a discussion of the impact of the murder and loss on the family, both pro- and anti-death penalty families of victims, the concept of closure, and the negative impacts of capital punishment specific to the criminal justice system, or 'secondary victimization'. For offenders' families, there is a discussion of the emotional impacts of having a loved one involved in a capital trial and on death row, as well as the financial and social impacts of this process and, finally, a discussion of the impact of the execution itself. Although there is more research on the families of murder victims than on the families of murder offenders (Vandiver, 2014), one thing that is common to research on both groups is the extreme pain they suffer as a result of their situation.

Capital Punishment and Victims' Families

The grief experienced by family members of murder victims is often greater than that experienced by family members of those who died in other ways (Bohm, 2013). The grief of these family members manifests itself in many ways, from feeling guilty to developing health problems (King, 2004), and a common theme is that the grief of homicide victims' families is particularly prolonged, not following a typical pattern of fading over time (King, 2004). The trauma of losing a loved one to murder is also associated with symptoms of posttraumatic stress disorder (PTSD), and can cause problems in other areas of the survivor's life, including marriage, relationship with children, friendships, and work (Vandiver, 2014).

Family members may feel guilty that they were not able to help their loved one or that they survived and the other person did not (Bohm, 2013). Family members will experience guilt years after the murder for things that may not truly be related to the murder, such as not calling the victim or being at work during the time of the murder (King, 2004). Family members may also experience changes in their social situation as they find their friends do not understand what they are going though, or their friends stop coming by. One father of a murdered daughter experienced employment problems as his coworkers would look at him with pity and he did not feel he could work with them (King, 2004). Survivors may also have employment-related problems associated with their emotional state and with time lost to attend legal proceedings (Bohm, 2013).

In addition to emotional and social issues associated with the murder of a loved one, some family members also have physical symptoms that begin after the murder or that, whether correctly or not, they attribute to the stress of the murder. Participants interviewed for King's (2004) study experienced "weight loss or weight gain, skin rashes, and headaches. In addition, several family members of murder victims suffered from persistent heartburn, irritable bowel syndrome, alcohol and prescription drug abuse, and chronic fatigue" (King, 2004, p. 203). The survivors may also experience a shift in their view of the world. As one grandmother whose first grandchild was shot and killed put it, "The world is not good, it's evil and nobody's safe" (King, 2004, p. 202).

Recovery from a trauma such as this, if it occurs, takes years, and the survivors will likely never be quite the same as before the loss. The criminal justice system does not necessarily help survivors and often harms them (Vandiver, 2014). As is discussed more fully in the section on secondary victimization, family members of murder victims may have trouble resolving their grief due to the police and court procedures associated with the murder. For instance, prolonged and repeated postmortem examinations and attending a trial may be upsetting to family members and increase the time needed to resolve grief (Riches & Dawson, 1998). When they participate in the legal proceedings, families often want to hear an apology and an expression of regret from the killer (Vandiver, 2014), which may or may not occur.

Death penalty supporters often cite the victims of murder and their survivors as a defense against abolitionists. This defense implies a number of things:

> that support for executions is based on selfless sympathy for the victims, that all families of victims of murder are entitled to (and find comfort in) the killing of the person convicted of murdering their loved one, that the abolitionists would be screaming for an execution if their loved ones had been brutally murdered.
>
> *(Costanzo, 1997, p. 143)*

Costanzo's points underscore the fact that there are a variety of reactions that the family members of murder victims may have. Despite the similar suffering (described earlier) that families experience, some are opposed to the death penalty for the perpetrator, and others favor it and want to witness the execution.

Victims' Family Members in Favor of the Death Penalty

When a family member is taken through murder, there are a variety of reactions by the surviving family members. The negative impact of a loved one's murder is discussed earlier; what the survivors would like to see happen to the perpetrator is discussed here. Some families of victims want revenge (Bohm, 2013). Revenge is "a visceral, personal desire to hurt the wrongdoer" while retribution is "a deep-felt desire to uphold society's values" (Lifton & Mitchell, 2002, p. 200). Regardless of whether the survivor seeks revenge or retribution, there are family members of murder victims who support the death penalty. In addition to wanting the offender to be executed, some victims' family members wish to witness the execution. Many states allow for the relatives of murder victims to witness the killer's execution (Acker, 2013).

Indeed, there are many anecdotal examples of family members who supported and were glad about the execution of their loved one's killer; however, there are no systematic studies of the impact of this outcome. Lifton and Mitchell (2002) provide many examples of pro-death penalty family members' statements, such as a mother's remarks regarding the man who murdered her two daughters. She said "she would have 'no problem injecting him myself. I could lie down and have a good night's sleep, knowing justice had been done'" (Lifton & Mitchell, 2002, p. 199). While she may not be sure she would feel that way after the execution, some family members have responded directly after an execution, such as a mother of a murdered daughter who said, "'I feel happy, I feel wonderful. I want you all to know I'm very glad'" (Lifton & Mitchell, 2002, p. 199). Again, this mother may not know if that reaction will persist days or weeks after the execution.

Many family members of murdered victims report that the execution was not enough to satisfy them or to see justice done, or that they anticipate that the type of execution carried out in the United States will not fulfill that need. For instance, a survivor of the Oklahoma City bombing perpetrated by Timothy McVeigh said he "wished the authorities would amputate one of Timothy McVeigh's legs and then suspend him over sharpened, growing bamboo shoots which would slowly penetrate his body" (Lifton & Mitchell, 2002, p. 199). Similarly, the brother of a black man tortured to death by a white racist said, after witnessing the perpetrator's execution, "'I would rather have had [him] in a ring one-on-one for fifteen rounds'. . . 'and whipped him the way he whipped my brother'" (Lifton & Mitchell, 2002, p. 199).

Vernon and Lizbeth Harvey witnessed the execution of Robert Willie, who murdered their daughter, Faith. Vernon is a strong supporter of the death penalty and believes every family member of a murder victim should be able to witness the execution of the offender. After witnessing the execution, he stated that he believed that the offender should have suffered more during the execution, as his daughter did. He continued to express this opinion months after the execution as well (Bedau, 2004), perhaps suggesting that the execution of his daughter's killer did not have the desired outcome for Vernon. As discussed later, one of the reasons that some family members of murder victims support the death penalty for the perpetrator is to achieve 'closure'.

The Harveys joined an organization called the National Organization for Parents of Murdered Children, Inc. (Bedau, 2004). The vision statement of the organization is "to provide support and assistance to all survivors of homicide victims while working to create a world free of murder" (National Organization of Parents of Murdered Children, n.d.). This organization has local chapters where survivors of a loved one's murder can meet, provides online support, and provides a number of programs to help remember loved ones, encourage the investigation of homicides, and block the parole of convicted murderers (National Organization of Parents of Murdered Children, n.d.). Bedau (2004) states that a review of the organization's newsletter suggests that most members support the death penalty; however, the organization does not have an official position on the death penalty (Elledge, 2017). The organization takes the stance that all survivors of a loved one's murder should be able to use the organization to express any emotion or opinion about the death penalty (Elledge, 2017). While there is not an official position on the death penalty, the organization is, understandably, punitive toward murderers, as the Parole Block Program it runs seeks to prevent convicted murderers from being released before their full sentence has been served and does so through writing and circulating petitions regarding particular convicted murderers who are facing a parole hearing. These petitions are requested by the survivors of that individual's victim(s) (Parole Block Program, n.d.). This lack of a position on the death penalty also allows for families who are not in support of the death penalty to participate.

Victims' Family Members Opposed to the Death Penalty

Bedau (2004) states that it is not surprising to hear that some family members of murder victims strongly support the death penalty, but it is amazing to find that there are more such family members who do not. There are many reasons for family members not to support the death penalty for their loved one's murderer, even outside of their general feelings about the death penalty. Most notably, the family may desire to avoid the public attention and the prolonged contact with the criminal justice system that is associated with a capital trial and seeking an execution (Bohm, 2013). One mother of a murdered son said "'most of my life I've been involved in the justice system. I can't go on with my life. I can't close that chapter until he's put to sleep. It's been twenty-two years'" (Lifton & Mitchell,

2002, p. 203). While this statement does reflect a desire to see the death sentence carried out, the main sentiment is despair over the great length of time the process has taken. A brother of a murdered man issued a similar remark, stating "'From the trial, which would be brief and simple without the ancillary issues raised by the death penalty, through the years of appeals, the death verdict forces the survivors to relive the experience'" (Lifton & Mitchell, 2002, p. 203).

While the practical reasons for opposing the death penalty for a loved one's killer may sway some to the anti-death penalty position, emotional reasons for this position are also quite compelling. Dennis Shepard, father of murder victim Matthew Shepard, said it was "'time to begin the healing process, to show mercy to someone who refused to show any mercy'" (Lifton & Mitchell, 2002, p. 205). The sister of a murder victim stated "'I had opposed the death penalty before my brother's murder. Afterwards my opposition grew stronger. I knew what killing looked like. And I felt, with my mother, that enough was enough'" (Bedau, 2004, p. 21).

Some families feel they are more likely to find peace through forgiveness of their loved one's killer. They believe their grief will not end if the killer is executed (Lifton & Mitchell, 2002). One father of an Oklahoma City bombing victim was opposed to the execution of Timothy McVeigh because that execution would not bring his daughter back. Indeed, he had been told by other murder victims' family members that execution did not end their grief, and he expected the same for himself (Lifton & Mitchell, 2002). People with feelings such as these formed an organization called Murder Victims' Families for Reconciliation (MVFR) (Bedau, 2004).

MVFR was founded by Marie Deans after her mother-in-law was murdered. The organization serves to support relatives of murder victims and also works against the death penalty (Lifton & Mitchell, 2002). The organization opposes capital punishment because it distracts the public from what victims' families and communities really need to "heal and become safer"; it diverts resources that could be used to help families with costs while they are grieving and toward support resources; it divides communities and victims' families; it delays the process of justice, which also delays healing as family members continue to be involved in the criminal justice system for decades; and damages the families of the person executed (Why We Oppose Capital Punishment, n.d.). For their own reasons, some victims' family members hope for mediation or reconciliation between the family of the victim and the offender (Bohm, 2013).

Still other victims' family members oppose the death penalty because they do not believe the sanction is punitive enough. Some people wish for the penalty of life in prison without the possibility of parole (LWOP) because that sanction seems harsher than that of death, with the perpetrator having to live with his or her actions for the rest of his or her life (Armour & Umbreit, 2007). They hope that the offender will spend the long sentence reflecting on the wrong he or she has done (Bohm, 2013). Victims' families who support the death penalty for the perpetrator often believe that the execution will bring them closure, while families who oppose the death penalty for the perpetrator often believe closure cannot come through execution. The next section discusses the concept of closure in more detail.

Closure

A discussion of whether the death penalty brings closure to family members of murder victims must necessarily begin with a discussion of what closure means. 'Closure' is a term that first began appearing in the media in 1989, and it has been used as reason for the public to support the death penalty (Zimring, 2003); however, it is difficult to define, and scholars have come up with varying definitions. Bandes (2009) notes that the term does not have a meaning within psychology, although it has taken on a number of meanings in research related to murder victims' families. In a study of families of capital victims who spoke to the media, Gross and Matheson (2003) found that closure was the most commonly mentioned concept and that it meant a variety of different things to different families. As summarized by Madeira (2010), closure can mean the finality in the sense of putting the murder, the proceedings, and a particular life stage behind them; it can mean that the offender is no longer a threatening presence; and it can mean something therapeutic such as the idea of healing. Zimring (2003) defines the term specifically in reference to the execution of the killer. He states that closure is different from revenge and satisfaction and that it is "something good that execution brings to those mourning the murder of a loved one" (Zimring, 2003, p. 59). This simple definition allows for the "something good" to mean a variety of different things to different families. Burkhead (2009) similarly relates closure to the execution, calling it "peace of mind and a sense that justice has been done" (p. 119).

Despite the difficulty in defining closure, the concept is used as a means of demonstrating public support for the death penalty. A 2001 ABC News/*Washington Post* poll had respondents address the following statement: "The death penalty is fair because it gives satisfaction and closure to the families of murder victims." Sixty percent of respondents strongly agreed or somewhat agreed with the statement (Zimring, 2003, p. 61), indicating that this concept is part of support for capital punishment. Indeed, players in the criminal justice system often encourage surviving family members to support the death penalty for their loved one's killer in the name of closure. Armour and Umbreit (2007) give an example of the way this can be presented to murder victims' family members.

> "When you have lost a child, you go into a state of insanity, and you think whatever they want you to think," says Aba Gayle . . . whose 19-year-old daughter was murdered in 1980. "They told me, 'We are going to catch this man. We're going to convict him, and when we have an execution, you will be healed.' The DA told me this, and the sheriff's department, also the media. And I believed them."
>
> (p. 396)

Some family members do "experience a lasting improvement in their emotional condition after the execution of their relative's killer" (Vandiver, 2014, p. 634). While the permanence of improvement after execution has not been systematically studied, there is anecdotal evidence that immediately after an execution, some family members express attitudes that suggest they have experienced something that might be described as closure. Remarkably, it appears that for many victims' families, the "closure" they are talking about is the closure of the legal proceedings. Gross and Matheson (2003) give examples from many survivors' statements that give this suggestion. For instance, a victim's brother said, after the killer's execution, "'We've been dealing with this for 21 years. It's a load off of our shoulders not to have to worry about any more appeals, trials'" (Gross & Matheson, 2003, p. 492). A husband of a murder victim expressed relief at the closure of the legal proceedings, without expressing relief in any other terms, by stating, "'I'm glad to get this over with . . . but I'm still very angry that he's taken my wife and my children's mother away'" (Gross & Matheson, 2003, p. 490).

There are other expressions of closure that do not relate specifically to the legal proceedings. For instance, a mother of a murdered son stated after the killer's execution, "'Mark can now rest in peace and our nightmares will end knowing Bill Hughes will not take another life'" (Gross and Matheson, p. 490). Some believe that even with offenders in prison, they may still "haunt" the families of the victims (Berns, 2009, p. 389) and that an execution is necessary to prevent that from occurring. A mother of a child victim stated, "'The only meaning this day [the execution] has for me is that tomorrow I will not get a phone call . . . that his conviction has been overturned and he's getting a new trial'" (Gross and Matheson, p. 492).

For others, the execution of the killer means they lose the object of their anger and end up feeling unfocused and empty (Vandiver, 2014). "If they had believed for years that the execution of their relative's killer would bring them substantial emotional relief and it does not, they may even feel worse after the execution" (Vandiver, 2014, p. 635). Lifton and Mitchell (2002) also discuss a man who wanted the execution of his son's murderer, specifically due to closure. The man wanted the killer back after he died, as he had no one upon whom to project his anger and began internalizing it. Execution only brings closure for a few family members of victims. "Having a loved one brutally murdered is a wound that never fully heals" (Bohm, 2013, p. 65). Even for survivors who are pro-death penalty and in support of or even attend the execution, "punishment does not necessarily bring peace" (Lifton & Mitchell, 2002, p. 203). Armour and Umbreit (2007) provide context:

> More often than not, families of murder victims do not experience the relief they expected to feel at the execution, says Lula Redmond, a Florida therapist who works with [survivor] families. "Taking a life doesn't fill the void, but it's generally not until after the execution [that the families] realize this. Not too many people will honestly [say] publicly that it didn't do much, though, because they've spend most of their lives trying to get someone to the death chamber."
>
> *(pp. 396–7)*

Berns (2009) also quotes the lack of relief, or closure, felt by a grandmother of a murdered grandchild upon the execution of the killer:

> as the execution spooled out in front of her last Sept. 27, something happened. Or rather, it didn't happen. Ms. Hamm felt . . . less than one might suppose. There was no flood of relief. There was no lifting of weight, no sense of turning a personal page. And today, months later, that is the message Mozelle Hamm has for the Oklahoma City bombing survivors and victim relatives who were to watch Timothy McVeigh's execution: Remember, closure is for doors.
>
> *(p. 392)*

Whatever closure is, we do not know if the death penalty helps bring it about.

> It is not known whether there are psychological advantages in mourning the loss of a loved one when that loss leads to an execution, nor is there any indication that the adjustment to loss of a loved one in a homicide is any different in death penalty states than in non-death penalty states.
>
> *(Zimring, 2003, p. 59)*

Indeed, if the execution of a murderer *does* help bring closure to the family, then capital punishment as we have it now cannot bring closure to most families. As Acker (2013) states, "more than 99 percent of murder victims' survivors will never see the murder of their loved one sentenced to death, let alone executed" (p. 257). For those who do see a death sentence, or even an execution, as a result of the murder of their loved one, the incredible amount of time between the murder and that outcome means that capital punishment is just as likely to extend the healing process for survivors as it is to bring them satisfaction (Acker, 2013). Indeed, as discussed later, the criminal justice process can victimize the survivors of murdered family members.

Secondary Victimization

Family members' experiences with the criminal justice system can be worse than the murder, such that it has been called "secondary victimization" (Bohm, 2013). A notable reason for this is the very long period of time it can take to reach a final outcome in a capital case. There are years of appeals, and each aspect of the proceedings can victimize the survivors over again. There are also other issues with the criminal justice system that may traumatize surviving family members, starting with the death notification and moving all the way through the process to the potential execution.

Police officers may not have the required sensitivity to deliver the very upsetting news of a loved one's death (Bohm, 2013). While this would apply to all homicides, and for that matter, all sudden deaths, not just capital homicides, there are guidelines for police officers to follow, such as using the victim's name and leaving no room for doubt regarding the death when delivering the news (Miller, 2008). They should not minimize the event or use cheerfulness to suggest recovery; they should express genuine concern, allow the family members to talk to them, and stay with the family members as long as desired (Miller, 2008). It should be noted that officers can find their encounters with death traumatic as well, sometimes using "gallows humor" to cope and sometimes becoming numb (Henry, 1995), which may lead to errors or improper behavior during a death notification. It should be noted that family members of a murder victim are often, at least initially, suspects in the crime (Bohm, 2013). Riches and Dawson (1998) tell of parents who were notified that their child had been murdered. They were then separated and interviewed as suspects, undoubtedly increasing the trauma associated with the loss. Not only were they unable to comfort each other, but they experienced the uncertainly associated with being suspected of the crime. This is understandable police procedure to the outsider, but certainly traumatic for the family members of a murder victim.

After the initial shock of finding out a loved one has been murdered, family members may also find that criminal justice personnel do not necessarily keep them informed of the progress of the case (Bohm, 2013). The way the murder victim's family is treated can depend on factors such as race and characteristics of the victim (Vandiver, 2014), with the police and DA visiting family members and hearing their wishes regarding the death penalty when the victim is white and noncriminal and ignoring families of black or criminal victims. If family members are going to serve as witnesses in the case, they are often excluded from the courtroom when the trial is going on (Vandiver, 2014). If they are in the courtroom, they may be uncomfortable being the presence of the defendant, and they will hear and see graphic descriptions of the crime (Vandiver, 2014). The time taken up by the court process, including hearings, the trial, and numerous appeals, also serves to victimize the survivors of a murdered victim. One victim's sister stated:

> "Every time there's another hearing, it's as if Timmy's corpse gets up out of the ground and walks into the courtroom. He truly has never been formally buried [and will not come to rest] until the case is closed one way or the other." She would have preferred a commutation over having to "relive her brother's death every time the case [came] up for another court review."
>
> *(Gross & Matheson, 2003, p. 493)*

While all this is done in the name of justice, Armour and Umbreit (2012) find that this concept of justice achieved through the criminal justice system was not related to the survivors' well-being, although catching the murderer increased feelings of personal safety. Of course, when justice, as defined by survivors as the offender getting the maximum sentence or the death penalty, was not achieved, this also served to increase suffering. Survivors found that the offender receiving a sentence they perceived to be minimal as devaluing their family member or themselves, and as evidence of the problems with society's priorities, with one survivor stating, "'You can kill a federally protected wildlife species [and] do life . . . whereas you can kill a human being and do 5, 6, 7, 8 years and be out on the street'" (Armour & Umbreit, 2012, p. 83). It seems that family members of murder victims can be put through the court process that can serve to victimize them and still not find satisfaction with the outcome. This feeling of injustice is maximized when the accused killer is exonerated. Most family members of the victim tend not to believe that the exonerated person is truly innocent. The family has invested so much emotional energy and time in believing that the accused is guilty that it is hard for them to change their perspective and believe in his innocence (Gross & Matheson, 2003).

A final aspect of capital punishment that may serve to victimize family members of the victim is the media. When capital punishment is carried out, the media may elevate the condemned to celebrity status, while the victim may not receive as much attention, leaving family members to feel betrayed by the media as well (Costanzo, 1997). When families are interviewed by the media, it is often about the killer or the execution rather than the victim, as most newspaper descriptions of executions include a statement from the victim's family, or note that no one was available or that they refused to speak (Gross & Matheson, 2003). While it would seem that victims' families are excluded from most of process related to seeking the death penalty for the killer, there is one area where they are specifically included. The use of victim impact statements at sentencing is discussed next.

Victim Impact Statements

Traditionally in Western democracies, the victim (or the victim's family) had been removed from the judicial system, with the wronged party being the public. This is changing as "victims are demanding that their voices be heard throughout the criminal process" (Sarat, 2001, p. 34). The victims' rights movement began in the 1960s with the establishment of victim compensation programs, continued into the 1970s as a response to what appeared to be an increase in defendants' rights in the 1960s, and continues today as part of the conservative agenda (Sarat, 2009). One aspect of victims' rights is the victim impact statement. A victim impact statement is a remark by the victim or (in the case of murder) a victim's family member given to the judge or jury that typically contains information regarding the impact of the crime on the family, including financial and psychological hardships that have been sustained as a result of the crime (Myers & Greene, 2004). The use of victim impact statements in capital trials has been challenged and reviewed by the Supreme Court.

In 1983, John Booth and William Reid broke into the home of Irvin and Rose Bronstein, intending to steal money. The Bronsteins were at home, and the pair murdered them. They were convicted of first-degree murder, and during the sentencing phase of the trial a victim impact statement was prepared as part of a presentencing report. This statement was based on interviews with the victims' son, daughter, son-in-law, and granddaughter (*Booth v. Maryland*, 1987). Booth was sentenced to death by a jury. He moved to have the victim impact statement suppressed as "irrelevant, unduly inflammatory, and therefore violative of the Eight Amendment" (*Booth v. Maryland*, 1987). The Supreme Court found that the information in the victim impact statement was indeed irrelevant to capital sentencing and that it created an "unacceptable risk that the jury may impose the death penalty in an arbitrary and capricious manner" (*Booth v. Maryland*, 1987). This ruling invalidated the Maryland statute that required the inclusion of a victim impact statement in sentencing and barred the use of victim impact statements in capital trials (Sarat, 2001).

The Supreme Court ruled on a similar issue in *South Carolina v. Gathers* (1989). Demetrius Gathers was convicted of murder and sentenced to death. During the prosecutor's closing argument during the sentencing phase of the trial, the prosecutor repeatedly referred to the victim, Richard Haynes, as being a religious person and a registered voter, which were comments about the victim's character (*South Carolina v. Gathers*, 1989). The Supreme Court concluded that, unless statements about the victim's character were relevant to the circumstances of the crime, and in this case they were not, that they could not be included. The court relied upon the ruling in *Booth* to reverse the death sentence and remanded the case for a new sentencing procedure (*South Carolina v. Gathers*, 1989).

Based on the two cases discussed here, it would seem that the type of information included in victim impact statements, as well as character information about the victim, cannot be introduced in the sentencing phase of a capital trial. The issue was, however, revisited. In 1987 Charisse Christopher, age 28, and her daughter, Lacie, age 2, were murdered, and Charisse's son, Nicholas, age 3, was seriously injured in the same attack. Pervis Payne was arrested for the crimes and subsequently convicted and sentenced to death (Sarat, 2009). During the sentencing phase of the trial, Nicholas' grandmother, who was his legal guardian, testified that Nicholas missed his mother and his sister. The prosecutor referenced the effect of the crime on Nicholas and the victims' family during his argument for the death penalty (*Payne v. Tennessee*, 1991). Payne argued that the grandmother's testimony and the prosecutor's closing argument violated his Eight Amendment rights, as held in *Booth* and *Gathers*. The Supreme Court overruled those cases, finding that the Eight Amendment does not prohibit a capital jury from considering victim impact evidence "relating to the victim's personal characteristics and the emotional impact of the murder on the victim's family" or a prosecutor from providing such arguments during the sentencing hearing (*Payne v. Tennessee*, 1991).

It seems a shift in the justices on the Supreme Court between *Booth* and *Payne* may be related to the different outcomes. Two members of the majority in *Booth*, Justices Brennan and Powell, had retired, and their replacements, Justices Souter and Kennedy, were with the majority in *Payne*, which came to the opposite conclusion regarding victim impact statements (Sarat, 2009). According to Sarat (2001), the use of victim impact statements in capital trials is evidence of the concept of revenge being used in the criminal justice system rather than the concept of retribution. Retribution involves "stern but controlled authority" (p. 39), whereas revenge is emotional. While it was previously discussed that much of the criminal justice process related to capital punishment is difficult for the victims' family members, victim impact statements may help with this. Research on victim impact statements' effect on victims in all types of trials where harm or loss was suffered by a specific individual suggests that victims may feel positive and empowered by their opportunity to have an impact (Erez, 1999). It should be noted that the family members of murder victims are not the only group of people impacted by capital punishment. In addition to numerous other groups associated with capital punishment in some way, the family members of the offenders are also negatively impacted by the system.

Capital Punishment and Offenders' Families

> There is another set of victims: the murderer's family. A sentence of death creates additional suffering for the family of the condemned prisoner. The convict is always someone's son, and he is often a brother, a husband, or a father. The relatives of the condemned prisoner—who are often innocent of any wrongdoing—are swept into the widening circle of suffering created by killing and counterkilling.
>
> (Costanzo, 1997, p. 146)

The entire criminal justice process associated with capital punishment, from the arrest of a family member all the way through his or her execution and beyond, impacts the family (Sharp, 2005). During the process, family members of accused capital offenders typically respond with withdrawal, anger, and joining supportive groups. Family members moved between responses throughout the process (Sharp, 2005). They experience something called an "ambiguous loss" and are stuck in a "repetitive cycle of hope and hopelessness" (Sharp, 2005, p. 18) similar to that of family members of someone with a terminal illness or a soldier who is missing, but the families of offenders lack the social support that others have, as they are often despised (Sharp, 2005). The following sections will discuss the emotional toll on the offender's family as well as the other impacts on the family related to the offender's arrest, trial, and execution.

Capital Offenders' Families' Emotional Response

There are many sources of emotional harm for family members of capital offenders, and the accumulation of these effects can result in mental health problems such as depression and PTSD (Beck, Blackwell, Leonard, & Mears, 2003). The stress comes from the understandable trauma of the situation and is impacted by outside forces such as the media, defense attorneys perceived as incompetent, and the procedures associated with prison visitation, among other sources (Beck et al., 2003). Mental and physical health problems attributed to the situation of having a loved one as a capital offender were commonly reported by family members (Beck et al., 2003; Sharp, 2005). In the Beck et al. (2003) study, all family members in whom mental health was assessed had symptoms of PTSD, and 11 out of 12 of them were diagnosed with major depression.

Procedures associated with the criminal justice system added to the distress of family members. Family members who lived with the offender found the search of their home associated with their loved one's arrest to be traumatic. They had things taken that they did not feel were associated with the crime and their possessions tossed around seemingly without care, and some had important keepsakes broken or destroyed during the search (Sharp, 2005). They also found prison visitation difficult.

> All the participants described the process of visiting an incarcerated relative as difficult and painful. One grandfather explained that the way he was treated during visits reminded him of the time that the spent as an Austrian dissenter of National Socialism in a Nazi work camp. He limited his visits as a direct result of this treatment and the memories it recalled.
> *(Beck et al., 2003, p. 403)*

In addition to the way they were treated, family members had difficulty seeing their loved ones behind glass and seeing them in what they perceived to be excessive restraints and shackles (Beck et al., 2003). While families understand the necessity of certain rules related to visitation, they perceive others as designed to harass them (Radelet, Vandiver, & Berardo, 1983).

The multiple trials and appeals associated with capital punishment victimize the families of offenders as well as the families of victims.

> Jim and Sharon have had a terrible ordeal because of the multiple trials. Their son's conviction has been overturned, followed by a new trial and a new conviction. Then, his sentence was overturned, followed by a new death sentence. Currently, the court has again overturned the sentence
> *(Sharp, 2005, p. 66)*

This situation, which was common for those Sharp (2005) interviewed, emphasizes the cyclical nature of the emotions associated with being the family member of a capital offender. The continued nature of capital trials and appeals also makes it difficult for family members to move on and keeps the offender in the public eye, potentially increasing the negative reactions they face from others. Sharp (2005) discusses a woman who "worries about what to tell her children about their uncle. Currently, he is facing a resentencing trial, so his name is again in the news" (Sharp, 2005, p. 40).

Many family members of capital offenders attribute mental and physical health problems they have developed to the stress associated with their situation.

> Alice and her husband have both experienced health problems as a result of their experiences. Her husband's blood pressure and blood sugar are, in her words, "out of control." Alice herself has experienced both physical and emotional health problems. "I have gained sixty lbs., take Prozac, see a shrink because I almost took my life. Doubled my smoking until I was hospitalized with lung disease. I stay in a state of depression."
> *(Sharp, 2005, p. 32)*

Sharp (2005) describes the mental health impact to another family member:

> After his brother was convicted, Matt developed severe depression and an anxiety disorder and was eventually declared disabled. For the three years prior to the interview, he had not been able to work. Matt blames his illness largely on the stress of dealing with his brother's death sentence. "It's put a lot of stress on my life from the point of I have panic attacks and all and I get so scared at times. I could just go and hide in the closet and I don't even want to face the world."
> *(Sharp, 2005, p. 40)*

The situation can also be associated with sleep disturbances, as one mother interviewed by Sharp (2005) describes:

> "There is nothing, not words or anything else, that can explain the terror of what I felt when I thought the state was going to kill my only child. I had nightmares, asleep or awake, trying to imagine me going into a chamber where my child was strapped down and being injected with poison."
>
> *(Sharp, 2005, p. 59)*

Another aspect of being the family members of a capital offender that causes distress is feeling that they do not have any control over the situation. Jim Fowler, the father of man who was eventually executed, said, "'It makes you realize you're not near as smart as you thought you were . . . . You just realize that you're not—that you just really don't have any control. And that's pretty terrifying when you stop to think about it'" (Sharp, 2005, p. 26). Sharp (2005) describes another family member who felt out of control.

> Naomi, who was fatalistic, believed that there was nothing she could do to change the outcome. She suffered from severe depression. Naomi told me, 'I don't have money, I don't know nothing about the law. What can someone like me do? I just go home and crawl into bed, hoping this will go away.'
>
> *(Sharp, 2005, p. 35)*

Some family members also feel guilt over not being able to prevent the crime that caused this situation. One mother was unable to take time of work to ensure her son was receiving mental health treatment, but dropped him off at an emergency room after he began hallucinating. There he was referred to a mental health clinic, where he sat in the waiting room for a few days without registering. He was arrested for murder shortly after. "His mother reported feeling guilty for her son's offense, but she believes things might have turned out differently had someone at the hospital or mental health clinic treated her son's mental illness" (Beck et al., 2003, p. 399).

Family members may try to join or become active in organizations such as their church or a support group for others in similar situations in order to ease the emotional toll. This proves difficult due to a number of problems. Some family members are asked to leave their churches or do not feel they are supported by the other members or the minister (Beck et al., 2003). "Many try joining prisoners' families support groups but end up dropping out. Support groups of prisoners' families are dealing, overall, with very different issues" (Sharp, 2005, pp. 36). There tend not to be support groups specific to those with loved ones on death row because they are too geographically spread out for this to work (Sharp, 2005). Finally, some join abolitionist groups to feel like they are contributing to a solution to the pain of capital punishment. Even after their son Mark's execution in 2001, the Fowlers were involved in abolition work for about two years as part of a promise to Mark (Sharp, 2005). Joining these types of groups is an attempt to ease their pain, but there are difficulties in doing so, including the reaction from others in the community.

Other Impacts on Capital Offenders' Families

In some ways, what the families of murder victims and capital offenders experience can be similar. Both groups may experience a loss of income that had been produced by the victim or offender, both groups have to deal with claiming the body of their loved one and funeral expenses, and both groups feel victimized by the criminal justice system due to the lengthy trial and appeals (King, 2004). The financial impact on the family of the offender is particularly harsh. The families of capital offenders often use all their resources to pay for defense attorneys for trials and appeals. Sharp (2005) gives several examples of families who used all they had and more to try to help their accused loved one. A mother of a capital offender took out a second mortgage on her and her husband's home to pay for the costs of her son's defense, and another family "mortgaged everything they owned to get the young man a good attorney, only to find that the $20,000 they raised was simply insufficient for retaining private counsel in a capital case" (Sharp, 2005, p. 65).

The financial hardships faced by all involved members of an offender's family can be severe, but some face more of an impact than others.

> Wives of death row prisoners face a particularly difficult situation, as they often must become the sole breadwinner for the family following the husband's arrest, find funds to help with legal assistance, and deal with their feelings alone. This may leave little time for involvement in support groups.
>
> *(Sharp, 2005, p. 44)*

While many family members experience problems within their community due to the reactions of others, Sharp (2005) tells of a wife who

> is too tired to worry about what people think or to try to fight the system. Twice a month she and her sons make the long drive to the prison. They used to go every week, but Linda finds that she is too tired and has too many responsibilities to go that often anymore.
>
> *(p. 44)*

This wife puts all her energy into supporting her two sons, without the assistance of her incarcerated husband (Sharp, 2005).

An additional expense faced by family members of capital offenders is for the travel associated with visiting their loved one. Most states only have one death row, while the families of those on death row can be from anywhere in the state, or even outside the state (Sharp, 2005). For many families, this means long journeys and a lot of resources spent on travel. "Lydia and her husband lived in Oklahoma but make frequent trips to see their son in jail" [in Fort Worth, Texas] (Sharp, 2005, p. 34). Additionally, they may have to take time off work to visit their loved one, further adding to the expense. They may also have to take time off work to attend multiple, lengthy legal proceedings, which may cause employment related problems. As one mother of a capital defendant said, "'My employer was anything but understanding. My supervisor would say he understood and do what I had to. Then if I ever called in he would have me written up'" (Sharp, 2005, p. 30).

Aside from the expense associated with being the family member of a capital offender, there are a number of other problems faced by the family as a result of the reaction of other people, either through outright hostility or unintentionally, as they do not know what to do or say. Friends, family members who do not support the offender, and supportive group members, such as church groups, may pull away from the family members and stop contacting them (Sharp, 2005). This unfortunately occurs at a time when the family members need the presence of their support system more than ever due to the strain they are facing.

The removal of a support system is damaging to the family members, as is the hostility they face from other community members. Sharp (2005) gives multiple examples of family members being targets within their community.

> Lisa, sister of a man executed in 1998 for the murder of a woman and her five-year-old child, described this [negative reactions from others] eloquently, stating, "Little did I know that the [victim's family's] pain turned into hatred not only for [her brother] but for my entire family. Everyone in [town where murders occurred] wrote nasty letters to the editor all the

time. There were blurbs on the television for the entire ten years. I can't tell you the hell it put my mother through and still is putting her through."

(Sharp, 2005, p. 36)

As Lisa noted, the impact of the media may intensify these reactions. One man stated, ""They showed right on TV where our house was. That's when the phone calls started. That's when people drove by and started honking their horns and making all kinds of obscene calls and shouts. . . . I have felt violated ever since then'" (Sharp, 2005, p. 61).

This can be particularly difficult for mothers of capital offenders, who may be held responsible for the behavior of their sons or daughters. One woman interviewed by Sharp (2005) said, "'Most people just flat out said I had raised the devil himself. This came from friends, family, and complete strangers'" (Sharp, 2005, p. 62). The negative response from others can be very intense and damaging.

> Paula [the mother of a defendant] and her family became the targets of severe harassment. Beloved pets were killed, tires were flattened, and harassing telephone calls were received. The family moved to reduce the harassment, but this lessened some of their support because they moved away from their staunchest supporters.

(Sharp, 2005, p. 29)

While the actions of strangers can be upsetting, some find that even people they know become hostile. Sharp (2005) tells of a conversation one mother had with a coworker:

> And during one of the breaks she said to me, "Oh, I'll bet you are really glad they have lethal injection in Oklahoma." I said, "I don't understand what you mean." And she said, "Well, that's a much easier way to go than other ways." So I think I said, "Well, [her son] hasn't been tried yet."

(Sharp, 2005, pp. 57–58)

As evidenced by these examples, the pain for all family members associated with a loved one being a capital offender is severe. The pain associated with the execution of that family member is even more destructive.

Execution

After suffering for years as the family member of someone on death row, for some, their loved one is eventually executed. It is very difficult for family members to accept that this is occurring. Even after appeals have been exhausted, there are still some procedures that may stop or delay the execution. Last minute requests for clemency or stays sometimes leave the family member with very little time, sometimes mere hours, to accept that their loved one is going to die (Sharp, 2005): "the likelihood of having a relative spared through the granting of clemency is miniscule. This does not deter family members from clinging to hope, however" (Sharp, 2005, p. 89). Sharp (2005) describes such a family member:

> Darlene refused to believe that her husband would be executed, holding on to the belief that the governor would issue a stay of execution. As her husband died, [she] was faced with the finality of his death. According to an article in a church newspaper, "Darlene beat the glass and screamed in pain. Her two young adult sons tried to help as they patted her and said, 'Mama, don't cry. Mama, we are so sorry.' Finally, she collapsed and was taken to a hospital to be treated for shock and exhaustion."

(Sharp, 2005, p. 87)

Although not all states allow for this, many family members choose to be present for the execution "so that their loved one will see the faces of people who do not hate him or her, not rejoicing in death" (Sharp, 2005, p. 85); however, when the family member and the condemned are close, this is very difficult for family members. Not only are they forced to face that their loved one will be put to death, but they are there to watch it happen. Journalist Leighanne Gideon, who had witnessed 52 executions, describes the pain she observed expressed by those who witness the execution of their sons:

> 'You'll never hear another sound like a mother wailing whenever she is watching her son be executed. There's no other sound like it. It is just this horrendous wail. You can't get away from it. That wail surrounds the room. It's definitely something you won't ever forget.'
>
> *(Sharp, 2005, p. 89)*

Another family member describes the aftermath of witnessing her son's execution: "'Since they killed [her son] life has been unbearable. I watched my boy draw his last breath, and it felt like it was my last breath'" (Sharp, 2005, p. 35). A cousin of an executed woman describes her reaction to witnessing the execution:

> "Her execution is something that is burned into my mind forever. The helplessness of sitting there watching a healthy forty-one-year-old mother of two die—and not even being able to cry because I'd promised her I would not cry. I was there because her mother, father, sisters, and brother said they could not bear to see her killed. I didn't want her to be alone and she asked me to be with her. I describe the execution procedure exactly as it is: OBSCENE. I didn't know the true meaning of the word 'obscene' until that night. There is anger, deep sorrow, helplessness—many emotions as you witness someone you love being killed. And you are powerless to stop it."
>
> *(Sharp, 2005, p. 97)*

There are some situations which may serve to increase the pain experienced by family members who witness an execution. When there is a problem with the way the execution is carried out, or it is 'botched', the family member witnesses not only a death, but suffering. Sharp (2005) interviewed a family member who witnessed such a botched execution:

> she related the traumatic experience of watching him struggle to breathe. He convulsed on the gurney and appeared to be straining against the restraints. Kendra and her mother were horrified. . . . "He was aware and he was terrified. I was devastated—I wanted to go through the window to help him. And there was nothing that I could do—nothing. I had to watch him suffer. It was the worst moment of my life."
>
> *(Sharp, 2005, p. 91)*

Kendra suffered additionally as she heard rumors about the way that execution was carried out. It was believed that the guards intentionally switched the order of the drugs being administered to ensure her brother's suffering (Sharp, 2005).

Family members use a variety of methods to cope after the execution of their loved one. It would seem that none of these coping mechanisms serve to alleviate the pain they feel. Some, like the Fowlers, try to be positive. "Jim coped with the immediate pain by reframing his son's death in a new light. No longer would his son have to live in a small, dim cell, counting the minutes and hours of his life" (Sharp, 2005, p. 93). In addition to this viewpoint, the Fowlers participated in abolitionist groups for two years, as they had promised their son they would. This coping mechanism eventually became too much for them:

> Finally, the Fowlers reached a point where they decided to pull back from their commitments and made a decision to quit attending abolitionist functions on a regular basis. Health problems and the need to spend more time with family contributed to the decision, but in part they had reached the end of their emotional resources and found that the pain of Mark's execution was still fresh.
>
> *(Sharp, 2005, p. 108)*

Other family members use clearly maladaptive coping mechanisms, such as drinking, and suffer consistently from the negative impact of the execution. One woman describes the negative impact on many different family members:

> "My youngest niece doesn't hold down a job. All she wants to do is sleep. If anyone says one word to her, she cusses them out and walks off. My sister just drinks all the time now. I am very worried about her. My oldest niece seems to be doing OK, except for her marriage. Myself, I have good days and bad days. I go through spells, especially around the holidays or the anniversary of his death. Sometimes I can't shut it off in my head."
>
> *(Sharp, 2005, p. 103)*

Some family members rely on their faith to help them get through the execution. Sharp (2005) describes one woman's reaction to her husband's execution:

> Family members who respond to tragedy with faith seem to fare better. Cheryl believes that she and her husband will be reunited in the afterlife. She has dealt well with the loss of her husband, and she came up with a unique way of feeling like he was still with her . . . she sewed his ashes into a teddy bear that travels with her. Now, when Cheryl is on the road, her husband is symbolically with her, which she says brings her comfort.
>
> *(Sharp, 2005, p. 107)*

Even with her faith, Cheryl has still experienced sleep and health problems after her husband's execution.

The family members of executed offenders put so much of their lives into following the trial and appeals, into trying to obtain adequate defense for their loved one, and into trying to gain clemency prior to execution. After the execution of a family member, it is difficult to let go of something that has been the focus of their life for so long (Sharp, 2005). It is clear that capital punishment has negative impacts on the family members of both the murder victims and the offenders. The full implications of capital punishment for both groups of families are not completely clear due to problems with research in these areas. The last section discusses suggestions for future research.

Future Research

The issues associated with capital punishment that affect the families of victims and offenders are clearly those that would be best understood using qualitative research. They are deep and complex emotional issues that require the human perspective given in qualitative research. Qualitative research is strong in that it can bring these issues to light; however, it often has weaknesses in terms of sampling and generalizability. Indeed, two of the studies cited here mention their weaknesses in that regard.

Sharp (2005) interviewed families of offenders who were more likely to be white than would be representative of the families of capital offenders. She also notes that research on family members of offenders can only be done with those who are still in contact with their offender family member and that research in this area often lacks comparison groups, such as family members of other types of offenders. Gross and Matheson (2003) used as their data statements made to the press by victims' families regarding the execution of their offender. They note: "The family members who make statements to the press are undoubtedly *not* a representative sample of victims' families at large, even among cases that do end in execution" (Gross & Matheson, 2003, p. 487).

What the studies here lack in rigorous sampling methods, they gain in terms of providing rich detail. But would it be possible to balance this with a study that does include a representative group of victims' or offenders' families, or even to carry out a study that is both representative and detailed? It would be very difficult to do so ethically. Of course, one cannot force victims' or offenders' family members to speak to researchers. Even if a representative sample were reached, those that agreed to participate in the research would undoubtedly be different in some ways from those who did not agree to participate, a phenomenon known as volunteer bias. It might be possible to increase response rate, and therefore reduce volunteer bias, by asking family members to participate in a quantitative study, wherein they regularly filled out an instrument with various measures of well-being, rather than a qualitative study, which would require more of their time and emotional energy. That, then, would give us an idea of the percentage of family members suffering particular effects and their degree but would not provide the rich detail of a qualitative study. For this topic area the addition of quantitative studies may help supplement the already rich qualitative detail that is available.

References

Acker, J. R. (2013). The myth of closure and capital punishment. In R. M. Bohm & J. T. Walker (Eds.), *Demystifying crime & criminal justice* (2nd ed., pp. 254–263). New York, NY: Oxford University Press.

Armour, M. P., & Umbreit, M. S. (2007). The ultimate penal sanction and "closure" for survivors of homicide victims. *Marquette Law Review, 91*(1), 381–424.

Armour, M. P., & Umbreit, M. S. (2012). Survivors of homicide victims: Factors that influence their well-being. *Journal of Forensic Social Work, 2,* 74–93.

Bandes, S. A. (2009). Victims, "closure," and the sociology of emotion. *Law and Contemporary Problems, 72*(2), 1–26.

Beck, E., Blackwell, B. S., Leonard, P. B., & Mears, M. (2003). Seeking sanctuary: Interviews with family members of capital defendants. *Cornell Law Review, 88*(2), 382–418.

Bedau, H. A. (2004). *Killing as punishment: Reflections on the death penalty in America.* Boston, MA: Northeastern University Press.

Berns, N. (2009). Contesting the victim card: Closure discourse and emotion in the death penalty rhetoric. *The Sociological Quarterly, 50*(3), 383–406.

Bohm, R. M. (2013). *Capital punishment's collateral damage.* Durham, NC: Carolina Academic Press.

Burkhead, M. D. (2009). *A life for a life: The American debate over the death penalty.* Jefferson, NC: McFarland & Company, Inc.

Costanzo, M. (1997). *Just revenge: Costs and consequences of the death penalty.* New York, NY: St. Martin's Press.

Elledge, M. (2017). Taking a stand on the death penalty. *Survivors, 35*(1), 6.

Erez, E. (1999). Who's afraid of the big bad victim? Victim impact statements as victim empowerment and enhancement of justice. *Criminal Law Review, 49,* 545–556.

Gross, S. R., & Matheson, D. J. (2003). What they say at the end: Capital victims' families and the press. *Cornell Law Review, 88*(2), 486–516.

Henry, V. E. (1995). The police officer as survivor: Death confrontations and the police subculture. *Behavioral Sciences and the Law, 13,* 93–112.

King, K. (2004). It hurts so bad: Comparing grieving patterns of the families of murder victims with those of families of death row inmates. *Criminal Justice Policy Review, 15*(2), 193–211.

Lifton, R. J., & Mitchell, G. (2002). *Who Owns death? Capital punishment, the American conscience, and the end of executions.* New York, NY: Perennial.

Madeira, J. L. (2010). Why rebottle the genie?: Capitalizing on closure in death penalty proceedings. *Indiana Law Journal, 85*(4), 1477–1525.

Miller, L. (2008). Death notification for families of homicide victims: Healing dimensions of a complex process. *OMEGA, 57*(4), 367–380.

Myers, B., & Greene, E. (2004). The prejudicial nature of victim impact statements: Implications for capital sentencing policy. *Psychology, Public Policy, and Law, 10*(4), 492–515.

National Organization of Parents of Murdered Children, Inc. (n.d.). Retrieved from www.pomc.org/

Parole Block Program. (n.d.) Retrieved from www.pomc.org/pbp.html

Radelet, M. L., Vandiver, M., & Berardo, F. M. (1983). Families, prisons, and men with death sentences: The human impact of structured uncertainty. *Journal of Family Issues, 4*(4), 593–612.

Riches, G., & Dawson, P. (1998). Spoiled memories: Problems of grief resolution in families bereaved through murder. *Mortality, 3*(2), 143–159.

Sarat, A. (2001). *When the state kills: Capital punishment and the American condition.* Princeton, NJ: Princeton University Press.

Sarat, A. (2009). The story of *Payne v. Tennessee*: Victims triumphant. In J. H. Blume & J. M. Steiker (Eds.), *Death penalty stories* (pp. 323–538). New York, NY: Thomson Reuters/Foundation Press.

Sharp, S. F. (2005). *Hidden victims: The effects of the death penalty on families of the accused.* New Brunswick, NJ: Rutgers University Press.

Vandiver, M. (2014). The impact of the death penalty on the families of homicide victims and of condemned prisoners. In J. R. Acker, R. M. Bohm, & C. S. Lanier (Eds.), *America's experiment with capital punishment: Reflections on the past, present and future of the ultimate penal sanction* (3rd ed., pp. 627–660). Durham, NC: Carolina Academic Press.

Why We Oppose Capital Punishment. (n.d.). Retrieved from www.mvfr.org/why_we_oppose_capital_punishment

Zimring, F. E. (2003). *The contradictions of American capital punishment.* New York, NY: Oxford University Press.

Cases Cited

Booth v. Maryland, 482 U.S. 496 (1987).

Payne v. Tennessee, 501 U.S. 808 (1991).

South Carolina v. Gathers, 490 U.S. 805 (1989).

35

CAPITAL PUNISHMENT'S
CO-VICTIMS

Kyle A. Burgason

Capital punishment in the United States is often viewed through the lens of constitutionality. Is it cruel and unusual punishment? Are inmates provided with adequate representation during capital trials? Is there disparity and discrimination in capital sentencing and the executions themselves? Indeed, for nearly 250 years scholars have debated these issues as well as whether there exists a deterrent effect to the death penalty, religious and retributive arguments, cost, administration, miscarriages of justice, and impact on surviving family. Although this list may appear at first glance to be exhaustive, it is omitting a large and often ignored collection of people, the co-victims of capital punishment: those individuals who feel the impact of capital punishment as a result of the duty they have to the criminal justice system. Any examination of the merit of capital punishment should also include a discussion of the emotional and psychological toll the death penalty process can have on the law enforcement, courtroom, and corrections personnel charged with carrying it out. As Mitchel (2013) stated, these individuals have been speaking out with greater force recently about how it feels when the responsibility of taking the life of another person falls on the shoulders of an individual.

Death penalty cases affect far more people than the perpetrator and the victim. This chapter examines a number of participants involved in capital punishment cases and is broken into three main sections: law enforcement, courtroom, and corrections. Within each of the sections lies the co-victims' thoughts and insights, and, maybe most important, the impact capital punishment has on them.

Law Enforcement

In general, a majority of law enforcement personnel have been zealous supporters of capital punishment, as the nature of the profession tends to appeal to individuals from blue collar, conservative backgrounds (Braswell, McCarthy, & McCarthy, 2017, p. 47). As Bohm (2013) argues, historically the police support the death penalty because of the belief that capital punishment provides a measure of security in their already dangerous profession and that it is the appropriate sanction for the worst of the worst offenders. However, recently, attitudes regarding the effectiveness of the death penalty as a deterrent to violent crime and simply serving as retribution have begun to alter.

According to a 1995 survey of U.S. police chiefs and sheriffs, a majority supported the death penalty even though they did not believe it was an effective law enforcement tool (Dieter, 1995). When these law enforcement executives were asked about what would be an effective way to reduce violent crime, only 1% of the nearly 400 executives answered with expanding the use of the death penalty. Additionally, when asked about the most cost-effective strategies for controlling crime, the death penalty was ranked last, with only 29% of law enforcement executives selecting capital punishment as cost effective. Furthermore, law enforcement executives were found to be more open to alternatives to capital punishment than were the first-line supervisors (lieutenants and sergeants). When they were given the choice of life in prison without the possibility of parole plus monetary restitution (LWOP+), death penalty support on the part of the executives dropped to approximately 50% (Dieter, 1995). A more recent survey of police chiefs seems to echo the results that were found in the 1995 survey in that police chiefs continue to rank the death penalty last among their priorities for effective crime reduction. The officers do not believe the death penalty acts as a deterrent to murder, and they rate it as one of most inefficient uses of taxpayer dollars in fighting crime. Similarly, many criminologists agree that the death penalty does not effectively reduce the number of murders or serve a general deterrent in any fashion (Dieter, 2009, pp. 9–10).

The impact of the death penalty process is not just affecting police in aggregate surveys, but specific jurisdictions, commissions, departments, and individual officers have begun to speak out about the collateral consequences of capital punishment. Recently, 30 law enforcement personnel, including police chiefs and other officers, signed a letter stating that "California's death penalty is broken." The letter cited multiple reasons why the state's death penalty system is not working, such as the excessive costs of capital cases, the risk of wrongful convictions, and the stress placed on victims' families (Death Penalty Focus, 2008). The signers noted that by seeking LWOP sentences instead of death, valuable resources now spent on the death penalty prosecutions and appeals could be better used in crime prevention and victim service programs.

In similar sentiments, a group of law enforcement officials at the World Congress against the Death Penalty with decades of experience in fighting crime in the United States and Europe opine that societies are better off without the death penalty. The panel members contended that the idea of capital punishment being a deterrent goes against their experiences. They also agreed that the cost of the death penalty, the risk of executing an innocent defendant, and the punishment's impact on co-victims are legitimate reasons for opposing the practice (Abbott, Cluny, Denmark, & Hampton, 2011). A strong point of contention against the traditional notion for the panel of officers came when they discussed the killing of police officers. In many segments of the law enforcement community and in actual law, the killing of police officers is considered an aggravating circumstance and acts as an automatic qualifier for the death penalty. It may be of some surprise when the panel came out against the execution of those who kill their brothers in arms, stating that some argue that the death penalty is needed to deter the killing of police officers. They continued, stating that if one of them were murdered, they would not want the perpetrator to receive the death penalty. The panel argued that the most important thing would be taking care of their families and helping them heal. The officers stated that they have seen how painful it is for families to go through years of death penalty trials and appeals and that would be the last thing they would want for their own families. The officers claimed that the idea that the death penalty provides "closure" for victims' families is a myth (Abbott et al., 2011).

Additionally, James Abbott spoke directly about the influence of capital punishment on co-victims that he had witnessed as a member of the New Jersey Death Penalty Study Commission, stating that he was greatly influenced by the stories of murder victims' families who testified during the commission's hearings. Abbott went into the commission as a supporter of capital punishment in theory and practice but was influenced by stories of collateral consequences, "I had no idea how much families suffer facing years of death penalty appeals and reversals. . . . For every person that had been sentenced to death, there was a family waiting for the promised punishment to be delivered" (Abbott, 2010, p. 1). Abbott contends that he still supports the death penalty as a means of retribution and a just sanction for some crimes, but states that in practice it does more harm than good and closes arguing that LWOP is a better alternative as it is harsh, it ensures public safety as well as eliminates the risk of an irreversible mistake, and most importantly it puts victims' families first. "I played a role in helping the state to repeal a policy that was ineffective and harmful to victims' families" (Abbott, 2010, p. 3).

Mirroring the attitudes of Abbott, May (2008), a former military police officer and Baltimore City police officer also changed his stance on the death penalty upon learning of innocent people who had been sentenced to death. During May's tours in Vietnam, working as a military police officer in Louisiana, as well as his tenure as an officer working in some of the poorest and most crime-ridden neighborhoods of Baltimore, he was exposed to violence on a routine basis, and he admitted that this only strengthened his feelings that some people were simply beyond redemption. May then became aware of the shift in public opinion concerning the death penalty, reading about the Kirk Bloodsworth case. Bloodsworth was sentenced to die in Maryland for a crime he did not commit (May, 2008). May struggled to imagine the horror of suffering on death row as an innocent man, then being hoisted onto a gurney, strapped down, and injected with lethal drugs, knowing the whole time that Bloodsworth did nothing wrong. His doubts about the death penalty continued to grow as he learned that human beings are not right 100% of the time and no amount of reforms, technological advances, or legal procedures could rectify that fact, and May's concerns about putting an innocent person coupled with his religious practices led to his change of opinion. He concluded that a single mistake could mean the execution of an innocent person, and as someone who dedicated his life to enforcing the law; he could not live with that (May, 2008). Consequently, May testified before the Maryland Commission on Capital Punishment, stating that the death penalty does not bring back or honor the deceased and does little to nothing to alleviate the sorrow of the victim's loved ones and actually contended the opposite is true in that capital punishment's uncertainty only brought more grief to victims' families (May, 2008).

Thus far we have seen how law enforcement personnel's feelings about the policy and practice of capital punishment can be affected via the death penalty process, but these next sections will focus on some of the issues that impact the officers themselves with regard to family, quality of life, and emotional and psychological well-being. In most communities, after a homicide has been reported, detectives arrive on the crime scene to investigate. Bohm (2013) states that one of the biggest concerns among officers investigating a capital case is not to screw up, as one homicide detective admitted: "When I know it's a death penalty case, there is extra scrutiny that goes into it. You're a little more meticulous, you might talk to more people than you normally would, there are differences" (p. 24). Homicide detectives do not treat all murders the same. A victim's status in the community usually determines the level of investigation. This can also be detrimental to the officer's psychological well-being: he or she knows that all cases should be treated equally, but higher profile cases generally bring with them more incentive, both monetarily and professionally, and more prestige than others, and officers are forced to live with this reality.

Officers also face certain pressures to solve a capital case, both internal and external. The interviewees in Bohm (2013) contend a majority of the pressure comes from the officer himself, as one detective has pictures of four of his unsolved cases at his desk. The officer stated "You do feel pressure from the families. There's a lot of nice people out there that have lost their sons and daughters, even if they weren't doing the right things at the time they're still somebody's son or daughter" (Bohm, 2013, p. 26). Additional sources of pressure, according to Bohm (2013), include the nightmare of screwing something up, notifying the next of kin in the homicide, the lack of physical evidence, dealing with the chain of command, and the time commitment.

Besides being stressful, investigations can affect officers in other ways as well: mentally, emotionally, and physically; Bohm (2013) identifies these as side-effects of the job. These include investigating homicides involving children or babies, courtroom proceedings where officers are forced to retell the horrific scene they encountered, and the time commitment, which takes away from the officer's family life. The time constraints of this job cause some officers their marriages and time spent with their children. In addition to the emotional stress and the pressures of family life, the job of detective is also physically demanding. "You are not eating and then when you do eat, you are eating poorly. You are eating on the run. The lack of sleep has a tremendous effect on your health" (Bohm, 2013, p. 31).

Living this lifestyle over a number of years has both a physical and mental toll on officers, to the point that they have been living such a poor lifestyle for so long that they forget what it feels like to live a healthy, active lifestyle (Braswell et al., 2017, p. 28). Consequently, officers often do not do enough to change the behavior until the detrimental impact has become the norm.

Some of the arrests can be extremely dangerous and counterproductive, as detectives must try to extract confessions from those they have just arrested. It is understandable in this situation that some offenders do not want to cooperate with an officer who has just ended their freedom (Bohm, 2013). Officers are given large amounts of discretion when extracting confessions and other evidence. They can fabricate stories, tell lies, and fabricate physical evidence and witness testimony to try to get a confession. This can then lead to a slippery slope concerning officers and their need to be truthful, upstanding servants of the community. It is difficult for officers to be underhanded and conniving in one part of their job and immediately turn around and be honest officers the remainder of the day (Braswell et al., 2017, p. 83).

Law enforcement personnel work closely with members of the courtroom group to bring perpetrators to justice. In the next section, we will look at the roles that some of the courtroom members play in the process, as well as how they affect and are affected by capital cases.

Courtroom

The courtroom attorneys, both the prosecutor and the defense, are the first members of the court to be involved in the death penalty process. Prosecutors are especially vital; they act as the gatekeepers of the process because it is their choice and their choice alone to charge a suspect with a capital crime (Bohm, 2013, p. 41). Almost immediately after deciding to pursue a death conviction, the prosecutors' work is resource intensive and time consuming, as they carry the burden of proof beyond a reasonable doubt that the defendant committed the crime for which he or she was charged. On the opposite side you have the defense attorneys, who as Bohm (2013) contends are often vilified from the onset of the case because they are taking on the task of defending an individual who has been charged with murdering a human being, leaving the victim's family and others to wonder how anyone could defend a brutal murderer (p. 83). As a majority of capital defendants are indigent and cannot afford private council, they are assigned a public defender or court-appointed counsel. These attorneys are often paid little if anything for their effort in a capital case, and similar to the prosecution, the time and effort that goes into making a case for their client can be astronomical. It is generally understood that many defense attorneys are not in favor of capital punishment, but similar to the change in attitudes of law enforcement personnel, some prosecutors are coming out in support of alternatives to the death penalty because of the impact the cases are having on the victims' families and themselves.

In California, District Attorney Bonnie Dumanis' decision not to seek the death penalty for the daughter of Charles King was "torturous," but so would have been a death penalty trial and the years of appeals that most certainly would have followed. Dumanis stated there was enough evidence to convict the suspect, but she agreed to LWOP in exchange for a confession because it was the only way to convict the suspect and find the victim's body (Figueroa & Walker, 2010). Dumanis explained that this was a difficult decision and called California's death penalty "a hollow promise." In line with Dumanis' thoughts, former district attorney of Los Angeles Gil Garcetti, who pursued numerous death sentences, recently said California's death penalty was dysfunctional and the resources spent on it should be diverted to more pressing needs (Garcetti, 2011). Garcetti (2011) contends the death penalty causes ongoing torment to family members and friends of murder victims, claiming that the living victims of such a crime may believe that the death sentence will provide closure, but for many it does not (Bohm, 2013, pp. 66–69).

These revelations on the part of prosecutors are not confined to the ultra-liberal state of California but have come from other states in the Northwest and even some more conservative jurisdictions in the Midwest. Kane County Illinois State's Attorney Joe McMahon recently opined that abolishing capital punishment in the Illinois meant that murder trials in the county could be decided more quickly. McMahon thoughts mirrored those of Dumanis and Garcetti in that, to the extent that officials can bring cases to resolution sooner, it may help the families of the victims get some small measure of closure and hopefully allow the healing process to commence sooner (Bilyk, 2011).

Similarly, in Lincoln County, Oregon, former district attorney Dan Glode recently criticized capital punishment not only for being an enormous expense but for the emotional fortitude it takes for the families of homicide victims (Glode, 2010). Glode was no stranger to violence and the death penalty, as he experienced both as a prosecutor and as a relative of a murder victim; a close relative of Glode's was murdered in the 1980s. It took several years for police to apprehend the suspect, which left Glode with a feeling of just wanting the case to end. As the suspect was tried and incarcerated, Glode contends that the justice system cannot make the victim's family whole again, but it can reduce the strain by not dragging things out incessantly (Glode, 2010). Glode argues that in capital cases, the process goes on and on, forcing family members to endure additional trials if the case is remanded, and the pain and suffering commence again, similar to a wound that never heals (Glode, 2010). Glode (2010) closed by stating that his change of opinion was not necessarily on moral or ethical grounds but rather on the way capital punishment was used (or not used) in Oregon, echoing again the enormous cost and emotional capital for the co-victims and their families.

Next we will focus on some of the issues that impact the prosecutors and defense attorneys with regard to emotional and psychological well-being, which can be impacted by the death penalty process. As one can imagine, trying a capital case takes more time and effort from both the prosecution and the defense than does a noncapital case. As stated earlier, the prosecutors' work begins almost immediately, as they must decide whether or not to charge the suspect with a capital crime. Complicating this task and adding more stress and anxiety to the process is the family of the victim. According to Bohm (2013), one prosecutor stated the wishes of the family were given a considerable amount of weight in determining a plea bargain, while another would take it under consideration but wouldn't necessarily do what the family wanted depending on how horrible the murder was (p. 44). Still another prosecutor claimed that "My client is the state" . . . not the victim or the victim's family (Bohm, 2013, p. 45). Prosecutors state that the time demands in capital case are the most difficult part of the ordeal because they are forced to be more meticulous and to get the job done right. When asked about the worst part of the process, one prosecutor cited achieving a good result for the victim's family and law enforcement (Bohm, 2013, p. 50).

Defense attorneys must deal with the knowledge that the more money spent on the defense the better chance the client has of not receiving a death sentence. This can weigh heavily on a public defender or court appointed counsel who knows he or she could do more with better financial backing. Bohm (2013) also states that there is no substitute for experience in a quality defense attorney, which again is going to cost more money, and an experienced capital-trained lawyer may well be a nonoption for indigent suspects. One attorney noted "If you're experienced at it, if you've done it before, you tend to get in better shape. . . . I will do whatever I can do to get my stamina up, otherwise, you get wiped out" (Bohm, 2013, p. 104). A former public defender stated "It's exhausting, it's stressful, it's weighty . . . it's a fabulous diet plan because I don't eat in trial so it's a guaranteed five pounds off" (Bohm, 2013, p. 104). Bohm (2013) cited another former public defender who described the mental and emotional aspects of handling a capital case as

> more of a challenge because you're dealing with issues that don't come up routinely. Emotionally, you've got the client and the client's family and the victim's family that you're dealing with, and your own feelings about the government killing one of its citizens.
>
> (p. 104)

A former public defender considers the penalty phase the more difficult phase of the trial, without question: "by the time you get into the penalty phase you are exhausted. You haven't gotten any sleep, all your nerves are on end, you've got your client's life right there in your hands. It's emotionally, physically, and intellectually demanding" (Bohm, 2013, p. 95).

Similar to defense attorneys, Bohm (2013) says, prosecutors also suffer significant, emotional, and physical effects. One prosecutor, when asked how handling a capital case affected her emotionally and physically, stated that:

> "It's a very weighing thing to do, and you have to know a life is at stake. It's not like you get a death recommendation and walk out of the courtroom and go, 'yee-haw'. Listening to a judge sentence someone to die: it's very sad. The bottom line is the victim is not coming back, and the victim's family is never going to have that feeling they think they are going to have."
>
> *(p. 60)*

Additionally, mirroring the physical ailments of the defense attorney, one lawyer was said to have lost 10–15 pounds during a capital case as a result of working out to increase his stamina.

The next courtroom members of note are judges. Judges manage the trial to ensure that each capital defendant receives a fair trial. According to Bohm (2013), they defend the integrity of the process by making sure all members of the court follow procedure, and with few exceptions, the capital trial is the only criminal trial where the judge is not required to sentence a guilty defendant. Both at the state and national level judges have taken an oath to uphold the law but may not agree with the policy of capital punishment per se. Judge Boyce Martin, in his final death penalty decision from the bench of the U.S. Court of Appeals, sharply criticized the capital punishment process in this country. While upholding the conviction and death sentence of the defendant, Harold Nichols, Judge Martin stated that he continues to condemn the use of the death penalty as an arbitrary, biased, and broken criminal justice tool. Martine noted that the many years since Nichols' conviction in 1990 have consumed numerous judicial hours, money, and legal resources, all while providing no closure for the families of the victims. He added that resources spent on the death penalty could be better utilized for other programs:

> The time, money, and energy spent trying to secure the death of this defendant would have been better spent improving this country's mental-health and educational institutions, which may help prevent crimes such as the ones we are presented with today.
>
> *(Nichols v. Heidle, 2013)*

Similarly, 17 current and former judges signed a letter to the California Commission on the Fair Administration of Justice professing their concerns about the current application and administration of the death penalty in California. The letter identifies the incredible strain capital cases have put on the entire judicial system. The judges conclude the letter by suggesting that any attempt to reform California's capital punishment policy must be comprehensive and must ensure a means of providing sustained and sufficient resources for the entire system (Death Penalty Focus, 2008). Additionally, the U.S. Supreme Court often gets contacted at the eleventh hour with requests for a stay of execution. Mitchell (2013) states that while condemned inmates typically request review by the high court at a few different points during the appeals process, the last-minute requests for a stay of execution often have a sense of gravity about them because the inmate's execution is scheduled to be carried out immediately if his stay is denied. Justice Ruth Bader Ginsburg stated that dealing with eve-of-execution stay applications is the hardest part of the job and that death penalty decisions were a "dreadful part of the business" (Mitchell, 2013). Echoing the sentiments of Ginsberg, retired Justice Sandra Day O'Connor contends that skepticism was growing concerning the administration of capital punishment in the United States. O'Connor stated that often some innocent defendants have been convicted and sentenced to death. In a speech to the Minnesota Women Lawyers, she remarked that with Minnesota having no death penalty, they must breathe a big sigh of relief every day (Mitchell, 2013). Mitchell (2013) opined that Justice O'Connor's words demonstrate the heavy weight of the decision the justices are charged with reaching in capital cases and the corresponding "big sigh of relief" that would come with never having to worry about reaching a wrong decision that resulted in the execution of an innocent person.

Next we will focus on some of the issues that impact the judges with regard to emotional and psychological well-being, which can be impacted by the death penalty process. According to Bohm (2013), the most important aspect of being a judge in a capital case is controlling the trial and making sure it is fundamentally fair for the defendant. The most difficult aspect of being a capital trial judge is "the decision; once you decide that the death penalty is appropriate, it ain't any fun to walk into the courtroom and tell somebody you are going to put them to death" (Bohm, 2013, p. 134). Both judges interviewed in Bohm (2013) agree that the worst aspect of being a capital trial judge was imposing the death sentence. Additionally, one judge stated that a "capital case ruins your docket. They don't just give me one case, and when I finish it say 'here's another one.' I have a case load to deal with, and the capital case takes up an enormous amount of time, energy, and resources" (Bohm, 2013, p. 135). Because capital trial judges in Florida have the added responsibility of sentencing, the effect on them mentally and emotionally can be more significant.

> "It's the most difficult, it's the most emotionally taxing trial that there is. There is just so many things to talk about, so many land mines you have to avoid, and of course, understanding the irrevocability of your decision. Ultimately, you want to get it right. A lot of pressure. A lot of stress on all of the participants, whether it's the police, the prosecutors, the defense, the witnesses, the jury, myself, my staff. There is a lot of tension that you undergo in a capital case that you don't see in a regular case."
>
> *(Bohm, 2013, p. 39)*

A final source of emotional stress can occur when actually handing down the sentence. Several judges contend they "make eye contact with the defendant. If I was imposing the death penalty, and I didn't have the backbone to look at the defendant while reading it, then I had no business passing his sentence" (Bohm, 2013, p. 141). Another judge related, "Imposing the death penalty is emotionally draining. Afterwards, I came back to my chambers, closed the door, and took a few moments to reflect." Another judge echoed those sentiments: "After I impose the death penalty, I was emotionally drained." Still another judge recalled, "It was both physically and emotionally draining. I felt weary inside" (Bohm, 2013, p. 132). The last members of the courtroom have arguably the greatest responsibility of the entire death penalty process: the jury.

Bohm (2013) states that jurors have the greatest responsibility in a capital case because they alone (with a few exceptions) decide whether a defendant lives or dies. As such, they are forced to live with that decision for the rest of their lives, as Slick (2011) agrees, arguing that jurors are the unrecognized victims of capital punishment. Whether or not jurors are up to the task of deciding on such a vital decision is arguable. In a perfect trial, jurors should be open-minded and assume that the defendant is innocent until proven guilty by the prosecution; however, jurors are ordinary citizens and human beings and therefore have prejudices and biases that may affect their judgment. An important strength of the American legal system is the gravity with which jurors view their charge to reach a decision based on the information presented; however, this is also one of the most difficult parts of serving on a jury (Mitchell, 2013). The defense and prosecution attorneys muddle this struggle by personalizing both the defendant and victim so that jurors emotionally connect with each of them. Witnesses may portray the defendants as spouse, parent, child and highlight positive things they have accomplished in their lifetime. Photos of the victim and statements of family members bring the victim's presence into the courtroom. This leads to an already present moral disengagement on the part of the jury. The core proposition behind moral disengagement is that individuals must morally disengage to perform actions and behaviors that run opposite and are counter to their individual values and personal moral standards (Osofsky, Bandura, & Zimbardo, 2005). Osofsky et al. (2005) state that capital punishment is a real-world example of this type of moral dilemma, where everyday people are forced to perform a legal and state-sanctioned action of ending the life of another human being, which poses an inherent moral conflict to basic human values.

Haney (1997) elaborated on this unique condition built into the sentencing process that enables jurors to sentence a person to death. As individuals who are absolutely opposed to the death penalty are eliminated from contention on the jury, the attorneys battle over the personalization and dehumaniza-tion of defendants. Diffusion and displacement of responsibility also figure prominently in the sentenc-ing process. Jurors view their decisions as a sentencing imperative rather than as a personal decision, aided by prosecutors who often present them with misleading and forced choices on capital sentencing (Bowers & Steiner, 1998). Jurors are then able to minimize their personal responsibility for their col-lective decision and sometimes rely on appellate judges to ultimately decide the fate of the accused.

Pretrial publicity is generally one of the first attempts to dehumanize the capital defendant, as potential jurors may be biased from the onset of a capital case because of exposure to the media's typi-cal one-sided coverage, which in turn makes it easier for the jury to view the defendant as the poten-tial "monster" or "animal" that he or she has been made out to be (Bohm, 2017). As research has identified, the media tend to focus on the most dramatic and heinous aspects of the crime. Rarely are the offender and his or her crime put in historical or social context, as the offender's personal history and background (factors that may "humanize" the offender) are generally ignored. Thus, research shows that the more negative information about a capital offender a potential juror was exposed to by the media, the more likely the potential juror was willing to convict the offender prior to his or her death penalty trial (Haney, 2005, p. 62), and it stands to reason that this negative information allows jurors to more easily implement moral disengagement techniques. This continues throughout the trial and sentencing as the attorneys introduce emotionally charged evidenced in the form of testimonies, graphic photographs, blood-stained clothing, and murder weapons. Additionally, the literature on the effect of such gruesome evidence demonstrates that, generally, mock jurors' judgments are more punitive when they consider highly emotional evidence, especially in the most serious cases such as those involving the death penalty (Bright & Goodman-Delahunty, 2004; Douglas, Lyon, & Ogloff, 1997; ForsterLee, Fox, ForsterLee, & Ho, 2004; Luginbuhl & Burkhead, 1995; Matsuo & Itoh, 2016; McGowen & Myers, 2004; Myers & Arbuthnot, 1999; Tsoudis & Smith-Lovin, 1998).

With each piece of evidence introduced, not only does moral disengagement become easier for the jury members to engage in, but the well-being of the jurors can be significantly affected. As was noted in the recent high profile cases of the Boston Marathon bomber and the Aurora, Colorado, theater shooting. Goldman (2015) opined that the jurors who were selected to hear these cases will have to watch and listen to graphic testimony, including pictures of wounded and dead victims at the crime scenes, and in the Boston bombing trial, jurors would likely have to watch security-video footage of the death of 8-year-old Martin Richard. Goldman's premonition was soon found to be true, as at the close of the Boston Marathon bombing trial, prosecutors pulled out the clothing and possessions of the 8-year-old. Item by item, the last shreds of a boy's life were introduced: a bloody jersey, bomb-melted shorts, metal, wood, and the devastating shrapnel that tore the breath away from a smiling child. The jurors wept openly in court (Ferguson, 2015). These facets of capital trials are particularly difficult for jurors to endure, as the guilt or evidence phase of a capital trial often include gory details about the killing and testimony from eyewitnesses or investigators. Researchers in one study found that jurors in murder cases were particularly upset by photographs of the victim and blood-tainted physical evidence, as well as having to sentence the defendant to death (Kaplan & Winget, 1992). In addition to the evidence and testimony, there are other factors that make sitting on a capital jury emo-tionally and psychologically draining, including the task of sentencing an offender to death.

For some jurors, the experience of having to decide whether the defendant should live or die can result in a variety of symptoms similar to posttraumatic stress, and the problems may remain with them for a long time. In fact, research has demonstrated that jurors who imposed a death sentence suffered greater PTSD symptoms compared to jurors who imposed a life sentence (Cusack, 1999). As such, it is not uncommon for jurors to suffer from other symptoms as a result of their jury service, including nightmares, nervousness, tension, and depression (Costanzo & Costanzo, 1994; Shuman, Hamilton, & Daley, 1994; Kaplan & Winget, 1992). Antonio (2008) found that over 60% of respondents (*n* = 711) found the experience of serving as a capital juror emotionally upsetting. Many of the themes identified in conversations with the jurors about serving on a capital trial concerned thoughts or feelings that developed after the trial concluded. Many jurors (38) reported long-term side effects such as chronic physical or emotional problems and difficulties relating to family, friends, or coworkers that occurred in the days, weeks, or months following the trial. Additionally, 40 jurors complained about dreams and nightmares, either general or specific in nature, relating to what they viewed or heard inside the courtroom, some even facing criticism from their own family regarding the decisions that were reached at trial (Antonio, 2008, pp. 400–401). Antonio (2008) echoed previous research in that it is not uncommon for jurors serving on capital cases to be exposed to graphic imagery or evidence during the trial and for them to be affected physically and emotionally by this evidence. He found 41 of the interviewed jurors reported being emotionally upset or shocked by eyewitness and expert testimony and by having to view the photographs presented at the trial (p. 402). One juror described the impact of the photographs of the victim's body:

> the picture of her dead, her eyes open. That was another shocking thing too. Part of the trial, when they presented the evidence, they had a slide show and they had this one slide of . . . showed the one victim, her eyes open. You thought for a minute that it was her at some time in her life when she was alive, but then they tell you, no, this is a morgue shot. You don't think of these things when you see a dead body on TV or in the movies or whatever. You usually don't see them with their eyes open, you see them closed. Here is this lifelike looking face, looking at you, but this person is dead. That kinda bothered me.
>
> *(Antonio, 2008, pp. 402–403)*

Jurors have reported a host of psychological and physiological symptoms resulting from their jury experience. In the current sample, the author found most comments concerned cognitive disturbances including dreaming or having nightmares about the trial, in addition to physical reactions including developing eating disorders, becoming physically ill, or needing drugs to cope with their stress (Antonio, 2008, p. 403). Altogether, 25 jurors reported specific dreams or nightmares concerning the manner in which the victim was killed or that related to the crime scene, although the nature of their dreams or nightmares varied in scope and intensity. Eleven jurors reported a loss of appetite during trial, while 14 engaged in smoking or drinking during the trial or were prescribed medication by a physician. Moreover, a few jurors from both life and death cases believed the defendant learned of their personal contact information, including names, addresses, and phone numbers, and were particularly fearful of retaliation from friends of the defendant if they had given the death penalty (Antonio, 2008, pp. 403–404). Some jurors even compared their experience of being sequestered with that of being imprisoned. A female juror from a different death case noted,

> First of all being sequestered is like prison. The juror is in a prison. A very padded and nice prison, but nevertheless a prison. It's very upsetting to have all contact with the outside world shut off. All the people that you care about, no connection with them.

In sum, 32 jurors mentioned that their jury experience felt isolating (Antonio, 2008, p. 405).

Additional research on juries supports prior findings in regard to the emotional and psychological toll a capital case can have on a juror. As stated earlier, one factor that causes juror trauma is the type of evidence, which is often graphic and gruesome, involving malice and brutality. This is outside the jurors' life experiences, and it exposes them to a difficult, even horrifying, view of the world (Slick, 2011); as one female jury member whose case—which dealt with the rape, beating, and murder of a young woman by a man who posed as a door-to-door salesman—described her flashbacks: "I'm paranoid," she said.

> I can't shake it. I went to the Smoky Mountains, and twice, I ran into a fellow who looked like him. I flipped out. I got hysterical, shook and just ran . . . I dreamed he broke into my apartment on several occasions.
>
> *(Pappas, 2015)*

Similarly, Pappas (2015) stated a woman who served on the jury in a death penalty trial in which the defendant wound up being sentenced to life in prison rather than getting the death penalty, stated that not long after the conclusion of the trial, the juror saw the victim's family in the grocery store and had a breakdown, fearing how the family would react to one of the people who'd spared the killer's life. Additionally, one juror who sat on a county's final death penalty case did not sleep for weeks afterward. Another juror claimed he could not get the images of the triple murder out of his head. Several jurors were so concerned about their safety after the trial that they fought their names and addresses being released to the *Beacon Journal*.

"I fear for my kids, my family, my wife," one juror said. "He's a pretty dangerous person" (War-smith, 2017). In describing the day after the jury made its sentencing decision, former capital juror Molly Wegler commented,

> I was crying driving home from the trial. It caused tension between my husband and myself and my friends. It's like you're in this one bizarre world, and then you go to this other bizarre world, and you can't talk about it. It's awful. I should have never taken that trip.

Former capital juror Wanda Nelson stated, "I had a part in it. I hate it. I hate that I had a part in it" (Fleury-Steiner, 2004, p. 1). Isolation and pressure from being a holdout were also identified as significant contributors of stress on some jurors. Some of the most anguished jurors interviewed for the Capital Jury Project were holdouts for life sentences who eventually caved to the pressure for a death sentence (Pappas, 2015).

Jurors indicate that a key factor causing them distress is the responsibility to make life-changing and (for death penalty cases) life-ending decisions, as jurors not only share the burden of imposing guilt (or even death) but are challenged with the loss of life that led to the case. Jurors recognize that their verdict and sentencing decision affects not only the defendant but also the victim and his or her family members. One juror who agonized over the decision of whether or not to sentence a defendant to death stated,

> I had emotional indigestion for a while. I kept recycling this thing in my mind over and over. I wondered what I could have done to have kept this from happening. What could society have done to prevent this? I couldn't do anything. I finally had to accept our decision.
>
> *(Bohm, 2013, p. 163)*

A female juror commented, "I lost it after the trial, I started crying. It was emotionally exhausting. I felt like I let the victim's family down." Another female on the same jury stated, "I really broke down afterwards. I felt bad for the family. I didn't know it'd be so difficult" (Bohm, 2013, p. 164). Bohm (2013) stated some jurors got physically ill, with one female juror experiencing sleep loss and becoming physically sick and actually vomiting. Most of the jurors who served on juries who returned a death sentence experienced lingering mental and emotional effects days, weeks, months, and years after the trial ended (p. 165). These effects are so great for some that about one quarter of all jurors either would refuse to serve in another capital trial or would try to get out of it, with another 40% serving reluctantly (Bohm, 2013, p. 166). During debriefings jurors regularly indicate how difficult it was to reach a decision and how troubled they were about whether it was the appropriate one (Slick, 2011). Paranoia was another feeling discussed by a former capital juror, as he became paranoid after the trial. He stated that he saw African American males in an older-model car near his home and wondered why they were there, claiming that it made him uneasy (the defendant was black; the juror is white). One female juror became so emotional talking about the toll the trial took on her during a hearing that she got teary, with the bailiff handing her a box of tissues. The juror stated she did not want to talk to the *Beacon Journal* because she did not want to relive the experience (Warsmith, 2017).

An estimated 70% of all jurors report some stress from jury service (Hannaford-Agor, n.d.). The Director of the Center for Jury Studies at the National Center for State Courts commented, almost mirroring the findings of the studies and interviews outlined in this chapter, that capital trials can provoke serious stress-related symptoms in jurors, including anxiety, depression, nightmares, and even physical symptoms such as nausea, elevated blood pressure, chest pain, and shortness of breath (Hannaford-Agor, n.d.). For most jurors, these symptoms disappear shortly after the trial, but some jurors continue to experience symptoms for weeks or even months after the trial has concluded. For some jurors, this experience of serving on a capital jury can result in a variety of symptoms related to post-traumatic stress, and the problems may remain with them for a long time. Further, the trauma is not mitigated and may even be exacerbated when the defendant's execution occurs (Slick, 2011). Slick (2011) concludes that jurors are unconsidered casualties in death penalty cases. The impact the death penalty has on them in the immediate and long term should be included in any consideration of ending it. Furthermore, in a similar vein to others sentiments in this chapter, he argues that abolishing the death penalty could help reduce this impact on jurors. Sending someone to life in prison would be an easier, less stressful decision and would still permit jurors to uphold their responsibility for providing public safety without having to "play God" with someone else's life. The final section of the death penalty process generally takes place in a correctional institution, where a number of individuals, from correctional guards to prison wardens, are affected by capital punishment.

Corrections

In this last section we will first turn our attention to prison wardens. Wardens are responsible for supervising and carrying out state-mandated executions and commonly do so with an outward professionalism; however, on the inside many are experiencing turmoil, as a number of prison wardens who have overseen executions were already, or have become, opponents of capital punishment (Bohm, 2013, p. 197). Unlike others discussed previously in the chapter, correctional staff, including wardens, are around the inmates for a number of years. As such, they get to know the prisoners as individuals, which makes the execution process even more emotionally and psychologically taxing. Similar to those involved in law enforcement and the courtroom, a number of corrections personnel are making their thoughts on capital punishment known.

Ron McAndrew, former warden of Starke Florida State Prison, testified in front of the Montana House Judiciary Committee about his experiences with the death penalty, stating that those who have lived through an execution know what the death penalty does to those who must perform it. In his tenure as warden, McAndrew performed three electrocutions in Florida and oversaw five lethal injections in Texas. In both places he witnessed staff traumatized by the duties they were asked to perform. He claimed that officers who had never even met the condemned fought tears and cowered in corners so as not to be seen (Mitchell, 2013). Some of McAndrew's colleagues turned to drugs and alcohol to numb the pain of knowing that a man had died by their hands, and he has received calls from distressed prison workers and executioners. Some corrections officers, he said, have committed suicide because of their guilt and regret. McAndrew concluded, "Being a corrections officer is supposed to be an honorable profession. The state dishonors us by putting us in this situation. This is premeditated, carefully thought out ceremonial killing" (Timmins, 2010). "I myself was haunted by the men I was asked to execute in the name of the State of Florida," McAndrew stated that he would wake up in the middle of the night to find former inmates lurking at the foot of his bed, as one had been cooked to death in a botched electrocution where he stood just four feet away, watching flames rise out of his head. McAndrew closed by arguing that the very notion that we need the death penalty to keep prisons safe is both professionally and personally offensive. He does not believe there is a single qualified prison warden in this country who would not trade the death penalty for more resources to keep his or her facility safe. McAndrew claims the death penalty system is just a drain on those resources, and it serves no purpose in the safety of the public or prisons (Mitchell, 2013).

Former warden Frank Thompson agrees; as someone who has led an execution team and given the order to "proceed," he is cognizant of the immeasurable burden that this process places on correctional officers, and he continues to be informed, by those who have been personally and directly involved in executing someone, of the awful, lifelong repercussions that can occur as a result of carrying out executions (Thompson, 2015). Thompson also testified in the House Judiciary Committee in Oregon on repealing the death penalty. Thompson told the committee the death penalty does not deter crime, fails to make the public safer, and places prison workers in an untenable position, stating that asking decent men and women to participate in the name of a failed public policy that takes human life is indefensible and rises to a level of immorality (Jung, 2013). Additionally, Thompson commented about what he had learned from his execution of two inmates while serving as the warden at the Oregon State Penitentiary. Because no one had been executed in over three decades, there was already a bit of pressure. Thompson stated that he really began to feel the weight of this undertaking while practicing for the executions. Teams rehearsed for more than a month. There was a full "run through" of the execution every week (Thompson, 2016). During the execution itself, correctional officers were responsible for everything, from strapping the prisoner's ankles and wrists to a gurney to administering the lethal chemicals. After each execution, Thompson had staff members who decided they did not want to be asked to serve in that capacity again. Others quietly sought employment elsewhere. A few told Thompson they were having trouble sleeping, and he worried they would develop posttraumatic stress disorder if they had to go through it another time (Thompson, 2016). Since retiring in 2010, Thompson has made it his mission to persuade people that capital punishment is a failed policy. Thompson (2016) contends that America should no longer accept the myth that capital punishment plays any constructive role in our criminal justice system, adding that it will be difficult to bring an end to the death penalty, but we will be a healthier society as a result.

Echoing the thoughts of Frank Thompson, Dr. Allen Ault, the former warden of the Georgia Diagnostic and Classifications Prison, appeared on MSNBC's *Rachel Maddow Show*, discussing the effects of carrying out executions on prison workers. Ault discussed the difficult questions prison officials face when participating in an execution. He stated that there is no denying that you are killing somebody. Add to that the fact that several inmates have been exonerated thanks to new scientific techniques, which made him question if the person about to be executed was even really guilty: that alone raised doubt for Ault. Ault also contended that the research indicates that capital punishment does not deter . . . arguing that it "seems so illogical to say to the public we do not want you to kill, and to demonstrate that, we are going to kill individuals" (The Rachel Maddow Show, 2011). Ault also recounted his experience with victims' family members after an execution:

> In every execution that I attended, I spent time with the victim's family. And most of the victims' families that I talked with, they thought they were going to get a lot of relief or closure from the execution. And in most cases, they did not.
>
> *(The Rachel Maddow Show, 2011)*

Former Oklahoma State Penitentiary warden Randy Workman was also critical of numerous aspects of capital punishment, stating that the death penalty fails the victims' families and wastes money: "We spend millions of dollars on these cases and going through the process and the end result is the family, do they feel vindicated? I'd say 90% of the time the people I've seen don't" (Fretland, 2014). Workman shared the advice he had given a murder victim's mother who requested his thoughts on seeking capital punishment:

> I said here's the deal, if you get the death penalty and you're successful, you're going to spend the next eight to 12 years back and forth in court and you're going to relive your son's death, because he has all these appeals. . . . I've seen some mothers that had some serious broken hearts that said this doesn't end it for me. This isn't justice to me. This doesn't do it
>
> *(Fretland, 2014)*

Workman closed by stating that during his tenure with the corrections department, he never directly pushed the button during a lethal injection, claiming that a guilty person would not be as much of an issue for him, but on the offhand chance that somebody was innocent, he would never take that chance with his life.

A final former warden worth noting is Donald Cabana. Cabana was a corrections officer for over 32 years in Missouri, Florida, and Mississippi, holding positions ranging from chief juvenile probation officer to prison warden for maximum-security facilities to commissioner of corrections (Bohm, 2013; Mitchell, 2013). After first being in favor of the death penalty, two executions in particular, those of Edward Earl Johnson and Connie Ray Stevens, started to change his mind and became a turning point for Cabana. Just four days after the execution of Edward Johnson, who was found guilty of killing a police officer but maintained his innocence until he was put to death, Cabana stated that he had a rather gut-wrenching meeting with a former high official who is now convinced that Johnson was in fact telling the truth (Mitchell, 2013). The Connie Ray Evans execution was even more emotional for Cabana. He had developed a relationship with Evans over the course of the four years Evans was on death row. Evans asked for permission to hug Cabana before taking the final walk to the death chamber, which forced Cabana to pray for a quick and easy death for his prisoner. As he stumbled through the reading of the death warrant with shaky hands and a quivering voice, Cabana realized how insane this whole process was and that he knew Connie Ray Evans, the man, and believed he was worth saving (Bohm, 2013, pp. 210–211). He realized killing Evans would not bring back his victims and wondering how killing Evans would end the lifelong pain they were experiencing. With his final words Evans asked if he could whisper something to Cabana, he leaned in, and Evans stated: "from one Christian to another, I love you" (Bohm, 2013, p. 211). Cabana was speechless and was shaken to the bone; since the execution of Edward Earl Johnson he "had slept with troubled dreams" . . . and wondered to himself if would ever sleep peacefully again. Claiming that there is a part of a warden that dies with his prisoner, Cabana came to realize that he was wrong about being able to carry out his job without it affecting him. In testifying before the Judiciary Committee of the Minnesota House of Representatives, he stated that "however we do it, in the name of justice, in the name of law and order, in the name of retribution, you . . . do not have the right to ask me, or any prison official, to bloody my hands with an innocent person's blood. Not in the name of justice, not in the name of fairness" (Mitchell, 2013).

As you have read in this section, wardens are not alone when supervising death row inmates and carrying out executions. They manage a number of correctional officers who serve as guards and/or execution staff who assist with the execution. These individuals are also affected by their roles in the death penalty process, and we will conclude with their views.

When we think about the people affected by the death penalty, we may not think about guards on death rows. But these officials, whether they oversee prisoners awaiting execution or participate in the execution itself, can be deeply affected by their role in helping to put a person to death (Long & Robertson, 2015). Mitchell (2013) argues that the last in the line of those who shoulder the heavy burden of carrying out a sentence of death on behalf of a state, in some individualized sense, are the corrections officers and executioners who carry out and oversee the actual killing of the inmate. The views of these individual are worth considering; while voters and legislators may support capital punishment in theory or as a policy, no one is closer to the death penalty or in a better position to comment on the impact of the policy than those who are charged with actually carrying it out. Corrections officers undoubtedly have stressful jobs. One recent report indicates that 31% of correctional officers have posttraumatic stress disorder (PTSD), like Craig Baxley, who was responsible for plunging the lethal injection syringe into at least eight prisoners, has himself attempted suicide, and is now on six types of medication for PTSD and depression (Pilkington, 2017)—compare that to the rate of PTSD among returning Iraq war veterans, which is 20% (Mitchell, 2013). Sadly, these individuals that work closest with the death penalty are often the most neglected group. Prison workers are forced to endure the reality of what it means to execute a human being, and this does not go without consequence. There are many reported cases of prison wardens and correctional officers suffering PSTD-like symptoms specifically as a result of their involvement with the death penalty. The harrowing experience can lead to emotional and physical distress such as mood swings, flashbacks, and nightmares as symptoms encouraged by feelings of shame and guilt that last long after the prison workers have resigned or retired (Martinez, 2014).

As Bohm (2013) outlines, the job of the death row corrections officer is no small feat and involves tending to the daily needs of death row inmates and keeping them alive until their execution date. This is a serious job, as no one ever intended the condemned inmates would wait for their demise in cages for an average of nearly 15 years, and as much as 30 years in some cases. This has become the norm for this dangerous, stressful, bleak environment where officers are forced to work. Because death row guards have shared the same environment with inmates for numerous years and sometimes have developed meaningful relationships with them, officers can develop empathy toward prisoners. As such, a separate team often conducts the execution. Giving small roles to different guards (such as walking the prisoner to the execution spot or putting a hood over the prisoner's head) aims to reduce the emotionally damaging effects of executions. Authorities can also try to disperse feelings of responsibility for the killing by having multiple guards involved (e.g., tie down team) with the focus on the process (Bohm, 2013; Long & Robertson, 2015). The emphasis on working 'efficiently' and 'professionally' also aims to reduce feelings of culpability, with execution teams trained to focus not on the meaning of their activity, but on performing the sub-functions proficiently. Despite such measures, guards can feel mentally tortured by their participation in executions both before and after. Many guards' experiences are consistent with acute stress disorder or posttraumatic stress disorder (PTSD). At the outset of his descent into PTSD, one guard began crying and shaking uncontrollably when (years later) the eyes of all the inmates he had executed began flashing before him (Long & Robertson, 2015, p. 2). Another who transported inmates to the execution chamber developed nightmares, cold sweats, and sleeplessness that led to a change in his personality. As one researcher noted "The inner lives of guards who execute become like those of battlefield veterans who suppress memories from themselves and others" (MacNair, 2002, p. 37). Though being a death row guard and serving on the execution team often requires tight lips, some members have spoken out about the impact the death penalty process has had on their mental well-being.

On aspect of the execution that several officers believed was significantly stressful was when a stay had been granted to the inmate. Bohm (2013) suggests that stays are difficult for these officers because it puts them on an emotional roller coaster. To perform an execution, officers must get their adrenaline going; when a stay is received, the team members often experience an emotional letdown. One member stated: "You crash. Your metabolism just drops. And then when it's back on, you got about a minute and thirty seconds to get up again. And you got to be professional about it and make no screw-ups. It's emotionally painful" (Bohm, 2013, p. 230). Some members do struggle more than others, as stated by one Utah team member who reported having second thoughts:

> I used to be gung-ho for the death penalty but now I'm not sure. It would be easier if he were a crud, but he is a nice, gentle person. I'm not sure we are doing the right thing by putting him to death
>
> *(Gillespie, 2003, p. 49)*

A death-chamber door guard at Louisiana's Angola State Prison shares parallel thoughts: "After it is over, you get to thinking about him. . . . You try to block it out, but you can't—his death is there" (Moseley, 2014).

Others have experienced far worse trauma, as one Texas tie-down member, who participated in approximately 120 executions, explained:

> "I was working in the shop and all of the sudden something just triggered in me and I started shaking, And then, I walked back into the house and my wife asked 'What's the matter?' and I said 'I don't feel good.' And tears, uncontrollable tears was coming out of my eyes. And she said 'What's the matter?' And I said 'I just thought about that execution that I did two days ago. And everybody else's that I was involved with.' And what it was was something triggered within and it just, everybody, all of these executions all of a sudden spring forward . . . . Just like taking slides in a film projector and having a button and just pushing a button and just watching, over and over: him, him, him. I don't know if it's a mental breakdown, I don't know if . . . probably would be classified more as a traumatic stress, similar to what individuals in war had. You know, they'd come back from war, it might be three months, it might be two years, it might be five years, all of the sudden they relive it again, and all that has come out. You see I can barely even talk because I'm thinking more and more of it. You know, there was just so many of 'em."
>
> *(Bohm, 2013, p. 234)*

Other members of execution teams seem to be affected very little if at all by the process; as one Missouri team member explained it:

> I don't know if it's the calloused individuals in us, or what . . . . it doesn't bother me. Sure, I take it for what it is. And I know where I'm at. And as a professional in the department of corrections, I know my duty. These people killed somebody. I didn't. All I'm doing is a job that the state says I should do.

Similarly, a Virginia team member stated

> I don't think about it, you know. The man is executed, the body is gone, and I clean the place up and close the books out, and, hey, I go home and eat me a hearty meal. I just block

it out, that's it. It's all blocked out until the next time. . . . We got a job to do. We did the job. Let's go about our business, you know, go home. So that's the way I look at it, you know.

(Bohm, 2013, p. 232)

Lastly, some officers have experienced what some might consider gains from this portion of the job, as psychological support team members bolster each other's confidence and receive assurance that they can do the job. One team member from Virginia claimed

I know death is my destiny. I find that now I can accept death. I won't look for it. But if it, you know, if it happens, I'd rather die than suffer. I try to enjoy life more. I try to get the full meaning out of life. I try to learn more, as far as, not so much as just about living, but just being a person.

(Bohm, 2013, p. 236)

As recently as April 2017 the topic of death row corrections officers' mental well-being has grabbed national attention, as the Arkansas Department of Corrections was set to have no fewer than eight executions over 11 days, a conveyor belt of killing dispensed at a clip not seen in the U.S. for at least half a century (Pilkington, 2017). Pilkington (2017) stated that 23 former corrections officials from 16 different states sent a joint letter to Arkansas Governor Asa Hutchinson urging him to reconsider. They warned, several on the basis of personal experience, that participating in executions can exact a "severe toll on corrections officers' wellbeing" and that by doing so many so quickly Arkansas was

needlessly exacerbating the strain and stress placed on these officers . . . as you are taking a totally defenseless person, planning, premeditating, even rehearsing, then killing him; any sane person other than a psychopath would be dramatically affected by that.

In prior statements, the governor's office has argued that it will be "more efficient and less stressful" for those involved in carrying out the killing to see them through in quick succession. Frank Thompson argues the exact opposite is true, citing several of the members of his own team who quit their jobs in the fallout of what they went through Oregon's first two executions in three decades. Despite the intensive training Thompson put them through, he said, he was ultimately unable to spare them the brutalizing consequences; as he stated:

There is absolutely no way to conduct a well-run execution without causing at least one person to lose a little bit of their humanity, or to start at least one person on the cumulative path to posttraumatic stress. So for Arkansas to do this eight times in 10 days, to me that is unimaginable—it is compounding the stress, laying traumatic experiences on top of each other.

(Pilkington, 2017)

As Pilkington (2017) contends, "the people who will make up the execution team will be called upon to take part in the killing of an otherwise healthy human being, under intense scrutiny and pressure, in a process that they have little to no prior experience with, using a drug that has not been used before for executions in this state. And then they are going to be asked to do it again. And then come back to work and do it again. And again. And again. And again. And again. And finally again, for the eighth time."

As you have seen throughout this chapter, capital punishment's affects are widespread and can significantly affect more than just the offender, the victim, and their respective families. As we have found, some participants in the death penalty process are adversely affected; indeed, some are seriously damaged by their participation. A number of individuals whose careers might lend others to believe that they must be staunch supporters of capital punishment are in actuality unhappy or dissatisfied with the current system or are possibly even opponents of the death penalty in theory and practice. As Bohm (2013) notes, many are not overly enthusiastic about their role in the process and view their participation as simply doing their jobs or being professionals, something they are prepared to do but would desire not to do. Like murder, execution inflicts emotional and psychological damage on those linked to it. This often begins with anticipatory trauma when law enforcement becomes aware they are investigating a capital crime scene or when the court sets an execution date, and the impact can remain for days, weeks, and even years after an execution. Those who work closely with the accused can often be affected the most, and law enforcement, the courtroom work group, and the corrections officer all fit under this category. Whatever the alternative to capital punishment may be will still possess negative effects for the individuals highlighted in this chapter; however, perhaps they will not be so great as to divert scarce resources from law enforcement and will eliminate the need for judges and lawyers to spend an inordinate amount of time and money on capital punishment, for jurors to be forced to make life and death decisions, and for prison wardens and corrections officers to be required to participate in the ritualized murder of a human being.

References

Abbott, J. (2010). *Testimony at the 4th World Congress against the Death Penalty.* Geneva, Switzerland, February 2010.

Abbott, J., Cluny, A., Denmark, B., & Hampton, R. (2011, January 8). Opinion: Police officials argue death penalty doesn't make us safer. *San Jose Mercury News.* Retrieved from http://www.mercurynews.com/2011/01/07/opinion-police-officials-argue-death-penalty-doesnt-make-us-safer/.

Antonio, M. E. (2008). Stress and the capital jury: How male and female jurors react to serving on a murder trial. *Justice System Journal, 29*(3), 396–407.

Bilyk, J. (2011, March 10). Death penalty abolition will have impact. *Kane County Chronicle.* Retrieved from http://www.kcchronicle.com/2011/03/09/death-penalty-abolition-will-have-impact/aukafil/.

Bohm, R. M. (2013). *Capital punishment's collateral damage.* Durham, NC: Carolina Academic Press.

Bohm, R. M. (2017). *Deathquest: An introduction to the theory and practice of capital punishment in the United States* (5th ed.). New York: Routledge.

Bowers, W. J., & Steiner, B. D. (1998). Death by default: An empirical demonstration of false and forced choices in capital sentencing. *Texas Law Review.*, 77, 605.

Braswell, M. C., McCarthy, B. R., & McCarthy, B. J. (2017). *Justice, crime, and ethics* (9th ed.). New York: Routledge.

Bright, D. A., & Goodman-Delahunty, J. (2004). The influence of gruesome verbal evidence on mock juror verdicts. *Psychiatry, Psychology, and Law, 11*, 154–166.

Costanzo, S., & Costanzo, M. (1994). Life or death decisions: An analysis of capital jury decision making under the special issues sentencing framework. *Law and Human Behavior, 18*(2), 151.

Cusack, R. M. (1999). *Stress and stress symptoms in capital murder jurors: Is jury duty hazardous to jurors' mental health?* Unpublished doctoral dissertation, St. Mary's University, San Antonio, Texas.

Death Penalty Focus. (2008). *47 members of law enforcement from California cite problems with the Death Penalty and call for reforms.* Press Release. Retrieved March 27, 2008 from https://deathpenaltyinfo.org/node/2337

Dieter, R. C. (1995). On the front line: Law enforcement views on the death penalty. *The Center.* Retrieved from https://deathpenaltyinfo.org/front-line-law-enforcement-views-death-penalty

Dieter, R. C. (2009). *Smart on crime: Reconsidering the Death Penalty in a time of economic crisis national poll of police chiefs puts capital punishment at bottom of law enforcement priorities.* Retrieved from https://deathpenaltyinfo.org/documents/CostsRptFinal.pdf

Douglas, K. S., Lyon, D. R., & Ogloff, J. R. P. (1997). The impact of graphic photographic evidence on mock jurors' decisions in a murder trial: Probative or prejudicial? *Law and Human Behavior, 21*, 485–501.

Ferguson, A. G. (2015). The trauma of jury duty. *The Atlantic.* Retrieved May 17, 2015 from www.theatlantic.com/politics/archive/2015/05/the-trauma-of-jury-duty/393479/

Figueroa, T., & Walker, M. (2010). State's death penalty lacks urgency. *North County Times.* Retrieved April 17, 2010 from www.sandiegouniontribune.com/sdut-region-states-death-penalty-lacks-urgency-2010apr17-story.html

Fleury-Steiner, B. (2004). *Jurors' stories of death: How America's death penalty invests in inequality.* Ann Arbor, MI: University of Michigan Press. Ann Arbor, MI.

ForsterLee, L., Fox, G. B., ForsterLee, R., & Ho, R. (2004). The effects of a victim impact statement and gender on juror information processing in a criminal trial: Does the punishment fit the crime? *Australian Psychologist, 39,* 57–67.

Fretland, K. (2014). Oklahoma former prison warden: Death penalty does not help families. *The Guardian.* Retrieved April 28, 2014 from www.theguardian.com/world/2014/apr/28/oklahoma-former-prison-warden-death-penalty-does-not-help-families

Garcetti, G. (2011). "California's death penalty doesn't serve justice," *Los Angeles Times,* March 25, 2011. Retrieved from http://opinion.latimes.com/opinionla/2011/03/gil-garcetti-californias-death-penalty-doesnt-serve-justice.html.

Gillespie, L. K. (2003). *Inside the death chamber: Exploring executions.* Boston: Pearson.

Glode, D. (2010). "Death penalty conflicts," *Newport News-Times,* June 25, 2010. Retrieved fromhttp://www.newportnewstimes.com/v2_news_articles.php?heading=0&story_id=23050&page=72.

Goldman, A. (2015). As bomb trial nears, Boston braces for a painful recounting. *The Washington Post.* Retrieved from www.washingtonpost.com/world/national-security/as-bomb-trial-nears-boston-braces-for-a-painful-recounting/2015/01/25/79fd7988-a0b9-11e4-903f-9f2faf7cd9fe_story.html?utm_term=.9783568080cf&wpmk=MK0000205

Haney, C. (1997). Violence and the capital jury: Mechanisms of moral disengagement and the impulse to condemn to death. *Stanford Law Review, 49,* 1447–1486.

Haney, C. (2005). *Death by design: Capital punishment as a social psychological system.* Oxford: Oxford University Press.

Hannaford-Agor, P. (n.d.). *Jury news.* Williamsburg, VA: Center for Jury Studies, National Center for State Courts.

Jung, H. (2013). Oregon death penalty "indefensible", says man who last carried it out. *The Oregonian.* Retrieved February 26, 2013 from www.oregonlive.com/politics/index.ssf/2013/02/oregon_death_penalty_indefensi.html

Kaplan, S. M., & Winget, C. (1992). The occupational hazards of jury duty. *Bulletin of the American Academy of Psychiatry and the Law, 20,* 325.

Long, W. C., & Robertson, O. (2015). *Prison guards and the death penalty.* London: Penal Reform International.

Luginbuhl, J., & Burkhead, M. (1995). Victim impact evidence in a capital trial: Encouraging votes for death. *American Journal of Criminal Justice, 20,* 1–16.

MacNair, R. (2002). *Perpetration-induced traumatic stress: The psychological consequences of killing.* Westport, CT: Greenwood Publishing Group.

Martinez, C. (2014). *The death penalty and its inexcusable burden on prison workers.* National Coalition to Abolish the Death Penalty. Retrieved October 30, 2014 from www.ncadp.org/blog/entry/the-death-penalty-and-its-inexcusable-burden-on-prison-workers

Matsuo, K., & Itoh, Y. (2016). Effects of emotional testimony and gruesome photographs on mock jurors' decisions and negative emotions. *Psychiatry, Psychology and Law, 23*(1), 85–101.

May, M. (2008). Time to end the death penalty in Maryland. *The Baltimore Examiner.* Retrieved December 1, 2008 from https://deathpenaltynews.blogspot.com/2008/12/time-to-end-death-penalty-in-maryland.html

McGowen, M. G., & Myers, B. (2004). Who is the victim anyway? The effects of bystander victim impact statements on mock juror sentencing decisions. *Violence and Victims, 19,* 357–374.

Mitchell, P. (2013). *The weight of capital punishment on jurors, justices, governors, and executioners.* Retrieved from https://verdict.justia.com/author/mitchell

Moseley, T. (2014). The enforces of the death penalty. *The Atlantic.* Retrieved October 1, 2014 from www.theatlantic.com/health/archive/2014/10/the-enforcers-of-the-death-penalty/379901/

Myers, B., & Arbuthnot, J. (1999). The effects of victim impact evidence on the verdicts and sentencing judgments of mock jurors. *Journal of Offender Rehabilitation, 29,* 95–112.

Nichols v. Heidle. (2013). No. 06–6495, 6th Cir. (July 25, 2013).

Osofsky, M. J., Bandura, A., & Zimbardo, P. G. (2005). The role of moral disengagement in the execution process. *Law and Human Behavior, 29*(4), 371.

Pappas, S. (2015). In Boston and Aurora, jurors may risk mental health for justice. *Live Science.* Retrieved January 28, 2015 from www.livescience.com/49607-boston-aurora-jury-selection-mental-health.html

Pilkington, E. (2017). Eight executions in 11 days: Arkansas order may endanger staff's mental Health. *The Guardian.* Retrieved March 29, 2017 from www.theguardian.com/world/2017/mar/29/arkansas-executioners-mental-health-allen-ault

The Rachel Maddow Show. (2011). *MSNBC.* September 22, 2011. Transcript retrieved fromhttp://www.nbcnews.com/id/44639338/ns/msnbc_tv-rachel_maddow_show/

Shuman, D. W., Hamilton, J. A., & Daley, C. E. (1994). The health effects of jury service. *Law & Psychology. Review., 18,* 267.

Slick, J. (2011). The weight of "playing god": In capital punishment cases, jurors are punished. *The Oregonian*. Retrieved from www.oregonlive.com/opinion/index.ssf/2011/10/the_weight_of_playing_god_in_c.html

Thompson, S. F. (2015). Ex-warden: Death penalty doesn't make guards safer. *The News Journal of Delaware*. Retrieved April 1, 2015 from www.delawareonline.com/story/opinion/contributors/2015/04/01/ex-warden-death-penalty-make-guards-safer/70791272/

Thompson, S. F. (2016). What I learned from executing two men. *The New York Times*. Retrieved September 15, 2016 from www.nytimes.com/2016/09/18/opinion/sunday/what-i-learned-from-executing-two-men.html

Timmins, A. (2010). Former warden "haunted" by executions, death penalty scars prison staff, he says. *The Concord Monitor*. Retrieved August 13, 2010 from https://deathpenaltyinfo.org/new-voices-former-warden-calls-executions-traumatic-prison-staff

Tsoudis, O., & Smith-Lovin, L. (1998). How bad was it? The effects of victim and perpetrator emotion on responses to criminal court vignettes. *Social Forces*, 77, 695–722.

Warsmith, S. (2017). Jurors on Summit County's last death penalty case detail difficult service. *Akron Beacon Journal*. Retrieved February 17, 2017 from www.ohio.com/news/local/jurors-on-summit-county-s-last-death-penalty-case-detail-difficult-service-1.748138

36

EXONERATION

Life After Death Row

Scott Vollum

We've all seen the headlines and television news clips: Death row inmate is shown jubilantly walking out the prison or courtroom a free man (or woman), finally free after years isolated in a small cell 23 hours a day. We are left to assume that their exoneration and release brings unmitigated joy and happiness as they embark on their new life as a free citizen. But this is not where the story ends. In fact, this is only the beginning for death row exonerees. Though the cameras and reporters may dissipate, the real story—a complex one of trauma, struggles, loss, and grief—and yes, of joy, happiness, and successes, too—is only beginning.

This story has become an increasingly common one, as the number of death row inmates found to be have been wrongly convicted and sentenced to death increased along with the increased use of the death penalty and the scrutiny that it brought over the years. According to the Death Penalty Information Center (2017), there have been 160 exonerations in the modern death penalty era (i.e., since 1973). During that same time, there have been 1,462 executions in the United States. That's about one exoneration for every nine executions during that time period. A recent study found that 4% of those sentenced to death are actually innocent of the crime (Gross, O'Brien, Hu, & Kennedy, 2014). The average time between wrongful conviction and exoneration is just over 11 years, with the longest time being 39 years. One of the consequences of these numbers is a growing population of exonerees who must find a way to navigate their new-found freedom in a world that has changed and from which they have been excluded and left behind.

Again, the story is not complete upon understanding these numbers and the reality they represent, upon understanding that, for these individuals, they have been exonerated and have found their freedom. No. Recovering from the wrongful conviction and death sentence, navigating the often cold and foreign world they are reentering, attempting to rebuild a previously defiled life, grieving losses that occurred over the years they were incarcerated, and beginning to manage the tasks of daily living prison had taken away from them all play out in the days, weeks, months, and years that follow exoneration. Westervelt and Cook (2012), who have produced the most complete and rich examination of death row exonerees and their struggles, eloquently state it this way:

> The story of the innocent does not end the day they are incarcerated for the crime or even the day their innocence is revealed and they are released. The impact of their wrongful conviction included more than their struggle to survive prison while fighting for their freedom. Their story, and their struggle, continues after they leave prison. For their stories to be more completely told, they must include what life is like the day *after* the day of their release, when

their new life begins, as they begin to confront and reconcile the impact of their wrongful conviction. Until this part of the journey of the innocent is examined and explained, the true meaning of what it is to be wrongly convicted is incomplete.

Counting the number of wrongly convicted—the number of "exonerees"—can easily mislead people into thinking that the day of release or exoneration is the end game, the end of this long journey to innocence reclaimed. . . . In a way, the day he or she becomes an exoneree is rather the beginning of another stage in his or her journey, another chapter in his or her story, a chapter that has yet to be written.

(pp. 5–6)

It is my objective here to offer insight into this part of the journey, into this "chapter" that follows exoneration, and into the experiences, reactions, policies, and practices that make up its proverbial pages.

In this chapter, I will shed light on these men and women's experiences of exoneration and life after exoneration and all that comes with it. I will discuss what, exactly, exoneration entails, the forms it takes, and how it comes to occur. I will also discuss the impacts, both short and long term, of the wrongful conviction and exoneration on the individuals who experience it. Importantly, I will also "give voice" to exoneration by offering the words of an exoneree, Damon Thibodeaux, and one of his postconviction attorneys, Steven Kaplan, in special capsules throughout this chapter. Damon Thibodeaux was wrongly convicted of the rape and murder of his 14-year-old cousin in 1996 and spent nearly 15 years on Louisiana's death row before being exonerated in 2012. Steve Kaplan is a tax attorney in Minneapolis, Minnesota, with previously little criminal law or appellate experience who took on Damon's case pro bono in 2001, unaware of exactly what he was getting into but determined to save Damon's life. Their story was recently highlighted in an article in the *Minneapolis StarTribune* (Smith, 2015), which can be freely accessed on their website. In each case, I present these words verbatim, based on personal correspondence. They have only been edited for grammatical clarity. I also present a profile of the case of Kerry Cook, an "exoneree" not fully represented among those to whom that term, and this chapter, refers. Though his conviction was overturned and he was released from death row, he has not been completely exonerated by the state of Texas (you can find his story in his 2007 book: *Chasing Justice*). I share his experiences, as they represent important realities about the difficulty of being truly exonerated.

GIVING VOICE: Death Row Exoneree Damon Thibodeaux

The thing that troubles me most about being wrongfully convicted and sentenced to death is that it happens way too often. I mean with all of the exonerations we have had in this country in the past 30 years, haven't we learned that the death penalty is not a viable punishment? It's bad enough that we incarcerate innocent people and the system swallows them and they get missed, so are we going to allow that same thing to happen where the death penalty is concerned? We are supposed to be an evolved civilized society. Aren't we smarter and better than that? How can we tell the world that our human rights record is better than most nations when we are one of the top five countries that still apply the death penalty in our criminal justice system? It troubles me greatly that the majority of our society has no problem executing an innocent man just to maintain the death penalty so that they can kill a truly guilty person.

GIVING VOICE: Steven Kaplan, Postconviction Attorney for Exoneree Damon Thibodeaux

Some 90% of all inmates who enter the Louisiana State Penitentiary at Angola will die there from natural causes because the lengths of their sentences are so great. Others, like Damon Thibodeaux, are sent to Angola's death row for the stated purpose of being executed in its death house.

At the age of 22, Damon was sentenced to death for the rape and murder of his 14-year-old cousin, Crystal. Indeed, he had confessed to those crimes after some nine hours of interrogation. Nonetheless, the forensic and timeline evidence flatly contradicted what he told his interrogators, and the content of the confession made absolutely no sense in light of it. Moreover, there was every reason to question the threats and tactics that detectives had employed to obtain his confession. Nonetheless, he faced execution unless his conviction could be overturned.

In early April 2005, Pam Wandzel, our law firm's pro bono director, and I traveled from Minneapolis to Angola to meet Damon for the first time. After being led into a small room, we spoke at length with Damon through a metal grating. What we saw and heard was an innocent, anxious, and articulate 31-year-old man who had by then already spent more than seven years on death row.

He had not hired us, knew nothing about us, but understood all too well that we and the other members of his legal team had his life in our collective hands. Shackled in chains and accompanied by a guard, he shuffled back slowly down the hallway and back to his cell following our conversation. As he did so, he glanced back at me with a nervous smile that I will never forget. From that day forward, Damon's case took on a personal imperative that equaled its legal importance.

Soon after that visit, Damon and I began speaking once, and sometimes twice, a week, and we corresponded frequently. Although we saw each other on other occasions, our relationship was primarily telephonic. He needed the ongoing contact with those trying to help him, and I needed the comfort of knowing that he was doing as well physically and emotionally as possible under the circumstances.

I and others in my office sent him books, music, and money to cover the costs of food and clothing from the prison canteen, eyewear, and long-distance calls. During our phone conversations, we spoke not only about his case but also about books, politics, world events, and his beloved New England Patriots and Houston Astros.

Our conversations offered me an insight into life on death row and the long-term effects of solitary confinement. Damon, like the others on death row, was housed in a 6-by-8-foot cell for 23 hours each day. He was allowed one hour per day outside of the cell to walk or exercise, make a phone call, or attend to any administrative detail that required his attention. On three of those days, Damon could spend that one hour exercising outdoors. In sum, during his 15 years on death row, Damon saw the sky three hours per week and never saw a star at night.

The food on death row is horrible and incompatible with good health. Medical and dental care is inadequate or non-existent. Over time, many on death row suffer the effects of heart disease and diabetes. Their physical and mental health declines from the continuing lack of activity in an environment where, at any time, they may be led from their cells and to their execution.

The monotony is unbroken and crushing. Death row inmates are given no jobs, educational services, or any other activity that would enable them to occupy their time in a meaningful way. After all, they are dead men walking or sitting, so why should the prison invest any more resources in them than is absolutely necessary to keep them alive long enough to execute them?

Many suffer from mental illness before they enter death row, and their conditions continue to degenerate over time. Shrieks and shouting from one or more inmates can be heard down the row of cells. The noise and lights make sleep difficult. The lack of exercise and mental stimulation, not to mention outside human contact, can reduce even the strongest to emotional rubble. They may lapse into a depression that keeps them in their cells even during the hour each day when they could leave it.

In the summer, the temperature inside Angola's death row often exceeds 100 degrees, while in the winter months the inmates need warm clothing. Conditions inside Angola's death row have been the subject of federal court litigation.

Damon, however, was unique. A born survivor, his sense of hope and good humor was unconquerable. His deep religious faith, determination to regain his freedom however long it took, and active mind sustained him. He read the Bible, books, newspapers, and magazines; stayed abreast of the news by watching television and listening to radio; exercised frequently in his cell; and maintained a daily routine to the extent that such was possible. His lived mentally outside of death row and suppressed any anger that crept into his consciousness. He fought despair and succeeded.

Exoneration

There are varying perspectives on what, exactly, it means for a death row inmate to be "exonerated." Some believe the label "exoneration" should only be applied to those who are 100% innocent of not only the capital crime but also any other criminal action involved in the particular incident of the victim's murder and for whom a legal disposition clearing the original conviction has been made (Bedau & Radelet, 1987; Gross & Shaffer, 2012; Risinger, 2007). Others take a more nuanced approach to defining exoneration, including anyone who is factually innocent of the capital murder (but who may have taken part in other crimes surrounding the incident), in some cases including those for whom no official disposition has exonerated them (see, for example, Cohen, 2003). The reality is that what it means to be exonerated exists on a continuum, taking on a variety of forms of exoneration and including a variety of paths by which a death row inmate becomes exonerated.

The *Death Penalty Information Center* (DPIC), which has the most comprehensive current database of death row exonerations and exonerees, requires one of the following for someone to be included among the exonerated:

- They have been acquitted of all charges related to the offense for which they were sentenced to death;
- The prosecution has dismissed all charges related to the offense for which they were sentenced to death;
- Or, they have been granted a pardon due to evidence of innocence.

(DPIC, 2017)

Others (Bedau & Radelet, 1987; Gross & Shaffer, 2012; Holmes, 2008) have produced more restrictive criteria for when a death sentence may be declared wrongful and thus warranting of "exoneration." Most notably, Bedau and Radelet (1987), in their pioneering work on cases of wrongful conviction and exoneration in capital cases, defined a "miscarriage of justice" in capital cases as occurring "when either (i) no such crime actually occurred, *or* (ii) the defendant was legally and physically uninvolved in the crime" (p. 45). Gross and Shaffer (2012) likewise restrict the designation of exoneree to those who are legally determined to have had nothing to do with the crime or other crimes that were committed in the same event, regardless of how minor any such offense might be. They also exclude "any case in which a conviction was vacated and charges dismissed for legal error without new evidence of innocence" (p. 7).

Holmes (2008) aligns his criteria more with DPIC, operationalizing wrongful conviction in capital cases as any in which the previously convicted person is, upon subsequent review, legally acquitted of the charges. He points out, however, the important distinction between one who is *illegally* convicted and one who is *wrongfully* convicted: "A person illegally convicted may or may not have actually done the crime for which he or she is charged, but a grievous legal defect in the process leads to his or her conviction. . . . Some of those whose illegal convictions are overturned are actually innocent . . . these are the individuals who have been wrongfully convicted" (pp. 100–101).

As illustrated in Figure 36.1, of the three criteria used by DPIC, dismissal of charges is the most frequent legal disposition for death row exonerees. Sixty-four percent of the 160 exonerees were released because, upon original charges being thrown out, the prosecutor refused to retry them. This typically occurs after the original conviction is successfully challenged on constitutional grounds such as ineffective assistance of counsel, violation of the equal protection clause of the Fourteenth Amendment, and a variety of due process violations. These cases are then usually returned back to the court of original jurisdiction, where the respective prosecutor is faced with a decision of whether or not to retry the case. Often due to new evidence or circumstances revealed in appellate review or in further investigation, the prosecution may decide to not retry the case, at which point the former death row

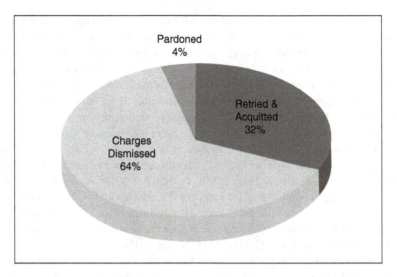

Figure 36.1   Basis of Exoneration: 1973–2017

inmate is considered exonerated and is, in most cases, released from prison (with the exception of cases where there are other charges for which the inmate was incarcerated).

In many cases (32% of those included in DPIC's list), the death row inmate is afforded a new trial when the prior conviction and sentence is overturned on appeal. In this case the inmate cum defendant is brought back to the court of original jurisdiction and the case is retried. If convicted, the inmate may be again sentenced to death and sent back to death row, sent to prison if sentenced to life, or even potentially freed if receiving a lesser sentence and being credited with time served. Or the defendant may be acquitted on retrial, in which case he or she becomes one of the exonerated. Though executive pardon may be ever present in popular perceptions and dramatic media representations of saving death row inmates from execution (Atwell, 2004), it is by far the rarest basis for exoneration of death row inmates. Indeed, only 7 of the 160 exonerations since 1973 were due to pardon.

Note that the DPIC criteria allow for the possibility that the exoneree was actually involved in the crime, but the evidence may not have been sufficient to either recharge or reconvict him in the wake of successful appeal. However, given the severity of the crime and the associated reluctance of public officials to allow an alleged perpetrator free if they believe him or her truly guilty, this possibility is likely very rare.

Regardless of the criteria used, there is no debate that a significant number of death row inmates have been found to be innocent over the history of the death penalty and, most notably, over the last four decades of its use. To be sure, the Death Penalty Information Center's database/list does not include all who are released from death row. Most significantly, it does not include those who make what's referred to as an Alford plea (see *North Carolina v. Alford*, 1970). An Alford plea (also referred to as the Alford doctrine) is a plea whereby the defendant maintains his innocence but pleads guilty as an admission that the prosecution would likely be successful in securing a guilty verdict if brought to trial. It is a form of "no contest" or "nolo contendere" plea usually accompanied by an agreement to lessen the sentence for the defendant or release him from incarceration (Bibas, 2002). In capital cases, it typically includes, at the least, removal of the death sentence and, in some cases, release from prison. One of the more famous cases in which this occurred is the case of Damien Echols, one of the "West Memphis Three" accused and convicted of brutally murdering three young boys in what was alleged to be a satanic ritual (Echols, 2012; Leveritt, 2014). Echols had spent more than 18 years on Arkansas' death row and was facing years of hearings to consider new evidence of innocence when offered the opportunity to be released immediately in exchange for an Alford plea. He (and his co-defendants Jason Baldwin and Jesse Misskelley, who had been sentenced to life in prison), took the plea to win his freedom (Echols, 2012; Leveritt, 2014). Though the evidence strongly establishes his innocence, he is nonetheless still guilty in the eyes of the law and not technically "exonerated" and, along with others who accepted Alford pleas, is not counted among the number of those considered to be death row exonerees.

Though it may be tempting to conclude that exoneration of an innocent death row inmate is evidence of success of the appellate courts and due process within the criminal justice system, most exonerations occur due to forces outside the formal system—some might say in spite of the system, not because of it (Findley & Golden, 2014; Westervelt & Cook, 2010; Zalman, 2006). Historically, exonerations have been more likely to occur due to the work of journalists (Westervelt & Cook, 2012), filmmakers (Adams, Hoffer, & Hoffer, 1991; Norris, 2017), and small groups of attorneys and law professors working pro bono to free the innocent (Findley & Golden, 2014). And it wasn't until the advent of DNA evidence and the publication of Barry Scheck and Peter Neufeld's book *Actual Innocence* in 2000 that the "innocence movement" began to coalesce into a broader collective network of advocates and activists (Findley & Golden, 2014; Norris, 2017).

It has been this collective network, and not DNA evidence alone, as some might presume, that has had the greatest sustained impact on the exoneration of death row inmates (Norris, 2017). In fact, DNA evidence has only played a role in 20 (12.5%) of the 160 exonerations since 1973, and only in 3 of the 23 exonerations since 2010. Nevertheless, the newfound DNA evidence and the cases it exposed as we moved into the twenty-first century drew a great amount of attention and catalyzed a much more far-reaching movement to exonerate death row inmates, as well as many others. In 2004, The Innocence Network (www.innocencenetwork.org), an ever-expanding affiliation of organizations and institutions devoted to working for exoneration of the innocent, was formed. Its members ranged from law schools and collectives of lawyers working pro bono to groups of investigative journalists to organizations working to help exonerees postrelease. It also became the centralized representative of a growing number of regional and local innocence projects modeled off the national Innocence Project founded in 1992 by Peter Neufeld and Barry Scheck. Today, virtually every death penalty state is served by either a state or regional innocence project (www.innocenceproject.org).

GIVING VOICE: Steven Kaplan, Postconviction Attorney for Exoneree Damon Thibodeaux

In mid-2007, Damon's legal team, comprised of the Capital Post-Conviction Project of Louisiana, the Innocence Project of New York, and my law firm, Fredrikson & Byron, presented to the district attorney and his staff a wealth of evidence demonstrating Damon's actual innocence. To their enduring credit, the district attorney and his people were willing to work jointly with us and reinvestigate the case. That process included several DNA tests and other forensic procedures, numerous witness contacts, internal law enforcement consideration, and legal memoranda that we submitted. It would not conclude for more than five years, but it would ultimately secure Damon's release and freedom.

As this reinvestigation was grinding to what we anticipated would be the desired conclusion, Damon and I began planning for his life after exoneration. During our conversations, it became evident that he was as interested in restarting his life in Minneapolis as we were in having him do so.

What he would need was far more available in the Twin Cities than in Louisiana or Texas, where members of his immediate family lived. Health care; educational, computer, and job training; psychological counseling; housing; employment; and continuing financial and personal support would be far more available here than there. In Minneapolis, he could have a fresh start with a host of people who were prepared to help him far from where his life had gone so horribly off the rails.

He would need immediate financial help for his everyday living expenses, funds that the state of Louisiana was not willing to provide. Indeed, Damon walked out of Angola with the clothes on his back and

whatever personal belongings fit into a pillow case. We had set aside money for him in a bank account,
but he would need ongoing and significant financial assistance before he could live independently.

Life After Death Row

The effects of being wrongfully convicted of a capital murder (by definition, a particularly "heinous" or brutal crime), sentenced to death, and spending time (often decades) incarcerated on death row as an innocent person are profound and pervasive. Most immediately, an exoneree must simultaneously recover from years of deprivation and trauma and cope with a new life in a world that is likely unfamiliar and, for some, downright frightening (Campbell & Denov, 2004; Grounds, 2004; Scott, 2010; Westervelt & Cook, 2012). But the ripple effects of wrongful conviction and death sentence continue over the years after release, with often severe social and psychological long-term effects, challenges, and struggles for death row exonerees (DeShay, 2016; Westervelt & Cook, 2008, 2012).

Much of what we know about the experience of death row exonerees has historically come from personal accounts, either in autobiographies/biographies (see, for example, Adams, Hoffer, & Hoffer, 1991; Cook, 2007; Echols, 2012; Junkin, 2005; Keine, 2011–2012; Melendez, 2008), news coverage, and informational campaigns from organizations such as the Innocence Project,[1] Witness to Innocence,[2] and Journey of Hope[3] or through both nonfictional and fictional television documentaries and films (see, for example, CNN's nonfictional series *Death Row Stories*, award winning Showtime documentary *After Innocence*, and Sundance Channel's fictional *Rectify*). Indeed, stories of the innocent surviving a death sentence and death row have captivated popular attention over the last few decades. The social research on exoneration and postexoneration life of those released from death row, on the other hand, has been scant and lagged behind the popular culture interest, with the notable exception of the work of Saundra Westervelt and Kimberly Cook (2008, 2010, 2012), who have produced the deepest and most complete analyses of the experiences of death row exonerees. Others have produced studies on the impact of wrongful conviction and postexoneration life more generally (Clow, Leach, & Ricciardelli, 2012; DeShay, 2016; Konvisser, 2012; Scott, 2010), and this is certainly valuable research that extends to those experiencing exoneration of capital murder and freedom from death row. But Westervelt and Cook's specific and rigorous attention to death row exonerees is to this point unparalleled in the social sciences.

What we find from these accounts is a complex mix of both short- and long-term effects of wrongful capital convictions and death sentences and associated experiences in the wake of exoneration. Of course, we find variation among the exonerated and their lives after death row, but we also find important commonalities that seem to pervade the experiences of all or most exonerees. These commonalities begin with the deprivations and solitary confinement commonly experienced on death row and extend through the often many years of separation from the outside world and loved ones and the losses experienced over this time; the lengthy and circuitous judicial process with its dead ends and false hopes; the often abrupt and jarring experience of being released; and years of adjustment as exonerees navigate life after death row.

One of the most dominant themes in death row exonerees' accounts reflects the most immediate impacts proximate to the experience of wrongful conviction and incarceration. Westervelt and Cook (2012), reflecting on the extant literature across disciplines, conclude that "trauma is at the core of the experience of a wrongful conviction" and that it presents "a primary explanatory framework for better understanding life after exoneration" (p. 9). Indeed, it is this early and ongoing trauma that sets the stage for postexoneration life and associated challenges and difficulties experienced by exonerees as they navigate their new-found freedom.

The trauma of experiencing wrongful conviction and incarceration on death row has been found to be similar to that experienced by soldiers in battle or individuals surviving natural disasters and to manifest in similar symptoms of posttraumatic stress disorder (PTSD) (Deshay, 2016; Westervelt

& Cook, 2012). The devastating impact of being wrongfully convicted and condemned by a justice system one may have previously trusted is one thing, but the deprivation and isolation of incarceration on death row in spite of being innocent is particularly and acutely traumatic. Some have declared these conditions, often of the "supermax" or solitary confinement variety, to be akin to torture (Arrigo & Bullock, 2008; Haney & Lynch, 1997; Westervelt & Cook, 2010). The psychological consequences are accordingly profound. One study found that the overwhelming majority of wrongfully convicted and incarcerated individuals studied exhibited long-term personality changes and met the diagnostic criteria of PTSD (Grounds, 2004). Others have found that depression and anxiety disorders are commonly manifested by those wrongfully imprisoned and that many experience forms of dissociation as they attempt to cope with their wrongful condemnation (Scott, 2010). In addition to the psychological trauma of deprivation and isolation, wrongfully condemned death row inmates must also come to terms with the stigma and defilement of their humanity that comes with being convicted of horrendous crimes, some involving rape of children (Scott, 2010; Westervelt & Cook, 2008). And some become violently (and sexually) preyed upon and brutalized by other inmates (Cook, 2007). These are experiences and traumas that follow exonerees throughout their post-death row lives. Westervelt and Cook (2008) articulate these experiences as "sustained catastrophe":

> If incarceration of an innocent person can be considered a sustained catastrophe, we can understand the human suffering experienced by exonerees just as we do other trauma survivors. Models of trauma, coping and stigma management help explain the "life after death" experiences of those we most often think of as surviving sustained catastrophes (cancer and AIDS patients, abuse victims). So, too, these ideas help us understand how death row exonerees negotiate trauma after release.
>
> *(p. 34)*

GIVING VOICE: *Death Row Exoneree Damon Thibodeaux*

The impact of spending so much time on death row is devastating. You not only lose your freedom but your life as well, even though you are still alive. If you have a family you miss their lives. You miss watching your children grow up. The passing of family members. And being locked in a cell for 23 hours a day takes a mental toll on you as well. Not to mention the fact that I had prepared myself for the possibility that I would be executed for something that I did not do. Can you imagine having to come to terms with your own death while still living? I often think about what my life might have been like. What did I miss? Where would I be? What would I have become? What did I not do that I could have done? Who would I be instead of Damon Thibodeaux, death row exoneree? And I come up with no answers.

The days immediately following exoneration and release from prison can be a tumultuous and conflicting experience for exonerees. Though there is indeed usually elation and joy, this can quickly become a frightening and overwhelming time. Sometimes the struggles and challenges come in the form of things most of us take for granted as relatively banal. I recently had a conversation with an Illinois death row exoneree who reflected on his early days of freedom after over two decades of incarceration: He recalled that one of his most troubling adjustments was safely crossing busy streets. After nearly getting hit by cars on several occasions, he finally resigned himself to following his pre-teen nephew until he regained his sense of timing in this world so removed from life on death row (Fields, personal communication, April 11, 2017). The point is that exonerees are faced with readjusting to a world that has passed them by. Geography, demography, and, perhaps most acutely in late modern society, technology often have changed profoundly over the years an exoneree wrongfully spent behind bars.

Another challenge in the early days following an exoneree's release from death row comes in reconnecting with family and loved ones, navigating the complex relationships interrupted and complicated by wrongful conviction and years of incarceration and condemnation at the hands of the state and the public. Westervelt and Cook (2012) point out that

> family members of exonerees watched while their loved ones were arrested and charged with unspeakable crimes. They often sat in the courtroom as witness after witness portrayed their child or sibling as a monster and heard jury and judge condemn them to extermination because they were no longer worthy of life
>
> *(p. 83)*

Interviews with family of the condemned reveal just how conflicting and traumatic these experiences can be and how they can make the ongoing relationship with the condemned exceedingly challenging (King, 2005). Add to this the fact that, as time passes, the very structure of the inmate's family and friend networks will inevitably transform, with the condemned being only a captive bystander to these transformations. Westervelt and Cook (2012), reporting on their interviews with exonerees, note the following:

> Loved ones were then left to build a life around periodic visits to prison, occasional letters, missed births and birthdays, and constant worry. Exonerees watched from prison as children were born and grew up, siblings and parents died, and spouses divorced them. Then, just as suddenly as they were taken away, our participants, one day, were released from prison and reinserted back into family dynamics that had become accustomed to their absence. They struggle to reestablish a place within the family unit. For better or worse, their relationships with those closest to them are never the same again.
>
> *(pp. 83–84)*

Typically, death row prisoners are not allowed physical contact, so they must get to know children through a glass partition if they are fortunate enough to have any contact at all. Likewise, they are not allowed to attend funerals for loved ones who die and thus are denied opportunities to mourn and grieve as they would if they were still free citizens. When released, then, they are faced with navigating new relationships with family members they hardly know as well as the losses and resulting gaps they have not yet fully grieved or reconciled with what they knew before their incarceration. Moreover, the co-existing trauma for all involved often creates tensions, as each person experiences different needs as they try to cope (Westervelt & Cook, 2012). This is exacerbated, of course, by the fact that the years of imprisonment should not have happened. Though this fact can be acknowledged and the exoneree can be freed, those years can never be regained nor the trauma simply abated.

GIVING VOICE: Death Row Exoneree Damon Thibodeaux

My first days free were kind of like a euphoric dream. I was walking into a world 15 years beyond the world I knew. It was different seeing the world progress on TV and now having to experience it and reintegrate into that world that I did not know. I spent a lot of time walking around New Orleans with my son Josh and getting to know him as a man. We talked and it was great. He is a fine young man and I am proud of who he has become. The biggest difficulty was learning about all the technology that I would have to learn how to use. Seeing all of these advances and now having to use it was daunting. I had a lot of help from family and friends and I am extremely grateful. The greatest joy I had was breathing air as a free man again. Being able to go wherever I chose freely without chains and shackles on me is the greatest feeling you can experience after having to live like a prisoner for so long. The biggest fear I had was not being able to stand on my own. In prison you have to rely on the state and the system to supply what you need. I have learned that EVERY exonerated person needs extensive help once released because it is so hard after being on death row. After fighting so hard to prove your innocence and doing so, it can be easy to be tired and afraid to live your life. After all you were just thrown back into a world that passed you by and that you know absolutely nothing about.

The weeks, months, and years in the wake of exoneration bring a perpetual flow of challenges for exonerees as they reenter free society. These range from practical matters such as housing, employment, and money to very personal matters such as forming and/or maintaining intimate relationships. Just as any other person reentering society after being incarcerated, death row exonerees are quickly faced with the realities of how they will live and provide for themselves. Though one might think that these would be mitigated by the fact that exonerees were actually innocent, it is sometimes quite the opposite. Though they experience the same basic needs, in many cases, exonerees are not afforded the services provided to guilty inmates who were released on parole. It may seem a cruel irony, but the fact that they are innocent removes their eligibility for reentry services such as assistance in seeking employment and housing, finding health care, or receiving psychological treatment or counseling (Scott, 2010; Westervelt & Cook, 2012). Though state compensation and services (discussed later in this chapter) are increasing as the number of exonerations rises, much of the practical support for exonerees still comes from private citizens and nonprofit organizations (Westervelt & Cook, 2010). Westervelt and Cook (2010) highlight just how problematic this reality is: "These practical problems become obstacles to social reintegration which ripple through their lifetimes: no home equity, no retirement funds, no prescription coverage, ruptured family relationships, and, in some cases, reincarceration or early death" (p. 266).

As previously mentioned, managing social and personal relationships proves particularly difficult for death row exonerees (Scott, 2010; Westervelt & Cook, 2012). First, there is the stigma carried by death row exonerees, leaving them with feelings of alienation and disconnection that impede their ability to form social relationships. Westervelt and Cook (2010) relay the story of one death row exoneree: "[He] was greeted with fear from his neighbors, suspicion from people he had known since childhood, and messages of hate written in the dirt on his truck—'child killer'" (p. 268). Another exoneree, who eventually took his own life, likened his wrongful conviction to a "scar" that was both permanent and seemingly visible to all (Scott, 2010, p. 11). There is also the inherent disconnect in awareness and familiarity of the world and culture. In a world dependent on emerging technology for making social connections, one can imagine the difficulty and alienation experienced by exonerees in attempting to relate to new-found peers and potential friends (Scott, 2010).

At a more personal, individual level, exonerees often struggle with intimate emotional and physical connection (Scott, 2010; Westervelt & Cook, 2012). Scott (2010) points out the similarities between exonerees and war veterans, noting that years cut off both physically and emotionally from family and loved ones may leave them with a diminished capacity for intimacy and emotional connection when they are reunited. This can be a strain on exonerees and their families as they attempt to rebuild their relationships and navigate the expectations they have of one another, a strain that tends to be more severe the longer the exoneree was incarcerated. With the average time between wrongful conviction and exoneration being just over 11 years, this is typically a significant problem for exonerated death row inmates as they reenter society.

Just as the emotional disconnection impacts exonerees' ability to rebuild and form new relationships, so does the physical disconnection. For many death row inmates, there is little or no physical interaction with others during their time in prison. Typically, death row inmates are only allowed no-contact visits with loved ones, often through a thick glass partition. And in many cases, they have been completely deprived of physical contact, as not even prison guards, chaplains, lawyers, or other inmates are allowed to be in physical contact with them. After years alone with little or no physical interaction with others, exonerees may struggle with the sensations of touching and embracing others and therefore experience difficulty either rebuilding intimate relationships with existing partners or engaging in new ones (Westervelt & Cook, 2012).

GIVING VOICE: *Death Row Exoneree Damon Thibodeaux*

I had a lot of help reentering. When I was released I had almost nothing. Steve Kaplan, one of the many lawyers on my case, invited me to his home and was a tremendous inspiration. He helped me get my first job at Fredrikson and Byron in the mail room, which Pitney Bowes handled and was given the chance by _____, who was the manager. I loved her positive attitude and that she was always there when I needed an ear or help understanding something that I was doing, and her team exemplified that attitude. When I started studying to get my CDL and be a long haul truck driver, she was sad but had nothing but encouragement to give. _____ of Interstate Truck Driving school was the one who convinced me to be a professional driver. He helped me get my CDL by putting me through his driving school. The list of people that have helped me is long. It takes a lot of people and resources to help an exoneree get his life back together as best he can, and even then you are still not whole. For most exonerees it's a hard struggle. I had a lot of help from people getting a job, an apartment, a car. Steve helped me get my license and helped with the car, along with The Innocence Project in New York. The Innocence Project also helped with my bills for a year as well as getting a car. At first I was a bit apprehensive when meeting people. I didn't know what I was going to say when someone asked about me. Then I met someone and developed a wonderful relationship, which I believed would NEVER happen given my situation, _____, a wonderful woman who has been so patient and understanding of my struggle to be a good partner after not being in a relationship with someone for so long. I get it wrong most times to be sure, but she is the best partner and friend that a man could want. I am fortunate and blessed to have met her, and I hope that she and I are together for a very long time.

While managing the personal and emotional terrain of their new world outside of prison, exonerees are also often faced with continuing judicial and legal processes. Sometimes exonerees are faced with defending themselves on new charges or secondary charges stemming from their capital case. In other cases, exonerees must engage a judicial or legal process to pursue compensation, expunge records, restore certain civil rights, sue the state for wrongful incarceration, or receive official certification of their innocence and exoneration. Not only are legal services lacking to assist exonerees with these processes, but as Westervelt and Cook (2010) point out, "[t]he state offers no post-exoneration aid to negotiate these difficulties, and in some ways, creates additional obstacles by requiring exonerees to secure their own legal services" (p. 266). These legal services do not come cheap, leaving the exoneree in a sort of Catch-22 where they cannot afford sufficient legal assistance to restore their full citizenry or receive compensation which is needed to afford legal assistance. They are typically left to fend for themselves in navigating the labyrinthine justice system and governmental bureaucracy, relying on friends, family, advocacy or nonprofit organizations, and, if they're lucky, attorneys willing to work pro bono. Fortunately there are a growing number of groups and advocates willing to help and, as will be discussed later, some states are beginning to develop compensation statutes that include legal assistance. However, such statutes typically do not apply to exonerees who have not been formally and officially exonerated, exonerees who often have the most challenging legal path to navigate.

Kerry Cook, who remains in the gray area of "pseudo-exoneration" due to a lack of official recognition of his innocence by the state of Texas, is a testament to the difficulties many experience as they attempt to obtain true exoneration and the tolls these take.[4] In his case, he has spent decades battling for exoneration since he was released from death row. In conversations and interviews with Kerry, the pain, anger and frustration are palpable. Since being released from death row in 1997, Cook has spent the last several decades free but not completely exonerated; his fight for justice has dominated his life over that period. And that fight has been with both those seeking to deny his innocence as well as supporters working to keep him free. His case attests to the fact that freedom is not the end of struggle for exonerees.

PROFILE: Death Row Exoneree Kerry Max Cook

Kerry Max Cook spent more than two decades on Texas' death row for the 1977 rape and murder of Linda Jo Edwards. His conviction was overturned in 1988, and a subsequent trial in 1992 ended in a mistrial. He was again convicted in 1994, but his conviction was again overturned by Texas' highest criminal court, this time citing police and prosecutorial misconduct. He was finally released on bail in 1997, with the state vowing to retry him once again. Kerry was eventually offered a plea deal in which he would be allowed to remain free for time served if he agreed to plead guilty. Never wavering from his claim of innocence, Kerry rejected the offer and instead sought DNA testing he was certain would exonerate him. As the trial approached, the district attorney offered him another plea deal—this time a dismissal of the case if Kerry would plead no-contest with no admission of guilt (often referred to as an "Alford plea"). Kerry accepted this deal and was finally freed in 1999. Several months later, the DNA of the semen on Linda Jo Edwards' underwear was revealed to have come from another man, a man who had been carrying on an affair with the victim.

During his time on death row, Kerry experienced unspeakable brutality at the hands of other inmates. He had been attacked, stabbed, cut, and repeatedly raped and today still carries the physical signs of these attacks. In addition to the more typical scars, words were carved into his body, forever marking the rapes and attacks he suffered. Determined not to become the violent killer he was accused of being, Kerry refused to fight back and was thus considered easy prey. The scars were not just physical ones. The psychological impact of Kerry's trauma led to suicidal and self-destructive impulses, resulting in the slitting of his own throat and horrific acts of self-mutilation.

The trauma followed Kerry outside the prison walls, where the symptoms of PTSD persisted. Over the years since his release, Kerry has continued to experience nightmares and difficulty sleeping, depression and suicidal thoughts, and physical health struggles associated with stress. He also struggled to find employment and a home, as his conviction for capital murder continued to follow him. He and his family (he eventually got married and had a son, aptly naming him "Kerry Justice") were forced to move numerous times, finding themselves shunned once members of their community found out about his previous conviction, one woman threatening to put up posters throughout the neighborhood. Knowing he would not be truly free until there was formal, official recognition of his innocence, Kerry found an attorney who agreed to represent him in his quest for true exoneration.

With the pro bono assistance of civil attorney Marc McPeak, Kerry began the process of appealing for a judicial finding of "actual innocence," the final recourse toward his being truly "exonerated." Soon, his case attracted the attention of Innocence Project attorneys who would join Kerry's battle for exoneration in Texas. His newfound legal team was able to convince the state's attorneys to offer Kerry a deal whereby they would set aside his conviction with the stipulation that he would drop his other claims, including those of prosecutorial misconduct. Though Kerry was frustrated that those responsible for his wrongful conviction and years of torture and torment would not be held accountable, after being cajoled by his attorneys, he reluctantly agreed with the understanding that he could still proceed with his request for a declaration of "actual innocence." With his attorneys working with the state's attorneys, Kerry's exoneration was finally within reach. And that was a problem for Kerry: his attorneys worked with, and even praised, the state's attorneys, effectively exonerating them along with him. To Kerry this was another in a long line of injustices. Frustrated, despondent and desperate, he did the unthinkable and fired the vaunted Innocence Project attorneys and went so far as to contemplate throwing out the agreement that had exonerated him, an agreement he felt weakened his chances of reaching his ultimate goal of being declared truly innocent and acknowledgment of the wrongs he had suffered. As of this writing, Kerry's case currently remains in limbo, his long struggle for exoneration, accountability, and some semblance of peace unfulfilled.

Needs and Reforms

The knowledge that has been produced about death row exonerees over the last few decades has shed important light on their postexoneration needs and highlighted the broad need for reform. The Innocence Project, a leading voice for reform and assistance for the wrongly convicted throughout the criminal justice system, has presented clear recommendations:

- Monetary Compensation, Based Upon a Set Minimum Amount For Each Year Served
- Provision of Immediate Services, Including:

  - Financial support for basic necessities, including subsistence funds, food, transportation;
  - Help securing affordable housing;
  - Provision of medical/dental care, and psychological and/or counseling services;
  - Assistance with education and the development of workforce skills; and
  - Legal services to obtain public benefits, expunge criminal records, and regain custody of children.

(Innocence Project, 2017)

One area of reform that has seen traction over recent decades is compensation. In 1989, only 11 states had compensation statutes for the wrongly convicted. By 2009, this number had reached 27 states (Norris, 2012), and today 32 states plus the District of Columbia and the federal government have compensation statutes (Innocence Project, 2017). Though, nationally, great gains have been made in compensation for those who have been wrongly convicted and exonerated, many states (15 of the 31 death penalty states) still have no compensation statutes[5] (Simms, 2016). Table 36.1 exhibits the compensation provided for in the statutes of death penalty states.

As can been seen from Table 36.1, wrongful conviction compensation statutes recognize some of the key needs of exonerees as they reenter free society. Of course, financial compensation is the paramount focus of these statutes, but they also include legal assistance, health and mental health care assistance, child support assistance, and assistance with college application or vocational training. All of the recommendations of the Innocence Project are represented somewhere across the variant statutes, but only one state's statute (Texas') covers all the listed compensations areas. With 16 of the 31 death penalty states having no compensation statutes at all and with most of the others only partially covering needed areas of assistance, many death row exonerees' needs go unmet after their release. In fact, only two of the 19 exonerees studied by Westervelt and Cook (2008, 2010, 2012) received compensation via statutory means. Others are left with only two other options: Litigation or pursuing a private bill with a state legislator. Both options have significant barriers for an exoneree. Litigation requires money and access to legal assistance, which is, of course, lacking without any compensation—another Catch-22 situation. And private bills require legislators to look past the possible political costs of advocating for someone who may still be seen as a convicted capital murderer by their constituents (Westervelt & Cook, 2012). Some, like Damon Thibodeaux, are fortunate enough to have people willing to assist them with the things they need to successfully reintegrate into society (see next). Most must rely on the prospects of this kind of fortune, meaning many simply go on with their needs unmet.

Table 36.1 Postexoneration Compensation and Support in Death Penalty States

State	Monetary Compensation	Other Compensation and Services						
		Lost Wages	Child Support	Legal	Health	Mental Health	College	Job Training/ Skills
Alabama	$50,000 per year incarcerated							
Arizona	None							
Arkansas	None							
California	$100 per day incarcerated							
Colorado	$70,000 per year incarcerated + $50,000 per year on death row	X	X				X	
Connecticut	Not specified						X	X
Delaware	None							
Florida	$50,000 per year incarcerated; $2,000,000 maximum		X				X	X
Georgia	None							
Idaho	None							
Illinois	< 5 years of incarceration: max $83,350; 5–14 years of incarceration: max $170,000; 14+ years of incarceration: max $199,150							
Indiana	None							
Kansas	None							
Kentucky	None							
Louisiana	$25,000 per year incarcerated; max $250,000				X	X	X	
Maryland	Not specified					X		
Mississippi	$50,000 per year incarcerated; max $500,000			X				
Missouri	$50 per day of postconviction incarceration							
Montana	None						X	
Nebraska	Max $500,000							
Nevada	None							
New Hampshire	Max $20,000			X				
New Jersey	Either twice the exoneree's income the year prior to incarceration OR $50,000 per year of incarceration (whichever is greater)	X	X		X	X	X	X

State	Monetary Compensation	Other Compensation and Services						
		Lost Wages	Child Support	Legal	Health	Mental Health	College	Job Training/Skills
New Mexico	None							
New York	Not specified							
North Carolina	$50,000 per year of incarceration; max $750,000						X	X
Ohio	$40,330 per year of incarceration	X		X				
Oklahoma	Max $175,000							
Oregon	None							
Pennsylvania	None							
South Carolina	None							
South Dakota	None							
Tennessee	Max $1,000,000							
Texas	$80,000 per year of incarceration	X	X	X	X	X	X	X
Utah	Avg. annual nonagricultural wage in Utah per year of incarceration, up to 15 years							
Virginia	90% of inflation adjusted per capita personal income in Virginia per year of incarceration							X
Washington	$50,000 per year incarcerated + $50,000 per year on death row		X	X		X		X
Wyoming	None							

GIVING VOICE: Steven Kaplan, Postconviction Attorney for Exoneree Damon Thibodeaux

After his release, we spent a few days in New Orleans, where he reunited with his mother, siblings, and a son whom he had not seen in some 17 years. We then drove to Minneapolis where he lived with my wife and me for about six weeks before he moved into his own apartment that he leased from Project for Pride in Living, a nonprofit organization that provides subsidized housing to those who are restarting their lives. He obtained much-needed medical care through a state of Minnesota health plan and his GED from the Project for Pride in Living Learning Center.

Our law firm secured employment for him with the company that provided our onsite office services. He obtained his driver's license, and through the generosity of the Innocence Project of New York, members of my law firm, and others who met him, Damon acquired a used car, furniture, kitchen equipment and utensils, and clothing.

He would also need legal counsel to sue in the state and federal courts in New Orleans for compensation and damages. More than four years after his release, the state of Louisiana continues to fight his claims under the state's wrongful conviction and incarceration statute and for violation of his civil rights.

The owner of a Twin Cities local truck-driving school gave Damon the opportunity to obtain the training, tuition-free, necessary to obtain a commercial driving license. In January 2014, Damon began driving commercially across the country for a trucking company, a job that he cherishes for the independence and income that it provides him. Our phone calls would then include his descriptions of seeing the sun rise over the Rockies and the snow fall in the Appalachians.

He and I often spoke to groups of high school, college, and law school students; lawyers; business people; and religious communities about his experiences with the justice system and capital punishment. Those occasions afforded him a way to give meaning to and make sense of his experiences. One of those speaking opportunities was before a subcommittee of the Senate Judiciary Committee examining the effects of solitary confinement. As he knows all too well, he can either lapse into anger or use what he has endured to inspire others and motivate himself. He has chosen the latter.

The struggles and needs of exonerees extend far beyond the immediate, practical needs and continue long after initial adjustments to life on the outside are made. These needs often are more hidden and insidious and are rooted in trauma, trauma that results from what Westervelt and Cook (2012) refer to as the "sustained catastrophe" of wrongful conviction and incarceration on death row. This is catastrophic trauma, according to Westervelt and Cook (2012), not unlike that experienced by prisoners of war, victims of sustained abuse and violence, and those who suffer atrocities such as genocide. They note that such "sustained catastrophes" are traumatic experiences in which "the danger and threats to life and self extend over a period of time when the catastrophe itself continues day after day, year after year with no discernible end" and further note that "trauma of this magnitude overwhelms the capacities for coping and adaptation used to manage more 'commonplace misfortunes'" (Westervelt & Cook, 2012, pp. 131–132). And because this trauma comes at the hands of the state and the justice system, additional needs related to stigma and a defiled identity are particularly acute as exonerees attempt to reclaim their innocence and remedy the harm by seeking "justice" (Westervelt & Cook, 2010). Though exonerees share many similarities in how the trauma of the "sustained catastrophe" impacts them, there is also great variation. Factors such as length of time incarcerated, nature of the offense they were wrongly convicted of, factors associated with their wrongful conviction, such as whether they falsely confessed, familial support while incarcerated, and social support when they are released all undoubtedly play a role in how, and to what extent, one is impacted by their experience and the associated trauma. For some, it is a trauma that will infect their lives thoroughly and pervasively, leading to continued struggles throughout life after death row. For others, it may be fleeting, waning, or sporadic in the years and decades after exoneration. But all death row exonerees, to some extent, experience this trauma and must find ways to cope with it.

Just as there are a variety of ways in which death row exonerees are impacted by their experiences, there are a variety of ways they cope with these experiences and their ongoing circumstances. It is around this necessary coping that the most profound needs of exonerees revolve. Westervelt and Cook (2012) identify key factors that facilitate and impede coping and adjustment in the wake of exoneration. The most potent facilitating factors cited by exonerees related to connection to and support from family, friends and their community, including acknowledgment of the trauma they experienced by those in their community. Conversely, the most potent factors cited to impede coping and adjustment related to hostile, negative, and stigmatizing responses toward exonerees and their experiences. It is these factors that seem to be the greatest predictors of how exonerees cope over the years after release from death row. As Westervelt and Cook (2012) point out, exonerees typically cope in one of two ways: 'avoidance' or 'incorporation'. Others have more generically labeled these two poles on the coping continuum for exonerees as "negative" and "positive" (DeShay, 2016).

Avoidance strategies include withdrawal from society and others and finding ways to numb the pain and suffering that comes with trauma. The latter often includes the use of drugs and alcohol and in some cases leads to destructive dependence and addiction (Westervelt & Cook, 2012). DeShay (2016) refers to this coping strategy as "negative or maladaptive," especially if engaged for a sustained amount of time. Indeed, given the cited importance of connection, the consequences of an avoidance strategy are often tragic. Westervelt and Cook (2012) tell of numerous exonerees who attempted to cope with their trauma through withdrawal. One, Gary Beeman, maintained a "substantial alcohol problem for almost twenty years after his release" (p. 156) and admitted that he "threw his life away with drugs and alcohol" (p. 159). Another, Greg Wilhoit, a death row exoneree who died in 2014 at the age of 59, suffered from severe PTSD after being wrongly convicted of murdering his wife, the mother of his two young daughters. After he was released, he moved to another state and attempted to escape his trauma. According to another exoneree,

> Greg was one of those men who suffered the greatest because of his death row conviction. He not only lost his wife but his kids as well as he sat on death row for a crime he did not commit . . . . Even after his release he never fully connected with his kids. This bothered him greatly.
>
> *(Love, 2014, p. 2)*

Many exonerees ultimately take a more 'positive' approach to coping with their trauma, an approach Westervelt and Cook (2012) refer to as a strategy of incorporation. Beyond simply finding ways to connect with their loved ones and their communities, incorporation refers to the attempt by exonerees to reach out and connect with the broader communities of other exonerees and associated advocates and organizations. It typically includes finding opportunities to share their trauma story and find meaning in their struggles, both on a personal and communal level. Konvisser and Werry (2017) note the substantial value to exonerees in telling their stories and speaking out about their cases, as it "helps them normalize the trauma and builds confidence through acknowledgment and affirmation, [giving] testimony to their resilience" (p. 54). Moreover, they note that many exonerees take this a step further and engage more overtly in policy and advocacy work. In addition to the personal motivations for healing their trauma, exonerees are often motivated to make broader social statements or bring about social change, fighting the injustices they have personally and acutely experienced. Attempting to inform the public and policy makers about these injustices, to ensure that others do not have to experience the miscarriages of justice and associate trauma they suffered, extends even greater meaning to their lives and produces a legacy as they reconstruct their identity. Kirk Bloodsworth, the first death row exoneree to be cleared with DNA evidence (Junkin, 2005), perhaps best exemplifies this approach (Westervelt & Cook, 2012). About his incorporation strategy, he notes "[it] is catharsis for me. This is why I do it. This is something I learned a long time ago, never keep it in because you're doing yourself a grave disservice if you do because you gotta get it out" (Westervelt & Cook, 2012, p. 143). He is also an exoneree who has played a key role in policy and legislation in the wake of his exoneration, becoming the face of the successful abolition of the death penalty in Maryland and continuing to testify in state legislatures around the country when bills to abolish the death penalty are being considered (Early, 2016; Wagner, 2013).

The personal catharsis along with the communal camaraderie produced by the incorporation strategy serves to meet some of the most essential needs of exonerated death row inmates. Though other steps are needed to assist exonerees with their mental health needs stemming from their trauma, many cite telling their stories and finding bonds with others who have experienced similar trauma as being of great emotional and psychological benefit. Moreover, it is through this process that they develop the connection and belonging Westervelt and Cook (2012) identify as so central to successful adjustment and adaptation to life after death row. They are seeking witness to their trauma and giving voice to the collective experiences of death row exonerees. They are being heard. But there is another paramount need being attended to here, and that is for a sense of justice, a justice that includes recognition and accountability on the part of those who had wrongly condemned them. This is not a desire for retribution or simply a need for someone to 'pay.' No; it is fundamental to exonerees' ability to fully reclaim and move forward with their life, to heal their trauma, and to once again identify as "innocent" (Westervelt & Cook, 2008). By engaging with organizations whose mission it is to inform about these miscarriages of justice and by advocating for social and policy change through speaking out, death row exonerees are able to play a role in trying to coax official recognition of the wrongs that have been exacted and the harms that have resulted. Unfortunately, as attested to by the case of Kerry Cook, profiled earlier in the chapter, and as noted by Westervelt and Cook (2008), achieving this recognition and accountability is all too often elusive:

> We seem unable to fully embrace the idea that justice for exonerees requires official recognition of responsibility to aid them in rebuilding a life. Our hesitancy in this regard may be entangled without competing need to believe in the efficacy of the system. To publicly acknowledge our responsibility to exonerees is also to acknowledge a flawed system—and the other innocent people in prison awaiting vindication.
>
> *(p. 37)*

To exonerees, the failure of the criminal justice system to acknowledge and attempt to rectify the harm done through wrongful conviction and incarceration adds another level of trauma and inhibits any attempt to become fully reintegrated into society (Westervelt & Cook, 2012).

It is appropriate that Westervelt and Cook (2012) conclude their penultimate study of death row exonerees and the book it produced with a discussion of the relevance of restorative justice to how we attend to the needs of this growing population. For it certainly provides the most salient paradigm for addressing the needs for connection and healing as well as for accountability on the part of those responsible for the wrongful conviction and incarceration. By making central the voices and perspectives of those who have experienced these injustices, it also aligns well with exonerees' needs to be heard and to share their stories of trauma and transformation. Finally, it incorporates the broader community and provides a potential path to reconciliation, and perhaps even apology and forgiveness, with those who perpetrated the harm brought upon them. In short, restorative justice provides a framework for developing what Westervelt and Cook (2012) call "reintegration networks." These would start with support circles that would include a variety of service providers, advocates, supporters and community members, other exonerees, and representatives of the state. These circles would build the foundation from which exonerees could proceed to best meet their postexoneration needs, which may then include legal processes, mental health care, seeking employment and housing, and possible community forums in which they can share their story and reach out to others in the community. With the increasing use of restorative justice programs and processes across the United States and the growth of advocacy groups for death row exonerees, it's not hard to imagine Westervelt and Cook's (2012) proposal being implemented in some form. We can perhaps allow ourselves to hope that change is on the horizon, that the needs of those experiencing one of the greatest injustices possible at the hands of the criminal justice system will be addressed, and that the trauma experienced by death row exonerees might be mitigated, if even only a little bit.

There are hundreds of death row exonerees navigating their life after death row, each with a unique story to tell. Some, like Damon Thibodeaux, have thrived. Others, like Kerry Cook, have struggled to even find true exoneration. Still others, like Greg Wilhoit, have become casualties of the weight of wrongful conviction, the death sentence, and imprisonment that preceded the years of freedom, the physical and psychological tolls having become for them a different form of death sentence. There are, undoubtedly, hundreds more remaining behind bars, yet to achieve exoneration. And then there are those who have been executed in spite of their innocence (see, for example, Liebman, 2014).

In this chapter, I have only been able to capture a few voices and to provide broad conclusions about the experience of exoneration and life after death row. What resonates loudly is the need for further attention on this growing phenomenon and population. While I was editing this final draft, another death row inmate was exonerated: Rickey Newman, number 160 on the Death Penalty Information Center's list. He is now navigating the terrain of postexoneration life, as have so many before him. It is for his sake, and the sake of those inevitably to come, that work needs to continue on understanding and attending to the needs of death row exonerees. Compensation statutes must expand and become the norm. This includes providing mental health services for those suffering from the constellation of symptoms and disorders stemming from the profound trauma they have experienced. Pathways to a justice that offer accountability and official recognition of wrongdoing must be forged. And, perhaps most importantly, assistance for exonerees needs to attend to the connection so important to effective coping and adjustment, to reconnection and reconciliation with loved ones and their communities, and to a reintegration that restores their sense of self and identity as whole, and innocent, members of society.

GIVING VOICE: *Death Row Exoneree Damon Thibodeaux*

Being an exoneree is an experience that no one should experience. The power and ability to take an innocent person's life should not be in our hands. Sadly, there are people that will commit those crimes that warrant such a punishment as death, but how we conduct ourselves when faced with such a person should be a testimony of our character as a people and as a society in saying that we are not going to put you to death because we are not like you.

GIVING VOICE: *Steven Kaplan, Postconviction Attorney for Exoneree Damon Thibodeaux*

In the spring of 2013, Damon attended a conference in Atlanta sponsored by a remarkable organization, Witness to Innocence. There, he met a highly intelligent and strong woman who continues to give him love and balance. Life has now taken him to Southern California, where lives with her and her family and continues to drive commercially. No one is more deserving of the happy and productive life he now leads. I have met only a few whom I call a hero. Damon is one of them.

Notes

1 www.innocenceproject.org
2 www.witnesstoinnocence.org
3 www.journeyofhope.org
4 For the complete story of Kerry Cook's experiences both on death row and in the years after release, see his book *Chasing Justice* (2007). See also *The Exonerated*, a play that includes Cook as one of several exonerees telling their stories (Blank & Jensen, 2004). Finally, for the most up-to-date information about his case, see Michael Hall's March 2017 article in Texas Monthly: http://features.texasmonthly.com/editorial/the-trouble-with-innocence/
5 As of February 2016, the date at which the most recent data were available.

References

Adams, R., Hoffer, W., & Hoffer, M. M. (1991). *Adams v. Texas*. New York, NY: St. Martin's Press.

Arrigo, B. A., & Bullock, J. L. (2008). The psychological effects of solitary confinement on prisoners in supermax units: Reviewing what we know and recommending what should change. *International Journal of Offender Therapy and Comparative Criminology, 52*(6), 622–640.

Atwell, M. W. (2004). *Evolving standards of decency: Popular culture and capital punishment*. New York, NY: Peter Lang.

Bedau, H. A., & Radelet, M. L. (1987). Miscarriages of justice in potentially capital cases. *Stanford Law Review,* *40,* 21–179.

Bibas, S. (2002). Harmonizing substantive-criminal law-values and criminal procedure: The case of Alford and nolo contendere pleas. *Cornell Law Review, 88,* 1361–1411.

Blank, J., & Jensen, E. (2004). *The exonerated.* New York: Faber & Faber, Inc.

Campbell, K., & Denov, M. (2004). The burden of innocence: Coping with a wrongful imprisonment. *Canadian Journal of Criminology and Criminal Justice, 46,* 139–163.

Clow, K. A., Leach, A., & Ricciardelli, R. (2012). Life after wrongful conviction. In B. L. Cutler (Ed.), *Conviction of the innocent: Lessons from psychological research* (pp. 327–341). Washington, DC: American Psychological Association.

Cohen, S. (2003). *The wrong men: America's epidemic of wrongful death row convictions.* New York: Carroll and Graf Publications.

Cook, K. M. (2007). *Chasing justice: My story of freeing myself after two decades on death row for a crime I didn't commit.* New York: William Morrow/Harper Collins.

Death Penalty Information Center. (2017). *Innocence and the death penalty.* Retrieved from www.deathpenaltyinfo. org/innocence-and-the-death-penalty

DeShay, R. A. (2016). "A lot of people go insane behind that": Coping with the trauma of being wrongfully convicted. *Criminal Justice Studies, 29*(3), 199–213.

Early, B. (September 27, 2016). Bloodsworth advocates for abolishing death penalty. Retrieved from Seacoastonline.com

Echols, D. (2012). *Life after death.* New York: Blue Rider Press.

Findley, K. A., & Golden, L. (2014). The innocence movement, the innocence network, and policy reform. In M. Zalman & J. Carrano (Eds.), *Wrongful conviction and criminal justice reform: Making justice* (pp. 93–110). New York, NY: Routledge.

Gross, S. R., O'Brien, B., Hu, C., & Kennedy, E. H. (2014). Rate of false conviction of criminal defendants who are sentenced to death. *Proceedings of the National Academy of Sciences, 111*(20), 7230–7235.

Gross, S. R., & Shaffer, M. (2012). *Exonerations in the United States, 1989–2012: Report by the National Registry of Exonerations.* Report of the National Registry of Exonerations, University of Michigan Law School, Ann Arbor, Michigan. Retrieved January 2017 @ www.law.umich.edu/special/exoneration/Documents/ exonerations_us_1989_2012_full_report.pdf

Grounds, A. (2004). Psychological consequences of wrongful conviction and imprisonment. *Canadian Journal of Criminology and Criminal Justice, 46,* 165–182.

Hall, M. (2017, March). The trouble with innocence. *Texas Monthly.* Retrieved from http://features.texasmonthly. com/editorial/the-trouble-with-innocence/

Haney, C., & Lynch, M. (1997). Regulating prisons of the future: A psychological analysis of supermax and solitary confinement. *New York University Review of Law and Social Change, 23,* 477–570.

Holmes, W. M. (2008). Who are the wrongfully convicted on death row? In S. D. Westervelt & J. A. Humphrey (Eds.), *Wrongly convicted: Perspectives on failed justice* (pp. 99–113). New Brunswick, NJ: Rutgers University Press.

Innocence Project. (2017). *Compensating the wrongly convicted.* Retrieved from www.innocenceproject.org/ compensating-wrongly-convicted/

Junkin, T. (2005). *Bloodsworth.* Chapel Hill, NC: Algonquin Books.

Keine, R. (2011–2012). When justice fails: Collateral damage. *Albany Law Review, 75,* 1501–1508.

King, R. (2005). *Capital consequences: Families of the condemned tell their stories.* Brunswick, NJ: Rutgers University Press.

Konvisser, Z. D. (2012). Psychological consequences of wrongful conviction in women and the possibility of positive change. *DePaul Journal for Social Justice, 5,* 221–293.

Konvisser, Z. D., & Werry, A. (2017). Exoneree engagement in policy reform work: An exploratory study of the innocence movement policy reform process. *Journal of Contemporary Criminal Justice, 33*(1), 43–60.

Leveritt, M. (2014). *Dark spell: Surviving the sentence.* North Charleston, SC: CreateSpace Independent Publishing.

Liebman, J. S. (2014). *The wrong Carlos: Anatomy of a wrongful execution.* New York, NY: Columbia University Press.

Love, D. (2014, April 21). A final farewell to Greg Wilhoit, who survived Oklahoma's death row. *Huffington Post.* Retrieved from www.huffingtonpost.com/david-a-love/a-final-farewell-to-greg-_b_4812785.html

Melendez, J. R. (2008). Presumed guilty: A death row exoneree shares his story of supreme injustice and reflections on the death penalty. *Texas Tech Law Review, 41,* 1–13.

Norris, R. J. (2012). Assessing compensation statutes for the wrongly convicted. *Criminal Justice Policy Review, 23*(3), 352–374.

Norris, R. J. (2017). Framing DNA: Social movement theory and the foundations of the innocence movement. *Journal of Contemporary Criminal Justice, 33*(1), 26–42.

Risinger, D. M. (2007). Innocents convicted: An empirically justified factual wrongful conviction rate. *The Journal of Criminal Law & Criminology, 97*(3), 761–806.

Scheck, B., Neufeld, P., & Dwyer, J. (2000). *Actual innocence: Five days to execution and other dispatches from the wrongly convicted.* New York: Doubleday.

Scott, L. (2010). "It never, ever ends": The psychological impact of wrongful conviction. *American University Criminal Law Brief, 5*(2), 10–22.

Simms, T. (2016). Statutory compensation for the wrongly imprisoned. *Social Work, 61*(2), 155–162.

Smith, M. L. (August 2, 2015). Life after death row: The resurrection of Damon Thibodeaux. *Minneapolis StarTribune.* Retrieved from www.startribune.com/life-after-death-row-damon-thibodeaux-s-resurrection/318969021/

Wagner, J. (2013, March 14). As Maryland votes on death penalty repeal, exonerated man becomes a living reminder. *Washington Post.* Retrieved from www.washingtonpost.com/local/md-politics/as-maryland-votes-on-death-penalty-repeal-exonerated-man-becomes-a-living-reminder/2013/03/14/8fb87e84-8ca8-11e2-9838-d62f083ba93f_story.html?utm_term=.7791d2d70d47

Westervelt, S. D., & Cook, K. J. (2008). Coping with innocence after death row. *Contexts, 7*(4), 32–37.

Westervelt, S. D., & Cook, K. J. (2010). Framing innocents: The wrongly convicted as victims of state harm, *Crime, Law, and Social Change, 53,* 259–275.

Westervelt, S. D., & Cook, K. J. (2012). *Life after death row: Exonerees' search for community and identity.* New Brunswick, NJ: Rutgers University Press.

Zalman, M. (2006). Criminal justice system reform and wrongful conviction: A research agenda. *Criminal Justice Policy Review, 17*(4), 468–492.

Case Cited

North Carolina v. Alford, 400 U.S. 25 (1970).

37

THE DEATH PENALTY'S DEMISE, WITH SPECIAL FOCUS ON THE UNITED STATES

Robert M. Bohm

For the last four decades, worldwide use of the death penalty has been trending toward extinction. Although pockets of heavy death penalty use endure, most countries of the world either have abolished the death penalty or no longer impose it. Until the 2016 elections, the United States was part of the trend, but as will be argued later, the election of Donald Trump and other recent developments likely have slowed, if not put a halt to, the abolitionist movement's hard-earned momentum in the United States. The purpose of this chapter is to examine the worldwide death penalty abolitionist effort, with special focus on the United States, and to evaluate the likelihood of the death penalty's demise in light of recent developments.

The chapter is divided into seven sections. The first section describes the status of the death penalty worldwide. Currently, two-thirds of the world's nations are abolitionist either in law or in practice. Section two examines the factors that have contributed to the worldwide trend toward abolition of the death penalty. Conceptualizing the death penalty as a human rights issue has been a key contributor, as has the involvement of the United Nations, the Council of Europe, the European Union, the Organization of American States, and the Catholic Church. The United States' recent experience with the death penalty, especially in light of the 2016 elections, is the focus of the third section. The election of Donald Trump, as well as referenda in California, Oklahoma, and Nebraska, put brakes on abolitionist efforts in those states and are likely to have wider repercussions. Section four presents data showing the pre-Trump success of the death penalty abolitionist movement in the United States. Four measures—the number of death sentences imposed, the number of executions conducted, the number of states that have abolished the death penalty, and the concentration of executions in a few states and counties—support the notion that momentum had swung to the abolitionists' side. Two legal arguments that challenge the death penalty on Eighth Amendment grounds are the subject of the fifth section. Neither argument is politically or legally radical; both arguments follow established legal precedent. The chapter concludes with a brief summary of the current status of the death penalty worldwide and in the United States and speculation about what the future may hold for the ultimate penal sanction.

Abolition of the Death Penalty Worldwide

In 1977—the year the United States resumed executions following a decades-long hiatus—only 16 countries in the world had abolished the death penalty for all crimes (Amnesty International, 2016, p. 4). By January 1, 2016, 102 countries in the world had abolished the death penalty for all crimes (Amnesty

International, 2016)—a more than 500% increase in about 40 years. The 2016 number marks the first time that a majority of the world's 196 countries are completely abolitionist (Amnesty International, 2016).

In addition to the 102 countries that are totally abolitionist, another six countries are abolitionist for ordinary crimes only (Amnesty International, 2016). Those six countries still allow the death penalty for exceptional crimes, such as those committed under military law (Amnesty International, 2016). Another 32 countries are abolitionist in practice (Amnesty International, 2016). These countries "have not executed anyone during the last 10 years and are believed to have a policy or established practice of not carrying out executions" (Amnesty International, 2016). In total, 140 countries, or more than 70% of all countries in the world, now are abolitionist either in law or practice (Amnesty International, 2016). Only 58 countries retain the death penalty and use it at least occasionally (Amnesty International, 2016).

Of the 58 retentionist countries—nearly 30% of the world's countries—84% of them are located in Africa, the Mideast, the Caribbean, and South or Southeast Asia (Amnesty International, 2016). In many of these countries where Islam is the dominant religion, death penalty abolition will prove difficult because Sharia law allows it (Penal Reform International, 2015). Africa has the largest number of reten- tionist countries, with about 28% of the total. The countries are Botswana, Chad, Comoros, Democratic Republic of the Congo, Egypt, Equatorial Guinea, Ethiopia, Gambia, Guinea, Lesotho, Nigeria, Somalia, South Sudan, Sudan, Uganda, and Zimbabwe (Amnesty International, 2016). The Mideast has the second most retentionist countries, with about 26% of the total. The countries are Afghanistan, Bahrain, Iran, Iraq, Jordan, Kuwait, Lebanon, Libya, Oman, Palestinian Authority, Qatar, Saudi Arabia, Syria, United Arab Emirates, and Yemen (Amnesty International, 2016). The region with the third most retentionist countries, with about 17% of the total, is the Caribbean. Countries are Antigua and Barbuda, Bahamas, Barbados, Cuba, Dominica, Jamaica, Saint Kitts and Nevis, Saint Lucia, Saint Vincent and the Grena- dines, and Trinidad and Tobago (Amnesty International, 2016). South and Southeast Asia have the fourth most retentionist countries, with about 14% of the total. The countries are Bangladesh, India, Indonesia, Malaysia, Pakistan, Singapore, Thailand, and Vietnam (Amnesty International, 2016). The remaining 16% of retentionist countries are spread among East Asia, with four (China, Japan, North Korea, and Taiwan); Central America, with two (Belize and Guatemala); and one each in Eastern Europe (Belarus), South America (Guyana), and North America (the United States) (Amnesty International, 2016).

Although 58 countries retain the death penalty, the number of countries that actually execute any- one in a given year is much smaller. In 2015, for example, Amnesty International confirmed that only 25 countries executed anyone. Those 25 countries conducted at least 1,634 executions—573 or 54% more than in 2014 (Amnesty International, 2016, pp. 3 and 5). The 1,634 executions do not include those conducted in China, which does not report death sentences or executions but is believed to have sentenced and executed thousands. Of the 1,634 known executions that took place in 2015, about 90% of them were carried out in only three countries: 60%+ in Iran, 20% in Pakistan, and 10%+ in Saudi Arabia (Amnesty International, 2016, p. 6)

An examination of worldwide execution trends from 2005 through 2014 found that the bulk of executions during this period were conducted in only a handful of the same countries (see Bohm, 2017, pp. 178–179). Outside of the Mideast (and the countries of Iran, Saudi Arabia, Iraq, Pakistan, and Yemen), only four other countries have ranked in the top five executing countries from 2005 through 2014: China, North Korea, Sudan, and the United States. The United States is notable for being the only Western country to regularly use capital punishment.

Factors Contributing to the Worldwide Trend Toward Abolition of the Death Penalty

The single most important factor in the acceleration of capital punishment abolition worldwide in the 1980s and 1990s appears to be its successful coupling with the issue of human rights (see, for example, Hood, 2002). The concept of human rights became institutionalized in 1948, when the

United Nations, without dissent, adopted the Universal Declaration of Human Rights. Article 3 of the declaration establishes that everyone has the right to life, while Article 5 provides that no one shall be subjected to cruel, inhuman, or degrading treatment or punishment. The death penalty is considered a violation of both of these human rights (Amnesty International, 2013; United Nations, 2013).

The United Nations, the Council of Europe, the European Union, the Organization of American States, and the Catholic Church have been at the forefront of the worldwide death penalty abolitionist movement. As early as 1966, for example, the UN adopted the International Covenant on Civil and Political Rights. Article 6 of the covenant asserts that "no one shall be arbitrarily deprived of his life" and that the death penalty shall not be imposed on pregnant women or on those who were under the age of 18 at the time of their crime (Amnesty International, 2013). Article 7 of the covenant affirms that "no one shall be subjected to torture or to cruel, inhuman or degrading treatment or punishment" (Amnesty International, 2013).

The Council of Europe adopted a key agreement in December 1982: Protocol No. 6 to the European Convention for the Protection of Human Rights and Fundamental Freedoms (known as the European Convention on Human Rights). This was the first legally binding instrument to abolish the death penalty in peacetime, though it still allows it in time of war or imminent threat of war (Council of Europe, n.d.). Its influence on the international debate about the death penalty is considered enormous because it has provided "the foundation for external judgments about the penal policies of other nations" (Zimring, 2003, p. 29). The agreement has been ratified by 46 European countries and signed but not ratified by one other (Amnesty International, 2016, p. 68).

The UN General Assembly took another preliminary step in 1984, when it endorsed by consensus the UN Economic and Social Council's "Safeguards Guaranteeing Protection of the Rights of Those Facing the Death Penalty." The safeguards declare that "no one under the age of 18 at the time of the crime shall be put to death and that anyone sentenced to death has the right to appeal and to petition for pardon or commutation of sentence" (Amnesty International, 2015).

In 1989, the UN General Assembly adopted the Second Optional Protocol to the International Covenant on Civil and Political Rights, which extends to the world the death penalty provisions of the European Convention on Human Rights, which, as noted, were adopted by the Council of Europe in 1982. Like the earlier agreement, the Second Optional Protocol provides for the total abolition of the death penalty in peacetime but allows countries wishing to do so to retain the death penalty in wartime as an exception. The protocol also contains the important stipulation that countries that have abolished the death penalty cannot reinstate it (Hood, 2002, p. 15). This agreement has been ratified by 81 countries and signed but not ratified by three more (Amnesty International, 2016, p. 67).

Toward the end of 1989 and 1991, respectively, the fall of the Berlin Wall and the breakup of the Soviet Union into 15 separate countries provided another important impetus to the worldwide death penalty abolitionist movement, as several postcommunist countries, including Azerbaijan, Bulgaria, Estonia, Georgia, Lithuania, Poland, Turkmenistan, and Ukraine, sought membership in the Council of Europe. Because of the Council of Europe's requirement that member countries relinquish capital punishment (discussed later), all of the aforementioned countries abolished their death penalties for all crimes in the late 1990s.

In 1990, in the Western Hemisphere, the General Assembly of the Organization of American states adopted the Protocol to the American Convention on Human Rights. Like the Second Optional Protocol to the International Covenant on Civil and Political Rights and the European Convention on Human Rights, this protocol requires the total abolition of the death penalty except during wartime (Amnesty International, 2013). Also, like the Second Optional Protocol, this protocol contains the condition that states that have abolished the death penalty must not reestablish it (Hood, 2002, p. 15). Thirteen countries have ratified this protocol (Amnesty International, 2016, p. 68).

Two important developments occurred in 1993 and 1994, when the International Criminal Tribunals for the former Yugoslavia and Rwanda, respectively, banned the death penalty as a possible option, "even for the most heinous crimes known to civilization, including genocide" (Amnesty International, 2013; Hood, 2002, p. 20). Both tribunals were established by the United Nations.

Another important event took place in 1994, when the Council of Europe made an immediate moratorium on executions and the intention to abolish the death penalty a precondition for membership (International Bar Association, 2008). As a result, since 1997, Europe has been a *de facto* death penalty free zone (Council of Europe, n.d.). Currently, all 47 countries in the Council of Europe—every European country except Belarus—have abolished the death penalty for all crimes (Death Penalty Worldwide, 2012).

In 1995, the UN Convention on the Rights of the Child went into effect. Article 37(a) of that convention prohibits the death penalty for persons under the age of 18 at the time of the crime (Amnesty International, 2013; Hood, 2002, p. 20).

Also in 1995, Pope John II issued the *Evangelium Vitae* (The Gospel of Life). The importance of this document to the worldwide death penalty abolitionist movement should not be underestimated. Not only has it influenced many Catholics, but it likely has swayed many non-Catholics as well. It was addressed to "the Bishops Priests and Deacons Men and Women religious lay Faithful and all People of Good Will on the Value and Inviolability of Human Life" (*Evangelium Vitae*, 1995). The document gave religious legitimacy to the abolition movement. The relevant part of the Gospel is reproduced here:

> On this matter [the death penalty] there is a growing tendency, both in the Church and in civil society, to demand that it be applied in a very limited way or even that it be abolished completely. The problem must be viewed in the context of a system of penal justice ever more in line with human dignity and thus, in the end, with God's plan for man and society. The primary purpose of the punishment which society inflicts is "to redress the disorder caused by the offense." Public authority must redress the violation of personal and social rights by imposing on the offender an adequate punishment for the crime, as a condition for the offender to regain the exercise of his or her freedom. In this way authority also fulfills the purpose of defending public order and ensuring people's safety, while at the same time offering the offender an incentive and help to change his or her behaviour and be rehabilitated. It is clear that, for these purposes to be achieved, the nature and extent of the punishment must be carefully evaluated and decided upon, and ought not go to the extreme of executing the offender except in cases of absolute necessity: in other words, when it would not be possible otherwise to defend society. Today however, as a result of steady improvements in the organization of the penal system, such cases are very rare if not practically nonexistent.
> In any event, the principle set forth in the new Catechism of the Catholic Church remains valid: "If bloodless means are sufficient to defend human lives against an aggressor and to protect public order and the safety of persons, public authority must limit itself to such means, because they better correspond to the concrete conditions of the common good and are more in conformity to the dignity of the human person."
>
> (*Evangelium Vitae, 1995*)

In 1998, the European Union, like the Council of Europe before it, made rejection of the death penalty a requisite for membership (International Bar Association, 2008). Article 2 of The Charter of Fundamental Rights of the European Union states that "no one shall be condemned to the death penalty, or executed" (Charter of Fundamental Rights of the European Union, 2007). All 27-member states of the EU have abolished the death penalty (Death Penalty Worldwide, 2012).

Also in 1998, 120 nations adopted the Rome Statute, the legal basis for the establishment of the permanent International Criminal Court (ICC), which is based at The Hague in the Netherlands. The court is an independent international organization and is not part of the United Nations

(International Criminal Court, 2015). When the court was established, the death penalty was excluded from the punishments it was authorized to impose, even for offenders convicted of genocide or crimes against humanity (Garland, 2010, p. 99).

The European Union also considers a universal moratorium on executions and the death penalty's abolition as key factors in relations between the European Union and third countries. Member countries are to take this into account when finalizing agreements with third countries. Consequently, some foreign businesses may make economic decisions based on a state's use of the death penalty. In a 1998 letter to then-Texas Governor George Bush, a European Union official wrote:

> We are concerned that the almost universal repugnance felt in Europe and elsewhere for the continued application of the death penalty in certain American states may also have economic consequences. Europe is the foremost foreign investor in Texas. Many companies, under pressure from shareholders and public opinion to apply ethical business practices, are beginning to consider the possibility of restricting the investment in the U.S. to states that do not apply the death penalty.
>
> *("Letter to Governor George Bush," 1998)*

Currently, European drug companies are refusing to export drugs to the United States that would be used in executions, such as sodium thiopental and pentobarbital. Such restrictions affect the use of the drugs for medical purposes (Death Penalty Information Center, 2013).

In 1999, The UN Commission on Human Rights passed a resolution calling for all death penalty countries to progressively limit the number of death-eligible offenses as a step toward total abolition (Death Penalty Information Center, 2013).

To this point, none of the aforementioned documents called for the complete abolition of the death penalty. That would change in 2002, when the Council of Europe adopted Protocol No. 13 to the European Convention for the Protection of Human Rights and Fundamental Freedoms (the European Convention on Human Rights). Protocol No. 13 provides for the total abolition of the death penalty in all circumstances, with no exceptions permitted (Amnesty International, 2016). Protocol 13 has been ratified by 44 countries and signed but not ratified by one other (Amnesty International, 2016, p. 68).

In addition, three human rights treaties that have been ratified by the United States ban arbitrary and discriminatory punishments. The International Covenant on Civil and Political Rights, mentioned earlier, prohibits any arbitrary use of the death penalty. The UN Convention Against Torture and Other Cruel, Inhuman or Degrading Treatment or Punishment bans torture and the infliction of severe pain or suffering based on any kind of discrimination. The International Convention on the Elimination of All Forms of Racial Discrimination (the Race Convention), as the name implies, forbids racial discrimination in the law's administration. International agencies and courts have found the United States in violation of each of these treaties. The United States, in turn, has adamantly denied the accusations (Dieter, 1999). The United States has taken reservations to the death penalty abolition provisions of treaties that it has ratified or signed. Reservations are statements that modify or exclude the applications or certain provisions for that country.

In December 2007, the UN General Assembly (UNGA) called for a worldwide death penalty moratorium, with the goal of abolishing executions. One hundred four member countries voted in favor of the resolution, 54 nations opposed it, and 29 nations abstained (Radelet, 2009, p. 19). In December 2008, the UNGA adopted a second resolution calling for a worldwide death penalty moratorium. This time 106 countries voted in favor of the resolution, 46 countries voted against it, and 34 countries abstained (Amnesty International, 2010). In November 2010, the UNGA adopted a third resolution calling for a worldwide moratorium, with 107 countries in favor, 38 countries opposed, and 36 abstentions (Amnesty International, 2010). The latest UNGA resolution calling for a worldwide death penalty moratorium was adopted in December 2014. This resolution was supported by 117 countries and opposed by 38 countries, with 34 abstentions, and four countries not present to vote (Amnesty International, 2014). The UNGA resolutions are not legally binding, but they do carry considerable moral and political weight. They also are indicative of the international trend to abolish the death penalty.

In sum, during the 1980s, 1990s, and the first decade and a half of the twenty-first century, the international death penalty abolitionist movement, led by the United Nations, the Council of Europe, the European Union, the Organization of American States, and the Catholic Church, has been relentless in its campaign against the death penalty. Many successes have been achieved. As noted previously, more than 70% of the countries in the world—140 of them—have abolished the death penalty in law or practice, and only 58 countries still retain it.

The United States is considered a retentionist country; however, its federalist structure of state legal autonomy makes that statement technically incorrect. While the U.S. government and the U.S. military retain the death penalty, only 31 states legislatively authorize capital punishment; 19 states and the District of Columbia are abolitionist jurisdictions (Death Penalty Information Center, 2017d). As noted previously, the United States was a part of the worldwide trend toward the death penalty's abolition until, that is, the 2016 election. The ramifications of that election are the subject of the next section.

Trumped!

Had Hillary Clinton won the election, the death penalty stood a good chance of being abolished during her presidential term. Even though Clinton supports the "very limited and rare" use of the death penalty (Chozick, 2015), she undoubtedly would have nominated a politically liberal-leaning justice, who likely would have joined the other four liberal justices on the United States Supreme Court (the "Court") and voted against the death penalty. But Clinton did not win the election, and the death penalty's demise in the entire United States may have been postponed for decades.

When President Trump, a death penalty proponent, nominated and the Senate confirmed Judge Neil Gorsuch, his likeminded choice for the late Justice Antonin Scalia's seat on the Supreme Court, the conservative majority was reconstituted. If President Trump has the opportunity to nominate one or more other justices for the possibly retiring elderly liberal Justices Ginsburg and Breyer, then he will be able to entrench a conservative majority on the Court for the foreseeable future. If that happens, it could be decades, if ever, before the Court finds the death penalty in violation of the Constitution.

That said, the possibility exists that whomever President Trump nominates to fill Court seats may surprise him and other political conservatives by voting contrary to his or her ideological reputation and against the death penalty. Other politically conservative Supreme Court justices, such as Nixon appointees Harry Blackman and Lewis Powell, repudiated the death penalty, albeit at the end of their careers. Both Blackmun and Powell had long supported the death penalty before finally opposing it. Each of them offered poignant mea culpas. David Souter, appointed to the Court by George H. W. Bush, also had a reputation as a political conservative and during his early years on the court established a moderately conservative record in death penalty cases. However, in the latter part of his career, Justice Souter has consistently aligned himself with the Court's liberal justices in death penalty cases, voting to abolish the death penalty in cases involving the intellectually challenged (mentally retarded), defendants under 18 years of age at the time their crimes were committed, and defendants convicted of child rape (Johnson, 2013). Perhaps any newly appointed politically conservative justices would have their death penalty conversions sooner in their careers than did either Blackmun, Powell, or Souter. The point is that just because a potential nominee to the Supreme Court has solid politically conservative credentials with regard to the death penalty, and is appointed to the Court by a Republican president does not mean that as a justice he or she will not alter his or her ideological beliefs about the death penalty.

However, short of such an improbable happenstance, the election year of 2016, may well be remembered as the year the death penalty abolition movement was slowed, if not stopped in its tracks. Not only was Donald Trump elected president in what is likely to go down as one of the greatest presidential election upsets of all time, a referendum in California to abolish the death penalty and replace it with life imprisonment without the possibility of parole plus restitution was defeated by a margin of 54% to 46%, while a companion referendum to impose time limits on state capital appeals passed 51% to 49% (Death Penalty Information Center, 2016b). Oklahoma voters by a margin of 66% to 34% approved a ballot measure that prevents Oklahoma's state courts from declaring the death penalty cruel and unusual punishment and empowers the state legislature to adopt any execution method not prohibited by the U.S. Constitution (Death Penalty Information Center, 2016b). Finally, in Nebraska, by a margin of 61% to 39%, voters reinstated the death penalty, overturning the state legislature's abolition of the death penalty in 2015 (Death Penalty Information Center, 2016b). Particularly disheartening to death penalty opponents, Nebraska was the first state to reinstate the death penalty after abolishing it since Kansas did it in 1994. Before Nebraska, Kansas was the last state to reinstate the death penalty in the modern era (Death Penalty Information Center, 2016a).

Toward the Death Penalty's Abolition in the United States

Until the election of 2016, death penalty abolitionists were on a roll, and a realistic path to the death penalty's complete abolition was in sight. The death penalty in the United States had been in decline for some time, as indicated by the number of death sentences imposed, the number of executions conducted, the number of states that had abolished the death penalty, and the concentration of executions in a few states and counties. Since 1976, and the death penalty's reinstatement in the United States, and through 2016, the number of death sentences imposed annually decreased approximately 90%, reaching a low of 30 in 2016, after having peaked at 315 in 1996 (Death Penalty Information Center, 2017a). Between 1996 and the end of 2016, the annual number of death sentences imposed in the United States decreased 15 times and increased only five times.

The annual number of executions followed a similar pattern. Since 1976, and through 2016, the number of executions conducted annually in the United States decreased about 80%, from a high of 98 in 1999, to a low of 20 in 2016 (Death Penalty Information Center, 2017b). Between 1999 and through 2016, the annual number of executions conducted in the United States decreased 13 times, increased only three times, and remained the same one time.

During the last decade, eight states abolished their death penalties: New Jersey and New York in 2007; New Mexico in 2009; Illinois in 2011; Connecticut in 2012; Maryland in 2013; Nebraska in 2015; and Delaware in 2016 (Death Penalty Information Center, 2016c). In four other states, governors had instituted moratoria: Oregon in 2011, Colorado in 2013, Washington in 2014, and Pennsylvania in 2015 (Death Penalty Information Center, 2016c). When New Jersey and New York abolished their death penalties in 2007, they were the first states to do so in more than 20 years, since Massachusetts and Rhode Island abolished their death penalties in 1984 (Death Penalty Information Center, 2016c). Currently, 19 states and the District of Columbia do not have death penalty statutes (Death Penalty Information Center, 2017d). Until Nebraska's reinstatement in 2016, 20 states did not have death penalty statutes.

Counting states that have abolished their death penalties, however, can be deceptive, because most death penalty states execute sparingly, if at all. Since executions resumed in 1977, following a decade-long moratorium, only five death penalty states have accounted for approximately two-thirds of all executions in the United States: Texas, Oklahoma, Virginia, Florida, and Missouri (Bohm, 2017, p. 370). The first three states—Texas, Oklahoma, and Virginia—have conducted more than half of all executions, and Texas alone has executed nearly 40% of the total (Bohm, 2017, p. 370).

Even these data conceal the concentration of executions within a limited number of U.S. counties. An examination of county-level data show that only 15% of all 3,143 U.S. counties or county-equivalents accounted for all of the executions in the United States since executions resumed in 1977, and only 2% of U.S. counties accounted for 52% of those executions (Dieter, 2013). By contrast, 85% of U.S. counties have not been responsible for a single execution in more than 45 years. The executing counties represent less than 16% of the U.S. population (Dieter, 2013).

The aforementioned data suggest that the death penalty in the United States simply might have withered away from disuse, and still may in most jurisdictions, despite Trump and whomever else he may appoint to the Supreme Court. Most prosecutors no longer may seek the death penalty, most jurors no longer may be willing to impose death sentences, or, alternatively, most death penalty states, the U.S. government, and the U.S. military may abolish their death penalties. However, even if the death penalty falls from favor in most jurisdictions, recalcitrant prosecutors and death-qualified jurors almost certainly will continue to seek it, and legislatures of some death penalty states, such as Texas, no doubt will remain defiant. If the goal is to be a nation without the death penalty, the U.S. Supreme Court probably will have to prohibit it. Based on the preceding analysis, that is not likely to occur anytime soon.

Legal Arguments for Death Penalty Abolition in the United States

The reasons for the decline in the number of death sentences and executions, as well as the recent state abolitions and moratoria, vary, but among them are the fear of executing an innocent person, the exorbitant costs of a capital punishment system, and problems with obtaining lethal-injection drugs. Regardless of the reasons, the dramatic changes in death penalty practice, until 2016, portended a coming reckoning—the death penalty's demise in the United States. Had Hillary Clinton been elected and appointed to the Supreme Court a politically liberal-leaning justice opposed to the death penalty, complete abolition stood a good chance. (It still may if Trump's Supreme Court appointee Neil Gorsuch surprises.) The case against the death penalty is a strong one based on established legal precedent. Following are descriptions of two legal arguments that challenge the death penalty on Eighth Amendment grounds. Before turning to the legal arguments, however, first consider legal precedent for how the Court could interpret the Eighth Amendment's prohibition of cruel and unusual punishment as it applies to the death penalty.

Justice Brennan in his *Furman* concurrence provided a reasoned framework for analyzing the constitutionality of the death penalty. Should the Court adopt this approach, at least two arguments for abolishing the death penalty follow. In his concurrence, Justice Brennan wrote,

> We know 'that the words of the [Cruel and Unusual Punishment Clause] are not precise, and that their scope is not static.' We know, therefore, that the Clause 'must draw its meaning from the evolving standards of decency that mark the progress of a maturing society' [*Trop v. Dulles*, 1958; also see *Weems v. United States*, 1910]. That knowledge, of course, is but the beginning of the inquiry.
>
> *(pp. 270–271)*

He added, "The basic concept underlying the [Clause] is nothing less than the dignity of man . . . . A punishment is 'cruel and unusual,' therefore, if it does not comport with human dignity" (p. 271).

Brennan then concedes that "[t]his formulation . . . does not of itself yield principles for assessing the constitutional validity of particular punishments" (p. 271). He notes, however, "there are principles recognized in our cases and inherent in the Clause sufficient to permit a judicial determination whether a challenged punishment comports with human dignity" (p. 271). Among those principles is that "the State must not arbitrarily inflict a severe punishment" (p. 275). He explains, "This principle derives from the notion that the State does not respect human dignity when, without reason, it inflicts upon some people a severe punishment that it does not inflict upon others" (p. 275).

Another principle inherent in the Clause, Brennan continues, "is that a severe punishment must not be unacceptable to contemporary society" (p. 278). He elaborates, "Rejection by society, of course, is a strong indication that a severe punishment does not comport with human dignity. In applying this principle, however, we must make certain that the judicial determination is as objective as possible" (p. 278). For Brennan:

> The question under this principle, then, is whether there are objective indicators from which a court can conclude that contemporary society considers a severe punishment unacceptable. Accordingly, the judicial . . . task is to review the history of a challenged punishment and to examine society's present practices with respect to its use. Legislative authorization, of course, does not establish acceptance. The acceptability of a severe punishment is measured, not by its availability, for it might become so offensive to society as never to be inflicted, but by its use.
>
> *(pp. 279–280)*

A final principle inherent in the Clause, according to Brennan, "is that a severe punishment must not be excessive" (p. 280). Brennan explains:

> A punishment is excessive under this principle if it is unnecessary: The infliction of a severe punishment by the State cannot comport with human dignity when it is nothing more than the pointless infliction of suffering. If there is a significantly less severe punishment adequate to achieve the purposes for which the punishment is inflicted, . . . the punishment inflicted is unnecessary and therefore excessive.
>
> *(p. 280)*

For Justice Brennan, then, the death penalty is cruel and unusual in violation of the Eighth Amendment if it does not comport with human dignity, that is, if it is imposed arbitrarily; is unacceptable to contemporary society, as measured by its use; and is excessive—that its purpose can be achieved by a less severe punishment. This standard and indicators of its violation have informed the arguments in the cases that have restricted the death penalty's use and, as argued here, could inform the arguments that lead to the death penalty's complete abolition in the United States.

Death Penalty Abolition: Two Legal Arguments

First, the Court could declare the death penalty unconstitutional for the same reason it declared the death penalty unconstitutional more than 40 years ago in *Furman v. Georgia* (1972): That unfettered jury discretion allowed the death penalty to be imposed arbitrarily, infrequently, and often selectively against minorities in violation of the Eighth and Fourteenth Amendments to the Constitution. The Court believed that the remedy for this problem was to guide jurors in their awesome responsibility of imposing death by having them consider aggravating and mitigating circumstances (see *Gregg v. Georgia*, 1976). As nearly four decades of research demonstrate, the Court was wrong. Thus, the Court could abolish the death penalty by conceding that its faith in the ability of "guided-discretion statutes" to adequately assist jurors in imposing the death penalty free of objectionable forms of arbitrariness and discrimination was mistaken. (Justice Brennan focused on arbitrary application of the death penalty and all but ignored discriminatory application or, perhaps, he confounded arbitrariness and discrimination.) Ironically, Justice Harlan anticipated this outcome less than a year before *Furman* was decided in his majority opinion in *McGautha v. California* (1971, p. 207):

Those who have come to grips with the hard task of actually attempting to draft means of channeling capital sentencing discretion have confirmed the lesson taught by . . . history. . . . To identify before the fact those characteristics of criminal homicides and their perpetrators which call for the death penalty, and to express these characteristics in language which can be fairly understood and applied by the sentencing authority, appear to be tasks which are beyond present human ability.

As noted, Justice Harlan's conjecture has been confirmed by decades of research showing that the death penalty continues to be imposed in constitutionally unacceptable arbitrary and discriminatory ways (see Bohm, 2017, Chapter 9, for examples of that research). The fact is that the death penalty in the United States always has been imposed in an arbitrary manner, and, short of abolishing it altogether, arbitrary application of the death penalty probably cannot be eliminated. The Court could acknowledge the validity of this fact and the research that supports it and rule that the death penalty, as it continues to be administered, is unconstitutional in violation of the Eighth Amendment. A possible problem with this strategy is that the Court has been notoriously leery of sophisticated statistical evidence, particularly as it pertains to the death penalty (see, for example, *McCleskey v. Kemp*, 1987). Also, whether all three of the criteria for determining whether a punishment is cruel and unusual—arbitrariness, unacceptability, and excessiveness—or whether finding only one will suffice is not clear. Thus, even with a liberal majority, the Court still may not have acted on the aforementioned argument.

A second legal argument and, for this author, the most likely way the Court could abolish the death penalty is for the Court to rule the death penalty unconstitutional for the same reason it has held as unconstitutional the death penalty for the rape of an adult woman (*Coker v. Georgia*, 1977), the rape of a child (*Kennedy v. Louisiana*, 2008), kidnapping (*Eberheart v. Georgia*, 1977), armed robbery (*Hooks v. Georgia*, 1977), participants in felony murders who did not kill or intend to kill (*Enmund v. Florida*, 1982), death row inmates who have literally gone crazy on death row (*Ford v. Wainwright*, 1986), the intellectually challenged (*Atkins v. Virginia*, 2002), and offenders who were younger than 18 years of age when their crimes were committed (*Roper v. Simmons*, 2005). In each of these cases, by a count of states and a consideration of momentum, that is, the number of states that had recently banned a specific death penalty application, the Court's majority concluded that the death penalty was in violation of the Constitution because it was grossly disproportionate and excessive in relation to the crime itself, the offender's role in the crime, or a specific characteristic of the offender based on "the evolving standards of decency that mark the progress of a maturing society." In short, the Court could declare the death penalty unconstitutional simply by following established legal precedent—by counting states and considering momentum.

While the Court traditionally has been leery about sophisticated statistical evidence, the Court has had no aversion to counting states. For the Court, the number of states that have or have not adopted a particular death penalty practice or, as will be argued here, even the death penalty itself, serves an indication of the will of the people as represented by the legislature, and is the principal way the Court determines the current "standards of decency that mark the progress of a maturing society." For example, when the Court reinstated the death penalty four years after *Furman*, in *Gregg v. Georgia* (1976), it was swayed by the 29 states that had enacted new death penalty statutes designed to remedy the problem the Court identified with pre-*Furman* death penalty statutes: unfettered jury discretion (number of states calculated from data in Death Penalty Information Center, 2017c).

Other, less important indicators of "the evolving standards of decency" are the number of death sentences imposed by juries, which, as noted previously, has been declining consistently and dramatically; international law, which, for a majority of countries, prohibits the death penalty; public opinion polls, which show a slow, long-term decline in death penalty support and increase in death penalty opposition; official positions of professional organizations and interest groups, many of which have taken positions against the death penalty; and the justices' own judgment (see, for example, *Coker v. Georgia*, 1977, p. 597; *Enmund v. Florida*, 1982, p. 801; *Atkins v. Virginia*, 2002, pp. 312, 316 n. 21, and 326). The justices' own judgment is brought to bear by asking "whether there is reason to disagree with the judgment reached by the citizenry and its legislators" (*Coker v. Georgia*, 1977, p. 597). Following are two examples of this approach.

In *Atkins v. Virginia* (2002), the Court decided that it was unconstitutional to execute the intellectually challenged ("mentally retarded"), in large part because, by then, 18 states had prohibited their execution. In *Atkins*, Justice Stevens, citing Chief Justice Warren in *Trop v. Dulles* and Justice Brennan in *Furman*, reiterated, "The basic concept underlying the Eighth Amendment is nothing less than the dignity of man . . . . The Amendment must draw its meaning from the evolving standards of decency that mark the progress of a maturing society" (pp. 311–312). He added, "We have pinpointed that the 'clearest and most reliable objective evidence of contemporary values is legislation enacted by the country's legislatures'" (p. 312). He noted, "*It is not so much the number of these States that is significant, but the consistency of the direction of change*" (i.e., momentum) (p. 315, emphasis added). "Given the well-known fact that anticrime legislation is far more popular than legislation providing protections for persons guilty of violent crime," Stevens continued,

> the large number of States prohibiting the execution of mentally retarded persons (and the complete absence of States passing legislation reinstating the power to conduct such executions) provides powerful evidence that today our society views mentally retarded offenders as categorically less culpable than the average criminal.
>
> *(pp. 315–316)*

He further stated, "The evidence carries even greater force when it is noted that the legislatures that have addressed the issue have voted overwhelmingly in favor of the prohibition" (p. 316). "Moreover, even in those States that allow the execution of mentally retarded offenders, the practice is uncommon" (p. 316), he observed. "Some States, for example New Hampshire and New Jersey," Stevens elaborated, "continue to authorize executions, but none have been carried out in decades. Thus there is little need to pursue legislation barring the execution of the mentally retarded in those States" (p. 316). "And it appears that even among those States that regularly execute offenders and that have no prohibition with regard to the mentally retarded," wrote Stevens, "only five have executed offenders possessing a known IQ less than 70 since we decided Penry" (p. 316) [referring to *Penry v. Lynaugh*, 1989, in which the Court upheld the execution of the mentally retarded]. "The practice, therefore, has become truly unusual," concluded Stevens, "and it is fair to say that a national consensus has developed against it" (p. 316).

In short, for Justice Stevens and the Court's majority in *Atkins*, the number of states that have prohibited a particular punishment and, more importantly, the consistency of the direction of that change (i.e., momentum) determines, at least in part, whether a punishment is cruel and unusual in violation of the Eighth Amendment. Other important considerations are whether any states legislatively reinstated the punishment following abolition, and whether states actually employ the punishment that is legislatively prescribed.

The Court's majority used the same argument it used in *Atkins* to determine whether the execution of juvenile offenders violated the Eighth Amendment. Writing for the majority, Justice Kennedy, citing *Trop v. Dulles*, framed his argument in familiar terms: "[W]e have established the propriety and affirmed the necessity of referring to 'the evolving standards of decency that mark the progress of a maturing society' to determine which punishments are so disproportionate as to be cruel and unusual" (pp. 560–561).

In *Roper v. Simmons* (2005), the Court ruled that it was unconstitutional to execute offenders who were younger than the age of 18 at the time their crimes were committed, again, in large part, because, by then, 18 death penalty states prohibited the death penalty for juveniles (joining the 12 states that had abolished the death penalty altogether), and the 20 death penalty states that had not prohibited it infrequently imposed it (pp. 564–565). The Court did note that "the rate of change in reducing the incidence of the juvenile death penalty, or in taking specific steps to abolish it [i.e., momentum] [had] been slower [than in *Atkins*]," but they were still significant (p. 565). The Court was impressed with the "consistency of direction of change" and the fact that "no State that previously prohibited capital punishment for juveniles [had] reinstated it" (p. 566). Justice Kennedy emphasized the salient point:

> As in *Atkins*, the objective indicia of consensus in this case—the rejection of the juvenile death penalty in the majority of States; the infrequency of its use even where it remains on the books; and the consistency in the trend toward abolition of the practice—provide sufficient evidence that today society views juveniles, in the words *Atkins* used respecting the mentally retarded, as "categorically less culpable than the average criminal."
>
> *(p. 567, citation omitted)*

In sum, by using the same logic and arguments used in a series of death penalty cases, including most notably *Atkins v. Virginia* (2002) and *Roper v. Simmons* (2005), a persuasive legal argument is available for an assault on the death penalty's constitutionality; specifically, that the death penalty is unacceptable to contemporary society, as measured by its use. By the end of 2016, 19 states and the District of Columbia had abolished their death penalties, and at least another dozen death penalty states, the U.S. government, and the U.S. military rarely execute (Death Penalty Information Center, 2017a). One state, Nebraska, had abolished its death penalty in 2015, but reinstated it in 2016. Based on the same reasoning the Court used in its *Atkins'* and *Simmons'* decisions, the Court's threshold to abolish the death penalty for the intellectually challenged ("mentally retarded") and juveniles already has been exceeded, even with Nebraska's reinstatement. And even if the Court reasoned that 19 states were not enough to abolish the death penalty, the Court might be hard pressed to retain the death penalty if a majority of states abolished it. Currently, only seven more states are needed to reach that threshold. Nebraska's reinstatement obviously puts a damper on the momentum argument.

Conclusion

Currently, only 58 countries in the world—less than 30% of all countries—employ the death penalty in their punishment systems. All of the other countries have abolished their death penalties either in law or practice—most of them since 1980. Many of the retentionist countries will not relinquish their death penalties easily, especially those countries whose legal systems are based on Sharia law. However, those countries that are not entirely resistant to death penalty abolition could be influenced in that direction by the example of the United States. If the United States were to abolish the death penalty nationwide, other countries likely would follow. The status of the death penalty in the United States, in short, may be the linchpin to worldwide abolition. If the current 58 retentionist countries are to be reduced significantly, then the example set by the United States could be pivotal.

Ironically, the rationale other countries might give for abolishing the death penalty is that it is a human rights violation. This is ironic because the United States is considered by much of the world (and itself) as a human rights champion, while at the same time some of its states—a majority of them—employ the death penalty, which is considered by most of the world (but obviously not by death penalty jurisdictions in the United States) as a human rights violation. The United States abolishing the death penalty nationwide would obviate that irony. The only way the United States could successfully abolish the death penalty nationwide is if the U.S. Supreme Court declares it in violation of the U.S. Constitution.

Had the elections turned out differently and Hillary Clinton won and appointed a politically liberal-leaning judge to the Court, then the Court likely would have been receptive to legal arguments based on well-established legal precedent and abolished the death penalty. The Court's majority likely would have found the following argument compelling: the death penalty is cruel and unusual in violation of the Eighth Amendment because it is applied arbitrarily; is unacceptable to contemporary society, as measured by its use; and is excessive, that is, its purpose can be achieved by a less severe punishment. As this chapter shows, each of these criterion has been met, with one possible caveat. Evidence shows that the death penalty is applied arbitrarily and probably always has been. Why this fact has not resonated with the Court is a mystery. Evidence also suggests that the death penalty is unacceptable to contemporary society, as measured by its use. The aforementioned caveat is that the Court might not consider the 19 states and the District of Columbia that have abolished the death penalty and the other approximately dozen death penalty states, the U.S. government, and the U.S. military that rarely execute as meeting the required threshold. The Court may want stronger proof that the death penalty is unacceptable to society by requiring that at least 26 states abolish it. If that is the case, as noted previously, only seven more states are needed to fulfill that requirement. Finally, the death penalty is an excessive punishment because its purpose can be achieved by a less severe punishment. Although many death penalty opponents are not enamored by the prospect, the public seems receptive to replacing the death penalty with life imprisonment without opportunity of parole (LWOP) or, especially, life imprisonment without opportunity of parole plus the offender working in prison to pay restitution to the victim's family or society in general (LWOP+).

Because of Trump's election and his appointment of Neil Gorsuch, a justice unsympathetic to death penalty abolition, the aforementioned legal argument cannot be expected to sway a majority of the Court. No argument could. Still, as noted previously, the death penalty simply may continue to wither away in most death penalty jurisdictions. For now, that may be all death penalty abolitionists can realistically anticipate.

Note

My thanks to Allie Bohm for her helpful comments.

References

Amnesty International. (2010). *UN moratorium on the use of the death penalty December 2008.* Retrieved November 24, 2010 from www.amnesty.org/en/death-penalty/international-law/moratorium/2008-resolution

Amnesty International. (2013). *Death penalty and human rights standards.* Retrieved January 24, 2017 from www.amnestyusa.org/our-work/issues/death-penalty/international-death-penalty/death-penalty-and-human-rights-standards

Amnesty International. (2014). *Record number of UN member states back call for global end to executions.* Retrieved January 24, 2017 from www.amnesty.or.jp/en/news/2014/1224_5046.html

Amnesty International. (2015). *Death Penalty: Ratification of international treaties.* Retrieved January 24, 2017 from www.amnesty.org/en/documents/ACT50/2305/2015/en/

Amnesty International. (2016). *Death sentences and executions 2015.* Retrieved September 5, 2016 from www.amnesty.org/en/latest/research/2016/04/death-sentences-executions-2015/

Bohm, R. M. (2017). *DeathQuest: An introduction to the theory and practice of the death penalty in the United States* (5th ed.). New York: Routledge.

Charter of Fundamental Rights of the European Union. (2007). Retrieved September 30, 2013 from http://eur-lex.europa.eu/en/treaties/dat/32007X1214/htm/C2007303EN.01000101.htm

Chozick, A. (2015). Hillary Clinton comes out against abolishing the death penalty. *FirstDraft* (October 28). Retrieved January 25, 2017 from www.nytimes.com/politics/first-draft/2015/10/28/hillary-clinton-comes-out-against-abolishing-the-death-penalty/

Council of Europe (no date). *Abolition of the Death Penalty.* Retrieved January 24, 2017 from www.coe.int/t/dghl/standardsetting/hrpolicy/Others_issues/Death_Penalty/default_en.asp

Death Penalty Worldwide. (2012). *Europe: An almost Death Penalty-free continent*. Retrieved January 24, 2017 from http://blog.law.northwestern.edu/cihr/2012/04/europe-an-almost-death-penalty-free-continent.html

Death Penalty Information Center. (2013). *Lethal injection: Many states changing lethal injection process*. Retrieved January 24, 2017 from www.deathpenaltyinfo.org/lethal-injection-many-states-changing-lethal-injection-process

Death Penalty Information Center. (2016a). *Kansas*. Retrieved November 15, 2016 from www.deathpenaltyinfo.org/kansas-1

Death Penalty Information Center. (2016b). *Latest news*. Retrieved November 15, 2016 from www.deathpenaltyinfo.org

Death Penalty Information Center. (2016c). *States with and without the Death Penalty*. Retrieved November 15, 2016 from www.deathpenaltyinfo.org/states-and-without-death-penalty

Death Penalty Information Center. (2017a). *Death sentences in the United States from 1977 by state and by year*. Retrieved January 17, 2017 from www.deathpenaltyinfo.org/death-sentences-united-states-1977-present

Death Penalty Information Center. (2017b). *Number of executions*. Retrieved January 17, 2017 from www.deathpenaltyinfo.org/executions-year

Death Penalty Information Center. (2017c). *State by state database*. Retrieved January 23, 2017 from www.deathpenaltyinfo.org/state_by_state

Death Penalty Information Center. (2017d). *States with and without the Death Penalty*. Retrieved January 23, 2017 from www.deathpenaltyinfo.org/states-and-without-death-penalty

Dieter, R. C. (1999). *International perspectives on the Death Penalty: A costly isolation for the U.S.* Death Penalty Information Center (October) www.deathpenaltyinfo.org/international-perspectives-death-penalty-costly-isolation-us#executivesummary. Retrieved January 24, 2017 from www.deathpenaltyinfo.org/international-perspectives-death-penalty-costly-isolation-us

Dieter, R. C. (2013). *The 2% Death Penalty: How a minority of counties produce most Death Penalty cases at enormous costs to all*. A Report from the Death Penalty Information Center (October). Retrieved January 24, 2017 from www.deathpenaltyinfo.org/documents/TwoPercentReport.pdf

Evangelium Vitae. (1995). Retrieved January 24, 2017 from www.vatican.va/holy_father/john_paul_ii/encyclicals/documents/hf_jp-ii_enc_25031995_evangelium-vitae_en.html (footnotes omitted).

Garland, D. (2010). *Peculiar institution: America's Death Penalty in an age of abolition*. Cambridge, MA: The Belknap Press.

Hood, R. (2002). *The death penalty: A worldwide perspective* (3rd ed.). New York: Oxford University Press.

International Bar Association. (2008). *The Death Penalty under international law: A background paper to the IBAHRI resolution on the abolition of the Death Penalty*. Retrieved September 30, 2013 from www.ibanet.org/Document/Default.aspx?DocumentUid=5482860b

International Criminal Court. (2015). Retrieved August 8, 2015 from www.icc-cpi.int/en_menus/icc/about%20the%20court/Pages/about%20the%20court.aspx

Johnson, S. P. (2013). The judicial career of justice David H. Souter and his impact on the rights of criminal defendants. *Wyoming Law Review, 13*, 263–302. Retrieved November 22, 2016 from www.uwyo.edu/law/_files/docs/wy%20law%20review/v13%20n1/johnson.pdf

"Letter to Governor George Bush by Alan J. Donnelly, MEP, Chairman, Delegation for the Relations with the United States, European Parliament, Interparliamentary Delegations, Division for Non-European Countries, June 25, 1998." Retrieved October 2, 2013 from www.eunitheus.org/. . .do/. . ./death-penalty/death-penalty. . ./eu-policy-on-t. . . .

Penal Reform International. (2015). *Sharia law and the Death Penalty: Would abolition of the Death Penalty be unfaithful to the message of Islam?* Retrieved January 30, 2017 from www.penalreform.org/wp-content/uploads/2015/07/Sharia-law-and-the-death-penalty.pdf

Radelet, M. L. (2009). The executioner's waning defenses. In C. J. Ogletree, Jr. & A. Sarat (Eds.), *The road to abolition? The future of capital punishment in the United States* (pp. 19–25). New York: New York University Press.

United Nations. (2013). *The universal declaration of human rights*. Retrieved January 24, 2017 from www.un.org/en/universal-declaration-human-rights/index.html

Zimring, F. E. (2003). *The contradictions of American capital punishment*. New York: Oxford University Press.

Cases Cited

Atkins v. Virginia, 536 U.S. 304 (2002).
Coker v. Georgia, 433 U.S. 584 (1977).
Eberheart v. Georgia, 433 U.S. 917 (1977).
Enmund v. Florida, 458 U.S. 782 (1982).
Ford v. Wainwright, 477 U.S. 399 (1986).

Furman v. Georgia, 408 U.S. 238 (1972).
Gregg v. Georgia, 428 U.S. 153 (1976).
Hooks v. Georgia, 433 U.S. 917 (1977).
Kennedy v. Louisiana, 544 U.S. 407 (2008).
McCleskey v. Kemp, 481 U.S. 279 (1987.
McGautha v. California, 602 U.S. 183 (1971).
Penry v. Lynaugh, 492 U.S. 302 (1989).
Roper v. Simmons, 543 U.S. 551 (2005).
Trop v. Dulles, 356 U.S. 86 (1958).
Weems v. United States, 217 U.S. 349 (1910).

INDEX

Page numbers in *italics* indicate a figure and page numbers in **bold** indicate a table.